SAWYER'S INTERNAL AUDITING

5th EDITION

The Practice of Modern Internal Auditing

by
Lawrence B. Sawyer, JD, CIA, PA
Mortimer A. Dittenhofer, Ph.D., CIA
James H. Scheiner, Ph.D.

With contributions by
Anne Graham, Ph.D.
Paul Makosz, CA

The Institute of Internal Auditors

Disclosure

The IIA publishes this document for informational and educational purposes. This document is intended to provide information, but is not a substitute for legal or accounting advice. The IIA does not provide such advice and makes no warranty as to any legal or accounting results through its publication of this document. When legal or accounting issues arise, professional assistance should be sought and retained.

The Professional Practices Framework for Internal Auditing (PPF) was designed by The IIA Board of Directors' Guidance Task Force to appropriately organize the full range of existing and developing practice guidance for the profession. Based on the definition of internal auditing, the PPF comprises *Ethics* and *Standards*, *Practice Advisories*, and *Development and Practice Aids*, and paves the way to world-class internal auditing.

This guidance fits into the Framework under the heading *Development and Practice Aids*.

ISBN 0-89413-509-0
03021 06/03 First Printing
05203 03/05 Second Printing

In Memoriam

Lawrence B. Sawyer, JD, CIA, PA
April 13, 1911 - September 18, 2002

One of my earliest opportunities to meet Larry Sawyer was on September 11, 1992, at The IIA's Altamonte Springs, Florida, global headquarters. I had just become president of The IIA, and Larry was visiting headquarters. He signed my copy of *Sawyer's Internal Auditing, 3rd Edition*. I still have that autographed book, and remember him saying that the publication was "a cornucopia of internal audit information."

Larry was always one with words. He authored 26 articles, 19 books, and two videos. That explains why he was The IIA's only four-time winner of the John B. Thurston Award for literary excellence; and why this publication is the number one internal audit textbook used by colleges and universities throughout the world. It can be found in virtually every audit shop library.

Larry, who joined The IIA in 1957, dedicated his entire life and career to advancing the role of internal auditors. He worked hard to encapsulate his vast knowledge, and shared it through his articles, speeches, and textbooks. He did more to impact future generations of auditors than any other individual, and was one of the profession's greatest emissaries.

Yes, he was duly rewarded for his achievements, with the coveted Bradford Cadmus Memorial Award and Victor Z. Brink Award for Distinguished Service, among others — but his greatest reward was having his wife, Esther, by his side.

I last saw Larry during The IIA's 2000 International Conference in New York City. Larry's motivation for attending the conference was to honor Esther's memory with a gift of $100,000 to The IIA Research Foundation, and a separate $35,000 donation by the Sawyer children for the establishment of an Esther R. Sawyer Scholarship Award. During the conference, The IIA honored Larry with a Lifetime Achievement Award for having singularly impacted the profession of internal auditing more than any other individual to date.

He was a man of honor, a man of many words, and a man, who even in memoriam, continues to give back to the profession in which he was revered as "the father of modern internal auditing." This textbook is Larry's lasting contribution to the profession. He gave The IIA rights to continue to use his name on upcoming editions, and the Sawyer estate directed The IIA to donate the royalties from the 4th and 5th Editions to The IIA Research Foundation and the Esther R. Sawyer Scholarship Award fund.

The written word found in this textbook, and the Sawyer family's continued contribution to The Foundation, mean that Larry's dream for internal auditors "to continue to grow, explore, and to welcome new concepts, ideas, and technology that will truly make a difference in our profession" lives on. There is no more suitable tribute to his memory.

William G. Bishop III, CIA
IIA President

Contents

Preface vii

The New Items in Sawyer ix

Acknowledgments xv

About the Authors xvii

PART 1 — INTRODUCTION TO INTERNAL AUDITING
   1   The Nature of Internal Auditing 3
   2   Control 57

PART 2 — TECHNIQUES OF INTERNAL AUDITING
   3   Risk Assessment 119
   4   Preliminary Surveys 169
   5   Audit Programs 219
   6   Field Work - I 259
   7   Field Work - II 297
   8   Audit Findings 347
   9   Working Papers 377
  10   Control Self-assessment 419

PART 3 — SAMPLING AND ANALYTICAL METHODS
  11   Sampling 437
  12   Analytical and Quantitative Methods 489

PART 4 — DATA PROCESSING
  13   Information Systems Auditing - I 539
  14   Information Systems Auditing - II 591
  15   Information Systems Auditing - III 631
  16   Using Personal Computers in Auditing 651

PART 5 — REPORTING
  17   Reports 687
  18   Audit Report Reviews and Replies 777
  19   Reports to Executive Management and the Board 803

PART 6 — ADMINISTRATION
20 Establishing the Auditing Activity 837
21 Selecting and Developing the Staff 879
22 Preparing Long-range Schedules 945
23 Controlling Audit Projects 975
24 Quality Assurance 1009

PART 7 — OTHER MATTERS RELATING TO INTERNAL AUDITING
25 Principles of Management 1053
26 Environmental Auditing 1113
27 Employee and Management Fraud 1163
28 Dealing with People 1223
29 Relationships with External Auditors 1271
30 Relationships with Boards of Directors and Audit Committees 1319
31 Standards for the Professional Practice of Internal Auditing
       and Code of Ethics 1349

Index 1391

Preface

In the sweep of current events, change is inevitable. In the field of modern internal auditing, change is a constant. New concepts, systems, and procedures keep flooding business and government. And to serve their clients, internal auditors must keep pace with all the changes that affect owners and managers. That is the reason for this new edition of *Sawyer's Internal Auditing*.

The original "Practice" was published in 1973 and comprised 13 chapters. The 2nd Edition was published in 1981 with 25 chapters. The 3rd Edition was published in 1988 and spanned 26 chapters. The title of that edition was changed from *The Practice of Modern Internal Auditing* to *Sawyer's Internal Auditing*. It also contained 26 chapters, but some of the subjects were either new or combined. The 4th Edition contained six parts divided by 26 chapters representing both combined and new chapters.

Although the roots of internal auditing haven't changed, the evolution of the profession is unfolding in directions that might not have been projected a few decades ago. This edition acknowledges these trends. It explains how a revised definition of internal auditing, a new competency framework for the profession, changes to the Certified Internal Auditor examination, and other developments are reshaping the profession and its practice. The book emphasizes the "added value" approach to internal auditing, which includes a stronger "customer orientation," as well as an emphasis on alignment with management and the achievement of organizational goals. The specter and implications of internal auditing outsourcing are considered, and new strategies and specialties that have become part of the internal auditor's vocabulary and practice are described.

This memorial edition is, however, substantially expanded as a result of a series of events. First, The IIA became more globally oriented and its philosophy was expanded to accommodate this broader approach. Also, the book abandoned its basic North American orientation. Second, The IIA's directors empaneled a task force with an international representation whose charter was to look at The IIA and define not only what it was, but also what it should be to reflect the evolutionary changes that commerce, governments, and the economy were experiencing. The result of the work of this group was an almost complete revision of the *Standards for the Professional Practice of Internal Auditing* to build on the original 1978 guidance. The recognition of the auditor's work in the field of consulting, the confirmation of what had been occurring in progressive audit activities, was one of the more important achievements. Another result was to emphasize the auditor's work to enhance governance in the organization and to expand the internal auditor's work to add value to the organization.

viii Sawyer's Internal Auditing, 5th Edition

Third, the organizational turbulence of the late 1990s and 2000s disclosed the need for more active and more incisive internal audit work. Numerous episodes of organization malfeasance were disclosed by enhanced internal audit activity and there was general recognition that a strong, independent internal auditing function could have had a deterrent result and that would have prevented much of the malaise that swept the commercial world.

Fourth, The IIA was maturing and looking at itself and saying, "Are we doing our best? Are we, in fact, providing the security and the foresight for greater efficiency and effectiveness that we should provide?" This self-evaluation led to a series of conferences that were dedicated to progressive methodologies and the exchange of ideas as to how to function more productively.

Finally, The IIA and internal auditing as a force was being recognized by industry and government. It was taking its place as a leader in the field and was no longer the "little brother" of the dominant public accounting profession. It developed stature and recognition, and a position of independence in the organization culture became assured.

These events and forces and probably many others have dominated the development of this edition of Larry Sawyer's significant professional contribution to the field. We have been careful to preserve the beauty and fluidity of Larry's outstanding descriptive style. We have made some clarifications resulting from evolutionary changes in the field, however we have tried not to interfere with Larry's fine descriptions. Because of the effect of Esther Sawyer's untimely passing and Larry's illness and subsequent death, we have tried to uphold the stature of the work. We were bereft of his wise counsel but we are responsible for the modifications and additions to this edition. There are about 130 new sections that are identified in the following preliminary unit, "The New Items in Sawyer."

This entire edition is dedicated to Larry Sawyer, a giant in the field, and our very dear friend and associate. We include his name in this Preface because this is really his book.

Larry Sawyer
Mort Dittenhofer
Jim Scheiner

The New Items in Sawyer

This memorial edition of *Sawyer's Internal Auditing* is almost two books in one. The broad area of internal auditing has become so dynamic that, in order to keep up with it, we have had to almost write another book. The corporate scandals during the late 1990s and early 2000s have had some significant impacts on both internal and external auditing. To cap it all, The IIA has expanded its position to become more global in its reach and to be more dedicated to the important area of organization governance.

Larry Sawyer was the moving force behind the design of this edition's content and we have tried to expand the coverage as he planned and envisaged it. Larry passed away as we were completing the final editing of the chapters.

One can consider the magnitude of the changes made in this edition in a number of ways, including the number of new chapters, the number of new sections, and/or the amount of new material added.

To begin, the book has expanded from 26 chapters to 31 chapters. The five new chapters are:

Field Work - II
Control Self-assessment
Information Systems Auditing - II
Using Personal Computers in Auditing
Environmental Auditing

Two new authors have assisted with this edition. Anne Graham, former editor-in-chief of *Internal Auditor*, revised and updated five chapters. Paul Makosz, founder and partner of PDK, developed and wrote the chapter on Control Self-assessment. These new authors add much to the editorial staff.

In all, this new edition has almost 130 new sections, most of which are new developments. Following are the important additions.

- Excerpts from the new *Standards for the Professional Practice of Internal Auditing (Standards)* appear throughout the book as they apply to each of the chapter's basic subject matter. The recently proposed modifications of the *Standards* appear in an Appendix to Chapter 31.

- An Appendix to Chapter 1 deals with the newly developed area of internal audit consulting.

- Much of the recent research on best methods in internal auditing appears in the various chapters.

- Twelve sections have been added to the Control chapter, including:
  - New definitions of control
  - Using the control method
  - The impact of reengineering on control
  - Reduction on control — the virtual organization
  - Auditing COSO

- The important subject of Risk Assessment also has 12 new sections. Several of them are:
  - Objectives of the risk management process
  - Planning for risk assessment and exposure
  - A risk inventory process
  - Bell Canada's risk management strategy
  - EDI risk
  - Risk disclosure considerations

- The Field Work chapters have 17 new sections. Included are:
  - SMART auditing
  - Benchmarking
  - Performance measurement
  - Stop-and-go auditing
  - Examination techniques for selected processes
  - Outsourcing and cosourcing
  - Integrated auditing
  - Handling sensitive evidence
  - Auditing in a high-technology environment
  - Using consultants

- The Working Papers chapter has two new sections. They are:
  - Proforma working papers
  - Automating working papers

- The Information Systems related chapters have nine new sections. Below are eight:
  - Enterprise software
  - Impact of e-business
  - High-level languages
  - Custom audit software
  - Obtaining information from the Web
  - Expanded controls in an Internet environment

- Working papers generated by the mainframe
- Network security assessment tools

• The Reports chapter has 10 new subjects:
  - Tips for audit report writing
  - Effective strategies for report writing
  - Elements of exceptional reports
  - Action on audit recommendations
  - Improving internal audit reports
  - Due diligence audit reports
  - "Short" reports
  - More prompt reports
  - Information security
  - Communications outside the organization

• The Audit Report Reviews and Replies chapter has two new sections:
  - Recommendations to augment GAO suggestions for follow-up on audit report items
  - Concurrent audit report reviews

• In Reports to Executive Management and the Board, three of the four new sections are especially interesting:
  - Factors for reporting to committees
  - Communications with the board
  - One-page audit reports

• In Establishing the Auditing Activity, six new sections are added, including:
  - Online auditing
  - The value-added concept
  - New organization strategy
  - Responsibility for non-audit functions
  - Acquisition and evaluation of external audit services

• Selecting and Developing the Staff. Three of the five sections are especially interesting:
  - The art of mentoring
  - Restructuring the human relations staff
  - The development of ethical cultures

• Preparing Long-range Schedules. The two items added are:
  - Integration with audit strategy
  - Impact of Enron-like results

- Controlling Audit Projects. Four of the five new sections are of special interest:
  - Controlling the time of internal audits
  - Integrating project control with payrolls
  - Computerized controls
  - The Texaco audit automation process

- Quality Assurance. All four of the new sections are of interest:
  - Southern California Edison's TQM Program
  - A current quality control survey
  - Productivity in internal auditing
  - A new look at external reviews

- In the Principles of Management, there is one especially new item of interest:
  - Managing to ensure an ethical environment

- Employee and Management Fraud has the largest number of new sections. This is understandable considering the recent occurrence of organizational malfeasance. The list of new subjects follows:
  - Expansion of treatment of computer fraud
  - Risk analysis related to fraud
  - Documentation of fraud instances
  - Three factors related to fraud
  - Verifying transactions through analytical methods
  - Behavioral aspects of fraud
  - Codes of conduct and hot lines
  - U.S. Sentencing Commission Guidelines
  - Audit programs for fraud examiners
  - Auditing for cyber fraud
  - Access device fraud
  - Forensics in fraud investigations
  - New approaches by AICPA

- Dealing with People has two important new sections. They are:
  - Effective use of interview questions
  - Managing conflict

- Relationships with External Auditors has four new sections. All are important:
  - Acquisition of external audit services
  - External auditor independence requirements for providing internal audit services
  - Outsourcing and cosourcing
  - Coordinating total audit coverage

- Relationships with Boards of Directors and Audit Committees has seven new sections. They are:
    - Current legal developments relating to audit committees
    - Recent SEC requirements relating to audit committees
    - A sample audit committee charter
    - IIA *Standards* update on audit committees, the board, and the chief audit executive
    - The Sarbanes-Oxley Act of 2002
    - Updates on the performance of audit committees
    - Audit committee reporting

Acknowledgments

To those who helped the authors with the previous four editions of the book, our gratitude continues. In this edition, two people, one a practitioner and prolific writer and the other an editorial specialist with a wealth of experience in internal auditing, gave us enormous assistance. The former, Paul Makosz, CA, added a chapter in a groundbreaking area; the latter, Anne Graham, Ph.D., made valuable revisions and updates to a series of chapters.

Gratitude is also due to Jim Fleishman, MACC, a graduate of Florida International University, who assisted with the questions at the end of the chapters; and to Jeorge Flores, MACC, also a graduate of Florida International University and Audit Director of the Bank of Costa Rica, who again updated the Supplementary Readings.

We also want to acknowledge the assistance and guidance provided by the staff at The Institute of Internal Auditors (IIA). Stacy Mantzaris, CIA, CCSA, CGAP, Assistant Vice President, Seminars Group, was the powerhouse behind this edition and contributed immeasurably to the update. Lee Ann Campbell, Senior Specialist, Print Publishing, committed endless hours to the editing and final production of this publication. Richard F. Chambers, CIA, CCSA, CGAP, Vice President, IIA Learning Center, Johanna S. Swauger, CIA, CCSA, CGAP, CFSA, Assistant Vice President, Research and Educational Products Group, and Susan B. Lione, CIA, CCSA, CGAP, CFSA, Assistant Vice President, Certification Group, provided valuable technical guidance. Michelle Entzminger, Administrator, Educational Products, and Evy Acevedo, Coordinator, Educational Products, provided the support and coordination needed to bring this edition to fruition.

We are also immeasurably indebted to several members of The IIA's Educational Products Committee: Philip D. Bahrman, CIA, John Vaughn, CIA, Jay R. Taylor, CIA, John C. Gazlay, Belinda Jo Finn, CIA, Marvin A. Stille Jr., CIA, John G. Sayers, CIA, David J. MacCabe, CIA, CGAP, Anna R. Nicodemus, CIA, and Daniel Pantera, CIA. This committee of volunteer practitioners provided technical guidance and suggestions in order to make *Sawyer's Internal Auditing, 5th Edition,* the giant in the field as envisioned by Larry Sawyer. It is definitely a better product, as Larry would have described it.

Finally, we want to acknowledge the loving material and spiritual assistance we received from our wives, Skeets Dittenhofer and Linda Scheiner, and the enthusiasm from our children. Without their help, the task would have been insurmountable.

Mort Dittenhofer
Jim Scheiner

About the Authors

The late **Lawrence B. Sawyer, JD, CIA, PA,** was widely known as one of the most articulate authorities on internal auditing. Indeed, he is often referred to as "the father of modern internal auditing." He gained his knowledge of audit practice in both government (with the U.S. General Accounting Office) and in the aerospace industry. He was the recipient of more major literary and professional awards than any other internal audit practitioner: four Thurston Awards, three Outstanding Contributor Awards, the Cadmus Award, and the Distinguished Service Award. He participated in early revisions of The IIA's *Code of Ethics* and the *Statement of Responsibilities*, and was instrumental in developing the first Certified Internal Auditor (CIA) examination and the original *Standards for the Professional Practice of Internal Auditing*. He continued to be a leader in the internal auditing profession. He published extensively in internal audit publications and wrote several other technical books, one of which (the second edition of *The Manager and the Internal Auditor*) was published in 1996. Mr. Sawyer was constantly in demand as a speaker on the subject of internal auditing. He was the first recipient of The IIA's Lifetime Achievement Award.

Mortimer A. Dittenhofer, Ph.D., CIA, was Professor of Accounting at Florida International University in Miami, Florida. He is a research fellow of The IIA and was the Director of the Master of Accounting Program in Internal Auditing at Florida International University. He has extensive internal auditing experience in industry at Sears and in the federal government at the Atomic Energy Commission. At the U.S. General Accounting Office, he chaired the work group that developed the first edition of the world-renowned Government Audit Standards. He was a two-term member of the committee that developed The IIA's *Standards for the Professional Practice of Internal Auditing*. He also was the second recipient of The IIA's Lifetime Achievement Award presented in 2002. He edited a two-volume annual government auditing and accounting update reference series and is coeditor of The IIA's two case study collections on ethics. He is currently developing a third edition of the case study collection.

James H. Scheiner, Ph.D., is Dean of the Walker L. Cisler College of Business and Professor of Business at Northern Michigan University. An award-winning teacher, his primary teaching interests are in auditing and accounting information systems. In addition, he has taught continuing education and staff training for auditors. He is a second-generation Certified Public Accountant. He has published in the leading accounting research journals, coauthored an auditing textbook, and coauthored an education monograph published by the American Accounting Association. He has served as a consultant to governmental and business entities.

Contributing Authors

Anne Graham, Ph.D., is Managing Director of Educational and Member Services at AACSB - International, the Association to Advance Collegiate Schools of Business. She was formerly Director of Publications at The Institute of Internal Auditors and Editor-in-Chief of *Internal Auditor.*

Paul Makosz, CA, is Chief Executive Officer of PDK Control Consulting International Ltd. PDK specializes and trains staff from all sectors in the self-assessment of control and risk. The company operates in North America, the UK, Australia, and Latin America. As General Auditor and Manager of Corporate Transformation of Gulf Canada from 1987 to 1995, he pioneered the process of control self-assessment (CSA) and developed it from simple employee meetings to technically sophisticated workshops, which assess the entire scope of control in a few hours. In 1995 he founded PDK.

Mr. Makosz has authored several articles on CSA and risk, has a strong interest in corporate ethics and psychology, and has spoken publicly in many countries on the risks associated with organizational change and techniques for raising ethical awareness. He believes that prevention is better than cure.

Mr. Makosz is the Chairman of the International Ethics Committee of The Institute of Internal Auditors and is a former Chair of the Criteria of Control Board (CoCo) of the Canadian Institute of Chartered Accountants. In 1999 he was honored by The IIA with the Bradford Cadmus Memorial Award for his international contribution to the profession.

PART 1

INTRODUCTION TO
INTERNAL AUDITING

Chapter 1
The Nature of Internal Auditing

The evolution and history of internal auditing. Internal auditors' achievement of identity. Differences between external and internal auditing. Definitions of internal auditing. Internal auditing as a profession. How professions differ from trades and crafts. Internal auditing's progress. IIA Statement of Responsibilities. IIA Code of Ethics. IIA Standards for the Professional Practice of Internal Auditing. The Common Body of Knowledge. A competency framework. Certified Internal Auditor program. Professional Recognition Credit. Specialty certifications. Internal auditing forms and approaches. Control self-assessment. Audit specialties. Outsourcing. A Core Function. Service to management. Independence in internal auditing. Whistleblowing. Appendix: The Internal Auditor as a Consultant.

• •

The Evolution of Internal Auditing

Internal auditing has evolved from an essentially accounting-oriented craft to a management-oriented profession. At one time, internal auditing functioned as a junior sibling to the independent accounting profession, and attesting to the accuracy of financial matters was the profession's paramount concern. Now, however, internal auditing has established itself as a distinctive discipline with a far broader focus.

Modern internal auditing provides services that include the examination and appraisal of controls, performance, risk, and governance throughout public and private entities. Financial matters represent only one aspect of internal auditing's purview. Once perceived as the client's adversary, internal auditors now pursue cooperative, productive working relationships with clients through value-adding activities. Since this broad-based auditing of all activities is a relatively recent occurrence, it is generally referred to as modern internal auditing.

Ancient Times

The history of internal auditing shows that the profession has evolved systematically, mirroring changes in the way commerce is conducted and managed. Audits began as far back as 3,500 B.C. The records of a Mesopotamian civilization show tiny marks beside numbers involved in financial transactions. The dots, checks, and tick marks portray a system of verification.

One scribe prepared summaries of transactions; another verified those assertions. Internal controls, systems of verification, and the concept of division of duties probably originated at that time.

Early Egyptian, Chinese, Persian, and Hebrew records indicate similar systems. The Egyptians, for example, required the actual witnessing of grain being brought to the granaries and demanded that receipts of grain be certified.

The Greeks were strong believers in control over finances. Their records show that transactions required authorization and verification. Their systems of control included peculiarly direct methods. They preferred slaves to freemen as record keepers because the Greeks regarded torture as a more trustworthy means of extracting information than the questioning of a freeman under oath.

Ancient Rome employed the "hearing of accounts." One official would compare his records with those of another. This oral verification was designed to keep officials in charge of funds from committing fraudulent acts. In fact, the task of hearing accounts gave rise to the term "audit," from the Latin *auditus* ("a hearing"). *Quaestors* ("those who inquire") would examine the accounts of provincial governors, seeking to detect fraud and the misuse of funds.

The Middle Ages

When Rome fell, so did monetary systems and financial controls. Not until the end of the Dark Ages did rulers demand proof that they were obtaining the revenues due them. Barons and justices made the first audits; appointed officials did so later.

An expanding Italian commerce during the 13th century demanded more sophisticated record keeping. Thus was born the double-entry system of bookkeeping, where every transaction is entered as both a debit and a credit. This system helped merchants control transactions with customers and suppliers and allowed them to monitor the work of employees. Auditing was taken seriously. In fact, an auditor representing Queen Isabella accompanied Columbus to the New World.

The Industrial Revolution

Auditing, as we now know it, began during the industrial revolution in England. Organizations hired accountants to check the financial records. More than a mere "hearing," audit verification became a matter of scrutinizing written records and comparing entries in the books of account with documentary evidence.

Recent Times

Auditing, along with British investments, crossed the seas to the United States during the 19th century. Wealthy Englishmen invested substantial amounts in United States enterprises, and they wanted an independent check on their investments. The English auditors brought with them methods and procedures that the Colonials adapted to their own needs.

The British requirements arose under the statutory dictates of the British Companies Act calling for accountability to investors. The United States had no such requirements; hence, auditing served the needs of the entrepreneur. These needs emphasized the balance-sheet audit, stressing a more analytical approach to accounts. Still, the need for outside capital remained the major impetus for audits.

Auditing in the United States

After World War I the United States economy escalated. Although they were not required to do so, many corporations published audited financial statements. By and large, however, auditing was for the benefit of the bankers who feared the overly optimistic balance sheets and needed an independent, reliable verification.

The railroads were among the first to adopt a far-flung internal audit program. Railroad executives needed assurances that their stationmasters across the country were handling receipts properly. The external audits were evidently considered inadequate for such operating matters.

The continued development of internal auditing can be attributed to the increased complexity and sophistication of business and government operations. Growth limited management's ability to monitor its operations and made internal auditing a more and more important function.

The Internal Auditor's Achievement of Identity

For many years, external auditors continued to influence the way internal audits were performed. Modern internal auditing began to evolve in 1941 when The Institute of Internal Auditors (IIA) was formed. Only then did internal auditors expand the scope of internal auditing to appraising all operations of the enterprise. Only then did internal auditors stand as equals to their external counterparts.

The terms *internal auditor* and *internal auditing* carried a nitpicking connotation to some of the founders of The IIA. They sought a term or phrase that would better describe the expanding role of the internal auditor, but none emerged. And so John B. Thurston, one of The IIA's founders, said in 1941:

> *You will recognize the unhappy inadequacy of the phrase "internal auditor." Years ago it was probably satisfactorily descriptive of our earlier predecessors in the profession. But today, auditing, in the precise meaning of the word, is only one of the functions of the internal auditor. Your organizing committee gave much thought to the possibility of using some other phrase or term and finally reached the conclusion that we must bow to historical precedent.[1]*

The founders hoped that the action rather than the description of the profession would help it achieve its separate identity. The year 1941, however, did not give birth to an Athena springing fully formed from the brow of Zeus. Rather, it sparked a glint in the eyes of the founders, who dreamed of a profession concerned with providing independent reviews of all entity activities, not merely with the verification of its financial affairs.

External Auditor and Internal Auditor

The activities of internal and external auditing may overlap in areas such as reviewing the adequacy of accounting controls, but the differences between the two fields are greater than the similarities because of divergent objectives. Accounting experience can provide important training in developing audit programs, evaluating systems, analyzing transactions, identifying defects, and preparing working papers; and many internal auditors are recruited from the ranks of the public accounting profession. In addition, many public accounting firms have begun to offer internal auditing services on an outsource basis. However, accountants who apply public accounting techniques without change to their internal auditing projects could miss the point of the entire audit.

Missions

The primary responsibility of external auditors is to report on the organization's financial statements. The external auditors' aim is to determine whether the statements fairly present the financial position of the organization and the results of its operations for the period. Also, they must satisfy themselves that the statements are prepared in conformity with generally accepted accounting principles; principles have been applied consistently with those of the previous year; and assets have been safeguarded.

Internal auditors furnish managers throughout the organization with information needed to effectively discharge their responsibilities. Internal auditing acts as an independent appraisal activity to review operations as a service to the organization by measuring and evaluating the adequacy of controls and the efficiency and effectiveness of performance. Internal auditors are vitally involved in all matters related to organizational governance and risks.

Differences

Internal reviews of accounting controls are important, and internal auditors must be involved with them; but that is not their entire mission. The losses resulting from poor production, engineering, marketing, or inventory management can be far greater than those suffered from financial peculations. Management controls over financial activities have greatly strengthened over the years. The same cannot always be said of controls elsewhere in the enterprise. Embezzlement can hurt a corporation; the inept management of its resources can bankrupt it. Therein lies one of the basic differences between external auditing and modern internal auditing. The first is narrowly focused, the second is comprehensive in scope.

Furthermore, the external auditor has not been overly concerned with fraud or waste that does not have a significant effect on, or is not material to, the financial statements. The internal auditor, however, is vitally concerned with all manner of waste and fraud, whatever the source and however small the size. The concern does not stem from the need to check every minor deviation. Rather, it is rooted in the understanding that the tiny cloud can mushroom into a tempest that may rock the pillars of the enterprise.

The principal distinctions between the internal and external auditors are summarized in the following table. The positions and concerns of the modern internal auditor are compared to the traditionally financially oriented external auditor:

Internal Auditor	External Auditor
Is an organization's employee, or can be an independent entity (outsource or co-source).	Is an independent contractor.
Serves needs of the organization, though the function must be managed by the organization.	Serves third parties who need reliable financial information.
Focuses on future events by evaluating controls designed to assure the accomplishment of entity goals and objectives.	Focuses on the accuracy and understandability of historical events as expressed in financial statements.
Is directly concerned with the prevention of fraud in any form or extent in any activity reviewed.	Is incidentally concerned with the prevention and detection of fraud in general, but is directly concerned when financial statements may be materially affected.

Internal Auditor	External Auditor
Is independent of the activities audited, but is ready to respond to the needs and desires of all elements of management.	Is independent of management and the board of directors both in fact and in mental attitude.
Reviews activities continually.	Reviews records supporting financial statements periodically — usually once a year.[2]

The internal auditor and the external auditor must coordinate their efforts. The techniques used in financial audits by both internal and external auditors may be similar; but their aims and intended outcomes vary. They represent two distinct professions that must respect each other and make use of each other's talents.

Toward a Definition of Internal Auditing

Internal auditors throughout the world practice their work differently, depending on the audit scope dictated by senior management. As a result, articulating one definition that embraces the varied activities those auditors pursue is difficult.

Several definitions of modern internal auditing have been promulgated. The American Accounting Association defines it as "a systematic process of objectively obtaining and evaluating assertions about economic actions and events to ascertain the degree of correspondence between these assertions and established criteria and communicating the results to interested users." This definition is intended to describe the process applied to all types of audits; but the term "economic actions and events" demonstrates that its thrust is toward financial or accounting matters.

The IIA introduced its original *Standards for the Professional Practice of Internal Auditing (Standards)* with the following definition:

> *Internal auditing is an independent appraisal function established within an organization to examine and evaluate its activities as a service to the organization.*[3]

This statement is more an introduction than a definition. It gives no indication of the internal auditor's responsibilities, nor does it underscore that auditing is no longer exclusively tied to books of account.

In 1998 The IIA established a Guidance Task Force (GTF) to consider possible changes to the *Standards* and other guidance. One of the first and most critical elements of the GTF mission was to develop a new definition of internal auditing that would capture the modern essence of the profession and record it in as clear and concise a manner as possible.

In its deliberations, the GTF took into account comments and suggestions from IIA members, as well as a new "competency-based" definition that emerged from preliminary drafts of the *Competency Framework for Internal Auditing (CFIA)*, published in 1999 by The IIA Research Foundation. *CFIA* defines internal auditing as "a process by which an organization gains assurance that the risk exposures it faces are understood and managed appropriately in dynamically changing contexts."

In the spring of 1999 the GTF submitted the following definition for exposure and comment by IIA members:

> *Internal auditing is an objective assurance and consulting activity that is independently managed within an organization and guided by a philosophy of adding value to improve the operations of the organization. It assists an organization in accomplishing its objectives by bringing a systematic and disciplined approach to evaluate and improve the effectiveness of the organization's risk management, control, and governance processes.*

> *Internal auditing is a dynamic and evolving profession that anticipates change in its operating environment and adapts to changes in organizational structures, processes, and technology. Professionalism and a commitment to excellence are facilitated by operating within a framework of professional practice established by The Institute of Internal Auditors.*

In July 1999 The IIA Board of Directors adopted the following definition:

> *Internal auditing is an independent, objective assurance and consulting activity designed to add value and improve an organization's operations. It helps an organization accomplish its objectives by bringing a systematic, disciplined approach to evaluate and improve the effectiveness of risk management, control, and governance processes.*

A resolution creating a new Professional Practices Framework was also passed by The IIA Board. IIA's Internal Auditing Standards Board has developed all recommended changes to the *Standards*.

For the purposes of this book, the following definition has been created to describe the broad, unrestricted scope of modern internal auditing:

> *Internal auditing is a systematic, objective appraisal by internal auditors of the diverse operations and controls within an organization to determine whether (1) financial and operating information is accurate and reliable; (2) risks to the enterprise are identified and minimized; (3) external regulations and acceptable internal policies and procedures are followed; (4) satisfactory operating criteria are met; (5) resources are used efficiently and economically; and (6) the organization's objectives are effectively achieved — all for the purpose of consulting with management and for assisting members of the organization in the effective discharge of their governance responsibilities.*

This definition not only spells out the internal auditor's role and purpose, but it identifies opportunities and responsibilities. In addition, the definition embodies significant requirements spelled out in the *Standards* and captures the modern internal auditor's broadening emphasis on adding value and on all matters related to risk, governance, and control.

The Profession of Internal Auditing

Many occupations strive for professional identification. That identification applies to doctors, lawyers, and similar practitioners; but it is also used to identify people in other careers who receive money for their contributions. Thus it is applied to an athlete, a seamstress, a chef, or to a building inspector. But in evaluating a learned discipline, as distinguished from a trade or craft, we must apply criteria of a different kind.

The following catalog of criteria is often used to judge the professional quality of any occupation:

1. **Service to the public.** Internal auditors provide service by promoting the efficient and effective use of resources. Their code of ethics requires members of The IIA to avoid being party to any illegal or improper activity. In addition, internal auditors serve the public through their work with audit committees, boards of directors, and other governance bodies.

2. **Long specialized training.** In some instances and in some areas of the world, internal audit departments accept people with varying degrees of training or learning. Only those who have demonstrated training, passed tests, and earned certification can properly regard themselves as professionals.

3. **Subscription to a code of ethics.** Members must subscribe to The IIA's *Code of Ethics*. They also must follow the *Standards*. These documents are reprinted later in this chapter or in the book.

4. **Membership in an association and attendance at meetings.** The IIA is unquestionably a professional association. Yet in many countries, including the United States, The IIA accepts members who may be practicing internal auditing, but who have not been certified. In other countries, such as Ireland and England, passing certain tests is a requirement for full membership. The IIA may eventually consider the establishment of a separate branch, restricted to Certified Internal Auditors, who are board certified and who must follow a prescribed continuing education program.

5. **Publication of journals aimed at upgrading practice.** The IIA publishes a technical journal, *Internal Auditor*, as well as technical books, research studies, monographs, audiovisual presentations, and other instructional materials. Contributions are submitted by practitioners as well as by respected academicians and other experts.

6. **Examinations to test entrants' knowledge.** The IIA began its certification program in 1974. Candidates must pass a rigorous two-day examination covering a wide range of subjects. Successful candidates receive the designation of Certified Internal Auditor (CIA). As a foundation for the examination The IIA established a *Common Body of Knowledge* for those seeking to prepare themselves for that examination. In 1999 a *Competency Framework for Internal Auditors* was published in lieu of a third iteration of the *Common Body of Knowledge*.

7. **Licensure by the state or certification by a board.** The practice of internal auditing is not limited to licensees. Anyone who can convince an employer of one's internal auditing capability can be hired, and in many organizations a lack of certification is not necessarily a bar. Anyone working as an internal auditor can sign an internal audit report and render an internal audit opinion.[4]

But there are glimmers of change on the horizon. Some internal auditing organizations now insist that all members be certified or be working toward certification. A uniform auditing act prepared for state governments by the U.S. General Accounting Office requires a state auditor general to be a CPA or a CIA.

Thus, many attributes of a profession apply to internal auditing: a common body of knowledge, a certification program, a continuing professional development program, a code of ethics, a statement of responsibilities, a set of standards, a professional journal, and an increasing flow of literature.

Internal Auditing's Progress

When contrasted to professions such as medicine and the law, internal auditing is quite young. Even public accountants, who are relatively recent additions to the ranks of professionals, have a considerable head start on internal auditing, as the following comparisons show:

	External	Internal
First training school	1881	—
First university school	1881	—
First professional organization		
AICPA (originally the American		
Association of Public Accountants)	1886	
The Institute of Internal Auditors		1941
First state licensing law and examination	1896	—
First CIA examination		1974
Professional journals first published		
Journal of Accountancy	1905	
Internal Auditor		1943
First educational treatises published		
Dicksee's Auditing (England)	1892	
Montgomery's Auditing (U.S.)	1914	
Brink's Internal Auditing (U.S.)		1941
Sawyer's Modern Internal Auditing (U.S.)		1973
Formal *Code of Ethics*	1917	1968
Statement of Responsibilities		1947
Standards for Professional Practice	1954	1978[5]

Internal auditors have some catching up to do. Yet they have made remarkable strides in a relatively short time.

Statements of Responsibilities of Internal Auditing

In 1947 The IIA published its first *Statement of Responsibilities of Internal Auditing*. It was a bold step forward for that time because it dared to show the internal auditor's concern for "matters of an operating nature," although its emphasis was still on "accounting and financial matters." As the years passed, the emphasis on accounting diminished, and audits of operations loomed larger. The five *Statements* issued after 1947 (1957, 1971, 1976, 1981, and 1990) show the progress in a changing, expanding discipline.

One significant change concerns the philosophy of the later changes. The 1947 *Statement* was the sole arbiter of internal audit responsibility; however, the 1981 and the 1990 *Statements* were issued after the adoption of the *Standards* and took a subordinate role to the *Standards*. The *Statements* were referred to as summaries, and readers were sent to the *Standards* for "more specific guidelines." With the new *Standards* effective January 1, 2002, the *Responsibilities* will no longer be in effect.

The original *Statement of Responsibilities of Internal Auditing* was issued by The Institute of Internal Auditors in 1947. The *Statement* (now being eliminated) was revised in 1990, embodied the concepts previously established, and included changes as were deemed advisable in light of the status of the profession at that time. From an evolutionary point of view, it is interesting to note some of the major changes that were made:

- The words "statement of" were added to the title in the 1957 *Statement*. In 1981 the title words "internal auditor" were changed to "internal auditing" to conform to the title of the *Standards*.

- The 1947 *Statement* contained a Foreword citing its approval by The IIA's Board of Directors and pointing to the constant evolution of the profession; then the Foreword was eliminated in the 1971 *Statement*.

- The words "as a service to management" were first added in the 1957 *Statement*, but the *Standards* later broadened the concept of the internal auditor's services to include policy-making bodies such as boards of directors. Accordingly, the word "management" was changed to "organization" in the 1981 *Statement*.

- In the 1971 *Statement*, the phrase "accounting, financial, and other operations" was replaced by the single word "operations" to denote the comprehensive nature of modern internal auditing. Financial and accounting matters became a part of internal auditing, not the primary reason for its existence.

- The 1957 *Statement* referred to "furnishing them (members of management) with objective analyses, appraisals, recommendations, and pertinent comments." The 1981 *Statement* added the significant word "counsel" to agree with the *Standards* and hence show the internal auditor as a counselor rather than a critic.

- The 1947 *Statement* referred to "reviewing and appraising performance under the policies, plans, and procedures." The 1957 *Statement* broadened this concept with "quality of performance in carrying out assigned responsibilities." This carries the internal auditor's responsibilities beyond reviewing solely for compliance with the rules.

- According to the 1971 *Statement*, "the responsibilities of internal auditing should be clearly established by management policy." The 1981 *Statement*, following the *Standards*, suggested that the internal audit charter should not only be approved by management but also accepted by the board.

- The first reference to the *Code of Ethics* appeared in the 1971 *Statement*. The 1981 *Statement* added reference also to the *Standards*.

- Coordinating the internal auditing work with that of others was first mentioned in the 1971 *Statement*. That statement did not single out external auditors since internal auditors should also coordinate their programs with other control groups such as security, safety, quality control, and industrial engineering.

- Organizational status and objectivity are first mentioned in the 1971 *Statement*, although the concepts were alluded to in prior statements.

Code of Ethics

Professional codes of ethics evolved as a result of the special relationship between members of the learned professions and their patients or clients. Professional practitioners do not keep those they serve at arm's length. The business principle of *caveat emptor* (buyer beware) does not apply when professionals provide their services to lay people. The client and patient must place their trust in the ethical behavior of the professional. This trust is enhanced when the professional is required to take an oath to serve the public honestly and diligently and to be governed by strict rules of ethical behavior. Trust is increased if the seeker of professional services can believe that professionals who violate their code of ethics will be taken to task by their own peers. Thus, in any discipline aspiring to professionalism, a code of ethics, enforced by a professional body, adds validity to the claim of professionalism.

The IIA's first *Code of Ethics*, which was adopted on December 13, 1968, affected all members of The IIA. When the CIA program was adopted, a separate code was designed for CIAs. However, CIAs who were not members of The IIA could not be forced to abide by the bylaws of that organization, so that the CIA *Code of Ethics* had fewer provisions. Also, the introduction and preface of the CIA code differed from the IIA code. One significant difference was that violation of the CIA code was grounds for forfeiture of the CIA certificate. Differences between the two codes were eliminated in 1988, when a new *Code of Ethics* was adopted. The new code applies to both CIAs and non-CIAs.

The International Ethics Committee issued a set of proposed new statements on ethics on October 1, 1999. A final version was approved by the Board of Directors on June 17, 2000. There are two major changes in the new Code.

1. The code is applied to all "internal auditing professionals" rather than to "IIA members and CIA's." This is to relate the Code to all individuals and organizations performing internal auditing, regardless of location or relationship to the organization.

2. The Code is divided into three major parts:
   Introduction
   Fundamental Principles
   Code of Conduct

   Within the two latter divisions the Code is reported into five elements
   Integrity
   Objectivity
   Confidentiality
   Professionalism
   Competency

Essentially there is little change in the basic thrust of the provisions of the old and new Codes.

The revised *Code of Ethics* is shown as Exhibit C in Chapter 31.

All internal auditing professionals are bound by the *Code of Ethics*, and violation of its terms is subject to forfeiture of membership and the CIA designation. A code is of special significance to internal auditors because it proclaims internal auditing's primary reason for being. Management must rest assured that it can trust its internal auditors implicitly. Management must have the secure feeling that if its internal auditors report something, then it just has to be true, valid, and objective. It has to be completely without bias.

These attributes must never be compromised. And internal auditors must guard jealously their reputation for objectivity and freedom from bias, not only in fact, but in perception. For example, internal auditors should not perform personal work for employees or managers; they should not be connected with suppliers or competing firms; they should not put their knowledge of the enterprise to personal use; and they should not accept gifts of any material value from entity employees. The prohibitions are many and impossible to catalog, but internal auditors should take steps to avoid even a hint that objectivity is being compromised. In such cases the perception is as important as the reality. Also, internal auditors must exhibit loyalty to their employers. They are members of the management team and should conduct themselves as senior managers would. Yet they must not knowingly be party to any illegal or improper activity. Where such activity is encountered, it should be reported to the proper authorities within the enterprise. Under the *Code of Ethics* internal auditors have no responsibility to report to agencies outside the enterprise unless they are specifically compelled to do so by law.

The *Common Body of Knowledge (CBOK)*

An essential building block in the structure of a profession is a common body of knowledge. It forms the conceptual foundation of the discipline and serves as the standard for education, training, recruiting, and testing the competence of those who aspire to enter the profession. The IIA's *Common Body of Knowledge (CBOK)* was adopted in 1972 and was revised and reissued in 1992. The revision cataloged 334 individual competencies allocated to 20 different disciplines.

CFIA was originally intended to be the third iteration of *CBOK*. However, it evolved into a comprehensive study that documents and defines internal auditing and its competencies on a global scale.

CFIA Findings

The mission of the *CFIA* research team, led by project director William Birkett, was to "find the essence" of the global profession of internal auditing and to update information on competencies needed for internal auditors throughout the world. The researchers surveyed the internal auditing profession from several perspectives: the global profession, internal auditing knowledge, the future of the profession, best practices, competency, and competency assessment. Answers to four key questions were sought:

1. What is to be understood by internal auditing in the future from a global perspective?
2. What are the attributes of a competent internal auditing function from a best-practice perspective?
3. What capabilities should be required of those in a competent internal audit function?
4. How is the competency of internal auditors and an internal audit function best assessed?

The *CFIA* study emphasizes that rampant change within business environments must be matched by changes within internal auditing, especially in terms of the expectations that organizations have of the profession, the way practitioners deliver their services, and the interaction between internal auditing and other service providers. The report advocates a "fuller context" for internal audit tasks, including:

- Maintaining relationships and communications throughout the organization.
- Assessing current and emerging risk exposures.
- Sharing expertise, knowledge, and ideas.
- Developing understanding in the organization about risk and control.
- Facilitating the adoption and implementation of control self-assessment.

The research team's four questions were integrated throughout the five modules of the study:

- *Internal Auditing: The Global Landscape*
- *Competency: Best Practices and Competent Practitioners*
- *Internal Auditing Knowledge: Global Perspectives*
- *The Future of Internal Auditing: A Delphi Study*
- *Assessing Competency in Internal Auditing: Structures and Methodologies*

Each module is a different study in terms of data sources, methodologies, and formats. While the modules are separate, they are interrelated and provide cross-validation for the research findings.

The *Competency: Best Practices and Competent Practitioners* module is divided into sections that include Field of Practice; Functional Definition; Units and Elements of Competency; and Performance Criteria, Cues, and Key Work Roles. The research is based on the assumption that elements of competency and their performance criteria together define competent practice for the function and provide the basis for its assessment. Elements of competency and individual attributes are defined according to the work roles of "entering internal auditor," "competent internal auditor," and "internal auditing management."

Exhibit 1-1
Competency: Best Practices and Competent Practitioners
Executive Summary

In early 1996 The Institute of Internal Auditors Research Foundation initiated a project designed to establish a Global Competency Framework for Internal Auditing. The centerpiece of the project was to be a study focused on the development of Competency Standards for Internal Auditing that would be applicable globally.

The use of a distinctive research methodology, together with a range of input from 200 expert practitioners around the world, justify the claim that the competency standards developed represent "best practice" globally.

The competency standards establish and elaborate a new definition (for its own purposes) of internal auditing:

Internal auditing is a process by which an organization gains assurance that the risk exposures it faces are understood and managed appropriately in dynamically changing contexts.

Exhibit 1-1 (Cont.)

With this point of reference, the competency standards then establish:

- The attributes of a competent internal auditing function, in the light of global "best practice."
- The capabilities required of key role-takers in a competent internal auditing function.

In this project "competency" refers to a relational notion — the way in which individual attributes (knowledge, skills, attitudes) are drawn on in performing tasks in particular work contexts. Competency is realized in performance. Hence, it can be defined by reference to particular types of contextual task performance, in terms of what is to be performed, and how well a performance is to be constituted. The performances thus defined are referred to as competency standards.

Competency standards establish an appropriate linkage between

- Tasks to be performed.
- The contexts in which tasks are to be performed.
- Specified performance criteria.
- Individual attributes entailed by the performance.

The following diagram is illustrative.

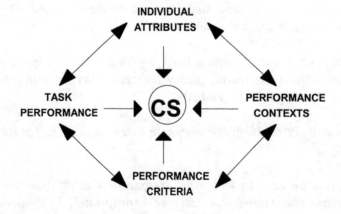

Exhibit 1-1 (Cont.)

In developing the competency standards, reference is made to a particular language for describing and structuring the components of competency.

Thus, internal auditing is delineated as a field of practice in terms of the function it serves within organizations. "Units of competency" is the label given to the set of tasks whose performance is both necessary and sufficient to meet the functional requirements of the field of practice. "Elements of competency" is a label used to refer to coherent and sensible clusters of sub-tasks whose performance is necessary and sufficient to meet the outcomes entailed by particular units of competency. "Performance criteria" refers to aspects of professional performance that are indicative of whether an element of competency was performed competently or not.

Units of competency and elements of competency were established for internal auditing as a field of practice, and performance criteria were defined for each element of competency (along with "cues" to guide the assessment of performance against them). The "individual attributes" associated with the field of practice were identified also, using a special taxonomy of cognitive and behavioral skills (both skills were seen as necessary to secure competent performance of internal auditing work).

As a result it was possible to define competency standards relating to competent practice in internal auditing by reference to both performance outcomes and the individual attributes drawn on selectively in producing such outcomes. The following diagram is illustrative.

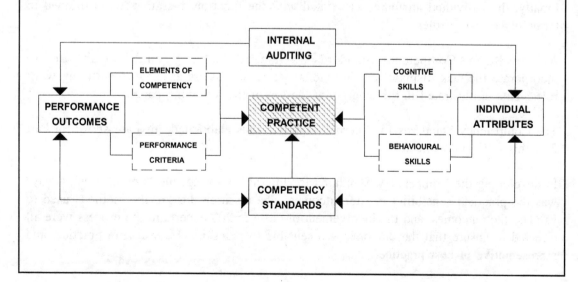

Exhibit 1-1 (Cont.)

The competency standards relating to competent internal auditing practice are shown in Part 2 of this document. (Not to be confused with the competency standards of the revised IIA *Standards*.)

In the study, a distinction is made between competent practice as an outcome secured through teamwork (for example, through the joint work of the entire staff of an internal auditing function) and the differentiated roles taken by individuals as part of the team. Thus, a distinction is drawn between competent practice as a team-produced outcome, and competent practitioners taking key roles in relation to that outcome.

Roles are defined in terms of the assignment of responsibilities and commensurate authority, and in terms of (mutual) expectations about performance. Also implicit in the specification of roles are expectations about the substantive understandings (knowledge) necessary for effective role performance.

Three key work roles were delineated in relation to an internal auditing function: Entering Internal Auditor; Competent Internal Auditor; and Internal Auditing Management. A competent internal auditing function was seen to be constituted through the interaction of these key roles. The three roles were specified in relation to each element of competency and as composites relating to the internal auditing function overall (in developing composite roles, the substantive understandings were drawn out separately to enhance their visibility and their accessibility for assessment purposes).

Finally, the individual attributes associated with the function overall were partitioned in terms of key work roles.

As a result, the Competency Standards for Internal Auditing could be elaborated to incorporate the task displays and individual attribute clusters associated with key work roles. This is illustrated in the diagram at the top of the following page.

The Competency Standards for Internal Auditing, thus elaborated, also are shown in Part 2 of this (*CFIA*) document.

In developing the Competency Standards for Internal Auditing, the "bottom line" always was the practical sensibility of the outcomes. The research design, the methods used to validate the outcomes, and the involvement of close to 200 experts in the process were all directed to ensure that the outcome was sensible to practitioners, useful in practice, and representative of best practice.

Exhibit 1-1 (Cont.)

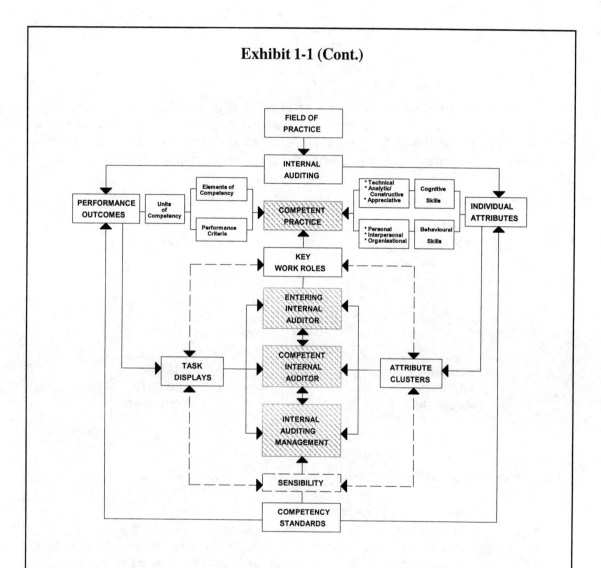

The Competency Standards for Internal Auditing stand as an independently produced, global point of reference or benchmark. Hence, they can be used in various ways by a range of interested parties.

Users (clients/consumers) of internal auditing services may use them to understand the nature of the service they are receiving and to evaluate its quality. Internal auditing managers may use them in assessing the structures, capabilities, and functioning of their own functions, and in the developmental needs of their functions and themselves personally. Internal auditing practitioners may use them to assess the contributions they could make

Exhibit 1-1 (Cont.)

to the work of the function and their own developmental needs. Professional associations (or other groups or authorities) may use them as a basis for peer/quality assurance reviews, and as a basis for admission to membership, certification of competence, and definition of continuing education needs or requirements. The following diagram is illustrative.

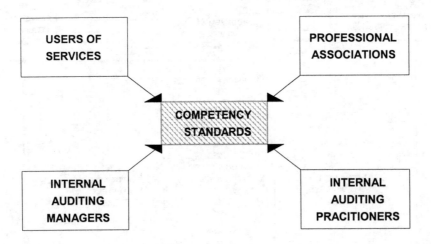

The Competency Standards for Internal Auditing can be used as:

- A benchmark of best practice.
- A resource for development within organizations.
- A framework for exploring relationships between practice, education, and training.
- A mode of facilitating communication globally between interested parties about internal auditing.

While the (*CFIA*) Competency Standards for Internal Auditing suit the field of practice generally, they still need to be suited to the circumstances of particular user contexts (applications, organizations, industries, sectors, countries). Thus, they serve both as an independent point of reference and as a resource that is adaptable for various uses.

Original *Standards for the Professional Practice of Internal Auditing*

The IIA formally adopted a set of standards for internal auditors worldwide in June 1978 at the International Conference in San Francisco. Five general standards provided a framework: Independence, Professional Proficiency, Scope of Work, Performance of Audit Work, and Management of the Internal Auditing Department. These five general standards were collectively followed by 25 specific standards. Accompanying each specific standard were guidelines showing appropriate means of meeting the standards. The original *Standards* are available from the 4th Edition of this work and from other publications of The Institute of Internal Auditors. The updated *Standards* effective January 1, 2002, are shown in Chapter 31. However, the introduction to the *Standards* follows as Exhibit 1-2.

Exhibit 1-2
Standards for the Professional Practice of Internal Auditing

INTRODUCTION

Internal auditing is an independent objective assurance and consulting activity designed to add value and improve an organization's operations. It helps an organization accomplish its objectives by bringing a systematic, disciplined approach to evaluate and improve the effectiveness of risk management, control, and governance processes.

Internal audit activities are performed in diverse legal and cultural environments; within organizations that vary in purpose, size, and structure; and by personas within or outside the organization. These differences may affect the practice of internal auditing in each environment. However, compliance with the *Standards for Professional Practice of Internal Auditing (Standards)* is essential if the responsibilities of internal auditors are to be met.

The purpose of the *Standards* is to:

1. Delineate basic principles that represent the practice of internal auditing as it should be.
2. Provide a framework for performing and promoting a broad range of value-added internal audit activities.
3. Establish the basis for the measurement of internal audit performance.
4. Foster improved organizational processes and operations.

Exhibit 1-2 (Cont.)

The *Standards* consist of Attribute Standards (the 1000 Series), Performance Standards (the 2000 Series), and Implementation Standards (nnnn.Xn). The Attribute Standards address the characteristics of organizations and individuals performing internal audit activities. The Performance Standards describe the nature of internal audit activities and provide quality criteria against which the performance of these services can be measured. The Attribute and Performance Standards apply to internal audit services in general. The Implementation Standards apply the Attribute and Performance Standards to specific types of engagement (for example, a compliance audit, a fraud investigation, or a control self-assessment project).

There is one set of Attribute and Performance Standards, however there may be multiple sets of Implementation Standards: a set for each of the major types of internal audit activity. Initially, the Implementation Standards are being established for assurance activities (noted by an "A" following the *Standard* number, e.g., 1130.A1) and consulting activities (noted by a "C" following the *Standard* number, e.g., nnnn.C1).

The *Standards* are part of the Professional Practices Framework. This framework was proposed by the Guidance Task Force and approved by The IIA's Board of Directors in June 1999. It includes the definition of internal auditing, the *Code of Ethics*, the *Standards*, and other guidance. The *Standards* incorporate the guidance previously contained in the "Red Book," recasting it into the new format proposed by the Guidance Task Force and updating it as recommended in the Task Force's report, *A Vision for the Future*.

The *Standards* employ terms that have been given specific meanings that are included in the Glossary.

The Internal Auditing Standards Board is committed to extensive consultation in the preparation of the *Standards*. Prior to issuing any document, the Standards Board issues exposure drafts internationally for public comment. The Standards Board also seeks those with special expertise or interest for consultation where necessary. The development of standards is an ongoing process. The Standards Board welcomes input from IIA members and other interested parties to identify emerging issues requiring new standards or revision to current standards.

Additional guidance regarding how the *Standards* might be put into practice can be found in Practice Advisories that are issued by the Professional Issues Committee.

Differences in *Standards* application. Internal auditors around the world practice their craft in different ways. Most of them work under the direction of senior managers, who hire and fire them and recommend their salaries, salary increases, and retention. These senior managers run the gamut from chief accountant to chief executive officer. Some internal auditors report directly to audit committees of the board of directors or to similar bodies.

Many practitioners have charters giving them access to all records, properties, and people within the entire organization. Others do not have charters at all. Currently, some are providing consulting services, risk analysis and assisting through their work in organizational governance. Still others are confined to making financial verifications within accounting departments. Such diverse environments obviously result in varied internal audit practice. As a result, The IIA sets consistent standards to constitute what is considered professional practice.

Certainly, no set of standards prepared by internal auditors can tell managers or board members how to use their internal audit operations. The *Standards*, therefore, carefully avoid imposing any criteria on managers or board members. Internal auditors may be bound by the restrictions management places upon them. But if these restrictions prevent them from complying with the *Standards*, then neither those auditors nor their superiors will have any basis for saying that the auditors are doing professional audit work. To be viewed by outsiders as performing professionally, an internal audit function would have to demonstrate that it is complying with the *Standards*.

No such document or body of standards could remain unaltered or unalterable over the years. Provision had been made for a formal method of changes, augmentation, and interpretations under the jurisdiction of what was once called the IIA Professional Standards Committee and is now called the Internal Auditing Standards Board (IASB).

Specific standards and guidelines. The original committee did anticipate changes in this area. When changes did occur, they addressed significant matters only and were titled *Statements on Internal Auditing Standards (SIASs)*. After several were issued, the original *Standards* were updated in a codification document. Any changes to the specific standards or guidelines represented the official IIA position, and were approved by The IIA's Board of Directors. These authoritative pronouncements were equal in force and effect to the original *Standards* as issued in 1978. *SIASs* were issued on the following subjects:

1. Control: Concepts and Responsibilities
2. Communicating Results
3. Deterrence, Detection, Investigation, and Reporting of Fraud
4. Quality Assurance
5. Internal Auditors' Relationships with Independent Outside Auditors

6. Audit Working Papers
7. Communication with the Board of Directors
8. Analytical Auditing Procedures
9. Risk Assessment
10. Evaluating the Accomplishment of Established Objectives and Goals for Operations or Programs
11. 1992 Omnibus Statement
12. Planning the Audit Assignment
13. Follow-up on Reported Audit Findings
14. Glossary
15. Supervision
16. Auditing Compliance with Policies, Plans, Procedures, Laws, Regulations, and Contracts
17. Assessment of Performance of External Auditors
18. Use of Outside Service Providers

The *SIASs* are not a part of the new *Standards* framework. A new structure is under consideration by the GTF.

Semi-authoritative pronouncements. From 1981 through 1989 The IIA issued a series of pronouncements called *Professional Standards Bulletins (PSBs),* which provided explanations of existing standards and guidelines. In 1996 and 1997 *Professional Standards Practices Releases (PSPRs),* another form of guidance, were also issued. These pronouncements are no longer being developed and are not a part of the new framework.

In accordance with previous practice, the IASB continues to respond to written questions about the *Standards.* Responses are researched and written by The IIA's Practices Center and then reviewed and endorsed by the IASB.

Certification Program

Once the first *Common Body of Knowledge* was adopted, the way was clear for a certification program. The Board of Directors adopted the program in 1972, and the first examination was held on August 16 and 17, 1974.

About 7,900 practicing internal auditors, out of about 8,500 who applied, received the CIA designation under the so-called "grandfather" clause. The successful candidates demonstrated that they had practiced internal auditing in a decision-making capacity and agreed to abide by The IIA's *Code of Ethics.* In October 1973 they were awarded certificates designating them as CIAs. In March 1975, the CIA designation was awarded to 122 out of 654 candidates who sat for the first CIA examination in 1974. By June 2002, more than 35,000 candidates who sat for the exam around the world became CIAs.

The CIA exam tests a candidate's knowledge and ability regarding the current practice of internal auditing. The exam addresses management skills, principles of management control, risk management, internal controls, information technology, emerging strategies for improving business and government, and other related topics.

Although the largest number of certifications has historically been awarded in the United States and Canada, the exam is also given in any other place in the world where sufficient applications are received to warrant holding the examination. As of 1999, the examination is offered in English, French, Hebrew, Mandarin Chinese, Spanish, German, Thai, and Italian. Candidates may sit for the exam in May and November of each year. The first examination was based on the original *CBOK*. When the *CBOK* was revised in 1992, the examination was restructured to conform. The latest version of the exam is also based on *CFIA*.

Plans are underway for computerization of the CIA exam. The electronic exam will take into account issues such as ease of translation and continuing enhancements regarding the statistical validity of the exam. Initial concepts call for an "exam-on-demand" that could be offered at various testing sites around the world.

Eligibility

Two years of work experience is required for the CIA designation. To satisfy this requirement, work as an internal or external auditor or as an auditor in public accounting is understood to mean the rendering of services such as those customarily performed by a full-time, regularly employed audit staff. Candidates' experience must be attested to by their supervisors, another appropriate member of their organization, or a CIA. The following conditions may also affect CIA eligibility:

- An advanced academic degree beyond the baccalaureate is considered as equivalent to one year of work experience.

- Auditing experience in public accounting qualifies as work experience in internal auditing.

- Full-time college or university-level teaching in the subject matter of the examination is considered as equivalent to work experience, on the basis of two years of teaching equaling one year of internal audit experience.

Competencies to be tested. Only those competencies that can be effectively tested by objective examinations are tested. Other competencies, such as effective listening skills, while significant for the working internal auditor, are not part of the exam.

Nature of questions. Although essay questions were included in the original exam, all four parts are now objective. Each part consists of 80 multiple-choice questions.

Non-disclosure. The exam is non-disclosed, which means that candidates must return their question booklets with their answer sheets at the conclusion of the examination. In addition, candidates must sign a statement asserting that they will not divulge questions and answers after the exam is administered.

Internationalization. The exam covers skills applicable to internal auditors regardless of the country or culture in which an internal auditor might practice. However, Part IV of the exam previously contained material, such as financial accounting, which was oriented to North America. The Board has now adopted a policy whereby it will work with National Institutes or regions that demonstrate a specific *CBOK* for their region. The Board has developed a framework for those regions to develop their own Part IV of the exam consistent with the current certification standards and objectives.

Transition for candidates in process. The exam's four-part structure has continued as revisions in the exam have occurred. Anyone who receives credit for any part of the exam prior to the implementation of the new exam receives credit for that same part on the new exam.

Evolutionary changes. As new material becomes established in practice, the exam reflects the new knowledge requirements that are important to internal auditing. Any major changes are announced to candidates.

Examination format. The difficulty of exam questions is structured. Each of the multiple-choice questions is assigned one of three levels of difficulty:

- **Proficiency.** Candidate exhibits the ability to understand and apply the subject matter in the workplace on a regular basis with skill and expertise.

- **Understanding.** Candidate exhibits sound understanding and ability to apply the competency. Candidates should understand relationships and problems involving the competency and apply the competency to new and different settings and the solution of problems.

- **Awareness.** Candidate exhibits basic awareness and knowledge. Candidate is able to define terms, recognize issues, and recall facts about the issues.

The material on which candidates are tested is divided into four general areas:

- **Part I, Internal Audit Process.** The theory and practice of internal auditing. Major topics include auditing, professionalism, and fraud.

- **Part II, Internal Audit Skills.** Problem solving and evaluating audit evidence; data gathering, documentation, and reporting; and sampling and mathematics.

- **Part III, Management Control and Information Technology.** Basic business disciplines essential to the practice of internal auditing. Major test areas include management control; operations management; and information technology.

- **Part IV, The Audit Environment.** Financial accounting; finance; managerial accounting; and the regulatory environment.

Professional Recognition Credit for Part IV

The IIA's Board of Regents (BOR), the volunteer group that provides guidance regarding the certification program, has recognized that regional and cultural differences and industry-specific needs require specialized audit knowledge, training, and professional development. Candidates who have received professional, non-IIA certifications that have been approved by the BOR may qualify for professional recognition credit (PRC) for Part IV of the CIA exam. Candidates who attain the PRC for Part IV and pass Parts I, II, and III will have satisfied the examination requirement for the CIA designation.

Specialty Certifications

Three separate new IIA examinations have been developed. The Certification in Control Self-assessment (CCSA) will test candidates' knowledge of control self-assessment fundamentals, process, and integration, as well as their understanding of important related topics such as risk, controls, and business objectives.

The Certified Government Auditing Professional (CGAP) designation is a global exam designed to test the knowledge and competency of governmental auditors. The Certified Financial Services Auditor (CFSA), the IIA's newest specialty certification, demonstrates competency in financial services auditing practices and methodologies. CIA candidates may submit either the CCSA, the CGAP, or the CFSA for Part IV PRC credit on the exam.

The Auditing Activity

Despite the breadth of modern internal auditing, the forms of audits practiced today fall into three fundamental categories: financial, compliance, and operational. Each of the three may receive varying emphasis in different organizations and countries; and structures and specific practices are often divergent.

Financial. The analysis of the economic activity of an entity as measured and reported by accounting methods.

Compliance. The review of both financial and operating controls and transactions to see how they conform with established laws, standards, regulations, and procedures.

Operational. The comprehensive review of the varied functions within an enterprise to appraise the efficiency and economy of operations and the effectiveness with which those functions achieve their objectives.

Both internal and external auditors (including outsourcing and cosourcing) may perform these types of audits. Once again, however, traditional external auditing emphasis is on fairness of financial representation, whereas internal auditing emphasis is on assisting managers and boards of directors or similar governing bodies in optimum governance and the proper discharge of their duties.

Approaches

To achieve their respective goals, internal auditors may rely on several different approaches. Comprehensive auditing, management-oriented auditing, participative auditing, and program auditing are among the most widely known approaches. Many of these terms overlap and they are likely to be conducted with some subtle variances; but all come under the rubric of the general term "internal auditing" when they are performed by employees of the entity.

Comprehensive Auditing — A term first used by the U.S. General Accounting Office (GAO) to encompass the audits of all activities within a government entity. Comprehensive auditing heralded the GAO's extension of auditing to operating activities.

Management-oriented Auditing — Reviews of all activities according to the perspectives of a manager or a management consultant. Management-oriented auditing is distinguished from other forms more by audit outlook than by audit procedures. Management-oriented auditing is clearly focused on helping the organization to achieve its objectives. A significant result is to help managers manage better and to make the manager, rather than the auditor, look good.

Management-oriented auditing should not be confused with "management auditing," which implies the audit of managers themselves. Professional auditors avoid such implication because the only true evaluators of managers are their own superiors.

Participative Auditing — A process that involves enlisting the aid of the client in gathering data, evaluating operations, and correcting problems. In effect, it is a problem-solving partnership; and it is sometimes called partnership auditing.

Program Auditing — The review of entire programs, public or private, to determine whether desired benefits are being achieved. In this sense, "program" means the composite of plans and procedures established to achieve some specific end. It differs from reviews of continuing activities within an enterprise.

Assurance and Consultative Auditing[6]

As a result of the work of the Guidance Task Force (GTF) two new approaches have been identified — Assurance and Consultative. The former relates to auditing where the internal auditor provides information relative to the status of the client organization as to the traditional areas such as financial, compliance, operational, economy and efficiency audits as well as newer forms such as control and risk management audits. They provide an assessment of the reliability and/or relevance of data and operations in specific areas. Consultative auditing consists of problem-solving methodologies seeking to make direct improvements in the circumstances or conditions of the client. Although the basic thrusts of the two approaches are different, audits can contain elements of both, i.e., defining the status quo and supplementing that with recommendations for change and improvement.

Control Self-assessment

During the past decade, control self-assessment (CSA), a nontraditional auditing approach, has been adopted in many organizations as a valuable governance tool. The methodology, which was initiated at Gulf Canada in 1987, is explained in detail in Chapter 10.

CSA workshops involve employees in assessing the adequacy of controls, identifying opportunities for improvement, evaluating risks, pinpointing strengths and weaknesses, determining the likelihood of achieving business objectives, and developing action plans. Internal auditors, acting as facilitators, bring together work teams that may represent multiple levels within an organization. In a group setting, auditors use questionnaires, electronic voting equipment, or other strategies to help gather information from participants. The facilitated workshops typically uncover valuable information that might not be revealed in traditional audits, especially in "soft control" areas such as control environment, morale, and communication. In addition, CSA enhances participants' skills in self-control and encourages workers' commitment to continuous process improvement.

CSA represents a dramatic change in mindset for many internal auditors, and it requires skill sets — in facilitating, negotiating, and communicating, for example — that have not historically been emphasized in more conventional internal auditing methods. Even the most ardent advocates of CSA do not suggest that it should replace other internal auditing strategies, however. It is considered as only one of the auditor's tools, albeit one with great potential.

In 1998 The IIA established a Control Self-assessment Center, which supports the development of knowledge surrounding the implementation of self-assessment workshops and techniques. Enrollment is open not only to internal auditors, but also to audit committee members, management, and internal control specialists.

The IIA has also established a Certification in Control Self-assessment, the first specialty certification to be offered by The IIA Board of Regents. The CCSA program identifies the skill sets needed by successful practitioners of CSA, measures understanding of CSA, and provides guidance for CSA initiatives.

Audit Specialties

"Audit specialties" in fields such as healthcare, utilities, information systems, government, universities, and gaming have evolved in recent years. Recognizing the unique and complex requirements of their niches, many internal auditors in these areas have sought more opportunities to establish communication and share specific information with colleagues in the same fields.

At the same time, approaches like CSA, forensic auditing, and environmental auditing have spawned a similar trend across industries. To support internal auditors with specialized interests, The IIA has developed targeted publications, Web sites and links, online forums, membership directories, seminars, conference offerings, and centers. These offerings respond to the needs of internal auditors who want to complement their professional competencies and knowledge base with additional expertise, either within industries or in other arenas. Internal auditors can now take advantage of The IIA's Gaming Audit Group, the Control Self-assessment Center, the Board of Environmental Auditor Certifications (BEAC), a Government Auditors Resource Center, and an online forum for healthcare auditors. The IIA has also established links with the Association of College and University Auditors and the Association of Credit Union Internal Auditors.

In some instances, The IIA's alliances with other groups have helped to strengthen and broaden specialty resources. BEAC, for example, is a cooperative effort of the Environmental Auditing Roundtable and The IIA. Its aim is to certify competency in environmental auditing and related scientific fields. The global risks associated with environmental auditing have made it a compelling concern for many corporations. Environmental standards developed by the International Standards Organization (ISO 14000) have provided guidelines that internal auditors and others can use to provide environmental audits.

Outsourcing

All forms of auditing might conceivably be performed by external service providers in an "outsourcing" arrangement. Also many external organizations perform cosourcing, strategic partnering, and loan staffing. Contract employees who are engaged to make such evaluations are not strictly internal auditors, however. The scope and nature of their work is generally defined by their contract of employment.

As a result of several factors, including organizational downsizing and aggressive marketing by external accounting firms, outsourced internal auditing has become more prevalent. In some instances, a core internal auditing function supplements its services by bringing in contract auditors with specialized skills in areas where expertise is needed only for short-term engagements.

A Core Function

The concept of core functions, those elements of an organization that are integral, essential, and unassignable, has frequently been explored within the context of internal auditing. Successful organizations obviously must coalesce its key internal constituencies; but declaring what are and aren't core functions has sometimes been arguable.

Mary Ellen Oliverio, professor of accounting at the Lubin School of Business of Pace University in New York City, has developed the following set of questions designed to help internal auditing departments determine whether or not theirs is a core function:

- Do the CEO's words and behavior reflect value added by the internal audit in implementing the tone at the top that unrelentingly supports a control environment of integrity and impeccable trust?

- Is the organization's culture one where the contribution of the internal auditors is perceived to have a positive and pervasive value?

- Is the head of internal audit one of the most astute and knowledgeable executives as far as the total organization's goals, operations, and strategic plans are concerned?

- Does the chief audit executive (CAE) provide the vision and leadership for the function's activities that are determined based on an independent review of what is best for the total company?

- Does the executive committee seek the observations, recommendations, and opinions of the internal audit department?

- Is experience as an internal auditor perceived to develop broad, insightful understanding of the total organization so that transfer to operational departments is a common practice?

- Is a strategy in place to ensure that the internal audit staff is responsive to contemporary developments such as risk assessment and cooperative participating with line management to maintain and monitor internal control (as identified in the COSO report)?

- Is the CAE free to meet with the audit committee where candidness about problems and issues is expected and the CEO and/or the executive committee are not present?

- Does the CAE meet with the audit committee without first getting approval for presentations from the CEO or the executive committee?

- Is the internal audit staff provided with training and carefully designed experience to meet the emerging needs of the entity on a timely basis?[7]

Oliverio maintains that if the answer to each of the questions is "yes," there is high probability that internal auditing is a core function. In such an organization, she asserts that the internal audit function is so broadly and deeply integrated into all that is happening in the entity that to outsource the function is to cut off a valuable dimension to the total organization.

How Internal Auditors Can Serve Management

Internal auditing evolved to satisfy management needs, and the most effective audit staffs keep management and organizational objectives at the forefront of their own planning and activities. Audit goals are aligned with those of management, so that internal auditors position themselves to produce the highest possible value in areas that management regards as most crucial to organizational success.

Internal auditing's contributions have become particularly important as business and government have become huge, complex systems. It is impossible for executives to monitor all the activities for which they are responsible. Yet the fact remains that the uninspected inevitably deteriorates. Unmonitored activities will most certainly lose their efficiency and their effectiveness. It has been said that the best fertilizer for the soil is the shadow of the owner, but for many activities the shadow is woefully short. The owners need surrogates who think like them and can be relied upon completely and utterly. In many cases that surrogate is the management-oriented internal auditor.

Unfortunately, some managers are unaware of the benefits awaiting them at their own doorsteps. Often the internal auditors themselves have not educated management to those benefits. Yet most internal audit organizations are equipped to perform much more than financial verifications. One internal audit organization, for example, was staffed with Certified Public Accountants (CPAs), attorneys, economists, industrial engineers, and mathematicians.

Thus their scope of expertise could encompass most management problems. In such situations the internal auditing department is well qualified to assist management in:

- **Monitoring activities top management cannot itself monitor.** Each year the CAE prepares a schedule of proposed audits that specify the activities to be monitored. These are presented to executive management and the board and are adjusted according to shifts in organizational strategies and the needs and wishes of senior officials. In addition, CAEs make certain that time and resources are available for audits that cannot be expected or projected when the annual plan is created. In volatile business environments, such audits become more and more common as internal auditors respond to management needs and concerns that surface quickly. In fact, some internal audit departments have adopted a "just-in-time" approach to audit scheduling so that they can maximize their responsiveness to management needs.

- **Identifying and minimizing risks.** At one time businesses relied on insurance policies to offset risks, but many of the world's largest organizations are now establishing proactive risk management functions. This holistic approach to risk encompasses all potential exposures to a company, from legal, political, and regulatory issues, to shareholder relations, the effects of competition, and management competence. Internal auditors are broadening their perception of risk management and expanding their efforts to assure management that organizational risks of all types are being properly evaluated and addressed.

- **Validating reports to senior management.** Senior managers typically make their decisions on the basis of reports they receive, rather than on personal knowledge. Accurate, timely reports are more likely to produce knowledgeable decisions. Some audit organizations make lists of such executive reports and reference them to scheduled audits. When such audits are made, the auditors review the reports for accuracy, timeliness, and meaningfulness. Management decisions are then more likely to be valid.

- **Protecting management in technical fields.** Technology has had a tremendous impact on what and how auditing is performed. Modern internal auditors must know how data originates, how it is processed, and where the security risks lie. As many traditional auditing procedures are replaced by electronic data processing, all internal auditors need at least some level of technical expertise. In fact, security of data has become one of the greatest risks faced by modern organizations.

The growing complexity of business and government affairs brings with it arcane matters that are often beyond the scope of the manager who must decide on them. Three examples show how internal auditors have been able to help in specific instances:

> The budget manager in a financial division proposed a method of developing overhead rates on the basis of a computer program using multiple regression analysis. The vice president of finance had no knowledge of the field and, therefore, no basis for approving or rejecting the plan. He called on the internal auditors, who processed the subordinates' calculations on a comparable program they developed. The initial process revealed errors that were corrected, and the budget manager's program then passed the test. As a result, the vice president was able to approve the proposed program with confidence.

> U.S. government auditors employed a new method of evaluating the productivity of indirect employees in certain departments of a large government contractor. The auditors made a series of random observations of employee activity that were plotted on a curve and then analyzed by employing the so-called "asymptote to the curve." Based on these observations the auditors calculated an annual cost avoidance for five departments at about $500,000, which the government auditor sought to recover.

> When faced with a potential loss of half a million dollars, management called on their internal auditors. The auditors fired up their own computer programs and also examined the literature on work sampling, probability theory, and least squares. They then pointed out to the government auditors that their curves and dollar projections were suspect; that observations during a deliberately selected two-week period could not be considered representative of a whole year; that projections of samples from a shifting population are not statistically supportable; and that the use of the asymptote as a measure of productivity is open to question. In the face of this defense the government auditors softened their tone and agreed to a mutually acceptable solution.[8]

- **Helping in the decision-making process.** Managers, not internal auditors, make operating decisions. But internal auditors can supply or validate the data on which those decisions are made. Also, they can evaluate the effect of decisions made and point out risks that were not anticipated. For example:

> In one organization, management decided to make a major change in a large product line. The change involved redesign of the product and the purchase of new parts to replace the old. The internal auditors, reviewing the results of the decision, learned that the purchasing agents had been instructed on what new parts to buy. But nobody had alerted them to cancel the orders for the old parts that were now obsolete. The

auditors immediately notified management, who promptly issued instructions to cancel orders for superseded parts.

- **Reviewing for the future — not just for the past.** The U.S. General Accounting Office has pioneered the so-called program audits. Under this approach they have assessed policies or programs still in the design phase, the implementation of a policy or program, and the actual results achieved by a policy or program. Also, internal auditors now appraise controls over proposed information systems before implementation, thereby helping to avoid the enormous costs of trying to correct defects after the fact. Most modern internal auditors acknowledge that audits of the present and the future have become far more valuable to management than audits of the past.

- **Helping managers manage.** Managers who are not in control of their activities develop problems. The internal auditors generally find the problems and suggest corrections. However, those corrections can either be "quick fixes," or they can reach the roots of the problems and improve management as well. Here are some examples that show both surface and root solutions.

  A planning problem. A claims department was failing to complete a number of plans on schedule and was overlooking others. On the surface the cause seemed to be people who weren't doing their jobs. But the root cause was that management had failed to establish a central log or register to keep track of all assignments in the department.

  An organizing problem. A production department experienced an excessive number of rejections of manufactured products. Ostensibly the cause seemed to be poor inspection practices, but the root cause was an unbalanced organization. The manager of quality control reported administratively to the director of manufacturing, who overruled the quality control people to maintain schedules and reduce costs.

  A directing problem. A data processing department issued reports recipients could not use. The apparent cause was perceived as the inability of the reporting employees to design effective reports. The root cause was the failure of the recipients to return the reports to the issuing unit with a statement indicating why the reports did not meet their needs.

  A controlling problem. An engineering department seemed unable to complete long-term projects on time. The superficial cause appeared to be people who did not apply themselves sufficiently. The root cause was failing to provide for interim assessment and reporting milestones on all projects that exceeded a given number of weeks.[9]

In each of these cases, addressing the surface cause will not cure the problem permanently. But when internal auditors identify the basic management principle violated, the corrective action will be effective. And, more important, the management of the unit will be improved.

The Internal Auditor's Dilemma

Claims of professionalism carry heavy responsibilities. It is not the work we do that makes us professionals, but the spirit in which we do it. The true professional subscribes to a code of conduct that may call for difficult personal decisions, a circumstance that is true in the professions of law, medicine, and accountancy, among others. It also applies to internal auditors who wish to lay claim to membership in a learned profession.

In some ways the choices between right and wrong may exact a harsher toll on the internal auditor than on other professions. The ethical attorney may refuse to participate in a case involving a conflict of interest and thereby lose a client. The ethical doctor may steadfastly "give no deadly drug to any, though it be asked of me, nor will I counsel such," as stated in the Hippocratic Oath, and consequently see a patient turn to another practitioner. The ethical public accountant may refuse to certify to an improper financial statement and watch a client seek the services of another accountant. This is professionalism; but it is not the end of a career or the loss of one's complete livelihood.

Professional internal auditors, however, face a different set of choices. Their immediate clients are senior management, boards of directors, or similar bodies. If internal auditors are asked to violate their code of ethics or the standards of professional practice, their choice can be an unhappy — indeed a terminal — one. Refusing the demands of an employer makes it almost impossible to keep one's job if the internal auditor does not have a guarantee of that central professional attribute: Independence.

The professional internal auditor must have the independence to fulfill a professional obligation; render an objective, unbiased, unrestricted opinion; and report matters as they are, rather than as some executive or body would like to see them. Internal auditors must be unfettered by restrictions on their audits — on what examinations they may make and how they make them. Only then can internal auditors be regarded as auditing professionally.

Can internal auditors ever attain complete independence? Probably not. Nor is it necessary. But, with regard to the matters they audit, internal auditors must be awarded sufficient independence to achieve objectivity, both in actuality and in perception.

Mautz and Sharaf, in their significant work, "The Philosophy of Auditing," give a number of indicators of professional independence. They speak chiefly of the public accountant, but the same concepts can be applied to internal auditors who seek to demonstrate real and perceived objectivity. The indicators are:

Programming Independence

1. Freedom from managerial interference with the audit program.
2. Freedom from any interference with audit procedures.
3. Freedom from any requirement for the review of the audit work other than that which normally accompanies an audit process.

Examining Independence

1. Free access to all records, properties, and personnel relevant to the audit.
2. Active cooperation from management personnel during the audit examination.
3. Freedom from any managerial attempt to specify activities to be examined or to establish the acceptability of evidential matter.
4. Freedom from personal interests on the part of the internal auditor leading to exclusion from or limitations on the audit examination.

Reporting Independence

1. Freedom from any feeling of obligation to modify the impact or significance of reported facts.
2. Freedom from pressures to exclude significant matters from internal audit reports.
3. Avoidance of intentional or unintentional use of ambiguous language in the statement of facts, opinions, and recommendations in their interpretation.
4. Freedom from any attempt to overrule the auditor's judgment as to either facts or opinions in the internal audit report.[10]

Many internal audit organizations can legitimately attest to having the freedom needed for independent, objective internal audit practice. But what of others? What of internal auditors who see improper activities but cannot get management to change them? Is the answer whistleblowing — going outside the organization structure to report what may be serious, proven deficiencies that go unheeded by management? What is the internal auditor's responsibility?

Many writers have attacked the subject. Some have defended the internal auditor's responsibilities to society. Others have seen the internal auditor as a member of management who owes loyalty only to the organization or agency. The IIA's perspective was addressed in 1988 in the following position paper on whistleblowing.

Exhibit 1-3
IIA Position Paper on Whistleblowing

Whistleblowing — The unauthorized dissemination by internal auditors of audit results, findings, opinions, or information acquired in the course of performing their duties to anyone outside the organization or to the general public.

The Institute of Internal Auditors' (IIA) *Code of Ethics* and *Standards for the Professional Practice of Internal Auditing* provide internal auditors with sufficient mechanisms for the reporting of audit results, findings, opinions, or information acquired in the course of performing their duties, without their bringing such matters to the attention of persons outside the organization. This reporting may involve violations of law, rules, or regulations, or damage to public health or safety.

Such mechanisms include reporting to the appropriate level of management, the audit committee of the board of directors (or its equivalent), or the board of directors as may be appropriate. Implicit in this process is the resolution of problems and improvement of internal controls. Accordingly, The IIA believes that for organizations with internal audit functions that adhere to the *Standards* and *Code of Ethics* of The IIA and that are headed by an audit director with full access to an active audit committee, there should be no need to report in an unauthorized manner to anyone outside the organization.

The IIA maintains a Professional Standards Committee (now the Internal Auditing Standards Board) to assure that The Institute's *Standards* and *Code of Ethics* provide the internal audit professional with guidelines and support for dealing with all issues that confront its members. Reporting to the board of directors satisfies the requirements of the professional *Standards*.

Some internal auditors, however, may not be afforded a means to deal appropriately with findings that involve violations of law, rules, or regulations, or damage to public health or safety. Internal auditors may find resolving such matters difficult if they do not have access to an audit committee comprised solely of independent directors with a written charter setting forth the duties and responsibilities of the committee, and with adequate resources and authority to discharge committee responsibilities. Also, the problems may be compounded if the internal audit organizations are not independent when they carry out their work and do not have organizational status sufficient to permit the accomplishment of their audit responsibilities in accordance with IIA *Standards*. In such situations, the auditor is obligated by The IIA *Standards* and *Code of Ethics* to report through the normal channels and ultimately, if necessary, to the board of directors; and to ensure that the matter is resolved satisfactorily within a reasonable period of time.

Exhibit 1-3 (Cont.)

If the matter is not resolved satisfactorily, or the auditor is terminated or subject to other retaliation, the auditor should secure the advice of outside counsel regarding further action.

This position paper is not to be interpreted to restrict any internal auditor from exercising rights granted to him or her under any state whistleblowing statute or any comparable federal law or rule.

In brief, the paper holds that internal audit functions that adhere to the *Standards* and *Code of Ethics* and have full access to an active audit committee should have no need to resort to whistleblowing. In the absence of these conditions, internal auditors should report through normal channels and ultimately, if necessary, to the board of directors. They should make sure that the matter at issue is resolved satisfactorily within a reasonable period of time. If the matter is not resolved satisfactorily, or the auditor is terminated or subjected to retaliation, the auditor should secure the advice of outside counsel regarding further action.

The IIA position paper does not restrict any internal auditor from exercising rights granted to him or her under any state whistleblowing statute or any comparable federal law or rule.

Appendix

The Internal Auditor as a Consultant

When the original standards for internal auditing were issued in 1978, the Scope portion of the standards included a provision that the internal auditor, in addition to considering the integrity of financial and operating information, also consider and report on the economy, efficiency, and effectiveness of the operation. This provision, though it did not specifically call for recommendations for improvement, certainly did infer that the auditor, when encountering less than optimum conditions, make recommendations for improvements in the subject operation. Thus, the concept of consulting, though not specifically identified was inferred.

When the Guidance Task Force and its predecessor-planning group met in 1997 and the years immediately following to consider The Institute's definition and associated standards, the concept of consultancy had increased in importance to the point where it was believed that it should be specifically identified. Though there were beliefs that consulting impinged on independence, it was suggested that to consult was not to direct, and the acceptance of the consulting recommendations was a decision by management. Also, in many cases, the consultancy projected a series of associated recommendations and the selection process was that of management.

However, in some cases, the internal auditor has been asked to render proactive services relative to reengineering of processes or the development of new or better operations or services. In those cases, because of the internal auditor's background, experience, and approach, the auditor, as a contributor to the well-being of the organization, serves in a capacity outside the usual assurance function, and where there is no conflict with the independence or objectivity aspect of traditional internal auditing.

Though The Institute planned to include standards for consulting as a counterpart to these for assurance, the latter took precedence, primarily because the preceding standards in The Institute's "Red Book" were essentially pointed toward the assurance concept. In October 2001, The Institute published a series of consulting engagement standards. The mandatory implementation date was July 1, 2002, as compared to January 1, 2002, for the previously issued standards. These new standards were supported by Practice Advisory 1000.C1-1: "Principles Guiding the Performance of Consulting Activities of Internal Auditors."

The consulting standards covered the following areas:

Attribute Standards

- Provision for consulting services where auditors *did* have previous responsibilities.

- Impairments of objectivity or independence to be communicated to clients prior to the engagement.

- Declining of engagements where skills, knowledge, or competence is lacking.

- Exercising of due professional care.

Performance Standards

- Planning for consulting engagements.

- Addressing risks consistent with the engagement objectives, during consulting engagements.

- To incorporate knowledge of risks gained from consulting into usual assurance functions.

- To address controls consistent with the engagement objectives during consulting engagements.

- Objectives should be consistent with values and goals of the organization.

- Reaching understandings with clients about objectives, scope, responsibilities, and expectations.

- Addressing risks, controls, and governance processes to extent agreed on with client.

- Reservations on continuance of scope of the engagement to be discussed with client.

- Work programs may vary in form and content.

- Development of policies covering custody and retention of records; also release of records to internal and external parties.

- Communication of progress and results may vary dependent on client's needs.

- Responsibility for communication of final results to clients.

- Risk management, control and governance issues, if significant, should be communicated to senior management and the board.

- Monitoring of disposition of results as agreed on with client.

The Practice Advisory 1000.C1-1 concerning the guiding principles of the consulting activities emphasizes that the intent is to "add value and improve an organization's operations." The advisory focuses on broad parameters to be considered in the engagements. It identifies the various types of engagements, including those that depart from normal or established procedures for consulting work. It then describes a series of guiding principles.

- The value proposition of the internal audit activity.

- Consistency with the internal audit definition.

- Acceptance of audit activities beyond assurance consulting.

- Interrelationship between assurance and consulting.

- Empowerment of consulting services through the internal audit charter.

- No impairment of objectivity through consulting activities.

Consulting Guiding Principles

Practice Advisory 1000 C1-1, "Principles Guiding the Performance of Consulting Activities of Internal Auditors," differs somewhat from most of the other advisories in that it is more definitive than directive. It describes audit activities beyond the usual assurance and consulting audits such as investigations and reviews related to mergers and acquisitions. Also, it describes the interrelationships between assurance activities and consulting and it specifies that though one type of audit might be the prime objective of the activity, the other type of audit might be the prime objective of the activity, that the other audit could normally be an important by-product. This approach was also described at the beginning of this Appendix.

The Advisory recommends that the charter of the internal audit activity identify consulting as a normal element of the audit activity and it suggests that the charter identify examples of such work and provide that such consultative activity should be conducted in a way that independence and conflicts of interest are considered.

The Advisory also reiterates a statement earlier in the Appendix that the recommendations from the activity be presented to management for its deliberations and decisions, and that the consulting is advisory and not a part of the management process. The internal audit activity is identified as an ideal participant in the project because of the background and experience of the audit staff and their investigations into risk management and into the development and conduct of strategies.

There is mention that the organization as a whole should have an awareness of the contribution that can be made by the internal audit staff and that the results should receive appropriate notice so that the audit activity can be considered by all levels as a valuable management tool. Thus, when the internal auditors are engaged in formal consulting assignments, the results of such extensive work should be considered by management at all levels, and the ensuing recommendations and findings should carry considerable weight.

The chief audit executive must have the experience and managerial acumen to design and direct the consulting activity and to evaluate its results and recommendations. Also, the executive should have the ability to communicate and discuss the consulting outcome with the appropriate levels of management.

The Advisory concludes with the provision that regardless of the uniqueness of the consulting activity, the auditors must be guided by The Institute's *Standards* and the *Code of Ethics*.

- Unique foundation of internal audit to conduct consulting through experience in assurance and investigative work.

- Communication of fundamental information on consulting to senior management and the audit committee.

- The codification of principles and ground rules that are understood by all members of the organization.

- The use of internal audit activity for formal consulting tasks using a systematic disciplined approach.

- The definition of the chief audit executive's responsibilities to address significant issues related to the engagement, including audit techniques and the rights of reporting to clients and management.

- Conflicts resolution and evolving issues should be resolved consistent with the *Code of Ethics* and the *Standards*.

Consulting services, whether performed as unique engagements or as a part of assurance work, should result as an added value to the internal audit activity's contribution to management and to the organization. The internal auditor, because of approach, experience, investigative skills, and analytical abilities, is eminently qualified to perform this service and thus to contribute to the basic objectives and the welfare of the organization.

Additional Considerations

Practice Advisory 1000.C1-2, "Additional Considerations for Formal Consulting Engagements," is a practical summary of the operational aspects of the consulting function. It discusses the concept of the "blended" engagement that includes both consulting and assurance activities into a single approach. It also provides for specific consulting arrangements. It recognizes the possibility of consulting activities being requested by management at all levels and it recommends that policies and procedures be developed for the various types of engagements, i.e.,

- Formal consulting engagements.

- Informal consulting engagements: routine activities as a part of participating in other functions that are non-audit activities.

- Special consulting engagements such as for mergers or acquisitions.

- Emergency consulting engagements.

It cautions that consulting engagements should not be conducted as a soporific to the conduct of an assurance audit.

The Advisory is quite specific as to the requirements for independence and objectivity. The substance of the discussion is closely related to that for assurance auditing and it cautions that assurance audits could be influenced by recent consulting engagements. Rotations of audit staff can resolve some of the independence problems. If impairments of independence or objectivity are actual or can be inferred, management should be alerted. Cautions should be taken to prevent ongoing or continuous consulting engagements that could result in the internal auditors' "inappropriately or unintentionally assuming management responsibilities that were not intended."

Due professional care is emphasized by ensuring that internal auditors conform to the requirements and understandings of these same facets emphasized in assurance type auditors. Examples are: extent of work needed, skills and resources required, management needs, potential impact on future assignments, and contributions to the organizational well-being. The auditor should also:

- Conduct informational activities to completely understand the work to be conducted.

- Determine that the consulting activities conform to the internal audit charter and that they will add value to and be in the best interest of the organization.

- Determine that the consulting work relates positively to the audit risk-based plans of engagements.

- Document key factors of the consulting work into a written agreement or plan.

There should be agreement as to the objectives and scope of the consulting engagement. The scope should ensure that professionalism, integrity, credibility, and reputation of the internal audit activity will be maintained.

The planning of the consulting engagement should be such as to meet the management needs of the officials receiving the services. Pursuit beyond the needs considered by management should be proposed, if appropriate, and if not agreed to by management, should be documented.

The Advisory provides for audit programs that generally conform to the programming activities of assurance-type internal audits. It also recommends attention to risk management considerations as would be normal for assurance audits. As a matter of fact, the unique activity of the consulting internal audit would have as an important objective a very complete review of the risk management aspects of the area being audited. Results of the audit should be communicated to all appropriate levels of management.

The Advisory identifies the reporting process as being designed to meet the needs of management and those requesting the audit and describes the characteristics it should contain. It also provides that the reporting can be communicated beyond those individuals and/or organizations. In those cases, it describes the steps the auditor should take relative to this expansion of the reporting in order to conform to the total organization's polices and procedures and to The Institute's *Standards* and *Code of Ethics*. The Advisory provides that there should be complete communication with the audit committee, board, and governing body as to the consulting activities, including descriptions of engagements and their significant recommendations.

The Advisory briefly covers documentation, record retention, and record ownership so as to provide adequate protection relative to legal, tax, regulatory, and accounting issues.

The Advisory concludes by recommending that the internal audit activity monitor the results of the consulting engagements "to the extent agreed on with the client considering managements' interest in the engagement, the risk aspects, and the value to the organization."

References

[1]Dooley, D.E., "Nothing New Under the Sun?," *The Internal Auditor*, Summer 1965, 10.
[2]Stettler, H.F., *Auditing Principles* (Englewood Cliffs, NJ: Prentice-Hall, 1982), 90-91.
[3]*Standards for the Professional Practice of Internal Auditing* (Altamonte Springs, FL: The Institute of Internal Auditors, 1978).
[4]Dierks, P.A., and E.A. Davis, "The Cruciality and Mystique of Internal Auditing: Last Prerequisites for Professionalism?," *The Internal Auditor*, April 1980, 36.
[5]Stettler, H.F., "Have the Internal Auditors Arrived?," *The Internal Auditor*, June 1979, 60-61.
[6]Krogstad, Jack L., Anthony J. Ridley, and Larry E. Rittenberg, "Where We're Going," *Internal Auditor*, October 1999, 31-32.
[7]Oliverio, M.O., "Is Internal Auditing a Core Function?," *Internal Auditing Alert*, September 1999, 6-7.
[8]Sawyer, L.B., "Consultant to Management: The Internal Auditor's Emerging Role," *The Internal Auditor*, June 1981, 31-32.
[9]Sawyer, L.B., "The Essence of Management-Oriented Internal Auditing," *The Internal Auditor*, June 1984, 43-44.
[10]Mautz, R.K., and H.A. Sharaf, "The Philosophy of Auditing," *American Accounting Association*, Monograph No. 6 (1982), 207.

Supplementary Readings

Bachman, Gregory A., "The Change Audit," *Internal Auditor*, June 1999, 40-43.

Black, Jonathan, "The Value of Adversity," *Internal Auditor*, August 2001, 96.

Bonisch, Peter, "*CFIA* Beams Up the Future," *Internal Auditor*, August 1999, 60-63.

Brink, Victor Z., "Forward from Fifty," *Internal Auditor*, June 1991, 8-16.

Burnaby, Priscilla, and Lawrence Klein, "Internal Auditor's Changing Roles," *Internal Auditing*, May/June 2000, 15-24.

Cashell, James D., and George R. Aldhizer, III, "An Examination of Internal Auditors' Emphasis on Value-added Services," *Internal Auditing*, September/October 2002, 19-31.

Chadwick, William E., "Keeping Internal Auditing In-House," *Internal Auditor*, June 2000, 88.

Chapman, Christy, "Accelerating Into the Millennium," *Internal Auditor*, February 1998, 26.

Colbert, Janet L., "Auditors or Advisors?," *Internal Auditor*, December 1999, 88.

Collins, Rod, "Auditing in the Knowledge Era," *Internal Auditor*, June 1999, 26-31.

Courtemanche, Gil, "How Has Internal Auditing Evolved Since 1941?," *Internal Auditor*, June 1991, 106, 109.

Efendi, Jap, Lawrence C. Smith, Jr., and L. Murphy Smith, "The Global Impact of Internal Auditing," *Internal Auditing*, January/February 2002, 3-11.

Fabrizius, Michael P., "A Passion for Excellence," *Internal Auditor*, October 1997, 22-27.

Garitte, Jean-Pierre, "Building Bridges," *Internal Auditor*, August 1998, 26-31.

Grand, Bernard, "Theoretical Approaches to Audits," *Internal Auditing*, November/December 1998, 14-19.

Haas, Lee D., "The Bottom Line," *Internal Auditor*, June 2001, 88.

Hall, John J., "Affirming Independence, Integrity, and Objectivity in Enron's Shadow," *Internal Auditing Report,* April 2002, 1, 4-6.

Harrington, Larry, "A New Vision," *Internal Auditor*, April 1997, 26-31.

Johnson, Howard, "Make It Unique," *Internal Auditor*, August 1999, 36-41.

Krogstad, Jack L., Anthony L. Ridley, and Larry E. Rittenberg, "Where We're Going," *Internal Auditor*, October 1999, 26-33.

MacDonald, Bill, and Lawrena Colombo, "Creating Value Through Human Capital Management," *Internal Auditor*, August 2001, 69-75.

McGreevy, Michael, Deborah Hopkins, and Clarence Lockett, "The Auditing Business," *Internal Auditor*, October 1996, 44-51.

McNamee, David, and Georges M. Selim, *Risk Management: Changing the Internal Auditor's Paradigm* (Altamonte Springs, FL: The Institute of Internal Auditors, 1998).

McNeil, Laura, "Career Internal Auditors," *Internal Auditor*, April 1997, 96.

Metzger, Lawrence, "The Art of Auditing," *Internal Auditor*, August 2000, 28-32.

Miller, Leah, "The Looking Glass," *Internal Auditor*, October 2000, 27-35.

O'Regan, David, "The Accounting Cornerstone," *Internal Auditor*, February 1999, 88.

Richards, Dave, "Envisioning the Future," *Internal Auditor*, August 2001, 60-67.

Ridley, Anthony J., "A Profession for the Twenty-first Century," *Internal Auditor*, October 1996, 20-25.

Rittenberg, Larry E., "A Guide for the Future," *Internal Auditor*, June 2001, 63-67.

Robertson, Kenda, "The Red Ribbon," *Internal Auditor*, June 1997, 60-65.

Sawyer, Lawrence B., and Fredric E. Mints, "The Genesis of the CIA Exam," *Internal Auditor*, August 1989, 14-20.

Sawyer, Lawrence B.," The Leadership Side of Internal Auditing," *Internal Auditor*, August 1990, 16-25.

Sawyer, Lawrence B., "The Political Side of Internal Auditing," *Internal Auditor*, February 1992, 26-33.

Sawyer, Lawrence B., "An Internal Audit Philosophy," *Internal Auditor*, August 1995, 46-55.

Sawyer, Lawrence B., "Performance Evaluators?," *Internal Auditor*, February 1998, 112.

Sears, Brian P., *Internal Auditing Manual* (New York: RIA, 2003). (See Chapter A1, "Auditing - An Overview," and Chapter A2, "Internal Auditing - Strategy and Approach.")

Tongren, John D., "A Magnificent Opportunity," *Internal Auditor*, August 1998, 96.

Wagner, Jacqueline K., "Leading the Way," *Internal Auditor*, August 2000, 34-39.

Multiple-choice Questions

1. An internal auditor engages in the preparation of income tax returns during the tax season. For which of the following activities might the auditor most likely be in violation of the *Code of Ethics*?
   a. Writing a tax guide that is intended for publication and sale to the general public.
   b. Preparing the personal tax return, for a fee, for one of the organization's division managers without the consent of senior management.
   c. Teaching an evening tax seminar, for a fee, at a local university.
   d. Preparing tax returns for elderly citizens, regardless of their associations, as a public service.

2. Under what circumstances would an internal auditor be required to forfeit the CIA designation?
   a. Upon leaving the internal auditing profession.
   b. After action by The IIA's International Ethics Committee.
   c. When found by The IIA's Board of Directors to be in violation of the *Code of Ethics*.
   d. Upon commission of a felony or other action resulting in serious criminal charges.

3. An audit of a foreign subsidiary disclosed payments to local government officials in return for orders. What action does the *Code of Ethics* suggest for internal auditors in such a case?
   a. Refrain from any action that might be detrimental to their employers.
   b. Report the incident to appropriate regulatory authorities.
   c. Inform appropriate organization officials.
   d. Report the practice to the Board of Directors of The IIA.

4. During the audit of one of its organization's nuclear power plants, an internal auditing team discovered serious instances of violations of safety procedures. The *Code of Ethics* requires the audit team to:
   a. Present sufficient factual evidence without revealing confidential information that could be detrimental to their organization.
   b. Disclose all material evidence obtained by the audit team as of the date of the audit report.
   c. Report factual evidence gathered within established time and budget restraints.
   d. Reveal material facts known to the audit team that could distort the report if not disclosed.

5. Which of the following would constitute a violation of the *Code of Ethics*?
   a. Discussing your organization's data processing control system at a trade convention.
   b. Purchasing stock in a target after overhearing an organization executive discussing a possible acquisition.

  c. Deleting sensitive information from a report at the request of senior management.

  d. Investigating executive expense reports based on rumors of padding.

6. Auditing to determine whether an entity is managing and using its resources economically and efficiently would most appropriately be classified as:
  a. Compliance auditing.
  b. Financial auditing.
  c. Operational auditing.
  d. Program results auditing.

7. According to the *Standards*, who is responsible for coordinating internal and external audit efforts?
  a. Chief audit executive.
  b. External auditors.
  c. Audit committee of the board of directors.
  d. Chief financial officer.

8. One of the purposes of the *Standards* is to:
  a. Establish the certification criteria for a CIA.
  b. Specify the content of the internal auditing department's charter.
  c. Serve as a guide in determining the reliance that can be placed on the organization's system of internal control.
  d. Establish a basis for measuring and guiding internal audit operations.

9. The purpose of governmental effectiveness or program results auditing is to determine if desired results of a program are being achieved. The first step in conducting such an audit should be to:
  a. Evaluate the system used to measure results.
  b. Determine the time frame to be audited.
  c. Collect quantifiable data on the program's success or failure.
  d. Identify the legislative intent of the program being audited.

10. In a broad sense, society benefits from internal auditing because the internal auditor:
  a. Enforces corporate compliance with the standards of public policy.
  b. Promotes the efficient and effective use of resources.
  c. Evaluates financial data against professional standards.
  d. Reviews systems established to ensure compliance with corporate policy.

11. An internal auditor who had been supervisor of the accounts payable section should not audit that section:
   a. Because there is no way to measure a reasonable period of time in which to establish independence.
   b. Until enough time has elapsed to allow the new supervisor to influence the system of controls over accounts payable.
   c. Until after the next annual review by the external auditors.
   d. Until it is clear that the new supervisor has assumed the responsibilities.

12. The function of internal auditing, as related to internal financial reports, would be to:
   a. Ensure compliance with reporting procedures.
   b. Review the expenditure items and match each item with the expenses incurred.
   c. Determine if there are any employees expending funds without authorization.
   d. Identify inadequate controls that increase the likelihood of unauthorized expenditures.

13. According to the *Standards*, due professional care calls for:
   a. Detailed audits of all transactions related to a particular function.
   b. Infallibility and extraordinary performance when the system of internal controls is known to be weak.
   c. Consideration of the possibility of material irregularities during every audit assignment.
   d. Testing in sufficient detail to give absolute assurance that noncompliance does not exist.

14. According to the *Standards*, the primary purpose for internal auditing's evaluation of the adequacy of an organization's system of internal controls is to determine:
   a. If controls are designed to insure that the organization's objectives will be met.
   b. The nature, extent, and timing of audit tests.
   c. The extent of compliance with key controls.
   d. If the application of due professional care will be sufficient to detect all material irregularities.

15. Which of the following actions would be a violation of auditor independence
   a. Continuing on an audit assignment at a division for which the auditor will soon be responsible as the result of a promotion.
   b. Reducing the scope of an audit due to budget restrictions.
   c. Participating on a task force which recommends standards for control of a new distribution system.
   d. Reviewing a purchasing agent's contract drafts prior to their execution.

16. Which of the items below would be a violation of The IIA's *Code of Ethics*?
    a. Certain facts evidenced in the auditor's working papers that helped to support the basic allegations made by the auditor as to a case of fraud were not included in the audit report.
    b. Evidence in the auditor's working papers that proved a criminal act was included in the auditor's report draft. The comments were later removed by audit management.
    c. To keep the audit effort within the budgeted time, the auditor was directed to and did curtail testing in an area that looked suspicious and later was proved to contain massive irregularities.
    d. A control system that had been recommended by the audit staff during the previous audit was found to be defective. The auditor reported the defective function as a client failure.

17. When required to select adequate operating standards to evaluate an activity, the internal auditors should:
    a. Seek client agreement on a set of appropriate standards.
    b. Conclude that internal control is not effective.
    c. Choose the standards used in the last audit of the activity.
    d. Develop an appropriate set of standards.

18. According to the *Standards*, an internal auditor's role with respect to operating objectives and goals includes:
    a. Approving the operating objectives or goals to be met.
    b. Determining whether underlying assumptions are appropriate.
    c. Developing and implementing control procedures.
    d. Accomplishing desired operating program results.

19. The best description of the purpose of internal auditing is that it:
    a. Furnishes members of the organization with information needed to effectively discharge their responsibilities.
    b. Reviews the reliability and integrity of financial and operating information.
    c. Reviews the means of safeguarding assets and, as appropriate, verifies the existence of such assets.
    d. Appraises the economy and efficiency with which resources are employed.

20. According to the *Standards*, the independence of internal auditors is achieved through:
    a. Staffing and supervision.
    b. Continuing education and due professional care.
    c. Human relations and communications.
    d. Organizational status and objectivity.

21. Which of the following actions by an auditor would violate the *Code of Ethics*?
    a. An audit of an activity managed by the auditor's spouse.
    b. A material financial investment in the organization.
    c. Use of an organization car.
    d. A significant ownership interest in a non-related business.

22. The *Standards* requires that the CAE seek the approval of management and acceptance by the board of a formal written charter for the internal auditing department. The purpose of this charter is to:
    a. Protect the internal auditing department from undue outside influence.
    b. Establish the purpose, authority, and responsibility of the internal auditing department.
    c. Clearly define the relationship between internal and external auditing.
    d. Establish the CAE's status as a staff executive.

23. An auditor often faces special problems when auditing a foreign subsidiary. Which of the following statements is false with respect to the conduct of international audits?
    a. The IIA *Standards* do not apply outside the U.S.
    b. The auditor should determine whether managers are in compliance with local laws.
    c. There may be justification for having different organization policies in force in foreign branches.
    d. It is preferable to have multilingual auditors conduct audits at branches in non-English-speaking nations.

24. Which of the following could be an organization factor that might adversely affect the ethical behavior of the CAE?
    a. The CAE reports directly to an independent audit committee of the board of directors.
    b. The CAE is not assigned any operational responsibilities.
    c. A CAE may not be appointed or approved without concurrence of the board of directors.
    d. The CAE's annual bonuses are based on dollar recoveries or recommended future savings as a result of audits.

25. As used by the internal auditing profession, the *Standards* refers to all of the following except:
    a. Criteria by which the operations of an internal audit department are evaluated and measured.
    b. Criteria which dictate the minimum level of ethical actions to be taken by internal auditors.
    c. Statements intended to represent the practice of internal auditing as it should be.
    d. Criteria that are applicable to all types of internal audit departments.

26. According to the *Standards*, internal auditors should possess the knowledge, skills, and disciplines essential to the performance of internal auditing. This means that all internal auditors should be proficient in applying:
    a. Internal auditing standards.
    b. Quantitative methods.
    c. Management principles.
    d. Structured systems analysis.

27. An auditor discovers some material inefficiencies in a purchasing function. The purchasing manager happens to be the auditor's next-door neighbor and best friend. In accordance with the *Code of Ethics*, the auditor should:
    a. Objectively include the facts of the case in the audit report.
    b. Not report the incident because of loyalty to the friend.
    c. Include the facts of the case in a special report submitted only to the friend.
    d. Not report the friend unless the activity is illegal.

28. An organization's new president meets the CAE for the first time, and asks him or her to briefly describe the department's overall responsibility. The CAE states that internal audit's overall responsibility is to:
    a. Act as an independent appraisal function to review operations as a service to management by measuring and evaluating the effectiveness of controls.
    b. Review the means of safeguarding assets and, as appropriate, verify the existence of such assets.
    c. Ensure compliance with policies, plans, procedures, laws, and regulations that could have a significant impact on operations and reports.
    d. Review the reliability and integrity of financial and operating information and the means used to identify, measure, classify, and report such information.

29. Which of the following activities would not be presumed to impair the independence of an internal auditor?
    I. Recommending standards of control for a new computer application.
    II. Drafting procedures for running a new computer application to ensure that proper controls are installed.
    III. Performing reviews of procedures for a new computer application before it is installed.
        a. I only.
        b. II only.
        c. III only.
        d. I and III only.

30. Which of the following activities is outside the scope of internal auditing?
    a. Assessing an operating department's effectiveness in achieving stated organizational goals.
    b. Safeguarding assets.
    c. Checking for compliance with laws and regulations.
    d. Evaluating established objectives and goals.

31. In recent years, control self-assessment has become a valuable auditing tool, especially in terms of:
    a. Determining the accuracy and understandability of financial events as expressed in financial documents.
    b. Identifying workers who may have been involved in fraudulent activities.
    c. Uncovering problems in areas such as organizational morale and communication.
    d. Conducting employee performance appraisals.

32. The mission of the 1999 *Competency Framework for Internal Auditing (CFIA)*, a research study commissioned by The IIA Research Foundation, was to:
    a. Design a new internal auditing educational program to be adopted by universities, IIA affiliates, and other training institutions around the world.
    b. Find the essence of the global profession of internal auditing and update information on the competencies that internal auditors need.
    c. Identify differences in internal auditing practices throughout the world and initiate actions that would require all internal auditors to become certified.
    d. Establish guidelines that would help internal auditors to maintain their current practices and high standards so that the profession is not compromised by importune changes in the business environment.

33. Risk management has become an element of ever-increasing importance for modern organizations. As a result, more and more internal auditors are:
    a. Reviewing all organizational insurance policies on regular-cycle basis.
    b. Concentrating on the regulatory aspects of risk management, since areas such as environmental risk have become so great that they can decimate a corporation.
    c. Adopting a holistic approach to risk management.
    d. Advising all audit customers to be more aware of the risks within their operations.

34. Upon obtaining factual documentation of unethical business conduct by the vice president in charge of internal auditing, the chief audit executive should:
    a. Conduct an investigation to determine the extent of the vice president's involvement in the unethical acts.
    b. Confront the vice president with the facts before proceeding.
    c. Schedule an audit of the business function involved.
    d. Report the facts to the chief executive officer and the audit committee.

Chapter 2
Control

Control, the internal auditor's "open sesame." Control, the noun and the verb, the two levels of every system. The bridge between auditor and client. Access and reporting on control. Definitions of control: origins, public accountants, internal auditors. SAS 78 expansion of concept of internal control. The purpose of control: to achieve objectives. Internal control models. The COSO concept. The CoCo model. Control defined by the SAC study. Prevention, detection, correction controls. Eliminating probability, not possibility of control. Benefits of control. Control systems. Open and closed systems. Objectives, standards, comparisons, corrective action. Closed loop or feedback systems. Elements of a system. Importance of control. Internal control standards. Management's responsibility for control. Means of achieving control. Characteristics of control. Problems with controls. The human element. How to achieve control: organization, policies, procedures, personnel, accounting, budgeting, and reporting. The impact of regulation on control. Canadian law. The internal auditor's role. Internal accounting controls — the cycle approach. The impact of reengineering on internal controls. Reduction of controls — the virtual organization. The audit of controls. Auditing COSO. Operating controls. The four management functions and control. Why control systems break down. Overcontrolling.

• •

The Importance of Control to the Internal Auditor

Comprehensive auditing leads internal auditors into unfamiliar territory. They find themselves confronted by disciplines and techniques outside their technical knowledge. They cannot possibly become instant experts in advertising, agriculture, customs duties, engineering, international trade, pensions, safety, pollution, transportation, and/or the myriad of other activities about which they must make objective and businesslike appraisals.

The key is control. Control, the verb, is a force. It sees that things get done or don't get done. Control, the noun, is the physical means through which the force is exerted. Both are used by managers to make sure that their operating objectives will be met.

Every activity within an organization works on two levels, within two systems. One is the operating system, which is designed to accomplish stated objectives like producing 100 items while meeting standards of cost, quality, and schedule. The other is the control systems, which is overlaid on the operating system. It is made up of procedures, rules, and instructions that are designed to make sure the operating system's objectives will be met. Control enhances the probability that management's objectives will be achieved.

Internal auditors may be unable to fully comprehend the operating system; and even if they did, they might not be able to appraise it objectively. Internal auditors are trained to objectively evaluate control systems. These are within the internal auditor's ability to comprehend and examine. This knowledge is the internal auditor's "open sesame."[1] For example, it might be impossible for an internal auditor to evaluate the methods by which employees produce 100 items. Those methods are part of an operating system that is technical and perhaps beyond audit evaluation. But professional internal auditors would have less difficulty evaluating a production control system that is designed to see that production meets its objectives. The auditors may not be able to determine whether machines have the proper settings, whether items have been produced in the most efficient manner, or whether the minimum amount of scrap has been generated. They can ascertain, however, the degree to which production control is fulfilling its role: planning and controlling production to meet the organization's objectives of good customer service, efficient plant operation, and low inventory investment. Thus, they can determine whether there are controls in effect to give reasonable assurance that machines are properly calibrated, efficient output is identified, and the normal amount of scrap generated is established.

Furthermore, when the clients see before them an emissary of high-level management — someone who knows what executive management is interested in and worried about, someone who understands top management's broad policies and procedures, someone who has had experience in examining the controls over many other operations of the enterprise, someone who is willing to share an understanding of internal control, someone who may be able to point out pitfalls and prevent unhappy surprises — then the clients begin to regard the internal auditor as an associate and not a police officer, a constructive business consultant and not a threat, a management-oriented evaluator and not a nitpicker.

After the original standards had been completed in 1978, one of the first activities in this area that The Institute performed was to expand the concept of auditing for controls. The subject was that of the first of the *Statements on Auditing Standards,* now encompassed in the current *Standards.* Its target was to treat control adequacy (properly designed), effectiveness (working as intended) and quality (the achievement of the organization's goals and objectives). There is a fourth quality, utility (being used). The new standard, 2120, describes the subject well and should be used as an introduction to this important subject.[2]

Standard 2120 — Control

The internal audit activity should assist the organization in maintaining effective controls by evaluating their effectiveness and efficiency and by promoting continuous improvement.

2120.A1 — Based on the results of the risk assessment, the internal audit activity should evaluate the adequacy and effectiveness of controls encompassing the organization's governance, operations, and information systems. This should include:

- Reliability and integrity of financial and operational information.
- Effectiveness and efficiency of operations.
- Safeguarding of assets.
- Compliance with laws, regulations, and contracts.

2120.A2 — Internal auditors should ascertain the extent to which operating and program goals and objectives have been established and conform to those of the organization.

2120.A3 — Internal auditors should review operations and programs to ascertain the extent to which results are consistent with established goals and objectives to determine whether operations and programs are being implemented or performed as intended.

2120.A4 — Adequate criteria are needed to evaluate controls. Internal auditors should ascertain the extent of which management has established adequate criteria to determine whether objectives and goals have been accomplished. If adequate, internal auditors should use such criteria in their evaluation. If inadequate, internal auditors should work with management to develop appropriate evaluation criteria.

2120.A4-1. The Practice Advisory augmenting this standard on Control Criteria expresses this well and provides more specific provisions.

Internal auditors should evaluate the established operating targets and expectations and should determine whether those operating standards are acceptable and are being met. When such management targets and criteria are vague, authoritative interpretations should be sought. If internal auditors are required to interpret or select operating standards, they should seek agreement with engagement clients as to the criteria needed to measure operating performance.

Access and Reporting on Control

Practice Advisory 2120.A1-1, "Accessing and Reporting on Control Processes," provides more detail relative to the determination of the adequacy and effectiveness of the control process and the responsibility of the chief audit executive to convey this assessment information to senior management and the audit committee. The Practice Advisory outlines the work of the chief audit executive to:

- Develop an audit plan to provide adequate and sufficient evidence.
- Consider relevant work that can be provided by others.
- Evaluate the proposed plan from two viewpoints:
  - Adequacy across organizational entities.
  - Inclusion of a variety of transaction and business process types.

The plan should provide for an audit that evaluates the effectiveness of the system of controls. The considerations in making this evaluation are:

- Were significant discrepancies or weaknesses found?
- If so, were corrections or improvements made?
- Do the discoveries and their consequences lead to a conclusion that there is an unacceptable level of business risk?

The report on the evaluation should identify the role played by the control process in achieving the organization's objectives and should state that:

- There were no weaknesses found.
- There are weaknesses — and their impact on the level of risk and the achievement of the organization's objectives.

The annual report should be clear, concise, informative, and understandable — considering the target audience. It should include recommendations for improvement and other information so as to make the report usable.

The Advisory also describes the "expectation gap" relative to the work of the internal auditor relative to the target group's high expectations about the value of the internal audit work and the disclosures as to the actual situations that exist.

Control Defined

Early Definitions

Control first appeared in the English lexicon around 1600 and was defined as "the copy of a roll [of account], a parallel [sic] of the same quality and content with the original." Samuel Johnson sums up this original meaning as "a register or account kept by another officer, that each may be examined by the other."

The importance of control to auditors (or "internal check" as it was first called) was recognized by L.R. Dicksee as early as 1905. He pointed out that a suitable system of internal check should eliminate the need for a detailed audit. He viewed control as a composite of three elements: division of work, the use of accounting records, and the rotation of personnel.[3]

In 1930 George E. Bennett more narrowly defined internal check this way:[4]

A system of internal check may be defined as the coordination of a system of accounts and related office procedures in such a manner that the work of one employee independently performing his own prescribed duties continually checks the work of another as to certain elements involving the possibility of fraud.

In 1949 a special report titled "Internal Control — Elements of a Coordinated System and Its Importance to Management and the Independent Accountant," by the American Institute of Certified Public Accountants (AICPA) Committee on Auditing Procedure, broadened the definition of internal control:

Internal control comprises the plan of organization and all of the coordinate methods and measures adopted within a business to safeguard its assets, check the accuracy and reliability of its accounting data, promote operational efficiency, and encourage adherence to prescribed managerial policies. This definition [continued the Committee] possibly is broader than the meaning sometimes attributed to the term. It recognizes that a system of internal control extends beyond those matters which relate directly to the functions of the accounting and financial department.

Definitions for Public Accountants

Independent auditors in the United States, however, saw the definition as too broad for their purposes. After all, they were primarily concerned with internal control as it relates to the reliability of financial statements or to the aims of authorization, accounting, and asset safeguarding. So internal control was subdivided into administrative control and accounting control. These were defined in Section 320.27-.28 (1973) of the AICPA's Professional Standards, taken from *Statement of Auditing Standards* (SAS) No. 1:

> Administrative control includes, but is not limited to, the plan of organization and the procedures and records that are concerned with the decision processes leading to management's authorization of transactions. Such authorization is a management function directly associated with the responsibility for achieving the objectives of the organization and is the starting point for establishing accounting control of transactions.
>
> Accounting control comprises the plan of organization and the procedures and records that are concerned with the safeguarding of assets and the reliability of financial records and consequently are designed to give reasonable assurance that:
>
> a. Transactions are executed in accordance with management's general or specific authorization.
>
> b. Transactions are recorded as necessary (1) to permit preparation of financial statements in conformity with generally accepted accounting principles or any other criteria applicable to such statements and (2) to maintain accountability for assets.
>
> c. Access to assets is permitted only in accordance with management's authorization.
>
> d. The recorded accountability for assets is compared with the existing assets at reasonable intervals and appropriate action is taken with respect to any differences.

It will be observed that the definition of administrative control links such control to management objectives; the definition of accounting control does not.

SAS 78 Expands AICPA Definition of Internal Control[5]

Effective for audits of financial statements for periods beginning on or after January 1, 1997, the American Institute of Certified Public Accountants has revised its statement of internal control as:

> "Internal control is a process affected by an activity's board of directors, management or other personnel — designed to provide reasonable assurance regarding the achievement of objectives in the following categories:

(a) reliability of financial reporting;
(b) effectiveness and efficiency of operations; and
(c) compliance with applicable laws and relations.

The three areas are subject to specific types of audit in the same order:

a. Annual auditing of financial statements.
b. Auditing of operations in relation to objectives and desired outcomes.
c. Auditing of compliance (presumably as a separate audit or in conjunction with audits in "a" and "b" above)."

The SAS also defines internal control as consisting of the five interrelated component parts of the COSO statement:

1. Control environment
2. Risk assessment
3. Control activities
4. Information and communications
5. Monitoring

There is direct relationship between objectives, which are what an entity strives to achieve, and components, which represent what is needed to achieve the objectives. Not all of these objectives and components are relevant to an audit of financial statements. Internal control, no matter how well designed and operated, can provide only reasonable assurance regarding achievement of an entity's objectives.

Definitions for Internal Auditors

The AICPA definition just given tends to blur the distinction between control as a verb and control as a noun. In the world of business and government, these words have developed specific meanings, and it is important to maintain the distinction between them: the verb represents the action of seeing to it that what should be done will be done and preventing what is prohibited, so that established management objectives will be met; the noun represents the means used to help the "controller" control.

Internal auditors, who should be management-oriented and objective-oriented, need a definition of their own — a definition that ties the management function of control and controlling to the means used to exercise that function in any activity of the organization. Thus, the internal auditor regarded control and controls as follows:[6]

Control is the employment of all the means devised in an enterprise to promote, direct, restrain, govern, and check upon its various activities for the purpose of seeing that enterprise objectives are met. These means of control include, but are not limited to, form of organization, policies, systems, procedures, instructions, standards, committees, charts of account, forecasts, budgets, schedules, reports, records, checklists, methods, devices, and internal auditing.

Definitions of control are, however, less significant than the purpose of control. What internal auditors must keep in mind is that controls are adequate and useful only if they are designed to attain an objective. Internal auditors must know the objective before they can properly evaluate the means of control.

Currently, control is defined by The IIA as:[7]

"... any action taken by management to enhance the likelihood that established objectives and goals will be achieved. Controls may be preventive (to deter undesirable events from occurring), detective (to detect and correct undesirable events which have occurred), or directive (to cause or encourage a desirable event to occur). The concept of a system of control is the integrated collection of control components and activities that are used by an organization to achieve its objectives and goals."

Controls exist and are to be used to assist management in the achievement of its primary objectives:[8]

Relevant, reliable, and credible financial and operating information.
Effective and efficient use of the organization's resources.
Safeguarding of the organization's assets.
Compliance with laws, regulations, ethical and business norms, and contracts.
Identification of risk exposures and use of effective strategies to control them.
Established objectives and goals for operations or programs.

The subsystems serving strategic planning and operating functions employ administrative controls. Senior management plans are at the strategic level. The means to carry out those plans are at the operating level. The concept of control remains the same. Only the objectives to which they apply are different. And as the "control used to evaluate other controls," internal auditors can make evaluations at all levels. (Are all the objectives being met efficiently, economically, and effectively?)

For the management-oriented internal auditor, even the objectives themselves are subject to review. Do they mesh with overall organization aims and philosophies? Are they based on accurate, useful information? Are they still relevant in a changing environment? Do they conform to the external controls of governmental rules and regulations? Do they meet the needs of society?

Internal Control Models

Traditionally auditors have used a series of internal control functions to determine if an organization's control functions were adequate. Within recent years questions have risen as to whether this pattern of control elements was adequate. Examples arose where organizations conformed to the requirements of the traditional controls, yet situations occurred that indicated there was something missing. Thus, a new look was taken, especially in the United States, Canada, and the United Kingdom, to determine what was missing. The result was the development of new control models: the Integrated Control - Integrated Framework model was developed in the United States by the Committee of Supporting Organizations of the Treadway Commission (the COSO report);[9] and the CoCo group in Canada (the Criteria of Control Board of the Canadian Institute of Chartered Accountants) developed a similar model which is reported to be more user friendly and in fact may be better structured for use as an audit tool. Also, the Cadbury Commission in the UK developed a model similar to COSO.

Internal control has many concepts. In an attempt to standardize the definition, the Committee of Sponsoring Organizations[10] recently defined and described internal control as:[11]

- Establishing a common definition for different groups.

- Providing a standard definition against which all entities can compare their control systems.

The Committee, using the acronym COSO, then gave this definition — it was to provide reasonable assurance of the achievement of objectives as to:

- The effectiveness and efficiency of operations.

- The reliability of financial information.

- The compliance with applicable laws and regulations.

Thus, the Committee postulated that the process could assist in achieving:

- Basic business and operating objectives.

- Safeguarding of assets.

- Reliable financial statements and reports.

- Compliance with applicable laws and regulations.

It is presumed that the reliability of operating statements is included in the first category relating to efficiency and effectiveness.

The COSO Model

The COSO model consists of five components of internal control:

1. Control Environment
2. Risk Assessment
3. Control Activities
4. Information and Communication
5. Monitoring

The traditional audit activities related to the determination of the efficiency and effectiveness are in the third component — Control Activities (separation of duties, authority and responsibility, authorization, documentation, etc.). The other four components appear to be new additions to the control function, but from an audit standpoint in many cases were considered by auditors, at least to a degree, especially in those cases where the controls did not seem to be effective. The new model requires the consideration of all five components. A brief description follows:

- **Control Environment** — This component includes the attitude of management at all levels toward operations in general and specifically the concept of controls. This included: ethics, competence, and integrity and a demonstrated interest in the well-being of the organization. It also includes the organization structure and management's policies and philosophy.

- **Risk Assessment** — This component is and has been a part of progressive internal audit activity. It involves identifying the risks in all areas of the organization and establishing the vulnerability of the organization through evaluating the risks. The COSO also added consideration of objectives in all aspects of the operation so as to assure that all parts of the organization are operating in concert.

- **Control Activities** — This component includes those activities that are traditionally associated with the concept of internal control. These activities include approvals, responsibilities and authorities, separation of duties, documentation, reconciliation, competent and honest personnel, internal check, and internal auditing. These activities should be risk evaluated throughout the entire organization considering the organization as a universe.

- **Information and Communication** — This component is an essential part of the management process. Management cannot function without current intelligence The communication of information relative to the operation of internal controls provides substance on which management can form its evaluations as to the control process effectiveness and to manage its operations.

- **Monitoring** — Monitoring is the provision of dynamic rational evaluation of the information supplied by the communication of information for the purpose of control management.

Another recent definition by an organization of top national government auditors from over 100 nations is simply:[12]

"...a management tool used to provide reasonable assurance that management's objectives are being met."

The definition then goes on to say that the following general objectives are to be achieved.[13]

- Promoting orderly, economical, efficient, and effective operations and quality products and services consistent with the organization's missions.

- Safeguarding resources against loss due to waste, abuse, mismanagement, errors, and fraud.

- Adhering to laws and management directives.

- Developing and maintaining reliable financial and management data and fairly disclosing that information in timely reports.

Though this statement was developed by the public sector, it has direct application to the private sector as well.

The CoCo Model[14]

The Canadians who started with the COSO model worked for several years before they could develop a model with which they were satisfied. The result is a model that is more oriented toward internal auditing procedures and that seems to be easier to understand and to serve as a guide for internal auditing activities.

The CoCo model includes four components. The components serve to classify 20 criteria, which can serve as the elements of auditing programs. The components and the 20 criteria follow:

Purpose

A1 Objectives should be established and communicated.

A2 The significant internal and external risks faced by an organization in the achievement of its objectives should be identified and assessed.

A3 Policies designed to support the achievement of an organization's objectives and the management of its risks should be established, communicated, and practiced so that people understand what is expected of them and the scope of their freedom to act.

A4 Plans to guide efforts in achieving the organization's objectives should be established and communicated.

A5 Objectives and related plans should include measurable performance targets and indicators.

Commitment

B1 Shared ethical values, including integrity, should be established, communicated, and practiced through the organization.

B2 Human resource policies and practices should be consistent with an organization's ethical values and with achievement of its objectives.

B3 Authority, responsibility, and accountability should be clearly defined and consistent with an organization's objectives so that decisions and actions are taken by the appropriate people.

B4 An atmosphere of mutual trust should be fostered to support the flow of information between people and their effective performance toward achieving the organization's objectives.

Capability

C1 People should have the necessary knowledge, skills, and tools to support the achievement of the organization's objectives.

C2 Communication processes should support the organization's values and the achievement of its objectives.

C3 Sufficient and relevant information should be identified and communicated in a timely manner to enable people to perform their assigned responsibilities.

C4 The decisions and actions of different parts of the organization should be coordinated.

C5 Control activities should be designed as an integral part of the organization, taking into consideration its objectives, the risks to their achievement, and the inter-relatedness of control elements.

Monitoring and Learning

D1 External and internal environments should be monitored to obtain information that may signal a need to reevaluate the organization's objectives or controls.

D2 Performance should be monitored against the targets and indicators identified in the organization's objectives and plans.

D3 The assumptions behind an organization's objectives and systems should be periodically challenged.

D4 Information needs and related information systems should be reassessed as objectives change or as reporting deficiencies are identified.

D5 Follow-up procedures should be established and performed to ensure appropriate change or action occurs.

D6 Management should periodically assess the effectiveness of control in its organization and communicate the results to those to whom it is accountable.

Using the Control Model in Internal Auditing

Both of the control models contain what has been termed "soft controls." These controls are not characterized by specific activities or procedures that can be observed and tested in a finite manner. The soft controls are related more to attitudes and philosophies. However, both types of controls can be identified with risks that can be described and measured as to the possibility of occurrence and significance of the situation if it does occur. The combination might be described as vulnerability. Thus, if we were to set up the situation algebraically we might use:

$$P \times S = V$$

P = Potential Occurrence
S = Significance
V = Vulnerability

These control models can form the substance of the internal auditing evaluations of control activities that are further described in this chapter.

The Systems Auditability and Control Study

In 1991 The Institute published a monumental study titled *Systems Auditability and Control (SAC).* Module 2 (of 12) of that study, "Audit and Control Environment," was to "provide a framework for the discussion of risks, controls, and audit considerations related to technology and information systems."[15] The study defined an organization's system of internal control as including:

The means established to provide reasonable assurance that the overall objectives and goals of the organization are achieved in an efficient, effective, and economical manner. . . . a set of processes, functions, activities, subsystems, and people who are grouped together or consciously segregated to ensure the effective achievement of objectives and goals.[16]

The study goes on to list three key concepts:

- Reasonable assurance is provided when cost effective controls are established to reduce the risk that overall objectives and goals will not be met to an acceptable level.

- Objectives are defined as a statement of the desired accomplishments of the organization.

- Goals are specific targets that should be identifiable, measurable, attainable, and consistent with objectives.[17]

The components of the system of internal control include:

- Control environment.

- Manual and automated systems.

- Control procedures.[18]

Control environment. Control environment includes:

- Organization structure — individual managers' responsibility for decision making and establishing organization policy and setting the limits of such authority.[19]

- Control framework elements include:
    - Segregation of incompatible duties; one person or organization should not control all stages of a process.
    - The competence and integrity of the people in an organization.
    - Appropriate levels of authority and responsibility.
    - The ability to trace each transaction to an accountable and responsible individual.
    - The availability of adequate resources, time, and knowledgeable personnel.
    - Supervision of staff and appropriate review of work.[20]

- Policies and procedures that are well documented and that describe the scope of the function, its activities, and interrelationships with other departments. Policies indicate direction; procedures tell how to implement and follow the policies.[21]

- External influences include fiduciary requirements, laws and regulations, contract provisions, customs, mores, union provisions, and the competitive environment.[22]

Manual and automated systems. This is the processing, reporting, storing, and transferring of information. Included are:

- Systems software.

- Application systems.
  - Core systems.
  - Operational systems.

- End-user and departmental systems.[23]

Control procedures. Control procedures include:

- General information system controls, "having a pervasive impact on the overall effectiveness of information systems functions," include:
  - Computer operations controls.
  - Physical and logical security controls.
  - Program change controls.
  - System development controls.
  - Telecommunications controls.

- Application controls are designed to, "ensure authorized, accurate, and complete processing of a transaction from input, through processing, to the output of information." They prevent, detect, and correct errors.

- Compensating controls "overcome or mitigate a weakness in another application of general control."[24]

Preventive, Detective, and Corrective Controls

Controls can be designed to carry out various functions. Some are installed to prevent undesirable outcomes before they happen (preventive controls). Others are designed to identify the undesirable outcomes when they do happen (detective controls). Still others are designed to make sure that corrective action is taken to reverse the undesirable outcomes or to see that they do not recur (corrective controls). All of them, in concert, function to see that some management objective or goal will be met.

Preventive controls are more cost-effective than detective controls. When built into a system, preventive controls forestall errors and thereby avoid the cost of correction. Preventive controls would include, for example: trustworthy, competent people; segregation of duties to prevent intentional wrongdoing; proper authorization to prevent improper use of organization resources; computerized edits to detect and prevent improper transactions; adequate documentation and records as well as proper record keeping procedures to deter improper transactions; and physical control over assets to prevent their improper conversion or use.

Detective controls are usually more expensive than preventive controls, but they too are essential. First, they measure the effectiveness of the preventive controls. Second, some errors cannot be effectively controlled through a system of prevention; they must be detected when they occur. Detective controls include reviews and comparisons, such as records of performance and independent checks on performance. They also include such control devices as bank reconciliations, confirmation of bank balances, cash counts, reconciliations of accounts receivable detail to accounts receivable control accounts, physical counts of inventories and analyses of variances, confirmation with suppliers of accounts payable, computerized techniques such as transaction limits, passwords, and edits, and systems of review like internal auditing.

Corrective controls take over when improper outcomes occur and are detected. All the detective controls in the world are valueless if the identified deficiency remains uncorrected or can be permitted to recur. So management must develop systems that keep the spotlight on an undesirable condition until it is corrected and, where appropriate, must set up procedures to prevent recurrence. Documentation and reporting systems keep problems under management surveillance until they have been solved or the defect is corrected. Corrective controls thus close the loop that starts with prevention and passes through detection to correction. Here is an example of the use of all three controls:

> Overhead cranes moving heavy materials from place to place in a manufacturing plant pose safety problems. Improperly loaded slings or jerky crane movements can accidentally release heavy weights from the slings and cause damage and injuries.

> To help prevent accidents, preventive controls were installed. All crane operators received safety instructions and training; their education was evidenced by a certificate in the form of a plastic identification card. This card had a metallic strip that would activate the crane's operating mechanism. Employees had to be retrained and recertified each year.

To make sure that cranes were operated only by properly certified operators, detective controls were installed. Safety engineers who roamed the plant looking for safety violations were required to determine that employees operating cranes only used their certificate card to operate the cranes.

To make sure any defects were corrected, corrective controls were installed. In the event of a crane-related accident, a special team was appointed to investigate the accident, determine the cause, recommend corrective action to operating management, and report the results to executive management.

Eliminating Probability Not Possibility of Controls

Internal auditors should understand that no system of control will eliminate the possibility of irregularities. Internal control is effected by people. A system of internal control is made up of people and procedures. People are expected to act and follow procedures in a normal and responsible fashion. But people are fallible and are subject to pressures. They may, on occasion, not act as intended. Then the system breaks down.

For example, an appeal based on sympathy or personal friendship may cause a superior to overlook an assistant's incompetence. Pressures from a higher-ranked employee may prevent an employee from reporting a suspicious transaction. An offer to help overcome a heavy workload or to double up on responsibilities during vacation time may circumvent a review procedure or eliminate a division of duties. Elimination of a time-consuming control may increase efficiency. Many events can contribute to the breakdown of an otherwise satisfactory control system. And so, the most that a seemingly satisfactory system of internal control can do is reduce the probability of irregularity to only a possibility — preferably a remote one. Never can it completely eliminate the possibility. Hence, internal auditors can rely reasonably, but not completely, on what seems to be an acceptable system of control.

Benefits of Control

Controls need not be exclusively restrictive. They do not have to be straitjackets or a catalog of "don'ts." They can aid managers. The view today is that controls should be a positive means of helping managers achieve objectives and goals.

Modern management philosophy regards control as an aid rather than a constriction. It looks at control as a means of integrating personal and enterprise objectives to help people meet their goals. It advocates inviting the person controlled to help devise the controls. It regards controls as the means of measuring oneself — determining whether standards have been met, whether one has accomplished the job intended.

Control devices thereby become the means of auto-control. They are used for self-measurement. They can also activate individuals to improve their performance — not just get by with what they are doing. Even from a restrictive view, controls can be beneficial. They can help to remove temptation. For example, it is well accepted that three conditions must exist before a person will embezzle an employer's funds: unusual need (actual or perceived), opportunity, and rationalization. Management can do little about how an employee perceives his or her needs. But by adequate control, the opportunity or temptation to embezzle can be removed or diminished. The need must become desperate, indeed, before an employee will seek to break a thoroughly controlled system. But where assets are left wide open to peculation, the employee can readily rationalize that he or she has been invited to partake of the feast.

Good controls not only protect the organization, they protect the employee as well. Management is morally obligated to see that temptation is not placed in the way. Most employees will respect a well-controlled operation. Control weaknesses breed contempt and make it easy for employees to rationalize: since management does not care, why not take what is there for the taking? For example, complete concentration of all parts of an operation in one individual's hands is dangerous — it is bad for the organization and just as bad for the individual.

Another benefit of control stems from the agency theory of management. Managers, as agents of owners, owe the owners a fiduciary responsibility. They must be able to prove that they have made proper use of the resources their principals have entrusted to them.

Through the exercise of control — through reports and the objective verifications by auditors — the principals can assure themselves that the fiduciary responsibility has been carried out. Further, by establishing appropriate systems of control, the agent manager can provide the owner with appropriate assurances of acceptable conduct.

Systems of Control

Elements

The means of control include people, rules, budgets, schedules, and a host of other components. Combined, these elements constitute systems of control. The systems may incorporate subsystems, and they may be parts of larger systems. All of these systems operate in concert to meet one or more common objectives. Systems may be closed or open. A closed system does not interact with its environment; an open system does. Closed systems were rare — but since the general use of computers they are more frequently used. Internal auditors will deal with both systems though they cannot ignore the effect of the environment on open system controls.

A well-known example of a closed system is the one used to regulate the temperature in the home. Here is how it works:

> The objective of the homeowner is to control the environment in the home — interact with it — by supplying cold or heat as needed. If the environment is excessively hot or cold, the air conditioner/furnace can be turned up or down to bring the temperature to a comfortable level. This control can be done manually or through some control device. One such device is a thermostat.
>
> The objective, as we have seen, is comfort. Deciding on an objective is the first step in the control process.
>
> The thermostat can be set to meet that objective. The precise setting is the standard — the second element of control.
>
> As the thermometer device in the thermostat rises above or falls below the standard, the device observes the difference between actual temperature and the temperature that will meet the homeowner's objective — the specific standard. This is the third element of control — comparing what is with what should be.
>
> When the comparison shows an unsatisfactory condition — standard (and therefore objective) not met — the thermostat device commands the heating or cooling element to turn on. This is the fourth element of control — corrective action.

Business systems, of course, are usually more complex, but they all work in the same way. The more common closed-loop systems, for instance inventory reorder systems, are commonly called feedback systems. As in the case of the thermostat, output (here, the environment) is compared with some standard so that an appropriate response is generated. All operating systems have the basic means of input, processing, and output:

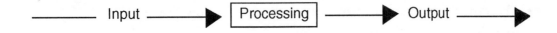

To control the process so that output continues to meet desired standards, two elements must be added — control and feedback:

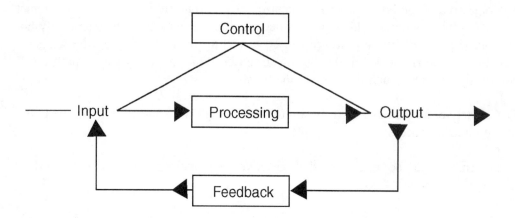

Thus, in a manufacturing system:

- Input includes people, machines, and raw materials.

- Processing converts raw material and labor into a product.

- Output is the finished product.

- The control system includes production control, which regulates the flow of input materials and services, and inspection of output.

- Control compares output with standards, through inspections or computerized observation.

- Feedback communicates variances to the processing element.

- Corrective action improves the process to better meet the standards of what is acceptable.

The closed-loop system — not to be confused with the open system — conforms to the classical management view of control: to see that intentions come to pass. Control, therefore, comprises the entire effort to achieve results that conform to plans, to see that objectives are met.

Importance of Controls

Control is especially important in large organizations. Managers are unable to personally oversee everything for which they will be held accountable. So they must delegate authority to subordinates who function in the manager's stead. Those subordinates will be assigned the responsibility for carrying out their tasks. Along with the assignment of responsibility comes accountability, which calls for evidence that assigned tasks have been accomplished as intended. The evidence is usually in the form of reports comparing actual outcomes with those planned. This is basic control.

Devising systems of control to see that tasks are accomplished and objectives are met is a management responsibility. Managers are responsible for installing controls, maintaining them, modifying those that need to be changed, and noting appropriately when aware of the information provided by the control system.

Managers use controls because they must. Plans may be unclear or poorly communicated. Employee objectives may differ from management objectives. Accidents and delays can occur, creating circumstances not planned. Detective controls constantly compare what is with what should be, communicate shortcomings to management, and permit managers to take needed corrective action.

Operating Standards

Operating standards may be key elements in the control process. Standards establish the kind of performance expected. They do double duty: identify objectives to be achieved and provide a basis for measurement.

To facilitate measurement, standards should be quantitative. Everyone understands numbers. Qualitative criteria are much more difficult to measure against. However, quantitative standards without a qualitative requirement can be misleading and can result in faulty management decisions. Operating standards should be specific, though they can contain a tolerance factor. Thus, a manager can readily measure against "completing the task by July 10," but have difficulty with "completing the task within a reasonable time." July 10 is July 10 for everyone. "A reasonable time" immediately raises the question of what is reasonable? And to whom?

Controls generally require operating standards. These standards can come from various sources, such as:

- Engineered standards.
- Cost accounting standards.
- Mandated standards.

- Industry standards.
- Historical standards.
- "Best estimate" standards.

Care must be taken that the standards are reasonable, contain appropriate tolerance factors, are current, and will, when complied with, produce their intended objective.

Internal Control Standards

Apart from the operating standards that are a part of the control systems, there is a body of standards to which the control systems themselves should conform. These standards are:[25]

General Standards

- **Reasonable Assurance** — Controls should give reasonable assurance that the internal control objectives will be achieved.

- **Supportive Attitude** — Managers and employees should maintain a supportive attitude toward internal controls.

- **Integrity and Competence** — Those involved in the operation of internal controls should have a level of professional and personal integrity and competence adequate to operate the controls so as to achieve the internal control objectives.

- **Control Objectives** — Specific, comprehensive, and reasonable control objectives are to be identified or developed for each organization activity.

- **Monitoring Controls** — Managers are to continually monitor the output of the control systems and to take appropriate action on deviations that warrant such action.

Detailed Standards

- **Documentation** — The structure, all transactions, and significant events are to be clearly documented. Such documentation is to be readily available.

- **Prompt and Proper Recording of Transactions and Events**

- **Authorization and Execution of Transactions and Events** — Such items are to be authorized and executed by properly designated persons.

- **Separation of Duties** — Authorizing, processing, recording, and reviewing transactions should be separated among individuals (and units).

- **Supervision** — Supervision should be competent and continuing so as to ensure the achievement of internal control objectives.

- **Access to and Accountability for Resources/and Records** — Access is to be limited to authorized individuals, some who are accountable for the custody and use of resources and others who maintain the records. This aspect should be periodically verified by comparing physical and recorded amounts.

Characteristics of Controls

Internal auditors can evaluate systems of control by finding out whether they meet certain criteria. Attributes that bespeak an acceptable system include:[26]

Timeliness. Controls should detect potential or actual deviations early enough to limit costly exposures. Controls should be timely, although cost effectiveness must also be considered. Managers should anticipate and provide for problems disclosed by the controls. But there are always the "unknown unknowns" — those for which there is just no experience. So, when the unexpected problems occur, they should be identified and dealt with in a timely manner.

Economy. Controls should provide "reasonable assurance" of achieving intended results at a minimum cost and with the fewest undesirable side effects.

Absolute control may be possible (though unlikely), but it may also outweigh the benefits to be gained. Controls should pay for themselves by reducing potential losses and expenses beyond the added costs. Thus, management should compare the cost of exposures to be prevented, detected, or corrected with the cost of related controls. Management must be concerned not only with effectiveness of controls, but also with their efficiency and economy. Controls should be increased only as long as the benefits they provide are greater than their incremental costs.

The balancing of exposure and protection may not always be easy or, indeed, objectively measurable. Some controls may be mandated by considerations of safety, the environment, sensitive situations, or enhanced reputation. So, in some cases, management may need to use subjective evaluations when establishing the rigor of particular control systems.

Accountability. Controls should help people demonstrate their accountability for tasks assigned. Managers need controls to help them meet their responsibilities. Managers should therefore be aware of the purpose and operation of controls to that end and be able to take advantage of them.

Placement. Controls should be positioned where they are most effective. They should be installed:

1. Before an expensive part of a project.
2. Before points of no (or difficult) return.
3. Where one phase of an operation ends and another begins.
4. Where measurement is most convenient.
5. Where corrective action is easier to take.
6. Where time is left for corrective action.
7. After a completed task or the completion of an error-prone activity.
8. Where accountability for resources changes.

Flexibility. Circumstances are bound to change. Plans and procedures are almost sure to be altered with time. Controls that will accommodate such changes without themselves requiring change are preferable to avoid the need to change. Changes in controls to match operation changes tend to bring about additional confusion. An example of a flexible control is a variable budget system where cost and operating quantities are provided for different levels of operation.

Cause identification. Prompt corrective action is facilitated if controls identify not only the problem but also the cause. Standard responses can be prepared in advance and readily put to use if the control points to the cause of the difficulty. No corrective action is truly effective unless the cause of the defect is addressed. An example is a cost accounting system where the various elements of cost and quantities are identified and compared to a standard. Thus, a variance in product cost or quantity can be traced to the individual element where there is a deviation from a standard.

Appropriateness. Controls should meet management's needs. They should help achieve the objectives of management's plans and they should fit into the personnel and organization structure of operations. The most efficient and useful controls are those that work on an exception basis, responding only to significant deviations.

Problems with controls. Controls certainly bring benefits. But they may also bring problems. They may keep a function on course, but at a price — both monetary and human. Excessive and redundant controls may cause confusion and frustration. As controls increase after a point, their effectiveness may actually decrease. They may cost more than the exposure they are designed to guard against. More on this later in the chapter.

Overemphasis on controls can make them an end rather than the means toward an end. Thus, people may work to satisfy procedural controls and lose sight of the operational objectives to be met. Controls can produce mental rigidity and reduce flexibility; slavish adherence to procedures may substitute for the application of reason and common sense.

Controls can become obsolete. The systems or the objectives for which they were devised may change, but the controls might not. So controls must be monitored for continued relevance. Controls may not respond to a need. In fact, they may become counterproductive. In addition, the information the control does provide may not be understood, or it may be transmitted to the wrong person, or it may be so complex as to be useless.

People generally resist controls. This is particularly true if they had no part in development of the controls or do not understand the objective to be met. Also, controls perceived as unreasonable can stifle creativity and initiative. Besides, when controls become a basis for reward or punishment, they may take on undue importance in the eyes of those affected.

Behavior must be taken into account in designing and enforcing controls. One way to do so is through communication to employees. Another way is to have affected employees participate in the design of the control operation. If people are to accept controls willingly, they should understand what the controls are seeking to achieve — they should understand the objectives. Employees may find controls excessively restrictive, a hindrance, or meaningless unless they understand the purpose of the controls. Here is an example of a perfectly reasonable control system that failed because behavioral aspects were not taken into account:

A manufacturing organization's production unit produced metal scrap, but its scrap sales yard was two miles away. Carts were filled with scrap at the plant, including such expensive metals as stainless steel, molybdenum, copper, titanium, and beryllium. Periodically, the carts were hooked to a tractor and hauled from the production plant to the scrap sales yard for sale to scrap dealers.

A control system was installed to safeguard the valuable scrap metal en route. The objective was to provide reasonable assurance that the transported scrap would reach its destination without loss. The standard established was the time it should reasonably take to haul the scrap, directly and without stops, from the production plant to the scrap sales yard. The information on whether the standard was met was to be included on tags accompanying the scrap.

As the tractor passed the guard at the gate of the production plant, the guard was to enter on the tags the exact time the driver left the plant. A guard at the scrap sales yard was to enter the exact time the tractor reached that point. The two entries were then to be compared. Any significant variances between the standard and the actual elapsed time were to be investigated. On paper, the control system contained all the elements of an adequate control system.

The audit, however, disclosed that the guards were not entering the times of departure and arrival on the tags. Without that information, the control system was valueless. The guards were asked if they had been instructed to enter the time on the tags and, if so, why they weren't doing so. Guards at both locations said that the instructions made no sense to them and that they were not about to spend time on nonsense.

Obviously, the guards had been ordered to gather the information without being told the objective of the control system. The auditors pointed out that, if the tractor driver stopped to hand over scrap illegally to a confederate, the difference between the standard time and the actual time would point up the improper stop. The guards' eyes widened and they agreed enthusiastically to gather the data. The information needed for the control system now made sense to them.

Because the objectives had not been explained to the guards, the information was not gathered, comparisons could not be made, variances could not be investigated, and any needed corrective action could not be taken. A control system, adequate in concept, was thus completely ineffective.

Means of Achieving Control

Some of the operational means by which managers can control functions within an enterprise are:[27]

- Organization.
- Policies.
- Procedures.
- Personnel.
- Accounting.
- Budgeting.
- Reporting.

For each of these means of control, there are some criteria that internal auditors can use to evaluate the adequacy and effectiveness of control systems. Some mention of these items was covered in the earlier section the SAC report.

Organization

Organization, as a means of control, is an approved intentional structuring of roles assigned to people within the enterprise so that the enterprise can achieve its objectives efficiently and economically.

- Responsibilities should be divided so that no one person will control all phases of any transaction.

- Managers should have the authority to take the action necessary to discharge their responsibilities.

- Individual responsibility should always be clearly defined so that it can be neither sidestepped nor exceeded.

- An official who assigns responsibility and delegates authority to subordinates should have an effective system of follow-up for making sure that tasks assigned are properly carried out.

- The individuals to whom authority is delegated should be required to exercise that authority without close supervision. But they should check with their superiors in case of exception.

- People should be required to account to their superiors for the manner in which they have discharged their responsibilities.

- The organization should be flexible enough to permit changes in its structure when operating plans, policies, and objectives change.

- Organizational structures should be as simple as possible.

- Organization charts and manuals should be prepared that will help plan and control changes in, as well as provide better understanding of, the organization, chain of authority, and assignment of responsibilities.

Policies

A policy is any stated principle that requires, guides, or restricts action. Policies should follow certain principles:

- Policies should be clearly stated in writing, systematically organized into handbooks, manuals, or other publications, and properly approved.

- Policies should be systematically communicated to all officials and appropriate employees of the organization.

- Policies must conform with applicable laws and regulations, and they should be consistent with objectives and general policies prescribed at higher levels.

- Policies should be designed to promote the conduct of authorized activities in an effective, efficient, and economical manner and to provide a satisfactory degree of assurance that the resources of the enterprise are suitably safeguarded.

- Policies should be periodically reviewed, and should be revised when circumstances change.

Procedures

Procedures are means employed to carry out activities in conformity with prescribed policies. The same principles applicable to policies are also applicable to procedures. In addition:

- To reduce the possibility of fraud and error, procedures should be so coordinated that one employee's work is automatically checked by another who is independently performing separate prescribed duties. In determining the extent to which automatic internal checks should be built into the system of control, such factors as degree of risk, cost of preventive procedures, availability of personnel, operational impact, and feasibility should be considered.

- For non-mechanical operations, prescribed procedures should not be so detailed as to stifle the use of judgment.

- To promote maximum efficiency and economy, prescribed procedures should be as simple and as inexpensive as possible.

- Procedures should not be overlapping, conflicting, or duplicative.

- Procedures should be periodically reviewed and improved as necessary.

Personnel

People hired or assigned should have the qualifications to do the jobs assigned to them. The best form of control over the performance of individuals is supervision. Hence, high standards of supervision should be established. The following practices help improve control:

- New employees should be investigated as to honesty and reliability.

- Employees should be given training and refresher courses that provide the opportunity for improvement and keep them informed of new policies and procedures.

- Employees should be given information on the duties and responsibilities of other segments of the organization so they may better understand how and where their jobs fit into the organization as a whole.

- The performance of all employees should be reviewed periodically to see whether all essential requirements of their jobs are being met. Superior performance should be given appropriate recognition. Shortcomings should be discussed with employees so that they are given an opportunity to improve their performance or upgrade their skills.

Accounting

Accounting is the indispensable means of financial control over activities and resources. It furnishes a framework that can be fitted to assignments of responsibility. Moreover, it is the financial scorekeeper of the organization. The problem lies in which scores to keep. Here are some basic principles for accounting systems:

- Accounting should fit the needs of managers for rational decision making rather than fit the dictates of some textbook or canned checklist.

- Accounting should be based on lines of responsibility.

- Financial reports of operating results should parallel the organizational units responsible for carrying out operations.

- Accounting should be such that controllable costs can be identified.

Budgeting

A budget is a statement of expected results expressed in numerical terms. As a control, it sets a standard for input of resources and what should be achieved as output and outcome.

- Those who are responsible for meeting a budget should participate in its preparation.

- Those responsible for meeting a budget should be provided with adequate information that compares budgets with actual events and shows reasons for any significant variances.

- All subsidiary budgets should tie into the overall budget for the organization.

- Budgets should set measurable objectives: they are meaningless unless managers know what they are budgeting for.

- Budgets should help sharpen the organizational structure because objective budgeting standards are difficult to set in a confused combination of subsystems. Budgeting is therefore a form of discipline and coordination.

Reporting

In most organizations, management functions and makes decisions on the basis of reports it receives. Therefore, reports should be timely, accurate, meaningful, and economical. Here are some principles for establishing a satisfactory internal reporting system:

- Reports should be made in accordance with assigned responsibilities.

- Individuals or units should be required to report only on those matters for which they are responsible.

- The cost of accumulating data and preparing reports should be weighed against the benefits to be obtained from them.

- Reports should be as simple as possible, and consistent with the nature of the subject matter. They should include only information that serves the needs of the readers. Common classifications and terminology should be used as much as possible to avoid confusion.

- When appropriate, performance reports should show comparisons with predetermined standards of cost, quality, and quantity. Controllable costs should be segregated.

- When performance cannot be reported in quantitative terms, the reports should be designed to emphasize exceptions or other matters requiring management attention.

- For maximum value, reports should be timely. Timely reports based partly on estimates may be more useful than delayed reports that are more precise.

- Report recipients should be polled periodically to see if they still need the reports they are receiving, or if the report could be improved.

The Impact of Regulation on Control

The Great Change

Internal controls were once an exclusive management prerogative and tool. Corporate executives decided what controls they did or did not need to carry on their business. If controls were deemed to be onerous, costly, or undesirable, management would either not install them or would eliminate them. If the situation brought on risks, management on its own initiative would decide whether to install the controls or take the risks.

The U.S. Foreign Corrupt Practices Act (FCPA) of 1977 (91 Stat. 1494), signed into law December 19, 1977, has curtailed management initiative in this country. Now, the ways in which publicly held United States enterprises are controlled, and how records are kept, are subject to legal constraints. Offenders may be fined or jailed under Section 32(a) of the U.S. Securities and Exchange Act.

The FCPA's most far-reaching implications for domestic firms are not the provisions prohibiting the corruption of foreign officials. Rather, they are the record-keeping requirements imposed on United States organizations. To that extent, the title of the Act is a misnomer. The Act in general says that internal accounting controls shall be examined and, if material weaknesses are found, controls must be strengthened or additional ones installed. Bribes or questionable conduct shall cease, and funds for such bribes and conduct must not be made available.

Internal auditors are concerned with both requirements of the law: bribery and accounting controls. But this chapter deals with controls. That part of the Act reads as follows:

. . . Every issuer which has a class of securities registered pursuant to section 12 of this title and every issuer which is required to file reports pursuant to section 15(d) of this title shall —

   (a) Make and keep books, records, and accounts, which, in reasonable detail, accurately and fairly reflect the transactions and dispositions of the assets of the issuer; and
   (b) Devise and maintain a system of internal accounting controls sufficient to provide reasonable assurances that —

   (i) Transactions are executed in accordance with management's general or specific authorization;
   (ii) Transactions are recorded as necessary: (I) to permit preparation of financial statements in conformity with generally accepted accounting principles or any other criteria applicable to such statements, and (II) to maintain accountability for assets;

(iii) Access to assets is permitted only in accordance with management's general or specific authorization; and

(iv) The recorded accountability for assets is compared with the existing assets at reasonable intervals and appropriate action is taken with respect to any difference.

Section 102(2)(b) of the Act is taken, without change, from the AICPA's *SAS No. 1,* Section 320.8. The Act has not broadened those responsibilities. *SAS No. 1* was issued to guide external auditors in the study of internal accounting control; it had one purpose, to serve as a basis for setting the scope of the financial statement examination. External auditors test only those controls on which they intend to rely; they are not concerned about controls on which they do not rely. But the Act gives management, and therefore internal auditors, a wider concern: devising and maintaining a system of internal accounting controls to provide reasonable assurance that transactions are authorized and accounted for and that assets are safeguarded.

Accounting Series Release 242 (U.S. SEC)

Following the enactment of the Foreign Corrupt Practices Act, the U.S. Securities and Exchange Commission issued Accounting Series Release No. 242 (ASR 242) on February 16, 1978 — Securities Exchange Act Release No. 14478, titled "Notification of Enactment of Foreign Corrupt Practices Act of 1977." The release said in part that:

> . . . because the Act became effective on signing, it is important that issuers subject to the new requirements review their accounting procedures, systems of internal accounting controls, and business practices in order that they may take any actions necessary to comply with the requirements contained in the Act.

The Canadian Law

The accounting provisions of the Foreign Corrupt Practices Act are not unique to the United States. For example, the Canadian Business Corporations Act laid down requirements similar to those now in effect in the United States. Section 20(2) of the Canadian Act states that, "A corporation shall prepare and maintain adequate accounting records," and Section 22(2) stated that, "A corporation and its agents shall take reasonable precautions to (a) prevent loss or destruction of, (b) prevent falsification of entries in, and (c) facilitate detection and correction of inaccuracies in the records and registers required by this Act to be prepared and maintained."

The Internal Auditor's Role

Internal auditors can become powerful aids for management by evaluating control systems and by pointing out weaknesses in internal control. But internal auditors, it should be remembered, assist management; they are not themselves managers. This difference raises a significant caveat in terms of compliance with the United States and Canadian acts regarding internal accounting controls.

Evidence of compliance with these acts resides in appropriate documentation. When systems of control are well documented, an organization can more readily demonstrate compliance with relevant statutes. Good documentation is an internal auditing stock in trade. Management is prone, therefore, to instruct its internal auditors to, "document our internal accounting control systems so we can prove to the government that we are complying with the law."

That is a trap, and the internal auditor should try to avoid it. Compliance with a statute is by definition a legal and not an audit matter. The internal auditor is not equipped to tell regulatory agencies, "We are complying with the law." That is a function of management with the advice and counsel of its legal people. Internal auditors can evaluate the control systems and the supporting documentation just as they can evaluate any other activity in the organization, but they are not responsible for rendering legal opinions on compliance with the law.

These acts apply to the United States and Canada. But internal auditors in other countries, though they may not be under legislative mandate, still have a responsibility for evaluating internal accounting controls and for pointing out weaknesses to management.

In evaluating both internal accounting controls and other internal controls of the organization, the internal auditor must heed the admonition: controls must be designed to achieve a management objective.

Internal Auditor Reports on Internal Controls

Internal auditors are expected to be experts in the aspects of controls. They are also expected to be intimately conversant with the principles of management, of which control is probably the dominant element. Consequently in internal auditing, the audit practitioner may not be familiar with the actual operations but the auditor is or should be intimately familiar with the management and control aspects of the client function. Thus, one could assume that in most audit reports that the internal control aspects of the operation would be a reportable subject. Even in those cases where there are no control aspects that require corrective action, that condition should be reported.

Thus, it would stand to reason that periodically the internal auditor would accumulate the control evaluations of the many internal audit reports and arrive at a conclusion as to the internal control environment, structure, and philosophy of the organization as a whole. This observation should be tempered by observations as to the position of management at various levels. Much of this evaluation can come from interviews with management.

The report should detail the objectives and scope of the examination and it should be accurate, objective, clear, concise, constructive, complete, and timely. It should detail the strength and weaknesses of the internal control philosophy and function. It should disclose any noncompliance with the *Standards*. It should also contain suggestions as to corrective action that could be taken to resolve the functional weaknesses. The report should also recite the corrective action that has or has not been taken following audit recommendations in previous audits, and the comment should identify the potential exposure and vulnerability from such inaction.

Input into this report emanating from control self-assessment workshops at various levels of management and from nonmanagerial personnel can add much realism to the report and can be coordinated with the results of traditional audit examination of the internal control elements reviewed in the various audit engagements.

The addressee of such a summary report would be the organization's audit committee and other appropriate individuals. It would follow that the chief audit executive would provide follow-up reports to the committee at appropriate subsequent intervals.

The Cycle Approach to Internal Accounting Controls

In 1979 the AICPA issued a "Report of the Special Advisory Committee on Internal Accounting Control." Although the committee was formed before the adoption of the Foreign Corrupt Practices Act of 1977, it believed that its report should be useful to management and to boards of directors when considering whether their organizations are complying with provisions of the Act.

The committee, as do many accounting firms, advocated the "cycle" approach to the evaluation of control procedures and techniques. The approach is eminently reasonable. It gives consideration to objectives and makes use of standards. It is linked to the cycles of business transactions, following such transactions throughout the organization's systems of control. For example, the "expenditure cycle" for goods purchased starts with the authorization to use certain suppliers, then covers the supplier selection process, the receipt of goods, and payments to suppliers, and then winds up with the recording of payments. The cycle approach has been applied to government operations and to the operations of specialized activities that do not use the standard cycles described on the following page.

The control objectives — authorization, accounting, and asset safeguarding — are those stated in the U.S. Foreign Corrupt Practices Act and in accounting literature. (Compliance could be a normal additive.)

The criteria are those appropriate for transactions that fall within each transaction cycle. The approach suggested three steps: (1) classify transactions according to the cycles into which they can be conveniently grouped; (2) identify the criteria (standards) of internal control appropriate for the transactions according to the objectives to be met; and (3) measure the existing control procedures and techniques and output against the criteria.

Cycles can vary from organization to organization. The committee suggests, however, that the transactions of most organizations can be grouped into these five cycles.

Cycles	Examples of Transactions
Revenues	Customer acceptance, credit, shipping, sales, sales deductions, cash receipts, receivables, warranties, allowance for doubtful accounts.
Expenditures	Purchasing, payroll, cash disbursements, accounts payable, accrued expenses.
Production or Conversion	Production, inventory planning, property and deferred cost accounting, and cost accounting.
Financing	Capital stock and debt, investments, treasury stock, stock options, dividends.
External Financial Reporting	Preparation of financial statements and related disclosures of other financial information, including, for example, controls over financial statement valuation and estimation decisions, selection of accounting principles, unusual or nonrecurring activities and decisions, and those that are not transactional in nature such as contingencies.

Criteria of acceptable internal controls for each of these types of transactions are set forth in the committee's report. These criteria are grouped according to the control objectives — authorization, accounting, and asset safeguarding. Each criterion has control procedures and techniques designed to see that the control objectives are met. Exhibit 2-1 shows examples for one of the five cycles — revenues.

Although the cycle approach tends to systemize the audit approach and help ensure that all areas of the organization are covered, a caveat exists in that areas where there is little risk to the well-being of the organization should not receive the same attention as those areas where there is greater risk. Risk evaluation is covered in Chapter 3.

Exhibit 2-1
Revenue Cycle

Criteria	Selected Control Procedures and Techniques

Authorization Objectives

The price and other terms of sale of goods and services should be properly authorized.	Approved sales catalogs or similar documents containing current price information and policies on matters such as discounts, sales, taxes, freight service, warranties, and returned goods. Use of appropriate control forms. Procedures for approval of individually priced sales.

Accounting Objectives

Cash receipts should be accounted for properly and on a timely basis.	Provision for comparing initial record of cash receipts with bank deposits and accounting entries and for investigating any unusual delays in depositing receipts.

Asset Safeguarding Objectives

Access to cash receipts and cash receipt records, accounts receivable records, and billing and shipping records should be suitably controlled to prevent, or detect within a timely period, the interception of unrecorded cash receipts or the abstraction of recorded cash receipts.	Independent control of cash upon receipt (through, for example, lock box arrangement, cash registers, prenumbered cash receipt forms). Restrictive endorsement of checks upon receipt. Segregation of duties between access to cash receipts and keeping records of sales, customer credits, cash receipts, and accounts receivable.

The Impact of Reengineering on Internal Controls[28]

The current drive of many managements to downsize their operations in the interest of economy and efficiency can have a substantial impact on the traditional internal control function. Auditors have always been sensitive to incidents where controls have been curtailed or modified in the interest of achieving greater efficiency and thus enhancing the appearance of an official's or an organization's performance. However, we are now in an era where it is conventional wisdom that downsizing through reengineering is the approved direction to take.

In the interest of determining the impact of this new approach to operations, The Institute of Internal Auditors conducted a recent study. The study discovered that:

- 72.7% of the participating businesses had completed reengineering in one or more processes.
- 88.4% of the participating businesses currently had reengineering underway in one or more processes.
- 82.4% had reengineering efforts planned for the next year.

The areas of operation most often targeted as to be targeted included:

Accounts payable/procurement	57.3%
Month-end closing	36.4%
Order-entry	32.4%
Accounts receivable	29.1%
Capital expenditures	24.7%

The study disclosed that there were substantial impacts on the elements of what have been long considered as the substance of internal controls and even on those covered in the internal control component of the COSO structure. The study disclosed that of the respondents:

- 58% indicated that reengineering resulted in the elimination of traditional control elements such as segregation of duties, accuracy cross checks, authorization and verification. Individually:

  40.8% segregation of duties
  34.8% accuracy cross checks
  33.6% verification
  30.9% authorization

It is possible that some of the vacuum from the elimination will be absorbed through the newly developed concept of the virtual organization where the control aspects are merely transferred. However, in those cases where the controls are completely eliminated, the future will have to tell whether there is actually cost/benefit in their absence. It is also possible that the development of computerized controls that act in lieu of manual controls can efficiently function as surrogate control elements. Internal auditing must consider this massive change and, in addition to being a part of the reengineering process, it must be an element of the evaluation to see if there is increased vulnerability of major proportions.

Reduction of Controls — The Virtual Organization[29]

With the institution of downsizing and reengineering of organizations, management has questioned the concept of traditional controls in those areas of operation where multiple controls have been traditional. These areas include accounts payable, inventories, accounts receivable, traffic, and sales. Even in those operations where transfers of funds are substantial, the "new look" is to design operations so as to replace the controls by a transfer of responsibility and accountability to another organization that performs such control as a part of its normal processing.

This new concept, termed "the virtual organization," is based on a position of mutual trust and assigns responsibility and accountability to the organizations that perform the functions they do best. Gibbs and Keating have identified four types of exposures that must be considered:

- Integrity: concerning inaccurate or poor quality data.
- Security: compromising the safety or privacy of assets.
- Availability: leading to the interruption of operations.
- Recovery: difficulty in restarting or continuing operations after they have been interrupted.

Once the exposures are identified, the next step is to design controls that are essential on a practical basis, emphasizing the use of automated controls that are discretionary and that are detective types. The emphasis is to employ activities of the organization's suppliers, assuming that the information by such controls is dependable. Periodic reviews can provide assurance, coupled with the knowledge provided to the supplier as to the importance of these contracts to the vulnerability of the organization to function. These writers describe the situation at the Ford Motor Company where the processing of vendor invoices has, through the elimination of the usual business papers, been reduced from 14 to three days. They cite the reduction of potential errors as well as the obvious elimination of clerical effort.

Each such application will indeed be the subject of engineering studies that identify the strong points and usable control functions of the associated organizations. Dependability and mutual trust are essential. This arrangement in its extreme application is exemplified by electronic data interchange (EDI) where there is a paperless process of activities that produce an automatic flow of electronic activities from inventory maintenance through finished goods production. This aspect of the operation, including the internal auditing aspects, is discussed in detail in Chapter 16, on the auditing of computer-produced information.

The Audit of Controls

The objective of the audit of controls is to determine that the: (1) controls are in place; (2) controls are structurally sound; (3) controls are designed to achieve a specific management objective or to achieve compliance with predetermined requirements, or to ensure accuracy and propriety of transactions; (4) controls are being utilized; (5) controls are efficiently serving their purpose; (6) controls are effective; and (7) management is using the output of the control system.

In more detail the auditor should:

- Review the control risk element.

- Determine the objectives of the control system.

- Review the objectives to determine if they are consistent with organization policy or are designed to ensure compliance with internal or external requirements.

- Examine and analyze the control system to determine whether its anatomy is sound; i.e., is there a criterion, a method of measurement of conditions, an evaluation of deviations, an evaluation of effectiveness, and a method of reporting?

- Determine if the output of the controls is designed to accomplish its intended purpose.

- Review the operation of the control system:
  - Is the output being used?
  - Is the input into the system valid, accurate, and reasonable? If statistical methods are used, is such use theoretically sound?
  - If the system is computerized, is it operating properly? (Use of test decks or other methods of computerized testing.)
  - Is the output of the control operation valid?

- Determine whether the control output is achieving management's objective in establishing the control.

- Determine if the control system has the required characteristics of:
  - Flexibility.
  - Timeliness.
  - Accountability.
  - Cause identification.
  - Appropriateness.
  - Placement.

Also determine that the control system is operating as intended.

The above recommendations are not exhaustive but will give the auditor a start on designing an audit program for control system audits.

Auditing COSO[30]

Internal auditing that is designed to consider the new COSO control concepts becomes much more complicated than the traditional internal control audits. Much of this increased difficulty stems from the need to consider the soft controls embodied in the COSO philosophy as well as the more traditional approach to control auditing. In an article in *Internal Auditor*, Mark Simmons outlined a series of steps that appear to be appropriate in accomplishing such an audit. His procedure recognizes the need to develop and use a unique approach to evaluate the soft controls. This method employs input from managers and workers who are associated with the area being audited. This technique is fully described in Chapter 10, "Control Self-assessment." Sufficient to say — it is the evaluation of, the status of, and handling of the soft control elements.

The operation includes procedures such as:

- What are the basic objectives of the unit or organization as a whole (based on the five COSO control components)?

- What are the sub-objectives of the basic objectives?

- What are the risks associated with the achievement of these sub-objectives?

- What is the degree of vulnerability of these risks?

- What are the strengths and weaknesses of these controls?

- Is there a consensus as to the results of the evaluations?

- What is the resolution of the preceding situation if there is no consensus?

Simmons then suggests:

1. "Confirm the presence and effectiveness of identified strengths in each of the control components.

2. "Confirm the weaknesses in each of the control components.

3. "Determine whether significant weaknesses are counterbalanced or mitigated by any outside independent controls.

4. "Determine where strengths have not been confirmed and where weaknesses are not independently balanced; whether or not any reportable conditions have occurred."

Simmons then concludes:

- If reportable conditions have occurred, further work is necessary.

- If reportable conditions have been resolved, it is likely that controls are present and effective.

- Thus, objectives can be achieved.

However, he states that operations are not under control when reportable conditions:

- "Have occurred and gone undetected.

- "Are persistent as evidenced by their appearance in current and prior periods or elsewhere in the organization.

- "Are pervasive thereby seriously imperiling the safeguarding of assets.

- "Have seriously jeopardized the achievement of operating, reporting, or compliance objectives."

The final step is to design corrective action and to improve system strengths. Such action can be most efficiently designed and installed through the work of auditor work "focus" groups.

Control Risk Audit Aspects

Control risk is a substantial element of the broad risk area. Control risk is the possibility that the controls that have been established will not detect a situation that violates the exposure for which the control was designed.

Control risk should be a consideration in the design of the control methodology. Control risk is a result of compromise between the actual review of all events and transactions and the review of representative samples. It also includes the consideration of control methods and the quality of personnel who are functioning in the control process.

The internal auditor, in reviewing the control operation, must consider the control risk aspect. This risk element will serve to influence the design of the audit process in that a high risk must cause a more stringent audit of the control operation. Thus, the review of control risk becomes one of the first elements in the audit program.

Internal Operating Controls

Controls, Criteria, and Objectives

Internal auditors should be as expert in dealing with operating controls as they are with accounting or financial controls. Indeed, inadequate or ineffective controls in a production or marketing department can result in greater dollar losses than those in the accounting department. Millions can be wasted in ineffective programs. Payment errors or abstractions of accounting or financial receipts rarely result in such large losses.

Operating controls are more difficult to assess. Financial controls have been written about and accepted for many years, but operating controls are not as clear or obvious. Often, no criteria or standards have been set for what constitutes appropriate control procedures and techniques. This, then, is where internal auditors can demonstrate their professional ability by recommending appropriate criteria and controls and reaching agreement with the client.

As with financial controls, controls over nonfinancial activities must be keyed to objectives and criteria. While financial controls are established in consonance with generally accepted accounting procedures, nonfinancial controls should be established in consonance with accepted management principles and techniques. Hence, in nonfinancial activities, the auditor who thinks like a manager will determine what control techniques and procedures the manager should have to help plan, organize, direct, and control the activity; these are the four functions of management.

Management Functions and Control

Within each of the four management functions, criteria of acceptable performance are needed which, if met, would give reasonable assurance that an objective would be achieved. Exhibit 2-2 gives some examples of the criteria and suggests control procedures in a research and development (R&D) activity. Through such techniques, the control system within an organization can be analyzed and evaluated. The means of control may often be similar for unrelated activities. For instance, some controls for R&D and for purchasing may be similar. Here are two examples:

In terms of planning, R&D activities call for formal procedures to control the creation of development plans; similarly, purchasing activities would call for formal procedures to control the selection of potential suppliers.

In terms of organizing, R&D personnel should have their responsibilities clearly assigned; in purchasing, procedures should explicitly spell out approval levels for purchase orders, based on the value of the orders.

Exhibit 2-2
Research and Development

Criteria	Selected Control Procedures and Techniques
Planning Function	
R&D work should be planned in adequate detail and the plans should be reduced in writing.	A formal procedure is used to create the development plan and consider inputs from all parts of the organization affected by R&D activities. Measurable goals are included in the plans for R&D. Each project is uniquely identified and budgeted in the plan, and project milestones are clearly set. The R&D budget is properly balanced as to new products, product maintenance, and cost reduction programs.

Exhibit 2-2 (Cont.)

Organization Function

The R&D department should be organized so as to be able to carry out its objectives to create new products or improve existing products.

Responsibility for R&D is clearly set forth in written job descriptions covering all personnel assigned to the activity. The technological requirements for development work have been identified and the personnel involved in R&D have the necessary knowledge and skills in these technologies.

Personnel records include complete data for each person assigned to R&D work. Where in-house technological capability is lacking, provision is made to use competent outside consultants. Special test facilities and equipment essential to R&D work have been identified and are available.

Directing Function

Personnel should be motivated to do imaginative, innovative work.

Personnel are promptly informed of the issuance of procedures and directives that affect their activities. Personnel are encouraged to participate in professional organizations. Personnel are encouraged to publish articles in professional journals. The atmosphere within the R&D unit is conducive to open and frank exchanges of opinion. "Rap" sessions are held to permit and encourage the airing of views.

Exhibit 2-2 (Cont.)

Controlling Function

The manager of R&D should be provided with adequate information to administer the department effectively.

The manager is supplied with timely, accurate, useful reports on R&D costs.

Comparisons are made between budgets and costs, and significant variances are investigated.

Provision is made for giving information on field operation performance to the R&D manager.

An adequate system of coordination is in force for R&D projects throughout the entire enterprise.

Records are maintained of the department's accomplishments.

A formal process exists for authorizing changes in scope of work or expenditures defined by plans.

Overcontrolling

One fear that followed passage of the U.S. Foreign Corrupt Practices Act of 1977 was the possibility of excessive, redundant, useless, and/or inordinately expensive controls. When a difficulty arises, the tendency sometimes is to throw money at it and hope that it will subside. But too much control can be as bad as too little. Expensive, restrictive controls can stifle performance and initiative. Protection is bought at the price of repression.

A mine superintendent who received a 200-page "cost sheet" made this wry comment: "You people slaved two weeks on this bundle of figures and all I ever look at are the first four [summary] pages. They tell me whether I'll keep my job. The rest is damn wasted motion."[31]

Perhaps, he was justified. Controls, in many instances, are being overdone. Control reports, which are supposed to help managers control their own activities, are often guilty of being:

- Too voluminous — they should be condensed to the bare essentials.

- Too complex — instructions should be easy to read, activities should be easy to perform, reports should be easy to interpret, and easy to understand.

- Too generalized — they should focus on one direction and not be guilty of "report sprawl."

- Too stereotyped — they should be elastic and, if uncommon matters are reported, these should be defined.

- Misleading — they should reach definite conclusions.

Why Controls Don't Work

Controls, even though meticulously set up, do not always achieve their intended purpose. Although the controls are set up to help managers do a better job, many managers see the controls as a threat, a challenge to be overcome. Aldag and Stearns identified four reactions to control systems.[32]

- **Game playing** — The controls are considered to be a challenge, something to be beaten, not a helpful adjunct to their management techniques.

- **Sabotage** — Employees attempt to damage the control system, create confusion, and design projects with complex characteristics. The objective is to make the system inoperable, lacking in credibility and unnecessarily complex. Or, one can ignore the system altogether.

- **Inaccurate information** — Managers manipulate information to make themselves and their units look better or to create data that are so false that the controls are inoperative.

- **Illusion of control** — Managers give the impression that control systems are in force and functioning. The systems are ignored or misinterpreted. Good results are credited to the system. Poor results are allegedly caused by unusual circumstances that were outside the system.

These dysfunctional effects are attributed to a mixture of technical, behavioral, and administrative processes such as:

- Personal differences.

- Overcontrol.

- Conflicting goals.

- Impact on power and status.

- Misplaced emphasis on the control system. It becomes the objective rather than the means to an end.

In addition, students of control operations have identified a series of more simplistic causes of the failure of control systems to operate as intended. These are:

- **Apathy** — Employees operating the system have no interest in its functioning and tend to become careless in making sure that the system functions as designed.

- **Fatigue** — The operation of the system induces fatigue, and rest periods or system simplification are not provided.

- **Executive override** — Executives grant permission to ignore the system in the (mistaken) interest of the organization or for personal reasons. Such allowances of override destroy the credibility not only of the system concerned, but of all established control systems.

- **Complexity** — The control system is so complex that employees are unable to cope with it.

- **Communication** — The control operation has not been well communicated to the people who are designated as the control operators.

- **Efficiency aspects** — Employees see the controls as impediments to efficient operations and in the absence of information as to their essential value to organizational well-being, the controls are altered or eliminated.

This list of dysfunctional aspects of control operations should be a checklist for auditors who are reviewing control systems. It is important to look for reasons why the systems are not operating as they should, thus performing proactive auditing.

Internal auditors have long claimed to be experts on control, and with good reason. They usually demonstrate their expertise during audits that focus on controls rather than on technical performance. Their claims are now more readily accepted by management. The penalties for poor controls are escalating and there are few other people in the organization to whom management can turn for expert, objective advice on control systems. With increased responsibility, however, comes increased accountability.

Internal auditors will be expected to be more aware of control weaknesses and control breakdowns. When losses occur because of poor control, internal auditors will be taken to task; management relied on them and took them at their word when they claimed to be the experts on control.

The Rule of Reason

Internal auditors must keep in mind that good auditing is not performed by rote. No two organizations are the same. Indeed, no organization is the same today as it was yesterday. Managers are replaced, supervisors are reassigned, new employees are hired, and procedures are revised. Good controls are dependent on good people, well motivated and well trained; people, their motivation, and their training can change.

Ostensibly, good controls can be circumvented either by employee collusion or management override. On the other hand, good controls may be too good. They may be more costly than the losses that they seek to control. The controls may be unnecessarily redundant, or they may be so ironclad that they restrict people's imagination, initiative, and innovativeness.

The internal auditor must review internal controls through the eyes of top management while giving consideration to the people, the times, the environment, the risks, and the circumstances.

References

[1]Sawyer, L.B, "Internal Control — The Internal Auditor's 'Open Sesame'," *The Internal Auditor*, January/February 1970, 36.

[2]*Standards for the Professional Practice of Internal Auditing* (Altamonte Springs, FL: The Institute of Internal Auditors, 2001).

[3]Montgomery, R.H., "Dicksee's Auditing," quoted in the *CPA Handbook* (American Institute of Certified Public Accountants, 1956).

[4]Bennett, G.E., *Fraud — Its Control Through Accounts* (New York: Appleton Century Co., 1930).

[5]*Internal Auditing Alert*, May 1996.

[6]Sawyer, L.B., "The Anatomy of Control," *The Internal Auditor,* Spring 1964, 15-16.

[7]Practice Advisory 2100-1.6, "Nature of Work."

[8]Ibid.

[9]The Treadway Commission (National Commission on Fraudulent Financial Reporting) reported in 1987. The report emphasized both internal control and internal auditing.

[10]Committee of Sponsoring Organizations of the Treadway Commission (COSO), *Internal Control - Integrated Framework* (New York: American Institute of Certified Public Accountants, 1992), Executive Summary, 1.

[11]COSO, Id., 2-3.

[12]Internal Control Standards Committee, International Organization of Supreme Audit Institutions (INTOSAI), *Guidelines for Internal Control Standards* (Vienna, Austria: International Organization of Supreme Audit Institutions, 1992), 7.

[13]Ibid., 7-8.

[14]Roth, James, *Control Model Implementation: Best Practices* (Altamonte Springs, FL: The Institute of Internal Auditors, 1997), 7.

[15]Price Waterhouse, *Systems Auditability and Control Report* (Altamonte Springs, FL: The Institute of Internal Auditors, 1991), 2-1.

[16]Ibid., 2-2.

[17]Ibid.

[18]Ibid., 2-3.

[19]Ibid.

[20]Ibid., 2-4.

[21]Ibid.

[22]Ibid., 2-4-5.

[23]Ibid., 2-5-6.

[24]Ibid., 2-7.

[25]INTOSAI, Id., 8-10.

[26]Neumann, Frederick L., "Internal Control Objectives," (Mimeograph), 19-21.

[27]U.S. General Accounting Office, "Comprehensive Audit Manual," Chapter 9.

[28]"The Impact of Business Process Reengineering on Internal Auditing," *Internal Auditing Alert,* December 1995.

[29]Gibbs, Jeff, and Patrick Keating, "Reengineering Controls," *Internal Auditor,* October 1995, 46-49.

[30]Simmons, Mark E., "COSO Based Auditing," *Internal Auditor,* December 1997, 68-73.

[31]Arnold, J.F., "The Dynamics of Internal Control," *The Internal Auditor,* May/June 1970, 29.

[32]Aldag, Raymon J., and Timothy M. Stearns, *Management* (Cincinnati, OH: Southwestern Publishing Co., 1987), 650-1.

Supplementary Readings

Aggarwal, Rajesh, and Zabihollah Rezaee, "Introduction to EDI Internal Controls," *The EDP Auditor Journal,* Volume II, 1994, 64-68.

Applegate, Dennis, and Ted Wills, "Integrating COSO," *Internal Auditor,* December 1999, 60-66.

Bean, LuAnn, and Karen Chambliss, "Preventing Revenue Recognition Problems: Internal Controls and Best Practices," *Internal Auditing*, May/June 2003.

Bishop III, William G., Richard M. Steinberg, and Delaine H. Gruber, "Everything You Always Wanted to Know About Internal Control But Were Afraid to Ask," *Internal Auditor,* December 1992.

Bishop III, William G., "Internal Control - What's That?," *Internal Auditor,* June 1991, 117-123.

Calhoun, Charles, "Internal Control for International Banks," *Internal Auditing Alert,* June 1998, 1-2.

Colbert, Janet L., "Reporting on Internal Control: IIA Guidance, the COSO Report, and SSAE 2," *Internal Auditing,* Winter 1996, 3-9.

Committee of Sponsoring Organizations of the Treadway Commission (COSO), *Internal Control - Integrated Framework* (Jersey City, NJ: AICPA, Two Volumes Edition, 1994).

Crawford, David B., "Levels of Control," *Internal Auditor,* October 2000, 42-45.

Fiorelli, Paul E., and Cynthia J. Rooney, "COSO and the Federal Sentencing Guidelines," *Internal Auditor,* April 1997, 57-60.

Gibbs, Jeff, and Susan Gibson, "Organizational Effectiveness," *Internal Auditor,* February 1998, 34-36.

Harrah, James E., "Internal Controls and Professional Sport Franchises," *Internal Auditing,* March/April 2000, 3-13.

Hawkins, Kyleen W., and Bill Huckaby, "Using CSA to Implement COSO," *Internal Auditor,* June 1998, 50-55.

Hermanson, Heather M., "Reporting on Internal Control," *Internal Auditing,* May/June 2001, 3-7.

The Institute of Internal Auditors, "Assessing and Reporting on Internal Control," Professional Practices Pamphlet 97-2 (Altamonte Springs, FL: 1997).

Jacka, Mike, "A Hard Look at Soft Controls," *Internal Auditor,* August 2001, 81-83.

Kring, Richard, "Systems Control Strategies," *Internal Auditor,* April 1998, 60-63.

Mills, John R., and Jeanne H. Yamamura, "Casinos and Controls," *Internal Auditor,* June 1996, 54-58.

Moore, Wayne G., and William W. Warrick, "Audit and Controls in a Transforming World: New Solutions Required!," *Internal Auditing,* November/December 1998, 29-34.

Palczewski, Thomas, "No Recipe for Control," *Internal Auditor,* October 1998, 88.

Perriam, Peter, "On-line Control Assessment," *Internal Auditor,* October 1998, 21-23.

Rogers, Violet, Donna Phillips Jackson, Treba Lilley Marsh, and Jack Ethridge, "Selling Internal Controls in Not-for-Profit Organizations," *Internal Auditing,* March/April 2000, 41-43.

Roth, Jim, "Taking a Hard Look at Soft Controls," *Internal Auditor,* February 1998, 30-33.

Sears, Brian P., *Internal Auditing Manual* (New York: RIA, 2003). (See Chapter I5, "Control Self-assessment.")

Simmons, Mark R., "COSO Based Auditing," *Internal Auditor,* December 1997, 68-73.

Simmons, Mark R., "The Standards and the Framework," *Internal Auditor,* April 1997, 50-55.

Sisaye, Seleshi, "Two Approaches to Internal Auditing and Control Systems: A Comparison of Reengineering and TQM," *Internal Auditing,* Spring 1996, 37-47.

Thornhill, William T., "The Importance of Internal Control in Fraud Prevention," *Internal Auditing,* Fall 1996, 50-54.

Thornhill, William T., "Working on a 'Risk-Based' Approach," *Internal Auditing,* Winter 1996, 40-44.

Verschoor, Curtis C., "Internal Control Reporting: It's Here and Now," *Internal Auditor,* June 1992, 39-42.

Verschoor, Curtis C., "Reporting on Internal Control: An Analysis of Empirical Evidence," *Internal Auditing,* Summer 1996, 43-45.

Verschoor, Curtis C., "Public Reporting on Internal Control: A New Perspective," *Internal Auditing,* Fall 1997, 31-46.

Wallace, Wanda A., *Handbook of Internal Accounting Controls* (Altamonte Springs, FL: The Institute of Internal Auditors, 1991).

Wallace, Wanda A., and G. Thomas White, *The Internal Auditor's Role in Management Reporting on Internal Control* (Altamonte Springs, FL: The Institute of Internal Auditors Research Foundation, 1994).

Multiple-choice Questions

1. An organization's labor distribution report requires extensive corrections each month because of labor hours charged to inactive jobs. Which of the following data processing input controls appear to be missing?
   a. Completeness test.
   b. Validity test.
   c. Limit test.
   d. Control total.

2. One operating department of an organization does not have adequate procedures for inspecting and verifying the quantities of goods received. To evaluate the materiality of this control deficiency, the auditor should review the department's:
   a. Year-end inventory balance.
   b. Annual inventory purchases.
   c. Year-end total assets.
   d. Annual operating expenses.

3. There is generally no incentive for efficiency or economy in a cost-plus construction contract for small, unique projects. There is a potential for inflated costs. An appropriate control to encourage efficiency and economy in these contracts is:
   a. Elimination of change orders to the contract.
   b. Provision for maximum costs and sharing any savings.
   c. Use of an agreed-upon price for each unit of work.
   d. A checklist approach to the audit of contract costs.

4. Upon receipt of purchased goods, receiving department personnel match the quantity received to the packing slip quantity and mark the retail price on the goods based on a master price list. The annotated packing slip is then forwarded to inventory control and goods are automatically moved to the retail sales area. The most significant control strength of this activity is:
   a. Immediately pricing goods for retail sale.
   b. Matching quantity received to the packing slip.
   c. Using a master price list for marking the sale price.
   d. Automatically moving goods to the retail sales area.

5. To minimize potential financial losses associated with property, plant, and equipment, physical assets should be covered by appropriate insurance in an amount that is:
   a. Supported by periodic appraisals.
   b. Determined by the board of directors.
   c. Automatically adjusted by the consumer price index.
   d. In agreement with the basis for property tax assessments.

6. One risk associated with the purchasing cycle is the possibility that quantities in excess of organizational needs may be ordered. Which of the following controls would address this exposure?
   a. A using department supervisor reviewing each purchase requisition prior to its being forwarded to the purchasing department.
   b. The purchasing department placing all orders when the computer indicates a low inventory level.

c. The receiving department delaying the unloading of each shipment presented for receipt until an originating purchase order is available.

d. The warehouse delaying the storage of all goods until the inspection department provides a receiving report that is consistent with the packing slip provided by the vendor.

7. Controls can be classified according to the function they are intended to perform; for example, to discover the occurrence of an unwanted event (detective), to avoid the occurrence of an unwanted event (preventive), or to ensure the occurrence of a desirable event (directive). Which of the following is a directive control?

a. Monthly bank statement reconciliations.

b. Dual signatures on all disbursements over a specific dollar amount.

c. Recording every transaction on the day it occurs.

d. Requiring all members of the internal audit department to be CIAs.

8. Maintaining a file of purchase orders in the receiving department for merchandise ordered but not yet received helps insure that:

a. Goods are delivered to the appropriate department in a timely manner.

b. Only authorized shipments are accepted.

c. Goods are properly counted when they arrive.

d. Goods received are not misappropriated.

9. The cash receipts function should be separated from the related record-keeping function in an organization to:

a. Physically safeguard the cash receipts.

b. Establish accountability when the cash is first received.

c. Prevent paying cash disbursements from cash receipts.

d. Minimize undetected misappropriations of cash receipts.

10. Which of the following controls would help prevent overpaying a vendor?

a. Reviewing and canceling supporting documents when a check is issued.

b. Requiring the check signer to mail the check directly to the vendor.

c. Reviewing the accounting distribution for the expenditure.

d. Approving the purchase before ordering from the vendor.

11. An audit of the payroll function revealed several instances where a payroll clerk had added fictitious employees to the payroll and deposited the checks in accounts of close relatives. What controls should have prevented such actions?

a. Using time cards and attendance records in the computation of employee gross earnings.

b. Establishing a policy to deal with close relatives working in the same department.

c. Having the treasurer's office sign payroll checks.

d. Allowing changes to the payroll to be authorized only by the personnel department.

12. Adequate internal controls are most likely to be present if:
    a. Management has planned and organized in a manner which provides reasonable assurance that the organization's objectives and goals will be achieved efficiently and economically.
    b. Management has exercised due professional care in the design of operating and functional systems.
    c. Operating and functional systems are designed, installed, and implemented in compliance with law.
    d. Management has designed, installed, and implemented efficient operating and functional systems.

13. Which method of evaluating internal controls during the preliminary review provides the auditor with the best visual grasp of a system and a means for analyzing complex operations?
    a. A flowcharting approach.
    b. A questionnaire approach.
    c. A matrix approach.
    d. A detailed narrative approach.

14. Which of the following situations would cause an internal auditor to question the adequacy of internal controls in a purchasing function?
    a. The original and one copy of the purchase order are mailed to the vendor. The copy, on which the vendor acknowledges acceptance, is returned to the purchasing department.
    b. Receiving reports are forwarded to purchasing where they are matched to purchase orders and sent to accounts payable.
    c. The accounts payable section prepares documentation for payments.
    d. Unpaid voucher files and perpetual inventory records are independently maintained.

15. Which of the following statements describes an internal control questionnaire? It:
    a. Provides detailed evidence regarding the substance of the control system.
    b. Takes less of the client's time to complete than other control evaluation devices.
    c. Requires that the auditor be in attendance to properly administer it.
    d. Provides indirect audit evidence that might need corroboration.

16. Internal controls are designed to provide reasonable assurance that:
    a. Material errors or irregularities would be prevented or detected and corrected within a timely period by employees in the course of performing their assigned duties.
    b. Management's plans have not been circumvented by worker collusion.
    c. The internal audit department's guidance and oversight of management's performance is accomplished economically and efficiently.
    d. Management's planning, organizing, and directing processes are properly evaluated.

17. An auditor begins an audit with a preliminary evaluation of internal control, the purpose of which is to decide upon the extent of future auditing activities. If the auditor's preliminary evaluation of internal control results in a finding that controls may be inadequate, the next step would be:
    a. An expansion of audit work prior to the preparation of an audit report.
    b. The preparation of a flowchart depicting the internal control system.
    c. An exception noted in the audit report if losses have occurred.
    d. To implement the desired controls.

18. The treasurer makes disbursements by check and reconciles the monthly bank statements to accounting records. Which of the following best describes the control impact of this arrangement?
    a. Internal control will be enhanced since these are duties that the treasurer should perform.
    b. The treasurer will be in a position to make and conceal unauthorized payments.
    c. The treasurer will be able to make unauthorized adjustments to the cash account.
    d. Controls will be enhanced because the treasurer will have two opportunities to discover inappropriate disbursements.

19. Control has been described as a closed system consisting of six elements. Identify one of the six elements:
    a. Setting performance standards.
    b. Adequately securing data files.
    c. Approval of audit charter.
    d. Establishment of independent audit function.

20. A payroll clerk working through a computerized payroll system increased the hourly pay rate for two employees and shared the resulting overpayments with the employees. Which of the following would have best served to prevent this illegal act?
    a. Requiring that all changes to pay records be recorded on a standard form.
    b. Limiting access to master payroll records to supervisory personnel in the payroll department.
    c. Reconciling pay rates per personnel records with those of the payroll system annually.
    d. Monitoring of payroll costs by department heads on a monthly basis.

21. Which of the following would provide an auditor with the least useful information in an evaluation of internal controls over finished goods inventory?
    a. Reviewing the physical inventory instructions used to count the inventory on hand.
    b. Completing an internal control questionnaire with management.
    c. Completing a flowchart of receiving and distributing procedures.
    d. Visiting the warehouse where the inventory is maintained.

22. A control that prevents purchasing agents from favoring certain suppliers in placing orders is:
    a. A monthly report of total dollars committed by each buyer.
    b. Requiring buyers to adhere to detailed product specifications.
    c. Periodic rotation of buyer assignments.
    d. Monitoring the number of orders placed by each buyer.

23. The most appropriate method to control the frequent movement of trailers loaded with valuable metal scrap from the manufacturing plant to the organization scrap yard about 10 miles away would be to:
    a. Perform complete physical inventory of the scrap trailers before leaving the plant and upon arrival at the scrap yard.
    b. Require existing security guards to log the time of plant departure and scrap yard arrival with the elapsed time reviewed by a supervisor for irregularities.
    c. Utilize armed guards to escort the movement of the trailers from the plant to the scrap yard.
    d. Contract with an independent hauler for the removal of scrap.

24. The most persuasive means of assessing production quality control is to:
    a. Evaluate the number and reasons for sales adjustments.
    b. Analyze labor efficiency variances.
    c. Analyze materials efficiency variances.
    d. Evaluate the production/inventory/sales mix.

25. A means of preventing production delays as a consequence of equipment breakdowns and repairs is to:
    a. Schedule production based on capacity utilization.
    b. Budget maintenance department activities based on an analysis of equipment work orders.
    c. Preauthorize maintenance department work orders and overtime pay.
    d. Establish a preventive maintenance program for all production equipment.

26. Which of the following control procedures would be the least effective in preventing frauds in which purchase orders are issued to bogus vendors?
    a. Require that all purchases be made from an authorized vendor list maintained independently of the individual placing the purchase order.
    b. Require that only approved vendors be paid for purchases, based on actual production.
    c. Require contracts with all major vendors from whom production components are purchased.
    d. Require that total purchases from all vendors for a month not exceed the total budgeted purchases for that month.

27. An internal auditor plans to conduct an audit of the adequacy of controls over investments in new financial instruments. Which of the following would not be required as part of such an audit?
    a. Determine if policies exist which describe the risks the treasurer may take and the types of instruments in which the treasurer may make investments.
    b. Determine the extent of management oversight over investments in sophisticated instruments.
    c. Determine whether the treasurer is getting higher or lower rates of return on investments than are treasurers in comparable organizations.
    d. Determine the nature of controls established by the treasurer to monitor the risks of the investments.

28. In which of the following situations would an auditor potentially lack objectivity?
    a. An auditor reviews the procedures for a new electronic data interchange connection to a major customer before it is implemented.
    b. A former purchasing assistant performs a review of internal controls over purchasing four months after being transferred to the internal auditing department.
    c. An auditor recommends standards of control and performance measures for a contract with a service organization for the processing of payroll and employee benefits.
    d. A payroll accounting employee assists an auditor in verifying the physical inventory of small motors.

29. Which of the following best describes an internal auditor's purpose in reviewing the adequacy of the system of internal control?
    a. To help determine the nature, timing, and extent of tests necessary to achieve audit objectives.
    b. To ensure that material weaknesses in the internal control system are corrected.
    c. To determine whether the internal control provides reasonable assurance that the organization's objectives and goals are met efficiently and economically.
    d. To determine whether the internal control system ensures that the accounting records are correct and that financial statements are fairly stated.

30. If an auditor's preliminary evaluation of internal controls results in a finding that controls may be inadequate, the next step would be to:
    a. Expand audit work prior to the preparation of an audit report.
    b. Prepare a flowchart depicting the internal control system.
    c. Note an exception in the audit report if losses have occurred.
    d. Implement the desired controls.

31. A perpetual inventory system uses a minimum quantity on hand to initiate procedures for restocking. In reviewing the appropriateness of the minimum quantity level established by the stores department, the audit would be least likely to consider:
    a. Stockout costs, including lost customers.
    b. Seasonal variations in forecasting inventory demand.
    c. Optimal order sizes determined by the economical order quantity model.
    d. The per-unit cost and potential obsolescence of the inventory.

32. The manager of a production line has the authority to order and receive replacement parts for all machinery that require periodic maintenance. The internal auditor received an anonymous tip that the manager ordered substantially more parts than were necessary from a family member in the parts supply business. The unneeded parts were never delivered. Instead, the manager processed receiving documents and charged the parts to machinery maintenance accounts. The payments for the undelivered parts were sent to the supplier, and the money was divided between the manager and the family member. Which of the following internal controls would have most likely prevented this fraud from occurring?
    a. Establishing predefined spending levels for all vendors during the bidding process.
    b. Segregating the receiving function from the authorization of parts purchases.
    c. Comparing the bill of lading for replacement parts to the approved purchase order.
    d. Using the company's inventory system to match quantities requested with quantities received.

33. The results of an audit of cash controls indicated that the bookkeeper signed expense checks and reconciled the checking account. If the cash account reconciliations were current and no cash shortages were found, an internal auditor should conclude that the system of internal controls over:
    a. Recording of cash receipts is adequate.
    b. Accounting for cash is inadequate.
    c. Reconciliations of the cash account are adequate.
    d. Physical safeguards of cash are adequate.

34. Which of the following exemplifies an inherent limitation of internal control?
    a. A controller both makes and records cash deposits.
    b. A security guard allows one of the warehouse employees to remove company assets from the premises without authorization.
    c. The company sells to customers on credit without proper credit approval.
    d. An employee who is unable to read is assigned custody of the company's tape library and run manuals.

35. The requirements that purchases be made from suppliers on an approved vendor list is an example of a:
   a. Preventive control.
   b. Detective control.
   c. Corrective control.
   d. Monitoring control.

36. A control that is likely to prevent purchasing agents from favoring specific suppliers is:
   a. Requiring management's review of a monthly report of the totals spent by each buyer.
   b. Requiring buyers to adhere to detailed material specifications.
   c. Rotating buyer assignments periodically.
   d. Monitoring the number of orders placed by each buyer.

37. The control that would most likely ensure that payroll checks are written only for authorized amounts is to:
   a. Conduct periodic floor verification of employees on the payroll.
   b. Require the return of undelivered checks to the cashier.
   c. Require supervisory approval of employee time cards.
   d. Periodically witness the distribution of payroll checks.

38. Which of the following controls would prevent disputes over the charges billed by independent contractors?
   a. Timely recording of both commitments and expenditures.
   b. A written agreement containing provisions for billing charges.
   c. Appropriate segregation of duties between the purchasing and accounts payable departments.
   d. A monthly report comparing actual expenditures with approved budgets.

39. Which of the following procedures is consistent with the effective administration of a company's insurance function?
   a. The insurance manager receives billings for insurance coverage and disburses payments.
   b. Insurance coverage is adjusted annually based on the appropriate price index.
   c. Final settlements are negotiated after claims are developed and submitted.
   d. Policies are always placed with the carrier offering the lowest rate for a specified level of coverage.

40. Which of the following controls would prevent the ordering of quantities in excess of an organization's needs?
    a. Review of all purchase requisitions by a supervisor in the user department prior to submitting them to the purchasing department.
    b. Automatic reorder by the purchasing department when low inventory level is indicated by the system.
    c. A policy requiring review of the purchase order before receiving a new shipment.
    d. A policy requiring agreement of the receiving report and packing slip before storage of new receipts.

41. Which of the following controls would be the most appropriate means to ensure that terminated employees are removed from the payroll?
    a. Mailing all checks to individual employee home addresses.
    b. Requiring direct deposit of all payroll checks.
    c. Reconciling payroll and timekeeping records.
    d. Establishing computerized limit checks on payroll rates.

42. Which of the following internal control procedures would minimize the misuse of corporate credit cards?
    a. Establishing a restrictive policy regarding the issuance of the cards.
    b. Reviewing the continued need for each card periodically.
    c. Reconciling the company's monthly credit card statements with cardholder charge slips.
    d. Subjecting credit card changes to the same controls applied to other expenses.

PART 2

TECHNIQUES OF INTERNAL AUDITING

Chapter 3
Risk Assessment

COSO philosophy. Who uses risk assessment? Planning for risk assessment and exposure. Expanding risk-based auditing. Organizations without a risk management process. Audit risk and its components in financial statement audits. A risk inventory. Basic questions on risk. Bell Canada's risk assessment strategy. Internal auditors and EC risks. EDI risk, risk of management. Building the risk assessment plan. Risk management. Objectives at the risk management process. Analytical methods. Flowcharting. Internal control questionnaires. Matrix analysis. Preventive and detective controls. COSO illustrative methodology. The Courtney Method. Another method of assigning value. Risk disclosure considerations. The need for several tools. Concluding comments.

• •

COSO Philosophy

Risk assessment is critical to management and the internal auditor. Federal law requires annual risk assessments for certain banks, and good management principles encourage it in other industries and sectors. The internal auditor must have an understanding of the risk assessment process and the tools used to make the assessment. The internal auditor must turn the output of the risk assessment into an audit program that makes sure needed controls are operating to reduce risk.

The COSO study, *Internal Control-Integrated Framework*,[1] begins its discussion of risk assessment with the following summary:

> Every entity faces a variety of risks from external and internal sources that must be assessed. A precondition to risk assessment is establishment of objectives, linked at different levels and internally consistent. Risk assessment is the identification and analysis of relevant risks to achievement of [an entity's] objectives, forming a basis for determining how the risks should be managed. Because economic, industry, regulatory and operating conditions will continue to change, mechanisms are needed to identify and deal with the special risks associated with change.

The assessment of risk is an integral and ongoing responsibility of management. It is integral because management cannot establish objectives and simply assume that they will be achieved. Many barriers will arise that will obstruct the path to objectives. Some barriers, or *risks*, will come from outside the entity; others from inside. For example:

- A new law or regulation diverts resources from operations required to meet other objectives.

- A competitor introduces a new product or service that requires immediate action and creates a new objective while lowering the priority of former objectives.

- A technological breakthrough makes one or more objectives obsolete.

- An incompetent manager puts empire building ahead of the organization's stated objectives.

The list of risks seems endless. The purpose of risk assessment is to bring sense, order, and limitation to that list. The number of risks is not static; there are new risks popping up all the time. Therefore, risk assessment is an ongoing function in the management process; it should be performed in an organized and orderly fashion. Thus, the risk assessment process is, itself, susceptible to audit.

Who Uses Risk Assessment?

Management uses risk assessment as part of the process of ensuring the success of the entity; that fact is clearly discussed in the COSO study. Management also uses risk assessment as an important tool in designing new systems. New systems, whether manual or computerized, are created to meet recognized objectives. An important part of the design and development process is the identification of all of the events and actions that might prevent the system from reaching its objectives.

Under recent legislation,[2] banks over a certain size are required to make an annual risk assessment to be used as a basis for making a public statement on the condition of the system of internal control. The bank's independent accountants are required to attest to the accuracy of that statement. There have been attempts since 1979 to require such statements by all entities that report under the Securities and Exchange Act of 1934. It is possible that through regulation or laws this reporting requirement will be imposed on more and more industries and public sector organizations.

Public accountants must make risk assessments to comply with their standards. *Statement on Auditing Standards (SAS) No. 55* of the American Institute of Certified Public Accountants (AICPA) discusses the accountant's responsibility to obtain an understanding of the control system. Public accountants also make risk assessments in planning their audits. What are the risks of failure to meet audit objectives? Which audit tests should be used to make sure that the audit objectives are met? One risk is selecting the wrong testing method; another, the use of improper sampling plans and techniques; and so forth.

Without question, internal auditors have engaged in risk assessment from the earliest days of the profession. Internal auditors have always asked, "What can go wrong?" The identification of potential errors and/or irregularities is an absolute requirement for determining what control procedures should be in place. After all, would there be a control if there were no risk? How can the auditor determine whether a particular control is an effective control — the right control — in the circumstance unless the risk is identified and evaluated? To deal with that question, The IIA issued *Statement on Internal Auditing Standards No. 9* on Risk Assessment in 1991. Currently the subject is treated in Standard 2210.A1 and further delineated in Practice Advisory 2210.A1-1.

In many entities, the internal audit department will be a key player in the risk assessment leading up to management's annual statement on the condition of the control system. The ongoing work of the internal auditors must be considered in the formulation of the statement. Special audits may be required in some entities to see that weaknesses found throughout the year have been corrected by the year-end reporting date.

Planning for Risk Assessment and Exposure

The audit plan should be designed to include a consideration of the organization's risks and exposures. Practice Advisory 2010-2. "Linking the Audit Plan to Risk and Exposure," infers that the organization's strategic plans should consider risks and exposures. The audit plan should assess the degree of attention in the strategic plans to these elements of risk priority and exposure. Thus, the audit universe can be influenced by the results of the risk management process. The advisory contains detailed methods of the audit activity such as the content of audit work schedules, approach to the audit, conduct of the audit, reporting content, and evaluation of the "internal controls to mitigate risks."

Expanding Risk-based Auditing[3]

The concept of risk-based auditing has traditionally started with the observation and analysis of controls, then proceeded to the determination of the risks associated with an operation, and finally the determination as to whether this activity was congruent with the organizational objectives. McNamee and Selim have faulted this approach because of the need to serve the objectives first, the objectives are the foundations of the operation and not always "cast in concrete," and they may be flexible and are — or should be — future oriented. The writers recommend an approach that first considers established organizational objectives and then assesses the risk through identification, measurement, and prioritization, and finally provides for the management of the risk by:

> Controlling and accepting the risk, or
> Avoiding or diversifying the risk, or
> Sharing and transferring parts of the risk to other units.

This concept of managing risk is becoming increasingly accepted because of the inevitability of risk in all types of operations and the need to accommodate it through multiple options of activity. The above options include:

>**Controlling** organizational activities to reduce the risk elements in size and number;
>**Accepting** risk by allowing prudent risk that is necessary for progress and profits;
>**Avoiding** risk that involves the redesign of the business process to change the risk pattern;
>**Diversifying** risk by spreading the total risk over a number of separate operations. An example: using multiple vendors for critical materials; and
>**Sharing and transferring** the risk by involving contractual arrangements with third parties to accept some or all of the risk. Insurance is an example.

The sign of the future is the expansion from risk recognition to risk management. It is an example of internal auditing leading the field in providing a "value-added" ingredient to a time-honored function, the concern with risk and the use of risk-based auditing.

Organizations Without a Risk Management Process

Much of this chapter has treated two aspects of risk: first, the internal auditors should review the risks in the areas being audited so as to develop an audit program. Second, if there is a risk management program, the internal auditor should evaluate it as a part of the audit. The IIA has recently issued two Practice Advisories related to risk management, Practice Advisory 2100-4, "Internal Audits Role in Organizations Without a Risk Management Process," and Practice Advisory 2110-1, "Assessing the Adequacy of the Risk Management Process." The latter Advisory treats the second of the audit aspects mentioned above. The former Advisory discusses a practice approach as a consulting service to audit clients. This Advisory recommends that internal auditors:

1. Assist the organization in identifying, evaluating, and implementing risk management and Board concerns and determine how they can be resolved by a risk management operations and controls.

2. Identify management and Board concerns and determine how they can be resolved by a risk management process.

3. Bring to managements' attention the lack of a risk management process and provide suggestions for establishing such a process.

4. Obtain an understanding of management and the Board's expectations as to internal audit assistance that can be provided in developing a risk management process.

5. Obtain from management its concepts of the role that internal auditing should play in the process.

6. Play a proactive role, if requested, in the development of a risk management process, keeping in mind the exposure to independence impairment.

7. Abstain from an "ownership of risks" role.

The chief audit executive must keep in mind the requirement that this assistance should not exceed the philosophy of normal assurance and consulting requirements.

Audit Risk and Its Components in Financial Statement Audits

Auditors and management are constantly questioning the extent and probability of risk. Extant is the amount exposed; probability is the likelihood of occurrence. There are a number of other issues that should be considered when assessing the impact of risk. A straightforward look at quantifying risk developed by Robert Courtney is presented later.

The AICPA has provided guidance in this area through several recent *Statement on Auditing Standards (No. 47, No. 53, and No. 55)*. Audit risk exists at two levels — the financial statement level and the account balance (or class of transactions level). At the financial statement level, audit risk is "the risk that the auditor may unknowingly fail to appropriately modify his opinion on financial statements that are materially misstated." An auditor is expected to plan the audit so that audit risk is limited to what in the auditor's judgment is an appropriately low level. In assessing audit risk at the financial statement level, auditing standards (*AU 316*) state that an auditor should consider management characteristics, operating and industry characteristics, and engagement characteristics. Factors such as the following may indicate situations with increased audit risk:

Management Characteristics

- Management decisions are dominated by a single individual.

- Management has an extremely aggressive attitude toward financial reporting.

- Management turnover is high.

- Management places extreme emphasis on meeting earnings projections.

- Management has a poor reputation in the business community.

Operating and Industry Characteristics

• Entity's profitability compared to its industry is inadequate or inconsistent.

• Entity's operating results are sensitive to various economic factors.

• Entity is in a declining industry.

• Entity's organization is decentralized without adequate monitoring of activities.

• Entity may not be a going concern.

Engagement Characteristics

• There are many contentious and/or difficult accounting issues.

• There are significant transactions or balances that are difficult to audit.

• There are significant and unusual related party transactions.

• There is either a prior history of significant misstatements detected during the audits or no prior history is available.

Factors such as these should not be considered in isolation. For example, the size, complexity, and ownership of the entity will heighten or mitigate these factors.

The auditor's conclusion about audit risk at the financial statement level will impact: (1) engagement staffing; (2) supervision required; (3) overall audit strategy; and (4) degree of professional skepticism. For example, in a situation in which an auditor feels that there is increased audit risk, the auditor may assign more experienced staff and apply more substantive procedures during interim and year-end work.

In considering audit risk at the account balance or class of transactions level, an auditor must consider financial statement assertions. Assertions are management representations that are included in an account balance, class of transactions and disclosures. *SAS* identifies five general management (or financial statement) assertions — existence or occurrence, completeness, rights and obligations, valuation or allocation, and presentation and disclosure. For example, management representing that accounts payable for a division at June 30 amounts to $85,000 is claiming that:

- The accounts payable existed at the balance sheet data (existence).

- All accounts payable are included (completeness).

- The accounts payable are legal obligations (obligation).

- The accounts payable are properly valued (valuation or allocation).

- All accounts payable are properly disclosed (presentation and disclosure).

At the account balance or class of transactions level, audit risk consists of (a) the risk that the balance or class and related assertions contain misstatements either by themselves or with others that could be material to the financial statements (called inherent and control risk) and (b) the risk that the auditor will not detect such misstatements if they exist (called detection risk). Hence audit risk at the balance or class level has three components — inherent risk, control risk, and detection risk. An auditor is expected to plan the audit so that audit risk at the balance or class level is limited to enable the auditor to render an opinion at an appropriately low audit risk at the financial statement level.

The *SAS* provides the following as examples of factors that an auditor should consider in evaluating audit risk at the balance or class level:

- Effect of risk factors identified at the financial statement level.

- Complex and contentious accounting issues.

- Frequent or significant difficult-to-audit transactions.

- Significant misstatements are likely, based upon information obtained from prior audits.

- Susceptibility of assets to misappropriation.

- Competence and experience of personnel who process data.

- Degree of judgment involved in determining an account balance or transactions.

- Size and volume of items included in an account balance or class.

- Complexity of calculations.

In many ways, the substance of the previously identified *SASs* is a landmark contribution to audit literature. It clearly defines a pathway for determining the audit work required to fulfill audit responsibilities.

Inherent Risk

Inherent risk is the susceptibility of an assertion to be a material misstatement, assuming no related internal control structure policy or procedures are established. Inherent risk is the risk that is intrinsic to the entity's business. The risk of such misstatement is greater for some assertions and balances or classes than for others. For example:

- Valuation and existence assertions relating to accounts receivable are more likely to be violated than the completeness assertion when an auditor is concerned about an entity's ability to continue as a going concern.

- Pension expense calculations are more likely to be misstated than depreciation expense calculations using the straight-line method (complex compared to simple calculations).

- Cash is more susceptible to theft than an inventory of limestone (amounts that are easier to steal with a higher value than items that are difficult to steal with a low value).

- Factors external to the entity such as technological change that may make specific inventory obsolete and potentially overvalued.

Factors identified at the financial statement level can impact the inherent risk at the balance or class level. For example, a going concern question identified at the financial statement level may cause inherent risk for the valuation of inventory to increase.

A few examples will be helpful in understanding the AICPA's observations on inherent risk:

- In a security trading firm, a simple interest calculation is less error-prone than a calculation based on the interest method.

- In a bank, the lapping of credits is more likely in deposits to savings accounts or payments on installment loans than deposits to checking accounts.

- In a department store, the balance of accounts receivable is more likely to be realistically stated than the balance of the bad debts reserve account.

- In a grocery store, increased demands for inventory control made simple cash registers and manual inventory counts/records obsolete when bar code readings at the point of sale terminals were introduced.

- In a diversified organization, emphasis on funding acquisitions through bank credits, rather than increased capital, puts pressure on earnings when interest rates rise; possibly leading to marginal sales prices and/or riskier receivable credits to obtain higher earnings.

The auditor is able to evaluate some of the inherent risk of a client/auditee by looking at the industry as a whole. Banks face a known set of inherent risks because they are in the credit and money handling business. An auto manufacturing organization faces known groups of inherent risk found both in manufacturing and the automobile business.

There is also inherent risk that an organization imposes on itself through the corporate culture it maintains. An organization tightly managed by a small group may have a philosophy: "We want to be free of constraining written policies and procedures in order to respond promptly and directly to events."

Such an organization faces risks not present in an organization with the philosophy: "We will have documented policies and procedures to provide instructions to employees on current operations and to provide guidance in responding to events at the lowest practical level in the organization."

Risks created by corporate cultural orientation are risks inherent to a management style.

When the inherent risks in the organization have been considered, the stage is set to assess the safeguards established to prevent or detect occurrences resulting from those risks. This consideration deals with control risk.

Control Risk

Control risk is the risk that a material misstatement that could occur in an assertion will not be prevented or detected on a timely basis by an entity's internal control structure, policies, or procedures. Some control risk will always exist because of inherent limitations of any internal control structure.

An auditor may assess control risk at the maximum level when either policy or procedures are unlikely to be effective or it is not worth the cost of evaluating their effectiveness. If the auditor assesses control risk below maximum, the auditor is expected to obtain evidence about the design and operation of the appropriate policies and procedures to justify such an assessment.

Detection Risk

Detection risk is the risk that the auditor will not detect a material misstatement that exists in an assertion. Detection risk can occur because an auditor decides not to examine 100 percent of the balances or transactions or because of other uncertainties. Included in these other uncertainties are selection of inappropriate audit procedures, misapplication of an audit procedure, or misinterpretation of the results of an audit procedure. Other uncertainties should be reduced to an acceptable level through appropriate audit planning and supervision.

Relationship Between the Risks

An auditor can evaluate these risks either quantitatively or qualitatively. The *SASs* provide the following formula:

Audit Risk = Inherent Risk x Control Risk x Detection Risk

In actually using the formula, an auditor may assess planned audit risk for an assertion, its inherent risk and control risk to determine the planned detection risk needed by solving for detection risk.

Detection Risk = Audit Risk/(Inherent Risk x Control Risk)

An auditor would select those audit procedures that in his or her opinion would reduce detection risk below the planned detection risk. This emphasizes the concept that inherent risk and control risk exist independent of the audit. In addition, changes in the internal control structure that are recommended and implemented after the period under audit will not change the auditor's assessment of control risk for the current period. Hence, for a particular level of planned audit risk, inherent risk and control risk are inversely related to detection risk. The greater the inherent risk and control risk associated with an assertion, the less the detection risk that can be accepted and the more audit evidence that must be accumulated. An auditor must perform some substantive tests when material misstatements could exist. In such cases the auditor cannot rely solely on assessments of control risk and inherent risk to justify not performing substantive tests.

An auditor will modify the nature, timing, and extent of planned audit procedures, staff assignment, and supervision required in considering reactions to changes in detection risk.

The concept of inherent risk is one that should be of particular concern to the internal auditor. The nature of the business or activities of the organization and the style of management create an atmosphere that has a great impact on the entity's inherent risks. Two municipal governments can have common inherent risks because they are municipal level organizations.

However, they can have different degrees of risk because one has a strong mayor and weak council structure while the other has a weak city manager and strong council structure. The risks can differ even more if there is strong citizen interest and open government in one, while the other is characterized by public apathy and political bosses.

Every entity is subject to its own inherent risks and the internal auditor should catalog them for use in risk assessment. The internal auditor's position as part of the organization offers an opportunity to observe inherent risks over an extended time period. The internal auditor should be aware of the differing inherent risks present in different parts of the organization. The inherent risks in manufacturing are different from those in finance. The risks in a clothing manufacture operation will be different from the risks in a chemical production organization.

The organization begins with inherent risks associated with its business and management style. The risks are countered by installing controls. Since there is no way to reduce risk to zero, there will be some risk even after the best controls are installed. That degree of risk is control risk. The concept of reasonable assurance comes into play at this point. Reasonable assurance is the level of control achieved when the cost of control and exposure and the benefits received are balanced. This can be viewed as the point at which control risk and the cost of control are in equilibrium.

A Risk Inventory[4]

Allstate's internal audit department developed a "business risk inventory" to assist it to:

- Provide a framework for identifying the risks that pose the greatest threats to the firm so that these risks would be considered in planning.

- Facilitate discussion about business risks.

- Establish an infrastructure for monitoring changes in business risks over time and for assistance in identifying new risks.

- Prepare management and internal auditing to take a proactive approach.

- Enhance audit staff's risk expertise.

The development of the risk inventory entailed a four-step process:

1. Identifying of "top of the mind risks."

2. Consolidating and organizing the risks.

3. Creating a prototype risk inventory and a risk glossary.

4. Refining the risk inventory.

The inventory was organized into two basic sections. External risks that included:

- Environment.
- Catastrophic.
- Financial market.
- Ratings.

Internal risks that included:

- Human resources.
- Integrity.
- Information and technology.
- Accounting and reporting.
- Financial.

The audit staff then developed specific risk inventories for each of the organizational units and for shared services and identified those that posed the greatest threats to the firm.

The audit staff then rated the risks as to significance and likelihood on a three-point scale; high, medium, and low. Those with the highest ratings were labeled "key" risks. The combination of "threat" and "key" risk then received the early audit and subsequently management attention.

Subsequently the audit staff developed a series of "Risk Triggers" for external risks and one for internal risks. Presumably, using a matrix approach with the triggers and the "key" risks, the auditor would be armed with the tools to develop the important areas to investigate.

Basic Questions on Risk

Entities are trying to maintain more control over their risk and hence audit those areas that involve higher levels of risk by asking a number of questions that have been determined to be significant. This has become especially important as management and internal auditors have come to realize that risk exposure has changed drastically with changes in business practice. For example, management has become increasingly concerned about market risk, the demand for entity's products. Alternatively, in the age of the Internet with its e-business and e-commerce components telecommuting risks drastically. Significant changes without recognition could have a devastating impact on a firm.

Organizations have been evaluating different ways to assess risk. Questions (risk factors) such as the following have been used in risk assessment:[5]

- Were there significant findings in previous audits?

- What was the scope of the last audit?

- How long ago was the last audit?

- What changes have occurred in the systems?

- What changes have occurred in personnel?

- What changes have occurred in products and/or services offered?

- What is the dollar value of the assets controlled?

- What is the dollar value of transactions through the entity?

- What is the entity's importance to the parent?

- How liquid are its assets?

- How is segregation of duties?

- How sensitive is the information in the entity?

- How are the pressures to meet goals or other business measures?

- How do laws and regulations impact the entity?

- How frequently are employees exposed to the potential for unethical conduct?

- What level of knowledge is required to perform the functions of the entity?

- How frequently do employees have contact with an entity's customers?

- How complex is the entity's operations?

Some organizations have basically established a list of questions that are to be addressed by the auditor in planning for engagements. Others have quantified answers to each of the questions by setting particular answers with associated values for the auditor to use. Based upon these answers a score is developed. This could be a simple sum of values to a weighting system based on expert systems. Once the scores are determined, the auditor can determine audit plans based upon relative scores. In any approach it is important for the auditor to evaluate the results of the audit relative to the prediction.

Some firms are developing sophisticated systems that will assign specific audit hours to specific engagements based upon their risk score. These systems will set audit hours and audit rotation using the risk evaluation. For example a score X would require 200 hours of audit work ever two years.

Bell Canada's Risk Assessment Strategy[6]

Bell Canada has used risk evaluation as an integral part of its audit planning process. A tool was developed to assist auditors in determining the type or level of risk to which each operation to be audited is exposed. Each operation being audited is divided into "key" subprocesses, functions, or activities. These items comprise one axis of a risk matrix. On the other axis the auditor lists the firm's 10 universal businesses risks. In each cell the auditor uses a simple scoring system where:

3	indicates a high probability of occurrence,
2	indicates a moderate probability of occurrence, and
1	indicates a low probability.

The business risks are:	Impact
1. Erroneous Financial Records	Financial statements and financial management records, recording, classification value, or time.
2. Unacceptable Accounting Principles	Procedures inconsistent with GAAP or inappropriate to the circumstances.
3. Business Interruption	Significant impairment to ability to provide service or to function.
4. Government Criticism or Legal Action	Penalties brought by judicial, regulatory, or government authorities.
5. Excessive Costs	Any expenditures, capital or expense, that could have been avoided or lessened.
6. Deficient Revenues	Loss of income or compensation to which entitled. Market share.
7. Destruction or Loss of Assets	Reduction in value or loss of facilities, equipment, material, cash, or claims to monies or data.

8. Competitive Disadvantage and Public/CustomerDissatisfaction	Inability to remain abreast of demands of the marketplace or to respond effectively to competitive challenge.
9. Fraud and Conflict of Interest	Intentional abuse of policies, rules or ethics, or erosion of basic honesty. Monetary aspects or misleading information.
10. Erroneous Management Policies or Decisions	Integrity of information for management decision-making causing inappropriate planning, organizing, directing, etc.

The auditors thus can attend to the targets with the highest level of inherent risk. The auditors develop a risk score for each corporate process and thus point the audit action in that direction. However, the risk areas should be evaluated as to their importance to the organization's functioning and well-being. Thus, a high-risk operation would not have a high priority if that operation would not be important to the ultimate well-being of the organization.

Internal Auditors and EC (Electronic Commerce) Risks[7]

The importance of internal auditing in this area is to determine where the various aspects of the EC function expose the organization to risks. Assuming that these risks can be identified, the auditor should, sometimes with expert IT assistance, determine and describe measures that can be taken to reduce the risks to acceptable rates. These recommended measures should include:

- The risks and their impacts on the organization.

- The modification or associated activity that is recommended.

- The impact of the risk modification on the operation.

- The degree of risk reduction that will be achieved.

- Financial exposures that are associated with the operation.

- Cost of the modification.

- Time elements.

- Probability aspects of success.

- Recommendations when more than one measure is presented.

Because of the dynamics of the EC functions, the reviews of these risk analyses should be conducted frequently. The internal auditors or associated IT experts, or both, must be familiar with new developments in the field as to:

- New technological IT changes.

- Recent publicized anecdotal situations.

- Changes in the organization's operations.

In a monograph published by The Institute of Internal Auditors, Xenia Lee Parker outlines the work of internal auditors in evaluating EC (electronic commerce) relative to the risk posed by the business processes. Parker states that basic IT internal auditing activity needs to perform the following so as to be able to make assertions as to risk in EC processing:

- "Understanding the system and infrastructure:

  ➢ Front-end Web servers;

  ➢ Transmission methods and protocol;

  ➢ Firewalls;

  ➢ Gateways;

  ➢ Back end;

  ➢ Middleware; and

  ➢ Possible links to back office systems.

- "Ascertaining which information is important, which data elements and programs affect the data, how distributed programs are, locations, servers, external parties, and processes are involved.

- "Recording and evaluating controls and procedures that handle critical or sensitive information;

- "Assessing monitoring procedures;

- "Obtaining possible external unification, as in assurances from a third party."

Parker states that, "certification from a trusted party is another way of providing verifiable factors to interested parties." She states that, "It is important to know who performed the work, their skills and qualifications, and the criteria used in the review."

EDI Risk[8]

Electronic data interchange (EDI) is an online computer-to-computer system of communication of the information on standardized business documents across organizational boundaries. Computers, databases, and information centers are linked by public or other communication networks.

Although computer aspects of internal auditing are more directly covered in Chapters 13 to 16, it is appropriate to introduce here some information on the risk assessment of that area of operation. The vulnerability of an EDI system is high because the failure of the system in any of its three stages — initiation, transmission, and destination will corrupt transactions.

There are six areas of risk factors; these factors and related internal controls are detailed in Figure 3-1. The six areas are:

1. Intruder accessing information
2. Loss of data integrity
3. Lack of transaction completeness
4. Unavailability of the EDI system
5. Inability to transmit transactions
6. Lack of legal guidance

The presence of several layers of internal controls has a multiplicative effect in reducing control risk. The control risk that the three layers of controls — administrative, physical, and software — will fail is computed with this equation:

$$CR_{EDI} = CR_A * CR_p * CR_s$$

where,

CR_{EDI} =   Control Risk of EDI system.
CR_A =   Control Risk that administrative procedures fail.
CR_p =   Control Risk that physical mechanisms fail.
CR_s =   Control Risk that software controls fail.

Thus, if the following assumptions are made:

Administrative procedures	0.10
Physical mechanisms	0.20
Software controls do not prevent penetration	0.05

Then, the vulnerability of a system with all three layers present will be 0.001.

The reference presents an excellent example of a situation where a potential problem related to inherent risk could result in a loss of $555,493. And that when the inherent risk is reduced using transaction completeness controls (with a risk reduction by $27,774) to $527,718.

The preference quotes the COSO report that internal auditors should make these steps a part of the assessment process:

1. Calculating the significance of the risk in monetary terms.
2. Assessing the probability that the risk will occur.
3. Determining how to mitigate the effects of the risk so that the exposure is reduced to an acceptable level.

The internal audit organization can contribute to the EDI risk assessment process by evaluating both inherent and internal control risks to determine if adequate and effective control activities are in place to manage risk.

Exhibit 3-1 Risk Factors and Control Activities	
Risk Factors	**Internal Controls**
1. Unauthorized intruder accessing information.	Access control.
a. Hacker accessing the system.	Password; dial-back mechanisms; user ID; storage lockout; different levels of access.
b. Interception during transmission.	Improving cable protection; routing message through secured medium; their fiber optics; encryptions; traffic padding; confidential electronic envelope.
c. Wiretapping.	Signal meters; leakage protectors; electromagnetic shielding; penetration resistant conduits.
2. Loss of data integrity.	Authentication.
a. Intruder modifying/fabricating.	Acknowledgment protocol.
b. Absence of paper audit trail.	Computerized log.
c. Physical signatures are missing.	Digital signatures; notarization mechanisms.
d. Errors introduced to the system.	Edit checks.
e. Corruption by authorized personnel.	Separation of duties; different levels of access.
3. Lack of transaction completeness.	Acknowledgment.
a. Transaction during transmission.	Batch totaling; sequential numbering.
b. Duplication of transaction due to retransmission.	One-for-one checking against the control file.
4. Unavailability of EDI system.	Fault tolerant systems.
a. Logical causes, such as virus, Trojan horses, programming errors, hardware and software errors.	Anti-virus packages; error free software and hardware.
b. Natural causes, such as fire, flood, earthquake, power failure, etc.	Off-site backup; RAID; disk mirroring.
c. Sabotage by authorized person.	Training; dissemination of procedure and policies on control.
5. Inability to transmit transactions.	Structured/standardized data format; adherence to ANSI/EDIFACT protocol.
6. Lack of legal guidance.	Agreement on legal definitions, responsibilities, and obligations.

Risks of Management Fraud[9]

A recent article on the risks associated with management fraud identified a fraud risk model for use by internal auditors. The writers propose the use of an analytical procedure:

1. Establishing a quantitative expectation for an account balance.
2. Establishing an investigative risk and a quantitative materiality balance.
3. Comparing the actual account balance with the auditor's expectation.

The writers then suggest a three-element structure to be used in the risk evaluation process. The three elements are:

1. **Conditions** that could allow management fraud.
2. **Motivations** that could underlay the conduct of fraud.
3. **Attitude** of management that could lead management to commit fraudulent acts.

In each of the above areas there are both internal and external risks. Examples are:

Conditions:
  Absent or weak internal controls
  Absent or weak audit committee
  Rapid growth
  Few predominant products
  Centralized decision-making
  Inexperienced management

Motivations:
  To encourage external investment
  To demonstrate increased earnings
  To dispel negative market perceptions
  To obtain financing
  To demonstrate compliance with financing covenants
  To meet goals and objectives
  To receive bonuses

Attitude:
  Dishonesty
  Lack of concern for rules and regulations
  Lack of commitment to ethics.

The auditor should set up a model consisting of all of the above potential indications of a fraudulent situation on one axis (the referenced article expands these lists materially), one of the frequently cited "red flags" lists on the other axis, and within each of the resultant cells to arrive at indications of potential areas of interest.

Building the Risk Assessment Plan

The COSO discussion of risk assessment points out that the objectives of the organization, the control system, and the risk assessment are inextricably tied together. It is impossible to determine risk if one does not know what is in danger. Once a risk has been identified, the only logical step is to create a means of controlling the risk.

The foundation of the risk assessment is contained in the definition of internal control. The COSO study is the source of a current and widely recognized definition of internal control.

Internal control is a process, effected by an entity's board of directors, management, and other personnel, designed to provide reasonable assurance regarding the achievement of objectives in the following categories:

- Effectiveness and efficiency of operations.
- Reliability of financial reporting.
- Compliance with applicable laws and regulations.

In its discussion of risk assessment, the COSO study observes:

Despite the diversity of objectives, certain broad categories can be established:

- *Operational Objectives* — These pertain to the effectiveness and efficiency of the entity's operations, including performance and profitability goals and safeguarding resources against loss. They vary based on management's choices about structure and performance.

- *Financial Reporting Objectives* — These pertain to the presentation of reliable published financial statements, including prevention of fraudulent public financial reporting. They are driven primarily by external requirements.

- *Compliance Objectives* — These objectives pertain to adherence to laws and regulations to which the entity is subject. They are dependent on external factors, such as environmental regulations, and tend to be similar across all entities in some cases and across an industry in others.

This definition of categories of objectives provides the starting point for the risk assessment. The broad objectives provide categories that can be refined to detailed objectives with identifiable risks. When the risks have been identified, various control options can be applied to the risks to determine the optimal control procedures to employ.

For example, assume that the auditor is looking at a cash receipts processing operation. Checks in amounts ranging from a few dollars to tens of thousands are received in payment of accounts receivable. The payments come to the organization's general post office box and are separated from other mail and delivered to the cash processing unit. This unit opens the mail and determines that checks and the accompanying payment stubs (remittance advices) agree in amount. Another unit prepares a deposit at the end of the day and delivers it to the bank in a night deposit bag. The deposit is made to an overnight investment or "sweep" account that earns interest. Use of a "lockbox" system would have the bank performing these functions.

The auditor begins by identifying operational, financial, and compliance objectives for the operation:

- To receive all payments on a timely basis (operational).

- To ensure the correctness of the document that will be passed to the accounts receivable accounting system (financial).

- To make sure that the negotiability of checks is limited by immediate endorsement (operational).

- To protect the checks from loss or misuse (operational).

- To make deposits in the bank on a timely basis to obtain maximum interest earnings (operational).

- To make sure the information posted to customer accounts will result in accurate credit records for aging of receivables and customers' credit histories (operational and compliance).

- To establish accountability for actions associated with handling checks to avoid any false accusations in the event of loss or fraud (operational and compliance).

- To provide methods for handling and approval of exception items (operational and financial).

- To provide measurements of performance of the unit and the personnel in it to reward high quality performance and to correct low quality and unacceptable performance (operational and compliance).

These detailed objectives are used to create a list of risks that would prevent the unit from reaching its objectives. Using two of the objectives as examples, the auditor prepares the list of risks:

Objective: To protect the checks from loss or misuse.

Risks

- The checks are exposed to loss, along with the general mail, between the post office and the organization's incoming mail room.

- Envelopes containing payments are vulnerable while being identified and sorted in the mail room before delivery to the processing unit.

- Checks are exposed in the processing area until the bank deposit is prepared.

- Exception items may be misplaced, lost, or mishandled during processing.

- The bank deposit may be lost or stolen during the trip from the processing area to the bank.

- An employee could be robbed during the trip to the bank with the deposit.

Objective: To make deposits in the bank on a timely basis to obtain maximum interest.

Risks

- Mail may not be gathered from the post office on a timely basis.

- Payments may not be separated in the mail room and delivered to the processing unit on a timely basis.

- Payments must be processed before the deposit is prepared, or the deposit will not reach the bank before the 2 p.m. cutoff time.

- Exception items may be held preventing some checks from being deposited until the next day or later.

- Equipment failures may slow the processing.

The auditor develops the list of risks by observing the activity and using an analytical approach, ingenuity, and imagination. The auditor determines what could stand in the way of achieving the objectives — what could go wrong. Once the risks are identified, the auditor can assess the controls that are in place and determine whether those controls are appropriate and adequate in light of the risks. If any risks are not adequately covered, the auditor will make recommendations on the weaknesses that are identified. The auditor will search for the optimum control structure.

Optimum is the best control structure in these circumstances and implies consideration of cost to benefits. The remainder of this chapter discusses the tools available to the auditor to identify and evaluate objectives, risks, and control activities.

Risk Management[10]

A recent article on risk has proposed the proposition that internal auditors should assist management by not only identifying the areas of risk but also assisting management in controlling the risks in a positive way. The writer states that risk is usually considered in a negative sense, yet risk is the essence of business and business-type functions. These functions normally use controls to neutralize excessive risk and attempt to set parameters where risk is established at a level where the positive aspects outweigh the negative. A simple example is the establishment of credit limits on sales: to set tight limits and eliminate risk would preclude marginal sales that potentially would be liquidated in the normal course of business.

The auditor assists management to take on profitable and prudent risks with "appropriate and efficient mitigants." The auditors evaluate management's employment of the mitigants to achieve the greatest benefits for the organization. Thus, audit becomes a positive control evaluator that assists to identify the risks that should be taken and the associated controls so as to enhance the operation from an income and profit position.

However, in addition to risk assessment and the assistance to management in converting risks to be an element of institutional income, the auditors should expand the area of audit interest to include risk control, risk financing, and risk administration. Thus:

Risk Control:
- Supports a proactive risk and loss control program.
- Provides maximum incentive for participation in the risk control program.
- Monitors the effectiveness of risk control activities.

Risk Financing:
- Considers all available financial resources.
- Maintains catastrophic protection.
- Allocates risk financing costs among operating units equitably.

Administration:
- Creates and sustains management commitment to risk management.
- Adopts a clearly defined risk management structure.
- Develops clearly targeted annual objectives.
- Maintains sound communications with all affected levels of management.

Thus, the internal auditor in the process of risk evaluation also is concerned with the positive aspect of risk management and causes the internal audit function to take a positive turn to contribute to improved management.

Objectives of the Risk Management Process

In evaluating the risk management process, the internal auditor should formulate an opinion as to the degree to which the process achieves the five key objectives listed in Practice Advisory 2110-1, "Assessing the Adequacy of Risk Management Processes." These objectives are:

- Risk arising from business strategies and activities are identified and prioritized.

- Management and the board have determined the level of risks acceptable to the organization, including the acceptance of risks designed to accomplish the organization's strategic plans.

- Risk mitigation activities are designed and implemented to reduce, or otherwise manage, risk at levels that were determined to be acceptable to management and the board.

- Ongoing monitoring activities are conducted to periodically reassess risk and the effectiveness of controls to manage risk.

- The board and management receive periodic reports of the results of the risk management processes. The corporate governance processes of the organization should provide periodic communication of risks, risk strategies, and controls to stakeholders.

Analytical Methods

The identification and use of risks to develop an optimum control structure employs an analytical method or combination of methods. These methods are:

- Flowcharting
- Internal control questionnaires
- Matrix analysis
- COSO illustrative methodology
- The Courtney Method

Flowcharting

Flowcharting is a method of analyzing operations for efficiency and control. Flowcharts are two-dimensional graphic representations of an operation in terms of the flow of activity through the process. They provide the ability to "see" the operation, to identify inefficiencies, missing steps, and control weaknesses. Flowcharts are excellent communication devices between the auditor and operating personnel; like a road map is a better communication device than a narrative of turns and traffic lights. Flowcharts also offer the opportunity to present in a comparable fashion a picture of alternative approaches to a process.

Flowcharting is a method that has not been used to its fullest potential until recently because it was so time-consuming. In the past, flowcharts were hand drawn on paper using a plastic template that contains the design of operational symbols. A final, hand drawn flowchart was often the end product of many false starts and much erasing. Hand drawn flowcharts did not lend themselves to easy amendment and modification. For all its virtue as an effective tool, flowcharting has not been fully used because of its lack of efficiency.

The advent of personal computers brought efficiency to flowcharting along with effectiveness. Flowcharts can be easily drawn, amended, and updated with little or no lost effort. A simple computer-processed flowchart of the current payment processing operation looks like this:

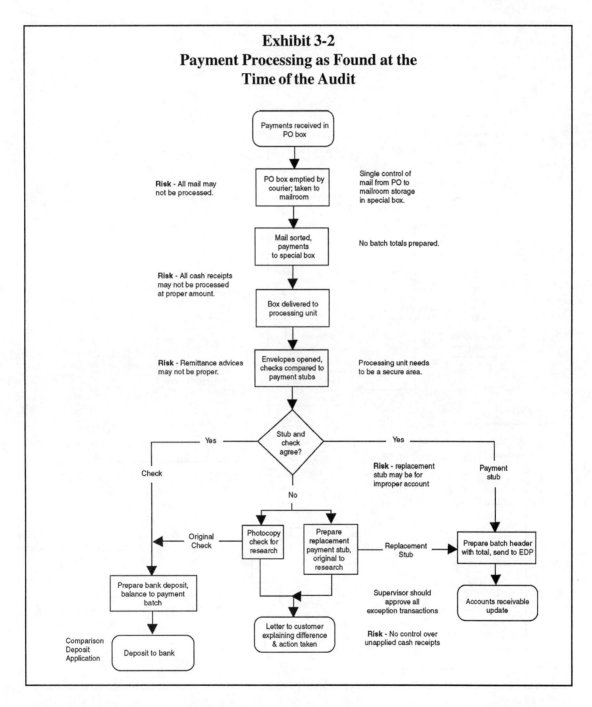

Exhibit 3-2
Payment Processing as Found at the
Time of the Audit

The auditor's notes are outside the flowchart symbols.

The auditor performs the initial analysis of the risks and uses alternative recommendation by superimposing the audit recommendations on the existing flowchart.

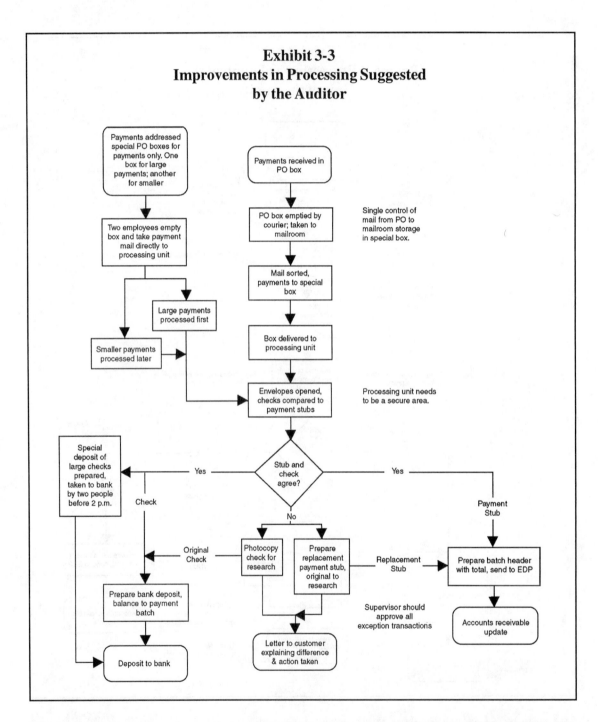

Exhibit 3-3
Improvements in Processing Suggested
by the Auditor

The auditor can make observations on methods, risks, and controls on the flowchart. The auditor can create alternative scenarios and try them out on the flowchart before they become audit recommendations. The alternatives can be more easily discussed with management when a picture of the old and the new can be compared side-by-side. Also, controls can be identified and discussed for efficiency and effectiveness.

Once a flowchart is prepared, it is available for review, analysis, and update in future audits. It also assists in the development and maintenance of audit programs. The updated flowcharts become part of the permanent file.

Internal Control Questionnaires

In the chapter on Preliminary Surveys, questionnaires are discussed as a means for eliciting information about the function to be surveyed and ultimately audited. There is another type of questionnaire commonly used by auditors. It is known as the internal control questionnaire or ICQ. It is different from the open-end questionnaire used in the preliminary survey.

The open-end questionnaire asks questions in a style requiring the respondent to supply a narrative response. The open-end questionnaire seeks information to broaden the auditor's understanding. The ICQ begins with a known or desired answer and seeks a "yes" or "no" answer with comment. The ICQ seeks very direct and precise answers about compliance with expected procedures.

ICQs are used for ongoing evaluation of existing controls and can be used in risk analysis. ICQs are usually developed *after* an activity or process has been analyzed and appropriate controls are in place. The ICQ is a compliance test intended to make sure that the controls are still in place and that risk can be evaluated. An ICQ can also be used as a reminder to the auditor of the controls that should be in place and tested in the course of the audit.

A segment of a typical ICQ contains the following elements:

Question	Answer	Comments	Method	Done By
Are checks compared to payment stubs?	Yes No	*This is part of assuring the amount received will be credited to the customer's account.*	Inquire Observe Test	JEL
Is the bank deposit balanced to the payment input before delivery to the bank?	Yes No	*If the two do not balance, the deposit is verified and sent to the bank for credit ASAP.*	Inquire Observe Test	MRE

Questions are answered (underlined) "Yes" or "No," and any modifying "Comments" are recorded by the auditor. The "Method" of determining the answer is recorded. An inquiry, that is asking the client, is not as desirable a source as is observing the event. Examining documentary evidence obtained through testing is more desirable than simply observing. Testing the records and transactions gives the opportunity to examine events and evaluate risk over a period of time instead of a short period of observation. This is necessary to evaluate functioning of "key" controls.

The "Done By" field should contain the name or initials of the person who performs the activity. By scanning this column, the supervising auditor can determine whether there are any incompatible duty assignments and can, through analysis, identify areas where this incompatibility results in risk.

The fact that an ICQ is a preconstructed array of questions emphasizes that it is used as a checklist to help with further evaluation after an initial risk assessment has been made. Conditions change, new technologies emerge, new laws and regulations are promulgated, and a host of events require the continuing assessment of risk. What *was* done and *is still* done may not be the best procedure for the organization. ICQs must be continually appraised to determine that the questions and the context in which they are answered remain relevant. The auditor must make sure the ICQ comprehends and responds to changes in the organization, in operating methods, and current objectives of the organization. Changes in any of these areas call for changes in the ICQ.

Matrix Analysis

Matrix analysis was introduced in *Computer Control and Audit*.[11] Though the methodology was introduced as an EDP audit concept, it can be used for control analysis in any activity.

A control matrix is a tool for matching controls to risks to assure that every risk is covered by an appropriate control. The control matrix also recognizes that a given control may provide protection over more than one risk. As an example, a lock protects assets against loss by restricting access. It also provides accountability for the handling of the asset because the person holding the key will be responsible if any asset behind the lock is missing. A budget sets down objectives and goals to be met and provides a yardstick to measure performance. It also establishes the authority of the manager to act within the financial constraints of the budget.

Each control (Control A) is designed to guard against a certain risk (Risk 1); the level of assurance is referred to as primary (P) because it is the primary defense against the risk.

The control (Control A) may also provide a degree of assurance in guarding against another risk (Risk 2), but the level of assurance is less than the control for which it was designed.

This level of assurance is referred to as secondary (S). Risk 2 has its own primary control (Control B) but Control A is a backup against Risk 2 while doing its job of protecting against Risk 1.

A control can provide a third level of assurance on another control (Risk 3). This level of assurance is referred to as useful (U). That level of assurance is not sufficient to rely on control to protect against Risk 3 but the control could raise a red flag on Risk 3 that should be investigated.

The matrix of risk and controls appears as:

	Control A	Control B	Control C
Risk 1	P		U
Risk 2	S	P	U
Risk 3			P

An example of the matrix method may help to clarify these principles. In a computerized operation, there are certain risks associated with access to the data files. Assume the following risks and their primary controls.

Risk	Primary Control
1. Unauthorized individuals inside the organization may gain access to computer records.	A. User IDs and passwords are required to gain access to computer systems.
2. Unauthorized individuals outside the organization may gain access to the organization's computer records.	B. Modem devices are connected only when known external users request access and are disconnected at the end of the session.
3. Unauthorized individuals may attempt to gain access to computer records, and may be successful in the future even though they have not yet gotten in.	C. Reports of unsuccessful attempts are generated by the security system, and the report is inspected daily by the data security officer.

What does this example say about the control system? User IDs and passwords (A) are a *primary* control to protect against unauthorized insiders who might try to gain access to the organization's computer records.

Disconnecting the modem when it is not in use (B) is the *primary* protection against outside intruders. They cannot gain access during the time the circuit is engaged with an approved user. If the modem is disconnected when legitimate sessions are complete, there is no way for the hacker to gain access. If the modem is still connected and the circuit is open, the next level of control — user IDs and passwords — would be available as a barrier to the hacker (secondary). That control can be relied on to protect against hackers even though it was created to protect against unauthorized insider users. (Primary) If the modem is connected and the hacker makes attempts over multiple days, the daily security report (C) will alert the data security officer of the attempts. (Useful)

The review of the daily security report is *useful* in protecting against unauthorized insiders because it will report someone trying to gain access with possible user IDs and passwords. With this knowledge, the data security officer can begin strenuous efforts to find the person who is trying to break in. Why is this only a *useful* control? The report has no value in preventing access to the computer. In addition, it displays unsuccessful attempts when a legitimate user is merely "fat fingered" on the computer and touches the wrong keys, which is a harmless error. Therefore, it cannot be considered reliable in detecting on an *immediate* basis or only access attempts with *malicious intent.*

The matrix recognizes control is needed in depth but the cost of redundant primary controls is too high. It is not cost effective to install several controls over the same risk in the fear that one may break down. If controls are installed singularly but can be used for more than one purpose and provide needed depth of controls, the system is stronger at no additional cost.

Preventive and Detective Controls

Another characteristic to be considered is the nature of each control — preventive or detective. A preventive control stops an undesirable event from occurring. A detective control uncovers it after the fact so corrective action can be taken. In the above matrix example, two controls — disconnecting the passwords and modem — are preventive controls. The "bad guys" cannot gain access because these controls are in place.

The daily security report is a detective control. It discloses the effort of unauthorized or clumsy individuals to enter the system. If the unauthorized user gains access on the first day, the review the next morning will provide information that can be used in chasing down the hacker, but after the access.

A detective control is characterized by after-the-fact activities and requires four units of action. The *first* action is a review, reconciliation, or search to determine where a problem or risk exists. The *second* action is identification and analysis of the undesirable event or condition to determine how it happened and what should be done about it. The *third* action is correction. The *final* action is a check on the corrective action to see that the undesirable event or risk has been reversed or neutralized.

There are two other aspects of detective controls that make them less effective than preventive controls. Detective controls, by their nature, are more easily overlooked or ignored. Reviews and analyses can be put off when other pressures build up, and they can be ignored when the person assigned to the task finds the work distasteful. Second, detective controls appear to be a waste of time if there is no undesirable event to be found. However, one cannot know that there is no undesirable event or risk until the search is complete. For all this, there are circumstances in which a detective control is the only option available. There is not a preventive control to guard against every possible risk. For example, the checkbook can be kept under lock and key — a preventive control. That will not eliminate the need to examine paid checks for alterations of legitimate checks and forgeries using counterfeit checks — a detective control.

A preventive control (p) is preferred over a detective control (d) because the preventive control is more efficient and because there is less likelihood that it can be compromised, overlooked, or ignored. So the matrix is enhanced when the nature of the control is added to the analysis. The previous example is used with the nature of the control shown in parentheses.

	Control A	Control B	Control C
Risk 1	P(p)		U(d)
Risk 2	S(p)	P(p)	U(d)
Risk 3			P(d)

In some uses of this approach, the (p) or (d) is placed at the head of the column with the control identification. This tends to remove it from the immediate area of consideration while the analysis is being conducted. Positioning the nature with the assurance level improves the efficiency and effectiveness of the analysis, particularly when the matrix is large with many columns and many rows.

COSO Illustrative Methodology

The COSO study includes one volume titled *Evaluation Tools*. In the Introduction to the volume is this statement:

> These tools are presented for *purely illustrative* purposes. They are not an integral part of the *Framework,* and their presentation here *in no way* suggests that all matters addressed in them need to be considered in evaluating an internal control system, or that all such matters must be present in order to conclude that a system is effective. Similarly, there is *no* suggestion that these tools are a preferred method to conduct and document an evaluation. (All emphasis is from the COSO study.)

Citing this statement is not intended to detract from the value of the Evaluation Tools. To the contrary, while the value and utility of these tools will be discussed here, there is a tendency to view an illustration contained in a seminal work like the COSO study as the "one and true word" in every aspect. However, these techniques have a good deal to say to internal auditors and others about how control systems can be analyzed and risks assessed.

The Evaluation Tools contain two general types of instruments. The first is *Component Tools;* the second, *Risk Assessment and Control Activities Worksheets.*

Component Tools refer to the analysis of the components of the control system. As a reminder, from the COSO study definition of control is:

Internal control is a process, effected by an entity's board of directors, management and other personnel, designed to provide reasonable assurance regarding the achievement of objectives in the following categories:

- Effectiveness and efficiency of operations.
- Reliability of financial reporting.
- Compliance with applicable laws and regulations.

The study goes on to say:

Internal control consists of five interrelated components. These are derived from the way management runs a business, and are integrated with the management process. The components are:

- *Control Environment* — The core of any business is its people — their individual attributes, including integrity, ethical values, and competence — and the environment in which they operate. They are the engine that drives the entity and the foundation on which everything rests.

- *Risk Assessment* — The entity must be aware of and deal with the risks it faces. It must set objectives, integrated with the sales, production, marketing, financial, and other activities so that the organization is operating in concert. It also must establish mechanisms to identify, analyze, and manage the related risks.

- *Control Activities* — Control policies and procedures must be established and executed to help make sure that the actions identified by management as necessary to address risks to achievement of the entity's objectives are effectively carried out.

- *Information and Communication* — Surrounding these activities are information and communication systems. These enable the entity's people to capture and exchange the information needed to conduct, manage, and control its operations.

- *Monitoring* — The entire process must be monitored, and modifications made as necessary. In this way, the system can react dynamically, changing as conditions warrant.

The Component Tools are designed to evaluate each of the above components in the entity's structure. Each component is subdivided into substantive issues referred to as "points of focus." These are further refined into specific examples of application that can be examined and commented on. An example of this approach is contained in a segment of the worksheet on the *control environment* under the heading *Commitment to Competence.*

The first stage of the Component Tool's worksheet control environment contains the substantive issue (commitment to competence) and the points of focus that are the means used to measure the achievement of the substantive issue. That worksheet looks like this:

Exhibit 3-4

Commitment to Competence
Management must specify the level of competence needed for particular jobs, and translate the desired levels of competence into requisite knowledge and skills.
- **Formal or informal job descriptions or other means of defining tasks that comprise particular jobs.** For example, consider whether:
  - Management has analyzed, on a formal or informal basis, the tasks comprising particular jobs, considering such factors as the extent to which individuals must exercise judgment and the extent of supervision required.
- **Analysis of the knowledge and skills needed to perform jobs adequately.** For example, consider whether:
  - Management has determined to an adequate extent the knowledge and skills needed to perform particular jobs.
  - Evidence exists indicating the employees appear to have the requisite knowledge and skills.

Conclusions/Actions Needed

When the auditor completes the evaluation of each of the points of focus, the findings are entered. Findings are entered on each point of focus and a summary conclusion and recommendation on the entire substantive issue. The completed sample on *Commitment to Competence* looks like this:

Exhibit 3-5	
Commitment to Competence Management must specify the level of competence needed for particular jobs, and translate the desired levels of competence into requisite knowledge and skills.	***Findings***
• **Formal or informal job descriptions or other means of defining tasks that comprise particular jobs.** For example, consider whether: • Management has analyzed, on a formal or informal basis, the tasks comprising particular jobs, considering such factors as the extent to which individuals must exercise judgment and the extent of supervision required.	*The company has formal written job descriptions for all supervisory personnel and, for jobs involving only few specific tasks, job duties are clearly communicated.*
• **Analysis of the knowledge and skills needed to perform jobs adequately.** For example, consider whether: • Management has determined to an adequate extent the knowledge and skills needed to perform particular jobs. • Evidence exists indicating the employees appear to have the requisite knowledge and skills.	*The job descriptions specify the knowledge and skills needed, either generally or in terms of the nature and extent of education, training, and promotion decisions.*
Conclusions/Actions Needed The existence of written job descriptions and defined tasks and parameters (e.g., education, training) demonstrates clear management commitment to competence. Management should consider more formal job descriptions for non-supervisory personnel.	

The Risk Assessment and Control Activities Worksheet is used to assess specific objectives, risks, and controls. The worksheet layout leads the preparer through the analytical process. It contains the following steps:

Exhibit 3-6	
Objectives	A statement of a finite objective that is specific enough to be analyzed.
O, F, C	The category(ies) of broad objectives: Operational, Financial, or Compliance that apply)ies) to this detailed objective.
Risk Analysis	
Risk Factors	Specific risks that could prevent the accomplishment of the detailed objective.
Likelihood	The likelihood of occurrence of the risk on a scale of Low, Medium, and High.
Actions/Control Activities/Comments	Specific control activities that can prevent of detect the risk if it occurs.
Other Objectives Affected	A cross-reference to any other objectives that will be affected by this risk or control activity.
Evaluation and Conclusion	A judgment of the effectiveness of the control in dealing with the risk that threatens achievement of the objective.

The application of this system of analysis can be best understood with an example. The following is taken from the COSO Evaluation Tools volume.[12]

Exhibit 3-7	
Objective	All materials received are accurately recorded. Operational, Financial, Compliance
Risk Analysis	
Risk Factors	Actual quantities received may not equal the quantities indicated on the purchase order or vendor shipping document.
Likelihood	Medium High
Actions/Control Activities/Comments	Goods received are counted, weighed, or otherwise verified as to quantity. Receipts are subject to a second count on a random basis by the receiving department supervisor. Quantities received according to the receiving report are matched to the vendor's shipping documentation and to the purchase order. Material shortages are noted on the receiving documentation and any excess material is refused. In the case of excess material, documentation is signed by the transportation organization representative for return to the vendor. Documentation is forwarded to accounts payable for further processing and control activities.
Other Objectives Affected	Production objective #10 (described in a previous step in the COSO Study).
Evaluation and Conclusion	Controls are sufficient to achieve the objective.

The application of this approach is reasonably straightforward. Each step flows logically from its predecessor.

- The objective is identified; the identification of risks becomes reasonably easy.

- When the risk is identified, historical likelihood of occurrence can be determined.

- When the risk is known, steps to guard against it — control activities — can be identified.

- The relationship of the risk and the control activities to other objectives is found by looking for the same risks or control activities in other objectives — similar to the matrix method.

- Finally, a conclusion is formulated on the effectiveness of the control. Auditors will recognize this because they reach a conclusion on each test of controls made in an audit.

When the analysis of objectives, risk, and control activities has been made, the audit program is put together to test the control activity. The effectiveness of the control activity is determined in the risk analysis. The audit is a test of performance; that is, whether the control activity is working as designed. The audit conclusion will be a measure of the quality of that performance.

The Courtney Method

One interesting and simple assessment technique relating to costs of control was developed by Robert Courtney when he was with IBM's System Communications Division.[13] The technique involves a computation whereby dollar values are assigned to potential risks, and estimates are made of the frequency with which those risks might create difficulties. If such an approach is used, internal auditors should try to reach agreement with management on the assigned values and estimated frequencies. These may be subjective, but a consensus can produce an acceptable degree of reliability. It can be argued that to use a method that explicitly requires one to make estimates is better than no estimates at all. The potential impact of an event is given a value (v) of from 1 to 7:

Amount		v
$ 10	=	1
100	=	2
1,000	=	3
10,000	=	4
100,000	=	5
1,000,000	=	6
10,000,000	=	7

The estimated frequency of occurrence is given a rating (p) of from 1 to 8:

Frequency		p
Once in 300 years	=	1
Once in 30 years	=	2
Once in 3 years	=	3
Once in 100 days	=	4
Once in 10 days	=	5
One per day	=	6
10 times a day	=	7
100 times a day	=	8

The following formula yields the estimated loss in dollars per year (E) for the assigned value and frequency if an undesirable event occurs:

$$E = \frac{10^{(p + v - 3)}}{3}$$

For example, it is assumed that some disastrous event could cost a company $1 million and that it might happen once in 30 years. Then v = 6 and p = 2. The solution, therefore, would be as follows:

$$E = \frac{10^{(2 + 6 - 3)}}{3}$$

$$= \frac{10^{5}}{3}$$

$$= \frac{100,000}{3}$$

$$= \$33,333$$

Thus, the control designed to guard against the risk should cost less than $33,333 a year.

If internal auditors or managers, or both together, can assign dollar values to the effect of an unwanted occurrence, and if they can estimate how often that occurrence might reasonably take place, they can arrive at the potential annual cost of the risk. This cost can then be compared with the cost of a control designed to reduce the risk. The decision to control or not to control, and how much to control, can then be supported mathematically.

Another Method of Assigning Value

Another, and simpler, method of assigning values takes into account only the estimated loss, not the risk of occurrence. It is termed "expected value."

Assume that the value of an asset is $100,000. There is sufficient control over the asset to ring bells and send up flares if a large percentage of the asset were lost. But there is a possibility that a smaller percentage could escape detection by existing controls. The auditor, perhaps with the assistance of operating management, estimates a five percent probability of a $15,000 loss, a 10 percent probability of a $10,000 loss, a 25 percent probability of a $5,000 loss, and a 50 percent probability of a $1,000 loss. Based on these estimates, the "expected value" of loss is $3,500, computed as follows:

Estimated Amount of Loss	Probability of Loss	Expected Value
$15,000	5%	$ 750
10,000	10%	1,000
5,000	25%	1,250
1,000	50%	500
Total Expected Value		$ 3,500

If an improved control can be installed for less than $3,500, it would be financially feasible. If it would cost more, a less expensive control should be sought or the risk accepted.

Risk Evaluation Systems

In order to reduce risk and improve efficiency, some organizations have developed a risk evaluation system based upon answers to questions that they have concluded are significant determinants of risk. Questions such as those presented earlier in the chapter are validated through past experience and through discussions with management and internal audit personnel. A key aspect of this is the determination of the specific answers and their weighting. For example, the organizations must consider what volumes of transactions are potential indicators. This can vary based upon organization size. Weights are assigned to these answers and a methodology to sum answers is determined. Depending on experience and current situations, some questions may have higher weighting than others. For example, sensitivity of information may have a higher weight than when the last digit was conducted.

The risk score for a particular situation is evaluated against all other risks scores and used to develop the audit plan. Some organizations are using these models to set hours on engagements. Organizations that are developing such programs believe that the benefits obtained clearly outweigh the cost and allow a more objective approach to risk assessment. However, there are organizations that believe otherwise and, while they use questionnaires, it is up to the auditor to make the determination based upon his or her evaluation of the answers to the questionnaire.

Risk Disclosure Considerations[14]

The writer analyzes FASB 5 and AcSEC SOP 94-6 in providing descriptive language that should be of interest to internal auditors.

Organizational risk should be separated into:

Operations risk,
Estimation risk, and
Concentration risk.

Operations risk relates to those risks incident to production, selling, and administering the organization. It includes both internal and external risks.

Estimation risk relates to the estimates used in the preparation of financial (and operating) statements and reports.

Concentration risk relates to concentration as to customers, vendors, lines of products, and markets.

There is substantial further detail relative to each of these areas; however, this detail is considered beyond the intent of this book. The reader is referred to the article quoted and to the large number of references quoted.

Probability of an event occurring is also treated. The writer quotes from another source in suggesting the use of the three terms:

	Range
Remote — chance is slight	0 – 15%
Reasonably Possible — more than remote, less than likely	20 – 50%
Probable — likely to occur	50 – 90%

The reference, used SOP 94-6, also introduces several new terms to the lexicon of accounting and auditing:

Near term — Not to exceed one year from the date of the statement (or report).
Severe impact — Used in reference to the vulnerability of the entity to certain concentrations. Though material can also disrupt the normal functioning of the organization, etc., it is, however, less than catastrophic.

The writer suggests that inasmuch as the above disclosure taxonomy is incident to organizational management, it would be desirable and useful to employ it in internal auditing so as to ensure a recognition of comparable degree and subjectivity.

The Need for Several Tools

There is no single, perfect tool for performing a risk assessment or measuring the effectiveness of controls. As the carpenter's toolbox contains many tools, each with a specific purpose, the auditor's toolbox must contain different tools for different purposes.

- *SAS* gives the auditor insight to evaluating the nature of risk and control in the entity.

- Flowcharting is most valuable during the preliminary survey when the auditor is seeking an understanding of the process. Having a picture of the controls and the placement of controls is vital to the development of a risk assessment.

- The COSO evaluation tools are valuable for assessing the risk in the control structure and assessing the risks in operations.

- Matrix analysis is a valuable tool for the next step in the assessment. It matches specific risks to controls and measures the depth of control coverage.

These four tools supply the base information to develop the audit program in the form of internal control questionnaires and test procedures.

Approaches such as the Courtney Method provide the auditor with quantitative techniques that may be useful in evaluating risk. A well-prepared auditor will have an appropriately equipped toolbox and the skill to use the several tools in the box.

Although the newly developed standards state that there should be evaluation of risks (Standard 2210.A1), there is little guidance in the standard nor in its Practice Advisory (2210.A1-1) as to methodology or procedure that should be followed. Guidance still is available in SIAS 9 on Risk Assessment and in current literature on risk assessment.

A Concluding Comment

Gregg R. Maynard sums up the positive approach to risk consideration by saying:[15]

> "Holistic risk management strategies have pushed aside internal auditors' traditional myopic focus on controlling the downside of risk. A fully integrated audit operation now understands and embraces risk as a source of profit."

As a result of empirical research in the field of finance, he has outlined 12 "best practices" that he believes could be adopted by any organization so as to develop a positive fully integrated management approach. The 12 best practices are:

- Combining objective and subjective analysis of the audit universe to reveal audit priorities.

- Analyzing management ability to achieve its stated goals and objectives in pre-audit narratives.

- Using questionnaires to examine internal controls from the top down.

- Analyzing the process for establishing and overseeing risk limits.

- Reviewing other risk management functions, such as treasury, compliance, and accounting control.

- Observing the strategic planning process and its results.

- Evaluating strategic initiatives.

- Integrating audit activities.

- Basing the audit process on the net effect of risk exposures and compensating controls.

- Partnering with management by providing consulting services and value added information.

- Reviewing ethics as a basic element of internal control.

- Conducting a comprehensive audit of the entire risk management program.

This pattern suggests that the entire fabric of risk management can serve as a productive value-added contribution to the organization's well-being and progress. The internal auditor plays a major part in the function.

References

[1]Committee of Sponsoring Organizations of the Treadway Commission, *Internal Control - Integrated Framework* (Jersey City, NJ: COSO, 1992), 29.

[2]The Federal Deposit Insurance Corporation Improvement Act of 1991.

[3]McNamee, David, and Georges Selim, "The Next Step in Risk Management," *Internal Auditor*, June 1999, 35-38.

[4]Reding, Kurt F., Craig H. Barber, and Kristine K. DiGirolamo, "Creating a Business Risk Inventory," *Internal Auditor*, February 2000, 47-51.

[5]Bellman, Carl E., and Richard D. Rees, "Reengineering Risk Assessment," *Internal Auditor*, October 1998, 24-31.

[6]Doyon, Michael, "Tuned-in to Management," *Internal Auditor*, December 1996, 36-41.

[7]Parker, Xenia Lay, *Primer on Risk Assessment* (Altamonte Springs, FL: The Institute of Internal Auditors, 2001).

[8]Aggarwal, Rajesh, and Zabihollah Pazaee, "EDI Risk Assessment," *Internal Auditor*, February 1996, 40-44.

[9]Green, Brian P., and Thomas G. Calderon, "Information Privity and the Internal Auditor's Assessment of Fraud Risk Factors, *Internal Auditing*, Spring 1996, 4-10.

[10]Bernens, Robert L., "The Biggest Little Chink in the Corporate Armor," *Internal Auditor*, February 1997, 38-46.

[11]Wood, D.R., W.C. Mair, and K.W. Davis, *Computer Control and Audit* (Altamonte Springs, FL: The Institute of Internal Auditors, 1972). Chapter 4.

[12]Op. Cit., 184-185.

[13]Courtney Jr., R.H., "Security Risk Assessment in Electronic Data Processing Systems," TR 21.700 (Kingston, NY: IBM System Communications Division, 1978).

[14]Baker, C. Richard, "Increased Disclosure About Risks and Uncertainties: Implications for Internal Auditors," *Internal Auditing*, November – December 1998, 3-13.

[15]Maynard, Gregg R., "Embracing Risk," *Internal Auditor*, February 1999, 24-28.

Supplementary Readings

Aerts, Luc, "A Framework for Managing Operational Risk," *Internal Auditor*, August 2001, 53-59.

Atwater, Geoffrey, "Culture of Assurance," *Internal Auditor*, June 2001, 56-61.

Baker, C. Richard, "Increased Disclosure About Risks and Uncertainties: Implications for Internal Auditors," *Internal Auditing*, November/December 1998, Volume 13, Number 8, 3-13.

Bellman, Carl E., and Richard D. Rees, "Reengineering Risk Assessment," *Internal Auditor*, October 1998, 24-31.

Bernens, Robert L., "The Biggest Little Chink in the Corporate Armor," *Internal Auditor*, February 1997, 38-46.

Chapman, Christy, "The Big Picture," *Internal Auditor*, June 2001, 30-37.

Foster, Sheila D., Mary B. Greenawalt, and Jason Collins, "Internal Auditors Add Value Via a Knack for Risk Analysis," *Internal Auditing,* September/October 1999, Volume 14, Number 5, 34-40.

Knight, Mitch, "More Isn't Always Better," *Internal Auditor*, August 2000, 96.

Lancefield, Larry, "The Unthinkable," *Internal Auditor*, April 1996, 44-46.

Leech, Tim J., "The Next Wave in Assurance Thinking," *Internal Auditor*, August 2000, 66-71.

Leithead, Barry S., "Managing 'Priority Conflict' Risks," *Internal Auditor*, October 1999, 66-67.

Leithead, Barry S., "Product Development Risks," *Internal Auditor*, October 2000, 59-61.

Leithead, Barry S., and David McNamee, "Assessing Organizational Risk," *Internal Auditor*, June 2000, 68-69.

Lemant, Oliver, "Risk as a Tripod," *Internal Auditor*, June 2001, 39-43.

Ley Parker, Xenia, "Understanding Risk," *Internal Auditor*, February 2001, 61-65.

McNamee, David, "Risk-Based Auditing," *Internal Auditor*, August 1997, 22-27.

McNamee, David, and Georges Selim, "The Next Step in Risk Management," *Internal Auditor*, June 1999, 35-38.

McNamee, David, "Targeting Business Risk," *Internal Auditor*, October 2000, 46-51.

Maynard, Gregg R., "Embracing Risk," *Internal Auditor*, February 1999, 24-28.

Reding, Kurt F., Craig H. Barber, and Kristine K. DiGirolamo, "Creating a Business Risk Inventory," *Internal Auditor*, February 2000, 47-51.

Saylor, Jimmy D., George R. Aldhizer, III, and James D. Cashell, "Incorporating Internal Audit into an Enterprisewide Risk Management Process," *Internal Auditing*, July/August 2001, 13-21.

Multiple-choice Questions

1. According to the COSO study, a precondition to risk assessment is:
   a. Establishing an internal audit department.
   b. Establishing control procedures or activities.
   c. Establishing objectives.
   d. Establishing a monitoring method.

2. Which of the following is a risk?
   a. A commitment to competence.
   b. A *Code of Ethics*.
   c. A personnel policy manual.
   d. A significant improvement in the competitor's products.

3. The COSO study defines the objectives of internal control in three broad categories. It also discusses five components that make up the system of control. Which of the following is an objective?
   a. Effectiveness and efficiency of operations.
   b. Risk assessment.
   c. Control activities.
   d. Information and communication.

4. Which of the following is defined as:
   "These objectives pertain to adherence to laws and regulations to which the entity is subject. They are dependent on external factors, such as environmental regulation, and tend to be similar across all entities in some cases and across an industry in others."
   a. Financial reporting objectives.
   b. Operational objectives.
   c. Control activities.
   d. Compliance objectives.

5. Which of the following comments is correct regarding the assessment of risk associated with two projects that are competing for limited audit resources?
   I. Activities that are requested by the audit committee should always be considered higher risk than those requested by management.
   II. Activities with higher dollar budgets should always be considered higher risk than those with lower dollar budgets.
   III. Risk should always be measured by the potential dollar or adverse exposure to the organization.
       a. I only.
       b. II only.
       c. III only.
       d. I and III only.

6. The personal computer has significantly improved the practicality of which of the following analytical methods?
   a. Flowcharting.
   b. Internal control questionnaires.
   c. Matrix analysis.
   d. Control index method.

7. Flowcharting helps the internal auditor in which of the following ways?
   a. Supplies an understanding of the sequence of events and activities in the process.
   b. Provides a means of communication between the auditor and the client.
   c. Allows the auditor to project the effects of recommended changes on the existing system.
   d. All of the above.

8. The internal auditor wants to make an initial risk assessment of the accounts payable department to determine what controls should be in place. Which of the following methods would NOT be used in that initial assessment?
   a. Flowcharting.
   b. Internal control questionnaires.
   c. A control matrix.
   d. *SAS No. 47.*

9. After an initial risk assessment is performed to determine the desired controls, which method is used to determine how well the controls are working?
   a. Flowcharting.
   b. Internal control questionnaires.
   c. The control index method.
   d. Both b and c, but not a.

Use this information to answer question 10.

	Control 1	Control 2	Control 3	Control 4	Control 5
Risk A	P(p)			U(d)	
Risk B	S(p)	S(d)	P(d)		
Risk C					P(p)
Risk D	U(p)	P(d)		S(d)	U(p)
Risk E		U(d)	S(d)		U(p)

The auditor prepares a control matrix showing the above information:

10. Which of the following is true?
    a. Risk E does not have a primary control aimed at guarding against that risk.
    b. Risk A has only detective type controls protecting against it.
    c. Risk D does not have sufficient backup if its primary control fails.
    d. Risk C has sufficient backup to protect against a failure of the primary control.

11. In an examination of receiving operations for a manufacturer of small appliances, an auditor will be most concerned with the risk that the function has:
    a. Failed to detect the receipt of substandard goods.
    b. Accepted goods in excess of current needs.
    c. Paid inflated prices for goods from related parties.
    d. Received goods that were not ordered.

12. The COSO study cites nine interrelated components of the control system. One is defined as:
    "The core of any business is its people — their individual attributes, including integrity, ethical values, and competence — and the environment in which they operate. They are the engine that drives the entity and the foundation on which everything rests."
    That component is:
    a. Monitoring.
    b. Risk assessment.
    c. Control environment.
    d. Information and communication.

13. The auditor is reviewing the control environment. Which of the following would be considered a weakness that calls for action by management?
    a. Job descriptions describing the tasks to be performed and the skills needed exist at the supervisory level and above.
    b. A Code of Conduct statement must be signed by all employees each year.
    c. Training programs are in place for every position in the organization.
    d. Police records are checked before a final hiring decision on all qualified applicants for positions handling cash, securities, and other valuables.

14. Which of the following explanations suggests the least amount of relative risk stemming from a failure to compare a purchased order to an approved price list?
    a. A temporary employee processed the purchase order.
    b. The comparison is not required by company policy.
    c. The vendor is one used often by the company.
    d. The director of the purchasing department approved the purchase order.

15. The current level of risk, considering the performance of the controls in place, is the:
    a. Inherent risk.
    b. Control risk.
    c. Achievable risk.
    d. Detection risk.

16. A public statement on internal control is made by:
    a. Management.
    b. Independent auditors.
    c. Internal auditors.
    d. Regulatory examiners.

17. According to the COSO study, how many components comprise the internal control system?
    a. 3.
    b. 5.
    c. 9.
    d. 15.

18. Which component is the foundation of all other components in the internal control structure?
    a. Control environment.
    b. Risk assessment.
    c. Control activities.
    d. Information and communication.

Chapter 4
Preliminary Surveys

Planning the internal audit at the home office. Preparing reminder lists, records of impressions, and questionnaires. Arranging for the initial meeting with clients and conducting interviews. Identifying objectives, goals, standards, controls, and risk. Risk assessment. The quality of management. The indicators of effective management. Signs of ineffective management. Constraints on effective management. Observing the quality of people. Carrying out physical observations and preparing flowcharts. Reporting on the results of the survey. Budgeting the preliminary survey.

• •

Introduction

The complex operations of today's enterprises can be difficult and frustrating to learn. Many auditors wistfully wish they had known as much about the intricacies of an audited operation when they began as they knew when the audit was completed. Preliminary surveys can be the auditor's best tool for gaining the insight, information, and perspective needed to support a successful audit.

But while a preliminary survey can be a well-considered analysis of people and systems, it can also be a haphazard fishing expedition. Internal auditors must make certain that the time and effort they spend on preliminary surveys are productive. A competent preliminary survey is likely to result in a competent audit program, and a competent audit program is likely to result in a competent audit. As a result, an audit's success or failure may well depend on the survey. When preliminary surveys are carefully planned and executed, they become more than an effective familiarization tactic; they also represent a powerful determinant for the success of the audit.

Audits may be part of a regular rotation, where standards and processes are known; or they may be the result of emerging issues, where new ground must be plowed or investigative techniques may be required. In fact, some internal auditing shops have established a "just-in-time" approach to audit scheduling, thereby making certain that internal auditing services are readily available. Audit scheduling processes have also been affected in other ways by the "value-added" approach many internal audit activities have adopted. In management-oriented internal auditing environments, those being audited are more and more likely to be considered as "customers" and "clients," and greater emphasis is being placed on satisfying audit's customers and demonstrating the benefits audit brings to the organization. In some situations, the added-value mindset has led to requests for audits by organizational units, so that many audits are not imposed, but invited by audit clients.

In the same way that auditing philosophies are shifting and evolving, special audit approaches such as control self-assessment are becoming more prevalent. The preliminary survey can help the auditor to decide what type of audit might be most effective.

Regardless of the audit approach, preliminary surveys are an essential device for familiarizing the auditor with objectives, processes, risks, and controls related to the audit. Internal auditors should approach the survey through seven basic steps: initial study, documenting, meeting, gathering information, observing, flowcharting, and reporting.

Initial Study

Much of the documentation and familiarization process is completed before the auditor ever arrives at the audit site. The internal auditor's initial study includes reviews of prior working papers, audit findings, organization charts, and other documents that will help to provide familiarity with the audit subject. In most instances the initial study will be conducted from the home office, although many internal auditors can now access information electronically from remote locations.

If the audit is one in a series of regularly assigned projects, the auditor will first look at the permanent file for the particular operation. (See Chapter 23, "Controlling Audit Projects.") The permanent file contains copies of prior audit reports and replies, as well as other relevant information on the activity to be audited. The file offers an overview of what the auditors can expect, the problems previously identified, and the steps taken or promised to solve them.

Working papers on prior engagements can show how other auditors approached the assignment, although the same approach might not be feasible or desirable in the current audit. New technology, systems, and approaches, or modifications in client operations may dictate a different course. Different auditing philosophies or staff strengths may also be factors. In any case, the review of prior working papers can represent a long step forward in the process of familiarization.

Whether the audit is part of a continuing series or a new project, a review of existing literature on the subject is essential. The literature on internal auditing is growing rapidly, and the coverage provided by auditing textbooks, research studies, and monographs is constantly expanding. Many auditors also seek out books and research on the audit area, especially if it is a new topic. For example, if the auditor is performing a first-time audit of some aspect of an advertising agency, research might include materials related to the advertising industry, as well as appropriate audit literature.

The Internet has also become an important new resource for auditors. The IIA has established an audit resource center on its Web site (www.theiia.org). The site provides a wealth of practical information, including a reference library, opportunities for electronic interaction with other auditors, samples of audit plans and checklists, professional guidance and position papers, and links to a steadily increasing number of related sites. Constant expansion and refinement help to assure more and more auditors of a rich, reliable resource.

The Institute's professional journal, *Internal Auditor*, has traditionally been a valuable source of information for auditors. Articles and departments, such as "Roundtable," may provide auditors with interesting and often remarkable insights into the activities they are preparing to audit. *Internal Auditor's* five-year index of topics is published annually in the journal and is also available on the Internet or on disk.

The initial study should also include careful reviews of relevant organizational charts and statements of authority and responsibility. Such documents can show where the client activity stands in the enterprise hierarchy, what senior management expects of client management, and what the operating manager has been authorized to do. A word of caution is appropriate, however. Statements of authority and responsibility are often drafted by those who perform the activity. To some degree, the statements may be window dressing and should be viewed with healthy skepticism.

Documenting

Documentation encompasses several steps that will eventually lead to the auditor's initial meeting with the client manager. Developing reminder lists and the initial table of contents for the working papers are among the key documentation tasks. In addition, the auditor composes questionnaires that will be used in interviews and discussions with the client manager and others.

Reminder List

At the start of any audit, the internal auditor is likely to wonder, "What do I do next?" Although every audit is different, certain initial steps are fairly common. These steps should be captured in a reminder list, thereby easing the launch of the job.

The reminder list is not designed to inhibit initiative or creativity. It merely simplifies the planning process by helping the auditor to quickly perform the mechanical chores needed to get the audit project going in an organized fashion and with a minimum of false starts. The reminder list helps auditors organize their working papers more methodically and makes the subsequent audit steps simpler to perform. A typical reminder list is shown in Exhibit 4-1.

Exhibit 4-1
Audit Project Reminder List

	Completed (Date) (NA)
Planning	
Permanent file review for:	
• Audit Analysis sheet (Exhibit 18-3) of prior examination	_____
• Prior audit report and related replies	_____
• Notes and comments	_____
Prepare a summary of the prior deficiencies and suggestions.	_____
Obtain Project Assignment Order (Exhibit 23-1)	_____
Review related reports from other auditing organizations within the company.	_____
Reviewed current research on the subject to be audited.	_____
Interviewed manager of organization(s) to be audited.	
Analyzed applicable organization charts, procedural instructions, and directives.	_____
Conducted preliminary survey.	_____
Prepared the audit program, making provision, where applicable, for	
• Examination of assigned ledger accounts	_____
• Review of applicable management reports	_____
• Determination whether computer-generated reports received by the organization are needed.	_____
• Determination whether input provided to data processing by the organization is accurate, authentic, and timely	_____
• Consideration of factors affecting income and other taxes	_____
• Allocation of project workdays to audit program segments	_____
• Use of statistical sampling	_____
• Plans for issuance of interim reports	_____
• Review of compliance with record retention provisions and security regulations	_____
• Use of flowcharts to evaluate control system	_____
Reviewed audit program and this checklist with the supervisor	_____
Field Work	
Posted project time record each day and reported time each week to the supervising auditor	_____
Forecasted calendar date of field work completion at midpoint of the field work	_____

Exhibit 4-1 (Cont.)

	Completed (Date) (NA)

Discussed with client management personnel their availability for review of findings and of draft reports so as to anticipate vacations and other absences   _____

Final

Completed record of audit findings and report outline, and reviewed them with the supervising auditor   _____

Prepared audit report draft and cross-referenced it to the working papers   _____

Transferred appropriate records to the permanent file   _____

Prepared Audit Analysis sheet (Exhibit 22-3)   _____

Described matters for consideration in other audit projects in writing and placed notes of such matters in the appropriate permanent files   _____

Scheduled reviews of the draft report with client personnel   _____

Confirmed status of completed and open findings either by test or by review with client personnel   _____

Performed final verification of the draft report, as modified by reviews with client or otherwise, before submitting it for final typing   _____

Table of Contents

Before auditors start to tackle the instructions in the list, it's a good idea to prepare a table of contents for the first part of their working papers. This step forges tangible inroads into the planning phase of the audit. It compels auditors to (1) provide for certain matters that need to be dealt with as the job progresses and (2) establish working paper references. With little variation, the table of contents and the documents and records to which they refer will be applicable to most internal audit projects. A sample table of contents with explanatory comments in parentheses is shown in Exhibit 4-2. Details on working papers are presented in Chapter 9.

Exhibit 4-2
Table of Contents

Subject	Working Paper Reference
Project closure form	A-1
(The final document in any audit; hence on top of the set of papers.)	
Replies to audit report	A-2
(The client's written response to the audit report and the findings requiring corrective action.)	
Copy of final, formal report	A-3
(Copy of the report submitted to the client.)	
Referenced report draft	A-4
(Copy of the draft from which the final audit report was prepared, with marginal references to the applicable supporting working papers.)	
Report outline	A-5
(The skeletal structure of the proposed report, to be reviewed by the supervisor before the report is drafted.)	
Review notes	A-6
(Notes on reviews of report drafts with the audited management personnel.)	
Assignment sheet	A-7
(The formal audit assignment.)	
Notes from permanent file	A-8
(Notes inserted in the permanent file, since the last audit, to indicate areas to be covered, problems encountered, people to talk to, etc.)	

Exhibit 4-2 (Cont.)

	Working Paper Reference
Audit instructions	A-9
(Notes on discussions with the supervisor or audit manager on the conduct of the audit.)	
Prior audit report and replies	A-10
(Removed from the permanent file for ready reference during the audit examination.)	
Time record	A-11
(Record of time budgeted and used.)	
Project reminder list	A-12
(List of steps to take in performing the audit project; see Exhibit 4-1.)	
Notes on preliminary contacts	A-13
(Record of discussions with or telephone calls to management personnel telling them of the proposed audit project.)	
Organization charts	A-14
(Copies of the major organization charts covering the audit area.)	
Policy statements, directives, procedures	A-15
Tentative audit program	A-16
(Primarily, a brief record of the intended purpose, scope, and theory of the proposed audit and a preliminary assessment of its thrust and course.)	
Audit program	A-17
(The formal audit program, prepared after the preliminary survey.)	
Summary of prior audit findings and suggestions	A-18
(A list of all such matters brought out by the prior audit. The purpose is to determine whether corrective action has been effective or whether deficient conditions have recurred.)	
Glossary of terms and abbreviations	A-19
(Each activity in an organization has its own jargon. The auditors will pick up the terms of abbreviations and sprinkle them throughout their working papers. A glossary is needed for the uninitiated reviewer of the papers.)	

Exhibit 4-2 (Cont.)

	Working Paper Reference
Questionnaires and responses (Formal or informal lists of question asked of or mailed to the clients, and the answers.)	B-1
Volume statistics (Data showing the volume of transactions or other values relevant to the audit.)	B-2
Flowcharts (New or updated charts — charts from prior audits can be used, either intact or with some updating.)	B-3
Records of audit findings (Reports of each individual deficiency finding and records of corrective action taken.)	B-4
Miscellaneous (Any other information not relevant to individual audit segments or tests.)	B-5

Cost Reductions

Cost reductions directly affect the enterprise's bottom line. Management generally expects internal auditing projects to result in reduced costs, as well as improved operations.

Some of the auditor's proposed cost reductions will stem from a combination of existing conditions, good luck, ingenuity, and a spark of insight. But the search for cost reductions can be methodically pursued if the auditor knows where to look. In many instances, cost reductions occur simply because a methodical auditor looked hard at a process, piece of equipment, form, computer report, or a register, and then asked questions such as:

- How can these activities be simplified?
- How can this process be improved?
- How can this form be eliminated or combined with another?
- How can this flow of work be rerouted and made more economical?
- How can this step be abolished entirely?
- How can duplications be eliminated?
- Can paper reports be replaced by electronic versions?
- To what extent is this report being used?
- Is this report really necessary?

The results from consistent, organized, methodical attacks on waste and duplication far exceed the rare flashes of genius. Educating the staff to direct their efforts and attention to records and activities where excessive cost may exist can have long-range benefits — for the organization and, for the auditor, in the eyes of management. A sample checklist for cost reduction is shown in Exhibit 4-3.

Exhibit 4-3 **Reminder List for Cost Reduction** (Indicate Matters Reviewed)							
Records	Eliminate	Combine	Simplify	Improve	Reroute	Eliminate Copying	W/P Ref.
Forms Tabulate reports Manually prepared reports Logs and registers Equipment usage							

Records of Impressions

Another checklist, one that records the auditor's observations and impressions during the audit, will not ordinarily appear in the auditor's formal report. However, this record can sometimes provide a special benefit to management. It accomplishes for senior managers what they themselves would do were they able to take a personal tour through the operations for which they are ultimately responsible. Exhibit 4-4 offers an example of such a form.

The information recorded on the record of impressions form does not represent the usual objective compilation of well-documented facts. Nevertheless, it is valuable because management is not only concerned with the hard facts of the audit, but also with its people. The auditor is in an advantageous position to provide such information.

Very often, poor performance cannot be traced solely to inoperative controls or inadequate instructions. Sometimes subpar work can be the result of slovenly habits, poor morale, fatigue, boredom, inappropriate organizational structure, inefficient work flow, indifferent supervision, clashes with interfacing organizations, badly maintained or inadequate facilities and equipment, and the general environment. Such inadequacies can have a profound effect on productivity. Where conditions like these exist — conditions that cannot be quantified — the auditor should bring them to management's attention.

Records of impressions are not created for formal submission to management. Instead, they function as a reminder list for auditors when they are engaged in confidential discussions with senior managers. At the same time, a combination of such lists, compiled for a large number of audit projects, can be summarized periodically to reveal undesirable trends that may pervade the entire organization. Records of impressions can help to identify symptoms of general malaise that deserve special attention and may lead to improvements in employee relations, working conditions, management, or supervision.

Exhibit 4-4
Record of Impressions

_____   _____
        Audit Project   Title

_____
                         Organization Audited

This record will serve to document your impressions of certain aspects of the organization you have reviewed. Complete it after each audit. Use it for each organization substantially involved in a functional review of many organizations. We plan to summarize the data so as to determine whether there are any general trends or problems throughout the organization that should be brought to management's attention. Thus, unless there is an impression that directly relates to a specific deficiency finding, do not discuss the record with client personnel. If you feel you do not have sufficient information to answer a question, so state beneath each question.

Yes or No

Employee Morale
Do employees seem to have a good attitude toward their fellow
    employees, their jobs, their supervisor, and the organization?   _____
Do they accept their assignments readily?   _____
Do they appear to support departmental and organization goals?   _____

Working Habits
Do people appear to be working at a reasonable tempo?   _____
Do they appear to be conducting an excessive amount of personal
    business at work?   _____
Are working hours, lunch hours, and coffee breaks observed?   _____
Is supervision sympathetic toward employee complaints?   _____
Is supervision willing to take appropriate corrective action?   _____
Does the manager seem to keep the employees informed?   _____

Exhibit 4-4 (Cont.)

	Yes or No

Organization and Staffing

Does the organization seem to be well organized to
accomplished objectives?

Are tasks segregated properly?

Does work appear to flow in an orderly and economical manner?

Do employees appear to be working within their job classifications?

Do new employees appear to be receiving sufficient orientation
and training?

Supervision

Do supervisors appear to know their jobs, and do they have the
respect of their employees?

Do supervisors seem to be exercising control and providing
direction to employees?

Interface with Other Organizations

Does the organization seem to communicate effectively with
interfacing organizations?

Are there any obvious conflicts?

Does there seem to be evidence of genuine cooperation?

Working Areas

Do working areas seem to be properly laid out and maintained?

Do location, noises levels, lighting, temperature, and housekeeping
seem adequate and lend themselves to an effective operation?

Does machinery and equipment seem to be properly maintained?

Do employees seem to have adequate equipment?

In the following space, explain any adverse ratings. If specific
deficiency findings appear relevant to any of the adverse ratings,
reference them.

_____   _____   _____
        Supervisor   Auditor-in-Charge   Date

Questionnaires

The initial reviews that internal auditors conduct in their own offices normally provide enough insight for auditors to generate intelligent questions about the entity being audited. Nobody expects internal auditors to be experts in the activity's affairs at the outset, but they are expected to have a general familiarity with where the activity stands in the organization and what it is supposed to be doing.

The in-office review will typically result in a list developed from the following records: the permanent file (see Chapter 23), the prior audit report and working papers, and management's charter for the activity that is to be reviewed. From this material, auditors can devise questions to (1) meet their audit objectives and (2) pose to the client manager at their first meeting. The "split page," with questions on the left-hand side and space for jotted responses on the right, provides a useful format and actually creates an agenda for the meeting. The pages can subsequently be inserted in the working papers without recopying them. Depending on the audit purpose, the following questions might be appropriate:

- How many sections exist within your activity?
- How many people are employed in this area?
- What activities do you carry out?
- Do you have written procedures for them?
- Which activities do you consider most important?
- Which are most troublesome?
- How do you exercise control over your organization?
- What control reports do you receive from your people?
- What standards do you set for your people?
- What is the source of your standards?
- How do you train your people?
- How do you evaluate their performance?
- How do supervisors help to improve employee performance?
- How do you set priorities for your work?
- What is the employee turnover rate?
- What is the extent and nature of your backlog?
- To whom do you report?
- What reports do you prepare for your own management, and how often are they generated?
- What is the source of the information on the reports?
- With what organizations do you interface?
- What kind of feedback do you get from them?
- What major changes have occurred since the last audit?
- What is the status of the audit findings last reported?
- Do you have any suggestions with regard to areas where we should place special attention?

This informal questionnaire may be expanded or contracted according to the circumstances. The nature of the questions will vary, depending on whether the proposed audit is organizational (completely within a single organizational unit) or functional (following a function or program from beginning to end and crossing organizational lines). In organizational audits, people-oriented questions will predominate. In the functional or program audit, the questions will deal more with work flow, interface with other organizations, and feedback.

Formal questionnaires, transmitted in advance of the auditor's arrival, may sometimes be useful, especially in distant locations. Questionnaires can trigger appropriate preparation for the auditor's arrival. They can also remove some of the apprehension and suspicion about the audit and involve the client's supervisory personnel in a sort of collegial approach. Questionnaires can give management personnel an opportunity to take a good hard look at themselves, since properly prepared questions can function as an effective self-evaluation form. Although recipients sometimes feel that answering all the questions represents an onerous task, the auditor's position is that the client-manager should have the requested information at hand to manage effectively.

Questionnaires can also represent substantial economies, since the legwork for the audit will have been conducted by those most qualified to complete the work rapidly. The auditors need only to analyze the answers and supporting data and then ask amplifying questions of the client personnel. In some instances, verification of responses may be in order.

When the audit is conducted at a remote location, questionnaires may be sent out under cover of a memorandum signed by the headquarters executive to whom the off-site manager reports. The letter will be designed to obtain and evidence the involvement of executive management and to add a touch of authority to the request. The memorandum, which should be drafted by the auditor for the executive to sign, will introduce the auditor or audit team, give the time of arrival, and ask for cooperation. The memorandum should also clearly communicate the executive's expectation that all questions will be answered fully and openly and supported by auditable copies of relevant reports and other pertinent document. Clients should also understand that the entire packet of information should be compiled and ready for the arrival of the auditor.

A sample transmittal memorandum is shown in Exhibit 4-5, and a sample questionnaire for a manufacturing plant is provided in Exhibit 4-6. The hypothetical plant highlighted in the exhibit is in a different location from company headquarters; however, most of its accounting functions are handled by the headquarters office.

Exhibit 4-5

To: Manager, Plant X
From: Vice President, Off-Site Plants
Subject: Audit of Plant X Activities

The internal audit activity is planning to perform its periodic audit of activities at Plant X in the very near future. The audit will be performed by two auditors: Jane A. Smith is the auditor-in-charge, and William B. Jones will assist her.

The auditors will arrive at Plant X on or about November 9. Ms. Smith will call you a few days before her arrival to tell you the exact date.

To save the time of both the auditors and your staff, they have developed a set of questionnaires that should elicit a good deal of the information they will need. The answers to the questions should be prepared in advance of their visit. This will simplify the audit and reduce the length of the auditors' stay at Plant X.

The questions are divided into the areas of Administration, Manufacturing Services, Production, and Quality Control — conforming to the Plant X organization — and so can be assigned to several people for response, thereby reducing the burden on any one individual. The auditors have asked that you attach any relevant reports and records to the answered questions to illustrate the documentation being used.

Please hold the answered questions pending the auditor's visit. After they have had an opportunity to review the replies and the supporting documentation, please assign someone to provide them with a "walk-through" of the Plant X facility, to answer any further questions they may have, and to assist them through the remainder of their audit.

I appreciate your giving the auditors your full cooperation and providing them with any assistance they may need.

Vice President, Off-site Plants

cc: J. A. Smith

Exhibit 4-6
Control Questionnaire

Administration

What means are used for recording employees' attendance?

What means are used for recording employees' time charges?

What means of monitoring are used to ensure the accuracy of the attendance records and time charges?

How are attendance and labor hours balanced?

What is the basis for redistributing labor charges from pool work orders to ultimate work orders?

What methods are used to control payments to suppliers?

What methods are used to safeguard assets and facilities?

How are the entrance and exit of personnel controlled?

How are the entrance and exit of materials controlled?

How are valuable documents controlled?

How is the need for repetitive reports determined?

How are telephone and telegram expenses controlled?

How are files kept up-to-date?

How are insurable valuables determined?

Production Services

What methods are used to schedule and control the manufacture of assemblies?

How are behind-schedule conditions determined and reported?

What assurance is provided that current, accurate planning documents (shop orders, tool orders, etc.) are used?

What provision is made for scheduling and taking cycle inventories?

What are the methods used to forecast needs for component parts and other materials and supplies?

What provision is made for scheduling and taking cycle inventories?

What methods are used to evaluate employee productivity?

What provisions have been made to procure materials and services at the most favorable prices?

What provisions have been made to account for and safeguard severable fixed assets?

What provisions have been made for issuing, safeguarding, and accounting for standard tools and supplies?

What provisions have been made to identify tools?

How are tools inventoried?

What provisions has been made for preventive and corrective maintenance?

Exhibit 4-6 (Cont.)

Production

What means are used to control vehicles and gasoline and to provide for appropriate maintenance?

What provisions have been made for the detection, accumulation, and disposition of scrapped and surplus materials?

What means are used to expedite the receipt of parts and the reporting of parts shortages?

What means are used to maintain parts and stock bins?

What provision has been made to detect the excess usage of material?

What are the methods employed to control high-value stock levels?

Quality Control

What methods are used in the inspection of assemblies to assure compliance with quality standards and engineering drawings and specifications?

What records of rejection are maintained?

What are the procedures for reviewing and evaluating discrepant parts and materials?

What provision has been made for the inspection of production parts and materials?

What provision has been made for the inspection of production tooling?

How are production and inspection stamps controlled?

What provision has been made for the certification of gauges and equipment?

To what extent is the TQM philosophy used?

Exhibit 4-7 offers examples of questionnaires for a purchasing department and a marketing department. Each question calls for a narrative response. "Yes" or "No" answers to structured questionnaires are usually of little value because the full burden is then placed on the internal auditors to support and evaluate the propriety of the responses. Also, the "correct" answers to such questions are usually dead giveaways. Narrative statements can be more readily documented and evaluated.

Exhibit 4-7
Questionnaire

Purchasing Operations

What proportion of the organization's purchases are "off-the-shelf" items, and what proportion is made to the organization's design?

What procedures have been developed for conducting surveys of suppliers operations and claims?

What procedures have been developed to cover negotiations with suppliers?

Which purchase negotiations, if any, have been delegated to other departments in the organizations?

What means are used to follow up on supplier deliveries?

What authority does the buyer have to expend additional funds to expedite delayed deliveries?

What kind of regular reports does the purchasing department issue on its follow-up activities?

How does the purchasing department judge the quality of supplier performance?

What standards of performance have been set?

What steps are taken to develop alternatives to sole source suppliers?

What controls have been installed to make sure that the organization receives credit for short shipments, rejected parts and materials, etc.?

What procedures have been developed on purchase order documentation?

What approvals are required before a purchase order may be issued?

Are there any reciprocal agreements with certain suppliers? If so, which suppliers, and what are the agreements?

What procedures govern supplier overshipments?

What procedures apply when invoice and purchase order prices differ?

What procedures apply when suppliers ship in advance of requested dates?

How are price and source files kept up to date?

How does the purchasing department participate in "make or buy" decisions?

What are the procedures for controlling, recording, and recalling organization-owned tools supplied to suppliers, or made by supplies and held at their plants?

What termination procedures have been developed for canceled orders?

What reports are prepared on the amounts of orders issued to various suppliers?

How is the purchasing department manual kept up to date?

What has been the ratio of purchasing department employees to total organization employees during the past three years?

What has been the volume of purchases per purchasing department employee during the past three years?

What purchasing department training programs are in effect?

Exhibit 4-7 (Cont.)

Purchasing Operations (Cont.)

What is the policy toward encouraging purchasing personnel to attend technical seminars and conferences?

To what extent has the purchasing department cooperated with suppliers to have them undertake cost reduction and value engineering programs of their own?

What are the three most important problems facing the organization — from the purchasing manager's viewpoint?

What type of assistance is received from corporate headquarters?

What additional type of assistance would the department like to receive?

Marketing Operations

List the major products sold and their approximate share of the market.

Give your ideas about each product's future.

Who are the organization's major customers, and what kinds of products are sold to each?

To what extent does the organization use dealers, agents, and distributors?

What are the strongest competitors in the organization's major product lines?

What was the sales and profit trend over the past three years, by important territorial, product, and customer groups?

Does marketing management systematically and regularly compare sales forecasts with performance, and does it attempt to determine the reason for the differences?

What kind of regular and current reports are prepared for marketing management that compare actual sales and profits with forecasted sales and profits for each marketed item?

What market analysis functions are now in use?

Are opportunities for electronic sales and commerce considered and, where appropriate, incorporated into marketing initiatives?

Which of the organization's product lines have required the most intensive marketing effort? Why?

To what extent has intensive marketing effort on weak product lines paid off in improved profitability?

How is your advertising program coordinated with other selling efforts?

On what basis is the overall advertising budget allocated so as to control spending for highest total profitability and allow monthly comparisons between actual expenditures and budgeted expenditures?

How is the organization's catalog kept up to date?

What training program does the marketing department have in effect?

How are prices set on organization products?

Exhibit 4-7 (Cont.)

Marketing Operations (Cont.)

How are prices set on spare parts?

What latitude do salespeople have in setting prices?

How is the performance of salespeople measured?

How frequently are the regular marketing publications issued, and to whom are they distributed?

What analyses are made of sales returns to determine causes?

What is the approximate number and value of items that are shipped but not billed?

What is marketing's procedure to review sales stock for excess and obsolete parts?

What are the amounts of inventory write-offs for excess and obsolete inventory for the past three years?

Do salespeople set delivery schedules? If so, on what basis?

To whom has the marketing manual been distributed?

What procedures have been developed for internal departmental operations?

What approvals are required to initiate changes in sales policies and procedures?

What are the two or three most important problems facing the organization — from the marketing manager's viewpoint?

What types of marketing assistance does the department receive from corporate headquarters?

What additional assistance would it like to have?

Meeting

The internal auditor's meeting with the client manager provides an opportunity for the auditor to explain the purpose and approach of the audit that will be performed. In some situations, the auditor may even want to discuss the overall role of internal auditing within the organization. However, the primary focus of the meeting will obviously be the audit at hand.

In discussions with the manager and supervisors, the auditor explores the objectives, goals, and standards of the operation, along with its inherent risks. The internal auditor also seeks to acquire insights into the style of management exercised. The meeting obviously represents a key point in the audit, and devoting attention to the various elements of the meeting can help to encourage positive results.

Arrangements

The time and place of the meeting should be arranged in advance. Whenever possible, surprise visits should be avoided, although unannounced audits may be necessary in situations involving cash audits, security audits, or other matters of extreme sensitivity. In the absence of such circumstances, advance notice is a courtesy that will be appreciated and should have no adverse effect on the audit. A prepared client can provide more information, and any deliberately misleading information submitted by the client would likely be detected during the actual audit.

The objection is sometimes raised that advance notice precipitates correction of defective conditions before the internal auditors arrive on the scene. The rejoinder to that objection is "that's fine." If this is the effect internal auditors have, it is a beneficial effect. Both the internal auditors and the operating people are working for the same employer and toward the same organizational goals. Whatever improves conditions is welcome. Seriously defective transactions probably could not escape a competent substantive test, and correction of inadequate control systems or minor deviations is desirable no matter when it is accomplished.

The preliminary meeting will most likely set the tone for the audit, and that tone should be one of cooperation. Internal auditors should be open and candid about their audit objectives. They should voice their questions with the tone of a seeker of information, rather than as an inquisitor. No disputes, discords, or challenges should mar this first meeting. By and large, client-managers wish only to be treated fairly and viewed objectively. They want to have findings placed in proper perspective, and they want to make sure that all deficiencies will be promptly reviewed with them. Auditors can do no less than to adopt and display a similar attitude of fairness and conciliation.

Of course, internal auditors should not let themselves be led down the garden path by false assurances. The airy comment from management that "we were fully aware of this condition and are working on it" should be challenged with: "Excellent, when did that work begin? Can you show us the plans or instructions to correct the difficulty? What is the time frame for correction? What has been accomplished to date?"

When the responses to those questions produce valid evidence of corrective action, the internal auditor should give management appropriate credit. If the matter is significant enough, it should be included in the internal audit report — not as an audit finding, but as a record of a problem solved. Where the assurances are merely attempts to avoid being tagged with deficiency findings, the matter should be reported as an audit finding.

Interviews

Perhaps no skill is so important to internal auditors as interviewing. Good interview techniques put people at ease, make them want to offer information, bring a cooperative tone to the audit, and augur well for a successful audit project. Poor interview techniques create hostility, cause people to withhold or give false information, and produce the real possibility of a failed audit project.

As the activities reviewed by internal auditors continue to become more complex and challenging, internal auditors need additional assistance in understanding the operations under review. They need someone to translate the peculiar argot that the clients use, for example. They need cooperation, not adversaries. Good interview techniques go a long way toward fulfilling these needs.

Internal auditors should be skilled in dealing with people and in communicating effectively. It is also important that internal auditors be skilled in oral and written communication so they can clearly and effectively convey such matters as audit objectives, evaluations, conclusions, and recommendations.

Since developing effective interview techniques is, in essence, a professional responsibility, internal auditors must understand the critical elements of interviews and master relevant techniques. Interviewing is not a single act, but part of a process. Successful interviews are based on careful implementation of six key steps: preparing, scheduling, opening, conducting, closing, and recording.

Preparing. Don't go in cold. Learn as much as possible about the client before the interview. Determine the objectives of the interview and prepare questions that are calculated to achieve those objectives.

Scheduling. Carefully plan logistical arrangements. Don't drop in uninvited — unless, of course, it is a legitimate surprise audit. Courtesy and common sense dictate calling the interviewee to arrange for a mutually acceptable time and place.

The location should be on the client's turf. The interview will then be more relaxed. Avoid Friday afternoons, the days before or after a holiday or vacation, or just before lunch or quitting time. If you have options with regard to time of day, choose morning or mid-afternoon.

The best interviews are one-on-one. Additional people can be distracting or inhibit frankness. Finding a way to limit interviews to the auditor plus one other person may be well worth any extra time and trouble.

Opening. Tell the interviewee honestly what the purpose of the interview is and how the results will be used. Present the forthcoming audit as an opportunity to provide a service, and ask how the auditor can be of help.

Make sure the interviewee understands that conversations alone rarely result in reportable findings; those will be the product of audit field work. Develop a good rapport at the outset. Let the greeting be friendly and the smile sincere. Learn the person's name and use it often; the sound of a person's name is music to his or her ears.

Be cordial and helpful; avoid the appearance of coming on as a threat. Say something complimentary if at all possible, and save criticism for later or only when it is absolutely necessary. Show a sincere interest in the interviewee and his or her problems. Show consideration for his or her time and assure the interviewee that you will strive to every extent possible to minimize disruptions to routines. Accept opinions respectfully, and acknowledge that you may not always be completely right.

Conducting. An interview is an exercise in communication, and internal auditors should be experts in the communication process. Every communication in every form follows the same process:

- A "sender" presents an idea through a message.
- The message is encoded in written or oral form or in nonverbal body language.
- The coded message is transmitted from sender to receiver through a channel, such as a letter or an oral presentation.
- The receiver decodes the message, based on the receiver's experience and ability to perceive the code.
- Depending on how the message is accepted, the receiver takes action by doing or responding.
- The receiver gives feedback to the sender in the form of words or actions.

As we know, the channel of communication is not always free and clear. Blockades to communication can halt, distort, or dilute what is being transmitted. An awareness of these impediments may help internal auditors avoid them and clear the channel for useful messages. The following strategies can help:

- Establish rapport. Communication barriers are numerous. If the auditor has a know-it-all attitude, the client will see no reason to provide information. If the client perceives the auditor as one who will "twist my words," the client will be reluctant to speak. The auditor's job is, therefore, to create a supportive atmosphere.

- Technical jargon can seem like a foreign language to the receiver — as accounting terms seem to a non-accountant. Learning about the interviewee's background can be well worth the effort. Auditors who know "where the interviewee is coming from" are less likely to present information in a form that will seem patronizing or won't be understood.

- Make sure that the preparatory list of questions or presentations flows logically. Poor organization — skipping back and forth among topics — may make the message confusing.

The way an auditor asks questions can affect the success or failure of an interview. Introductory questions should put people at ease. The initial queries should not raise problems or hackles. Rather, they should lower the interviewee's defenses, create an informal setting, develop a "we" rather than a "you" situation, and produce a positive tone for the meeting.

- Avoid prejudicial or biased statements. Intemperate or insensitive remarks can abruptly block the communication channel.

- Make sure the message is transmitted at an appropriate time. If you wait until right before lunch or late on Friday, it goes unheard.

- Try to prevent defensiveness on the part of the client. Don't get personal. Adopt a positive attitude and try to head off personality conflicts.

- Avoid jumping to conclusions. Don't neglect to ask the right questions, and make sure you comprehend what the interviewee means. Periodic feedback to the client can help ensure reasonable communication: "Do I understand you to say... ?"

- Physical noise or distraction can ruin an interview. Set the place carefully. If noise occurs anyway, move the meeting or postpone it.

- Don't get overloaded with information; there is a limit to what the human mind can absorb.

- Be on the lookout for nonverbal cues that belie the actual words spoken.

- Develop good listening habits. Perhaps more than any other factor, ineffective listening can destroy an interview. Use active listening techniques that convey interest and understanding to the speaker. For example:
  - Keep the conversation going with noncommittal phrases such as "that's interesting," "I see," or even "uh-huh;" but don't agree or disagree — you do not yet know the facts.

  - Show you understand the speaker — or avoid misunderstanding — by restating the speaker's statements and asking for agreement.

  - Reach out to the speaker with empathy by mirroring his or her feelings: "I guess you were rather upset by this," or "That must have made you feel good."

  - Summarize the dialogue before ending the interview: "The way I see it, these are the key ideas about the situation," or, "As I understand it, this is how you feel about this proposition."

Asking questions. The way an auditor asks questions can affect the success or failure of an interview. Introductory questions should put people at ease. The initial queries should not raise problems or hackles. Rather, they should lower the interviewee's defenses, create an informal setting, develop a "we" rather than a "you" situation, and produce a positive tone for the meeting.

- Don't lead interviewees. That is, don't give them the answers in the questions. For instance, don't say, "You lock the storeroom at night, don't you?" Better questions start with what, when, where, who, why, and how. "How do you protect stores at night?" for example.

- Don't load the question by requiring a self-incriminating reply: "When did you stop leaving the storeroom unlocked?"

- Don't ask questions that call for a "yes" or "no" answer. If you do, follow up with an open-ended question: "Have you completed the new inventory system" "How is it different from the old one?"

Closing. Don't drag out the interview. Look for nonverbal signs that the interviewee has had enough. Try to end the interview on a positive note by summarizing agreements or recognizing laudable actions. If all the significant questions have not been asked, schedule another meeting. The last few minutes of the meeting may be important for interpersonal relations and future meetings.

Recording. An unrecorded interview is a waste of time. Researchers tell us that within 24 hours we forget 50 percent of what we've heard. In two weeks, we'll forget another 25 percent. The mind is a wonderful instrument, but it does not have the retentive ability of our computers. Auditors must, therefore, develop techniques that allow them to capture, as soon as possible, what is said and what they learn in an interview.

Some auditors successfully use tape recorders during interviews. However, interviewees can be intimidated by recorders; and, in such instances, they become an intrusive element that may inhibit openness and full disclosures. In addition, transcribing the tapes can be a lengthy process; and it's a task than can't always be easily delegated because of confidentiality issues.

One tactic that is useful and not too distracting to the interviewee is to list the questions on a "split page." Then, as information is gathered, brief notes, words, phrases, and numbers can be jotted down. As soon as possible after the interview, the auditor should expand on the information captured. Notes should never be allowed to get cold; they're too important to lose.

In fact, good notes can be a treasure. It is comforting to be able to say to a recalcitrant manager, when challenged: "If you will recall, on April 13 when we discussed this matter, you agreed with both the facts and our conclusions. I have your comments recorded here. May I refresh your memory?"

An internal auditor who can't interview productively is like a trial attorney who can't cross-examine. Neither will get to the truth. Unlike the trial attorney, however, the auditor wants to create a collegial, rather than an adversarial, relationship.

We are not born with compelling interviewing ability, but we can develop it. Interviewing can be as important to the management-oriented auditor as developing professional working papers.

Gathering Information

Preliminary surveys will move along swiftly, smoothly, and systematically if internal auditors have a clear idea of what they want to achieve. In most audits, the essential information can be readily classified under the basic functions of management: planning, organizing, directing, and controlling. Each category of information includes several steps:

Planning

- Identify the objectives of the activity or organization, both long range and short range.
- Obtain copies of policies, directives, and procedures.
- Obtain copies of budgets.
- Determine what special projects or studies are underway.
- Determine whether plans for the future have been developed.
- Ask if any ideas for improvement remain undeveloped.
- Determine how goals are set and who developed or helped develop them.

Organizing

- Obtain copies of organization charts.
- Obtain copies of position descriptions.
- Inquire about relationships with interfacing organizations.
- Review the physical layout, the equipment records, and the location and condition of assets.
- Determine what organizational changes were made recently or since the last audit.
- Obtain information on the authority delegated and responsibility assigned.
- Obtain information on the location, nature, and size of field offices.

Directing

- Obtain copies of operating instructions to employees.
- Ask employees if instructions are clear and understandable.
- Determine whether the spans of management and supervisory control permit adequate direction of the work.
- Determine whether authority equals responsibility.
- In government agencies, identify important problems that would interest the legislature or the public.
- Identify any restrictions on the organization's ability to carry out its assigned duties.

Controlling

- Obtain copies of written standards and performance guides.
- Review systems and work flow. Be alert to signs of waste and extravagance, backlogs, excess equipment or material, idle personnel, extensive repair and rework, excessive scrap, and poor working conditions.
- Review historical financial data, seeking to identify trends.

- Review financial operating reports: (1) budgets compared with revenues and expenditures; (2) progress with regard to time and cost objectives; (3) increasing or decreasing productivity — units produced compared with number of employees; and (4) receipts and expenditures, indicating trends. If managers do not have this information, ask what other means they use to control the work in their departments.
- Identify the specific activities or procedures to be illustrated by flowcharts, such as awarding contracts, examining loan applications, approving or disapproving loans, selling assets, entering into leases, advertising, fixing prices, hiring employees, borrowing money, and selecting suppliers. These actions or procedures should be representative of the activities under review. Representation is more important than volume.

General

Merely cataloging information mechanically is not enough. Experienced internal auditors seek not only to list and array data, but also to understand its implications. One activity is clerical, the other is professional. As auditors gather information during the preliminary survey, they are alert to obvious and potential difficulties. These problem areas will become the focus of the audit program. Internal auditors are typically looking for:

- Duplication of effort and records.
- Unbudgeted purchases.
- Not accepting responsibility for duties assigned.
- Not receiving authority to do the job.
- Not exercising control over activities.
- Cumbersome or extravagant organizational patterns.
- People without the background, education, or training to do the work.
- Ineffective use of people or resources.
- Records or reports seldom consulted or serving no useful purpose, unnecessary reporting, or excessive copies of reports.
- Excessive backlogs or no backlogs at all where some would be expected. The possibility of using data processing instead of manual methods.
- Standards, goals, and budgets employed as a working guide.
- Unclear instructions.
- Customer complaints. Poor inventory ratios. Prolonged poor quality from suppliers. Time delays between receipt of unsatisfactory materials and the issuance of debit memos.
- Increases in the volume of returns and allowances. Critical field service reports.
- Excessive rework costs.

When a significant number of these items or deficiencies seem evident, they are recorded for inclusion in the audit program and developed during the field work. Seeking to develop them during the survey defeats its purpose and slows it down; but if management appears amenable to suggestions and is willing to take corrective action, there is no point in withholding the information.

Observing

Observing, in its broadest sense, continues throughout the entire preliminary survey. By persistent observation and diligent inquiry, the internal auditor is able to:

- Determine objectives, goals, and standards.
- Assess controls to achieve these aims.
- Evaluate risks.
- Identify controls to minimize risks.
- Make statistical risk assessments.
- Assess management style.

The auditor's awareness of each of these critical elements will help to assure a sound preliminary survey and an effective audit.

Objectives, Goals, and Standards

During preliminary surveys, internal auditors should determine the objectives of the activity under audit — not the audit objectives, which come later, but the objectives of the activity itself. Unless these objectives are clearly understood, the audit may miss its mark. Acquiring a clear, precise picture of the activity's objective and how its mission aligns with the strategic goals of the enterprise is the hallmark of professional internal auditors.

The auditor's sharp image will not be swayed or influenced by descriptions in statements of function and responsibility. Such documents may be obsolete or self-serving declarations designed to elevate status. In any case, they frequently do not get to the heart of the activity.

Internal auditors should differentiate among objectives, goals, and standards. Objectives come from the Latin *objectum*, literally a thing thrown before (the mind). It is the thing aimed at, the purpose or end. The derivation has nothing quantitative about it.

Goal, on the other hand, comes from the French *gaule*, a pole or stick. It brings to mind goal posts on a playing field, where points are given for hurling some object between the two poles. It has a quantitative flavor. In sports, the objective is to win the game. The goals are milestones along the path to that end.

Standards are authoritative, recognized examples of correctness, perfection, quantity, or some definite degree of quality. They provide levels of excellence and attainment, a prescribed target or a measure of what is adequate for some purpose. Standards can sometimes do double duty, both as goals to be achieved and as measures of excellence.

For example, service is the objective of a department of water and power. Installing 1,000 new water meters in the coming year might be a goal. Keeping the cost of the average installation under $25, the time of installation under an hour, and improper installations under one percent can be standards.

Objectives are more difficult to identify than are goals or standards. For example, a statement of function and responsibility may declare that the accounts payable department shall process invoices for payment. While the statement is quite true, it doesn't really hit the mark. All it calls for is seeing that invoices are supported by evidence of terms, such as contracts or purchase orders, and evidence of receipt or quality, through memos or signed approvals. Actually, the objective of accounts payable is to approve for payment what is due, when due, while at the same time achieving maximum conservation of organization funds and charging the proper accounts. Perceiving that type of objective will lead internal auditors into more productive examinations than the type that merely calls for comparing pieces of paper.

During the preliminary survey, internal auditors should evaluate objectives and goals. Are they set forth formally? Are they understood by those charged with meeting them? Do they incorporate standards of excellence? Do all involved understand precisely what is expected of them? If the internal auditors can't measure accomplishment, how can the manager or the manager's people do so? Oh yes, the manager can obtain a general impression of whether things are going badly or well, but this can be affected by bias, unreasonable demands, or how the manager happens to be feeling that day.

Internal auditors should know the goals of the activities they intend to review before proceeding to programming and field work. If goals and standards can't be satisfactorily established, detailed review during the audit may become a chancy exercise.

In audits of economy and efficiency, goals are generally implied. All organizations are expected to keep costs down and schedules in line without sacrificing effective performance. But even here goals and standards can provide reasonably precise performance gauges. How many cases should a welfare caseworker handle in a month? How many invoices should an accounts payable clerk process in a week? How many telephones should be installed per day? How many catalogs should be produced in a year? How long should it take to develop a web site? In seeking out standards, auditors may often obtain useful data from other organizations doing similar work. Other sources might include cost accounting standards, historical standards, and similar documents.

For program results, goals usually represent what the authorizing body, such as the legislature, board of directors, or chief executive officer, intends to accomplish. Information about these goals is critical. An internal audit that does not report the extent to which objectives and goals have been met does not measure up to an effective management-oriented audit.

Defining goals and standards is not a simple task. In some units of the organization, objectives may be imprecisely stated or not stated at all. Quantitative indicators or standards for measuring performance may not have been established. Data for measuring performance may not be available. When these conditions exist, internal auditors owe it to executive management to seek out the reasons so that objectives, goals, and standards can be improved. Here are some of the causes of imprecisely stated aims:

- Enabling legislation or management policies and procedures did not identify program objectives clearly.

- Goals and standards may not have been properly understood by those responsible for meeting them.

- Premises, such as sociological, economical, or human factors, were not thoroughly examined in setting goals and standards.

- The original objectives and goals may have changed, but formal statements about the changes have never been altered.

Internal auditors must remember that they are staff, not line, and have neither the authority nor the responsibility to set objectives, goals, or standards for operating people. Yet, without a clear understanding and agreement of this managerial area, an audit might be fruitless.

Due professional care includes evaluating established operating standards and determining whether those standards are acceptable and are being met. When such standards are vague, authoritative interpretations should be sought. If internal auditors are required to interpret or select operating standards, they should seek agreement with clients as to the standards needed to measure operating performance.

The guideline suggests that the work of internal auditors should involve identifying goals and standards and gaining their acceptance, rather than dictating them. If the client agrees to them, they become the goals and the standards of the client and not of the auditor.

When goals and standards have not been set and no agreement on them can be reached, that condition in itself is a deficiency. Establishing goals and standards by which management can be measured or measure itself is basic to good business practice and to accepted principles of management. Managers have a responsibility to set goals and standards for themselves and their people. When they do not, the internal auditor must recognize that a primary management function has been abrogated.

Throughout their survey, internal auditors will be sorting out in their minds precisely what objectives, goals, and standards the client organization should be or is working toward. Auditors should seek to determine if:

- Formal statements of objectives have been prepared for the client organization.
- The objectives agree with the strategic plan of the organization — the entity's grand design.
- Those who will be bound by objectives, goals, and standards participated in setting them.
- The objectives are known to all who will participate in their achievement.
- The objectives realistically consider the activity's available resources.
- The objectives may run the activity aground on the shoals of external constraints and controls.
- Established goals and standards will motivate people to reach beyond what they think is within their grasp.
- Periodic, formal reports are being prepared to show to what degree the objectives are being achieved and the goals and standards are being met.
- Objectives, goals, and standards are periodically reevaluated and redefined.

The controls applicable to a system are directly related to the objectives, goals, and standards of the system. For example, if the primary objective of an activity is to process something promptly, the controls should center around ensuring timeliness and meeting established schedules. If, on the other hand, the objective of timeliness is secondary, the controls should be concerned with accuracy and adherence to established standards of quality.

Controls to Achieve Aims

Once objectives, goals, and standards have been identified and agreed upon during the preliminary survey, the next step is to determine what controls are, or should be, in effect to make sure that the desired results will be achieved. Although the topic of control was covered extensively in Chapter 2, some points are especially relevant to the preliminary survey.

Internal auditors are faced with a host of potential controls when they conduct a preliminary survey: organization or agency policies, procedures, manuals, special instructions, reports, logs, registers, forms, division of duties, approval systems, supervision, and others. Attempting to read and comprehend them all can blur the eyes and stultify the brain. Seeking to absorb the literature on a myriad of controls is often a waste of time. When read without relevance to a particular problem, all these controls appear unconnected to reality.

When a control is sought out, because the internal auditor sees a need for it, it will appear to have some meaning. So the most productive way to identify and evaluate controls is to look, first, for the problem areas and then for the controls that should have identified or prevented those problems, or for the controls that should reduce a perceived risk.

One way of identifying problem areas is through conversations with people in the activity being audited, or with people in downstream activities who bear the brunt of difficulties flowing from their upstream neighbor. Skimming through production and performance reports also provides indicators of actual or potential problems.

Once these problems have been brought to light, internal auditors can study the procedures in effect and determine why the procedures did not prevent the improper actions. Perhaps people were not following the procedures or systems. In that case, either supervision or training — two significant means of control — was probably inadequate or ineffective; or perhaps the procedures and systems were inadequate for the job. In any event, the defects should be brought to the attention of management.

Another way of linking the problem to the control is to focus on risk. Wherever a risk is known to exist, a control should be in effect to help prevent the adverse effects of that risk. Determining the adequacy of the control is a matter of professional competence. Based on experience, training, and sound business judgment, the professional internal auditor should be able to judge whether an existing control is sufficient to diminish or guard against the risk.

Determining the actual existence of controls, that is, whether purported controls are in effect and are working, is a function of the "walk-through." Determining the effectiveness of the controls — whether they are actually doing the job for which they were designed — is a function of the tests carried out during the field work.

Risks

Internal auditors' roles and responsibilities with regard to risk have been a familiar topic of professional discussion in recent years (see Chapter 3). While internal auditors do not manage risks or make decisions about resource allocations involved in risk management, closer relationships between risk management and internal auditing have been advocated in some quarters. In fact, some observers advocate that the starting point of internal auditing planning should be organizational risks, or threats to achievement of business objectives.

Actions by The IIA Standards Board have guided the profession toward an even greater involvement in the business risk environment. (Practice Advisory 2210.A1-1 and Standard 2210.A1, "Risk Assessment in Engagement Planning") See Chapter 3, Risk Assessment.

The *Standards* currently call for professional care — the kind expected of a reasonably prudent and competent internal auditor. These standards do not require internal auditors to be omniscient or to be insurers against any and all noncompliance or wrongdoing that might be occurring. The *Standards* require reasonable care and compliance, but not infallibility or extraordinary performance.

Professional care does include consideration of material irregularities or noncompliance. Whenever internal auditors undertake audit assignments, they must be aware of the risks, the potential traps — the stones under which lie scorpions poised to strike. Infinite awareness and insight, no; professional competence, yes. Lay people may see no harm in the same employee ordering and receiving supplies, but the professional internal auditor must immediately perceive the inherent risk.

In the same way that the competent physician will detect the telltale signs of illness with a single glance at a patient, or an able attorney will recognize the dangers in the language of a homemade will after a quick scanning, the professional internal auditor will be able to clearly identify the hazards that lurk in some activities.

Deliberate wrongdoing is not the only, or the most significant, hazard to organizations. Records or transactions are mishandled less because of dishonesty or malice than because people make mistakes. They may not follow the rules, understand instructions, or take appropriate care; and they may not be properly monitored.

When improprieties are deliberate, the losses are generally attributable more to employees who misuse systems than to outsiders who gain unlawful entry. Those who steal from inventory usually have access to inventory control. Those who work in payroll do not usually steal from inventory or from accounts receivable. Most improprieties involving property are committed by people who work in the activities where the thefts or embezzlements occur.

Internal auditors look for the safeguards that will help prevent losses from such risks. They must not be swayed by the employees' tenure, past history of sterling behavior, or the high repute in which they are held by others. Individual personal integrity is not a constant. It varies with time and circumstances and changes as conflicts arise. The desire to be honest may yield when a child urgently requires an operation. Highly motivated employees — pillars of probity who feel they were passed over for promotion — may decide to get those increases in a manner of their own choosing.

Internal auditors place their reliance on adequate systems, effective monitoring, and competent management. They are responsible for identifying inadequate controls, for appraising managerial effectiveness, for assessing the quality of people, and for pinpointing the common risks.

Cataloging all such risks will be difficult, especially since risks emerge as constantly as business practices change. However, many common risks have been defined in standard texts on accounting, auditing, and management. Some risks are obvious and well known to professional auditors. For example, failure to separate significant duties will create a risk, whether in the accounting department or the medical department. The person who receives cash should not also record receipts in the books of account. Similarly, the person who orders medical supplies should not also receive them, record them, inventory them, or make record adjustments.

In the preliminary survey, potential exposures for the particular activity should be identified; and the controls required to protect against those exposures should be identified and evaluated. If controls are absent or inadequate, conditions may warrant reporting to management. Examples of such exposures might include the following areas:

Blank check inventory. Blank-check stock left unprotected is a fertile source of forgeries. The exposure is obvious. Controls should include master records of check numbers, checks kept under lock and key, keys available only to authorized personnel, up-to-date tallies of checks used, and periodic inventories of stock on hand.

Signature plates. Facsimile signature plates can be improperly used to sign checks, and such plates should obviously be under strict control. They should, for example, be kept in a locked box, with keys given only to a restricted number of people. The box should be kept in a safe, and the combination should be known only by designated people.

Plant security. When the assignment of guards is not periodically rotated, the guards can become apathetic and inattentive. They may become so accustomed to their posts that they relax their vigilance. A formal schedule of guard rotation should be prepared and enforced.

Scrap and salvage generation. Failure to segregate scrap into separate containers for each category of scrap can reduce the prices obtained from scrap dealers. If scrap is contaminated — that is, if a container of valuable scrap like titanium contains but a few pieces of less valuable scrap such as aluminum — the scrap dealers often allow only the value of the cheaper metal in the container. A good system of control requires scrap to be segregated at the source in containers properly labeled. In addition, the scrap yard should report to operating management any instances of contaminated scrap, so that the problem will not continue to recur.

Uncapitalized Test Equipment. This equipment, whose cost may have been charged to testing or research expense, may not be under any type of control.

The internal auditor should be vigilant regarding uncontrolled exposures that create the kinds of risks that auditors must report to management. In some cases, exposure to risk can be assessed during an audit that is directed exclusively to the identified risk. That is, the risk or risks may be the subject of the complete audit. In other cases, exposures could be reviewed during an audit of a broader subject that includes both those risks and other matters as well.

Each organization has its unique problems. In a manufacturing organization, for example, product changes are accompanied by significant risks. When purchased parts that are incorporated into a product are changed, there is a real risk that purchase orders for the superseded parts will not be canceled. As a result, unneeded parts will be received and paid for. In an insurance organization, changes to policy provisions present a risk when claims processors or insurance agents are not promptly instructed about how to handle the changes. Each situation carries its own potential exposures.

Controls Over Risks

When internal auditors perceive risks, they should search out the controls designed to protect against them. Controls that are inadequate or ineffective should be discussed immediately with the client-manager. If agreement on corrective action is reached and adequate corrective action is taken, further audit effort would be pointless. If, however, the manager remains unconvinced and needs proof that the risks are real and the controls are weak, the auditor should program a purposive test — rather than a test by random sample — to support both the experience and significance of the risks.

The preliminary survey provides a firm foundation for the preparation of a thoughtful audit program — one that concentrates on matters of vital interest to management: Have the key risks been identified? Are the key risks being monitored? Are inadequate controls being brought to light and corrected? Which unmonitored hazards should be audited in depth?

Exhibit 4-8 provides a simple illustration of how controls can reduce risks in two familiar audit areas: purchasing and payroll. Internal auditors should take a similar approach when they identify a risk to an operation. They should determine the kind of controls that have been installed or should be installed to reduce or eliminate the risk exposure.

Exhibit 4-8
Controls to Reduce Risk

Risks	Controls
	Purchasing
Receipt of substandard supplies.	Suppliers' quality control systems are to be reviewed by quality assurance engineers. Inspection of all receipts by receiving inspectors.
Purchases made from suppliers related to buyers or other organization people.	An approved vendor file. Supervisory approval of bidders lists. Conflict of interest program.
Purchases of supplies in violation of import quotas.	Legal approval of foreign purchases Written procedures and instructions on foreign purchases. Supervising approval or review of all foreign purchases.
Purchases in excess of need.	Provision that only materials on bills of material will be ordered, and quantities of materials ordered should not result in on-hand inventory exceeding stated levels. Using department, not buyers, should determine quantities to be ordered except where quantity discounts become a factor.
Goods purchased far in advance, straining working capital and warehouse facilities.	Analysis of lead time experienced vs. lead time desired. Requirement for using department to show need dates on requisitions.

Exhibit 4-8 (Cont.)

Risks	Controls
	Payroll

Risks	**Controls**
Employees hired for sensitive positions without checking backgrounds.	Statements of criteria for each job and formal job descriptions. Verification of applications for positions by obtaining credit reports, checking references, or contacting former employers.
Nonexistent employees added to the payroll.	Payroll additions only by written authorization of personnel department. Payroll checks delivered to employees by a paymaster or through electronic transfer to verified accounts. Periodic floor checks of employees on payroll.
Separated employees still on payroll.	Reconciliation of payroll and timekeeping records. Undelivered checks returned to cashier. Witnessing of check distributions.
Laws and government regulations not followed.	Documented and up-to-date payroll tax tables. Schedules of voluntary deductions supported by signed authorizations. Requirement that legal department inform payroll department of all relevant new or revised laws and regulations.
Payments in amounts not authorized.	Reconciliation of hours between time cards and attendance logs. Reasonableness tests or computerized limit checks for such conditions as excessive hours worked, higher than expected payroll taxes, and deductions that exceed gross pay or a given percentage of gross pay.

Risk Assessment

Internal auditors can't demand controls that would cost more than the risks to be guarded against. This concept is called "reasonable assurance" by the American Institute of Certified Public Accountants (AICPA). A control costing $100,000 a year should not be recommended to prevent a hazard that could not exceed $10,000 a year. While the premise sounds simple, comparing potential risks and costs can be perplexing.

Chapter 3, "Risk Assessment," provides formulas for mathematically evaluating the potential risks faced in management activities. A number of software programs are also available to help assess risks.

The U.S. Foreign Corrupt Practices Act requires organizations bound by the law to maintain systems of "internal accounting controls sufficient to provide reasonable assurances..." What is "reasonable" calls for a management decision, but those decisions must be documented. Management should be prepared to demonstrate that a neglected control was deliberately omitted for valid reasons. For example, one reason could be that the cost of the control exceeded the cost of the risk. Demonstrating that fact mathematically would be a powerful argument for the soundness of the management decision.

Effective Management

During the preliminary survey, and especially during the interviews with operating management, internal auditors may be able to take the measure of the manager. There is no better control than knowledgeable, accessible, all-seeing management. When that kind of management exists, the manager is, in effect, an internal auditor. Where such management is effective, the internal auditor can safely reduce the extent of audit.

Sometimes, management problems are not the fault of the operating managers. These people may be working under constraints that prevent them from doing an effective job. Their complaints about restrictions imposed on them may be falling on deaf ears at the executive management level. When internal auditors detect deficient conditions that have occurred because of such constraints, they should present the conditions and their causes to higher management. The auditor's objective appraisal might get a better hearing than the complaints of operating managers.

The following conditions may indicate untenable constraints:

- Requiring managers to spend their time correcting problems rather than planning for the prevention of problems.
- Withholding resources needed to do an acceptable job.

- Assigning responsibility without delegating the necessary authority.
- Emphasizing schedule over everything, including quality, cost, safety, ecology, and the needs of people.
- Excluding operating management and supervision from the setting of goals and objectives.
- Generating the fear syndrome throughout the enterprise.
- Stifling creativity.
- Not providing operating managers with the information needed to measure their own productivity.
- Not informing operating managers about the future plans, objectives, and goals of the enterprise.
- Not putting the right manager in the right job.

Chapter 25 provides further details on management aspects.

People

People are the muscle of every organization. Good controls, in and of themselves, can't guarantee that an activity will be successfully carried out unless competent people in adequate numbers are there to do the work. Internal auditors seek objectivity in expressing their opinions; but, while surveying an activity and determining the extent of their audit, they must consider the people engaged in an activity.

As a result, the preliminary survey may include, in appropriate cases, a review of personnel records and practices. The review may not permit auditors to make definitive determinations, but it may raise danger signals and influence the audit program. Internal auditors may want to raise the following questions, for example:

- Has there been a rapid turnover of personnel?
- Is the organization staffed with new and inexperienced people?
- Is the educational background appropriate for the kind of work performed?
- Is the training program for new employees adequate?
- Is there a mix of ages so that at no time in the near future will the staff be decimated by retirements?
- Does each key position, including the manager's, have a backup in the event of disability or retirement?
- Is there a system of rotation so that each person knows more than one job?
- Is there a formal system of on-the-job training for high-level positions?
- Are people kept informed about what is happening in the organization?
- Is the requirement to take vacations enforced so that improper practices are not kept hidden?
- Is there an unusual level of overtime?

The answers obtained through questions such as these may have a significant effect on the size of the samples the auditors examine during their field work. When answers indicate a satisfactory condition, the auditors may reduce the high level of sample reliability that they might otherwise demand from test results. In other words, they may be justified in examining smaller samples. Where the survey indicates unsatisfactory personnel practices, auditors may need to test more rigorously, expand their samples, and be on the lookout for ineffective, inefficient job performance.

Physical Observations

Abstractions can be difficult to comprehend and impossible to picture. Someone else's description cannot substitute for personal observation by the auditor. Descriptions have gaps and flaws. They can't portray everything; and, besides, they are secondhand. Observation — personal observation — creates pictures that are impressed on the mind.

Internal auditors must go out and see for themselves the facilities, physical layouts, processes, flow of materials, and documents. Personal observation reveals what is going on and how it is going on. It also proves whether what was purported to exist corresponds to reality.

Physical observations should occur in two phases. In the first phase, internal auditors should tour facilities to obtain a better understanding of location, conditions, and layout. The objective is to acquire a bird's-eye view — a frame of reference for policies, procedures, and organization charts. At this point, people will be met, introductions will be made, and questions such as the following may be raised:

- Is the work coming to you on schedule, and is it of acceptable quality?
- Are there any informal reports or records of difficulties with the work received?
- What corrective action was taken on problems encountered?
- Has the action proved effective? If not, why not?
- Are there any safety problems? Have there been any reviews by Occupational Safety and Health administration or insurance inspectors?
- Are there any security problems relating to documents and assets?
- Is work flow and document flow reasonable and efficient?
- What is the condition of equipment facilities?
- What is the quantity and quality of scrap and surplus?

In relatively simple operations, this tour may be enough of an inspection. In complex operations, internal auditors may find it necessary to go on to the next phase, which is often referred to as a "walk-through." During the walk-through, auditors may review a few representative work activities from beginning to end, and the preparation of flowcharts may be warranted. By examining acts, steps, processes, and work, and then tracing their flow through the system, internal auditors can gain practical working information regarding:

- How the program or activity is actually carried out.
- The need or usefulness of the various steps of a process.
- The results of the work in terms of organization or agency objectives, legal requirements, and plain common sense.
- The existence or the absence of needed management controls.

The walk-through helps internal auditors assess compliance with policies and procedures and determine whether or not control measures are really functioning. It will not disclose how well transactions are being processed; that must await substantive tests. Nonetheless, a walk-through is far more effective than a general review of manuals and operating instructions. Besides, it provides a faster and more efficient identification of weaknesses and potential problem areas.

Internal auditors should not walk through every type of document processed by the auditor organization. They should test only those they believe to be significant to the organization's objectives.

Flowcharting

A flowchart portrays a process. Although flowcharting contains elements of both science and art, it is chiefly an art. As with most other art forms, developing a facility for flowcharting takes time. With practice, it can become a useful instrument for all auditors. Flowcharts provide a visual grasp of the system and a means for analyzing complex operations — analysis that cannot always be achieved by detailed narratives.

Formal flowcharting should be standardized within an auditing department. All auditors should use the same templates and follow the same basic instructions. It is usually helpful to coordinate flowcharting with the external auditor — the independent accountant — so that each can use the work of the other. Certain standardized flowchart symbols, along with a legend describing each one, are shown in Exhibit 4-9.

Not all flowcharts need be detailed, formal, or extensive. Some auditors may find that a simple layout providing an easy-to-read overview of the system meets their needs. Exhibits 4-10 and 4-11 provide examples of the key steps involved in a process that starts with procurement and ends with the storage of purchased materials. These steps may be adequate in some circumstances.

Software programs are available for developing more formal flowcharts. These are discussed in Chapters 13 and 14, "Information Systems Auditing, I and II."

Exhibit 4-9
Standard Flowchart Symbols

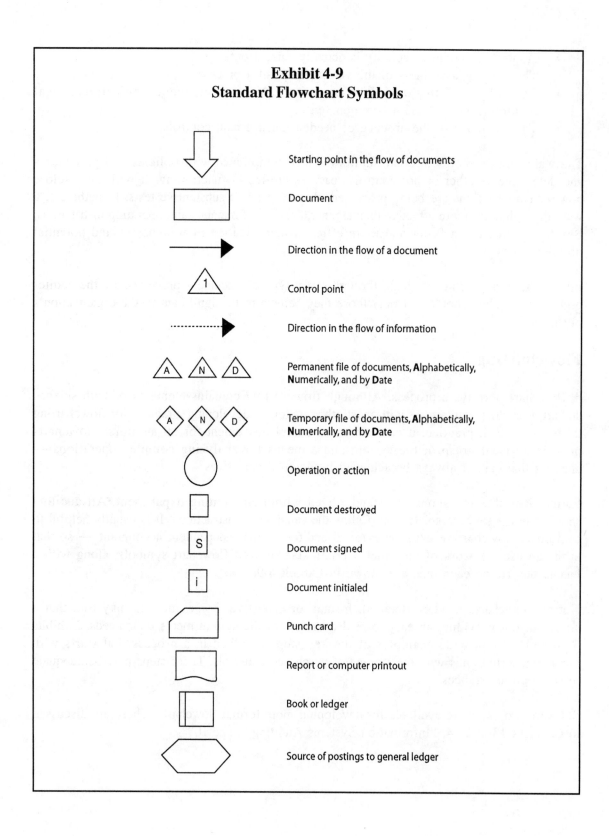

Symbol	Description
	Starting point in the flow of documents
	Document
	Direction in the flow of a document
	Control point
	Direction in the flow of information
	Permanent file of documents, **A**lphabetically, **N**umerically, and by **D**ate
	Temporary file of documents, **A**lphabetically, **N**umerically, and by **D**ate
	Operation or action
	Document destroyed
	Document signed
	Document initialed
	Punch card
	Report or computer printout
	Book or ledger
	Source of postings to general ledger

Exhibit 4-10
Informal Flowchart

Procurement of Materials

| Purch. Department | Receiving Department | | | A/C Payable | Inspection | Stores |
	Office	Dock	Hold Area			
Purchase orders and changes are prepared and sent to: 1. Supplier 2. Accounts Payable 3. Receiving Dept. 4. Buyer 5. Purchasing Files	The master P.O. is held in temporary files awaiting receipt of materials and shipping notice. Upon receipt of shipping notice, the receiving information is added to the ditto master of the P.O. to create the Receiving Memo.	Materials and shipping notice are received. The shipping notice is sent to receiving office. The materials are sent to the hold area.	Materials are held until the Receiving Memo is prepared. Thereupon the materials are sent to inspection.	Evidence of receipt is matched with copy of P.O. No invoice is required. If match is satisfactory, payment to supplier is approved.	Material is inspected. Unsatisfactory material is sent to hold area. Satisfactory material is sent to stores.	Materials are stored awaiting requisitions from using departments.

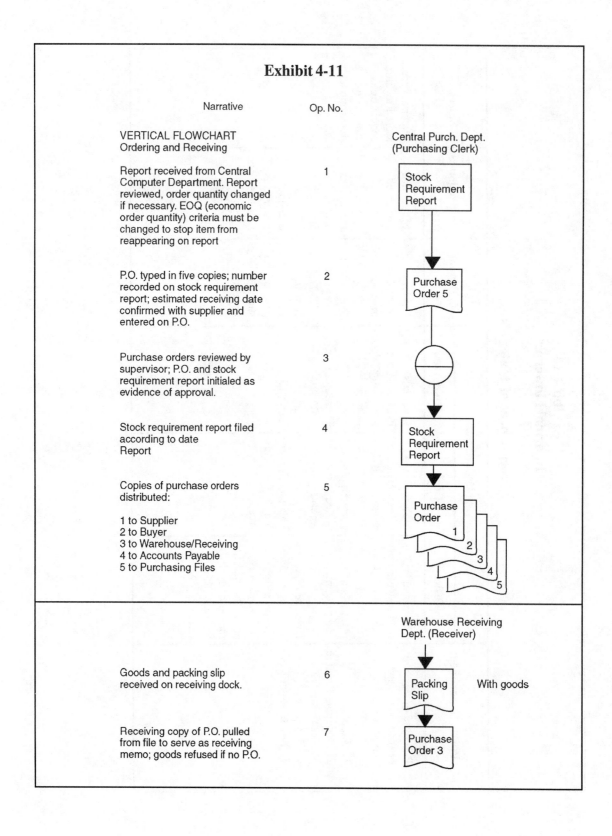

Exhibit 4-11

Narrative | Op. No. | Central Purch. Dept. (Purchasing Clerk)

VERTICAL FLOWCHART
Ordering and Receiving

Report received from Central Computer Department. Report reviewed, order quantity changed if necessary. EOQ (economic order quantity) criteria must be changed to stop item from reappearing on report — 1 — Stock Requirement Report

P.O. typed in five copies; number recorded on stock requirement report; estimated receiving date confirmed with supplier and entered on P.O. — 2 — Purchase Order 5

Purchase orders reviewed by supervisor; P.O. and stock requirement report initialed as evidence of approval. — 3

Stock requirement report filed according to date Report — 4 — Stock Requirement Report

Copies of purchase orders distributed:

1 to Supplier
2 to Buyer
3 to Warehouse/Receiving
4 to Accounts Payable
5 to Purchasing Files — 5 — Purchase Order

Warehouse Receiving Dept. (Receiver)

Goods and packing slip received on receiving dock. — 6 — Packing Slip — With goods

Receiving copy of P.O. pulled from file to serve as receiving memo; goods refused if no P.O. — 7 — Purchase Order 3

Reporting

A properly conducted survey usually produces a considerable amount of useful information. The collected data can identify important issues and problem areas and help the auditor decide whether or not further investigation is needed.

If the survey provides assurances of good systems, controls, surveillance, and management, it may form the basis for a "no audit" decision. Audit resources are usually scarce, and most internal audit organizations have more audit projects on tap than they have auditors to perform them. It makes no sense to waste precious audit hours doggedly pursuing the testing of transactions when it is likely that the control system itself will bring all materially deficient transactions to light.

At the same time, most internal auditors consider it advisable to issue an audit report even if they contemplate no audit beyond the survey. With the information gleaned during the survey, a respectable report can probably be prepared. It would be wise, however, to carefully delineate the scope of such a limited audit, concentrating on the adequacy — not the effectiveness — of the controls and pointing to the basis for the decision to proceed no further with the audit.

Even in situations where an audit program will be prepared and field work will be performed, it may be useful to summarize the survey results and report them informally to management. Sometimes, enough information will be obtained during a survey to recommend improvements even before substantive tests are made. In such cases, the internal auditor's preliminary observations should be discussed with the client-manager before the audit program is prepared. If the manager is satisfied with the auditor's analysis and is willing to take corrective action, those survey results may be considered final, subject to the normal follow-up for any corrective action.

During review of the survey results with management, reporting both positive and negative findings can be conducive to good auditor-client relations. This approach communicates what all internal auditors seek to convey: a healthy, objective, unbiased, cooperative attitude toward the appraisal of operations.

When survey results dictate further auditing, audit summaries should include suggested audit steps and the rationale for them. Auditors should also identify activities that will not be audited and explain the reasons for the decision. Preliminary estimates of time and resource requirements should be provided, along with target dates for the field work and reporting phase of the audit.

Budgeting the Survey

Projecting the auditor's time is a key factor in budgeting for the preliminary survey. The amount of time to be allotted will depend on a number of factors. The purpose of the survey is familiarization. The more familiar auditors are with the activity at the outset, the less time needed for the survey. Also, if the audit is a rotational one and the prior working papers provide a good description of the operation's objectives, goals, standards, and controls, along with flowcharts, organization charts, and similar material, updating the information may be all that is needed.

Significant changes in objectives, procedures, operating systems, automation, organization, management, and people will also affect the time needed for familiarization and problem identification. People are most comfortable with established routines; significant changes have an upsetting effect. Changes always present a risk.

All such factors should be taken into account in budgeting for the survey. But even when auditors feel quite familiar with an activity, they must always be conscious of two factors that can change: people and their attitudes. There is no assurance that either the people or their attitudes will remain the same year after year. So an illusion of familiarity may be just that.

There is no excuse for diving into the verification work of any operation without some form of preliminary survey, even if it only asks what changes have occurred since the last audit. There are no standards for preliminary survey budgets. Based on informal surveys of practitioners, a reasonable estimate may be about 10 percent to 20 percent of the total budget for the audit project.

Supplementary Readings

Bellman, Carl E., and Richard D. Rees, "Reengineering Risk Assessment," *Internal Auditor,* October 1998, 24-31.

Carcello, Joseph V., and Dana R. Hermanson, "Enhancing Internal Audit Department Credibility: Internal Auditors' Perceptions of Serving Two Customers," *Internal Auditing,* Spring 1997, Volume 12, Number 4, 27-34.

Ewert, George A., "How to Sell Internal Auditing," *Internal Auditor,* October 1997, 54-57

Flagg, James D., David S. Kerr, and L. Murphy Smith, "Conducting Effective Interviews," *Internal Auditing,* Winter 1995, 41-46.

Gladden Burke, Kimberly, and Stacy E. Kovar, "The Power of Persuasion: Negotiation Strategies for Internal Auditors," *Internal Auditing*, March/April 1999, Volume 14, Number 2, 11-15.

Harmeyer, W.J., S.P. Golen, and G.E. Sumners, *Conducting Internal Audit Interviews* (Altamonte Springs, FL: The Institute of Internal Auditors, 1984).

Hays, Richard D., "Internal Service Excellence," *Internal Auditor*, August 1997, 20-21.

Johnson, Gene H., Tom Means, and Joe Pullis, "Managing Conflict," *Internal Auditor,* December 1998, 54- 59.

Kimbrough, Jr., Ralph B., "Facilitating Trust," *Internal Auditor*, August 1997, 64-66.

Neck, Christopher P., "Managing Your Mind," *Internal Auditor*, June 1996, 60-63.

Rubinstein Bennett, Amy, "Management 'Soft Skills' Importance in the Audit Environment," *Internal Auditing*, May/June 1998, Volume 13, Number 5, 45-47.

Sawyer, Lawrence B., "When the Problem is Management," *Internal Auditor,* August 1998, 33-38.

Sears, Brian P., *Internal Auditing Manual* (New York: RIA, 2003.) (See Chapter D3, "Performing Preliminary Work.")

Thevenin, Stephen R., "Teaching an Old Audit New Tricks," *Internal Auditor*, October 1997, 58-65.

Vinten, Gerald, "The Questioning Auditor," *Internal Auditor,* August 1993, 57-58.

Ward, Raymond C., *Interviewing Dynamics for Internal Auditors* (Altamonte Springs, FL: The Institute of Internal Auditors, 1996); workbook with videotape and discussion guide.

Multiple-choice Questions

1. While planning an audit, an internal auditor establishes audit objectives to describe what is to be accomplished. Which of the following matters is a key issue to consider in developing audit objectives?
   a. The qualifications of the audit staff selected for the engagement.
   b. The client's objectives and control structure.
   c. Recommendations of the client's employees.
   d. The recipients of the audit report.

2. The primary purpose of an internal control questionnaire is to:
   a. Make preliminary appraisals of controls to be tested.
   b. Establish the level of compliance with controls.
   c. Determine the control environment in the department.
   d. Establish the time budget for the audit.

3. Which of the following elements in the audit planning process typically takes a long-term perspective?
   a. Objectives.
   b. Staffing.
   c. Programs.
   d. Procedures.

4. The auditor-in-charge has just been informed of the next audit assignment and the audit team has been assigned. Select the appropriate phase for completing the audit budget.
   a. During the formulation of the long-range plan.
   b. After the preliminary survey.
   c. During the initial planning meeting.
   d. After the completion of all the field work.

5. During a preliminary survey of the accounts receivable function, an internal auditor discovered a potentially major control deficiency while preparing a flowchart. What immediate action should the auditor take regarding the weakness?
   a. Perform sufficient testing to determine its cause and effect.
   b. Report it to the level of management responsible for corrective action.
   c. Schedule a separate audit of that segment of the accounts receivable function.
   d. Highlight the weakness to insure that work steps to test it are included in the audit program.

6. Which of the following is the primary advantage of using an internal control questionnaire?
   a. It provides a clear picture of the interrelationships that exist between the various controls.
   b. It reduces the risk of overlooking important aspects of the system.
   c. It forces an auditor to acquire a full understanding of the system.
   d. The negative responses indicate the only areas needing further audit work.

7. A preliminary survey of the purchasing function indicates that:
   - department managers initiate purchase requests that must be approved by the plant superintendent.
   - buyers regularly update the official vendor listing as new sources of supply become known.
   - rush orders can be placed with a vendor by telephone but must be followed by a written purchase order before delivery can be accepted, and
   - vendor invoice payment requests must be accompanied by a purchase order and receiving report. One possible fault of this system is that:
   a. Purchases could be made from a vendor controlled by a buyer at prices higher than normal.
   b. Unnecessary supplies can be purchased by department managers.
   c. Payment can be made for supplies not received.
   d. Payment can be made for supplies received but not ordered by the purchasing department.

8. Flowcharting would most likely be used in the evaluation of controls in:
   a. An application involving the joint efforts of both internal and external auditing.
   b. A simple but well documented system.
   c. A complex system.
   d. An internal audit department with limited experience in the evaluation of internal control systems.

9. Which of the following observations, made during the preliminary survey of a local department store's disbursement cycle, reflect a control strength?
   a. Individual department managers use prenumbered forms to order merchandise from vendors.
   b. The receiving department is given a copy of the purchase order complete with a description of goods, quantity ordered, and extended price for all merchandise ordered.
   c. The treasurer's office prepares checks for suppliers based on vouchers prepared by the accounts payable department.
   d. Individual department managers are responsible for the movement of merchandise from the receiving dock to storage or sales areas as appropriate.

10. During which phase of the internal audit would the auditor identify the objectives and related controls of the activity being examined?
    a. Preliminary survey.
    b. Staff selection.
    c. Audit program preparation.
    d. Audit report issuance.

11. During a preliminary survey an auditor found that several accounts payable vouchers for major suppliers required adjustments for duplicate payment of prior invoices. This would indicate:
    a. A need for additional testing to determine related controls and the current exposure to duplicate payments made to suppliers.
    b. The possibility of unrecorded liabilities for the amount of the overpayments.
    c. Insufficient controls in the receiving area to ensure timely notice to the accounts payable area that goods have been received and inspected.
    d. The existence of a sophisticated accounts payable system that correlates overpayments to open invoices and therefore requires no further audit concern.

12. Which of the following best describes a preliminary survey?
    a. A standardized questionnaire used to obtain an understanding of management objectives.
    b. A statistical sample to review key employee attitudes, skills, and knowledge.
    c. A "walk-through" of the financial control system to identify risks and the controls that can address those risks.
    d. A process used to become familiar with activities and risks in order to identify areas for audit emphasis.

13. Which of the following procedures should be performed as part of preliminary review in an audit of a bank's investing and lending activities?
    a. Review reports of audits performed by regulatory and outside auditors since the last internal audit.
    b. Interview management to identify changes made in policies regarding investments or loans.
    c. Review minutes of the board of directors' meetings to identify changes in policies affecting investments and loans.
    d. All of the above.

14. Compared to a vertical flowchart, which of the following is true of horizontal flowchart?
    a. It provides more room for written descriptions that parallel the symbols.
    b. It brings into sharper focus the assignment of duties and independent checks on performance.
    c. It is usually longer.
    d. It does not cross departmental lines.

15. Which of the following is not an advantage of sending an internal control questionnaire prior to an audit visit?
    a. The manager of the audited area can use the questionnaire for self-evaluation prior to the auditor's visit.
    b. The questionnaire will help the manager of the audited area understand the scope of the audit.
    c. Preparing the questionnaire will help the auditor plan the scope of the audit and organize the information to be gathered.
    d. The manager of the audited area will respond only to the questions asked without volunteering additional information.

Chapter 5
Audit Programs

The audit program. Guide and means of self-control. Telling the what, when, how, and who. The benefits of a proper program. When to prepare programs. Internal auditing responsibilities. Stress on risks, controls, standards. Audit scope — from compliance to effectiveness. Defining economy, efficiency, and effectiveness. Audit objectives and procedures. Comparison with operating objectives and procedures. Examples of varied auditing procedures. How to prepare the audit program. Using background information gained during the preliminary survey. Identifying objectives, risks, and controls. Programs as a defensive tool. Examples of purchasing and marketing audit programs. Comprehensive audit programs: Traffic. Example of a pro forma *program: Safe deposit boxes. Ambiguities in program language. Relationships to the final audit report. Program mechanics. Small audit staffs. Guidelines for preparing audit programs. Criteria for audit programs.*

●●

Introduction

Purpose

The internal audit program is a guide to the auditor and a compact with audit supervision that certain audit steps will be taken. The audit steps are designed (1) to gather audit evidence and (2) to permit internal auditors to express opinions on the efficiency, economy, and effectiveness of the activities to be reviewed. The program lists directions for the examination and evaluation of the information needed to meet audit objectives within the scope of the audit assignment.

In short, the program is designed to tell the internal auditor:

- What is to be done.
- When it is to be done.
- How it is to be done.
- Who will do it.
- How long it will take.

The audit program is the link between the preliminary survey and the field work. In the preliminary survey internal auditors identify operating objectives, risks, operating conditions, and controls. In the field work they gather evidence about the effectiveness of control systems, the efficiency of operations, the accomplishment of objectives, and the effects of risks on the enterprise.

Benefits

Well-constructed audit programs may offer many benefits. These audit programs:

- Set forth a systematic plan for each phase of the audit work, a plan that can be communicated both to audit supervision and to audit staff.

- Provide a basis for assigning work to auditors.

- Provide a means, through time budgets, of controlling and evaluating the progress of the audit work.

- Permit audit supervisors and managers to compare what was performed with what was planned.

- Assist in training inexperienced staff members in the work steps of an audit.

- Provide a summary record of work done.

- Help familiarize subsequent auditors, through programs for past audits, with the kind of audit work carried out and how long it took.

- Benefit supervisors by reducing the amount of direct supervision needed.

- Present appraisers of the internal audit function with a starting point from which to evaluate the audit effort.

These potential benefits should not lead internal auditors into a slavish adherence to specific audit steps — a checklist form of audit. Audit programs should never stifle initiative, imagination, or resourcefulness. The program should tell what is to be accomplished. An ounce of common sense is better than a pound of specific instruction. And the law of the situation will always prevail; when reality differs from what was anticipated, adjustments may have to be made.

This chapter presents traditional audit program development. Audit programs generated through software that are based upon risk evaluation are discussed later in this text. Likewise audit programs generated in a high technology environment are also discussed later.

When to Prepare the Audit Program

Internal auditors should prepare their audit programs immediately after the preliminary survey. Programs prepared too late may have gaps and inadequacies and may fail to establish proper priorities. But even carefully prepared audit programs may omit important matters the auditors are unaware of until they become deeply involved in the field work. So, all audit programs should be considered tentative until the audit is completed. Of course, all changes to the drafted audit program require the same approval as the original program.

The *pro forma* program, used on repeated audits of similar operations, often evolves over a period of years and gradually is accommodated to problems encountered in the field. It should not be so inflexible as to fail to accommodate changes or unusual situations. At other times, the program may be developed in advance to obtain particular information at many localities or to fit new or changing circumstances.

New *pro forma* programs intended for use at many locations should be prepared enough in advance to allow time to purge them of errors, unreasonable demands, and unnecessary steps. What is conceived in the ivory tower often fails in the arena. So new *pro forma* programs should be given trials or pilot runs to prevent confusion. The trials permit defects to surface early and to be corrected before the programs are put to broad use.

Some firms are developing software that prepares audit programs as a direct result of their risk assessment. These programs are based upon past experience, input from management, and seasoned audit judgment.

Audit Responsibilities

Internal auditors should be responsible for planning audit assignments. Planning should be documented and should include:

.1 Establishing audit objectives and scope of work.
.2 Obtaining background information about the activities to be audited.
.3 Determining the resources necessary to perform the audit.
.4 Communicating with all who need to know about the audit.
.5 Performing, as appropriate, an on-site survey to become familiar with the activities and controls to be audited, to identify areas for audit emphasis, and to invite client comments and suggestions.
.6 Writing the audit program.
.7 Determining how, when, and to whom audit results will be communicated.
.8 Obtaining approval of the audit work plan.

Currently, Audit Standard 2201, "Planning Considerations," states:

In planning the engagement, internal auditors should consider:

- The objectives of the activity being reviewed and the means by which the activity controls its performance.

- The significant risks to the activity, its objectives, resources, and operations and the means by which the potential impact of risk is kept to an acceptable level.

- The adequacy and effectiveness of the activity's risk management and control systems compared to a relevant control framework or model.

- The opportunities for making significant improvements to the activities risk management and control systems.

The related Practice Advisory 2200-1, "Engagement Planning," provides that the internal auditor is responsible for planning and conducting the engagement assignment, subject to supervisory review and approval. The engagement program should:

- Document the internal auditor's procedures for collecting, analyzing, interpreting, and documenting information during the engagement.

- State the objective of the engagement.

- Set forth the scope and degree of testing required to achieve the engagement objectives in each phase of the engagement.

- Identify technical aspects, risks, processes, and transactions that should be examined.

- State the nature and extent of testing required.

- Be prepared prior to the commencement of engagement work and modify, as appropriate, during the course of the engagement.

All those in management who need to know about the engagement should be informed. Meetings should be held with management responsible for the activity being examined. A summary of matters discussed at meetings and any conclusions reached should be prepared, distributed to individuals, as appropriate, and retained in the engagement working papers. Topics of discussion may include:

- Planned engagement objectives and scope of work.

- The timing of engagement work.

- Internal auditors assigned to the engagement.

- The process of communicating throughout the engagement, including the method, time frames, and individuals who will be responsible.

- Business conditions and operations of the activity being reviewed, including recent changes in management or major systems.

- Concerns of any request of management.

- Matters of particular interest or concern to the internal auditor.

- Description of the internal auditing activity's reporting procedures and follow-up process.

Audit Scope

The audit program should indicate the scope of the audit work. It should make clear what is to be covered in the audit and what is not. The audit objectives should govern the scope of the work.

The *Standards* hold professional internal auditors responsible for examining and evaluating the effectiveness of their organization's system of internal control and the quality of performance in carrying out assigned responsibilities. The primary objectives of these internal control systems are to ensure:

.1 The reliability and integrity of information.
.2 Compliance with policies, plans, procedures, laws, and regulations.
.3 The safeguarding of assets.
.4 The economical and efficient use of resources.
.5 The accomplishment of established objectives and goals for operations and programs.

A comprehensive, unrestricted internal audit may cover all these objectives; certainly, internal auditors should prepare their audit programs with these responsibilities in mind. But they should not overlook the audit authority vested in them by their superiors. The audit scope may not exceed what senior management has authorized the auditors to do.

In an audit of an expenditure cycle — the business cycle that runs from the ordering of, to the subsequent receipt of and payment for, goods and services — all primary objectives may be examined. For example:

- Distribution to the appropriate accounts of expenditures for goods and services.

- Compliance by buyers with rules regarding selection of suppliers and approval of purchases, and with relevant government regulations.

- Safeguarding of goods on the receiving docks and in storerooms or warehouses.

- Purchase of economical order quantities and efficient operation of a value engineering program.

- Authorization and accountability controls for access to systems and data.

- System controls for assuring data integrity, availability, and confidentiality.

- Assistance in meeting production goals by obtaining goods and services on time, but also meeting financial and storage objectives by not bringing goods in too early.

Improved audit ability is needed as internal auditors progress from relatively simple financial and compliance audits to the comprehensive audits of the economy, efficiency, and effectiveness of operations.

Defining Economy, Efficiency, and Effectiveness

The terms *economy, efficiency,* and *effectiveness* are often used interchangeably, although there are subtle distinctions among them.

Economy is often used to mean thriftiness; but it can imply more than saving. Its chief implication is "prudent management" or "use to the best advantage without waste" — meanings that can also apply to efficiency. It is more widely applicable than thrifty, which refers only to persons or their expenditures. For example: Sea power is the most mobile and therefore the most economical form of military force. In that sentence, the term *economical* could probably be replaced by *efficient* without doing violence to the intent of the statement. Webster defines *economical* as, "the prudent use of things to their best advantage." At the same time, Webster defines an efficient operation as being, "one which is measured by a comparison of actual results with the energy expended to achieve those results." Not too wide a chasm separates the two terms.

Efficiency implies minimizing the loss or the waste of energy when effecting, producing, or functioning. When referring to people, the term *efficient* suggests exercising skill, taking pains, and keeping vigilance; it often becomes synonymous with capable and competent. In some cases the term *efficient* can be applied to a person or operation that is competent and capable of producing desired results with minimum effort.

Effectiveness emphasizes the actual production of an effect or the power to produce a given effect. Something may be effective without being efficient or economical. Yet a program to make a system more efficient or economical may also turn out to be more effective.

The overlap is there, but with careful writing and reading, one may be able to distinguish among the three terms. A system of processing records may be effective in producing accurate and properly approved documents, but the route the records take from desk to desk may be inefficient because it involves unnecessary backtracking. Besides, the operation may be uneconomical because six copies of the documents are produced when only five are needed.

Since audit programs usually address all three concepts, internal auditors should keep the definitions and differentiations in mind when developing their programs.

Objectives and Procedures

Objectives are what one aims at — a purpose or end. Procedures are the techniques employed to achieve one's objectives. Internal auditors deal with different sets of objectives and different sets of procedures in their work. These include operating objectives and procedures and audit objectives and procedures. They must learn to differentiate among them if they are to carry out their own responsibilities.

Operating Objectives and Procedures

Operating objectives are the ends to be achieved by operating managers and their people. Among the operating objectives of a procurement activity are those of purchasing the right goods or services at the right price at the right time and of the right quality. Each of these objectives is pursued through procedures or techniques. For example, among the procedures used to make sure the right goods are purchased would be the use of requisitions from ordering departments spelling out precisely what goods are to be procured.

Internal auditors are unable to evaluate an operation if they do not understand fully what that operation is designed to achieve — its objectives. Nor would they be able to determine whether the objectives are being met efficiently, economically, and effectively if they did not examine the procedures employed by operating personnel in achieving their ends.

All audit programs, therefore, should identify the operating objectives whose accomplishment auditors seek to evaluate.

Audit Objectives and Procedures

Audit objectives can be general or specific. General audit objectives are pursued in all engagements and are governed by the audit scope that management and the board grants to the chief audit executive. For example, internal auditors may be restricted to accounting and financial matters only. In that event their general audit objectives may be directed solely to determining the reliability and integrity of financial information; compliance with policies, plans, procedures, laws, and regulations; and the safeguarding of assets.

If their audit scope is comprehensive, however, then their general audit objectives would be increased to include reviewing operating reports as well as evaluating the economical and efficient use of resources and the accomplishment of established objectives and goals for operations and programs.

Specific audit objectives are linked to the operating objectives. For example, if the procurement objective is to purchase the right goods, the audit objective is to determine whether systems are designed to see that the operating objective has been achieved and whether the right goods have indeed been purchased.

Audit procedures are the techniques the auditor employs to determine whether operating objectives have been met. For example, the audit program would specify that the auditors would examine a sample of purchase orders and determine whether they are supported by required requisitions.

Determining which operating objectives warrant audit examination, and therefore should become audit objectives and be included in an audit program, becomes a matter of audit judgment based on study and experience. The professional internal auditor usually has a background that permits discrimination between the audit objectives that should be met in evaluating a proposition and those that may be irrelevant or unimportant to that end. The audit program, then, should be designed to tell auditors which audit procedures to perform to meet the audit objectives.

Similarly, experience and logic will determine which audit procedures apply to which audit objectives. Procedures should be relevant to the selected objectives. Irrelevant procedures, no matter how applicable to the audit as a whole, will be useless if they do not produce evidence about the operating objectives selected for review.

Each of the multitude of operating activities in the great variety of entities, both public and private, presents challenges to internal auditors when deciding what to include and what to exclude from an audit program. The same is true for the audit objectives and the audit procedures needed to meet the audit objectives. There is probably no compendium of all the audit procedures needed to meet all audit objectives. Still, an analysis of some audit objectives and procedures, selected at random from CIA examinations, may shed some light on the approach professional internal auditors take.

Advertising. Advertising is usually contracted to an agency. The agency normally bills for the costs it incurs plus a commission based on those costs. The best assurance the auditor has for determining whether the costs are documented and reasonable — the audit objective — is to audit, in the field, the agency's records and operating procedures. Other operating procedures, such as developing the advertising budget, selecting the right media, or establishing financial controls for the agency are clearly outside the audit scope.

Asset disposals. In an audit of controls over the disposal of assets, auditors are generally in over their heads if they try to determine on their own whether particular disposals were made properly. Only reviews of the written approvals of people responsible for the disposals, given in accordance with established procedures, or determining if disposals followed prescribed procedures would satisfy the audit objective.

Employee medical contributions. An audit objective could be to determine the validity of deductions from employee payroll for contributions to medical insurance options. Whether employee contributions cover the cost of the options is a good question, but irrelevant to the audit objective. An audit procedure to determine whether the payroll deductions are supported by written authorization forms is both appropriate and relevant.

Environmental protection and alarm devices. An internal auditor is seeking to determine whether such devices are installed and operating. Audit procedures that might be interesting, but irrelevant, would be reviewing the architect's alarm specification documents, examining invoices for the devices, or interviewing the plant safety officer. The only procedure that would provide assurance of installation and operation would be an observation of the placement of the alarms and of actual testing.

Inventories. An audit objective is to determine whether significant inventories have been correctly stated. Some audit procedures might be relevant but ineffective, such as obtaining statements from management, or flowcharting the inventory cycle, or interviewing personnel. An effective procedure would be to conduct or review physical inventories and obtain expert valuations.

Land acquisitions. The proposition is to verify legal ownership of land considered for acquisition. Examining the existing deed and title documents would be interesting but not conclusive; these might have been superseded. The surest way of determining legal ownership is to inspect the current records at the local courthouse.

Not-for-profit activity. Many audit objectives may enter into the audit of a not-for-profit organization. A management-oriented audit will seek to determine whether the activity is doing the job for which it was established. Hence, appropriate audit procedures would be to determine the mission of the organization, what standards have been established to measure performance toward that mission, and the extent to which the standards were met.

Payables. An audit is being performed of potential overpayments of payables. Under the existing system, payments are made on the basis of matching documents evidencing orders, receipts, and billings. Partial payments occur often. Comparing the records of every payment would be onerous. It is more productive to zero in on potential overpayments. An appropriate procedure, to that end, is to sample and compare amounts paid with the purchase order limits. Working from the purchase order, receiving report, or invoice records would not be conclusive. Automated analyses and comparisons should be used where appropriate.

Payrolls. Assume an audit objective of verifying appropriate payroll cost distributions to specific accounts. Many audit procedures may be perfectly valid in a payroll audit, but not relevant to the objective cited. For example, it would be irrelevant here to reconcile total payroll costs to the payroll cost distribution, to review time cards for supervisory approval, or to compare labor cost distributions to standard labor hours. For the cited objective, the appropriate procedure would be to trace the payroll cost distribution to job time tickets to determine whether the account or contract charged was actually the one on which the employee worked, and to verify that the work performed pertained to the job (for instance, charging costs of fixed price work to time and material contracts).

If the audit objective is to test for payments to unauthorized recipients, the most appropriate audit procedure would be to review and verify by field check the distribution of paychecks. Reviewing authorizations to put new employees on the payroll, calculating payroll payments, or reviewing approvals of hours worked are interesting but not relevant.

An audit objective in a payroll audit may be to make sure that salaried employees are not taking more paid vacation time then that earned. The most effective audit procedure would be to observe physically or from the vacation records which employees were absent because of vacations. Then the internal auditor would be able to trace those absences through the payroll records to deductions from accumulated vacation time.

The question is whether persons on the payroll of a particular department actually work there. Reviewing time cards, observing paycheck deliveries, or discussing the matter with departmental supervision would not be conclusive; but a surprise departmental floor check would.

To find out whether individuals are actual employees, the appropriate procedure would be to cross-reference individual payroll time cards to personnel department records and reports.

Comparing current departmental staffing with industry standards could lead to assessing department performance. The comparisons would provide no information on identifying bogus employees or evaluating internal controls or compliance with laws and regulations.

Pricing. To determine whether the markup applied to an organization's products varies improperly among customers, an appropriate procedure would be to determine that all prices are set objectively and followed. Analyzing costs would be ineffective in this case.

Production. An audit objective is to assist management in its evaluation of the effectiveness and efficiency of the production process. An appropriate procedure would be to compare actual costs with standard costs.

Purchasing. An audit objective is to determine whether an organization is purchasing excess/ raw materials. To decide whether standards are established for the quality, quantity, and sourcing of raw materials would not address the question of excess materials. What could shed light on the subject would be to determine whether production budgets, job orders, standard inventory levels, and economic order quantities are meshed and used in determining the quantities to be purchased. Analyzing surplus account disposals could help.

If an audit objective is to determine whether purchase transactions are authorized, the audit procedures should include verifying that the documentation the purchasing agents received contained signed approvals. Reviewing other documentation, such as receiving memos and vendor invoices, would be irrelevant.

Quality. If an auditor is seeking to learn whether and why excessive rejection rates are being experienced, the audit procedure calculated to bring the matter to light would be to evaluate how well the sales department is communicating on product returns with the production department. Looking into the volume of sales or the credit ratings of customers would be entirely irrelevant. Also, analyzing scrap accounts and accumulations could help.

A reasonable audit objective is to evaluate the propriety of quality control standards. A relevant procedure would be to review the appropriateness and accuracy of the data that management used to document the development of the standards. Determining whether the standards were being met is wholly irrelevant to the given audit objective. That would be another part of the audit and another audit objective.

Rental property. In an audit of an organization that owns, maintains, and operates rental property, an audit objective would be to determine the propriety of recorded maintenance expense. An appropriate audit procedure would be to trace selected entries in the maintenance expense account to their supporting work orders. Other procedures, such as discussions with maintenance people or checking arithmetical accuracy and authorization of work orders might be relevant but not as definitive as an examination of the completed work orders themselves.

Research and development. Research and development projects must be planned like any other project. Such plans should include standards for measuring performance. Without appropriate and quantifiable standards, management has no yardstick by which to measure R & D results. Certainly, internal auditors cannot set standards in such a technical environment. But they can determine whether standards exist and test the validity of the process used for setting them.

Sales. The audit objective may be to determine whether sales commissions are too big. A procedure to determine the accuracy of the recorded commission expense for individual salespersons is best determined by recomputing selected sales commissions. Other techniques, like calculating commission ratios, using analytical procedures, or assessing overall reasonableness, would be of no value for this audit objective.

An auditor wants to determine whether all credit sales are recorded in accounts receivable. An audit procedure would be to trace the records from a sample of shipping documents to the related sales invoices and subsidiary ledger. The only procedure in a case like this must start with the documents showing actual shipments and working backward.

Tax revenues for a state government. An audit objective is to ascertain whether taxpayers are properly reporting their sales taxes. Of the various options available to internal auditors, the most likely procedure for achieving the objective involves field examination of selected taxpayers. Much less definitive would be testing selected sales tax returns for proper computations, confirming sample sales tax receipts with organizations that file returns, comparing the names of organizations filing returns with those who are licensed, and comparing sales tax revenues received with sales tax receipts budgeted.

Preparing the Audit Program

Background Information

The background information gained through the preliminary survey will help dictate the programmed audit coverage. Any broad operation with its many interrelationships and processes could keep an audit team occupied for a long time if it decided to examine every activity being carried out. But effective, economical programs focus on what is essential to meet the operation's key objectives and not on what is merely interesting.

At the same time, internal auditors must look to their professional responsibilities in deciding what to audit and what not to audit. Internal auditors cannot be held responsible for the prevention of fraud, misconduct, or error. These are management's responsibilities. Yet internal auditors are held responsible for identifying those matters that permitted or fomented undesirable actions. When fraud or misconduct surfaces, internal auditors have but one defense: Their methods and procedures were professional and were calculated to identify and explore the risks within the enterprise.

But saying so is not enough. The auditors must be able to produce documentation to that end. And that is one of the functions of a professional internal auditing program: To demonstrate that the program is effective — addressing only what is significant; and to give proof to the fact that significant risks and controls were identified and evaluated.

That is why tailor-made programs will be more relevant to an operation than generalized programs. The latter do not necessarily take into account the variations resulting from changing circumstances, varied conditions, and different people. But a careful analysis — made with the assistance of operating managers — can spell out the operating objectives, identify the actual or potential risks, and determine the controls appropriate to the circumstances. And the assistance of operating management affords protection against any criticism that the auditors were not interested in what interested management.

Analyses such as these can produce thoughtful, relevant, effective, and economical audit programs. Such programs make good sense to an organization or agency executive because they are management-oriented. They also deal with the larger issues — the issues that executives would take into account if they themselves would review their own activities or programs.

Such programs are economical for another reason as well. While they may be time-consuming when first constructed, they will address key, continuing risks that need to be reviewed during every audit. Therefore, follow-on audit programs would only add new risks or delete those that are no longer significant.

Some examples will help explain this approach more clearly than a written description. Let us examine how this analytical approach to objectives, risks, and controls applies to the functions of purchasing and marketing.

Purchasing

The generally accepted management objectives of a purchasing operation are to obtain the right goods or services: (1) at the right price, (2) at the right time, (3) in the right quantity, (4) of the right quality, and (5) in the right place.

These objectives can form the framework of the audit program. Each can head a separate segment of the program. For example, obtaining goods and services at the right price can represent a separate part of the audit program and the audit work. Then the auditor can list any actual or potential risks disclosed during the preliminary survey relating to establishing the right prices for goods and services inherent in any purchasing operation.

Exhibit 5-1 shows part of an audit devoted to prices. It does not list every conceivable risk and control; such a comprehensive audit program could be unnecessarily expensive. Instead, it spells out those risks that are applicable to a particular purchasing organization at the time of audit, as determined by the preliminary survey. For example, assume that the preliminary survey documented close adherence to excellent bidding procedures. To expend an inordinate amount of audit effort on bidding practices would be wasteful. Instead, the program identifies existing and potential problems and concentrates on them.

In any audit of operations, internal auditors must go beyond the six kinds of operating objectives enumerated for the purchasing function. Another significant objective exists in any activity or department: that it be well managed. Accordingly, one segment of a program for procurement would be related to the administration of the activity. The administrative risks revealed during the preliminary survey might be:

- Organization charts for the purchasing department have not been prepared. (May result in confusion as to which buyer is responsible for purchasing particular products or services.)

- Lack of a directive covering the purchasing department's authority and responsibility. (Other organizations [line units] may assume the authority to deal directly with suppliers.)

- Lack of a purchasing department manual. (Buyers may perform in accordance with their personal desires rather than in a consistent, approved fashion.)

- Absence of a procedure by which people are authorized to sign requisitions for supplies and services. (Orders may be issued by people for their own use or for the wrong materials or quantities.)

Exhibit 5-1
Excerpts from an Audit Program for a Purchasing Department

Audit Segment: Costs and goods and service

Objective of Operation: To obtain goods and services at the right price.

Audit Budget: 5 days

*The letters in parentheses indicate the degree of risk, running from high risk (A) to low risk (G).

Risks	Controls	Tests-(Recommendations)	W/P Ref.	Comments
Make or Buy Committee does not have a written charter or set of procedures. (F)*	Committees should include people from Manufacturing, Quality Control, Engineering, and Procurement. They should meet regularly to arrive at make-or-buy decisions on new products and programs. Decisions should be based on plant capacity, continual cost information, and appropriate trade-offs.	Examine records of Committee to determine whether principal procurements have been considered and adequate support has been provided for the decisions.		
Absence of quantitative and qualitative yardsticks on purchasing activities. No information or standards by which management can judge procurement activity. Uncontrolled buying. Higher prices and possible deterioration of buyer discipline. (E)	Monthly commitment reports by each buyer on such matters as: Total dollars committed. Commitments based on competitive bids. Reasons for no competition. Dollars spent on non-competitive buys.	Determine by sample the volume of noncompetitive bids. Ask for reasons. Inquire of buyers the procedures they follow in obtaining reduced prices. (Recommend system of reporting to provide management with such information.)		

Exhibit 5-1 (Cont.)

Risks	Controls	Tests-(Recommendations)	W/P Ref.	Comments
	Savings achieved through competitive bids, negotiation, new supply sources, and substitute materials.			
Lack of provision for rotation of buyer assignments. Permitting buyers to have long-term dealings with particular suppliers and favoring them. (C)	Provision for periodic rotation of assignments. Requirement that all buyers take vacations. Formal rotation and vacation schedules.	Examine rotation and vacation schedules. Investigate any instances where vacations were not taken or assignments were not rotated.		
Purchasing made aware of new equipment requirements on receipt of completed engineering drawings. Thus, Purchasing does not have time to obtain competitive bids on long lead time items. (D)	A committee, including Purchasing people, to establish schedules for equipment items to deal with long lead time procurements. Purchasing should be party to establishing schedules on such items.	For a sample of long lead time items, determine whether schedules were set, were realistic, and provided ample time for soliciting competitive bids.		
Absence of a value analysis program whereby goods are investigated to relate to function, not cost. (G)	System by which items procured must pass tests as to appropriate form. Is cost proportionate to usefulness? Is there a need for all the features the item has? Availability of standard parts, etc.	Determine who is responsible for value analysis. Review reports on savings. From a sample, determine whether items were subjected to value analysis.		

Exhibit 5-1 (Cont.)

Risks	Controls	Tests-(Recommendations)	W/P Ref.	Comments
Excessive number of confirming orders, meaning that using departments instead of Purchasing are selecting suppliers and ordering goods, thereby evading procurement controls and leading to favoritism and higher prices. (A)	Provision for reports on such orders, determining reasons, and taking appropriate disciplinary action. Management directive giving Purchasing sole authority to commit organization funds for services and supplies obtained from suppliers.	Determine ratio of confirming orders to total orders. Determine what is done to reduce their number. From a sample, inquire of buyers and using departments the reasons for the confirming orders.		
No provision for records showing prior purchases for same products, thereby withholding valuable information from buyers in assessing bids and quotations. (B)	System for recording on cards or on electronic equipment the procurement activity on each individual item on which there are repeated purchases.	For purchase orders sampled, trace prior purchases for same items. Investigate significant variances. (Recommend maintenance of price history records.)		

Risks vary in degree of intensity. Obviously, auditors should be sure to review those risks presenting the greatest danger before dealing with those that are less hazardous. Internal auditors may find it burdensome to prepare a program that lists risks in the order of decreasing perceived intensity. But once the risks, controls, and program steps have been put into the program, auditors should be able to review what they listed and indicate the severity of the risk.

Accordingly, internal auditors may rate the intensity by placing some form of indicator after the listed risk. For example, "A" might indicate the greatest risk, "B" the next, and so forth. In that way, auditors will be alerted to review major risks before they work on minor ones. Thus, they would not put themselves in the unfortunate position of failing to examine a serious risk before the audit budget was exhausted.

Marketing

Some of the more important objectives of a marketing organization might be to (1) determine the market potential for the organization's products and/or services (market research); (2) impart information, develop consumer attitudes, and induce action beneficial to the organization (advertising); and (3) induce distributors to give extra attention to the sales of organization products and persuade customers to buy those products (sales promotion).

Thus, market research, advertising, and sales promotion might each be a separate segment of a marketing function audit. Some of the risks, related controls, and suggested tests associated with an advertising activity are found in Exhibit 5-2.

Both programs illustrated in the exhibits provide a column for reference to the working papers ("W/P Ref."), which are the records of tests and reviews. This reference is extremely important for ready access to the evidence of work done. Audit supervisors, external auditors, and other reviewers will generally use the audit program as a starting point for appraising the adequacy of the audit work accomplished.

The program also provides a column for the auditors' comments. These can be brief statements indicating the results of the audit work, and can be very useful in providing an overview of audit results. The comments should be brief, such as "controls adequate," "no exceptions," "excellent system," "substantially correct," or they should make reference to a record of an audit finding such as "RAF-7" (see Chapter 8).

Exhibit 5-2
Excerpts from an Audit Program for a Marketing Department

Audit Segment: Advertising

Objective of Operation: To impart information, develop consumer attitudes, and induce action beneficial to the organization.

Audit Budget: 10 days

• The letters in parentheses indicate the degree of risk, running from high risk (A) to low risk (G).

Risks	Controls	Tests-(Recommendations)	W/P Ref.	Comments
Organization is advertising in various media but has a single expense account. Hence budgets become useless as a control device. (F)*	Establish separate budgets and accounts for such matters as magazine and newspaper space, television and radio, television talent and production with written descriptions on what should be charged to each account.	Compare budgets and costs. Investigate significant differences. Determine that overruns have been properly approved. (Recommend separate accounts.)		
Complete comparisons between budgets and actual advertising costs are made at the end of a fiscal year. Thus, advertising trends are not identified in time to take corrective action. (G)	Prompt recording of both commitments and expenditures; monthly reports comparing budgets and actuals.	Review reports for accuracy, timeliness, and meaningfulness. Determine what action was taken on adverse trends. (Recommend monthly comparisons.)		
Absence of written agreement with advertising agency. Leads to uncertainty and disputes. No right to review agency records. (A)	Written agreement containing provision as to charges and expenses billable, records to be maintained, and right of audit of systems and records.	Review agency charges for reasonableness and applicability to advertising work. (Recommend written agreement.)		

Exhibit 5-2 (Cont.)

Risks	Controls	Tests–(Recommendations)	W/P Ref.	Comments
Absence of a detailed estimate of charges for each advertising project. Hence, agency may make expenditures exceeding budget. Lack of information on adverse cost trends. (D)	Provision for costs of individual jobs or projects to be itemized on the estimates and subjected to frequent comparisons with actual costs incurred.	Without estimates, tests may be meaningless. Examine whatever means management used to determine propriety of charges. (Recommend provision for written estimates and comparison of charges with the estimates.)		
The same agency employee is responsible for placing advertising orders and also verifying related charges. Hence, excessive authority given to one individual; potential for manipulation. (E)	Separation of duties. It is as important in an advertising agency as it is in the auditor's organization.	Review system. See what supervision the employee receives. Test transaction from ordering to receipt. (Recommend separation of duties.)		
Artwork and organization property left with agency for photographic sets. Hence, possible loss of valuable materials. (C)	Provision for inventory records of all property with sufficient value to warrant control. Insurance coverage for valuable property.	Test system of control exercised by the advertising group. Trace records of items shipped to agency. Compare records and physical items. Question retention by agency of property for unreasonable lengths of time.		

Exhibit 5-2 (Cont.)

Risks	Controls	Tests–(Recommendations)	W/P Ref.	Comments
For non-media purchases, the advertising group deals directly with suppliers and contracts with them for supplies. (B)	Purchasing department must have the responsibility and the authority to make all commitments for supplies. For repetitive purchases of items needed expeditiously, the purchasing department should negotiate blanket orders for the advertising group.	Examine a sample of transactions. Determine whether appropriate bidding, ordering, and receiving practices were used. (Recommend that Advertising deal with Purchasing for all supplies.)		

Comprehensive Audits

Under some circumstances, internal auditors may want to make comprehensive audits of an operation. Perhaps the first audit of an operation may warrant an audit of all activities, whether or not they present serious risks or hazards. Or the auditors may want to document an entire system to determine whether it conforms to the internal accounting control requirements of the U.S. Foreign Corrupt Practices Act of 1977 or other requirements that have been established.

The tailor-made audit program may still be the best course but, in such cases, the focus will be on controls since the risks are not the primary basis for the extent and approach of the audit. The audit will be directed toward determining what controls exist or should exist to see that the operation's objectives will be met. Exhibit 5-3 provides an excerpt from one segment of such a program for a traffic department.

Exhibit 5-3
Excerpts from an Audit Program for a Traffic Department

Audit Segment:	Routine Inbound and Outbound Shipments
Objective of Operation:	To select carriers and routes that will provide the most economical and timely shipments of supplies and finished goods.
Audit Budget:	8 days

Optimum Means of Control	Risks	Audit Tests	W/P Ref.	Comments
Inbound Shipments		Select at random documents covering a representative number of routings and determine whether:		
Provision for close coordination with the purchasing department and for review by traffic personnel of requests to purchase.	Inefficient and uneconomical routings.	Routing was approved by traffic.		
Requirement for special approvals for premium transportation.	Excessive use of more costly transportation.	Premium traffic was properly authorized.		
Provision to consolidate shipments to obtain carload rates.	Unnecessarily expensive shipments.	Items received in large quantities and subject to carload rates, were received in carload lots and not LCL (less than carload).		
Standard time spans for the ordering of goods to allow adequate time for nonpremium routings.	Excessive premium routings to meet production schedules.	Sufficient time was allowed by ordering and purchasing departments between shipping and required dates.		

Exhibit 5-3 (Cont.)

Optimum Means of Control	Risks	Audit Tests	W/P Ref.	Comments
Preparation by traffic for purchasing of information on routings and rates for major suppliers.	Purchase orders providing uneconomical routing instructions.	Suppliers made allowances for transportation costs when purchase orders provided for carload shipments and part of shipment was LCL.		
Outbound Shipments		Determine whether:		
Provision for traffic to specify means of shipment.	Best means of shipment might not be used.	Routing was specified by traffic.		
Maintenance of current routing and rate guides.	Errors in routing.	Routing and rate guides were up to date.		
Provision to charge customers for more expensive routing when such routing is requested.	Customer may not be billed for requested routing.	Customer was billed for more expensive routing requested.		
Provision for adequate support for premium shipments.	Unauthorized premium shipments.	Premium rates were supported by: • Reason for routing. • Authorization for premium shipment. • Appropriate accounting distribution.		
Provision to review and report on the use of premium shipments.	Failure to detect any unfavorable trends. Excessive premium shipments.	Results anticipated by premium transportation were actually gained.		

Pro Forma Programs

Pro forma programs are useful, even essential, when audits will be carried out by inexperienced auditors whose work must be closely monitored. They are also useful if (1) the same kind of audit will be performed at a number of different locations; (2) comparable information is needed for each location; (3) similar reports or consolidated reports will be issued; and (4) operations being audited are relatively similar.

An example of such a program, for the audit of safety deposit boxes in a bank, is shown as Exhibit 5-4. The program focuses on detailed verifications and also provides the auditors with background information that indicates the objectives of the operation and the prescribed system of control. It is a useful audit program, helpful to the auditors and capable of producing all the information needed for a comprehensive evaluation of the activity under review.

**Exhibit 5-4
Excerpts From Audit Program for
Safe Deposit Department**

General Information
Boxes are rented to customers for the safekeeping of personal property. Each safe deposit box has two separate locks. The box can be opened only when the key to each of these locks is used at the same time. When a box is rented, two keys to one of these locks are given to the customer. There are no duplicates available. The keys to the other lock, which are called "Guard Keys," are kept by the bank. No customer can gain admittance to a box without proper identification.

Purpose of Audit
To determine if all boxes that are indicated as being rented are actually rented and that proper rental fees are being received. To determine if there is strict adherence to operating procedures. To determine if rental collections are credited to the proper income account.

Lease Agreements
Review exceptions noted in the last audit. Prepare a list of all safe numbers in the vault. If a prepared list is included with the working papers, make a visual check to verify the numbers. Review lease agreements for rented boxes. Place audit mark opposite the number on the list for each agreement held. If the agreement is new since the previous audit, check for proper completion and correctness of form used. Show initial and date on the agreement to the left of the safe number. (An alteration of safe number on the rental agreement should be initialed by the renter.) Check all court orders of guardianship and trusteeship covering new lease agreements. If a box is subject to restricted access because of a deceased depositor, two or more should be present or, if there is an attachment, list the number on a worksheet.
  • Check to see that the agreement card is jacketed.
  • Check to see that there is a plug in the lock of the customer's box.

Exhibit 5-4 (Cont.)

- Test-check access slips for boxes requiring two or more to be present by comparing signatures with the agreement card. Review customer access procedure with the safe deposit attendant.
- Ask attendant to outline procedure followed in admitting customer to box.
- Review current access slips for proper processing and filing.

At offices where a separate audit is made of the safe deposit department, indicate on the office rating sheet the number of boxes available and number of boxes rented. For example: "Of the 5,268 total number of boxes, 4,183 were rented on the date of our audit."

Additional segments of audit program include: Keys • Annual Rental Cards • Contents of Drilled Boxes • Storage • Night Depository • Articles Found on Bank Premises • Vacant Boxes.

Ambiguities

Precise instructions are most likely to produce precise audit information. Words like adequate, sufficient, and thorough mean different things to different people. Telling an auditor to "determine whether adequate competition was obtained" is to say nothing and to invite different responses from different auditors.

For example, assume that an audit program is to be carried out by audit teams in different locations. Assume further that their audit program tells them to "determine whether the installation has an adequate payroll system."

Some staffs might appraise every single part of the system, doing more work than was intended. Other staffs might decide to determine only that employees were properly paid — and no more. Still others, in their tests of payments to employees, may see errors in paid vacations or reimbursement of travel expenses. They might decide to concentrate on these known hazards and do very little auditing of the payroll system. In addition, staff auditors might be confused and spend unnecessary time discussing ambiguous program steps when they could be devoting their time to productive audits.

Instead of broad ambiguous instructions about "an adequate payroll system," the program could call for these specific steps:

- Determine if payments to employees are in accordance with approved time cards.
- Determine if employees are paid the correct amounts due.
- Determine if total salaries and wages paid are in agreement with the direct and indirect labor charged to appropriate contracts and accounts.

Most auditors would be likely to get answers to such program steps without further instructions, and they still would have plenty of latitude to decide how they would meet these program objectives.

Ambiguities are reduced if internal audit activities adopt uniform meanings for the various terms used in audit programs. Here are some definitions that can help eliminate confusion and build a sound bridge between the audit program writer and the staff auditor:

- **Analyze** — To break into significant component parts and determine the nature of something.

- **Check** — To compare or recalculate, as necessary, to establish accuracy or reasonableness.

- **Confirm** — To prove to be true or accurate, usually by written inquiry or by inspection.

- **Evaluate** — To reach a conclusion as to worth, effectiveness, or usefulness.

- **Examine** — To look at or into closely and carefully for the purpose of arriving at accurate, proper, and appropriate opinions.

- **Inspect** — To examine physically.

- **Investigate** — To ascertain facts about suspected or alleged conditions.

- **Review** — To study critically.

- **Scan** — To look over rapidly for the purpose of testing general conformity to pattern, noting apparent irregularities, unusual items, or other circumstances appearing to require further study.

- **Substantiate** — To prove conclusively.

- **Test** — To examine representative items or samples for the purpose of arriving at a conclusion regarding the population from which the sample is selected.

- **Verify** — To establish accuracy.

The term *audit* is too general to use in referring to a work step.

Relationship to the Final Audit Report

Audit steps are usually wasteful if they produce information that will not be reported. The audit program stage is not too soon to think about the final audit report. Some organizations even develop a standard report outline — a sort of digest — to indicate the subjects to be covered in the final report. This provides a useful discipline and sense of direction while carrying out the review and eliminates unnecessary audit work. Even if no such digest is prepared, auditors should keep in mind the general structure of the report and the programmed scope of audit. Economy and efficiency are also qualities desirable in internal auditing.

Some internal auditors find it efficient and helpful to write segments of their audit reports as the audit progresses. In large audit projects, progress reports provide early information to clients and make the final audit report easier to write. And if the audit report is kept in mind as the program is written, the format of the program itself will make the outline of the formal report easier to prepare.

Program Mechanics

The audit program should include estimates of the time required to carry out each of the segments of the audit. These are preliminary estimates, of course, but they help the auditor in charge and the audit supervisor to control and review the progress of the work. The estimates also help determine how many staff people should be assigned to the audit to complete the work in a reasonable time.

Adjustments to the estimates may be necessary, as the audit progresses, if circumstances differ markedly from those anticipated.

Audit supervisors or managers should approve all audit programs. They should also approve all significant changes. Audit programs tend to be evolutionary. It is rare indeed for the programmer to anticipate every circumstance or condition that will be encountered in the audit. A small rock seen in the preliminary survey may turn out to be the tip of a huge boulder when the auditors start digging.

In actual practice, the audit evolves from the initial programmed step. Audit programs should be updated periodically as the work progresses. If actual conditions are not those foreseen, it may be necessary to revise plans or even to discontinue the audit. Any significant changes should be reduced to writing with the reasons for the changes shown. Such changes should be approved at the same level of authority that approved the original program. Experience has shown that important information is overlooked when changes in audit scope or direction are not recorded.

The audit program should document the progress of the audit work. When tests are carried out, a simple method is to make reference in the audit program to the working papers. Each programmed audit step should bear a working paper reference. This will show what work was done and what still remains to be done. Also, it helps the auditor to avoid omitting steps inadvertently. If a step is deliberately omitted, the reason should be shown.

Small Audit Staffs

Audit staffs composed of one or two auditors may object to the time required to prepare audit programs. These objections have no merit.

An audit report is usually written by one person. A good report writer will prepare a careful outline before writing the report. The outline is the program for the written report. Similarly, even a one-person audit department should prepare programs for the audit projects. It is just as easy for that individual to forget or omit significant audit steps as it is for junior members in large audit departments. Also, the concept of association assists in more complete coverage.

Besides, even small organizations will want external auditors to make use of the work of their internal auditors to reduce external audit costs. But external auditors will have little respect for internal auditors whose audit work is not programmed and whose audit scope and objectives are not defined (see Chapter 24).

Obviously, an audit program prepared by the same internal auditor who will carry it out in its entirety need not be as detailed as one written for a junior auditor. It should, however, set forth the objectives of the operation being audited and show the audit procedures to be followed. These can be combined with the audit objectives. (For example: "Determine the adequacy and effectiveness of the controls to see that the names of people leaving the organization are promptly removed from the payroll.") Whichever way auditors decide to show the audit procedures, they should list them and carry them out.

Guidelines for Preparing Audit Programs

The preparation of an audit program is closely linked to the information gained during the preliminary survey. One phases into the other. Guidelines for preparing the program will take into account the results of the steps taken during the survey. As a summary of both survey and programming steps, here are some guidelines for carrying out the steps and the reasons for them:

Guideline	Reason
Review prior reports, audit programs and working papers, and other documents from preceding audits, and list any open items requiring action.	To gain the background and determine the results of past reviews to better decide on the scope of the current audit.
Perform a preliminary survey.	To determine the objectives of the activity to be reviewed, the actual or potential risks, and the existing systems of controls.
Review policies and procedures for the audited function, its operating manuals, organization charts, chart of authority, long-range and short-range objectives and goals.	To determine the areas that can be measured and appraised, and whether the function is operating in accordance with the intentions of management.
Review current internal auditing literature about the area under audit.	To obtain the latest information on techniques for auditing the activity under review.
Prepare a flowchart of the key operations of the audited function.	To identify any control weaknesses and to obtain a visual analysis of the transaction flow.
Review performance standards that have been established by management and, if possible, compare these with industry-wide standards.	To obtain a yardstick by which to measure and evaluate the efficiency and effectiveness of the operation and to determine whether they are meeting reasonable standards.
Interview the client and discuss the scope of the audit and the objectives the auditor seeks to achieve.	To obtain agreement from the auditee and to avoid any misunderstanding about the purpose and scope of the audit.
Prepare a budget detailing the resources it will take to complete the audit engagement.	To establish estimates for the number of auditors and time needed so as to ensure the efficiency of the audit process.
Interview key people who have an interface with the audited function.	To obtain an insight into the operation and the efficiency and effectiveness of the operation and to identify any problems in co-operation and coordination.

Guideline (Cont.)	**Reason (Cont.)**
List the material risks that must be considered.	To make sure that matters of the greatest vulnerability are addressed and receive appropriate attention.
For each of the identified risks, determine what controls are in effect and whether they are adequate.	To see if existing controls can eliminate or sufficiently reduce the identified risks.
Determine the substance of major problems and opportunities.	To identify the major areas of difficulty and determine the causes and possible remedies.

Criteria for Audit Programs

Audit programs should conform to certain criteria if they are to meet the objectives of the internal audit department. For example:

- The objectives of the operation under review should be stated carefully and agreed to by the client.

- Programs should be tailor-made to the audit assignment unless compelling reasons dictate otherwise.

- Each programmed work step should show the reason behind it, i.e., the objective of the operation and the controls to be tested.

- Work steps should include positive instructions. They should not be stated in the form of questions. General questions, particularly those calling for yes or no answers, do not lead to effective auditing. They usually result in superficial answers rather than in-depth analyses and evaluations. Moreover, the way that the questions are framed may call for answers with an undesirable slant or bias. This rule does not reject the use of yes or no questions as mind-joggers to help the auditor make certain that no significant audit objective is overlooked. As a practical matter, experienced auditors will jot down such questions to make sure they look at all important aspects of an operation. But the work steps leading to an objective, unbiased audit opinion should be positive.

- Whenever practicable, the audit program should indicate the relative priority of the work steps. Thus, the more important parts of the program will be completed within the allotted time or other restrictions.

- Audit programs should be flexible and permit the use of initiative and sound judgment in deviating from prescribed procedures or extending the work done. But audit supervisors should be informed promptly of major deviations.

- Programs should not be cluttered with material from sources readily available to the staff. Incorporate by reference if feasible.

- Unnecessary information should be avoided. Include only what is needed to perform the audit work. Excessive detail wastes the time of those who prepare the program and those who read it.

- Audit programs should bear evidence of supervisory approval before they are carried out. Significant changes should also be approved in advance.

- When client management asks the auditor to perform certain tests, these should be included in the audit program if the audit budget permits (or the budget should be modified if appropriate).

Supplementary Readings

Applegate, Dennis B., "Best Practices in Joint Venture Audits," *Internal Auditor*, April 1998, 50-54.

Barrow, John Henry, "Preaward Audits," *Internal Auditor*, February 1998, 50-52.

Brown, Doug S., "Auditing Contracts for Control and Cost Recovery," *Internal Auditing*, Fall 1997, Volume 13, Number 2, 9-14.

Cashell, James D., George R. Aldhizer III, and Rick Eichman, "Construction Contract Auditing," *Internal Auditor*, February 1999, 30-34.

Cerullo, Virginia, and Michael J. Cerullo, "Factors Considered in EDP Operational Reviews," *The EDP Auditor Journal*, Volume III, 1992, 53-66.

Cerullo, M. Virginia, Michael J. Cerullo, and Tracy Hardin, "Auditing the Purchasing Function," *Internal Auditor*, December 1997, 58-64.

Chesney, Linda, "The Heart of the Matter," *Internal Auditor*, February 1999, 48-52.

Christensen, David L., "Inventory Reviews," *Internal Auditor*, October 1997, 50-53.

Dame, Don R., "Auditing Commodity Payments," *Internal Auditor*, August 1998, 68-70.

Fargason, James Scott, and John J. Price, "Workers' Compensation," *Internal Auditor*, June 1994, 66-71.

Jacobson, Alan, "Tenant Lease Reviews," *Internal Auditor*, August 1996, 44-47.

Ladd, William H., and Edward J. Blocher, "Auditing Advertising Agencies," *Internal Auditor*, December 1991, 42-47.

Luizzo, Anthony J., "Auditing Warehouse and Loading Dock Security," *Internal Auditing*, March/April 2001, Volume 16, Number 2, 32-35.

Luizzo, Anthony J., "Developing Security-Related Audit Programs," *Internal Auditing Report,* April 2003, 6-8.

Mize Jr., B. Ray, "Vendor Audits," *Internal Auditor*, August 1992, 47-52.

McNeil, Laura J., "Unsuspecting Lease Encounters," *Internal Auditor*, August 1996, 48-53.

Nelson, Karen, "Auditing a Telecommunications System: A Primer," *The EDP Auditor Journal,* Volume II, 1992, 61-76.

Ngo, Huong Q., "Claims Fraud Auditing," *Internal Auditor*, June 1997, 44-46.

Parkinson, Ken (ed.), *Modern Accounting and Auditing Checklists* (New York: RIA, 2003).

Powell, Rodney, "Auditing Electronic Funds Transfer," *The EDP Auditor Journal,* Volume II, 1994, 48-53.

Reed Jr., Roy E., "Auditing Pension Plan Investments," *Internal Auditor*, October 1993, 60-64.

Servage, John A., "The Last One to Know," *Internal Auditor*, June 1998, 104.

Siotas, Chris, "Cooperative Auditing," *Internal Auditor*, April 1999, 88.

Stohl, Richard M., "Ten Ways to Control Health Benefits Costs," *Internal Auditor*, April 1998, 48-49.

Turman, Keith G., "Evaluating a Bank's Loan Loss Reserve Adequacy," *Internal Auditor*, February 1991, 52-59.

Multiple-choice Questions

1. During an audit of your organization's purchasing function, you learned that buyers were allowed to develop long-term relationships with particular suppliers. Such a policy will have the impact of increasing:
   a. Confidence dispersion.
   b. Cost of purchases.
   c. Materiality.
   d. Risk.

2. You are the internal auditor for an organization with more than 10,000 employees. You want to test for payroll payments to unauthorized recipients. The best procedure would be to examine:
   a. Authorizations of newly hired employees by the human resources department.
   b. Procedures for internal verification of the accuracy of payroll calculations.
   c. Departmental supervisor approvals of hours worked.
   d. Procedures for distribution of paychecks.

3. Which of the following would not be generally considered an essential criterion for developing audit programs?
    a. Description of the objective of the client operation as agreed to by the client.
    b. Specificity as to the controls to be tested.
    c. Specificity as to audit work steps to be followed.
    d. Specificity as to the methodology to be used for the audit steps.

4. An internal audit supervisor reviewed the system of controls and the organizational objectives of the purchasing department. What facet of audit planning was the supervisor developing?
    a. Internal audit policy manual.
    b. Audit work schedule.
    c. Audit program.
    d. Internal audit budget.

5. The *Standards* require that internal auditors establish plans to carry out audit assignments. Such plans include:
    a. Reviewing the reliability and integrity of financial and operating information.
    b. Establishing audit objectives and scope of work to be performed.
    c. Determining whether assets are properly safeguarded.
    d. Appraising the economy and efficiency with which resources are employed.

6. An organization manufacturing special-order products is experiencing excessive rates of rejection of finished products. An audit procedure to identify the source of the problem would be:
    a. Evaluating communication from the sales department to the production department.
    b. Evaluating communication from the production department to the sales department.
    c. Analyzing customer demand for the product.
    d. Testing whether supply of the product is sufficient to meet customer demand.

7. The markup applied to an organization's products has varied between customers. An audit procedure most likely to uncover this is:
    a. Checking to see if sales have been made to customers with inadequate credit ratings.
    b. Checking to see if salespeople were able to set prices without clearance from the central office.
    c. Determining if production costs have been excessive.
    d. Analyzing selling costs for excessiveness.

8. In a payables application, checks are authorized and paid based on matching purchase orders, receiving reports, and vendor invoices. Partial payments are common. An appropriate audit procedure for verifying that a purchase order has not been paid twice is to:
   a. Sort the receiving report file by purchase order, compute total amounts received by purchase order, compare total amounts received with purchase order amounts, and investigate any discrepancies between the total amounts received and purchase order amounts.
   b. Sort the vendor invoice file by purchase order, compute total amounts invoiced by purchase order, compare total amounts invoiced with purchase order amounts, and investigate any discrepancies between the total amounts invoiced and purchase order amounts.
   c. Sort the receiving report file by vendor invoice amounts, and investigate any discrepancies between the total amounts received and vendor invoice amounts.
   d. Sort the check register file by purchase order, compute total amounts paid by purchase order, compare total amounts paid with purchase order amounts, and investigate any discrepancies between the total amounts paid with the purchase order amounts.

9. To ascertain that all credit sales are recorded in accounts receivable, an auditor should:
   a. Confirm selected accounts receivable balances by direct correspondence with customers.
   b. Trace from a sample of subsidiary ledger entries to related sales invoices and to related shipping documents.
   c. Trace from a sample of customer purchase orders to related shipping documents.
   d. Trace from a sample of shipping documents to related sales invoices and subsidiary ledger.

10. To determine if an organization is purchasing excess raw materials, an internal auditor should:
    a. Be sure that standards are established for quality, quantity, and sourcing of raw materials.
    b. Ascertain that production budgets and economic order quantities are integrated and have been used in determining quantities purchased.
    c. Obtain assurance that purchasing agent assignments are rotated periodically.
    d. Determine that the purchasing department has a written charter with a set of procedures and guidelines covering purchasing operations.

11. An internal auditor wishes to determine if salaried employees in the division being audited are taking more paid vacation time than they have earned. Which of the following audit procedures would be most effective?
    a. Observing which employees were absent because of vacation and tracing those absences through the payroll records to subtractions from accumulated vacation time.
    b. Comparing total vacation time taken by selected employees in the most recent 12 months per payroll records to the time taken by the same employees in the preceding 12 months.
    c. Sending confirmations to selected employees, asking them to verify the accuracy of the number of days of vacation used during the year and the number of remaining unused days as obtained from the payroll records.
    d. Comparing the accrued vacation pay liability as computed for the firm's most recent balance sheet with the corresponding amount for one year earlier, and investigating any significant change.

12. An auditor wants to perform a test to determine if people on the payroll of a particular department actually work there. Which of the following would be the best source of evidence for the audit test?
    a. The physical presence of properly identified employees observed during the distribution of paychecks in the department.
    b. Testimonials obtained by discussing the performance of each employee with the department manager.
    c. The physical presence of properly identified employees observed during a surprise departmental floor check.
    d. Time cards documenting reported work time that can be reviewed for employee and supervisor signatures.

13. The cross-reference of individual payroll time cards to personnel department records and reports allows an auditor to conclude that:
    a. Individuals were paid only for time worked.
    b. Individuals are bona fide employees.
    c. Individuals were paid at the proper rate.
    d. Personnel department records agree with payroll accounting records.

14. In a comprehensive audit of a not-for-profit activity, an internal auditor would be primarily concerned with the:
    a. Extent of compliance with policies and procedures.
    b. Procedures related to the budgeting process.
    c. Extent of achievement of the organization's mission.
    d. Accuracy of reports on the source and use of funds.

15. What action should an internal auditor take upon discovering that an audit area was omitted from the audit program?
    a. Document the problem in the workpapers and take no further action until instructed to do so.
    b. Perform the additional work needed without regard to the added time required to complete the audit.
    c. Continue the audit as planned and include the unforeseen problem in a subsequent audit.
    d. Evaluate whether completion of the audit as planned will be adequate.

16. Which of the following audit techniques would be most persuasive in determining that significant inventory values on the books of an organization being acquired are correctly stated?
    a. Obtain a management representation letter stating that inventory values are correctly stated.
    b. Flowchart the inventory and warehousing cycle and form an opinion based on the quality of internal controls.
    c. Conduct a physical inventory and bring in an independent expert if necessary to value the inventory items.
    d. Interview purchasing and materials control personnel to ascertain the quality of internal controls over inventory.

17. You are an internal auditor who has been assigned to an audit of the material acquisition cycle of an organization. To satisfy an audit objective of verifying that purchase transactions are categorized and are for needed materials, you should:
    a. Review signatures on a sample of receiving reports.
    b. Discuss a sample of transactions with the purchasing agent.
    c. Review a sample of purchase orders and their related purchase requisitions for proper approval signatures.
    d. Examine a sample of vendor invoices.

18. During an operational audit, the auditor compared the current staffing of a department with established industry standards to:
    a. Identify bogus employees on the department's payroll.
    b. Assess the current performance of the department and make appropriate recommendations for improvement.
    c. Evaluate the adequacy of the established internal controls for the department.
    d. Determine whether the department has complied with all laws and regulations governing its personnel.

19. Manufacturing operations that use just-in-time (JIT) inventory delivery must develop a system of total quality control (TQC) over parts and material. The objective of TQC is to:
    a. Provide an early warning system that detects and eliminates defective items.
    b. Statistically estimate the potential number of defective items.
    c. Detect and eliminate maintenance and processing problems that cause bottlenecks.
    d. Insure that the "pull" exerted by each assembly stage includes correct quantities and specifications.

20. An operational audit of the production function includes an audit procedure to compare actual costs to standard costs. The purpose of this operational audit procedure is to:
    a. Determine the accuracy of the system used to record actual costs.
    b. Measure the effectiveness of the standard cost system.
    c. Assess the reasonableness of standard costs.
    d. Assist management in its evaluation of effectiveness and efficiency.

21. Management believes that some specific sales commissions for the year were too large. The accuracy of the recorded commission expense for specific salespersons is best determined by:
    a. Computing selected sales commissions.
    b. Calculating commission ratios.
    c. Using analytical procedures.
    d. Testing overall reasonableness.

22. Which of the following factors would be considered the least important in deciding whether existing internal audit resources should be moved from an ongoing compliance audit to a division audit requested by management?
    a. A financial audit of the division performed by the external auditor a year ago.
    b. The potential for fraud associated with the ongoing audit.
    c. An increase in the level of expenditures experienced by the division for the past year.
    d. The potential for significant regulatory fines associated with the ongoing audit.

23. When faced with an imposed scope limitation, the chief audit executive should:
    a. Delay the audit until the scope limitation is removed.
    b. Communicate the potential effects of the scope limitation to the audit committee of the board of directors.
    c. Increase the frequency of auditing the activity in question.
    d. Assign more experienced personnel to the engagement.

24. A standardized internal audit program would not be appropriate for which of the following situations?
    a. A stable operating environment undergoing only minimal changes.
    b. A complex or changing operating environment.
    c. Multiple locations with similar operations.
    d. Subsequent inventory audits performed at the same location.

25. A determination of cost savings is most likely to be an objective of:
    a. Program audits.
    b. Financial audits.
    c. Compliance audits.
    d. Operational audits.

26. In deciding whether to schedule the purchasing or the personnel department for an audit, which of the following would be the least important factor?
    a. There have been major changes in operations in one of the departments.
    b. The audit staff has recently added an individual with expertise in one of the areas.
    c. There are more opportunities to achieve operating benefits in one of the departments than in the other.
    d. The potential for loss is significantly greater in one department than in the other.

27. Which of the following is an appropriate statement of an audit objective?
    a. To observe the physical inventory count.
    b. To determine whether inventory stocks are sufficient to meet projected sales.
    c. To search for the existence of obsolete inventory by computing inventory turnover by product line.
    d. To include information about stockouts in the audit report.

28. An auditor, nearly finished with an audit, discovers that the director of marketing has a gambling habit. The gambling issue is not directly related to the existing audit and there is pressure to complete the current audit. The auditor notes the problem and forwards the information to the chief audit executive but does no further follow-up. The auditor's actions would:
    a. Be in violation of The IIA's *Code of Ethics* for withholding meaningful information.
    b. Be in violation of the *Standards* because the auditor did not properly follow up on a red flag that might indicate the existence of fraud.
    c. Not be in violation of either The IIA's *Code of Ethics* or *Standards*.
    d. Both a and b.

29. The internal auditing department of a large corporation has established its operating plan and budget for the coming year. The operating plan is restricted to the following categories: a prioritized listing of all audits, staffing, a detailed expense budget, and the commencement date of each audit. Which of the following best describes the major deficiency of this operating plan?
    a. Requests by management for special projects are not considered.
    b. Opportunities to achieve operating benefits are ignored.
    c. Measurability criteria and targeted dates of completion are not provided.
    d. Knowledge, skills, and disciplines required to perform work are ignored.

30. Which of the following is the best means of determining if an internal audit department's goals are being met?
    a. Having the audit committee periodically review the quality of the department's goals being met.
    b. Developing measurement criteria to accompany departmental goals.
    c. Scheduling an outside peer review of the department every three years.
    d. Having the external auditors review and evaluate the work of the department.

Chapter 6
Field Work - I

Field work — a systematic process and a professional discipline. Healthy skepticism. Strategy for field work. Self-directed audit teams. Stop-and-go auditing. Control self-assessment. Elements of field work. Audit objectives and operating objectives. SMART auditing. Performance measurement. Applying and developing standards. Benchmarking. Evaluation testing. Techniques for examining selected transactions or processes: observing, questioning, analyzing, verifying, investigating, and evaluating.

• •

The Process and Purpose of Field Work

The Process

Field work is a systematic assurance process of objectively gathering evidence about an entity's operations, evaluating it, and (1) finding out whether those operations meet acceptable standards and achieve established objectives; and (2) providing information for management decisions.

The term "systematic process" implies planned audit steps that are designed to meet audit objectives. It also implies that the internal auditor will employ professional discipline in the audit, as well as the appropriate research, while gathering, arraying, recording, and evaluating audit evidence.

"Professional discipline" implies complete freedom from any bias that would affect the gathering and evaluating of evidence. Freedom from bias is attained through independence and objectivity, both actual and perceived. Actual objectivity stems from an impartial mental attitude, one that is based on knowledge and that views evidence apart from oneself — judging it in purely factual terms. Such judgments must be arrived at without reference to one's personal feelings, prejudices, opinions, and interests, as well as pressures from external sources.

All audit evidence must be approached with a healthy professional skepticism. All evidence must be viewed with doubt until the doubt has been resolved through unbiased verification. Thus, a well-disciplined mind is an essential ingredient to professional internal auditing. Such a mind does not accept evidence on its face; it seeks to go behind surface assertions and numbers to find the truth.

Professional auditors approach all assertions with uncertainty — with an uneasy and questioning state of mind. To arrive at a professional opinion, internal auditors must gather objective evidence. Only such evidence will permit them to pass from the state of uncertainty into a state of belief that is sufficiently strong and supportable.

This uncertainty, this skepticism is important, but it must be used wisely. If the auditor continues to doubt after a reasonable, prudent person would be persuaded by the accumulated evidence, then skepticism is no longer productive. It accepts no proof at all. It can come to no useful result. It will impel the auditor to pile facts upon facts beyond a foregone conclusion and after a reasonable audit effort has been exhausted will still arrive at no conclusion.

The Purpose

The purpose of field work is to assist in assurance by performing the audit procedures that are spelled out in the audit program, in response to the audit objectives. Audit objectives are related to but are quite different from operating objectives. More on this relationship later. When reduced to its barest essentials, fieldwork is simply the gathering of evidence for measurement and evaluation. The concept of measurement has a special significance for internal auditors. When they have fully grasped this concept, internal auditors can successfully examine virtually any operation in the organization. Professional internal auditors should not engage in casual or haphazard auditing. They must understand that they:

- Cannot provide assurance by auditing an operation in a vacuum.
- Cannot observe a process and offhandedly decide whether it is good or bad.
- Must look at the operation in terms of units of measurement and standards.

The units of measurement are derived from quantification of the discrete elements that apply to the operation — the dollars, days, pounds, degrees, people, documents, machines, or other quantifiable elements of defined quality by which the activity can be objectively gauged. The operating standards are those qualities of acceptable performance — the frame of reference — against which the measured operating elements will be compared to judge the degree of success or failure.

Under these circumstances, internal auditors can measure operations objectively and effectively. But where they cannot measure, they had better tread lightly; they will be able to produce only a subjective observation, not an objective conclusion.

Developing Strategy for Field Work

Preparing for the field work phase requires the same attention and rigorous planning as does the preparation for the overall audit. At this point, the preliminary survey has been completed and the audit program has been prepared. Auditors must direct their attention to the work itself and how it is to be done. The elements of the strategic plan would include:

1. Personnel requirements.
2. Need for outside resources.*
3. Audit staff organization.
4. Authority and responsibility.
5. Structuring of field work.
6. Timing of field work.
7. Methods of field work.
8. Method of documentation.
9. Report preparation.
10. Contingency plans.

This concept of audit strategy, an integral part of the planning process, applies to all audit organizations regardless of size. In small organizations, staff aspects such as staff organization, authority and responsibility, and personnel requirements have minimum applicability.

There may be other elements, but those just listed are the most important. They should be developed in sufficient detail at the start of the work and they should be flexible enough to be modified as the work proceeds. These elements described in some detail are:

Personnel requirements. It is important to plan for the numbers and qualifications of the staff who will perform the audit. This includes the identification of the skills, experiences, and disciplines needed to properly perform the audit. Included also should be the internal source of these assets and the particular work that they will perform. Especially important is the identification of specialty support that is required from the support staff such as statistics, actuary science, and advanced IT expertise.

Need for outside resources. If the indigenous audit staff does not contain unique specialty expertise, it must be obtained from outside sources. Included in this element would be such expertise as engineering, economics, medicine, social work, psychology, education, and operations analysis, as well as outsourcing and cosourcing. The sources should be identified and an estimate made of the extent these resources will be needed and, as far as possible, an estimate as to cost and when and where these services will be required as well as their fit into the budget.

Audit staff organization. An organization plan of the audit line function is needed here. The plan should be identified as a *flat* (limited layers of supervision) or *silo* (many layers of

---

*outsourcing, cosourcing, use of experts, loan staffing, etc.

supervision) plan depending on the complexity of the work and the needed span of control. The plan should identify which part of the audit organization will perform different modes of the audit such as financial, efficiency, effectiveness, asset safety, and compliance as well as the plan of audit structure such as: by function, by product, by location, or by organization. If the audit is to have its own special audit staff support, this aspect of the audit organization should be designed as to specialty skills and numbers.

Authority and responsibility. This element relates to the command structure of the audit team. It is closely tied to the prior element and it defines the various aspects of responsibility such as personnel management, technical functions, administrative aspects, and fiscal items. It also contains the concomitant flow of authority and specifically describes the authorizations that are delegated to each line and staff official on the audit team.

Structuring of field work. Here, the audit program is planned as to sequence. The sequential activities are related to each other to assure that there is an orderly flow of work. Thus, staff members assigned to a particular activity will not have to wait for another group to complete its activity as a necessary prerequisite. An analytical system such as the Program Evaluation and Review Technique (PERT or CPM) can be used. The activities are identified in a diagram with symbols that are connected to indicate sequence. The connector should include an estimate as to the time needed for the activity and can also include costs. This procedure is needed for the next strategic element.

Timing of the field work. The process of structuring the field work gives rise to the timing of the field work operation. As many activities will be performed concurrently with other activities, it is essential that a technique such as PERT be used to arrive at the estimate of the sequence of work and overall time. The time estimates should contain allowances for administrative aspects such as inter and intra group liaison, nonoperating allowances and for the documentation and writing of the field drafts of the audit reports. The activity estimates of necessity will be based on experience and hopefully on operational standards for different types of audit work, when such can be identified. If the PERT operation is computerized, as most of them are, changes in the estimates or actual times can be fed into the program and instantly a modified overall estimate will be produced.

Methods of field work. There are six regularly used methods of field work, which will be described later in this chapter. They are:

- Observation
- Confirmation
- Verification
- Investigation
- Analysis
- Evaluation

It is appropriate to identify the method or methods that are most likely to be used in the field work process. Some of the methods such as confirmation may require advance preparations. For example, they may require the development of methodology for selection of participating population, the preparation of a confirmation instrument, and the construction of software for the processing of the results. Some field work may call for more than one method and the planning must integrate the several methods.

Methods of documentation. This element involves the accumulation of evidence and the preparation of working papers. It requires the anticipation of the results of the field work methods and also the ultimate use of the audit. Although care is always required in the documentation process, if there is a possibility of litigation or some type of legal action, the evidence must be in a form that is legally usable and handling by methods that are legally acceptable. Also, the evidence must be able to support the recommendations resulting from the audit findings. The auditor must anticipate resistance to these recommendations and have adequate ammunition to overcome this resistance. Evidence is discussed later in Chapter 9, Working Papers.

If computer working papers are to be used, an appropriate software program must be used. It must be able to accommodate the type of evidence that is being accumulated and the electronic and/or hard copy format that is to be required.

Report preparation. The report structure is frequently designed early in the audit process. The preliminary survey often will identify the important areas to which the audit will be directed. The survey will also give some indication of what is to be found. On the other hand, some mandated audits are structured to examine specific issues, activities, or conditions. In this case, the organization of the audit may provide an outline of the audit report.

The macrostructure of the report must be planned. This is the sequence of presentation of the audit findings and the rough outline of the report elements. Also, the microstructure of the report, or the method of presentation of individual audit findings, must be planned. Not all findings will need the complete anatomy of finding elements. In some cases, such elements as background, criteria, and impact may be marginal. Surprisingly, in many cases, the report is planned almost completely during the early part of the audit.

The report must be designed with the reader and user in mind. Consideration of the readers' capability and reactions must be a major item in its design and content. It is possible that more than one report may be appropriate for use by the operating echelons of the organization or when classified material is being presented. Quantity of detail, needed by the operating echelons, may be dull reading for management.

Contingency plans. It is probably axiomatic that very few activities proceed as planned. Thus, the plans should provide for contingencies. The plans should provide for the best case, the average case, and the worst case.

Contingencies should be anticipated and an outline should be prepared for such situations as:

- Shortage of staff (illness, withdrawal, transfers, etc.).
- Unavailability of auditable material.
- Indication that a projected condition is immaterial.
- Sudden indication that there may be fraud, malfeasance, nonfeasance, or misfeasance.
- Material obstruction by the client (lack of interest, refusal to cooperate, withholding of evidential material).
- Computer failure or software problems.
- Top management interference (as to scope of the audit, access to material or people, or method of audit).
- Withdrawal of audit resources.
- Work progress is such that it appears that projected audit work will exceed budget.

The audit should be planned so that any of the above situations that might occur has an immediate set of alternative actions that can be taken, again considering an average situation and a bad situation.

Self-directed Audit Teams[1]

Organizations in both the public and the private sector are going through the process of reengineering with the intent of improvements in service to customers, clients, and users, and also with the intent of functioning more efficiently and economically. The self-directed team departs from the silo form of traditional management of directors, deputy directors, assistant directors, supervisors, managers, and workers. The team is an operational unit, frequently consisting of specialists in various audit areas, and has leadership on a rotating or selected basis. The team makes its own decisions, frequently with the assistance of a coach who with the team leader provides expertise and assistance in the decision-making process.

Early experiments with the process indicate that there are improvements in productivity, audit quality, and customer service that exceed the savings from the downsizing of the auditing staff. The team accepts the responsibility of its work and shares the blame for poor work — also the praise and bonuses, if any, for good work. The fact that the team works closely with the client tends to improve auditor-client relationships. There is, however, not complete abandonment by audit top management. There must be resolution of basic organization objectives, independence, poor audit work, and inadequate decision-making.

Pay increases for the normal audit career path are abandoned. In their absence, pay raises are given for specific demonstrated audit performance such as the usual audit functions of programming, reporting, scheduling audit examination types of performance, and leadership. The age-old philosophy of salary administration, that the organization must share some of the innovation's cost saving with the worker who makes it possible, operates here. Also, unusual events may result in onetime bonuses. Examples — large cost savings and large fraud recoveries. Thus, to operate effectively, the team must be comprised of members who exhibit selflessness and agree to shared leadership.

Some of the problems faced with the innovation are:[2]

- Lack of positive feedback by a manager.
- Lack of corrective feedback by a manager.
- Difficulty to come to consensus/conflict resolution.
- No focal point of accountability.
- Difficulty of assigning hiring, firing, and promotion decisions.
- Reluctance to seek guidance.
- Unclear definitions of authority.
- No official external liaison.
- Unclear line for training needs.
- No clear career path.
- No clear system of quality assurance.

Regardless of these drawbacks, organizations are continuing to use the concept, especially where the teams are reasonably large (about eight members). The coach (who may coach more than one team) is assigned many of the administrative responsibilities. Because of its greater productivity and effectiveness it is being given emphasis as a new potential operational asset.

Stop-and-Go Auditing[3]

Edison's audit activity routinely screens proposed audit assignments to eliminate audits with low-return potential and to rank the remainder according to risk and to known concerns. The "stop-and-go audit" technique helps to eliminate the low-return audits that slip through this initial screening process. The basic concept behind the stop-and-go approach is to empower the field auditor to stop the audit during the preliminary survey, or at any other time, if indications of substantial risks or potential adverse findings are absent. Once the audit is stopped, the auditor moves on to the next audit contained in the department's annual audit plan. In this manner, each auditor can perform more audits each year than under the traditional audit approach of spending all of the available time budget on each audit regardless of the results of the preliminary work.

For example, if an auditor with 1,800 available hours per year is requested to conduct 10 audits, each lasting 180 hours, he or she will perform only those 10 audits when using the traditional audit approach of spending 180 hours on each audit. However, if the stop-and-go audit technique is employed, the auditor may average only 40 hours on three or four audits where the business activities under review do not display high risk or potential adverse findings, thereby freeing up 360 to 480 audit hours per year. The result from utilizing stop-and-go auditing is improved auditor efficiency and the performance of 13 or 14 audits each year instead of just the 10 originally planned. Of course, if concerns are discovered during the preliminary review, or at any other time, the auditor stays with the audit and uses the amount of time planned for the audit and even spends extra time, if necessary.

The Audit Committee of the Board of Directors at Edison was introduced to the stop-and-go audit technique and embraced it because stop-and-go auditing:

- Reinforces the audits activity's objective to concentrate its resources on high-risk areas and activities of the company (i.e., to operate at a high point on the priority curve) and provides the Audit Committee with assurance that more audit effort is spent on such areas rather than on low risk-areas.

- Allows the auditor flexibility to stop or go, to reduce or increase the audit scope, and motivates him or her to focus on activities of the company that will produce the most beneficial findings and provide the most value to the organization.

- Increases the number of audits beyond the minimum audit coverage, because the auditors perform shorter but more audits each year. For example, 600 audits may be performed in one year, instead of the routine 500.

Control Self-assessment[4]

Control self-assessment is a relatively recent innovation that is being used by many large organizations to supplement and in some cases to supplant their internal auditing process. The proponents of this technique are careful to state that there is no intent for completely supplanting the internal auditing function. The new technique is important and quite involved. Thus, Chapter 10 is dedicated exclusively to it; however, because it impinges substantially on fieldwork, it is believed appropriate to give it some attention in this chapter.

Internal auditing has long promoted the concept of "participative auditing," a process that employs various degrees of partnering between the auditor and the client. Where employed with reason and sincerity it has proved to be effective and it has provided for efficiency and greater effectiveness in carrying out audit objectives. Control self-assessment is a type of participative auditing. In its simplest form it is not completely new. Auditors in both the public and the private sectors have practiced it to a degree. It is being used to gain information that has proved difficult for the traditional audit staffs to gather.

Probably the event that propelled this innovation into prominence was the development of the COSO concept of internal control. This concept identified aspects of internal control that were less substantive than the traditional methods that were being considered. Thus, this measurement and evaluation defied the usual methodologies employed by internal audit staffs. Control self-assessment remedies this deficiency by using indigenous staffs to evaluate these ephemeral aspects of internal control based on what they see, experience, and practice.

The method being used is to develop workshops conducted by the audit staff, but consisting of client personnel who will evaluate and measure the "soft" aspects of internal controls. The internal audit participants develop questions and subject matter for discussion. The client participants discuss the material and come to conclusions relative to presence of and effectiveness of the internal control aspects under discussion. They also attempt to arrive at causes of problems and potential remedial activity.

During the workshops there is a discussion of the primary objective provided by the client business unit and of the supporting objective. Also discussed are control successes, obstacles, and recommendations. These discussions are converted into ratings as to the organizations' actual and desired levels of control effectiveness. The differences become the opportunity for improvement.

Participants are protected from retribution through the use of keypads that transmit opinions and comments without identification.

The results of this phase of the audit can be made a part of the scheduled audit report or they can be reported separately. This phase of reporting is frequently carried out through graphics that relate to the primary objective and to the basic objective.

Elements of Field Work

Audit Objectives

Audit objectives differ from operating objectives, just as audit procedures differ from operating procedures.

Operating objectives are the results sought by operating managers, for example:

- Obtaining the right goods at the right place at the right time and at the right price.
- Accepting only those suppliers' products that meet specifications and are in the quantities ordered.
- Processing insurance claims promptly, correctly, and in accordance with policy terms.

The list is endless.

Operating procedures are designed to see that the operating objectives will be achieved. Examples might include:

- Clear and explicit specifications for goods.
- Use of appropriate statistical methods of determining quantities received.
- Technical inspection operations.

Audit objectives are keyed to operating objectives, but they have different purposes. The audit objectives are designed to determine whether the particular operating objectives are being met. They are achieved by applying audit procedures to determine whether operating procedures function as intended and are accomplishing operating objectives. Operating objectives are set by management. Audit objectives are set by the auditors.

Audit procedures are the means by which the auditor meets the audit objectives. They are steps in the audit process that guide the auditor in carrying out the planned reviews, based on the established audit objectives.

Exhibit 6-1 shows the relationship among operating objectives and procedures and audit objectives and procedures in some purchasing, claims processing, and receiving activities. The matters listed are merely illustrative: no attempt has been made to compile an exhaustive catalog.

Audit objectives must be specified for everything the auditor needs to do. All audit procedures must be relevant to the audit objectives. An audit procedure may seem appropriate in an audit of a particular operation, but if it is not designed to carry out an approved audit objective, it may be of little value in helping meet the audit mission. The catalog of audit objectives and procedures for all operations of all enterprises is practically endless because of the variety of activities and the means by which they are accomplished. We know of no comprehensive listing of such matters. It is up to the internal auditor to exercise the audit judgment needed to make sure that audit objectives are complete and that the audit procedures carry out the audit objectives set forth in the audit program.

The practitioner, therefore, must not select audit objectives or apply audit procedures, by rote, mindless of the circumstances. Rather, the practitioner must devise procedures that are relevant to the audit objective selected. This text can do no more than provide some examples as guides.

Exhibit 6-1
Objectives and Procedures (Operating vs. Audit)

Operating Objectives	Operating Procedures	Audit Objectives	Audit Procedures
Purchasing To obtain the right goods.	User departments, not buyers, shall prepare approved requisitions, specifying products needed.	To determine whether purchase orders were issued to purchase only those products the organization needs.	Review a sample of purchase orders to see if orders were supported by approved requisitions and whether the nature of purchased goods, in the quantity ordered, are relevant to the organization's needs.
To obtain goods at the right price.	Buyers shall use competitive bidding for all purchases over a stipulated amount, justifying in writing the failure to obtain bids.	To determine whether competition was solicited when required and whether failure to obtain bids was properly explained, whether purchase orders are mathematically correct and received the proper approvals. In either case, determine whether purchase order was properly executed.	For sample selected, verify evidence of bidding where required, whether explanation for failure to bid was reasonable.
Claims Processing To process claims promptly.	All claims are to be logged in. Processing is monitored through periodic reports.	To determine whether all claims received are logged in and monitored during processing cycle and whether management has been alerted to unreasonable delays.	Review a sample of paid claims to determine whether they have been logged in and whether they have been processed within a reasonable time. Examine reports to management on claims processing for accuracy and timeliness.
To process claims correctly.	Management specifies precise steps to take in examining claims, including comparison with policy terms. Also provides for a review system and levels of approval, depending on value of the claim.	To determine whether valid claims are paid in amounts due.	For sample selected, determine whether payments are mathematically correct, meet policy terms, show evidence of appraisals where required, and bear evidence of review and approval.

Exhibit 6-1 (Cont.)
Objectives and Procedures (Operating vs. Audit)

Operating Objectives	Operating Procedures	Audit Objectives	Audit Procedures
Receiving To accept only goods ordered.	Management provides for counting, weighing, and measuring products received and signing therefore. Specified sampling procedures are permitted where appropriate.	To determine whether only the goods ordered are received, and in the amounts ordered.	Review a representative sample of receiving reports for evidence of counts, weights, and measurements. Compare store's records with quantities shown on receiving reports.
To accept only those goods that meet specifications.	Management provides for inspection of goods ordered, comparing samples of goods received with specifications. All changes to specifications must be sent promptly to the receiving inspection department.	To determine whether products of prescribed quality only are accepted, and whether rejected products are charged back to suppliers.	For the sample selected, review evidence of inspection. Review evidence of charge-backs for rejected receipts. Analyze records of scrapped materials to determine whether inferior products have been ordered or accepted.

The following examples have been selected from CIA examinations. The selections connect audit objectives and audit procedures for different activities in a variety of organizations.

- *Hospitals.* An audit objective is to evaluate the quality of housekeeping services in a hospital. Reviews of records would probably not help the auditor determine the quality of the service. Observation and interviews with a random sample of medical personnel and patients would be more likely to point up any serious problems. Another audit objective is to ascertain the completeness and validity of patient insurance claims. Confirmation with patients, comparisons with prior years' claims, and the cost of processing claims may provide useful information. These do not meet the objective, however, because only an actual review of claim completeness and validity would be effective.

- *Inventories.* Supplies are transferred from inventory to a department that ordered the supplies. An audit objective is to evaluate controls over the transfer of accountability for those supplies. The most appropriate documents to show physical delivery of the supplies would be signed receipts or stock requisition forms. Although receiving reports, shipping lists, and vendors' invoices deal with supplies, they are irrelevant to this audit objective.

  Another audit objective is to determine whether inventory is released only after receipt of an authorized request form. The surest test to meet that objective is to select a random sample of perpetual inventory credits and trace them to properly authorized request forms. Other tests, such as reviewing requisitions for authorized signatures and tracing release forms to perpetual inventory records or to cost accumulation records do not provide assurance that every inventory credit has been properly authorized.

  An audit objective might be to ascertain whether retail inventory thefts are occurring. Observing inventory removal and testing pricing might meet other inventory audit objectives, but not this one. The most appropriate procedure would be to investigate significant differences between physical inventory totals and retail inventory computed amounts — what is versus what should be.

- *Manufacturing.* An audit objective is to evaluate the effectiveness of production quality control. A relevant audit procedure would be to evaluate the number and reasons for sales adjustments; the fewer the adjustments the higher the quality. Other procedures, like the number of products rejected during processing, might deal more with purchasing problems than with production quality.

  An audit objective might be to determine the reasonableness of labor-efficiency standards. Asking management about the reasonableness of the standards would most likely produce subjective judgments. Factory wage rate authorizations might be based on other factors. Comparison of historical gross profit percentages might yield information that is interesting, but it would not be directly relevant to labor standards. The most objective tests would be to trace those standards to the time and motion studies on which they were based, or to industry-wide standards.

The audit objective is to ascertain the quality of manufacturing operations. One direct reflection of that efficiency is excessive rework and scrap. Comparisons of current and historical outputs, costs of materials purchased, and fulfillment of production quotas are of interest, but irrelevant.

The audit objective is to review the effects of a learning curve developed from accounting and production records for a new process. In testing the accuracy of the curve, the auditor would have to take into account certain conditions that would adversely affect the learning curve and reduce its accuracy as a production indicator. Some such conditions are: charging overtime hours to overhead, increasing the number of preassembled parts and skilled higher-paid workers, and using newly developed equipment. All of these items affect the process on which the curve was based.

- *Personnel.* The audit objective in a personnel department is to review controls over the termination process. The greatest risks in the termination process lie in the lack of coordination about termination pay between the personnel and payroll departments. Other procedures such as comparing turnover rates, reviewing exit interviews, and inquiring about reasons for dismissals are of interest but not relevant to implementation of the termination process itself.

- *Program results.* The audit objective is to determine the effectiveness of a particular program or project. Such audits are approached by identifying the operating objectives and finding out if they have been met. The audit procedures used are the same as those used in other comparable audits and can be performed by both internal and external auditors.

- *Research and development.* The audit objective is to determine whether R&D projects were properly authorized. The audit procedure would be to examine project authorization documents — not to evaluate the R&D department's effectiveness, assess costs, or evaluate priorities.

- *Scrap.* The audit objective for a scrap disposal function is to determine whether only properly designated material is being sold as scrap. Many audit procedures are employed in a scrap audit: (1) review transfer procedures; (2) determine whether competitive bids were received; (3) trace selected items from perpetual inventory records to the scrap storage area. But these audit steps are irrelevant to this audit objective. What is relevant is the review of scrap transfer and disposal documents for properly authorized approvals.

Audit objectives for modern internal auditors span a broad field. Today, internal auditors concern themselves with audits that run the gamut from reliability of financial information to organizational compliance with laws and regulations, to economy and efficiency in the use of resources, to effectiveness of performance. But there are limits to this scope — areas where internal auditors may have no authority to tread. Chief among these is the evaluation of long-range strategic planning by management or by boards of directors. Internal auditors may be called upon to assure that there is such planning or to validate the information on which such plans are based. But the adequacy of the plan or the methods used is usually within the sole province of the board.

SMART Auditing[5]

The concept of SMART auditing was developed by the auditing operation of Carolina Power and Light, one of the largest public utilities in the United States. The acronym stands for Selective Monitoring and Assessment of Risks and Trends. The method seems to be a combination of risk assessment and analytical auditing. It is intended to "...reflect the effectiveness of the system of internal controls and enables auditors to quickly identify potential problems, unfavorable trends and abnormal fluctuations." It uses "key indicators" as the basic element of the audit process. There are four phases:

- Selecting key areas to monitor and assess
- Developing key indicators to monitor and assess
- Implementation
- Maintenance of SMART auditing techniques

The selection of key areas to monitor or assess is based on the following criteria:

- Risks to the organization
- Control environment (weak)
- Changes or new initiatives
- Known problem areas
- Ability to use computer assisted audit techniques (CART) in a cost effective manner
- Quality of information
- Liquidity of assets/fraud potential
- Major contracts
- Management (strength and focus)
- Oversight activities by others

The key indicators to monitor and assess will, "...focus on an organization's systems, processes, or key financial, operational, managerial, and information technology of controls." The characteristics are:

- Meaningfulness
- Timeliness
- Sensitivity
- Reliability
- Measurability
- Practicality

The tools and techniques that are used are those frequently employed in analytical auditing such as periodic observation, statistical analysis, regression analysis, etc. The procedures may be employed as monetary amounts, quantities, ratios, or percentages. The frequency of measuring should be often enough to provide early warning of problems. "The reporting method and frequency varies depending upon the functional area of the SMART auditing objectives and the risks involved."

Implementation is the carrying out of the audit plans, including review of the information and follow-up activities where appropriate.

The maintenance of the SMART auditing techniques includes these elements.

- Assignment of the SMART auditing activities to individual team members
- Maintenance of appropriate documentation and centralized storage
- Periodic evaluation of the audit activity
- Consideration of its use during the annual audit planning process

Carolina Power and Light cites the outcome of the innovation as a cost effective adjunct to the traditional internal auditing process. Listed as major benefits are:

- "Improved usage of limited audit methods,
- Increased audit presence,
- More effective audits,
- Timely problem identification,
- Improved fraud detection,
- Enhanced annual audit planning."

Performance Measurement

An example of a routine examination will illustrate the concept of audit measurement. Suppose auditors want to evaluate the promptness with which purchased materials clear receiving and inspection. Promptness implies that the units of measurement are hours or days. The standard rate per unit of time may be (1) what management considers acceptable, as stated in operating instructions; (2) the needs of the production department as set out in production schedules; or (3) some other logical criterion that is keyed to an organization objective. The auditors will measure the time required to process each transaction — each delivered shipment in the audit sample. They will then compare the results with the standard. Finally, they will evaluate the results of their measurement and determine whether their findings portray a good or bad condition.

Now let us take a less common audit situation. Assume that internal auditors want to determine whether test pilots are reporting, when they should, defects they find in the aircraft they are testing. As they fly, pilots read the instruments before them and fill in check sheets. Some entries relate to pressure readings. The pressure instruments are calibrated in pounds per square inch. The pilot is asked to read a particular instrument, at a given altitude and power setting, and enter the reading on the check sheet. If the reading is outside acceptable limits, the pilot must prepare a "squawk" sheet that will trigger an investigation into the reason for the unacceptable reading.

Standards bring meaning to measurements. To make their determination about the pilots' responsiveness, the auditors will read the pilots' check sheets. The units of measurement are there — the pounds per square inch shown on the instruments and on the pilots' check sheets. Yet, if the auditors were to examine the pilots' readings without reference to a standard, they would be wasting their time. The auditors could draw no acceptable conclusions. A reading of 80, 100, or 120 pounds might all seem equally appropriate.

But if the auditors consulted engineering specifications and found that, at 20,000 feet and a power setting of 85 percent, fuel pressure should be between 90 and 100 pounds, they have a standard. Then, if the pilot's entry on the check sheet is 100 pounds, the auditors could be quite satisfied that no action was needed. If the entry showed 130 pounds, then the auditors would expect to see a squawk sheet. If one had not been prepared, they would record a deficient condition and they could do so confidently.

To make a meaningful examination, auditors look for a unit of measurement and then for a standard. The standards can be found in job instructions, organization directives, budgets, product specifications, trade practices, minimum standards of internal control, generally accepted accounting principles, contracts, statutes, sound business practices, or even in the multiplication tables. Then, by comparing their findings of fact with the standards, they can arrive at an objective conclusion.

Developing Standards

Internal auditors are wading deeper and deeper into the stream of operations. Also, they are beginning to evaluate management functions for which standards have not been established. As they do, they find themselves faced with the need to find authoritative standards, or to develop standards with the client. This may not be a simple task but, if done with care, it can lead to audit results previously thought to be beyond the auditor's reach.

The standards should match the objectives of the operation reviewed. If the subject is technical, the standards should be validated by an expert who is technically qualified before they are accepted by client management. An example of this approach involves an audit of an organization's safety control system.

No standards existed, so the auditors constructed standards. Then, to obtain adequate assurance that the standards were reasonable and relevant, they asked a local representative of the National Safety Council to review the standards. The validated standards were discussed with client management and accepted. The auditors then used those standards with confidence for comparing their measurements.

Relevant excerpts from the resulting audit report follow, demonstrating the auditors' methods: To evaluate the adequacy of the organizational structure as a means for dealing with potential disasters and with matters of safety, we constructed a set of criteria to use as a yardstick in measuring the adequacy of the control system. Our criteria covered matters of industrial safety:

Committee structure, composition, and operation
- Have appropriate committees been constituted to provide policy guidance and direction over disaster and safety control?
- Are line organizations that are responsible for industrial safety operations adequately represented on the committees?
- Are committee activities carried out in a businesslike manner, including the advance scheduling of meetings, the provision for detailed agendas, the recording, assigning, and resolution of action items, and the preparation and distribution of minutes?
- Is there assurance that safety problems at the hourly employee level will receive proper attention and will be followed to a satisfactory conclusion?
- Is there a means of obtaining interface among the various committees for handling related problems?

Plans, programs, practices, and implementation instructions
- Have emergency and/or disaster plans been developed?
- Have appropriate instructions been issued to implement the plans?

- Have industrial safety programs been established for the promotion of safety through accident prevention?
- Have adequate provisions been made for the implementation of the requirements of the Occupational Safety and Health Act that became effective April 29, 1971?

Monitoring, inspecting, and reporting activities
- Have specific hazards been identified and has provision been made to monitor them?
- Are physical inspections of plants and facilities being made, and are reports on the inspections being distributed?
- Is the workmen's compensation insurance organization with which our organization deals represented at general safety meetings?
- Is the insurance organization provided with minutes of all safety meetings and reports of the inspections?
- Is corrective action being taken on deficiencies reported as a result of inspections?

To obtain assurance that our criteria have provided us with adequate yardsticks, we submitted them to the Occupational Safety Director of the local chapter of the National Safety Council. He informed us that, in his judgment, our criteria were both reasonable and complete and that an organizational structure, together with appropriate plans and programs that measure up to those criteria, would represent an adequate system of control. The criteria were accepted by the client.

An alternative method could have been to work *with* the client to develop adequate safety control standards.

Benchmarking[6]

Benchmarking is really the selection of best practices conducted by other organizations or by parts of the organization itself that are intended to assist in achieving objectives. The development of the benchmarks is usually the result of a study process. Arthur Andersen is reported to have conducted a Global Best Practices study that identified eleven actions that were appropriate for the determination of activities that would enhance the organization's effort. These activities classified into four phases were:

- Analyzing audit processes
  - Identify and map internal audit processes.
  - Develop relationships with other internal audit units that are known for quality and progress.
  - Conduct documentary research.
  - Attend conferences on subjects likely to describe new developments.

- Planning the study
  - Define the scope of the benchmarking study; identify uses it should cover.
  - Identify benchmarking partners; request site visits.
  - Develop a methodology for capturing the new data.

- Conducting the study
  - Identify, understand, and analyze best practices.
  - Identify and analyze existing and potential performance gaps.

- Gaining insight
  - Organize, adapt, and incorporate best practices.
  - Recalibrate and improve processes.

This study identified eight best practices of the internal auditing activities as follows:

1. Understand customers so that their expectations can be met.
2. View internal auditing on a for-profit business or organization service line.
3. Use quality concepts to improve audit processes, including establishing performance measures.
4. Audit the business (operations) as well as its controls to help maximize the organization's performance.
5. Establish a new role for internal auditing as an agent of organizational change.
6. Communicate on a regular basis within the internal audit activity and with customers and shareholders.
7. Integrate technology issues and applications into the audit process.
8. Emphasize the importance of professional staff satisfaction in internal auditing.

Benchmarking has probably become important because of the dynamics of the field of internal auditing and the need of all auditing organizations to become aware of new developments that are making the function more important and more valuable to corporate and government management. Benchmarking is simply an auditing process applied to the complete discipline of internal auditing to identify methods that are innovative and productive and that will result in a more efficient internal auditing operation.

Benchmarking can be used to enhance all levels of the internal auditing function. It can be applied to the basic philosophy of internal auditing's relationship to the organization; to the organization of the auditing function; to the planning process, including risk assessment and self evaluation processes; to field work, including methods of examination and evaluation; to the reporting processes; and to relationships with external auditors and boards of directors. The important thing is that change be made not just to use new methods, but also to result in substantial improvements in the audit operation.

Evaluation

Measurement with comparison with standards is only one of the two phases of field work. Having made their measurements, internal auditors must then evaluate their findings to arrive at professional judgments.

Evaluation suggests an intent to arrive at a mathematically correct judgment, and to express that judgment in terms of what is known. Evaluation seldom suggests determination of monetary worth but, rather, a finding of the numbered equivalent in more familiar terms — such as the timeliness with which invoices are processed, or their mathematical accuracy, or the accuracy with which receipts are inspected. However, evaluation involves more than just a comparison of measurements with standards. It calls for a judgment on both the standards and the results of the comparisons. It also requires that the standards and the measurement process employ congruent concepts.

The numerical connotation permits measurement and evaluation, the two keys to field work, to walk side by side down the audit trail with perfect compatibility. Numerical evaluation represents the ability to turn raw data into reasoned assessments.

As they apply operational standards throughout their field work, internal auditors should not fail to evaluate the standards themselves. The fact that such standards have been established and approved as satisfactory performance criteria does not necessarily raise them above reproach. Standards developed yesterday may not be applicable today. Changing circumstances may require new or revised statutes, contracts, regulations, procedures, or instructions. Standards, too, should be evaluated as the yardstick to their appropriateness and adequacy in measuring progress toward the organization's objectives and goals, and the applicability of the standards in the world of today.

Aspects of an Operation

The internal auditor's measurements will normally be directed to three principal aspects of an organization. These are: Quality, Cost, and Schedule. As a simple example, assume that the auditor is examining controls over the purchasing operation. Included among the measurements are:

Quality. Determine whether purchase orders have been properly approved and contain all required specifications and terms. Determine whether changes in specifications have been submitted to the supplier.

Cost. Determine whether bidders' lists have been approved by buying supervisors. Determine whether competitive bids are used whenever possible.

Schedule. Determine whether dates when goods are needed are shown on the purchase orders and whether the dates agree with those requested by the using organization. Determine whether buyers follow up regularly with suppliers to obtain purchased products on time.

Testing

The Purpose of Testing

Auditors achieve audit objectives by a process known as testing. Testing implies placing activities or transactions on trial by putting selected items to the proof and revealing their inherent qualities or characteristics.

To the internal auditor, testing implies the measurement of representative items and comparison of the results with established standards or criteria. The purpose is to help provide the auditor with a basis for forming an audit opinion.

The audit test usually implies evaluation of transactions, records, activities, functions, and assertions by examining all or part of them. In today's complex world, the examination of an entire entity in detail is usually impracticable or uneconomical. But testing — when viewed as putting something to proof — does not necessarily exclude a complete examination. Testing is any activity that supplies the auditor with sufficient proof to support an audit opinion. Computer Assisted Audit Techniques (CAAT) can, under certain circumstances, place the entire population under test. The software conducts the test and exceptions to preestablished criteria are identified for audit examination.

The Objectives of Testing

Audit testing comprises the methods of examining, comparing, analyzing, and evaluating subject data, material, and transactions in terms of some type of standards or criteria. The objective of the testing processes is to determine:

- Validity, i.e., propriety, genuineness, reasonableness.
- Accuracy, i.e., quantity, quality, classification.
- Compliance with applicable procedures, regulations, laws, etc.
- Competence of controls, i.e., the degree that risks are neutralized.

The testing should be responsive to one or more of the above objectives, depending on the directive, implicit or explicit, conveyed to the audit organization in making the assignment of the audit project.

Simply put, testing determines whether something is as it should be.

Planning for the Testing

Like any substantive element of the audit process, testing should be preceded by planning. The plan should be formalized by documentation and should include:

- Defining the objective of the testing.
- Identifying the type of testing that will be responsive to the objectives.
- Identifying the personnel needs as to: skills and disciplines, experience qualification, numbers.
- Determining the sequence of the testing processes.
- Defining the standards or criteria.
- Defining the test population.
- Deciding on the methodology of sampling to be used.
- Examining the selected transactions or processes.

The first four elements above are an extension of the strategic planning discussed previously. However, the last four elements require further treatment.

The use of Computer Assisted Audit Techniques (CAAT) has supplanted much of the traditional manual testing. Here, the software automatically, using the entire population as a "sample," identifies those items that the auditor would have produced if the whole population had been tested.

Defining the Performance Standards or Criteria

Performance standards or criteria are explicit or implicit. They are explicit when they are set forth clearly in directives, job instructions, specifications, or laws. Instructions may state categorically, for example, that time spans shall not exceed five days, or that competitive bids must be obtained on all procurements exceeding $1,000, or that production lots must be rejected when error rates exceed five percent, or that the advertising budget may not exceed one percent of projected sales. Auditors in such cases have well-calibrated measuring sticks for their comparisons: units of measurement and established standards.

Standards are implicit when management may have established, or may be working toward, objectives and goals, but has not explicitly set forth how they will be achieved. In those cases, auditors, after reviewing the objectives and goals and determining the controls established or needed, will have to consult with management on what it considers to be satisfactory performance. To make tests without coming to agreement on units of measurement and on standards of acceptability may result in wasted work and fruitless argument. There can be no meaningful measurement without agreed upon standards; without measurement, field work becomes conjecture and not fact.

Defining the Test Population

The population to be tested must be considered in terms of the audit objectives. If the objective is to form an opinion on the transactions that took place since the last audit, the totality of those transactions represents the population. If the objective is to form an opinion on the adequacy, effectiveness, and efficiency of existing systems of control, the population may be more restricted. Under the latter circumstances, management is not interested in past history. It is concerned with the here and now. Is the system working the way it should? If not, how can we improve it?

In either event, auditors should seek to obtain reasonable ideas of the number and materiality of transactions involved: purchase orders, receiving memos, invoices, billings, shipping tickets, shop orders, rejections, sales slips, contracts, travel vouchers, blueprints, change orders, and manifests. Auditors should determine the character and location of the population to see if any documents are missing and to decide on the appropriate selection plan. How are the documents filed? Are they in random order? Are file receipts supposed to be substituted for all items removed from the files? Is there good control over the files? Are the transactions stratified according to value or other quality? Are the documents serially numbered? Also, are the transactions computerized where they can be called out by using computerized techniques? What should be done about missing items?

Methodology of Sampling to be Used

Sample selection should follow the plan that best fits the audit objectives: judgmental or statistical. The most reliable selections are made from lists that are separate from the records of transactions themselves. In that way, the auditors have better assurance that items that may have been removed from the files will not be overlooked (see Chapter 11).

The Techniques for Examining Selected Transactions or Processes

Auditors examine documents, transactions, conditions, and processes to get the facts and to reach conclusions. The term examination includes both measurement and evaluation. Auditors have many techniques at their disposal to help them achieve this audit objective. Just what those techniques should be called is a moot point among auditors. They are grouped here under six headings that can carry the auditors from the beginning to the end of their field work.

The definitions of these headings are relevant to audit examinations rather than to common usage. Of the six forms of field work, the first five may be considered part of the measurement process. The last — evaluating — gives meaning to the information that the auditor has gathered. They are:

- Observing
- Questioning
- Analyzing
- Verifying
- Investigating
- Evaluating

Observing. To the auditor, observing means seeing, noticing, not passing over. It implies a careful, knowledgeable look at people, facilities, processes, and things. It means a visual examination with a purpose, a mental comparison with standards, an evaluative sighting.

Observing differs from analysis because analysis implies setting down, arraying, and interpreting data. Observation, on the other hand, means seeing and making mental notes and judgments. These observations can be committed to documented notes, diagrams, charts, etc. Since all auditing, including observing, is largely measurement, proper observation is probably one of the most difficult of audit techniques. Auditors are measuring what they see against what they have in their minds. The broader their experience, the more standards and patterns they retain, the more alert they are to deviations from the norm, the better observers they become.

While observing is important, it is generally preliminary to other techniques. It usually requires confirmation through analysis or investigation. It takes place during the preliminary survey when auditors familiarize themselves with the physical plant and with workflows and systems and processes. But it can also take place during questioning and interviewing, when auditors note the reactions and behavior of those with whom they deal. It can take place, as well, when auditors are obtaining impressions of work tempo, facilities, staffing, and plant or office layout and conditions.

Observations can be useful in noting clerical filing practices or workflow steps that lead to unnecessary effort or tortuous routing. Auditors can observe the condition of rejected material as a first step in backtracking for causes. They can tour a plant and observe idle equipment or idle facilities or idle workers. They can observe security precautions on the perimeter of a plant or inside a bank or store. They can observe dangerous conditions and safety violations. They can observe cluttered stockrooms and evidence of backlogs. They can observe poorly stored or dangerously stacked materials. They can observe storerooms left unlocked. They can observe lack of adequate maintenance. They can observe trucks leaving the plant without being stopped by guards. The list is endless.

Knowledgeable observations can provide keen insights, but auditors must be careful how they use observations when citing deficient conditions. If visual examinations are reported without confirmation, they should be clearly labeled as observations and impressions.

Observations will seldom withstand a frontal attack by the client. If the client agrees with the observations and takes corrective action, they need not be followed up with detailed analysis.

Here is an example of how auditors followed through with a thoughtful imaginative analysis of an observation made during an audit examination:[7]

> Everybody knows about cases of collusive tendering where the companies bidding for a job meet secretly and decide who will win. It's called a Losers' Club — for a job that ought to cost about £100,000 they agree that four companies will bid £125,000, and one will bid just £120,000. Naturally, the "cheap" company gets the job and either splits the profits with the members of the club, or takes its turn to be a loser on the next bid.

> Of course, Losers' Clubs aren't easy to run. They lead to a lot of surreptitious phone calls, arguments about how much to overbid, where the extra costs are to be hidden, and not least, whose turn it is to win!

> This internal auditor came across one Losers' Club involving carpet contractors who got around all those problems, quite ingeniously, to swindle a chain of street restaurants. Three carpet contractors were involved, two of whom were more interested in residential rather than commercial work. They entrusted their only rival with a supply of their letterheads. Whenever the two were asked to tender for commercial carpet requirements, they simply sent the details to the rival contractor. The rival would go and measure up for its own tender and take two employees along, supposedly representing the other two contractors, to measure up for them. The rival contractor would send off three bids, each accompanied by a letter on the appropriate letterhead, and win every contract, at an excessive price.

> The two residential carpet contractors received an appropriate sweetener occasionally, and the swindle would never have been detected, but for their carelessness and the auditor's alertness. The commercial carpet contractor was using different words and layouts for each of the three bids, but made the mistake of using the same printer. Although most typed characters look pretty much the same, there are a few fonts that have very distinctive characteristics. One is the lowercase "m" that may have serifs on all three feet, two feet, or none of the feet. Another is the lowercase "g" with the top right squiggle sometimes pointing down, up, or to the side. All three bids had the same printed characteristics.

> After detecting this similarity, the auditor dug further and uncovered the swindle. The auditor also suggested that looking for similarities in signatures, paper, postmarks,

envelopes, and the way the address appears on envelopes will help uncover Losers' Clubs such as this one.

Here is another example of audit observation resulting in substantial savings.[8]

During a review of inventory procedures at the warehouse, the internal auditors noticed that empty pallets were conspicuous by their absence. This was surprising because the warehouse received a delivery of 600 new pallets each week. When asked about the dearth of empty pallets, the warehouse manager stated, "Them pallets don't last too long around here. When they break, we throw 'em out."

The auditors recommended a formal pallet recycling procedure be adopted. Management implemented the recommendation by requiring that broken pallets be repaired by warehouse employees during slack periods. During the follow-up audit, the auditors found that the warehouse's budget for pallets had been reduced by $64,000 (40 percent) annually.

Questioning. Questioning is probably the most pervasive technique of the auditor who is reviewing operations. Questioning continues throughout the audit and may be oral or written.

Oral questions are usually the most common, yet are probably the most difficult to pose. The act of obtaining information can be raised to the level of an art. To get the facts, and to do so without upsetting the client, is sometimes not an easy task. If auditees detect an inquisitorial tone or feel they are being cross-examined, they may raise their defenses and be reluctant to part with the truth. The information they give may be wrong or incomplete; answers may not be forthcoming at all. So, if auditors can understand how the average auditee sees them — as a potential threat to job security — and can modify their manner to allay fears, the chances for obtaining useful information will improve.

At the same time, the auditors' concern for the auditees' feelings should not deter them from insisting on getting the facts. To that end, the auditor should not put words in the auditee's mouth. A question such as, "Do you always keep the doors to the storeroom locked?" will usually produce an affirmative response, true or not. A question such as "How do you protect stores?" might bring a more satisfactory and complete answer. When audit decisions depend on answers to oral questions, there is a good rule to follow: Confirm the information by putting the same question to at least two people. Good reporters never believe what the first person tells them. Here is an example of the result of some persistent questioning.[9]

In this age of technology, are surprise cash counts still used? According to most internal auditors, they are — although not necessarily to the client's advantage.

The internal auditors, by reviewing prior audit workpapers, determined that surprise cash counts had uncovered defalcation schemes in the past, but none had been performed for some time. The auditors decided that the time was ripe for a count on the client's cash register and coin change machine, which together involved an imprest fund of $700. The surprise cash count found that the fund was short by $60.

The following morning, the employee responsible for the fund brought in $60 that had been "inadvertently taken home." The auditors then performed a more detailed audit of the area and uncovered more monies missing from the fund.

After the auditors reported their findings to management, the employee brought in $1,200 in cash and $2,200 in checks that the employee claimed were collected from sales during the prior month. The employee had, "put the funds under my bed for safekeeping and forgot they were there."

The auditors determined that the employee had been able to perpetrate the defalcation because of the lack of separation of duties. The employee was responsible for collecting cash from sales and also performing the bookkeeping duties.

During a prior audit, the manager of the operation had been informed about the risks of having one employee perform both duties and had promised to perform frequent checks to ensure early detection of any dishonesty. This was not done consistently, and the employee was able to exploit the weak controls.

Subsequently, the auditors determined that as much as $7,500 was taken by the employee. The employee was charged with grand theft and fired. The manager promised to perform surprise cash counts in the future to prevent a recurrence.

Questions may sometimes be the most satisfactory way of determining how well or how poorly an activity is being conducted. The test of whether a service is acceptable rests on the opinions of those served. This is especially true of technical operations, where only the technicians are qualified to evaluate the manner in which a service or product meets their own expectations or standards.

Questions can be asked with two purposes in mind: to help the auditor and to help the client. James Binns proposes a "standard operating procedure" questionnaire that is designed to help both. His theory is based on the proposition that the usual procedure manual is voluminous, not always easy to read and comprehend, and almost impossible to remember.[10]

Binns' questionnaire system is designed to elicit information for the auditor and, at the same time, simplify the client's use of procedure manuals. Very often, procedures are not followed because the operating employee is too busy to read the manual or to understand it after the quick reading accorded most documents in an employee's busy day.

The internal auditors' bread and butter is the reading, appraising, and understanding of written procedures to determine whether they are relevant, valid, up-to-date, and complied with. Hence, as a part of the audit process, the auditor asks the client to answer a questionnaire that is both a quiz and an education. The questions are taken from, and referenced to, specific significant procedures in the standard operating procedure (SOP) manuals. To simplify the process, a guide to the answers is included in the question. If the clients are fully acquainted with a particular procedure, they can answer questions without difficulty. If the procedure is a mystery to them, the questionnaire becomes an educational tool. Moreover, if the client uses the questionnaire periodically to check on whether employee practices conform to organization procedures, the questionnaire becomes a useful vehicle for self-audits.

Here are two examples of an SOP questionnaire, the first relating to financial matters and the second to operational matters. (The SOP numbers are fictional.)

1. What do all invoices covering operating expenses indicate? (SOP Reference 015)
   a. Approval by the function's manager?
   b. Date paid?
   c. Expense account number charged?
   d. Number of expense check issued in payment?
   e. Amount of discount taken?
   f. Correct amount paid?

2. What employment notices are posted on the bulletin board? (SOP Reference 156.1)
   a. Notice to employees: Minimum Wage, Overtime Pay, Equal Pay for Equal Work?
   b. Equal Employment Opportunity poster?
   c. Age Discrimination poster?
   d. State rules to be observed by employers?
   e. Occupational Safety and Health poster?
   f. A current policy statement on Equal Employment Opportunity?

Obviously, the drafting of such questionnaires takes a considerable amount of work on the part of the internal auditor. The questionnaires should therefore be restricted to matters of significance. Also, there may be a question concerning sensitive matters such as cash audits, securities, and the like. Should they be handled through questionnaires? To assure cooperation by the client, questionnaires should probably be cleared with client management. Most likely, they will also need periodic updating. But properly used, questionnaires could ease the auditor's job and improve the operating managers' ability to monitor the operations for which they are responsible.

Analyzing. Analyzing implies a detailed examination. It means dividing a complex entity into parts for the purpose of determining its true nature. It connotes laying bare the inner working of some function, activity, or mass of transactions and determining the relationships among the individual parts.

Analyzing suggests the intent to discover or uncover qualities, causes, effects, motives, and possibilities, often as a springboard to a further search or as a basis of judgment. By analyzing an account, auditors who examine financial records separate, array, and spread out the individual elements that constitute the account. In this way, they can see which elements are significant, which recur, which are minimal, which need further attention, and which should not be there.

Internal auditors who examine operations do much the same thing. The principles are no different, only the subject matter. Auditors can see significant relationships and make precise measurements by parading before their audit microscopes the individual elements that make up the activity they examine. In contrast, when the entities are examined as a whole, the mind cannot perceive the intricate interrelationships among the diverse and varied elements that make up a complex function or a large population.

In audits of operations, the subject matter can span a broad spectrum; so can the types of analyses that modern internal auditors may use in making evaluations. Auditors can list a sample of purchase orders on a spreadsheet and analyze each one in terms of bids, sole source procurements, approvals, past history of particular purchases, freight routing, cost analysis, schedules, accurate purchase order preparation, make-or-buy decisions, and other matters. The use of artificial intelligence methods can assist.

Similarly, auditors can analyze a directive, a statute, a contract, or a statement of policy. They can spread out the document, read each word, underline what is significant, measure it in terms of good business practice or real-world conditions, or measure existing practices against the requirements of the document. A simple reading is not enough. Auditors must identify and highlight significant elements and determine what each one means.

Also, auditors may analyze the work of committees having related functions that are part of broad programs. An organization's safety program is an example. In any large organization, a number of committees can have responsibilities for different aspects of organization and employee safety. Auditors might analyze the program by arraying the functions of the committees in a matrix — one that shows where each committee gets its authority, what its precise functions are, its areas of responsibility, who the chairperson and vice chairperson are, to whom it reports, how often it meets, who prepares the minutes and what happens to them, how action items are assigned and monitored, and how the various committees interface. Auditors can thus observe administrative failings, if any, decide whether there is overlap among committees, and see whether some essential function has somehow been overlooked.

Any composite can be analyzed by division — by breaking it into elements, observing trends, making comparisons, and isolating aberrant transactions or conditions. Auditors do it by arraying data on work sheets, verifying the validity of the data, and evaluating the results. This is the essence of the auditor's art. Auditors step into modern internal auditing, a far cry from account analysis, when they apply these techniques to operating matters. This precise analysis, this ability to isolate, identify, quantify, and measure, makes the audit results useful, sound, and unassailable.

Here are examples of developing standards or benchmarks, gathering data, comparing what is with what should be, and investigating variances:[11, 12]

The company had a facility responsible for selling retired office equipment and furniture. The customary audit consisted of evaluating the bidding process and cash receipting as well as conducting a physical inventory. The audit usually resulted in minor findings. This time, the internal auditors decided to review the facility's profitability to see whether changing the way the audit was done would be really worth it.

They found that the facility stated its operating costs as $200,000 and income, over book value, as $250,000 — a seemingly profitable operation. Especially where revenue exceeded incremental costs, one method of value added. However, when the auditors determined that only the direct expenses were included in the $200,000, incremental overheads such as pensions, health care, and other benefits were excluded from the $200,000 cost figure. The actual costs were $310,000. Quite a difference!

The auditors' finding resulted in consolidation of two similar facilities located in close proximity to one another and the elimination of one full-time employee — an estimated savings of $90,000. Changing the way the audit was usually done was really worth it.

During the normal operation of a chemical plant, some spillage of raw material or finished product is to be expected. What the auditors found in this case appeared to be the mother of all spills.

From the records, the auditors determined that 2,500 tons of raw material valued at $1.2 million had been spilled over a two-year period at the plant. Spills of that magnitude would have filled the plant grounds up to the employees' knees; however, there was no evidence of such a large spill.

Further investigation by the auditors revealed that employees had removed raw material from inventory without recording the movement. At the month-end reconciliation, all of the missing inventory was booked to the spillage account.

Consequently, it appeared that an inordinate amount of raw material had been spilled. Controls were tightened to help ensure that written documentation supported all raw material requisitions.

Verifying. Verifying suggests confirming the truth, accuracy, genuineness, or validity of something. It is the auditor's oldest tool. It is most often used in establishing that facts or details given in an account or in a statement are true. It implies a deliberate effort to establish the accuracy or validity of some statement or writing by putting it to the test, such as comparing it with known facts, with an original, or with some standard.

Verification includes corroboration and comparison; statements of one person are confirmed by discussions with others, or one document is compared with a substantiating document or documents. It also includes confirmation, which implies the removal of all doubts through independent validations by objective parties.

Auditors verify an accounting entry by comparing it with supporting detail. They verify an amount due by confirming it with a creditor. They verify an approval by consulting directives that establish levels of approval and by comparing the approval signatures with those on signature cards. They also verify that the approval was based on conformance to required conditions. They verify the propriety of a purchase by assuring themselves that:

- The requirement for the purchased item was established by someone other than the buyer.
- The number of items processed did not exceed those called for in a bill of materials or a requisition (or an allowed average).
- The items were procured on time, but not materially in advance of need by referring to production or construction schedules and to statements of inventory levels.
- The items were actually received and conformed to specifications (by referring to a receiving memo, by visiting the stores department, or by examining the end product).

Verifying not only has certain unique qualities of its own; it has some of the attributes of other techniques the auditor uses. Here are two examples:[13, 14]

"With our tight controls, duplicate payments just can't happen," the manager told the internal auditor. The auditor's first test proved the manager wrong.

The manager of the accounts payable group told the auditor, "We never pay any bill unless it is accompanied by a copy of the purchase order with the notation 'OK TO PAY' and the initials of one of the purchasing representatives." The auditor asked what happened when the associated purchase order was missing from a bill received by the accounts payable group. "We'd send the bill to the purchasing group for a copy of the associated purchase order," replied the manager.

Therein lay the control weakness that caused the duplicate payments found by the auditor. If no copy of the original purchase order could be located, the accounts payable clerks did send the bill to the purchasing group and verbally requested that a copy of the noted and initialed purchase order be attached and the bill returned for payment. The auditor found that if the purchasing group could not find the related purchase order, one was generated with no requisition, authorization, need for the purchase, nor investigation, thereby duplicating payments. After the audit, the purchasing group was warned about issuing unauthorized purchase orders, and a memo was issued to all managers to be more careful of what bills were "OK TO PAY."

The internal auditor was verifying a sample of bills from health care providers. The bills had been paid for health care services rendered to clients. Of the 70 verification notices mailed, two came back marked "RETURN TO SENDER: ADDRESSEE UNKNOWN." Seeking an explanation, the auditor asked the manager in charge of paying health care providers about the returned verification notices. "Well, I knew it couldn't last forever. They don't exist." The manager then confessed to writing checks payable to fictitious health care providers and depositing the checks into a personal bank account.

The manager, a trusted employee and compulsive gambler, confessed to stealing $4 million over a two-year period and losing most of it at casinos in Atlantic City and Las Vegas. A pang of conscience caused him to return 1.2 million dollars to help cover his tracks. The judge sentenced him to a 10-year prison term after he was arrested and tried for grand larceny.

The auditor is still amazed that no controls existed to prevent, or at least detect, the embezzlement.

Investigating. Investigating is a term that generally applies to an inquiry aimed at uncovering the hidden facts and establishing the truth. It implies a systematic track-down of information the auditor hopes to discover or needs to know. It includes, but is not limited to, probing — investigations that search deeply and extensively with the intent to detect wrongdoing.

Auditors may investigate, but investigating is different from auditing. Audits imply objectivity. Investigations seek to establish evidence of impropriety. Investigations, therefore, have more pointed direction than do analyses and verifications, which imply the review of data that have relatively unknown qualities — until examined. This book will treat investigations as dealing with conditions that are suspect.

Probes are specifically related to wrongdoing, and here auditors must be careful not to go beyond their depth. Probes often involve legal and criminal considerations. After obtaining some inkling of serious impropriety, auditors should refer the matter to those who are experienced in these matters. Auditors who do not heed such warnings may find themselves violating an individual's rights and laying their organization open to prosecution for libel, slander, defamation of character, malicious prosecution, or false imprisonment. In such matters, therefore, it is wise to consult with their organization's security people or legal counsel (see Chapter 27).

Here are examples of investigating:[15, 16]

During a review to make sure the organization was in compliance with federal, state, and local environmental laws, the internal auditors found things in just a bit of disarray. Eight noncompliance issues were identified — issues that could subject the company to potential penalties of $725,000.

The auditors found inaccurate and untimely annual and quarterly PCB inspection reports. In addition, they found improper handling, labeling, and storing of hazardous wastes, as well as retention of an outdated contingency plan. The auditors also found that the company did not have a program to control 55-gallon drums used to store and dispose of hazardous wastes. (Evidence included 200 drums of hazardous wastes that had no labels and were not encased in concrete containment areas as required.)

As a result of the audit, management established comprehensive training programs and issued written instructions for the personnel responsible for handling hazardous wastes.

The internal auditors found that $3,250 in repairs were made to a truck that was sold for scrap three months later. The inquiries about this apparent waste of company money unearthed rather convoluted thinking on the part of many of the company's plant personnel.

The information about the truck repairs was presented to the plant manager for an explanation. The manager told the auditors the money was actually used, with company management's full knowledge, to purchase a used truck to replace the one that had been scrapped. The manager was asked to produce a list of similar purchases. The list included $162,000 worth of repairs and spare parts purchased since 1985. In reality, the "repairs and spare parts" turned out to be 39 used vehicles purchased to replace vehicles that had deteriorated to the point that repairs were no longer feasible.

After further digging, the auditor determined that the practice of charging the capital expense of vehicle purchases to the account for repairs and spare parts had been going on for 30 years — with company management's approval. The practice was intended to be an interim step to provide the plant with a vehicle until the capital approval process could be executed. However, the auditor could find no evidence that the vehicle purchases were ever approved through the process. Annual depreciation was also in question.

Management concurred with the auditors that a cultural revolution was needed to emphasize the "accurate books and accounts" section of the company's business conduct policy. A program was begun that would not only emphasize the proper accounting for purchases, but give employees a firm understanding of why the purchasing policies exist in the first place.

There is an old adage that says, "When the goats guard the cabbage, will any cabbage be left for the farmer?" Complete control by one employee over any significant operation is a sign of serious control weakness and the possibility of wrongdoing.

Evaluating. Evaluating, as well as its kindred term appraising, implies estimation of worth. In auditing, it means arriving at a judgment. It means weighing what has been analyzed and determining its adequacy, its efficiency, and its effectiveness. It is the step between analysis and verification on the one hand and an audit opinion on the other. It represents the conclusions the auditors draw from the facts they have accumulated.

Evaluation implies professional judgment, and it is the thread that runs through the entire fabric of the audit. In the early stages of an audit examination, auditors must evaluate a special risk — the risk of eliminating an activity from their review, compared with the cost of examining it (audit risk). In their programs, auditors must evaluate the need for a detailed test in place of a survey or a walk-through. In their sampling procedures, auditors must evaluate the precision and confidence level required to achieve the sample reliability they believe they need. As they compare a transaction with a standard and find a variance, they must evaluate the significance of the variance and determine whether corrective action is necessary. As they summarize the results of the audit examination, they must evaluate what those results imply.

Fact-finding without evaluation becomes a clerical function. Proper evaluations lift the audit from what may be a detailed check to a management appraisal. It becomes a part of the internal auditor's consulting responsibility. Auditors first observe the facts through the bottom part of their bifocals, the verification half, and then evaluate them through the top, the management half.

No auditor can become a full professional without evaluating everything audited in terms of objectives and standards. Arrayed data, no matter how artfully arranged, is merely rough ore until it has been transformed into something useful through evaluation.

Evaluation, obviously, calls for judgment. The mature, experienced auditor — the veteran of many audit examinations, the participant of many a report draft review, the wise observer of the organization's course and objectives — evaluates audit findings almost intuitively and usually is correct. But even such auditors can benefit from a structured, organized approach to the evaluation of the findings. For example, in evaluating deviations from the norm — the failure to meet standards — they might ask themselves these questions:

- How significant are these deviations?
- Who or what has been hurt or could be hurt?
- How bad was or could be the damage?
- Have the deviations prevented the organization or function from achieving its objectives and goals?
- If corrective action is not taken, is the deviation likely to recur?
- Why and how did the deviation take place?
- What is the cause? What event or combination of events threw the process off its track?
- Has the cause been truly ascertained and precisely described? Will the event or combination of events cause the observed result every time? Does the cause satisfactorily explain every aspect of the deviation?

Clearly, auditors must think about how to alleviate ailments as they diagnose them. To consider their proposals in an organized manner, they might ask themselves these questions:

- What course of action will most practically and economically cure the defect?
- What objectives should we keep in mind in recommending corrective action?
- What should management be trying to achieve in setting forth an improved course of action?
- What choices are open? How do they measure up when compared with the objectives?
- What tentative alternative has been selected and what injurious side effects might be expected?
- Which is the best choice with the least unsatisfactory side effects?
- What mechanism should be suggested to control the corrective action after it is taken? How can one make sure that the corrective action is taken; that it will be carried to a conclusion; that future deviations will be referred back to someone authorized to remove impediments to the proper fulfillment of the suggested course of action?

The auditor owes management a duty not only to suggest corrective action, but also to point the way to the continued efficacy of that action.

Here is a situation in which auditors discovered some relatively minor defects. Their evaluation of the activity, which included those defects, disclosed a significant problem that needed management attention.[17]

> The contractor provided cost-plus engineering services to the company, along with data processing services on a break-even basis. The internal auditor noted in reading the contract that the rates charged for the data processing services were supposed to be reviewed each year by the contractor and adjusted to ensure operation on the break-even basis. What the auditor found was very different.
>
> The auditor's review of the data center's books disclosed that revenues had exceeded expenses for years, but the rates had never been reduced. The auditor also determined that some of the data center's overhead costs had already been billed in the overhead rate applied to labor charges for the cost-plus engineering services performed for the company.
>
> After these findings were presented by company management to the contractor, lengthy negotiations ensued before $7,000,000 was refunded to the company. An additional $12,000,000 is expected to be saved over the next two years.

References

[1]"Developing a Self-Directed Audit Team," *Internal Auditing Alert* (Boston, MA: Warren Gorham and Lamont, September 1993), 6-8.

[2]Ibid., October 1993, 2-4.

[3]Written for *Sawyer's Internal Auditing* by David Z. Halasi, Senior Auditor, Edison International.

[4]*Internal Auditing Alert* (Boston, MA: Warren Gorham & Lamont, June 1997).

[5]Rose, C. Wayne, and Becky Hirte, "SMART Auditing" in *Enhancing Internal Auditing Through Innovative Practices* (Altamonte Springs, FL: The Institute of Internal Auditors, 1996), ed. Glen L. Gray and Maryann J. Gray, 47-57.

[6]"Benchmarking as Related to Internal Auditing," *Internal Auditing Alert* (Boston, MA: Warren Gorham & Lamont, 1993), 2-4.

[7]"The Round Table," *Internal Auditor,* December 1992, 78.

[8]"The Round Table," April 1992, 78.

[9]"The Round Table," April 1993, 69.

[10]Binns, James, "Designing a Standard Operating Procedure Questionnaire," *The Internal Auditor,* October 1982, 23-25.

[11]"The Round Table," April 1993, 66-7.
[12]"The Round Table," February 1993, 63.
[13]"The Round Table," October 1992, 70-71.
[14]"The Round Table," June 1992, 74.
[15]"The Round Table," February 1992, 61.
[16]"The Round Table," February 1993, 64-65.
[17]"The Round Table," February 1992, 60.

Supplemental Readings and Multiple-choice Questions for "Field Work - I" follow Chapter 7, Field Work - II.

Chapter 7
Field Work – II

Applying the audit technique, functional audits, organizational audits, management studies and consulting, program audits, contract audits. Integrated auditing, using consultants, outsourcing and cosourcing. Analytical reviews: trend analysis, ratio analysis, regression analysis, other analytical techniques. Legal evidence. Audit evidence. The handling of sensitive evidence. Field work in a high technology environment. Continuous auditing. Internal audit issues relative to risk, e-commerce/e-business, and continuous auditing.

Applying the Audit Techniques

The Techniques

The techniques of observing, questioning, analyzing, verifying, investigating, and evaluating are applied under varied circumstances. They are used, singly or in combination, whenever auditors perform examinations. By and large, however, these techniques are applied within certain frameworks, depending on the subject matter of the audit. The end results are the same: audit opinions and recommendations. But the approach will differ according to the auditor's mission and particular plan of attack.

Most audit projects will be carried out under one of four different modes: functional audits, organizational audits, management studies, and program audits. In addition, many internal auditors also engage in audits of costs generated under contracts with outside organizations. What follows is a discussion of each of these five forms of audit assignments.

Functional Audits

As discussed here, a functional audit is one that follows a process from beginning to end, crossing organizational lines. Functional audits tend to concentrate more on operations and processes than on administration and people. They seek to determine how well all the organizations concerned with a function will interface and cooperate. Will the function be carried out effectively and efficiently? Functional audits that can be of value in an organization include audits of:

- The ordering of, receiving, and paying for materials and supplies.
- Direct deliveries of supplies or services to using departments.

- The incorporation of changes into products.
- Scrap accumulation, segregation, and sale.
- Safety controls and practices.
- Programs to detect conflicts of interest.
- The management of capital assets.
- Budget formulation.
- The marketing functions.

Functional audits present special difficulties because of their breadth and scope. Auditors are required to define the parameters of the job and keep it within reasonable bounds, yet cover all significant aspects of the function. They must deal with a number of subordinate organizations, each with objectives that might be different from the objective of other downstream, upstream, or lateral organizations.

Yet functional audits can provide special benefits to management: Varying viewpoints can be identified. Bottlenecks can be exposed. Differing objectives can be reconciled. Duplications can be highlighted. Accountability can be defined. The following example of a case history provides an example of the benefits of a functional audit.

A manufacturing organization developed procedures and assigned responsibilities for the accumulation, segregation, and sale of scrap metals. In general, the responsibilities were as follows:

The *machine shops* where the scrap metal was generated were responsible for segregating the scrap according to types of metals.

The *reclamation department* was charged with supplying carts bearing signs to show the categories of scrap to be deposited in the carts. Reclamation was to identify the scrap and to ticket the carts when the carts were ready to be transported to the salvage sales yard or to truck bodies supplied by scrap dealers under contract with the organization.

The *transportation department* was responsible for transporting the carts either to the organization's salvage sales yard (mixed metals) or to the truck bodies (large volumes of metal turnings or chips).

The *salvage sales yard* was responsible for obtaining the best prices for scrap, rejecting those carts that contained improperly segregated scrap, and returning the carts used for the mixed scrap to the scrap-generating departments. It also conducted the sale.

The *procurement department* was to issue sales reports on the different types of scrap, showing the prices received for each.

The auditors followed the process from the point of scrap generation to the point of sale. They examined scrap placed in the carts, rode in trucks, talked to people, and compared the receipts for scrap with prices listed in a technical publication dealing with metals. As they carried on their examination, they became aware of a considerable amount of parochialism; there was excessive concern for individual department goals and indifference to, or lack of understanding for, the needs of other organizations or of the organization. For example:

At the *machine shop* scrap generating points, production supervisors gave little thought to the need for scrap segregation. They were not aware of the value of properly segregated scrap as compared with the value of contaminated (mixed) scrap. They were resentful of having to segregate scrap when reclamation refused to accept carts with contaminated scrap or when salvage sales returned carts containing improperly mixed metals.

Reclamation supplied carts, but did not always supply the identifying signs that would facilitate segregation.

Salvage sales was concerned solely with obtaining the highest dollar return for scrap and rejected any carts that carried contaminated scrap.

Procurement prepared reports on scrap sales, but submitted the reports only to its own management.

As a result of conflicting goals, poor communication, and failure to understand the goals of others and the objectives of the organization as a whole, the auditors found the following conditions:

- The cost of segregation in some instances exceeded the value of the segregated metals.
- Rejected carts were shuttled back and forth because salvage sales was concerned only with cash returns, not with the cost of resegregating scrap.
- Since procurement sent reports of sales receipts to its own management only, other departments were not aware of the cash return for properly segregated scrap.

At the conclusion of the audit, the auditors held meetings with the managers responsible for the processing and sale of scrap metals. As a result, the following corrective action was taken:

- Organization procedures were revised to emphasize total organization objectives and to establish reasonable rules for scrap segregation, accumulation, and sale.

- Carts were properly identified.
- Scrap generating departments were supplied with reports of scrap sales and were given the authority to segregate or to not segregate metals, based on the volume of scrap generated and the potential return.
- The shuttling back and forth of carts was discontinued, but to keep scrap generating departments informed of their derelictions, *salvage sales* issued memos informing those departments of the revenue losses suffered because of improperly segregated scrap.

The auditors managed to resolve conflicts, reconcile differences, and generate a better net return for scrap. They conducted a follow-up review about six months after the new procedures went into effect. They were amazed at the turnabout in attitude, cooperation, and results. People were willingly following policies that made sense to them. The system was functioning smoothly, effectively, and economically.

The functional audit can achieve similar results for other systems and processes in the organization. To do so, however, auditors must keep their eyes on the overall organization objectives and manage to bridge the gaps between the various units concerned with the function. In carrying out functional audits, and other audits as well, internal auditors should also be aware of what senior management expects from its internal auditors. Every organization is guided and led by management decisions. Good decisions are dependent on good information. Management needs information on economic trends, on the behavior of the competition, on the attitudes of its customers, and on the effectiveness of its people. Management develops policies and procedures based on this information. It sets up systems of control and feedback to make sure its decisions and systems are valid and working.

In all their audits, internal auditors, as consultants to and partners with management, must evaluate the information on which the management decisions are made. They must make sure that control systems are functioning as intended. At the same time, internal auditors should be on guard for overcontrol — for excessive control that makes people prisoners of job instructions, unable to use common sense to solve day-to-day problems.

In making internal audits, whatever the mode, internal auditors should be generalists rather than specialists. They should be comfortable in their dealings with a production supervisor, a research scientist, or even senior management. Certainly, top management expects internal auditors to exercise that sixth sense that identifies the possibility of a problem. But before a solution is presented, the auditor must be buttressed by unassailable facts and figures. Once the auditors are sure of the problem and of their facts, they must adhere to strict rules of conduct and inform management of all serious infringements that may hurt the organization.

Yet internal auditors must not let their authority breed arrogance. They must be careful not to overstep bounds or the limits of their jurisdiction and take on operating responsibilities or managerial attitudes. Humility founded on strength and professional competence is a persuasive quality. Auditors should not let their efforts be compromised by antagonistic behavior that turns people off. Change will not occur easily in such an environment.

Senior management, therefore, expects its auditors, in all their assignments, to have the following attributes:[1]

- A mastery of internal audit techniques
- The ability to establish sources of factual information
- The capacity to thoroughly analyze the information received
- The capability to make recommendations based on hard evidence
- The qualities of sincerity, integrity, and humility in carrying out all audit duties

Organizational Audits (and Productivity Evaluations)

Organizational audits are concerned not only with the activities performed within an organization but also with the administrative controls used to make sure they will be carried out. The auditor is interested, therefore, in how well the organization's manager is meeting the objectives of the organization with the resources at hand. An incisive organizational approach can often provide broad insights into operations that transcend those insights obtained solely by testing of transactions.

Especially in large organizations with a multiplicity of operations and functions, the auditor is better advised to determine how well management is managing them — how well transactions flow or trickle through the organization's pipeline. The audit measuring stick, or the body of standards applied to an organization's operations, is constructed from the elements that make up acceptable administrative control.

It is a rare organization indeed that operates in accordance with all or even most of the theoretical precepts of good administrative control. Yet internal auditors, in performing organizational audits, should have those precepts in mind. Often, an unsatisfactory condition can be the direct result of the violation of an accepted principle of good administration. If auditors keep these principles in mind, they will begin to function at the consultative or management level. They should have a working knowledge of administrative or management control within a business. As auditors carry out organizational audits, they will be putting the principles of management control to work. They should be able to "flesh out" the skeletal structure or the organization. A clear picture of the completed structure, engraved on the mind's eye, can have a profound effect both on how auditors view the administration of the organization and on the questions they ask when they perform their audits. The nature of those questions will mightily increase the auditor's stature in the eyes of operating management.

Internal auditors should be conversant with the principles of planning — with setting objectives, developing policies and procedures, maintaining continuity, and reappraising plans and goals in the light of changed conditions. They should be conversant with the principles of organizing — with the assignment of responsibility, the delegation of authority, and the development of staff.

Internal auditors should be conversant with the principles of directing — with leadership, motivation, and communication. They should be conversant with the principles of controlling — with setting standards, maintaining standards, training people to comply with standards, prescribing an approval and review system, ensuring compliance with standards, devising systems of records, reports, and master control, and monitoring the entire ongoing process.

Each organization should also be reviewed for productivity — for the efficient and effective use of resources entrusted to the manager. Improving productivity is the key to an organization's survival in a competitive environment.

To assess productivity, the internal auditor must learn the organization's productivity objectives — the kind of improved productivity the organization is trying to achieve. Is it to reduce rework? Reduce the time required to process the receipts of purchased goods? Reduce outstanding receivables? Improve output from a word-processing pool? Reduce the time required to process claims? Increase market penetration? Develop new products? Increase the volume of sales? The list is practically endless.

First, therefore, productivity objectives must be identified. If such objectives have not been set, the operating manager may be persuaded to do so in partnership with the internal auditor.

The next step, after deciding on the objectives, is to set quantifiable goals against which productivity can be objectively measured. Where are we? Where should we be? How can we tell where we stand in relation to the goals we have set? This last question calls for productivity measurement. Without productivity measurement, an organization cannot control.[2]

And so, in concert with the auditors, managers can devise suitable measurements and decide on the information they need to determine how they are doing. This might require coordination with the accounting department or the data processing department. But once management has established productivity objectives and goals and the means of measuring productivity, the road to improvement becomes unblocked. Self-appraisal and self-assessment are possible and encouraged. The manager, not the internal auditors, has ownership of the operation. The internal auditor is the facilitator, but the manager gets the credit and reaps the rewards.

Yet, the numbers are not enough. Internal auditors must go behind the numbers to determine what is preventing improved productivity. For example, scrap and rework are generally measured in the manufacturing function, so that is where the numbers originate. Internal auditors, however, should go behind the numbers to identify the reasons for increased scrap and rework. The real cause may be in the purchasing department, where substandard materials are purchased, or in receiving and inspection, where the materials are accepted from suppliers. Or, the problem may be in the excessive number of design changes developed by the engineering department, either to keep redundant engineers employed or because plans are released prematurely. Finally, the problem may be in emphasis on output of product regardless of scrap generation.

And so, in making professional internal audits, the auditors must keep in mind that the very survival of the enterprise may depend on the productivity of each of its parts. Innovative internal audit suggestions will help keep the whole entity moving forward.[3]

Management Studies and Consulting

Functional and organizational audits form the framework of the long-range audit program. These individual audits, generally repeated at appropriate intervals, represent the meat and potatoes of the auditor's fare. Another aspect of auditing may well be the caviar and champagne: the audit directed toward solving problems for (usually not *of*) management.

Many organizations call upon outside consultants to perform management studies, make evaluations, and offer recommendations for improving problem areas of the organization. Some of these organizations have benefited from the experience and knowledge that consultants bring to bear. Others have not. The disappointments can result from a number of factors. Some of them are:

- Employees may regard the consultants as strangers who have no feel for the organization's lifestyle or personality. Both employees and managers may be resentful and secretive, preventing the consultants from obtaining a complete understanding of the problems they are engaged to solve.

- The consultants have a long and expensive training period to go through. No matter how experienced they may be, they still have to learn the organization's geography, its organizational structure, its ingrained methods and procedures, its philosophies, and the personalities, strengths, weaknesses, and predilections of its management.

- The outside consultant's recommendations, usually communicated in an exit interview or in an elaborate report, may get a defensive reaction. Organization personnel may spend more time in defending entrenched operations than in implementing what may very well be worthwhile suggestions.

- The outside consultants generally charge sizable fees that, in many cases, would exceed the cost of using existing talent already in the organization.

A top-notch internal audit staff, experienced in audits of operations and familiar with the organization's objectives, policies, organization, and people, is a natural source of talent for this kind of consulting work. Internal auditors are already well versed in the techniques needed for problem solving: i.e., fact gathering, analysis, and objective evaluation. The auditors develop these techniques in their regular audits. These are the same techniques needed for solving management problems. (See Definition of Internal Auditing in Chapter 1.)

Implementation Standard 2010.C1 states that:

> "The chief audit executive should consider accepting proposed consulting engagements based on the engagement's potential to improve management of risks, add value, and improve the organization's operations..."

A series of subsequent Standards and Practice Advisories further defines the specifics of the internal auditing consulting practices and procedures. The reader is referred to the Appendix to Chapter 1 that contains the substance of this material.

Further, the internal auditors will have developed an understanding of management philosophy and principles essential to the dissection and evaluation of matters concerning management. If they have developed a proper image within the organization, they have the reputation for objectivity, fairness, and personal concern for the organization's interests. They will not feel impelled to generate a host of recommendations — warranted or not — merely to justify a fee.

Internal auditors who feel competent to take on special studies within the organization, then, should accept the opportunity when it is presented to them. Indeed, they should be close enough to the councils of management to know when the opportunity arises and to offer their services in appropriate circumstances and under appropriate conditions.

Of course, the problem should be one that internal auditors have a chance of solving. Matters that are completely technical, or that depend entirely on executive judgment, should probably be avoided. They may not yield to the tools internal auditors possess or have available.

On the other hand, the fact that the problem is difficult or extensive should be an inducement and not a deterrent. If some aspects of the engagement are technical, they may be dealt with through the assistance of outside technicians assigned to help the auditor over the technical hurdles, or through specialized cosourcing.

These management engagements should be requested and endorsed by executive management. Their scope and breadth will usually require backing at that level. It must be made clear to all employees and operating managers that this is a management project operating under a special management charter. In fact, the project will function best as a task force, nominally headed by a vice president or another executive manager, with the audit manager and the audit staff conducting the actual work.

The auditors should, from the outset and throughout the engagement, employ all the techniques of influencing they possess. They should keep management informed and obtain recommendations at the grassroots level before presenting the recommendations to management.

As soon as possible after they have taken the measure of the situation, internal auditors should make a formal presentation to management on how they view the problem and how they propose to attack it. This presentation can be enhanced by using presentation software flip charts or some other type of visual presentation. It should be carefully thought through and carried out in a professional fashion.

The presentation of the parameters of the problem, and the theory of the case as the auditor sees it, can have several benefits. It may force management to consider the problem in a light it had not considered before, because the problem had not been laid out visibly and in a logical manner. It can save the auditor from pursuing matters or running down avenues that are of no special interest to management. It can lead to better rapport with management and draw executive management more solidly into a problem-solving partnership.

The study itself must be in-depth. It cannot be a broad-stroke pass at the problem. It will require extensive review and thorough research. It must produce authoritative answers to any relevant questions management may pose. It must be able to provide a stout defense for any recommendations that are made. It must be based on a thorough understanding of the following matters, among others:

- What is the basic problem? (Not necessarily what management thought it was, but what it really is.)

- What are the relevant facts? (The data, the processes, the systems, the procedures, the policies, the organizations, the people, the past, the present, the probable future, what has been written on the subject, and what is being done at other organizations.)

- What are the causes? (The number and variety of causes, the root causes and the surface cause, when they began to affect the problem.)

- What are the possible solutions? (The alternatives, the costs, the answers to associated local problems within affected operating organizations, the solution or solutions to the generic problem with organization-wide implications, the possible side effects of proposed solutions.)

A management study of broad scope will have a general cleansing effect. As the audit teams probe and query and analyze, they may find system and performance defects. They should promptly reduce each of these matters to writing, discuss them with the people concerned, and issue a memorandum that identifies the particular problems, provides adequate detail, sets forth the views of those interviewed, and proposes solutions. It may be appropriate to issue a follow-on memorandum on a single study. If so, the Memorandum Number should have a letter suffix, i.e., 123A. Such follow-on memos should be limited to material modifications in one or more of the memo segments. A format for such a memorandum is shown in Exhibit 7-1. Each memorandum would identify an individual problem, indicate the people with whom the problem was discussed, set out their views, and offer solutions.

Exhibit 7-1
Management Study Memorandum

No: _____

Date: _____

Organization Concerned: (Show all the organizations involved in or affected by the condition or its solution.)

Summary of Condition: (Provide a capsule comment that identifies the condition.)

Details of Condition: (Describe the condition in sufficient detail to explain its significance, its causes, and its actual or probable effect.)

Proposed Solution: (Supply the various alternatives that are available to cure the condition.)

Discussed with: (List the names and identities of all management and supervisory personnel with whom the matter was discussed.)

Results of Discussions: (Summarize the comments of each person with whom the matter was discussed, indicating whether he or she agreed with the statement of condition and/or the solution.)

Distributed to: (Distribute the memo to all management personnel with whom the condition was discussed, and their superiors, as well as to the executives responsible for the task force.)

Each week, or every two weeks, appropriate management personnel should be provided with a summary showing the status of the management study memorandums. Separate summaries should be prepared for each major organization. Using the procurement organization as an example, the form for such a summary might be Exhibit 7-2:

			Status		
MSM No.	**Date**	**Summary of Condition**	**Initiated**	**Completed**	**Under Development**

Exhibit 7-2
Record of Management Study Memorandums

PROCUREMENT

The Record of Management Study Memorandums keeps the study in the forefront of management's attention. Those matters requiring action remain flagged until corrected. The study is not permitted to fade into the background.

Every month, the audit manager may give a progress report to executive management on the status of the study. That report may:

- Identify the major management studies in progress.
- Summarize the number of management study memorandums issued and their status.
- Identify the more significant problems that either have been solved or remain unsolved.
- Discuss in general terms the progress of the work.
- Provide an estimate of the time required to complete the studies. Show the number of people, both auditors and technicians, who are involved in the study and the number of teams to which they are assigned. (Only if requested.)

When each task is completed, the results should be incorporated in a final report. The report should be a professional piece of work, giving the matter the aura of importance that it deserves. The detail may very well be a listing of the management study memorandums, as shown in the Record of Management Study Memorandums, minus the final three columns (initiated, completed, under development), supported by copies of the memorandums themselves. The report should discuss the matters that have been corrected and those remaining uncorrected. (If the task can be considered complete with some elements uncorrected, their status should be described.)

Program Audits

Of their own volition or at the request of executive management, internal auditors may undertake special reviews of ongoing programs. "Program" is a broad term that encompasses any funded effort that is collateral to the normal ongoing activities of an organization — an expansion program, a new employee benefit program, a new contract, a governmental health or training program, a new computer application, or a program that is germane to the objective of the organization.

The audit goal is to provide management with information on the costs, the conduct, and the results of the program and to make the evaluations as informative, useful, and objective as possible. In such reviews, it is helpful for all concerned to have a common understanding of the terms used. Here are some:

- *Evaluation* — Ascertaining the value of something by comparing accomplishment with a standard or goal.

- *Program evaluation* — In the broadest sense, evaluating what is being accomplished, in relation to the resources used, and, beyond that, whether the objectives of the program are proper and suitable. Auditors would want a special authorization to question the latter.

- *Cost benefit study* — Considering the relationship between resources used and costs (inputs) and benefits (outputs or outcomes). Auditors may have to explore alternative ways of achieving a program objective. The auditors' aim is to identify the best choice in terms of dollars — the greatest benefits for a given cost or the required level of benefits at the lowest cost.

- *Cost effectiveness study* — Considering the benefits (outcomes) that cannot be measured in terms of dollars — the benefits of a new apprenticeship program, for example, or the teaching of handicapped students.

Essentially, internal auditors want to determine three things in a program audit: What was accomplished? Was the program successful? Is there an adequate system to ensure future success? In the private sector, accomplishment is generally measured in terms of revenues and profits. In the public sector, internal auditors would be concerned with outputs, benefits or outcomes, and impacts:

Outputs. Outputs include such matters as services rendered, goods produced, and assistance given. Examples are students taught, cases processed, investigations conducted, reports completed, and examinations conducted. It sometimes takes considerable imagination to develop and apply standards and criteria for measurement. Quality may become a problem.

Benefits or Outcomes. Benefits represent the effect of the outputs. For example, the number of students taught is an output. But the increased knowledge, skills, motivation, and aspiration levels of students are benefits. Benefits or outcomes are more difficult to measure than outputs but, obviously, they are more relevant to the evaluation of a program.

Impacts. Impacts are the effects of the program on a community, society, or even the world. These are extremely difficult to measure. They represent the lasting effect of a program, and it is a challenge to devise standards of measurement or means of appraisal.

Clearly, objectives, goals, and standards must be identified quite specifically in program reviews. Otherwise, auditors will have nothing to measure against, and the audit results would be opinions subject to dispute, rather than well-supported conclusions. These objectives, goals, and standards are not easy to identify when:

- Management, the board of directors, or the legislature has not clearly defined the objectives.
- Objectives overlap or are interdependent.
- The people responsible for achieving the objectives, goals, or standards do not really understand them.
- The apparent intent of management, the directors, or the legislature has not been followed.
- The real program objectives have not been identified or have changed even though the stated ones remain constant.

When such difficulties arise, auditors must understand that they cannot make an objective evaluation until the definition problems have been resolved. When no reasonable understanding of objectives, goals, and standards can be reached, it may be best to report that an evaluation would be fruitless. The yardsticks must be clear and concrete and agreed upon. This condition may become an audit finding. However, it may be that the auditors will be asked to report on output, outcome, or impact, leaving the evaluation process to management or to the legislature.

The responsibility for continually evaluating programs lies with operating and program management. Essentially, the auditor is concerned with determining the quality of the information being provided to management, and how well the managers are carrying out that evaluation function. All programs are different, but certain common threads run through them. Internal auditors, in their program evaluations, seek answers to these questions:

- Are program objectives sufficiently clear to permit program managers to determine whether they are accomplishing the desired results? Are component program objectives in gear with overall program objectives?
- How valid were the data used in justifying the program to top management or to the legislature?

- How valid is the input, output, and outcome information?
- To what extent is the program accomplishing intended results? How closely is it meeting its schedules?
- How well is the program succeeding within the costs budgeted or appropriated?
- What variances are there between expenditures made and expenditures authorized?
- What kind of information system (reports and the like) is in effect to keep top management informed about the program?
- What is the quality of the information?
- What form of internal monitoring system is in effect to keep program managers informed of program accomplishments and problems?
- What conflicts, if any, exist between the program being evaluated and similar or parallel programs?
- How closely related are program costs to program benefits?
- To what extent were alternative programs considered to achieve the same benefits?
- What might happen if the program were to be discontinued?
- How accurate are the results being reported to top management or the legislature?

Contract Audits

Construction or operating contracts often involve large amounts of money; construction contracts are not usually part of the regular business of the organization that is having the construction work done; operating contracts may provide services or programmatic operations. Management may not be as familiar with construction costs and operations as it is with in-house production. Internal auditors can, therefore, be particularly helpful in auditing such contracts. (Some examples follow at the end of this section.)

Contracts generally fall into one of three categories: lump-sum, cost-plus, and unit-price.

Under *lump-sum* (fixed price) contracts, contractors agree to perform work for a fixed amount. If the work is done according to the agreement, there is little for the auditor to review. Rarely are large lump-sum contracts that simple. They often contain escalation clauses, progress payments, incentive provisions, and adjustments for field labor costs. If actual field labor exceeds that agreed upon, any additional cost may be borne by the organization letting the contract. Also, lump-sum contracts may call for reimbursement of "premium time" to obtain a sufficient labor supply.

Changes can be the most vexing. Large construction contracts are seldom completed without a host of changes (change orders). These, as well as other collateral matters, call for close audit surveillance, especially for the fee related to the change.

Cost-plus type contracts may be the most economical way of dealing with a construction or operation project, because of the many unknowns that attend such projects. Cost-plus contracts do not require built-in hedges for the unknowns. They may be written to reimburse the contractor for costs plus a fixed fee or costs plus a fee based on percentage of costs. The latter type is prohibited in many organizations because of the motivation to escalate costs so as to increase the fee. Some cost-plus contracts provide for maximum costs and splitting of any savings. Cost-plus contracts are not self-policed with an incentive for efficiency or economy, so the costs the contractor is required to record need close surveillance. This type of contract may also have incentive (time) provisions.

Unit-price contracts are useful when a project requires large amounts of uniform work. Examples are clearing land by the acre, removing earth by the cubic yard, and driving pilings by the foot or performing operational functions such as providing surveillance of buildings or operations. A price is agreed upon for each unit. The problem is one of keeping proper records on the amount of work accomplished.

All these forms of contracts, cost-plus type in particular, can benefit from audit surveillance. Internal auditors should not wait until the project is underway to protect their organization's interests. Early participation is vital to evaluate bidding procedures, cost estimates, contractors' accounting and management systems, budgeting, financial condition, financial forecasting, tax treatments, cost control, financial reporting, systems of internal control, sources of funding, and even contract terms.

Of crucial importance is provision in the construction contract for system review, progress reviews, and cost audits.   Without these activities, the organization is at the mercy of the contractor — especially under cost-plus type contracts. It is true that the organization will usually have a project engineer and even an accountant on the job. But these people may not be conversant with the fine points of contract auditing. Also, continued attendance on the job, while working closely with the contractor, can diminish objectivity.

Construction and operating projects are seldom alike, so a checklist approach to contract audits generally results in sterile reviews. As in other audits, experienced internal auditors are aware of the hazards that exist in a particular project or can exist in any project. The auditors focus on protecting their organizations from potential risks rather than on checking numbers and documents.

Here are some of the risks and risk areas in contract agreements that should concern internal auditors:

In lump-sum contracts
- Inadequate competition
- Inadequate insurance and bond coverage
- Certification of completion when work is not completed
- Charges for equipment or activities that are not received

- Escalation provisions
- Changes in specifications or prices
- Authorization for extras and revisions
- Extras, changes, and revisions that are already part of the original contract
- Overhead items included as additional charges
- Content of change orders, including inappropriate fees
- Inadequate inspection relative to specifications

In cost-plus type contracts
- Overhead costs also billed directly
- Inadequate internal controls by contractor over charges for people, materials, and services
- Unreasonable charges for use of contractor-owned equipment
- Excessive manning of project
- No effort to obtain best prices for materials and equipment
- Billings in excess of the amounts the contractor pays for labor or material
- Failure to credit project for discounts, insurance rate refunds, returned or salvaged material
- Duplication of effort or costs between headquarters and field offices
- Inadequate job-site supervision or inspection by contractor or by architect-engineers
- Inadequate communication and follow-up from headquarters office
- Unreliable cost accounting and reporting procedures by contractor
- Billing supervision as direct labor in violation of contract terms
- Idle rented equipment
- Poor work practices
- Poor quality
- Extravagant use or early arrival of materials and supplies
- Excessively high standards for materials and equipment
- Poor physical protection of materials and equipment
- Lack of control over absences of contractor employees
- Cost-plus type work of contractor going on simultaneously with fixed-type work
- Excessive costs incurred because of contractor's negligence
- Uncontrolled overtime

In unit-price contracts
- Excessive progress payments
- Improper reporting of units completed
- Prices bearing no relation to cost
- Improper changes to the original contract
- Unauthorized escalation adjustments
- Inaccurate field records
- Inaccurate extension of unit prices

Auditing literature has documented a wide variety of improvements or recoveries made as a result of contract audits. Here are a few:

The internal auditor was reviewing a repair shop's records for time and material charges billed to the auditor's company. The auditor noticed that the bookkeeper had a basket full of unpaid invoices for work completed for the auditor's company. Some of the invoices covered repair work that had been completed up to a year ago, and the repaired items were sitting in the repair shop gathering dust. The shop's manager was reluctant to explain the unpaid invoices and told the auditor, "Your company is one of our biggest customers, and I don't want to make waves."

After much persuasion, the shop manager finally told the auditor that the company's plant supervisor had told him that there was no money in the budget to pay for the repairs and he probably wouldn't request delivery until he absolutely needed the repaired items. The supervisor also told the shop manager if he didn't go along, someone else would get the business.

The auditor expanded the scope and visited other repair shops serving the company and found the same situation. The auditor's discussions with the plant supervisor were fruitless. The plant supervisor told the auditor that the practice was improving the company's cash flow and it was just plain good business practice. The auditor didn't think so and told the supervisor a report would be issued regarding the practice.

The auditor included in the report that the supervisor's practice precluded timely recognition of liabilities and related expense ($400,000 at the time of the audit), as required by GAAP and violated the Securities Exchange Act and related SEC regulations. Further, the auditor warned, the practice might subject the company's management to injunctive or criminal proceedings.

Initially, company management didn't take the report seriously. They did take it seriously when the audit committee of the board of directors demanded that the plant supervisor's practice cease immediately.[4]

During an analysis of change orders for a completed major construction project, the internal auditors found that the cost of change orders was 14.6 percent of the value of the entire contract. Applying this percentage to the base value of another contract, recently awarded, the auditors estimated that change orders would increase the cost of that contract by $806,000. When the auditors presented their findings to management, management started placing special emphasis on the review of change orders before they were approved for the new contract. As a result, the number of change orders for the new contract was reduced and the cost of the contract increased by only $290,000 — a potential savings of $516,000.[5]

While reviewing costs under a cost-plus contract, the internal auditors observed that a payroll load factor was applied to direct labor costs to recover actual payroll taxes (FICA, FUI, and SUI). The auditors found that the factor was applied to the entire gross wages for the year, not merely to the statutory wage limits. Since there was significant overtime work on the project, a substantial number of workers wages exceeded the limits and resulted in $84,000 in tax overbillings. The auditors also found that Workers' Compensation Insurance rates were calculated on total wages and not on the fixed-wage limit set by the insurance organization. This resulted in an additional $122,500 in insurance overbillings. The contractor concurred in these findings and refunded the total $206,500 for both overbillings.[6]

Integrated Auditing[7]

Integrated auditing currently is considered a major element of the internal auditing function. However, portions of the integration philosophy have a history of being employed in internal audits of the 1940s. These early audits combined aspects of financial auditing with performance auditing, a procedure that resulted in portions of the year-end financial audit being completed during the preceding operational audit year.

The concept of integration can be broad and can include such aspects as providing for the audit to serve as:

- The continuing of elements of a balance sheet and an operational audit during a performance audit.
- The conduct of audits of variance phases of the client's operation that would normally be audited separately.
- An exercise in participative auditing where the client:
  — Assists in the planning of the audit, and/or
  — Participates with staff in the conduct of the audit

- An audit that actually combines diverse phases of internal auditing such as:
  — Financial auditing
  — Performance auditing
  — Information systems auditing

Obviously the degree of integration is dependent on:

- The size of the audit staff.
- The skills represented on the staff or that are available through outside sources.
- The audit philosophy held by the organization management and by the auditing organization.
- The level of technological activity at the client and the auditing organizations.
- The cost-benefit of such an auditing operation.

In a 1993 study of this aspect of auditing, The Institute of Internal Auditors pointed out that the objective, strategic and operational plans for this audit function should tie into the organization's strategic plan and should have input from management, the audit committee, the external auditors, technological elements of the organization and the clients and other users.[8]

Consultants

Some of the above mentioned programs and activities are quite technical or have technical aspects. Currently much of this work is described as "outsourcing or cosourcing (see next section)." A thorough audit evaluation may require the services of technical consultants. Auditors must remember that consultants assist; they do not take over the evaluation or shoulder the auditor's responsibilities. Hence, there are some rules internal auditors should follow in dealing with consultants:

- The consultant must be credible and have demonstrated competence for the work to be performed.
- The consultant and the auditors must have complete agreement on program scope and objectives before they prepare the audit or work program.
- Staff should be assigned to work with consultants, monitor their activities, and discuss problems with them.
- Auditors must understand the nature of the consultant's work — the reasoning underlying their analytical choices, the risks inherent in their data and analyses, and whether work done by the consultant conforms with what was intended.
- The final audit report is the internal auditor's. It expresses the auditor's opinion, even though it is buttressed by the results of the consultant's studies. The consultant's opinions should be quoted only when the subject matter is clearly beyond the competence of the internal auditor and relates to completely technical matters.
- Currently consultants must not be allowed to direct or take management prerogatives.

Technical assistance may be solicited for the duration of an assignment or on an as-needed basis. The internal auditor must be in charge. The technical consultant is needed to clarify technical or esoteric matters, point toward the areas that need probing, and protect the auditors from inaccurate information or self-serving declarations by line personnel; but technicians may not have the ability to gather evidence, array facts, and examine data so as to reach logical conclusions.

Outsourcing and Cosourcing[9]

This subject will be discussed extensively in Chapter 29. However, there are some aspects of field work where outsourcing, or the use of experts who are not organic to the function, becomes an important aspect of the audit operation. Cosourcing, considered an element of outsourcing, is generally understood to be an audit operation where the outsider performs part of the internal audit along with the organization's audit activity. Internal auditors generally are educated and trained to perform audits. They are generally specialists in the aspects of controls and of the management processes. Much of their auditing is dedicated to these important elements of the organization's operations. However, in many organizations, efficient, economical, and effective operations entail the consideration of technical operations that impact materially on the operations. For instance, an operation cannot be performed more efficiently if the change would react unfavorably on the technical aspects of the operation. An example might be a case where aggregate (crushed stone) used as the integral element of concrete in a reactor containment vessel could be used without impacting on the strength of the construction, but the specialist states that the radioactive shielding would be diminished.

Outsourcing and cosourcing are important in many specialized areas. Examples are engineering, physics, health services, education, medicine, chemistry, veterinary medicine, actuarial service, advertising and selling, investments, and many others. The field work staff must be complete and have the disciplines and skills necessary to produce audit findings and recommendations based on solid facts and considering all aspects of the present and recommended actions.

The chief audit executive is responsible for the quality of the outsourced services. The evaluation of the quality of the engaged staff, whether from the organization itself or from an external organization, must be as comprehensive as would be that of the normal employment function.

Outsourced or cosourced assistance should, where needed, be used in the planning process as well as in the evaluative audit activities. It should also play an important part in the reporting activity and should be used in conferencing with the clients. There is always an element of confrontation between the specialists on the audit staff and those organic to the client operation. A method of reducing the noise level of this type of a situation might be to bring the client into the outsourcing selection process, in a concurring capacity.

Well-structured and intelligently employed outsourcing and cosourcing will bring technical value and credibility to the internal auditing operation.

Analytical Reviews

Analytical reviews have long been used to determine the reasonableness of certain data. Traditionally, these reviews have related to financial matters. For example:

- Comparing financial information for a current period with that of prior periods.

- Comparing current financial information with what is expected, i.e., budgets, forecasts, and industry experience.
- Investigating the relationship between financial and nonfinancial information.

Some of the methodologies used to conduct these reviews are:

Trend analysis. This is a test that compares current data with previous data. Previous data provide a prediction of what current data should be. Abnormal variances are investigated. A number of mathematical models are used, such as exponential smoothing, weighted average, and simple linear trend. Auditors are cautioned about certain weaknesses in trend analysis: there can be no assurance that past trends will continue into current activities. New variables not previously applicable may affect the predictions. The numbers may be used subjectively and include the auditor's biases.

Ratio analysis. Financial ratios, such as profitability, solvency, and efficiency, can be used to determine the reasonableness of current information. As in trend analysis, unexpected variables can affect results and provide distorted information.

Regression analysis. This technique is used to examine the relationship among certain variables. It measures the extent to which variables increase together or one increases as the other decreases. Regression analysis is a richer source of relationships than either trend or ratio analysis because (1) it permits the use of multiple independent variables; (2) auditors can explore relationships between financial statements and nonbalance-sheet indicators; and (3) seasonal fluctuations, trends, and ratios can be included.

With the advent of analytical oriented computer software and the use of personal computers, more sophisticated analytical reviews are made easier.[10]

Internal auditors can use analytical reviews when examining operating as well as financial data. Analytical reviews can highlight trouble spots and point the way for more intensive audits to determine both the degree of abnormality and, what is more important, the reasons for it. Below are some examples.

Fixed Assets Maintenance

In examining the controls over fixed assets, internal auditors would want to know whether property has been aged by class and whether the cost of maintenance is shown for each class. Do the reports show where the maintenance people spend the bulk of their time? Have analyses been made of the relative economics of purchase versus lease? Do the reports show machine hours between breakdowns? Do they show maintenance hours and cost of major repairs related to replacement cost? Such analysis may disclose excessively liberal replacement policies, abnormal repair costs, or excessive preventive maintenance.

Personnel Statistics

Reports can be analyzed to show various relationships between numbers of employees and other organization trends — for example, ratios of hourly to salary personnel, direct to indirect personnel, sales to nonsales personnel, truck drivers to shipping personnel, supervisory to the nonsupervisory personnel, total personnel to sales, and total personnel to profit.

Reports of different branches can be studied to disclose variances in procedures or the efficiency of personnel deployment. The results of the analyses may not be an end in themselves, but rather indicators for more studies in depth.

Inventory Turnover

Turnover is generally reported as a lump sum figure, often embracing a number of accounts or store areas. But even within a single account or store, unfortunate conditions can be hidden. For example, unless inventories are periodically aged by class of item, many individual slow-moving or obsolete items can be overlooked. An overall turnover rate of four times a year, say, may conceal the fact that 30 percent of the items turn over only two times a year or less.

An analysis of turnover rates, including the records of specific items, may disclose how many inventory items are more than a year old. It may point to buying errors that are hidden in inventory and protected by a satisfactory overall turnover ratio. Also, an excessively low ratio may point to fraud in false inventory charges.

Employment Costs and Employee Turnover

The cost and time involved in the average hire, by class of employee, is often a matter of interest. Also of interest is the turnover rate by department or branch, and the organization's turnover rate compared with that in similar organizations.

Rolling Stock

Of importance are computations of the relationship between mileage traveled and the average life of tires, batteries, and plugs; analyses of the comparative cost of using personal versus organization cars; and comparisons of manpower or of dock and warehouse space with loading and unloading times, standby time, and delivery time between points.

Stationery and Supply Stores

It is often interesting to compare usage and stock balances. It is also useful to compare usage with the number of using personnel, particularly when items are attractive for home use and where physical control over the stock leaves something to be desired.

Material Records

To distribute material costs, the auditor can analyze reports that show the number of storeroom requisitions processed. In some cases, however, the average unit prices may be too low to warrant the extensive paper flow. Why spend $50,000 to distribute $500,000 worth of material costs a year when approximations based on samples can accomplish the same results at far less cost?

Telephones and Personal Computers

The auditor could determine and analyze the ratios of the number of people to the number of telephone instruments, the number of outside calls made, the number of toll calls, the average length of calls, and the number of restricted phones in each department. Periodic reports to management on the results of these analyses can have a salutary effect and reduce the number and length of calls.

Auditors must use caution in making any such analyses; the analysis may produce data that impel false or superficial conclusions. Auditors should seek to measure their findings against norms — norms that may already have been developed in the organization or in an industry. Statistics in a vacuum are meaningless. Used, however, to show deviations from norms, variances between similar operations, or adverse trends, they may be significant and can point the way to further investigation that will establish causes and effects. A similar type of analysis may be made of personal computers.

For an extended discussion on analytical reviews, see Chapter 12.

Legal Evidence

Relationship to Audit Evidence

Legal evidence and audit evidence have much in common. They have the same objective — to provide proof, to foster an honest belief about the truth or falsity of any proposition at issue. Belief is produced by the consideration of information. The information thus presented, in whatever shape it may take, is evidence.

The focus of audit evidence differs somewhat from that of legal evidence. Legal evidence relies heavily on oral testimony. Audit evidence relies more on documentary evidence. Legal evidence permits certain presumptions; for example, it is conclusively presumed at law (meaning no evidence, no matter how strong, can be brought in to the contrary) that facts recited in a written instrument, between parties and successors of interest, are true. Auditors, however, are not bound by any presumptions; they should question any evidence until they, themselves, are satisfied with its truth or falsity.

Internal auditors should know the common forms of legal evidence. This knowledge will be useful to them in fraud cases, in any situations where they gather facts for legal counsel, and even in their routine audit work. What follows is a brief commentary on some of the forms of legal evidence.

Best Evidence

Best evidence, often referred to as primary evidence, is the evidence that is the most natural — the most satisfactory proof of the fact under investigation. It has a strong relationship to reliability. It is confined, generally, to documentary evidence and applies mostly to proof of the content of a writing. If the original writing is available, the best evidence rule prevents a party from proving the content of a writing by oral testimony.

The rule is designed to foreclose possible erroneous interpretations of a writing; it requires that the original writing be produced when it is available. Oral evidence, for example, may not be used to dispute a written instrument such as a contract or a deed; however, oral evidence can be used to explain the meaning of the instrument where such instrument is reasonably capable of more than one interpretation.

Secondary Evidence

Secondary evidence is inferior to primary evidence and cannot be given the same reliance. Secondary evidence may include a copy of a writing or oral evidence of its contents. A copy of a writing is admissible, generally, if (1) the original writing is lost or has been destroyed without fraudulent intent on the part of the proponent of the copy; (2) the writing is not reasonably procurable by the proponent of the copy by use of legal process or other available means; or (3) the writing is controlled by a public entity. It must be shown that the copy is a proper representation of the original writing.

Oral testimony or written summaries are generally considered inferior to copies of writings. These inferior forms of evidence are not barred by the best evidence rule if (1) the writing consists of numerous accounts or other writings; (2) the accounts cannot be examined in court without a great loss of time; or (3) the accounts or other writings are produced for inspection by an adverse party if the court, in its discretion, requires such production.

Direct Evidence

Direct evidence proves a fact without having to use presumptions or inference to establish that proof. The testimony of a witness to a fact is direct evidence — no inference is required. For example, a witness who states that he or she observed a receiving inspector sign for the receipt of goods, when in fact the goods received were less than those signed for, is giving direct evidence.

Circumstantial Evidence

Circumstantial evidence proves an intermediate fact, or group of facts, from which one can infer the existence of some primary fact that is significant to the issue under consideration. It does not directly prove the existence of the primary fact, but merely gives rise to a logical inference that it exists. Short receipts that have been cleared through the receiving department, with an inspector's stamp on the receiving memo, are circumstantial evidence that the receiving inspector was negligent.

Internal auditors must always be wary of circumstantial evidence. For example, in the case of the receiving inspector, it is possible that the inspector was not on duty the day the goods were received and that someone else used the inspector's stamp.

Conclusive Evidence

Conclusive evidence is incontrovertible evidence, irrespective of its nature. It is so strong that it overbears all other evidence. It is evidence from which only one reasonable conclusion can be drawn. It cannot be contradicted and needs no corroboration. As Thoreau said, "Some circumstantial evidence is very strong, as when you find a trout in the milk." It can be conclusively presumed that the trout did not come from a cow.

Corroborative Evidence

Corroborative evidence is additional evidence of a different character concerning the same point. It is evidence supplementary to that already given and tends to strengthen or confirm it. For example, oral evidence consistent with a written instrument, and offered merely to confirm the written instrument or show the truth of the matter contained in it, is corroborative evidence and is considered acceptable. Oral evidence, given by an inspection supervisor, that the receiving inspector was on duty the day of the short receipts and that nobody else had access to the inspector's stamp, corroborates the circumstantial evidence of the receiving stamp.

Opinion Evidence

The opinion rule holds that witnesses must ordinarily testify to fact only — to what they actually saw or heard. Auditors should likewise filter out opinions and gather and evaluate facts only — those items that tend to prove truth or falsity. Opinions offered by others may be useful in pointing out the right direction for fact gathering, but opinions may also be biased, self-serving, or uninformed.

There is an exception to the opinion rule, however, that relates to the testimony of experts. Under that exception, an expert is permitted to offer an opinion on the facts; it is the only way the jury or administrative judge will understand the facts and the only way the jury will get to the truth.

Some safeguards have been set up with respect to opinion testimony, however. These safeguards require two elements to be present: First, the subject on which the opinion is expressed must be distinctly related to some science, profession, business, or occupation that is beyond the understanding of the average layperson. Second, the expert witness must have such skill, knowledge, or experience in that field or calling that his or her opinion will probably help the jurors or the court in their search for the truth.

Auditors should keep the opinion rule in mind when they encounter matters outside their ken. They should understand that the opinions of others are valid when those opinions come within the scope of the expert opinion rule, but are *not* valid unless they include essential elements: (1) a subject beyond the understanding of the auditor; and (2) an acknowledged expert in the field.

As a practical matter, the auditor should include a third element: freedom from potential bias. In business situations, the expert is often an organization employee. The auditor should, if possible, select one who is outside the department or division involved in the audit. An engineer whose opinion is solicited on a matter involving Project A should be selected from Project B or C. In some organizations, of course, the only expert may be working on the project under review. In that case, the auditor must consider the possibility that the expert's testimony may not be completely free from bias.

Hearsay Evidence

The hearsay rule renders objectionable any statements made by someone, other than a witness, to prove the truth of the matter stated. Put another way, it refers to any oral or written evidence brought into court and offered as proof of things said out of court. It is secondhand evidence.

Hearsay is generally inadmissible because one of the best ways to get at the truth or falsity of an assertion is to put witnesses under oath and cross-examine them about what they personally saw or heard. Cross-examination has a way of bringing to light the untrustworthiness and the many possible deficiencies, suppressions, and sources of error that lie under the bare, untested assertions of a witness.

Internal auditors must put themselves in the position of the court as they ask questions and examine records. If Smith says to the auditor, "I personally saw Jones sign the receiving memo," it is direct evidence and not hearsay. Smith is in the presence of the auditor, who can "cross-examine" him by asking questions that will tend to prove the truth or falsity of Smith's statement. The auditor could ask, "Do you know Jones when you see her? Were you able to see Jones signing the receiving memo? How do you know this is the same receiving memo? When did she sign it?" and so forth.

If Smith were to tell the auditor "Thompson told me he saw Jones signing the receiving memo," that is hearsay. Thompson is not there to answer the auditor's questions. The auditor is unable to query Thompson as to the truth or falsity of the statement. All the auditor can be sure of is whether Smith heard Thompson's words exactly: "Is that word-for-word what Thompson said? Where were you at the time? What brought up the conversation? How can you remember so precisely?" As to the truth or falsity of Thompson's statement, however, that is hearsay.

What about a written statement — a sales slip, a purchase order, a discrepancy report, or any of the myriad business documents that are prepared, signed, and processed by people? They, too, are hearsay. They also represent statements by people not in court (or not in the presence of the internal auditor).

Business documents, however, come under one of the various exceptions to the hearsay rule. The exception holds that business records made during the ordinary course of business are admissible in court as evidence. That is because records made during regular business routines are usually trustworthy. Such business entries as sales slips, purchase orders, and discrepancy reports are therefore considered admissible evidence. But there should be testimony from the custodian of the records or from some other qualified witness who can identify the record and describe its mode of preparation. The testimony should show that the record was prepared in the regular course of business at or near the time of the event recorded.

The trend in the courts today follows the methods of ordinary business by assuming the validity of records kept as daily commercial routine until they are actually discredited. In other words, the validity of the business record is rebuttable — the document is not unassailable merely because it is a so-called business record. With proper proof it can be found to be invalid or incorrect. Thus, when auditors find that the document or record represents critical evidence, they would wish to discuss it with the person responsible for preparing it and satisfy themselves about its truth or falsity by "cross-examination."

Photographs also represent hearsay evidence, but they will be considered admissible if properly authenticated. Photographs may be authenticated by one or more witnesses who are familiar with the subject portrayed and can testify that the photograph is a good representation of the person, place, object, or condition.

Auditors who observe the act of photographing, or take the photographs themselves are competent witnesses. If they have someone else take the picture, they should have the photographer sign the reverse of the photograph and record the date, the time, a brief description of the subject matter — in fact, anything that would help authenticate the photograph at a later date after memory has grown dim.

Audit Evidence

Nature of Audit Evidence

Audit evidence is the information internal auditors obtain through observing conditions, interviewing people, and examining records. Audit evidence should provide a factual basis for audit opinions, conclusions, and recommendations. Audit evidence has been categorized as physical, testimonial, documentary, and analytical.

Physical Evidence

Physical evidence is obtained by observing people, property, and events. The evidence can take the form of statements of observation by the observer, or by photographs, charts, maps, graphs, or other pictorial representations. Graphic evidence is persuasive.

A picture of an unsafe condition is far more compelling than a written description. All observations should, if possible, be supported by documented examples. When the observation is the sole evidence, it is preferable to have two or more auditors make important physical observations. If possible, representatives of the client should accompany the auditors on such inspections.

Testimonial Evidence

Testimonial evidence takes the form of letters or statements in response to inquiries or interviews. These, standing alone, are not conclusive; they should be supported by documentation if possible. Client statements can be important leads not always obtainable by independent audit testing.

Documentary Evidence

Documentary evidence is the most common form of audit evidence. It may be external or internal. External documentary evidence includes letters or memorandums received by the client, suppliers' invoices, and packing sheets. Internal documentary evidence originates within the client organization. It includes accounting records, copies of outgoing correspondence, e-mail receiving reports, and the like.

The source of documentary evidence will affect its reliability. An external document obtained directly from its source (a confirmation, for example) is more reliable than a document obtained from the client. The possibility always exists that internal documents can be altered, for instance, by surreptitious computer programs. Other matters affecting reliability include the circulation of documents through outside parties (canceled checks, satisfactory internal review procedures, and corroboration by other evidence).

Internal procedures have an important effect. For example, the reliability of a time card is significantly improved if employees are forbidden from punching a fellow employee's card, supervisors review the cards, the payroll section checks time cards against job tickets, and surprise floor checks are made. Computer editing programs can also help.

Analytical Evidence

Analytical evidence stems from analysis and verification. The sources of such evidence are computations: comparisons with prescribed standards, past operations, similar operations, and laws or regulations; reasoning; and information that has been broken down into its components.

Standards of Audit Evidence

All audit evidence should stand the tests of sufficiency, competence, and relevance.

Sufficiency. Evidence is sufficient if it is so factual, adequate, and convincing that it would lead a prudent person to the same conclusions as the auditor. This, of course, would be a matter of judgment; but the judgment should be objective. Hence, when samples are used, the samples should be the result of objective, acceptable sampling methods. The samples selected should provide reasonable assurance that they are representative of the population from which they were selected.

Competence. Competent evidence is reliable evidence. It should be the best that is reasonably obtainable. An original document is more competent than a copy. A corroborated oral statement is more competent than one standing alone. Direct evidence is superior to hearsay evidence.

The best evidence rule should apply to audit evidence as well. Computer-produced evidence should be carefully evaluated.

Relevance. Relevance refers to the relationship of the information to its use. The facts and opinions used to prove or disprove an issue must have a logical, sensible relationship to that issue. An original purchase order, properly approved and issued, has no relevance to whether the goods procured have been received. A receiving memorandum certifying to the receipt of a certain number of items has no relevance to whether those items met stipulated specifications.

Whenever evidence does not meet the standards of sufficiency, competence, and relevance, the auditor's work remains unfinished. Corroboration or additional evidence may be required. When the internal auditor expresses an opinion, it must be based on incontrovertible evidence.

The Handling of Sensitive Evidence[11]

The chapter on working papers, Chapter 9, describes generally the maintenance and care of working papers. However, in a discussion of evidence such as appears above, it seems appropriate to discuss the aspect of handling sensitive evidence. There should be a plan developed for the handling and security of this sensitive material. This plan should include methods for preserving the integrity of documents that should be abstracted from the normal working paper files and should be stored in locked cabinets or safe deposit boxes or safes. It may be appropriate to store them in off-site locations.

It is also necessary to safely secure computerized evidential information so as to deny access to it in its original state. An added method of presentation would be to develop backup files that are stored at a location other than that of the original records or documents.

It is also necessary to maintain records to show a clear chain of custody of the evidence to show that it was not compromised. Also, obsolete documents should be shredded. (Along with certificates of destruction.)

The evidence database should be organized through the use of a document management system, preferably computerized chronologically and by subject. This type of database can provide inestimable assistance in the support of the audit report, but also can prove valuable for developing the chronology of activities that are the subject of the audit report.

In very sensitive situations that ultimately could result in legal activity, legal counsel should be consulted as to the care of the evidence in the light of potential actions. The accumulated file should be known to all concerned and all meetings and activities in addition to those resulting from audit effort should also be reflected in the evidence accumulation.

Legal and security advice should be obtained relative to handling during discovery procedures in criminal or civil use situations.

Working Papers

Audit working papers, which are more completely discussed in Chapter 9, contain the basic substance of the work performed by auditors during the entire audit but especially during the field work phase of the activity. The working papers are the foundation on which the evidence is built. There are several generic types of working papers; all are important. They include:

- Excerpts from authoritative sources for criteria and standards.
- Summarizations of interviews, meetings, conversations.
- Detail resulting from observations, including diagrams, photographs, flowcharts, etc.
- The substance of verifications and vouching, i.e., comparisons of substantive material to criteria or authorizing documentation.
- Analyses of findings from other working papers or observations.
- Analytical computations relating to the audit.

These working papers are the substance of the audit. They should be given careful supervisory examination to determine that they are valid and that they leave no questions open; also, that the material on some working papers does not conflict with that on other working papers.

Field Work in a High Technology Environment

As information systems have become more closely linked and have provided for real time processing, auditors are faced with complications that have not typically been found in older systems. These complications are expanded when firms install enterprise-wide systems that have the potential of integrating an entity's business functions from marketing to manufacturing and logistics to human resources and financial reporting.

Enterprise-wide systems

Increasingly larger firms are using well-established enterprise-wide systems, also called enterprise resource planning systems. These systems, such as SAP, PeopleSoft, Baan, and J. D. Edwards, provide a significant potential for more efficient and effective operations for an entity by using a standard system which is flexible enough to deal with different business components in different countries and produce needed information for appropriate management levels. These systems can handle wide ranges of businesses and functions, including those involved in substantial amounts of e-commerce. In addition to penetrating most large firms, these systems are being targeted to medium-sized businesses. Hence, over time they are liable to be the standard for most firms that are large enough to have their own internal audit area.

While there have been discussions in the popular business press about a number of installation problems, it is clear that the firms are continuing their installation of these systems. Furthermore, firms in the "second tier" are investing in the software. The amount of investment required for even these firms is significant. A firm with two manufacturing plants and three sales offices reported that it planned to spend almost $10 million dollars on its enterprise-wide computing system to complete its installation and maintain the system for three years. Firms typically expect to spend from three to 10 times hardware and software costs on technology consulting services. Large firms have reported spending as much as $1 million a day to install their system.

Given the amount of money spent on these systems and the risks associated with implementation, the internal auditor should be fully involved in the process, including installation. This is critical because traditional controls that are relied upon by auditors are typically eliminated and no other controls exist to replace them. If these controls are not properly addressed during initial implementation, the firm may face high costs of modifying the system or face unacceptable levels of risks. This is because systems such as SAP require the entity to modify their business processes. Hence the entity could very well be changing its basic business structure.

One approach to dealing with this problem is to develop a database for processes and another for internal controls.[12] One large chemical company reports over 1,200 business processes in such a database. Indeed such a method would require coordination among systems analysts and functional area specialists.

This control is critical because the system is designed around the theory that singly entry of information is the most desired situation. Approvals tend to be built into the system rather than requiring individual intervention. Hence separation of duties, which is a problem in information system applications, becomes a larger problem in enterprise-wide systems. For example, rather than having a purchasing clerk enter data which is approved by a purchasing agent, purchases may be approved based only on potential need and an approved vendor list maintained in the information system.

The emphasis on data entry in such a system may have a substantial impact on employees. It has been reported that some entities have experienced higher turnover among employees because employees who exercised judgment in their previous positions were dissatisfied with the enterprise-wide system where they felt they had become data entry clerks. In fact, a firm has reported that the general quality of employees has declined in most of its first-line positions.

A substantial part of the controls built into the system are based upon password protection. In general an auditor needs to be concerned about whether a control (firewall) provided in the system can be overridden and whether an alternative transaction or transactions can override the control. This is especially important given the emphasis on authorization in these systems.

Continuous Auditing

The nature of a system such as provided in an enterprise-wide system may make continuous auditing desirable. The Canadian Institute of Chartered Accountants and the AICPA define continuous audit as:

> ...a methodology that enables independent auditors to provide written assurance on a subject matter using a series of auditors' reports issued simultaneously with, or a short period after, the occurrence of events underlying the subject matter.[13]

The research study concludes that the following conditions are necessary for a continuous audit:

- Subject matter with suitable characteristics
- Reliability of systems providing the subject matter
- Audit evidence provided by highly automated audit procedures
- Reliable means of obtaining the results of audit procedures on a timely basis
- High degree of auditor proficiency in information technology and the subject matter[14]

Later the study goes on to address specific issues that an external auditor should consider about the internal auditor in a continuous audit. Issues of primary concern which may impact the field work and reporting of the internal auditor are:

- The internal auditors' involvement with the subject matter. When the internal auditor has extensive involvement, the internal auditor would be the prime source of information about the characteristics of the subject matter.
- The internal auditors' knowledge of the reliability of the subject matter.
- The internal auditors' involvement in reporting and evaluating management's responses to reports.
- The internal auditors' proficiency with information technology and the matters under audit.[15]

While the work of the internal auditor may be used by the external auditor, in most situations the risks associated with the possibilities errors or fraud require that the internal auditor have such knowledge and involvement. Without such knowledge and involvement the entity may be exposing itself to unacceptable levels of risk. Hence it becomes paramount for the internal auditor to develop such activities that would fall under the definition of continuous auditing.

One of the key components in a continuous audit would be the design and implementation of "automated controls and alarm triggers."[16] Such alarms triggers would be warnings to the internal auditor and management that one of the following has occurred:

- Controls are functioning and they have identified an error that must be investigated and or corrected, and
- Controls are not functioning based upon information identified.

It is clear that in enterprise-wide systems, the internal auditor must play a key role in reducing risk to an acceptable level. This is especially important because typically management and the auditor should be alerted to potential problems that could result in errors or be the result of fraud and action must be taken with a short timeframe.

Internal Audit Issues Relative to Risk

Given the internal auditor's role in reducing risk to an acceptable level, several significant issues must be addressed. As enterprise-wide systems are modified, these issues may have to be changed.

A clear distinction must be made between what is reported to what level of management and what is reported to internal audit. For example, if management is alerted to a potential inconsistency that they have in fact caused, such reporting could allow them to develop answers to and changes in data, which would potentially be a plausible explanation to cover a fraud. Similarly if management knows the criteria used by internal auditors to investigate transactions or to consider that controls are not working, a fraud could be conducted, which potentially would not be investigated. Specific frauds might not be significant in and of themselves but combined they may have a potentially dramatic impact on the entity.

However, in an environment that collects sales, distribution, manufacturing, and financial performance data, the internal auditor can be in a position to use this performance data to measure against traditional financial data to detect whether errors or frauds are occurring or whether there is a control breakdown. For example, most enterprise-wide systems allow someone with proper authorization to "drill down" or look at various levels of detail for unusually large transactions. Or an auditor could examine sales by area based upon the time the sales were entered. In addition, the auditor may have to carefully evaluate such traditional audit alert factors such as changes in personnel to determine whether additional procedures need to be performed.

In enterprise-wide systems, there tends to be a wealth of data available to the auditor who has appropriate knowledge of the system. Since all data is stored in a database, the auditor has access to a great deal of information that can be used for comparison purposes. This data can be used to make comparisons across time periods, across similar components, and/ or using various industry and demographic information.

Further, the internal auditor can review the information in a real time environment. Hence the potential to be diminished for timing differences causing the appearance of an error or fraud when none exists.

As enterprise-wide systems proliferate and entities move toward a continuous audit approach consistent with their evaluation of risk, the auditor's traditional field work will change, especially for high risk areas. The field work will not be in a discrete time period but will be a continuous one in which reports will be issued as exception reports for ongoing audits and summary reports at the end of specific periods. In addition, field work may be performed at central audit locations rather than at specific regional or plant sites.

The internal auditor in the future may have assigned responsibilities to monitor specific areas or segments for a long period of time. In fact, by having such assigned responsibilities, the auditor may become familiar with the areas so that situations that need further investigation are developed based upon various audit procedures and auditor knowledge. The internal auditor in such a position may be able to provide assistance to areas to improve efficiency and effectiveness.

As enterprise-wide systems connect to suppliers and customers' systems, the internal auditor will need to further consider changes in field work that will be needed because of the close coupling of the systems. For example, could customer personnel in conjunction with client personnel be in a position to commit a substantial fraud in a short period of time and cover up the fraud and leave the entities?

Specific procedures used to evaluate controls and types of controls will need to be evaluated on a continuous basis. Types of controls are discussed in Chapters 13 through 15. In such systems, these controls are extremely important in evaluating risk. Types of audit procedures that may be used are discussed in Chapter 16. Analytical procedures, which may indicate the potential for errors or frauds, are discussed in more detail in Chapter 12.

E-commerce/E-business and Continuous Auditing

As firms move more toward e-commerce and e-business, continuous auditing may be required to reduce risks to acceptable levels. If an entity is using e-commerce to sell to consumers, there are several risks that an auditor must consider in planning field work. These risks include the potential for fictitious sales and returns and the potential that competitors may be able to access critical information from the entity.

In a similar manner, when an entity deals with other businesses, fictitious sales, purchases, returns, and payments can be made which could result in substantial losses to the entity. Continuous auditing can help alert the auditor to potential problems and their discovery. In addition the entity must make sure that sensitive information about purchasing and other activities is not compromised. The entity must make sure that the portal used does not allow access to unauthorized information. This is especially critical when using an enterprise-wide system that is designed to allow access from key partners. In a highly competitive environment, entity critical information can be available to others.

References

[1]Phillips, Roger, "What Management Expects and Needs from Internal Auditors," *The Internal Auditor,* December 1982, 33-35.

[2]Drucker, Peter, *Management: Tasks, Responsibilities, Practices* (New York: Harper & Row, 1977), 112.

[3]Phillips, Roger, "What Management Expects and Needs from Internal Auditors," *The Internal Auditor,* December 1982, 33-35.

[4]"The Round Table," April 1993, 68-69.

[5]"The Round Table," June 1985, 72.

[6]"The Round Table," December 1984, 65.I.

[7]*Internal Auditing Alert* (Boston, MA: Warren Gorham & Lamont, April 1993).

[8]*Adapting the Integrated Audit* (Altamonte Springs, FL: The Institute of Internal Auditors, 1993).

[9]*Internal Auditing Alert* (Boston, MA: Warren Gorham & Lamont), January 1996, March 1996, December 1997, June 1997.

[10]Albrecht, W. S., "Analytical Reviews for Internal Auditors," *The Internal Auditor,* August 1980, 20-25; K. R. Ferris and K. L. Tennant, "New Tools for Analytical Reviews," *The Internal Auditor,* December 1982, 14-17; *Modern Analytical Auditing* by McKee (New York: Quorum Books, 1987).

[11]Ehlers, Helen, "Building a Case," *Internal Auditor,* October 1996, 37-43.

[12]Bui, A., "Staying in Control," *Internal Auditor,* August 1999, 25-27.

[13]*Continuous Auditing,* Canadian Institute of Chartered Accountants, Toronto, Canada, 1999, 5.

[14]Ibid., 5-18.

[15]Ibid., 67-69.

[16]Ibid., 31.

Supplementary Readings

Adamec, Bruce A., "Using Process Engineering in Operational Auditing," *Internal Auditing*, Summer 1994, 3-13.

Ames, Gary Adna, Deborah L. Lindberg, and Khalid A. Razaki, "Web Advertising Exposures," *Internal Auditor*, October 1999, 51-54.

Attaway Sr., Morris C., "What Every Auditor Needs to Know About E-Commerce," *Internal Auditor*, June 2000, 56-60.

Attaway, Morris C., "Billing Risks & SAP R/3," *Internal Auditor*, August 1999, 42-47.

Bachman, Gregory A., "The Change Audit," *Internal Auditor*, June 1999, 40-41.

Bergstein, Warren M., "Audit Program for Pension and Other Postretirement Employee Benefits," *Internal Auditing Alert*, January 1999, 1-3.

Bergstein, Warren M., "Audit Programs for Fixed Assets," *Internal Auditing Alert*, March 1998, 7-8.

Bjork, R. Scott, "Inventory Management Systems," *Internal Auditor*, December 2000, 40-44.

Burke, Joe, "Due Diligence in Mergers and Acquisitions," *Internal Auditor*, October 2000, 37-41.

Calhoun, Charles, "Audit Program for Cash," *Internal Auditing Alert*, December 1998, 7.

Calhoun, Charles, "Auditing Accounts Receivable," *Internal Auditing Alert*, January 1998, 4-5.

Calhoun, Charles, "Payroll Audit Program," *Internal Auditing Alert*, August 1997, 6.

Cashell, James D., and George R. Aldhizer III, "A Seal of Approval," *Internal Auditor*, June 1999, 50-53.

Crisp, Gregory, "A Warrant for Savings," *Internal Auditing Alert*, August 1999, 1-3.

Fargason, James Scott, *Law and the Internal Auditing Profession* (Altamonte Springs, FL: The Institute of Internal Auditors, 1992).

Figg, Jonathan, "Partnering with IT," *Internal Auditor*, August 2000, 73-75.

Hicks, Richard C., and William A. Newman, "Multiple Database Access Tools for Audit Testing," *Internal Auditing*, Winter 1997, 22-27.

Huberty, Peter J., "Worldwide Audit Automation," *Internal Auditor*, December 2000, 25-27.

Jeffords, Raymond, Greg Thibadoux, and Marsha Scheidt, "Utilizing Questions in the Audit Interview," *Internal Auditing,* January/February 2003, 14-20.

Jenne, Stanley Earl, "Audits of End-user Computing," *Internal Auditor*, December 1996, 30-34.

Kastner, Ryan, "Automating Bank Audits," *Internal Auditor*, October 1999, 23-25.

Keller, Paulette J., and J. Mike Jacka, "Process Mapping," *Internal Auditor*, October 1999, 60-64.

Kilpatrick, Teresa, "Auditing Manufacturing Costs," *Internal Auditor*, June 2000, 25-27.

Levy, Joel F., and Abba Z. Krebs, "Performance Audits that will Save Money: Hospital and Medical Surgical Bill Audits," *Internal Auditing Alert*, October 1998, 3-5.

Luizzo, Anthony J., "Auditing Retail Security Programs," *Internal Auditing Alert*, May 1999, 5-7.

Luizzo, Anthony J., "Auditing Hospital Security," *Internal Auditing Alert*, December 1998, 4-6.

Luizzo, Anthony J., "A Checklist to Audit the Security Survey," *Internal Auditing Alert*, October 1998, 5-8.

Luizzo, Anthony J., "Auditing Proactive Security Programs," *Internal Auditing Alert*, September 1998, 5-7.

Luizzo, Anthony J., "Auditing Security Policies and Procedures," *Internal Auditing Alert*, August 1998, 4-5.

Luizzo, Anthony J., "Auditing General Security," *Internal Auditing Alert*, July 1998, 5-7.

Luizzo, Anthony J., "Auditing the Hiring Process," *Internal Auditing Alert*, June 1998, 5-7.

Mautz, R.K., and H.A. Sharaf, "The Philosophy of Auditing," Monograph No. 6 (Sarasota, FL: American Accounting Association, 1982), Chapters 4 and 5.

Miller, Curtis, "A Look at European Shared Service Centers," *Internal Auditor*, October 1999, 44-48.

Pyzik, Kenneth P., "Building a Better Toolbox," *Internal Auditor*, April 1997, 32-35.

Rezaee, Zabihollah, William Ford, and Rick Elam, "Real-Time Accounting Systems," *Internal Auditor*, April 2000, 62-67.

Rice, Tammy, Stacey McKendree, and Kathy Kennedy, "Automating Health-care Audits," *Internal Auditor*, June 2001, 25-27.

Scantlebury, D.L., and R.B. Raum, "Operational Auditing," AGA Monograph, Series Number One (Arlington, VA: Association of Government Accountants, 1978), vii.

Sears, Brian P., *Internal Auditing Manual* (New York: RIA, 2003). (See Chapter D4, "Working Effectively in the Field.")

White, Scott, Walter Fuller, and Timothy Dugan, "Uncharted Waters," *Internal Auditor*, February 1999, 55-58.

Whitham, Robert B., "Auditing Fleet Maintenance Operations," *Internal Auditing Alert*, July 1997, 5-6.

Zhang, Charles, "The Art of Coordination," *Internal Auditor*, April 1998, 56-58.

Multiple-choice Questions

1. Shipments are made from the warehouse based on customer purchase orders. The matched shipping documents and purchase orders are then forwarded to the billing department for sales invoice preparation. The shipping documents are neither accounted for nor prenumbered. Which of the following substantive tests should be extended as a result of this control weakness?
   a. Select sales invoices from the sales register and examine the related shipping documents.
   b. Select bills of lading from the warehouse and trace the shipments to the related sales invoices.
   c. Foot the sales register and trace the total to the general ledger.
   d. Trace quantities and prices on the sales invoices to the customer purchase order and test extensions and footings.

Use the following information to answer questions 2 and 3:
An internal audit department plans to begin an audit of manufacturing operations. The audit objectives are to: (1) evaluate the quality of performance in carrying out assigned responsibilities; (2) determine whether all legal and regulatory requirements concerning employee safety are being properly implemented; and (3) determine whether fixed assets employed in manufacturing are properly reflected in the accounting records.

2. In meeting objective (2), which of the following audit approaches is likely to be most useful?
   a. Interviewing members of the executive management team.
   b. Examining documentation concerning the design and operation of the relevant systems and observing operations for compliance.
   c. Requesting an inspection by government regulators.
   d. Reviewing accident reports.

3. In meeting objective (3), which of the following audit approaches is likely to be most useful?
   a. Interviewing members of the accounting department.
   b. Examining documentation concerning the cost of fixed assets used in the manufacturing process.
   c. Inspecting fixed assets used in the manufacturing process and tracing to the asset subsidiary ledger.
   d. Selecting items from asset subsidiary ledger and recalculating depreciation.

4. A large manufacturing organization has a transportation division that supplies gasoline for the organization's vehicles. Gasoline is dispensed by an attendant who records the amount issued on a serially prenumbered gasoline disbursement form that is then given to the accounting department for proper recording. When the quantity of gasoline falls to a certain level, the service station attendant prepares a purchase requisition and sends it to the purchasing department where a purchase order is prepared and recorded in a gasoline purchases journal. Which of the following audit procedures would best determine if there is full and complete recording of gasoline disbursements?
   a. Compare the gasoline purchase requisitions with the gasoline disbursement records.
   b. Select a number of gasoline purchases from the gasoline purchases journal and compare them with their corresponding purchase orders and ascertain that they are serially prenumbered, are matched with purchase requisitions, and are authorized by someone independent of employees of the service station.
   c. Perform analytical procedures comparing this period's gasoline consumption with prior periods.
   d. Match the quantity of gasoline disbursed according to disbursement forms with an independent reading of quantity disbursed at the pump.

5. In an audit of a nonprofit organization's special fund, the primary audit objective would be to determine if the entity:
   a. Complied with existing fund requirements and performed specified activities.
   b. Managed its resources economically and efficiently.
   c. Prepared its financial statements in accordance with generally accepted accounting principles.
   d. Applied the funds in a way that would benefit the greatest number of people.

6. Interviewing operating personnel, identifying the objectives of the client, identifying standards used to evaluate performance, and assessing the risks inherent in the client's operations are activities typically performed in which phase of an internal audit?
   a. The field work phase.
   b. The preliminary survey phase.
   c. The audit programming phase.
   d. The reporting phase.

7. An organization recently entered into a cost-plus contract to build a new and larger manufacturing plant. Which of the following auditing procedures would be of most importance to the auditor reviewing this contract?
   a. Review the contract to ascertain that it contains a provision for the right of system review and cost audits of the contractor.
   b. Review the contract for a specific date of completion.
   c. Review the contract and all of the related bids received to ascertain that the organization selected the contractor with the lowest bid.
   d. Review the business integrity of the contractor through direct inquiry.

8. In the performance of an audit, audit risk is best defined as the risk that an auditor:
   a. Might not select documents that are in error as part of the examination.
   b. May not be able to properly evaluate an activity because of its poor internal accounting controls.
   c. May fail to detect a significant error or weakness during an examination.
   d. May not have the expertise to adequately audit a specific activity.

9. Which of the following tests can help the auditor evaluate the adequacy of the organization's allowance for doubtful accounts?
   a. Reconciling the accounts receivable subsidiary ledgers with the control account.
   b. Preparing an aging analysis.
   c. Reviewing authorization of credit terms.
   d. Tracing a sample of credit memos to the accounts receivable subsidiary ledger.

10. An internal auditor has just completed an on-site survey to become familiar with the organization's payroll operations. Which of the following should be performed next?
    a. Assign audit personnel.
    b. Establish initial audit objectives.
    c. Write the audit program.
    d. Conduct field work.

11. To identify shortages of specific items in an inventory of expensive goods held for retail sale, the most appropriate audit work step is to:
    a. Apply the retail method of inventory valuation.
    b. Compare physical inventory counts to perpetual records.
    c. Develop inventory estimates based on the gross profit percentage method.
    d. Analyze current and previous inventory turnover rates.

12. Which of the substantive field work procedures presented below provides the best evidence about the completeness of recorded revenues?
    a. Reconciling the sales journal to the general ledger control account.
    b. Vouching charges made to the accounts receivable subsidiary ledger to supporting shipping records.
    c. Vouching shipping records to the customer order file.
    d. Reconciling shipping records to recorded sales.

13. The scope of an internal audit is initially defined by the:
    a. Audit objectives.
    b. Scheduling and time estimates.
    c. Preliminary survey.
    d. Audit program.

14. The primary audit objective for a compliance audit of restricted funds at a government-supported university would be the determination of:
    a. Compliance with accepted accounting principles.
    b. Adequacy of the institution's budget process.
    c. Accuracy of financial reports.
    d. Approval for expenditure of restricted funds.

15. An audit of the purchasing function disclosed that orders were placed for materials which at that time were being disposed of as surplus. What corrective action should be recommended?
    a. Have all purchase requisitions approved by the responsible purchasing agent.
    b. Confirm all orders for replacement material with the user department.
    c. Employ a historical reorder point system.
    d. Develop and distribute periodic reports of surplus stocks.

16. An internal auditor would trace copies of sales invoices to shipping documents to determine that:
    a. Customer shipments were billed.
    b. Sales that are billed were also shipped.
    c. Shipments to customers were also recorded as receivables.
    d. The subsidiary accounts receivable ledger was updated.

17. Which technique is most appropriate for testing the quality of the preaudit of payment vouchers described in an internal control questionnaire?
    a. Analysis.
    b. Evaluation.
    c. Verification.
    d. Observation.

18. The internal audit department of a large corporation has established its operating plan and budget for the coming year. The operating plan is restricted to the following categories: a prioritized listing of all audits, staffing, a detailed expense budget, and the commencement date of each audit. Which of the following best describes the major deficiency of this operating plan?
    a. Requests by management for special projects are not considered.
    b. Opportunities to achieve operating benefits are ignored.
    c. Measurability criteria and targeted dates of completed are not provided.
    d. Knowledge, skills, and disciplines required to perform work are ignored.

19. A clerk's duties included comparing goods received with vendor shipping documents, authorizing payment for goods received, and updating online inventory totals. From time to time, the clerk removed small valuable items from the goods received, authorized payment for all items shipped, and manipulated inventory totals to match the goods actually added to inventory. The best preventive control over the clerk's unauthorized actions is:
    a. Separating the incompatible functions of access to goods received and authorization of payment of vouchers.
    b. Periodically reconciling quantities received with inventory transactions.
    c. Authorizing payment based on vendors' shipping documents.
    d. Requiring passwords for access to the online inventory system.

20. An operational audit of the production function includes an audit procedure to compare actual costs to standard costs. The purpose of this operational audit procedure is to:
    a. Determine the accuracy of the system used to record actual costs.
    b. Measure the effectiveness of the standard cost system.
    c. Assess the reasonableness of standard costs.
    d. Assist management in its evaluation of effectiveness and efficiency.

21. Management believes that some specific sales commissions for the year were too large. The accuracy of the recorded commission expense for specific salespersons is best determined by:
    a. Computation of selected sales commissions.
    b. Calculating commission ratios.
    c. Use of analytical procedures.
    d. Tests of overall reasonableness.

22. Factors that should be considered when evaluating audit risk in a functional area include:
    1. Volume of transactions.
    2. Degree of system integration.
    3. Years since last audit.
    4. Significant management turnover.
    5. (Dollar) value of "assets at risk."
    6. Average value per transaction.
    7. Results of last audit.
    Factors that **best** define materiality of audit risk are:
    a. 1 through 7.
    b. 2, 4, and 7.
    c. 1, 5, and 6.
    d. 3, 4, and 6.

23. Assuming all of the procedures below are satisfactorily performed, to test the valuation of receivables, the auditor should rely most on:
    a. Mailing positive confirmation requests.
    b. Completing an aging schedule of accounts receivable.
    c. Comparing the accounts receivable total with totals from prior periods.
    d. Recalculating the value of selected individual accounts receivable.

24. Analytical procedures, in which current financial statements are compared with budgets or previous statements, are primarily intended to determine:
    a. Adequacy of financial statement disclosure.
    b. Existence of specific errors or omissions.
    c. Overall reasonableness of statement contents.
    d. Use of an erroneous cutoff date.

25. To obtain evidence that no duplicate payments of accounts payable are made, an internal auditor would examine:
    a. Purchase orders for proper approval.
    b. Receiving documents to see whether goods were received.
    c. Approved vendor price lists to see whether the company paid the proper amount.
    d. Supporting documentation for cancellation when the check is written to the vendor.

Use the following information for questions 26 through 31.
Each audit objective listed in questions 26-31 is independent of the other audit objectives. Fill in the blank space with the letter designating the **single** best audit technique for meeting the audit objective specified. Make your selection from the audit techniques listed below.

Audit Techniques
a. Inspection of documents
b. Observation
c. Inquiry
d. Analytical review

Audit Objectives
26. Ascertain the reasonableness of the increases in rental revenue resulting from operating costs passed on to the lessee by the landlord. The auditor has already inspected the lease contract to determine that such costs are allowed.

    _____

27. Identify the existence of personality conflicts that are detrimental to productivity.

    _____

28. Determine whether research and development projects were properly authorized.

    _____

29. Ascertain compliance with city ordinance forbidding city purchasing from vendors affiliated with elected city officials.

    _____

30. Determine whether planned rate of return on investment in international operations has been achieved.

    _____

31. Determine whether mail room staff is fully utilized.

    _____

32. Directors may use a tool called "risk analysis" in preparing work schedules. Which of the following would not be considered in performing a risk analysis?
    a. Financial exposure and potential loss.
    b. Skills available on the audit staff.
    c. Results of prior audits.
    d. Major operating changes.

33. Which of the following audit objectives would be accomplished by tracing a sample of accounts receivable debit entries to customer invoices and related shipping documents?
    a. Sales are properly recorded.
    b. Sales are billed at the correct prices.
    c. Accounts receivable represent valid sales.
    d. Customer credit is approved.

34. An activity appropriately performed by the internal auditing department is:
    a. Designing systems of control.
    b. Crafting procedures for systems of control.
    c. Reviewing systems of control before implementation.
    d. Installing systems or control.

35. Divisional management stated that a recent gross margin increase was due to increased efficiency in manufacturing operations. Which of the following audit procedures would be most relevant to that assertion?
    a. Obtain a physical count of inventory.
    b. Select a sample of products and then compare costs-per-unit this year to those of last year, test cost buildups, and analyze standard cost variances.
    c. Take a physical inventory of equipment to determine if there were significant changes.
    d. Select a sample of finished goods inventory and trace raw materials cost back to purchase prices in order to determine the accuracy of the recorded raw materials price.

36. Which of the following measures would be most appropriate for an auditor to use in an audit of the efficiency of a motor vehicle inspection facility?
    a. The number of cars inspected per hour.
    b. The ratio of cars rejected to total cars inspected.
    c. The number of cars inspected per inspection agent.
    d. The average amount of fees collected per cashier.

37. Which of the following is not likely to be included as an audit step when assessing vendor performance?
    a. Determine whether vendors delivered desired lot sizes.
    b. Determine whether only authorized items were received from vendors.
    c. Determine whether the balances owed to vendors are correct.
    d. Determine whether the quality of the goods purchased from vendors has been satisfactory.

38. If a department's operating standards are vague and thus subject to interpretation, an auditor should:
    a. Seek agreement with the departmental manager as to the standards to be used to measure operating performance.
    b. Determine best practices in the area and use them as the standard.
    c. Interpret the standards in their strictest sense because standards are otherwise only minimum measures of acceptance.
    d. Omit any comments on standards and the department's performance in relationship to those standards, because such an analysis would be meaningless.

39. Which of the following is more likely to occur if receiving reports are not matched with purchase orders and invoices prior to payment for goods?
    a. Purchases might be made from unauthorized vendors.
    b. Available purchase discounts might not be taken.
    c. Untimely purchases might result in stockouts or oversupply.
    d. Payments might be made for goods that were not received.

40. Which of the following procedures would provide the best evidence of the effectiveness of a credit granting function?
    a. Observe the process.
    b. Review the trend in receivables write-offs.
    c. Ask the credit manager about the effectiveness of the function.
    d. Check for evidence of credit approval on a sample of customer orders.

41. An auditor plans to evaluate the adequacy of a company's insurance coverage. What is the most likely source of information for a detailed schedule of insurance policies in force?
    a. Original journal entries found in the cash disbursements journal and supported by canceled checks.
    b. The corporate charter prescribing the insurance staff's objectives, authority, and responsibilities.
    c. The current fiscal year's budget for prepaid insurance together with the beginning balance of the account.
    d. The files containing insurance polices with various carriers.

42. Which of the following statements is true about audit evidence?
   a. Physical observation provides the most reliable evidence of the existence of accounts receivable.
   b. Purchase orders are relevant evidence that goods paid for have been received.
   c. An appropriate conclusion about a population based on a sample requires that the sample be representative of the population.
   d. A copy of an original document is as reliable as the original document.

43. Competent evidence is best defined as evidence which:
   a. Is reasonably free from error and bias and faithfully represents that which it purports to represent.
   b. Is obtained by observing people, property, and events.
   c. Is supplementary to other evidence already gathered and which tends to strengthen or confirm it.
   d. Proves an intermediate fact, or group of facts, from which still other facts can be inferred.

44. An operational audit report that deals with the scrap disposal function in a manufacturing company should address:
   a. The efficiency and effectiveness of the scrap disposal function and include any findings requiring collective action.
   b. Whether the scrap material inventory is reported as a current asset.
   c. Whether the physical inventory count of scrap material agrees with the recorded amount.
   d. Whether the scrap material inventory is valued at the lower of cost or market.

45. To identify the amount of obsolete inventory that might exist, an internal auditor would probably collect evidence using all of the following except:
   a. Confirmation.
   b. Scanning.
   c. Recomputation.
   d. Analytical review.

46. In evaluating the validity of different types of audit evidence, which of the following conclusions is incorrect?
   a. Recomputation, though valid, is restricted in its usefulness due to its limited scope.
   b. The validity of documentary evidence is independent of the effectiveness of the control system in which it was created.
   c. Internally created documentary evidence is considered less valid than externally created documentary evidence.
   d. The validity of confirmations varies directly with the independence of the party receiving the confirmation.

47. Which type of evidence would be most convincing when evaluating the collectibility of accounts receivable?
    a. Positive accounts receivable confirmations.
    b. Negative accounts receivable confirmations.
    c. Aged accounts receivable listings.
    d. Shipping documents.

48. What is the appropriate source of information for determining if all goods shipped are billed to the customer?
    a. Prenumbered customer invoices.
    b. Accounts receivable files.
    c. Prenumbered shipping documents.
    d. Customer purchase orders.

49. To assess the quality of a preaudit of payroll vouchers, an auditor would most likely use:
    a. Analysis.
    b. Evaluation.
    c. Verification.
    d. Observation.

50. To be sufficient, audit evidence should be:
    a. Well-documented and cross-referenced in the workpapers.
    b. Based on references that are considered reliable.
    c. Directly related to the finding and include all of the elements of a finding.
    d. Convincing enough for a prudent person to reach the same conclusion as the auditor.

51. A letter in response to an auditor's inquiry is an example of:
    a. Physical evidence.
    b. Testimonial evidence.
    c. Documentary evidence.
    d. Analytical evidence.

52. Which of the following could contribute to discrepancies between receiving reports and the number of units in a shipment?
    a. Using inadequate vendor selection procedures.
    b. Showing quantities ordered on the receiving department's copy of purchase orders.
    c. Failing to compare the quality of goods received with specifications.
    d. Accepting improper authorization of purchases.

53. An auditor would most likely judge an error in an account balance to be material if the error involves:
    a. A clerical mistake that is unlikely to occur again.
    b. A large percentage of net income.
    c. An unverified routine transaction.
    d. An unusual transaction for the organization.

54. Which of the following is an example of internal documentary evidence?
    a. A carrier's bill of lading.
    b. A sales invoice copy.
    c. A customer's purchase order.
    d. A vendor's month-end statement.

55. In evaluating the quality of housekeeping services performed in a large hospital, the most reliable source of evidence would be:
    a. Interviews with a sample of medical personnel.
    b. A review of survey forms returned by medical personnel directly to the manager of housekeeping services.
    c. A review of housekeeping records maintained by the medical records department of the hospital.
    d. Interviews with top hospital officials.

56. While interviewing a data input clerk, an auditor identifies a potentially significant weakness in a system. The auditor should:
    a. Avoid any further mention of the weakness.
    b. Ask indirect questions that will help elicit more factual information relating to the potential weakness.
    c. Ask the clerk about the weakness and determine immediately if the finding should be reported.
    d. Schedule a second interview and use other means to determine if the weakness actually exists.

57. Data gathering activities such as interviewing operating personnel, identifying standards to be used to evaluate performance, and assessing risks inherent in a department's operations are typically performed in which phase of an audit?
    a. Field work.
    b. Preliminary survey.
    c. Audit program development.
    d. Examining and evaluating evidence.

58. Which of the following would not be considered a primary objective of a closing or exit conference?
   a. To resolve conflicts.
   b. To discuss the audit findings.
   c. To identify concerns for future audits.
   d. To identify management's actions and responses to the findings.

Chapter 8
Audit Findings

The nature of audit findings. Standards. Suggestions for improvement. Reportable audit findings. Approach to finding construction. Adding value. Degrees of significance. Elements of an audit finding. Discussing findings. Record of audit findings. Communication skills. Supervisory reviews. Reporting audit findings. Follow-up. Adequacy of corrective action. Authority and audit status.

• •

The Nature of Audit Findings

During the course of their work, internal auditors identify conditions that require corrective action. These deviations from norms or acceptable criteria are called audit findings.

Audit findings come in all shapes and sizes. For example, they can describe:

- Actions that should have been taken, but were not, such as shipments that were made but not billed.

- Prohibited actions, such as an employee's diversion of rented equipment to a personal contracting firm for his own benefit.

- Improper actions, such as paying for goods and supplies at rates that had been superseded by a more favorable contract specifying lower rates.

- Unsatisfactory systems, such as processes whereby uncollected insurance claims receive equal follow-up action despite wide variances in amount and significance.

- Risk exposures that should be considered.

Although audit findings are sometimes referred to as "deficiencies," many internal audit organizations find that term too negative; and the original *Standards* seemed to agree (see 430.04.). In fact, even the term "findings" is considered too negative in some environments. Words like "conditions" are considered to be less threatening and much less likely to evoke a defensive attitude on the part of the client.

While the appellations may vary from one organization to another, the basic concepts are universal. Whatever name it is given, an audit finding describes something that was or is wrong, or something that is likely to go wrong.

Standards

The *Standards for the Professional Practice of Internal Auditing* in Standard 2310 state:

> Internal auditors should identify sufficient, reliable, relevant, and useful information to achieve the engagements objective.

The *Standards'* Practice Advisory 2410-1, "Communication Criteria," expands this directive in the following:

2. Engagement final communications may include background information and summaries. Background information may identify the organizational units and activities reviewed and provide relevant explanatory information. They may also include the status of observations, conclusions, and recommendations from prior reports. There may also be an indication of whether the report covers a scheduled engagement or the response to a request. Summaries, if included, should be balanced representations of the engagement communication's content.

5. Results should include observations, conclusions (opinions), recommendations, and action plans.

6. Observations are pertinent statements of fact. Those observations necessary to support or prevent misunderstanding of the internal auditor's conclusions and recommendations should be included in the final engagement communications. Less significant observations or recommendations may be communicated informally.

7. Engagement observations and recommendations emerge by a process of comparing what should be with what is. Whether or not there is a difference, the internal auditor has a foundation on which to build the report. When conditions meet the criteria, acknowledgment in the engagement communications of satisfactory performance may be appropriate. Observations and recommendations should be based on the following attributes:

   - Criteria: The standards, measures, or expectations used in making an evaluation and/or verification (what should exist).

   - Condition: The factual evidence that the internal auditor found in the course of the examination (what does exist).

- Cause: The reason for the difference between the expected and actual conditions (why the difference exists).

- Effect: The risk or exposure the organization and/or others encounter because the condition is not the same as the criteria (the impact of the difference). In determining the degree of risk or exposure, internal auditors should consider the effect their engagement observations and recommendations may have on the organization's financial statements.

- Observations and recommendations may also include engagement client accomplishments, related issues, and supportive information if not included elsewhere.

Relative to the actual reporting, the *Standards'* Practice Advisory 2420-1, "Quality of Communication Criteria," has this to say:

1. Objective communications are factual, unbiased, and free from distortion. Observations, conclusions, and recommendations should be included without prejudice.

2. Clear communications are easily understood and logical. Clarity can be improved by avoiding unnecessary technical language and providing sufficient supportive information.

3. Concise communications are to the point and avoid unnecessary detail. They express thoughts completely in the fewest possible words.

4. Constructive communications are those which, as a result of their content and tone, help the engagement client and the organization and lead to improvements where needed.

5. Timely communications are those that are issued without undue delay and enable prompt effective action.

Suggestions for Improvement

Auditors also encounter transactions or conditions that may not be intrinsically wrong, but could be improved. Paying for products that were never received is just plain wrong, for example. If enough money is involved, it is clearly a reportable audit finding. On the other hand, a receiving memo form that could be simplified should not be considered defective — and hence is not an audit finding — especially when the internal auditor cannot point to errors in the processing of receipts.

Operating managers would find it hard to dispute that payments for goods not received must be considered as valid audit findings. It would be unfair, however, to apply the same label to suggestions for simplifying the receiving memo that had caused no errors. Such improvements should come under a separate classification. In some organizations these are reported as "suggestions for improvement." They do not warrant recommendations for the correction of defects and do not carry the faultfinding connotation of audit findings.

In distinguishing audit findings from suggestions for improvement, the auditor must ask whether the condition is contrary to some acceptable criteria, or if it is acceptable but capable of being improved because new knowledge about the subject has come to light. The dividing line between the two is not always easy to draw. Operating managers may seek to persuade the internal auditor that a particular finding merely represents an opportunity to improve an otherwise satisfactory condition, whereas the internal auditor may see it as a defect and hence an audit finding. The decision is a matter of professional judgment, and that judgment may not be relinquished to operating managers.

Audit findings require corrective action. The operating manager can be given no option on whether or not to take the action. On the other hand, a suggestion to improve a condition, one that does not violate some established rule or criterion, is another matter. In such cases managers should have the right to decide whether or not to implement the suggestion.

Reportable Audit Findings

Not every defect identified by an internal auditor should be reported. Some are minor and not worthy of management attention. All reportable audit findings should be:

- Significant enough to deserve being reported to management.
- Documented by facts, not opinions, and by evidence that is sufficient, competent, and relevant.
- Objectively developed without bias or preconceived ideas.
- Relevant to the issue involved.
- Convincing enough to compel action to correct the defective condition.

Obviously these characteristics will be interpreted subjectively. What seems to be a significant deviation to one individual may appear to be insignificant to another. Words like objective, convincing, reasonable, and logical have different connotations to different people.

The test is to project how the defect would be regarded by a reasonable, prudent person under the same or similar circumstances. As they appraise a deficient condition, internal auditors must ask themselves: "If this were my organization or agency, and if I were its president or director appraising this condition, what would I do about it?"

Approach to Finding Construction

Developing facts and details into a significant, reportable audit finding is an acquired skill. It requires discrimination based on experience. What may seem like a serious shortcoming to a layperson may be a trifling deviation to a professional internal auditor.

Finding minor deviations in any ongoing process is relatively simple. Perfection is rare and its price is often far too high. The effort needed to achieve the last five percent of purity can well exceed the cost of achieving the first 95 percent. Internal auditors must be realistic and fair in their judgments and conclusions. They must bring good business sense to the development of their findings. As they pursue the development and reporting of audit findings, internal auditors should consider these factors:

- Applying hindsight to management decisions can be unfair and unrealistic. Internal auditors should consider the circumstances existing at the time the defect occurred. Management decisions are based on currently available facts. Internal auditors should not criticize a decision merely because they disagree with it or because they have new information that was not available to the decision maker. Internal auditors should not substitute audit judgment for management judgment.

- The auditor, not the client, must assume the burden of proof. If an audit finding has not been thoroughly proved to the satisfaction of an objective, reasonable person, it is not reportable.

- Internal auditors should certainly be interested in improvements in performance, but performance does not necessarily deserve reported criticism because it is less than 100 percent.

- Internal auditors should play the devil's advocate with developed audit findings. They should scrutinize their discovery for possible flaws and fallacious reasoning. Internal auditors, like any other proponents of a proposition, are tempted to rationalize interpretations that will support their findings. After investing a great deal of time and effort, the auditor tends to protect the investment and defend the finding against perfectly logical questions. But those findings may not stand the test of time or rigorous questioning.

Adding Value

In every aspect of business, the concept of adding value has taken on new and emphatic meaning. The recent definition of internal auditing is specific in its mention of adding value. Functions that are perceived as non-value-adding are at risk of being downsized, or even eliminated. One of the ways internal auditors add value is by making sure that the findings and recommendations they present clearly have a positive impact on the organization. Not only must internal auditors be certain that their work contributes in meaningful ways to the goals and success of the organization, they must also be sure that those contributions are understood and valued by others.

Findings that result from "front-end" reviews are likely to be especially beneficial. If internal auditors are able to detect potential control problems in a new computerized inventory-tracking system before — rather than after — it is designed and implemented, the organization gains big dividends. Findings that generate the greatest value often unleash the power of technology, promote positive change, and are future-oriented. They help the organization to move forward and attain its goals.

Sound audit findings can result in hard dollar recoveries, or improved service, or they can improve organizational structures and processes. In both cases, internal auditors will enhance their image as value-adders, rather than as resource consumers. Throughout the audit finding phase, it is important for internal auditors to maintain focus on providing high-value activities and services.

Degrees of Significance

No two findings are exactly the same. Each will represent a unique degree of actual or potential loss or risk. Placing the same emphasis on random clerical errors as on an overpayment of $100,000 is clearly illogical. So internal auditors should consider the degree of damage a deficient condition can cause or has caused before communicating that condition to management. For most purposes, audit findings can be classified as insignificant, minor, or major.

Insignificant Findings

An insignificant finding — the sort of clerical misstep that all organizations experience — does not warrant formal action. In fact, including such a finding in a formal audit report would be counterproductive because it would tarnish the truly significant findings in the report, implying that the internal auditor could not discern the difference between a mere flyspeck and a spreading blot. It would also perpetuate an undesirable stereotype: the internal auditor as a nitpicker.

Insignificant items should not be hidden or overlooked. The acceptable course of action is to (1) discuss the item with the individual responsible; (2) see that the situation is corrected; (3) note the matter in the working papers; and (4) keep such slight deviations out of the formal internal audit report. The failure of an accounts payable clerk, who knows better, to take a few random discounts here and there could be considered an insignificant error.

This is not to suggest that random clerical errors should never be reported. If those errors are symptomatic of a larger problem, reporting might be warranted. The errors might indicate poor employee training, ineffective supervision, or unclear written instructions. In such cases it is these control deficiencies that constitute the audit finding. The random errors are merely evidence that the deficiency exists and needs management attention.

Minor Findings

A minor audit finding requires reporting because it is more than a random human error. If not corrected, it will continue to have adverse effects; and while it may not thwart a major operating objective of the organization, it is of sufficient significance to bring to the attention of management. Some minor findings would be better reported in what is termed a Management Letter.

An employee who has commingled personal and organization petty cash violates both organization rules and good business practice. Certainly the matter should be reported and corrected; otherwise, it might continue or become widespread.

Major Findings

A major finding is one that would prevent an organization or a unit within an organization from meeting a major objective. For example, a major objective for an accounts payable department is to pay only what is rightfully due. A defective system of control that resulted in, or could result in, payment errors totaling $500,000 represents a defect that could bar the department from meeting a major objective. Therefore, it is a major audit finding and should be so reported.

The line between major and minor findings can become exceedingly fine. Good audit judgment is required to discriminate between the two. But if the benchmarks just described are reasonably applied, internal auditors should be able to defend their classification of findings. And since audit judgment is involved, the final decision about whether a finding should be classified as major or minor lies with the internal auditor. This is not a determination to be relinquished to management.

Elements of an Audit Finding

Internal auditors are not omniscient, and they cannot be expected to know all there is to know about the operations being audited. Knowledge about a reportable audit finding is something else again, since the internal auditors are disputing the propriety of the status quo. They are singling out some system or transaction that did not meet acceptable operating standards. Internal auditors can expect to be challenged, however; and they should know as much about their findings as anyone else. Internal auditors' facts should be unassailable; their criteria should be acceptable; and their logic should be convincing.

The propriety of any action is best measured by comparing it with some criterion of acceptability. The development of an audit finding is no different. If the developed finding meets all acceptable audit standards, it will be logical, reasonable, and compelling. It will provide a stimulus for motivating corrective action. If something is missing from the reported finding, it may be disputed and result in grudging action or even no action at all.

Most reportable audit findings should include certain elements, including background, criteria, condition, cause, effect, conclusions, and recommendation. Any audit finding that properly includes these elements, either explicitly or implicitly, will present a strong argument for corrective action. It will demonstrate that no stone was left unturned in demonstrating the problem and proposing a solution. In some unique cases, the element, "cause" may not be appropriate. A problem may be the result of a specific condition.

Background

The reader must be provided with enough general information relative to the situation to completely understand the reasons why the auditor believes the finding should be reported. Background can also identify the players, the organization's relationships, and even, to a degree, objectives and goals concerned. It should describe, in a general sense, the environment surrounding the operation and the gravity of the situation that prompts the auditor to report the finding.

Criteria

The development of an audit finding must include two key elements in the concept of criteria:

(1) Goals and objectives, possibly including operating standards, that represent what management wants the audited operation to accomplish.

(2) The quality of the accomplishment.

Not understanding the goals or objectives of an operation is like appraising a sculpture while blindfolded. It's possible to have some appreciation for the part touched, but there is no sense of context. In developing an audit finding, internal auditors must clearly see and understand the big picture, as well as its elements.

In any audit of an activity, the goals of propriety, efficiency, economy, and effectiveness are implied: All resources should be used with a minimum of waste. To determine how proper, how efficient, how economical, and how effective an operation is, internal auditors must have yardsticks — standards of measurement. They must identify valid standards or criteria of performance. Before they can criticize what is, they must know what should be.

Operating standards may already exist in some areas of the organization. For example, management may have decreed that the rejection rate for certain products should not exceed two percent. Before accepting the standard, however, the internal auditor should appraise its validity. The basis for the standard may need to be researched; and the auditor may want to compare standards with those in similar organizations and examine their reasonableness in meeting enterprise goals.

On the other hand, management may not yet have established standards. In that case, the internal auditors can be guided by a former standard which suggested:

> Due professional care includes evaluating established operating standards and determining whether those standards are acceptable and are being met. When such standards are vague, authoritative interpretations should be sought. If internal auditors are required to interpret or select operating standards, they should seek agreement with clients as to the standards needed to measure operating performance.

Sources of standards may include engineered, industry, historical, or mandated standards. In addition, expert opinions and cost accounting studies may provide standards. The following example illustrates an established operating standard:

> Water meters in a community are installed to measure water. To obtain the revenue needed to maintain the water distribution system, the meters should be accurate and charge customers for the right amount of water used. Water meters in use should not vary from a master meter by more than a stated percentage. In this case, the percentage was set forth in legal requirements.

Standards are closely linked with procedures and practices. Procedures are management instructions, which are generally in written form, while practices are the way things are being done, whether right or wrong. Poor procedures may contribute to an unsatisfactory condition, or poor practices may violate an adequate procedure. In developing audit findings, internal auditors should seek to determine what the practices and procedures are or should be.

The existence of faulty procedures or the absence of proper procedures may be the reason behind the need for corrective action. Yet it takes considerable skill to write about them without making dull reading. Only the highlights should be reported, leaving out unessential detail. For example:

The auditors found no written operating procedures against which they could compare conditions, but the operating practices violated good business practice. People spent only part days on the job. Supervision was poor, and the functioning of the meters was not being checked. Accordingly, the auditors developed their own standards, based on acceptable administrative procedures and information gleaned from other organizations in the same field. Their audit was then dedicated to showing the results of inadequate procedures and recommending ways of improving them.

Condition

The term "condition" refers to the facts determined by the internal auditor's observation, questions, analysis, verification, and investigation. The condition is the heart of the finding, and the information about it should be sufficient, competent, and relevant. It must be able to withstand any attack. It must be representative of the total population or system under review; or, if an isolated instance, it should be a significant defect. The clients should agree with the facts presented, though they may dispute the significance the auditor attaches to them.

Clients may disagree with audit conclusions and interpretations, but there should never be any disagreement with the facts on which the conclusions are based. A finding may not be considered properly developed if the client can validly assert that the internal auditors did not get their facts right. All else becomes irrelevant. Thus, conditions should be discussed early on with those in a position to know the facts. Any disputes about the facts should be resolved before the finding is reported. Internal auditors must maintain a reputation for accuracy and live up to the observation that "If the internal auditor says it, then it must be true."

The following example illustrates a reported condition:

> Internal auditors used random sampling to select meters for testing. The meters selected were replaced and were then subjected to laboratory tests. The tests showed that 17 percent of the tested meters did not work at all and that an additional 23 percent ran slower than the standards specified by legal requirements.

Cause

The underlying cause explains why there are deviations from the criteria, why goals are not met, and why objectives are not attained. Identification of the cause is essential to the cure. Every audit finding can be traced to a departure from what is expected. Only when the departures are identified and their causes are known can the problem be solved.

Determining cause is a problem-solving exercise, and the process follows classic steps:

- Gather the facts.
- Identify the problem; look for the deviation.
- Specify the particulars of the problem. What is the deviation? Where is the deviation? When did it occur? How significant is it? Was it caused by some action or some inaction?
- Test for possible causes — those that completely explain the deviation, make it happen every time, and answer all parts of the deviations. Look for causes that are basic, not merely on the surface.
- Set out the objectives of potential corrective action.
- Compare alternative actions with the objectives and tentatively select the best.
- Think of the adverse circumstances that the selected corrective action triggers.
- Consider the "what ifs." For example, what effect would it have if supervisors were sent out to see that inspectors stay on the job until the proper quitting time?
- Are there any mitigating circumstances?
- Recommend controls to make sure that the best action is actually carried out.

The following example targets the cause of an improper condition:

Using multiple regression analysis, the auditors established a definite correlation between the operating conditions of the meters and their age. When the meters had been in operation for a certain number of years, they had a tendency to slow down and gradually fail. After talking to managers of other utility organizations, the auditors determined that the practices followed in their organization were not calculated to focus on aging meters, make the best use of inspectors, make inspectors alert to meters that were failing, or provide needed supervision.

Effect

Effect answers the "so what" question. Assuming that all the facts are as represented, so what? Who or what gets hurt, and how badly? What are the consequences? Those adverse results should be significant — not merely some deviation from procedures. Effect is the element needed to convince clients and higher management that the undesirable condition, if permitted to continue, will cause serious harm and would cost more than the action needed to correct the problem.

In economy and efficiency findings, the effect is usually measured in dollars. In effectiveness findings, the effect is usually the inability to accomplish some desired or mandated end result. Effect is the convincer. It is indispensable to an audit finding. If it is not adequately presented to management the chances are slim that corrective action will be taken.

The following example shows a significant effect:

> The internal auditors were able to demonstrate by their sample that $2 million in revenues were being lost each year. They were also able to show that water rates were unnecessarily high, resulting in excess revenue of at least $1.5 million annually.

Conclusions

Conclusions must be buttressed by the facts; but they are professional judgments, not a recitation of details. In developing their conclusions, internal auditors clearly have an opportunity to demonstrate their unique contributions to the organization. When internal auditors consistently present conclusions that can lead to new and higher levels of performance, reduce costs and improve production quality, eliminate needless work, exploit the power of technology, elevate customer satisfaction, improve service, and enhance the competitive position of the organization, the value of internal auditing is obvious. Conclusions can underscore the auditor's understanding of the business of the organization and the relationship of the audited function to the entire enterprise.

Conclusions can and should present potential courses of action and point out that the cost of correcting the defects will be exceeded by the benefits. The extent of losses shown in the effects are a springboard to the need for corrective action. For example:

> The findings led the auditors to conclude that the procedures should be improved. Meters over a certain age should be monitored, and those that do not meet standards should be replaced. Instruction and surveillance should be provided for inspectors so their performance can be boosted.

Recommendations

Recommendations describe the course of action management might consider to rectify conditions that have gone awry, and to strengthen weaknesses in systems of control. Recommendations should be positive and as specific as possible. They should also identify who is to act on them.

Audit recommendations carry the seeds of danger, however. If management is told that the course recommended by the auditors is the course to take, the action when taken can return to haunt the auditors. Identifying an unsatisfactory condition is an audit responsibility. Correcting that condition is a management responsibility.

It is preferable that internal auditors propose methods of corrective action for management's consideration. Audit recommendations should not be blindly taken, but considered, along with other possible courses. Internal auditors do not dictate to management; and, in the end, management, not the internal auditor, must live with the corrective action.

The most satisfactory means of resolving an audit finding is to discuss it with operating management before the written audit report is published. At that time, agreement should be reached on the facts and on some reasonable course of action to correct the defect. Thereafter, the formal report could contain a statement along these lines: "We discussed our findings with management; and, as a result, action was taken that we believe is calculated to correct the condition described (or action was taken that corrected the condition described)." This approach takes nothing away from the auditor, and it builds a problem-solving partnership between auditor and client.

We are firmly convinced that this form of reporting is preferable to a set of audit recommendations that seem to emphasize client derelictions and display the auditor as some superior, omniscient creature issuing proclamations engraved in granite. For example:

> We discussed our findings and conclusions with management personnel. As a result, management took action to replace 25,000 aging or inoperative meters at a cost of $1 million. Management was satisfied that this action would yield $2 million a year in additional revenue and, at the same time, reduce water rates revenue by about $1.5 million annually.

> Also, management took steps to dispatch a team to several utility organizations, where they were to study the methods employed in inspecting meters, supervising meter inspection, and monitoring meters to detect those that were beginning to deteriorate.

Discussing Findings

When they develop their audit findings and contemplate their recommendations, internal auditors must be aware of their own fallibility. They may not have interpreted conditions correctly, or they may not have read procedures as intended. To check their understanding of what they found, internal auditors should talk with those most likely to know the facts. They should seek the client's interpretations and note them in the working papers.

The opinions of managers and experienced employees concerning the results of recommended action are especially welcome. The experienced internal auditor will seek out knowledgeable people in the organization — people with a wide-ranging grasp of the operations in question — and say: "Here's the problem. The condition needs correction or improvement. What would happen if we recommended this course of action?" Many a veteran auditor can recount tales of how such questions saved them embarrassment.

Record of Audit Findings

Internal auditors who want to make sure they have fully considered the elements of an audit finding may want to rely on a form or some other device for keeping themselves on track. The form can also provide supervisors with a means for determining whether all steps needed to produce a properly developed audit finding were taken.

The Internal Audit Activity Record of Audit Finding shown in Exhibit 8-1 provides one example of such a form. It serves the purposes described and provides space for:

- Identifying the organization responsible.
- Providing an identifying number for the particular finding and a reference to the supporting working papers.
- Giving a brief statement of condition.
- Identifying the standards criteria applied in assessing the condition.
- Indicating whether the finding was a repetition of something found in a prior audit.
- Citing the directive, procedure, or job instruction involved in the finding.
- Summarizing the audit tests and the number of discrepancies found.
- Showing the causes — why the deviation occurred.
- Explaining the effect, actual or potential, of the condition.
- Stating the corrective action proposed and/or taken.
- Recording the discussions with client personnel and noting their comments (agree, disagree), and the nature of the action, if any, they propose to take.

The Record of Audit Findings (RAF) form provides flexibility in that a number of RAFs can be sorted and re-sorted to facilitate formal reporting. The form also provides a ready reference for discussion, since it captures on one sheet most of the information needed to describe the problem. It also functions as a guide to remind auditors of all that is necessary to obtain the information for a thoroughly developed finding. The RAF should be completed in the field so that any elements that are missing or incomplete can be corrected without requiring a return visit to the audit site.

Some organizations have expanded the use of the RAF beyond a working paper document. They use it to communicate the finding promptly to the client and to obtain written comments. In this way, disagreements can be more readily resolved, and promises of corrective action can be made a matter of record. The client's response and the record of action taken or promised are contained in an attachment to the RAF (Exhibit 8-2).

Exhibit 8-1
Internal Audit Activity Record of Audit Findings
Example 1

Organization _____   RAF No. _____
                                                           W/P Ref. _____

Condition _____
_____
_____

Standards _____
_____
_____

Same finding last examination: Yes _____   No _____

Procedures or practices _____
_____
_____

Method of sample selection _____

Pop. size _____   Sample size _____   No. of discrepancies _____   % of sample _____

Causes _____
_____

Effect _____
_____

Recommendation _____
_____

Corrective action _____
_____

Discussions:

	Name	Title	Department	Date	Auditor
(1)					
Comments					
(2)					
Comments					
(3)					
Comments					
(4)					
Comments					

_____   _____
                    Auditor   Date

_____   _____
                   Supervisor   Date

Exhibit 8-1
Internal Audit Activity Record of Audit Findings
Example 2

INTERNAL AUDIT ACTIVITY

Subject: Automated Underwriting System
Area of Responsibility: Personal Lines Underwriting

Responsible Officers:
Ron Smith, John Miller

Auditors: Frank Bossle,   **Hours:** 400
Ed McCaulley

Scope:
◆ Reviewed the system development process used in the development and implementation of the Automated Underwriting System (AUS).
◆ Reviewed processing of new business, renewal, and endorsement transactions through the AUS, including the underwriting procedures for accepting, modifying, or rejecting risks suspended by the AUS to an underwriter.
◆ Reviewed the testing and implementation of programming changes required by the AUS to the Personal Lines system (IMPACT).
◆ Reviewed system interfaces with IMPACT affecting AUS (e.g., ordering of VAP, MVR, and CLUE reports).
◆ Reviewed the development, testing, implementation, and change control process for the tables containing the underwriting rules by state.

Overall Risk Exposure:
(After Considering Controls)

■ LOW
☐ Moderate
☐ High

Audit Conclusion:

☐ Exemplary
☐ Satisfactory
■ SATISFACTORY, NEEDS IMPROVEMENT
☐ Unsatisfactory

Audit Comments:
◆ The AUS Implementation Team has delivered the AUS two weeks ahead of schedule and within budget.
◆ The corporate system development process was followed closely during system development. The final version of the AUS system and all programming changes to IMPACT were thoroughly tested before being moved into production.
◆ New business, renewal, and endorsement transactions are being filtered through the AUS. The AUS is appropriately suspending transactions to underwriters which violate the defined underwriting templates. Underwriters follow well-defined procedures for accepting, modifying, or rejecting these risks.
◆ System interfaces with IMPACT affecting AUS are working as designed.

Significant Audit Recommendations:
◆ The underwriting tables need to be moved into a secure production environment. Additionally, change control authority over the tables needs to be defined by Personal Lines Underwriting management. Refer to Corrective Action Plan (CAP) 95-11 for further details.

Management Response:

■ ACCEPTS   **Date all recommendations will be implemented:** 12/31/95
☐ Disagrees

Planned Follow-up by Management and Internal Audit:
Internal audit will check to see that AUS tables are moved into a secure production environment and that change control procedures over them are defined.

Reprinted with permission from *Internal Auditor*, April 1997.

Exhibit 8-2
Internal Audit Activity
Record of Audit Finding
Comments and Action

Management Comments

(Use reverse side for additional comments)

Name: Title: Date:

Corrective action:

Effective date of corrective action _____

Name: Title: Date:

Auditor's appraisal:
Proposed action satisfactory _____   Unsatisfactory _____

Auditor: Date:

Follow-up of corrective action:

Auditor: Date:

Results of corrective action (evaluated during subsequent audit)

Auditor Supervisor: Date:

Exhibit 8-3
Abstract of Findings

Office: Northeast District
Subject: Travel Expenses
Report Title: Fiscal Accounting

Condition: Travel advances exceeded prescribed maximum amounts allowed. We found that 133 of 175 accounts exceeded the allowable maximum advance of $2,500. These excessive balances ranged from $2,640 to $4,750. The excess totaled about $300,000.

Criteria: Company policy provides advance travel funds to employees authorized to travel. Advances are not to exceed expenses anticipated for a period of 45 days. Normal per diem rates are $50. Thus, the maximum for 45 days is $2,250. An additional amount up to $250 may be included to over estimated mileage when travelers use their personally owned automobiles.

Cause: Company procedures do not require specific justification for large travel advances. The Fiscal Accounting Office relies primarily on employees' supervisors to make sure advances do not exceed needs. Inconsistencies can occur because requests are approved by different supervisors, and none of them follow the same rules.

Effect: Employees can and do accumulate large, unneeded advances. These accumulations can adversely affect the company's cash position. In addition, collections become difficult when employees holding large advances leave the company. Fiscal Accounting is now in the process of trying to collect over $15,000 from employees no longer with the company.

Management's response   The accounting activity will compare travel claims with outstanding advances to identify employees with advances in excess of needs. Those employees will be required to justify the amounts advanced to them or reduce the advances to the amounts of their actual expenses. Supervisors will be given specific instruction about the amounts of advances they are authorized to approve.

_____
Audit Manager

Some organizations issue a memorandum for each significant audit finding to report condition, criteria, cause, effect, and management's response. The "Abstract of Finding," reproduced in Exhibit 8-3, for example, was adapted from a government agency report on a contractor audit. These memorandums are given wide distribution throughout the agency. Proponents of such abstracts report that they offer many benefits:

- Senior managers are given a quick means of learning about current problems and the action taken or needed to resolve them.

- Managers in field offices are kept informed of problems likely to affect them as well; thus, internal auditing is able to reach several areas with the same expenditure of resources.

- The abstracts are analyzed periodically to disclose trends. When brought to senior management's attention, overall action can be taken to reverse adverse trends. A relatively minor problem in one office may become serious if it crops up in many offices.

- The discipline of preparing abstracts before writing the audit report helps internal auditors pinpoint any shortcomings in the development of their audit findings. Care in preparing abstracts eases the subsequent preparation of the final audit report.

- A central review of abstracts helps to maintain a quality assurance program designed to improve internal auditing.

Communication Skills

Even brief statements such as those that appear in the RAF should be well written, and problems must be clearly defined in concise, precise terms. When possible, the language of the RAF should be couched in positive tones, and terms that incite emotional or defensive reactions should be avoided. Of course, the same attitude should also prevail in day-to-day verbal communication and interim presentations of audit results.

At the same time, auditors must often deal with sensitive, negative issues. Serious control problems, fraud, or illegal acts will always be regarded as bad news, regardless of the auditor's communication abilities or the objectivity of the RAF.

Supervisory Reviews

Audit supervision remains the key control over the professional development of audit findings. Each reportable finding should be subjected to close supervisory review, either manual or electronic, and the review should be evidenced by the supervisor's signature or electronic indication of approval.

Nothing reduces the credibility of an internal audit activity so much as an ineptly developed finding that collapses under attack. An audit finding is by definition a criticism. The natural defensive mechanism of those criticized often prompts a counterattack on the critic. Audit findings must therefore be beyond reproach. Audit supervisors can see that the desired end is accomplished by approaching any audit finding with these questions:

- Are any elements of the finding missing? Why? What can be done to seek out the missing elements? Are these defects a result of poor presentation or of incomplete audit work?

- Are the elements so mixed up that clarity is clouded? Are opinions substituted for facts? Are causes confused with effect? Are recommendations simply a recital of facts?

- When procedures have not been followed, are recommendations merely a lame statement that the procedures should be followed? Or do they show why the procedures were not followed? In other words, would it be more useful to recommend clearer instructions, closer supervision, more constant monitoring, or other means of control that will promptly identify deviations from procedures?

- Are the audit criteria credible, clear, convincing, and objective? Are they designed to meet a management goal? Do they make good sense?

- Is information on the causes complete, or is it superficial? Is the cause a logical conclusion? Does it go to the heart of the problem? Will the cause trigger the same undesirable effect each time? Is the cause superficial, or is it basic?

- Is the effect exaggerated? Is it logical? Is it understated? Is it sufficiently quantified? Are intangibles adequately recognized and sufficiently explained? Does operating management agree with the reported effect? If not, what is its position?

- Are there mitigating circumstances that could render the finding null and void? Can these circumstances be neutralized?

- Is the recommendation useful and specific, or does it merely say "improve controls"? Is it too rigid, insisting on the internal auditor's course of action? Does it address the past but ignore the future? Is it punitive rather than constructive? Is it out of harmony with the cause? Does it include a means of monitoring conditions so that the adverse effects will not recur?

- Do the methods of presentation agree with the *Standards*?

Reporting Audit Findings

RAFs and abstracts have been put to uses beyond recording a finding or communicating it to the client. In fact, some audit organizations have made these summaries the primary basis for the internal audit report. They are accumulated in a logical order grouped by subject, location, or audited unit and then submitted to management by means of a one-page executive summary. The summary briefly describes the scope of the audit, offers an overall audit opinion, and provides the auditor's assessment of the operation audited. The executive summary also briefly lists the reportable findings. The documented findings are represented by the RAFs or abstracts.

This form of reporting concentrates on defects. It does offer the advantage of prompt reporting after the field work has been completed, but what is gained in speedy reporting may be lost in unfavorable auditor-client relations. The auditor may take on the aspect of a carping critic, rather than an objective observer who is concerned with both the good and the bad. This adverse effect could be balanced by overall objective comments in the executive summary. It could also be neutralized by interim discussions of the RAF with the client.

Follow-up

Views are not unanimous about auditors' responsibility with regard to follow-up. Some writers and practitioners take the position that internal auditors identify deficient conditions and that it is up to management to take the corrective action, determine its adequacy, and monitor its effectiveness. However, this view is not consistent with the broader description of internal audit responsibilities as stated in the introduction to the *Standards*:

Internal auditing is an independent, objective assurance and consulting activity designed to add value and improve an organization's operation.

Implicit in that statement is the responsibility to identify and report on both actual and potential risks to the enterprise. Internal auditors who are aware of defects and risks are required to report them to appropriate levels of management.

The current *Standards* 2500.A1 state that:

> The chief audit executive should establish a follow-up process to monitor and ensure that management actions have been effectively implemented or that senior management has accepted the risk of not taking action.

The *Standards'* Practice Advisory 2500.A1-1, "Follow-up Process," further states:

2. Follow-up by internal auditors is defined as a process by which they determine the adequacy, effectiveness, and timeliness of actions taken by management on reported engagement observations and recommendations. Such observations and recommendations also include those made by external auditors and others. *(Source: Red Book* 440.01.1)

3. Responsibility for follow-up should be defined in the internal audit activity's written charter. The nature, timing, and extent of follow-up should be determined by the chief audit executive. Factors that should be considered in determining appropriate follow-up procedures are:

   - The significance of the reported observation or recommendation.
   - The degree of effort and cost needed to correct the reported condition.
   - The risks that may occur should the corrective action fail.
   - The complexity of the corrective action.
   - The time period involved.

A reported deficiency, accepted as valid by management, has obviously described a risk to the enterprise. The condition remains a risk until it has been fully corrected. Failing to monitor that risk until it is corrected, or until senior management or the board has stated it will assume the risk, must be regarded as the abandonment of an audit responsibility.

Another argument against allowing auditors to follow up on corrective action is that they are staff and not line. The statement is obviously true, and internal auditors should not take on line functions. But following up on corrective action is not a line function. It is a staff function designed to assess the actions of the line functions. Internal auditors are carrying out their own responsibility by appraising the performance of the line function in reducing risks to the enterprise.

Adequacy of Corrective Action

Audit findings and the action needed to implement them come in such a great variety of shapes and sizes that no rigid rules for the appropriateness of corrective action would apply in all instances. In general, corrective action should be:

- Responsive to the reported defect.
- Complete in correcting all material aspects of the defect.
- Continuing in its effectiveness.
- Monitored to prevent recurrence.

In the following example, corrective action did not meet these four criteria:

An organization used various forms of explosives in its operations. The handling of explosives, as one might expect, required care and experience. That lesson was learned when a careless, untrained worker blew off his own arm and blinded a co-worker.

Thereafter it became organization policy for all explosives handlers to complete a course on the subject, acquire certification in explosives handling, and carry a card attesting to their certification. The handlers were to be recertified each year after being tested for their knowledge and ability in dealing with explosives.

Internal auditors examined the certification procedures and the status of certification for a number of the handlers. They found that no system existed to inform the handlers or their supervisors that their annual examinations were due. In addition, they questioned 30 of the 100 explosives handlers and found that two had not been certified at all and that the certification of three others had expired. All five were engaged in daily explosives handling.

The internal auditors promptly reported their findings. In response, the production manager had the five employees tested and certified. He then reported that information to the internal auditors, stating that he had thereby corrected the deficient condition.

The corrective action was inadequate on all counts and was rejected by the internal auditors for the following reasons:

- **It was not responsive.** It did not deal with the controls over certification.

- **It was not complete.** Only the handlers in the auditor's tests were considered.

- **It was not continuing.** No system had been installed to make sure that handlers and their supervisors were notified about pending expirations of their certificates.

- **It was not monitored.** There was no provision, other than periodic internal audits, to make sure that people handling explosives were trained and certified.

The auditors explained the defects in the corrective action to operating management. As a result, the following additional steps were taken:

- A card record listing the names and the certification expiration dates for each handler was set up in a date "tickler file" in the personnel department, which was responsible for training and certification. The card was then placed in a "pending" file and removed only upon receipt of evidence of recertification.

- All 100 handlers were checked for valid, up-to-date certification cards.

- One month before the expiration of a handler's certification, the manager of each handler was to be notified that recertification was due. They were also to be notified if any handler's certification had been allowed to expire even though notification of recertification dates had been given.

- The chief safety engineer instructed his engineers, who toured the plant in search of safety violations, to verify that anyone seen handling explosives had a current card evidencing certification.

Authority and Audit Status

Responsibility cannot be carried out without corresponding authority. The audit responsibility for appraising the adequacy and effectiveness of corrective action is meaningless if the auditor is not authorized to do so. Busy operating managers are likely to respond to auditors' objections by saying: "I'm running my shop. I took the action I felt was appropriate. It satisfies me. Who are you to tell me differently?"

These are the responses internal auditors will hear unless senior management clearly provides them with the authority to judge whether actual or proposed corrective action will correct reported deficiencies. This authority must be spelled out clearly in the internal audit charter. All operating managers should be fully aware that corrective action must be real and effective. The auditors will always have the authority to review the action and, if it does not properly correct the condition, to report it.

However, it is more desirable to sell than to tell. And the selling process should start early on. At the preliminary meeting, auditors should assure clients that: (1) they will be told promptly of every finding the auditors encounter; (2) both the finding and the support for it will be thoroughly discussed; (3) any questions regarding the facts will be resolved before the matter is reported; (4) the client will be allowed to present a position adverse to the finding; and (5) the client will be given every opportunity to initiate corrective action.

In the final audit report, prominent notice should be given to any corrective action started or completed. No audit finding should be given any more weight or stress than it deserves. Insignificant findings should not be formally reported at all, so long as they are properly corrected.

The desirability of selling a finding to the client should never deter the auditors from their primary purpose, which is to see that the condition is corrected. Despite the best efforts of the auditors, some operating managers, may be recalcitrant and unconvinced. In such circumstances, the auditors may have to contact the client's superiors. Very often, the higher the auditors have to climb up the management ladder, the more objectively their findings will be regarded.

Auditors should prepare their cases for the higher levels of management with special care. Senior management may not have the operating managers' intimate knowledge of conditions; so the presentation should be clear, understandable, and convincing. Flip-chart and electronic presentations have been found useful in explaining the problems and demonstrating the need for corrective action. It is especially important that the presentation properly explain the goals and the standards of the operation in question, the conditions, the procedures and practices, the cause and effect, and the conclusions and recommendations.

Internal auditors will be assured that they have done their job professionally if either operating managers or senior management request additional audits or special studies.

Supplementary Readings

Aldridge, Ashlee, "Just Another Audit Finding?," *Internal Auditor*, August 2000, 77-79.
Bossle, Francis X., and Alfred R. Michenzi, "The Single Page Audit Report," *Internal Auditor*, April 1997, 37-41.
Didis, Stephen K., "Communicating Audit Results," *Internal Auditor*, October 1997, 37-38.
Flaherty, J.J., and Judy Stein, "Solution-Focused Audit Reporting," *Internal Auditor*, October 1991, 58-61.
Hubbard, Larry D., "What's a Good Audit Finding," *Internal Auditor*, February 2001, 104.
Jacka, J. Mike, "Door Number Three," *Internal Auditor*, December 1997, 54-57.
Johns, G.F., "Audit Recommendations: Overcoming Implementation Frustration," *Internal Auditor*, April 1989, 30-33.
Marks, Norman, "Dismissed Audit Findings," *Internal Auditor*, June 2001, 69-71.
Qureshi, Anique Ahmed, "How to Evaluate a Specialist's Findings," *Internal Auditing*, Spring 1996, 48-53.
Ratliff, Richard L., and I. Richard Johnson, "Evidence," *Internal Auditor*, August 1998, 56-61.
Sawyer, L.B., "The Human Side of Internal Auditing," *Internal Auditor*, August 1988, 40-44.

Schwartz, Brian M., "Documenting Audit Findings," *Internal Auditor*, April 1999, 48-49.

Sears, Brian P., *Internal Auditing Manual* (New York: RIA, 2003). (See Chapter D1, "Evidential Matter.")

Sprakman, Gary, and Mohamed Ibrahim, "Cost-Economizing Superiority of Operational Audit Findings to Financial Audit Findings," *Internal Auditing*, May/June 1998, 34-43.

Walz, Anthony, "Adding Value," *Internal Auditor*, February 1997, 51-54.

Multiple-choice Questions

1. Which of the following situations best describes an appropriate role for internal auditing?
   a. The chief audit executive is responsible for the internal audit budget as well as the budgetary program of his or her organization as a whole.
   b. Internal auditors suggest alternatives for decision makers, and management selects the best alternative.
   c. Internal auditors develop and install the organization's system of internal control, and the controller's office reviews the adequacy of those systems.
   d. The chief audit executive is responsible for installing the accounting system used by the firm, and the controller is responsible for assuring these systems are properly implemented.

2. If an internal auditor finds that no corrective action has been taken on a prior audit finding that is still valid, the *Standards* state that the internal auditors should:
   a. Restate the prior finding along with the findings of the current audit.
   b. Determine whether management or the board has assumed the risk of not taking corrective action.
   c. Seek the board's approval to initiate corrective action.
   d. Schedule a future audit of the specific area involved.

3. According to the *Standards,* audit findings are the result of:
   a. Comparing what should be with what is and analyzing the impact.
   b. Determining the impact on the organization of what should be.
   c. Communicating the impact on the organization of what should be.
   d. Analyzing differences between organizational and departmental objectives.

4. Management is beginning to take corrective action on personnel department deficiencies that were reported during the last internal audit. According to the *Standards,* the internal auditor should:
   a. Oversee the corrective action.
   b. Postpone the next audit of the personnel department until the corrective action is completed.
   c. Refrain from judging whether the corrective action will remedy the deficiencies.
   d. Follow up to see that the action corrects the deficiencies.

Use the following audit finding to answer questions 5 and 6:

PARAGRAPH 1: The production department has the newest production equipment available because of a fire that required the replacement of all equipment.

PARAGRAPH 2: The members of the production department have become completely comfortable with the state-of-the-art technology over the past year and a half. As a result, the production department has become an industry leader in production efficiency and effectiveness.

PARAGRAPH 3: The production department produces an average of 25 units per worker per shift. The defect rate is one percent.

PARAGRAPH 4: The industry average productivity is 20 units per shift. The industry defect rate is three percent.

5. Which paragraph would be characterized as the attribute described in the *Standards* as "Criteria" ?
   a. 1.
   b. 2.
   c. 3.
   d. 4.

6. Which paragraph would be characterized as the attribute described in the *Standards* as "Condition"?
   a. 1.
   b. 2.
   c. 3.
   d. 4.

7. In beginning an audit, an internal auditor reviews written procedures that detail segregations of responsibility adopted by management to strengthen internal controls. These written procedures should be viewed as the following attribute of a finding:
   a. Criteria.
   b. Condition.
   c. Cause.
   d. Effect.

8. According to the *Standards,* the chief audit executive should ensure follow-up of proper audit findings and recommendations:
   a. To determine if corrective action was taken and is achieving the desired results.
   b. Unless management rejected the recommendation in its initial response.
   c. Unless the audit schedule does not allow time for follow-up.
   d. Unless management has accepted the recommendation.

9. During an operational audit, the auditor compares the current staffing of a department with established industry standards to:
   a. Identify bogus employees on the department's payroll.
   b. Assess the current performance of the department, and make appropriate recommendations for improvement.
   c. Evaluate the adequacy of the established internal controls for the department.
   d. Determine whether the department has complied with all laws and regulations governing its personnel.

10. The *Standards* require that internal auditors discuss conclusions and recommendations at appropriate levels of management before issuing final written reports. Which of the following is the primary reason that a closing conference should be documented by the auditor?
    a. The information may be needed if a dispute arises.
    b. The *Standards* require that closing conferences be documented.
    c. The information may be needed to revise future audit programs.
    d. Closing conference documentation becomes a basis for future audits.

11. Why should organizations require clients to promptly reply and outline the corrective action that has been implemented on reported deficiencies?
    a. To remove items from the "pending" list as soon as possible.
    b. To effect savings or to institute compliance as early as possible.
    c. To indicate concurrence with the audit findings.
    d. To insure that the audit schedule is kept up to date.

12. The preliminary survey shows that a prior audit deficiency was never corrected. Subsequent field work confirms that the deficiency still exists. Which of the following courses of action should the internal auditor pursue?
    a. Take no action. To do otherwise would be an exercise of operational control.
    b. Discuss the issue with the chief audit executive. The problem requires an ad hoc solution.
    c. Discuss the issue with the person(s) responsible for the problem. They should know how to solve the problem.
    d. Order the person(s) responsible to correct the problem. They have had long enough to do so.

13. An internal audit supervisor, when reviewing a staff member's working papers, identified an unsupported statement that "the client unit was operating inefficiently." What action should the supervisor direct the auditor to take?
    a. Remove the comment from the working paper file.
    b. Obtain the client's concurrence with the statement.
    c. Research and identify criteria to measure operating efficiency.
    d. Explain that it is the opinion of the staff member.

14. Management asserted that the performance standards the auditors used to evaluate operating performance were inappropriate. Written performance standards that had been established by management were vague and had to be interpreted by the auditor. In such case auditors may meet their due care responsibility by:
    a. Assuring themselves that their interpretations are reasonable.
    b. Assuring themselves that their interpretations are in line with industry practices.
    c. Establishing agreement with clients as to the standards needed to measure performance.
    d. Incorporating management's objections in the audit report.

15. When audit findings are challenged, auditor's factual rebuttal is best facilitated by:
    a. Summaries in the audit program.
    b. *Pro forma* working papers.
    c. Cross-referencing the findings to the working papers.
    d. Explicit procedures in the audit program.

Use the following information to answer questions 16 through 19.

The following data was gathered during an internal auditor's investigation of the reason for a material increase in bad debts expenses. In preparing a report of the finding, each of the items might be classified as criteria, cause, condition, effect, or background information.
 1. Very large orders require management's approval of credit.
 2. Audit tests showed that sales personnel regularly disregard credit guidelines when dealing with established customers.
 3. A monthly report of write-offs is prepared but distributed only to the accounting department.
 4. Credit reports are used only on new accounts.
 5. Accounting department records suggest that uncollectible accounts could increase by five percent for the current year.
 6. The bad debts loss increased by $100,000 during the last fiscal year.
 7. Even though procedures and criteria were changed to reduce the amount of bad-debt write-offs, the loss of commissions due to written-off accounts has increased for some sales personnel.

8. Credit department policy requires the review of credit references for all new accounts.
9. Current payment records are to be reviewed before extending additional credit to open accounts.
10. To reduce costs, the use of outside credit reports was suspended on several occasions.
11. Since several staff positions in the credit department were eliminated to reduce costs, some new accounts have received only cursory review.
12. According to the new credit manager, strict adherence to established credit policy is not necessary.

16. Criteria are best illustrated by items numbered:
    a.   1, 8, 9.
    b.   2, 10, 11.
    c.   3, 4, 12.
    d.   5, 6, 7.

17. Cause is best illustrated by items numbered:
    a.   2, 10, 11.
    b.   3, 4, 12.
    c.   5, 6, 7.
    d.   1, 8, 9.

18. Condition is best illustrated by items numbered:
    a.   5, 6, 7.
    b.   1, 8, 9.
    c.   2, 10, 11.
    d.   3, 4, 12.

19. Effect is best illustrated by items numbered:
    a.   3, 4, 12.
    b.   5, 6, 7.
    c.   1, 8, 9.
    d.   2, 10, 11.

20. According to the *Standards*, the findings in an internal audit report should include:
    a.   Statements of opinion about the cause of a finding.
    b.   Statements of fact concerning the control weaknesses which were identified during the course of the audit.
    c.   Statements of both fact and opinion developed during the course of the audit.
    d.   Statements that may deal with potential future events and might be helpful to the audited department.

Chapter 9
Working Papers

What working papers are, what they do. Documentation. Working paper summaries. Indexing and cross-referencing. Pro forma working papers. Automating working papers. Nations Bank. Electronic working papers. Supervisory reviews of working papers. Control over working papers. Sample working papers. Ownership of working papers.

Introduction

What They Are

Working papers document the audit. They record the information obtained and the analyses made during the audit process. Working papers are prepared from the time the auditors first launch their assignment until they review corrective action and close the audit project. They document the following steps in the audit process:

- The plans for the audit, including the audit program.
- The examination and the evaluation of the adequacy and effectiveness of the systems of internal control.
- The audit procedures followed, the information obtained, and the conclusions reached.
- The supervisory reviews.
- The audit reports.
- The follow-up of corrective action.

This chapter includes and builds on the guidelines for audit working paper preparation set forth in Practice Advisory 2330-1, "Recording Information," of the *Standards*.

What They Do

Internal auditors prepare working papers for a number of different purposes:

- To provide support for audit reports. Well-structured working papers make it easier to transfer the material written during the audit to the pages of interim and final audit reports. Besides, the experienced auditor keeps one eye on the final report throughout the entire audit project. This keeps the field work relevant and pointed in the right direction. Whatever is not suitable for reporting may not be relevant for review.

- To record information obtained through the questioning of people, the review of instructions and directives, the analysis of systems and processes, the observation of conditions, and the examination of transactions.

- To identify and document audit findings, accumulating the evidence needed to determine the existence and extent of deficient conditions.

- To lend support for discussions with operating personnel. Operations are often quite complex and difficult to remember. Well-documented explanations and charts in the working papers, indexed for ready access, can put the internal auditor on an equal footing with the people who live with the operations and understand them intimately. Thus, good working papers can be a line of defense when audit conclusions and recommendations are challenged.

- To offer a basis for supervisory review of the audit's progress and accomplishments. Reviews of documented work are more productive than conversations between audit supervisor and auditor. The supervisor's review, also documented in the working papers, is a means of control over the audit and an integral part of it.

- To provide support and evidence for matters involving fraud, lawsuits, and insurance claims.

- To provide a means by which external auditors can evaluate the internal audit work and then use it in their own assessment of the organization's system of internal control.

- To create background and reference data for subsequent reviews. Audit projects are often repeated or followed up. Professional working papers make the repeat audit easier and more efficient.

- To help facilitate peer reviews. More and more internal audit organizations are becoming involved in quality control programs and self-evaluations. Either external auditors or consultants are called upon to evaluate the internal audit activity. Working papers form a basis for evaluating the internal audit department's quality assurance program, demonstrating compliance with the *Standards*.

- To serve as part of the documentation required by the U.S. Foreign Corrupt Practices Act. The Act requires an issuer to, "devise and maintain a system of internal accounting controls sufficient to provide reasonable assurances" that certain objectives relating to management authorization, recording of transactions, access to assets, and accountability for assets are being met. Evidence of compliance must be documented.

Part of that documentation can well be the working papers of internal auditors; so such documents must be capable of standing the sharpest scrutiny.

The arguments for professional working papers are numerous and compelling. Internal auditors must prepare papers that are accurate, clear, organized, and professional, taking the following matters into account:

- Documentation, including working paper arrangement
- Summaries, including records of audit findings
- Indexing and cross-referencing
- *Pro forma* working papers
- Supervisory review of working papers
- Ownership of and control over working papers
- Criteria for ideal working papers
- Writing the working papers as the audit progresses
- Retention of working papers

Documentation

Working papers should follow a reasonably consistent form and arrangement, not only within individual audit projects but also throughout the internal audit department. Thus, the chief audit executive should establish policies for the types of audit working paper files to be maintained, the stationery to be used, the indexing systems to follow, and other related matters.

Once they become accustomed to a workable format, internal auditors can give less thought to how the working papers are laid out and more to what needs to be recorded. Among other things, working papers may include:

- Planning documents and audit programs.
- Control questionnaires, flowcharts, checklists, and the results of control evaluations.
- Notes of interviews.
- Organization charts, policy and procedures statements, and job descriptions.
- Copies of important contracts and agreements.
- Letters of confirmation and representation.
- Photographs, diagrams, and other graphic displays.
- Tests and analyses of transactions.
- Results of analytical review procedures.
- Audit reports and management replies.
- Relevant audit correspondence.

In general, internal auditors should keep working papers neat, uniform, understandable, relevant, economical, reasonably complete, simple, and logically arranged. More specifically:

Keep Papers Neat

Neat papers mirror neat thinking. They give an immediate impression of care and professionalism.

All names and titles should be printed clearly and legibly. Only one side of a worksheet should be used; material on the reverse side can easily be overlooked. Working papers have been known to end up in courts of law. Sloppy papers lose their worth as evidence.

Keep Papers Uniform

All working papers should be prepared on paper of uniform size and appearance. Smaller pieces of paper should be fastened to a standard sheet. Larger pieces of paper should be folded in a manner that simplifies later review.

Three-ringed binders are used successfully for audit working papers. They keep the papers from getting lost. And the papers can be sorted, re-sorted, added to, or removed without difficulty. Dividers can be inserted to separate segments of the audit documents. Computer printouts and electronic records should be provided for.

Keep Papers Understandable

Working papers should be clear and understandable. They should need no supplementary information. Anyone reading the papers should be able to determine what the auditors set out to do, what they did, what they found, what they concluded, and what they decided not to do. Conciseness is important, of course; but clarity should not be sacrificed to save time and paper.

Information obtained orally is rarely recorded verbatim. Auditors who paraphrase client comments should also record their own interpretation of what the client meant. To make sure there is no misunderstanding, the client should be asked to confirm the auditor's interpretations. If recorded voice material is used, interpretive notes may be appropriate.

Keep Papers Relevant

Working papers should be restricted to matters that are relevant and material; they should be directly related to the audit objectives. Records that may be interesting but not directly relevant should be eliminated. Well-organized audit programs and effective supervisory instructions can help ensure the inclusion of relevant documents only.

Having clear statements of purpose in the papers helps assure relevance. If the purpose of the particular audit cannot be spelled out, the information gained is likely to be irrelevant. Background material may be important.

Forms and directives should be included only when they are relevant to the audit and to the audit findings. Written directives may often contain much information that is not germane to the audit; only a few lines may be directly related to the audit purposes. Those lines should be highlighted so that they stand out in subsequent review. Where the precise wording of a procedure is not needed to support a finding, it may be referred to in the working papers without reproducing it.

If an audit approach contemplated in the audit program was abandoned, explain the reason for abandonment and retain the related working papers.

Keep Papers Economical

Auditors should avoid unnecessary listing and scheduling. To this end, use copies of client's records or computer printouts. These can show by distinctive tick marks what audit steps were carried out, also recording audit comments in the margins.

Cover as many tests as feasible on one worksheet. The same sample can thus be used for a number of analyses.

Internal auditors should not try to answer every conceivable question that can be raised. This is particularly true when tests indicate satisfactory conditions.

Make full use of the working papers developed in the prior audit, if there was a prior audit. Flowcharts, system descriptions, and other data may still be valid. Those papers that remain useful should be transferred to the current working papers. They should be updated with current information, renumbered, rereferenced, and then initialed and dated by the current auditors. The updated working papers are now the current auditors' working papers and they bear full responsibility for those papers. The fact that the papers were taken from the prior file should be noted in that file.

Keep Papers Reasonably Complete

Working papers should leave nothing hanging. No questions asked should go unanswered. If a space has been left for a cross reference, it should be filled in. If a question is raised, it should be answered — or the reason for not answering it should be provided.

Auditors should keep a "to do" list with their papers. On it they may note matters still to be covered, new thoughts worth pursuing, and any other items not specifically set forth in the audit program but warranting audit action. Then, each item on the "to do" list should be answered or otherwise commented on and referenced. The "to do" list becomes a part of the working paper file.

Every time supervisors review working papers, they should date and record their review notes or questions, preferably on the left-hand side of a fresh worksheet. The auditors should answer each note, recording their answering comments on the other side of the sheet. The supervisor's "to do" list and the notes also become a part of the auditor's working papers.

Prior audit findings, at least those from the prior audit, should be followed up. Management is generally quite interested in whether deficiencies previously reported have again come to light. The working papers should contain summaries of prior audit findings as well as notes on their current status.

If the internal auditor is reporting on financial information, the audit working papers should show whether the accounting records agree or reconcile with such financial information.

Keep the Writing Simple

Working papers should be readily understandable to an uninitiated reviewer. Jargon should be avoided. If it is used, it should be explained in a separate part of the working papers — in a Glossary of Terms — along with all the other technical and arcane terms used in the activity and in the working papers.

Simplicity and clarity in the working papers do not demand perfect syntax. Brief telegraphic sentences can get the ideas across and save time.

The final test of a set of good working papers is whether another internal auditor, who had nothing to do with the assignment, could step into the audit project in midstream, understand what was done, and proceed with the examination without wasted effort.

Use a Logical Working Paper Arrangement

Working papers should be arranged in a manner that makes them parallel with the audit program. Each distinct subject should be included in a separate segment of the papers. The parallel relationship between the program and the working papers will afford ready reference during and after the audit.

For each segment of the audit, the auditor should provide general information in narrative form at the beginning of that part of the papers. Such information should include the objective of the operation being audited and background information: organization, volume statistics, and the control system.

For each audit segment, the auditor should spell out the detailed purposes of the segment, including and, where necessary, expanding on the related matters set out in the audit program.

Also, auditors should explain in the working papers the scope of their audit: what was covered and what was not covered. In this part of their papers, the auditors will discuss the sample selection methods they used and the size of the sample and confidence levels — or if computers were used, the methodology used to replace sampling.

Following the statements of purpose and scope, the auditors record their tests and findings. These should be restricted to the facts — the good as well as the bad. After the facts are recorded the auditors will draw their conclusions from what they found. Supported by their findings on control and performance, the auditors should state whether the conditions they found are satisfactory or unsatisfactory. That is, whether the operation's goals were or were not being met. These conclusions, in the aggregate, will support the auditor's opinion on the entire organization or function reviewed.

Finally, the auditors should document their recommendations to correct the conditions they found and the corrective action taken by the client.

Behind the narrative comments will be the records of the audit: the flowcharts of the control system, the schedules of audit tests, and the summaries of the findings. Each worksheet would generally contain:

A descriptive heading. The heading should identify the company, organization, or function audited, indicate the nature of the data contained in the paper, and show the date or period of the audit.

A reference to the audit project. This identifies the reference number of the audit assignment.

Tick marks and other symbols. Tick marks and other symbols should be uniform throughout the audit. They should be small and neatly placed, useful but unobtrusive. They should be explained in footnotes.

The date of preparation and the auditor's initials. The date should indicate when the worksheet was completed. The auditor's initials should appear on each worksheet. A separate sheet in the working papers should list the names of all the auditors and other personnel on the audit project and their initials.

The reference number of the working papers. Working papers should be referenced as they are prepared and should be kept in logical groupings. There is nothing so discouraging — both to the auditor and to the reviewer — as a mass of working papers unnumbered and uncontrolled.

Sources of data.   Sources of data should be clearly identified.

Working papers may be prepared in pencil, pen, and/or with computer software and printed. Pencil is preferred for schedules containing figures that may be changed. Narrative comments are neater when written in ink. Some internal auditors give their working papers a special look of professionalism by writing the worksheet and column headings in ink — these rarely change — and the remainder of the schedules in pencil.

Sources of the information appearing on a worksheet should be clearly identified. An independent reviewer should be able to retrace the auditor's steps — from basic schedules to summaries and comments — without needing to ask for supplemental information. To that end, worksheets should be cross-referenced to other related working papers and to the audit program. Effective cross-referencing often reduces the need to duplicate data. Where the data is especially important, column totals, cross-footed totals, and computations should be independently verified by someone not assigned to work on the audit project.

The cover of each file of working papers should show project number and code number, name of organization or function, subject matter, audit period or other applicable date, security classification if applicable, and volume number if more than one volume.

Each working paper file should contain a table of contents. The first file should also contain a summary table of contents, identifying all the files.

Working Paper Summaries

Although we have touched on summarization in Chapter 8, Audit Findings, it is worth special mention here because of its importance in working paper presentation.

Auditors, in their dash down the audit trail, are often reluctant to disrupt the tempo of the audit to summarize. Failure to summarize often and currently is a mistake. What the auditors think they have grasped fully may be dispelled by the passage of time. The mind can be a rebellious servant, often retaining what it wishes rather than what is.

The process of summarizing, then, provides an objective overview. It hauls the mind back to hard facts. It helps put findings in perspective. It focuses on what is important and relevant and helps put the trivial and irrelevant in their proper places. Auditors who periodically summarize their findings, both the good and the bad, retain firm control over their audit projects.

Summaries are beneficial, also, in tying together groups of working papers that relate to a particular point. Summaries can provide an orderly and logical flow for the various related papers and can facilitate review of particular work segments. Here are some forms of summaries that can be helpful:

Summaries of Audit Segments

Each segment of an audit should be summarized in narrative form to show the audit subject, the audit purpose and scope, the findings, the conclusions and recommendations of the auditor, and any corrective action the client takes. Summaries should have references to their support. This type of summary was discussed earlier in connection with logical working paper arrangement.

Statistical Summaries

Auditors often use statistical summaries that bring together the results of audit tests. Data scattered through the test schedules can be built into a cohesive unit that is easy to read, understand, and deal with.

These summaries should be treated as a pyramid, with the final, compacted data gradually expanding out into the test schedules. The secret of good statistical summaries is the ease with which reviewers can move from the top summary to the individual test items without using a pencil. The auditors will have done it for them.

Summaries of Meetings

Discussions with the clients — their observations, agreements, disagreements, and suggestions — should be summarized completely and promptly. Summaries can be used to record these matters exactly as they were said, not as they seem, filtered through diminished recollection. The dates and the hours of the discussions may be valuable in the case of later dispute.

Summaries in the Audit Programs

As auditors complete a segment of their audit, they should make appropriate comments in the audit programs about their findings — comments that briefly state their conclusions about the audited activity.

As they read through the audit program thereafter, the auditors will be aware of the course the audit is taking. This process will tell them where they have been and where they must still go. It can tune them into the quality of the operations' controls and performance. It can help them control the audit. It can also be a cumulative thumbnail sketch of how they feel about the operation they are reviewing. Here are some brief examples:

Program Steps	W/P Ref.	Comments
Examine a representative number of engineering drawings to see whether they are:		
Being properly checked	C-8	Unsatisfactory at Project A. See RAF-1.* Satisfactory at Projects B and C.
Meeting specifications	C-8	Unsatisfactory at Project A. See RAF-2. Satisfactory at Projects B and C.
Meeting schedules	C-8	Unsatisfactory at Projects A and C. See RAFs 3 and 4. Satisfactory at Project B.

*RAF refers to Record of Audit Findings.

Summaries of Findings

Perhaps the most important summary is that of the audit findings. These matters need the most support since they usually result in the most discussion. The summary should place the relevant and significant facts about a finding at the auditor's fingertips. A completed Record of Audit Findings is shown in Exhibit 9-1.

Indexing and Cross-referencing

Good cross-referencing serves many purposes. First, it simplifies supervisory review of the working papers. Although the internal auditor may have all relevant facts about an issue clearly in mind, the relationships between facts may not be that clear to someone else. References should lead reviewers easily to the related facts in other parts of the working papers.

Second, cross-referencing eases the path of the next auditor who uses the working papers for a follow-up review.

Exhibit 9-1
Record of Audit Findings

RAF No.   4
W/P Ref: C5, C8, C9

Organization: Eng. Branch - Project C

Condition: No provision had been made to monitor drawings sent to the Checking Dept. As a result, a large percentage of the drawing included in our test had been held in Checking beyond the prescribed 20-day period.

Same finding last examination: Yes _____   No ___X___

Criteria: Eng. Proc. D-79 permits only 20 working days from drawing completion to release to the Manufacturing Branch.

Method of Sample Selection: Random sampling using random numbers

Pop. Size 140   **Sample Size** 30   **No. of Errors** 10   **% of sample** 33

Cause: Project management failed to consider need for control.

Effect: Expensive delays, missed schedules, irate customers.

Recommendation: Monitor all drawings sent to check until release.

Corrective action: Controls established to use the same system of monitoring as that used on Project B. See C-15 and C-16.

Discussions:

	Name	Title	Dept.	Date	Auditor
(1)	R. Roe	Administrator	Eng. Proj. C.	2/3/0X	LBS
(2)	L. Snow	Project Eng.	Eng. Proj. C.	2/3/0X	LBS
(3)					
(4)					

Client comments:

(1) Roe corroborated the accuracy of the findings and their cause.

(2) Snow agreed with the need for corrective action. Said he'd install the same kind of monitoring controls used in Proj. B.

(3)

(4)

LBS   2/3/0X
Auditor   **Date**
PEH   2/7/0X
Supervisor   **Date**

Third, cross-referencing simplifies later reviews of the papers. In a heated review with the client, good cross-referencing helps prevent fumbling and bumbling — those mortifying "stage waits" after the client has asked a pertinent and pointed question while the auditor frantically flips through worksheets as the whole room sits in impatient silence.

And fourth, cross-referencing improves the final product: the internal audit report. As the auditor prepares the draft of the report, the well-referenced papers reveal their supporting information readily and helpfully. The ill-referenced papers tend to hide their secrets.

The system of indexing should be simple and flexible. Different kinds of reviews will call for different indexing patterns, but certain principles should apply. The system to be used in a particular examination should be considered and devised as soon as the audit program has been developed. By doing this the working papers can be referenced as the audit proceeds. The auditor thus avoids dealing with a mass of unreferenced papers in which it is almost impossible to find anything.

One simple index system uses capital letters to designate broad segments of the audit and Arabic numerals for the worksheets within the segments. Some auditors use Roman numerals. This may be satisfactory for external broad divisions of a large audit project, but when the numbers go beyond I, II, and III, auditors accustomed to Arabic numerals must translate the Roman numerals in their minds. Indexing and cross-referencing are tedious enough without the added burden of translation.

Thus, capital letters and Arabic numerals are usually sufficient. They stand the test of good indexing systems: simplicity and infinite expansion. The capital letters can be repeated if the series of A, B, C, etc., is exhausted. For the next series, the auditor can use AA, BB, CC, and so on. The Arabic numerals can also be readily expanded: A1 can become A1.1 or A1.1.1 or A1.1.1.1. This simple system is much preferable to some forms of indexing that begin to look like algebraic formulas. For example:

$$\underline{IX - A - 1 - a}$$
$$(a) - (1)$$

The auditor in charge should expect assistants to keep their working papers currently referenced. Assistants should be assigned a symbol at the same time they are assigned a task. The number of assignments should be planned in the audit program. The letters of the alphabet can be assigned to the segments in the program. When assistants are given the appropriate symbol, D or D.1, for example, they can then be held responsible for indexing their papers and cross-referencing them within their segments or sections.

Cross-referencing should show the source of information if taken from another working paper and, if the information is used on another working paper, different colors can be used, i.e., red — from a working paper; blue — to a working paper.

Thorough cross-referencing takes time, of course. But in the final analysis it saves time when the auditors discuss matters with clients or when the final report is being prepared and verified.

Pro Forma **Working Papers**

Budgets and schedule often combine to tempt all auditors to cut corners in working-paper presentation.

Recognizing the dilemma, some audit organizations have developed working paper templates that contain standard information, reminding the auditor of the key points to be covered in the audit. One internal audit organization developed some *pro forma* working papers that can be helpful.[1] In the following example, an index sheet identifies the segments of the audit and provides the initial reference number for each segment:

Item	Description	Ref.[2]
Reports	Transmittal letter, audit report, replies	A
Plans	Audit objectives, steps to meet objectives, executive contact letter, and pre-audit meeting	B
Flowcharts	Flowcharts and sampling plans	C
References	Written procedures and operating practices	D
Prior audit	Reports, replies, and prior audit findings	E
Final meeting	Records and flip charts	F
Time records	Estimated and actual	G
Administration	Audit control sheet, draft report, etc.	H

Forms were also developed for the audit program. Each sheet of the program is in two parts: The first provides space for the audit objective; the second provides space for the steps needed to achieve the objective. By using the form, auditors must state what they are setting out to achieve and the steps they take to that end.

The audit worksheets provide space for three sets of narrative comments. They are headed: Purpose of the Work, Work Done, and What the Auditor Concluded. Here again the auditors are compelled to show why they took certain steps, what the steps were, and what was the auditor's opinion.

Separate *pro forma* sheets are used for interviews. The head of each sheet provides spaces for information on the people interviewed: their names, titles, and functions. Spaces are also provided for the location of the interview, the date, and the start/stop time. The sheet has a heading for the Record of Interview, and one for Key Points to Bring Up. The record sheet for the final audit meeting provides space to show the location, date, and start/stop times; the people attending; and the record of discussion.

Each audit organization using *pro forma* working papers has to develop forms most suitable to its needs. The forms should be helpful and not restrictive. They should guide the auditors and make sure that all significant points are covered — that the auditors do not just follow routines because the *pro forma* worksheets demand them. Used properly, such working papers can be useful, ensure proper coverage, and save time.

Automating Working Papers — Nations Bank[2]

A report published by The Institute of Internal Auditors on innovation practices in internal auditing discussed automation of the internal auditing operation. The report described a particular procedure of Nations Bank and identified Lotus Notes as the medium through which the process was operated. It identified a series of 10 characteristics of the groupware application. These characteristics and their application to the working papers, as described by the authors, follow:

Reflection of Information: Allows auditors to maintain up-to-date copies of databases and working papers without the need to return to the office. Also results in improved real-time review of working papers.

Standardization: Working papers are preformatted and administrative working papers are pre-composed (achieves consistency in the audit process).

Convenience: Eliminates the need to manually head up working papers using Lotus Notes filters.

Document References: Electronic connections automatically take the auditor from one workpaper to another document and back again. Thus, working papers do not need to be numbered and auditors can easily flip between working papers and their supporting documents.

Views: Allows auditors and supervisors to see the entire audit at any time by providing views of document databases, current year working papers, permanent file working papers, and findings forms. Audit progress can be tracked as the audit progresses.

Imaging: Allows for the incorporation of nonelectronic media into automated working papers, through optical scanners.

Communications: Note's e-mail can interface with most other PC, LAN, and mainframe e-mail systems.

Served as a Control Point: Working papers are stored in one or more servers. These working papers cannot be lost and auditors have a copy of their working papers on a local basis (e.g., notebook computers). This becomes a built-in contingency plan.

Application Integration: Automated working paper environment does not mean elimination or modifying existing applications. For example, any Windows-compatible product can be integrated with Lotus Notes to provide auditors working papers.

Access Rights Security: Through access rights, only those people who need to read, edit, or delete working papers can do so. Others can be assigned reading access only, thus providing more security than paper files.

The authors described the development of the automated working process as the need to review and evaluate audit processes and methodologies. Then it was necessary to move auditing forms and manual processes into a database template that contained all the necessary preformatted documents already used in the audit process. One of the most difficult challenges was to consolidate the diversity of the different forms and procedures of a division of 300 auditors. It was believed that standardization kept the automation process simple, especially for training.

Chapters 7 and 13 to 16 on computer and information systems operations contain more basic information on the application of computers to internal auditing. Various portions of these chapters describe computer aspects of the internal audit process that would be incorporated into the audit working papers and that would provide specificity as to the computerized application process.

Electronic Working Papers

Audit working papers may take forms other than traditional paper: tapes, disks, diskettes, film, or other media. The use of electronic workpapers assist in reducing the complexity and increasing the flexibility of documentation. System generated workpapers allows greater capacity for review and design changes, quicker development when used with Computer Assisted Audit Techniques (CAAT) and Computer Aided System Engineering (CASE) tools, and provides more reasonable documentation.

System techniques for documentation and analysis of the content of workpapers allows greater flexibility for the evaluation of internal controls through the use of structured questionnaires, analytical systems flow charts, and data flow diagrams. Program flowcharts, decision tables, and control matrices can all be developed using these tools.

Audit evidence can be more readily retrievable, easily stored, and backed up and may be accessed using online utilities. Since the early 1990s there has been increased use of electronic media to record audit results.[3]

With electronic working papers, the material is entered directly into the computer; in some cases the material can be downloaded from the client's records onto the working papers. Cross-referencing as described in the preceding sections of the chapter is used, and material from earlier completed and referenced working papers can be simultaneously used while composing the subject working papers. Working papers may be converted to hard copy although they may be kept in electronic form and used in that form for client conferences and for supervisory reviews.

The working paper pages can be automatically headed up by the audit working paper computer program and the audit program can be updated and cross referenced by the auditors as the work progresses.

The actual structure of the working paper will appear much like those of the manually constructed working papers with the exception of the spreadsheets, flowcharts and other specialty formats that are a part of the working paper computer program.

Access to the working papers should be controlled by the use of passwords. The working papers must be protected against intruders from obtaining confidential or other sensitive information contained therein. Care must also be taken that unauthorized persons cannot use the directives contained in the audit programs to obtain information or to cause unauthorized activities to the detriment of the organization.

More entities are using software workpaper packages which contain templates and allow the auditor to develop the audit program and workpaper templates at the same time.

Supervisory Reviews of Working Papers

As in many other activities, the best control is surveillance by knowledgeable supervisors. Such reviews should be evidenced on each worksheet by the name or initials of the supervisor and the date reviewed. Questions raised should be included with each related group of working papers, and the papers should not be considered completed until the questions have been answered to the supervisor's satisfaction.

As supervisors review working papers, they should be concerned with making sure that:

- The audit program was followed and specific instructions to the auditors were followed.

- The papers were accurate and reliable — that they evidenced adequate work performed — and that they demonstrably support the audit findings.

- The conclusions reached were reasonable, logical, and valid.

- There were no planned steps that had not been examined.

- Reviews with clients were carried out and adequately recorded and that disputes were resolved.

- The audit department's rules on working papers were followed.

Supervisors should review working papers as soon as possible after they are completed. Thus, disruption to the work is reduced and problems are resolved before reports are written and auditors are reassigned.

One audit organization uses a special form to conduct the final review of audit working papers. Here are some of the standards that are listed on the form:

Reports
- Reported findings sufficiently cross-referenced to adequate supporting documentation.
- Evidence supplied that full scope of the audit was carried out.

Plans
- Adequate audit program developed.
- Pre-audit planning documented.
- Omissions of steps called for in the audit program adequately explained.
- Estimated and actual audit time adequately documented.

General
- Flowcharts prepared, or carried forward from prior audits and updated.
- Sampling plans sufficiently documented and informative.
- Reference material (policies, procedures, etc.) retained served a constructive purpose.
- Prior audit reports and replies included.
- Prior audit findings investigated.
- Post-audit meeting documented.
- Administrative data completed.

Field Work
- Each working paper section summarized as to work done and findings developed.
- Summaries cross-referenced to appropriate supporting material.
- Purpose, scope, and nature of work properly identified.
- Auditor's conclusions shown.

Supervision
- Supervisor's questions all answered.
- Quality of work appraised.

Control Over Working Papers

Working papers are the auditors' property and should be kept under their control. Auditors should know exactly where the papers are during the conduct of the audit. If there is any risk of loss, the papers should be kept in a locked file or a locked desk during lunch hours and overnight. If they are taken to a hotel room, they should be kept in padlocked briefcases or in locked suitcases. They should not be made available to people who have no authority to have or use them. To do so invites misuse; people may remove, change, or read information not for their eyes.

This does not mean that auditors may not show their working papers to clients under appropriate circumstances. Where there are no damaging comments or indications of fraud, auditors may find it useful to spread out the results of their review before the client.

Access to audit working papers and reports may be allowed to external auditors and to people within the organization other than the clients. But this must be with the approval of the chief audit executive. Where people outside the organization seek access to working papers, the chief audit executive should obtain the approval of senior management and/or legal counsel.

Audit management must take a direct interest in the control of the auditors' working papers. There have been instances where a set of working papers has been lost in the middle of the audit. Audit management should also be concerned with whether a substitute auditor can pick up the work done by an auditor who suddenly becomes unavailable. The rule should be: Keep your working papers so guarded, so organized, and so indexed and cross-referenced that the audit job can be continued by the next auditor with a minimum of program interruption.

Good control over electronic working papers dictates that they be changed only by the auditor who created them.

Sample Working Papers

Exhibits 9-2 through 9-11 are a sample segment of working papers whose format is usable in any operational audit and where the computerized working papers would be quite similar. The exhibits illustrate the audit of an engineering function, but they are usable in any operational audit. The segment deals with the release of engineering drawings after they have been prepared.

These papers were taken from an actual audit. Yet, some audit organizations might find such detailed preparation too onerous. They should therefore be regarded as an ideal rather than as a specific requirement. But the subjects mentioned should be dealt with in every audit before working papers can be accepted as being professional. Actual working papers will usually be prepared in pencil. They are shown in print here for greater clarity and ease in reading.

Under "General Information" (Exhibit 9-2) will be found the objectives of the activity, background information, and a discussion of the control system. The objectives of the activity will dictate the approach the auditors take in their review. The background information contains only enough to provide an understanding of the tests. The explanation of the control system is supported by a simple flowchart.

The "Purpose" statement can be related to the objectives of the activity because obviously the auditors are mainly interested in whether the activity's objectives are being carried out. The "Scope" statement shows the source of information or records used in tests and the sample selection technique employed.

The "Findings" answer each item in the Purpose. They provide factual information only, since it is important in subsequent reviews to distinguish between provable facts and matters of audit judgment. The "Opinion" covers all the findings and provides the auditor's assessment of the findings. The "Recommendations" cover all significant defects found in the audit and indicate the action taken by the client to improve conditions requiring correction.

The supporting schedules describe the tests (Exhibits 9-7 through 9-9) and highlight the deficient items (Exhibit 9-6). The schedules are then summarized in workable form (Exhibit 9-5). The corrective action is documented at the end of the working papers (Exhibits 9-10 and 9-11).

By following a standard working paper arrangement, the auditors will be able to complete one segment of the audit before going on to another. They will know just what each segment requires. They will leave no trailing ends. Even when they must wait for additional information, the practice of completing sections as much as possible makes the return much easier.

Exhibit 9-2
Sample Working Papers: Release of
Engineering Drawings

Sample Working Papers
Release of Engineering Drawings
General Information

Objective of Activity
To prepare engineering drawings that are accurate and will meet specification requirements, and to release them in time to meet factory needs.

Background
Three separate engineering project organizations prepare and release drawings: Projects A, B, and C. Each project works under a project engineer. All three project engineers report to the Chief Engineer. A separate checking department, under a Chief Checker, also reports directly to the Chief Engineer and is therefore not under the control of the people whose drawings he checked. See organization chart on C5.

LBS 2/1/02

Each project has its own procedures for controlling the preparation, checking, approval, and release of drawings.

Each project provides for a span of 20 factory days from completion of drawings to release to the factory. [Factory dates are numbered from 1 to 1000 (going back to 1 when they reach 1000) and exclude weekends and holidays.] The 20 days are to cover checking the drawings, correcting them, and obtaining approvals.

LBS 2/1/02   C1

Exhibit 9-2 (Cont.)

<u>**Control System**</u>
1) To assure accuracy of drawings, each one is to be verified by a checker using different color checks: yellow to indicate accuracy, red to indicate an error. All errors are to be corrected or, if not corrected, the reasons for release without correction are to be shown.
2) To make sure that the drawings meet contract specification, they must be approved in writing by the:

Engineering Supervisor
Project Engineer
Production Engineer
Quality Engineer

Projects B and C have a system for reviewing all drawings for evidence of check and approval before release to the shop. Project A does not.
3) To assure the release of drawings in time to meet factory needs, schedules covering

LBS 2/1/02

drafting provide for completion of the drawings within 20 days of factory need dates. Project B has a follow-up system. Projects A and C do not.
4) All projects use registers to record completed drawings. All projects show release dates. Only Project B shows receipt dates. (See flowchart on C5)

<u>**Purpose**</u>
To determine whether control system is adequate to meet objectives of:
1. Accuracy
2. Meeting specification requirements
3. Meeting schedules
    To determine whether performance is effective in that:
    • All drawings are checked and corrected
    • All drawings bear evidence of

LBS 2/1/02   C2

Exhibit 9-2 (Cont.)

approval
All drawings are released within 20 days of completion.

Scope

We took a judgment sample for our preliminary review of drawings released during the last half of 190X. We made a selection at random, using the interval selection technique, from the registers of released drawings maintained at each project. We decided to take a sample of 20 drawings as a preliminary test and expand our test if necessary. Since our findings were conclusive at each project, we decided not to expand the tests.

Findings

Controls

1) Accuracy
2) Meeting Specs

Project A had no provision for reviewing drawings before release

LBS 2/4/02

or for evidence of check and of approvals. Projects B and C did. C9

3) Schedule

Projects A and C had no follow-up system for drawings in process of checking. Project B did. C9.

Performance

1) Accuracy
2) Meeting Specs

At Project A: 4 drawings bypassed the checkers; total of 7 uncorrected errors; 3 drawings did not have the signatures of the Production Engineer.
At Projects B & C, we found no errors. C10

3) Schedule

At Project A — 5 out of 20 drawings were 21 to 50 days late.
At Project C — 8 out of 50 drawings were 10 to 50 days late.
At Project B — all

LBS 2/4/02

C3

Exhibit 9-2 (Cont.)

drawings in sample were released on time.
C10

<u>Opinion</u>

Project A — Controls over accuracy, meeting specs and schedule inadequate

Project B — Controls satisfactory

Project C — Controls over schedule inadequate

<u>Recommendations</u>

Install at Projects A and C the same system of control in effect at Project B.
The Project Engineers at A and C agreed with our recommendation. They issued
instructions to their administrative assistants to that effect. See C 12 and C 13.
Subsequent reviews showed that the new controls were in actual operation.

LBS 2/4/02   C4

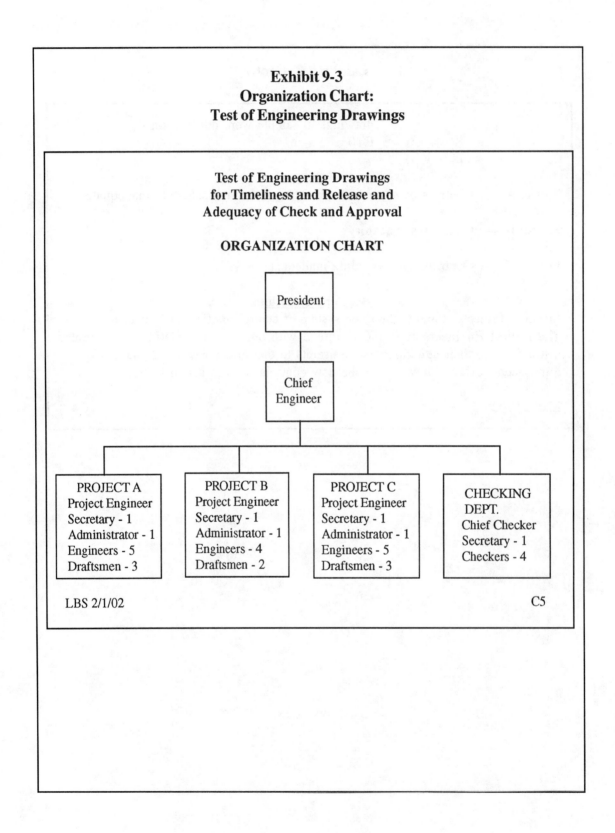

**Exhibit 9-3
Organization Chart:
Test of Engineering Drawings**

Test of Engineering Drawings
for Timeliness and Release and
Adequacy of Check and Approval

ORGANIZATION CHART

President

Chief Engineer

PROJECT A
Project Engineer
Secretary - 1
Administrator - 1
Engineers - 5
Draftsmen - 3

PROJECT B
Project Engineer
Secretary - 1
Administrator - 1
Engineers - 4
Draftsmen - 2

PROJECT C
Project Engineer
Secretary - 1
Administrator - 1
Engineers - 5
Draftsmen - 3

CHECKING DEPT.
Chief Checker
Secretary - 1
Checkers - 4

LBS 2/1/02   C5

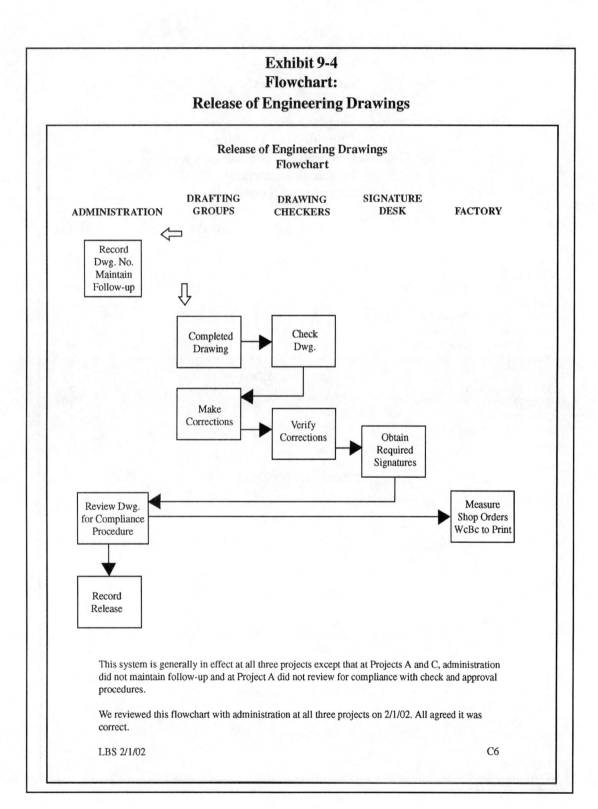

Exhibit 9-4
Flowchart:
Release of Engineering Drawings

Release of Engineering Drawings
Flowchart

This system is generally in effect at all three projects except that at Projects A and C, administration did not maintain follow-up and at Project A did not review for compliance with check and approval procedures.

We reviewed this flowchart with administration at all three projects on 2/1/02. All agreed it was correct.

LBS 2/1/02   C6

Exhibit 9-5
Summary of Tests
of Engineering Drawings

Test of Engineering Drawings
for Timeliness of Release and Adequacy of
Check and Approval
Summary of Tests

	PROJECTS			TOTAL
	A	B	C	
Population:				
Dwgs. issued last 6 mos., 190X	150	130	140	420
Sample:				
Judgment Sample Selected at				
Random by Internal Sampling				
from Drawing Release Registers	20	20	20	60
Selected Every Nth Starting with:	#3	#6	#1	
	Delays			
10 to 20 Days Late	--	--	2	2
21 to 30 Days Late	1	--	2	3
31 to 40 Days Late	1	--	3	4
41 to 50 Days Late	3	--	1	4
	5		8	13

Drawings Bypassing Check
4

Uncorrected Errors
No. Dwgs.	No. Errors
3	7

Unobtained Signatures
No. Dwgs.	No. Sigs.
3	3

Reasons for Deficiencies
Delays } Projects A & C had no system of follow-up control
Project B had an effective system

Bypassing
Checkers
Uncorrected Errors } Project A did not provide for a review of drawings before release to factory
Projects B and C had an effective system.
No Signatures

Refer to C11

LBS 2/3/02   C7

**Exhibit 9-6
List of Discrepant Items:
Test of Engineering Drawings**

**Test of Engineering Drawings
for Timeliness of Release and Adequacy of
Check and Approval
List of Discrepant Items**

Delays
(Drawings Requiring More than 20 Days)

Project A		Project B		Project C	
Drawing	No. of Days	Drawing	No. of Days	Drawing	No. of Days
A-1219	65 - 20* = 45	None		C-325	50 - 20* = 30
A-1105-1	62 - 20 = 42			C-331	60 - 20 = 40
A-1232	58 - 20 = 38			C-334	63 - 20 = 43
A-1250	70 - 20 = 50			C-338	53 - 20 = 33
A-1283	50 - 20 = 30			C-350	48 - 20 = 28
				C-359	30 - 20 = 10
*20 Days Considered to be Standard Flow Time				C-376	53 - 20 = 33
				C-389	40 - 20 = 20

Drawings Bypassed Check

Project A	Project B	Project C
A-1222	None	None
A-1260		
A-1266		
A-1283		

Uncorrected Errors

Project A		Project B		Project C	
Drawing	No. of Errors	Drawing	No. of Errors	Drawing	No. of Errors
A-1105-1	2	None		None	
A-1247	2				
A-1285	3				

Signatures Not Obtained

Project A		Project B		Project C	
Drawing	Missing Sigs.	Drawing	Missing Sigs.	Drawing	Missing Sigs.
A-1227	Prod. Eng.	None		None	
A-1253	Prod. Eng.				
A-1279	Prod. Eng.				

See C9	See C10	See C11

LBS 2/3/02   C8

Exhibit 9-7
Project A:
Test of Engineering Drawings

Test of Engineering Drawings
for Timeliness of Release and Adequacy of
Check and Approval
Project A

Drawing Number	Dwg. Prep	Was Rel	No. of Days Between Prep & Rel	No. of Defects Per Checker	Cor-rected	Required Approvals Shown	Comments
A-1206	605	615	10	3	3	Yes	
A-1219	550	615	65	7	7	Yes	Dwg. delayed in check
A-1222	600	616	16	0	0	Yes	Dwg. bypassed check in error
A-1105-1	555	617	62	4	2	Yes	Dwg. delayed in check. 2 errors uncorrected (no reason shown)
A-1227	607	617	10	4	4	No	Prod. Eng. did not sign
A-1232	560	618	58	5	5	Yes	Dwg. delayed in check
A-1240	604	618	14	3	3	Yes	
A-1247	605	618	13	6	4	Yes	2 errors uncorrected (no reason shown)
A-1250	549	619	70	9	9	Yes	Dwg. delayed in check
A-1253	612	621	9	2	2	No	Prod. Eng. did not sign
A-1260	614	622	8	0	0	Yes	Dwg. bypassed check in error
A-1266	612	622	10	0	0	Yes	Dwg. bypassed check in error
A-1270	610	622	12	3	3	Yes	
A-1274	611	622	11	4	4	Yes	
A-1279	612	624	12	3	3	No	Prod. Eng. did not sign
A-1283	575	625	50	6	6	Yes	Dwg. bypassed check (no reason shown) Prod. Eng. did not sign
A-1285	615	625	10	4	1	Yes	3 errors uncorrected (no reason)
A-1290	617	627	10	3	3	Yes	
A-1292	618	627	9	3	3	Yes	
A-1296	619	628	9	2	2	Yes	

All differences reviewed with administrator John Doe 2/3/02.
He agreed with our findings.

LBS 2/2/02

C9

Exhibit 9-8
Project B:
Test of Engineering Drawings

Test of Engineering Drawings
for Timeliness of Release and Adequacy of
Check and Approval
Project B

Drawing Number	Factory Date Dwg. Prep	Was Rel	No. of Days Between Prep & Rel	No. of Defects Per Checker	Cor- rected	Required Approvals Shown	Comments
B-614	606	616	10	4	4	Yes	
B-615	614	617	3	5	5	Yes	
B-619	610	620	10	5	5	Yes	
B-622	609	620	11	6	6	Yes	
B-626	609	620	11	3	3	Yes	
B-629	612	623	11	2	2	Yes	
B-632	620	627	7	7	7	Yes	
B-639	621	627	6	2	2	Yes	
B-642	620	627	7	2	2	Yes	
B-645	619	630	11	5	5	Yes	
B-647	619	630	11	5	5	Yes	
B-649	626	632	6	5	5	Yes	
B-661	626	632	6	3	3	Yes	
B-662	622	632	10	2	2	Yes	
B-671	624	634	10	7	7	Yes	
B-680	627	634	7	6	6	Yes	
B-692	628	635	7	8	8	Yes	
B-693	628	636	8	3	3	Yes	
B-695	626	636	10	4	4	Yes	
B-698	625	636	11	2	2	Yes	

LBS 2/2/02

C10

Exhibit 9-9
Project C:
Test of Engineering Drawings

Test of Engineering Drawings
for Timeliness of Release and Adequacy of
Check and Approval
Project C

Drawing Number	Factory Date Dwg. Prep	Was Rel	No. of Days Between Prep & Rel	No. of Defects Per Checker	Cor-rected	Required Approvals Shown	Comments
C-325	570	620	50	4	4	Yes	Delayed in check (no follow-up)
C-327	610	622	12	4	4	Yes	
C-331	562	622	60	7	7	Yes	Ditto
C-334	562	625	63	2	2	Yes	Ditto
C-338	572	625	53	2	2	Yes	Ditto
C-341	606	625	19	4	4	Yes	
C-344	612	625	13	3	3	Yes	
C-346	615	629	14	6	6	Yes	
C-350	581	629	48	5	5	Yes	Ditto
C-352	620	630	10	5	5	Yes	
C-359	601	631	30	4	4	Yes	Ditto
C-365	619	631	12	4	4	Yes	
C-370	623	633	10	3	3	Yes	
C-372	623	633	10	2	2	Yes	
C-376	580	633	53	2	2	Yes	Ditto
C-381	617	636	19	3	3	Yes	
C-383	620	636	16	4	4	Yes	
C-389	596	636	40	4	4	Yes	Ditto
C-392	616	636	20	5	5	Yes	
C-397	620	640	20	5	5	Yes	

All differences reviewed with administrator Richard Roe 2/3/02.
He agreed with our findings.

LBS 2/2/02   C11

Exhibit 9-10

To: Administrator, Project A
From: Project Engineer, Project A
Subject: Control over Drawings — Check, Approvals, Follow-up

An audit of our operations has disclosed that:
    Some drawings had bypassed the checkers;
    Some drawings did not bear all required approvals; and
    Some drawings had been delayed in check without proper follow-up.

The following procedures will be put into effect immediately, pending the issuance of suitable job instructions covering these matters:
    All drawings being released to production shall clear over the administrator's desk. He shall initial and date the release document to show that he has reviewed the document for evidence of: (1) check and (2) appropriate approvals. All documents not checked or approved shall be returned to the responsible individual by a brief memo, with copy to this office.

    The administrator shall establish and maintain a record of all drawings sent to check, showing the dates of release to and from check. Each week, the administrator shall prepare a report listing all drawings in check for more than 20 days. One copy of the report shall be sent to this office and one copy to the Chief Checker.

/s/P. Snow
Project Engineer
Project A   C12

Exhibit 9-11

To: Administrator, Project C
From: Project Engineer, Project C
Subject: Control over Drawings in Check

An audit of our administrative procedures has shown that drawings were delayed in the checking process without adequate follow-up.

Please install the following procedures immediately, pending the issuance of a job instruction:

    The administrator shall establish and maintain a record of all drawings sent to check, showing the dates of release to and from check. Each week, the administrator shall prepare a report listing all drawings in check for more than 20 days. One copy of the report shall be sent to this office and one copy to the Chief Checker.

/s/T. Blow
Project Engineer
Project C   C13

Writing as the Audit Progresses

Internal auditors who are constantly pressed for time may doubt their ability to turn out working papers such as those illustrated in the exhibits. But good field work organization will help. The secret is to record comments while performing the field work.

The initial comments about objectives, background, controls, purpose, and scope can be prepared as soon as the auditors have made an initial review of the operation. They do not have to wait until the end of their audit of the segment. By that time, the chore becomes far too heavy and many of the facts become blurred in their minds. The findings can be summarized right after the tests have been made. The results are then immediately usable in discussions with the client. In some organizations the material to be considered for the audit report is also constructed and may even be reviewed with the client at that time. This is especially useful when the client has started work to implement the auditor recommendations.

Many internal auditors, working under heavy pressures of budget and schedule, object to preparing the kinds of working papers illustrated in this chapter. Obviously, jotted notes on scraps of paper take less time to prepare. In some cases, preparing working papers can be made easier through the use of *pro forma* worksheets that have the headings and some segments already prepared. In other cases, particularly in audits of operational matters where the examinations are not repetitive, or where the auditor may be making an initial audit of a new subject, *pro forma* papers may be inapplicable.

In any case, working papers that meet professional standards must show what the internal auditors intended to do, what they did, what their sources were, and what audit steps they took, what they found, and what they concluded from their findings.

Another argument against jotted notes on scraps of paper is that the added time taken to write the audit report would probably exceed the time saved through scratch notes. And the trauma of unsupported findings is avoided by working papers that stand the test of professionalism and compel belief from an objective observer.

Retention of Working Papers

Working papers should be disposed of when they are of no further use. Once the subsequent audit of an operation has been completed, auditors should make a determination, approved by their supervisors, as to whether the prior papers should be retained or destroyed. When working papers contain documentation or other material of continuing use, those sections of the papers should be carried forward to the current papers. Contractual or legal provisions may demand retention. A retention procedure and schedule for the internal audit department should therefore be prepared by the chief audit executive and approved by legal counsel.

Documentation evidencing compliance with the U.S. Foreign Corrupt Practices Act may have to be kept in separate files.

Some audit working papers contain information of continuing importance, often referred to as permanent files. Auditors should identify such papers at the conclusion of the audit. Supervisors should approve retention by initialing and dating the auditor's determination. Permanent files are discussed more completely in Chapter 23, Controlling Audit Projects.

Ownership of Working Papers

When it comes to restricting outsiders to any access to internal audit working papers, internal auditors are the victims of their own success. As their work products and effectiveness become better known and accepted, demands for their working papers become more widespread. A collateral question is the ownership of internal audit documentation. Does it belong to management, the shareholders, or the internal audit department? In many cases, the way a corporation's articles, bylaws, and audit charter are written can determine the outcome.[4]

Unfortunately, the rights of outsiders to internal audit papers have not been clearly established in law. By and large, demands by government agencies are permitted by the courts or are spelled out in contracts. The demands by private persons or organizations are subject to conflicting rules. Also, the nature of the evidence requested will dictate its accessibility. The whole matter is complicated by the fact that in some cases access rights are being determined by trial courts rather than appellate courts, leading to inconsistent applications.[5]

In certain cases, internal audit working papers must be surrendered to the Internal Revenue Service (IRS). In U.S. vs. Powell 85 S.Ct. 248, 379 U.S. 48 (1964), the court established a four-part test to determine when an IRS summons for such working papers will be enforced.

- The investigation is for a legitimate purpose.
- The inquiry is relevant.
- The information is not already in the IRS's possession.
- The administrative steps in the Internal Revenue Code have been followed.

The Powell decision was affirmed in subsequent court decisions involving the government as plaintiff: U.S. vs. Noall, 587 F.2d 123 (1978); U.S. vs. Leaseway Transportation Corporation, 523 F. Supp. 1333 (1981); Stuart vs. U.S., 813 F.2d 243 (1987); and U. S. vs. Abrahams, 905 F.2d 1276 (1990), among others.

In the cases after Powell, the courts reduced the threshold of relevance. The arguments advanced about relevancy were dismissed. The government did not have to show that the inquiry was relevant — only that it *might* be relevant.

The court also rejected policy considerations: that the internal audit reports are designed to improve operations and that people would be reluctant to speak to the internal auditors if they knew that their statements would come under the scrutiny of the IRS.

In the Leaseway case, an expert witness testified that the internal audit reports were almost entirely operational; they dealt almost exclusively with internal controls, compliance with policies, and the efficiency of subsidiaries. Some of the reports, however, did refer to specific transactions and contained one or two corrective entries, timing adjustments, and other items that could have an impact on the financial statements from which the tax return was prepared. The court determined that it was not required to decide whether the internal audit reports were relevant; only that they might be relevant to the audit. The decision is an almost unlimited endorsement of the IRS's right to obtain internal audit working papers.

Other government agencies have been equally successful in obtaining audit reports and working papers. In Federal Trade Commission vs. TRW, Inc., 628 F.2d 207 (1980), the FTC sought to subpoena documents as part of an investigation under the Fair Credit Reporting Act (15 U.S.C. Sections 1681-1681t. 1976 & Supp IV 1980). Because TRW was convinced that a complaint under the Act would be filed, it instituted an audit to determine the adequacy of its procedures under the so-called "self-evaluative" privilege. The court rejected that argument, saying that whatever status that privilege may have in private litigation, it was not applicable to government agencies. See also U.S. vs . The Dexter Corporation, 132 F.R.D. 8 (1990) where the TRW decision was followed.

The self-evaluative privilege, sometimes referred to by the courts as the "self-critical analysis," has it roots in Bredice vs. Doctors Hospital 50 F.R.D. 249 (1970). There, a plaintiff attempted to obtain documents relating to a peer review of hospital staff for the purpose of improving practices and procedures. The court held that the needs of society to promote self-improvement outweighed the need of the plaintiff to obtain information.

But Bredice has not been uniformly followed. Indeed, in TRW, the court held that the self-evaluative privilege "at the most, remains largely undefined and has not generally been recognized." It further held that whatever status the privilege may have in private litigation, it has uniformly been rejected where documents are sought by government agencies.

Hence, the outlook in private litigation is not quite as bleak as it is in cases involving government communications. It must meet certain standards, however. These can be found in Wigmore on Evidence, Section 2285, page 527, speaking about privileged communication in general:

- Communications must originate in a confidence that they will not be disclosed.
- The element of confidentiality must be essential to the full and satisfactory maintenance of the relation between parties.

- The relation must be one that in the opinion of the community ought sedulously to be fostered.
- The injury that would inure to the relation by the communication must be greater than the benefits that would inure therefrom for the correct disposal of litigation.

Courts have applied these concepts in refusing plaintiffs access to reports of internal reviews. In Banks vs. Lockheed-Georgia, 53 F.R.D. 283 (1971), plaintiffs asked for reports by a team appointed by Lockheed to study Lockheed's equal employment problems. The court refused the plaintiff access to the reports on the grounds that such access to outsiders would inhibit frank self-criticism and evaluation. See, also, where documents have been shielded: Scott vs. McDonald, 70 F.R.D. 568 (1976); Keyes vs. Lenoir Rhyne College, 555 F.2d 579 (1977); and New York Stock Exchange vs. Sloan, 22 F.R.Serv. 2d (1976).

Yet self-evaluative privilege is no automatic shield against records of self-appraisal. In the case of In Re Burlington Northern, Inc., 679 F.2d 762 (1982), the court said:

> A number of other courts have relied on a "self evaluation" privilege in diverse factual settings. More recently, however, courts have appeared reluctant to enforce even a qualified "self-evaluation" privilege. They typically concede its possible application in some situations, but then proceed to find a reason why the documents in question do not fall within its scope.

Zeroing in more closely on where self-evaluation privilege may pertain, the court in Webb vs. Westinghouse Electric Corporation et al., 81 F.R.D. 431, 434 (1978) in an employment discrimination suit.

> In reviewing all of the cases, several factors emerge as potential guideposts for the application of the "self-critical" analysis defense. First, materials protected have generally been prepared for mandatory government reports. Second, only subjective, evaluative materials have been protected; objective data contained in those same reports in no case have been protected. Finally, courts have been sensitive to the need of the plaintiffs for such materials, and have denied discovery only where the policy favoring exclusion of the materials clearly outweighed the plaintiff's needs.

In Hardy vs. New York News, Inc., 114 F.R.D. 633 (1987), the court refused to shield documents, voluntarily drafted by the employer, from discovery by the plaintiff. The court observed that in the area of employment discrimination virtually every court has limited the self-critical privilege to information mandated by statute or regulations. It further noted:

> Those courts that have recognized a privilege for self-critical analysis have nonetheless held that the privilege is qualified and that the application is subject to a balancing of general policy interests against the interests of the individual plaintiff.

In Granger vs. National Railroad Passenger Corporation, 116 F.R.D. 507 (1987), an injured employee sought to obtain the results of Amtrak's Investigation Committee Report. The court held that those sections of the report captioned "Accident Analysis" and "Committee Recommendation" were protected against disclosure. But the sections captioned "Cause" and "Contributing Factors" were not so protected. Dowling vs. American Hawaii Cruises, Inc., 133 F.R.D. 150 (1990) is to the same effect. Apparently the privilege is to be judged on a case-by-case basis.

What then is the internal auditor to do in the face of potential requests by plaintiffs for internal audit reports and working papers? Suggestions will be found in The IIA's "Report of the Subcommittee on Access to Internal Auditing Products":[6]

- Internal auditors should make sure that before they develop any policy on access, the board, management, the attorneys, and the chief audit executive are involved.

- Internal auditors should educate themselves about the access rights in their industries. They should also educate the board and management about the risks of access, and educate audit staff on both the risks of access and the organization's policy on access.

- Internal auditors should develop a written access policy. The policy should be documented and approved by counsel and by the audit committee of the board of directors or equivalent government body in the non-private sector. A sample policy, suggested by the "Report of the Subcommittee on Access to Internal Auditing Work Products,"[7] is shown in Exhibit 9-12.

More recently internal audit reports and working papers on environmental conditions have come to the attention of the courts. This situation is discussed in Chapter 26 on Environmental Auditing.

Schnee and Taylor suggest dividing into separate files the information internal auditors gather.[8] Statistical and other objective data would be held in files that are separated from those containing the internal auditor's subjective appraisals and judgments. The objective data is more likely to be unprotected from disclosure.

Another possibility is to limit the audit scope or to assign different auditors to review different subjects. Neither is a perfect solution, for logical reasons. Perhaps a more workable solution is to review and destroy internal audit working papers frequently. This activity may also pose legal problems.

Murphy suggests closer involvement with legal counsel in those situations where the self-evaluation privilege is not available to the internal auditors.[9] Where self-evaluations are channeled through counsel, the internal auditor's working papers and reports may benefit from attorney-client privilege. Counsel's reviews may also benefit the audit results. But too much leaning on counsel may be counterproductive. Counsel does not know as much about the inner workings of the corporation as does management or the internal auditors. Murphy's excellent article includes a long-range solution to court acceptance of privilege by proposing legislation that would provide for the privilege in appropriate cases.

In the meantime, internal auditors should be aware of the potential protection afforded to their evaluations, the need for advice from counsel in appropriate cases, and the fact that, while factual data may not be shielded, subjective evaluations, opinions, and recommendations may under proper conditions be protected by the self-evaluation privilege.

Exhibit 9-12
A Sample Access Policy

It is the policy of the XYZ Organization to restrict assess to the work product of its internal auditors to those persons with a "need to know" or to those who have a right of access by virtue of law, contract provision, power of subpoena, or court order.

The chief audit executive is authorized to restrict access to those persons falling into one or more of the categories set forth in this policy. Persons who do not satisfy the criteria for access set forth herein may request permission to gain access to internal auditing work products following procedures established by the chief audit executive for such purpose.

Permission to gain access to the work products of internal auditors will be granted under the following terms and conditions:

- The objective is to gain an understanding of particular processes, functions, or controls within the organization or to gain an understanding of the internal audit function.
- Access is part of a joint undertaking between the internal audit activity and other auditors, such as the organization's external auditors, for their mutual benefit.

Permission to gain access to the work products of internal auditing will not be routinely granted under the following terms and conditions.

- The organization is a target in a criminal investigation.

Exhibit 9-12 (Cont.)

- The purpose is to gather evidence to assert claims or damages against the organization.
- The purpose is to make public disclosure of portions of the internal audit activity's work product.

Requests such as these must be submitted in writing to an appeals committee that is composed of external parties (board members and external auditors), and internal parties (management, legal, and internal auditors).

References

[1]Cater Jr., C.W., "Standards for Working Papers," *The Internal Auditor,* April 1978, 68-75.

[2]Gray, Glen L., and Maryann Jacobi Gray, *Enhancing Internal Auditing Through Innovative Practices* (Altamonte Springs, FL: The Institute of Internal Auditors, 1996), 84-87.

[3]Office of the Auditor General of Canada, "Internal Auditing in Changing Management Culture," 1992, 34-36.

[4]Fargason, J.S., "Law and the Internal Auditing Profession," *Internal Audit Briefings* (Altamonte Springs, FL: The Institute of Internal Auditors, 1992), 27.

[5]The Institute of Internal Auditors, "Report of the Subcommittee on Access to Internal Auditing Work Products," 1991-1992, 10.

[6]"Report of the Subcommittee," 11, 12.

[7]Ibid, 18, 19.

[8]Schnee, E.J., and M.E. Taylor, "The IRS Has Been Gaining Access to Working Papers," *The Internal Auditor,* October 1983, 26-29.

[9]Murphy, J.E., "The Self-Evaluative Privilege," *The Journal of Corporation Law,* Spring 1982, 489-502.

Supplementary Readings

Bodnar, George H., "Nonrepudiation of "Paperless" Workpapers," *Internal Auditing*, Fall 1991, 77-81.

Flesher, Dale L., and Roberto De Magalhaes, "Electronic Workpapers," *Internal Auditor*, August 1995, 38-45.

Swalley, Michael C., and Charles K. Trible, "Enough is Enough," *Internal Auditor*, December 1991, 39-41.

Urbancic, Frank R., "Documenting the Application of Analytical Auditing Procedures," *Internal Auditing*, Fall 1993, 48-52.

Multiple-choice Questions

1. An adequately documented working paper should:
   a. Be concise but complete.
   b. Follow a unique form and arrangement.
   c. Contain examples of all forms and procedures used by the client.
   d. Not contain copies of client records.

2. Working papers are the property of the auditors. Good controls over working papers:
   a. Preclude showing working papers to clients.
   b. Require retention of working papers for at least three years.
   c. Require that electronic working papers be changed only by the auditor who created the working papers.
   d. Prevent surrender to a summons issued by a governmental agency.

3. Working papers should be disposed of when they are of no further use. Retention policies:
   a. Should specify a minimum retention period of three years.
   b. Should be prepared by the audit committee.
   c. Should be approved by legal counsel.
   d. Should be approved by the external auditor.

4. Internal auditors often include summaries within their working papers. Which of the following best describes the purpose of summaries?
   a. Summaries are prepared to conform to the *Standards*.
   b. Summaries are usually required for the completion of each section of an audit program.
   c. Summaries distill the most useful information from several working papers into a more usable form.
   d. Summaries are used to document the fact that the auditor has considered all relevant evidence.

5. A working paper is complete when it:
   a. Complies with the auditing department's format requirements.
   b. Contains all the elements of a finding.
   c. Is clear, concise, and accurate.
   d. Satisfies the audit objective for which it is developed.

6. According to the *Standards,* audit working papers should be reviewed to insure that:
   a. They are properly cross-referenced to the audit report.
   b. No issues are open at the conclusion of the field work.
   c. They meet or exceed the work standards of the organization's independent outside auditors.
   d. They are properly referenced for easy follow-up within the next year.

7. According to the *Standards,* the chief audit executive should establish policies for:
   a. Indexing and the type of working-paper files maintained.
   b. Defining the audit hours available for individual audits.
   c. Defining standardized tick marks and ensuring compliance with them.
   d. Ensuring the written documentation of all conversations held throughout the audit.

8. Which of the following does not describe one of the functions of audit working papers?
   a. Facilitates third-party review.
   b. Aids in the planning, performance, and review of audits.
   c. Provides the principal evidential support for the auditor's report.
   d. Aids in the professional development of the operating staff.

9. Working papers have the following characteristic:
   a. They are the property of the organization and are available to all organization employees.
   b. They document the auditing procedures performed, the information obtained, and the conclusions reached.
   c. They become the property of the independent outside auditors when completed.
   d. They should be retained permanently in the organization's records.

10. Each individual working paper should, at a minimum, contain:
    a. An expression of an audit opinion.
    b. A tick mark legend.
    c. A complete flowchart of the system of internal controls for the area being reviewed.
    d. A descriptive heading.

11. Working papers serve the following purpose for the internal auditor:
    a. Provide the client a place to make responses to audit recommendations.
    b. Make the audit report readable by providing a place to append exhibits.
    c. Provide the principal evidential support for the internal auditor's report.
    d. Provide a place to summarize overall audit recommendations.

12. Working papers should include:
    a. Documentation of the examination and evaluation of the adequacy and effectiveness of the system of internal control.
    b. Copies of all source documents examined in the course of the audit.
    c. Copies of all procedures that were reviewed during the audit.
    d. All working papers prepared during a previous audit of the same activity.

13. The primary criteria for determining the adequacy of working papers can be found in the:
    a. *Standards*.
    b. *Code of Ethics*.
    c. *Statement of Responsibilities of Internal Auditing*.
    d. U.S. Foreign Corrupt Practices Act.

14. Audit working papers are indexed by means of reference numbers. The primary purpose of indexing is to:
    a. Permit cross-referencing and simplify supervisory review.
    b. Support the audit report.
    c. Eliminate the need for follow-up reviews.
    d. Determine that working papers adequately support findings, conclusions, and reports.

15. An internal auditor's responsibility regarding control over audit working papers is best typified by:
    a. A requirement of full disclosure, including copies to cognizant government auditors.
    b. An obligation to provide the external auditors with copies of those pertaining to financial audits.
    c. A ban against allowing clients to view any portion that was auditor developed.
    d. A posture of restricting access to only those who have a legitimate need to know.

16. Which of the following statements is correct regarding internal audit workpaper documentation for a fraud investigation?
    I. All incriminating evidence should be included in the workpapers.
    II. All important testimonial evidence should be reviewed to ensure that it provides sufficient basis for the conclusions reached.
    III. If interviews are held with a suspected perpetrator, written transcripts or statements should be included in the workpapers.
    a. I only.
    b. II only.
    c. II and III only.
    d. I, II, and III.

17. Workpaper summaries, if prepared, can be used to:
    a. Promote efficient workpaper review by internal audit supervisors.
    b. Replace the detailed workpaper files for permanent retention.
    c. Serve as an internal audit report to senior management.
    d. Document the full development of audit findings.

18. Which of the following most completely describes the appropriate content of workpapers?
    a. Audit objectives, procedures, and conclusions.
    b. Purpose, criteria, techniques, and conclusions.
    c. Objectives, procedures, facts, conclusions, and recommendations.
    d. Audit subject, purpose, sampling information, and analysis.

19. Which of the following is a disadvantage of electronic workpapers?
    a. Each member of the audit staff must have a personal computer.
    b. Critical workpapers must still be printed and filed.
    c. Cross-referencing is more difficult.
    d. Specific technical training may be required.

20. Which of the following concepts distinguishes the retention of computerized audit workpapers from the traditional hard-copy form?
    a. Analyses, conclusions, and recommendations are filed on electronic media and are therefore subject to computer system controls and security procedures.
    b. Evidential support for all findings is copied and provided to local management during the closing conference and to each person receiving the final report.
    c. Computerized data files can be used in information systems audit procedures.
    d. Audit programs can be standardized to eliminate the need for a preliminary survey at each location.

Chapter 10
Control Self-assessment
by
Paul Makosz

Control self-assessment — why is it needed? Change, another driving force. New tools for a different world — the Gulf Canada contribution. What is control self-assessment? Tools and techniques. RSA, QSA, ESA, and other variations on the self-assessment theme. Implications for employees, management, auditors, and boards. Independence, objectivity, and facilitator ethics. The relationship between CSA and other internal audit activities. Necessary qualities for the CSA facilitation team. Pitfalls. Reflections.

● ●

Control Self-assessment — Why is it Needed?

In the post-Watergate era in the United States of the 1970s, many large multinational corporations were investigated to find out if they had been channeling funds illegally. It soon became apparent that many organizations maintained secret bank accounts from which they made payments not only to U.S. political parties but also to domestic and foreign government officials to support corrupt procurement of contracts. A political scandal had spilled over and revealed an unattractive side of big business.

Despite the Foreign Corrupt Practices Act, effective 1978, which forbade corporations to make payments that could be considered as bribes to government officials, but more importantly, imposed a requirement to maintain effective internal control, corporate failures continued in the 1980s. Five sponsors emerged to create the National Commission on Fraudulent Financial Reporting. These sponsors were:

1. American Institute of Certified Public Accountants
2. The Institute of Internal Auditors
3. American Accounting Association
4. Financial Executives Institute
5. Institute of Management Accountants

In 1987, after extensive research, the Commission published its findings, now known as the Treadway Report. Some very significant discoveries were made.

"Too often, [control] has been considered from a narrow perspective."

"We believe a realistic potential exists for reducing the risk of fraudulent financial reporting, provided the problem is considered and addressed as multidimensional."

"Internal control is effected by people...at every level of the organization."

As a result, the Commission created an organization, the Committee of Sponsoring Organizations (COSO), with members from each of the sponsors and a supporting staff. The Committee agreed to collaborate in developing an integrated control framework to help refocus the oversight capabilities of management, auditors, and directors. The resulting document, now known as the COSO report, was published five years later, changing forever the definition of internal control and thereby the approach of auditors, both internal and external.

Treadway and COSO had discovered that audit processes were too narrowly focused on financial accounting and ignored the broader *"control environment"* in which management and accounting decisions were formed. They noted that the control environment had a "pervasive effect" on the way financial statements were prepared. Clean audit reports had been issued to organizations whose accounting processes were sound and compliant but whose managements condoned unethical operating practices. Sooner or later such practices would come to light and result in massive fines or even corporate collapse. COSO recommended that auditors review and take into account these people-related factors before forming their opinions.

Suddenly, auditors found themselves challenged to evaluate tone at the top, ethics, competency, communication, human resource policies, even culture.

> *"Official policies specify what management wants to happen. Corporate culture determines what actually happens, and which rules are obeyed, bent, or ignored."*

The auditor's standard kit included many tools to dig deeply and identify weaknesses in procedure and breaches in compliance and in control activities, but the strength of these tools was based upon clarity, focus, and specificity. All of these could be independently verified against an established standard, template, or benchmark. Where was the guide for a healthy culture? Who could make a judgment call as to whether a new business strategy was unethical or just fiercely competitive or whether a culture was unhealthy? What audit tool could reliably assess the effectiveness of communication or the leadership of the CEO? Was an auditor's training adequate to support such tasks?

Change — Another Driving Force

The 1980s and 1990s saw another and more massive driving force that would compel auditors to broaden their approach and skills. These were the decades of deep and widespread corporate cutbacks, de-layering, sweeping corporate programs for total quality management and reengineering, enormous investment in radical technological solutions, and in many cases the elimination of the time honored control processes. According to Peter Drucker, in 1985 the Fortune 500 companies employed 30 percent of the American workforce, whereas in 1995 that figure had shrunk to 13 percent. More recent statistics show that the pace of corporate change has not noticeably slowed down. The spate of massive multinational mergers may even be accelerating the pace.

Does it make sense to spend six weeks auditing a system when many of the people who operate it may be changed within a few months and the system itself or parts of it may be replaced within a year? Not only will the audit results have a short shelf life, but perhaps the opportunity cost of the audit is too high. What other areas of risk were neglected? It might be more valuable to spend time auditing the impacts from widespread introduction of risk created by corporate turmoil. Again, the people-related component is significant. It is likely that managers and employees who know their job tenure may be short will think and act differently from those who confidently expect to work for one company for 30 years. What are the risks, the opportunities, and the consequences? And again, how do we audit them?

New Tools for a Different World — the Gulf Canada Contribution

Surprisingly an answer had emerged in the internal audit department of a Canadian oil and gas company based in Calgary, Alberta — Gulf Canada Resources Ltd. Having observed the reaction of Gulf Oil to the post-Watergate revelations and dismayed by the failure of conventional auditing techniques (even when well executed) to detect fraud, Gulf Canada's internal audit team had devised a new approach they called control self-assessment or CSA. Teams of employees and managers would attend a one-day workshop, facilitated by senior internal audit staff. In these workshops the teams openly identified what was working well, what was not working well, and what action needed to be taken.

Even in the earliest clumsy CSA workshops in 1987, two startling facts emerged:

1. In team workshops, with facilitators who have no hidden agenda, people tend to be very frank and truthful.

2. When people discover for themselves what their problems are, they become much more involved and committed to resolving them than if the problems are identified in an audit report.

In the second year of CSA workshops at Gulf Canada, two more important discoveries were made:

3. As long as the facilitator does not too narrowly prescribe what "control" means, people will identify and analyze the impact of *any significant factor* that affects their ability to achieve their objectives.

4. The factors that people describe as having the most impact are different from and much broader in scope than anything found in older models of internal control: they frequently cite issues regarding culture, communication, trust, ethics, and leadership.

By the time COSO was published in 1992, Gulf Canada's CSA process was routinely uncovering the full scope of issues prescribed in the new model. The company exemplified the business paradigm of the current era, having undergone several downsizings and reorganizations, a takeover, and comprehensive reengineering. Throughout these processes, CSA continued to provide reliable, up-to-date information on the full scope of the company's activities. Often, major risks were identified as they emerged, before any damage became widespread and in time for the company's top management to take corrective action.

In the meantime, Gulf Canada managers had written articles and made many presentations on CSA, attracting the attention of The IIA and corporate internal audit groups worldwide, many of whom visited Gulf Canada to participate in CSA training courses or simply to seek out best practices. By the end of 1994, more than 300 workshops had been conducted in over eight years. Although the company's CSA program was discontinued in 1995 following yet another takeover and drastic change in new management's attitude to governance, many internal audit groups across the world had adopted Gulf's original CSA philosophy and were experimenting with or building their own CSA programs.

What is Control Self-assessment?

The original Gulf approach encouraged experimentation in a quest for continuous improvement of CSA methodology. As a result, many organizations tried different approaches to CSA, some more successful than others. As this chapter goes to press there are many processes that bear the name of CSA or CRSA (control risk self-assessment) but not all of them are true to its guiding principles. To understand what CSA is, it is necessary first to understand these principles.

"Control" means a broad integrated framework that takes into account all major internal factors that influence the achievement of the organization's objectives. It aims to be holistic or systemic in scope. To date, the only published frameworks comfortably fitting that definition are those of COSO in the U.S., Cadbury in the UK, and CoCo (the Criteria of

Control) published by the Canadian Institute of Chartered Accountants. All of these models see people as the most important factor affecting control. COSO and Cadbury, both published in 1992, are essentially similar although significant further refinement of the Cadbury model has taken place in the UK. Only CoCo, published three years later, recognizes the emergence of CSA and its usefulness through actively engaging all levels of personnel in the assessment. The CoCo board, building upon the enormous contribution of COSO, devoted considerable effort to simplifying concepts and language so that the full scope of control could be discussed as easily on the factory floor as in the boardroom. The board sought to devise a language also accessible to all those who might attend CSA workshops.

The "self" in self-assessment is also a fundamental criterion for CSA. It distinguishes CSA from other audit processes. An auditor is presumed to have sufficient knowledge and expertise to independently form an accurate assessment of control. CSA presumes the opposite: that the scope of control is so broad and the pace of change is so great that to form an accurate assessment of the current state of control, it will require all the knowledge and expertise of those who perform the tasks. Unlike audit, where in addition to audit investigation the client donates information to the auditor so that the latter can form an assessment, *the participants in the CSA process form their own assessment*. It is vital to understand this distinction and yet some traditional auditors have failed to grasp the point, simply sending out their usual internal control questionnaires for clients to complete and return so that the auditor can then form an opinion. Clearly such approaches involve no control assessment by oneself, just answering questions posed by an external assessor.

"Assessment" is a more accurate term than measurement when it comes to evaluation of control. So many factors combine to influence the outcome of an organization's endeavors that mathematical precision inevitably yields to intuition and judgment. Even the very best risk assessment tools are ultimately dependent on the exercise of subjective judgment, sometimes of one or two key individuals. CSA mitigates the risk associated with subjectivity by gathering the subjective opinions of many different observers, usually in a group setting, seeking to identify common patterns before arriving at a judgment. Note that CSA is not a survey that can be gathered quickly and remotely from many individuals. Such surveys gather data that experts subsequently process to form an external opinion. However, in CSA the information is gathered and discussed interactively by those who are close to the action, before opinions are formed. Although numbers are used to depict CSA results graphically, the graphs are merely an invitation or portal to the discussion and analysis that has taken place.

To be faithful to the foregoing principles, CSA must involve a systemic framework and extensive, interactive discussion of observed strengths and weaknesses that affect the achievement of an organization's objective by those whose function it is to achieve them. Accuracy will be improved if participants are in a setting that rewards open, truthful communication. Objectivity will be improved if an independent outsider facilitates the process. Corrective action will more likely ensue if participants discover for themselves the source of the problem and make any decisions to resolve it.

Given the foregoing, CSA may be described as follows:

> *A process whereby employee teams and management, at local and at executive levels, continuously maintain awareness of all material factors affecting the likelihood of achieving the organization's objectives, thereby enabling them to make appropriate adjustments. To promote independence, objectivity, and quality within the process, as well as effective governance, it is desirable that internal auditors are involved in the process and that they independently report results to senior management and board committees.*

Tools and Techniques

Although there are now many providers of CSA services and tools, the best results are obtained by following the above principles. Some approaches are much more likely to achieve success with lower risk to participants and auditors alike. The CSA workshop approach, whereby auditors with specialized training facilitate workshops across the organization, has been particularly successful over a relatively long period of time.

If, as COSO and CoCo state, people are at the heart of all control issues, then it is important to reach them in a forum that allows for full freedom of expression and also ensures that all relevant ground has been covered. Most people enjoy participating in CSA workshops. Even those of a quiet or shy disposition will find it useful and interesting to spend a day with their colleagues discussing how their work could be accomplished more smoothly or faster or more reliably. However, to go beyond running a pleasurable retreat and gain optimal value from the day requires hard work and advance preparation by the facilitation team.

There are five key components to a successful workshop, four of which are primarily the responsibility of the facilitation team. First, the facilitators will interview management and other participants before the workshop begins. They will gain an understanding of the team's primary purpose, current objectives, and significance in relation to the organization's overall strategy. They will research any available documentation to try to understand the team's function, processes, and dynamics. This activity makes it more likely that the discussion will flow evenly without frequent interruption to explain terminology to the facilitators, and it reduces the risk that the facilitators will miss important verbal cues that signal the need for deeper discussion of a sensitive topic. The facilitators must also be prepared to avoid the risk that they may form strong early opinions that could threaten their objectivity during the workshop.

Secondly, the team attending the workshop needs time to brainstorm and develop ideas that are currently prominent in their thinking. They need time to discuss these ideas and they need to see that their thoughts are accepted by the facilitators. Naturally, any group of people will want to talk about its own ideas first before listening to any outside agenda. Therefore, after a brief introduction, a good workshop begins with brainstorming about what operations are working well for the team and what are the major obstacles they encounter in trying to achieve their objectives or primary purpose. Not surprisingly, during the first half-hour of a workshop, the team identifies issues that are a significant barrier to its efficiency and effectiveness. Discussion of these issues and of group strengths and weakness may take two hours or more. During this process the team starts to identify root causes rather than just symptoms and often comes to a realization that its own internal strengths are sufficient to address some of the issues. The facilitators also note those aspects that will require outside assistance so that help can be offered after the workshop.

The third component can commence when participants are satisfied that their concerns have been identified and discussed. Using one of the control frameworks as a guide, the participants can answer a series of questions that ensure that the whole spectrum of control issues receives scrutiny in the workshop. Many CSA teams use electronic voting technology to gather votes on these issues and a laptop computer to capture the key elements of the discussion. The equipment speeds up the process of gathering information, provides numbers from which graphs can be prepared, and is fun for the participants. The equipment cost may be prohibitive for small audit departments but they should not feel discouraged. They can take heart from the fact that Gulf's team ran more then 150 workshops with great success over several years before becoming the first to experiment with electronic voting in 1991. Genuinely listening to participants and accepting their comments is ultimately far more important than technology.

The fourth critical component is to quickly return a summary of the discussion and votes, if any, to the participants. This is very different from the process for preparing and distributing an audit report. First of all, the summary and the assessment contained therein belong to the participating team; it is a record of their discussion and should be returned to them at the earliest possible opportunity, preferably the following day. They need the record of their thoughts so they can begin taking corrective action on key issues. If the facilitation team spends days tidying up the document and wordsmithing, as is common with audit reports, two very destructive things happen: first, the participants return to their desks, become consumed with pressing tasks, forget what was discussed, and put off taking action; secondly, when the document does finally appear, pride of authorship and ownership of the findings has evaporated and it is treated as a report by an outsider.

The fifth and final component that determines success is action. The participant team and managers must decide which actions to undertake first as they rarely have time to immediately do everything they discussed. Typically, the items that have the biggest payoff and that are within the team's own authority and immediate resource capacity will be done first. Very often there will be other potentially valuable actions that require either the application of resources beyond the team's capacity or cooperation from other teams. In these cases, the auditor can help the team and local management by drawing the attention of senior management or by arranging for the teams to get together. Occasionally the issue may appear very significant but require deeper analysis or investigation to define the extent of the problem. In these cases, other audit tools may be helpful.

As with material findings from a conventional audit there may be a need to report findings to top management and the audit committee if the risk to the organization is significant. While such findings may emerge from a single workshop, it is more likely that they will come from a comparison of results from several workshops, all of which reveal a disturbing pattern or trend. As with audit, it is important that these issues are brought first to senior management (unless that is the source of the problem) so they can take immediate action.

Variations on a Theme

In the late 1990s the concept of risk management was widely adopted. Unlike the internal control frameworks, the concept of risk includes external factors which can affect the organization's ability to achieve its objectives. Many CSA practitioners simply adapted their existing CSA process to take account of the external factors included in risk. The overlap between the two frameworks is very high. Similarly, proponents of quality management also discovered an overlap with frameworks such as the Baldridge model. As a result there are now several forms of self-assessment — CSA, QSA, RSA, MSA, GSA, ESA — using the same methodology and similar indicators to track control, quality, risk, management, governance, and ethics.

Sometimes it may make sense to invite individuals from different parts of the organization who may not even know each other but who are all significant links in a process chain, e.g., sourcing, procurement, receiving dock, inventory control, production parts, and accounts payable are all part of the purchasing chain. In such sessions the participants typically discover significant opportunities to remedy overlaps, gaps, and costly failures in communication.

The success of CSA workshops creates a demand from the organization. People find the tool useful and tell their peers. Often teams that have just been through a workshop ask the facilitators to come back and run another workshop in which they hope to delve deeper into a problem area and devise a solution. Although this may create a resource headache for audit managers, it means that the audit team is visibly adding value to the organization. The same facilitators and hardware and software tools that are useful in CSA workshops can be applied in these sessions also.

Most of the time it is desirable for CSA to be provided internally, as it is an integral learning process of the organization. However, in three situations it may be desirable to seek outside resources. The first of these is in initial training and implementation when stakes are very high and skills are at their lowest: using experienced professional assistance can bridge the gap. The second is when top management, boards, or board committees decide to have a CSA workshop. Again the stakes are very high, independence and objectivity are critical, and there may also be interest in informal benchmark comparisons with similar external groups. The third situation occurs when well-established CSA programs need a tune-up or outside review. This is a good idea periodically because CSA practice and technology are still evolving rapidly as we improve our understanding of control, psychology, and application of technology.

Implications for Employees, Management, Auditors, and Boards

From the standpoint of the auditee or client, the CSA auditor is primarily a facilitator providing a helpful forum and agenda whereby the clients can discover for themselves the true state of affairs and decide what changes are necessary. The independence and objectivity of the auditor are viewed as assets that will bring added focus to bear on the most critical issues requiring resolution or support. This is welcomed as future-oriented and consultative, adding value to executive and employee teams alike. As a consequence CSA workshops are often requested by clients and conducted on an annual basis across the entire organization.

To senior management, CSA offers an exceptionally well-informed and constantly up-to-date overview of emerging risks and opportunities. This gives management the opportunity to compare their strategy with current reality and make the necessary adjustments to ensure that objectives are realistic and will be achieved — the primary purpose of control.

For directors, audit committees, and others responsible for governance, CSA has significant implications. The external auditing profession's narrow focus on financial reporting has frequently resulted in shock and embarrassment when corporate catastrophes occurred unexpectedly because major control factors were left unexamined. COSO, CoCo, Cadbury, and various risk frameworks have broadened the internal audit scope of review to include any factor that significantly affects operational efficiency, effectiveness, or legality. Directors will now gain a much more comprehensive overview. However, those who volunteer to serve on audit committees because of their financial or managerial acumen may be startled to find themselves reviewing reports on environmental management deficiencies or inequitable application of human resource policies. As a result, more board committees may be formed and auditors may find themselves reporting not only to audit committees but also to other standing committees such as Safety and Environment, Ethics, Governance, or even to the board itself.

Independence, Objectivity, and Facilitator Ethics

Although CSA typically brings the auditor/facilitator into a closer relationship with clients or auditees, it is extremely important to maintain independence and objectivity. Workshop participants are often more frank in their disclosures because they trust the facilitator as a reliable outsider whose voice, if added to their own, will be influential in bringing about change. For this reason the pre-workshop research phase is vitally important as the facilitator gains some independent external benchmarks to use for comparison. Teams usually understand the audit role quite well and, despite the closer relationship produced by the workshop, they respect the auditor's independence.

Facilitators must also mind their own ethics in two crucial respects. First it is important to acknowledge that CSA is dependent upon participants speaking out frankly and being honest about individuals. Occasionally they may risk inviting criticism or damage to their careers in doing so — from their manager, from their peers, or from an inexperienced facilitator. This could be because they discuss their concerns about inappropriate behavior by themselves or more importantly by others or simply because they disregard a cultural taboo. If facilitators condone or encourage such comment, they may have betrayed the trust of the forthright participant. Also, when the other participants observe this they quickly learn that, while the facilitators encourage frankness and open disclosure, they take no responsibility for the consequences. Open communication quickly dies. The correct approach is to set opinion and judgment of the action of individuals aside and explore the root cause of the problems, asking the group what they can do to eliminate the problem. Major problems are usually rooted in culture or a system, not an individual.

The second aspect facilitators must recognize is that they too are human and fallible and so need to manage their own potential for conflict of interest. A facilitator may be tempted to take a significant issue to senior management before the team has had adequate time to address it. Another facilitator may be conscious of a personal career objective to join the very team in the workshop and so may be overly gentle, or may overcompensate by being too tough, or may simply grandstand to display talent. Unlike most audits where written work may be produced in a calm atmosphere, free from distraction and subject to supervisory review before a report is issued, facilitation is immediate, interactive, and highly visible. Career prospects of participants and facilitators alike can be altered by a chance remark. Facilitators should review their potential for conflict of interest with their supervisors and take the appropriate action prior to undertaking the assignment.

The Relationship Between CSA and Other Internal Audit Activities

In contrast to most conventional audit activities, CSA has a very broad scope, gathers material information quickly and interactively, and spends little time in verification and reporting.

From an audit manager's perspective it provides a fast and usually reliable macro-level assessment of risk but, unlike some audit tools, it is not designed to dig deeply. Where CSA is performed continuously across an organization it is an ideal tool to identify risks and high value areas where it would be beneficial to conduct an audit. Workshop participants are usually thoughtful in identifying the major problem areas.

If the nature of the problem is clear and the organization is moving swiftly to address it, there may be no need to carry out an audit, because detection, acceptance, and remedial action have already taken place. However, when the problem seems big but ill-defined, or the nature of the problem is of such sensitivity that it must be investigated more deeply, or if it is not being taken seriously, it makes sense to use other audit tools to fill the gap. The effect is dramatic. Every audit brings major results. For this reason CSA is a gift to auditors. The hit-or-miss element of traditional auditing is reduced and all the subsequent audit findings produce value for the organization, as opposed to just providing assurance.

Some CSA consultants advise using audits to verify or validate what has been disclosed in workshops. Unless the situation is similar to those described in the preceding paragraph, most workshop participants will regard this as insulting and feel the workshop was a waste of time since they will then have undergone both a workshop and an audit. Auditors must use common sense in these situations. Workshops distill group opinions and it is very rare for a whole group of workshop participants to lie. [Author's note: This has happened to me only once in hundreds of workshops and was easily detectable because it clearly conflicted with pre-workshop research findings.]

Of course the group's perceptions may be in error, but this is rarely the case when they are discussing their own close area of expertise. It is much more likely when they are expressing opinions as to situations outside their area of activity. It is common for groups to express derogatory opinions as to the competency or motives of another team or management when their own work is being impaired by the actions or decisions of others. If the facilitator questions the certainty of the group's opinions in such instances, most will admit that they are making presumptions; hence the need for sensitivity and interactive questioning.

Necessary Qualities for the CSA Facilitation Team

Although training and technology can greatly assist facilitators, neither of these assets is of any value if fundamental personal qualities are lacking. Honesty, empathy, and respect for others are far more important than techniques. Workshop participants will readily forgive a little clumsiness in technique if they believe the facilitators are honest and trying to do their best for the team. However, if they believe they are being treated disrespectfully or worse, that the facilitators have a hidden agenda, workshops can be disastrous. Trust is earned slowly, through open communication and multiple demonstrations of good faith; it is lost quickly through a careless or insincere remark.

All facilitators must have a genuine respect for other people, have high interpersonal skills, be curious, listen carefully, and be driven by a desire to provide value to the client and the organization. Good facilitators add to these fundamental qualities a deep knowledge of systemic control, healthy skepticism, skill in facilitation, organizational ability, and expert knowledge of any software or hardware used in the workshop or reporting process. The best facilitators have, in addition, good (and quick) analytical and learning skills that they use to understand what they have gathered and convert it into meaningful conclusions for the organization.

Pitfalls

CSA is both simple and amazingly complex. It is simple because it involves a group of people with a common purpose and shared experiences coming together to identify opportunities for improvement. However, any process involving people is complex and affected by recent and historical events beyond the knowledge of the facilitator. Consequently there are many pitfalls to trap the unwary and inexperienced. Some of the most common pitfalls have been identified above: inadequate pre-workshop preparation; failure to give the group its own time to brainstorm before introducing the auditor's agenda; ignoring the "self" in self-assessment; conflicting interests of the facilitator; and distrusting the truthfulness of the group. Some other common pitfalls are listed below.

Too many workshops and not enough analysis is a common failing, especially when audit teams first implement CSA. Workshops are exciting and provide a rich stream of information, so it is tempting to run as many as possible. If CSA teams do not set aside a generous allocation of time to review the results, learn from them, refine their subsequent questioning, and communicate back to the organization, they have seriously failed to achieve potential value. The workshop participants have benefited but not the rest of the organization; 75 percent or more of the benefit from CSA has been lost.

Not keeping promises or making too many is another common failing. Facilitators will learn that it is important to only make promises on which they can deliver, e.g., they can promise to communicate issues fully to senior management but not that action will be taken by senior management, unless that firm commitment has been obtained in advance. Each workshop generates its own bundle of raised expectations and promises made; if there is no visible subsequent action, the result is demoralization and distrust.

Insensitivity to participants' need and fears is also a common failing with junior facilitators. When working with any group it helps to be aware of socioeconomic factors. Not everyone in the group will be functioning at peak performance: someone may be having family problems; another may be in financial difficulties; another may have a substance abuse problem or be experiencing a midlife crisis. Most workshops have a few participants who are afraid that what they say may damage their careers. This is simply how people are. Awareness of these possibilities will help facilitators temper their remarks and be sensitive in their requests for frankness.

Questionnaires, with a few exceptions, are not self-assessment. Many organizations use excellent questionnaires for employee surveys but the assessment is made by a third party who interprets the data. For the respondents, there is no sense of ownership, no sense of personal commitment to making change happen, no sense of teamwork in the face of difficulty. Often there is no input from those who are exceptionally busy or exceptionally critical. If your audit budget or resources are small, it may be necessary to gather data through questionnaires but it is essential to augment the data so gathered by going out and talking to people, seeking to understand why they voted as they did, and seeking out those who may not have contributed. Extraverts are another large group in the population who dislike questionnaires but will enjoy talking in an interview.

Jumping in at the deep end without knowing how to swim may be a reasonable approach in an entirely new field. This is what the pioneering efforts at Gulf were all about — those first stumbling attempts took place in 1987, many years ago. We now know a lot more about CSA and this information is available through some excellent training courses, the CSA Center at The IIA, and a growing, though still patchy, body of literature. As professional auditors we have a duty to learn as much as we can before offering services to our organizations.

Reflections

In the years since it first started, CSA has spread rapidly across the world and now appears in a number of guises such as RSA, QSA, etc. It is being practiced in industry, government, health, education, international multilateral bodies, and not-for-profit agencies. In all of these sectors it has been well received by thousands of clients who see it as a breath of fresh air. Why? Perhaps it is because we are now asking them about issues in their world — the real world — and recognizing their expertise. Perhaps, also, because we are beginning to understand that people, not procedures, are the root cause of organizational success.

Suggested Readings

Baker, Larry L., and Rodger D. Graham, "Control Self-assessment," *Internal Auditor*, April 1996, 52-57.
Bjelke, Sten I., and Kjell M. Nilsson, "Automating the Self-assessment Process," *Internal Auditor*, August 1997, 16-19.
Calhoun, Charles, "Validating CSA," *Internal Auditing Alert*, May 1998, 1-3.
Calhoun, Charles, "CSA: Avoiding the Pitfalls," *Internal Auditing Alert*, April 1998, 6-8.

Figg, Jonathan, "The Power of CSA," *Internal Auditor*, August 1999, 28-35.

Fritsch, Kurt P., "A Revolution in Our Midst?" *Internal Auditor*, June 1996, 85-86.

Hawkins, Kyleen W., and Bill Huckaby, "Using CSA to Implement COSO," *Internal Auditor*, June 1998, 50-55.

McCuaig, Bruce, "Auditing, Assurance, and CSA," *Internal Auditor*, June 1998, 43-48.

Marden, Ronald, and Randy Edwards, "Using Control Self-assessment to Maintain Growth," *Internal Auditing,* Fall 1997, 15-19.

Summerell, Mike, "The Way of the Dinosaur," *Internal Auditor*, February 2000, 96.

Multiple-choice Questions

1. Conflict of interest for facilitator.

Q. You notice that you have been scheduled to run a CSA workshop for a team you are eager to join in a few months when your term in the audit department is completed. You:
   a. Commence preparations for this workshop as you would for any other.
   b. Before doing anything, disclose your interest in this team to your supervisor.
   c. Suggest that a different facilitator be scheduled for this client.
   d. Make special preparations to ensure that your work will be outstanding.
   e. Conduct some early interviews to find out if the workshop may threaten your plans.

Rank your actions from more appropriate to least appropriate, giving explanations for each choice.

A. Suggested answer: b, c, a, d, e.
   Like it or not, you have a significant conflict of interest as this workshop and its results could significantly affect your future career prospects.
   Unless other factors are involved, (b) represents the safe, most open and honest choice. If you cannot disclose your interest, then (c) is still safe and honest.
   Option (a) might be appropriate if your supervisor and CSA team have already discussed how all of your workshops can have such conflicts as you near the end of your term.
   In (d), despite your good intentions, your conflict is already affecting your approach, without your team and supervisor's knowledge.
   In (e), you have begun to put your own interests ahead of those of the client and the CSA team.

2. Preparation for the workshop — establishing a relationship.

Q. Rank, from most to least important, the following sample of actions to be taken in preparing for a CSA workshop with a new client, Team X:
   a. Interview the manager.
   b. Read through past audit reports relating to the area.
   c. Review other CSA workshops for any comments on Team X's area.
   d. Understand the team's objectives.

e.   Interview some of the proposed attendees.

f.   Review Team X performance statistics, e.g., budget/actual reports.

Explain the principles underlying your rationale.

A.   Suggested answer: a, d, e, f, b, c.

First, get to know the client and the client's business (a, d, e).

Second, establish a relationship of trust and mutual respect before the workshop (a, e).

Third, explain the workshop purpose and process to the client (a, e).

Fourth, identify team and personal concerns and expectations regarding the workshop (a, e, d).

Fifth, review evidence of how X is perceived elsewhere in the organization (f, b, c).

Sixth, understand how the client, based on past experience, sees you (b, a, e).

3.   Control activities vs. control environment.

Q.   Your supervisor, who has not yet received any CSA training, has pointed out to you that only 15 percent of the questions you plan to ask in a forthcoming CSA workshop deal with compliance issues such as policies and procedures. She suggests that you substitute more of these "audit-related" questions in place of ones that deal with "HR" or "soft" control factors, such as ethics, communication, and culture.

You:

a.   Agree to make the changes proposed by your manager.

b.   Agree to add in some more questions dealing with control activities.

c.   Leave the balance of questions as they are and point out that CoCo and COSO were developed in response to audit failure to detect catastrophic issues, largely because of ignoring control environment factors.

Rank these choices from most to least appropriate and explain the relevant factors.

A.   Suggested answer: c, b, a.

Although control activities such as setting procedures and policies are important factors in maintaining effective control, they are far less powerful than culture, tone at the top, ethics and competency, which form the essence of control environment as defined in COSO. It is extremely important that auditors broaden their scope to assess these factors. Because they are all people-related, it becomes important to access the observations of a wide range of employees, using tools such as CSA.

(b) is often adopted as a compromise measure but is far less satisfactory than (a) because it puts disproportionate emphasis on less material factors, overburdens the participants and lessens the opportunity for due discussion of major issues. (c) is not an adequate answer, as it ignores the lessons learned in the Treadway study, adoption of COSO by The IIA, and may well cause false assurance to be given to senior management and audit committees, because scope of review has been too limited.

4. Distribution of CSA findings.

Q. In the course of the CSA process you are asked by one of the participants, "Who will receive the 'report' produced from this process?"

You reply:

a. Only the immediate CSA participants.

b. Only senior management and the audit department.

c. Anyone in the organization who asks for a copy.

d. Findings will be shared with any other person or group in the organization, if it will help them or the participating team to accomplish the organization's objectives more effectively.

A. In the first place, such an important rule of process should never be left to a chance question in the workshop. The protocol should be stated explicitly before the workshop discussion commences. This means that participants know in advance who will have access to their comments and can apply the appropriate level of thought before speaking out on a topic. Secondly, the word "report" is less accurate than "summary" in a true self-assessment process, where the opinions being offered are those of the participants, not the auditor alone.

Given the foregoing comments, (d) is the most effective protocol. It ensures that the process is fairly described beforehand and that key findings can be shared wherever necessary, without breaching any agreement as to confidentiality. (a) may protect sensitive participants but robs the institution of an opportunity to learn and robs the participants of an opportunity to gain external support. (b) is unsatisfactory in that participants have no opportunity to audit the document and ensure that it fairly represents their discussion; this in turn breeds suspicion and distrust of the process. Because the discussion in CSA is often exploratory, far-reaching, and blunt, (c) represents a major risk to the organization: competitors can use this information to their advantage, and the media, by publishing flaws disclosed in CSA, can unfairly damage the reputation of an institution which is openly self-assessing in order to make improvements.

5. Which of the following are reasons to involve employees in the control self-assessment process?

I. Employees become more motivated to do their jobs correctly.

II. Employees are objective about their jobs.

III. Employees can provide an independent assessment of internal controls.

IV. Managers want feedback from their employees.

a. I and II only.

b. III and IV only.

c. I and IV only.

d. II and IV only.

PART 3

SAMPLING AND ANALYTICAL METHODS

Chapter 11
Sampling

Introduction to sampling. Sample selection and how to take the sample. The various sample selection techniques: Random numbers, interval, stratified, and cluster. Haphazard and judgment sampling defined. Sample sizes. Statistical sampling theory simplified. Various sampling plans: sampling for attributes, stop-and-go sampling, discovery sampling. Variables sampling and the variables sampling techniques: mean-per unit, difference estimation, and ratio estimation. Formula for use in variables sampling. Dollar Unit Sampling (DUS), also called Monetary Unit Sampling. When judgment sampling is appropriate. Contrasting statistical and nonstatistical sampling. Evaluating sample results. Population proportions in known and unknown populations. Summary of sampling rules. Various selection techniques and sampling plans and when to use them.

• •

Introduction

Sampling is the process of applying audit procedures to less than an entire population to draw conclusions about the totality. Sampling theory assumes that a demonstrated quality of a representative sample can be extrapolated to the population.

Sampling, in essence, is the process of learning about a great deal by looking at a little. At the same time, by sampling the auditor must accept the risk that the sample selected does not truly represent the population; that is, that the characteristics projected from the sample are not the same as those that would be found if the entire population — or a larger sample — were audited.

Sampling is not an end in itself; it is only a means to an end. The sample and the sample results are merely raw data — data that must be weighed and sifted. That data must be analyzed for materiality, reasons, causes, and actual or potential effect. The sample is but the first step to an informed audit opinion.

With the increasing use of information technology, the auditor must decide whether sampling is the most efficient and effective way to obtain evidence. With data warehouses and information retrieval approaches, it may be more efficient to perform computer-assisted tests on the whole population. Given the movement toward enterprise-wide software and other integrated software, an auditor may decide not to sample from a population but to audit 100 percent of the population.

Generalized audit software and other techniques may allow an auditor to more efficiently audit 100 percent of a population than to select a sample and audit the sample. This is especially the case where the entity has eliminated manual documents.

This chapter will explain how the auditor decides: (1) which sampling approach to use; (2) how many units (or sample items) to select; (3) how to select the units; and (4) how to evaluate the results in terms of the objectives of the audit procedures.

Sampling terminology often varies in textbooks and in certification examinations. Accordingly, the CIA examination questions at the end of this chapter were used as written, without attempting to establish consistent terminology. But the reader needs to be aware of the variations to be able to deal effectively with sampling terminology.

This book presents a survey of key sampling techniques and plans. For a more detailed discussion of specific sampling methods, see the supplementary reading list at the end of the chapter.

Sample Selection

When auditors select samples, they may take at least two paths. The first leads to the directed sample; the second leads to the random sample.

The directed or purposeful sample is used when auditors suspect serious errors or manipulation and want either to obtain evidence to support their suspicions or to find as many of the suspected items as they can. This process has nothing to do with statistical sampling. It is pure detective work. And the better a sleuth the auditor is the more useful his or her sample will be. But auditors may not draw conclusions about a population from a directed sample. Such a conclusion would be completely unwarranted, because the sample did not represent the population.

The random sample seeks to represent, as closely as possible, the population from which it was drawn. When auditors take a random sample, they are trying to take a picture, in miniature, of the great mass of records or data that make up the population from which the sample is selected. The larger the sample, the more closely it depicts the population. In audit argot, the sample is then termed "representative."

Statistical sampling permits internal auditors to measure sampling risk — that is the risk that a sample will not represent the population. To measure that risk statistically the sample selection must be random. Random selection means that every item in the population has an equal chance of being selected.

Nonstatistical sampling does not permit the auditor to measure the sampling risk objectively, since each population item did not have an equal chance of being selected. Nevertheless, nonstatistical sampling can be of value in such sampling plans as purposive (directed) or other forms of judgmental sampling.

It is possible, of course, for an auditor to select items at random without attempting to draw statistical inferences about the entire population. But by using random selection the auditor could reject any imputation of bias and, also, feel more comfortable that the sample selected is more likely to represent the values of the population.

Taking the Sample

There are certain rules for taking a representative sample. Here are three fundamental principles of selection that apply in any sampling procedure:

1. Know your population because audit conclusions may be based only on the sample taken from that population.

2. Define the sampling unit in terms of the audit objectives.

3. Let every item (sampling unit) in the population have an equal (or known) chance of being selected.

The mass of data, records, or documents from which the auditor selects a sample is variously referred to as population, universe, and field. They all mean the same thing. They also imply something that is central to good sampling: Know what you are testing. Clearly define the audit objective. Establish the population to be tested. Identify the sampling unit to be examined. The initial questions must be: "What are the objectives of my audit?" "What is the population I want to test?" "What are the sampling units I need to examine?" These are significant questions, having to do as much with good audit practice as with statistical sampling.

If the three principles above are violated, the tests are open to serious questions on technical grounds, and conclusions are without objective support. Consider, for example, the auditor who wishes to estimate the annual fuel consumption of the organization's automotive fleet. The fleet is made up of the following 750 pieces of automotive equipment:

50	12-wheel trucks
100	pickup trucks
100	forklift trucks
200	passenger cars
300	motor scooters

Let us assume in this example that the fleet has been well maintained and that there are no "gas guzzlers" within each group. Since the motor scooters were the most numerous, the auditor decided to select a sample of 50 motor scooters, examine fuel consumption for these 50, and project the finding to all 750 pieces of equipment. Stated this way, the results would be clearly ludicrous. Yet auditors fall into similar traps in their sampling every day. For example, in their audits they might:

- Select a sample of invoices for all those paid in July and use that test to form an opinion of all invoices paid during the year.

- Select a sample of travel vouchers of domestic travel only and project their findings to a population that includes foreign travel as well.

- Select a sample of purchase orders from a population that excludes all orders under $5,000 and express opinions on all purchase orders issued — from $1 on up.

- Sample inventory records in one tool crib and express an opinion on the records of tool cribs in all the many locations within the organization.

Each of these opinions and projections — unless properly qualified — is without support and just plain wrong. In the case of the motor vehicles, the auditor either should have sampled from all the various types of equipment or should have restricted the audit opinion solely to the scooters sampled.

Hence, auditors must always remember to define the population and the sampling unit in terms of the audit objectives. For example, the population of the 750 vehicles can have a different meaning, depending on the audit objective. If the objective were to determine whether all vehicles are maintained regularly — and let us assume that every item of equipment, be it scooter or truck, must be periodically maintained — the population assumes a different character than if the audit objective were to estimate fuel consumption. When the population or the sampling unit is improperly defined in the light of the audit objective, the result is bad sampling and bad auditing.

When the population and sampling unit are properly defined, the whole audit thrust and approach improve. A good technique is to plot the population *before* sampling to identify subpopulations or strata.

The principles on which scientific sampling is based operate only if the sample is selected at random. There are several ways in which random selection can be accomplished. Each method has its advantages and disadvantages. The three common methods are referred to as: (1) random number sampling; (2) interval (systematic) sampling; and (3) stratified random sampling. In addition, three nonrandom sampling techniques are discussed: cluster sampling, haphazard sampling, and judgment sampling.

Random Number Sampling

Random number sampling is generally considered the most likely to result in a representative sample. It makes use of computer algorithms or tables of digits that have been scientifically "randomized." The algorithms or tables provide substantially complete assurance that every item in a population has an equal chance of being selected. Many such tables have been compiled.

In general, the tables are easy to use if some simple rules are followed:

- Enter the tables by opening them at random and, with eyes averted, place a pencil point on the page. Start the number selection with the digit closest to the pencil point.

- Use as many digits in a line as there are digits in the reference numbers of the documents being selected. For example, if receiving memos being tested have a maximum of seven digits in their numbers, use seven adjoining numbers from the tables.

- Once a starting point has been selected, proceed through the tables in a predetermined order — down the columns or across the rows — without deviation, because deviation implies personal bias.

- If an applicable number does not appear, continue on to the next.

The numbers selected can then be arranged in numerical order for ease in locating the documents bearing those numbers, assuming the documents themselves are filed in numerical sequence.

Random number sampling can sometimes be difficult to use. Documents may not be numbered or may resist ready identification, or the identification numbers assigned may be quite long; thus it would be an almost impossible task to match random digits with the identification numbers.

The selection job is simplified, however, if the population of items is listed on a printout. Then, the random number tables could be used to select a page and a line. For example, assume a printout of 250 pages with 52 lines to a page. The auditor might want to use the first three digits of a column of random digits to identify a page and the last two digits to identify a line.

Random number software can also be used. Most such software gives the reader the option to place the selected items in numerical order. An auditor can also use the random number function available in most spreadsheets.

Interval Sampling

Some auditors use interval sampling — sometimes referred to as systematic sampling.

Interval sampling simply means selecting items at intervals. It is a relatively simple method but, in using it, the auditor must remember basic selection principles: Because the audit opinion may properly be based only on the population sampled, no items should be missing from the population. Also, because every item must have an equal chance of being selected, the first item in the selection process must be picked at random. Finally, because no pattern in the population should affect the selection, the auditor should make two or more passes through the population, each with a random start.

The concept of interval sampling is simple. As an example, suppose the auditor wants to draw a sample of 40 items from a population of 2,000 unnumbered documents. Divide the population of 2,000 by the sample size of 40. The sample interval is thus 50. Start the selection with a random number of say, 15, which is less than 50, and the sample items would be the fifteenth item, the sixty-fifth items, the one-hundred and fifteenth item, the one-hundred and sixth-fifth item, and so forth — every fiftieth item until 40 items are selected.

But the auditor must always be concerned with bias; for example, say every tenth item has a different characteristic from the others. This might happen if every tenth name on a payroll represented a supervisor. Then it would be necessary to make multiple starts — at random, of course — and hence multiple passes through the population.

To accomplish three passes through the population, take the following steps:

- Multiply the interval of 50 by 3 to get 150.

- From the random number tables select three random starting points, all less than 150. They are, say, 39, 66, and 91 — all under 150. The selection would then be:

First item	Second item	Third item	Etc.
39	189	339	(Last item + 150)
66	216	366	(Last item + 150)
91	241	391	(Last item + 150)

Because the total sample involves three series of selections, it will be slightly larger than a sample with only one series. Interval sampling is the simplest selection technique to use and, if it is used with care, can provide adequate assurance that the sample has been selected at random.

Stratified Random Sampling

In every population we should look for wide variations in size — the amount or characteristics of the items making up the population. When we see wide variations, we should consider stratification. Stratified sampling arranges the population so as to provide greater sampling efficiency. Properly used, stratified sampling will result in a smaller variance within a given sample than simple random sampling.

In stratified sampling we separate the population into two or more strata — in effect, separate populations — and then take samples from each. Auditors have always used the principles of stratification. Usually, they set aside the largest or more expensive or most significant items in a population for complete examination and then select a sample from the remainder.

It may sometimes be desirable to allocate the population to many strata so as to reduce the number of items needed to obtain a representative sample of the population. As we shall see, it is variability in the population, not its size, that causes sharp increases in the number of samples needed to give a good picture of the population.

Obviously, if the population were composed of identical items, a sample of only one of them would be representative of the whole. For example, if we wished to estimate fuel consumption for a fleet of 1,000 cars, and each automotive unit in the fleet was exactly the same as the others, all we would need to do is study the consumption of one unit and multiply by 1,000. We would have fairly good assurance that the projection would be a pretty reliable indicator of the true condition. If, however, the fleet were made up of tiny scooters, huge trailer trucks, and many different types of units in between, we would have to select samples from each type; in other words, we would have to stratify the population.

In real-life situations, the quality of the population usually varies widely. The more the quality or character of the individual items differs in the characteristic under study, the greater the number of items we must select to obtain a fair representation of the population. We are seeking to obtain a good picture of the population through our sample. The picture tends to become distorted by unusual items or wide swings of variability. Usually the only way to get that picture is through stratification.

Stratification, then, helps the auditor in two important ways: It controls distortion and it permits smaller sample sizes.

Just how to stratify, how many strata to develop, and what items to group together, call for audit judgment. It can be done with available software programs; however, in most cases sound audit judgment will suffice. Any reasonable stratification is better than none.

Once the population has been stratified, the sample items can be selected through random number sampling or interval sampling, depending on the circumstances.

Cluster Sampling

Cluster sampling, also called block sampling, acknowledges the shortness of life. Sometimes documents or records to be sampled are so scattered or dispersed that it is too time consuming and costly to use simple random number sampling. In such cases, auditors can use the technique of cluster sampling — even though it is less efficient than random number sampling or interval sampling in typical audit situations.

Cluster sampling is what the name implies. Clusters of items are selected at random, and then the clusters either are examined in their entirety or are themselves sampled. The latter method is referred to as multistage sampling. So long as each selection is at random — first the clusters and then, if necessary, the items within the clusters — no rules are violated; each item has been afforded an equal chance of being selected.

Clusters may be natural — that is, all the documents in a file cabinet drawer or in a bundle of records. Or the clusters may be artificial; the auditor may decide that each half-inch group of cards represents a cluster at, say, 10-inch intervals. Cluster sampling can be used to select:

- A sample of tool cribs and then a sample of tools in each crib.

- A sample of stockrooms and a sample of the inventory records for each of the rooms.

- A sample of file drawers and all or some of the documents filed in those drawers.

- A sample of months, weeks, or days, and a sample of the documents processed during the sample periods.

Haphazard Sampling

Haphazard sampling involves selecting items without being concerned about bias toward any feature of the sampling unit. For example, in the haphazard sampling of invoices, the auditor would take whatever invoices are readily at hand and disregard in the selection such information as invoice number, customer, location of sale, dollar amount of sale, number of items in the sale, or any other feature. Haphazard sampling takes the easy approach rather than a reasoned one.

Judgment Sampling

Judgment sampling involves selecting sample items based on the auditor's personal reasoning or suspicions. For example, an auditor may examine only those invoices processed by accounts payable clerks newly assigned to their jobs. Or the auditor might concentrate on invoices for products or services delivered directly to using departments without clearing through the normal receiving process. Further discussion of judgment sampling will be found later in this chapter.

Sample Sizes

Sample sizes can be determined judgmentally or statistically. The decision depends on the audit objective. In many audit situations, a large audit sample or a statistically determined sample size is unnecessary. Often, after a preliminary survey, auditors may be so impressed with the quality of a control system and of the management of the activity that they will be content with a review of handpicked items to assure themselves that the system is actually in operation.

In such circumstances, how many items are examined? If the system is being used to process three separate types of transactions, one sample of each of the three types is walked through the system, touching each of the control points. It can then be declared that the system does, indeed, have the purported control points and that they are, in fact, operating. Since the system satisfied us that aberrant items would be detected and corrected automatically, further sampling may be wasteful.

Suppose, however, that we want to feel reasonably sure in our minds that the system is working with substantial effectiveness. What is the smallest sample we can take to give us that assurance? That is hard to say without knowing the system and the quality of the population; but we should not place undue reliance on a sample of under 30 items. Only at 30 may the sample begin to adopt the characteristics of the population. In many situations, a statistical sample of 30 or 40 items will give sufficient assurance that the system is working with reasonable effectiveness. Auditors should be aware, however, that they are counting on the system to detect errors rather than on their small sample.

What if auditors want to be able to objectively measure the reliability of their sample results? Now they are making a quantum jump. Now they must be willing to step into statistical sampling. With an open mind and a few basic concepts, they will soon find that they can grasp this important subject.

Statistical Sampling Theory

Auditors must understand that when they deal with sampling, they are seeking a reliable estimate, not an exact answer. For instance, let us say we examine 100 items out of a population of 1,000 — a sample of one tenth of the population. Let us assume that we have found five errors. May we then multiply the number of errors by 10 and say with certainty that the population contains 50 errors? No! We may say, if the selection was at random, that we have a certain degree of confidence that our estimate, our projection, comes within a certain range or tolerance — that is, plus or minus some determinable percentage.

This brings us to two concepts that are pivotal to an understanding of scientific sampling: confidence level and precision.

Confidence level, also called reliability level, is the degree to which we are justified in believing that the estimate based on a sample drawn at random will fall within a specified range. A confidence level is usually expressed as a percentage. For instance, a confidence level of 95 percent means that there are 95 chances out of 100 that the sample results will not vary from the true characteristics of the whole population by more than a certain specified amount; there are 5 chances out of 100 that they will.

The confidence level for a sample can never be 100 percent. For that degree of confidence, the auditor will have to examine the entire population.

Precision, also called confidence interval, is the range within which the estimate of the population characteristic will fall at the stipulated confidence level. Precision, being a range or tolerance, is usually expressed as a plus-or-minus percentage, such as ±2 percent, or as an amount, such as ±$5,000.

Thus the estimate obtained from a sample may permit us to say that we are 95 percent confident that the value of a population is:

$$X \text{ dollars} \pm Y \text{ dollars.}$$

Confidence level and precision are inescapably related. Each has an effect on the other. The meaning of sample results cannot be understood without understanding that relationship. A simple example will go much further in showing this relationship than any definitions.

Assume that a baseball pitcher is given 100 balls and is asked to throw them over the center of home plate. Home plate is 17 inches wide and looks like this:

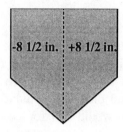

Let us assume that the pitcher can regularly get 95 out of the 100 balls over the plate. It could then be said that he or she has a 95 percent chance (confidence level) of getting a ball over the centerline ±8 1/2 inches (precision).

But then let us say that we widen the plate to 20 inches, like this:

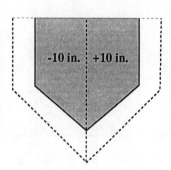

Now, with a broader range, the confidence level improves. Most likely the pitcher could get 98 or 99 balls over the center of the plate ±10 inches.

Pursuing the analogy further, let us reduce the size of the plate to 10 inches:

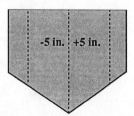

Now perhaps the pitcher can get only 80 balls over the center of the plate ±5 inches. The analogy is rough, but it points out the relationship between confidence level and precision. A change in one must change the other.

Another concept that must be understood in determining sample size is variability. Variability determines how large the sample must be to provide the acceptable level of confidence and range of precision. Many auditors have long believed that the size of the sample must bear a direct relationship to the size of the population. In earlier days, the percentage usually employed was 10 percent. Under that theory, a population of 100 would call for a sample of 10, and a population of one million would call for a sample of 100,000. In truth 10 percent of 100 is too small and 10 percent of a million is far too large.

Another simple example will bring the picture into sharper focus. Assume three lengths of cloth, each with a different design. The owner wishes to take a swatch from each so as to match them at the store and purchase more cloth of the same designs. This is how the lengths of cloth look:

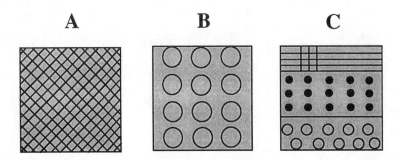

It becomes immediately apparent that although all three lengths are the same size, different sample sizes will have to be taken from each to obtain a good representation of the total design — in effect, the population. From A, a very small sample will be representative. From B, a much larger sample would be necessary to represent the total design. From C, unless a sample is taken from each of the four design patterns — in effect, stratification — a very large sample would be needed.

So sample size depends on four factors: confidence level, precision, population variability, and population size. The first two are under our control. But deciding how much reliability is needed from the sample calls for sound judgment based on the audit objectives and the nature of the associated system of internal control.

Although we may sometimes reduce variability by stratifying the population, variability is outside our control once the population to be sampled has been defined. It is part of the nature and character of the population we must deal with. That is why it is so important to "know your population."

Once the confidence level and precision have been decided, and once the variability of the population and its size have been measured, we are in a good position to determine how large a sample we will need to give us sample results which are sufficiently reliable for our purpose. In other words, we will be able to predict how close to the true population values (determined precisely only by examining the entire population) are the values of our sample.

This ability to predict is based on principles that have been developed mathematically. The principle, referred to as the Central Limit Theorem, roughly states that the measurements of the values of many similar objects — when arrayed according to value or size — tend to take the shape of a bell, also known as the normal curve. And if one were to select from any population, at random, any infinite number of samples of the same size of about 30 or more units, the frequency distribution of the means (averages) of all those samples would inevitably take the shape of a bell-shaped curve — no matter how the values of the population were distributed. Further, the mean of all the sample means would be the same as the population mean. This latter concept is important because it permits a prediction of population values based on sample values.

To visualize — so as to show how natural that shape is — assume a huge funnel, closed at the bottom and filled with gravel, suspended over a flat surface. As the gravel is released from the funnel, it will invariably assume a shape somewhat like:

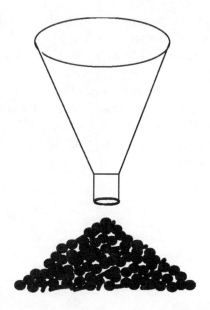

Viewed in silhouette, the pile of sand seems to have a bell-shaped curve. This shape seems natural to the viewer. Any other shape under the same circumstances might seem unnatural.

That is how the measurements of a great number of objects could be pictured. Assume the measurement of the shoe size of 2,000 men selected at random, plotted on a graph. The results could be:

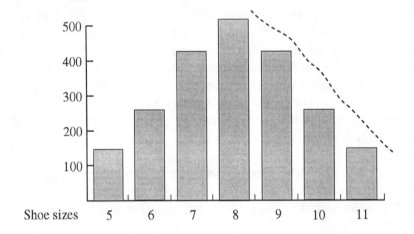

Again, we see the frequency of the measurements tending to take the form of a bell-shaped curve. The shape of the curve will depict the variability of the population. A high, narrow curve will illustrate little variability; a flat, wide curve will illustrate great variability.

Variability within a population can be measured. Just as coal can be weighed by the ton, speed can be measured by miles per hour, length can be measured by yards, and time can be measured by hours, so can variability be measured by what is known as the standard deviation. This formidable term means simply, "the measure of the variability of a particular population or of a sample from that population."

Let us break it down into its components. The standard deviation, technically, is the square root of the average of the squared deviations from the mean. It is portrayed in the following formula for a determination from a statistical sample:

$$s = \sqrt{\frac{\Sigma(x-\bar{x})^2}{n-1}}$$

where:

s	=	standard deviation
Σ	=	the sum of
x	=	each observation — the characteristic or value of each sample item
$\bar{x}$	=	the average (arithmetical mean} of the sample item values
n	=	the size of the sample

To determine the standard deviation:

- Obtain the mean (average) of the sample items
- Subtract the mean from each item
- Square the results and sum them
- Divide that sum by the number of sample items — minus 1
- Extract that square root

The result is the standard deviation of the sample or the measure of variability of the sample — hence, an estimate of the variability of the population.

Let us determine the standard deviation, through this method, of two groups of numbers. Each has the same mean, but different variability. The resulting standard deviations will show how this measure portrays variability, whereas the mean or average does not:

A	Sample Values		Mean†		Difference	Difference Squared
	17	-	20	=	-3	9
	20	-	20	=	0	0
	23	-	20	=	+3	<u>9</u>
						18

$$s = \sqrt{\frac{18}{2}}$$

$$s = \sqrt{9}$$

$$s = 3$$

*Sample size of 3 minus 1 = 2.

B	Sample Values		Mean†		Difference	Difference Squared
	11	-	20	=	-9	81
	20	-	20	=	0	0
	<u>29</u>	-	20	=	+9	<u>81</u>
						162

$$s = \sqrt{\frac{162}{2}}$$

$$s = \sqrt{81}$$

$$s = 9$$

*Sample size of 3 minus 1 = 2.

Although both groups of numbers have a common mean, the standard deviation of the one with the greater variability is three times that with the smaller variability.

The relationship between the bell curve, or normal distribution, and the standard deviation is an interesting one. It has been determined that in any normal distribution, the mean of the distribution, plus or minus one standard deviation, includes about 68 percent of the area under the normal curve; the mean plus or minus two deviations includes 95.5 percent of the area; and the mean plus or minus three standard deviations includes about 99.7 percent of the area. The relationships between standard deviations and the curve can be shown as:

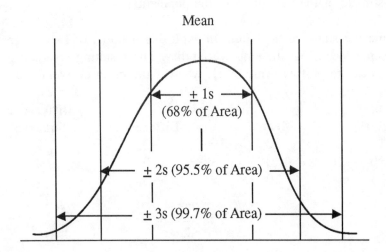

Unlike fixed units of measurement, such as an inch or a minute, the standard deviation will be different for each sample or each population because the standard deviation is the measure of variability of individual samples or populations. But regardless of the nature of the population, if we select at random a large number of samples of the same size, the distribution of the means of all those samples approximates a normal curve, and the average of the sample averages equals the average of the population.

Now let us see how this helps us in a sampling problem. Based on the principles of the normal curve, we could say that any item selected at random would fall — 68 percent of the time — within the range measured by the sample mean, plus or minus one standard deviation. Let us put it another way: Assuming a sample of invoices, "normally distributed," with an arithmetic mean of $100 and a standard deviation of $10, we could say that 68 percent of the sample units will fall within the value of $100 plus or minus one standard deviation of $10 — from $90 to $110 at a confidence level of 68 percent.

If we wished to increase our confidence level to 95.5 percent, we must now be satisfied with a wider range — plus or minus two standard deviations. Thus:

$80 to $120 at a confidence level of 95.5 percent.

If we wished to increase our confidence level still further to 99.7 percent, we would have to be satisfied with a still wider range — plus or minus three standard deviations. Thus:

$70 to $130 at a confidence level of 99.7 percent.

Or if we wished a confidence level of 95 percent — plus or minus 1.96 standard deviations — our range would be $80.40 to $119.60. On the normal curve, the results just enumerated could be pictured as:

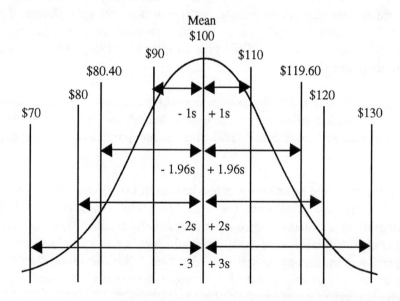

Recapitulating, then, the sample size is largely dependent on the confidence level and precision stipulated for the sample results and the variability found in the population.

One other factor affects sample size: the audit objective — what the auditors seek to determine by their tests. The objective may call for any one of several plans:

- Sampling for attributes. Determining "how many."

- Stop-and-go sampling. An economical sampling approach.

- Discovery sampling. Seeking to find a single suspected item.

- Variable sampling. Determining "how much."

- Dollar unit sampling. A combination of attribute and variable sampling.

- Judgment. When sample results are not to be attributed to the entire population.

Each of these plans will be discussed in the following pages.

Sampling for Attributes

Sampling for attributes calls for yes-or-no, right-or-wrong answers. It is usually applied to testing systems of internal control. It is concerned with estimating the number of errors or other characteristics in a population. It can provide an estimate of the number of engineering drawings received late by production people, but it will not give an estimate of how late — that is a function of variables sampling. It can provide an estimate of the number of purchase orders issued to sole sources, but it will not give an estimate of their value — that too is the function of variables sampling.

Determining sample sizes is relatively easy when tables are used, and the method of using tables is set forth in the sampling literature. Briefly stated, the auditor first determines the population size, the desired confidence level, the desired precision, and the expected error rate.

The principle of the expected error rate was touched on in the discussion of variability — the more variable the items in a population, the larger the sample size needed. Obviously, there is no great variability in a situation where the characteristic is either "yes" or "no," — that is, binary. If all the characteristics were "yes," it would take a test of only one to then predict that all the other items in the population were also "yes." But the more "no's" — up to 50 percent of the items — that are sprinkled throughout the population, the larger the sample needed to obtain a good representation of that population.

Estimating the error rate calls for judgment, but methods are available to give reasonably sound basis for an estimate:

- Examine a pilot of about 25 or 30 items.

- Review prior working papers for past experience.

- Discuss the estimated number of errors being encountered with knowledgeable people.

- Estimate the percentage of error it would take to automatically alert management that something is wrong.

Once the necessary decisions are made, we can proceed to the tables without difficulty, finding the one that shows the population size, confidence level, precision, and expected error rate in which we are interested.

But the available tables may not always fit the auditor's specifications. Doing so would take an enormous number of tables, and the auditors should never change their specifications merely to fit the tables at hand. That would be like the tail wagging the dog.

A simple formula can solve the dilemma. It adjusts to any confidence level, precision, and error rate. It also adjusts to any population by applying a simple supplemental formula. It uses the standard deviation factors — here called Z factors (often referred to as *t* factors). The values include:

Confidence Level	Z Factors
99	2.5758
95.5	2.0000
95	1.9600
90	1.6449
85	1.4395
80	1.2816

The formula has two parts, and both are simple. Neither requires the extraction of square roots. The first formula is used to obtain the sample for an infinite population. The second adjusts the formula for the population being considered.

The first formula (the normal approximation of a binomial distribution) is:

$$n_{(e)} = \frac{Z^2(p)(1-p)}{A^2}$$

where:

$n_{(e)}$ = First estimate of sample size
Z = Standard deviation factor
p = Occurrence rate
A = Desired precision

The second formula uses the first estimate of sample size and adjusts it to fit the population:

$$n_{(f)} = \frac{n_{(e)}}{1 + (n_{(e)}/N)}$$

where:

$n_{(f)}$ = Final sample size
$n_{(e)}$ = First estimate of sample size
N = Population

Using these formulas, here is the computation for the sample size where the population (N) is 1,000, the desired precision (A) is ±2 percent, the desired confidence level (Z) is 95 percent, and the estimated error rate (p) is not to exceed five percent:

1. $n_{(e)}$ = $\dfrac{1.96^2 \text{ x } .05 \text{ x } (1-.05)}{.02^2}$

   = $\dfrac{3.8416 \text{ x } .05 \text{ x } (.95)}{.0004}$

   = $\dfrac{.182476}{.0004}$

   = 456

2. $n_{(f)}$ = $\dfrac{n_{(e)}}{1 + (n_{(e)}/N)}$

     = $\dfrac{456}{1 + (456/1000)}$

     = $\dfrac{456}{1.456}$

     =   313

The second formula, representing a "finite population correction factor," can generally be omitted if the first sample estimate is less than five percent of the universe size. The second formula, in such cases, has little effect on the sample size — merely making it slightly smaller.

If we examine the sample of 313 items and find that there is indeed an error rate of five percent, then we can declare that we are 95 percent sure that our population of 1000 contains 950 error-free items, plus or minus two percent of 1000, or plus or minus 20 items. In other words, the number of satisfactory items in the population can be estimated to be anywhere from 930 to 970 — at a 95 percent confidence level.

If it turned out that the error rate in our sample is actually somewhat higher, say six or seven percent, we would recompute the formula, using the new error rate, and determine how many more items we would have to examine to obtain an estimate with the required confidence level and precision. If the actual error rate is much higher, say 10 percent or more, the sampling could well be finished — since 10 percent of 313 items would be sufficient to indicate a real problem that needs correcting.

Stop-and-Go Sampling

Stop-and-go sampling was devised to permit audit decisions, with appropriate reliability, that are based on relatively small samples. It is used in testing for attributes. It applies, by and large, to fairly "clean" populations — those in which auditors want to do as little sampling as possible. Based on their knowledge of the system, the auditors may conclude that the population is relatively error-free; but they want statistical support without extensive testing.

So if they can examine a small sample and find few or no errors, they will have a measurable assurance that they can discontinue their tests and accept the reasonable accuracy of the population.

Stop-and-go sampling tables and software are available. In a stop-and-go sampling table as illustrated below, the first column shows the size of the sample. The second column shows the number of errors brought to light by the auditor's analysis of the sample. The other columns, headed by various possible maximum error rates, show different levels of probability (the number of times out of 100) that the true error rates in the population will be less than the indicated maximum error rates in the headings.

A simple example can show how stop-and-go sampling works. Let us say that we are interested in whether receiving memorandums bear evidence that the materials received have been inspected. We shall assume that all items must be inspected. The absence of an inspector's stamp indicates no inspection.

Employees appear to be well trained. Supervisors watch the operations carefully. The manager periodically checks completed receiving memos to see that the rules are being followed. Clearly, under such a system, extensive testing would be wasteful. We take a sample of 50 items out of a population of 20,000. We stipulate that we would be satisfied if we have adequate assurance that the population has an error rate no higher than five percent.

Probability that error rate in universe of size over 2,000 is less than:

Sample Size	# of Errors Found	1%	2%	3%	4%	5%	6%	...
50	0	39.50	63.58	78.19	87.01	92.31	95.47	...
	1	8.94	26.42	44.47	59.95	72.06	81.00	...
	...	...	...	...	...	...	...	...
...	...	...	...	...	...	...	...	...
100	0	63.40	86.74	95.25	98.31	99.41	99.80	...
	1	26.42	59.67	80.54	91.28	96.29	98.48	...
	...	...	...	...	...	...	...	...

Let us say that we examine the 50 items and find no errors. The condition is therefore as shown in the first line of the table: a 92.31 percent assurance (probability) that the population contains no more than a five percent error rate. If we are satisfied with that assurance, we could discontinue our tests.

But let us say that we found one error in our sample of 50. Now, the condition is as in the second line: 72.06 percent assurance that the population contains no more than a five percent error rate. If this does not satisfy us, we might take a sample of 50 more receiving memos — a total of 100. Assume that we find no more errors. The condition is then as in the second line for a sample size of 100: 96.29 percent assurance. If we consider that to be adequate — taking into account the excellent system of internal control — we may discontinue our test. Otherwise, we will take additional samples.

If errors keep showing up in a small sample size, the auditor should not continue with stop-and-go sampling for sample sizes. At that point, the auditor will want to obtain an estimate of the error rate in the population within a plus-or-minus range of precision at an appropriate confidence level.

Discovery Sampling

Discovery sampling is used when the auditor is examining populations where the existence of fraud or gross error is suspected. Such populations might include fictitious employees on the payroll, duplicate payments, unauthorized shipments of goods, or nonexistent collateral for loans.

We would not try to express an opinion on the population as a whole. We are trying, through sampling, to find at least one item with a particular characteristic — assuming a stipulated number of those items in the population. The stipulation is significant. The population would require examination, item by item, until the one such item was found. There would be no other choice if the item of interest were a single unique unit. But if we are willing to specify some limited, assumed number of items, we may use discovery sampling to obtain a measurable assurance that we will find at least one of that number, if the actual quantity in the population is equal to or greater than the assumed quantity.

A sample of part of a table follows.

Probability, in percent, of finding at least one error if total number of errors in universe is as indicated:

Total errors in universe size of 10,000

Sample Size	1	2	3	4	...	50	75	...
5	0.1	0.1	0.1	0.2	...	2.5	3.7	...
10	0.1	0.2	0.3	0.4	...	4.9	7.3	...
...	...	...	...	...	...	...	...	...
600	6.0	11.6	16.9	21.9	...	95.5	99.1	...
...	...	...	...	...	...	...	...	...

Here is how the tables are used: We are examining the organization records on conflict of interest. Every employee is required to complete a record designed to disclose any such conflict. There are 10,000 employees on the rolls and we want to be 95 percent certain that we would locate at least one instance of impropriety — no record, wrong record, or an uninvestigated record of potential conflict.

By consulting the previous table for a population size of 10,000, we see that if we were to stipulate 50 errors in the population, we would have to examine a sample of 600 items to be 95.5 percent sure that our sample would include one of the erroneous items. If our sample contained none of the errors, we would be 95.5 percent sure that the population included fewer than 50 erroneous items.

How many erroneous items to stipulate is a matter of judgment, taking into account the seriousness of the errors under consideration. The only alternative to discovery sampling is the examination of each item until an example has been found or the entire population has been examined. The auditor will have to evaluate the impact of the undiscovered errors in the population.

Variables Sampling

This form of sampling is sometimes called dollar estimation, since it usually deals with dollar values. It can also be used for any other kind of values, like time periods or weights.

Variables sampling can be used to obtain estimates based on a sample of the value of inventories, the value of disallowances of travel vouchers, the value of aged accounts receivable, and the like. Computing sample sizes and sample results is simplified by the use of tables. Such tables can be found in the sampling literature previously mentioned. Here we shall make use of an alternative set of tables that allows a certain degree of flexibility often desirable in computing sample sizes.

To establish suitable sample sizes, we must determine, as we did for attributes sampling, the population size, the desired confidence level, and the desired precision. Instead of an expected error rate, however, we must determine the standard deviation.

As we pointed out in attributes sampling, the expected error rate is a measure of variability that is needed to work out the formulas for sample sizes. In variables sampling, the standard deviation does the same thing.

Accordingly, for the first step in establishing the sample size needed to provide the desired degree of reliability, we must estimate the standard deviation of the population. We do that by determining the standard deviation of the sample. Just as we may take a pilot sample in attributes sampling to estimate the error rate, so we must take a pilot sample in variables sampling to determine the standard deviation.

The sample for that purpose should not be fewer than 100 units. Fewer than that number may not be representative of the population and, therefore, may not give a correct reading. The sample must be drawn at random, and even though it is termed a pilot sample, all the items selected can be used with the additional sample items that may be required to achieve desired sample reliability.

In dealing with so many numbers, it is best to use a simplified computation in determining the standard deviation. This computation does not require subtracting the mean from the value of each sample item. The results are the same as those obtained from the formula described earlier in this chapter. The simpler formula (easier to compute, even though it looks more complicated) is:

$$s = \sqrt{\frac{\Sigma(x^2) - (\Sigma x)^2/n}{n-1}}$$

where:

s = Standard deviation of the sample
Σ = Sum of
x = Value of each sample item
n = Sample size

Using the figures in example 2 shown previously in determining the standard deviation:

x = Sample Values	$\Sigma(x^2)$ = Sum of Squared Sample Values	(Σx) = Sum of Sample Values
11	121	11
20	400	20
29	841	29
Totals	**1362**	**60**

and substituting these values in the formula, we have:

$$s = \sqrt{\frac{1362 - \frac{60^2}{3}}{3-1}}$$

$$= \sqrt{\frac{1362 - 1200}{2}}$$

$$= \sqrt{81}$$

$$= 9$$

Variables Sampling Techniques

There are three classical variables sampling plans used to calculate the population estimate: mean-per-unit, difference estimation, and ratio estimation. These three techniques will be demonstrated through the use of the following example:

The accounts receivable balance of $5,000,000 is composed of 4,000 customer accounts. The auditor selects a sample of 200 accounts with a book value of $250,000. After applying audit procedures, the audit value of the sample is determined to be $265,000.

1. *Mean-per-unit.* By this method, the auditor calculates the average audit value ($265,000 ÷ 200 = $1,325) and multiplies this mean-per-unit value by the population units ($1,325 x 4,000 = $5,300,000) to estimate the correct accounts receivable balance. This method is also referred to as simple extension.

2. *Difference Estimation.* Difference estimation may be appropriate when the following conditions are present:

   - There are sufficient errors in the population to generate a reliable sample estimate and the differences are not proportional to recorded book value. If the number of differences between the audit value and book value is small, a relatively large sample would be required to provide a representative difference between audit and book values.

   - The following information is available:
     BV = Book value of the population
     N   = Number of units in the population
     UBV = Book value of each unit
     UAV = Audit value of each sample unit
     S   = Size of sample

The following steps are followed in difference estimation:

   - Determine the average "difference" between audit value and book value for the sample (UAV − UBV) ÷ S = average difference [($265,000 − $250,000) ÷ 200 = $75].
   - Multiply the average difference by the number of population units to obtain a total difference estimate ($75 x 4,000 = $300,000).
   - The difference is combined with the population book value to obtain an estimate of the population value ($300,000 + $5,000,000 = $5,300,000).

3. *Ratio Estimation.* Ratio estimation is similar to difference estimation and is appropriate when the differences are approximately proportional to the book values. The following steps are used to generate a ratio estimate of the population value.

- Determine the sample audit value ($265,000).
- Determine the sample book value ($250,000).
- Compute the "ratio" of the audit value to the book value ($265,000 ÷ $250,000 = 1.06).
- Multiply the ratio by the book value of the population (1.06 x $5,000,000 = $5,300,000).

These simplified examples illustrate the differences among the three methods. The following section provides a formula for the use of the more common method — mean-per-unit.

Variables Sampling— Formula

As in attributes sampling, fairly simple formulas can be used to determine sample sizes and precision (sampling error). Using the same example shown for the tables:

Population size	5,000
Population value	$500,000
Standard deviation of 200 items	
selected at random	$40
Desired confidence level	90%
Desired precision per unit of population	±$4

Here is the first formula for mean-per-unit:

$$n_{(e)} = \left(\frac{Zs}{A}\right)^2$$

where:

$n_{(e)}$ = First estimate of sample size
Z = Standard deviation factor
s = Standard deviation of the sample
A = Precision (sampling error)

The second is the same adjustment formula shown previously and uses the first estimate of sample size and adjusts it to fit the population:

$$n_{(f)} = \frac{n_{(e)}}{1 + (n_{(e)}/N)}$$

Using these formulas, here is the computation for the sample size:

1.

$$n_{(e)} = \left(\frac{1.645 \times 40}{4}\right)^2$$

$$= \left(\frac{65.8}{4}\right)^2$$

$$= 16.45^2$$

$$= 271$$

2.

$$n_{(f)} = \frac{271}{1 + (271/5,000)}$$

$$= \frac{271}{1.0542}$$

$$= 257$$

Also, as in attributes sampling, the second formula is generally not needed if the first sample is less than five percent of the population.

As a result of the computations, the internal auditor will select at random another 57 items to bring the total to 257. Let us assume that the examination of the sample of 257 items shows the standard deviation remains at $40. Let us also assume that the value of the sample items is as follows:

Book value	$27,000
Value determined by physical verification	$23,130

The average value of the inventory items is $90 ($23,130 ÷ 257). The estimated actual inventory would be $450,000 ($90 x 5,000). The next questions are: How reliable is that projection? What is the precision (sampling error) at a 90 percent confidence level? What is the range within which the estimated actual inventory value can be projected at the desired confidence level? A formula can provide that answer:

$$A = Z\frac{S}{\sqrt{n}}\left(\sqrt{1-\frac{n}{N}}\right)$$

where:

A = Precision
Z = Standard deviation factor
s = Standard deviation of the sample
n = Sample size
N = Population size

Substituting the values determined by the audit and by the desired confidence level, the value of the sampling error is reached as:

$$A = 1.645 \left(\frac{40}{\sqrt{257}} \right) \sqrt{1 - \frac{257}{5000}}$$

$$= 1.645 \left(\frac{40}{16.03} \right) \sqrt{1 - .0514}$$

$$= 1.645 \times 2.4953 \times .97396$$

$$= \$4.00$$

The precision of ±$4 for each unit computes to ±$20,000 for 5,000 units. The projected value of the entire inventory is therefore $450,000 plus or minus $20,000. In other words, at a confidence level of 90 percent, the actual value of the inventory would lie within a range of $430,000 to $470,000.

Dollar-unit Sampling (Monetary Unit Sampling)

The internal auditor has many statistical sampling models at his or her disposal. The attribute and variables sampling are often referred to as the classical statistical sampling models.

A relatively new form of dollar estimation has been gaining increased acceptance in recent years. It goes by many names and lacks common terminology. It has been referred to as probability proportional to size (PPS) — in essence, a sampling selection procedure. It is also referred to as dollar-unit sampling (DUS), which is a unique statistical approach based on a PPS selection process. Other terms for this method include Monetary Unit Sampling (MUS), cumulative monetary amount (CMA) sampling, combined attributes variables (CAV) sampling, monetary-unit sampling (MUS), and sampling proportionate to size (SPS). The differences and variations of the separate but closely related topics are beyond the scope of this text. Owing to their similarities, however, we will refer to the entire concept as dollar-unit sampling or DUS.

DUS is actually a hybrid that combines attribute and variable sampling methodology, as expressed in the term CAV. DUS relies on an attribute sampling approach (Poisson distribution) to express a conclusion in dollar amounts (variables) rather than as a deviation rate. DUS provides an alternative to stratification and combines the advantages of both attribute and variable sampling. It can be used for both compliance and substantive testing.

Classical sampling approaches designate physical items (vouchers, invoices, checks, etc.) as the sampling unit. Each of the physical items is likely to have a different value; hence, they are variable. Any selection of such "audit units" may include large amounts and small amounts. It is quite possible for significant items to be overlooked in the sample selection process unless considerable stratification is employed. DUS avoids this problem by defining units that do not vary. Each one has the same value because each one is one dollar; thus, the sample is composed of random dollars, not random items.

DUS avoids the difficulty of determining standard deviations of the sample by removing the variability of the sampling unit. DUS does not look at an account receivable population as totaling $5,000,000, for example, and comprising 2,000 customer accounts that range, say, from $1 to $100,000. Instead, it looks at the population as comprising 5,000,000 dollar bills, stretched out — dollar bill after dollar bill — for almost 500 miles.

In selecting a random sample of 60 dollars (see example that follows) from the population, each dollar must have an equal chance of being selected for inclusion in the sample. Although dollars are the units for sample selection, the auditor does not actually examine individual dollar bills. The auditor examines the item, account, transaction, or document associated with the dollar selected. The individual dollar selected is generally described as "hooking" the entire item with which it is associated. If one dollar is selected from an account receivable balance, it will not relinquish its companion dollars, say customer No. 5 (in the example that follows) with an account balance of $81,897, within which the dollar resides. The item snagged is termed the "logical sampling unit."

In applying DUS, the author is automatically stratifying the population for selection. The probability of any one item being selected for detailed verification is proportional to the size of the item — therefore the terms PPS and SPS. In the example given, the probability that customer account No. 9 ($10,000) is selected is 10 times greater than that of customer account No. 8 ($1,000). DUS provides an alternative to stratifying and is somewhat simpler. This characteristic, and its use where differences between audited and book amounts are rare, has popularized DUS in audit practice.

DUS has audit appeal, since large-value items are generally of greater concern than small-value items. DUS provides an estimate of the maximum amount of overstatement of a recorded amount with measurable levels of risk of making a decision error. It allows the auditor to make the following general conclusion:[1]

Based on the sample's evidence, I am x percent confident that the dollar amount of error in the account (related to the attribute) does not exceed $Z (where $Z depends on the sample's outcome).

DUS is appropriate where the audit objective is to detect overstatements and is not appropriate in testing understatements. Since basic audit philosophy is to audit assets for potential overstatement and liabilities for understatement, DUS is appropriate to test asset account balances. Frequent applications include the test of accounts receivable, investments, inventory, and fixed assets.

Before using the DUS model, the auditor should determine that the two assumptions incorporated in the model are valid for the population being tested:[2]

1. The error rate in the population should be small (less than 10 percent) and the population should contain 2,000 or more items. (The use of the Poisson probability distribution for evaluation of the sample requires this feature.)

2. The amount of error in any item of the population cannot be more than the reported book value of the item. That is, if the book value of a customer's balance is $100, the amount of error in the balance cannot exceed $100.

As noted, DUS is generally not appropriate in testing for understatement of liabilities since the more a balance is understated, the less is its chance of being included in the sample. Ironically, the presence of an understatement error limits the probability of its detection and adjustment. Also, unrecorded items obviously will not be selected by DUS. Zero and negative balances should be excluded from the population being tested because they have no probability of being selected for inclusion in the sample. These items are generally handled as a separate population for testing, using a classical selection process.

A few of the other advantages and disadvantages of DUS are:

Advantages
- It can be applied to a group of accounts, since the sampling units (dollars) are homogenous.
- It is an efficient model for establishing that a low error rate population is not materially misstated.
- It does not require consideration of the standard deviation to determine the sample size or to evaluate the results.
- It does not require the normal approximations required by variables sampling.
- It permits a statistically valid sample selection that includes more high-dollar balances for "dollar coverage" of the population being tested.

Disadvantages
- It requires that the population be cumulatively totaled to identify the random dollars selected. This disadvantage is generally offset with a software package.
- As the errors increase, it requires a larger sample size than that required when using classical statistics.
- It may overstate the allowance for sampling risk when errors are found and thereby cause the auditor to reject an acceptable book value.

Two methods are available for use in selecting sample items for DUS:

1. *Random DUS.* If this method were used in the following example, the auditor would select 60 random numbers from a random digit table or through the use of a random number generator. The next step would be to arrange the random numbers in ascending order and select the account balance whose cumulative amount included the number.

2. *Systematic DUS.* This is a more widely used method and is illustrated in the following example.

The more complex applications of DUS are beyond the scope of this text. A simplified step-by-step example is presented to provide a conceptual understanding that can serve as a foundation for more sophisticated applications.

Example: Ricky Roderick, a staff auditor of Petro, Inc., elects to use DUS to test for overstatement of the organization's accounts receivable book balance of $5,000,000. He has determined that the DUS assumptions are satisfied and that DUS is valid to achieve the audit objective. Roderick has decided that a five percent error in the book value is material. Five percent of $5,000,000 is $250,000. He also decides to use a 95 percent confidence level and expects no errors. Hence, the parameters are:

BV	(book value)	=	$5,000,000
N	(population units)	=	2,000
M	(maximum tolerable error)	=	$250,000
CL	(confidence level)	=	95%

Determine the reliability factor given a 95 percent confidence level and zero expected overstatement errors. An Error Factor (F) of 3.0 is available from a Poisson DUS Cumulative Evaluation Table (Table of Error Factors).

DUS Reliability Factors

Reliability Required	Reliability Factors
99%	4.605
95%	2.996 (rounded to 3.0)
90%	2.300

The sample size (n) is calculated as:

$$n = \frac{BV \times F}{M}$$

$$n = \frac{\$5,000,000 \times 3.0}{\$250,000}$$

$$n = 60$$

Alternative calculation:

$$n = \frac{Error\ Factor}{Materiality\ Percentage}$$

$$n = \frac{3}{5\%}$$

$$n = 60$$

Calculate the sample interval (I):

$$I = \frac{BV}{n}$$

$$I = \frac{\$5,000,000}{60}$$

$$I = \$83,333$$

Select the sample. The first dollar is selected through the use of a random number (say 1,000). The second number is determined by adding the random start to the skip interval. The third number is determined by adding the random start to two times the skip interval, and so on through the entire population.

Sample Units	Calculation	Unit Selected
#1	Random start	1,000
#2	1,000 + $83,333 x 1 (first skip interval)	84,333
#3	1,000 + $83,333 x 2 (second skip interval)	167,666
#60	1,000 + $83,333 x-59 (last skip interval)	4,916,647

The auditor must accumulate the cumulative dollar total of items in the population (therefore the term CMA). The worksheet for this DUS example is shown in Exhibit 11-1.

Evaluate sample results.

Assuming no errors, Roderick can state that he is 95 percent sure that the error rate for the population does not exceed $250,000. Alternatively stated, the auditor can say that he is 95 percent sure that the book value of $5,000,000 is not overstated by more than $250,000. The reader is referred to the February 1982 issue of *The Internal Auditor* for the evaluation of sample results with errors present.[3]

Given the appropriate situation, there are good reasons for the auditor to select DUS over classical statistical sampling. DUS is particularly efficient and effective when the auditor: (1) wants to maximize dollar coverage; (2) wishes to calculate the maximum dollar overstatement; and (3) expects the overstatement to be low. The auditor must exercise professional judgment to determine if the use of DUS is valid for the population being tested and if the model conclusions are consistent with the audit objectives.

Judgment Sampling

Judgment sampling usually receives poor notices whenever statisticians deign to speak of it. But auditors have used it from time immemorial and still find that it performs signal service when statistical sampling is neither needed nor warranted. Judgment sampling remains a significant part of the auditor's sample selection and evaluation procedures. But auditors should know when and how to use it.

Judgment sampling may be used to select examples of deficiencies to support the auditors' contention that the system is weak. They may make a purposive search for defective or improperly processed items to confirm their suspicions or support their position that the system is not capable of identifying improprieties. This is a valid use of judgment sampling. But it should not be used to estimate the number or value of such items in the total population. The auditors had not given every item in the population an equal chance of selection. The test was subjective, not objective. Hence the auditor definitely may not statistically extrapolate sample results to the entire population.

Judgment sampling can be used where it is known that the population has no variability. In an information system, for example, each item may be treated exactly the same by the system. The transactions would be either all wrong or all right. The examination of a single judgment sample will provide the auditor with adequate assurance of the propriety or impropriety of all the items the information system processed.

Exhibit 11-1
Worksheet for DUS Selection

Customer No. (Logical Sampling Unit)	Balance (Book Value)	Cumulative Total	Related Dollar Units (Sample Units)	Unit Selected (See Separate Calculations)	Logical Sampling Unit ("Hooked" Unit Value)
001	$ 1,798	$ 1,798	1 - 1,798	$ 1,000	$ 1,798
002	563	2,361	1,799 - 2,361		
003	974	3,335	2,363 - 3,335		
004	4,621	7,956	3,336 - 7,956		
005	81,897	89,853	7,957 - 89,853	84,333	81,897
006	421	90,274	89,854 - 90,274		
007	8,109	98,383	90,275 - 98,383		
008	1,000	99,383	98,384 - 99,383		
009	10,000	109,383	99,384 - 109,383		
010	67,705	177,088	109,384 - 177,088	167,666	67,705
·	·	·	·		
·	·	·	·		
·	·	·	·		
2,000	5,974	5,000,000	4,994,025 - 5,000,000		
	$5,000,000 (100%)	5,000,000			**$2,897,427 (58%)**

NOTE: A sample of 60 units from 2,000 resulted in a 58% "dollar coverage."

Judgment sampling can provide auditors with some clues as to whether to proceed with a statistical sample. If they encounter a well-designed, well-controlled system, good management, well-trained employees, and a feedback mechanism that highlights errors, it would be extravagant to spend a great deal of time performing extensive transaction tests. A small sample — too small for stop-and-go sampling but nevertheless selected at random to obtain some reasonable representation of the population — might suffice.

If the auditors find no errors, they may be able to say that they see no basis for examining the population further or for suspecting any material error. They may not say that they have adequate assurance that the population is truly error-free or even reasonably error-free. They have no statistical basis for such a statement. But what they can say about the functioning of the system may be sufficient for their audit purposes.

Judgment sampling has its place, so long as the auditor is aware of its limitations. Where the audit objectives are fully met by a judgment sample, there would be no valid reason to insist on the discipline of added statistical support.

Statistical and Nonstatistical Sampling

The internal auditor who elects to use audit sampling may select statistical sampling, nonstatistical sampling, or a combination of the two. The selection process is essentially the result of a cost-benefit decision and does not affect the audit procedures performed.

Two criteria are required for a sampling approach to be classified as statistical: (1) The sampling units must be randomly selected; (2) They must be quantitatively evaluated through the application of probability theory. The absence of either requirement defines the approach as nonstatistical (traditionally referred to as judgmental sampling). With nonstatistical sampling, the internal auditor determines the sample size and evaluates the results on the basis of subjective audit experience.

Statistical and nonstatistical sampling both project the characteristics of the sample to the population. Representativeness is generally required by both statistical and nonstatistical sampling unless directed sampling is used (directed sampling involves a search for specified items to prove a hypothesis). Every sample presents a risk that it does not reliably represent the population. Statistical sampling, however, uses the laws of probability to measure sampling risk. However, if the auditor randomly selects a sample but elects not to express the results in statistical terms, the sampling procedure is classified as nonstatistical.

As shown in Exhibit 11-2, there is no difference between statistical sampling and nonstatistical sampling in the execution of a sampling plan, nor does the approach affect the competence of the evidence obtained or the auditor's response to detected errors. Selection between statistical and nonstatistical sampling should be made after a careful evaluation of the advantages and disadvantages of each.

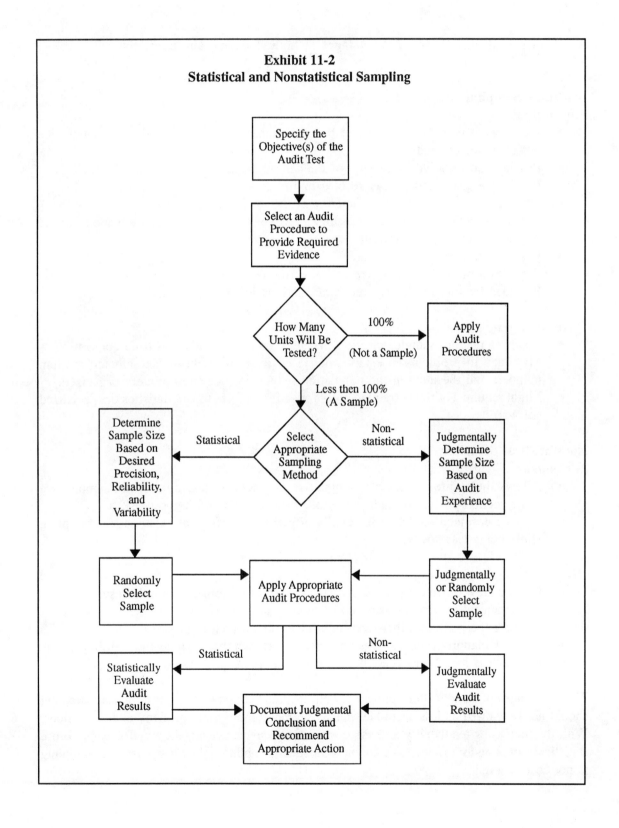

Exhibit 11-2
Statistical and Nonstatistical Sampling

A few of the advantages and disadvantages of both statistical and nonstatistical sampling are:

Statistical Sampling

Advantages

- Provides an opportunity to select the minimum sample size required to satisfy the objectives of the audit tests.
- Provides quantitative expression of the sample results.
- Provides a quantitative measure of sampling risk.
- Provides a measure of the sufficiency of the evidence gathered.
- Permits the auditor to explicitly specify a level of reliability (confidence) and a desired degree of precision (materiality).
- Is simple to apply with software.
- Provides a more defensible expression of the test results.
- Provides for more objective recommendations for management.

Disadvantages

- Requires random sample selection that may be more costly and time consuming.
- May lead to problems in establishing a correlation between the selected random numbers and the units in the population if they are not appropriately organized.
- Might require additional training costs for staff members to use statistics or specialized software.

Nonstatistical Sampling

Advantages

- Allows the auditor to inject a subjective judgment in determining the sample size and selection process to audit items of greatest value and highest risk.
- May be designed so that it is equally effective and efficient as statistical sampling while being less costly.

Disadvantages

- Cannot draw objectively valid statistical inferences from the sample results.
- Cannot quantitatively measure and express sampling risk.
- Presents the risks of either over-auditing or under-auditing.
- May be inappropriate for inexperienced staff members, since the validity of the approach is based on experience with the sampling process.

The advantages of statistical sampling are well documented; however, nonstatistical sampling should not be viewed as less desirable. It may be more appropriate in many audit situations. With the increasing availability and use of audit software, however, the trend may be to use statistical sampling as a first choice and nonstatistical sampling only when statistical sampling is not cost beneficial.

Evaluating Sample Results

Internal auditors cannot content themselves with the mathematical results of their audit samples. True, these results will provide them with a measurable assurance that the sample is a facsimile, in miniature, of the audited population. The results will provide them with an objective estimate of the number of errors in the population or of the true value of the population. However, this is not necessarily what management needs.

When variances occur, management wants to know why they occurred. If the book value of an inventory is $500,000, and the auditor can demonstrate that the physical inventory represented by the books is only $450,000, management wants to know — or should want to know — where the $50,000 went.

Statistical sampling helps provide the auditors with assurance that they have found out what has happened; it cannot tell them why it happened. Thus when samples point to differences, auditors must determine whether the differences are material, how they happened, and what can be done to prevent their recurrence.

The audit objective of modern internal auditors transcends mere scorekeeping — the number of erroneous items they find in a sample. Their objective is to determine what the score means, whether it indicates a system failure, whether it points to poor supervision, whether it is highlighting adverse trends, or whether it hints of manipulation. So unless the sample results provide assurance of satisfactory conditions, the sample is merely a prologue to the real audit task.

A shrewd appraisal of the audit results and surrounding circumstances may give those results an entirely different character. Also, the appraisal may point to the direction the audit report should take. Here are some examples:

- An examination of 200 items discloses only one error. But that error represents a significant item of a material amount. The sample results may not portray a trend, but the individual matter is of sufficient materiality to require reporting to management without reference to the sample. In other words, management may be told that the control system is functioning adequately, although this one matter needs correcting.

- An examination of 100 items discloses 10 errors. The errors resulted from a control breakdown. The sample, taken from a population of 20,000, does not provide good statistical reliability. The auditor, however, feels that the job has been performed and proposes to test no further. The report to management should emphasize the control aspect, buttressed by the fact that 10 percent of the items were in error. There should be no implication that the error rate may reliably be projected to the entire population.

- An examination of 150 items discloses only three errors. But each of the errors is traced back to one clerk who has not been adequately trained. The auditors may then make a purposive test, in addition to their random sample, examining a substantial number of the transactions processed by that clerk to determine the seriousness of the deficiency. The results of the purposive test should not be combined with those of the random sample for the purpose of projecting results to the entire population.

- An auditor selects and examines an attributes sample of 796 items out of a population of 10,000 items and finds a 10 percent error rate. The projection of that rate to the total population carries a 95 percent confidence level with a precision of ±2 percent. This is extremely high reliability. The errors can be attributed to poor supervision. The auditor feels that the population should be purged of error. Management is not mathematically sophisticated and has no conception of the measurement of sample reliability. The auditor may recommend an operating review of the entire population, stating that in his or her opinion the population contains approximately 1,000 erroneous items. But the auditor would be well advised not to discuss confidence levels and precision, since this may do little more than complicate an issue that is better left simple.

Population Proportions

Auditors may have occasion to estimate the proportion of a population that possesses some property of interest. They are not concerned with error rates or sample variability; they merely wish to project the item or items of interest, found in a sample, to the entire population with some measurable degree of reliability.

For example, let us assume that certain purchases are made only after the receipt of competitive bids. Others are not. Still others are made from selected suppliers at the direction of the organization's customers. It may be significant to estimate for management — with adequate reliability — what the proportions are.

There are a variety of formulas that will provide the measure of reliability for such estimates. The use of the binomial probability distribution, or the hypergeometric probability distribution for a finite universe, would define the confidence limits with maximum accuracy. But confidence limits based on these distributions would involve computations so complex that they would not ordinarily be feasible without the use of software.

Fortunately, the formula for the standard deviation of the binomial distribution can readily be used by the auditor to determine the confidence limits with a reasonably acceptable degree of accuracy. We shall discuss here two formulas based on the standard deviation of the binomial distribution: The first applies when the size of the population is known. The second applies when it is not.

Known Populations

Let us assume a population of 40,000 purchase orders. Let us further assume that the auditor selected a random sample of 4,000 purchase orders — every tenth order with a random start — and distributed them to the three categories just enumerated. The results of the sample are:

A. Competitive bids	2,000	50%
B. No competitive bids	1,600	40%
C. Customer direction	400	10%
	4,000	100%

By simple projection, or "blow up" (multiplying each sample group by 10), the auditor estimates that the population contains 20,000 of A, 16,000 of B, and 4,000 of C. But how reliable is the estimate? In other words, what is the precision range for the estimate at a stipulated confidence level? The auditor can obtain that statement of reliability through the following formula:

$$A = ZN \sqrt{\frac{N - n}{N \times n}} \quad x \quad \sqrt{p(1 - p)}$$

where:

A = Precision
Z = Normal deviate for the desire level of confidence
N = Population size
n = Sample size
p = Proportion of items of interest to sample

The computation of the range of precision, assuming a stipulated confidence level of 95.5 percent, is as follows:

Number in population	40,000
Number in sample	4,000
Z at 95.5% confidence level	2,000
Proportions of items with a particular characteristic	
A. 2,000/4,000	.50
B. 1,600/4,000	.40
C. 400/4,000	.10

First solve:

$$ZN \sqrt{\frac{N - n}{N \times n}}$$

$$2 \times 40,000 \sqrt{\frac{40,000 - 4,000}{40,000 \times 4,000}}$$

$$80,000 \sqrt{\frac{36,000}{160,000,000}}$$

$$80,000 \sqrt{.000225}$$

$$80,000 \times .015 = 1,200$$

Then solve, for each class:

$$\sqrt{p(1-p) \times 1,200}$$

Class	p	1 - p	p(1 - p)	p(1 - p)	x	1,200 = A Precision (±) at 95% Confidence Level
A	.50	.50	.25	.5000		600
B	.40	.60	.24	.4900		588
C	.10	.90	.09	.3000		360

Estimated Proportions and Reliability Statements

	Classification	Sample POs	% of Total	Estimated POs in Population	Precision (±) at 95% Confidence Level POs	%
A.	Competitive bids	2,000	50	20,000	600	3.0
B.	No competitive bids	1,600	40	16,000	588	3.7
C.	Customer direction	400	10	4,000	360	9.0

It will be observed that the formula provides the best reliability when the item of interest represents a relatively high proportion of the sample.

Unknown Populations

Let us assume a large but unknown population of purchased tools. Auditors want to estimate with reasonable reliability how many cost $100 and over. Assume a sample of 400 tools with the division as:

Under $100	320
$100 and over	80
	400

Without an idea of population size, the auditors will be unable to estimate how many tools cost $100 or more. But they can estimate the proportion of items of interest. In this case, they can estimate that 20 percent of the population contains tools costing $100 or more. They will then seek to determine the reliability of that estimate to help decide whether they have taken a large enough sample for their purposes. The formula used to determine the precision of the estimated proportion is:

$$A = \pm Z \sqrt{\frac{p(1-p)}{n}}$$

where:

A = Precision
p = Proportion
n = sample size
Z = Normal deviation for the desired level of confidence

The computation of the reliability statement for the estimate of tools at a 95 percent confidence level is:

$$A = \pm 1.96 \sqrt{\frac{.20(1-.20)}{400}}$$

$$= \pm 1.96 \sqrt{\frac{.20 \times .80}{400}}$$

$$= \pm 1.96 \sqrt{\frac{.16}{400}}$$

$$= \pm 1.96 \sqrt{.0004}$$

$$= \pm 1.96 \times .02$$

$$= \pm .0392$$

Thus, the precision is .20 ±.0392, or approximately from 16 to 24 percent. In other words, at a 95 percent confidence level, between 16 and 24 percent of the tools cost $100 or more.

If the auditors want a more precise result, they might increase their sample size. Assuming that the sample size is doubled to 800 and the sample results remain the same, the precision would be computed:

$$A = \pm 1.96 \sqrt{\frac{.20 (1 - .20)}{800}}$$

$$= \pm 1.96 \sqrt{\frac{.16}{800}}$$

$$= \pm 1.96 \sqrt{.0002}$$

$$= \pm 1.96 \times .01414$$

$$= \pm .0277$$

Now, the precision, at a 95 percent confidence level, is ±2.77 and the range is approximately from 17 to 23 percent. If this is sufficient reliability in the auditors' judgment, they may stop sampling.

Summary

In dealing with audit sampling, the auditor should keep these 10 commandments in mind:

1. Know the principles of scientific sampling, but use them only when they best fit the audit objectives.
2. Know the population, and base audit opinions only on the population sampled.
3. Let every item in the population have an equal chance of being selected.
4. Do not let personal bias affect the sample.
5. Do not permit patterns in the population to affect the randomness of the sample.
6. Do not draw conclusions about the entire population from the purposive or directed (judgment) sample, even though it does have its place.
7. Base estimates of maximum error rates on what is reasonable in the real world; try to determine at what point alarms would automatically go off.
8. Stratify wherever it would appear to reduce variability in the sample.

9. Do not set needlessly high reliability goals (confidence level and precision). Controls, supervision, feedback, self-correcting devices, and management awareness and surveillance should all be considered in seeking to reduce the extent of the audit tests.

10. Do not stop with the statistical results; know why the variances occurred.

In deciding which selection or sampling plan to use, the auditor should consider these applications:

Recommended Selection Technique

Random Numbers. Where each of the items in the population is or can readily be numbered or is included in lists or registers that are or can be numbered.

Interval. Where items are not or cannot readily be numbered, or where random number sampling would be excessively expensive. (Steps must be taken to avoid any bias that may be introduced by patterns in the population or by items missing from the population.)

Stratification. Where the population is composed of items that may vary considerably in value or in other characteristics of interest, and where sample size can be reduced by separating the population into groups of items with reasonably similar values or characteristics.

Cluster or Multistage. Where the population is so dispersed that random number or interval sampling would be burdensome. It must be remembered that there usually may be a loss of sample reliability when cluster or multistage sampling is used, as compared with random number or internal sampling, and that a larger sample size may usually be required to offset that loss.

Recommended Sampling Plan

Attributes. To estimate the attributes or characteristics of a population — obtaining "yes or no" answers — with a measurable degree of reliability.

Stop-and-Go. To estimate error rates or similar attributes from the smallest possible sample — discontinuing the sampling when a definitive answer is obtained.

Discovery. To identify through sampling at least one suspected item — assuming some given number of such items in the population — and discontinuing sampling when at least one item is identified.

Variable. To estimate the value of a population — dollars, weights, time spans, or other variable values — with a measurable degree of reliability.

Judgment. To use samples for the purpose of obtaining information that may not be attributed to the entire population with measured reliability.

References

[1]Andrews Jr., W.T., and A.G. Mayper, "Dollar-Unit Sampling," *The Internal Auditor,* April 1983, 31.

[2]Guy, D.M., and D.R. Carmichael, *Audit Sampling: An Introduction to Statistical Sampling in Auditing,* 2nd Ed. (New York: John Wiley & Sons, 1986).

[3]Harwood, G.B., R.E. Schiffler, and J.M. Woods, Jr., "Putting Dollar-Unit Sampling to Work," *The Internal Auditor,* February 1982, 50-55.

Supplementary Readings

Apostolou, Barbara, and Francine Alleman, *Internal Audit Sampling* (Altamonte Springs, FL: The Institute of Internal Auditors, 1991).

Braun, Gary P., and Patricia M. Myers, "The Use of Statistical Sampling by Internal Auditors: Current Practices," *Internal Auditing*, September/October 2000, 13-16.

Calhoun, Charles, "International Guidance on Audit Sampling," *Internal Auditing Alert*, April 1998, 5-6.

Colbert, Janet, "Audit Sampling," *Internal Auditor*, February 2001, 27-29.

Hitzig, Neal B., "Audit Sampling: A Survey of Current Practice," *The CPA Journal*, July 1995, 54-57.

Sears, Brian P., *Internal Auditing Manual* (New York: RIA, 2003.) (See Chapter D5, "Testing and Sampling.")

Wendell, John P., "The Dual-Risk Method for Calculating Attribute Sampling Sizes," *Internal Auditing,* January/February 1998, 19-22.

Multiple-choice Questions

1. A sampling plan is needed to test for overstatement of a $3 million accounts payable book balance. The auditor determines that a $100,000 error is material and a 95 percent confidence level is appropriate. Based on these determinations, the sample size of 90 is needed. The sampling plan *most* likely to be used is:
   a. Stop-and-go sampling.
   b. Cluster sampling.
   c. Dollar unit sampling.
   d. Attributes sampling.

2. To use stratified sampling to evaluate a large, heterogeneous inventory, which of the following would least likely be used as criteria to classify inventory items into strata?
   a. Dollar values.
   b. Number of items.
   c. Turnover volume.
   d. Storage location.

3. Assuming no change in sample standard deviation, how would sample size and achieved precision be affected by a change in confidence level from 95.5 percent to 99.7 percent?
   a. Sample size would be smaller, but achieved precision would be larger.
   b. Sample size would be larger, but achieved precision would not change.
   c. Sample size would be smaller, but achieved precision would not change.
   d. Sample size would be larger, but achieved precision would be smaller.

4. An internal auditor is preparing to sample accounts receivable for overstatement. A statistical sampling method that automatically provides stratification when using systematic selection is:
   a. Attributes sampling.
   b. Ratio-estimation sampling.
   c. Dollar unit sampling.
   d. Mean-per-unit sampling.

5. In the audit of a health insurance claims processing department, a sample is taken to test for the presence of fictitious payees, though none are suspected. The most appropriate sampling plan would be:
   a. Attributes sampling.
   b. Discovery sampling.
   c. Variable sampling.
   d. Stop-and-go sampling.

6. An auditor wishes to sample 200 sales receipts from a population of 5,000 receipts issued during the last year. The receipts have preprinted serial numbers and are arranged in chronological (and thus serial number) order. The auditor randomly chooses a receipt from the first 25 receipts and then selects every twenty-fifth receipt thereafter. The sampling procedure described here is called:
   a. Systematic random sampling.
   b. Dollar unit sampling.
   c. Judgmental interval sampling.
   d. Variable sampling.

7. Each time an internal auditor draws a conclusion based on evidence drawn from a sample, an additional risk, sampling risk, is introduced. An example of sampling risk is:
   a. Projecting the results of sampling beyond the population tested.
   b. Using an improper audit procedure with a sample.
   c. Incorrectly applying an audit procedure to sample data.
   d. Drawing an erroneous conclusion from sample data.

8. A confidence level of 90 percent means that:
   a. The expected error rate is equal to 10 percent.
   b. The point estimate obtained is within 10 percent of the true population value.
   c. There are 90 chances out of 100 that the sample results will not vary from the true characteristics of the population by more than a specified amount.
   d. A larger sample size is required than if the desired confidence level were equal to 95 percent.

9. Internal auditing is conducting an operational audit of the organization's mail room activities to determine whether the use of express mail service is limited to cases of necessity. To test cost-effectiveness, the auditor selects the 100 most recent express mail transactions for review. A major limitation of such a sampling technique is that it:
   a. Does not allow a statistical generalization about all express-mail transactions.
   b. Results in a sample size that is too small to project the population.
   c. Does not evaluate existing controls in this area.
   d. Does not describe the population from which it is drawn.

10. A statistical sampling technique that will minimize sample size whenever a low rate of noncompliance is expected is:
    a. Ratio-estimation sampling.
    b. Difference-estimation sampling.
    c. Stratified mean-per-unit sampling.
    d. Stop-and-go sampling.

11. In a regional survey of suburban households to obtain data on television viewing habits, a statistical sample of suburban areas is first selected. Within the chosen areas, statistical samples of whole blocks are selected, and within the selected blocks, random samples of households are selected. This type of sample selection can best be described as:
    a. Attributes sampling.
    b. Stratified sampling.
    c. Cluster sampling.
    d. Interval sampling.

12. Using random numbers to select a sample:
    a. Is required for a variables sampling plan.
    b. Is likely to result in an unbiased sample.
    c. Results in a representative sample.
    d. Allows auditors to use smaller samples.

13. An auditor tested a population by examining 60 items selected judgmentally and found one error. The main limitation of the auditor's sample is the inability to:
    a. Quantify sampling risk.
    b. Quantify the acceptable error rate.
    c. Project the population's error rate.
    d. Determine whether the sample is random.

14. A sample from a population of over 10,000 bills of lading is needed to estimate an error rate. Since a sample size of 250 will satisfy precision and confidence level needs, a sampling interval of 40 is chosen. For ease of implementation, the auditor randomly selected a number between 1 and 40, and then selected each succeeding 40th item. Which of the following is true?
    a. The sample lacks randomness and will not be correct.
    b. Interval sampling is not an acceptable statistical method.
    c. If the population lacks bias, the sample is statistically valid.
    d. Interval sampling eliminates the use of auditor judgment.

15. The supervisor of claims processing for a health insurance firm selects all claims processed in the past two days by a particular employee for audit. From this sample, the supervisor can develop:
    a. An overall representative view of employee work for the year.
    b. A quantification of sampling error.
    c. Conclusions about the correctness of processing for the department.
    d. Understanding the details contained in the processing task.

16. To audit invoices paid over the past year, an auditor selects the two busiest months that account for 60 percent of invoices. Following a random start, every tenth invoice is chosen, yielding a sample of 116 invoices. This sample may not be valid because it is not a:
    a. Representative sample.
    b. Random sample.
    c. Large enough sample.
    d. None of the above — sample is valid.

17. An internal auditor with an international shipping organization needs to sample shipping records over the past six months. To do so, the auditor draws a random sample for ships operating in the Mediterranean and a separate sample for those operating in the North Atlantic. This method of sampling is called:
    a. Cluster sampling.
    b. Haphazard.
    c. Interval sampling.
    d. Stratified sampling.

18. By statistically projecting the population value based on the average value of sampled subsidiary accounts, the auditor has estimated the value of the total equipment account to be $2,800,000. This is an example of:
    a. Dollar unit sampling.
    b. Mean-per-unit sampling.
    c. Attributes sampling.
    d. Statistical difference estimation.

19. An inventory listing consisting of approximately 2,050 unnumbered items is arranged by category, with 10 items in each category. Within each category the most expensive (per unit) items are listed first. An auditor wants to use an interval sampling plan to select a representative sample of at least 100 items from the population. The best technique is to:
    a. Select a random number from 1 to 20 as the starting point and then select every 20th item, moving through the entire population.
    b. Select a random number from 1 to 15 as the starting point and then select every 15th item until he or she has 100 items.
    c. Select seven random digits from 1 to 135 as the starting points and then select every 135th item per pass, moving the entire population seven times.
    d. Select the 50 largest items (i.e., extensions with the highest dollar amounts); then excluding the 50 largest items already selected, select a random number from 1 to 37 as the starting point and select every 37th item, moving through the entire population.

20. Using organization policies to establish when approval is needed, an auditor has sampled accounts receivable balances exceeding $1,000 to determine whether the credit department is requiring a credit check for credit sales when appropriate. This is an example of:
    a. Dollar unit sampling.
    b. Mean-per-unit sampling.
    c. Attributes sampling.
    d. Variables sampling.

21. The probability that an estimate based on a random sample falls within a specified range is known as the:
    a. Error rate.
    b. Lower precision limit.
    c. Confidence level.
    d. Standard error of the mean.

22. One objective of an audit of the purchasing function is to determine the cost of late payment of invoices containing trade discounts. The appropriate population from which a sample would be drawn is the file of:
    a. Receiving reports.
    b. Purchase orders.
    c. Canceled checks.
    d. Paid vendor invoices.

23. A sample of 100 items was taken from a population of 5,000 items. The mean value was $200 and the standard deviation was $30. The computed confidence interval for a 95 percent confidence level (z = 1.96) is:
    a. $970,600 to $1,029,400.
    b. $706,000 to $1,294,000.
    c. $996,733 to $1,003,267.
    d. $997,060 to $1,002,940.

24. The range into which an estimate of a population characteristic is expected to fall at a stated confidence level is known as the:
    a. Precision.
    b. Measure of central tendency.
    c. Standard deviation.
    d. Sampling field.

25. An internal auditor suspects that the invoices from a small number of vendors contain serious errors and therefore limits the sample to only those vendors. A major disadvantage of selecting such directed sample of items to examine is the:
    a. Difficulty in obtaining sample items.
    b. Inability to quantify the sampling error related to the total population of vendor invoices.
    c. Absence of a normal distribution.
    d. Tendency to sample a greater number of units.

Chapter 12
Analytical and Quantitative Methods

Learning from operations research and models. Analytical auditing procedures. Nature and use of analytical procedures. Unexpected results or relationships. Trend analysis. Ratio analysis. Regression analysis. A study of trends and relationships. Scatter diagrams. Least squares. Simple and multiple regression analysis. Computer programs. Regression analysis of hospital services. Mathematics and common sense. Operations research — a practical tool. Models classified. Uses of models. Linear programming. The optimum allocation of resources. Uses of linear programming. Steps in linear programming. An application. A practical use in business. Probability theory. Networks. Gantt chart. Inventory models. Queuing theory. Sensitivity analysis. Game theory. Learning curves. Simulation. Decision trees. Dynamic programming. Exponential smoothing. Audit model applications. Standards to use. Data validity. Operational validity. Verifying computer models. Using consultants.

• •

Learning from Operations Research and Models

Purpose

Owing to the increased ease of analysis through information technology, internal auditors are becoming more involved in the use of quantitative techniques to which managers turn for assistance in making business decisions. Where management goes, the internal auditor should be prepared to follow; but if management doesn't know the path, the internal auditor should be able to point the way.

The field of analytical auditing makes extensive use of quantitative techniques that have come from the realm of operations research (OR). OR makes use of mathematical and statistical models designed to simulate reality and assist in decision-making.

A model is a depiction of the interrelationships among recognized factors. In business, mathematical models seek to depict the whole business or any part of it. For example, the balance sheet and the income statement may be considered models. The balance sheet is a "static" model representing the listing of the assets and liabilities of the business at a specified point in time. The income statement is a "dynamic" model of the stream of revenues and expenses flowing through the business. Other models may include the entire accounting system, the production control system, the quality control system, organization charts, and plant layout.

The model concept — to represent but not actually be, the real thing — is not new. After all, a map describes the terrain; it is not the terrain itself. What we are beginning to see is a myriad of variations, including statistical models as the means of analysis.

A Planning Tool

Operations research was developed during World War II. Teams of mathematicians, statisticians, physicists, chemists, military personnel, and others pooled their talents to solve difficult problems that would not yield to current knowledge, individual experience, and intuition. These problems required disciplined, structured approaches. They included such applications as the search for optimum road and water convoy sizes, repair schedules for airplane engines, and the deployment of ships and armored equipment to avoid or reduce losses from enemy attack.

The advent of computer techniques to handle the vast computations required permitted OR to become a practical tool for management and the internal auditor. The manager and auditor could use it as a disciplined means for discovering feasible alternatives, evaluating them, and making the best choice from among them. Thus, OR is essentially a planning and analysis tool and a means of control.

Operations Research (OR) Models

OR models can be classified by their intended use, their subject matter, how they deal with time, how close they are to reality, or the techniques used in their construction. Models are used to do many things and are identified in terms of their intended use:

- Descriptive
- Predictive
- Planning

Descriptive. Classify variables and show their relationship.

Predictive. Predict on the basis of relationships how the variables will behave when one or more of them are changed.

Planning. Decide the best way of combining or changing relationships to achieve some desired result.

As pointed out, financial statements can be considered to be models. Here is an example of how such models can be used in management decision-making:

> A corporation wants to know its financial status so as to be able to borrow money for investments. To demonstrate to prospective lenders the financial performance and the condition of the corporation at a given time, management directs its controller to develop a projected balance sheet and earnings statement, using the following descriptive model (formula):

$$\text{Assets} = \text{Liabilities} + \text{Net Worth}$$

> A prospective lender asks an independent auditor to test the descriptive model for accuracy and reasonableness. Having the auditor's statement based on the test, the lender uses a predictive model to compute the probability that the borrower will be able to pay periodic interest and to repay the loan. The predictive model includes the various ratios used in evaluating financial condition.

> Meanwhile, with the information provided by the descriptive model, the borrower/investor develops a planning model to identify the alternative effect on the current and future balance sheets and earnings statements of investments in securities or facilities.

Internal auditors find many opportunities to use models in their own work. The U.S. General Accounting Office (GAO) has used these methods for many years and with great effect. GAO used models to compute airline costs to support deregulation, forecast postal service volume, revenue, and cost; measure the benefits of auto safety standards; and determine the cost-effectiveness of military physician procurement.[1] The GAO has also audited the models used by other government agencies to analyze:

- Alternatives to achieve energy independence and to determine the technical aspects of synthetic fuel development. (Energy)

- National economic policies to localize economic issues. (Economics)

- Interstate highway systems to develop integrated transportation plans for metropolitan areas. (Transportation)

- The interactions of many factors affecting the total environment and the water quality in individual rivers. (Environment)

The following sections discuss analytical auditing and a few of the quantitative techniques that are commonly used by the profession or have potential use. In selecting topics to include, consideration was also given to recent coverage of quantitative techniques in the CIA exam.

Analytical Auditing Procedures

The internal auditing profession has made increasing use of analytical techniques. As with many of the advances in the profession, the formal recognition of a technique comes after practitioners have molded its use and acceptability informally. In internal auditing, the formalizing of analytical auditing techniques came with the promulgation of *Statement on Internal Auditing Standards No. 8.*

SIAS 8 is titled "Analytical Auditing Procedures." It interpreted Guideline 420.01.1 — *Collecting Information. SIAS 8* discussed three general areas: the nature of analytical auditing procedures; the use of analytical auditing procedures; and dealing with unexpected results.

Guideline 420.01.1 said, "Information should be collected on all matters related to the audit objectives and scope of work." The interpretation in *SIAS 8* dealt with methods of placing the information under a microscope to see what the information is saying.

Practice Advisory 2320-1, "Analysis and Evaluation," captures the substance of the original Guideline 420 and is the basis of much of the material that follows.

Nature and Use of Analytical Procedures

Analytical Auditing Procedures (AAP), also called analytical procedures, are the study and comparison of the relationships of information, both financial and nonfinancial. One of the simplest illustrations is the comparison of a single line item in an expense budget to the total and comparing the current year proportion to the prior year.

	FYE 12-31-x5		FYE 12-31-x6	
	Expense	**% of total exp**	**Expense**	**% of total exp**
Salaries	1,500,000	8.82%	2,000,000	10.26%
Fringes	300,000	1.76%	500,000	2.56%
Total expenses	17,000,000		19,500,000	
Fringes as a percentage of Salaries			20.0%	25.0%
Growth rate in Salaries			33.3%	
Growth rate in Fringes			66.7%	
Growth rate in Total Expenses			14.7%	

AAP is based on a simple — deceptively simple — premise:

". . . Absent any known conditions to the contrary, relationships among information may reasonably be expected to exist and continue." In our illustration, we would expect the growth rate of salaries to maintain a fixed relationship to the growth of expenses. This is obviously not true. The growth of salaries is more than twice the growth of total expenses. Not only that, the growth of fringe benefits is twice the growth rate of salaries — a condition that does not appear *reasonable* and the rate of growth in fringes is 4.5 times the growth rate in total expenses. This short and simple analysis is doing exactly what AAP is expected to do, identify:

- Differences that are not expected.

- The absence of differences when they are expected. Once alerted, the auditor must investigate why the situation has occurred. These could be the result of:

  - Errors.
  - Irregularities.
  - Illegal acts.
  - Unusual events or transactions.
  - Method of accounting.

If the auditor did not have knowledge of any material change in the fringe benefits program, or any increase in staff or compensation rates, the facts clearly fall in the "differences that are not expected" category. That can mean: (a) the auditor did not know facts that should have been known; (b) there were differences that need attention; (c) some irregularity may have occurred; or (d) some combination of these causes. Whatever the case, the auditor has more work to do.

AAP offers an efficient and very effective tool for evaluating information gathered in an audit. The key concepts in using AAP are: (a) identifying the relationships between various pieces of data and (b) identifying expected results. The relationship concept addresses itself in understanding how aspects of the organization work together. If a production plan calls for a constant level of output of the same products from one year to the next and no material changes in production methods occur, the relationship of personnel and raw material to output should remain *reasonably* constant.

One of the most basic ideas in AAP is reasonableness; it implies sensible and rational explanations of change or constancy. Things do not change unless there is some cause. Payroll fringe costs would increase faster than salaries if:

- Health insurance premiums rose faster than the growth of salaries.

- The rate of employer paid taxes increased.

- A new retirement plan was introduced, and so on.

Conversely, if an auditor knew that health insurance premiums increased substantially this year and fringe benefit expense as a percentage of salaries had not changed, the auditor would have to investigate the reasons why.

If there were no changes in the relationship of fringes to salaries, the growth rate of salaries and fringes should be approximately the same. Therefore, there is an obvious issue for exploration by the auditor. What other audit procedure could have surfaced these issues so quickly and clearly? No amount of transaction testing would have uncovered a condition of this type as economically.

There are a number of approaches to AAP that were suggested in *SIAS 8*, and though they were not all-inclusive, they provided considerable insight into the possibility for the use of AAP. Being compared were:

- Current period information to similar information in prior periods.

- Current period financial and operational information to budgets and forecasts.

- Information with similar information in other organizational functions.

- Relationships of financial information with appropriate nonfinancial information (e.g., salary expense to number of employees).

- Relationships among elements of information (e.g., changes in interest expense to changes in daily outstanding debt).

AAP may involve ratios, percentages, monetary amounts, quantities, or other means of comparison of one factor to another. The comparison does not have to employ the same unit of measure. A comparison of units of output to cost of materials from one period to another may use mixed units of measurement in a consistent fashion to identify changes.

AAP may involve:

- Trend analysis.
- Ratio analysis.

- Regression analysis.
- Reasonableness tests.
- Period-to-period comparisons.
- Comparisons with budgets, forecasts, and economic information.
- Comparisons with independent causal or related factors.

In the planning process that was set out in Section 410 of the *Standards,* AAP can be used to help establish the scope of the audit by identifying conditions for further inquiry. During the course of the field work, AAP can be used to examine and evaluate information to support audit findings. According to *SIAS 8,* the auditor should consider a number of factors when using AAP:

- The significance of the area being examined.

- The adequacy of the control system.

- The availability and reliability of financial and nonfinancial information.

- The precision with which results of such procedures can be predicted.

- The availability of comparative information regarding the industry.

- The extent to which other procedures provide support to audit results.

A recent article on analytical auditing procedures quotes from a very early study by Professor Littleton who described analytical ability as the presence of four components.[3]

- Ability to comprehend
- Ability to associate
- Facility in manipulating figures
- Facility in communicating ideas

This combination of skills that was identified by A.C. Littleton in 1944 comprises the list of abilities that internal auditors must have to perform effectively in the analytical auditing process.

Analyzing nonfinancial and even non-quantitative or soft information could reveal important business opportunities or control deficiencies that would be of management interest. Attention could be pointed toward business risks of which it is unaware.[4] As a matter of fact; there is a close relationship between analytical auditing procedure and risk assessment.

Unexpected Results or Relationships

Analytical auditing procedures are like reconciliation procedures — if there is nothing wrong, it would appear to have been a big waste of time; however, one does not know there is nothing wrong until the procedure is carried out. For example, a count of the cashier drawer would seem to be a waste of time if it is found to be in balance — neither over or short. On the other hand, there is no way to know that the drawer is or is not short (or over) without counting the cash and comparing it to the control total.

If an AAP generates unexpected results, the auditor seeks to clarify the meaning of the results. This usually requires audit procedures that are *not* analytical in nature. The follow-on procedures will be inquiries and discussion with managerial and supervisor personnel, transaction review, and other substantive tests.

The auditor must be constantly sensitive to the fact that fraudulent activity as well as simple errors can surface through AAP. The auditor must also keep in mind that some results or relationships will not be properly explained in the audit work. These cases should be reported to management. The auditor may recommend that action be taken if the circumstances dictate.

Auditors use any number of AAP techniques to lead them to further inquires. For example:

- An auditor questioned the fact that a joint venture was booking 5,000 feet of casing pipe each for two oil wells that were only 3,400 feet deep.[5]

- An auditor was reviewing a construction project and noted that cost per square foot was exceeding the industry average.[6]

- While examining seller-provided financing, where the auditor's firm was the seller, the auditor found that interest rates charged were well below the rates of local competitors. Each point of interest rate resulted in a loss of $1 million over the seven-year life of the loans in the portfolio.[7]

- An alert auditor in a supermarket chain observed that the inventory turnover in the produce department of a single store was less than the turnover of any of its departments. It resulted from unbooked inventory acquired from the manager's mother and father with sales paid to them.[8]

- Auditors in India compared prices paid for identical items of machinery spare parts in auto factories in different divisions. They found that the prices paid by some divisions were more than three times the prices in other divisions.[9]

- Bank auditors compared fees collected in one branch to the same fees in other branches as they related to the volume of changeable transactions and found a substantial loss of fee income.[10]

The quantitative techniques discussed in this chapter are used as tools in the analytical auditing process. The auditor must be familiar with these available procedures to choose the proper tool for the task at hand.

Trend Analysis

Trend analysis is a specialized form of AAP used primarily to analyze the changes in account balances, other financial information, or operational information over time. It is the most commonly used quantitative technique and has application for both substantive and compliance testing. It is often used to identify performance indicators (profitability factors), highlight significant changes, and assess how past performance has led to the present position.

Trend analysis is often referred to as "horizontal analysis," since its primary use is tracing an account balance or operating element over time, thereby adding a needed perspective to the internal auditor's analysis. Since trend analysis focuses on the changes in account balances or other information over time, it is more useful in analyzing income statement accounts than balance sheet accounts, or in analyzing operating activities. Regression analysis, which is subsequently discussed, is a more sophisticated version of trend analysis for determining factor relationships.

Ratio Analysis

Ratio analysis is a discrete subset of trend analysis that is used primarily to compare relationships among financial statement accounts at a point in time. Ratio analysis can be used for examining both income statement accounts and balance sheet accounts. It is most effective, however, in evaluating the variations in the income statement accounts, because of the greater cause-effect relationships.

Two methods of ratio analysis are commonly employed by internal auditors.

1. Common-Size Statement. This approach converts each account balance to a percent of another relevant aggregate balance. The most common example is relating all income statement accounts as a percent of sales. This type of comparison is often classified as "vertical analysis."

2. Financial Ratios. This approach expresses the relationship between account balances to reflect useful measures of position or change. An example would be the division of

average inventory into costs of goods sold to generate the inventory turnover. These ratios are also generally classified as activity, liquidity, leverage, or profitability ratios. Common financial ratios are available from various sources such as Dun & Bradstreet and Robert Morse Associates. Financial ratios and common-size statements can also be classified as either time-series analysis or cross-sectional analysis (comparison across organizations).

An auditor may also use ratio analysis to make comparisons within an entity. For example, an auditor may make comparisons of key financial information between divisions. An auditor would investigate the fact that payroll as a percentage of sales is three percent higher for the division under audit than it is for any other division. In addition, an auditor could decide to investigate a higher return rate for goods manufactured by Plant A than for Plant B. These comparisons can also be made historically. However, such comparisons require that such prior information be available to the auditor.

Audits of model applications provide a useful service to managers who would like to use modeling techniques to improve their decision-making but would like assurance that the models and their results can be relied upon. Two more sophisticated OR, or modeling, techniques with which some internal auditing organizations are becoming involved are regression analysis and linear programming.

Regression Analysis

Regression analysis is used to examine relationships among two or more variables. It measures the extent that a change in one of the quantities is accompanied by a change in another or others. Simple regression analysis uses only two variables. For example, the increases in the ages of children tend to be accompanied by increases in their heights. One of the variables is called the independent variable. In the example of the children, the age is the independent variable. The other variable is called the dependent variable. It is associated with the independent variable — the heights of the children tend to depend on their ages.

This relationship can be plotted on a graph called a scatter diagram. The items plotted disclose the trend or historical information. In Exhibit 12-1, a simple linear regression for the heights of children is plotted. The independent variable is normally plotted on the horizontal axis while the dependent variable is plotted on the vertical axis. The line fitted to the scattered dots represents the relationship between the heights of the children at various ages (the dependent, or Y variable) and their ages (the independent, or X variable) as shown by regression analysis.

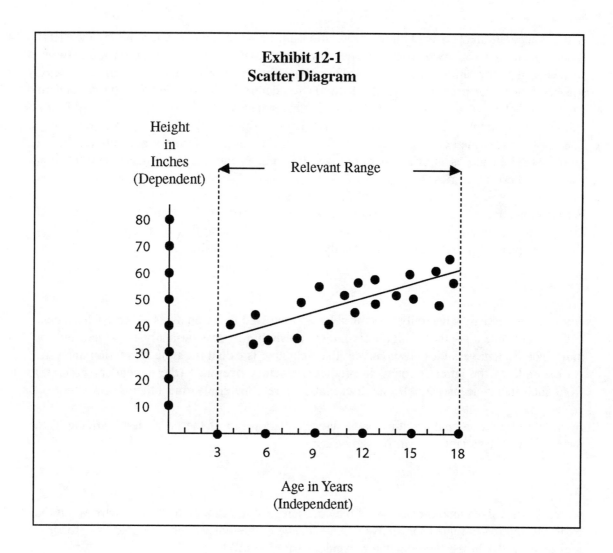

Exhibit 12-1
Scatter Diagram

Children's heights tend to level off after 18 years, so projections about heights past 18 cannot be made with this model. The "relevant" range for the model becomes three to 18 years. This caveat must be taken into account for all models, so the operating range must be strictly defined.

Least Squares

Merely looking at the points on a scatter diagram is not the most accurate way of defining the relationship between two variables. Looking does not reveal which is the best fit for the line or the curve threading its way through the scattered points.

A more accurate method is to show the relationship between the two variables by the "least squares method." This method is a mathematical tool used to study the relationship between variables. If that relationship is truly linear — or close to linear — the result of using least squares is a better prediction. In the formula for determining the best fit, the dependent variable — the one we want to predict — is designated as the Y variable (the children's heights, for example). The independent variable is designated the X variable (their ages). The least squares method is based on the idea that the value that best represents (or fits) a given set of quantities is one that minimizes the sum of the squared differences between itself and these quantities.

For example, according to the least squares principle, the arithmetic mean of a set of repeated experimental measurements subject to random error is the value that best represents the set. Computer programs are available for easily performing regression analysis.

Variables

As stated previously, when only two variables are involved in the analysis — one independent and one dependent — the technique is known as simple regression analysis. Where two or more independent variables are involved, the technique is called multiple regression analysis. An example of the latter is found in predicting factory overhead (the dependent variable) from such independent variables as direct labor, direct materials, and other direct charges.

In simple regression analysis, the mathematical relationship of the dependent variable Y to the independent variable X can be shown as:

$$Y = a + bX$$

where "a" is a fixed amount and "b" is the coefficient of the change in X. This carries out the basic assumption of regression analysis: Any change in the independent variable (X) produces a change of "b" in the value of the dependent variable (Y).

When the number of the independent variables is greater than one, the relationship between the dependent and the independent variables becomes much more complex. The relationship is shown as:

$$Y = a + b_1X_1 + b_2X_2 + \ldots + b_nX_n$$

In simple terms, the value of Y depends on "a" (a fixed amount) and "b" (the coefficient of change) for each of the independent variables.

Correlation

As we learned from sampling, projections are not necessarily 100 percent accurate. The projections will lie within some range of reliability. The corresponding question is: How closely are the variables related? This relationship can be quantified with a number called the correlation coefficient r. The number r ranges from +1.00 (perfect positive — heights of children and foot sizes) through 0.00 (perfect random correlation — sets of two children selected at random from a school yard) to -1.00 (perfect negative correlation — ascending ages of children and amounts of baby fat).

The mathematical basis for the least squares method and regression analysis is explained in standard statistics textbooks.

The reader should be aware that the numbers must stand the test of reason. A high degree of mathematical correlation could be plotted between the amount of beer consumed in the City of X and the number of teachers in the City of X. But reason tells us that one is not really related to the other. Regression in and of itself does not assure a cause and effect relationship.

Uses of Regression Analysis

Regression analysis can be employed to predict the expected. It is being used increasingly in business to disclose trends and identify aberrations. Internal auditors can use it to help managers make predictions or to test management's predictions. Some uses of regression analysis are to analyze supply and demand, predict customer receivables, forecast burden rates, analyze markets, study price behavior, and study advance reservations and predict account balances.

Internal auditors can use regression analysis in their audit or investigative work. They can tell where trends may be leading and whether those trends point to aberrant conditions. They may also point to a dependent variable that is not being achieved. Thus, indicators so plotted might point to matters that ordinary operating reports do not identify, or the trends may point to potential danger spots.

Software is available to determine the relationship between variables. For example, the program could be fed two variables: the accounts payable balances for the last 12 months and, for each of these months, the cost of direct material charged to work in progress. The program would then determine the coefficients for individual values of the dependent variable and predict what the dependent variable would be for given independent variables. If it were known that actual material costs charged were, say, $100,000 for a particular month, the software would predict the expected accounts payable for that month. The accounts payable prediction shown for $100,000 of material might be, for example, from $125,800 to $144,500. This might be useful to management in forecasting, among other things, cash flow or estimating cash available for investment. It could also point to a fraud situation where invisible vendors were being paid. An auditor may wish to investigate Accounts Payable if substantially above or below this range.

Predicting Hospital Costs

An epic case involving audits of hospital costs underscores the value of regression analysis to management decision-making.[11] The nature of this case and its use of regression are as valid in current audit practice as when it was carried out.

Government auditors were asked to study the cost of constructing and operating health facilities. The main question was whether the expense of recent innovations would reduce health costs. In some cases, the costly initial expense of innovative procedures could be less costly over the long run because of greater efficiency. But this might be true only in large hospitals. So the question involved the relationship between the volume of the hospital activity (the independent variable) and the initial investment plus lifetime operation and maintenance (dependent variable) for hospitals of different sizes.

The audit team selected a number of departments and activities for their study, including these:

Department or Activity	Methods Compared
Dietary	Conventional
	Convenience foods
Material handling	Manual
	Semi-automated
	Automated
Pharmacy	Conventional medication distribution
	Unit dose distribution

The team gathered information from 67 hospitals, 39 manufacturers of health care systems and equipment, and six trade associations. That data included initial investment costs, annual operation and maintenance costs, and volume of activity. The data was used in a computer program that performed regression analysis.

The application to the pharmacy department illustrates the use of regression analysis. In a conventional system, the pharmacy simply purchases medication and distributes it to nursing stations. But there are other elements of a total medication distribution system: filling physicians' medication orders, administering the proper dosage to patients, and recording results of patient therapy.

The unit dose system calls on the pharmacy people to do more. They maintain medication records, interpret physicians' orders, provide unit dose packages of medication at the time they are to be administered, and, in certain instances, administer medication to patients. A unit dosage package contains the exact dose, such as one tablet or one capsule, ordered by the patient's physician to be administered at a specified time.

In each analysis, the number of prescriptions filled annually was the independent variable and the lifetime cost (20 years) for that category was the dependent variable. For each of the alternative approaches, a separate regression analysis was performed for certain cost categories:

- Annual personnel costs
- Annual medication costs
- Annual supply costs
- Equipment and maintenance costs
- Space and maintenance costs

The regression analyses showed that the unit dose distribution system resulted in lower life cycle costs than conventional distribution for annual prescriptions over 250,000. The major factor was the reduction in nursing time for administering unit dose medication.

Limitations

Regression analysis doesn't answer "why?" It does not prove cause and effect. The statistical determination of a relationship does not explain the reason — it merely establishes a fact. So, as in everything else, when the auditors obtain the facts they must then apply judgment.

In any mathematical technique, the procedure cannot be carried out mechanically; the assumptions must be valid and the results must make sense. For example, enamored with the numbers they generate, people sometimes follow the numbers by rote and stub their toes in the process. More important is the possibility of making the wrong assumption that relationships between variables will persist in the same way over periods of time. This assumption is not always valid.

Linear Programming

Nature

Linear programming is employed to make the best use of scarce resources. Materials, work hours, space, products, facilities, machines, and money are invariably limited. These limitations are referred to as constraints or restraints. In business one needs to make the most out of what one has. The question is: Which mixture of resources will provide the greatest return for the lowest allocation of available resources? But the variety of available mixes may at times boggle the mind, and intuition will almost certainly produce invalid answers.

Linear programming, however, provides the best mix of available resources to meet an objective — for example, to maximize profits or minimize costs. It derives its name from the linear algebraic equations used to describe the mix. The equations describe the relationship between variables — a relationship in which the change in one variable is accompanied by a proportional change in another or others. An example is the relationship between transportation costs and the distance traveled.

Properly used, linear programming can be employed to determine the best way to locate retail stores, achieve optimum product or material mixes, select machine and worker combinations, select the best media mix for advertising, schedule flight crews, select transportation routes, determine the least expensive routes for salespeople, blend chemical products, use storage facilities, and other applications.

Linear Programming Illustrated

Mathematicians use a number of steps to solve problems of resource allocations, but the problems must have certain characteristics. These characteristics and a simple example of each are:

A stated objective. The objective is to reduce transportation costs between scattered factories and customers.

Limited resources that can be put to alternative uses. A number of factories, each with maximum capacity, must deliver goods to a number of customers, each with minimum requirements.

Problems that are subject to quantitative measurement. The factory outputs are known in quantitative terms. The customer needs are similarly known. The transportation costs between each factory and each customer can be determined.

Linear relationships. In our transportation problem, the elements are proportional to each other: generally, the longer the distance between a factory and a customer, the greater the cost. A percentage increase in distance results in a percentage increase in transportation costs.

The mathematical formulas are beyond the scope of this book; texts on OR provide them. In fact, any linear programming problem involving many variables needs a computer program for solution. A simple application of linear programming to a transportation problem will illustrate the procedure:

An organization is engaged in producing items in four different plants throughout the country — Plants 1, 2, 3, and 4. The organization also has four customers for the items — Customers A, B, C, and D. The plant capacities and the customer requirements each month are:

Plant		Customer	
Identification	Capacity	Identification	Needs
1	30	A	70
2	50	B	50
3	80	C	40
4	60	D	60
Totals	**220**		**220**

The plants and customers are scattered all over the country. Transportation costs differ. For example, it costs $5 to ship an item from Plant 1 to Customer B. But it costs $8 to ship from Plant 3 to Customer B. To juggle all the varying costs in one's head would be impossible, but a matrix helps lay out all the variable choices of this relatively simple problem. In the following matrix, the dollar amounts represent transportation costs from any plant to any customer; the units represent the items:

	Customer				Plant
Plants	A	B	C	D	Capacities
1	$5	$2	$2	$4	30 units
2	3	6	3	2	50 units
3	7	8	5	3	80 units
4	4	2	3	6	60 units

Customer Requirements:

	A	B	C	D	
	70	**50**	**40**	**60**	**220 units**

By using appropriate mathematical formulas, the best combinations for the matrix are determined — combinations that would lead to the lowest total transportation costs. The matrix shows the number of units transported and the destinations.

Plants	Customer				Plant Capacity
	A	B	C	D	
1		$2 10	$2 20		30
2	$3 50				50
3			$5 20	$3 60	80
4	$4 20	$2 40			60
Totals	70	50	40	60	220

The total costs are then determined as follows:

Plant to Customer	Units Number of Units	Units Transportation Cost ($)	Total Transportation Cost ($)
1-B	10	2	20
1-C	20	2	40
2-A	50	3	150
3-C	20	5	100
3-D	60	3	180
4-A	20	4	80
4-B	40	2	80
Totals	220		650

Because the calculations for the preceding problem are simple, they can be carried out using matrix algebra. For complicated business problems, software can easily be used to sort out all the combinations and to point to the best one. Internal auditors may wish to use linear programming in evaluating the efficiency of various resource allocations or in evaluating compliance with an entity's policies and procedures if such policies require the use of linear programming. If internal auditors are asked to evaluate or develop a complex problem, they would be well advised to call upon qualified mathematicians for guidance.

Other OR Methods

Probability Theory

This theory refers to the probability that some event will occur or refers to the frequency with which an event will occur in an infinite number of trials. The expected ratio of the probable occurrences, on the one hand, to the total trials, on the other, may be based on data obtained from experience.

The probability ratio is a percentage between zero at one end (impossibility) and unity at the other (certainty). For example, the probability that the sun will rise in the east is certainty (unity or 1). The probability that it will set in the east is impossibility (or 0). The probability that the sun, rising in the east, will be obscured by clouds is somewhere in between.

Probability theory may be used to refine estimates of revenues and costs. It is also the basis for the sampling plans and techniques used in audit tests.

Networks

Networks assist managers in visualizing the required operations, resource requirement, time requirements, costs, and the sequence of events in large complex projects. Networks provide diagrammatic representations of the sequence of events and the critical steps in the project. Network analysis assists management in understanding how the project must proceed and in identifying possible ways to revise or shorten the sequence of activities to expedite the project and/or lower the costs. Chief audit executives often use network analysis in planning and scheduling the complex audit process. In certain industries such as construction and aircraft manufacturing, an understanding of networks is critical to an internal auditor.

The best known network decision aids are PERT (Program Evaluation and Review Technique) and CPM (Critical Path Method). These two methods are similar but were developed independently. PERT can best be explained through the use of an example that also shows how it differs from CPM:

> Lee Corporation is considering the introduction of a new information system. The marketing research department has informed management that two major competitors are also working on models that will compare very favorably in both quality and price. As with many high technology products, the amount of lead time from the drawing board to delivery to customers is crucial.

Management has several questions, including:

- What is the expected time to complete the project?

- What are the critical tasks that have to be completed on time to deliver the product as scheduled?

- Can resources be allocated from other tasks to expedite completion of the critical tasks?

Management has decided to use PERT as a decision aid to analyze the project and has developed a schematic of the tasks involved (Exhibit 12-2). The main components of PERT network — activities, events, and arrows (for direction and interrelationships) — are present in the schematic.

A few definitions are needed before the solution is presented.

- *Activity* — A task or operation that consumes resources over time. The activities are represented in Exhibit 12-2 by the lines labeled A through J.

- *Event* — Discrete points in time, represented by the numbers 1 through 7, that indicate the completion of one activity and the start of another.

- *Path* — Sequence of activities that connect the start event (1) to the end event (7).

- *Critical path* — The longest path through the network.

- *Slack* — The amount of additional time that an activity can consume without delaying the project past the expected completion date. Slack is the difference between the earliest expected time and the latest allowable time for each event.

- *Earliest expected time* — The earliest expected time that all activities leading to an event can be completed.

- *Latest allowable time* — The latest time that all activities leading to an event can be completed without delaying the project.

Exhibit 12-2
Network

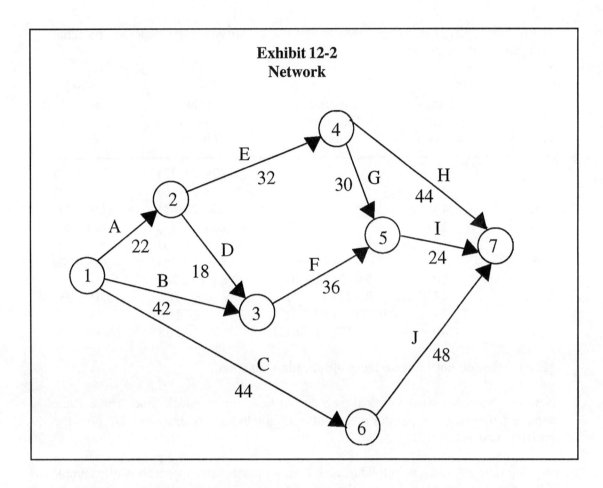

The first step in solving the problem is to identify the paths in the network:

$$
\begin{array}{rcl}
1\text{-}2\text{-}4\text{-}7 & = & 98 \text{ days} \\
1\text{-}3\text{-}5\text{-}7 & = & 102 \text{ days} \\
1\text{-}6\text{-}7 & = & 92 \text{ days} \\
1\text{-}2\text{-}3\text{-}5\text{-}7 & = & 100 \text{ days} \\
1\text{-}2\text{-}4\text{-}5\text{-}7 & = & 108 \text{ days}
\end{array}
$$

Path 1-2-4-5-7 is the critical path because it has the longest time (108 days). This provides the expected time to complete and identifies the critical tasks. These tasks will merit close monitoring to assure scheduled completion. Resources may be shifted from noncritical activities (3 and 6) to critical activities (1, 2, 4, 5, and 7) to expedite the completion of the activities and, thereby, shorten the expected completion time.

The following data can be generated to assist in identifying slack time and potential reallocation of resources:

Activity	Time for Activity	Earliest Expected Time*	Latest Allowable Time*	Slack (Col 4 Minus Col 3)
A	22	22	22(108-24-32)	0
B	42	42	48(108-24-36)	6(48-42)
C	44	44	60(108-48)	16(60-44)
D	18	40(22+18)	48(108-24-36)	8(48-40)
E	32	54(22+32)	54(108-24-30)	0
F	36	78(42+36)	84(108-24)	6(84-78)
G	30	84(22+32+30)	84(108-24)	0
H	44	98(22+32+44)	108	10(108-98)
I	24	108(22+32+30+24)	108	0
J	48	92(44+48)	108	16(108-92)

*Parentheses do not indicate the multiplication function.

Note that activities on the critical path do not have related slack time. The earliest expected time for completion of activity "D" includes the time for "D" plus the previous network activity "A."

In assigning time estimates to individual activities, a probabilistic approach is often employed in PERT. CPM uses activity cost estimates and assumes a single time estimate for each activity. The PERT time estimates are weighted (X4) for the most likely time. For example, in arriving at the time estimate of activity "A" in the preceding example, the following calculations were made:

$$12 \text{ days} = \text{Optimistic Time (0)}$$
$$20 \text{ days} = \text{Likely Time (l)}$$
$$40 \text{ days} = \text{Pessimistic Time (P)}$$

The usual formula for Expected Time (ET) is:

$$ET = 1/6[0 + 4(L) + P]$$
$$ET = 1/6[12 + 4(20) + 40]$$

Since the times are estimates, sensitivity analysis may be employed to determine the sensitivity of the time estimates to varying conditions.

Network methods, particularly PERT and CPM, have been used to address significant industry and government projects as an aid to management in organizing, planning, monitoring, and controlling large onetime projects. These methods are even more powerful when used with a computer program. Internal auditors may be called upon to use PERT or CPM in evaluating efficiency and adherence to an entity's policies and procedures.

Gantt Chart

A Gantt chart is a project scheduling technique that divides each project into activities with estimated start and completion times. The Gantt chart allows the decision-maker to visually review a schematic presentation of the project time budget and allows for subsequent comparison with actual times. Its simplicity allows for easy schedule modification.

As indicated in Exhibit 12-3, the Gantt chart is easy to use and modify and does not require sophisticated tools or techniques.

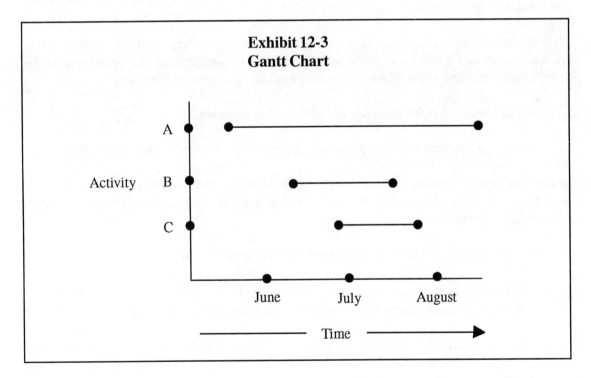

Exhibit 12-3
Gantt Chart

A Gantt chart is probably appropriate for internal audit scheduling because the audit process does not frequently lend itself to sequence revisions. However, problems may arise that require a continuous rescheduling of audit resources.

Inventory Models

The materiality of inventories in many organizations initiated the early development and application of related OR models. Most organizations find it necessary to maintain inventories that are either sold to customers or consumed within the organization. Improvement in inventory management and control is, therefore, important at all stages of operation (purchasing, production, distribution, and sales). Many complex models have been developed to address the need for more effective and efficient inventory management. This section will present only the classic model that serves as the basis for the more complex adaptations.

Inventory theory is not restricted to inventories alone but, broadly defined, applies also to such matters as accounts receivable, cash, staffing, workloads, and parking facilities. In fact, the concept can be applied to any economic resource that has the basic characteristics of inventory (investment of resources, holding cost, etc.). The most common uses, however, are for inventory control and production scheduling. Accordingly, only the classic economic order quantity (EOQ) model will be discussed.

Characteristic of all models, the classic EOQ model has several assumptions. Although they are too restrictive for most real-world applications, these assumptions can be relaxed in the development of more sophisticated inventory models. The assumptions are:

1. Inventory demand is known with certainty and is constant.

2. Inventory is instantaneously replenished at zero level (no lead time and no stockouts).

In addition to these assumptions, the model is restricted to one item at a time and does not consider the priority of the inventory item. Inventory computer programs are often used to address these problems.

The costs considered in the inventory model are classified as follows:

- *Ordering costs* include all incremental costs associated with placing an order, such as requisitioning, receiving, inspecting, handling, and accounting.

- *Carrying costs* include all incremental costs associated with holding inventory, such as cost-of-capital (opportunity costs), warehouse, insurance, taxes, and direct storage costs.

- *Shortage costs* (stock-out costs) include such costs as lost sales, lost future sales, and lost customer goodwill.

Obviously, there are trade-offs between the advantages of large inventories and the related costs. The objective of the EOQ model is to minimize the conflicting costs by determining the optimal order quantity that balances ordering and carrying costs. Exhibit 12-4 illustrates that, as the number of items ordered increases, the ordering cost decreases because fewer orders are placed. As the number of items ordered increases, however, the carrying costs increase as the inventory level rises. The impact of the above trade-offs on total cost is an initial decrease, but an increase at some point. The EOQ point is the low point on the total cost curve where the ordering cost and carrying cost curves intersect.

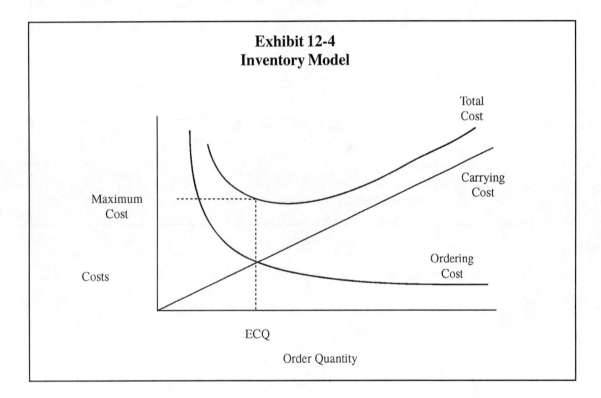

Exhibit 12-4
Inventory Model

The impact of following an EOQ model, modified for safety stock and lead time, is diagrammed in Exhibit 12-5.

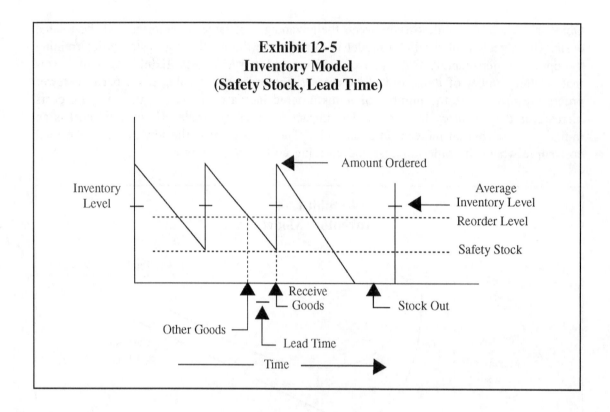

Exhibit 12-5
Inventory Model
(Safety Stock, Lead Time)

The EOQ formula that results in the optimal order quantity is:

$$EOQ = \sqrt{\frac{2\ AR \times OC}{CC}}$$

where:

AR	=	Annual Requirement
OC	=	Order Cost per order
CC	=	Carrying Cost per unit

As illustrated in Exhibit 12-4, this formula will indicate the economic order quantity that will minimize total costs in the following equation:

Total Cost (TC) = Total OC + Total CC

As this elementary example will indicate, once the cost parameters are estimated, the formula can be used for a general solution:

Roy Company is attempting to reduce the inventory costs of a stock item with an annual demand of 2,000 units, order cost of $8 per order, and carrying cost of $20 per unit.

$$EOQ = \sqrt{\frac{2(2000) \times (\$8)}{\$20}}$$

$$EOQ = \ 40 \text{ units}$$

Since many of the cost parameters in the model are estimated, sensitivity analysis, which involves the use of other potential values for variables, often plays an important role in inventory models. Inventory models are useful to auditors in evaluating the efficiency of organizations that have substantial inventory.

Queuing Theory

Most organizations need to provide a variety of services to customers or internal users. Queuing theory offers a decision tool for distributing a system of service units. It describes how users arrive for service, the waiting process, the service process, and other relevant data. Queuing theory has been used in the initial design of service centers and in evaluating the cost/ benefit of alternative service levels. The primary objective of queuing theory is to provide the information necessary to minimize total cost while providing timely service.

As illustrated in Exhibit 12-6, queuing theory involves two costs:

1. The service cost, which includes the operating cost and the facility costs.
2. The waiting cost, which may include either idle time cost or lost customer cost.

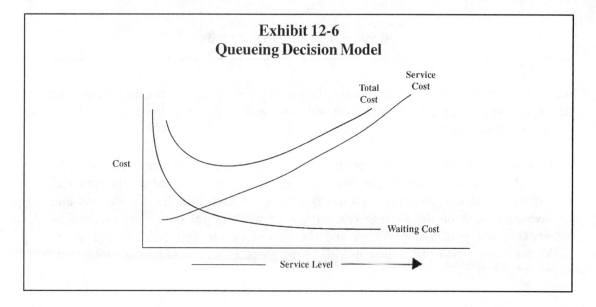

Exhibit 12-6
Queueing Decision Model

As the level of service is increased, the related service cost will increase while waiting cost diminishes; there is an inverse relationship between service cost and waiting cost. Thus, the decision is a trade-off between waiting-time costs and service-level costs in attempting to lower total costs.

Exhibit 12-7 illustrates a simple queuing system with one queue and one service system. The actual number of conceivable queuing systems is almost infinite, i.e., multiple queues, multiple servers, multiple service stations, multiple queue stations, etc. Also, the first step (arrival) and the last step (departure) in the process can have a variety of scenarios. Most studies use arrivals and departures that have a Poisson distribution This statistical distribution will not be addressed here.

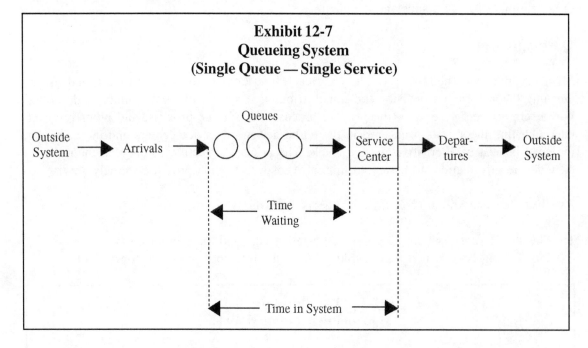

Exhibit 12-7
Queueing System
(Single Queue — Single Service)

Suffice it to say that users generally arrive in a random manner, wait for the service, receive the service, and depart. A simple problem with one waiting line and one server will provide a better understanding of queuing theory:

> Brenner Manufacturing Company has production workers who must periodically stop their machines and obtain raw materials from stores. Based on the material requisition records, 10 workers on the average arrive each hour for service, and one inventory clerk on the average can service 15 workers per hour. The production workers are paid $10 per hour and the inventory clerk is paid $5 per hour. Management would like to determine if hiring another clerk would reduce total cost.

Before the solution is demonstrated, a few formulas will be presented that provide additional solutions to queuing problems. For ease of recognition, the abbreviations used will be "user-friendly" instead of the typical Greek notations.

SR = Service Rate (15 per hour). The service rate is the mean number of workers serviced in one hour.

AR = Arrival Rate (10 per hour). The arrival rate is the mean number of workers arriving for service per hour.

AS = Average number of workers in the system waiting in the queue or being served.

$$AS = \frac{AR}{SR - AR} = 2 \text{ workers}$$

ST = Average worker time in the system either waiting or being served.

$$ST = \frac{1}{SR - AR} = \frac{1}{5} \text{ hour (12 minutes)}$$

QT = Average time workers spend waiting in the queue.

$$QT = \frac{AR}{SR(SR - AR)} = \frac{1}{7.5} \text{ hour (8 minutes)}$$

AQ = Average number of workers in the queue.

$$AQ = \frac{AR^2}{SR(SR - AR)} = 1.33 \text{ workers waiting}$$

PQ = The probability that the server is busy and that a queue is created.

$$PQ = \frac{AR}{SR} = 67\%$$

IT = The percent of server idle time.

$$IT = 1 - \frac{AR}{SR} = 33\%$$

To continue the example, assume the following:
Workers rate of pay = $10 per hour
Inventory clerk rate of pay = $5 per hour
Mean system time

1 clerk	=	12 minutes	($\frac{1}{5}$ hour)
2 clerks	=	4 minutes	
3 clerks	=	3 minutes	

(1)

Worker Lost - Time Cost (WC)	=	**Arrival Rate (AR)**	x	**Mean Time Spent in System (ST)**	x	**Pay Rate (PR)**
WC	=	AR	x	ST	x	PR
WC	=	10	x	.2 hour	x	$10/hour
WC	=	$20/hour				

(2)

Worker Total Cost per Hour (TC)	=	**Clerical Cost per Hour (CC)**	+	**Lost-Time Cost per Hour (WC)**
TC	=	CC	+	WC
TC	=	$5	+	$20
TC	=	$25		

Using an incremental cost approach, management wishes to determine the cost/benefit of having two inventory clerks.

(3) WC = AR x ST x PR
WC = 10 per hour x 1/15 hour x $10 per hour
WC = $6.67

(4) TC = CC + WC
TC = 2 x $5 + $6.67
TC = $16.67

It is apparent from this analysis that the cost of workers waiting time outweighs the cost of server idle time and that total cost is reduced by hiring a second clerk.

Management must go one step further and determine if using three clerks would lower the total cost.

(5)   WC = AR x ST x PR
       WC = 10 per hour x 1/20 hour x $10 per hour
       WC = $5

(6)   TC = CC + WC
       TC = 3 x $5 + $5
       TC = $20

The total cost increases with the hiring of the third clerk. Since the number of servers is discrete (i.e., management can hire two or three clerks but cannot hire two and one-half clerks), the lowest cost results from using two clerks.

Given an almost infinite variety of waiting-line situations, queuing models can become quite complex and require simulation to test. A computer simulation model can imitate the real-life system and yield useful results for decision-making.

Internal auditors can use queuing theory to evaluate the efficiency of service organizations.

Sensitivity Analysis

Sensitivity analysis is used to test a model's behavior to changing conditions. More specifically, it is concerned with how the model solution changes as a result of changes in the problem parameters. Model parameters are generally not known with certainty, since some degree of uncertainty usually exists in real-world situations. Therefore, it is often advantageous to know how changes in the parameters change the optimal solution.

In formulating and solving linear programming problems, certain initial assumptions are made that all values of the coefficients are derived from the analysis of data and that they represent average values or best estimate values. Accordingly, it is important to analyze the sensitivity of the solution to variations in these coefficients or in the estimates of the coefficients. Stated another way, one seeks to determine the variation ranges of the coefficients over which the solution will remain optimal. With available software an internal auditor can easily rerun a model with different estimates and evaluate changes in the solution.

If the given situation is not sensitive to changes in the parameter values, then the solution is considered more reliable than that in a highly sensitive situation. Given a solution that is sensitive to changes, special attention should be given to forecasting future parameter values. On the other hand, a solution with little sensitivity to change does not merit the effort and resources necessary to estimate the values of the parameters more accurately.

Given that many decision problems utilize estimated parameter values in formulating a model, sensitivity analysis becomes an integral part of decision analysis.

Learning Curves

Learning curves (Exhibit 12-8) illustrate that as people acquire experience, they can reduce the time required to complete a given task. Alternatively stated, production increases with task experience.

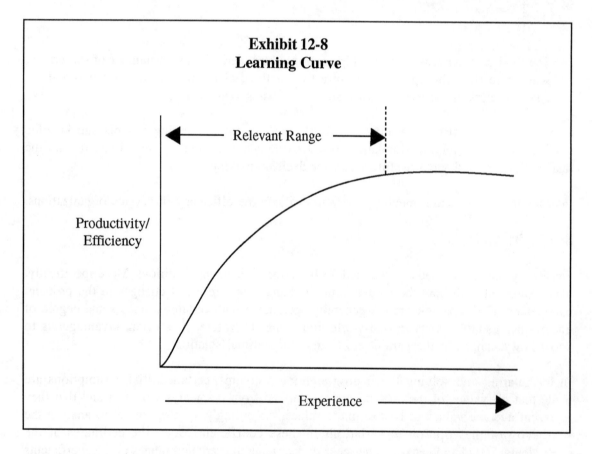

Exhibit 12-8
Learning Curve

This technique has a relevant range only in the initial stages of an activity since the curve "flattens" out, reflecting diminishing marginal returns for experience. Learning curves are useful in evaluating alternatives or in predicting start-up or training costs.

Learning curves are generally described by the time required to double the production level. A 50 percent learning curve means that each time the production is doubled, the time required for production will be 50 percent of the prior production time. A simple example will illustrate the procedure:

Chris' Marine production records reflected the following labor hours for new airboats:

Airboat Number	Labor Hours Per Unit	Calculations
1	1000	
2	700	
4	490	(700 x 70%)
8	343	(490 x 70%)
16		

The data indicates that a 70 percent learning curve is present (700 hours for No. 2 divided by 1000 hours for No. 1 = 70 percent). As indicated, this information can be used to predict the time to complete Airboat No. 4. If management believed that the 70 percent learning curve would still be present, internal auditors can use this to evaluate efficiency for new products. This information can be plotted to generate future production estimates. Alternatively, computer programs can be used.

Simulation

The term *simulation* is defined as the process of deriving system performance measures by conducting sampling experiments on the system model. It is a technique employed to develop measures of performance for decision problems where various components of the problem are random. This technique involves defining the objective of the model, formulating the model, validating the model, designing the experiment, and conducting the simulation.

The process of simulation involves sampling from the designed model to obtain operational information. Since some assurance is necessary to determine that the results of the sampling process provide realistic information, validation is required. This step involves determining if the model results represent the true system and if the program correctly simulates the original model. This is usually accomplished through comparison with historical data. Simulation has many uses and may be applied to problems too difficult to model or solve by analytical means. Often, parallel simulation is employed where the model results are compared to historical information for substantive testing. Other uses include:

- Inventory simulation.
- Queueing simulation.
- Network simulation.
- Alternative choice simulation.
- New-product simulation.
- Internal control simulation.

Many complex real-world decision problems involving random activities are easily handled by simulation procedures. In fact, it is in these complex situations that simulation proves most useful.

One of the limitations of simulation is that the technique only provides a method of generating representative samples of the performance variable. Thus, it has the limitations inherent in any probabilistic model. In other words, the sample values yield statistics that are only estimates of the true values and are subject to sampling variability. Thus, simulation requires the ability to model and a certain amount of statistical expertise. There are many simulation languages, however, that have decreased the work necessary and have increased the application.

Monte Carlo simulation is often used when the characteristics of a system are too complex to be solved analytically. With this technique, the relevant characteristics of the system are defined as random variables and constitute an integral part of the model. The random variables in the model are represented by probability distributions. In effect, Monte Carlo simulation is a procedure for sampling from the probability distribution(s) to generalize the individual values for a random variable for use in a particular run or simulation study. With sufficient replication, the sample results will conform to the designated probability distribution. Simulation can be used by internal auditors to evaluate efficiency and effectiveness.

Decision Trees

Decision trees are useful when the solution requires a sequential decision-making process. The use of a decision tree diagram allows the decision-maker to visually review each possible decision strategy and the probability of the possible subsequent events. The objective of the decision tree is to select the appropriate set of strategies that will yield the highest expected value. Decision trees are useful to internal auditors in their own decision-making. For example, an auditor's decision on whether to perform substantive testing or tests of controls can be viewed using a decision tree.

Dynamic Programming

Dynamic programming is termed a "maximization theory." It is used where a whole series of states (conditions) or actions take place and where a decision in each state is dependent on the decision made in a preceding state. It permits one to determine mathematically the period-by-period consequences of decisions.

It can be used to calculate the desirability of incurring temporary losses for the sake of long-term gains. For example, through dynamic programming, one could calculate the benefits of expending large sums on research and development and incurring losses during immediate periods in the hope of making much greater profits in later periods.

Exponential Smoothing

The exponential smoothing technique is used to correlate later values with earlier ones in the same series. It is used to base predictions on past observations, giving the greatest weight to the latest observation. It can be applied to determine the production of optimum lot sizes to meet forecasted sales.

Game Theory

Game theory can be differentiated from other decision tools since it is applied under conditions of conflict. It is a mathematical decision-making approach used when confronted with one or more rational, intelligent competitors. It takes into account the consequences of the action by one party upon the actions of an opponent who is choosing from among alternatives.

Game theory goes beyond the classical theory of probability, which is limited to pure chance. In game theory, strategic aspects are stressed — that is, aspects controlled by the participants. It is therefore well adapted to the study of competition where several common factors are present, such as conflicting interests, incomplete information, the interplay of rational decisions, and chance.

Game theory has limited application in business but can be used in competitive bidding, marketing strategies, and personnel recruiting. Still, a theoretical understanding of game theory is important, since many business situations involve competition. A conceptual understanding of game theory provides valuable insights that may lead to better decisions.

Game theory cases are classified by the number of participants and the sum of the payoffs. A two-person game is called a zero-sum game if the payoff to the winner is taken from the loser. A positive-sum game is one in which both players benefit. Games with more than two players are referred to as n-person games. An internal auditor can use game theory to evaluate the bargaining of independent business units.

Auditing OR Models

Standards

Standards for acceptable models are available to help internal auditors make a knowledgeable assessment of an OR model.[12] Some standards the internal auditor can apply in assessing model building include:

- The documentation for the model should clearly set forth the model's assumptions, uncertainties, limitations, and capabilities.

- The documentation should also disclose whether the model is understood and can be operated and maintained, and whether the model can be evaluated by an independent person or group.
- The model should be developed to answer the needs of the user. The developer and user should coordinate development effort; the user should participate in the planning process; and the model should be what the user needs — no more, no less.
- Model development should be adequately monitored.
- Provision should be made to update the model for future use, so as not to produce outdated information.
- The data needed for input into the model should be available.
- The costs of building the model should be justified in terms of usefulness. How closely does the model mirror reality; that is, has the model's validity been established? Has the model's credibility been established; that is, does the documentation include, as an absolute minimum, the intended purpose of the model, the key assumptions made, a discussion of the reasonableness of the assumptions, and the basic structure of the model?

Data Validity
- Does the data identify and measure the desired problem elements?
- Are the data sources clearly defined and are the responsibilities for data collection established?
- Are the procedures for the collection and updating of data workable?
- Is the data obtainable within reasonable time spans and at reasonable cost?
- Do the data collection procedures lead to impartiality in the accurate recording of the data?
- Is the resulting data representative?
- Are there audit procedures for the data collection activity?
- Is the data current?

Operational Validity
- To what extent do the assumptions made for the model differ from actual conditions?
- Would the cost of gathering the data and the need for timeliness and accuracy prevent the accumulation of needed information?
- Do the logic and numerical elements of the program as transformed into the computer program result in an invalid computational process?
- Are the accuracy ranges of the model's answers so wide as to make results unusable?
- Are trial results inconsistent with user expectations? If so, are changes planned?
- Are expected cost savings attributed to the model sufficient to justify the model? Have the costs been accurately computed? Have all elements of cost been considered?

- What determination has been made of the model's responses to changes in parameter values? Is the user aware of model outputs for different possible ranges of data?
- What has been done to see that the final operational environment for the model is the same as that which was assumed in the original and modified development plans?

Computer Model Verification
- Are the mathematical and logical relationships internally consistent?
- Are the results accurate?
- Are the flow of data and the intermediate results logical and correct?
- Have all important variables and relationships been included?
- Does the computer program, as written, accurately describe the model as designed?
- Is the program properly debugged on the computer?
- Does the program run as expected?

The computer model verification cannot be overlooked if the internal auditor is to express an opinion on the OR model. As stated in GAO's *Guidelines for Model Evaluation*:

Experience has shown that in the absence of computer model verification — at least main program flow, critical parameters, and program modules — the odds are that no one will really know what is going on. If the evaluators do not have sufficient evidence that the model has been properly verified, then they may decide to so report and to suspend their evaluation effort until the developer has satisfied the deficiency.

Employing Experts

These standards and audit questions illustrate that auditing a model is not a simple process. The auditors must have experience with operations research and computers. Where these talents are not available within the internal audit department, expert assistance may have to be procured from outside the department. But the internal auditor must heed this caveat: The final report on the evaluation is the internal auditor's opinion. Management is looking to the internal auditor's opinion, not the consultant's opinion.

It is not enough to simply hand the consultant a job to do. The internal auditors must monitor the consultant's work. They must do whatever is necessary to satisfy themselves that they and the consultants fully understand and agree on the objectives and scope of the work. The internal audit involvement should take the following forms:

1. Understand the nature of the work, the assumptions the consultants made, the reasoning behind their analytical choices, and the risks inherent in their data and analyses.

2. Make sure that the consultants' work benefits the internal auditor.

3. Be sure that the work the consultants do is what was intended.

If information developed by consultants is used in an internal audit report, the internal auditors should, to the extent practicable, have the consultants furnish them with sufficient supporting documentation so that they can independently satisfy themselves and others as to the accuracy and validity of the consultants' work.

References

[1]U.S. General Accounting Office, *Models and Their Role in GAO* (Washington, DC: U.S. General Accounting Office, October 1978), PAD-78-84.

[2]The Institute of Internal Auditors, *Statement on Internal Auditing Standards No. 8.* (Altamonte Springs, FL: The Institute of Internal Auditors, 1992).

[3]Myers, Patricia M., and Sridhar Ramamoorti, "Educating and Training Internal Auditors in the Use of Analytical Auditing Procedures," *Internal Auditing*, September/October, 1998, 15-20.

[4]Ibid.

[5]*Internal Auditor*, Roundtable, *Invisible Equipment* (Altamonte Springs, FL: The Institute of Internal Auditors, August 1992).

[6]*Internal Auditor*, Roundtable, *Prevent Construction Cost Overruns* (Altamonte Springs, FL: The Institute of Internal Auditors, August 1989).

[7]*Internal Auditor*, Roundtable, *Alertness equals $1,000,000* (Altamonte Springs, FL: The Institute of Internal Auditors, October 1988).

[8]*Internal Auditor*, Roundtable, *Ma and Pa (and Son) Operation* (Altamonte Springs, FL: The Institute of Internal Auditors, October 1988).

[9]*Internal Auditor*, Roundtable, *Fraud Findings, Machinery Spare Purchases* (Altamonte Springs, FL: The Institute of Internal Auditors, October 1989).

[10]*Internal Auditor*, Roundtable, *Fee Waived* (Altamonte Springs, FL: The Institute of Internal Auditors, October 1989).

[11]U.S. General Accounting Office, Division of General Management Studies, Case Study (CS 5), *Using Regression Analysis to Estimate Costs: A Case Study* (Washington, DC: U.S. General Accounting Office, August 1974).

[12]U.S. General Accounting Office, *Guidelines for Model Evaluation* (Washington, DC: U.S. General Accounting Office, January 1979), PAD-79-17.

Suggested Readings

Bergquist, Robert K., "Audit Risk Analysis: An Experiment Using Data Envelopment Analysis," *Internal Auditing*, Fall 1996, 3-12.

Crusoe, John, George Schmelzle, and Thomas E. Buttross, "Auditing JIT Implementations," *Internal Auditing,* September/October 1999, 21-24.

Forrest, Edward, and Jonathan S. Forrest, "Integrating the Balanced Scorecard and ABM," *Internal Auditing*, March/April 2000, 20-25.

Forrest, Edward, and Jonathan S. Forrest, "Decision Making as Easy as ABM," *Internal Auditing*, March/April 2000, 46-48.

Forrest, Jonathan S., and Edward Forrest, "Internal Audit and the Activity-Based Management Connection," *Internal Auditing,* September/October 1999, 36-38.

Gauntt, Jr., James E., and William Glezen, "Analytical Auditing Procedures," *Internal Auditor*, February 1997, 56-60.

Gribbin, Donald W., James B. King II, and Ching-chao Tseng, "A Process Approach for Internal Auditing in an ABC Environment," *Internal Auditing*, Summer 1996, 10-15.

Haskin, Daniel L., "Using ABC to Allocate Audit Costs," *Internal Auditor*, December 1999, 56-58.

Lambert III, S. J., Kung H. Chen, and Joyce C. Lambert, "Overhead Cost Pools," *Internal Auditor*, October 1996, 62-67.

Lanza, Richard B., "Performing a Process Improvement Study," *Internal Auditor*, August 1997, 58-62.

Matherly, C. Michele, and Thomas A. Gavin, "What is Costing Us? An Operational Audit Perspective," *Internal Auditing*, July/August 1998, 3-15.

Moore, Wayne G., and William W. Warrick, "Audit and Control in a Transforming Worlds: New Solutions Required!" *Internal Auditing*, November/December 1998, 29-34.

Myers, Patricia M., and Sridhar Ramamoorti, "Educating and Training Internal Auditors in the Use of Analytical Auditing Procedures," *Internal Auditing*, September/October 1998, 15-20.

Ottenheimer, Jack L., "How Are We Doing?" *Journal of Accountancy*," February 1999, 35-37.

Sampson, Wesley C., "Transaction Index: A Tool for Auditors," *Internal Auditing*, Spring 1996, 16-24.

Wong, Jeff, "Data Mining as a Tool for Internal Auditors," *Internal Auditing*, January/February 2001, 21-25.

Wong, Jeff, "The Role of the Balanced Scorecard in Operational Auditing," *Internal Auditing*, July/August 2000, 33-36.

Multiple-choice Questions

1. In regression analysis, the coefficient of correlation is a measure of:
   a. The amount of variation in the dependent variable explained by the independent variables.
   b. The amount of variation in the dependent variable unexplained by the independent variables.
   c. The slope of the regression line.
   d. The predicted value of the dependent variable.

2. What is the critical path for the PERT network given below?
   a. A-D-G.
   b. A-D-E-H.
   c. A-C-F-H.
   d. B-F-H.

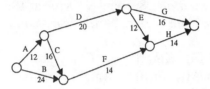

3. An organization produces two products. One of the material inputs required for each of these products is in short supply. In addition, production capacity is limited by the availability of machine capacity. What is the appropriate method for determining the most profitable product mix?
   a. Linear programming.
   b. Reciprocal cost allocation.
   c. Queuing analysis.
   d. Least squares analysis.

4. Bank management would like to determine the effects of policy changes (these changes would change some of the constraints) on the optimal mix for its portfolio of earning assets. The appropriate technique for doing so is:
   a. Regression analysis.
   b. Cost-volume-profit analysis.
   c. Sensitivity analysis.
   d. Queuing analysis.

5. An organization uses CPM/PERT for planning the construction of a new manufacturing facility. The primary purpose of determining the "critical path" related to this project is:
   a. To identify the optimal mix of products to be produced in the new facility.
   b. To determine the maximum production capacity of the new facility.
   c. To identify those activities that must be completed as scheduled if the new facility is to be completed on time.
   d. To determine the maximum amount of time an activity in the critical path may be delayed without delaying the scheduled completion of the new facility.

6. An organization has several departments that conduct technical studies and prepare reports for clients. Recently, there have been long delays in having these reports copied at the organization's centralized copy center because of the dramatic increase in business. Management is considering decentralizing copy services to reduce the turnaround and provide clients with timely reports. An appropriate technique for minimizing turnaround time and the cost of providing copy services is:
   a. Queuing theory.
   b. Linear programming.
   c. Regression analysis.
   d. Game theory.

7. To facilitate planning and budgeting, management of a travel service organization wants to develop forecasts of monthly sales for the next 24 months. Based on past data, management has observed an upward trend in the level of sales. There are also seasonal variations with high sales in June, July, and August, and low sales in January, February, and March. An appropriate technique for forecasting the organization's sales is:
   a. Time series analysis.
   b. Queuing theory.
   c. Linear programming.
   d. Sensitivity analysis.

8. The network below shows the interrelationships of several activities necessary to complete a project. The arrows represent the activities and are labeled alphabetically. The numbers in parentheses indicate the number of weeks to complete each activity. The shortest time to complete the project is:

   a. 18 weeks.
   b. 17 weeks.
   c. 16 weeks.
   d. 14 weeks.

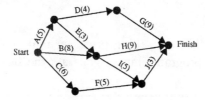

9. The marketing department of your organization is deciding on the price to charge for a key product. In setting this price, marketing needs to consider the price that a major competitor will charge for a similar product because the competitor's price will affect the demand for your organization's product. Similarly, in setting its price, the competitor will consider what your organization will charge. An appropriate mathematical technique for analyzing such a decision is:
   a. Game theory.
   b. Probability theory.
   c. Linear programming.
   d. Sensitivity analysis.

10. An internal audit department developed the formula, Total Audit Cost (TC) = a + bX = cX2, where X was internal audit resources. The director wanted to minimize TC with respect to X. The appropriate technique to use is:
    a. Linear programming.
    b. Least squares.
    c. Differential calculus.
    d. Integral calculus.

Use the following information to answer questions 11-18.
An organization produces three products, A, B, and C, using three different machines, X, Y, and Z. Management has decided that at least 100 units of product A must be manufactured. Marketing research indicates that the organization's maximum market share for product C is 150 units.

Each product uses different amounts of machine time (hours per unit) and each machine has different capacities (hours per year), as summarized in the next column.

	MACHINE TIME (HOURS)		
PRODUCT	X	Y	Z
A	2	4	3
B	3	2	5
C	4	3	2
CAPACITY	1,400	1,650	2,100

Each product also has a different selling price per unit and different cost per unit. Management used linear programming to generate the following solution:

	PRODUCT		
	A	B	C
Selling price per unit	$7	$6	$5
Variable cost per unit	5	3	1
Fixed cost per unit	1	1	2

PRODUCT	VALUE	REDUCED VALUE
A	100	8
B	?	2
C	150	0
CONSTRAINT	VALUE	SHADOW PRICE
Machine X	-0-	?
Machine Y	400	-0-
Machine Z	500	-0-
Machine A	100	-0-
Machine C	150	-0-

Table of Values

a.	0	g.	6
b.	1	h.	7
c.	2	i.	8
d.	3	j.	1,400
e.	4	k.	1,650
f.	5	l.	2,100

For each of the questions (11-18) select the appropriate answer from the above table of values ("a" through "l").

11. How many constraints were involved in determining the optimal mix of products A, B, and C? _____

12. What is the coefficient for product B in the objective function for machine X? _____

13. What is the coefficient for product A in the constraints involving machine Y? _____

14. What is the maximum number of machine hours available for the following constraint: 2A + 3B + 4C? _____

15. How many surplus constraints are involved in the linear programming solution to this problem? _____

16. If one additional unit of product A were produced and sold, the net income of the organization would decrease by: _____

17. What is the opportunity cost of obtaining an additional machine hour for X? _____

18. How many units (in hundreds) of product B should be produced? _____

19. An auditor's preliminary analysis of accounts receivable revealed the following turnover rates:

19x2	19x3	19x0
4.3	6.2	7.3

Which of the following is the most likely cause of the decrease in accounts-receivable turnover?
   a. Increase in the cash discount offered.
   b. Liberalization of credit policy.
   c. Shortening of due-date terms.
   d. Increased case sales.

Use the following information to answer questions 20-23.
An auditor frequently performs analytical review procedures to obtain audit evidence relating to audits of inventories, receivables, and other accounts.

20. Which of the following would be the best example of analytical evidence?
   a. Comparison of organization financial information with industry averages.
   b. Comparison of recorded amounts with appropriate invoices.
   c. Statistical sampling results.
   d. Computation of gross margin.

21. What form of analytical review might uncover the existence of obsolete merchandise?
   a. Inventory turnover rates.
   b. Decrease in the ratio of gross profit to sales.
   c. Ratio of inventory to accounts payable.
   d. Comparison of inventory values to purchase invoices.

22. Which of the following analytical audit findings would most likely indicate a possible problem?
   a. A material decrease in the receivables turnover.
   b. A material increase in inventory turnover.
   c. A material decrease in days-sales-outstanding.
   d. A material increase in the acid-test ratio.

23. Analytical review procedures can best be categorized as:
   a. Substantive tests.
   b. Compliance tests.
   c. Qualitative tests.
   d. Budget comparisons.

24. Which of the following would be the best type of evidence of the reasonableness of various sales-related expenses?
    a. Analytical evidence obtained by comparing such expenses to some standard such as budget or historical data.
    b. Documentary evidence obtained by vouching selected specific expenditures to supporting documentation.
    c. Oral evidence obtained by discussing such expenses with managers who have authorized sales-related expenditures.
    d. Recomputation of selected specific expenditures from data on supporting documentation and approval forms.

25. An audit of an international nonprofit organization established to finance medical research revealed the following amounts (in millions):

	Current Year	Past Year
Revenue	$500	$425
Investments (average balances)	$210	$185
Medical research grants made	$418	$325
Investment income	$16	$20
Administrative expense	$10	$8

Which of the following analytical review procedures should an auditor use to determine if the change in investment income during the current year was due to changes in investment strategy, changes in portfolio mix, or other factors?
    a. Simple linear regression of investment income changes over the past five years to determine the nature of the changes.
    b. Ratio analysis of changes in the investment portfolio on a monthly basis.
    c. Trend analysis of changes in investment income as a percentage of total assets and of investment assets over the past five years.
    d. Multiple regression analysis using independent variables related to the nature of the investment portfolio and market conditions.

26. A sales department has been giving away expensive items in conjunction with new product sales to stimulate demand. The promotion seems successful, but management believes the cost may be too high. Which of the following audit procedures would be the **least** useful to determine the effectiveness of the promotion?
    a. Comparing product sales during the promotion period with sales during a similar non-promotion period.
    b. Comparing the unit cost of the products sold before and during the promotion period.
    c. Performing an analysis of marginal revenue and marginal cost for the promotion period, compared to the period before the promotion.
    d. Performing a review of the sales department's benchmarks used to determine the success of a promotion.

27. A production manager ordered excessive raw materials for delivery to a separate company owned by the manager. The manager falsified receiving documents and approved the invoices for payment. Which of the following audit procedures would most likely detect this fraud?
    a. Select a sample of cash disbursements and compare purchase orders, receiving reports invoices, and check copies.
    b. Select a sample of cash disbursements and confirm the amount purchased, purchase price, and date of shipment with the vendors.
    c. Observe the receiving dock and count materials received; compare the counts to receiving reports completed by receiving personnel.
    d. Perform analytical tests comparing production, materials purchased and raw materials inventory levels and investigate differences.

28. As used in the verification of an accounts payable schedule, which of the following is best described as an analytical test?
    a. Comparing the items and the schedule with the accounts payable ledger or unpaid voucher file.
    b. Comparing the balance on the schedule with the balances of prior years.
    c. Comparing confirmations received from selected creditors with the accounts payable ledger.
    d. Examining vendors' invoices in support of selected items on the schedule.

29. Which of the following procedures would be appropriate for testing whether cost overruns on a construction project were caused by the contractor improperly accounting for costs related to contract change orders?
    I. Verify that the contractor has not charged change orders with costs that have already been billed to the original contract.
    II. Determine if the contractor has billed for original contract work that was canceled as a result of change orders.

III. Verify that the change orders were properly approved by management.
a. I and III only.
b. I only.
c. III only.
d. I and II only.

30. The use of analytical review to verify the correctness of various operating expenses would not be a preferred approach if:
a. An auditor notes strong indicators of a specific fraud involving these accounts.
b. Operations are relatively stable and have not changed much over the past year.
c. An auditor would like to identify large, unusual, or nonrecurring transactions during the year.
d. Operating expenses vary in relation to other operating expenses, but not in relation to revenue.

31. All of an organization's employees must select a financial institution to which their monthly payroll checks will be deposited. The organization sends its bank an electronic file containing each employee's financial institution selection, account number, and the dollar amount to be paid. Sorting the file by account number would help the organization's internal auditors test for:
a. Invalid account numbers.
b. Accuracy and completeness of the electronic file.
c. Fictitious employees.
d. Excessive dollar payments.

32. The manager of a production line has the authority to order and receive replacement parts for all machinery that require periodic maintenance. The internal auditor received an anonymous tip that the manager ordered substantially more parts than were necessary from a family member in the parts supply business. The unneeded parts were never delivered. Instead, the manager processed receiving documents and charged the parts to machinery maintenance accounts. The payments for the undelivered parts were sent to the supplier and the money was divided between the manager and the family member. Which of the following tests would best assist the auditor in deciding whether to investigate this anonymous tip further?
a. Comparison of the current quarter's maintenance expense with prior-period activity.
b. Physical inventory testing of replacement parts for existence and valuation.
c. Analysis of repair parts charged to maintenance to review the reasonableness of the number of items replaced.
d. Review of a test sample of parts invoices for proper authorization and receipt.

33. An internal auditor is conducting an audit of the use of corporate credit cards. Which of the following are major audit concerns regarding the use of credit cards?
    I.   Segregation of duties is insufficient.
    II. The purchasing function is impaired.
    III. Cards may be used for personal benefit.
    IV. The company is required to make one large payment instead of many small ones.
    a. I and III only.
    b. II and IV only.
    c. III only.
    d. I, II, Ill, and IV.

34. During an operational audit, an auditor compared the inventory turnover rate of a subsidiary with established industry standards in order to:
    a. Evaluate the accuracy of internal financial reports.
    b. Test controls designed to safeguard assets.
    c. Determine compliance with corporate procedures regarding inventory levels.
    d. Assess performance and indicate where additional audit work may be needed.

35. The following represents accounts receivable information for a corporation for the most recent three-year period:

Description	2002	2001	2000
Net accounts receivable as a percentage of total assets	30.8%	27.3%	23.4%
Accounts receivable turnover ratio	5.21	6.05	6.98

All of the following are plausible explanations for these changes except:
    a. Fictitious sales may have been recorded.
    b. Credit and collection procedures have become ineffective.
    c. Allowance for bad debts is understated.
    d. Sales returns for credit have been overstated.

PART 4

DATA PROCESSING

Chapter 13
Information Systems Auditing - I

The internal auditor's responsibility. Information system components. Data organization and processing methods. Information systems controls. System development life cycle. General controls. Data security. Physical security. Contingency planning and disaster recovery. Storage. The operating system. Telecommunications. Program changes. Hardware.

● ●

The Internal Auditor's Responsibility

Information system's (IS) understanding, once a "nice to have," is now essential for the internal auditor. Information technology (IT) continues to permeate the fabric of business life. The internal auditor's need to understand and evaluate risks and opportunities related to information technology has heightened for a number of reasons:

- The explosive growth of technology.

- The broader use of information systems in every organizational function which are more closely tied together.

- The use of mainframe, distributed processing, and personal computers by an increasing percentage of an organization's staff and managers.

- The vast increase of information available to managers.

- The decrease in skepticism about the accuracy of data that have been processed by a information system.

- The shift of systems management from the discipline of professional programmers to the end user.

- The increase of information system literacy in the general population leading to more widespread ability to manipulate the data.

- The increasing use of Local Area Networks (LANS) and distributed computing environments.

- The increasing use of personal databases.

- The increasing use of enterprise-wide systems.

Internal auditors must be able to understand and work with complex information systems. Business and nonprofit are supported by what at times are potentially bewildering systems that initiate transactions without human intervention, make decisions based on highly complicated logical models, transmit and store data in myriad electronic forms, interactively communicate with customers and suppliers, operate machinery, and create financial statements. "Expert" systems replicate their human counterparts and make significant business decisions. Systems using artificial intelligence even learn from their mistakes — or the mistakes of their human operators — and refine their programming for improved performance. The importance of information technology has been recognized by The IIA through the publication of *Systems Auditability and Control (SAC)*. For further information on topics covered in this and the next three chapters, the reader is encouraged to review *SAC*.

For internal auditors to make a significant contribution to the organization, they must be able to use the information systems and understand the risks associated with their use. Achieving this understanding requires technical education and hands-on use. Internal auditors must be comfortable with information technology terminology, concepts, and practical applications. Those who neglect this education will be relegated to trivial applications within the organization. Auditing "around the computer" becomes a meaningless term when nearly all records, transactions, and processing decisions are automated. To maintain their independence, internal auditors must be able to deal with these systems.

Executives and operating managers look to the internal audit staff to assist in providing a realistic assessment of the risks in their organization. With the proliferation of distributed processing (computing) and personal computers or PCs (microcomputers), layer upon layer of networking, vast data storage, decreasing levels of human review of transactions, and rapidly evolving application systems, management desperately needs internal auditors who can see the "big picture."

The proliferation of information systems, including systems of all sizes and capabilities, makes a comprehensive treatment of information technology concepts and controls impractical in a few chapters. For example, the software delivered with a large "mainframe" computer may easily be accompanied by a thousand manuals describing all of its components. As a result, only the highlights of hardware, software, and systems controls can be presented. Hardware and software concepts as well as processing methods are discussed to establish a technical background for the description of systems controls. Common data processing functions, related controls, and internal audit responsibilities are treated in two sections:

1. General controls, which encompass environmental controls common to all information systems within the organization.

2. Application controls, which apply to specific business applications.

    The advances in software and hardware require several special topics to cover them:
    *   Vendor-supplied software
    *   Personal computers and end-user computing
    *   Distributed data processing
    *   Systems effectiveness and efficiency
    *   Documentation
    *   Legal requirements

Each segment of the chapter contains: (1) a description of the subject, with a discussion of related controls, and (2) suggestions for auditing those controls.

Information System Components

Traditionally, information system components can be divided into hardware and software.

Hardware

System hardware used in business can be categorized into four groups: servers, PCs, minicomputers, and mainframes. These divisions are not based on physical size of the systems as much as on their processing capability — speed, storage, and capacity to process sophisticated applications. In recent years, the categories have been blurred because of significant technology changes. For example, some PCs now routinely execute more "MIPS" (millions of instructions per second) than mainframes of 20 years ago.

A server is a system that receives requests from other systems, called clients, and processes those requests. These systems are discussed in the next chapter.

PCs are smaller systems that have a small number of attached input/output devices. Unlike mainframes and minicomputers, it is economical to devote a PC to a single user (hence the term "personal computer"). Larger PCs are often shared within a department and may be linked in a "local area network" or LAN (i.e., a network with maximum distance between two points, usually less than one mile). Typically, a PC will consist of a processor, a keyboard, a display monitor, a "hard" (non-removable) disk, one "floppy" (removable) diskette drive, a CD-ROM drive, and a printer. PCs may also have a scanner, upgraded monitors that produce picture quality images, a microphone and speakers for multimedia applications, a tape drive or high density drive for backing up of data and/or modem or fax modem to communicate with other systems. Through time, PCs have tended to become more powerful at less cost. Notebook computers and handheld devices have increased in prominence.

Minicomputers vary greatly in physical size and processing capability. Typically, they have a large "memory," along with several terminals, printers, and large capacity disk drives. Minicomputers often serve as a central computer for small to mid-sized businesses. These machines are also used for departments or divisions of larger organizations to meet specialized demands such as scientific analysis or machine intensive departmental accounting that would not be efficient on the mainframe. Minicomputers are used as servers to control software costs by allowing a maximum number of licenses in use at a time.

Mainframes, often costing millions of dollars, generally have a large number of terminals/users, storage devices such as hard disks and tape drives, high volume printers, very large processor memories, and complex applications. Mainframes are historically the backbone of the data processing industry and are the central repository of data for most medium-to-large corporations. Some of the basic components of an information system are the central processing unit, communications devices, magnetic tape drive, disk drives, impact printers, non-impact printers, console, and terminals. As the technology changes, the distinction between these groups is being blurred.

Central processing unit. The central processing unit (CPU) functions as the brain of the computer. It accepts input from a variety of peripheral devices, processes the data in accordance with instructions provided by one or more computer programs, and provides output in a variety of forms (e.g., printouts, data displayed on a terminal, or an updated master file). In spite of the vast complexity of modern systems, all their functions are derived from the simple ability to perform arithmetic operations and make predetermined logical comparisons (e.g., if A is greater than B, perform calculation X). The logical units of the CPU are buried in a series of computer "chips" that process instructions in nanoseconds (i.e., billionths of a second).

Magnetic tape drives. Tape drives read and write data, in sequential order, onto a magnetic tape. This is probably the most common (and most inexpensive) means of storing large amounts of data. Systems commonly use disk storage for rapid access to current files but store copies of those files on tape for backup and historical retention. Magnetic tapes are also a reliable means of transporting data from one system to another. Financial institutions, for example, can submit tax information to the Internal Revenue Service on magnetic tape. This eliminates error-prone and expensive data entering from source documents. Typical "magnetic tape drives" are more commonly used with mainframes, while most servers and minicomputers use smaller backup devices such as CD-RW drives, tape backup drives, and archive servers (which are discussed later in the text).

The storage capacity of a tape reel depends on its length and the "density" used to record the data. Density is a measure of how much data can be packed into an inch of computer tape. Not all tape drives will read all tape densities. In addition, all systems do not handle data in the same format. Some computers use Extended Binary Coded Decimal Interchange Code (EBCDIC); others use American Standard Code for Information Interchange (ASCII). The EBCDIC structure is limited to some mainframe systems while ASCII is found in all PCs and a number of systems performing mainframe duties. A tape file created on one system may or may not be "readable" on another because of the density of data or data format. An auditor considering copying files onto tape at one location for use at another should verify compatibility first.

Disk drives. While tape storage is reliable and inexpensive, its major disadvantage is the fact that data must be read sequentially — from the beginning to the end of the tape. For example, assume a parts inventory is maintained only on tape. During the day, the reorder clerk may inquire on part numbers 001, 888, and 555. If the tape is in part-number sequence, the system could quickly access the first record, but the second and third requests would require rewinding and searching through the tape to find the desired records. Disk drives, because of their physical construction and associated software, can directly access data.

Impact printers. These are peripheral devices that vary greatly in speed, appearance of output, and capacity. One class of impact printers, called line printers, strike a ribbon and print the page a line at a time. They are considered "impact" printers because they physically strike the paper and they are capable of printing on multipart forms.

A much slower class of impact printers uses "daisy wheels" to strike a ribbon and create type very much like that created by a typewriter (hence the term "letter quality").

The dot matrix printer uses small metal pins to create an approximation of the characters and symbols used in text, as well as graphics. Dot matrix printers are slower than line printers. These printers perform their work without physically touching the paper.

Non-impact printers. A common member of this class of printer is the laser printer, which can print very high volumes of nearly flawless text or graphics. Common types of non-impact printers are the ink-jet and bubble jet printers. These printers spray the page with ink for each character.

Other non-impact printers are based on electrothermal or electrostatic principles in which heated or charged rods create images on special paper. Printer technology has changed rapidly, which has created increased access to color, graphics, and quality at lower cost.

Console. A mainframe or minicomputer console is a terminal (or series of terminals) that functions as the command center for human interaction to control the system. Operators enter commands, respond to questions from the operating system, and generally monitor the system from the console. In the early days of data processing, access to the console was a primary concern because so much processing was dependent on manual responses from the human operator. Operating systems and applications are now far more operator independent. Console access controls, while still important for physical security reasons, are less critical because of their limited role in applications processing (at least for mainframes and minicomputers). In networks the console may be an unattended personal computer having a high capacity disk drive. Logical access to the system is controlled by passwords authorized by the network administrator.

Terminals. The terminal device, commonly called a cathode-ray tube or video display terminal, is one of the most widely used forms of input/output hardware. It consists of a keyboard for input, and a screen for displaying output. The screen is often called a monitor. The PC is the primary user workstation where data and instructions to the system are entered. The versatile PC has become the workhorse of the industry replacing the CRT though much data is entered into systems via optical and magnetic-ink readers, and decreasingly through key-to-tape and key-to-disk machines. The PC is used not only for data entry and inquiry, but serves programmers in systems development and displays electronic mail messages and graphics.

Software

Software instructs the system's processor. The investment in software, including purchased packages, staff salaries to develop and maintain programs, and maintenance fees paid to vendors, often substantially exceeds the cost of hardware. Medium-to-large data processing centers can easily have hundreds of thousands of program instructions for their business applications. In addition, computers of all sizes require a vendor-supplied set of programs, called the "operating system and systems software," which manages the system's resources, permitting the applications programs to do useful work. There is a trend for operating system software to become more user-friendly by using a graphical user interface. Typically, operating systems for mainframes contain millions of instructions. Much of the internal auditor's review of data processing centers around controls over software.

Application software. Consisting of a series of programs, application software performs the organization's business processing. A multitude of computers are in commercial use today. Systems can be developed from specifications (in-house) or be purchased from vendors and modified. Vendor packages usually have "system control files" that permit tailoring the programs to fit the needs of a particular organization. For example, a payroll system may provide for insertion of specific local and state income tax rates into a generic tax table.

In addition to traditional languages such as COBOL (programs written in such languages are referred to as legacy programs), retrieval languages are increasingly used by both users and professional programmers to extract data from master files and create ad hoc reports. Programs coded in retrieval languages (also called fourth-generation languages) are relatively easy to develop and modify. For example, an entire "program" to summarize national sales year-to-date by region might be written:

SUM YR-TO-DATE-SALES ACROSS REGION
FOR NATION = 'USA'

In spite of their simplicity, fourth-generation languages use a relatively large share of the CPU's processing power. As a result, they are not often used for basic processing such as posting and routine data validation (although they could be used for these purposes).

Even though a program is written with symbols that appear logical to its programmer, the system actually executes only a form of the program, called the "object" program. Computers are, at their core, a vast series of electronic switches. These switches are either off or on like a light switch. Programs that the system can read must be written in on-and-off switch settings displayed as 1 (on) and 0 (off) for designated switches. One can imagine how tedious and error-prone programming would be if every instruction were written in 1's and 0's. In fact, the earliest programming was done in exactly that fashion. Early computer scientists realized they could group a series of those 1's and 0's together and express them in a fashion that was easier to deal with.

It is important to recognize that, while *source code* and *object code* should always correspond, the computer does not require them to. It is possible to make a copy of the source code, change the instructions, compile the modified version, and destroy the modified source after the creation of the new object code. The new object is then cataloged into the operating library on the computer and data is then processed under the new version of the program. Though the executable object program would reflect the instructions embedded in the changed source code, it would not match the authorized source code. Without adequate controls over compiling and cataloging activities, this weakness can be used to perpetrate computer fraud.

Systems software. Operating system software manages the internal operation of the computer itself. Provided by the hardware vendor or an independent software organization, operating system software provides the ability to schedule jobs, manage multiple simultaneous users, read and write files, transmit data between various devices, perform certain security checks, handle certain errors, provide a mechanism for program development, and support interactive online communications. Powerful "utility" programs perform many of the routine chores of a data processing installation. Some of these functions include sorting, copying data from disk to tape or vice versa, printing, and even modifying data within files.

The modification of data within files is a particular concern. The Data Handling Utilities or Data File Utilities (DHUs or DFUs) are powerful tools and potentially dangerous. The DFU can be used to go into a data file and change the data in place without the need for a processing program. Imagine that someone went into the file of checking accounts in a bank and reduced one account balance by $1,000 and increased another by the same amount. The overall file total would stay in balance and there would be no record of a "transaction" in the reports or accumulated transactions files that are built during the normal processing runs. These utilities are necessary to correct some errors that occur in conversions of computer systems, when abnormal endings (ABENDS) or crashes occur, and when files become corrupted. However, because of the power in these utilities, they must be carefully controlled.

Since system software interfaces between specific hardware (such as disk drives or tape drives) and application software (such as accounts receivable) when it is operating, it tends to be "machine specific." Even in a PC environment, operating systems typically will only work on the hardware configuration for which they were designed.

Data Organization and Processing Methods

The control structure required for an organization's information system varies widely according to the type of processing performed and the level of technology used. To effectively review information systems controls, the auditor should understand the concepts and controls found in each processing method. Here are three basic processing methods in common use today:

Batch Processing

The oldest technique to process data is batch processing. Classes of transactions (e.g., accounts receivable payments) are grouped together and processed by the system at one time. This is the traditional method for processing large volumes and offers the greatest degree of control. Manual totals of items and dollars can be compared to machine-generated totals. In many applications, the batches are read by a front-end edit program that validates the data and computes a total. If the totals are wrong, the sources of error are identified, and the batches are corrected and reentered. When both manual and system totals agree, processing continues and files are updated.

Online Entry/Batch Processing (Memo Post)

Memo posting applications provide online data entry, inquiry, and editing, but update the master files with batch processing. After the master files have been updated (usually at night after business hours), a "memo" copy of the current master files is created. The memo file is updated by data entry and used for inquiry during the day. After balancing, the memo file can be used to post transactions to the master during batch processing the following night.

In practice, organizations may use several types of processing in the same application. Banks, for example, frequently process maintenance (e.g., customer address changes) online real time. Dollar transactions, on the other hand, are memo posted during business hours and batch processed at night. By memo posting dollar transactions during the day, banks maintain each customer's current balance and can monitor cash withdrawals. The real (i.e., permanent) posting of dollars to the accounts occurs when paper documents such as checks and deposit tickets are read into the bank's sorters and are batch processed along with electronic transactions. This permits the use of traditional controls over dollar transactions, including batch totals and signature verification.

Online Real Time

Online real time applications update system files immediately as the data is entered into the terminal. As a result, the data is always up-to-date. For example, in an online real-time purchase order and receiving system, the latest purchase orders and receiving data are available to determine the status of vendor shipments. Unlike batch processing, online real-time processing does not lend itself to control totaling. Updates can come one at a time from any terminal connected to the mainframe. These systems may present a higher risk to the organization than the older batch-oriented applications. Strong controls are important, including audit trails with the identification of the terminal operator, special passwords for sensitive transactions, intelligent cards, and restriction of terminal functions.

In evaluating a system, an auditor needs to consider the inherent risk of the segment(s) included in the system. In evaluating inherent risk, the auditor needs to consider:

- The risk of fraud.
- The operational importance of the system.
- The competitive advantage provided by the system.
- The technology used by the system.

The first of these involves consideration of whether assets can be stolen or assets/liabilities intentionally misstated. The second relates to the ability of the entity to function without the system in operation. As the system becomes more important to its operation, there is higher inherent risk. Likewise, as a system provides the entity with more of a competitive advantage, the higher the inherent risk. Finally, it is generally believed that as more technologically advanced the system, the higher the inherent risk.

An auditor is alert to controls that impact control risk. Since these controls vary substantially across systems, a number of these chapters cover these controls.

Information Systems Controls

Most records are kept on magnetic devices. The millions of records processed each day flow invisibly and without human intervention. Exposure to accident, error, and loss of data exists in every segment of an application — when data is transcribed from one medium to another, when data is transmitted from one location to another, while data is being processed, when data is rejected and reentered, and when data is stored.

Controls in an information system are the means used to manage these exposures and to help achieve management's objectives. These means differ from those in a manual environment because:

- Sources of data are sometimes independent of the users of the data.

- Transaction trails from input to output are seldom visible to the human eye.

- The need exists to be explicit in the absence of human judgment.

- Documentation must be accurate and usable.

- Responsibility for the user's information is shared with IS processing facilities.

To compound the difficulties, a number of factors combine to keep an adequate control system from being developed:

- Fact gathering and evaluation may be incomplete.

- Users are more and more inclined to believe whatever they find in system reports just because they come from an information system; they do not skeptically examine the report to see "if the data make sense."

- Strong, unified direction may be lacking.

- Senior management may not exercise its responsibility for the control system on the grounds that the subject is too technical.

- Errors may occur in the system design.

- Communication is often poor among systems people, users, and management, so users fail to specify which controls are needed to handle transactions, process data, and receive information output.

- Unscrupulous programmers can incorporate instructions into the system to divert assets to their own use.

Controls must be incorporated into every system and application to reduce the ever-present exposures to poor records, improper accounting, interruptions of business, bad decision-making, fraud and embezzlement, violations of statutory or regulatory requirements, increased costs, loss of assets, and loss of competitive position in the marketplace.

Management must therefore be aware of the controls needed to keep the system from being used for improper purposes, to reduce the incidence of error, and to obtain the best results from system operations. Management cannot shirk its responsibility for seeing that the controls are, in fact, established and working. These controls can be grouped into two broad categories: (1) general controls and (2) application controls. With the advent of enterprise-wide systems, this distinction becomes less relevant. However, the controls discussed under these categories are still relevant.

General Controls

General controls consist of those controls in the IS and user environment that are pervasive over all or most applications. They include such controls as segregation of incompatible duties, systems development procedures, data security, all administrative controls, and disaster-recovery capabilities. A discussion of the major general controls found in most data processing environments follows.

Organizational Controls

Description

Organizational controls include adequate responsibility and authority for the EDP activity. Such responsibility should be sufficient to permit the IS activity to meet organizational objectives efficiently and effectively.

The IS activity should report to a high enough level of authority to escape the domination of the organizational units it serves. In that way, it will not be compelled to carry out programs which, in its judgment, have low priority.

Within the IS activity, efficiency is enhanced by appropriate functional groupings. The major groupings are:

- **Operations and production:** Converting written source documents to machine-readable form (such as key-to-disk or key-to-tape); operating consoles, peripheral devices, and auxiliary equipment; maintaining a library for data files and programs;

and establishing a control group that monitors production, keeps records, balances input and output, and sees that schedules are met.

- **Project development:** Developing systems and designing new methods and requirements; devising procedures, forms, and instruction manuals; and applying mathematical logic and modeling techniques (including operations research) to appropriate activities within the organization.

- **Technical services:** Selecting software and providing maintenance; analyzing equipment and comparing capabilities of new equipment; developing and maintaining IS standards for projects, hardware software, and operations; maintaining quality control over operations; preparing detailed coding instructions for processing applications.

A significant form of control over system operations is the separation of duties within the IS activity. In small IS organizations, separation of all incompatible functions may not be feasible. But managers and internal auditors must be aware of the dangers in combining incompatible functions and put them under greater surveillance. For example:

- The IS activity should be independent of the users who authorize transactions to be processed. Similarly, IS should never initiate any entries or transactions.

- Systems and programming should be independent of computer operations.

- Both systems and programming should be independent of the file library and the input/output control functions.

- Programmers should not be permitted to operate the system (this control is more frequently violated on weekends and off hours than during regular processing times). When tests or assemblies require programmers to operate the system, the production programs and data files should be made secure against accidental or intentional manipulation. Programmers should work with copies of records (unless access to disk files is "read only"). They should not be able to change original records or files.

- System operators should neither have access to the file library or program documentation nor should they control input/output functions.

- The IS librarian should be independent of system operations. At the same time, the librarian should not transport files or programs to off-site storage locations or into the computer room.

- As few people as possible should know the location of off-site storage facilities.

- Data processing personnel should not have custody of, or access to, any of the organization's assets that are accounted for in the computer system.

- Responsibility for sensitive applications should be rotated, and all system personnel should be required to take vacations.

- People in the systems control function — not computer operators — should be responsible for the detection and correction of errors.

- Knowledge of applications, programming, and documentation should be restricted to authorized and qualified people. Those people should then be given access to data files or the computer only for those activities for which they are specifically authorized.

- The test environment should be separated from the production environment with formal procedures for moving from one to the other.

Internal Audit

The review of organizational controls normally starts with familiarization of the system. Internal auditors can gain this familiarity by reviewing management policies, organization charts, job descriptions, manpower and overtime reports, system-operator procedures, library and storage facility operations, input/output controls, and data conversion.

All job positions, particularly those for librarians, system operators, control groups, and data-entry operators, should be adequately described so that there is no question as to who is responsible for what. Conversely, identifying who should not perform certain duties is important in IS-related job descriptions. These prohibitions, along with specific authorizations, form the basis for logical security, including password-related control systems.

Internal auditors will have to observe operations to determine whether purported separations of duties are in effect. Often, organizational controls are not documented. Internal auditors, therefore, would want to know if departments are physically segregated, if machine-readable media contain external and internal labels, if the library is not open to just anyone who wants access, if supervisors maintain reasonable surveillance, and if only authorized people are in the computer room using files needed for operations.

Internal auditors should review records of job rotation and vacation schedules. They should make sure that everyone in the IS activity actually takes a vacation each year and is physically away from the operation.

The review of the IS control group is designed to determine whether the group is accountable for data from the time it is received through data conversion, processing, error correction, and reentry, to the time the data are formally distributed as output to users.

Systems Development Life Cycle

Description

In the early days of applications, the IS soufflé had a tendency to fall as soon as it was taken out of the oven. The absence of a single ingredient was the reason — involvement by executive and user managers. They avoided feasibility studies, setting of policies and objectives, development of standards, and testing of the application. They regarded the computer as a mysterious and unmanageable beast, and they left its handling to IS specialists.

Over the years, systems have been demystified by several factors.

- The fact that information technology permeates every aspect of business and government has forced managers, employees — and auditors — to learn how to interact with information systems.

- The "graying" of the computer resistant population has removed many who could not adapt to the information systems environment.

- The increased teaching of computers in all levels of the education process has created generations of new workers who are as comfortable with their computers as programming their VCRs.

- The increasing drive to automate functions and the associated job security has provided incentives for many managers and workers to master system usage.

Changes in technology have led managers to control system resources as they would control human resources. The days when the programmer/analyst dictated what information system resources management would have is diminishing in favor of management's specifying the resources it needs. The process of systems development has created a life of its own — a methodology and a discipline. The formalization of this process grew from the need to solve practical business problems. The objectives of management and data professionals have been brought together by organizational necessity.

The systems development life cycle (SDLC) should involve all stakeholders in the system being created or overhauled. Stakeholders are those who have an organizational interest in the day-to-day operations of the system. They are marshaled through *group design sessions*[1] that identify and define user requirements. The involvement of this broader group is supported by more disciplined and rigorous testing procedures to make sure the system will meet the design requirements. There are a number of testing steps in the development process.[2] The users' acceptance testing is a requisite part of the integrated development process.

There are significant issues and opportunities for the internal auditor to deal with in the course of the systems development life cycle. Not the least among these is the assurance that the stakeholders' interests are always at the forefront of the development objectives. The internal auditor is also involved in assuring that the development project follows the organization's standards for systems development. The auditor can use structured techniques for the audit of systems development projects. One such technique was developed by Drs. David Gelprin and William Hetzel; it is called the Systematic Test and Evaluation Process (STEP).[3]

Beyond the development process, the ongoing oversight of the data processing function is increasingly a group activity. The data processing function is now viewed as an organizational enterprise requiring organization-wide coordination. An IS steering committee is a key factor in management's involvement in and oversight of the IS function.

A member of top management should serve on the steering committee as should IS users.[4] Steering committees must meet regularly. Their functions should include:

- Approving IS policies.

- Approving long-term and short-term plans for systems, monitoring the progress of systems design, and development.

- Broad oversight of implementation, training, and operation of new systems.

- Ongoing monitoring of the adequacy and accuracy of software and hardware in use.

- Assessment of the effects of new technology on the organization's IS operations.

Management policies should be developed during the all-important feasibility studies. These studies should be able to show the benefits to be obtained from a proposed application. They should also show the impact of the new application on operations in the user department and should specify the actual budget reductions to be experienced.

Management policies should provide for and protect the user. They should prescribe the formal system for requesting IS assistance. They should also provide for a master plan encompassing all approved development projects and should define user needs and prepare sound cost-benefit analyses for new applications. They should call for active user participation in both system definition and user approval of design.

Management may not be able to appraise the technical adequacy of standards but, through the steering committee, it should make sure that these have been developed.

Depending on the IS project, they may be in many different stages of the life cycle: full systems development, small project maintenance, and emergency maintenance. Following are key phases and related controls over the systems development life cycle:

Request for systems design. A written request should be submitted by authorized users stating the business need (not the perceived solution). The requests should be appropriately cataloged and reviewed by a steering committee or other manpower allocation committee. In practice, small requests or routine maintenance requests (e.g., changing payroll tax tables at year end) may not go through the committee process. If the request is approved, a (relatively) small allocation of resources is provided for the feasibility phase. The bulk of the work-hours needed to complete the project is allocated if the feasibility study indicates that the business, technical, and cost factors are favorable.

Feasibility study. In this phase, basic questions regarding cost/benefit are answered. Some of the considerations are as follows: (1) Is vendor-supplied software available to do the job? (2) Will the system provide an adequate and timely payback? (3) Will it fit into the existing software environment? (4) Will it run efficiently on existing hardware — in particular, will other storage media be required? (5) Will a system hardware upgrade be needed to process the new system in a timely manner? (6) Will implementation of the proposed project divert resources that are needed for more critical projects? (7) Does the application use technology that would require extensive user or programmer training and/or a search for specialized expertise? (8) What effect would the proposed system implementation have on existing systems? (9) How does this proposal relate to trends in technology?

A study of the current system and an analysis of needs, costs, implementation times, and potential risks should be included in the feasibility study. At its conclusion, users, the steering committee (if the project is large enough), and IS management should give written approval or disapproval of the project. All appropriate parties — users, management, IS professionals — should be included in the feasibility study. A seriously flawed project is much cheaper to terminate at this early stage than later on when major expenditures have occurred and political fortunes are tied to its success or failure.

The feasibility study should consider the impact of major technology trends. For example, increased electronics storage and memory requirements have increased dramatically with increased functionality and presentation capabilities of software packages and operating systems.

High-level systems design. Projects that are accepted and funded beyond the feasibility phase proceed into the high-level (general) systems design phase. Major steps include:

- *Analysis of inputs, processing, and outputs (reports, screens) of the existing system.*

- *Detailed breakdown of user requirements.* For example, it is not enough to say that an inventory system should be able to cost items using various inventory valuation methods. LIFO, FIFO, averaging, or other specific valuation methods should be specifically listed in the systems development documentation.

- *Functional specifications listing exactly what the system is supposed to accomplish, from a business perspective.* For example, specifications for a purchase order system may require the ability to list, by vendor, those purchase orders still outstanding. Note that this is not a technical specification at this point. It does not, for example, indicate the screen layout of the open-purchase-order inquiry program.

- *Alternatives.* The system design should outline alternative methods of achieving the functional specifications. "Make or buy" is a typical alternative when vendor packages are available that approximate the needs of the user. Packages from well-established vendors can often provide a quicker implementation time and a better quality system than those obtainable from in-house effort. On the other hand, if extensive modifications are required, the package may not prove worth the cost. In some cases, a rigorous analysis may reveal that the system would be implemented more efficiently (or more quickly) on a local area network or on a single PC. Some vendors provide a "turnkey" service in which all software, hardware, and training are provided by the vendor.

Detailed systems design. With the general specifications in hand, the systems analysts, with the assistance of users, create a technical blueprint of the system. Various types of design methodologies are used. The following items are often included in the detailed systems design:

- Detailed program specifications
- File layouts
- Report and online screen layouts
- System flowcharts
- Overall system narrative
- Data-conversion procedures
- Test plans
- Data-element definitions (i.e., each field in each file is listed and defined)

Program coding and testing. In this phase, programs are coded according to the particular program specifications developed in the detailed systems-design phase. Testing is formalized and reviewed by users and project management. Testing usually occurs in two stages: (1) unit testing, in which the individual program is tested in isolation; (2) system testing, in which a series of programs (or even all the programs in the application) are run in sequence, as they would be after implementation. Testing should be the responsibility of an independent group that tries to make the system fail during testing instead of in actual operation. Purchased packages should also be tested with equal rigor since virtually no source code is "bug" free.

Testing is one of the most important parts of systems development and maintenance. It is the final quality check to make sure that the system performs as intended. Yet, it is frequently given inadequate attention due to its technical complexity, the level of detail and time required, and a lack of understanding of its importance.

Conversion. If an older system is being replaced, the data files must be converted to the new format. This process is the "Bermuda triangle" of systems development. Codes may be incorrectly converted, records can be dropped, and fields can be truncated (i.e., shortened). The most insidious errors are those with effects that show up after conversion.

For example, a large regional bank in the southeast converted its Certificate of Deposit system from one manufacturer's mainframe to a similar system from another manufacturer. During the conversion, the interest rates were converted correctly. Unfortunately, hidden from the user's sight (because it never appeared on a report) an obscure field called "daily interest accrual factor" was converted incorrectly for eight certificates. This field was derived from the interest rate and was used to perform the actual interest calculations. It is essential that the conversion processes and results be thoroughly tested and documented. For the eight certificates, the daily factor was too large by a factor of 100. Five months after the conversion, a routine analysis of gross corporate interest expense by the finance department revealed an inexplicable increase in interest expense. Further research identified the eight certificates. The total over-accrual exceeded $1 million. If one more month had passed before the error was detected, the entity IS financial statements would have had to be restated and the entity would have been publicly embarrassed. Problems that occur in processing must be documented to see that these problems will be tested for and considered in subsequent changes.

If conversion is manual, a percentage of the file may be corrupted because of data entry errors. Controls such as record counts, visual review of reports, hash totals, and other forms of reconciliation should be included in any conversion. In many cases, a percentage of the old system data is incorrect. Time should be allocated in the project budget for file scrubbing prior to conversion so that old data errors do not corrupt the new system.

Implementation. Prior to implementation, final reviews of conversion results and end-user management signoff should be obtained. Various types of implementation should be considered, including phased, pilot, and cutover. If at all possible, old/new system parallel processing should be maintained for a reasonable period of time (normally several weeks) so that bugs can be identified before they become critical. Also, if there are serious flaws in the new system, the old system provides a fallback option of the organization. If the old system cannot be paralleled, the need for review the first few days after implementation becomes even more critical. The possibility of returning to the old system diminishes with each passing day. Regardless of the approach used, the entity should be able to back out in case of failure and revert to the old system.

Maintenance. After implementation, the system remains in the maintenance phase until it is replaced. Change controls will prevent or lessen the deterioration of system quality over time. Modifications of the system should be: (1) authorized by user management, (2) made in accordance with the organization's development standards; and (3) tested and approved by the user as well as IS management (project managers). High risk, major projects should be approved by senior management. The degree to which changes must be tested depends on the risk. Small changes such as adding a new column to an existing report require only minimal testing.

Some organizations use the internal release method for making non-emergency changes. It is possible for even a relatively innocuous change to cause a serious problem. Thus, in theory, the acceptance test group should perform a full systems test to make sure any changes, however minor, work correctly and do not introduce unintentional results.

Formal procedures should be implemented to move approved and tested changes into production. Once tested and approved, the changes should be introduced into the live system on the same day. Even organizations that do not formally use the internal-release method achieve some control by restricting application changes to a particular day of the week or time of the month (except, of course, for emergency changes to resolve immediate processing errors). For example, assume a large data processing organization prints payroll checks on the last business day of the month. A logical policy for that organization would be to restrict implementation of payroll program changes to the first three weeks of the month. Changes during the last week of the month would be prohibited. As a result, the last week of the month serves as a grace period to detect programming errors before they show up on employee paychecks.

Internal Audit

The internal auditor's role in the feasibility and system study is not an enviable one. Internal auditors are dealing with specialists in a specialized undertaking. They must be knowledgeable, tactful, and helpful — yet they must maintain their independence and be watchful of the organization's broader goals. Not always will they be able to carry out their own function as they wish, but they will do it much better if they have a definite plan of action in mind. Here are some of the things they should try to be assured of when they participate in and review the feasibility and system study:

- The study should be made by a team composed of representatives of all departments whose interests should be considered.

- At least one member of the team should be an expert in the capabilities of the hardware and software.

- The study should start with a thorough analysis of the preexisting manual or automated system. Sometimes the only thing wrong with the prior system is that it needed to have its problems identified and corrected.

- Consideration should be given to control deficiencies identified through audits.

- Specifications for the new system should not show current volume only; they should consider contemplated growth.

- Consideration should be given to the risk of fraud or the loss of control.

- The users should agree to the proposed system.

- The budget estimates should be reasonable and supportable.

- Input and output requirements should be clearly defined. The system flow should offer logical processing procedures and should be clearly presented.

- Reasonable conversion plans should be formulated.

- Proper written authorization should be obtained for each phase of the systems development life cycle.

If any of these standards are not met and if the internal auditors find the IS specialists reluctant to take corrective action, they have no alternative but to report their findings to top management.

If a development methodology has not been implemented in the organization, the internal auditor should relentlessly campaign for its introduction. A strong systems development life cycle can drastically improve the quality of systems, reduce long-term maintenance costs, and increase user service levels.

An auditor should also be alert to management's failure to recognize and take action on projects that appear to be unsuccessful. Typical evidence of potential problems includes substantial delays and/or substantial cost overruns.

Data Security

Description

Data may be an organization's most critical asset. The controls over access to data determine the organization's vulnerability to accidental or fraudulent manipulation of assets.

Files are protected through a logical security system;[5] this is also referred to as "logical access controls." Logical access differs from physical access control. Physical access controls prevent people from having access to the hardware, tape vault, etc. Logical access refers to a logical or programmatic system for identifying authorized users. Logical access uses special files to determine whether a person attempting access should be allowed into the system and what the user can do on the system. So logical access both prevents unauthorized access and authorizes the actions of those who are given access. An effective data security system should provide assurance that:

- Only authorized users have access to data.
- The level of access is appropriate to the need.
- Modifications to data are accompanied by a complete audit trail.
- Unauthorized access is denied and the attempt is reported.

There are numerous approaches to data security. Prior to widespread use of online terminals, data input was entered almost exclusively through batch transactions of paper, card, tape, disk, etc. Application controls over the input and strong physical controls in the data center provided effective barriers against most unauthorized changes to files. With online systems, however, access spreads throughout the organization and the data is far more vulnerable to manipulation.

The most important — and difficult — function of a data-security system is authentication of the user. Unlike a signature, which is unique and can be verified, the same key strokes on a keyboard by user A and user B look alike to the system. If employee A tapes a password in the drawer under the terminal, employee B could find and use the password and appear to the system to be employee A.

Passwords are by far the most common means of authenticating users in business applications. A user typically has a user ID (e.g., "MPJ" for Michael P. Jones) that is known and often displayed on audit trail report. The user also has a password (e.g., "XYZ213"), which is kept secret.

Some data security software is supplied by hardware vendors in the operating system for their hardware. Independent vendors have developed general-purpose security software that, among other functions, enhances the effectiveness of password controls. Data security software may include features such as:

- Encryption of passwords so they cannot be browsed, even by programmers.

- Forced change of passwords after a designated number of days.

- Required password structure. For example, the password may be required to be at least four characters, contain no vowels, and include one or more numbers. Passwords should never be constructed so others can easily figure them out. The last four digits of a phone number, a child's name, an anniversary date, or other information that others can deduce make for vulnerable passwords. Employees should be cautioned to avoid such passwords.

In addition to password controls, data-security software monitors and controls access to a variety of resources. Following are some common features of a full-scope mainframe data-security package:

- Access to files and online transactions can be tailored to individuals and departments. For example, the security package can permit only accounts payable employees to access or update file names beginning with the letters "AP."

- A user ID can be suspended if too many attempts are made to sign on with an invalid password. This prevents unlimited password guessing.

- Transactions can be restricted to particular terminals and/or employees. For example, modifications to employee rates of pay may be restricted to terminals physically located in the payroll department. Thus, even if the password to access payroll files is stolen, payroll transactions cannot be entered on terminals outside the payroll department.

- Operation of terminals can be restricted by time of day or day of the week. If an organization's hours are 8:00 a.m. to 5:00 p.m. Monday through Friday, the data security package can prevent terminal access during all other hours.

- "Time out" limits can be established that force the terminal to sign off after a specified period of inactivity. This reduces the likelihood that an unauthorized person can use the sign-on of an authorized user who has temporarily left the area.

- The security system displays the last time and date an ID was used when the user signs on. Assume an employee has been on vacation for two weeks. Upon signing on to the system, a last week's date is displayed as the last sign-on date. The employee then knows that his or her ID has been compromised.

- The system can be set to require the entry of the password on every transaction when the transactions cover highly sensitive information. This prevents the use of an idle terminal even during the few minutes the authorized user leaves for a break.

"Global" security systems (so called because they cover most or all applications in a data center) have many of the features listed above. Such systems provide a strong level of control in a mainframe or minicomputer environment. However, there are many installations that have no comprehensive security package and must rely on "application level security." Generally, small systems rely on application security and some limited security provided by the operating system.

Properly implemented, application-level security can usually prevent unauthorized activities related to a specific application. For example, consider a three-tiered security system in a payroll application:

- The first level permits inquiry on all data except salary.
- The second level permits inquiry into all payroll data.
- The third level permits update of data such as hourly rate of pay.

Each level requires a different identification code and related password. For example, Byron C. Smith has an ID of "BCS" and a password of "124QRVF." "BCS" is assigned Level 2 security so he can enter the application system and examine all data on the payroll master file but he cannot change any data. Unfortunately, though application-level security usually provides strong security over user access, its control over knowledgeable programmers is weak.

Internal Audit

Organizations vary in the extent to which they have implemented data security. However, there are a number of basic rules for a proper security environment.

First, and foremost, the responsibility for information system security rests with senior management of the organization.

Senior management should see that:

- Exposures are assessed.
- Organizational policy is established.
- A compliance structure is implemented.[6]

Senior and middle managers are no longer ignorant of the need for security and the mechanisms available to maintain security. The improvement of management knowledge has created an environment within which the simplicity of security can be addressed. Managers can now understand the important elements of security.

Internal auditors are challenged to become technically competent to perform reviews of operating system security controls. The great diversity of hardware platforms and their associated strengths and weaknesses creates a need for more detailed and continuous training.

Physical security is generally well understood because it is easily compared to the storeroom, the cash vault, research laboratory, or other high security areas of the organization.

A major role of the internal auditor is to evaluate the effectiveness of the current security system(s) and, if weaknesses are found, to recommend the strongest system compatible with the organization's business practices and risk factors. It is not enough, for example, to state in a management report that an unauthorized person could access a particular system. The auditor must show management the exposures that result from inadequate access controls. If the internal auditor finds that user access decisions are being exercised by the data processing staff, the auditor must emphasize the need for control by the unit that owns the data. Data processing personnel may not be aware of what access is appropriate.

After the organization has established the direction of its data-security program, the auditor should continuously monitor its effectiveness. For example, as a part of every specific application review, the internal auditor should review password administration, levels of authority assigned in the security system, appropriateness of such authority, and number of violations of security policy over a period of time. Some specific review areas are:

- Classification and ownership
- Operational policies
- Organization and resources
- User awareness
- Security administration procedures[7]

Physical Security

Description

Physical security is perhaps the most basic control in an organization. In the early days of data processing, before the widespread use of online terminals, computer-room access controls were vitally important. While the burden of data security has now shifted toward sophisticated logical access software controls, physical security still remains a key safeguard against a host of risks such as fire, power outage, willful destruction, and theft of information. The areas of sensitivity can be categorized into three general areas of:

- Physical access.
- Environmental hazards.
- Fire and flood protection.[8]

Listed below are some of the major exposure areas and related physical security controls.

Unauthorized access. A data center and/or secured operations building with significant processing activities should limit access to only authorized individuals. Some of the specific techniques used to enforce this control include:[9]

- **Card access:** A magnetically encoded card, issued to authorized individuals, is inserted into a slot that reads the information on the card and transmits it to a security computer (usually a PC). Access is granted or denied based on the security records in the computer. Usually an audit trail — time, date, and ID — is maintained for later review. The security system, if not connected to a UPS (uninterruptible power supply), should have a backup mechanism such as mechanical door locks.

Time and location zoning is another important feature of a security system. For example, a computer operator may be authorized to enter the computer room but not the tape vault. By establishing "zones," access can be selectively assigned by the security officer. Time zoning works in a similar manner, limiting access to certain days and/or times.

Based on newer technology, the proximity sensing card automatically recognizes the physical card (inside a wallet or purse) at distances up to several feet. This reduces the congestion and temptation to "tailgate" in high traffic areas.

- **Biometric access systems:** These technologies are appropriate when rigorous physical security is required. These systems rely on physical characteristics to authenticate the individual requesting access. One such system, the retina scanner, relies on the uniqueness of blood vessel patterns in the eye. The person requesting access looks into a narrow screen while the scanner compares the individual's blood vessel pattern with those previously recorded. If there is a match, the individual is granted access. Owing to the time-consuming nature of this authentication procedure, it is not suitable for high-traffic or low-security-risk areas. Also, a small percentage (usually less than one percent) of authorized persons will be improperly rejected and a percentage of unauthorized persons will be accepted. Combined with other controls, these may be acceptable error rates in most organizations. Other biometric access devices include hand geometry recognition, electronic signature verification (based on hand motion as the signature is written), and voice recognition.

Computer center design. A significant level of physical security can be achieved simply by good planning. Here are some of the factors that should be considered in a computer center:

- The data center should be in an inconspicuous location.

- The data center in areas subject to earthquakes, flooding, or other natural disasters should have appropriate procedures to allow the system to operate during and/or after a natural disaster.

- The computer room itself should have only interior walls.

- Tape vaults or other media storage areas should be fire rated.

- The number of doors entering the computer room should be minimized (within fire code regulations).

- For highly sensitive areas (such as data centers housing industrial secrets), slab-to-slab construction may be justified. This prevents an intruder from penetrating an area via a false ceiling or raised crawl space.

- Emergency exits should be locked from the outside and alarmed.

- Visitor controls using closed-circuit TV monitors may be justified in some organizations.

- In tape vaults with highly sensitive data, motion detectors can be used to detect unauthorized activity during nonbusiness hours.

- Air conditioning capacity should be adequate. Humidity and temperature should be monitored.

- Exposed wiring should be minimized.

Fire prevention. While it is important for an organization to develop disaster-recovery capability, it is even more important to prevent a disaster. Since fire and smoke are a frequent source of damage, an organization should address protection needs in this area first. Fire-prevention safeguards for a data center are:[10]

- A fire alarm system should be tied to a manned security center, or the fire department if the security center is not manned 24 hours a day. The fire alarm system should be periodically tested and fire drills should be held to ensure an orderly evacuation of the building in the event of an actual fire.

- Smoke detectors should be in place throughout the building. Smoke damage to the computer can result from a fire in any office of a building, even if it is distant from the computer room. An appropriate fire suppression system should be installed.

Power supply. Public utility organizations cannot be relied upon to supply totally uninterrupted power to a data center. Organizations that do not provide for an alternate power source are subject to loss of power and brownouts. Two basic approaches to power backup systems in common use are: (1) custom diesel or other form of independent, long-term power generation (that can power a data center for days or even weeks); (2) short-term systems (which permit an orderly shutdown of the computer system before batteries are depleted of energy). Independent power generation has a higher cost, both for setup and maintenance, and is most often used for larger systems or mission-critical applications.

The proliferation of PCs and minicomputers has resulted in a number of small UPS (uninterruptible power supply) systems that permit continued processing for a limited period of time. One benefit is that current work is not lost when a brief power outage occurs. More important, however, is the use of a surge protector (combined with the UPS) to filter out large voltage spikes that can (and do) damage systems. The spikes are often the result of lightning striking a building. Surge protection for PCs is relatively inexpensive and should be used routinely unless power is filtered for the entire building.

Miscellaneous threats. A number of threats arise from day-to-day activities in the computer center. These include the following potential hazards:

- Water from burst pipes, leaks, or fire-fighting efforts can cause short circuits or deposit residues that are difficult or impossible to remove.

- Electrical devices, like pencil sharpeners and floor polishers, operating near tapes, disks, and computer processors and not fitted with suppressors, may emit electromagnetic "noise" that interferes with accurate data processing.

- Static electricity resulting from poor grounding, floor covering not equipped with static takeoff qualities, or poor humidity control, can interfere with accurate processing.

- Using steel wool for buffing can release tiny steel particles into electronic circuitry. (In one case, an employee left a cheese sandwich on the central processing unit. The heat caused the cheese to melt and ooze. Cleaning people tried to remove the mess with steel wool. The steel fibers from the wool entered the CPU and required its complete replacement.)[11]

- Using hard water in humidifiers can permit metallic dust to be sprayed into the equipment. Dust can affect the accuracy of tapes.

- Cigarette, pipe, and cigar smoke will leave a sticky residue on any surface inside or outside the computer.

Maintenance and housekeeping are critical aspects of the IS operation and should receive attention by management and the auditor. Controls are available that reduce the chances of equipment breakdown or hardware-engendered inaccurate processing. Examples are:

- Written procedures for operators in the event of unanticipated equipment failure.

- A written schedule of preventive maintenance procedures.

- Preventive maintenance programs providing for periodic maintenance according to manufacturer's recommendations.

- Provision for cleaning drive read/write heads, capstans, and vacuum columns at regular intervals as specified by the equipment manufacturer.

- Malfunctions described in console logs or an "incident reporting system" that notifies IS management of all errors occurring on each shift.

When hardware errors occur, they should be reported. Advanced operating systems keep an internal hardware log (separate and distinct from the console log) that permits field engineers to determine many hardware errors that have occurred. Some suggested steps for an adequate preventive maintenance program are:

- Equipment malfunctions should be logged.

- The malfunctions should be reported to vendor service people.

- Reported malfunctions should be followed up to see if they have been investigated and corrected.

- Intermittent malfunctions should be investigated until resolved.

The program status at the appropriate restart point should be shown by the files for each hardware failure. Accordingly, a history log should contain before-and-after images of updated disks. Software packages are available that not only record malfunctions but also prescribe diagnostic routines.

Internal Audit

Internal auditors should make sure hardware controls are in force and working. Some of the audit steps they can take are:

- Interview operators and users about the reliability of equipment. Between the two, the auditor should be able to obtain reliable information.

- Determine what action is taken by computer operators (or by software) in the event of a hardware malfunction.

- Check downtime reports, machine-error logs, and maintenance reports to confirm the oral statements. Logs kept by maintenance engineers are a good source for determining which components failed, how often, why, and what was done to correct the difficulties.

- Determine if temperature-control and humidity-control devices are installed and functioning, and conform to manufacturer's environmental specifications.

- Review logs generated by temperature and humidity equipment and operating statistics to ascertain the extent of equipment downtime and the extent of reruns because of equipment failure.

- Review daily computer logs and periodic equipment utilization reports to see if manufacturer's preventive maintenance schedules are being followed.

- Compare actual downtime with what would be considered normal.

- Determine whether equipment is released for preventive maintenance at the most appropriate times.

- Determine whether fire detection and fire suppressing devices are in place and have been checked for operation as required.

The fact that provisions have been made for hardware maintenance is no guarantee that it will be done. Internal auditors cannot rely on what should be, but on what is. In one example, an auditor was reviewing requests for system repairs and maintenance and found these deficiencies:

- Twenty-two percent of the time, source requests for maintenance took more than 10 days.

- Although requests for maintenance were required to be in writing, they were sometimes oral.

- System failure records designed to call attention to chronic problems were not always used.

- The service request procedure was not made routine and took an excessive amount of clerical time.

- Preventive maintenance objectives were orally agreed to, and even these were not being met.

- No objectives had been set for maintenance of tape drive units even though service requests for these units represented 43 percent to 50 percent of the total requirements for maintenance.

- Discrepancies between nonchargeable rerun, maintenance time shown on the computer operations machine logs, and the machine maintenance logs sent to the supplier for credits on computer equipment billing had been running generally in favor of the supplier.

The internal auditor suggested several improvements in the system, recommended the establishment of preventive maintenance objectives for all hardware, and followed up to see that controls were established to eliminate incorrect credits to the suppliers.[12]

Contingency Planning and Disaster Recovery

Description

Since the early 1960s, most organizations have automated previously manual functions. In addition, online services are now an integral part of the day-to-day routine. As a result, the availability of IS is critical to the continuity of many organizations. The internal auditor should review both contingency planning and backup capability to determine if the organization can continue to process vital transactions in the event of fire, earthquake, flood, bomb attack, or other disasters affecting the data center.

Generally, an organization with an adequate capability to recover from a disaster will be equipped with:

- Off-site storage of key data, programs, operating systems, and documentation.

- A planning document containing detailed steps to be taken in the event of a disaster — for example, off-site processing locations, listings of critical applications, run documentation, telecommunications information, names and phone numbers of key employees (both user and IS personnel), and software-hardware vendor information.

- Backup agreements with alternative sites.

"Hot sites" are popular. These are fully equipped, manned information system's sites — often provided for a fee by outside vendors — which are on standby 24 hours a day. In the event of a disaster, an organization's files can be loaded onto the hot site systems and vital processing can continue until the damaged data center can be repaired. Hot sites are usually equipped with extensive telecommunications hookups, since online processing is so crucial to many businesses.

Another alternative is the reciprocal agreement in which two or more businesses agree to share system resources (usually in off hours) if a disaster occurs. This alternative is less desirable for high transaction volume organizations. It also requires that the participating firms stay technically "in sync."

Finally, the "cold site" is sometimes used when a quick recovery is not essential. Cold sites are buildings with power, air conditioning, telecommunications hookups, raised flooring for computer equipment, and other environmental requirements. Usually, no computer equipment is stored in a cold site until a disaster occurs. Reliance is placed on equipment vendors to prioritize shipment and installation of replacement computers and peripherals. Because of the technical complexity of even a modest data center, fully activating a cold site can take from three days to several weeks, depending on equipment availability.

Many organizations rely on a cold and hot site combination. After a major disaster, the hot site is used to provide critical services while the cold site is being prepared. Typically, hourly usage rates for the hot site are substantial. In addition, the hot site, by design, is often a significant physical distance from the original data center. Personnel and data must be shuttled back and forth between the organization's business locations and the hot site. Thus, every effort is made to prepare the cold site (which is often physically closer to the organization's business locations) for longer-term processing. Eventually, the original data center is rebuilt and normal processing is resumed.

A test run of critical applications, conducted at least semiannually, will reveal any flaws or bottlenecks in the plan. In practice, disaster recovery planning is a complex endeavor, requiring significant technical and business acumen. The alternative, however, is to risk severe losses or even termination of the business.

Internal Audit

The internal auditor must answer two fundamental questions for executive management: Could the organization survive a major information system disaster? If so, what is the likely extent and effect of the disaster?

Because systems and organizations vary so much, it is impossible to present a checklist of all the steps needed to review an organization's disaster recovery capability. To get started, however, the internal auditor can use the following list of concerns:

- What is the extent of the business's dependence on IS? An airline is totally dependent on immediate availability of vast system resources. A retail chain may be able to survive a little longer without a central processing site — particularly if IS is decentralized. A questionnaire to the organization's operating department heads may be the best means for the internal auditor to assess the number of vital system applications in the organization.

- Has a disaster recovery plan been developed? The plan should consider both data processing and user needs. Is there adequate provision for transportation of the organization's work to the new site? Are critical applications listed? Are technical details listed such as alternative JCL (Job Control Language), special jobs, and any operating system peculiarities? Is there an escalation procedure? Occasionally a "disaster" may not be completely obvious. A small water leakage into some of the hardware may appear initially to be a problem that could be corrected by vendor maintenance engineers. As time goes on, the situation gets more critical but the data processing manager is unsure whether to sound the alarm. An escalation procedure makes sure that the organization will have adequate notice if the situation continues to deteriorate. Above all, the disaster recovery plan should be practical, tested, and up-to-date. For example, telephone numbers two years out of date can be worse than useless.

- What is the organization's current disaster recovery capacity? Note that a disaster recovery *capacity* is different from a disaster recovery *plan*. Off-site storage of critical data, a hot/cold site, reciprocal agreement, or a redundant data center would indicate (but not demonstrate) a disaster recovery capability. A signed intent to "rush the next available computer to the organization in the event of a disaster" by the hardware vendor is not adequate. For management to have comfort that the organization can recover from a disaster, regular testing of the disaster plan is required. Operating systems must be loaded, applications processed, and output balanced back to the organization's general ledger or other control totals.

- Have the critical applications been defined? During a disaster, there will be little time for debate. IS personnel must quickly begin processing, and know what applications must be executed first and what applications are to be omitted.

- Are backup telecommunications facilities adequate? For some industries, telecommunications is vital. If alternative methods of data transmission are not available, the organization may be able to restore the data center but will not be able to communicate with the customer or outlying business units. The auditor should determine the extent to which telecommunications are used and the availability of dial-up lines (and related telecommunications equipment).

- The internal auditor should observe the off-site testing process. It is important to be realistic in this area — mainframe systems do not "port" well. Subtle differences in the way operating systems are implemented, even on identical hardware and software, may cause baffling technical problems that delay start-up. Mainframe systems were not intended to be brought up from scratch overnight. The auditor should look for progress rather than instant success. The frequency of testing can be reduced somewhat after one or two successful tests. The testing should be conducted with typical volumes, and processing times should be carefully noted.

Storage

Description

It is usual for a modern data center to output thousands of disk and/or tape files in a week's time. These files include backups of current data to be used in case of a disaster and archive files for permanent storage. Program controls are needed to make sure that these files are correctly labeled and stored. Otherwise, incorrect files can be input to applications or good files can be inadvertently deleted.

The file management system should include security considerations as well as managing rotation of files to and from off-site storage. Many organizations now transmit backup files to remote, possibly unmanned, backup sites due to recent advances in telecommunications, including expanded bandwidth and fiber optics.

External labels are tags physically attached to removable volumes such as a reel of tape, a disk pack, or a diskette. Use of external labels is a simple process to implement but may result in occasional mislabeling, since it depends on the diligence of the computer operator. Without additional controls, files could easily get lost (particularly when the same file is created repeatedly, with each version different from the next only in terms of its creation date).

Most applications use internal labels to provide accurate identification of files. These labels exist in the first inches of the readable portion of the magnetic tapes or a fixed location on a removable disk pack. Information such as file name, time and date created, record length, and other technical specifications are maintained within the label record (sometimes called a "header"). If, for example, a computer operator accidentally mounts an accounts-payable tape with the internal (i.e., machine-readable) name "AP.TP.DAILY" instead of the correct fixed assets tape "FA.TP.WEEKLY," the operating system will not permit continued processing until the correct tape is mounted on the tape drive.

Tape management systems that regulate the use of all tapes in a data center are commercially available. Most applications are set up using the grandfather/father/son concept. For example, assume an organization has a monthly payroll:

- At the end of January, the first copy of the payroll master is created; it becomes the (0) generation.

- At the end of February, a second payroll master is created. The January master becomes the (-1) generation, i.e., father, and the February master is the (0) generation, i.e., son.

- At the end of March, another master is created, becoming the (0) generation and bumping the prior generations to (-1) and (-2). The (-2) generation is the grandfather.

Assuming that the tape management system has been instructed to keep three "generations," the January payroll master would "fall off" at the end of April. At that point, the data would physically remain on the January master but the tape management system would notify the tape librarian that the physical reel of tape was available as a "scratch" tape — i.e., to be written over as new data.

In very large data centers, external tape labels are not used and complete reliance is placed on the tape management system. (The only external identifier is a tape serial number that remains the same throughout the physical life of the tape. The operating system tells the operator, via a console message, which tape number to mount.) The tape management catalog itself must be backed up; otherwise, massive disruption of processing could occur because the identity of tapes may have been lost.

Files on fixed or non-removable disks are normally managed by the operating system, which tracks all files in a VTOC (volume table of contents). Sophisticated databases and more complex files are usually controlled via special system catalogs.

In a data center nearing maximum capacity of disk space, processing can be disrupted when insufficient room is available for all the necessary files. Typically, as an organization nears period end, transactions and master files tend to become bloated with records that are eventually purged. Disk space will be closely monitored in a well-run data processing organization. Special vendor-supplied software is often available for regulating disk space utilization. Any files not used for more than X months will be migrated to tape storage (which is far cheaper for long-term storage).

File naming standards play an important role in disk file management. Assume, for example, that an organization is running year-end processing. Programmers have left test files on the disk packs. If all test file names are prefixed with "TEST," operators (or a disk-file management system) can easily delete noncritical test files so that essential production processing can continue without disk-space shortage. Without such conventions, it is difficult to know which files are test and which are production; which can be erased and which cannot.

Tapes, disk packs, and other storage media are subject to periodic breakdowns from normal usage. For example, when tape drives start and stop, stress is placed on the tape's magnetic-oxide coating which houses the data. Eventually, the tape weakens in one or more places and becomes unreadable, i.e., the data can no longer be accessed. Disk packs can also break down (sometimes catastrophically in the form of a "head crash"), although less commonly now than in the past. As a result of these risks, it is important for the organization to always store critical data on at least two separate media (e.g., tape and disk or two tapes). A file and its backup should never be placed on the same disk pack. A common procedure is to keep the most current, working file on disk, retain an on-site tape backup, and periodically send a second tape copy off-site.

Internal Audit

Loss of data can be a serious and immediate problem for an organization. The concentration of information on magnetic media compounds the problem. The internal auditor should pose the following questions:

- How are internal labels used?

- Are external labels used where appropriate?

- Is a tape management or disk management or file management system available?

- Have there been "abnormal terminations" due to inadequate disk space? An excessive number (some will be expected in normal operations) indicates either inadequate disk space or poor management of that space.

- Are generation data sets (i.e., grandfather/father/son file concept) maintained? Are enough generations maintained so that if a file becomes corrupted, the previous generation can be used to restore data to current status?

- Are tapes and other media housed appropriately? Are copies kept off-site as well as on-site?

- Are appropriate environmental factors (temperature and humidity) monitored and controlled? Are tapes cleaned periodically?

- Are files named according to standards? This is far more than a "nice to have." With thousands or perhaps hundreds of thousands of files in a large data center, poor naming conventions can result in inadvertent deletion of files by operators seeking new disk space.

The auditor should not lose sight of the fact that computer tapes may contain organizational information even after they have outlived their usefulness. The internal auditor of a financial institution noted that several thousand magnetic tapes formerly used for backup of data files were being sold to the highest bidder. The auditor urged that the tapes be erased because they contained important and often confidential information. Management contended the files could only be read by someone who knew the institution's file structures, but they grudgingly agreed to erase all of them. In one of those classic moments every auditor dreams of, the last laugh was the auditor's. The high bidder was a programmer recently terminated from the institution who knew how to read the tapes.[13] In this case a simple procedure of using a magnet erased the information.

The Operating System

Description

The operating system is the heart of the computer. Without adequate controls over its implementation and maintenance, the organization will be subject to excessive down time, incorrect processing, and hard-to-detect computer fraud.

The operating system and related systems software are a series of interlocking systems with a large number of options chosen by the systems programmer. The options enable the operating system to exactly match the organization's hardware and software environment. For example, the number, ID, and type of display terminals are specified when the operating system is installed (called a "SYSGEN"). Installation of systems software should follow its own life cycle, including approvals, documentation, appropriate testing, and signoff by computer operations and general IS management. Operating system changes tend to carry relatively high risk since they affect the entire data center and network. Changes should be made during off hours and a backout plan should be available. All changes should be logged and be available for review.

When any software is considered for purchase, the systems programmer (operating system specialist) should determine if any "hooks" to the operating system are required. If so, the package will have to be reinstalled with each new release of the operating system — since the hooks modify the operating system to allow the particular software to work.

A medium-to-large data center will usually have many systems packages, most of which are supplied by the hardware vendor. Examples of these include:

- The operating system itself.

- Utilities for copying, printing, browsing, and otherwise manipulating data.

- Compilers to convert human-readable program source code to machine executable programs.

- Database management software.

It is important for these software components of the operating system to be kept up-to-date (i.e., releases should be current). Eventually, the vendor drops support on old operating system releases. Organizations processing under old operating systems risk excessive down time since the source of an operating system failure is sometimes very difficult to identify without the aid of vendor specialists.

While all computers require an operating system, popular mainframes and minicomputers have a plethora of efficiency and monitoring software packages to choose from. Cost-benefit studies should be performed prior to purchasing these packages, since they can be relatively expensive. For example, report distribution software can be purchased that intercepts all output directed to the printer. The output is stored on tape or other magnetic media. If a report is lost, the report distribution management system (RDMS) can recreate the report without a lengthy rerun of the entire application. Also, if several organizations are being processed together in one application, RDMS can segregate the printouts and print banner pages between each organization's work. This assists printer personnel in the physical distribution of the work and reduces the likelihood of improperly routing sensitive reports.

These and other capabilities should be considered in light of the package cost (note that packages are generally sold with a yearly maintenance fee, which is often a percentage of the purchase price). In contrast to applications, major systems software is rarely developed in-house. A single organization cannot usually justify the time and costly expertise required for the development.

Data security and operating system controls are closely linked. Certain powerful operating system utilities, sometimes called "ZAP" programs, can bypass many security safeguards and modify both data and programs without an audit trail. Availability of these utilities should be restricted to systems programmers, and authorizing documentation should accompany each use. In recent years, data security software has become more adept at detecting unauthorized use of such utilities, but security packages are not an absolute control.

Given the great technical knowledge of systems programmers, proper segregation of duties assumes a vital role in controlling the access these individuals have to the organization's assets. Systems programmers should have no *applications* responsibilities. For example, responsibility for installation of a new purchase order system combined with operating system maintenance responsibilities would be an improper segregation of duties. Such a combination would provide an individual with the technical means and business knowledge to both perpetrate and conceal a fraud.

Internal Audit

Operating system controls, because of their complexity, are perhaps the most difficult for the internal auditor to review. An in-depth analysis of operating system controls requires the aid of a highly trained IS audit specialist. Nevertheless, many of the controls over the operating system and its maintenance reflect traditional control practices. Here are some questions internal auditors should ask:

- Are appropriate change control procedures used? Are operating system changes documented, approved by an independent technical services manager and/or computer operations manager, and installed at low-risk times of the day or week?

- Are operating system releases kept up-to-date?

- Are certain powerful utilities kept restricted to only personnel that need to use them? Is their use recorded?

- Are duties properly segregated? Do systems programmers have applications responsibilities?

- Are systems programmers adequately trained? Is technical backup available if they leave the organization?

- Are operating system tables that contain employee or terminal information kept up-to-date?

- Has any redundant operating system software been purchased? Is the organization paying maintenance on software that is no longer being used?

- Are appropriate studies performed when new systems software is requested?

- Is there a system to track and summarize errors related to the operating system and its components?

Telecommunications

Description

Information systems routinely transmit large quantities of data from one point to another. Internal auditors must assess the integrity, security, reliability, and performance of the organization's network to determine if the data is accurate and timely.

Many organizations are heavily dependent on telecommunications. Airline reservation systems, for example, must be continuously online during business hours. Any telecommunications breakdown means immediate loss of revenues. Another example is the transmission of inventory or sales data from regional to central data centers. Regardless of the application, here are some common exposures in all the telecommunications systems:

- Data can be dropped, changed, or duplicated during transmission.

- The network (e.g., telephone system) can be inoperable for a period of time.

- Confidential information can be extracted by various eavesdropping techniques (passive wiretapping).

- Transmission response time can be so slow that customers are irritated or business functions are adversely affected.

- Unauthorized individuals can insert fraudulent messages into the network (active wiretapping).

- A poorly designed telecommunications network can result in excessive costs if incompatible equipment is purchased.

Fortunately, technical controls are now available that significantly reduce the risks associated with transmitting data. As in manual systems, the cost of controls should match the risk. For example, large dollar sums are transferred from one bank account to another account in a different bank. The customer initiates the transfer via a telephone call to the bank. Most banks "call back" customers at pre-designated telephone numbers to verify the identity of the caller. Even though this is a time-consuming procedure, the risks (losses of millions) justify the additional controls. Listed below are some of the common telecommunications controls in use today:

- **Sequencing of messages:** A message number is inserted in each record transmitted. Each message number is incremented by one more than the last one sent. The receiving computer detects when a gap or duplicate has occurred.

- **Encryption:** The transmitted data is "scrambled" by using a complex mathematical algorithm to encode the data. Only with the proper algorithm and other "key" information can the data be unencrypted.

- **Self-checking algorithms:** Various sophisticated mathematical techniques such as "cyclical redundancy checking" are used to determine if any information has been changed during transmission. Any detected errors result in a retransmission of the data in question.

- **Network-monitoring software:** Transmissions travel through many public and private relays and other telecommunications equipment. Often, it is difficult to pinpoint which specific equipment has malfunctioned. Monitoring software permits operators at a central location to both identify and anticipate weak points in the telecommunications network.

- **Automatic dial-back:** Numerous commercial databases have been accessed and, in some cases, vandalized or fraudulently changed by "hackers." Dial-back systems accept incoming calls from modems but disconnect and automatically call back a prearranged telephone number to establish a permanent connection for data transfer or inquiry. The incoming caller must supply an ID and a password so that the dial-back system knows which prearranged number to call.

- **Dedicated lines:** For organizations transferring significant volumes of data on a routine basis, a dedicated line provides a higher level of security and transmission quality. Dedicated lines are leased by public carriers to specific organizations. These lines are available only to that organization, are "up" 24 hours a day, and have relatively little "noise." Dial-up lines, on the other hand, have an inconsistent level of quality and can only carry data at relatively slow speeds. While the cost of a dedicated line is significantly more than dial-up connect charges, the organization benefits from greater reliability and control over data transmissions.

- **Restart/recovery procedures:** Telecommunications can fail without warning. Construction near telephone wiring, an electrical surge from lightning, and even a programming blunder on the mainframe can result in sudden loss of telecommunications support. Without proper restart/recovery procedures and controls, data entered earlier in the day can be lost. Data ambiguity can be even more damaging. If it is unclear just what data have been preserved and what have been lost, the users do not know what to reenter. As a result, data could be lost or duplicated.

Fortunately, good restart/recovery procedures in the data center can assist users when the system returns "online." If the system keeps a backup "journal" of all data input, the database(s) can be returned to the status they were in just prior to the problem. Also, an organization without good restart procedures may have technical problems when bringing the system online again.

Internal Audit

The extent to which the auditor reviews telecommunications controls will of course depend upon the organization's level of dependence on telecommunications. If telecommunications are used primarily for inquiry, simple hardware-related controls may be sufficient. If funds are being transferred or asset balances changed through remote communications, additional controls (manual and technical) may be needed.

Following are some questions that the internal auditor should ask regarding telecommunications:

- Are standards and policies for network control in force? For example, is new telecommunications equipment required to conform to protocol standards? If other firms are serviced by the organization, are they limited to a number of standard protocols? (This reduces ongoing maintenance effort for the organization.)

- For critical network applications, are appropriate user controls installed, e.g., callbacks?

- Is there an audit trail for all transactions transmitted over the network?

- Has the network experienced sufficient noise and other problems to justify monitoring software?

- Is encryption used for sensitive data?

- Have cables, modems, control units, and other telecommunications been appropriately labeled so that repair service can be expedited? Note that "fault isolation" (i.e., identifying the problem) can be a difficult task in large telecommunications systems.

- Is the network adequately documented? Locations and users of terminals, control units, and other equipment should be documented. Otherwise, it may be necessary for network personnel to *physically* visit sites to make changes to the network.

- Where sensitive data are transmitted, are telephone closets and other network access points locked or otherwise protected?

- Are backup lines available when the primary lines are down?

- Have adequate restart/recovery procedures been developed?

- The introduction of LANs and WANs has caused some of the networking hardware to be located outside the bounds of data centers, causing concern for physical and logical security of the network. Furthermore, telecommunications "closets" should be secured and cleaned of debris since many times these are used for storage and other non-IT purposes. If racks are used to contain the hubs, routers, or switches, ensure that the rack is bolted to the floor to ensure that it is not knocked over inadvertently.

As organizations transfer data electronically to other organizations, electronic data interchange (EDI) becomes more important. EDI is designed with standardized formats that allow the consistent and accurate processing of data. Mechanisms available include physical exchange media, point-to-point communications and third-party services, such as a value-added network (VAN). VANs are private networks that sell capacity to other third parties.

Program Changes

Description

In the typical IS environment, program changes are often frequent and major in scope. The internal auditor must assess whether changes are authorized, tested, and properly implemented. Without an adequate change control system, it is impossible to rely on the processing integrity of individual applications.

For example, consider the effect of a fraudulent program change on the following accounts payable application:

When payments to vendors are generated, the name and address of each vendor residing on a vendor file is accessed during the check run. The organization requires written authorization for any vendor name and address change. Furthermore, online access to the accounts payable system requires a special supervisory password, which is regularly changed. Finally, the accounts payable vendor name-and-address list is printed out and compared with authorizing source documents on a quarterly basis.

Such controls would appear to be strong. Unfortunately, the programmer responsible for maintaining the check-printing program could insert fraudulent logic to appropriate organization funds through the following scheme:

For the first check greater than $200,000, change the address to be printed on the check to P.O. Box 1111, Anytown, USA.

The programmer could set up a business account at a local bank with a name similar or identical to the name of the firm that should have received the check. After the check is mailed to the programmer's post office box, it could be deposited without drawing suspicion.

Traditional controls, at least in a large accounts payable system where computer-printed checks are not individually reviewed by knowledgeable employees, would detect this fraud only well after the fact. Since the dollars were not changed, the check run would be in balance. The check register would show that the check was issued to the original (authorized) vendor. The vendor file would show no changes. The programmer, by "recompiling" the check-printing program, could erase all evidence of the fraudulent program change. The vendor would, of course, eventually complain; but several months might be required to determine the source of the problem. Only a strong change control system can effectively prevent such unauthorized program modifications. Without such a system, application controls can be circumvented.

Computer fraud, though sensational when it occurs, is not the primary impetus for strong change controls. Computer fraud occurs only occasionally, whereas data processing errors and omissions occur every day. Over time, organizations lose significant amounts due to changes that are: (1) improperly tested; (2) improperly implemented, i.e., installed at the wrong time; (3) implemented without adequate user notification and training; and (4) implemented without adequate supervisory review of the business/technical impact of the change. An organization should develop consistent procedures for initiation, testing, approval, and implementation of program changes.

A sound change control program includes these elements:[14]

- **Security:** The programmer may make changes to a test copy of a computer program but only the librarian can actually move the test program (and associated changes) into the production environment. Security software should routinely be used to "lock out" programmers from production libraries.

- **Audit trail:** A detailed history of all program and JCL (Job Control Language) changes should be maintained. Individuals authorizing, initiating, and implementing the changes are listed on the audit trail. In addition, the audit trail should include the disposition of the change, i.e., whether it was successful or had to be "backed out" due to technical or logic flaws. Both the librarian and supervisory personnel should review the audit trail to make sure all "moves" were completed as scheduled and nothing was moved into production without authorization.

- **Quality assurance:** The change-control system provides the framework for an IS quality review system. An organization may have standards that require reviews and written authorizations by users, IS programming supervisors, computer operations supervisors, and even internal auditors. Without proper signatures, the librarian will not implement the change. For example, if a programmer carelessly implements a system that uses all available drives at the same time, daily production could be hampered due to drive contention with other applications. Computer operations, provided it is part of the change control/review process, should not sign off on a system that does not conform to standards.

- **Provision for emergency changes:** Irrespective of the efforts devoted to testing and quality assurance, programs will occasionally stop running (often referred to as "blowing up" or "bombing") or produce incorrect results. When these problems occur in time-sensitive applications, there is usually insufficient time for the formal approval process to correct the situation. The programmer in charge of the application is called in to correct the problem immediately so production can continue. The change control system must have a method to handle such changes. Typically, computer operations supervisors provide temporary authorization for the change and users/IS management review and authorize the changes at a later time. Technical procedures are also available that flag temporary changes so management is fully aware of and can subsequently validate all changes.

- **Source code and JCL change tracking:** In addition to an audit trail that indicates what program was changed and when, detailed listings of each line of source code that has been changed should be available. Some vendor-supplied change control systems provide such information automatically. For example, these systems can list the last one hundred changes made to a particular program. In less sophisticated (and less reliable) change control systems, programmers are required to place the date and their initials near the lines of source codes that have been changed. The system relies on programmer diligence and, as a result, does not capture 100 percent of the changes. When programs function incorrectly, it is often due to a recently introduced change. Hence, as a practical matter, it is important to flag changes and retain the prior version of the changed code so that the probable cause of the error can be quickly identified.

Changes to vendor packages represent a special problem. Software vendors usually send their customers one or more "releases" (i.e., a series of program changes to update the application) per year. If the organization has not customized the vendor package, installation of the new release after testing is typically straightforward. Frequently, however, packages are modified by the organization to perform some new function or process the data in a manner not envisioned by the vendor. These "in-house" changes must be identified and reinstalled on top of any new releases by the vendor. If a good audit trail of program changes has not been maintained, it is very difficult to reinstall custom changes. The programmer, visually comparing new and old source code, cannot readily determine whether differences in the lines of code are the result of vendor changes or in-house changes. Thus, in data processing organizations with poor change controls, it is common for some customized changes to mysteriously disappear when a new vendor release is installed. Another concern is that these changes can impact the ability of the software to function properly when new releases are installed.

Internal Audit

No one — users, management, programmers, nor operators — is served by an atmosphere of uncontrolled changes and constant surprises. While change control may be perceived by some as needless overhead, it in fact reduces programming hours spent in maintenance. If the organization does have a change control system, the internal auditor can perform the following tests (among others) to determine if the system is working and effective:

- Examine change authorization documents. Determine if they are properly signed and authorized.

- Determine if program and JCL libraries are protected by systems controls (very difficult to circumvent) or merely administrative procedures.

- Compare "executable" versions of programs from one time period to the next. This step is technically difficult for the nonspecialist, but it provides the most objective and independent evidence of program change. Trace changed programs back to authorizing documents.

- Examine emergency change procedures. If there is no follow-up and subsequent review of these changes, the value of the entire change control system is greatly reduced.

- Determine if management reports are produced that indicate the number of emergency fixes and the number of changes that had to be backed out due to technical/quality problems.

Hardware

Description

The reliability of hardware has significantly increased with each new generation of hardware. Nevertheless, hardware will continue to be a potential source of systems error in the foreseeable future. Following are basic hardware controls that reduce the likelihood of such errors:[15]

- **Redundant character check:** Although this control takes many forms in specific vendor's hardware configurations, it is always based on the principle of redundancy. Each piece of data transmitted or moved inside the computer carries an extra character (or "bit") that has a mathematical relationship with the preceding data. If the data is altered, there will no longer be a mathematical match between the data and the redundant character. This allows the system to detect corrupted or missing data.

- **Duplicate process check:** A particular function is performed twice and the results compared. Any differences are flagged as a hardware error.

- **Equipment check:** Electronic controls are built into the circuitry to detect errors and provide for automatic retry.

Internal Audit

The internal auditor should be aware of the need for basic hardware controls, particularly in the telecommunications area. If a vendor does not provide adequate hardware controls (more often the case with antiquated systems or very small systems), the auditor should review compensating user and software controls to make sure some capability exists to capture hardware errors. Even in state-of-the-art systems, it is possible to have occasional hardware errors. Particularly in the IS field, the internal auditor should avoid "Maginot line" thinking, i.e., relying on a powerful control to stop 100 percent of the errors from a particular source.

References

[1]*Systems Auditability and Control* (Altamonte Springs, FL: The Institute of Internal Auditors Research Foundation, 1994 Edition), 5-55.

[2]Ibid., 5-70.

[3]Durant, Jerry E., "Applying Systematic Testing to Application Development Audits," *Internal Auditor,* February 1991, 38-44.

[4]*Systems Auditability and Control* (Altamonte Springs, FL: The Institute of Internal Auditors Research Foundation, 1994 Edition), 5-10.

[5]Ibid., 9-29 through 9-60.

[6]Ibid., 9-2 through 9-4.

[7]Ibid., 9-7 through 9-23.

[8]Ibid., 9-25 through 9-29.

[9]Strauchs, John, *Designing the Computer Room for Security DataPro Security* (Delran, NJ: DataPro Research Corporation, 1987), 101-104.

[10]Mair, William E., D.R. Wood, and K.W. Davis, *Computer Control and Audit* (Altamonte Springs, FL: The Institute of Internal Auditors, 1976), 322.

[11]*Systems Auditability and Control,* (Altamonte Springs, FL: The Institute of Internal Auditors Research Foundation, 1994 Edition), 4-36 through 4-44.

[12]Minterm, H.J., ed., *How to Save $14,500,000 Through Internal Auditing* (Altamonte Springs, FL: The Institute of Internal Auditors, 1975), 78-79.

[13]"The Round Table," *Internal Auditor,* April 1993, 70.

[14]Yarberry Jr., William A., "Auditing the Change Control System," *EDPACS,* June 1984, 1-4.

[15]Watne, Donald A., and Peter B. Turney, *Auditing EDP Systems* (Englewood Cliffs, NJ: Prentice-Hall, 1984), 227-232.

Supplementary Readings

Arlinghaus, Barry P., "Internal Audit's Role in the Implementation of Enterprise and Other Major Systems," *Internal Auditing,* November/December 2002, 32-38.

Attaway, Morris C., "Wired Business," *Internal Auditor*, April 1999, 50-57.

Baumer, David L., Robert P. Moffie, and Acie L. Ward, "Cyberlaw and E-Commerce: An Internal Audit Perspective," *Internal Auditing,* November/December 2002, 24-30.

Bean, LuAnn, and Steven A. Harrast, "Thin and Ultra Thin Clients: Fat Issues for Internal Auditors," *Internal Auditing*, November/December 2000, 3-12.

Bhattachayra, Somnath, "IT Failure: Can the Internal Auditor Mitigate the Damage?" *Internal Auditing*, November/December 1998, 35-39.

Bodnar, George H., "Trends in Data Security," *Internal Auditing*, Summer 1995, 51-56.

Bodnar, George H., "The Effect of Pervasive IS Controls," *Internal Auditing*, May/June 2001, 39-43.

Bodnar, George H., "TAKO: An Instance of Computer-Aided IT Education," *Internal Auditing*, January/February 2001, 26-30.

Bogusky, Clay, and Stanley Halper, "Control and Security Issues in Electronic Document Imaging," *The EDP Auditor Journal,* 1991, 33-50.

Bou-Raad, Giselle, and Carmel Capitanio, "The Implications of Computer Hacking on the Internal Audit Function: A Banking Industry Study," *Internal Auditing*, May/June 1999, 36-41.

Bradley, Rodney J., and E. Perrin Garsombke, "Electronic Data Interchange: Controlling the Risk," *Internal Auditing*, Spring 1993, 51-56.

Brockie Leonard, Barbara, "Data Security: Internal and External Control Issues," *Internal Auditing*, Winter 1997, 3-9.

Cerullo, Michael J., and Virginia Cerullo, "The Internal Auditor's Role in Developing and Implementing Enterprise Resource Planning Systems," *Internal Auditing*, May/June 2000, 25-34.

Champlain, Jack, *Practical IT Auditing Manual, 2nd ed.* (New York: RIA, 2002).

Gaston, S.J., *Audit of Small Computer Systems Including LANs* (Toronto, Canada: The Canadian Institute of Chartered Accountants, 1993).

Gilhooley, Ian A., *Information Systems Management, Control, and Audit* (Altamonte Springs, FL: The Institute of Internal Auditors, 1991).

Glover, Steven, Prawitt Douglas, and Marshall Romney, "Software Showcase," *Internal Auditor*, August 1999, 49-59.

Higgins, Leta Fee, *Guidelines for Establishing an Information Systems Audit Function* (Altamonte Springs, FL: The Institute of Internal Auditors, 1990).

The Institute of Internal Auditors Research Foundation and the Information Systems Audit and Control Foundation, *UNIX: Its Use, Control, and Audit* (Altamonte Springs, FL: The Institute of Internal Auditors Research Foundation, 1995).

Luo, Dongxin, and Jack L. Armitage, "A Risk Analysis Approach to Control and Audit in a Network Environment," *Internal Auditing*, Fall 1996, 13-22.

The Proceedings of The IIA Research Foundation and Advanced Technology Committee's 1993 Advanced Technology Forum, *Advanced Technology Forum: Audit, Control, and Security Issues in Networks* (Altamonte Springs, FL: The Institute of Internal Auditors Research Foundation, 1993).

Sears, Brian P., *Internal Auditing Manual* (New York: RIA, 2003). (See Chapter G3, "IS Auditing Techniques.")

Tener, William T., *Adapting the Integrated Audit Approach* (Altamonte Springs, FL: The Institute of Internal Auditors Research Foundation, 1992).

Valente, George, "Hackers, Crackers, and Sniffers," *Internal Auditor*, October 1996, 52-55.

Weatherholt, Nancy D., Arthur H. Gilbert, Jr., and David W. Cornell, "UNIX: In with the New," *Internal Auditing*, Winter 1996, 34-38.

Weaver, Michelle, Somnath Bhattacharya, and Stuart Galup, "Effective Software Management: Its Time Has Come in Internal Auditing," *Internal Auditing*, May/June 2000, 3-13.

Multiple-choice Questions

1. A series of instructions telling a computer how to process data or files is defined as a:
   a. Network.
   b. System.
   c. Program.
   d. Modem.

2. Software that directs and assists the execution of application programs is referred to as the:
   a. Operating system.
   b. Utility program system.
   c. Database management system.
   d. Compiler system.

3. Which of the following control features is the most effective protection against unauthorized access to an online system?
   a. Online access unavailable except during normal working hours.
   b. Backup and recovery procedures.
   c. Policy prohibiting unauthorized access.
   d. Passwords.

4. A savings and loan association wants an information system that allows members to make transfers and inquiries over the phone. For this, the system must be capable of:
   a. Online processing.
   b. Multiprocessing.
   c. Batch processing.
   d. Distributed processing.

5. Which of the following statements would be an appropriate reason for the internal audit department not to participate in the systems development process?
   a. Participation would affect audit independence, and the auditor would not be able to perform an objective review after the system is implemented.
   b. Participation would delay project implementation.
   c. Participation would cause the auditor to be labeled as a partial owner of the application, and the auditor would then have to share the blame for any problems that remain in the system.
   d. None of the above.

6. In one company, the application systems must be in service 24 hours a day. The company's senior management and information systems management have worked hard to ensure that the information systems recovery plan supports the business disaster recovery plan. A crucial aspect of recovery planning for the company is ensuring that:
   a. Organizational and operational changes are reflected in the recovery plans.
   b. Changes to systems are tested thoroughly before being placed into production.
   c. Management personnel can fill in for operations staff should the need arise.
   d. Capacity planning procedures accurately predict workload changes.

7. Which of the following is necessary to determine what would constitute a disaster for an organization?
   a. Risk analysis.
   b. File and equipment backup requirements analysis.
   c. Vendor supply agreement analysis.
   d. Contingent facility contract analysis.

8. A program that edits a group of source language statements for syntax errors and translates the statements into an object program is a(n):
   a. Interpreter.
   b. Compiler.
   c. Debugger.
   d. Encrypter.

9. Corrosion of electrical contacts in computer equipment is most likely the result of a(n):
   a. Buildup of static electricity.
   b. High humidity level.
   c. Intermittent power failure.
   d. Excessive dust level.

10. An organization's IS help-desk function is usually a responsibility of the:
    a. Applications development unit.
    b. Systems programming unit.
    c. IS operations unit.
    d. User departments.

11. Which of the following would not be appropriate to consider in the physical design of a data center?
    a. Evaluation of potential risks from railroad lines and highways.
    b. Use of biometric access systems.
    c. Design of authorization tables for operating system access.
    d. Inclusion of an uninterruptible power supply system and surge protection.

12. Minimizing the likelihood of unauthorized editing of production programs, job control language, and operating system software can best be accomplished by:
    a. Database access reviews.
    b. Compliance reviews.
    c. Good change control procedures.
    d. Effective network security software.

13. Users in one department of a company developed a batch mainframe program to obtain financial information for their cost center. The program extracts data from the general ledger system master file backup tape. The program calls for the current generation of the tape backup. Which of the following error conditions are the users most likely to become aware of?
    a. A preliminary monthly closing file was used.
    b. The job did not complete successfully.
    c. The wrong program version was used.
    d. The program contained errors in its processing logic.

Chapter 14
Information Systems Auditing - II

Application controls. Input controls. Processing controls. Output controls. Audit trails. Impact of e-business. Vendor-supplied software. Personal and end-user computing. Distributed processing. Documentation. Efficiency in information systems. Legal requirements.

• •

Application Controls

Application controls are those controls that provide assurance that specific applications will be processed in accordance with management's specifications and that processing will be accurate, timely, authorized, and complete. Following is a list of exposures arising from application processing and related controls — input, processing, and output — that reduce those exposures:

- **Loss of input:** Transactions transmitted from one location to another are particularly subject to loss.

- **Duplication of input:** This may occur when an input item is erroneously thought to be lost.

- **Inaccurate recording of input:** Wrong numbers or misspellings are common examples.

- **Missing information:** This, obviously, makes input incomplete.

- **Unrecorded transactions:** These include not only accidental failures but are also the result of theft and embezzlement.

- **Authorizations:** Authorizations covering a composite mass of transactions may be necessary because of the sheer volume of transactions, but the absence of management focus on individual items can let some improper transactions slip through.

- **Transactions:** Transactions initiated by the system include automatic stock reorders and payments to suppliers. If all is normal, the program acts as a control. But situations not anticipated in the design can cause serious difficulties.

- **Output sent incorrectly:** Output information is sent to the wrong people. Output is sent to its destination too late to be of value. Output is incorrect.

- **Large volumes of detected errors:** Complete analysis is physically impossible and/ or backlogs are frustrating.

- **Incomplete processing:** Programming errors or clerical errors.

- **Processing performed too late:** The processing may be correct, but the recognition of the items may not be timely.

- **Loss:** File lost during processing. The loss of knowledgeable people, coupled with the absence of adequate documentation.

Input Controls

Description

Input controls help strengthen the weak link in the chain of information systems (IS) events. All manner of checks and balances can be built into a program to assure proper processing, storage, and retrieval of data, but all of this is to no avail if the computer is presented with erroneous or incomplete data at the onset. Input controls can be devised to help. There should be assurance that whatever is received by the machine is complete. If controls are established close to the point of preparation of transactions, losses will be minimized.

A system of batch controls can provide assurance that no data is lost as it travels from place to place before it reaches the computer. One way of achieving batch control is to process all transactions for a specified period of time, total their values as part of a terminal or processing feature, and record and reconcile those totals on logs at different transfer points.

Real-time systems do not readily lend themselves to batch controls. At remote-terminal systems, items entered sporadically and by different people into the terminals are not easily batched. Whether batched or not, however, each entry can be displayed on the screen for visual verification. The displayed entry can be checked against corroborative data extracted from the database for visual tests. For example, entering an account number results in the system displaying a customer name and asking for verification. Also, each entry can be subjected to an edit program to make sure that each field has the proper numeric, alphabetic, or alphanumeric format. Finally, each entry can be checked for reasonableness or logic. For example, items showing more than 24 hours to a day may be rejected, or certain types of items may be originated by a particular department only.

When items have been rejected, there should be some method of ensuring the reentry of such material after it has been corrected.

Other input controls include:

- **Hash totals:** These are meaningless but highly useful because they add up numerical amounts of nonmonetary information to prevent loss during application processing. It is the change in the hash total that indicates if a file has been updated.

- **Format checks:** These indicate that data is entered in the proper mode and within designated fields.

- **Limit checks:** These make sure that input does not exceed a given numeric range, such as a maximum hourly workweek.

- **Reasonableness checks:** These are performed by comparing input with other information available within existing records. They can detect wildly erroneous data.

- **Field checks:** These indicate completeness of information, such as an address for a new customer.

- **Numerical checks:** These make sure that alphabetic data are not included in fields reserved for numeric data.

- **Historical comparisons:** These indicate whether current information is comparable with previous information.

- **Sequence checking:** This verifies the alphanumeric sequence of the key field in an item to be processed.

- **Overflow checking:** This is a programmatic check to prevent exceeding the capacity of a memory or field length to accept data (usually numeric). For example, a two-byte numeric field may only be able to contain a maximum value of 99. Adding 1 to this field would result in a value of 00.

- **Check digits:** This control is a function of other digits within a number and permits a mathematical algorithm to determine if the number has been keyed incorrectly (particularly helpful in detecting transposition errors). Popular examples of using check digits include credit card and bank account numbers.

- **Keystroke verification:** By entering data into keyboards a second time (and preferably by a different person), erroneous input can be detected via a mechanical signal.

- **Authorizations and approvals:** There are two types of authorizations. The first is advance permission. The second occurs after the fact and assumes that some edit or review took place.

- **Reconciliation and balancing:** There are two types of reconciliation. The first is to analyze differences; the second is to make tests of equality.

- **File labels:** These identify transactions, files, and outputs.

Input controls should have the following design criteria:

- **Updating transactions:** These processes involve large amounts of data and are usually repetitive. Such techniques as reasonableness checks and application program logic help control the input.

- **Inquiry:** These transactions do not change a file, but they may result in updating or file maintenance as a result of an inquiry. Inquiry logs usually control such access to the computer.

- **Error correction:** These transactions cause the most difficulty and are the hardest to control. Obviously, a problem already exists if error correction must take place. Also, error corrections often result in additional errors. Correction calls for analysis of the error reports, determination of the action required, need for new input, updating of files, entry of data into the proper files, and readjustment of balances to take the corrections into account.

Internal Audit

The majority of all errors introduced into systems are the result of input errors. Internal auditors should budget a significant portion of total staff hours to a review of input controls.

Some specific review steps are:

- Determine what program controls, such as online edits, have been included in the system. This can be accomplished through interviews with programmers, direct source code review (this can be very time-consuming), review of program abstracts, and examination of edit reports.

- Use an integrated test facility (see the next chapter for an explanation of this technique) to test the application for adequate input controls.

- Substantively test existing data on master and transaction files. If data have been accepted that are obviously incorrect (e.g., an incomplete social security number), input-control weaknesses can be assumed.

- For batch systems, observe balancing procedures.

- Examine documents for evidence of authorizations and approvals.

- Using audit software (see the next chapter), determine the relative percentage of transactions that represent corrections to previous input. Usually, application systems will have specific reversing transactions whose accumulated total may be used as a barometer of application input control strength.

- Determine if data entry personnel are making inappropriate business decisions by correcting important data without consulting the originator.

- Determine if re-keying or verification of data entry is used for highly critical data.

Processing Controls

Description

Traditionally, processing controls have been applied to the machine room. Their object has been to prevent or discourage the improper manipulation of data and to ensure the continued, satisfactory operation of both hardware and software. Increasingly, these controls are moving outside the room where the computer equipment is located.

Access to the computer should be limited to those authorized to operate the equipment. Object programs should be accessible only to the equipment operators. This separation renders it difficult to make unauthorized modifications to the program. Similarly, programmers should not have uncontrolled access to the computer locations, files, or records. Their knowledge of IS programs makes data manipulation particularly easy.

Operators should not have unlimited access to the system. They should be allowed access only to the program information needed to set up the equipment and respond to programmed halts. The data processing supervisor should respond to any unprogrammed "abends" (ABnormal ENDS or halts) for programs that have already been tested and approved for use.

Any operator intervention should be made a matter of record. Indeed, most modern systems have a console log that lists all operator intervention within the system. Because of the ever-present possibility of wrongful manipulation, these additional precautions should be considered:

- Require the presence of at least two trained operators during the equipment operations.
- Rotate assignments among operators.

The systems should have sufficient built-in controls. For example, if a system builds a series of temporary files as it processes the data, each succeeding step should check a control total built by the previous step in a "system control file." If the control total does not agree with the sum of the input records on that step, the system should flag the error (probable hardware error or software bug) and terminate processing. These controls are ideal because they require no operator review or balancing by humans — but they are performed consistently during the many steps of processing.

Another control feature is a date and file total check. Well-controlled systems will retain totals from the previous run (dollars and count) as well as the date and time of the last run of the application. If the application is submitted in error the same day, an error message will be issued, since the system knows that the application is not supposed to be run twice in one day. Also, if duplicate data are read into the system, an error message will be generated. The reasoning behind this is that it is extremely unlikely that input totals for two different days will be *exactly* the same.

The use of appropriate internal labels is almost a required processing control in a large data processing environment. Applications can easily have 200 programs that read related files during processing. Reading the correct file (and version of that file) is essential and should be routinely handled by a tape- or disk-management system.

Error-handling procedures should be well documented. Error messages should be clear and should indicate appropriate corrective action. Operators should be prohibited from overriding label or device errors.

In a growing number of minicomputer and LAN server installations, the computer operator is more a baby-sitter than a technician. "Turnkey systems" include a combination of integrated application software and prescheduled operating system software that remove a great deal of the human factor from the day-to-day operations of the computer. The operator is relegated to a servant function that must:

- See that the hardware is properly turned on and the initial program load (IPL) performed.
- See that appropriate media paper is loaded in the printer for statements or checks.
- See that tapes are mounted for backup of transaction and master files.
- See that computer room maintenance (vacuuming of the printer, installing new printer ribbons or toner, etc.) is performed.

The turnkey system manager function typically has a schedule of applications to be run and the correct order of execution. The operator has little ability to intervene in the processing and to access data in the files.

In turnkey systems, a great deal of the processing is governed by parameter files (called control records, specification files, organizational control files, and a number of other names). These files are provided by the software vendor to allow the user organization to customize the system to the business objectives of the organization. These files will contain a number of options for the same activity and the user organization will select the one that fits the way the user wants to operate. For example:

- In a bank, the software vendor provides the ability to perform interest calculations on deposits by compounding annually, semiannually, quarterly, monthly, or daily or to pay simple interest.
- In a finance company, interest can be calculated on a 365-day calendar (actual days in the year) or a 360-day calendar (12 thirty-day months per year).
- In a sales organization, 2%, 10, Net 30, or no discount; FOB our dock or the customers.
- In a manufacturing organization, inventory accounting can be chosen as FIFO, LIFO, weighted average, or discrete item.

These processing parameters and myriad like them are controlled by designated management personnel. The people controlling these factors have far more control now than computer operators had in the past. This control approach is commonly found in a PC processing environment.

Internal Audit

The internal auditor's goal in reviewing processing controls is to assess whether the application processes input data in an accurate and timely manner, in accordance with management's intent, and with no unauthorized modifications of data.

Some specific review steps are:

- Determine whether proper segregation of duties has been maintained, i.e., individuals with processing responsibilities do not input data, distribute reports, or reconcile control totals. If segregation of duties is inadequate, the internal auditor should determine if compensating controls exist.

- Determine if transactions are retained so data files may be reconstructed, if necessary (e.g., if a tape breaks in the middle, can the file be easily reconstructed?).

- Determine if transaction trails are adequate to trace data back to the point of origin.

- Determine if internal labels, system-control files, and date checks are used in the application.

- Verify processing accuracy of critical transactions using the "test data" or "test base" method (see next chapter for explanation).

- Determine if run-to-run totals are maintained by a data-control group.

- Observe routine processing of the system and note whether console or operator input is required for processing. If online system-control files are maintained, determine what controls exist to make sure that processing options are set correctly. For example, a bank savings-account system might have a system-control file that specifies the dates for interest posting. Without proper controls, those dates could be set incorrectly, resulting in incorrect processing, customer irritation, and public embarrassment for the bank.

- Determine if "before and after" update images are printed when data is modified on files.

- Determine if the date, terminal ID, and responsible individual are shown on transaction trails (particularly important for online real-time systems).

- Determine procedures for reprocessing transactions previously found in error. If a suspense file is used, examine dates on the file to determine if suspense items are being cleared in a timely manner.

- Examine rerun/restart procedures for the application. Controls should exist to verify that the files, once reconstructed, are correct.

- Review operators' run instructions for completeness and accuracy. If, for example, the sequence of "jobs" is listed incorrectly, an operator unfamiliar with the application may submit jobs in the wrong order, resulting in incorrect output.

- Examine records showing entries into parameter files.

- Examine any records maintained by computer operations that show processing errors by application.

- If the assistance of an IS audit specialist is available, determine if summaries of program operation are available.

Output Controls

Description

Output controls govern the accuracy and reasonableness of the information processed. Output controls also cover the retention of output reports. The totals of records processed should agree with the total record input. Prenumbered forms can help control output since these can be accounted for. As an example, the number of payroll check forms can be checked against input records.

In some organizations, piles of paper are printed in every cycle and the piles are discarded at specified periods. Millions of trees are sacrificed on the altar of printed reports. Some organizations print only reports that must be acted on while reports used for research (audit trails) are recorded on other media. Action reports include new account journals that should be reviewed, past due receivables listing, changes of customer addresses, etc. Research reports include transaction listings, posting journals and trial balances that are referred to only when a transaction has to be traced through the system. Research reports can be stored on Computer Originated Microfiche (COM or just fiche), on WORM optical disks (Write Once, Read Multiple) or CD-ROM (Compact Disk-Read Only Memory). These media are permanent, unchangeable storage systems.

- **Microfiche** is produced by writing the report on a terminal screen and taking a picture of the screen onto film in a very reduced size. A 4" by 6" sheet of film will contain 100 or more pages of system reports. This entire process takes place within a sealed unit at very high speed. The reports on fiche can be seen full size on a special viewer and a photographic copy can be produced.

- **Optical disks** (WORM and CD-ROM) are broadly related to the compact disks used for music recording. The data is physically burned into the surface rather than magnetically encoded as on a magnetic disk. The data is a digital "picture" of the report as it would have been printed on paper (a PRN or print file). The optical drive is often attached to a PC where it can be viewed on the monitor or printed on the PC's printer.[1]

Output controls also include the proper handling of exceptions. When valid data are rejected, the fault may lie with machine malfunction or with operator error. Console typewriter sheets, a form of output, should be maintained to show the reason for valid data rejection and the steps taken to correct errors. Larger, more modern mainframe systems will not have hard copy console output, but store the equivalent on disk. These logs can be printed as needed.

System output should conform to the following standards:

- **Reports:** These should be timely, accurate, and meaningful. Confidentiality should be assured. Format should be useful to the reader. Large amounts of data should be summarized. Recipients should be polled periodically to see whether they still need the reports.

- **Working documents:** These take the form of checks, savings bonds, purchase orders, etc. Security is obviously an important matter to consider, along with assurance that input is balanced with output.

- **Reference documents:** These are used to show what was in the computer if computer services were interrupted. This kind of output is typically magnetic.

- **Error reports:** While usually small in volume, these may be complex and difficult to deal with. They are sent to the right people for corrective action, and they should be controlled to make sure the action is taken and the corrected reports are returned. Follow-up is essential. If errors exceed a critical level, the problem should be reported to an appropriate level of management.

Internal Audit

Some specific review steps are:

- Determine whether a control group or the user balances and reconciles outputs.

- Determine if exceptions are flagged on reports.

- Examine totals on reports for reasonableness. Independent testing of critical field totals may be necessary.

- Determine if reports are relevant (or even used), timely, reliable, and organized (sorted) properly.

- Determine if an output log and distribution list are maintained. Determine if reports are lost or misrouted.

- Determine if a user control group uses a checklist to decide whether all reports have been received.

- Determine if the application has a mechanism for creating extra copies of the reports without actually rerunning the entire processing stream.

- Determine if report headings are meaningful, if the report is numbered, dated, and if it shows the organizational entity for which the report was printed.

- Determine if a report list, which summarizes all reports created during a batch run, is available to users.

- Determine if dual-custody and other controls are in force to protect negotiable/sensitive outputs such as checks, stock certificates, or payroll listings.

- Determine if appropriate retention policies have been established for application output such as hard copy reports and microfiche.

- Determine if reporting standards are being met.

The internal auditor should also determine that output reports are properly disposed of. An alert and inquisitive auditor observed a truck parked beside a trash container with a man loading printout paper from the container into the truck. The man responded to the auditor's question saying that the paper was being taken for recycling. The auditor pursued the issue with the security manager who found that no such activity was scheduled. Because the auditor noted the tag number on the truck, the truck was traced to a former employee of the organization who was now working for a competitor.[2]

Audit Trails

Description

Transactions should be traceable from their initiation through all intermediate steps to final reporting and archival. This ability permits verification of transactions and correction of errors. In the days of manual systems, the trail was visible and continuous. Today, information systems have rendered those trails invisible. There is no one-to-one relation between the entry and the exit of a transaction.

Auditors auditing around the computer are put at a disadvantage. They depend on the integrity of the trail through the computer. With that dependence, they cannot assume that what went into the systems came out uncontaminated, because programmers can easily disguise the trail within the computer.

Other problems compound the difficulty. Suppose a person is in the process of initiating a transaction and the system fails during that process. That person may not know whether the transaction was ever completed. The absence of a transaction trail may prevent correction or corroboration of results.

Trails and controls do not exist solely for the convenience of the auditor; neither are they necessarily a management tool. Their function is to trace and correct exceptions. The trail helps personnel correct errors and control the quality of the transactions.[3]

At the same time, the review of all the transactions processed through the information system is burdensome and expensive. Computerized edits are more desirable. No system is perfect. Therefore some form of assurance of continuity from input to output is needed — even obligatory. This assurance is required to support tax transactions. Indeed, the IRS recognized the desirability of machine-readable transaction trails in Revenue Ruling 71.20, holding that "machine-sensible data media may be considered records within the meaning of the revenue code."

Internal Audit

Internal auditors must contribute to the incorporation of transaction trails. They should not dictate the particular trail; that would affect their independence. But they must be able to satisfy themselves and management that needed transaction trails and controls are in force. They cannot hold themselves out as "authorizing" the system; they should evaluate the proposed system and, if needed controls are lacking, report the absence to management. Internal auditors are an important user of every system.

The internal auditor also should keep in mind the needs of other users. For example, those in the accounting department may need certain transaction trails and controls so that they can rely upon the accuracy of the information they may need for financial reports.

In terms of transaction verification, internal auditors have historically been more comfortable when they can walk a visible trail — from account balance to the record of an event, from the record of an event to the account balance, and from any point within the process. Non-accounting activities are no different.

In online systems, however, hard copy source documents are often lacking; transaction trails are not visible and palpable. The auditor must therefore look to the system to provide assurance that normal transactions are properly processed and that abnormal transactions are detected, rejected (and possibly placed on a suspense file), and brought up for review.

Since the system is to be relied upon, changes in it become critical to the auditor — changes in the ways data are processed within the system, changes in the environment in which the system operates, and changes in those sensors that observe the input material. For this reason, an event concept may be employed.

The event concept refers to the review of the entire system at a particular point or period of time — the audit determination of the aggregate effectiveness of all controls as the system responds to events that enter and flow through it. If the system is reliable, it does not necessarily follow that the transactions flowing through it must be acceptable. Clearly, a reliance on the system is conditioned on the continuity of the system. So discontinuities and changes must be given careful audit review.

For the internal auditors to be able to rely on a system as a basis for accepting the validity of transactions, they must be capable of analyzing the system and its controls. This calls for expertise in evaluating data processing systems. If the auditors are not themselves expert, they must be able to recruit such expertise.

Impact of E-business

The main difference between traditional business and e-business is that the customer is not physically present or in joint communication with a representative when the transaction takes place. The transaction occurs on the Internet. E-business is considered by many to be the most significant change in business in the century. While different individuals may define terms differently, it is clear that e-business has its roots in EDI. Some consider e-business to be only business-to-business transactions and e-commerce to be only business-to-consumer transactions. However, we will use the terms interchangeably.

Entities may make use of e-commerce to sell to, provide information to, and/or to communication with consumers. In doing so the firm must consider the costs involved, the controls present to ensure the validity of transactions, and the protection security of data. In dealing with e-business, a firm must consider many of the same issues as well as the amount of data that it will allow its "partners" to have access to and the portal(s) that will be used. For example, as "bidding" for goods and the demands for scheduling information becomes more prevalent, management and the internal auditor must consider the risk that competitors and others will obtain access to this information. This is especially critical when firms do business internationally. In some cultures it is expected that firms will have employees attempt to "crack" into competitors' systems and obtain confidential information.

Vendor-supplied Software

Description

In many industries, applications used by different organizations are sufficiently similar to permit development of software "packages" by outside vendors. These packages usually consist of a series of programs and related documentation. Increasingly, software vendors provide a multitude of options that permit the organization to tailor the package to its business environment.

For example, a payroll system will invoke one of many tax tables in its net pay computations, depending on the location of the organization. Another option may be the specification of a particular currency to be used for all or part of the firm's employees. Generally, these options do not require programming changes and are initiated entirely by the user department.

The trend toward powerful and flexible "off-the-shelf" software has resulted in a number of benefits and concerns:

- Documentation of packaged software is often (but not always) superior to that of in-house systems.

- Testing, at least for well-known major packages, is generally more thorough than in-house systems.

- If key IS personnel are lost (in a disaster or from turnover), vendor personnel — as a last resort — can be used to resolve immediate processing problems.

- The flexibility of vendor-supplied systems can itself become a concern. Less-skilled or diligent users can inadvertently set parameters incorrectly and cause erroneous processing.

- The burden of detailed application knowledge may be shifted from IS personnel to the user. Users new to the system or to automation in general may not anticipate the time and dedication required to understand and control a complex system.

- Most software vendors issue "releases" (system changes) annually or more frequently. If these changes are required for period-end processing, but are not given to customer organizations well in advance, the programmers will be under extreme pressure to quickly install the changes. The risk of error increases significantly under these conditions due to inadequate testing.

- The flexibility of vendor packages sometimes comes at a price — possibly as decreased processing speed or massive increases in disk-storage needs. Any package should be "benchmarked" with transaction volumes comparable to the organization's usual workload. In some cases, packages have been purchased and never implemented because the system hardware was not sufficiently powerful to process the application in a timely manner. (Applications programmed in fourth-generation languages have been particularly vulnerable to this deficiency. Forth-generation languages, while flexible and easy to use, are often inefficient for routine processing of large data volumes.)

- There is often pressure from user departments to modify vendor packages. Wise IS management will resist such pressure and place the burden of proof on the user to demonstrate the need for any changes. The accumulation of changes to a vendor-supplied system can eventually destroy its integrity, increasing the risk of subsequent changes. In addition, retrofitting custom changes is necessary for each new vendor release.

Enterprise-wide Software

Enterprise-wide software is one type of vendor-supplied software that has been of significant interest to the largest firms and is becoming increasingly of interest to many large- and medium-size firms. These systems typically provide single entry into the system and the elimination of the "stovepipe" mentality. Hence a sale entry will update credit, purchasing, and manufacturing scheduling as needed in a real-time environment. The internal auditor needs to be closely involved in such applications because of the extensive reengineering that is typically involved and the costs of implementation.

The reengineering required usually substantially reduces all traditional controls that the internal auditor has typically relied upon. In addition the auditor should monitor the customization of the software to his or her situation. While such customization at first appears to be desirable, it may present substantial problems in future upgrades. While such vendors have historically supported all releases (versions) of their software, it appears that they may not do so in the future. The more customization the less likely the firm will realize the benefit of relatively easy upgrades.

The use of enterprise-wide software requires the entity to carefully consider the systems development life cycle. This is especially important given the need to devote full-time functional area personnel to the project. Such applications typically involve the extensive use of consultants and the internal auditor should take an active role in evaluating the credentials and abilities of the proposed team.

Other areas that are critical that should be considered by the auditor include the general plan to train personnel, how the auditor will audit the systems, and the conversion plans. The conversion plan is especially critical because of the integrated nature of the system.

Internal Audit

The internal auditor should focus on two key factors when reviewing vendor-supplied software packages: (1) the evaluation and selection process, and (2) the maintenance of the integrity of the package over time.

Any vendor package to be purchased should go through a rigorous evaluation. Some of the factors to be considered include:

- Stability of vendor.
- Installed base of users.
- Age of system.
- Satisfaction of current users.
- Quality control standards of vendor.
- Processing speed on the organization's system(s).
- Adequacy of documentation.
- Availability of vendor hot line/help desk.
- Flexibility of system (e.g., does system have a report writer that allows users to develop reports without the aid of the programming department?).

The second key control factor considered by the internal auditor should be maintenance procedures. Releases issued by the vendor should be installed on a timely basis. Data processing management should know at all times what software releases are currently running on the system, as well as the version numbers of the most current release available from the vendor. For example, an organization may be running release 1.1 of XYZ accounts payable system. Release 1.2 is waiting to be installed and the vendor has just released version 1.4. The risk to the organization is that, at some point, the vendor will drop support on the earlier releases and the newer releases correct problems or provide additional information. It is very important for a data processing organization to stay current on all software releases (including operating-system software, which nearly always is supplied by vendors).

In organizations with integrated software (usually from the same vendor), releases must be kept "in sync." For example, a bank may have a customer information system linked to a check-accounting system. Version 1.5 of the customer information system corresponds (in time) to version 4.2 of the check accounting system. If the two releases of the customer information system are installed (i.e., to version 1.7) while the check accounting system is not upgraded, the two systems may no longer interface properly. For example, one system may create an interface file that in a previous release was 200 characters per record but is now 225 characters. The other system, expecting a 200-character record, would "abend" and issue the error message "wrong length record."

Many of the day-to-day processing errors found in organizations using vendor-supplied software can be traced to custom changes of vendor source code. If the changes are not properly reinstalled on top of new releases, erroneous processing will result. The internal auditor should review the organization's change controls to verify that a separately maintained "patch deck" properly identifies all custom changes.

The most damaging practice in software maintenance — heavy modification of vendor code with no intention of installing new vendor releases — often begins when IS management is in a "fire fighting" mode. Installation of new releases is repeatedly postponed and vendor code is so heavily modified that the system goes beyond the point of no return. It becomes, at that point, an essentially in-house system without the benefit of vendor support.

Personal and End-user Computing

Description

The rapid development of information technology has stimulated information-processing activities at the end-user level. With storage capacities in the hundreds and even thousands of megabytes (i.e., a megabyte is a million characters of data) and processing speeds in the millions of instructions per second, PCs can now process large volumes of transactions in reasonable time periods. Increasingly, data that is specific to one department or organizational unit is being processed on small systems. Often, packaged application software for the PC can be obtained at a fraction of the cost of comparable mainframe software. In addition, the user has the advantage of greater responsiveness and control over the application (i.e., no need to wait months for the data processing department to provide a report). Many PC applications can create a data-exchange file that can be used by popular spreadsheet or database programs for analysis.

End-user processing with PCs does, however, potentially expose the organization to loss or corruption of data, errors in programming logic, loss of processing services, and fraudulent alteration of programs and data. Some specific control issues are:

- Mainframe environments are generally organized with incompatible duties segregated. Computer operations, data entry, programming, and balancing are performed by separate employees. End-user computing, on the other hand, usually has at least data entry and operations combined. Frequently, there is no segregation of duties at all.

- PCs are often kept in areas that are not physically secured, permitting data or program tampering in off-hours.

- Unlike most mainframe operating systems, PC operating systems are notoriously easy to manipulate. In the absence of special software/hardware controls, data can be easily modified without an audit trail.

- Decades of development on mainframes has resulted in certain basic controls that are usually in force in a data center. End users typically do not have such a background and fail to provide safeguards such as regular backups of important files and supervisory reviews of spreadsheet and database programming.

- Unless a central PC department (sometimes called an information center) coordinates purchases, end users may buy hardware/software that is not compatible with the rest of the organization. This has practical results:

  (1) The PCs may not be able to "talk" to the mainframe.
  (2) Files on one PC may not be readable by other PCs in the organization.
  (3) The user department may not receive adequate technical assistance if their software is not used elsewhere.

- The number of people in society that understand the operation and programming of PCs is increasing dramatically. Whereas mainframe knowledge is usually restricted to a small number of specialists, PC hobbyists abound.

- There is a pernicious tendency among users to regard computer-printed materials as always correct; some refer to this as Garbage In, Gospel Out. Experienced data processing personnel, living with the daily reality of software "bugs," tend to regard results from the system with skepticism. Users should be made aware that even popular, well-established software can have subtle errors that only surface under unusual conditions.

- PC hardware and software vendors may lack the stability of mainframe vendors. Should the vendor supplying the hardware or software go out of business, users may be saddled with unsupported and often unmodifiable software or hardware.

It would appear from the above discussion that end-user computing is extremely difficult to control. In practice, however, there are a number of safeguards that can promote secure and accurate processing in a PC environment:

- Commercial backup software is available that can back up a hard disk in a matter of minutes onto CD-ROM or other media.

- Sensitive data can be "encrypted" on the hard disk (or on CD-ROMs or floppy diskettes). This process uses a mathematical algorithm to scramble data into a format that cannot be readily deciphered. A password is entered when the data are encrypted. The same password is required when the data are decrypted (i.e., converted to clear text). For very sensitive applications, the safest procedure is to store data on removable media — which is subsequently locked up. All files stored on the hard disk leave residual data, even after deletion of the file. Unless special precautions are taken (using "wipe disk" utilities that overlay unused portions of the disk with all zeros), "hacker" software can retrieve this residual data.

- Security "cards" are available for PCs. These devices slip into an available slot and take control of the PC operating system. Anyone using the PC must sign on with an ID and a password. The date, time, duration of the session, and ID of the user are recorded continually on memory stored on the card. The security administrator alone can access this card's memory and print out the audit trail. A midnight session on a personal computer, for example, might indicate the need for scrutiny of a particular employee. Security bolts for the outside of the PC make removal of the card difficult. In addition, security cannot be bypassed by "booting" off a floppy diskette.

- The integrity of software used by several departments can be maintained by the use of a master version. The master is periodically copied to each PC using the software. This promotes uniformity (and accuracy) of processing. For example, assume a sophisticated spreadsheet model is used to price commercial loans in a bank. If factors built into the model, such as prime rate, loan risks, and cost per hour to service the loan, are altered, the loan decision could be incorrect, reducing overall profitability. New copies of the pricing model, created from the master copy, make sure that no errors are made from inadvertent changes to the spreadsheet.

- Manual controls should be very strong when transactions are processed by a PC. Daily balancing, manual review of reports, examination of individual checks and other negotiable instruments created on the PC, reasonableness checks, and other such procedures prevent accidental or intentional alteration of data.

As the use of local-area networks increases, these networks have the potential of compensating for weaker stand-alone PC controls.

The network server (host computer) may provide file management, backup and recovery, program version control, access control, and other security features. Network servers can control the software usage and memory configuration of individual users.

As in other areas of the organization, PC controls should match the risks. If the PC is used only for word processing or noncritical applications, simple backups of the files may be the only formal controls needed. If, on the other hand, complex lease-or-buy decisions involving millions of dollars are made on the basis of a PC model, controls should be strengthened accordingly.

Internal Audit

The internal auditor's review of end-user computing should be directed toward the higher-risk applications. If a personal computer is used simply for non-confidential memorandum preparation, the level of review should be minimal, if any. On the other hand, if a PC system is used to bill customers for millions of dollars, the internal auditor should target the system for detailed review.

Specific review steps are:

- Determine if policies have been written for the acquisition of PC hardware and software. Determine if these policies result in increased organization-wide compatibility.

- Determine if, for important applications, files are backed up regularly.

- Determine if users (including mainframe, fourth-generation language users) are properly trained.

- Determine if physical security over vulnerable PC applications is adequate.

- Determine if data security controls have been established. Determine if sensitive data can be inappropriately accessed.

- Determine if standards have been established for spreadsheet construction and documentation, when such applications provide input for major decisions.

- Examine vendor programs on PCs and compare with invoices in order to determine if illegal copies are being used.

- Determine if encryption of highly sensitive PC files is used in vulnerable areas.

- Determine if custom software has been programmed for user departments. If so, determine whether the vendor has provided adequate documentation. Assess the risks to the organization if the vendor goes out of business.

- Check the operation of security "cards."

Distributed Processing

Description

Information technology has evolved substantially in the past 30 years. In the early days of data processing, the majority of organizations processed all significant transactions on a central mainframe and performed no significant processing on smaller (distributed) computers. Starting in the early 1970s, however, minicomputers began moving from the factory floor into the white-collar office environment. These early machines were used to augment or, in some cases, replace the central computer. As networks grew, the strain on the central computer became more and more obvious. Users experienced increasingly slow online terminal response and applications (running under a smaller slice of the CPU pie) took longer and longer to process. Minicomputers, with gigabytes (1,000 megabytes) of disk storage and increasingly large main memories, were able to control up to several hundred terminals and thus reduce the overhead on the central computer.

Currently distributed processing takes many forms. Following is a sampling (by no means comprehensive) of DP (distributed processing) configurations and applications:

- Online terminals are connected to a minicomputer that is responsible for editing data entry and storing transactions for later (batch) transmissions to a central mainframe where corporate databases are updated. The transmission could be via short- or long-distance telecommunications or through physical transfer of a magnetic tape.

- Minicomputers are used to completely process the data (including posting to accounts). Summary information is transmitted to a central computer for consolidated reporting and control.

- PCs with programmed editing capabilities are linked to the mainframe (usually via a board with coaxial cable thin wire (Ethernet) co-ax, twisted pair or optical fiber, but sometimes via high-speed modem). Data are edited at the PC. After validation, input data are transmitted to the central computer for processing. The PCs sometimes double as terminals for online inquiry.

- A remote printer is used to print checks or other time-sensitive information. In this rather prosaic form of DP, print files are transmitted via telephone lines to a location distant from the central site. Checks are sometimes printed in such areas to take advantage of the "float." Controls are maintained to prevent print files from being transmitted more than once and creating duplicate checks.

- PCs are linked together over a short distance (usually less than one mile) into an integrated network, called a local-area network (LAN). Inquiry, data entry, and processing are shared by the PCs. One PC is usually dedicated to network administration, and handles common disk storage and file access. This dedicated PC is often called a "file server." Entire LANs can be connected to a minicomputer, the central mainframe, and/or to other LANs. There are many configurations of these networks.[4]

The network software used for PC-based LANs is much more than simple communications software. In most cases, it is an operating system that supersedes the traditional single user operating system and contains complex options, including security. The level of knowledge of the LAN administrator is critical to the sound operation of the LAN.

Following is a list of risk factors found in a typical distributed data processing network:

- Segregation of duties may be lacking.[5] In many distributed computing environments, one person performs data entry, computer operations, limited programming, and other incompatible duties. Under such conditions, it is essential that an independent reconciliation and review of critical data be performed.

- Adequate program change controls may be lacking.[6] In a distributed system using minicomputers with stand-alone programs, undocumented and uncontrolled program changes can reduce the overall integrity of the distributed system. Assume, for example, that an organization has 10 minicomputer sites. Each site has a data-entry program that is responsible for editing. Nonuniform changes to individual site programs could lead to varying levels of editing and potentially incorrect changes to data transmitted to the host system (i.e., central computer). Without safeguards, computer fraud could be easily perpetrated at the local site level. Even without the fraud exposure, the practical burden of maintaining 10 versions of the same software could become a maintenance nightmare. Organizations are now implementing central PC LAN support groups to provide centralized control, relieving users of technical responsibilities. The tendency to centralize controls while decentralizing computing and information management is an essential element in empowering IS users. Vendors are recognizing this by including control options as features in their system software.

- Software often have powerful utility programs that can modify data on hard disk or tape without an audit trail. If users become proficient with these utilities, they can modify data for fraudulent purposes or (more likely) to correct data felt to be in error. Unfortunately, using a utility to modify data will often throw an application system out of balance or cause internal processing errors, since the application may not recognize that changes have been made outside the normal data-entry process. In addition, the lack of an audit trail is a serious control problem.

- Interpretive languages may be used to modify data. Like utility programs, interpretive languages such as BASIC permit the user to modify data outside the control of the application. High-level languages are even more powerful than the utilities because their function is not restricted to "housekeeping" chores. If the organization's applications are written in an interpretive language, modifications to these programs can be readily performed by knowledgeable users. Ideally, only object code should be used to process critical applications in a distributed environment. Though it is technically possible to modify object code, the technical skill required is beyond most users and, indeed, beyond the capability of most application programmers. It is desirable that compiling of source code be performed on another computer (a so-called "development" computer) and only object code catalogued into the minicomputer.

- Access controls may be lacking in minicomputer systems and likely will be missing in PC systems. A full-scope data-security package, as described earlier in this chapter, is often used in the mainframe environment to control terminal access. In a distributed environment, however, such controls may be less effective or missing altogether. While most commercial systems today have at least a veneer of data-security features (e.g., require a password to sign on), some important features may be missing. For example, passwords may not be internally encrypted so that a user can browse the password file with a utility. The password hierarchy may not be properly segregated between browse, update, and highly sensitive functions. Probably the greatest exposure, however, is lack of user concern for data security and access controls. Over the years since mainframe computers were introduced, most mainframe data processing organizations have been stung by one or more access-control breakdowns. Inexperienced users operating a minicomputer/PC in a distributed environment often will not have such experiences to provide them with a sense of caution. This market is beginning to provide the traditional systems control elements, as described in *Systems Auditability and Control (SAC)*. However, such controls have a cost that may include additional software, reduced performance of the system, and complicated management procedures. However, in general these costs are justified when considered from a cost-benefit perspective.

Internal Audit

Distributed processing presents a significant challenge to the internal auditor. The systems may be geographically separate, have different vendors, and be difficult to audit from a technical perspective. Some of the areas to be reviewed by the internal auditor include:

- **Segregation of duties:** For example, if a minicomputer accumulates daily stock issues, the same person should not approve issues, authorize adjustments to totals accumulated by the system, and also operate the equipment.

- **Programming standards:** If minicomputer programs are prepared by organization programmers, a manual of programming standards should be prepared and enforced. The programs should be as carefully documented as the programs used on large computers. If PCs are used, commercial software such as spreadsheets and database management systems, should be subject to programming controls. The programming of spreadsheets and databases should be reviewed by knowledgeable supervisors or co-workers.

- **Program-change control:** The internal auditor should review the procedures for authorizing and installing program changes. There should be a means to periodically make sure programs that are required to be the same at various points in the DP network are in fact the same.

- **Procedural controls:** If the DP system is used for business applications, the procedural controls (input, processing, and output) should be reviewed to make sure standard control techniques are used (such as file balancing).

- **Data security and access controls:** The internal auditor should be thoroughly familiar with the access controls built into the system and should evaluate them in terms of the risk to the organization. Password administration, in particular, should be reviewed by the auditor. Passwords that are shared by an entire department, rather than being unique to each individual, are basically worthless, since transactions cannot be traced to specific individuals. In addition to passwords, badges and plastic cards can also be used. Of increasing interest are fingerprints, voiceprints, and retinal scans. The auditor needs to be familiar with the threats to data through the system. A way suggested by Cohen to organize these threats in order to evaluate them is to consider a two-by-two matrix, which has the nature of the threat for the columns (whether accidental or deliberate) and the source of the threat (whether internal or external) as rows.[7]

- **Database integrity:** If databases or portions of databases are downloaded from a central computer to various minicomputers or PCs in the network, controls should be in force to ensure uniformity among the various sites. For example, if one site has a price list from Monday's database and another site has a price list from Tuesday's database, customers may be quoted two different prices for the same item.

- **"Peer-coupled" distributed databases:** When a distributed system does not have a central mainframe as the center of the network but, instead, relies on a series of smaller but equal minicomputers or PCs, it is referred to as a peer-coupled system. This is a potentially difficult configuration for the internal auditor to address. The auditor must determine which machine has the "real" database and how the databases are kept in "sync."

- **Backup and disaster recovery:** The internal auditor should review the organization's ability to recover from a damaged DP system. As discussed in a preceding section, off-site storage of programs and data and alternative processing capabilities are vital.

- **User expertise:** The internal auditor should review the user's expertise with respect to the system. The user must understand the operational and control functions of the system. For example, some minicomputer systems require a periodic "reorganization" of the database. If this is not performed with sufficient frequency, processing can become onerously slow and interfere with day-to-day business activities.

- **Telecommunications:** Many distributed systems use telecommunications extensively. Whether dial-up or dedicated lines are used, the internal auditor should review controls to make sure both technical and manual controls exist to see that data is transmitted from one point to another without duplication, deletion, or change. Appropriate transmission protocols, balancing controls, and front-end edits are examples of telecommunications controls that could be used in a DDP system.

Documentation

Description

Documentation should define the process to be performed by programs in the system. It should identify the data files and fields within those files to be processed. It should describe the reports to be prepared for users. It should include any online screens. It should set forth the operating instructions for system operators (particularly for reruns in the event of an abnormal termination). It should tell users about the preparation and control of data. In short, documentation should let a reviewer, auditor, or manager know what reliance can be placed on a system.

Good documentation is a sign of a well-run data processing facility. Unfortunately, many programmers and computer specialists find the chore of documenting their work mundane and not to their liking. They would rather finish the system or application they are working on and go on to the next.

Documentation is essential. It is frequently needed by management to determine the functional adequacy of a program; by programmers who have reason to make changes in a computer program; and by auditors, both internal and external, to review controls and develop audit software. In the absence of adequate documentation, it is not uncommon to find that complex and expensive programs had to be substantially rewritten to introduce minor changes. Only one or two people — usually the original programmers no longer on the scene — were aware in detail of what the program was supposed to do; management was not informed of the specifics it needed to review the adequacy of programs. Finally, unauthorized changes could be inserted in the program for fraudulent purposes.

Both the manual and the computerized systems should be documented. Documentation for the manual system should describe the functions and activities for which the system was responsible, the specific clerical functions carried out, the input-output documents, and the forms, screens, and records in use. It should contain a flowchart of the system and should describe all records and fields. The documentation should also describe the security features and any backup capabilities (i.e., off-site tapes or other storage media).

A comprehensive documentation program for computerized systems includes these forms of documentation:

System documentation: System objectives, flowcharts linking the manual and computer steps, system specifications for design and development, input forms and procedures, record formats, descriptions of transaction trails, and balancing and control procedures.

Program documentation: Program narratives needed to facilitate maintenance after initial installation, job control language descriptions, parameter cards, program test data, a testing log, input/output distribution instructions, data retention instructions, appropriate change-control information (often maintained in a separate library and controlled by a library control system), and copies of program-change requests.

Operations documentation: Instructions needed to run an application accurately and efficiently, to balance inputs and outputs, to distribute reports, and to facilitate restart and recovery.

Library documentation: Procedures for backup and retention, restrictions on access to sensitive data, and inventory record keeping.

User documentation: Narrative description of the systems documentation and a general flow diagram; instructions on completing input forms and transactions, including all necessary code values; control procedures on balancing, reconciling, and maintaining overall control transactions, master files, and processing results. (User documentation is, in effect, a contract between users and IS personnel. It covers what the user is to do, what decision rules to apply, what the IS personnel have set out to do for the user, and how the two parties to the contract will interact.)

Control documentation: A narrative of specific points in application systems telling where the user, the internal auditor, and the data processing people can expect to find controls and the methods by which their adequacy and effectiveness can be verified.

In sum, adequate documentation has characteristics of prevention, detection, and correction. By preparing the documentation, the preparer can prevent errors through the self-checking opportunities arising from putting prescribed procedures on paper. By communicating procedures to others, detection is permitted because a medium is provided for subsequent inspection. The availability of adequate application documentation permits correction and reconstruction of practically any application process.

Internal Audit

IS personnel are often lax in preparing adequate documentation, which is an additional reason for internal auditors to become involved early enough in system and application development processes to counteract that tendency. Management has or should have a vital interest in adequate documentation, but rarely can it afford the time for a detailed review. The responsibility, therefore, will fall on the internal auditor, an unbiased surrogate, to perform those reviews for management and to inform top managers of their findings.

Internal auditors should review existing procedures for documentation preparation. In their testing, they should be concerned with program documentation, system documentation, operations documentation, and user procedures documentation. Internal auditors should be particularly concerned with documentation of change control procedures, where manipulation may take place.

Auditors should first assess the adequacy of prescribed documentation controls within the organization. Documentation requirements can be the basis for compliance audits.

In terms of proposed systems, the internal auditor should review planning documentation to see if it contains information on:

- The objectives and goals of the system.
- System flowcharts.

- Descriptions of both clerical and mechanical functions.
- The general (macro) logic of the programs for the new application.
- A description of input data.
- Copies of source documents.
- A description of the output of the new system.
- A catalog of controls to be included.
- Exception reporting and the action to be taken on exceptions.
- A list of the files to be maintained — both manual and machine-readable (e.g., tape files and disk files).
- File-retention schedules.
- Minimum documentation standards for programs.

Adequate documentation certainly simplifies an internal auditor's job, but what if the documentation is inadequate? Auditors will, of course, evaluate risk and report this defect to management. But they may still have to move ahead to determine whether the undocumented system is adequate, efficient, and effective. They may find that people working with the system have prepared their own informal notes and descriptions for their own use. The auditors may ask for those notes that the IS personnel and users have in their possession. They can then fill in gaps in the system that were not otherwise documented.

If even those notes and descriptions are lacking, the internal auditor might have to make assumptions of what the system should be and test for it. Obviously, internal auditors do not draw conclusions or express opinions on the basis of assumptions; these should be based on their testing.[8]

The internal audit documentation can prevent future difficulties. Here is an example:[9]

> Internal auditors found that the only documentation of certain control programs were the programs themselves, and these were quite complicated. They therefore recommended that a statement be prepared describing the control procedures. The recommendations resulted in two benefits. First, the programs were documented for future use. Second, the documentation provided a training tool for computer programmers. In addition, a copy of the test file, developed by the information system audit staff, was turned over to the user to conduct independent tests of the system.

Efficiency in Information Systems

Description

The more money spent on an activity, the greater the payback if efficiency and economy are proportionately increased. The huge sums invested in IS make it a fruitful source of savings that result from careful management. For that reason, management should see that feasibility studies are carried out objectively and in-depth, that a clear statement of objectives and needs is developed for each system and application, that cost-benefit analyses look without bias at costs to be incurred and the benefits to be obtained, that the IS organization deploys its resources efficiently, and that good administrative procedures are developed and followed.

Feasibility studies for IS must take this concept into account. The operations will be efficient and economical if the systems and applications help management guide the organization toward established objectives and goals without wasting time, energy, and money. Hence, the feasibility study should look beyond the computer room. It should look to the needs of users and the effect on peripheral organizations. Reports that are not summarized are useless to operating managers. Designers of systems and applications must recognize that data and information are not the same. Data are the flower petals. Information is the distilled nectar. Management needs information, not data.

Systems are rarely efficient and economical when management has not presented a sound statement of goals, when it does not supply the needed resources, when it does not develop a master plan for an IS system, and when it does not support and become involved in the design effort. Similarly, efficiency and economy suffer when the design group does not adequately review the entire relevant organizational structure, analyze information requirements, adequately evaluate hardware and software requirements, and provide a maintainable system. Finally, to achieve economy and efficiency, users must involve themselves in the design and suggest appropriate changes to see that their needs are met. All three groups must remember that the system has for its chief objective the ability to provide service at a cost that compares favorably with alternate methods.

IS activities need adequate cost-accounting systems. These should define the specific work projects required to meet management goals. They should establish detailed methods and cost centers to track and control the progress of projects or tasks. They should accumulate data to measure cost, decide on how to establish billing rates, and assign costs to users. The cost system should meet three separate needs:

1. Those of the IS managers, to measure their own cost effectiveness and efficiency, to plan future workloads, to justify the resources assigned, and to transfer costs to user units.

2. Those of senior managers, to keep abreast of costs of the information system and to know whether its results are helping meet organization goals.

3. Those of users to give them information on the cost of IS services, to help them decide whether they can afford the services, to determine how these services relate to their own activities, and to show them how they are in a position to control those costs.

Efficiency can be improved by charging user departments for IS time used, but they should be charged only for what they can be held responsible.

For example, they should not be charged for reruns that are the fault of the IS department. Proper charges tend to force users to be more efficient; users will learn to do manually what will help reduce running time if manual operation is more economical. But economy is not enough. The IS department should also be responsible for user satisfaction. In sum, the object is to provide computer facilities only for those applications that are cost justified, and to hold the IS department responsible for efficient and effective processing.

The enormous sums invested in hardware, software, and personnel demand well-controlled deployment of these resources. Just as inept production control can escalate manufacturing costs, so can poor scheduling erode the hoped-for benefits from the system or increase the costs of running it.

The scheduling function should be separate from other data processing activities and should not be under the domination of one particular user. The scheduling supervisor should be in a position to balance equipment capability with the user's demands on the equipment and, at the same time, be aware of broad organization needs to make sure essential jobs, like payroll or production control, are not shunted aside for rush jobs having less organization-wide emphasis. Most organizations use automated schedulers that permit routine processing to be scheduled by the system. This tends to reduce the frequency of "rush" jobs and makes sure infrequently run jobs will not be inadvertently omitted.

The records, logs, and other documentation should support and justify scheduling decisions. They should establish conformance to scheduling procedures and demonstrate whether scheduling objectives have been met.

Scheduling procedures should account for all uses of equipment and data and they should indicate the running time for each job. The procedures should require logs to report processing, completed jobs, machine down time, uncompleted jobs and the reasons for them, summary performance statistics, IS payroll and overtime, operator rotation and vacation schedules, and analytical comparisons between budgeted and actual costs. Many of these functions may be automated using vendor-supplied software.

Internal Audit

An important function of internal auditors is to assure management that systems and applications will operate or are operating as intended, alerting management to any failures. Senior managers do not have the time for close and constant surveillance of the IS function. That is why the internal auditor must therefore be management's surrogate.

Internal auditors should seek to determine whether resources of personnel, property, and space are being used efficiently and economically. They would want to know if operations produce the desired results. They would review the adequacy of the statement of mission needs and system objectives, the feasibility study and evaluation of alternative designs, the cost-benefit analysis and whether these attribute specific benefits and costs to system alternatives.

Here are some questions internal auditors can ask:

- Is the basis for equipment selection well supported? Has consideration been given to lowest cost, program and system reliability, and service?

- Has a study been made of new equipment, new operating systems, new programming languages (including fourth-generation languages), online programs, databases, and telecommunications applications and considerations?

- Has appropriate consideration been given to lease or purchase, including provision for (or calculation of) depreciation? Cost of capital? Cash flow? Timing? Opportunity costs? (Lease implies steady disbursement over the years. Purchase implies large initial cash outlay.) Obsolescence? Preparing the site? Providing power facilities, air conditioning, humidity control, soundproofing, raised floors to house cables and wiring, reinforced floors and foundations, uniform and independent sources of power and security? Storage facilities for tapes, diskettes, system libraries? Standby equipment in the event of equipment failure? Adequate protection, such as off-site storage of vital information so it can be reproduced if necessary?

- Does the study establish objectives for cost savings? Efficiency? Improved information? And are these objectives sufficiently detailed so they may serve to measure system performance?

- Have time-phased plans been established for site preparation? Equipment delivery? Development operating procedures? Programming and testing? Orientation of operating personnel? Disaster recovery?

- Have provisions been made for the multiple use of common source data? Has provision been made for management by exception?

With respect to scheduling, internal auditors need to satisfy themselves that the rules regarding scheduling have been reduced to writing and that they are well understood and uniformly applied by all schedulers. Auditors would also want to know how well actual schedules agree with forecasted needs. They will be particularly interested in the basis for accepting nonscheduled work and how often established schedules are disrupted by special jobs.

Legal Requirements

Description

Legal requirements can make significant impacts on IS systems and applications. In addition to the needs of management and users, statutory and regulatory requirements must be taken into account.

In the public sector, privacy statutes have been enacted at state and federal levels. These restrict the collection and use of certain types of information. Under the Privacy Act of 1974, federal agencies falling within the purview of the statute are required to establish appropriate administrative, technical, and physical safeguards to ensure the privacy of personal information.[10]

To comply with the 1974 government privacy statutes, each government agency is required to: (1) establish appropriate safeguards to assure the security and confidentiality of records, and (2) protect against anticipated threats or hazards to their security or integrity that could result in substantial harm, embarrassment, inconvenience, or unfairness to any individual about whom information is obtained.

One of the major threats to security comes from individuals already having authorized access to the system. Once authorized, they are permitted to browse unchallenged through personal or sensitive files. A secondary threat is from those unauthorized to have access to the system, but who have the technical ability and the resources needed to circumvent security measures.

The 1974 Act and a growing list of others are primarily applicable to the federal government, but it may also apply to government contractors. There is also a growing list of laws at the state and federal level in the United States and many other countries that are designed to protect computers from invasion.[11] The invasion of systems is a key method of invading the privacy of the individuals whose information is contained in the systems' records.

The risk to sensitive information varies with the type of data involved, the effectiveness of the controls exercised, and the configuration of the computer network. The potential risk increases as more personal data are centralized, the number of users proliferate, and more common data are shared.

Absolute security is a will-o'-the-wisp. But if senior management sets security as a key objective and sees that systems are monitored, the chances of reasonable success improve. The major problem is the trade-off between the economies achievable through IS, on the one hand, and the cost of obtaining the level of protection for personal information that is appropriate to the threats faced, on the other. By addressing the problem rationally and using oversight, as provided in the Privacy Act of 1974, a balance can be drawn.[12] On the other side of the coin are the requirements of the Freedom of Information Act. Systems should have the capability of providing prompt responses to legitimate requests under the statute.

Care should be taken to address specific industry issues. For example, the Health Insurance Portability and Accountability Act of 1996 (HIPAA) contains privacy provisions regarding health information maintained by specific health-care providers, insurance carriers, and clearinghouses.

In the private sector, some of the government statutes and regulations that have their impact on information systems include the Security and Exchange Commission's requirement for quarterly reviews, affirmative action programs, new rules for pension reporting, and consumer protection laws. The related reports are often different from those required for managers.

Internal Audit

The primary function of the internal auditor in this area is communication. For example:

> A state law, recently enacted, establishes strict rules for the purchase and use of commercial hypodermic syringes. These are often used to place drops of bonding liquid in inaccessible places on assemblies and subassemblies. Inquiries of buyers who procured the syringes and of operating people who stored, issued, and used them disclosed a vast ignorance of the subject, yet the penalties were severe. The corporation was subject to stiff fines for violation.

> The internal auditor (one of the authors) asked the company attorneys what the law required. They then passed that information on to the procedure writers and the people responsible for compliance with the statute. Violations were thus prevented and fines were avoided.

The internal audit function with respect to other statutory and regulatory requirements is much the same. Auditors will have to make sure that all such requirements are known; they will have to consult legal counsel to become aware of the requirements and the steps that must be taken under those requirements. Then they will have to make sure that the requirements are considered in the feasibility study and the systems design. After the installation or application is approved and working, they will have to determine whether the statutes and regulations are in fact being complied with.

Internal auditors will be concerned not only with actual compliance but also with how such compliance can be proved if questions are asked.

The answer lies, in part, in documentation. Such documentation should demonstrate that the applicable statutes and regulations were considered. It should substantiate the incorporation of appropriate routines and controls, and should contain copies for references to the required reports. The answer also lies in tests that make certain that statutes and regulations governing the application are in fact incorporated into the software and that the software is functioning only as intended.

Probably the most extensive job of documentation will be to evidence compliance with the U.S. Foreign Corrupt Practices Act. There, the system of control, like a complete human nervous system, extends through the entire body corporate. The penalties for failing to show compliance are serious. Here the internal auditors would be well advised to work jointly with external auditors and present a common front and a unified approach to statutory compliance.

Turning once more to privacy acts, fear of violation may stampede management into excessively expensive controls. For example, cryptography can be employed to secure communication links. Cryptography in a computer network calls for the use of an encryption device at the point of data transmission and a decryption device at the point of data reception. Such devices have to be incorporated at all remote terminals, or terminal controllers, as well as at the central computer facility.

The National Bureau of Standards published a standard for data encryption on January 15, 1977 (Federal Information Processing Standard Publication 46). This standard (known as the Data Encryptions Standard or DES) specifies a step-by-step procedure, an algorithm, to be implemented in electronic devices to protect information system data.

Encryption is expensive (at least for routine telecommunications), so a definite need should be established before employing this technique. Internal auditors would want to examine a threat analysis to see if the threats to privacy warrant the cost of the devices. They would also want to know if other security safeguards, such as identification, access controls, callbacks, and access auditing can be implemented before sophisticated encryption devices are procured to protect personal data. Internal auditors must always balance the cost of control with the cost of loss before taking exception to a system or making recommendations to improve it.

As more and more data becomes readily available because of decreases in the cost of information technology, the internal auditor needs to be alert to the potential for either accidental or intentional disclosure and use of data. Hence the auditor needs to be familiar with specific statutes that cover the entity and their impact on disclosure and determine that the entity is in fact in compliance with legal requirements. The auditor also needs to make sure that the auditor and their staff comply with disclosure requirements.

References

[1]"The Round Table," *Internal Auditor,* April 1993, 70.

[2]*Systems Auditability and Control* (Altamonte Springs, FL: The Institute of Internal Auditors Research Foundation, 1994 Edition), 2-22, and 9-13, 9-47, through 48.

[3]Ibid., 4-75 through 84.

[4]Ibid.

[5]Ibid., 4-81.

[6]Ibid., 4-78.

[7]Cohen, Fred, "Information System Attacks: A Preliminary Classification Scheme," *Computers & Security* 16(1), 29-46 (1997).

[8]Mair, et al., 88.

[9]"The Round Table," *The Internal Auditor,* October 1978, 97.

[10]National Bureau of Standards Special Publication 500.19, Audit and Evaluation of Computer Security, October 1977, 4-5.

[11]*Systems Auditability and Control* (Altamonte Springs, FL: The Institute of Internal Auditors Research Foundation, 1994 Edition), 9-79 through 84.

[12]Report to Congress by the Comptroller General of the United States, *Challenges of Protecting Personal Information in an Expanding Federal Computer Network Environment,* B-146864, 28 April 1978, 2, 17, 28.

Supplementary Readings

Aggarwal, Rajeesh, and Cary T. Hughes, "Internal Control Structure in System Development with Computer-Aided Software Engineering," *Internal Auditing*, Winter 1996, 26-33.

Bacon, Chris N., "Auditing 401(k)s with CAATs," *Internal Auditor*, October 2001, 27-29.

Bodnar, George H., "Trends in Data Security," *Internal Auditing*, Summer 1995, 51-56.

Bodnar, George H., "CAATs at the Millennium," *Internal Auditing*, January/February 2000, 3-8.

Bodnar, George H., "Internet and Intranets: Network Accounting," *Internal Auditing*, July/August 1998, 43-47.

Bodnar, George H., "Focusing on Firewalls," *Internal Auditing*, Fall 1996, Volume 12, 59-63.

Bogusky, Clay, and Stanley Halper, "Control and Security Issues in Electronic Document Imaging," *The EDP Auditor Journal,* 33-50.

Bradley, Rodney J., and E. Perrin Garsombke, "Electronic Data Interchange: Controlling the Risk," *Internal Auditing*, Spring 1993, 51-56.

Cerullo, Michael J., M. Virginia Cerullo, and Tracy Hardin, "Computer Techniques Used to Audit the Purchasing Function," *Internal Auditing,* March/April 1999, 17-25.

Coderre, Dave, "Testing Application Controls," *Internal Auditor*, December 1996, 18-20.

Gaston, S.J., *Audit of Small Computer Systems Including LANs* (Toronto, Canada: The Canadian Institute of Chartered Accountants, 1993).

Gilhooley, Ian A., *Information Systems Management, Control, and Audit* (Altamonte Springs, FL: The Institute of Internal Auditors, 1991).

Gin, Doris D., "Controls Testing," *Internal Auditor*, April 1996, 12-14.

Gray, Glen L., and Maryann Jacobi Gray, "Internal Auditors and the Webtrust," *Internal Auditor*, June 1999, 54-57.

Hicks, Richard C., and William A. Newman, "Multiple Database Access Tools for Audit Testing," *Internal Auditing*, Winter 1997, 22-27.

Higgins, Leta Fee, *Guidelines for Establishing an Information Systems Audit Function* (Altamonte Springs, FL: The Institute of Internal Auditors, 1990).

The Institute of Internal Auditors Research Foundation and the Information Systems Audit and Control Foundation, *UNIX: Its Use, Control, and Audit* (Altamonte Springs, FL: The Institute of Internal Auditors Research Foundation, 1995).

The Institute of Internal Auditors Research Foundation, *Systems Auditability and Control* (Altamonte Springs, FL: The Institute of Internal Auditors Research Foundation, 1994 Edition).

Lanza, Richard B., "Audit Raw, Not 'Cooked,' Data," *Internal Auditor*, December 1997, 23-25.

Leonard, Barbara, and Charles Werner, "Examining Accounting and Integrated Web-Based Accounting Systems," *Internal Auditing*, March/April 2000, 14-19.

Paukowits, Frank, "Mainstreaming CAATs," *Internal Auditor*, February 1998, 19-21.

Pfaltzgraff, Renée, and H. Perrin Garsombke, "Risks and Implications of Client/Server Technology for Auditors," *Internal Auditing*, May/June 1998, 26-33.

The Proceedings of The IIA Research Foundation and Advanced Technology Committee's 1993 Advanced Technology Forum, *Advanced Technology Forum: Audit, Control, and Security Issues in Networks* (Altamonte Springs, FL: The Institute of Internal Auditors Research Foundation, 1993).

Roesch Laura, and Laurie J. Henry, "Client/Server Systems," *Internal Auditor*, August 1997, 40-43.

Stone, William A., "Electronic Commerce," *Internal Auditor*, December 1997, 26-34.

Tener, William T., *Adapting the Integrated Audit Approach* (Altamonte Springs, FL: The Institute of Internal Auditors Research Foundation, 1992).

Warigon, Slemo, "Data Warehouse Control & Security," *Internal Auditor*, February 1998, 54-60.

Weber, Ron, *Information Systems Control and Audit* (Upper Saddle River, NJ: Prentice Hall, 1998).

Wiggins, Jr., Casper E., and Uday S. Murthy, "Audit Implications of Future Database Systems," *Internal Auditing*, January/February 1998, 8-18.

Multiple-choice Questions

1. The purpose of a decision support system is to provide:
   a. All information necessary for a decision.
   b. Quick and easy access to models and data.
   c. Regular reports to decision makers.
   d. A consensus on a decision.

2. A computer-based system for sending, forwarding, receiving, and storing messages would be called:
   a. A data bank.
   b. Electronic mail.
   c. Office automation.
   d. Document distribution.

3. A series of instructions telling a computer how to process data or files is defined as a:
   a. Network.
   b. System.
   c. Program.
   d. Modem.

4. Computer software that directs and assists the execution of application programs is referred to as the:
   a. Operating system.
   b. Utility program system.
   c. Database management system.
   d. Compiler system.

5. The primary purpose of a computer database management system is to:
   a. Enable the processing of two or more application programs by interleaving the execution of individual instructions.
   b. Accept computer instructions in a symbolic code and convert them to machine language instruction.
   c. Provide storage used to compensate for differences in rates of data transfer or in timing of data transmission between devices.
   d. Act as a software controller enabling different applications to access large numbers of distinct data files stored on direct access devices.

6. Which of the following control features is the most effective protection against unauthorized access to an online computerized system?
   a. Online access unavailable except during normal working hours.
   b. Backup and recovery procedures.
   c. Policy prohibiting unauthorized access.
   d. Passwords.

7. Many organizations have developed decision support systems (DSS), a class of information systems that address the relationships between management decisions and information. Which of the following **best** describes the objective of a DSS?
   a. To automate a manager's problem-solving process.
   b. To provide interactive assistance during the process of problem solving.
   c. To impose a predefined sequence of analysis during the process of problem solving.
   d. To impose a predefined sequence of analysis during the process of problem solving.
   e. To minimize a manager's use of judgment in the process of problem solving.

8. Traditional information systems development procedures that ensure proper consideration of controls may not be followed by users developing end-user computing (EUC) applications. Which of the following is a prevalent risk in the development of EUC applications?
   a. Management decision-making may be impaired due to diminished responsiveness to management's requests for computerized information.
   b. Management may be less capable of reacting quickly to competitive pressures due to increased application development time.
   c. Management may place the same degree of reliance on reports produced by EUC applications as it does on reports produced under traditional systems development procedures.
   d. Management may incur increased application development and maintenance costs for EUC systems, compared to traditional (mainframe) systems.

9. Traditional information systems development and operational procedures typically involve four functional areas. The systems analysis function focuses on identifying and designing systems to satisfy organizational requirements. The programming function is responsible for the design, coding, testing, and debugging of computer programs necessary to implement the systems designed by the analysis function. The computer operations function is responsible for data preparation, program/job execution, and system maintenance. The user function provides the input and receives the output of the system. Which of these four functions is often poorly implemented or improperly omitted in the development of a new end-user computing (EUC) application?
   a. Systems analysis function.
   b. Programming function.
   c. Computer operations function.
   d. User function.

10. An auditor is planning an audit of a customer information system that uses a local-area network (LAN) with personal computers (PCs). Increased risks associated with the company's use of a LAN and PCs, as opposed to use of a mainframe, could include all of the following **except**:
    a. Lack of documentation of procedures to ensure the complete capture of data.
    b. Poor security of data residing on the PCs.
    c. Problems with failures of the hardware used for processing data.
    d. Incomplete data communications.

11. Which of the following areas will usually experience an increase in risk as microcomputers proliferate?
    1. Backup and recovery.
    2. Application development costs.
    3. Batch updating of records.
    4. Access security.
    5. Copyright violations.

    a. 1, 2, and 3.
    b. 2, 3, and 4.
    c. 3, 4, and 5.
    d. 1, 4, and 5.

12. An organization currently creates sequential log files of database transactions on tape. This practice appears to be degrading response time for online users of other applications. The **best** approach for improving response time would be to replace the sequential tape file with:
    a. A sequential disk file.
    b. An indexed sequential tape file.
    c. A direct access disk file.
    d. An indexed sequential disk file.

13. In some audits of computer applications, it is appropriate to review the program code to determine whether it satisfies its processing objectives. The code reviewed is the:
    a. Object code.
    b. Source code.
    c. Hash code.
    d. Access code.

14. A work flow analysis determined that employees in a department needed the following: access to departmental laser printers, electronic mail with each other and employees in other departments and other plants, and file inquiring and downloading of corporate files. The **most** appropriate computer configuration for employees in this department is:
    a. A self-contained minicomputer with terminals.
    b. Personal computers with a terminal emulator.
    c. Personal computers in a stand-alone local-area network (LAN).
    d. Personal computers in a LAN with a gateway.

15. After a security review, an organization determined that all employees in the bid preparation department should have access to common data such as current costs, but that access to data pertaining to specific bids should be restricted to employees working only on that bid. The organization keeps all bid-related data together in an integrated database. To enable selective access to bid data, the organization needs data security software that restricts access to records based on:
    a. The type of resource.
    b. Statistical summaries.
    c. The age of the records.
    d. Data item contents.

16. A hospital is evaluating the purchase of software to integrate a new cost accounting system with its existing financial accounting system. Which of the following describes the **most** effective way for internal audit to be involved in the procurement process?
    a. Evaluate whether performance specifications are consistent with the hospital's needs.
    b. Evaluate whether the application design meets internal development and documentation standards.
    c. Determine whether the prototyped model is validated and reviewed with users before production use begins.
    d. Internal audit has no involvement since the system has already been developed externally.

Chapter 15
Information Systems Auditing – III

Introduction. Using mainframe systems in auditing. Generalized audit software. High-level languages. Custom audit software. Objectives of computer-assisted auditing. Test data techniques. Integrated test facility. Parallel simulation. Mapping. Snapshot. Obtaining information from the Web. Database management. Expanded controls in an Internet environment. Working papers generated by the mainframe. Network security assessment tools. Increasing use of analytical procedures and expert systems.

• •

Introduction

The previous two chapters discussed information systems basics and controls and tests of controls that should be considered in evaluating an information system. This chapter covers software that can be used to perform audit tests.

Using Mainframe Systems in Auditing

The use of the mainframe as an audit device is not new. In the 1960s, when the use of computer technology gained wide acceptance, internal auditors and their colleagues in public accounting realized that if the data to be audited were stored in the computer, the auditor would have to test it. In the early stages, auditors tended to audit outside the computer. That is, they watched data go into the computer and determined how the data would look if it were manually processed. Then they went to the output side of the process and tested the data to see that the data met their manual expectations. This is referred to as auditing *around* the computer.

Auditors rapidly learned that the process was not so simple even in the early days when processing was less complicated. The computer was creating new data through the synthesis of various data that were input. Some of the most crucial decisions effecting the profitability and viability of the organization were solely dependent on the accuracy of this information.

For example, a bank's computer would calculate the interest on a certificate of deposit using simple interest = principal x rate x time (I=PRT) formulas. However, the money managers wanted to have more information. They wanted the rolling average cost of funds to determine how best to invest the money on deposit. So the data were accumulated and programs written to build new files about:

- The sources of funds received (certificates of deposit, checking accounts, and savings accounts).
- The rates paid for the funds.
- The maturity schedules of mixed types of deposits.

These records had to be matched to investment and loans — the uses of funds to see that the earnings rates and the liquidity, ability to meet cash demands, are matched.

The volume of data, complexity of the calculations, and the daily changes made manual calculations so time-consuming that the auditor could not stand on the outside of the system to test the accuracy of this data. There are similar examples in production operations with raw material mixes and staffing requirements compared to orders received and anticipated.

Increasingly, input to the computer system was coming from outside the organization's staff. A bank customer goes to an automated teller machine (ATM), enters a specially designed card, presses a few buttons, and out pops money. At the same time an electronic entry goes to the bank deposit accounts and the general ledger cash account.

A customer of a manufacturing organization sends a computerized order to the manufacturer's computer. At the manufacturer's site the computer translates the order into units in the production schedule, accounts receivable entries, and inventory orders to replenish the stock of materials that will fulfill the customer's order. The manufacturer may even create an electronic draft on the customer's bank account timed to charge the customer on the day the order is delivered.

Now the auditor cannot stand outside the system and watch the input and output; the auditor must go inside the computer to look at the data and its processing. In sophisticated systems the auditor must audit *through* the computer.

A new set of audit skills and a new type of auditor appeared — the EDP auditor. These auditors used a new box of tools to perform their work, and they wore several hats. They were responsible, among other things, for:

- Auditing events, transactions, and records *within* the organization's computer systems.

- Auditing the programming activities that provided the processing instructions to the computer.

- Auditing the security systems that restricted access to and actions on the data assets of the organization.

- Auditing the physical operations in the computer room and related activities.

- Auditing the disaster and recovery planning, records retention, and backup activities.

- Providing advice and guidance on internal control to programmers and others involved in the creation of new systems and modification of existing ones.

- Providing the rest of the audit staff with information extracted from the computer system for testing in non-computer files and operations.

Generalized Audit Software

Generalized audit software (GAS) is one of the most widely used tools of the EDP auditor. *Systems Auditability and Control (SAC)* says, "Generalized Audit Software, designed specifically for use by auditors, includes features such as summarizations, stratification, sampling routines, and general information retrieval capabilities and can be used to accomplish. . .basic auditing tasks."[1]

GAS is available from a number of vendors, but all of them provide the auditor with the means to:

- Read files.

- Examine records based on criteria specified by the auditor.

- Test calculations and make independent calculations.

- Compare data in separate files.

- Select and print audit samples.

- Summarize or re-sequence data and perform analyses.

- Compare data obtained through other audit procedures to data in the entity's records.[2]

All of these facilities give the EDP auditor the ability to perform standard audit work. Efficiency is gained because the complex programming work has been completed for the auditor. The auditor gives the software the specific information about audit objectives and the GAS supplies the standard routines to summarize, examine, and compare the information.

GAS can be used to specify the selection of transactions for manual examination. For example: An auditor can take a statistical sample of accounts receivable and prepare confirmation letters within the software. The accounts payable file can be examined and working papers prepared to record manual examination of paper files of purchase orders and voucher approvals.

GAS can also be used to prepare independent trial balances to compare the results to the trial balances created by the production applications. An auditor can prepare an independent trial balance of the payroll records to make sure that all employees are being reported in the payroll register. GAS can be used to extract sensitive information such as past due receivables to test the collection reports generated by the production programs. An independent listing and aging of accounts receivable can be prepared to test the data used by the collection and credit departments.

The use of GAS software to test data and information found in computer files and standard operating reports is as broad as the auditor's imagination.

High-level Languages

Many auditors use fourth-generation languages and generalized statistical software to obtain audit information that traditionally would have been obtained through generalized audit software. Fourth-generation software typically provide more user-friendly capabilities, have similar capabilities to GAS, and — depending upon their use within an organization — are able to obtain better support than GAS.

With increasing use of analytical procedures, auditors have expanded their use of statistical software that allow the use of user-friendly complex statistical methods. The use of high-level languages has expanded with the development of personal computer versions of statistical packages and fourth-generation languages. With appropriate utility software an auditor can download data and perform audit procedures in a known environment.

Custom Audit Software

EDP auditors will find occasions when they are not able to use generalized audit software. There may be limitations imposed by hardware, system configuration, or the complexity of processing or output requirements.[3] In these circumstances, the auditor may use customized software solutions. These may be developed with in-house programming resources, or external experts may be employed to create specialized software to examine, collate, and extract information. The *Systems Auditability and Control (SAC)* report describes a software system created by U.S. government agencies to extract data from records of state government alcohol and drug-related traffic offenses and Federal Aviation Administration Active Medical

Files to validate the representations by members of the armed services concerning their records of alcohol and drug use.[4]

This effort involved varied computer hardware systems, with different file structures created for different purposes. The files contained elements of data that could be matched directly or within predictable ranges of values (birth dates, social security numbers, addresses and former addresses, bank electronic transfer numbers, etc.). Software of this complexity has to be developed in highly specific and controlled circumstances to meet its objectives and to assure its accuracy and integrity.

The Objectives of Computer-assisted Auditing

When using the system as an audit tool, the testing of data may use direct mathematical techniques such as footing and cross footing of files, or recalculation of accruals and other computations. A payroll file may be tested by recomputing net pay amounts based on hours worked, wage rates, deduction values, etc.

Other tests may be analytical in nature. An aging of accounts receivable or an analysis of inventory turnover can be performed by the system in a fraction of the time required for a comparable manual study. Once the software has been created and validated, its use in future audits is even more efficient.

Auditors may also embed audit routines in production software to capture explicit transactions or data about special conditions into special files for examination by auditors. If a new customer's credit account balance rises to a high percentage of the approved credit limit within a short period of time, the audit software may highlight the account for special examination. If a buyer in the purchasing department is concentrating a high percentage of orders with a single or smaller number of vendors, the audit software can report this so the auditor can determine whether a special review is warranted. These automated monitors can be embedded in the regular processing software like a post-transaction auditor who never sleeps and never loses interest in the task at hand.

In these cases, the auditor should question why these control checks are being created as audit tests. If these are valid conditions for an audit inquiry, it is reasonable to suggest that they should be standard tests built into the system for management review. Therefore, the auditor should structure these embedded control tests for audit purposes, but he or she should be careful to determine whether the ongoing use of the output of these routines is an audit task or a control task. The auditor's role is to *test* the control, not to *be* the control.

Tests of Processing

Simply extracting and examining data is important, but it is an after-the-fact test. It assumes that the processing must be correct because no errors were found in the data that successfully passed through the processing steps. This assumption may be inaccurate because: (a) potential error conditions have not yet been encountered in processing, or (b) errors that did occur were not detected by current edit routines. The audit approach should test *processing* in addition to testing data. These are referred to as test transaction techniques.[5]

Test Data Techniques[6]

Test data are auditor-designed input data that present a variety of transactions to the system for processing through the normal application software. Sometimes auditors use the terminology "test deck" to mean test data. Typically, the auditor prepares both good data (i.e., should be accepted) and bad data (i.e., should be rejected) for processing through the system. In order to reduce the potential impact of updating actual data and records, the data are entered in test mode and the output is examined to see that expected results are achieved. Any exceptions to expected results are reviewed further. Test mode refers to running the normal application software in isolation from the regular production processing to avoid contamination to the production files. This is often done by setting up a "dummy" organization and using the files for that organization to process the test data. In this approach, the dummy organization is a parallel operation with the same processing requirements but a separate set of files.

Test data techniques depend on the "expected results" concept. For transactions that will result in computations (e.g., application of a payment to principal and interest for a short-term note), the results of the transactions are precomputed, usually by hand, and compared with the results of the test run. For invalid data (e.g., a transaction to pay someone not listed on the payroll master file), it is expected that the transaction will be rejected and appear on an exception report.

For complex systems, the implementation of test data techniques is a significant effort. There are numerous combinations of inputs, and the total number of transactions can quickly run into the thousands. As a practical matter, only the most critical transactions are usually included. It is essential that the internal auditor make sure that no "live" files are updated.

Test data generators, available in some generalized audit software packages, are often used to randomly enter both valid and invalid data into the system. While not as effective as an elaborate expected results table, they are a quick way to review the basic edit capabilities of the application. Test data generators can also be used to volume-test the system (i.e., see that it functions properly with a large number of input records). The volume of transactions is used to overload the system to determine if it will "crash" or take too long to process.

Integrated Test Facility[7]

Some systems have an integrated test facility (ITF) built in. This permits "live" changes to certain test records on the master file. For example, an auditor can use an ITF to set up a fictitious person in the human resources database. These test records are usually included in a special department or segregated in some way so that they do not interfere with normal processing. The same program processes all the transactions so both test and production transactions will be logically processed in the same manner. Using an ITF requires consideration of the method that will be used to enter the test data and the method that will be used to remove the test data. Without strong general controls to assure that only authorized programs are allowed, this technique can be invalidated — the program tested today may not be the one run in "production" tomorrow.

Parallel Simulation[8]

Parallel simulation uses a separate program to duplicate normal processing of the computations that are important to the auditor. It performs the same function carried out by the application program used for regular processing.

Using the simulation program with the same input data and the same files, the same results are expected. The results of the simulation program are compared with those of the live program. The technique is similar to auditing around the computer, but it does not require manual audit trails or manual processing. The auditor obtains better results from parallel simulation programs than by manual processing because computer programs perform consistently; human beings do not.

In performing parallel simulation, auditors can introduce transactions involving large amounts, transactions subject to error or manipulation, and other conditions of audit interest. The speed of the computer permits the simulation of many transactions; it does not restrict the number of items to be tested to a number that will fit into the audit budget.

The steps in a simulation program include:[9]

1. Defining the audit objective.

2. Understanding the computer application being audited.

3. Specifying the logic to be followed.

4. Coding the instructions to be followed.

5. Obtaining files representative of the population being examined.

6. Debugging the simulation program.

7. Processing the application.

8. Evaluating the results.

To summarize: auditors can extract relevant data or samples of data from a live file, then run those data through a simulation program that parallels the live program. They compare results and investigate any differences. They can assume that the transactions with no differences are acceptable.

Parallel simulation provides an excellent independent tool for evaluating application systems. Although this technique can be time-consuming for very complex applications, it can often be performed quickly and accurately for moderate to small-size applications. It is also important to note that the entire application need not be paralleled — only that portion being tested. For example, if the auditor is only interested in determining that a payroll system correctly computes net pay, it is not necessary to include departmental transfer reporting in the simulation.

An online auditing variant of parallel simulation is continuous and intermittent simulation (CIS). In a CIS environment, requests to the database management system from the application program are passed through the CIS to determine if the CIS is to act. CIS might act if the transaction has been selected statistically or is outside of parameters selected by the audit. If the transaction is selected, the CIS replicates processing and determines whether a difference exists.

Mapping

Another, less widely used computer-assisted audit technique is mapping. It shows what portion of a program is being used and what part will never be executed. It isolates "dead" program codes and can flag codes that may be used fraudulently. This technique is frequently employed with extremely large and/or poorly documented programs.[10] Mapping produces a report of the lines of program code used to produce the input, update records, and produce the output. If there is a code that is not used, it will be missing from the report of code used. All unused codes are examined, and the purpose of an unused code is evaluated to determine if it should stay in the program or be removed.

Snapshot

The objective of the snapshot technique is to "take a picture" of a transaction as it travels through the application. The auditor can then determine if the transaction flows through the logic required for correct processing. Generally, the transaction is "tagged" by a special code in an unused portion of the record. Programs in the system recognize the code and generate a special audit trail indicating its path. One disadvantage of this technique is that it usually requires special programming as the system is being developed.[11]

The extended record technique is a variant of the snapshot. Instead of writing a record for each snapshot, under the extended record technique data is appended to a record for each point.

In selecting a technique, the auditor should follow the systems development process discussed previously. However, the use of concurrent techniques allows the auditor to avoid after-the-fact auditing or auditing around the computer. But these methods do have high cost. In an age of the rapidly disappearing paper trail, the potential for errors and irregularities to occur quickly, and the difficulty of doing a walk-through, the auditor must carefully consider these alternatives.

Obtaining Information from the Web

With the need for additional information for analytical procedures in a real-time environment, an auditor may need data that is as up-to-date as possible. For example, an auditor may want to develop a regression model for sales in a territory based upon macroeconomic data for the area. Information, such as this may have been difficult or time-consuming to obtain. However, with the Internet, firms and organizations are making information available faster. For example, SEC filings can be found on the Web within a day of filing.

With the expanding use of the Web as a data source, the auditor must be able to search for appropriate data. Currently there are four fundamental types of search engines available. Hierarchical indexes, such as Yahoo, are based upon categorization done by professionals, such as librarians and indexers.

Another type of search engine, referred to by many people as "standard search engines," searches based upon the occurrence of keywords. This type includes Alta Vista, Excite, and Go Network. These typically report how relevant these pages are based upon such factors as frequency of keywords and placement of keywords.

Meta search engines search other search engines. This type includes Dogpile and MetaCrawler. A problem with these types of searches is their historical inability to perform Boolean searches. The final type of search engine involves various alternatives and is currently referred to as alternative search engines. This category includes various groups that do not fit conveniently into the other three categories. For example, Northern Lights would be included in this group. Northern Lights performs a search as does the standard search engines but combines the results into similar groupings. Ask Jeeves is based upon questions asked. It has a database of questions and cites for answers. Clearly, as the Web matures the search engines will also mature.

Database Management

Database management systems have changed drastically over recent years. Until recently, database management systems required substantial programming skills to be used effectively. That meant significant training and regular practice to acquire and maintain those skills. Recently, non-procedural databases have been introduced to the market. These systems do not require the programming skills of previous database systems. This progress allows end users to create practical solutions to their business needs without having to learn complex database programming languages and conventions. Examples will be presented using an audit situation and then expanded to other systems.

Auditors use database systems for a number of purposes. Some uses will be flat databases. A flat database can be visualized as a spreadsheet where every record (row) has the same elements of data (columns). This was previously demonstrated with the example of a phone directory where all of the data is in a single database and no external data sources are needed. However, this is not always practical because it leads to large databases and redundant data when the same data are needed in more than one database.

A relational database, like the one presented below, allows the sharing of data between two or more databases. Imagine a database on the training of the audit staff. The overall database has several distinct parts, each one of which stands on its own.

Personnel Data Fields	Record 1	Record 2
Employee number	77	48
Name	Smith, Joe	Jones, Sue
Current position	Senior auditor	Supervising auditor
Employment date	1-1-90	1-1-87
Date promoted to current level	1-1-94	1-1-93

Curriculum Data Fields	Course Number	Required for Level
Accounting	01	Trainee
Writing skills	02	Trainee
Statistical sampling	10	Staff auditor
Computer proficiency	11	Staff auditor
Fraud auditing	21	Senior auditor
Analytical review techniques	22	Senior auditor
Supervisory skills	31	Senior auditor

Suppliers Data Field	Supplier #	Courses offered 1	Courses offered 2
State University	11	01	10
Internal training classes	21	11	31
Professional association	31	31	21
Computer-based training	41	22	02

Courses Taken Data Field	Record 1	Record 2
Employee number	48	48
Course taken	01	21
Date completed	5-31-91	3-1-95
Course provider	11	31
Grade	4.0	Pass

Sue Jones, who is carried in the **People** database, will take the courses in the **Curriculum** database required for her level. The courses will be obtained from the providers in the **Suppliers** database, and her completion will be recorded in the **Courses taken** database. Each employee's record in the **People** database cannot carry all of the possible variants of courses required, courses taken, and suppliers. It will not be a manageable database if it carries all of the information on all of the courses taken by all of the employees.

The relational database allows the user to enter data once and use it as many times as needed in as many relationships as needed. For example, Sue Jones and Joe Smith will both take Accounting and Statistical Sampling courses. They may take them from the same provider or different providers. Because Sue is a supervisor and Joe is a senior, she is in the supervisory curriculum (not shown) while Joe is still in the senior curriculum. The various databases are related to each other by "keys" or shared fields in the databases. By entering a course code of 21, all of the information on Fraud Auditing can be obtained. Provider code 31 identifies the Professional Society as the course provider.

Auditors also use databases to maintain or create:

- Audit programs.
- Risk and control inventories.
- Personnel data related to staff members.
- Departmental or organizational fixed assets.
- Records retention control.
- Histories of audit findings.
- Data on organizational units or audit sites.

Databases are becoming increasingly important in applications, especially in real-time systems. In these cases data is entered only once in a database instead of having separate databases for accounts receivable. As improvements in technology occur, one can find (1) increasingly large databases that store multiple years of data, and (2) storage of graphics, audio, and video in addition to text. Large databases that contain multiple-year data, which typically contain transactions, are referred to as data warehouses. Data mining is the process concerned with extracting reliable information or patterns of data from a data warehouse. The database management system used with an enterprise-wide system is in fact a decision that must be determined for each system.

Expanded Controls in an Internet Environment

Many entities are using intranets to deliver information to internal users. The term intranet refers to the fact that the Web (or other Internet applications) are being run completely in a private network without being connected to the Internet. The Internet, or external Web, provides a way for organizations to communicate with parties.

With the increasing use of the Internet, an auditor needs to be alert to the potential for unauthorized entry into the information system. Entry, which could have a significant impact on a firm, includes obtaining important propriety information, the destruction of important software through viruses, and the destruction of the firm's business through changing critical site information.

A firm must establish security procedures based upon its risk assessments of where authorized entry can occur. Traditionally, one of the first lines of defense is a firewall. A firewall is a computer that (1) all traffic from inside to outside and outside to inside must pass, and (2) allows only authorized traffic to pass. The auditor should carefully evaluate the security policies that are used in the firewall. The computer itself should only contain the operating system and protection software.

Currently there are three types of firewalls. Packet filter firewalls examine the source and destination addresses of all information. Based upon established rules, the software denies or allows information to flow. Gateway firewalls filter traffic based on the application that they select. For example, rules may be established that prohibit access to applications such as Telenet and FTP. Proxy servers are firewalls that communicate on behalf of the private network.

Other issues in an Internet environment include:

1. Is appropriate usage of the Internet being made (are resources being wasted by individuals using the Internet for pleasure or, worse, are employees violating laws by conducting illegal activities)?
2. Is software downloaded from the Internet and used reliable and is the entity complying with copyright issues?
3. Is information that is transmitted secure?

Working Papers Generated by the Mainframe

The extracting of information from files through generalized audit software or custom software was discussed earlier. The rules that apply to manually generated working papers apply to computer-generated working papers as well. The form of the papers should be governed by all of the rules found in earlier chapters. The security and preservation of physical papers is equally important.

A new set of concerns appears when the working papers are in electronic form. The form of the papers can comply with the professional conventions whether the papers are in printed form or reside solely on the computer. The security for working papers may, in fact, be better controlled on the computer if the security system on the computer is properly used. On the other hand, failure to maintain proper security on electronic working papers can create serious problems. If an auditor's working papers can be accessed and changed by others, changes can be made without any "footprints" being left behind. After all, a change of data on a computer leaves no eraser marks or "liquid paper" spots. These concerns will be discussed in the next chapter in the section on security of personal computer working papers.

Network Security Assessment Tools

Software is available to test for security weaknesses in network hardware and software. Depending on the software selected, a novice can be up and running in less than 15 minutes. Typically the software must be updated frequently to recognize changes in hardware and software.

Increasing Use of Analytical Procedures and Expert Systems in Enterprise-wide and Real-time Systems

With the advent of enterprise-wide and other tightly linked real-time systems, internal auditors and/or management must increasingly use analytical procedures on a real-time basis. The risk that material errors or irregularities can occur in a sort time frame must be carefully evaluated. For example, could a clerk enter fictitious sales in order to purchase goods from a vendor and have them returned and credited to a special account? This could happen in a relatively short period of time, a matter of hours or days, and the clerk could be long gone before anyone might discover it.

A recent survey by the Manufacturers Alliance/MAPI points out that of 106 companies, 76% were installing or had completed installing at least one module of an enterprise-wide system.[12] Of those responding that had or were installing this software, 84% responded that internal audit was not involved in selecting the software vendor.[13] Over 30% of 69 responding expressed a lack of satisfaction with their control environment.[14]

Negative comments about controls included:

> ..."The problem is that transaction-level security is difficult to deploy and manage in the real world. The result is that very few people, including those responsible, understand how the software functions from a control perspective."

> ..."New systems typically lack traditional controls, which must evolve. We are not yet familiar with all of the available controls and are not getting much help from the software originator."

> ..."The defaults seemed weak in most areas, but OK in a few. We had to customize heavily."

Positive comments about controls included:

...."The controls seem to be very comprehensive."

...."Yes, we are satisfied with the software. However, we need strong security and management review in our type of company structure."[15]

As the study notes, "we found some parties reticent for lack of experience to date."[16]

Given these initial comments, an auditor should carefully consider the use of analytical procedures and expert systems in such systems.

In addition there should be regular monitoring for abnormal activity. For example, extensive use of systems after "normal" working hours may be an indication of potential problems. Similarly, sales recorded by east coast sales personnel late in the night may be an indication of someone recording fictitious sales. Another analytical procedure might involve a comparison of sales by salesperson for a specific period of time. While such an analytical procedure might have been performed by firms before they adopted a closely tied real-time system, after adoption it must be done on a regular basis for short time periods in order to identify potential problems/issues on a timely basis.

An expert system is a computer application that incorporates a set of rules that interpret input data in the same way an expert would interpret the data if the expert was present at the audit site. Expert systems ensure consistent interpretation of data.

Expert systems have been used for tasks from geological assessments to credit scoring. Geologists have developed systems that predict the probability of the presence of oil based on a large number of variables from seismic responses to physical attributes of the terrain and a number of other factors. Lending organizations can input various data about a potential borrower and obtain a prediction of the likelihood that the borrower will repay the loan. In both of these cases, the "experts" have accumulated data gained from experience over a number of years and developed that into a set of "rules." The rules are usually expressed in terms like, "If condition A exists and condition B exists, then the likely outcome is C."

As an example, the software has been developed to calculate the inherent risk and control risk that exist in audited operations. The "experts"— audit managers — determine a rule such as the importance of the control that will be tested. Based on that value of importance, the inherent risk can be determined; that is, how much risk exists if the control does not work at all. The best protection that can be expected can be determined if the control is working as designed. These are values the experts can set down in a theoretical discussion. The expert system enables the staff auditor to take those values into the field and automatically apply them to the results of the tests of the controls. The auditor enters the results of testing and the expert system, using the rules, produces a control risk value between 100 percent (if the control was not working at all) and the best achievable level (if the control was working as designed). Any point between these two extremes is established based on the results of testing.

Procedures that might be performed include using an expert system to monitor for unusual numbers or volumes of transactions. Expert systems monitor the log in/log off of employees to determine whether, in fact, employees properly log off the system during breaks, lunch, and at the end of the day. While one might argue that this is ingrained in personnel, "horror" stories are consistently reported by security personnel that indicate that one of the easiest ways to enter a system is to find a PC terminal that is still connected to the system. It is amazing that no matter how often employees and management are told, turning off the monitor is used as a replacement for logging off the system.

Software is available which will allow one to look for anomalies in data. For example, Benford's Law, adopted from mathematics, states that individual digits in a set of random numbers will have an expected distribution. Software is available that will use Benford's Law to search out unusual patterns and report them for further analysis. Internal auditors can also search for data that is inconsistent with entity operations; for example, a firm's office in one city selling to a company located in another city. Auditors are also using continuous monitoring software to monitor high-risk transactions and identify situations in which fraud is likely. For example, auditors might monitor sales for transactions occurring at the end of the day or a large number during the last day of the month.

It would be ideal for a number of these procedures to be performed by management on a regular basis. This would allow the auditor to evaluate the procedures performed. If they are not performed by management, the internal auditor must perform them on a regular basis. Failure to do so may expose the firm to an unacceptable level of risk without its realization. The need to monitor for abnormal activity also extends to e-business.

References

[1] *Systems Auditability and Control* (Altamonte Springs, FL: The Institute of Internal Auditors Research Foundation, 1994 Edition), 3-36.
[2] Ibid.
[3] Ibid., 3-38.
[4] Ibid., Focus Box 5.2
[5] Ibid., 3-41 FF. and 3-111.
[6] Ibid., e-43 and 3-107.
[7] Ibid., 3-43 and 3-108.
[8] Ibid., 3-47 and 3-111.
[9] Mair, W.C., D.R. Wood, and K.W. Davis, *Computer Control and Audit* (Altamonte Springs, FL: The Institute of Internal Auditors, 1976), 153.

[10]*Systems Auditability and Control* (Altamonte Springs, FL: The Institute of Internal Auditors Research Foundation, 1994 Edition), 3-114.
[11]Ibid., 3-112.
[12]Manufacturers Alliance/MAPI, Survey of General Audit 2000 (Arlington, VA), 144.
[13]Ibid., 147.
[14]Ibid., 148.
[15]These represent a selection of 34 responses from Manufacturers Alliance/MAPI, Survey of General Audit 2000 (Arlington, VA), 148-9.
[16]Ibid., 148.

Supplementary Readings

Antoine, Robert, "Automating the Audit Function," *Internal Auditing*, Winter 1995, 53-56.

Bigler, Mark, "Computer Forensics," *Internal Auditor*, February 2000, 53-55.

Bigler, Mark, "Computer Forensics Gear," *Internal Auditor*, August 2001, 27-31.

Coderre, David G., "Seven Easy CAATT," *Internal Auditor*, August 1994, 28-33.

Coderre, David G., "Computer Assisted Fraud Detection," *Internal Auditor*, August 2000, 25-27.

Crowell, David A., "Equipping a Mobile Audit Staff," Internal Auditor, August 1997, 50-56.

Everest-Hill, Deborah, and David Young, "Automating Risk Assessment," *Internal Auditor*, June 1999, 23-25.

Gillevet, Joe, "Utilizing CAATs to Determine Input Errors," *The EDP Auditor Journal,* 19-24.

Glover, Steven M., and Marshall Romney, "Out in Front," *Internal Auditor*, February 1998, 44-48.

Glover, Steven, Douglas Prawitt, and Marshall Romney, "Software Showcase," Internal Auditor, August 1999, 49-59.

Glover, Steven M., Douglas Prawitt, and Marshall Romney, "The Software Scene," *Internal Auditor*, August 2000, 49-57.

Lin, Thomas W., David C. Yang, and Carolyn L. Hartwell, "How Internal Auditors Use Microcomputers in Practice," *Internal Auditing*, Winter 1993, 24-33.

Oxner, Thomas H., and Richard Rivers, "Computer Usage by Internal Auditors," *Internal Auditing*, Spring 1994, 40-45.

Salierno, David, "Tools of the Trade," *Internal Auditor*, August 2001, 32-42.

Schneider, Gary P., and James T. Perry, *Electronic Commerce*, Course Technologies, 1999.

Stewart, Trevor R., and Rodger A. Geel, "Integrated Audit Teamware," *Internal Auditor*, February 1994, 56-59.

Thompson, Courtenay, "CAAT Can Do," *Internal Auditor*, June 2001, 73-75.

Varney, Thomas, "Computer Forensics," *Internal Auditing*, November/December 2000, 31-33.

Weber, Ron, *Information Systems Control and Audit* (New York: Prentice Hall, 1999).

Multiple-choice Questions

1. In order to test whether data currently within the automated system are correct, the auditor should:
   a. Use test data and determine whether all the data entered are captured correctly in the updated database.
   b. Take a sample of data to be entered for a few days and trace the data to the updated database to determine the correctness of the updates.
   c. Use generalized audit software to provide a printout of all employees with invalid job descriptions. Investigate the causes of the problems.
   d. Use generalized audit software to select a sample of employees from the database and verify the data fields.

2. The auditor is concerned that retired employees are not receiving the correct benefits. Which of the following auditing procedures would be the least effective in addressing this concern?
   a. Take a sample of employees added to the retirement list for a specified time period, for example, a day or a week, and determine that they are scheduled for the appropriate benefits.
   b. Use an integrated test facility and submit transactions over a period of time to determine if the system is paying the appropriate benefits.
   c. Use generalized audit software to take a classical variables sample of retired employees on the database. Verify that all benefit payments are appropriate.
   d. Use generalized audit software to take a variables sample stratified on years since retirement and size of benefit payments. Verify that all benefit payments are appropriate.

3. The production line has experienced shutdowns because needed production parts were not on hand. Management wants to know the cause of this problem. Which of the following audit procedures best addresses this objective?
   a. Determine if access controls are sufficient to restrict the input of incorrect data into the production database.
   b. Use generalized audit software to develop a complete list of the parts shortages that caused each of the production shutdowns and analyze this data.
   c. Take a random sample of parts on hand per the personal computer databases and compare with actual parts on hand.
   d. Take a random sample of production information for selected days and trace input into the production database maintained on the LAN.

4. Which of the following statements are correct regarding the Internet as a commercially viable network?
   I.   Organizations must use firewalls if they wish to maintain security over internal data.
   II. Companies must apply to the Internet to gain permission to create a home page to engage in electronic commerce.
   III. Companies that wish to engage in electronic commerce on the Internet must meet required security standards established by the coalition of Internet providers.
   a. I only.
   b. II only.
   c. III only.
   d. I and III.

5. Which of the following is one purpose of an embedded audit module?
   a. Enable continuous monitoring of transaction processing.
   b. Identify program code that may have been inserted for unauthorized purposes.
   c. Verify the correctness of account balances on a master file.
   d. Review the contents of a specific portion of computer memory.

6. Which of the following is not a tool that could be used by an internal auditor in performing substantive tests?
   a. Embedded audit module.
   b. Parallel simulation.
   c. Test data.
   d. None of the above.

7. When an auditor uses his or her own designed input data, the auditor is using:
   a. Test data.
   b. Parallel simulation.
   c. Code review.
   d. Mapping.

8. When an auditor produces a report of the lines of program code used to produce the input, update records, and produce the output, the auditor is using:
   a. Test data.
   b. Parallel simulation.
   c. Code review.
   d. Mapping.

9. An accounting clerk developed a scheme to input fraudulent invoices for nonexistent vendors. All the payments were sent to the same address. The auditor suspects a possible fraud. The most effective computer audit technique to investigate the fraud would be to:
   a. Use test data for multiple vendors and investigate unexpected results.
   b. Perform a complete audit of computer program changes.
   c. Use generalized audit software to compare addresses across multiple files and print out duplicates for investigation.
   d. Test application controls through an integrated test facility and investigate unexpected results.

10. To determine whether there have been any unauthorized program changes since the last authorized program update, the best EDP audit technique is for the auditor to conduct a(n):
   a. Code comparison.
   b. Code review.
   c. Test data run.
   d. Analytical review.

11. Generalized audit software (GAS) is designed to allow auditors to:
   a. Monitor the execution of application programs.
   b. Process test data against master files that contain real and fictitious entities.
   c. Select sample data from files and check computations.
   d. Insert special audit routines into regular application programs.

12. An internal auditor was assigned to confirm whether operating personnel had corrected several errors in transaction files that were discovered during a recent audit. Which of the following automated tools is the auditor most likely to use?
   a. Online inquiry.
   b. Parallel simulation.
   c. Mapping.
   d. Tracing.

Chapter 16
Using Personal Computers in Auditing

Personal computers: Types of personal computer. Operating environments. Spreadsheets. Word processing. Flowcharting. Audit project management software. Scanning and optical character recognition. Graphics. Presentation software. Desktop publishing. Combinations of mainframe and personal computers. Special considerations in the electronic audit environment. Audit program integrity. Working paper integrity and accountability for work performed. Working paper review and control of review notes. Managing the audit project. Backups in the field. Archiving working papers. Risk analysis considerations.

Introduction

In the past, auditors used only a No. 2 pencil and a columnar pad to perform their assignments. The adding machine appeared on the business scene and auditors adopted it as a tool to improve productivity. Portable typewriters, calculators, and copying machines all became opportunities for improvement of efficiency. In the 1960s, mainframe computers became the newest tool for auditors. At that point, auditors began to seek ways to improve their efficiency and, ultimately, their effectiveness through the use of these machines as audit tools.

Previously the auditor had "audited around the computer." Typically in this mode, the auditor selected a sample of records and made manual calculations to test the accuracy of the records. These tests included interest on investment securities in a brokerage house, extensions on invoices in a sales organization, and so on. The auditors began to analyze the efficiency and effectiveness of using purely manual methods to check on records processed by the system.

A series of questions began to flow from the analysis of the audit work.

- Can the system test the calculations with an independent calculation constructed by the auditor?

- Can the system select the items to be tested based on selection criteria established by the auditor?

- Can multistage selections be made so a general sample can be taken and unique transactions identified for special examination?

- Can the entire file be examined rather than relying on sampling?

- Can the file be presented to the auditor in different views to facilitate more probing examination of transactions?

The list of questions can go on and on, and more often than not, the answer to each will be "Yes." The system can be programmed to do almost anything the mind can imagine, if the problem can be reduced to a set of logical instructions. Those questions and responses were largely geared to mainframe computer systems. In the 1980s, microcomputers or personal computers (PCs) became a growing part of the auditor's tool kit.

Using Personal Computers in Auditing

The rush of technological change has had its effect on audit practice just like every other facet of the organization. The use of PCs, laptops, handheld devices, and other Internet appliances seems to expand daily. It is not an overstatement to say that PCs and the software used on them constitute one of the most significant changes in the execution of day-to-day audit work in the history of the profession. These devices offer the opportunity to bring together theory and practice in an efficient and effective tool.

The PC is used for learning, audit testing, documentation, audit project management, access to information, writing, presentations, and a number of other applications. Most important, PCs are bringing the knowledge of experts into the field so the work of the field auditor can be seamlessly blended with the expert's knowledge. All of these PC uses will be discussed in the following segments.

Types of Personal Computers

One of the first issues auditors try to tackle is the type of PC they should use. This subject is too often attacked in discussions of brand name, processor identification, and instruction speed. Sometimes it becomes a contest of who has the most "gee whiz" PC. Other users will say that they are waiting for the next technological advancement; they fear obsolescence. There are a couple of truisms that the auditor should keep in mind.

- Any machine bought today will be superseded by new technology in the next 12 to 18 months. However, today's machine will not cease to function just because new technology is introduced.

- No user will realize all of the productivity of any given machine before the end of its useful life.

The real consideration in acquiring any technology — hardware or software — is the productivity that will be achieved during its useful life. Simply stated, if the salary of a staff auditor is $50,000 plus 20 percent fringes, and a purchase of $3,000 will improve that auditor's productivity 25 percent, it will pay for itself in the first year. The annual cost of a staff auditor is $50,000 + $10,000 = $60,000 multiplied by 25 percent = $15,000; $3,000 is 20 percent of the expected productivity increase in the first year.

The issue in buying PCs is not the price of the hardware and software; it is utility. The beginning of utility is allowing the computer to produce. If the computer assigned to the auditor is on the desk in the office while the auditor is in the field, the major benefit is lost before the process ever starts.

Major productivity gains are missed if the auditor records information on hard copy in the field and brings it back to the office to record it on a computer. Computers are at their best when information is entered at once and used whenever and wherever it is needed. A majority of the computer needs of the auditor must be addressed in the field. This means that the computer must be available wherever the auditor is. Also, the computer can be integrated with the client's record system and it can be used to actually obtain information for the audit.

Laptops are becoming standard devices for auditors. They have virtually all the capabilities of their physically larger siblings that sit on desktops. They have random access memory (RAM) and data storage (hard disk) capacities equal to desktop models. They have display and keyboards incorporated into one convenient package for use in the field. They are able to perform all of the work that the auditor needs despite their deceptively small size. The issue of laptop versus desktop is far more important than processor speeds or brand names. It is impossible to predict at the time of this writing what the average processor speed will be when this book is published.

Operating Environments

The operating environment of the auditor's computer is more important than the speed. The operating environment will determine how fast the auditor produces results, and the speed of results is more important than the speed of the computer itself. The operating environment is the ease-of-use factor. Personal computers have become increasingly sophisticated in their ability to respond to the needs of users — generally referred to as user friendly. Three characteristics have driven the increase in user productivity; they are multitasking, application interaction, and graphic user interface.

Multitasking. Multitasking (literally, performing multiple tasks at one time) has been performed by mainframe computers for decades. Historically, personal computers have not actually been performing several tasks at the same time. However, the speed with which the computer changes from one task to another gives the appearance that it is doing several tasks at once. This is important in auditing because the auditor uses a number of tools almost simultaneously. If we explore the low-tech audit bag and the auditor's computer, we will find:

Low-tech Audit Bag	Auditor's Computer
• Columnar pads	• Spreadsheet application
• Legal pads	• Word processing
• Plastic templates	• Flowcharting application
• Date book/diary	• Computerized date book
• Calculators	• Spreadsheet application or calculator utility
• Portable typewriters	• Report writing and creation of confirmation letters, scanning
• Reference books	• CD-ROMs or disk files with regulations, GAAP, and other regulatory rules
• Flip chart with pens	• Presentation tools
• Hard work	• Data extraction

Prior to the introduction of personal computers, the low-tech audit bag had considerable utility. The auditor could have the columnar pad, the legal pad, the flowchart template, and the calculator on the desk at the same time. This allowed the auditor to quickly reach the tool when it was needed.

However, in older operating environments on the PC, the auditor could not easily move from one tool to the next. It was necessary to close the word processing application to open the spreadsheet. If there was information in the spreadsheet that was needed for a report, the spreadsheet had to be printed and the data typed onto the word processing document.

In the newer multitasking environment, several applications can be operating at the same time. Data can be moved from one application to another through computerized "cut-and-paste" operations. Data can also be shared through linking facilities (interaction of applications) in the operating environment software. These capabilities do not simply match the "several tools on the desktop" manual environment. They improve operations because data can be moved from one source to another destination without having to rewrite the data. For example, data can be moved from a spreadsheet workpaper to a word processing report without retyping.

Multitasking environments are found in Windows on DOS PCs and the Macintosh operating system. This software is the most rapidly expanding product line in the PC environment. In the near future, a number of computers will have pen input like legal and columnar pads and voice input like dictating machines. As these changes in input sources occur, the multitasking environment will expand even more.

Speed of learning. Another clear advantage of a multitasking operating environment is the increasing standardization of the way the software is presented to the user. To operate in a multitasking environment software, the developer must abide by certain conventions. Drop-down menus require the developer to place the menu bar in a certain position and the menu items must react in a certain fashion. This means that the user finds many similarities between applications and learns each new application more quickly. Rather than having very different command sequences as found in the single application environment, the user can expect significant commonalty among applications in the multitasking environment.

The use of a multitasking environment provides more productivity for auditors through greater use of computer resources and quicker passage through the learning curve. This environment encourages the auditor to use more of the tools available in the PC because of the ease of use. The tools include spreadsheets, word processing, database management, flowcharting, and advanced statistical and modeling software — all of which are more easily mastered in the graphic user interface environment.

Interaction of applications. The sharing of data between applications is available in multitasking environments. This facility eliminates many of the cut-and-paste operations. Data linking is used when the user knows that data in one file will be used in another and both must be kept up-to-date. Imagine that the time records of an auditor are maintained in a spreadsheet and that information must be shown in a monthly narrative report. The detail or a summary section in the spreadsheet can be linked to a word processing document containing the monthly report form. As the spreadsheet is updated, the word processing document will be automatically updated — no cut-and-paste required.

Other applications allow the auditor to improve efficiency and effectiveness. For example, an auditor can scan documents to facilitate the entry of data. The auditor can also use information from e-mail and the Internet to obtain necessary information to incorporate into working papers.

Graphic user interface. An added feature in most of the multitasking systems is the graphic user interface. In this environment, the user employs an electronic pointing device referred to as a *mouse* and pictures called *icons* to initiate actions on the computer.

Personal Computer Software Used in Auditing

The auditor has access to a variety of software tools, and there are a number of organizations writing or "publishing" software applications. This means that the auditor can find several auditor-friendly word processing systems, several spreadsheet systems, and so on. The following exploration of software applications does not advocate any particular publisher's product. The intention is to comment on features that facilitate the auditor's work. These characteristics are found in a number of products in the marketplace.

Spreadsheets

If any single software application can be described as the auditor's most used tool, it has to be the electronic spreadsheet. It is the columnar pad on the computer as well as the calculator. It is used for accounting schedules, "flat" database files, graphic presentation of numeric values, and "what if" modeling. The spreadsheet should be the first application that the auditor should master.

The spreadsheet is laid out in columns and rows. Each intersection of a column and a row is called a **cell.** A cell may contain data or a formula, which is an instruction to perform a calculation or a logical analysis. Cells can be linked to other cells to provide for automated updating.

To obtain maximum utility from the spreadsheet system, the auditor must look for a number of features that will enhance productivity. (With the rapid advances being made in technology, there may be additional features available that did not exist at the time of this writing.) In this listing, the term "package" will be used to refer to the spreadsheet system that can be purchased and installed on one machine as a single unit. The features are:

- **Multitasking environment:** The package must be able to operate while the word processing, flowcharting, and other applications are open.

- **Multiple spreadsheets and spreadsheet linking:** The package must allow the user to have more than one spreadsheet open at the same time. The package must allow the linking of data between spreadsheets in the same fashion that links are made between cells within a single spreadsheet. Data changes in one spreadsheet will cause changes in dependent spreadsheets at the same time. This feature is important because it allows spreadsheets to be smaller and discrete to a specific task and still carry the results to other spreadsheets with different but related objectives. Many mistakes come from the use of extremely large spreadsheets where the user is actually trying to do several interactive tasks at the same time on a single spreadsheet.

- **Macro programming:** Macros are small programs created by the user that allow the user to perform recurrent activities at the press of a button. The package should contain a macro recorder that works like a tape recorder. The user starts the recorder, performs the task, and stops the recorder. The resulting record is saved as a file or unit on a macro sheet that can be recalled and "played" or run at any time.

- **Charts and graphs:** The package should have extensive but easy to use charting capabilities. There are many situations where the auditor wants to show information in both tabular form and in a picture or chart that rapidly and clearly communicates the information. In many cases, an auditor may display information in both formats because some readers digest facts faster and more accurately in different formats.

- **Hot links to other applications:** The spreadsheet package should allow the user to perform hot links connections to other applications such as word processing. Hot links are a step beyond simple copy and paste. If the data are copied from the spreadsheet and pasted with a hot link to a word processing document, the word processing document will be automatically updated if the spreadsheet is changed. This is particularly valuable when the spreadsheet data are being used in a report. If the spreadsheet data are changed at the last minute and a hot link was established, the report will be automatically updated.

- **Spelling checker:** Auditors very often present copies of their spreadsheets to their clients. Just as their reports should be free of spelling errors, so should their spreadsheets.

- **Integrated printing options:** The package should allow the user to print in portrait or landscape as an option within the system. Portrait is the top-to-bottom presentation that is standard in word processing and many accounting reports. However, many spreadsheets prepared by auditors are wider than they are tall, so landscape or sideways printing is required. The user should be able to make single instruction requests for scaling to reduce an oversized spreadsheet to a single page for printing.

- **Built-in analytical functions and procedures:** The package should be delivered with a broad selection of analytical tools. These are found in functions and pre-developed macros that are included in the cost of the package. They will include tools for auditing spreadsheets; solvers that allow reverse what-if analysis starting at the end and going back to the beginning; regression, correlation, break-even analysis, and others.

- **Tutorial:** The package should include a full featured, online tutorial and "help" system to facilitate learning and to constantly improve the user's skills.

- **Drag and drop editing:** Drag and drop editing is faster than conventional cut-and-paste editing. The user highlights the text to be moved with a pointing device such as a mouse and drags it to its new location. If the new location turns out not to be what the writer wants, an immediate "undo" command will return it to the original position.

- **Quick click totaling:** One of the most common commands used in spreadsheets is the "=SUM(x:y)" command, where x:y is a range of cells. If this command can be executed in a click of the mouse button or a minimum number of key and mouse movements, greater accuracy and faster output are achieved.

- **Intuitive filling or spreading:** Another common task is spreading or filling a formula or value to a number of contiguous cells. Sometimes this is a formula as we saw in the invoice test. Sometimes it is a progression of values such as January 1, February 1,. . .December 1. The spreadsheet program should be able to spread these values over a range specified by the user with only a minimum of instructions. If the process of spreading data is automatic, time is used more efficiently and the likelihood of error is reduced.

- **Annotations and notes:** Annotations are special inserts in documents that attach at a specified place but remain separate from the actual text of the document. They are like an electronic post-it note. This feature is invaluable in working paper review. It allows reviewers to attach questions and comments without disrupting the original text. In some packages, the annotation can be attached to a cell by a single command. Some packages allow the reviewer to record spoken comments that the author or other reader plays back like a tape recorder.

- **Conversion capability:** The system must include the capability to read and open spreadsheets or databases developed in other packages and to write spreadsheets or databases to the format of those packages.

Word Processing

If spreadsheets are the auditor's most commonly used tool, word processing is the auditor's window to the rest of the world. Word processing is where the auditor prepares his or her findings, sends letters and memos, and publishes administrative policies and procedures. In many cases, auditors write their audit programs in word processing systems. In other situations an auditor may use a special audit program generator.

Word processing software is more than an electronic typewriter. Word processing software provides facilities to assure the quality and efficiency of output and to manage archives.

There is a material portion of each audit report that is repeated in report after report with only minor changes. This "boilerplate" includes covers, letters of transmittal, and common statistical tables. These forms can be held in electronic files to be copied into a current report when needed. This technique makes sure that the material is accurate and efficiently entered in the report. It also means that the material will be consistent from report to report. But it also embodies the danger that boilerplate will be used when it is not appropriate or totally accurate. The use of boilerplate must be carefully and thoughtfully controlled by audit management.

Audit policies and procedures are an important part of the operation of the audit organization. They can be easily written by using a word processing system just like any other document. More importantly, when all auditors are using personal computers, the policy and procedures manual can be easily carried in computer readable form and can be consulted by every auditor. The true value of a policy and procedures manual is found in the degree of access and ease of use. Electronic files in a computer are more convenient to carry, and the ease of referring to the electronic form encourages the auditor to consult them.

There are many word processing packages on the market. When a decision is being made about buying one or more packages for the audit organization, there are a number of attributes to be considered.

- **Multitasking environment:** The package must be able to operate while the spreadsheet, flowcharting, and other applications are open.

- **Spelling checker:** Audit reports, correspondence, and other documents should be free of spelling errors. Spelling errors in reports and other documents often undermine the most thoughtful and well-researched logic.

- **Grammar checking:** Good word processing programs contain grammar-checking capabilities to ensure the correctness and power of wording. Grammar checkers identify passive wording, mixed tenses, and mixed numbers. Having the computer perform portions of the proofreading work improves productivity and ensures consistency. Most grammar checkers can measure the grade level required to read the document, the fog factor, and the average sentence length.

- **Thesaurus:** Searching for the "right word" can be a time consuming process and using the "same old words" makes for boring documents. A computerized thesaurus is an automated version of the widely used little book that many auditors carry with them.

- **Multiple files and file linking:** The package must allow the user to have more than one document open at the same time. The package must allow the linking of data between files.

- **Macro programming:** Macros are small programs that allow the user to perform recurrent activities at the press of a button.

- **Charts and graphs:** It is desirable to have easy-to-use charting capabilities in a word processing program. There are many situations where the auditor will want to show information in both tabular form and in a picture or chart that rapidly communicates the information. Many of these displays are relatively simple and should not require exiting to a spreadsheet to do simple calculations.

- **Hot links to other applications:** The word processing package should allow the user to perform hot link connections to other applications such as spreadsheets, flowcharting, and graphics packages.

- **Tutorial:** The package should include a full featured, online tutorial and help system to assist the user in learning the system and to constantly improve the user's skill.

- **Conversion capability:** The system must include the capability to read documents developed in other packages and to write documents to those packages. At the time of this writing, there are a number of widely used word processing packages. Auditors will encounter situations where packages other than their own are in use. Auditors often need to obtain information from client files or give their documents to someone who uses another package. Auditors should always be prepared to make these exchanges without having to reenter data on either side of the exchange.

- **Integrated printing options:** The package should allow the user to print in portrait or landscape as an option within the system. The user should be able to make single instruct requests for scaling to reduce an oversized document to a single page for printing.

- **Outlining:** An outlining feature allows the user to prepare an outline of the document, rearrange elements, and change into the writing process without reentering any of the data. The production process is significantly improved when the outline is prepared in the planning process with convenient rearrangement to polish the outline. When the outline is finished, the writer should be able to shift gears directly into detail writing without superfluous restarts and reentry of information.

- **Drag and drop editing:** Drag and drop editing is faster than conventional cut-and-paste editing. The user highlights the text to be moved with a pointing device such as a mouse and drags it to its new location. If the new location turns out not to be what the writer wants, an immediate "undo" command will return it to the original position.

- **Table functions:** Auditors regularly use columns of figures and comparative lists of texts. Using conventional "type and tab" entry of information makes this a laborious and error-prone effort. A table function allows the user to set up an array of columns and rows resembling a spreadsheet. The system will wrap text within each cell so the user has only to type the text and let the computer take care of all the alignment problems.

- **Mail merging:** Auditors use merging capabilities for a number of standard procedures. One of the most common is the creation of confirmation letters. The basic letter is prepared with variable spaces for data such as name, address, account number, balance, and so on. The variables are loaded on a separate file containing only the variable data. The merge function will create multiple letters, each having the data for one account. The merge function can also be used for a number of other efficiency applications in auditing. Standard letters such as "prepared by client" requests, advance arrangements, and other communications can be more easily prepared. The basic letter can be constructed with questions planted in the text. The questions prompt the auditor to enter the variable data on the keyboard and the completed letter is presented immediately. This is an advanced approach to boilerplating.

- **Annotations:** Annotations are special inserts in documents that attach at a specified place but remain separate from the actual text of the document. They are like an electronic post-it note. This feature is invaluable in report review and clearance. It allows reviewers to attach questions and comments without disrupting the original text. In some packages, the annotation can be inserted into the actual text by a single command. If the review suggests alternative language that the writer likes, it can be immediately incorporated in the text. Some packages allow the reviewer to record spoken comments that the author or other reader plays back like a tape recorder.

- **File searching:** As the auditor builds an increasing volume of files, the ability to find the one needed becomes a drain on time. A file search feature allows the user to command a search of files for identification numbers, key words, subject matter, or other criteria. This is much faster than opening and closing files until the desired document is located.

- **Automatic tables of contents, indexes, and footnotes:** In larger documents, the writer often needs to prepare a table of contents or an index. The word processing package should provide this as an automatic function. A simple code or symbol flags the text to be included in the contents or index. This facility is also valuable in extracting language from the detail of an audit report to compile a summary of findings in an audit report. Footnotes are often needed in reports and research documents and it should be an easy step for the user. The package should allow footnotes at the bottom of the page, at the end of a chapter, or at the end of the document with a single step selection. Changes in footnotes also must be automatically accommodated.

Flowcharting

One of the most important tools that the auditor should have in the computer is a flowcharting package. Flowcharting is a basic audit tool that has not been used to its fullest capability because the manual preparation of flowcharts is cumbersome. Manual flowcharts often require many restarts before a final chart is constructed. Any significant mistake or change may require a complete redrawing of the chart.

Electronic flowchart packages have eliminated that problem and made flowcharting the convenient tool it should always have been. A flowcharting package allows the auditor to move, delete, and insert symbols with ease.

There are two general types of flowcharting packages — flat and hierarchical. The hierarchical can be used as a flat flowchart — a two-dimensional form customarily seen in manual flowcharting. This can result in some very large flowcharts that are intimidating to people reading the chart.

The hierarchical type is three-dimensional. The top layer is a broad view of the entire process reduced to a few — ideally no more than nine — major functions or activities. Each of the major functions has its own flowchart at the next lower level. If any of these function flowcharts is too complex, they can be further detailed in lower levels of charts. The result is an uncluttered, easy-to-read chart at each level. The auditor can also use these subsequent levels for write-ups of procedures, rules, controls, or other information.

Flowcharting packages are also excellent for maintaining organizational charts. They allow easy revision from audit to audit as duties and reporting lines are modified and personnel are changed.

The issue of compatibility between computer operating environments has been discussed before but it bears additional consideration here. The internal and external auditors will often share files of flowcharts as well as accounting schedules and memoranda. These two groups may not be using the same software. Flowcharting is considerably more difficult to transfer between different software packages than word processing or spreadsheets. If an auditor has any plans to share flowcharts with others, the parties should discuss the compatibility issues. There are only a few packages that will interchange files.

The flowchart in Exhibit 16-1 illustrates current technology for processing transactions in a procurement operation. A student group, led by Peder Shalin working in Dr. Alan H. Friedberg's EDP Audit class at Florida Atlantic University, used Patton & Patton's FLOWCHARTING 3 to create this flowchart.

It becomes readily apparent that this flowchart is not restricted to a single entity; instead it shows the transaction processing of three independent entities working together. In electronic data interchange (EDI) situations like this, internal auditors are concerned not only with the processing within their own entity; they also must be concerned with the controls existing within trading partners' systems as well as third-party service providers.

There are several reasons for concerns about extra-entity controls. The relationship among trading partners is evolving from a competitive environment to one of mutual cooperation. We are beginning to rely on vendors'/purchasers' controls as well as our own. By relaxing internal manual reviews that require paper handling and physical evidence of authorization, we are able to reduce costs and speed the rate of commerce. The increased profits are assumed to be worth the risk of relying on trade agreements and partners' controls. Nevertheless, even among the most cooperative trading partners (not to mention adversarial parties who may become interested, such as the IRS and unions), disputes may occur. So to be admissible as evidence, in the event of disputes, electronically processed transactions are best supported by independent, producible, outside records.

The exhibit demonstrates three parties to an EDI transaction for the purchase of goods and services: the entity making the purchase, the supplier, and the trusted third party (TTP). The TTP is a vendor of wide-area-network services that supplies not only communication services but also translation software, a secure location to store transactions in transit (mailbox), and control features within a standardized processing environment.

Essentially, EDI, paperless transaction processing, is advantageous because it reduces the time, cost, and errors associated with processing a transaction. To understand how EDI and paper-based systems differ, consider three scenarios: a paper-based environment, a theoretical EDI environment, and a practical environment.

In the paper-based world, the need for a purchase is documented, and approval is indicated on the document, along with the authorization to make a purchase. A purchase order is prepared (the first opportunity for a transcription error) and approved. An additional transcription is made by the vendor on an order form that is endorsed after credit approval is made. The approved order is the basis for preparing a packing list that is annotated to show which items have actually been shipped and which have been back-ordered. Shipping documents are prepared based on the order form information, as is an invoice based on a

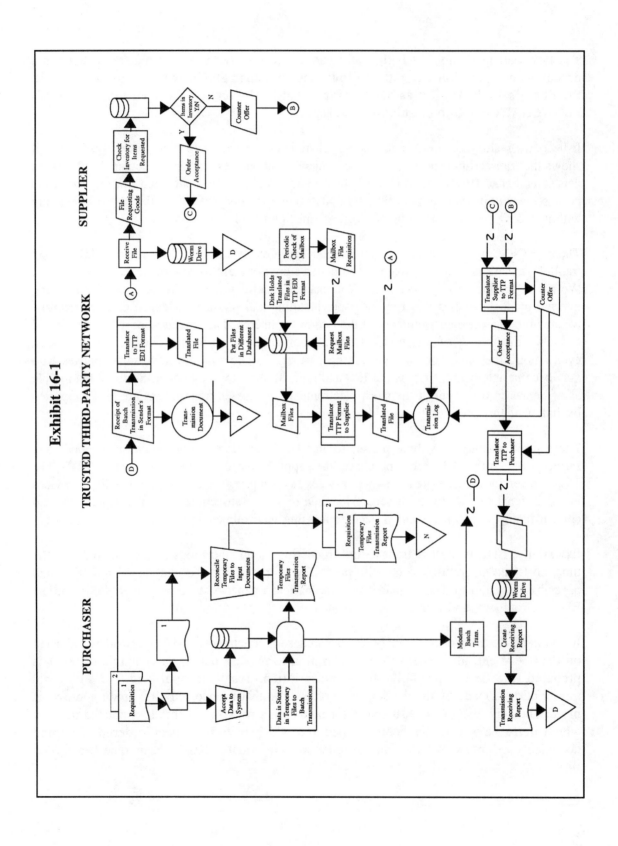

Exhibit 16-1

shipping report. The process continues with many levels of clerical transcription and review. Because there are so many opportunities for errors, we add the requirement of separation of duties to review the work of others for accuracy and completeness.

In the ultimate (probably unattainable) EDI world, a series of computer programs and controls would whisk the transaction along from initial need through payment without slowing down for printing hard copy and for multiple levels of human approval and authorization along the way. Authorization would be achieved by programmed controls and agreements.

In the current, practical environment, many organizations have created programs that automate transaction processing within their organizations. Controls over approval and authorization have shifted from separation of clerical duties to programmed computer authorization. But most of these systems still produce paper documents for processing between entities. This is where the most common type of EDI is used. Instead of passing documents between entities, electronic messages are passed instead. Two trading partners will employ a TTP network to reduce the logistical costs of electronically connecting multiple trading partners. Moreover, the TTP network can afford to provide significant controls for accuracy, completeness, and privacy of transactions that may be beyond the economical and/or technical means of the trading partners individually. The TTP network can also afford to provide translation software much more economically than can individual trading partners.

When a partner wishes to send an EDI transaction to a vendor, the format of the message must meet strict standards agreed to by industry associations or dictated by government agreements. The standards include the contents of documents such as purchase orders (POs). The PO format specifies fields of information included, the order, the way the information is coded in the fields, how repeating fields are managed, and control information for accuracy, completeness, and authorization. The translation software is necessary because businesses do not create their transaction processing software to meet the EDI standards. For example, a small retailer X, the purchaser in our flowchart, might purchase goods from any number of suppliers not all of whom use or meet the same EDI standards. When the purchaser completes a purchase order (either on paper or as an output from his or her own computer system) shown as a requisition on the flowchart, his or her computer system generates a computer file containing many orders, including those intended for a specific supplier, Y. X's file is sent via modem to the TTP network. The TTP network submits that file to a program that translates X's requisitions to the EDI standard and distributes the standard form to the mailboxes (databases) of various vendors, including Y. When Y's computer is ready, it tells the TTP network to collect its mail and translate it into the form that Y's computer and software understand. The physical transmission and transcription of X's output into Y's input is completed by the computer. Acknowledgments, shipping documents, receiving reports, payments, and other parts of the transaction cycle can be programmed to reference and agree with the original order to reduce clerical error and speed processing. If authorization by computer program is too difficult or undesirable for other reasons, it can be designed into interactive terminal programs, and authentication can be achieved via electronic signature.

In such an environment, the primary concerns include general and transaction controls. Examples of general controls are: (1) program development and change controls — making sure the software does what it should and only what it should; (2) access control — adequate protection against unauthorized access or modification of data or programs; (3) manual follow-up of errors detected by programmed controls; (4) backup and recovery controls; and (5) audit trails. Transaction controls, such as (1) accuracy controls; (2) completeness controls; and (3) user controls are implemented in all phases (input, processing, and output) of transaction processing.

It is important to note, also, that EDI would normally provide for payment of invoices electronically via an automated clearinghouse that would likely function as a trusted third party between the respective banks of the purchaser and supplier. Payment processing systems and the related transaction controls are not illustrated on the flowchart and may or may not be included in an auditor's review of a procurement processing system.

In a review of controls for a purchasing system in an EDI environment, auditors would be concerned with how the computer systems and networks meet standard control objectives. Examples of major control points are:

Association controls. At data entry time, the system will make sure the data entry person is duly authorized. Operator identifiers and passwords, terminal identifiers, authorized hours of operations, sequence numbers, batch authorizations, and write-only access rights are examples of authentication controls that could be built into the system. Authentication controls are important because the transactions entered will result in a binding contract (the purchase order) with a supplier.

Application system controls. The purchasing application, including its data entry components, will provide edits such as assuring only numerical data in numeric fields, legitimate requisition numbers, appropriate levels of user authority, checks for duplicate records or back-ordered items, and batch counts and totals. In addition to edits, the purchasing application will provide other controls depending on its degree of sophistication. Application controls could include combining orders for similar items, applying economic reorder quantities, checking against existing inventory levels, and preventing the issuance of orders for obsolete, discontinued, or unprofitable items. Again, the objective is to make sure that only legitimate items are ordered. More sophisticated applications may automatically generate purchase orders based on items approaching the economic reorder point, items of seasonal demand, or items temporarily available at a low cost. As application systems become more sophisticated, the control structure — including human review of machine-generated transactions or other monitoring types of controls — must also be improved.

Transmission controls. The system components and networks for transmitting transactions to suppliers must also meet basic control objectives. Controls should make sure that only authorized transactions are transmitted. The sending device and location should be authenticated by the receiving network services provider. Transaction record items must meet prescribed formats and standards including all required fields and authorization codes. Standard communications systems controls make sure that all messages are received in their entirety and data are not corrupted during transmission. Technical controls in the communication environment should also protect against electronic intruders, provide privacy for sensitive records (such as encryption for passwords or authentication cones), and make sure record contents are unchanged.

Trusted third-party network controls. The third-party network would complete the link for transmission controls. Additionally, the TTP network would make sure that records meet the required formats, are complete, and match the batch or control totals sent with the records. The TTP would then distribute transaction items to the appropriate recipients, reformatting data as necessary to match the different standards used by different participants in the network. Balancing controls would guard against the loss of transactions during distribution. Any control breakdowns identified would have to be communicated immediately back to the parties concerned.

We have listed only brief examples of the types of controls needed for purchasing systems in an EDI environment. The auditor's appraisal of controls would begin with: (1) understanding management objectives for the systems, including an appraisal of risks relevant to the system; (2) addressing any mandated controls such as those prescribed by regulators or industry standards; and (3) looking for control elements related to effectiveness and efficiency, security, competitive advantage, or other considerations within the scope of the auditor's review.

In all cases the controls should be continuous throughout the processing cycle, giving reasonable assurance that any breakdowns in controls at any step within the cycle would be detected by the controls in the next step.

Audit Project Management Software

Every auditor who has been in charge of an audit project has acted as a project manager. A typical audit project is made up of some or all of the following tasks:

- Reviewing the prior audit report and working papers on this audit subject
- Determining the staff resources needed for this audit
- Establishing the audit work program
- Making assignments of personnel
- Making advance arrangements with the client

- Making travel and lodging plans
- Supervising on-site work
- Reviewing working papers and preparing review notes
- Drafting the report (continuous)
- Following up to see that review notes are cleared
- Discussing the draft report with client management
- Completing the report
- Sending the report to the client
- Holding a conference with the client
- Archiving the working papers

All of these tasks must be carried out in the proper order if the project is to be effective and efficient. Travel arrangements cannot be made until the staffing of the job is known. Advance arrangements cannot be made with the client until a date is set. A date cannot be set until the staff and their availability have been established.

This process of sequencing is critical. The tasks that must come first — called predecessors — have to be completed before later tasks — called successors — can take place. In classical project management, the relationship of these various tasks is mapped out in a project diagram. The diagrams, called network charts, are used to make sure that the right things happen in the right order. The charts also reduce the likelihood of unexpected events because of incorrect sequencing.

Experienced project managers know that sequence is not the only problem. Time is also a problem — and usually the larger one. Projects generally have two time constraints (1) resource time and (2) lapse time.

Resource time is the sum of all of the time of the personnel assigned to the project. If five people are assigned to a project for five days each, there are 25 person days available. The project manager determines the time required to complete each task. If the sum of the required task times is 30 person days and the resources available are 25 days, the project is in trouble.

Lapse time is the planned calendar time from the beginning of the project to the end. If the project is to begin on March 1 and be completed by March 5, the lapse time is five days. If the resource time is 30 person days, the project will need some combination like six people for five days to complete the project within the lapse time requirement. This was discussed in Chapter 12, "Analytical and Quantitative Methods."

These two issues — resource time and lapse time — are further complicated by the skills of the people and the skill requirements of the project. Suppose the project required 10 days of engineering time, 15 days of accounting time, and five days of programming time. If the personnel assigned to the project are two engineers for five days each, two accountants for five days each, and two programmers for five days each, the project is in trouble. There is a mismatch of accounting and programming talent on the project.

Audit project management software handles all of the many complex calculations that are required for project scheduling. The constraints described above are only some of the complicated calculations that lead to successful project management. Until recently, only large mainframe computers could handle the complex calculations for project management. Now personal computers perform all these functions and do a superior job of displaying the results in a graphic form. Graphic representation of task sequences and resource allocations makes it easier to understand and deal with the project.

Scanning and Optical Character Recognition Software

One of the auditor's nightmares is transcribing information that is obtained during the course of an audit. The answer in the past has always been a trip to the nearest copying machine with the resulting increase in paper files. An environmentally sensitive auditor refers to this as "arborcide." If an audit department is to change to a paperless audit operation, it must find efficient means of capturing outside information onto the auditor's computer. This reduces the paper load and makes reference to the information easier.

Auditors need policy and procedures manuals in their computer files for handy reference. They also need reference materials on GAAP and regulatory requirements within easy access. In some cases, such as policy manuals, the files are probably on computers in the organization because they were done on word processing applications in other departments. The auditors can ask for copies of these files for their use.

In many cases, the auditor does not have access to original word processing or spreadsheet files and the alternative is a laborious job of typing that information into the computer. Modern technology has solved that problem. Scanners are available to "read" documents and put them into the computer in lieu of manual typing. Auditors are using this technology every day to replace the traditional copying machine.

Scanners come in two general types. The first is the flatbed scanner. It looks like a truncated version of a copying machine. The document to be copied is placed on a flat glass plate and a light source passes back and forth over it. As the light source passes, an electronic image is taken and passed to the computer as a "picture" of the document. The picture can be stored or it can be scanned into the computer with *optical character recognition* (OCR) software.

The OCR software will examine the shapes in the picture and compare them to tables that recognize the letters in the picture. If the scanner sees the shape "r" it will recognize it to be a lowercase letter r and the shape "R" will be seen as an uppercase letter R. Once the character has been identified, it can be converted to its ASCII equivalent — that is, the mathematical code that a personal computer system recognizes as a lowercase r or uppercase R. Then, the document is a computer file that can be noted, cross-referenced, even quoted by copy and paste procedures.

Flatbed scanners are lightweight but they are rather delicate instruments and awkward to carry around to field sites. For use in the field, auditors use hand scanners, the second type. A typical hand scanner is slightly larger than a normal person's hand. It contains a light source and the scanner is passed over the document that is being copied. In most configurations, the hand scanner is a combination of hardware and software. The hand scanner device takes the picture and sends it to the computer.

The OCR software in the computer examines the "picture" and converts it to ASCII text automatically. Since the hand scanner may require several passes over a document to cover the entire surface, the OCR software also recognizes the overlaps that occur and eliminates those duplications. In some hand scanning systems, the user can tell the system that the information is being loaded into a spreadsheet and the software will recognize blanks in the "picture" as the distance between columns and will lay out the ASCII picture into the rows and columns of a spreadsheet. This is particularly valuable when the auditor wants to take data from computer reports into the personal computer and no downloading facilities are available. The auditor must be sensitive to the fact that the data on the printout is not the computer's raw data, but the result of a report creation process.

Even the slower, but more portable hand scanner is described by one vendor as: ". . .typing 500 wpm. . .," which is a bit faster than most auditors can keyboard process information.

Scanners are also used by auditors to get pictures into workpapers. Photographs can be scanned into computer files and pasted into word processing documents with comments. They can be placed in reports, also.

Graphics Software

Graphics software is employed by auditors for a number of uses. Examples are: a floor plan of an office to show physical workflow; a computer room plan to show physical access; fire hazards and device locations; and a grounds plan to show where buildings are located on campus. All of these may be recorded in computer files for reference and further use in audits and reports.

In general, graphics software works well only in the graphical user interface (GUI) environment. The GUI environment supports the use of the mouse and other pointing devices that are needed in the graphics or drawing environment. As with other packages, the graphics package should have hot links capabilities.

Presentation Software

Auditors are often required to make formal presentations. There are preliminary presentations to clients; presentations of audit findings to the people audited, senior management, and the audit committee; "sales" presentations to explain the value of the auditors' services; and so on. Presentation systems such as PowerPoint are used to make overheads, handouts, and speaker's notes. Connected to the speaker's personal computer, they are used to project the slides from the computer system to a movie screen.

Presentation systems provide another tool for the auditor to use in delivering messages to various audiences. The professional quality of the presentation may prove to be one of the critical factors in delivering it. It has been accurately observed that the medium is often the message. The best message content improperly delivered may be a major negative.

Automated Workpapers Software

Internal audits are increasingly using automated workpapers which perform risk assessment, audit scheduling, generate workpapers and reports, allow the tracking of unresolved issues and expenses. Such software also typically provides security features to limit access to the data.

Other Software

Auditors should include **virus protection software** on their computers and make sure that entity systems are properly protected. Without up-to-date software, there is clearly a risk of loss or corruption of data and programs. Given the propensity for the development of viruses by individuals, the software needs to be updated on a regular basis to provide up-to-date protection.

Auditors should regularly back up their data. This is also true for the entity as a whole. While high capacity drives have lessened the need for **backup software,** the discipline of regular backups is important. In addition to regular backups, utility programs can be used to provide protection in case of certain sudden hard disk crashes. These utility programs frequently will also monitor system performance.

For those auditors who regularly connect their systems to an Internet provider, a **firewall program** should also be used. This is especially important if the connection is made through a cable modem because the connection is technically alive constantly.

Desktop Publishing Software

Auditors often circulate newsletters within the organization and to clients outside the immediate location. These newsletters can be very informal, using word processing software. On the other hand, the auditor may be quite concerned that the appearance should be as professional as the message.

Desktop publishing software has considerable similarity to word processing. Its primary difference is the ability to place information where the writer wants it. Everyone reads newspapers, newsletters, and magazines. Articles often start on one page and are continued several pages later. Two or more articles start on the first page and are concluded on later pages. Sidebars are placed along the side, bottom, or top of a page to emphasize a particular point. All of these features enliven a newsletter or a major audit report and cannot typically be easily achieved with a standard word processing program.

Desktop publishing software, also referred to as page layout software, enables the writer/publisher to accomplish all of these visual effects without having to employ specialists or send the work out to specialty houses. However, as word processing programs become more sophisticated, they can provide many of the benefits of desktop publishing software without the substantial additional cost.

Expert Systems

Personal computer technology is advancing rapidly, and it is impossible to anticipate all of the tools that will be available in the future. One tool that is sure to become important for auditors in the near future is expert systems.

Expert systems are not widely available as "off-the-shelf" software. These applications are usually custom programmed for each specific user. That is likely to change in the future. Framework models within which expert systems can be written are appearing and will be increasingly available. The next extension of the expert system — **artificial intelligence systems** — will also become more available. Artificial intelligence systems are able to change the rules in the expert system as more and better information is available. Credit scoring systems can improve themselves as the performance of current borrowers is tracked. The historical basis that made up the beginning rules is updated and the rules are modified by the system.

Artificial intelligence is already available in systems that are as basic as word processing. The word processing system "watches" the errors that are detected by the spelling checker. When a given error is identified as a frequent problem, the word processing system will start to look for it as it occurs and will make the correction "on-the-fly" rather than waiting for the run of the spell checker.

Audit systems will be developed to bring the experience and insight of experts to bear on the work of the auditor in the field. These systems will include artificial intelligence "engines" that will constantly update the rules of the experts to keep the software current with the changing circumstances encountered by the field audit and by the organizations within which they work.

Combinations of Mainframe and Personal Computers

The ultimate in audit resources is the mainframe or networked computers or minicomputers to personal computer connection that allows the auditor to extract data from the mainframe and work with the data inside the auditor's computer. Some auditors have been accustomed to using generalized audit software (GAS) to obtain data in printed reports. That was a major step forward for the auditor. The movement of masses of data from the mainframe to the PC is an advancement that rivals or surpasses GAS as an advancement in audit efficiency and effectiveness.

The mass download method does not attempt to use the mainframe to classify, examine, or analyze data. The extract from the mainframe is the most time consuming part of the process. Therefore, auditors use their GAS to define all of the fields found in the data records. Then the fields needed can be extracted and a mass download dump of the data is made to the PC. All sorting, classification, and analysis is performed in the auditor's PC. This is usually carried out in spreadsheet, database, or statistical analysis software. In other cases, the auditor uses the mainframe's power to extract records for analysis on the auditor's system.

Special Considerations in the Electronic Audit Environment

As the auditor changes the working environment from paper to computer, there are new issues that must be considered. These include the preservation of the audit work recorded on computers and maintaining the integrity of audit programs, review notes, and working papers. In many cases, there are analogies in the pencil and paper environment. However, there are new wrinkles in some of these issues and there are new challenges to face.

Audit Program Integrity

The integrity of the audit program is a greater concern in the electronic environment than in the pencil and paper environment. In the paper environment, the program was drawn up and approved by the audit manager. If a standard program was used, the master was photocopied. If the field auditor decided to take out a step, the removal had to be signed off or a portion of the printed page had to be cut off. Such changes tended to be rather obvious. In the electronic world, the deletion of a section of a document is both easy to do and hard to identify. How then does the audit manager make sure that the integrity of the approved program is maintained?

There are several tools available to see that the full, approved program is carried out or that incomplete work is identified. One method is the use of a database system with password security to manage the program. The audit program is entered in a database designed for this purpose where the load and delete functions are under password security. This prevents the field auditor or anyone else from deleting or modifying any steps.

A second method is to place audit programs in read-only files. The field auditor can read the files but cannot change or delete them. This is less desirable because the ability to tie working paper references to the audit program is lost. Efficiency is lost to security, because variances must be resolved on a post-field work basis.

Another method is proofreading the audit program file when it is turned in by the field auditor. The proofreading is a comparison of the file returned by the field auditor against a copy of the approved original. Again, efficiency is lost to security. This can be improved by using programs that compare different files for changes.

There are other methods that audit management may develop, but the objective is to provide audit management with a stated and understood plan to determine program integrity.

Working Paper Integrity and Accountability for Work Performed

The preceding section discussed audit management's vulnerability to manipulation by the field auditor. The next logical question is, "What protection is there to assure the integrity of the work of the field auditor?" In the past, an erasure in the working papers was reasonably obvious. So, also, was the use of whitening liquids on the paper. Not so with computer files.

If the field auditor turns in working papers containing schedules on a spreadsheet, data can be changed without leaving erasures. So how is the field auditor protected from charges that he or she might be held accountable for in the future? Passwords work both ways. The auditor can password-protect the original working papers; however, there must be a system of central storage of passwords in case they are needed at a future time.

Password protection should be used only in the cell structure of a spreadsheet, NOT on the document itself. Protection of the cell structure prevents changes to the data in the cells — and that is the objective. Protection of the entire file means that the file cannot be opened without the password. If the password is forgotten or the auditor is not available, the file is useless unless special security-breaking utility programs are used.

Completed workpapers can be saved to a CD-R (write once, read many) and the CD can be subject to appropriate physical security. Likewise, once completed and reviewed, workpapers can be moved to another protected area on the network.

A word of caution. Some audit managers rely on the creation date in the directory to make sure the original files have not been changed. This is not a completely reliable method. Remember that changing the system date and time can be a convenient way to mask a change to the data files. In addition, some movements of files from the original computer to a floppy disk to an audit manager's computer for review and then to an archive device will result in changes in the creation date.

Working Paper Review and Control of Review Notes

How does the reviewing supervisor make sure that all review notes are maintained and none are deleted? The same security concerns that were covered in the audit program discussion apply to the review notes. The same advantages and disadvantages of various security techniques apply to review notes as to the audit program. The incorporation of the review notes under password access in the database system along with the audit program is a blending of security and efficiency.

The use of a database system also offers the ability to automate some of the review process. For example, the database system can report automatically on all steps that the auditor marks "not applicable" or "N/A." The audit supervisor can quickly evaluate whether the field auditor's explanation of nonapplicability makes sense.

If the system requires the field auditor to draw a conclusion on each control tested, there is another automatic review step available. Suppose the auditor has the following options when concluding a test of control:

- Satisfactory operation
- Minor weakness
- Major weakness
- Control is not operating

Any conclusion other than satisfactory operation should result in a finding and recommendation for improvement. If the database provides a place to record the finding and the recommendation, the system can be programmed to look for any case where the conclusion is other than satisfactory operation and there is *no* recommendation. This saves the supervisor from looking for this condition.

With current technology, all review work cannot be automated. However, a number of critical tests can be performed by the computer. If the review notes are recorded in the same system and the auditor is required to answer the notes in the system, further review can be automated. The items with review notes can be automatically presented to the field auditor so time is not wasted in searching for the notes. The reviewer can follow up with an automatic call for all review notes and their answers. An automated report can be produced for all unanswered notes. The supervisor and managerial levels are highly paid and their expertise is needed in many activities. Any operations such as those described above that free more of their time to train, mentor, coach, and develop the staff should produce valuable returns to the organization.

Managing the Audit Project

The computer can provide additional resources to improve the efficiency and effectiveness of the audit process. First, it can provide the audit steps in priority order to make sure the important steps are done first and the unimportant steps last. It can ensure that the issue of importance is established by audit management, not by the field auditor who may perceive different priorities. Management can code the steps with defined levels of priority and the system can offer all of the highest priority items before those at the second priority level and so on.

The system can also provide an ongoing to-do list to help the auditor project time requirements. If standard programs are used, the system can carry advisory times for each step to help the auditor with time management. The system can also provide for the auditor to enter the time used on each step to establish data for time budgeting on future audits.

Some firms are having auditors electronically transmit their working papers back on a regular basis. This allows the supervisor to answer questions or to review progress made on a regular basis. Some use updating software to make sure that only the most recent versions are kept.

Backups in the Field

A new issue has surfaced with the advent of the personal computer as an audit tool. Imagine that the auditor has put all of the paper working papers in the audit bag and checked it through on the flight home. At the destination, the bag is missing. Now imagine that the modern auditor has all of the working papers in electronic form on the laptop computer. Recent stories of the theft of computers in security lines reminds one to back up all important data and not to put it into the same bag as the computer. While the new x-ray systems have effectively minimized the potential of losing data, there is still some chance of data loss.

Some still prefer to ask that the computer be hand checked at air terminals. The wise auditor will also perform another simple but effective procedure — copy the working papers to floppy disks and mail the copy to the audit office before starting the trip home. This will make sure that one copy is traveling with the auditor in the computer's hard disk and another is traveling independently via the mail. This procedure is equally important when the auditor is traveling by other means, such as by automobile.

Archiving Working Papers

Now that the working papers are in electronic form, how shall we archive them? One way is to print them out and store them in the same musty warehouses where paper records have been stored for years. If an auditor found that condition in an audited organization, the findings and reports would fly. The auditor should be equally enlightened about audit operations and files.

When audit papers have been reduced to electronic files they should be stored in that form to preserve space and to provide ready access and security. Audit management should consider the media on which the audit information will be stored and the possible issues that surround that information.

Audit papers may be called to court at some future time. This means that the auditor must be able to say that the electronic files, in fact, present the original information from the audit. As discussed earlier, the ability to change electronic files could be an immediate and important issue in a trial, particularly a criminal trial, such as a fraud case. If the auditor stores the papers on a medium such as floppy disks or magnetic tape, the issue of possible alteration could be critical. Provision should also be made for the storage of working papers that contain classified data that requires increased security levels. In addition, magnetic media have a limited shelf life before deterioration sets in and they are vulnerable to corruption if they are in the vicinity of a magnetic field or temperature extremes. So, how can the auditor store audit files for long periods of time in conditions that will prevent intentional or accidental changes?

As mentioned earlier, a CD-ROM is the answer. It can store information equivalent to 350,000 or more letter size pages of paper. When an audit will generate 2 to 10 megabytes or more of electronic working papers, the cost of the optical drive or CD drive is amortized rather rapidly.

Risk Analysis Considerations

There is an entire chapter on risk analysis earlier in this book. At this point, a few remarks should be made. Formalized risk analysis has been rather limited in the past because it is labor intensive when performed manually. However, the availability and speed of personal computers has made some very complex risk analysis systems more practical.

Auditors also have ability to collect data from many different analyses in many parts of the organization into a single analytical database. If the controls tested are divided into categories (e.g., authorization controls, accounting controls, and safeguarding controls), a broad analysis might show that more weaknesses are found in the controls related to authorization than to accounting or safeguarding. This would lead to further examination of the organization's methods for assigning and communicating authorities.

Suppose the data also shows whether the failures were control or performance failures. If the analysis shows widespread weakness in control failures *and* the authority category, there is an indication that the communication of authorities is weak. On the other hand, if the weaknesses are performance failures in the authorities area, it would indicate people are not reading the communications and/or not abiding by the direction in the communications.

Using computer technology, the auditor is able to develop a number of views of the findings of an audit to make the best recommendations for control improvements. The auditor can look at the control weaknesses in the following ways:

- By method of operation: detective controls vs. preventive controls

- By control type: authorization controls vs. safeguarding controls vs. accounting controls vs. compliance controls, etc.

- By control objective: operations, financial or compliance or a combination

- By combinations of any or all of these characteristics

This ability to analyze the underlying reasons for the control problems provides the auditor with the ability to improve and support the organization. It helps the auditor identify the root causes and not just the resulting "symptoms" of those causes. This makes the auditor a far more valuable resource to the organization.

The advances in computer technology for auditors are just beginning. The future will bring greater opportunities to improve audit techniques and audit productivity. The auditor will be able to reduce the burden of uninteresting, repetitious tasks and open new fields of work and greater contributions to the organization, the basic concept of "value added."

Supplementary Readings

Antoine, Robert, "Automating the Audit Function," *Internal Auditing*, Winter 1995, 53-56.
Calderon, Tomas G., and Brian Patrick Green, "Neural Networks as Risk Assessment Tools in Internal Auditing," *Internal Auditing,* November/December 2001, 3-16.
Chung, Cynthia L. K., "Elements of an Effective Internal Audit Intranet Website," *Internal Auditing,* January/February 2003, 3-13.
Coderre, David G., "Computer-assisted Audit Tools and Techniques," *Internal Auditor*, February 1993, 24-30.
Coderre, David G., "Seven Easy CAATT," *Internal Auditor*, August 1994, 28-33.

Crowell, David A., "Equipping a Mobile Audit Staff," *Internal Auditor*, August 1997, 50-56.

Daigle, Ronald J., and James C. Lampe, "Continuous Online Assurance: Expanding Internal Audit's Scope," *Internal Auditing,* September/October 2002, 8-17.

Gillevet, Joe, "Utilizing CAATs to Determine Input Errors," *The EDP Auditor Journal,* Volume IV, 1995, 19-24.

Glover, Steven, Douglas Prawitt, and Marshall Romney, "Software Showcase," *Internal Auditor*, August 1999, 49-59.

Lampe, James C., and Andy Garcia, "Using Data Mining as an Audit Tool," *Internal Auditing,* May/June 2002, 3-11.

Leitch, Robert A., and Yining Chen, "Natural Database Structure and Audit Activities," *Internal Auditing,* September/October 2001, 35-39.

Lin, Thomas W., David C. Yang, and Carolyn L. Hartwell, "How Internal Auditors Use Microcomputers in Practice," *Internal Auditing*, Winter 1993, 24-33.

Oxner, Thomas H., and Richard Rivers, "Computer Usage by Internal Auditors," *Internal Auditing*, Spring 1994, 40-45.

Stewart, Trevor R., and Rodger A. Geel, "Integrated Audit Teamware," *Internal Auditor*, February 1994, 56-59.

Multiple-choice Questions

1. Passwords for microcomputer software programs are designed to prevent:
   a. Inaccurate processing of data.
   b. Unauthorized access to the computer.
   c. Incomplete updating of data files.
   d. Unauthorized use of the software.

2. Your firm has recently converted its purchasing cycle from a manual process to an online computer system. Which of the following is a probable result associated with conversion to the new automatic system?
   a. Processing errors are increased.
   b. The nature of the firm's risk exposure is reduced.
   c. Processing time is increased.
   d. Traditional duties are less segregated.

3. The best approach for making sure that only authorized employees receive computer output is:
   a. Place the output in bins early in the day rather than late in the day.
   b. Load the output in a file to print at local workstations.
   c. Hold the output in a secure area until it is picked up by authorized employees.
   d. Make printouts available only at specified times.

4. Each day, after all processing is finished, a bank performs a backup of its online deposit files and retains it for seven days. Copies of each day's transaction files are not retained. This approach is:
   a. Valid, in that having a week's worth of backups permits recovery even if one backup is unreadable.
   b. Risky, in that restoring from the most recent backup file would omit subsequent transactions.
   c. Valid, in that it minimizes the complexity of backup/recovery procedures if the online file has to be restored.
   d. Risky, in that no checkpoint/restart information is kept with the backup files.

5. Your firm has recently converted its purchasing cycle from a manual to an online computer system. You have been placed in charge of the first post-implementation audit of the new system and have access to a generalized audit software package. One of your objectives is to determine whether all material liabilities for trade accounts payable have been recorded. Which of the following would most help you achieve this objective?
   a. A listing of all purchase transactions processed after the cutoff date.
   b. A listing of all accounts payable ledger accounts with a post office box given as the vendor mailing address.
   c. A listing of all duplicate: (1) purchase orders, (2) receiving reports, and (3) vendor invoices.
   d. A listing of all vendors with a debit balance in the accounts payable ledgers.

6. A construction organization uses a spreadsheet program to prepare estimates for bids on new projects. The best approach for making sure that its spreadsheet calculations are correct is to:
   a. Protect all cells except those specifically intended for data entry.
   b. Inspect the documentation to verify the approach used by the model developer.
   c. Perform sensitivity analysis on the major output results.
   d. Map the spreadsheet model with spreadsheet analysis software.

7. Which of the following database controls would be most effective in maintaining a segregation of duties appropriate to the users' reporting structure within an organization?
   a. Access security features.
   b. Software change control procedures.
   c. Dependency checks.
   d. Backup and recovery procedures.

8. Which of the following microcomputer applications would be least helpful in preparing audit working papers?
   a. Spreadsheet software.
   b. Word processing software.

c. Utilities software.

d. Database software.

9. Encryption protection is least likely to be used in which of the following situations?

a. When transactions are transmitted over local area networks.

b. When wire transfers are made between banks.

c. When confidential data are sent by satellite transmission.

d. When financial data are sent over dedicated, leased lines.

10. At the end of the day, an internal auditor uses the client's microcomputer and word processing program to draft a working paper that contains the day's findings. Which of the following would be the best thing to do before leaving the office?

a. Print the working paper and save the file on a floppy disk.

b. Print the working paper and save the file on a hard disk.

c. Print the working paper, save the file on the hard disk, and save a backup copy of the file on a floppy disk.

d. Save the file on the hard disk.

11. Which of the following is the least efficient and most error prone method for transferring large amounts of data from a mainframe to a microcomputer?

a. Transfer by downloading.

b. Transfer by diskette.

c. Transfer using an optical scanner.

d. Transfer from a tape drive through specialized software.

12. Which of the following is not true? Relational databases:

a. Are flexible and useful for unplanned, ad hoc queries.

b. Store data in table form.

c. Use trees to store data in a hierarchical structure.

d. Are maintained on direct access devices.

13. Organizations now can use electronic transfers to conduct regular business transactions. Which of the following terms best describes a system where an agreement is made between two or more parties to electronically transfer purchase orders, sales orders, invoices, and/or other financial documents?

a. Electronic mail (e-mail).

b. Electronic funds transfer (EFT).

c. Electronic data interchange (EDI).

d. Electronic data processing (EDP).

14. Using test data, an auditor has processed both normal and a typical transaction through a computerized payroll system to test calculation of regular and overtime hours. Sufficient competent evidence of controls exists if:
    a. No other tests are performed.
    b. Test data results are compared to predetermined expectations.
    c. Exceptions are mapped to identify the control logic executed.
    d. Test result data are tagged to instigate creation of an audit data file.

15. Which of the following concepts distinguishes the retention of computerized audit working papers from the traditional hard copy form?
    a. Analyses, conclusions, and recommendations are filed on electronic media and are therefore subject to computer system controls and security procedures.
    b. Evidential support for all findings is copied and provided to local management during the closing conference and to each person receiving the final report.
    c. Computerized data files can be used in EDP audit procedures.
    d. Audit programs can be standardized to eliminate the need for a preliminary survey at each location.

16. Which of the following most significantly encouraged the development of electronic funds transfer systems?
    1. Response to competition.
    2. Cost containment.
    3. Advances in information technology.
    4. Improvements in automated control techniques.
    5. The development of data encryption standards.

    a. 1, 2, & 4.
    b. 2, 3, & 4.
    c. 2, 4, & 5.
    d. 1, 2, & 3.

17. Of the techniques available to an auditor, which is the most valuable in providing a summary outline and overall description of the process of transactions in an information system?
    a. Flowcharts.
    b. Transaction retrievals.
    c. Test decks.
    d. Software code comparisons.

18. Enabling users to have different views of the same data is a function of:
    a. The operating system.
    b. A program library management system.
    c. The database management system.
    d. A utility program.

19. Which of the following is not a benefit of using information technology in solving audit problems?
    a. It helps reduce audit risk.
    b. It improves the timeliness of the audit.
    c. It increases audit opportunities.
    d. It improves the auditor's judgment.

20. Which of the following is an indication that a computer virus of this category is present?
    a. Frequent power surges that harm computer equipment.
    b. Unexplainable losses of or changes to data.
    c. Inadequate backup, recovery, and contingency plans.
    d. Numerous copyright violations due to unauthorized use of purchased software.

21. Which of the following operating procedures increases an organization's exposure to computer viruses?
    a. Encryption of data files.
    b. Frequent backup of files.
    c. Downloading public-domain software from electronic bulletin boards.
    d. Installing original copies of purchased software on hard disk drives.

22. Which of the following is a risk that is higher when an electronic funds transfer (EFT) system is used?
    a. Improper change control procedures.
    b. Unauthorized access and activity.
    c. Insufficient online edit checks.
    d. Inadequate backups and disaster recovery procedures.

23. Which of the following concepts distinguishes the retention of computerized audit workpapers from that of the traditional hard copy form?
    a. Analyses, conclusions, and recommendations are filed on electronic media and are therefore subject to computer system controls and security procedures.
    b. Evidential support for all findings is copied and provided to local management during the closing conference and to each person receiving the final report.
    c. Computerized data files can be used in EDP audit procedures.
    d. Audit programs can be standardized to eliminate the need for a preliminary survey at each location.

PART 5

REPORTING

Chapter 17
Reports

Getting management's attention. The philosophy of reporting. Report writing friction. Proposed solutions. Marketing the audit report. Action on audit recommendations. Improving internal audit report timing. The ingredients of communication: report procedures, communication, discussions, factual reports, perspective, precision, clarity, background support, technical discussion, organization, constructive tone, timeliness, recommendations, clients' views, director's responsibilities. Graphics. Informal reports. Due diligence audit report. Communications outside the organization. Oral reports and flip charts. Good writing and good thinking: outlines, prior reports, getting started. Language. Physical characteristics. Tips for audit report writing. Effective strategies for report writing. Elements of exceptional reports. Short reports, More prompt reports. Information security. Editing. Proofreading. Three sample reports.

• •

What They Are and What They Do

Reports are the internal auditor's opportunity to get management's complete attention. That is how auditors should regard reporting — as an opportunity, not dreary drudgery — a perfect occasion to show management how auditors can help.

Much too often, auditors clearly throw away this golden chance to open management's eyes, to show management what they have accomplished and what they can accomplish, to explain what management needs to know and what it needs to do. Internal auditors throw away this opportunity by using pallid prose, by making mountains out of rubbish heaps, by being content with uninviting report formats, by making allegations that won't withstand assault, by drawing unsupported and illogical conclusions, and by reporting findings without solutions.

The auditors should regard their reports in the same light that a vendor regards an opportunity to present his or her products to the president of an organization; an opening for a well-rehearsed, well-tested, well-conceived presentation. In this light, the audit report has three functions: first, to communicate; second, to explain; and third, to persuade and, when necessary, sound a call to action. As Dudley E. Brown said 40 years ago: "We have, on the whole, an admirable story to tell — buttressed by facts and figures, and supported by analysis and reason — and it surely is one that deserves to be told often and in the right places"[1] (and with vigor).

Audit findings and opinions are important to management. The dispassionate, objective conclusions may ease management's mind about well-functioning activities, and the recommendations may alert management to matters needing improvement.

But management must want to read or hear the reports. For communication to be effective the channels must be clear and the medium must be incisive and easily understood. The story must be worthy of the material; much skillful and constructive audit effort flounders in the murky waters of poor reporting. Auditors who sharpen their auditing techniques but leave their reporting dull will be unable to penetrate the management circles where their story should be told.

When management gives them an audience, internal auditors must never forget that they are marketing. So they must be consciously persuasive — by the techniques of motivation and by the style they use. They must highlight what is management-oriented. They must downplay or omit what is immaterial. They must adroitly translate the technical into the readily understandable. They must point skillfully to the need for taking action, describe that action, and explain the advantages of the action and the penalties for avoiding action.

Then management will begin to appreciate the significance of the audit product, see the valuable insights it can obtain, and learn to expect the accuracy, the objectivity, and the plain good sense of what the auditor has to say. Then, and not until then, will the internal audit report become required reading for management. This development will help auditors achieve one of their own objectives: to contribute to the organization's well being, to be a part of the councils of management, and to have access to management's ear.

There is small likelihood that auditors were born with the word mastery of a Shakespeare or the crisp, lean style of a Hemingway. If they were, they would probably be writers instead of auditors. But what writing talent they have can be forged into an effective tool — with the right effort, with the right desire, with the right standards, and with the right techniques.

Report Philosophy

Internal audit reports can be powerful instruments when they are well used and constructed. They can create the impression of audit professionalism. They can tell their clients — senior management — about important events they would otherwise not know about. They can change thinking. They can impel action.

The audit report as mentioned before, has three major purposes. If internal auditors do not achieve these purposes, their reports are a waste of time. In their reports, internal auditors should seek to:[2]

Inform	Tell what they found.
Persuade	Convince management of the worth and validity of the audit findings.
Get results	Move management toward change and improvement.

Thus, the reports should present audit findings clearly and simply. They should support conclusions with persuasive evidence. They must provide direction to management for decision-making by offering recommendations for improvement. These ends can be achieved by the following means:

Objectives	Means
Inform	Create awareness.
Persuade	Obtain acceptance; create support.
Get results	Impel action.

The purpose of the audit report is to provide these means. The report should create in the reader the assurance that (1) what is reported can be relied on, and (2) what is recommended is valid and worthwhile.

To carry out the means, the following elements are needed in the audit report:

Means	Elements
Awareness	A clear and understandable identification of the difficulties, or of an opportunity for improvement.
Acceptance/ Support	Real and persuasive support for conclusions and evidence of their importance.
Action	Providing constructive and practical means of achieving the needed change.

To develop awareness, the report should explain the conditions found and compare them with some criterion of acceptable action. To achieve acceptance by management, the report must convincingly show the actual effect of the conditions or their potential effect. To help management take adequate corrective action, the report should show the cause of the difficulty; not only the surface cause, but also the basic problem. And to improve the chance of taking action, the report should provide recommendations — some means of solving the problems. Later on in this chapter we provide an example of applying these methods.

Report Writing Friction

Few sources of friction within the audit activity exceed that caused by the process of report writing. The most brilliant analyses and the most productive audit findings seem to be forgotten during the trauma of report writing. The reasons are many:[3]

- *Supervisory rewriting.* When an experienced, professional auditor finishes the draft of a report, it usually represents a best effort. The auditor is not very pleased to see a supervisor tear it to shreds with a blue pencil or, even worse, without explanation, disregard that hard work entirely and start rewriting the report from scratch.

- R*eporting under pressure.* Internal auditors do not seem to enjoy report writing in the first place. Yet they try to anticipate supervisory comments and structure the report to answer previous criticisms. This takes time. And the pressures to rush the draft are a constant source of irritation. Operating managers and executives are concerned with the results of the audit and impatiently await the finished audit report. They pressure the chief audit executive for the final draft. Exasperation mounts.

- *Too much time spent on reports.* In an effort to turn out a product that meets professional standards and eliminates errors and misconceptions, chief audit executives set up review procedures to produce the best possible product. That, too, can take time. So a great deal of available audit time and budget are spent on the reporting process.

- *Poor drafts.* Most auditors are more concerned with auditing than with writing. They see their objectives met when they unearth serious defects and have them corrected. The report strikes them as a means to an end. And so the drafts of reports submitted to supervisors may be slipshod products. Other auditors feel that, since the supervisor is going to rewrite it anyway, there is no reason to spend too much of their own time budget on it.

- *Poor writing skills. Many* internal auditors are not skillful writers. Schools today are trying to help correct the problem. In the past, little time was spent learning how to turn out clear and unambiguous prose. Computers today are helping to cure this deficiency.

- *Disagreements between auditors and their supervisors.* Disagreements run the gamut from grammar and spelling, to logic and the interpretation of discovered conditions.

- *Writing the reports far from the site of the audit.* Many audit reports are written in the office after the field work has been completed. Time tends to dull memories even though working papers may provide a degree of support. Writing the segments of the reports in the field provides realism and attention to detail that may or may not be in the working papers. When it is not, there is a tendency to omit or to curtail the complete finding. Here again, computers are assisting by allowing field writing with concurrent real-time supervision during the process.

- *Lack of client interest.* Where reports are poorly written and difficult to understand, where their structure is difficult to follow, and worst of all, where clients have no obligation to respond to them, hard-working auditors find nothing but frustration in the difficult audit report process.

Proposed Solutions

What seems to be the answer? Unfortunately, there are no easy solutions. Courses in report writing concentrate on word choice, sentence length, paragraph structure, and similar matters that reside between the covers of grammar texts. However, tools are becoming available in word processing software. They cannot teach judgment, empathy, perspective, or analytical ability. The sources of audit report problems can often be found, however, in the process itself. This process can be improved, if not completely corrected, by some of the following steps:

- Develop a style manual for the audit activity. A style manual can set standards of grammar, spelling, capitalization, and the like, so as to remove some of the petty sources of disagreement among the audit staff and achieve some measure of standardization and excellence within the audit organization.

- For larger internal audit activities, an editor to review reports before they are submitted to the supervisors should be considered for several reasons. The petty grammatical and obvious logical problems are solved before there is any confrontation between auditor and audit supervisor. A central editing function provides for more consistency in both the report writing and the report format. Care must be taken that this does not become a bottleneck.

- Conduct training in the writing and processing of reports within the audit organization — if possible, by the auditors themselves. The training can communicate the standards that are acceptable to the chief audit executive. Independent editing can reinforce the training and make sure the standards *are met.*

- The use of a format to ensure the presence of all elements of a finding. This format should be completed in the field regardless of where the report is drafted.

In short, to improve the report-writing process:

- Set minimum standards of acceptability through a style manual.

- Communicate those standards to staff through training.

- Reinforce the established standards by independent editing or by evaluating all reports against those standards.

- Ensure the presence of all elements of findings.

The problem of getting clients to accept reports is part policy and part process. Clients must be required, by organization policy, to respond to all reports containing findings that have not been corrected. That policy establishes senior management's position on the power of the audit report. By an appropriate report-writing process, the reports can be made readable and complete and can help achieve client acceptance.

Marketing the Audit Report

One of the reasons why some recipients of audit reports from client management to top management and the audit committee and board of directors often do not read or appreciate audit reports is because they see little value in them. The audit organization, with the encouragement and sponsorship of the audit committee, should conduct a program on "Marketing the Audit Report." This program is essentially an orientation program that is aimed at motivating the report recipient to *want* the report. This "want" can be fostered by:

- Explaining the audit process as a participative adjunct to management.

- Describing the professionalism of the audit staff.

- Simply identifying the anatomy of an audit finding.

- Listing the advantages to each level of management resulting from using the report.

- Explaining how management can obtain the aid of the audit staff to solve management problems — objectively.

Action on Audit Recommendations

Earlier in this chapter it was stated that one of the objectives of audit reports is to persuade or to stimulate action. It was said that the factual reporting of situations that need changing is not enough; that the readers' inertia will result in passivity or in no action at all. The U.S. General Accounting Office in 1991 issued an action paper resulting from research in this area.[4] Discussed were certain characteristics that it suggested would ensure action on most audit recommendations. The report classified its suggestions into four groups:

- Action-oriented effective recommendations

- Commitment to results

- Monitoring and follow-up systems

- Special attention to key recommendations

Each of these groups will be briefly discussed. For complete coverage, the reader would do well to obtain a copy of the report.

1. Action-Oriented Effective Recommendations
   - Action-Oriented Recommendations
     - Properly directed
     - Hard hitting
     - Specific
     - Convincing
     - Significant
     - Positive in tone and content
   - Effective Recommendation; Must:
     - Deal with underlying causes
     - Be feasible
     - Be cost effective
     - Consider alternatives
     - Be matters for concern by governing bodies

2. Commitment to Results
   - Commitment making improvements happen
   - Staff commitment:
     - Believing in their recommendations
     - Promoting action
     - Understanding the client (or the client environment)
     - Cooperating and helping
     - Believing in the need for change
   - Organizational commitment
     - Job management systems
     - Resource allocation and staffing decisions
     - Training programs
     - Performance reward systems

3. Monitoring and Follow-up Systems
   - Ensuring improvements: aggressive monitoring and follow-up
   - Basic elements of monitoring and follow-up systems
     - Firm basis for monitoring and follow-up
     - Active status monitoring
       - Determine progress
       - Take additional steps to get recommendations implemented
     - Determining the adequacy of actions taken on recommendations
     - Reporting accomplishment
     - Recognizing the basic responsibility of clients

4. Special Attention to Key Recommendations
   - Identifying key recommendations
   - Early and continuing emphasis
   - Examples of ways to highlight key recommendations
     - Impact of policies
     - Impact of procedures
     - Impact of laws and regulations
     - Attention of key organizational officials

The above "bare bones" outline constitutes a summary checklist for the measuring of internal audit recommendations. Audit organizations should expand them with narrative to accommodate their own environment, organizational culture, and policies. There is probably no universal methodology. Each organization is unique.

Improving Internal Audit Report Timing

The development and writing of internal audit reports has usually been a slow laborious process. Reports typically were issued in some cases between three and six months after the auditors had completed the field work and the formal exit conference. The result was twofold. First, management was prevented from an early full knowledge of situations that called for prompt actions, frequently of a policy or procedure nature. Second, it slowed down the implementation of audit recommendations that usually had an efficiency or effectiveness nature and thus resulted in an adverse financial or operational result.

The delays were caused by several factors, all of which were traditionally considered to be an element of good auditing procedure — but which were patently time-consuming. Several of these were:

- Withholding the presenting of all findings until the exit conference
- Providing clients with a reasonable period to comment: usually 30 to 60 days
- Writing the report draft in the office from the audit working papers

- Accommodating to the clients comments:
  - Positively — this could result in report restructuring
  - Negatively — here additional writing was usually necessary
- Editing the report drafts at two or three levels
- Reviewing the reports:
  - As to legality
  - As to audit policy
  - As to audit procedure
- Final review by the chief audit executive

This situation has been a difficult and unpleasant problem in many internal audit shops. Pressure is being continually exerted to speed up the report issuance — but not to eliminate any of the elements of the reporting process. The flattening of the audit organization with the concurrent delegation of report issuance to a lower level has been one result. Also, the increased accountability for policy and procedure compliance at a lower and decentralized level has been another. However, one of the most effective changes was one instituted by TRW Inc., the development and use of the IAM, the Interim Audit Memorandum.[5]

This procedure utilizes methods that are not new but it puts them into a combination that is logical and efficient. The procedure is to issue an IAM as soon as a reportable audit finding is disclosed and to describe the situation and suggest recommended activity. The client is asked to respond in writing or verbally in a few days. Each IAM is limited to one finding and in this way closure of the finding can be achieved promptly while the audit is in process. If the IAMs are constructed properly, they can be used as substantial parts of the audit report. An interesting innovation is that the audit working papers relative to the finding are available for client review, which allows the client to "present new information that may alter the audit finding or offer alternative recommendations or solutions."[6]

Thus, the audit report is being *completed* on an interim basis and during the field work phase. Completion of the report is not only expedited, but the clients' reactions and their impact on the report are crystallized. Not all IAMs are used in the final report; materiality and importance determine the usage. Excluded IAMs are held until the next audit and if the client's planned implementation has not taken place, the items then become a reportable finding.

This method has reduced the report preparation time from five weeks to one week and according to the writer, "The quality of the reports has been enhanced by the improved communication between clients and auditors."[7]

Communication

Reports seek to communicate. If they do not achieve communication, they are without value. The individual who understands the ingredients of communication, however, is unusual. Many auditors take the position that if they have put it in writing, they have achieved communication. More often, they have thwarted communication. They've spawned words, but they have not constructed a bridge between the mind of the writer and the mind of the reader.

The difficulty begins with thought: the report writers have thought more about the writing than about the reading. They have failed to comprehend that communication does not take place only with the writer, the utterer; it happens also in the mind of the recipient. Until the recipient perceives the message, there is no communication — only words on paper. Perception is the key. So all report writers must ask themselves, as they put words to paper: "Is this within the scope of my reader's comprehension and perception?"

The writer must remember that he or she is very familiar with the background and circumstances surrounding the material that is being presented. Normally, the reader is not. Thus, the material should be introduced with enough background so that the reader can comprehend the message completely.

What is beyond the reader's perception cannot be understood. What the mind does not expect, it will not receive. A mind slanted in one direction will reject what comes from another direction.

The main rule in report writing is to know the readers. What can they perceive? What do they expect? What are they led to expect? What do they need? Once these questions are answered, the auditor can hope to achieve some measurement of communication.

Top management can best perceive general concepts. They can perceive those matters that affect the organization as a whole. They expect to be told about matters of significance. They expect either to have their concerns allayed or to take action on some risk that can be avoided or some significant defect that can be corrected.

Operating management can perceive the details of its operations. It can comprehend discussions couched in its own familiar language. It can fully understand the details of defective conditions. But it has the right to not be surprised. It has the right to see, in the audit report, those matters that have been discussed as the audit progressed.

So internal auditors must know that communication ultimately resides in the recipient and that it is composed of perceptions and expectations. The best field work and the most brilliant analyses will remain moldering in the working papers until they are communicated.

In seeking to communicate, internal auditors must remember their principal objectives: (1) to provide useful and timely information, both oral and written, on significant matters; and (2) to promote improvements in control and performance of organization operations.

Report Procedure

The *Standards for the Professional Practice of Internal Auditing* (2400) provide guidance on the internal auditor's responsibilities for reporting the results of audits. The standard is produced below.

2400 – Communicating Results
Internal auditors should communicate the engagement results promptly.

2410 – Criteria for Communicating
Communications should include the engagement's objectives and scope as well as applicable conclusions, recommendations, and action plans.

2410.A1 – The final communication of results should, where appropriate, contain the internal auditor's overall opinion.
2410.A2 – Engagement communications should acknowledge satisfactory performance.

2420 – Quality of Communications
Communications should be accurate, objective, clear, concise, constructive, complete, and timely.

2421 – Errors and Omissions
If a final communication contains a significant error or omission, the chief audit executive should communicate corrected information to all individuals who received the original communication.

2430 – Engagement Disclosure of Noncompliance with the *Standards*
When noncompliance with the *Standards* impacts a specific engagement, communication of the results should disclose the:
- *Standards(s)* with which full compliance was not achieved,
- Reason(s) for noncompliance, and
- Impact of noncompliance on the engagement.

2440 – Disseminating Results
The chief audit executive should disseminate results to the appropriate individuals.

2440.A1 – The chief audit executive is responsible for communicating the final results to individuals who can ensure that the results are given due consideration.

Interim reports. It is recommended that interim reports be used where early information is needed, but they should not be substituted for a final report. Findings discussed in an interim report, and satisfactorily disposed of before the final report is issued, need not be included in the final report. An exception can be made where the findings are material and have importance in the client's operations. We suggest caution in eliminating any significant findings from the final report.

The interim report can minimize report writing time. Ongoing descriptions of findings and supervisory reviews can reduce the time it takes to prepare reports after field work is completed. Interim reports are further discussed later in the chapter.

Summary reports. An important objective of internal auditing is to get senior management interested in auditing and in reading audit reports. Audit reports can supply objective information about the organization that is usually not available elsewhere. One difficulty in achieving this objective is the time busy executives must spend perusing long reports that provide operating managers with the information needed to take corrective action. In large audit projects, the audit reports can be, and properly are, extended and detailed.

Senior management should know about significant findings of the audit activity on a timely basis. Which audited units are doing well and need no top-level attention. Which matters unearthed by the auditors need prompt and/or continued attention. Such information can be provided to busy executives through summary reports of one page or two, at the most.

Internal auditors should give serious consideration to what senior management needs and wants to know about completed audit projects. Such information can be obtained by polling executives and asking them what they need.

However, internal auditors should also put themselves in the shoes of the busy executive and ask themselves what they would want under such circumstances. Here are some suggestions for a one-page executive summary:

- A brief description of what was audited
- The auditors' conclusions
- Capsule statements of truly significant findings, referencing the pages where the detail can be found
- A brief description of the action taken by clients on these findings
- An overall statement that puts findings and conclusions in proper perspective

Exhibit 17-1 is an example of such an executive summary. The audit covered the entire marketing branch, but each segment of the audit was large enough to warrant a separate conclusion. The auditors used adjectival ratings for each of the segments, explaining in a footnote the meaning of those ratings.

Exhibit 17-1

Executive Summary
Marketing Division

Activity Reviewed	Auditors' Opinions
Marketing Research	Fair (1)
Advertising	Good (2)
Sales Promotion	Poor (3), (4)
Credit	Excellent
Customer Service	Good (5)

Findings

(1) The data costing Marketing Research $100,000 to gain through field polls on Program Q was available in trade publications.

(2) The advertising department instead of the purchasing department dealt directly with suppliers in a number of instances.

(3) Orders for sales promotion material were not issued on time, resulting in excessive overtime and premium transportation costs.

(4) Costs were not monitored, hence the sales promotion manager was not informed that the costs of programs exceeded budgets by $63,000 (38 percent).

(5) Instructions to customers on using organization products were written in technical terms not understandable to the layperson.

Corrective Action

Corrective action was completed on Findings (1) and (2) through revised procedures. Findings (3) and (4) were corrected through improved instructions to employees and closer supervisory review. Corrective action was initiated but not yet completed on Finding (5); a written reply is requested.

Comments

Despite the five deficiencies we observed, we believe that people in the marketing division were highly motivated and technically proficient. Both advertising and sales promotion are of high quality and have received commendations of merit in trade publications. Prompt action was instituted to correct the reported conditions. While some represent serious deviations from good practice, they are not material in the light of the division's overall mission. The marketing director is now devoting increased attention to administration.

Legend

Excellent — No deficiencies. Good — Relatively minor deficiency. Fair — Relatively major deficiency. Poor — More than one major deficiency. Unsatisfactory — Failure to accomplish major missions of the activity.

Discussions with clients. Internal auditors should be careful to avoid the possibility of replies to audit reports that dispute the reported facts. Such comments, whether true or not, cast doubt on the audit credibility. Accordingly, auditors should review all findings with client personnel and with management during the course of the audit to assure there is no disagreement on the facts. Where differences in interpretation are encountered, the client's views should be incorporated into the report.

Similarly, it is useful to discuss with the client not only the impact of the findings on operations — their cause and effect — but also the auditor's recommendations for corrective action. However, the internal auditor should not forget, particularly in operational audits, that the client's experience and knowledge of operations far exceeds that of the auditor. Hence, what may seem to the auditor to be a perfectly logical recommendation may be shown by the client to be impractical or have severe side effects.

Agreement on the course of corrective action is extremely important. A mutually accepted means of correcting a shortcoming will have the client's backing. This attitude can be reinforced by giving full credit in the audit report to the course of action agreed to by the client. For example, the following statement in the report, after the statement of the finding, is sure to sit well with the client and receive a more enthusiastic acceptance: "We discussed the matter with the manager of the operation, who promptly modified the procedures so as to preclude repetition of the situations that were found."

Differences of opinion as to interpretation of fact and as to appropriate corrective action are understandable. Where these occur, the auditor should identify both sides of the issue together with the arguments for and against. Since the audit report is the instrument of the auditor, the auditor can refute the client's position. It is possible that the client in the reply letter may also refute the auditor's position. This letter should be an appendix to the audit report. The adverse effects of undiscussed findings can be so serious as to hamper future audits.

The oral review of draft reports or segments of a draft reports has so much to commend it that there can be no argument for releasing a report without such reviews. The reviews can counter misperceptions. They can be a source of gaining additional information. They can highlight wording and phrasing that are either incorrect or irritate the client. They can lead to recommendations that have the best opportunity to correct the difficulty with the least adverse side effects.

Discussion participants. The chief audit executive can ensure some uniformity in draft reviews by issuing written instructions to guide auditors and audit supervisors. Yet the instructions should not be so inflexible that they fail to take into account the human element. Most large organizations have several levels of hierarchy — for example: operating manager, division chief, branch director, vice president, president, and board of directors. In most instances, reviews with the operating manager and the division chief should suffice; the first is responsible for taking action, the second for making sure it is taken.

But often, people higher up the hierarchic ladder recognize the importance of keeping current on what is going on and of getting involved in the audits within their areas of responsibility. Some clients like to review draft reports with the auditors in attendance. Others merely want an opportunity to read the draft at their leisure before it is issued. Still others prefer that internal auditors provide an oral presentation of audit findings. This gives such managers an opportunity to discuss not only the matters to be reported, but also the auditor's impressions of supervision, training, morale, and other matters that do not appear in formal reports but which can be of great interest to higher management.

Factual reports. The report must be completely and scrupulously factual. Every categorical statement, every figure, every reference must be based on hard evidence. The internal audit organization, through unremitting effort, must develop a reputation for reliability — utter reliability must become the hallmark of the internal audit report. It should be written and documented so as to compel belief and reliance and ultimately endorsement. It should have character. It should speak with authority. Whatever is said, particularly in operating areas outside the auditor's normally accepted scope, must be supported or supportable. The reader must be able to rely upon the report because of its well-documented facts and inescapable logic.

Statements of fact must carry the assurance that the auditors personally observed or validated the fact. If they say there was an excessive backlog of work, it means that they personally know this to be a fact. It means they know what backlogs are considered normal and the extent of the backlog they observed.

There may be conditions that the auditors have not personally observed but of which management should be made aware. A statement to that effect in a report should show the source: "The department manager told us that the backlog was excessive." The reported statement is completely factual — the auditor personally heard the statement from the department manager, but the auditors themselves are not certifying to the existence or to the extent of the conditions.

Perspective. Objectivity also implies perspective — objective, observations, refraining from puffing up that which is not material or relevant. Senior management generally gives serious attention to audit reports. Conditions reported to be deficient may become the subject of executive wrath. It is a form of inaccuracy, therefore, to hold up as deficient one of a dozen related activities without showing how the one activity fits into the mosaic of overall function or organization. For instance, if an operating manager is fiercely and successfully fighting the battle of quality, schedule, and cost in his or her organization, producing an acceptable product, delivering it on time, making it within budget constraints, and training people well while knowing what they are doing — wouldn't it be a lack of perspective to highlight in an audit report that written job instructions could stand updating? The suggestion could be handled informally either orally or in an informal memo.

Objectivity implies that what is reported is material — a matter worthy of a busy manager's attention. Matters should not be included in a report as filler or merely to expand the volume of audit findings. It must be demonstrated that, if a reported condition is permitted to continue, there will be significant harm. A prudent person reading the finding should be impelled to say, "Yes, here is a condition that needs attention and requires correction. It cannot be overlooked."

Precision. Objectivity implies precision. Imprecise words leave a reader confused. Specificity conveys ideas more accurately than broad generalities. It is much more precise to say "of the 100 items we examined, 30 were received three to five days late and 20 were six to 15 days late" than to say "not all items were received on time."

Reporting that "not all items were received on time" is weak and confusing. It raises vague warnings but says nothing. It is a model of imprecision and is therefore misleading. It conveys different thoughts to different people. It does not say what the auditor may have meant. How much is "not all?" Is utter perfection the standard? If only one item out of a thousand were a few hours late, then certainly "not all were received on time." Similarly, if 500 out of the thousand were between two and five days late, that condition could also be described as "not all were received on time." The first is *de minimis* while the second would shock a prudent person.

Some words are too imprecise to appear without specific quantification in a self-respecting audit report: *several, a few, many, almost all, hardly ever, sometimes, a good deal.* These words may be acceptable in a lead sentence that summarizes a condition, but they should be immediately followed by the specific numbers — the population, the sample size, and the specific number or percentages of items that are unacceptable.

Clarity. Clarity implies many things. Chiefly, it indicates transferring to the mind of the reader or listener what was in the mind of the auditor. There are a host of impediments to this hoped-for clear transfer of thought. Auditors should be aware of them and they must consciously try to remove them.

Lack of clarity in the mind of the auditor is the prime impediment to clear writing. One cannot write clearly what one does not understand clearly. If we do not have a firm grasp of our subject, we are not ready to write. Until auditors know precisely what they are talking about, they should do more field work or research before starting to record.

Dull and tedious writing is another impediment to clarity. Dreary, stilted prose makes the mind turn to other things. Consider: "Reconciliation of the accounts was effected by the accounting personnel." Note how much clearer this is when we say: "The accounting staff reconciled the accounts."

Poorly structured reports are impediments to clarity. An orderly processing of ideas enhances clarity. Some auditors start their reports in the middle and then go off in all directions. They may well be hiding excellent findings and recommendations in a morass of tangled sentences and paragraphs. The ideas that client management desperately needs may never be communicated. For the want of structure, the audit is lost.

Technical terms and jargon are impediments. Skillful translations clear the way. This means more than just substituting "rejections by inspectors" for "I-tags." It also means conveying ideas in terms that mean something to the reader. It is one thing to say that receiving memos are not being matched with invoices. It is quite another to say that there was no assurance that the organization received the goods it was paying for. The first statement is factual, but it paints no pictures. The second is no more factual, but it will sound sirens and galvanize management into action.

Proper background support. Reporting on findings without setting the stage is an impediment. Giving the proper background information is sometimes essential to the understanding of a process or a condition, or to an appreciation of its significance. If auditors are recommending a new procedure, they should first describe the existing one, what's wrong with it, and the probable effect of its continued use. Then management will be more receptive to the relevance of the auditor's proposal, and yet be in a position to make its own considered decision.

Technical discussions. Long discussions of technical matters, like the interrelationships of many different amounts, are impediments to understanding. Well-designed schedules, tabulations, charts, and graphs can bring clarity. One picture can make clear what a thousand words can only obscure.

Clarity is a condition precedent to persuasiveness. Auditors must be able to convince client managers of the validity of their positions, so findings must be presented convincingly. The conclusions and recommendations must flow clearly and logically from the facts presented. The reports must convince an objective reader that the findings are significant, that the conclusions are reasonable, and that the recommendations are workable and acceptable.

Proper organization. Poor organization of reported material is an impediment to clarity. Reports should flow easily from beginning to end. They should not contain closely related material in different sections. Many reports deal with complex subjects. Some report sections bear a relationship to others. To the extent possible, each audit report should be so organized that all the auditor has to say on a given subject appears in only one place in the report. Summaries and digests, of course, are understandable exceptions. There should also be logical bridges from subject to subject.

Conciseness. Conciseness means cutting out what is superfluous. This does not necessarily mean making all reports short; the subject matter may demand extended discussion. Brevity that does not inform is not a virtue. Conciseness does mean eliminating what is irrelevant and immaterial. Conciseness means eliminating the ideas, the findings, the words, the sentences, and the paragraphs that do not help get across the central theme of the report.

At the same time, conciseness should not become such a fetish that writing is reduced to an abrupt, telegraphic style. There must still be a continuity of thought, an ease of reading, and a comfortable, integrated flow of ideas.

Auditors sometimes fall into the trap of long sentences that leave the reader puzzled and weary. If auditors really put their minds to it, they can cut the long sentences into digestible bite sizes. They can overcome abruptness through words or thoughts of transition.

Also, conciseness does not mean using only short sentences. An uninterrupted series of short sentences creates its own sameness and dullness. A few well-constructed long sentences, sprinkled among the short ones, provide a much-needed variety and tend to break the tedium.

Constructive tone. The audit report must have a proper tone, it should be courteous, and it should consider the report's effect upon subordinate operating people. It should not, therefore, identify individuals or highlight the mistakes of individuals. It should avoid pettiness and not concern itself with trivia, and should sound like the voice of management.

The tone should be constructive. Criticism of things past may be necessary, but the emphasis should be placed on needed improvements. The report should be dignified without being stodgy. It should avoid slang on the one hand and high-blown language on the other; these do not stand the test of time.

The client executive, pressed from all quarters by operating reports and arguments — often self-serving declarations that put the best face on questionable matters — should be able to see in the audit report a calm, objective, thoughtful, dispassionate exposition on which to rely.

Timeliness. The final, formal report is not designed to be a historical document though it can serve as such. It is a call to action and answers client management's needs for current information. Its effect is lost, therefore, if it is not timely. Yet it must be carefully thought out, be impregnable, and incapable of being misunderstood. And these needs cannot be met with a stroke of the pen.

These sometimes conflicting needs — thoughtfulness and promptness — must both be met. The informal interim progress report, issued while the audit is still going on, may be one answer.

Interim reports. Interim reports convey in writing the need for prompt action. What is written, in most big organizations, produces action where the spoken word may not. As the Chinese proverb says: "The mouth is wind. The pen leaves tracks."

Interim reports can be brief, addressing themselves to only one or two ideas. They can be labeled "interim reports" and contain written caveats against accepting them as the final word; operating management is permitted to act expeditiously while the auditors reserve the right to polish and revise. The transmittal letter or memo for the interim report can start by saying: "This interim report is designed to provide current information on conditions needing prompt management attention. Our final report will include the matter discussed here, along with other information obtained during the remainder of our field work."

The interim report can have other salutary results. It can serve to set auditors straight on their facts or to sharpen their perspective, since the response evoked by the interim report can confirm or deny the auditor's findings to date. The studies, action, and/or replies of operating management may have a significant effect on what the auditor will finally report.

Where the audit organization employs many young and still inexperienced auditors to perform audits away from headquarters, there may be an understandable concern about permitting them to draft and release interim reports without supervisory review. Yet prompt notice to operating management about deficient conditions — in writing — may be important. In those cases, it may be advisable to develop a form, similar to the Record of Audit Findings (see Chapter 8), which compels the auditor to cover all significant aspects of a deficient condition: a concise statement of condition, size of sample, extent of deficiency, causes and effects, applicable written procedures, and discussions with operating personnel.

This material is covered by Practice Advisory 2420-1, "Quality of Communications," related to *Standard 2420*, "Quality of Communications."

Audit format. The format of the report depends much on the kind of report being issued: formal versus informal, final versus interim, written versus oral, overall opinion versus findings only, or financial versus performance. The format of the report will also depend on the readers: what the readers expect and how much time they can devote to reading the report.

Further, the format of the report will depend on the nature and the seasoning of the audit activity. An audit organization just beginning to review nonfinancial operating areas will feel impelled to give abundant support for its opinions and conclusions — to overcome reluctance on the part of the reader to accept audit opinions on matters that are far afield from accounting activities.

Hence, different audit organizations will employ different report formats and divide their reports into different subsections. Whichever format is found most appropriate should be useful with reasonable consistency. The *Standards* does not require standard report formats. But management will feel more comfortable if it becomes accustomed to the report format and can readily turn to whatever is of interest. Consistent forms of reporting are also more efficient. They permit the auditors to use comparable wording in similar situations and eliminate the need to continually reword the same messages.

Audit report summary. Summaries come in many shapes and sizes. A summary may be a simple transmittal memorandum that sends the report to the president or other executives of the organization. Properly drafted, such a summary may be ideal for harried executives who want to read no more than they absolutely have to while reserving the right to dip into pertinent detail.

Summaries should be useful devices. But they may present pitfalls to unwary report writers who must be careful, as they compress the report into a brief summation, that they do not distort meaning, materiality, or perspective.

An example of a brief transmittal follows:

> This is our report on receiving department activities. In general, the department has provided an adequate system of controls for its receiving functions. Activities were being carried out effectively and efficiently, with the following exception:

> No comparisons were being made between chemicals received and billed. Comparisons showed that tank cars were not being completely emptied. As a result, variances of over eight percent were found. After the matter was discussed with operating management, systems were improved and negotiations with the supplier resulted in recoveries of about $40,000.

An additional example of a summary was presented in Exhibit 17-1. A simpler, less formal summary is illustrated in Exhibit 17-2. It is used to transmit a copy of the report to executive management and provides the barest summary of the audit results. If the recipients of the report are interested in further information, they can refer to the detailed findings supporting the summary.

Exhibit 17-2

Executive Summary

To: Audit Committee of the Board of Directors
        Chief Executive Officer
        Executive Vice President
        Director of Financial Operations

From: Chief Audit Executive

Here is our report on the audit of the marketing division. Our audit covered the reviews of controls over marketing research, advertising, sales promotion, credit, and customer service.

Controls were generally adequate and effective except for some shortcomings in the use of field polls, unsatisfactory purchasing practices, untimely orders for sales promotion material, absence of cost controls, and unclear instructions to customers. The details of these conditions will be found in the attached report. Overall, however, the division appears to be meeting its major objectives.

Corrective action has been initiated and is continuing to correct all reported conditions.

                                                    _____
                                                    Signed

Background information. Background information on the audit is provided in sections labeled "Introduction" or "Foreword." This section is the first to meet the reader's eye, so it should be written crisply and clearly. It is usually a stage-setter and can be used to:

- Identify the audit as a regular examination or as the response to a special management request.

- Identify the organizations, programs, or functions reviewed.

- Refer to relevant prior examinations.

- Comment on findings or recommendations in prior reports and on their current status.

- Provide explanatory information needed to acquaint the reader with the subject under examination. (A report on shipping or receiving needs no more introduction than the title of the report itself. A report on special test equipment, however, may deserve some explanatory comment.)

- Set forth briefly the value or volume of transactions processed, so as to give the reader an idea of the significance of the function.

Here is an example of a foreword section:

> This report covers the regular audit of the engineering property control department. The 2000 audit reported four deficiency findings. None of the deficient conditions then reported has recurred. The department is responsible for tools and equipment, valued at $7 million, which are used in the engineering branch.

Audit objectives. The objective should be described. It should be in sufficient detail to help readers understand what to expect from the rest of the report. When the objective is spelled out with some precision, and when the discussions of findings address themselves to each statement in the objective, then it serves as a road map — making it easier for readers to find their way through the report.

Here is an example of a detailed statement of objective:

> The audit was directed toward determining whether an adequate and effective system of control has been provided over the activities of the credit department. The audit was concerned specifically with the following activities of the department:

- Performing credit investigations and determining the financial responsibility of both suppliers and customers.

- Establishing credit terms for sales to commercial customers.

- Establishing control over payments to assignees.

- Investigating new suppliers.

Audit scope. The scope statement is sometimes combined with the objective. The description of scope can be of particular importance in identifying the breadth or the limitations of the examination. It should specifically point to areas that were not covered — areas that, because of the very title of the report, readers would expect to be covered in the audit unless told differently.

The scope is particularly important when normal auditing techniques are dispensed with and other techniques are relied upon.

Here are examples of two scope statements:

- The review of receiving activities was confined to those carried out in the central receiving department. Controls over direct deliveries, which bypass central receiving, were not reviewed. A separate examination of direct deliveries is planned.

- The preliminary survey disclosed an excellent system of control over the shipping department's activities. All job instructions were up to date. The department's supervisors were required to make periodic examinations of selected transactions and report their findings to the manager, who sees that deficient conditions are corrected. Shipping activities were discussed with representatives of peripheral organizations, and it was found that they uniformly held the shipping operations in high regard. As a result, the tests of transactions were considerably reduced from the tests normally made as a basis for opinions.

Auditors should avoid giving a detailed account of the audit steps they take. For some activities of a sensitive nature, such disclosure may provide potential malefactors with a blueprint to follow in manipulating transactions for personal gain.

Elements of audit results. Audit reports should include scope and results of the audit; but they also may include findings, conclusions (opinions), and recommendations. We believe that formal reports on the results of an internal audit should include all six elements (background, criteria, condition, impact, cause, and recommendation) if they are to provide client management with the information needed to show the internal auditor's assessment of the activities audited and if they are to provide guidance and counsel to management on needed corrective action.

Some internal audit organizations never supply overall opinions on the grounds that management is interested in only those matters that require action. We submit that only by including all elements of a report in its message to the various levels of management can the internal auditor truly communicate the complete results of the audit.

Attributes of a finding. The four basic attributes of a finding were discussed in Chapter 8, Audit Findings. These attributes are:

- **Criteria**. Standards, measures, or expectations used in making an evaluation and/or verification.

- **Condition.** The factual evidence as to what was found.

- **Cause.** The reason for a difference between the criteria and the condition.

- **Effect.** The impact on the organization or the difference between the criteria and the condition.

Background and a **recommendation** may also be a part of a finding when it is believed appropriate.

The first two attributes, criteria and condition, are equally applicable to positive findings. In other words, internal auditors may not arrive at a conclusion that some activity is working satisfactorily unless they have some standard or criterion against which to measure client accomplishment. An intuitive feeling is not enough; it cannot be objectively demonstrated. But where a standard of conduct or performance is established and agreed to by management and/or the client, then the internal auditors can with confidence declare — after appropriate comparisons have been made — the degree of propriety with which such activities are being carried out.

By employing these four attributes when reporting unsatisfactory findings, internal auditors can accomplish the three important audit objectives previously discussed: (1) to create awareness of a problem; (2) to achieve acknowledgment of the reported condition; and (3) to impel action to correct the condition. Thus, a comment work sheet can be useful to the auditor to make sure that none of the attributes are overlooked when reporting the finding.

The work sheet shown in Exhibit 17-3 provides internal auditors with a simple means of determining whether all the important attributes were considered.[8] In the work sheet, we have included two other elements: a summary to encapsulate the finding and a recommendation to guide the reader and manager toward effective action.

Exhibit 17-3

Comment Work Sheet

Summary (to create awareness)
Condition (to reinforce awareness)
Criteria (to create awareness and acceptance)
Cause (to create acceptance and impel action)
Effect (to create acceptance)
Recommendation (to facilitate action)

* * * * *

An example of an executed comment sheet that can facilitate the reporting of a finding:

Attribute	Statement
Summary	Losses from sales to poor credit risks were excessive for the last year.
Condition	Lack of objective credit evaluations of customers resulted in losses of over $75,000.
Criteria	Sales and credit have two different objectives; one is to promote a sale, the other is to ensure payment for the sale.
Effect	There is a tendency to allow credit to promote a sale without considering whether the customer is creditworthy and will be able to pay for the sale.
Recommendation	Transfer the credit manager from the office of the marketing director to the office of the director of financial operations.

The outline in Exhibit 17-3 readily permits itself to be transformed into a finding in the audit report:

> Losses from sales to poor credit risks were excessive. Credit evaluations of potential customers were not always objective, resulting in losses of more than $75,000 in the last year. The credit department manager reports administratively to the marketing director. But sales and credit should have different objectives: one is to promote sales, and the other is to ensure payment for those sales. Hence, there is a tendency to allow credit solely to promote a sale without considering whether the customer is creditworthy and whether payment for the sale will be received. The matter was discussed with all parties concerned and, before the audit was completed, an agreement was reached to transfer the credit department to the office of the director of financial operations.

It will be observed that the recommendation was actually made during the oral discussion of the finding. Since agreement had been reached on the corrective action to be taken, credit for such action is, in effect, given to the client rather than the auditor. This approach has a positive effect on relations between the two. As one executive is reputed to have said: "There is nothing in the world people cannot accomplish if they do not insist on taking credit for it."

By rigorously following the dictates of the *Standards* (Practice Advisory 2410-1) in addressing all the attributes of a finding, the internal auditor is more likely to get acceptance of the finding and the means of correcting it. Of course, all auditors must be certain that the supporting evidence for reported findings is both competent and relevant. Not only should findings be persuasively stated, they must also be able to withstand any frontal attack by some disgruntled client bound to get rid of the auditor instead of the unsatisfactory condition.

Audit conclusions (opinions). The opinion is the auditor's professional judgment of the activities reviewed. It provides a capsule comment on the assessment of the conditions found. Not all auditing organizations provide overall opinions on the results of their examinations, but many progressive auditing organizations believe that the failure to do so deprives client management of a significant knowledgeable service.

It would be most natural for a president of an organization who meets an auditor after the completion of an audit assignment to ask: "Well, what do you think of the activity you just reviewed?" A responsive answer would represent an overall opinion: "The activity is operating quite well," or "I believe they could improve their operation, because. . .," or "Except for some minor matters which they quickly corrected, they're doing a reasonably good job."

Judgments along these lines are what executives expect from their auditing organizations. They are entitled to receive such judgments. Certainly, auditors should not express opinions they are not capable of supporting. And, certainly, they must weigh carefully the factors supporting their opinions. An opinion should say exactly what the auditor means, include only what can be justified, and be adequately supported by the facts. Finally, it should encompass, and be responsive to, the objectives of the audit as set out in the purpose statement. Three examples of opinions on audits of operations are:

- Based on the results of our audit, we believe that an adequate system of control has been established over the activities of the sales department and that the department's assigned responsibilities were being carried out effectively and efficiently.

- In our opinion, the activities concerned with the layoff and recall of employees were well controlled and, except for inadequate explanations for monetary settlements of grievances, were performed effectively and efficiently.

- In our opinion, the system designed to ensure the timely calibration of test equipment was inadequate because no provision had been made to identify all of the equipment subject to calibration.

In expressing their opinions, auditors should not hesitate to be complimentary if the compliment is deserved. If they find a well-controlled, well-organized, well-managed, and smoothly functioning operation, they should say so — it will give evidence that they do not seek deficiencies only. There should, of course, be adequate support for a complimentary opinion. Auditors would not wish to see an opinion invalidated by activities not covered or events that should have been foreseen; but if they are certain of their grounds, they should have the courage of their convictions. Here is an example of a richly deserved compliment:

> Based on the results of our review, we are of the opinion that adequate controls had been provided over the activities of the production services department, and that the controls were working effectively and efficiently. In fact, we consider this department to be highly effective in accomplishing its assigned mission. We believe this can be attributed to well-motivated and knowledgeable supervision and key personnel; good communication and feedback between management and subordinates; thorough on-the-job training of the individual employees, reinforced by a sound rotational assignment policy; up-to-date, comprehensive job instructions; constant vigilance on the part of supervision and alternates to monitor workload schedules and performance and to minimize errors; good rapport and loyalty between the manager and the group supervisors; and the participation by the manager and her supervisors in arriving at management decisions.

An overall audit opinion provides a focus for a report. Everything that follows should be relevant to and support the overall opinion. Some authors take the position that the conclusions should be the starting point of the report writing process. All that follows is designed to support the opinion and explain it.[9]

It is not easy to arrive at a good conclusion — to try to embody in one sentence all that the auditor has determined about a significant operation. But the one-sentence rule can help identify the conclusion with which to start writing. Developing a workable conclusion is simplified by meeting the following standards:

- The conclusion should answer the questions raised by the audit's purpose.

- The conclusion should include a statement of the subject the report deals with.

- The conclusion should include the writer's opinion on what was found.

Most of the following material is provided for and discussed by Practice Advisory 2410-1 related to *Standard 2410*, "Criteria for Communicating," and related *Standard 2410.A1*. (The material appeared in *Sawyer's 4th Edition* but has been revised and updated to reflect current thinking and technological advances. It covers footnotes 13 to 18 of that edition.)

Following are some techniques for writing audit reports that use the above conclusion as the point of departure. These suggested techniques, not sequential, can be useful rules to follow in outlining the proposed audit report:

1. Start with conclusions.
2. Place important issues first.
3. Make direct statements of conclusions and conditions.
4. State management concerns and opportunities for improvement.
5. Include information needed to prove a point.
6. Eliminate unnecessary information or procedural descriptions.
7. Identify the effects of the problems that cause management concern.
8. Identify the cause of the problem so that it can be resolved.
9. Recommend action that is directly tied to the cause.
10. Emphasize solutions and results, not detailed procedures.

Good report writing does not come easily. It will not flow from the mere reading of instructions. It needs time, practice, and teaching. We have never seen a report that came out perfectly at the first writing. Trying to write fast is as nonproductive as trying to sleep fast. It just cannot be done. But with effort, training, and the insistence on meeting high standards, the reports are bound to improve.

Audit recommendations. Auditors should not tell operating managers how they must correct unsatisfactory conditions. The most they can do is recommend. Even then, the recommendations must not be considered the only courses the client could take. They should be regarded as options to be considered among others. Hence, it is a good idea to discuss recommendations during the audit, rather than to bring them in as a surprise in the audit report.

During the audit, both client and auditor can explore the avenues available to correct conditions or improve methods and processes. At that time, the client may be able to explain the side effects of the recommendations. The client has a broader understanding of operations that are beyond the auditor's knowledge and thus can often predict results to proposed measures.

When the recommended action is agreed upon, it helps foster auditor-client relations to make the proposed action the idea of the client. The auditors do not need the credit. After all, they are the ones who brought the matter to light. But the client can save face if the audit report says something like: "The matter was discussed with the operating manager and this is what was done to correct the condition." This consideration for others helps change the stereotyped image of internal auditors held by many clients.

When auditors make recommendations, they must consider the cost of improving a condition. To install controls that far exceed the value of that which is being controlled is not normally productive. Internal auditors must view their recommendations as if they owned the organization and as if the cost of the improved controls or other means of correction came out of their pockets.

At the same time, it must be understood that some controls must be installed and enforced without regard to cost. Included are such matters as service, organization image, ecology, safety, and product liability. In such cases, it may be necessary to carry the recommendations to the highest authority — the policy makers of the organization.

In general, a recommendation for corrective action must relate directly to a specific audit finding. It is a call for action when the auditor finds a difference between actual conditions and expected results. This rule does not prevent an auditor from making a recommendation on matters outside the normal audit scope. This may occur when auditors are called upon to give opinions on operations that may not be the subject of an audit. Internal auditors should be prepared to provide members of the organization with analyses, appraisals, recommendations, and counsel about the organization's activities.

In addition, internal auditors may find, during their audits, certain methods that can be improved but that do not stem from an improper condition. This fact should not prevent the internal auditor from suggesting an improved method of performance. Yet it would be unfair to the client to consider it the result of a defect. Some auditors separate recommendations for corrective action from suggestions for improving otherwise blameless activities. These two categories are separately summarized in the audit report under the headings of "Findings Requiring Corrective Action" and "Suggestions for Improvement." The latter may also be covered in a "Management Letter" from the auditor to the client.

Client accomplishments. The tendency in many internal audit departments is to make the audit report as simple and easy to write as possible. As a result, most audit reports are negative. They list only the defects found because these require attention by executives and action by the client manager. Yet audit reports should be objective. Objectivity implies an unbiased view. And anyone reading a completely negative report will perceive no redeeming qualities mentioned in the report of the operation audited.

Certainly, it is not necessary to give equal space to positive as well as negative findings. But the entire audit can be put in perspective by a single paragraph or by adjectival ratings. Exhibits 17-1 or 17-2 show how it is possible, briefly, to give a balanced view of audit results and not leave the impression that everything the auditor touched was unsatisfactory.

Putting things in perspective helps the auditor's image, and it makes the auditor's return much more welcome. Not only that, it keeps the clients from feeling that everything they say will be used against them. It may take a little effort to inject perspective and understanding in an audit report, but the dividends are substantial.

Clients' position. During discussions of individual findings or of the final audit report, disagreements between auditor and client may arise. When those disagreements concern factual material, there is no reason why the facts cannot be resolved so that there is no quarrel about evidence and proof. Conclusions and interpretations are another matter. On these, there can be honest disagreements — even in the highest of circles. Consider U.S. Supreme Court decisions with five jurists on one side and four on the other.

In such circumstances, the clients should be given adequate space in the audit report to present their views. The client's written comments may be included as an appendix to the audit report. Such disagreements may call for executive intervention and decision. And higher client management should have both views to make an informed decision.

As much as possible, however, the client and the auditor should avoid using the audit report as a forum for debate through rebuttals and surrebuttals. Firm positions should be stated and presented to higher management for decision.

Most of the above material is provided for and discussed by Practice Advisory 2410-1 related to *Standard 2410*, "Criteria for Communicating," and related *Standard 2410.A1*.

Approving and signing the report. There is no specificity as to signers of internal audit reports. Too many variables enter the report-signing equation. Some internal audit activities are quite large and have locations throughout the world. Any attempt by the audit executive to see or sign all the reports before they are issued would cause inordinate delays. Delegation of both the report approval and report signing authority may be essential to achieve timely reporting.

In smaller internal audit organizations, or those where all auditors are stationed in the headquarters office, delegation becomes the chief audit executive's decision. If the internal audit organization is small and the reporting process is evolving, the chief audit executive may wish to review and approve all reports before they are issued.

In seasoned internal audit departments, the executives may feel comfortable delegating the signing function to others and maintaining control by reviewing reports after they are issued.

Frequent practice has the auditor-in-charge, supervisor, or lead auditor sign the report. When possible, the chief audit executive or designee approves the report before it is issued, but the approval does not have to be evidenced by a signature of a qualified professional on the report itself.

Report distribution. To ensure uniformity in report distribution, internal audit executives should (with management approval) develop a distribution list for all normal audit reports. Any deviations from the standard distribution should be approved by the chief audit executive or designee. The report should go to those in a position to take corrective action or to see that corrective action is taken. It should also be distributed to client officials. The distribution of reports to others who may request a copy of the report should likewise be approved by the chief audit executive or designee. These restrictions prevent an indiscriminate broadcasting of reported information to people without a need to know.

Even after an audit report is issued, it is possible for new information to come to light that may require alteration of what was reported. When it is found that the substantive information published in a final report is incorrect, the chief audit executive should issue a new report that clearly highlights the information being corrected. The erroneous information may have an effect on the auditors' recommendations, management's actions, or both. The amended audit report should be distributed to all individuals who received the audit report being corrected (see *Standard 2421*).

Restricted information. In their reporting, Certified Internal Auditors and members of The IIA are required by their codes of ethics (as approved on June 17, 2000) to reveal all material facts known to them that would distort the report if not revealed. Materiality is not relevant. Also, all illegal acts are to be reported by the internal auditor.

Certain information may not be appropriate to be included in audit reports because of being security related, privileged, proprietary, or related to improper or illegal acts. Such information must be reported in separate reports appropriate for the character of the restricted information.

Where internal auditors encounter abuses by executives, they have no choice but to report such matters. But they can choose the manner of their reporting. They can state their findings in the audit report and include comments by the executives involved. They can state their finding without incorporating those executive comments — assuming, of course, that they are certain of their facts. They can eliminate the finding from the regular report, but report the details in a confidential communication to the organization's top executive or to an audit committee, noting this confidential report in the original audit report.

Of course, if the top executive is involved in an irregularity, it is appropriate to report the matter to the audit committee of the board of directors or a similar body.

Some internal audit organizations may consider that audits of economy and efficiency should be subjects of separate reports. But presenting these audits separately, such as in a special memorandum, may suggest that the findings are not presented objectively or that reporting on the economical and efficient use of resources is not within the scope of normal audit activity. The *Standards* specifically states that, "Internal auditors should appraise the economy and efficiency with which resources are employed." So communicating the results of audit procedures concerned with economy and efficiency should be no different from reporting other audit results.

Most of the above material is provided for and discussed by Practice Advisory 2440-1, "Disseminating Results," and related *Standard 2440*.

Graphics

Even the most professionally written audit reports can use illustrations that clarify concepts and highlight interrelationships. Illustrations can establish believability in ways that words cannot.

Matters that can be portrayed in graphics and appended to reports include:

- Bar charts showing relationships between two or more kindred sets of statistics (Exhibit 17-4).

- Flowcharts explaining complex processes (Exhibit 17-5).

- Pictures clearly showing the existence and extent of hazardous conditions or wasteful practices (Exhibit 17-6).

Informal Reports

Every audit activity needs an informal reporting system to complement its formal system. Matters may be encountered during the audit engagement that: (1) require the prompt attention of management to supplement oral reports on an ongoing project; (2) bear no relationship to an ongoing project but warrant reporting to management; or (3) require the postponement or abandonment of a project. These and other matters can be made the subject of written interim (or progress) reports.

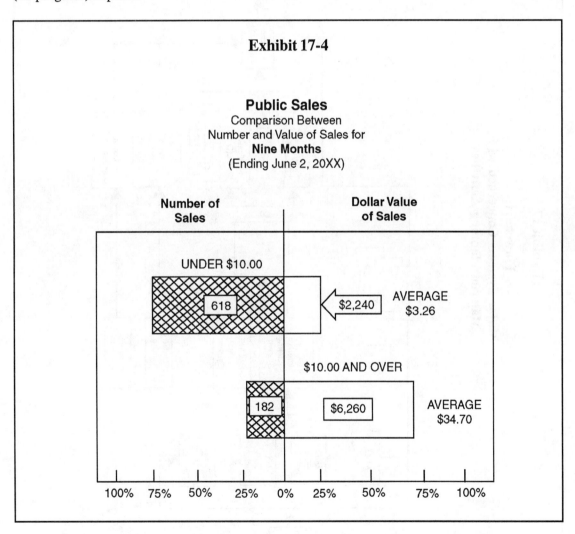

Exhibit 17-4

Public Sales
Comparison Between
Number and Value of Sales for
Nine Months
(Ending June 2, 20XX)

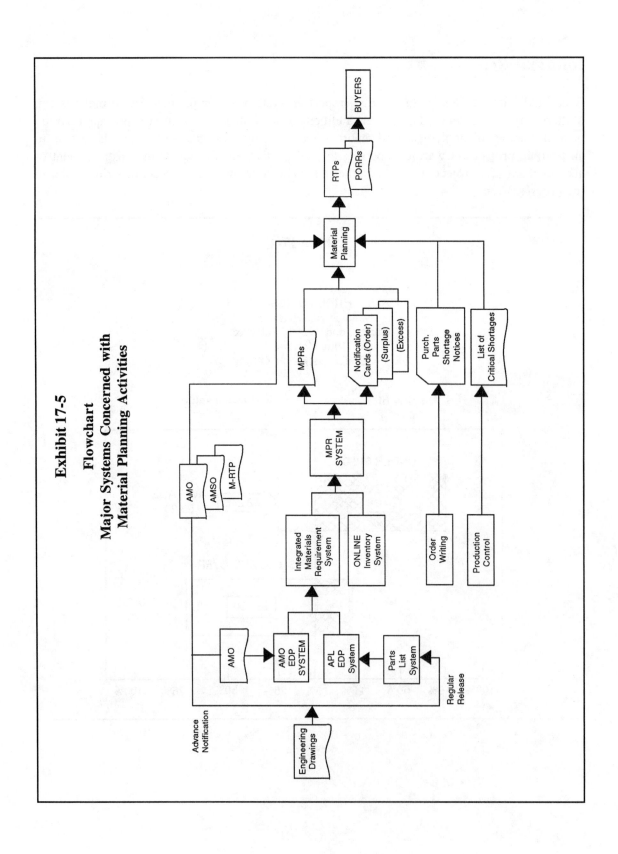

Exhibit 17-5

Flowchart

Major Systems Concerned with
Material Planning Activities

Exhibit 17-6

Warehouse open to elements (note daylight through open wall). Also, product damaged in handling.

Customer's warehouse containing company's consigned products. Deterioration on the outside indicates conditions inside.

Bulk product stored in tank with evidence of corrosion at top of tank. Impurities can materially damage the product.

Open burning at plant site. Potential violation of pollution standards.

As with other informal reports that keep communication timely, interim reports should occupy an official position in the audit function. Readers will become accustomed to these informal reports if they follow a regular pattern, are referred to by a common designation, and are subject to some form of numerical control.

They may be designated "Informal Audit Reports" and may be given consecutive numbers for each year. The first report for the year could be designated "IAR XX-1."

The report may be of any length, depending on the subject to be covered. If it is brief, it may be presented on a single typed page. If it exceeds one page, it is preferable that a brief summary act as a transmittal and outline, with the fully discussed material contained in an attachment to the informal report.

As an example, assume that information on the supply departments is being reported informally to client management. The full discussion could be incorporated in an attachment. The transmittal report could be as shown in Exhibit 17-7. Through the use of e-mail, copies can be sent simultaneously to appropriate officials.

Exhibit 17-7

IAR 8X-10

To: Manager
From: Auditor
Subject: Bethany Supply Department

This informal report is sent to you to keep you informed on a matter that we found in our audit now in progress of the Bethany supply department.

Inventory records are not being kept up to date. As a result, the supply department recently purchased unneeded material costing $75,000. The matter is discussed in detail in the attachment to this report.

The matter will be covered in our formal report on the Bethany supply department. We would like to receive your comments and will acknowledge any corrective action that you take before we issue that report. Please let us know, therefore, of any action you take or intend to take. Our field work will be completed in about two or three weeks.

Due Diligence Audit Reporting

The objective of due diligence auditing is to collect information, pro and con, for client management to use in decision-making relative to joint ventures, mergers, consolidations, and other types of acquisitions. Usually the due diligence audit is a joint three-way project involving the external auditors, lawyers, and internal auditors. Each of these three organizations has specific areas of interest. Yet, there must be coordination. Examples might be:

Areas	Outside Auditor	Lawyer	Internal Auditor
Accounts Receivable	Validity of Accounts	Collections, Litigation	Aging of Accounts, Collection Policies
Inventories	Validity of Accounts	Hypothication, Bailments	Condition of Stockage, Obsolescence

All three of the investigating teams should use similar computer programming to enter any findings relating to a previously established list of areas of interest. Lotus Notes has software that will allow input such as this. The result during the audit can be an association device that alerts one of the other teams to potential subjects of interest. It can also be very helpful in the preparation of the due diligence audit report.

The final element of the due diligence audit project is the preparation of the report. Management will be sensitive to the tone and content of the report. Thus, report writers must scrupulously adhere to report only factual material and exclude as much subjectivity as possible. Suggestions from a recent article include:[10]

- "Include an executive summary with bullet points highlighting aspects that could favor the negotiation of a better deal."

- "Structure the report by cycles of business as defined by the acquiring organization; for example, categories could include finance and administration, sales and marketing, human resources, management, purchasing, production, and treasury." (We might also add classes of balance sheet items.)

- "Index all supporting documents and working papers."

- "Back up all work sheets and other data on disks."

A carefully coordinated audit, properly reported, can well serve the decision makers and can serve to enhance management's perception of the internal audit process.

Communications Outside the Organization

Internal auditors may be called upon to provide information outside the organization. Practice Advisory 2440-2 addresses this subject. It suggests that formal guidance be available as to the policies for such activity to include necessary authorizations, the process for seeking approvals, guidelines as to types of information, outside persons authorized to receive such information, privacy, regulatory, and legal restrictions, and the peripheral content of the information as to advice, opinions, and assurances included.

The advisory also provides the mechanics suggested for the providing process such as written agreements; processors of the information; objectives, scope, and procedures in the generating process; nature of the communications; and copyright issues.

Oral Reports

Oral reports should not, in our opinion, replace written reports. But they do have their place, and a valuable place it is. They are being used more and more because:

- They are immediate. They give management prompt assurances or current information for corrective action.

- They evoke face-to-face responses. They can reveal attitudes and convictions.

- They permit the auditors to counter arguments and provide additional information that the report recipients may require.

- They can bring out inaccuracies in the auditors' thinking.

- They can develop improved rapport with the client.

Oral reports should not be off-the-cuff. They should be prepared with care. They should show that the auditors have done their homework.

It does not follow, however, that the auditors should make gold-plated presentations that go beyond the needs of the subject or the audience. Oral reports can be presented economically without the appearance of excessively expensive preparation.

Desktop flip charts can be eminently effective for small groups. The charts can be prepared through computer facilities without too much effort and are extremely effective in keeping the auditors in charge of the meeting, keeping the clients focused on what is being said, and keeping the auditors themselves on track.

The flip charts can be prepared on 8 1/2 x 11-inch cards and should not be wordy, which only serves to distract attention rather than focus it. One means of achieving brevity is to print the material first on 3x5-inch slips of paper — there just is not sufficient room for extended comments. A series of charts for the audit of a supply department, giving background, pointing out the problem, and recommending action, might be as shown in Exhibit 17-8.

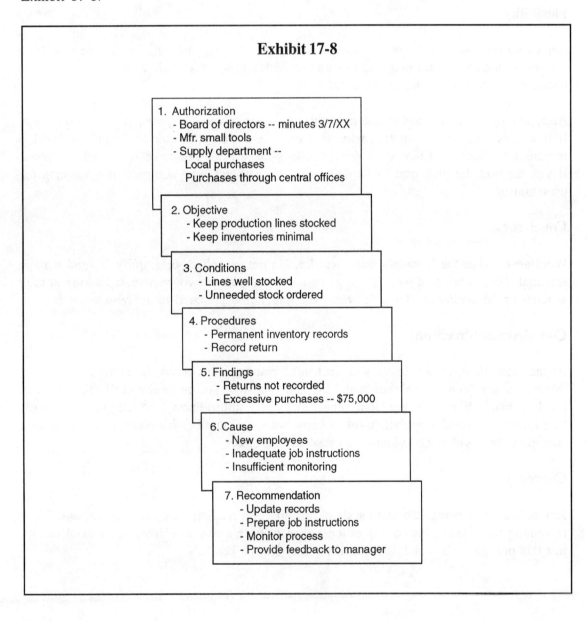

Exhibit 17-8

1. Authorization
   - Board of directors -- minutes 3/7/XX
   - Mfr. small tools
   - Supply department --
     Local purchases
     Purchases through central offices

2. Objective
   - Keep production lines stocked
   - Keep inventories minimal

3. Conditions
   - Lines well stocked
   - Unneeded stock ordered

4. Procedures
   - Permanent inventory records
   - Record return

5. Findings
   - Returns not recorded
   - Excessive purchases -- $75,000

6. Cause
   - New employees
   - Inadequate job instructions
   - Insufficient monitoring

7. Recommendation
   - Update records
   - Prepare job instructions
   - Monitor process
   - Provide feedback to manager

The informal, desktop presentation may not always suit the auditor's needs. A formal oral presentation may be called for. The audience may be at a level that requires auditors to give considerable thought to their talk and prepare carefully for it. This situation should not be regarded as a catastrophe, but rather as a splendid opportunity to present another facet of the auditor's ability: the articulate, practiced speaker. In this instance, PowerPoint or transparencies or slides can be used.

These presentations deserve effort. Here are some of the possibilities to take into account.

Flexibility

Keep your options open as you proceed toward your oral presentation. Be capable of cutting the presentation short. Be prepared to skip material, amplify material, or do whatever else is necessary to keep the listener interested.

Also, be prepared to respond to questions that are not an element of your planned presentation. It is a good idea to set up scenarios that include anticipated questions and to develop responses to them. You may even develop charts that can be presented if needed. However, if you do this, be prepared to explain why this subject was not part of your original presentation.

Conciseness

Wordiness makes the listener's mind wander. Do not embellish or amplify beyond what is essential. Do not bring in what is not germane. When you see your listeners looking at their watches or drumming on the table with their fingers, be prepared to abbreviate the talk.

Completeness/Precision

At the same time, do not leave a subject until you have answered the obvious questions. When you say "considerable amount," the audience will not be happy until you tell them just how much. When you say "long time," they will want to know how long. When you say "a number of errors," they will want to know what that number is. When you talk about a condition, they will want to know its cause and its effect.

Currency

Just before the meeting, the auditor should try to get a reading on current conditions. There is nothing more satisfying to a questioner than to hear a response like: "I checked on that just this morning. The condition is still the way I described it."

Preparation

The oral report should have the same analytical attention as would be given to a written report. In outline form, these are the elements of the preparatory phase.

- Set objectives:
    Interim reporting
    Progress reporting
    Calling attention to a specific finding

- Determine the audience. Based on the objective, identify the most appropriate audience. Or is the audience mandated? Determine the characteristics of the audience so as to fit the presentation to its interests.

- Based on the objective, the audience, and the material to be presented, establish an outline of the report. Include:
    Introductory material
    Substantive material (each element should be organized within itself)
    Conclusion

- Make sure that each segment of the material is complete as to any of the following that are appropriate:
    Background
    Criteria
    Condition
    Impact
    Cause
    Recommendation

- Use visual aids as much as possible. Each segment of the report should be outlined visually so that the attendees can follow visually as well as by listening.

- Assuming that there is time, conduct a "dry run" of the material before a critical internal audit audience to ensure completeness, clarity, and flow.

- Anticipate questions and have prepared responses. Use 5" x 8" cards containing the anticipated questions and potential answers including references to the audit working papers and to outside sources if appropriate.

Good Writing

Let us emphasize once more that good writing calls for good thinking. There is no escaping it. If concepts are confused and tangled, if thoughts are muddy, and if no logical relationship has been established between cause and effect, between the important and the insignificant, then the report that rises from this accumulation is bound to be an ineffectual piece of work. So before starting to write, straighten out your thinking, put things in place, and get your findings in proper perspective.

Outlines

One way of sorting things out, making sure of a logical and reasonable flow of ideas, is through the report outline. The drafting of the outline is simplified if the audit organization has developed a reasonably standardized format for its regular reports.

Standardization usually spells economy. It makes the writer, reader, speaker, and audience feel comfortable. Both know the general path the report will take. Filling in the information needed to fit a particular set of circumstances becomes simplified to a considerable extent.

Outlining takes discipline. Many an auditor, instructed to outline a report, presented a completed draft with the statement, "I started to outline, but when I began writing I just couldn't stop." Compassionate reviewers wind up outlining the report themselves. Hard-nosed (and probably the more effective) reviewers toss the draft back with a terse comment: "When I ask for an outline, I want an outline."

What the reviewer really wants is a crisp, simple skeleton of the report — a word or a phrase — to make sure that the thoughts flow logically and that nothing has been omitted. Here is a sample outline:

Summary

A. Foreword
   1. First regular audit
   2. Covered supply department
   3. Procures, maintains supplies
      a. Locally
      b. Through headquarters
   4. Total value — amount
B. Purpose
   Evaluate:
   1. Procurement
   2. Physical inventory
   3. Records

C. Scope
  1. Test purchase documents
  2. Observe inventory-taking
  3. Examine records
D. Opinion
  1. Satisfactory on —
    a. Procurements
    b. Physical inventories
  2. Unsatisfactory on —
    a. Records
E. Findings
  1. Procurements
    a. Written bids
    b. Approvals
    c. Follow-up system
  2. Physical inventories
    a. Security
    b. Arrangement of stock
    c. Bin cards
  3. Records
    a. Perpetual inventory records
    b. Returns from production
      (1) Not recorded
      (2) Over-procurement

Details

A. Summary statement re over-procurement
B. Procedures — criteria
  Enter returns on records
C. Results of tests — facts
  Returns not entered
D. Effect
  Over-procurement — amount
E. Cause
  Employees not instructed
  Inadequate supervision
F. Recommendation
  Update records
  Issue instructions
  Monitor performance
G. Action
  All steps taken

Prior Reports

The auditor should not overlook or fail to take counsel from any previous reports. Much thought probably went into those reports. Shades of meaning were considered. Difficult wording may have been drafted and polished. Reporting policies were probably observed. A proper format was no doubt employed.

But the prior report should be relied upon with discretion. Conditions may have changed. Procedures may have been revised. Reporting styles may have been changed. With these caveats, using the prior report may be a great time saver.

The First Draft

No writer who ever held a pen or sat before a computer did not, at one time or another, get stuck. The gears slip into neutral and nothing moves. The auditor, too, may wait for inspiration — for that perfect beginning that will give character and interest to all that follows.

We may wait forever before that sterling sentence forms itself on paper. Somehow we must develop the discipline that says: "I must write. Therefore I shall."

Andre Gide, in his *Journal,* June 4, 1930, said, "Too often I wait for the sentence to finish taking shape in my mind before setting it down. It is better to seize it by the end that first offers itself, head or foot, though not knowing the rest, then pull: the rest will follow."

The writer, therefore, needs some spur to getting words down on paper. The outline helps. It shows where to begin and what will come after. The next step is to boldly violate the purity of the blank page with the thrust of the pen or the inscription of the computer. Some mark, some line, some word. Perhaps the title. Perhaps a heading. But something to prime the pump and get the words flowing.

The material is there. The working papers are full of facts and figures. All it takes is a dogged persistence for the draft to grow. Little matter that the first words are trite or poorly phrased. No one waits to cart them away and put them in print. They will be revised and reshaped before they reach their final form; for there is no such thing as good writing — just good rewriting. The first draft is a lump of clay to be pummeled and mauled — to be cut away here and added to there until it emerges as a monument to the auditor's persistence.

When the first draft has been written, hacked at, and interlineated, if not on a computer, have it typed or retyped. In the interim, the ideas within the subconscious will marinate and become more palatable. Then when the new draft is available and perused, new thoughts, better thoughts, and better phrases will come. The draft will be seen with new eyes. New ways of getting ideas across will emerge, and gradually the report will take the desired form and give the hoped-for message.

Then, after dozens and dozens of painstakingly written reports, the writing improves, the chore becomes less painful, and the product becomes more professional. But at the beginning, the answer lies in good field work, good working papers, supporting evidence, a well-structured outline, and dogged persistence.

Language

No language is easy to master. It takes a long, hard apprenticeship and a flair for words. But as in any craft, there are techniques that keep the writing from being inept and amateurish. Three basic rules can help any report writer: Keep your writing simple; keep your writing clear; keep your writing alive.

Within the compass of these rules are a number of sub-rules, which, if followed, can reward the efforts of even the poorest of writers:

Keep your writing simple. Use short sentences. It is easy for the reader to get lost in the labyrinth of a long sentence, but add some well-constructed long sentences for variety.

Use common words. Do not try to send the reader to the dictionary. If an unusual word is the only one that fits, define it.

- Omit needless words.
- Do not include any unnecessary ideas, phrases, or words in a sentence or a paragraph.
- Keep all the thoughts relevant and related.
- Make the ideas flow in a logical succession. Do not force the reader to mentally rearrange the ideas to understand them.
- Avoid contradictory ideas or thoughts that violate logic. What is said should make sense.
- Avoid beginning a sentence with verb-form modifiers that require the passive tense. "The completed audit occurred in September" is improved by saying, "We completed the audit in September."

732 Part 5: Reporting

Keep your writing clear. Write to communicate your findings and express your ideas, not to impress someone with your knowledge.

Use common words.

Don't use:	**When you can use:**
terminate	stop, end
optimum	best
institute	begin
initiate	start
initial	first
purchase	buy
facilitate	ease, simplify
demonstrate	show
subsequent	next
expedite	hasten, speed
prior to	before
numerous, innumerable	many
velocity	speed
accordingly, consequently	so
furthermore	then, also
nevertheless	but, however
adhere	stick, follow
likewise	and, also
conducted, effected	made
utilize	use
informed, indicated	told
implemented	carried out
reflect	show

Consider the reader's experience. Give enough information to supply background, but not so much as to belabor the obvious or be patronizing.

Express coordinate ideas in similar form. Keep related expressions in parallel. Switching between different forms for comparable thoughts troubles and confuses the reader.

Not: We made our audit by observing receipts, examining, documentation, and we interviewed inspectors.

But: During the audit we observed receipts, examined documentation, and interviewed inspectors.

Some further ideas:

- Make it clear which of two or more things just mentioned is being referred to or discussed.

- Define clearly any technical or unfamiliar subject.

- Make it clear when something happened and where it happened.

- Be specific about quantities. A "substantial percentage" is not as clear as "20 out of 50."

- Use the right word. Rarely do two English words mean the same thing. Use the one that best describes what you have in mind.

- Avoid ambiguous words and phrases. Good writing should be susceptible to only one meaning. If a word or phrase can possibly be misunderstood, it most likely will be.

- Put words in the right place. "We only wish to improve procedures" is different from "We wish only to improve procedures."

- Do not omit important details. If a finding states that, "The checks did not bear two signatures," it should be shown by what authority two signatures are required.

- Carry out promises. If an introductory sentence says, "We shall discuss three controls over the accuracy of engineering drawings," make sure all three are discussed. On the other hand, if a heading states, "Accuracy of Engineering Drawings," do not discuss under that heading the timeliness with which drawings are prepared.

- Lists of items should include words belonging to the same categories.

- Do not use the same word in different senses in the same sentence. Avoid, for example: "There was a material amount of rubbish mixed with the scrap material."

- Avoid ambiguous references. Make sure there can be no doubt about what the referent is when you use such words as "it," "they," "that," "these," and "which."

- Avoid dangling modifiers.

Not: Having reported our finding, the manager took corrective action.
But: After we reported our finding to him, the manager took corrective action.

Keep your writing alive. Use action words. They command attention. They give writing spice. The active voice is preferable, but the passive may sometimes be used for variety.

Use words that draw pictures. Avoid vague and fuzzy generalities. "Envelopes and writing paper" draws a clearer picture than "stationery."

Avoid sentences that begin with "As a result of," "Although," "Despite," "In view of," and the like. The sentences tend to get long and dreary.

Physical Characteristics

Appearance

Like any other product on the market, the report should be attractively packaged. It should have a dignified and tasteful appearance. At the same time it should not indicate excessive expense in the preparation. An expensive looking package is inconsistent with exhortations by the auditor to practice greater economy.

Most organizations follow fairly consistent formats in their report presentation, covers, and distribution sheets. Some of the reports are transmitted by memoranda. Others have the distribution sheet as the first page. Some are placed within covers with varying types and colors of bindings.

In the main, audit reports show a good deal of "white space." Paragraphs are generally short. There is an abundant use of headings to indicate what follows and to break up the crowded lines.

Some reports are double-spaced, but the majority are single-spaced. For still others, the summaries are double-spaced and the detail is single-spaced.

Length

Reports come in all lengths. Long reports are generally summarized to give executive management the gist of the audit results. Longer reports will generally have tables of contents to make their contents more accessible.

Quality Ratings

Some organizations have adopted a plan that calls for an adjective or numerical rating for each organization audited. This idea faces opposition from many auditors. They feel that it is very difficult for the auditor to produce logically comparable ratings for the many diverse operations they review.

In most instances, the rating would merely represent the auditor's subjective opinion, vulnerable to dispute and argument. To be reasonably objective, the following two factors should apply. First, the operations to be rated should be similar. Only under such conditions could standards be developed that are equally applicable to the different operations and equally applied by different auditors in the same audit department. Second, the conditions should be quantifiable — numbers of errors or differences in inventories, for example. Where audit opinions become the significant factor, ratings may be difficult to apply fairly. This is particularly true in large audit organizations with many auditors, each with different views and audit approaches.

In one organization, the first item in the report is a rating (A, B, C, D) for the current audit and, for purposes of comparison, the rating for the previous audit. An explanation follows these ratings. For example:

> Rating for this audit ....C Minus
> Rating for last audit (June 28, 19XX) .... B Plus
> This unsatisfactory rating shows a serious deterioration in controls, irregularities in the handling of estimates, and a poor credit routine performance. In addition, the work in a number of other sections is far from satisfactory.

In another firm, audit rating sheets are included in the reports on wholesale sales regions. The sheet lists the activities to be examined and shows, for each activity, the number of points that indicate the standard for top performance. Another column shows the number of points assigned in the current audit. The third and last column shows the percentage relationship between the current rating and the standard. An overall rating is then developed and reported in the first paragraph of the transmittal letter.

Titles

Titles of reports deserve careful consideration. They should be sufficiently descriptive to clearly convey the subject matter of the report. They should not be so long as to be a report in themselves. Yet they should not imply coverage that is not contemplated. For example:

"Review of Warranties" is so broad that it can be construed to cover both warranties to customers and warranties from suppliers.

"Review of Warranties from Suppliers" restricts the field, but implies coverage of warranties on productive equipment as well as nonproductive equipment such as computers and other office equipment.

"Review of Warranties from Productive Equipment Suppliers" may accurately convey the entire extent of the audit coverage.

Tips for Audit Report Writing

An article in *Internal Auditor* listed a series of general "DO's" and specific tips for audit report writing and editing.[12] They follow:

1. Slow down. Think before you write. Write what it is you want to say.
2. Write for your least informed reader. Simplify what you are trying to say.
3. If something doesn't seem clear to you when you write it, rewrite it until it is clear.
4. Aim your writing at your audience.
5. Use a good style manual and refer to it often. Always have one available.
6. Try to write and edit in the mornings when your mind is relatively clear.
7. When editing, review each document at least three times:
   - To get a general understanding of what is being said.
   - To determine that each sentence is needed and says precisely what it intends to say.
   - To judge style, syntax, and grammar.
8. Trust in your judgment regardless of how painful it may be.
9. Explain why you are making changes in the report. It becomes an educational process
10. Keep giving your best effort.

Some additional comments to enhance the writing would include:[13]

- Content and flow of logic are the most important criteria in a first draft.
- Let it lie for fresh eyes. Reread after a reasonable time to see if it still conveys the intended thoughts.
- If in doubt, take the item out.
- Keep it simple, clear and brief.
- Edit for grammar, appearance, and consistency.

Effective Strategies for Report Writing

A series of effective strategies for internal audit report writing was described in a recent *Internal Auditing* newsletter by Warren Gorham & Lamont.[14] In substance, these items were emphasized.

- Full wording of acronyms should be given when first used in a report. If there are many, use an appendix for all.
- Recommendations should precisely describe the procedures that will resolve problems.
- Recommendations should address basic problems, not surface problems nor symptoms.

- Recommendations should be made to the client organization segment that has the authority to implement them.
- Client responses to findings should be included in the report.
- An audit finding should present only one situation.
- Language should be objective and nonjudgmental.
- Use a good updated dictionary.
- Make an outline of the report before starting to construct and write it.
- Use short paragraphs.
- List short items rather than using sentences.
- Put long tables in appendices.
- Group similar findings together.
- Place the most important finding at the beginning of the report.
- Include an executive summary of the findings and recommendations.
- For emphasis, use bullets, sidebars, and bold or italic type.

The writer should try to develop innovative approaches such as using simplified descriptions of analytical processes. However, the context must remain objective and factual.

Elements of Exceptional Internal Audit Reports

Exceptional internal audit reports should contain the following four sections:

- Purpose
- Overview
- Body
- Findings and Recommendations

So says a current article in *Internal Auditing Alert.* The article discussed the elements as a distillation of *Standard 2410* of The IIA's *Standards.*[15]

- Purpose
  - Nature
  - Objective
  - Scope (depth of work):
    Areas under review
    Extent of sampling
- Overview
  - Client functions
  - Size and budget of the client organization
  - Volume produced
  - Recent changes in operation

- - Reporting structure
  - Changes in client management
- Body
  - The audit work performed
  - The results of the audit work
- Findings and Recommendations
  - Criteria
  - Conditions
  - Cause
  Impact
  - Recommendations

During the audit process, the auditor should develop documentation as to:

- The audit process.
- Descriptive material on the client.
- Descriptive material on targeted systems.
- Documentation of testing performed.
- Documentation of the results of the testing.
- The findings and the results.

The secret to good audit report writing is the capturing of the above elements at the earliest possible time in the audit process. "Day-to-day writing and the updating of the report draft is a must."

Short Reports

Many senior managers are constrained by the normal pressures of their position from devoting the time necessary to read the usual lengthy audit report. Because of this, some audit activities have developed a "short report." This report is limited to five pages; in some cases to one or two pages. The material is summarized, usually into a single paragraph for each audit finding. Background material is limited and the essence of the treatment is confined to identifying the risk related to operating objectives, the exposure resulting from current controls, and the remedial action that should be taken, has been taken, or will be taken to resolve the problem. An appendix for each finding supports the short report. The appendix provides detailed information (including client's position, if appropriate), though this could be covered in a phrase in the report's treatment of the matter.

Another type of "short reporting" is to make an oral report using PowerPoint or the usual overhead transparencies with a copy for the executives attending the presentation. The auditor makes the presentation using a laser pointer for emphasis and having supporting plates available to respond to anticipated questions. There are definite advantages in this type of presentation in that the auditor has the complete attention of the executive and can normally get some type of reaction relative to the situation described. This approach is also useful in reporting on follow-up activities. The method can be supported by actual photographs or by charts or graphs that pictorialize the situation. This method gains from the old adage "a picture is worth a thousand words."

The material should be retained in either electronic or hard copy form for historical use and reference. The presentation, together with executive questions and comments, should be recorded and retained. In sensitive situations it may be a good idea to have legal counsel review the presentation and the support to ensure that there are no problems relative to libel or slander or where there might be potential damage issues in environmental audit reporting where remediation payments, fines, or penalties could result.

See Chapter 30 for a description of One-Page Reports using colors for emphasis for executives and members of boards of directors.

More Prompt Reports — Another Option

Another method of achieving a minimum of time between the close of field work and the issuance of the audit report is through the use of computers to transmit the current status of findings to clients and supervisors. Editing and clarification by supervisors are currently fed by computer to the staff auditors. Also, questions as to facts and to presentation are also currently input into the computer by clients. Thus, the audit findings are consistently in a state of being perfected so that at the end of the field work, the exit conferences are primarily formalities.

The entire communication process is through the use of voice messages coupled with the use of screens by the participants at both ends. Printouts are available and supervisors can continually check the progress of the work by accessing the field auditors' computers to review working papers and observe their summarization into a findings section.

As has been described in the chapter on planning, the supervisors and managers have a preliminary idea as to the substance that will probably be in the report. This outline material based on risk evaluation and other planning devices can be used as report development criteria against which the computerized working papers and finding summaries can be compared.

Information Security

Information security is a management responsibility. The internal audit activity should determine that:

- Management recognizes this responsibility.
- There is no risk of breaching the information security function.
- If there are situations where security provisions are faulty, management is aware of them.
- Corrective measures are taken to resolve any and all problems of information security.
- Preventive, detective, and mitigative measures are in place to ensure information security.

The internal audit activity may act in consultative capacity to ensure that the organization's information security function is appropriate to its relationship with outside entities (Practice Advisory 2100-2, "Information Security").

Editing Reports

Reviews

In most internal audit activities, audit reports are edited with great care. They are drafted by the auditor and reviewed in detail by an editor, a supervisor, an audit manager, or any combination of the three. This review is conducted to put reported findings in perspective, to make sure the audit organization's policies are followed, and to ensure accuracy, logic, and acceptable style.

The review process is a training ground for the auditor. It should point up any weaknesses in thought or in the development of facts. It should highlight the matters the auditor ought to keep in mind in the next audit. The reviewer owes it to the auditor to explain the changes and improvements made so that weaknesses can be strengthened. The reviewer should have, therefore, a thorough understanding of the factors that contribute to reporting.

Current philosophy and practice in many internal audit activities is to enhance the skill of field managers and supervisors so as to eliminate the need for time-consuming reviews of policy, logic, and accuracy.

Basically, the reviewer, regardless of position, is concerned with the report's readability, correctness, and appropriateness:

Readability. The reviewer will try to determine how clearly the report will come across to the reader. Does it lay a proper foundation and background? Are the sentences well constructed? Do the paragraphs have topic sentences and are they short? Is the language clear and free from jargon? Do the thoughts flow freely and logically? Is the message clear?

Correctness. Are the grammar and punctuation correct? Are the department's reporting policies followed? Are the audit thoughts properly connected? Are ideas and conclusions summarized yet properly supported? Does the report stick to its purpose? Does it make use of all the significant data accumulated in the field work? Do the working papers support the reported statements?

Appropriateness. Is the tone tactful? Are opinions separated from facts? Is the attitude objective? Are minor deficiencies given too much space — and are major deficiencies given too little? Does the report do a proper job on the ideas that need selling, while not wasting time on matters of little importance?

Reviewers can use the Written Performance Inventory (Exhibit 17-9) to evaluate report drafts. The inventory identifies common reporting mistakes. It clarifies precisely what reviewers don't like about a particular report. When the auditor asks in outrage, "What do you mean, I can't write?," the reviewer can answer with authority.[16]

Proofreading

When the report is ready to be put in final form, it must be free of errors. It is unfortunate but true that one relatively insignificant mechanical flaw, a typographical or spelling error, can cruelly blemish and downgrade a well-written, soundly documented report. The very nature of audit reports — finding fault, exposing deficiencies, suggesting changes — magnifies in the eyes of the reader any defects within the report itself.

Typographical errors and other minor mistakes divert the reader's attention from the text and thereby lessen the force of the subject matter. Readers may begin thinking about the writer rather than about what is written. They may begin to wonder whether errors in the text may be an indication of substantive blunders in the work or in the document itself.

Internal auditors must therefore be exceptionally careful not only in what they say and how they say it, but also in how successfully they have purged their reports of even the slightest errors. This is not easy to do. Sometimes we cannot trust our own eyes. In reading our own reports, we would like to see them without flaws. As a result, our eyes may slip over errors because we don't really want to see them.

Also, the intelligence that makes us good internal auditors may be the very thing that blinds us to the blemishes in our own work. Intelligent people need fewer details to perceive the whole; hence, the less likely they are to plod doggedly through the individual words and letters that express a thought — a thought that they have grasped at a glance, or with which they are completely familiar.

Exhibit 17-9
Written Performance Inventory

I. READABILITY
Reader's Level
- Too specialized in approach
- Assumes too great a knowledge of subject
- So underestimates the reader that it belabors the obvious

Sentence Construction
- Unnecessarily long in difficult material
- Subject-verb-object word order too rarely used
- Choppy, overly simple style (in simple material)

Paragraph Construction
- Lack of topic sentences
- Too many ideas in single paragraph
- Too long

Familiarity of Words
- Inappropriate jargon
- Pretentious language
- Unnecessarily abstract

Reader Direction
- Lack of "framing" (i.e., failure to tell the reader about purpose and direction of forthcoming discussion)
- Inadequate transitions between paragraphs, thoughts, and conclusions
- Absence of subconclusions to summarize reader's progress at end of divisions in the discussion

Focus
- Unclear as to subject of communication
- Unclear as to purpose of message

II. CORRECTNESS
Mechanics
- Shaky grammar
- Faulty punctuation

Format
- Careless appearance of documents
- Use of unacceptable form

Coherence
- Sentences seem awkward owing to illogical and ungrammatical yoking of unrelated ideas
- Failure to develop a logical progression of ideas through coherent, logically juxtaposed paragraphs

Supporting Detail
- Inadequate support for recommendations
- Too much undigested detail for busy executive

Preparation
- Inadequate thought given to purpose of communication prior to its final completion
- Inadequate preparation or use of data
- Failure to stick to job assigned

Analysis
- Superficial examination of data leading to unconscious overlooking of important evidence
- Failure to draw obvious conclusions from data presented
- Presentation of conclusions unjustified by evidence
- Failure to qualify tenuous assertions
- Failure to identify and justify assumptions used
- Bias, conscious or unconscious, that leads to distorted interpretation of data

III. APPROPRIATENESS
Tact
- Failure to recognize differences in position between writer and receiver
- Impolite tone — too brusque, argumentative, or insulting
- Context includes unnecessary sharpness or implications
- Overbearing attitude toward subordinates
- Insulting and/or personal references

Opinion
- Adequate research but too great an intrusion of opinions
- Too few facts (and too little research) to entitle drawing of conclusions
- Opinions not clearly identified as opinions

Attitude
- Too obvious a desire to please recipients
- Too defensive in face of authority
- Too fearful of recipients to be able to do best work

Persuasiveness
- Seems more convincing than facts warrant
- Seems less convincing than facts warrant
- Too obvious an attempt to sell ideas
- Lacks action-orientation and managerial viewpoint
- Too blunt an approach where subtlety and finesse are called for
- Failure to identify cost/benefit relationship of recommendations

Auditors who are proofreading must therefore slow down and follow a careful regimen before signing reports and sending them off. The audit executive should establish a routine that makes sure all reasonable steps have been taken to assure complete accuracy. The following routine can prove helpful:

Comparison. After the report has been completed, the report should be compared with the draft by reading it aloud. If the person who completed the final report is also proofreading, he or she should read the rough draft and have someone else read the final report — it is hard to detect a flaw in one's own offspring. Both people who do the proofing should initial the report, or a form prepared for the purpose, to evidence their work.

Reference check. The auditor should "tick" on a copy of the final report every factual statement, every number, every title, and every date. The tick marks bear evidence that each item has been referenced back to basic data — to directives, organization charts, working papers, computations, and the like. Drafts must carry marginal references to working papers. This is useful during reviews with clients, for investigations and court cases, and in checking the final report.

The whole picture. Auditors should focus their attention on the report's overall organization. This becomes quite simple if they spread out the pages of the report before them like a game of solitaire. Any inconsistencies in format, headings, and indentation will practically leap out at the auditor. This step will also simplify the verification of references within the report or between the report and supporting schedules.

Auditors should also, at this time, read the report for sense and flow. Often, what sounded completely logical and reasonable and what appeared in perfect sequence assumes a most discouraging aspect in final form when read in rough draft. Auditors who read the final report aloud may reap benefits by having to slow down and hear how the report sounds to others.

The detailed picture. After auditors have satisfied themselves with the organization, sense, and flow of the report, they should then focus on detecting the maddening typographical errors that so easily elude the eye. Here they had better have some assistance, some device to force them to focus, to keep them from reading too rapidly, and to help them concentrate on letters and not on word pictures.

One such device can be made from a sheet of blank paper or cardboard. Cut a strip from the center of the sheet — a strip that is long enough and wide enough to reveal one line of type, but no more. Lay this scanner over the line and read each line slowly, undistracted by the lines before or after it. Finally, if the report is of such significance that a single typographical or mechanical error is utterly unthinkable, read the report backwards through the scanner, thereby focusing on individual words, letters, and punctuation, undiverted by the sense of what was written.

Included in the techniques of the professional proofreader is a mental list of the kinds of errors that most easily escape detection. With these in mind, the auditor is less likely to overlook them. Here are a few of the many errors to watch for:

- Letters omitted (omited) or added (ommitted).
- Doublets or repeaters (allocable).
- Words spelled two ways in the same report (travelled, traveled).
- Improper or inconsistent capitalization.
- Incorrect indentation.
- Wrong division of words.
- Transposition of letters (form for from).
- Inconsistent compounding ("14-foot extrusions and 7 gauge sheet stock").
- Poor spacing (f. o. b. should be f.o.b.).
- Headings that do not relate to the subject matter.
- Showing open quotes or parentheses, but no closed quotes or parentheses.
- Disagreement between subject and predicate in person or number.
- Disagreement between pronoun and its antecedent in person or number.
- Pronoun with unclear referent.
- Using "above" or "below" when matter referred to is on another page (use foregoing, previously, following).
- Day of week does not agree with date.
- Incorrect use of homonyms (principal, principle; compliment, complement; course, coarse; stationary, stationery).
- Using hyphens between adverbs and adjectives (recently-revised instructions).
- Using percent and % both ways in same text.
- Failing to place commas before and after etc., e.g., i.e., when they are in the middle of a sentence.
- Disagreement between the total of a list of items and the specific number mentioned (we have discussed the following five deficiency findings, etc.).
- Failing to put words in quotations that might otherwise be misunderstood (removing the bugs from the system).
- Using both the singular and the plural when referring to the same noun.

Joseph Lasky's monumental work on proofreading gives many more.[17] Word processing software tools may accomplish many of the above checks.

Sample Reports

There are audit reports and there are audit reports. They come in every conceivable size and style. There is not, and there probably never will be, a standard form. Some have acquired their present form from a gradual evolution. Others retain their present form because that is what people have become accustomed to — they are reluctant to see the report changed.

We believe that the internal audit report is much too important to continue in an accustomed form year after year without considering improvements. New needs, new technology, and new insights into what will attract or influence the reader should be periodically evaluated by the audit staff — not change for change's sake, but change that will further meet management's needs and the auditor's objectives.

Exhibit 17-10 is a comprehensive report from a Highway Transportation Department. The distribution sheet shows the broad dissemination given to the report. It specifically identifies the people who will have to take corrective action and those who are to see that the action is taken. An "Audit Highlights" section provides a brief summary of the report for executive consumption. The Summary Report gives background information, sets forth the purpose of the audit, offers an overall opinion, and summarizes the audit findings, both good and bad. The findings are keyed to the objectives of the operation; they are documented by showing how the auditors were able to arrive at their conclusions.

Exhibit 17-10

XYZ Corporation
Internal Audit Report

Audit Project R8X-18   Date: August 26, 20XX

DISTRIBUTION	TAKE ACTION	SECURE ACTION	INFOR- MATION	REVIEWED PRIOR TO RELEASE
President			X	
Executive Vice President		X	X	
Vice President- Controller			X	
Director of Material		X	X	
Manager, Procurement	X			X
Manager, Highway Transportation Department	X			X
Director of Industrial Relations				X
Chief Security Division				X
Chief Plant Protection				X

AUDIT HIGHLIGHTS

	Highway Transportation Department (A Regularly Scheduled Review)
Prior Audit:	No deficiency findings.
Audit Coverage:	1. Equipment maintenance and vehicle dispatching.
	2. Fuel, parts, and repair services.
	3. General administrative activities.
Overall Opinion:	In general, the operation was functioning in a reasonably satisfactory manner.
	We did find some control weaknesses. The most serious involved the lack of separation of duties in the procurement of parts and services. Steps are being taken to correct these weaknesses. Despite the weaknesses, however, the department's activities were being performed satisfactorily.
Executive Action Required:	None.

Exhibit 17-10 (Cont.)

SUMMARY REPORT
Foreword
This report covers the results of our regularly scheduled audit of the activities of the Highway Transportation Department. Our last review of the department's activities disclosed no deficiencies.

The department's primary responsibilities are (1) to transport personnel and materials, and (2) to maintain and repair automotive equipment.

At the time of our audit there were about 50 employees assigned to the department. Operating costs (not including labor) for equipment rental, repair parts and services, and fuel and oil, are projected to reach about $900,000 for 20XX. Mileage for the year will total about 5 million miles.

During this audit we issued one progress report to bring to management's attention certain matters requiring prompt corrective action.

Purpose
We have made an examination of the Highway Transportation Department's principal activities to determine whether they were being controlled adequately and effectively. In performing our audit, we examined the system of controls concerned with the following activities:
(1) Equipment maintenance and vehicle dispatching, including (a) scheduling preventive maintenance inspections, (b) performing regular maintenance and repairs, and (c) dispatching cars and trucks.
(2) Ordering, receiving, and disbursing fuel and parts and obtaining automotive repair services.
(3) General administrative activities concerned with (a) property accountability, (b) plant protection, (c) accident reporting, (d) insurable value reporting, (e) gasoline credit cards, and (f) petty cash dispursing.

Opinions and Findings
We formed the opinion that adequate controls had been provided over the activities we reviewed, except for a lack of separation of duties in the procurement of parts and services. Three other matters of lesser significance likewise involved control weaknesses.

We also formed the opinion that, despite the control weaknesses we had detected, the functions we reviewed were being performed in a generally satisfactory manner.

Our conclusions and findings on each of the three groups of activities covered in our examination are summarized in the following paragraphs.

Equipment Maintenance and Vehicle Dispatching
The department has designed adequate controls to make sure that (1) automotive equipment would receive inspection and preventive maintenance in accordance with the manufacturers' recommendations, and (2) truck and car dispatching would be accomplished in accordance with established procedures.

Exhibit 17-10 (Cont.)

We examined preventive maintenance reports and related control records and satisfied ourselves that maintenance was being properly scheduled, monitored, and performed. We also examined documentation supporting vehicle dispatching and observed the dispatching operations; we concluded that dispatching was being adequately controlled and performed.

Ordering, Receiving, and Disbursing Fuel and Parts, and Obtaining Vehicle Repair Services
Controls had been provided that were designed to make sure that fuel, parts, and outside repair services were: (1) ordered when needed; (2) recorded upon receipt; and (3) properly approved for payment; and that the disbursement of fuel and parts was adequately documented.

We found, however, that there was: (1) a lack of appropriate separation of duties in the procurement of parts and services, and (2) what we considered to be inadequate surveillance over the withdrawal of gasoline and oil by vehicle operators. These matters are discussed more fully in the Supplement to this Summary Report.

We examined representative samples of: (1) reports, records, and blanket purchase orders covering the procurement and receipt of supplies and services; and (2) the logs and records covering fuel withdrawals. Despite the control weaknesses referred to, we concluded on the basis of our tests that the functions were being performed in a reasonably satisfactory manner. We made an analysis of the fuel pump meter records and compared them with the amounts of fuel recorded by vehicle operators. The results showed little variance between the two, indicating that fuel withdrawals were in the main being properly recorded.

General Administrative Activities
Controls had been devised to provide assurance that: (1) property accountability records would be complete and accurate; (2) accidents to licensed vehicles would be reported promptly; (3) gasoline credit cards would be used for the purpose issued and only when vehicles were operated away from organization-owned fuel supplies; and (4) petty cash would be properly safeguarded and used only for the purpose for which the petty cash fund was established.

The Highway Transportation Department was inadequately protected, and we found that there was no provision for reporting the insurable values of repair parts and inventories. These matters are also discussed further in the Supplement.

We tested: (1) equipment information cards; (2) facilities location control cards; (3) acquisition and retirement fixed asset work orders; (4) the department's accident register; (5) the organization insurance administrators control number assignment log covering vehicle and other accidents; (6) a gasoline credit card assignment register; (7) credit card delivery tickets; (8) petty cash reimbursement request; and (9) vouchers covering petty cash disbursements, making a petty cash count as well. Based on our tests, we concluded that except for the lack of reports on insurable values, the activities we examined were carried out in a satisfactory manner.

* * *

Exhibit 17-10 (Cont.)

The four deficiency findings previously mentioned are discussed in the Supplement that follows and are summarized at the end of the Supplement, along with the referrals for completion of corrective action.

Before we completed our review, provision was made to report insurable values, and steps were initiated to correct the remaining three control weaknesses.

_____ Auditor-in-Charge
_____ Supervising Auditor
_____ Chief Audit Executive

SUPPLEMENT TO SUMMARY REPORT

DETAILS OF DEFICIENCY FINDINGS
1. There was no separation of functional authority in the procurement of parts and services, and effective administration of labor-hour agreements was beyond the Highway Transportation Department's resources.

Blanket Purchase Orders (BPOs) have been issued for the procurement of parts and services. The cognizant purchasing department has assigned to the Highway Transportation Department all authority and responsibility for controlling: (a) releases of orders under the BPOs to suppliers; (b) receipt, inspection, and acceptance upon delivery; and (c) approvals of invoices for payment.

In practice, all of these functions are performed by the department manager or by one or two people under his direct control and supervision. Thus, there is none of the protection normally afforded by the separation of such functions among personnel of independent departments; such as establishing requirements, ordering, receiving, inspection, and approving for payment.

There are about 70 currently active BPOs that require suppliers to furnish automotive parts and/or services, as requested. Expenditures for the year are budgeted at about $230,000. Many of the BPOs specify labor-hour rates for the repair of automotive equipment. In effect, these BPOs are Time and Material (T and M) agreements since no fixed number of hours is established for the orders released. Thus, the scope of work is undefined. Yet, the BPOs do not include clauses providing the organization with the right of audit, something normally included in T and M agreements.

In our opinion, these labor-hour BPOs do not appear to meet the intent of Procurement Instruction 501, in that they do not ensure the establishment of a fixed price for the order involved at the time of delivery. Furthermore, adequate and effective contract administration of these agreements is beyond the present resources of the Highway Transportation Department.

Exhibit 17-10 (Cont.)

SUPPLEMENT TO SUMMARY REPORT (Cont.)

Because of the lack of separation of duties and the nature of the agreements, we made an extensive examination of the system and of transactions, but we found no basis for questioning any of the charges. Nevertheless, we recommend that branch management review this condition with a view toward implementing some reasonable control through assignment of some of the key functions to other departments. Further, we recommend that management implement appropriate controls to preclude the use of T and M BPOs without an audit clause.

We discussed this matter with management personnel and they informed us that they intended to review the methods used at other major divisions of the organization to determine whether any of their practices may warrant adoption.

2. Gasoline and oil were being withdrawn by organization employees without adequate surveillance. Since our last examination, the department reassigned elsewhere the service station attendant who had recorded gasoline and oil disbursements on the form provided for that purpose. Under present practice the vehicle operator serves himself and records his own withdrawals of gasoline and oil, without surveillance. There is no assurance, therefore, that the records are maintained accurately or that the information is always entered. Hence the potential for misappropriation are increased. We estimate that the total yearly gasoline withdrawal will approximate 300,000 gallons at a cost of about $450,000.

We recognize that there must be a weighing of the benefits versus the costs of control. Nevertheless, we recommend that management consider some means of surveillance — even on a spot check basis — to provide minimum elements of control.

We discussed this matter with management personnel and they indicated that appropriate surveillance would be conducted over fuel pump operations.

3. The area in which the Highway Transportation Department is located was not adequately protected. Area 10, the site of the Highway Transportation Department, is used to house vehicles, fuel pumps, oil, repair parts, and the garage. The area is completely fenced. But it has two large gates, one at the northwest corner and one at the southeast corner. At the time we began our review both gates were kept open during the regular and swing shifts. A sign at the southeast gate warned that entrance is for the organization vehicles only. No such sign appeared at the other gate.

We observed that departmental employees, as well as other organization employees, were allowed to park their private vehicles within the area. No guards were posted at the gates; plant protection personnel informed us that guards were not available for that purpose.

Exhibit 17-10 (Cont.)

SUPPLEMENT TO SUMMARY REPORT (Cont.)

After we discussed this matter with the department manager, he closed the northwest gate to strengthen security somewhat. We believe that further action should be considered, however. While there is an adequate number of employees on hand during the day shift to provide some protection for property, it is doubtful that the reduced swing shift staff can do the same. Also, permitting private cars in the area violates the posted instructions and increases the danger of losses.

We recognize that the unavailability of Plant Protection guards creates some problems. But we believe that management should consider some substitute safeguards, particularly on swing shift.

During discussions with management personnel, they indicated that additional measures to strengthen plant protection would be considered.

4. The insurable value of repair parts on hand was not being reported.
We found that the value of repair parts on hand in the Highway Transportation Department had not been reported for insurance purposes since the inventory records were decontrolled in 20XX. The value of these repair parts is about $4,500.

We called the matter to the attention of the Insurance Administrator, and he requested the highway Transportation Department to report the estimated dollar value as of the end of June 20XX. He has also taken action to revise the Company Insurance Manual to show this requirement.

The Highway Transportation Department informed the Insurance Administrator of the insurable value on July 16, 20XX. Corrective action on this matter is considered complete.

SUMMARY OF FINDINGS REQUIRING CORRECTIVE ACTION
The four matters requiring corrective action are summarized:
1. There was no separation of functional authority in the procurement of parts and services and effective administration of labor-hour agreements was beyond the Highway Transportation Department's resources.
2. Gasoline and oil were being withdrawn by organization employees without adequate surveillance.
3. The area in which the Highway Transportation Department is located was not adequately protected.
4. The insurable value of repair parts on hand was not being reported.

Finding 1 is jointly referred to the manager of the Procurement Department and the manager of the Highway Transportation Department for completion of corrective action. Findings 2 and 3 are referred to the manager of the Highway Transportation Department for completion of corrective action. Finding 4 has been corrected.

A supplement to the report explains in detail the four findings the internal auditors reported. The report concludes with a summary of findings requiring corrective action. Findings for which corrective action was not completed at the end of the audit are referred to specific individuals for action.

Exhibit 17-11 presents an interesting form of report prepared by the internal auditors of a bank. Because of its length, we have used excerpts from the report to show the approach and the format. The report is bound in a paperback cover. Inside the cover are standard printed instructions, "How to Read This Report." The full report contains:

- A distribution sheet.

- A transmittal letter to the audit committees of the various boards of directors.

- A table of contents.

- A statement of audit scope.

- The auditor's conclusion running from Excellent to Substandard (the meanings of these adjectival ratings are explained in the instructions on the cover).

- A summary of the major findings disclosed by the audit.

- A digest of recommendations summarized under three headings: Loans, Assets, Liabilities. The digest defines both repeat findings and those recommendations that were previously made but that were not implemented because of limitations of staff and/or facilities. The digest shows which recommendations had been met, which had not been carried out, and which had been agreed to and would be carried out by a given target date.

- The details of the findings supporting the recommendations. Actions taken are shown in italics.

- Appendices provide statistical and financial data. Among the appendices is a list of related-party transactions showing the names of the directors or officers involved, the names of the borrowers, and other pertinent information.

Exhibit 17-11
How to Read This Report*

This report is structured to afford you ease in identifying the seriousness of the findings of the auditor. A quick overview of the findings will be obtained by reading the CONCLUSION and SUMMARY REPORT (2 minutes). The definition of CONCLUSION statements is found below. The DIGEST (1-3 minutes) that follows the SUMMARY will give you a listing of all of the recommendations made, their status, and the date by which implementation should be completed.

The SUMMARY is divided into two primary sections: MAJOR FINDINGS and OTHER FINDINGS. While no recommendations should be ignored, this division is intended to help the reader gain a feel for the relative importance of weaknesses found by the auditors in the course of their examination. The MAJOR FINDINGS section is subdivided into CONTROL and COMPLIANCE subsections.

Findings in the CONTROL subsection indicate exposure to internal or external fraud, or exposures to error that can be costly and have material probability of occurrence.

Findings in the COMPLIANCE subsection indicate exposures created through failure to comply with laws, regulations and legal requirements that expose the bank to penalties, suits and/or judgments or that would require the bank to resort to costly legal action to maintain its rights.

Key factors to watch in the DIGEST are:

(1) The words "see comments" in the status column refers the reader to the DETAIL OF RECOMMENDATIONS section for a discussion of the two sides of an unresolved recommendation.
(2) The symbol *** in the left margin that indicates that the recommendation was made and agreed to in the previous audit and the condition still existed at the time of this audit.
(3) When the symbol @@@ is found in the left margin of the DIGEST it denotes that this recommendation is repeated because of limitations of staff size and/or physical facilities. In such case, the most desirable control procedure will be described in the recommendation. Any alternative, cost-effective control will be described in the response by management following the recommendation.

The section titled DETAIL OF RECOMMENDATIONS is for study at your convenience and contains a detailed discussion of each recommendation and a response from management stating their intentions or actions on the implementation of the recommendations. An APPENDIX section may be placed at the end of the report that contains certain analytical and exposure information that is of interest to management and directors.

*Inside front cover

Exhibit 17-11 (Cont.)

CONCLUSION STATEMENTS

The following terminology is used in the conclusion statements of XYZ Bank Holding Co. internal audit reports and is defined as:

EXCELLENT: Virtually all desired controls are in operation, only very minor exceptions were noted and backup controls exist for all weaknesses noted.

GOOD: Most material controls are in operation and the exposures found are minor in extent and nature, usually backed up by other controls.

STANDARD: Attention should be given to some exposures in protective and compliance controls; however, reasonable assurance exists that current controls afford the bank adequate protection.

MARGINAL: Early attention should be given to exposures in protective and compliance controls; any deterioration in current controls can lead to serious exposures.

SUBSTANDARD*: Requires immediate attention to serious exposures in protective and compliance controls; exposures exist that could make the bank vulnerable to significant losses.

*MAY BE MODIFIED AS **SERIOUSLY** OR **DANGEROUSLY SUBSTANDARD** WHERE CONDITIONS WARRANT.

THE AUDIT COMMITTEES OF THE BOARD OF DIRECTORS OF XYZ BANK HOLDING CO. AND THE SUBSIDIARY BANK.*

Committee Members:

Attached is the report on our recent audit of _____that began August 16, 20XX. This audit covered all departments of the bank and the major areas of three branches. All recommendations, suggestions, and observations arising from the audit have been discussed in detail on December 19, 20XX, with _____. These discussions were held to assure a complete understanding of the contents and emphasis of the items in this report.

It should be understood that no matters in this report are intended to reflect on the honesty or integrity of any officer or employee of the bank. All recommendations have been offered as constructive suggestions for the improvement of internal control in the bank. We are sure that you will be pleased to know that we received the complete cooperation of each concerned member of the bank's staff.

ASSIGNED AUDITORS: SENIOR AUDIT OFFICER
Supervising Auditors   CHIEF AUDIT EXECUTIVE
Senior Staff Auditors
Staff Auditors

Exhibit 17-11 (Cont.)

REPORT DISTRIBUTION

AUDIT COMMITTEES
AUDIT COMMITTEE - XYZ BANK HOLDING CO.
AUDIT COMMITTEE - SUBSIDIARY BANK

CORPORATE MANAGEMENT
CHAIRMAN & CHIEF EXECUTIVE OFFICER - XYZ BANK HOLDING CO.
PRESIDENT - XYZ BANK HOLDING CO.
EXECUTIVE VICE PRESIDENTS - XYZ BANK HOLDING CO.

LINE MANAGEMENT
CHAIRMAN - SUBSIDIARY BANK
PRESIDENT & CHIEF EXECUTIVE OFFICER - SUBSIDIARY BANK
CASHIER - SUBSIDIARY BANK

INFORMATIONAL COPIES
SENIOR VICE PRESIDENT, SYSTEMS & PROCEDURES - XYZ BANK HOLDING CO.
SENIOR VICE PRESIDENT, CREDIT ADMINISTRATION & LOAN REVIEW - XYZ
BANK HOLDING CO.
INDEPENDENT ACCOUNTANTS
AUDIT DEPARTMENT FILES

TABLE OF CONTENTS

ITEM	PAGE
SCOPE OF AUDIT AND CONCLUSION OF AUDITOR	1
SUMMARY OF REPORT	2
DIGEST OF RECOMMENDATIONS	3-5
DETAIL OF RECOMMENDATIONS	
SECTION 1 - LOANS	6-8
SECTION 2 - ASSETS	8-12
SECTION 3 - LIABILITIES	12-14
SECTION 4 - PAYROLL & PERSONNEL	14-15
SECTION 5 - NON-GENERAL LEDGER ITEMS	15-18
APPENDIX I - PAST DUE COMMERCIAL LOANS	19
APPENDIX I - PAST DUE INSTALLMENT LOANS	20
APPENDIX II - OVERDRAFT ANALYSIS	21
APPENDIX III - RELATED PARTY TRANSACTIONS	22-26

Exhibit 17-11 (Cont.)

SCOPE OF AUDIT

The scope of our audit was consistent with generally accepted standards of internal auditing in major banks. We reviewed operations and accounting records in all areas of the Main Office and three branch locations. Our audit tests were made to the extent we deemed necessary to establish our conclusions on the internal control structure of the bank. In several areas, we relied upon the audits that were performed and records that were maintained by the bank's independent accountants,_____, whom we determined was independent of the routine banking operations and bookkeeping record keeping. The audit programs used in these audits were our standard audit programs that have been reviewed by the independent accountants of XYZ Bank Holding Co.

CONCLUSION OF AUDITOR

In our opinion, at the time of our audit the level of internal control was GOOD at the Main Office location and STANDARD at the three branch locations. Accompanying recommendations are submitted to further enhance the bank's existing system of internal control and to establish several controls that do not now exist.

SUMMARY OF REPORT
MAJOR FINDINGS

CONTROL

TELLER FUNCTIONS AND BRANCHES: Effective dual control has not been established over a number of negotiable items at the branches: vault cash, travelers checks, Series E Bonds, official checks, certificates of deposit, night deposit safe, preparation of night deposits, and safe deposit boxes holding branch contents. A separation of duties was not being exercised over several branch functions: deposit account opening/cash handling and approval of loans/proceeds disbursement. In general, a number of cash and teller operations controls were not functioning effectively, due primarily to high turnover and lack of proper training. In addition, night deposit records do not assure the proper disposition of each bag handled by bank personnel.

MAIN OFFICE OPERATIONS AND LOANS: Dormant account signature cards and reserve supplies of official checks and certificates were not strictly controlled at Main Office because of an occasional lack of protection to keys. Work in transit between the bank's locations and the commercial note files are not controlled to ensure accountability for missing documents. Approval for payment of expenses is sometimes not documented, and the insider overdraft policy has not been reduced to written terms. Proper identification of new depositors is sometimes not obtained, and this sometimes results in not obtaining corporate resolutions. Nonmonetary changes to deposit account records are not being signed by the employee responsible for such changes, and no log of customer complaints is maintained. Customer safekeeping items and the supporting records do not agree with one another. Several note agreements are not accurately completed regarding purchase money security interests and collateral descriptions, and collateral documentation and information is occasionally not in file: hazard insurance, inspection reports, and UCC-1 financing statements.

Exhibit 17-11 (Cont.)

COMPLIANCE

Borrowers are not required to sign agreements when their loans are extended and a fee is charged. Some denials of credit are not made in writing if the application is taken orally, and two branches have not posted FDI C signs at teller windows. Standard performance review forms are not utilized, and this could result in using different criteria to judge the work performance of each bank employee.

OTHER FINDINGS

Review and documented approval controls do not exist for waiver of late charges on installment loans, and the fixed asset acquisition and employee loan policies have not been reduced to writing. Cash items were not carried in locked bags when being transported between bank locations, and some guarantors of industrial revenue bond issues do not have current financial statements in file. Approval for overtime pay is not documented, and specimen signatures are not obtained from customers when accepting items to be sent for collection. A number of security procedures could be strengthened to enhance protection to employees and bank assets.

The bank's staff was most helpful and cordial during the course of our audit, and we appreciate their assistance. We also feel that bank personnel should be commended for their conscientious efforts in promptly correcting deficiencies found during the course of our audit and in correcting previous audit recommendations.

DIGEST OF RECOMMENDATIONS

RECOMMENDATION	STATUS	TARGET DATE
SECTION 1- LOANS		
1.1 Note Completion and Credit Documentation.		
C/L*** A. Protect the bank's collateral by obtaining proper documentation.	done	
B. Complete note forms properly.	done	
1.2 Require customers to sign extension agreements.	done	
1.3 Internal and Record Keeping Controls.		
C/L*** A. Assign the responsibility for the commercial note files to designated employees.	done	
B. Document all denials of credit in writing.	done	

Exhibit 17-11 (Cont.)

@@@	C. Establish a separation of duties between approval of loans and disbursement of proceeds at the branches.	see comments
	D. Establish a written lending policy on employee loans.	done
	E. Enhance the control over late charges waived on installment loans.	done

SECTION 2 - ASSETS

2.1   Cash

@@@	A. Provide adequate controls over large supplies of cash.	see comments	
***	B. Make sure that tellers can be held accountable for assigned cash funds and transactions bearing their stamp.	see comments	
	C. Strengthen and strictly enforce the established administrative guidelines over tellers.	done	
	D. Strengthen the teller training program.	agreed	2-15-20XX

DETAIL OF RECOMMENDATIONS
SECTION 1
LOANS

The recommendations in this section apply to both commercial and installment loans. If the recommendation is preceded by C/L***, it will indicate that the audit suggestion has been made in previous audit(s) to commercial loan management only. Asterisk notations without any identifying letters are explained inside the front cover of this report.

1.1 Note Completion and Credit Documentation.

C/L***   **A. Protect the bank's collateral by obtaining proper documentation.**

To perfect its interest in personal property taken as collateral, the bank must either file a UCC-1 financing statement, obtain non-filing insurance, or in the case of 19XX or newer vehicles, obtain a title. The bank should further make sure that its tangible collateral is protected by requiring hazard insurance from the borrower, and in certain cases, a bill of sale should be obtained for personal property that is purchased with loan proceeds and taken as collateral. Our sample review of secured loans disclosed the following conditions: many loans had no hazard insurance, nor were there bills of sale to support tangible property collateral; several loans did not have collateral inspection reports, UCC-1 financing statements or evidence of non-filing insurance coverage. To adequately secure and protect the bank's interest in personal property, we recommend that procedures be established to make sure that all collateral documentation is acquired and maintained.

Exhibit 17-11 (Cont.)

B. Complete note forms properly.
The bank's note forms have been prepared by Legal Counsel of XYZ Bank Holding Co. to assure close compliance with federal and state laws and regulations and to ensure a proper interest in collateral for secured notes. It is management's responsibility to properly complete all note forms before the customer executes the note. During a sample review of notes, we found a number of notes whose purchase money sections were not completed, and several notes had incomplete purpose of collateral sections or inadequate collateral descriptions of accounts receivable. To properly state the legal relationship between the bank and its borrowers, we recommend that all note agreements be accurately and fully completed.

Action Taken

* agreed to implement these suggestions.
also stated that the commercial loan area does not handle typical auto financing and that it was not normally bank policy to acquire bills of sale in these situations.

1.2 Require customers to sign extension agreements.
Granting loan extensions is a lending function and should be treated as such. Regulation Z also governs disclosure of extension fees to borrowers. In our review of extension procedures, we found that customer signatures are not required on extension agreements. To provide a better control over extensions and to be in compliance with applicable laws, we recommend that borrowers sign all extension agreements.

Action Taken

*indicated that this has now been corrected.
1.3 Internal and Recordkeeping Controls.
C/L*** **A. Assign the responsibility for the commercial note file to designated employees.**
The responsibility for the commercial notes should be assigned to a designated employee(s) in order that the responsibility can be fixed for all notes. During our audit we observed that loan officers enter the note window and pull notes for review. This condition can lead to notes that are unaccounted for. We therefore recommend that a designated individual(s) be placed in charge of the commercial notes. These persons can maintain a sign-out sheet for notes that must be removed from the commercial loan department and will help to eliminate the officers' direct access to the note records.

Exhibit 17-11 (Cont.)

B. Document all denials of credit in writing.
The Equal Credit Opportunity Act states that all denials of credit must
be made in writing. The notice must contain a statement of specific reason for the
action taken or disclosure that the reasons can be obtained. During our audit we
learned that some details of credit are made orally when loan applications are taken
orally. To comply with the Equal Credit Opportunity Act, we recommend that all
denials of credit be communicated with the customer in writing, using forms designed
for this purpose by the holding organization's legal staff.

@@@ **C. Establish a separation of duties between approval of loans and disbursement of
proceeds at the branches.**
Basic internal control is provided by a separation of duties so that no one person can
handle a transaction from inception to disposition. During our audit of one branch, we
noted that the loan officer responsible for making a loan is also responsible for the
preparation of the cashier's check for disbursement of the loan proceeds. To help
provide adequate internal control, we recommend that a person who is independent of
loan approval prepare the cashier's check for loan disbursement.

D. Establish a written lending policy on employee loans.
The bank should define its lending parameters and criteria through written policies
and procedures. Such written policies will help to make sure that loans can be made
within established guidelines set by senior management and approved by the board of
Directors. During our review of the bank's lending policy, we found that there are no
written policies for employee loans. To provide guidelines for employee loans, we
recommend that a written policy be prepared by management.

E. Enhance the control over late charges waived on installment loans.
An effective means for management to monitor income from waiver of late charges on
installment loans is to be aware of all late charges waived by each officer. We were
informed that late charge waivers are not approved by an officer. To provide a better
control over late charges waived and loss of potential income, we recommend that a
lending officer be responsible for waiving late charges and that this approval be made
in writing.

Action Taken

*stated that approvals of late charge waivers will be properly controlled in the future.
said that Assistant Branch Managers will prepare the cashier's checks for disbursement
of loan proceeds after the Branch Managers approve loans, whenever possible;
however, there will be times when this control cannot be exercised because of the
small staff sizes. According to the bank now has an employee loan policy, and
management agreed to implement the remainder of the suggestions.*

Exhibit 17-11 (Cont.)

SECTION 2
ASSETS

2.1 Cash.

@@@ **A. Provide adequate controls over large supplies of cash.**

Banking authorities feel that reserve cash and large currency shipments are best protected if maintained under the joint custody of two individuals because it is the bank's most vulnerable asset. During our audit we learned that the combination to the outer vault door is known by each officer at the main office. At several branches, we noted that the vault and reserve cash is not under joint custody, and at one branch the coin vault is left open at all times during the day. To help ensure proper custodial control to vault cash supplies, we encourage management to establish effective dual control over such funds.

*** **B. Make sure that tellers can be held accountable for assigned cash funds and transactions bearing their stamps.**

Cash funds are assigned to tellers and each teller should then be able to be held accountable for all funds charged to her responsibility. Further, identification stamps and keys to tellers' machines should be equally protected to make sure that no unauthorized transaction validations are allowed to occur. During our audit we found that tellers sometimes leave their working and reserve cash, teller identification stamps, and teller machine keys unprotected when away from the teller window area; combinations and locks to the tellers' boxes and the vault have not been changed recently; and duplicate keys to teller boxes are not held under joint custody at several branches. We also noted at one branch that a large amount of cash was placed on a portable table behind the teller lines. To make sure that tellers can be held accountable for their assigned cash funds, we recommend that all cash, machine keys, and identification stamps be locked away when unattended, combinations and locks to the tellers' boxes be changed periodically, duplicate keys to teller boxes be held under joint custody, and tellers be prohibited from placing currency in an area that is visible to customers and not adequately safeguarded.

C. Strengthen and strictly enforce the established administrative guidelines over tellers.

Policies and procedures are established to assist bank personnel in performing their jobs in accordance with management's desires and with sound business practices. Further, periodic management reviews should be made to make sure that personnel are abiding by established guidelines and to review work performance and accountability for negotiable items assigned. During our audit we observed that cash limits appeared to be rather informally established and communicated to officers and tellers. Further, nearly all tellers continually exceeded these cash limits. We also noted at one of the branches that tellers do not obtain the customers' signatures or initials of approval when making out deposit slips for them. To ensure customer approval of transactions

---

Exhibit 17-11 (Cont.)

prepared by bank personnel, we suggest that they sign or initial deposit slips. We also recommend that cash limits be formally communicated to all tellers to help ensure their ability to properly comply with them.

D. Strengthen the teller training program.

Tellers provide a vitally important service at the bank since they are frequently the only personal contact customers have with the bank. Tellers should be trained to operate effectively and efficiently and also be able to sufficiently handle depositors' needs. During our audit we observed that several tellers did not observe a number of proper cash controls; tellers' recap sheets were not legible; and tellers were frequently out of balance and in general did not seem to have an understanding of controls surrounding the cash function. To help protect the bank, tellers, and depositors from loss, we recommend that a more adequate training program be established for the teller function.

Action Taken

and stated that the main office vault door only has a three number combination; it is therefore difficult to split the combination between two teams of people to ensure effective dual control. However, nothing is exposed when vault door is open due to the effective dual control of contents inside the vault.

also stated that a $10,000 cash limit has been established, and tellers sell their excess currency to the vault after closing; this is usually denoted on the bottom of the cash recap sheets. The bank is now in the process of hiring more mature and experienced tellers to improve the teller turnover situation and hopefully, some of the existing control problems will then correct themselves when stability of teller personnel occurs. Due to small branch staffs, rotating days off and Saturday banking hours, it is impossible to establish effective dual control of negotiable items at the branches; in these cases, management is ensuring effective sole control of reserve cash supplies, minimizing the amount of such cash on hand, and surprise counting of these supplies on a monthly basis. Due to the expense involved, management wishes to continue consideration of changing locks throughout the bank and will implement this suggestion at a later date. All other recommendations either have been or will be implemented.

Many audit departments prefer a simpler form of report, in memorandum form, concentrating on findings. Exhibit 17-12 is an example of such a report. It describes an audit in a retail chain. Although the detailed report section deals exclusively with deficiencies and the recommendations to correct them, the "Summary of Audit Results" seeks to put the findings in perspective. It provides a digest of both the good and the bad. The objective comments are useful to executives and face-saving to the clients. It is interesting to observe that the reports are distributed to the very highest levels in the corporation, including the chairman of the board and the audit committee. We were told that these people actually read and comment on the audit reports.

Exhibit 17-12
Memorandum

DATE: January 8, 20XX
TO: Senior Vice President, Administration
FROM: Chief Audit Executive
SUBJECT: BUYING CONTROLS AND ADVERTISING ALLOWANCES —
            AUTOMOTIVE

EXECUTIVE SUMMARY

We have completed an audit of Buying Controls and Advertising Allowances. Our audit objectives and findings are summarized below. The detailed report was discussed with and issued to division management.

PURPOSE AND SCOPE
Our purpose was twofold: First, to review the procurement procedures and practices used in product and vendor selection and in the ordering of selected products. Second, to review procedures designed to ensure the receipt and timely recording of cooperative advertising revenues.

SUMMARY OF AUDIT RESULTS
Procedures and practices employed in both the procurement of automotive products and in the receipt and recording of cooperative advertising revenues were in compliance with Organization and Division objectives. Some conditions required improvement, however. These included excessive slow-moving items; lack of procedures for regular competitive price checks and returns of superseded lines of merchandise, and lack of segregation of duties for billing, accounting, and collecting advertising allowances.
These conditions, along with some administrative weaknesses and our recommendations on corrective action, were discussed at our closing conference. Division management agreed with our findings and recommendations and plans to reply to our report by January 31, 20XX.

cc: President of Division
      President of Corporation
      Chief Financial Officer
      Chairman of the Board
      Chairman of the Audit Committee
      Independent Accountant

Exhibit 17-12 (Cont.)

AUTOMOTIVE DIVISION
BUYING CONTROLS AND ADVERTISING ALLOWANCES

November 1, 20XX

FINDINGS AND RECOMMENDATIONS

1. *Inventories include excessive amounts of discontinued and slow moving items.*

    A computer-generated analysis of inventory by line item identified $5.4 million of automotive products that had a turnover of less than once per year. Four turnovers a year is considered an optimum standard. In addition, 24 percent of all line items had dollar balances under $25. Over five percent is considered excessive. The monitoring of discontinued inventory is at the sole discretion of the buyers. But no procedures have been issued to guide them in monitoring and classifying inventory.

    Recommendations:

    Consider expanding test marketing for new items.

    Define and regularly summarize and review excessive inventory.

    Issue written procedures for timely monitoring and disposition of discontinued and excessive items.

2. *There are no formal procedures for competitive price checks.*

    Retail prices for new items are based on market conditions and gross margin considerations. No formal procedures, however, have been established to compare and document competitors' prices for those items that are price sensitive. This lack of adequate information impairs the ability to respond promptly to market changes.

    Recommendation:

    Develop regular retail price-check procedures for high-value and competitive items.

3. *Procedures have not been established for sending discontinued merchandise to new vendors.*

    New vendors have claimed numerous discrepancies in the shipments of old merchandise to them. Losses during a six-month period are estimated at over $50,000. This has been attributed to the absence of adequate instruction to the people responsible for identifying and shipping such merchandise. New procedures have been contemplated but not prepared. The lack of clear and specific instructions increases the possibility of errors and losses.

Exhibit 17-12 (Cont.)

Recommendation:

Prepare written procedures for determining the dollar amounts of inventory, establishing counting methods, obtaining vendor participation, and processing paperwork for the exchange of merchandise with new vendors.

4. *One person in the Advertising Accounting Department is responsible for receipts, collections, reconciliations, and billings.*

One person in the Advertising Accounting Department performs the following advertising-allowance functions:

- Prepare and mail debit memos.
- Maintain accounts receivable records.
- Prepare journal entries to record debit memos and collect checks.
- Receive checks.
- Reconcile bank statements with general ledger accounts.

Permitting one person to be responsible for all such activities increases the possibility of undetected errors and misappropriations.

Recommendations:

Separate responsibilities for accounts receivable, collections, and reconciliations from those of billings.

Instruct all vendors to send checks directly to cash receipts department.

5. *Debit memos are not prepared promptly.*

The Advertising Accounting Department prepares debit memos for advertising allowances after it obtains proof of performance. The standard interval between receipt of proof of performance and debit memo preparation is one week. Yet a review of 30 debit memos prepared during the second quarter of this year disclosed an average interval of four weeks. Such delays, of course, have an adverse effect on cash flow.

Recommendation:

The department manager should establish goals both for more timely billings and for reduction of current backlog. Also, a control log should be maintained. Before we completed our audit, considerable reductions were made in the debit memo backlog.

References

[1]Browne, D.E., "Patterns for Progress in Internal Auditing," *The Internal Auditor,* Spring 1966, 18.
[2]Maniak, A.J., *Presenting Audit Results — Logic, Content, and Form,* Monograph Series (Altamonte Springs, FL: The Institute of Internal Auditors Research Foundation, 1985), 5-6.
[3]Maniak, 1-2.
[4]U.S. General Accounting Office, How to Get Action on Audit Recommendations (Washington, DC: U.S. General Accounting Office, 1991). [GAO/OP 9.2.1]
[5]Johnston, Warren M., in *Enhancing Internal Auditing Through Innovative Practices* (Altamonte Springs, FL: The Institute of Internal Auditors, 1996), 121-5.
[6]Ibid.
[7]Ibid.
[8]Maniak, 6.
[9]Maniak, 23-24.
[10]Zhang, Charles, "The Art of Coordination," *Internal Auditor*, Apr. 1998, 58.
[11]Research Committee Report No. 10, *Internal Audit Reporting Practices* (Altamonte Springs, FL: The Institute of Internal Auditors, 1961), 22.
[12]Bates, David A., "When Good Writing Goes Bad," *Internal Auditor*, Apr. 1996, 36-38.
[13]Ibid.
[14]*Internal Auditing Alert* (Boston, Mass: Warren Gorham & Lamont, Oct. 1995), 6.
[15]Ibid., Sept. 1997.
[16]Felden, J.S., "What Do You Mean I Can't Write?" *Harvard Business Review,* May-June 1984, 147.
[17]Lasky, Joseph, *Proofreading and Copy-presentation* (New York: Mentor Press, 1941), 88-176.

Supplementary Readings

Avishai, Roma, "The Power of the Pen," *Internal Auditor*, April 1999, 31-34.
Bates, David A., "When Good Writing Goes Bad," *Internal Auditor*, February 1996, 36-38.
Becker, Michael W., and Julius Byars, "Audit Reports That Get the Right Results," *Internal Auditor*, October 1989, 30-37.
Bergman, F.L., et al., *From Auditing to Editing* (Washington, DC: U.S. Government Printing Office, 1976).
Burr, Thomas H., "Low-Fat Audit Reporting," *Internal Auditing Report,* December 2001, 8-9.
Calhoun, Charles, "Communication Skill Resources on the Internet," *Internal Auditing Alert*, November 1997, 4-5.

Calhoun, Charles, "Proposed Auditing Standard Highlights Restricted Reports," *Internal Auditing Alert*, July 1998, 1-5.

Danzinger, Elizabeth, "Writing in Plain English," *Journal of Accountancy*, July 1997, 71-74.

Fleming, Mark, "Video Presentations for Auditors," *Internal Auditor*, October 1991, 50-57.

Gladden Burke, Kimberly, and Stacy E. Kovar, "The Power of Persuasion: Negotiation Strategies for Internal Auditors," *Internal Auditing*, March/April 1999, 11-15.

Goldstein, Leslie M., "High Impact Reports," *Internal Auditor*, December 1991, 18-25.

Maniak, Angela J., *Report Writing for Internal Auditors* (Bankers Publishing Company, 1990).

Ponemon, Lawrence A., "Internal Auditor Objectivity and the Disclosure of Sensitive Issues," *Internal Auditing*, Summer 1991, 36-43.

Ratliff, Richard L., and I. Richard Johnson, "Evidence," *Internal Auditor*, August 1998, 56-61.

Sears, Brian P., *Internal Auditing Manual* (New York: RIA, 2003). (See Chapter D7, "Communicating Results.")

Sloane, David E., "Power Writing: Plain Language, Simple Words," *Internal Auditing Alert*, June 1997, 6-7.

Sloane, David E., "Power Writing: Fixing Those Long, Dull, Confused Sentences," *Internal Auditing Alert*, March 1997, 2-3.

Sloane, David E., "Power Writing: Clear Subjects," *Internal Auditing Alert*, February 1997, 5-6.

Sloane, David E., "Power Writers' Corner: The Internet and E-mail," *Internal Auditing Alert*, November 1996, 5.

Sloane, David E., "Power Writers' Corner," *Internal Auditing Alert*, October 1996, 8.

Stokes, Deborah, "Communicating Results," *Internal Auditor*, December 1989, 15-20.

Whitham, Robert B., "Writing Strategies for Effective Internal Audit Reports," *Internal Auditing*, Winter 1996, 60-62.

Multiple-choice Questions

1. The internal audit unit has recently completed an operational audit of its organization's accounts payable function. The audit director decided to issue a summary report in conjunction with the final report. Who would be the most likely recipient(s) of just the summary audit report?
    a. Accounts payable manager.
    b. External auditor.
    c. Controller.
    d. Audit committee of the board of directors.

2. The internal audit department for a chain of retail stores recently concluded an audit of sales adjustments in all stores in the Southeast region. The audit revealed that several stores are costing the organization an estimated $85,000 per quarter in duplicate credits to customers' charge accounts.

   The audit report, published eight weeks after the audit was concluded, included the internal auditors' recommendations to store management that should prevent duplicate credits to customers' accounts. Which of the following standards for reporting has been disregarded in the above case?
   a. The follow-up actions were not adequate.
   b. The auditors should have implemented appropriate corrective action as soon as the duplicate credits were discovered.
   c. Auditor recommendations should not be included in the report.
   d. The report was not timely.

3. An internal auditor has just completed an audit of a division and is in the process of preparing the audit report. According to the *Standards*, the findings in the audit report should include:
   a. Statements of opinion about the cause of a finding.
   b. Pertinent factual statements concerning the control weaknesses that were uncovered during the course of the audit.
   c. Statements of both fact and opinion developed during the course of the audit.
   d. Statements that may deal with potential future events that may be helpful to the audited division.

4. Which of the following is not an advantage of issuing an interim report?
   a. Final report-writing time can be minimized.
   b. An interim report allows information requiring immediate attention to be communicated.
   c. An interim report can be conducted on an informal basis, and may be communicated only verbally.
   d. A formal, written interim report may negate the need for a final report in certain circumstances.

5. Which of the following would not be considered an objective of the audit closing or exit conference?
   a. To resolve conflicts.
   b. To discuss the findings.
   c. To identify concerns for future audits.
   d. To identify management's actions and responses to the findings.

6. Internal audit reports should contain the purpose, scope, and results. The audit results should contain the criteria, condition, effect, and cause of the finding. The cause can best be described as:
   a. Factual evidence that the internal auditor found.
   b. Reason for the difference between the expected and actual conditions.
   c. The risk or exposure because of the condition found.
   d. Resultant evaluations of the effects of the findings.

7. According to the *Standards*, internal audit reports should be distributed to those members of the organization who are able to make sure that audit results are given due consideration. For higher-level members of the organization, that requirement can usually be satisfied with:
   a. Interim reports.
   b. Summary reports.
   c. Oral reports.
   d. Final written reports only.

8. Which of the following best defines an audit opinion?
   a. A summary of the significant audit findings.
   b. The auditor's professional judgment of the situation that was reviewed.
   c. Conclusions that must be included in the audit report.
   d. Recommendations for corrective action.

9. Exit conferences serve to ensure the accuracy of the information used by an internal auditor. A secondary purpose of an exit conference is:
   a. Get immediate action on a recommendation.
   b. Improve relations with clients.
   c. Agree to the appropriate distribution of the final report.
   d. Brief senior management on the results of the audit.

Use the following information to answer questions 10 and 11.
You are the chief audit executive of a parent organization that has foreign subsidiaries. Independent external audits performed for the parent organization are not conducted by the same firm that conducts the foreign subsidiary audits. Since your department occasionally provides direct assistance to both external firms, you have copies of audit programs and selected working papers produced by each firm.

10. The foreign subsidiary's audit firm would like to rely on some of the work performed by the parent organization's audit firm, but they need to review the working papers first. They have asked you for copies of the parent organization's audit firm working papers. Select the most appropriate response to the foreign subsidiary's auditors:

a. Provide copies of the working papers without notifying the parent organization's audit firm.
b. Notify the parent organization's audit firm of the situation and request that either they provide the working papers or authorize you to do so.
c. Provide copies of the working papers and notify the parent organization's audit firm that you have done so.
d. Refuse to provide the working papers under any circumstances.

11. The foreign subsidiary's audit firm wants to rely on an audit of a function at the parent organization. The audit was conducted by the internal audit department. To place reliance on the work performed, the foreign subsidiary's auditors have requested copies of the working papers. Select the most appropriate response to the foreign subsidiary's auditors:
a. Provide copies of the working papers.
b. Ask the parent organization's audit firm if it is appropriate to release the working papers.
c. Ask the audit committee for permission to release the working papers.
d. Refuse to provide the working papers under any circumstances.

12. During the course of an audit, an auditor discovers that a valued employee has been patenting new developments that are unrelated to the basic business of the company. The company does not have a specific policy regarding patents on developments that are not related to the basic business. Although all new discoveries by employees are the property of the company, division management condoned the employee's actions. The auditor's decision not to report the employee's action would be:
a. A violation of The IIA's *Code of Ethics*.
b. A violation of the reporting requirements in the *Standards*.
c. Justified because divisional management is aware of the practice, and it is not in violation of company policies.
d. Both a and b.

Use the following information to answer questions 13 through 16.
The following data was gathered during an internal auditor's investigation of the reason for a material increase in bad debts expenses. In preparing a report of the finding, each of the items might be classified as criteria, cause, condition, effect, or background information.

1. Very large orders require management's approval of credit.
2. Audit tests showed that sales personnel regularly disregard credit guidelines when dealing with established customers.
3. A monthly report of write-offs is prepared but distributed only to the accounting department.
4. Credit reports are used only on new accounts.

5. Accounting department records suggest that uncollectible accounts could increase by five percent for the current year.
6. The bad debts loss increased by $100,000 during the last fiscal year.
7. Even though procedures and criteria were changed to reduce the amount of bad debt write-offs, the loss of commissions due to written-off accounts has increased for some sales personnel.
8. Credit department policy requires the review of credit references for all new accounts.
9. Current payment records are to be reviewed before extending additional credit to open accounts.
10. To reduce costs, the use of outside credit reports was suspended on several occasions.
11. Since several staff positions in the credit department were eliminated to reduce costs, some new accounts have received only cursory review.
12. According to the new credit manager, strict adherence to established credit policy is not necessary.

13. Criteria is best illustrated by items numbered:
   a. 1, 8, and 9.
   b. 2, 10, and 11.
   c. 3, 4, and 12.
   d. 5, 6, and 7.

14. Cause is best illustrated by items numbered:
   a. 2, 10, and 11.
   b. 3, 4, and 12.
   c. 5, 6, and 7.
   d. 8, and 9.

15. Condition is best illustrated by items numbered:
   a. 5, 6, and 7.
   b. 1, 8, and 9.
   c. 2, 10, and 11.
   d. 3, 4, and 12.

16. Effect is best illustrated by items numbered:
   a. 3, 4, and 12.
   b. 5, 6, and 7.
   c. 1, 8, and 9.
   d. 2, 10, and 11.

17. An internal audit department is conducting an audit of the payroll and accounts receivable departments. Significant problems related to the approval of overtime have been noted. While the audit is still in process, which of the following audit reports is appropriate?
    a. A summary report.
    b. A written report.
    c. A questionnaire-type report.
    d. An oral report.

18. During an audit of sales representatives' travel expenses, it was discovered that 152 of 200 travel advances issued to sales representatives in the past year exceeded the prescribed maximum amount allowed. Which of the following statements is a justifiable audit opinion?
    a. The majority of travel advances in the organization exceed the prescribed maximum.
    b. Travel advances are not controlled in accordance with existing policy.
    c. The prescribed maximum travel advance is too low.
    d. Seventy-six percent of all travel advances exceeds the management-prescribed maximum.

19. The person responsible for audit report distribution should be:
    a. The chief audit executive or designee.
    b. The audit committee of the board of directors.
    c. The vice president responsible for the area being audited.
    d. The audit supervisor of the audit being performed.

20. Select the most appropriate solution to resolve staff communication problems with clients:
    a. Provide staff with sufficient training to enhance communication skills.
    b. Avoid unnecessary communication with clients.
    c. Discuss communication problems with staff auditors.
    d. Meet with clients to resolve communication problems.

21. Which one of the following elements of an audit report is not always required?
    a. A statement that describes the audit objectives.
    b. A statement that identifies the audited activities.
    c. Pertinent statements of fact.
    d. An evaluation of the impact of the findings on the activities reviewed.

22. Summary written audit reports are generally intended for:
    a. Local operating management.
    b. Review by other auditors only.
    c. High-level management and/or the audit committee.
    d. Mid-level staff management.

23. An oral audit report may be most appropriate when:
   a. A permanent record of the report is needed.
   b. Emergency action is needed.
   c. A summary of individual audits is needed by higher-level management.
   d. It is used only for internal reporting within the internal audit department.

24. In the course of performing an audit, an internal auditor becomes aware of illegal acts being performed by several of the highest ranking officers of the organization. To whom should the findings of the audit report be addressed?
   a. Line-level supervision.
   b. Members of the news media.
   c. The officers involved in the illegal acts.
   d. The audit committee of the board of directors.

25. According to the *Standards*, which of the following best describes the nature of opinions that are appropriate for internal audit reports?
   a. Opinions are generally the auditor's subjective judgments concerning why deficiencies exist.
   b. Opinions are the auditor's evaluations of the effects of the findings on the activities reviewed.
   c. Opinions are conclusions that the auditor has reached concerning the appropriateness of the client's objectives.
   d. Opinions should only involve the fairness of the client's financial statements.

26. Which of the following relationships best depicts the appropriate dual reporting responsibility of the internal auditor? Administratively to the:
   a. Board of directors, functionally to the chief executive officer.
   b. Controller, functionally to the chief financial officer.
   c. Chief executive officer, functionally to the board of directors.
   d. Chief executive officer, functionally to the external auditor.

27. The scope statement of an audit report should:
   a. Describe the audit objectives and tell the reader why the audit was conducted.
   b. Identify the audited activities and describe the nature and extent of auditing performed.
   c. Define the standards, measures, or expectations used in evaluating audit findings.
   d. Communicate the internal auditor's evaluation of the effect of the findings on the activities reviewed.

28. An internal audit of sales contracts revealed that a bribe had been paid to secure a major contract. It was considered quite possible that a senior executive had authorized the bribe. Which of the following **best** describes the proper distribution of the completed audit report?
    a. The report should be distributed to the chief executive officer and the appropriate regulatory agency.
    b. The report should be distributed to the board of directors, the chief executive officer, and the independent auditor.
    c. The chief audit executive should provide the board of directors with a copy of the report and decide whether further distribution is appropriate.
    d. The report should be distributed to the board of directors, the appropriate law enforcement agency, and the appropriate regulatory agency.

29. During a review of purchasing operations, an auditor found that procedures in use did not agree with stated company procedures. However, audit tests revealed that the procedures in use represented an increase in efficiency and a decrease in processing time, without a discernible decrease in control. The auditor should:
    a. Report the lack of adherence to documented procedures as an operational deficiency.
    b. Develop a flowchart of the new procedure and include it in the report to management.
    c. Report the change and suggest that the change in procedures be documented.
    d. Suspend the completion of the audit until the client documents the new procedures.

30. The primary reason for having written formal audit reports is to:
    a. Provide an opportunity for auditee response.
    b. Document the corrective actions required of senior management.
    c. Provide a formal means by which the external auditor assesses potential reliance on the internal audit department.
    d. Record findings and recommended courses of action.

31. Internal auditors occasionally express opinions as well as state facts in audit reports. Due professional care requires that the auditor's opinions be:
    a. Limited to the effectiveness of controls.
    b. Expressed only when requested by top management or management of the audited function.
    c. Based on experience and free from all bias.
    d. Based on sufficient factual evidence that warrants the expression of the opinions.

32. Which of the following situations is most likely to be the subject of a written interim report to management of a department being audited?
    a. Seventy percent of the planned audit work has been completed with no significant adverse findings.
    b. The auditors have decided to substitute survey procedures for some of the planned detailed review of certain records.
    c. The audit program has been expanded because of indications of possible fraud.
    d. Open burning at a subsidiary plant poses a prospective violation of pollution regulations.

Chapter 18
Audit Report Reviews
and Replies

Report reviews: insurance and courtesy. Responsibility for assessing the adequacy of replies. Policy statement for the internal audit department. The objectives of report reviews. Who reviews drafts of audit reports. Documenting the reviews. The dilemma of sufficient reviews versus prompt issuance of audit reports. Concurrent audit report reviews. Setting the stage for report reviews. Preparing for the hard questions. Referencing the working papers. Rules for avoiding conflicts. Methods of improving responses. Accommodating the client with wording changes. Audit opinions are nonnegotiable. Determining the causes of deficient conditions. Estimating the dollar effect of deficiencies. Allowing reviews of revisions to report drafts. The right to obtain replies to audit reports. Assessing the adequacy of replies to audit reports. Policy statement on assessing replies.

Introduction

(***Note:*** Some of the material in this chapter is discussed in Practice Advisory 2440-1, "Disseminating Results," related to Standard 2440, "Disseminating Results.")

Reviewing report drafts with clients is both a form of insurance and a form of courtesy. Due concern for client replies to published audit reports is an assumption of proper audit responsibility.

Some audit organizations — probably a minority — still refrain from reviewing drafts of audit reports with clients before issuing the reports in final form. This is a kind of arrogance. It assumes omniscience on the part of the auditor. One thing the auditor is certainly not, particularly in operational matters, is omniscient.

Auditors in the field spend but a minute portion of the time that clients spend on their operations. Auditors can, within that short span, isolate and identify problems. They cannot possibly be aware, however, of all the nuances, the historical backgrounds and reasons, the oral executive mandates, the delicate interfaces with peripheral and other organizations, and the conflicting forces throughout the organization that are usually involved in organization operations. The auditors may have resolved problems at the working levels — or they may think they have — during their development of the audit findings. But they may not have obtained the views of line management or middle management.

People at those levels may have significant information to offer that can lend perspective or a new view to reported findings. They may add an ingredient to the findings that the auditors themselves may not be able to supply — the mature experience of the operating managers and their better understanding of the many facets of the problem.

If they cannot be omniscient, the auditors can at least be courteous. Showing line and middle management the draft of the report, which will find its way to the executive desk, is a gesture of courtesy (and sometimes safety). Auditors do not owe it to the client to be soft and tender. They should not gloss over what is adverse and significant. But they do owe fairness, candor, and consideration of others as covered in Practice Advisory 2440.1-3.

Often, the regard clients have for the auditors will affect how clients react to what is said about them in the draft report. If they see the auditors as fair, honest, competent individuals doing their job without rancor or an axe to grind, then the clients may gulp and accept the description of the most serious of findings. Their sole response should be to take corrective action.

But if the clients see the findings in print for the first time when they read the final report, and if they do not regard the auditor personally in a favorable light, they may be resentful, defensive, and arbitrary. They may respond to the report with denials and excuses instead of with constructive, corrective action.

So, even in addition to any consideration of the client's feelings, auditors must look at draft reviews in the light of their own self-achievement — as a way of getting their audit job done without unfortunate repercussions.

When audit reports call for replies and for both assurance and evidence of corrective action, internal auditors have a further obligation. Auditors must assume — with executive blessing — the responsibility for obtaining, reviewing, and assessing the adequacy of written client replies to those reports. If written replies are not mandated by executive management, busy line management may see no reason to take the time to consider the reports and respond to them.

Clearly, the auditor who has reported the conditions and made the recommendations is in the best position to assess the reasonableness and adequacy of the response. The auditor has no right to dictate line management's course of action, but does have the responsibility for determining if the conditions are corrected, if management so directs — irrespective of whether the audit recommendations are followed to the letter. Put simply, then, the objectives of report reviews are:

- To provide information on the audit.
- To resolve conflicts.
- To reach agreement on the facts.

- To prevent argumentative replies.
- To permit the client to see the written work in advance — which sometimes will be different from the spoken word.
- To provide early action on findings.

When reviewing and evaluating clients' written replies to reports, the auditor's objectives are to: (1) ensure the clients' proper consideration of the auditors' findings and recommendations, and (2) provide assurance that matters reported remain monitored until corrected.

Report Reviews

Who Reviews Report Drafts

There are four types of audit report reviews that can be conducted. Each has a specific purpose and unique characteristics. The four are reviews of:

- Audit report segments
- Draft audit reports
- Audit reports that have been completed and issued
- Open recommendations

The early reviews of report drafts are constructive in that the auditor and the client meet to establish facts, evaluate recommendations, and set the tone of the report. The reviews of issued final audit report drafts are to react to recommendations and may be defensive in approach. Reviews of open items are investigatory and explanatory in nature.

Who reviews report drafts depends on the nature of the report itself and on the interest or concern of the individual managers and executives.

Draft reviews of a completely satisfactory report — a report that covers some relatively small and well-defined area or function and has no findings or recommendations — can be limited to the line manager and his or her superior.

Although some believe totally satisfactory reports either should not be written at all or do not warrant the review time, such reports demonstrate audit objectivity. They give credit where due. They raise the auditor from the level of deficiency finder to that of objective analyst. They present a permanent record of audit coverage that management can see. They bring management and auditor together under pleasant circumstances and cement the understanding between the two. Therefore, the time devoted to drafting such a report and reviewing the draft with the client is time well spent. *Standard 2440* provides for the issuance of an audit report to appropriate individuals.

After a usual report has been drafted, the review by the client becomes appropriate (*Standard 2440.A1*). It is insurance — to make sure the report has not overlooked significant aspects of the operation under audit. The draft review may point up the need for a shift of audit emphasis — of which the auditors themselves are unaware. It may raise questions about the nature and adequacy of the audit coverage. It may stimulate needed face-to-face discussions between auditors and management — discussions that establish a good rapport for the future, when different circumstances may make that rapport a significant foundation on which to build. It may construct a desirable image of the auditor in the eyes of management.

The review of a report that describes deficient conditions call for a different approach. It should be reviewed with anyone who may be able to object with validity to its contents. Or it should be reviewed with anyone required to take action. Or it should be reviewed with anyone who has a responsibility for the area or condition reported to need corrective action — whether or not they personally would take that action or would be affected by the action.

Where the conditions are restricted to specific areas, the matter presents relatively few problems. But in functional audits crossing many lines, and in organizational audits bringing broad significant defects to light or calling for extensive system overhauls, the report may require reviews that go through many organizations to the executive level.

Audit organizations should furnish their staffs with written instructions on draft reviews. In large organizations, it may be easy to forget who should review what and in what order the reviews should take place (see Exhibit 18-1).

In general, reviews should be made with the client manager and his or her superior. Yet some branch directors may wish to see all drafts of reports affecting their branches. Auditors should be pleased to comply; but they should also tactfully point to the need for promptness, so that the reviews will not delay the issuance of the final report.

Reports calling for systems changes should also be reviewed with the procedures staff or with systems analysts such as the industrial engineers or information system specialists. In instances where the auditor has conducted a report review at the line level, it may be well to determine whether reviews at higher levels are necessary. Line clients generally have a good idea how their superiors regard audit reports. Their views on whether or not to go higher should be given full consideration. Where line or middle management people say that no further reviews are needed, those comments should be carefully considered and recorded in the working papers. These records can defend the auditor if he or she is accused of withholding information. However, report review protocol should be carefully developed in advance to consider the requirements of client management. After the final report is issued, the auditor should not receive a call from higher management asking why the report was not reviewed in draft form at that level. Having taken the proper steps, the auditor can respond by explaining understood normal practices and stating exactly who said that further reviews were unnecessary, giving the time and date of the statement.

Exhibit 18-1

**ABC Corporation Internal Audit Department
Reviews of Draft Reports**

Policy
It is the policy of internal auditing to review drafts of audit reports with the management personnel responsible for the activities examined — in advance of the formal release of the reports.

Order
The review should begin with responsible line management and proceed, as necessary, through the branch level of management. As a minimum, the draft should be reviewed with the manager responsible for the activity and with his or her superior. Reviews may be held at levels beyond the branch director when circumstances warrant or when management so provides. Such reviews should be approved in advance by the audit manager.

Form of Review
The individual drafts should be reviewed to the extent necessary — in whole or in part; or through the oral or the written work, or a combination of the two. To this end the auditor should remember that the purpose of these reviews is to obtain agreement on the facts and to make sure management people understand the key statements in the report: The report is the responsibility of the auditor, not the client; hence, the review process is designed to ensure a proper interpretation of what the auditor has written, not what the client would like to see written.

Disagreement as to interpretations is another matter. The auditor should make an earnest effort to resolve such disagreements. But if all reasonable attempts at reconciling differences have proved fruitless, the report should clearly set forth the positions of both the auditor and the operating manager for the benefit of higher management.

Experienced auditors are usually aware of those people with whom they have trouble in draft reviews. The reviews may be dreaded and the sessions may be unpleasant experiences. Sometimes these confrontations just cannot be helped, but they may be alleviated. For example, the auditor may use informal interim oral reports of potentially troublesome issues or may try to include the superior of the troublesome individual in the review conference. This may tend to keep the meeting less turbulent.

In all cases, the report reviews should be carefully documented. Results of the review should be recorded in the working papers during or immediately after the conference so that no significant matter, comment, or decision is lost. These notes can be very important in any later dispute or situation as to the adequacy of the audit coverage.

Timing the Reviews

Obviously, the greater the number of draft reviews, the longer the delay in issuing the final report. This fact places auditors in a dilemma. On the one hand, they wish to afford all those who have a "need to know" the opportunity to review the draft. On the other hand, they are aware of the need for current reporting.

The problem is not insuperable, however. It does require pressure and the setting of deadlines, both for the auditors and the reviewers. There should be a definite protocol. After drafting their reports, auditors should prepare a list of distributees. Together with audit supervisors, they should decide which people should review the report draft and what the order of those reviews should be. Computers should be used to the greatest degree possible.

The order is important. The list of draft reviewers should begin with those who are most closely involved in or affected by the report. They are the ones most likely to have suggestions for changes, objections to phrasing, or disputes as to facts. They are the ones with whom the report should be reviewed face-to-face, if possible, to iron out differences and obtain agreement on the facts.

Thereafter, the draft can be duplicated and sent to all other concerned individuals for review. The transmittal memo should identify the report, indicate with whom it has been reviewed, include an offer to discuss the report in person, and set a date for its return (see Exhibit 18-2).

This memorandum can be used to submit draft reports to reviewers in other cities. Distance should not prevent draft reviews. Reviewers in other cities should be afforded the same courtesy as those in the central offices.

Concurrent Audit Report Reviews

In order to expedite the review of audit reports, some organizations use a technique of interim reports to the client. The finding report is prepared by the audit staff as soon as possible after the finding is firm, using the language that will be in the audit report and supplementing it with the detail that will be in the full audit report package. If the internal audit organization uses a one-page audit report, that page, or the excerpt relating to the finding that will be used as an abbreviated short description of the subject audit, should also be used.

The client will be given a reasonable time to respond to the factual aspects of the finding. Elements of the finding such as cause and impact also will be described and the client will be requested to concur or to provide substantive support for disagreement.

Elements of the concurrent audit review request will include:

- Operation being audited
- Accountable official
- Audit liaison
- Date audit started
- Date of this current request for review
- Details of the findings: (see enclosed material for support)
  - Criteria Used
  - Conditions Found
  - Cause
  - Impact
  - Recommendations
- Lead auditor (to whom reply should be addressed)

The early receipt from the client of the interim report allows adequate time to resolve differences, while other aspects of the audit are in progress. It also provides the client with an opportunity to help design the recommendations and also to have their implementation in progress when the report is ultimately issued. Language to be used in the final report should be used.

The Review Conference

The draft review can be either a grim confrontation or an open and courteous discussion. True, the auditor presumably has discussed all findings with the client. But a comprehensive written draft, showing the language of the distribution to executive client management, somehow has a different impact from informal reports or oral discussions.

It is the auditor's conference. The auditor can — and should — influence its course. No matter how serious the findings, the auditor who is sensitive to the feelings of others can put the draft language in a perspective that takes out much of the harshness. A copy of the draft should be distributed to all attendees for a reasonable period of time before the conference.

Exhibit 18-2
Transmittal Memorandum

TO: Draft Reviewer

FROM: Auditor

SUBJECT: Draft Report — Review of Controls Over Conflicts of Interest

Enclosed is the subject audit report draft for your review. It has already been reviewed with A.B. See, E.F. Gee, and H.I. Jay. They were in agreement with the matters described in the draft and it reflects changes resulting from their reviews. If you have any questions on the draft or wish to discuss it, please call me. Otherwise, kindly return the draft, noting your approval, after your review. We would appreciate you giving the draft your prompt attention, since we plan to put it in final form on Wednesday, July 10, 20XX.

                                      _____ Internal Auditor

No draft review conference should be started abruptly. There should be a setting of the stage. There should be an attempt to bring about a pleasant atmosphere. The more critical the report, the more attention is needed for proper preliminaries. The feeling should be developed that what is reported is not said with rancor but in the spirit of assisting to improve conditions. Some of the matters to consider in orally setting the stage include:

- The scope of the examination.

- The significance of the matters to be reviewed.

- An acknowledgment of the difficulties that face the client in carrying out his or her responsibilities.

- A willingness to discuss all matters in whatever detail is necessary.

- The fact that the report contains no surprises — that all aspects of the findings were discussed during the field work. (If the auditor has not done so, there is no one else to blame for difficulty during the draft review.)

- Comments on how many matters are already corrected, how many are in the process of correction, and how many are still to be corrected.

- The cooperation obtained during the audit.

- An assurance that the client will be given credit in the report for all corrective action suggested, instituted, and/or completed.

More detailed information on the conduct of conferences can be found in Chapter 28, Dealing with People. It should be remembered that the objectives of the conference are to:

- Provide information.

- Obtain agreement on facts.

- Set the stage for implementation of recommendations.

Avoiding and Resolving Conflicts

It would be wishful thinking for the auditor to expect every draft review to be conducted without conflict, no matter how well the internal audit function may be accepted in the organization. Indeed, the stronger the auditor's position, the greater the client's concern with what the report has to say to superiors.

Auditors must therefore be prepared — thoroughly prepared — for conflict and dispute. They must be able to retrieve information, support facts, and amplify findings without difficulty or delay. It is embarrassing to the auditor and unnerving to his or her supervisor when the auditor must fumble through volumes of audit working papers to find evidence that will back up statements in the report. However, a report well referenced to working papers can provide instant support.

Auditors can avoid some of these awful moments by being aware that every critical comment may evoke objections and call for additional proof. Auditors can rise to the challenge with forethought and preparation. Their own copy of the report draft should be copiously annotated in the margin with references to the supporting detail. This simple preparation pays big dividends. It is a good idea to develop a list of potential points of contention and to prepare responses, including copies of the working papers and other support. Flip charts or PowerPoint presentations illustrating this information also can be prepared.

Suppose the client said, "I can't believe that this function you're talking about is my responsibility." Internal auditors who are prepared look for the proper marginal notation in the draft. They can turn immediately to the copy of the appropriate directive in the working

786 Part 5: Reporting

papers. If they have done their homework, there is the particular statement — underlined in red for all to see — which assigned responsibility to the client.

Suppose the client asks, "Are you sure there are no procedures on the subject?" The auditors — again, if they have done their homework — promptly turn to a work paper that shows that, on a particular date, they spoke to the individual responsible for preparing such instructions and learned that, indeed, no procedure had been issued, and why such a condition existed.

References to records of audit findings (see Chapter 8) that show all relevant details can be invaluable. They can give ready information on the population sampled, the manner of sample selection, the proof that the sample was representative, the citations to directives, the causes, the effects, and the people with whom the conditions were discussed and the substance of such discussions.

When auditors must go through the agony of fumbling for each piece of information needed to support their position, their credibility and the integrity of their report declines. When, on the other hand, they are able to answer each question promptly and fully, when their working papers appear to be a readily accessible storehouse of easily retrieved information, the stream of objections and questions can quickly dry up.

There are several other reasons why there are disagreements and conflicts. These reasons are related to the aspect of change. The client is:

- Concerned about any unknown adverse effect that the recommendation will bring.

- Concerned by the dislocations and bureaucratic confusion that will be caused by complying with the recommendation.

- Upset by the recommendation implying that the present methods are not adequate.

These issues for concern and conflict can be neutralized by the auditor's positive constructive comments that clearly demonstrate:

- The positive and the negative results that will result from complying with the recommendation.

- The specific changes necessary to carry out the recommendation and how they can be effected.

- That the recommendation is evolutionary, not revolutionary, and how it will improve the operation.

Auditors must recognize that the client is on the defensive. Somehow that defensive barrier must be removed and agreement reached. Here are some rules that might help.

Have good manners. It is just plain bad manners to say bluntly, "I disagree with you" or "You're wrong." It is worse to use such words as "idiotic," "ridiculous," or "nonsense." Besides, it is poor judgment. Under this kind of attack, the client either lashes back or withdraws. More important, communication is destroyed and the auditor's objectives may not be met. Equally important, the auditor must be prepared to absorb such language from the client without angry response.

Use nonpersonal phrases. In disagreeing, avoid starting a sentence with "you." That implies disagreeing with the individual rather than with the concept or idea. Use neutral phrases: "It might be worth considering. . .," "There might be a possibility that. . .," or "Perhaps it might be useful to explore. . ." These phrases, being impersonal, are less likely to arouse emotions — certainly not the emotions caused by "You haven't thought of. . .," "You've forgotten. . .," "You don't realize. . .," or "You don't know about. . . ." Never underestimate the emotional impact of accusatory words.

Get on common ground. Where an impasse appears to have been reached, step back until some point can be agreed upon — even if it is just agreement that the problem is not an easy one to solve. Stand on that ground until tempers are calmed and the client is comfortable enough to reasonably discuss the matters at issue.

Don't back anyone into a corner. Do not press clients for a clear statement that they have reversed themselves. If they finally go along with a point, resist the temptation. Don't say something like, "I'm glad you finally see things my way." The auditors' objective is to get their conclusions and recommendations across. It doesn't really matter whether or not the clients changed their minds. The auditor wins when the recommendation is accepted, not when the client is overcome.

Don't mistake the airing of views with disagreement. Often, all that is necessary is to let the clients talk themselves out. Perhaps they do not really disagree but merely want a chance to justify their position or to explain the reasons for the conditions. After they have made their point, they might be perfectly willing to let the wording of the draft stand as written.

When there is an irreconcilable disagreement, when no mutual ground can be reached, auditors have a responsibility to give the client's views equal prominence with their own. The auditors may then point out that they will report the client's views as well.

In some situations, the mere offer to quote the client will reconcile the disagreement. If clients realize that they are in an untenable position, they would not want that position paraded before their superiors in an audit report. But when there is an honest disagreement on interpretations — never on the facts since they must be agreed upon — the client's views should be incorporated into the report.

It is common courtesy, of course, to ask clients to read the added material so they can make sure they were not misquoted.

Auditors should not be inflexible. They must recognize that people are understandably defensive and that audit reports may cause executive wrath to descend on the head of the client.

Auditors must understand that the same words may mean different things to different people. Auditors must also be sufficiently realistic to recognize that they may describe situations in what the client considers a derogatory manner. Hence, they should be willing to substitute the client's suggestion of words and phrases that do not change the meaning they wish to convey.

Auditors should also heed the client in matters of perspective or relevance. It may well be that what the auditor considers to be the heart of a function was really only a side issue. It may also be that what the auditor was told at the working level failed to take into account matters not known at that level. Auditors must be prepared to adjust accordingly. They must try to maintain a reputation for fairness, for objectivity, and for concern solely with what is factual and significant. To that end, they should not be averse to changes that make for better reports.

Gaining Acceptance of Recommendations

An interesting method of reducing the conflicts that often accompany auditors' recommendations for corrective action has been suggested by Kendig.[1] Instead of the auditors making recommendations to the client, the client would be asked to make recommendations to the auditors. This approach would apply to complex audits in industry or to program audits in government — audits that take a good deal of time to complete.

Kendig's method is to issue the report with the audit findings but with no audit recommendations. In the transmittal letter for the report, the client would be asked to propose at least two alternative ways of dealing with each finding or group of findings. The client would be asked to declare which is considered the better alternative and why.

On receipt of the recommendations, the auditors would have the right to evaluate the recommended approaches and agree or disagree. If the auditors reject a recommendation, they would have to explain why they believe the recommended action is irrelevant, unworkable, or unfeasible.

This procedure reverses the usual methods under which an auditor makes a recommendation and then is required to defend it. The client might acquiesce to the auditors' recommendations but not wholeheartedly embrace them and carry them out with any degree of enthusiasm. When the recommendations are made by the client, however, there would be pride of authorship, which would impel the client to do whatever is needed to take corrective action. Also, the not-voiced but often-thought grumble, "Those auditors don't know how to solve problems in my program," is eliminated.

Obviously, for this procedure to work effectively, the client would have to respond in a timely manner. Where the client fails to respond within a reasonable time, the auditors are no worse off than they were in the beginning; they would have to make recommendations of their own. But at least the clients would know that they had the opportunity to prescribe the corrective action themselves. And they would be aware that, if the client has not provided the proposed corrective action, the auditors would probably point this out to higher management if their own recommendations are challenged.

Kendig proposed this approach as a desirable experiment. We are not aware of any organizations that make use of this procedure. It is an interesting proposal and we assume he used it. But one organization with which we are familiar has a comparable way to getting the client involved in the corrective action.

On the other hand, Campfield has some suggestions for improving management's responses to audit findings and recommendations:[2]

1. Recommendations should be problem-specific and corrective action should be measurable.

    Identify the activity involved. Point to problems, not symptoms. Provide recommendations that are so specific that corrective action can easily be measured against them.

2. Recommended action should be subject to implementation at frontline operating levels.

    Work out the problems and the solutions with line management. Do not rely on upper management to resolve routine matters. Where complex issues are involved and there is disagreement between auditor and client, the two should clearly identify the issues before referring them to senior management.

3. Auditors and client management must develop a tolerance for each other.

    Each should be fully aware of the other's strengths. The client has the strength of intimate knowledge of ongoing operations. The auditor has the strength of independence and objectivity as well as a unique perspective of overall entity goals and objectives. Each should learn to respect the other's contributions. Then, and only then, will concluding conferences turn into a problem-solving partnership and corrective action be worthwhile and permanent.

4. Auditing must be a timely, ongoing activity of assistance to operating management.

Internal auditors must never interfere with the responsibility and decision-making authority of management. But auditors should be keyed into events as they unfold: review plans, changes, new procedures, and new operations. Then they can be available, or make themselves available, to assist management in assuring proper controls for new activities before the procedures are hardened into concrete.

5. Auditors must write understandable, action-oriented reports.

Reports should tell a story in as few words as necessary to convey key ideas. Those ideas should be presented in a way that moves the ideas into the reader's mind in the exact shape, depth, and meaning intended by the writer. And the reports should not include conclusions that lack proof or plausibility or data that is petty. Each report should contain only worthwhile information that is factual, significant, and pertinent to the client's responsibilities.

The U.S. General Accounting Office (GAO), in a publication titled "How To Get Action on Audit Recommendations," proposed four basic principles that it believes will get action on audit recommendations. It stated that this problem has been persistent over the years and that it has "limited the effectiveness of audit organizations." The principles, highlighted, are:[3]

(This subject was discussed in more detail in Chapter 17 on Reports.)

- **Quality recommendations:** Basic to effective audit work are recommendations that, when adequately implemented, accomplish a defined and worthwhile result. They must state a clear, convincing, and workable basis for implementation. Their utility and continued relevance should be reevaluated as follow-up actions progress.

- **Commitment:** Auditors and audit organizations must be committed to identifying and bringing about needed change. The auditor's commitment should be personal and professional. The audit organization should be supportive and reinforce the commitment to its staff.

- **Monitoring and follow-up system:** The audit organization should have a system that provides the structure and discipline needed to promote action on audit recommendations. It should make sure that recommendations are aggressively pursued until they have been resolved and successfully implemented. Also, auditors should assess whether the agencies they audit have a follow-up system that adequately meets their basic responsibility for resolving and implementing audit recommendations.

- **Special attention to key recommendations:** Auditors should make sure that key recommendations are fairly considered when effective use of the first three principles has not done so. They should reassess strategies to get positive action on those recommendations. Outside intervention should be considered when it would help to get necessary action on key recommendations of great significance.

  The GAO "Action-Oriented Recommendations" should be: (1) properly directed; (2) hard hitting; (3) specific; (4) convincing; (5) significant; and (6) positive in tone and content. To be effective, the recommendations should: (1) deal with underlying causes; (2) be feasible; (3) be cost effective; and (4) consider alternatives.[4]

Relative to the third GAO recommendation above, techniques that are suggested by Practice Advisory 2500-1: (*Standard 2500*, "Monitoring Progress") for follow-up include:

- Addressing engagement observations and recommendations to the appropriate levels of management responsible for taking corrective action.

- Receiving and evaluating management responses to engagement observations and recommendations during the engagement or within a reasonable time period after the communication of engagement results is issued. Responses are more useful if they include sufficient information for the chief audit executive to evaluate the adequacy and timelines of corrective action.

- Receiving periodic updates from management in order to evaluate the status of management's efforts to correct previously communicated conditions.

- Receiving and evaluating information from other organizational units assigned responsibility for procedures of a follow-up nature.

- Reporting to senior management or the board on the status of responses to engagement observations and recommendations.

Audit Opinions

There are some suggestions for change with which the auditor cannot agree: those affecting the audit opinion. Audit opinions cannot be delegated or compromised. An audit opinion can be given only when the auditor can defend and support it and is willing to attest to it by his or her signature. Auditors cannot substitute someone else's opinion for their own.

Auditors' professional opinions cannot be negotiated. Those opinions are either what they honestly believe, based on what they have seen, or they are nothing. Thus, it must be clearly understood that, while the auditors will discuss facts and the meaning of facts, the audit opinion is not subject to give and take. Of course, new facts that are brought to light may have an effect on the audit opinion, but it is still the auditor's opinion, based on all the facts.

Cause and Effect

Senior management is vitally concerned with both the causes and effects of the conditions that the auditor reports. Understanding cause and effect may be a significant factor in making client executive decisions. It is good, therefore, for the auditor to explore these matters during the draft review. Very often, line management is in the best position to explain the reasons for deficient or unusual conditions, and the operating manager's views should be sought and carefully considered.

Auditors should probe for the reasons so they can be sure that proposed corrective action is aimed at the causes, not the symptoms. For example:

- Was management aware of the problem?

- Was the problem traceable to inadequate instruction or insufficient training of personnel?

- Did the condition occur because supervisors were not adequately monitoring the ongoing process?

- Were improper priorities assigned?

- Were insufficient resources provided?

- Did the need for controls go unrecognized?

- Was there lack of coordination with an interfacing organization?

- Were conditions caused by human error?

- Were the defects attributable to the attitudes of the employees? Of the supervisors? Of the manager?

One potential source of conflict in the audit report is the auditor's statement concerning the effect of deficient conditions. The auditor's estimate of the monetary amounts lost or possibly lost, or of services that are not provided can be a source of irritation to the client, whose superiors readily understand such numbers. If the client considers them inflated, the estimates will just be another point for dispute. Hence, it is important during the draft reviews to gain agreement on the impact of deficiencies. In that vein, the auditor should come to the draft review prepared to demonstrate the validity of such estimates.

Reviewing Revisions

As the draft report goes through its reviews, some changes may be made. The significance of those changes becomes a matter of judgment. So does the need to review the changed wording with those who have not seen the revisions.

Certainly, if clients are now called upon to take action not discussed in the first review, they are entitled to see the draft again as modified. They are especially entitled when, as a result of subsequent reviews, the draft places the client in a less favorable light, or quotes the client, or attributes an action to the client.

Sometimes the changes can be communicated by telephone, fax, or e-mail. Auditors, in the interest of prompt report release, should try those methods. Sometimes those changes are merely word substitutions that do not call for reviews. The chief criterion must be maintenance of the auditor's reputation for fairness and objectivity and the assurance that the auditor is being independent.

Replies to Reports

Internal audit activities that do not have the authority to demand replies to their reported findings, or to evaluate the adequacy of the corrective action, have their effectiveness diminished. Management directives or policy statements must spell out clearly that audit reports calling for corrective action must be responded to in writing. Usually, these directives and statements establish time limits for submitting replies. The audit distribution sheet from senior management in one organization bears this statement regarding replies:

> An "X" following your name in the column "For Securing Action" means that you are responsible for seeing that satisfactory action is taken with respect to the findings that are referred for action to persons under your jurisdiction.

> Management Directive XX requires you to see that an adequate reply, describing the action taken, is sent to the vice president, finance and controller within 30 days after the audit report release date, with a copy to the chief audit executive. If action cannot be completed within this time limit, the vice president, finance and controller should be informed of the reason for the delay and when the final report may be expected.

It is desirable for each operating branch or division to have its own instructions regarding replies to audit reports. These instructions should state: Who should prepare the reply. Who should sign it. How the reply should be written (straightforward, addressing itself to the findings and not trying to justify the status quo). What steps should be taken if corrective action cannot be completed within the established time span.

The internal auditors should let it be known that they will be willing to discuss corrective action and review drafts of client replies. At the same time, the auditors should scrupulously respect the difference between staff and line. Line people must live with the corrective action they take. The auditors are responsible for pointing out situations and recommending courses of action — not *the* course of action. Still, auditors must have the responsibility to evaluate proposed corrective action directed by management and to determine whether it does or does not cure the situation.

Management may direct that audit reports should remain open until the auditing organization considers the replies satisfactory, that is, that action has been or will be taken to resolve the situation. Some auditing organizations thus will not be satisfied solely with the statement or description of corrective action from the client. Subsequent to the issuing of the audit report, the auditors may be required to return to the audit site to satisfy themselves that effective action has indeed been taken. They may also be directed to schedule interim follow-up examinations within a period of six months or a year to make sure the reported deficiencies have not recurred.

When replies are unsatisfactory, and agreement cannot be reached orally with the client, the reply should be formally rejected by memorandum. The memorandum should specifically spell out why — in what respects — the reply is deficient. Copies of the reply should be addressed to whatever level of management is needed to see that the matter is satisfactorily resolved.

The audit activity should have a formal method of closing reports that have a satisfactory response. This may be in the form of a memorandum to the audit executive bearing the signature of the auditor. The memorandum should state that the auditor is satisfied with the response and that the report may now be closed. Exhibit 18-3 is an example of such a memorandum to be completed.

Different organizations follow different reporting practices. But there seems to be a uniform feeling about the need for follow-up procedures — with management's interest and support. Exhibit 18-4 is an example of a procedure covering replies to audit reports.

Exhibit 18-3
Formal Closing Memorandum

TO: Internal Auditing Executive
FROM: Auditor
SUBJECT: Replies to report dated _____, Project No. _____
              Title _____
Ref: Replies:

          Date   From

      _____   _____

      _____   _____

      _____   _____

We have received the referenced replies describing the action taken on findings discussed in the subject report. Our evaluation of this action is as follows:

	Reference to
Evaluation	findings

Considered an Interim Reply:
   Appears satisfactory. Awaiting final reply.

   Does not appear satisfactory. We are investigating.

Considered a Final Reply:
   Appears satisfactory. Finding closed.

   Appears satisfactory; but the action described needs
   confirmation before the finding can be closed.

   Appears unsatisfactory; needs further investigation.

The action indicated in the reference replies does _____ does not _____ constitute completion of satisfactory action on all the findings described in the subject report. Accordingly, we recommend that Project No. _____ be _____ _____ not be _____ closed at this time.

                                    _____Auditor

Exhibit 18-4
ABC Corporation
Internal Auditing Activity
Reviews of Draft Reports

Policy
Internal auditors are responsible for bringing to the attention of senior management any significant risks to the organization. A reported deficiency that has not adequately been corrected is regarded as such a risk. At the same time, the responsibility for seeing that unsatisfactory conditions are properly corrected is assigned to operating management. The responsibility to evaluate the corrective action and to determine whether it is both responsive and effective is assigned to the internal audit activity.

So as to have some assurance that operating managers will take corrective action promptly, they are asked in the instructions on the report distribution sheet to reply to the executive vice president in writing when there are findings requiring corrective action. The reply must outline action taken to correct the unsatisfactory conditions reported and must bear the approval of all persons responsible for securing action. If any of the corrective actions described in the reply are merely proposed and not completed, or are deferred to some future date, the reply must indicate the date when corrective action will be completed. A final reply must be made when all the corrective action has been completed.

Action Required
When replies are received they will be reviewed by the auditor in charge and the audit manager. If the reply seems likely to dispose satisfactorily of the findings reported, the in-charge auditor should inform the internal auditing executive on the form provided for that purpose. The auditor should describe any matters subsequently discussed with operating management, such as action taken that is not clearly described in the reply, or action that does not conform to recommendations but which is felt to be worth a trial. This form should close the project.

If the corrective action described in the reply does not seem likely to correct the conditions reported, further action on the part of the in-charge auditor or supervisor is necessary. This may take the form of discussion with the operating manager in order to clear up any questions or misunderstandings that may not have been cleared up in the review of the draft report, and to clear up any questions regarding action taken or to be taken that may not have been expressed clearly enough in the reply.

Exhibit 18-4 (Cont.)

In any event, the objective is to secure some agreement or understanding as to an acceptable course of action with a minimum of further correspondence. It is therefore important to have clearly in mind what is meant by an acceptable course of action. This does not necessarily mean the adoption of all the recommendations made in a report in precisely the manner set forth. As operating management has the responsibility for correcting unsatisfactory conditions, it also has been given the authority to decide how it should be done. Accordingly, in the absence of considerations of such importance as to cause the executive vice president or other members of top management to intervene, operating management will be free to accept, to accept with modifications, or to reject any recommendations made. What is meant then is some course that at least does not seem so objectionable that it should not be given a trial.

Where no action is taken or the action taken or proposed seems clearly unsatisfactory and operating management seems unwilling to take any action that will satisfactorily dispose of the matter, a letter should be prepared for the signature of the executive vice president. It should state the auditor's position on the unsatisfactory conditions.

Monitoring Replies
The audit manager will have the responsibility for keeping a record of replies required but not received.

When a reply has not been received within one month after the date of the report, the person responsible for keeping the record will notify the supervisor responsible. The supervisor will then make, or will have the auditor make, whatever inquiries seem to be necessary to determine when the reply might be expected. Thereafter, further inquiries will be made at intervals until different action is desirable.

At this point the supervisor may prepare a formal letter or inquiry for the signature of the executive vice president. The letter should be addressed to the person from whom the auditor's report requested the reply and should be forwarded through the chief audit executive for the executive vice president. From that point on, the nature of any further action will depend on the kind of response received from operating management, or on the nature of any instructions received from the executive vice president.

The audit manager will submit a monthly report not later than the tenth of each month showing the status of replies. Copies should be provided for the executive vice president, the chief audit executive, and the audit manager.

References

[1]Kendig, W.L., "Findings Without Recommendations," *The Internal Auditor,* June 1983, 45-47.
[2]Campfield, W.M., "A Look at Responses to Audit Findings," *The Internal Auditor,* October 1983, 49-52.
[3]Comptroller General of the United States, *How to Get Action on Audit Recommendations* (Washington, DC: U.S. Government Printing Office, 1992), 8-9.
[4]Ibid., 10-13.

Supplementary Readings

Bates, David A., "When Good Writing Goes Bad," *Internal Auditor*, February 1996, 36-38.
Calhoun, Charles, "Elements of Exceptional Audit Reports," *Internal Auditing Alert*, September 1997, 5-6.
Crocket, James R., *Conducting the Post-audit Conference* (Altamonte Springs, FL: The Institute of Internal Auditors, 1992).
De Vos Binder, Elena, "Giving Useful Feedback About Writing," *Internal Auditor*, August 1993, 54-56.
Didis, Stephen K., "Communicating Audit Results," *Internal Auditor*, October 1997, 36-38.
Fischer, Michael J., "Fitting the Medium to the Message: Choosing Effective Communications Media," *Internal Auditing*, January/February1998, 43-47.
Flaherty, John J., and Judy Stein, "Solution-focused Audit Reporting," *Internal Auditor*, October 1991, 58-61.
Flesher, Dale L., and Jeff Zanzig, "A Survey of Internal Audit Follow-up Procedures," *Internal Auditing*, September/October 1998, 27-34.
Jeffords, Raymond, Melinda Carter, and Annette Hixon, "Assessing Internal Auditors' Negotiation Skills," *Internal Auditor*, February 1993, 41-45.
Keating, Gerald, "The Art of the Follow Up," *Internal Auditor*, April 1995, 59-62.
Sloane, David E., "SEC Promotes a 'Plain English' Handbook," *Internal Auditing Alert*, May 1997, 3-4.
Stern, Gary M., "Improving Verbal Communications," *Internal Auditor*, August 1993, 49-53.
Wycoff, Edgar B., "The Language of Listening," *Internal Auditor*, April 1994, 26-29.

Multiple-choice Questions

1. One purpose of the exit conference is for the internal auditor to:
   a. Require corrective action for deficiencies found.
   b. Review and verify the appropriateness of the audit report based upon client input.
   c. Review the performance of audit personnel assigned to the engagement.
   d. Present the final audit report to management.

2. An audit of an automated accounts receivable function for a single plant furniture manufacturing organization has just been completed. Significant findings include late posting of customers' payments, late mailing of monthly invoices, and erratic follow-up on past-due accounts. Which of the following managers should attend the exit conference for this audit?
   a. Chief audit executive, chief operating officer, and controller.
   b. Head of the audit team, controller, and vice president of information systems.
   c. Head of the audit team, manager of the accounts receivable department, and manager of the data processing department.
   d. Chief audit executive, chief financial officer, chief executive officer, and vice president of information systems.

3. The *Standards* require that internal auditors discuss conclusions and recommendations at appropriate levels of management before issuing final written reports. Which of the following is the primary reason that a closing conference should be documented by the auditor?
   a. The information may be needed if a dispute arises.
   b. The *Standards* require that closing conferences be documented.
   c. The information may be needed to review future audit programs.
   d. Closing conference documentation becomes a basis for future audits.

4. Why should organizations require clients to promptly reply and outline the corrective action that has been implemented on reported deficiencies?
   a. To remove items from the "pending" list as soon as possible.
   b. To effect savings or to institute compliance as early as possible.
   c. To indicate concurrence with the audit findings.
   d. To ensure that the audit schedule is kept up to date.

5. The preliminary survey discloses a prior audit deficiency was never corrected. Subsequent field work confirms that the deficiency still exists. Which of the following courses of action should the internal auditor pursue?
   a. Take no action. To do otherwise would be an exercise of operational control.
   b. Discuss the issue with the chief audit executive. The problem requires an ad hoc solution.
   c. Discuss the issue with the person(s) responsible for the problem. They should know how to solve the problem.
   d. Order the person(s) responsible to correct the problem. They have had long enough to do so.

6. An exit conference helps insure that:
   a. The objectives of the audit and the scope of the audit work are known by the client.
   b. The client understands the audit program.
   c. There have been no misunderstandings or misinterpretations of fact.
   d. The list of persons who are to receive the final report are identified.

7. According to the *Standards*, the chief audit executive should ensure follow-up of prior audit findings and recommendations:
   a. To determine if corrective action was taken and is achieving the desired results.
   b. Unless management rejected the recommendation in their initial response.
   c. Unless the audit schedule does not allow time for follow-up.
   d. Unless management has accepted the recommendation.

8. Which of the following is the most appropriate method of reporting disagreement between the auditor and the client concerning audit findings and recommendations?
   a. State the auditor's position because the report is designed to provide the auditor's independent view.
   b. State the client's position because management is ultimately responsible for the activities reported.
   c. State both positions and identify the reasons for the disagreement.
   d. State neither position. If the disagreement is ultimately resolved, there will be no reason to report the previous disagreement. If the disagreement is never resolved, the disagreement should not be reported, because there is no mechanism to resolve it.

9. A primary purpose of the closing conference is to:
   a. Implement audit findings.
   b. Gather audit evidence.
   c. Resolve remaining issues.
   d. Determine the scope of the audit.

10. An audit report recommendation should address what attribute of an audit finding?
    a. Cause.
    b. Statement of condition.
    c. Criteria.
    d. Effect.

11. After an audit report with adverse findings has been communicated to appropriate client personnel, proper action is to:
    a. Schedule a follow-up review.
    b. Implement corrective action indicated by the findings.
    c. Examine further the data supporting the findings.
    d. Assemble new data to support the findings.

12. An internal auditor can use oral reports to:
    a. Give immediate information to management and more accurately exchange thoughts with a face-to-face discussion.
    b. Report interim findings more efficiently by eliminating the preparation time for a written report.
    c. Eliminate the need for a lengthy final report by reaching verbal agreement on the handling of significant findings with the clients.
    d. Impress the client with a polished presentation using graphics to enhance the credibility of audit findings.

13. The *Standards* require auditors to discuss conclusions and recommendations at appropriate levels of management before issuing final written reports. Auditors usually accomplish this by conducting exit conferences. Which of the following best describes the purpose of exit conferences?
    a. To allow clients to get started implementing recommendations as soon as possible.
    b. To allow auditors to explain complicated findings before a written report is issued.
    c. To allow auditors to "sell" findings and recommendations to management.
    d. To insure that there have been no misunderstandings or misinterpretations of facts.

14. During an audit of purchasing, internal auditors found several violations of organization policy concerning competitive bidding. The same condition had been reported in an audit report last year and corrective action had not been taken. Which of the following best describes the appropriate action concerning this repeat finding?
    a. The audit report should note that this same condition had been reported in the prior audit.
    b. During the exit interview, management should be made aware that a finding from the prior report had not been corrected.
    c. The chief audit executive should determine whether management or the board has assumed the risk of not taking corrective action.
    d. The chief audit executive should determine whether this condition should be reported to the independent auditor and any regulatory agency.

15. Which of the following combination of participants would be **most** appropriate to attend an exit conference?
    a. The responsible internal auditor and representatives from management who are knowledgeable of detailed operations and those who can authorize implementation of corrective action.
    b. The chief audit executive and the executive in charge of the activity or function audited.
    c. Staff auditors who conducted the field work and operating personnel in charge of the daily performance of the activity or function audited.
    d. Staff auditors who conducted the field work and the executive in charge of the activity or function audited.

16. Recommendations in audit reports may, or may not, actually be implemented. Which of the following **best** describes the role of internal auditing in follow-up on audit recommendations? Internal auditing:
    a. Has no role; follow-up is management's responsibility.
    b. Should be charged with the responsibility for implementing audit recommendations.
    c. Should follow up to ascertain that appropriate action is taken on audit recommendations.
    d. Should request that independent auditors follow up on audit recommendations.

17. Which of the following describes the most appropriate action to be taken concerning a repeat finding of violations of company policy pertaining to competitive bidding policies?
    a. The audit report should note that this same condition had been reported in the prior audit.
    b. During the exit interview management should be made aware that a finding from the prior report had not been corrected.
    c. The chief audit executive should determine whether management or the board has assumed the risk of not taking corrective action.
    d. The chief audit executive should determine whether this condition should be reported to the external auditor and any regulatory agency.

Chapter 19
Reports to Executive
Management and the Board

Summary and activity reports. Factors for reporting to committees. Communication with the board. Reporting requirements of the Standards. *Administrative records and forms to help in preparing summary and activity reports. Reports of recoveries and savings. Audit productivity. Example of a summary report. Reporting various types of audit activities. Graphic reports. Activity reports on the administrative health of the enterprise. Evaluation reports. Summarizing the various types of findings: major versus minor and control versus performance. Reporting causes of findings. Reporting on the nature of findings encountered. One-page audit reports. Special communications. Care in reporting certain data.*

• •

What Reports Do

(*Note:* Material in this chapter is discussed in Practice Advisory 2020-1, "Communication and Approval," related to *Standard 2020* and to *2060*, "Reporting to the Board and to Senior Management," and to Practice Advisory 2060-1, Same title.)

Reports to senior management and to the board of directors through the audit committee have two purposes. One is to communicate what internal auditing has accomplished. The other is to describe what internal auditing has observed. In this book, we shall call the former activity reports and the latter evaluation reports.

Activity reports tell the extent to which internal auditing managed to meet its goals. They describe the scope and the depth of the internal audit effort. They summarize corrective action taken as a result of internal audits. They demonstrate how the audits have helped protect the enterprise by monitoring the adequacy and effectiveness of the various systems of control.

Evaluation reports supply management and the board with information about the enterprise not available elsewhere. Financial reports, audited by the independent accountants, supply objective information on the financial health of the enterprise. Operating reports describe operations from the standpoint of operating managers, and may or may not be completely objective. Evaluation reports by internal auditors, however, supply objective information on the operating health of the enterprise and serve to supplement external auditors' reports and management letters.

Activity and evaluation reports have been used by many internal audit activities for some time, but rarely have they been mandated. Usually, they were another service to management and the board that internal auditors, of their own volition, provided. An air of urgency, however, was created by the *Standards for the Professional Practice of Internal Auditing (Standards)*. Practice Advisory 2060-1, "Reporting to the Board and Senior Management," which spelled out the obligation of chief audit executives to submit such reports, follows:

1. The chief audit executive should submit activity reports to senior management and to the board annually or more frequently as necessary. Activity reports should highlight significant engagement observations and recommendations and should inform senior management and the board of any significant deviations from approved engagement work schedules, staffing plans, and financial budgets, and the reasons for them. *(Source: Red Book 110.01.6b)*

2. Significant engagement observations are those conditions that, in the judgment of the chief audit executive, could adversely affect the organization. Significant engagement observations may include conditions dealing with irregularities, illegal acts, errors, inefficiency, waste, ineffectiveness, conflicts of interest, and control weaknesses. After reviewing such conditions with senior management, the chief audit executive should communicate significant engagement observations and recommendations to the board, whether or not they have been satisfactory resolved. *(Source: Red Book 110.01.6b)*

Boards of directors are becoming more and more sophisticated. They are also becoming increasingly aware of their accountability for whatever is happening in the corporation.

Board members are far removed from organizational operations, yet they can be held accountable for whatever occurs there. The board's chief lifeline to accurate, objective, unbiased information on operations is contact with and information from the internal auditors. Board members may not be able to read all the reports on internal audit examinations, but they would be extremely interested in summary reports on overall organization controls and performance:

- Summaries of audit findings and conclusions
- Status of the organization's internal controls
- Opinions internal auditors expressed on the activities reviewed
- Material findings not corrected
- Trends in the magnitude and severity of reported deficiencies
- Coordination between internal and external auditors
- Risks that remain unguarded

And so, periodic reports on what internal auditors have accomplished and what they have found, as well as reports on the internal auditors' evaluations of the administrative and operational health of the organization, can be of vital interest to the audit committee of the board of directors.

Factors for Committee Reporting[1]

Karen Grandstand, vice president of the Minneapolis Federal Reserve Bank, describes a series of elements that directors and senior managers believe should exist in the internal audit functions. They are:

- **Structure:** Placement so as to be independent.
- **Management, staffing, and audit quality:** The responsibility should be one manager's responsibility.
- **Scope:** Review and testing should reflect nature, complexity and risk of on and off-balance sheet activities.
- **Communications:** Senior management should foster forthright communications and critical examination of issues, creating awareness of the internal auditor's findings and operating management's solutions to identified internal control weaknesses.

Communication with the Board[2]

Internal auditing should through its reports be a major source of information for the board. Also, the internal auditing executive should have a direct line of communication with the audit committee.

The board and its audit committee must expect and the auditor must deliver candid communication about the quality of the company's financial reporting. (Public Oversight Board's report, Sept. 1995)[3]

Some lessons could be learned from a review of the AICPA's SAS 61, "Communications with Audit Committees." This statement discusses communication requirements to include the following areas:

- Fraud and illegal acts
- Deficiencies in internal control
- Significant accounting policies
- Accounting estimates
- Significant audit adjustments
- Disagreements with management
- Difficulties in performing the audit

The internal auditing executive should discuss each of the above as appropriate with the audit committee. Details of each that should be a concern to the committee should be described in detail, outlining the adverse implications of the deficiencies.

Activity Reports

Prior to Practice Advisory 2060-1, some internal auditors take the position that activity reports are unnecessary; their current internal audit reports — those issued to show the results of specific audits — are the best evidence of audit accomplishment. Current internal audit reports do provide valuable information and point to matters needing corrective action, but they are like yesterday's newspaper. They are obscured by the rush of time and events, and rarely are they read in their entirety by board members. Also, they are usually specific as to their orientation. These current audit reports need to be summarized so as to present a totality of internal audit accomplishment. When summarization is done artfully, it seizes and retains the interest of both executive management and the board.

Internal audit accomplishments can often boast a dollar sign, capturing more attention than most other accomplishments. When internal auditors save or recover more than their services cost, they offer a potent reason to retain or even expand the audit department. Certainly, such savings and recoveries should have a prominent place in activity reports.

But dollar return is only one of the audit accomplishments — often it can be the least of them in terms of service to the organization. When a dry year passes with little or no dollar recovery, internal auditors who rely exclusively on the dollar sign may be embarrassed. Preferably the consultive and the constructive and protective aspects of their work are also stressed.   The use of dollar return also obscures audits that are productive through the recommendations that add value and that improve service to various clients of the organization and its integral parts and functions. The Foreign Corrupt Practices Act in the United States, for example, makes systems improvement and integrity powerful objectives for internal auditing and a matter of serious concern to senior management and the board.

Internal auditors should periodically call attention by executives and the board to these summaries of accomplishments, both monetary and other, to demonstrate the value of internal audit contributions. When they put their minds to it, auditors can report an impressive array of steps taken and benefits provided. Here are some subjects these activity reports can address:

- Comparison of work programmed with work accomplished
- Number and diversity of activities audited
- Number and kinds of reports issued
- Number of other communications to management
- Cost of operating the auditing department
- Amounts of recoveries and savings
- Status of risk exposure

- Number and types of special management studies
- Quantification, if possible, of improved services to inside units or to outside individuals or organizations
- Effectiveness of the audit work
- Quality of external audit activities

In addition, internal auditors should be alert to those matters in which management or the board have exhibited special interest: activities subject to highest risk; coordination of internal and external audit activities so as to minimize total audit expense; and comprehensiveness of coverage.

To provide information for summary or activity reports (see Exhibit 19-2), the input for several reports which is discussed in the next several pages, the internal audit activity should develop and maintain administrative records designed to permit ready accumulation of source data.

Comparisons between work programmed and accomplished. For each internal audit project, audit days programmed and expended can be compared. Programmed days can be taken from the long-range audit schedule (see Exhibits 22-1 and 22-2). Audit days expended can be summarized for each project on registers posted from individual time reports (see Exhibit 23-3).

Activities audited. Information on the number and diversity of activities audited can be accumulated on a form prepared after each audit project is completed. The form would have many purposes. It would provide space for overall audit opinions on the entire project, yet provide for segmented opinions also. Each project is often subdivided into specific operating functions or areas. This is particularly true in functional audits. There, the audit may cross many organizational lines. Each organization, therefore, may be considered separately on the form even though the several organizations were involved in the same project.

Some large organizational audits embrace a number of significant activities. Each activity may itself be larger than some other activities that constitute a single audit project. For example, an audit of returnable containers covers one subject. An audit of purchasing may cover many different subjects: selecting suppliers, controls over competitive bidding, approvals of purchase orders, following up on the receipt of items ordered, etc. Hence, to achieve some measure of equality, the form should provide for a subdivision of the elements covered by the audit project. The form should also permit a classification of audit findings into major and minor rankings.

A suggested form is shown as Exhibit 19-1. The format of the form can be used both for reports on audit activities and for reports on the organization's operations. For other reports and communications to management, information can be extracted from Exhibit 19-1 and from registers of informal reports.

Exhibit 19-1
Classification of Report Opinions and Findings

Audit Project No. _____   Report Date _____

Title _____

		Opinions	**OVERALL**		**OPINIONS**	
			Controls		Performance	
			Sat.	Unsat.	Sat.	Unsat.
		Overall				
Organization	Function		Detailed Opinions			
_____	_____		__	__	__	__
_____	_____		__	__	__	__
_____	_____		__	__	__	__
_____	_____		__	__	__	__
_____	_____		__	__	__	__
_____	_____		__	__	__	__
_____	_____		__	__	__	__
_____	_____		__	__	__	__
_____	_____		__	__	__	__

Deficiencies

		Controls		Performance	
		Major	Minor	Major	Minor
Organization	Finding No. (R)				
_____	_____	__	__	__	__
_____	_____	__	__	__	__
_____	_____	__	__	__	__
_____	_____	__	__	__	__
_____	_____	__	__	__	__

Totals

Open Findings _____

(R) Repeat Findings _____

Date _____   Supervisor _____

Cost of operating the auditing department. Incremental costs can be accumulated by recording salaries, fringe benefits, and allowances for vacations and estimated sick leave, travel, and other direct costs. The added overhead can be determined by discussions each year with the budget department. However, nonincremental costs should be shown separately. Audit costs can be computed and reported on each audit report. Activity based costing can produce a more precise cost of each audit.

Amounts of recoveries and savings. These amounts should be accumulated on a special record that identifies the project and analyzes the recoveries and savings. The record would show estimated recoveries at the end of the reporting period and actual recoveries after they have been finally determined. Projected information should also be computed and reported.

Reports of dollar savings can be a sensitive issue. The matter is relatively simple where an overpayment is recovered; the amount is usually beyond dispute. But savings because of improved systems or elimination of unnecessary work can be given different interpretations by auditor and client. What are the savings when a person is taken off unproductive work but not removed from the payroll? A wise course of action is to calculate such savings conservatively and to obtain agreement with the client on the amount of savings to be reported. Time and motion studies add strong support.

Audit Productivity

Productivity is usually considered as the comparison between resource input and product or service output. In a sense it is comparable to the concept of efficiency. However, productivity can go further than the mere count of units produced or services rendered, in that it also can measure the outcome of the audit effort. Outcomes are the results of the outputs. They are the improvements achieved by the organization or by society that were gained through the exercise of the audit activity.

Outcomes are often difficult to measure because they relate to conditions such as better community relations, improved personnel relations, a reduction in morbidity (illness), an improvement in the education process, or better customer or client relations.

The ultimate test of audit success is its productivity. To determine if an audit is productive, the audit must have an objective. This objective should be stated in terms of the expected output or outcome of the audit effort, or both. It should be stated in terms such as, "To increase the output of a certain client effort by 'X' percent." Or it could be stated as, "To improve the service provided to the manufacturing division by the engineering organization." This latter measurement is difficult to come by because outcome measurements frequently defy precision.

The ideal situation would be for the audit directive to contain not only the objective of the audit but also specifications as to how the achievement of this objective can be measured. When these conditions are present, audit productivity can be determined, and when identified, can be reported as a part of the audit activity report.

Too frequently audit productivity is incorrectly reported as:

- The number of audits completed.
- The number of workdays devoted to auditing.
- The comparison of audit costs incurred to the audit budget.
- The costs eliminated (savings) or funds collected.

Items such as these are important as quantitative statistics relative to the audit operation. They do not measure in a true sense the real productivity of the organization that is the degree of achievement of the individual audit objectives. As an example, an audit that is directed as an investigation into a suspected unsatisfactory functional activity may provide information that will improve that function's contribution to the organization's activity or well-being. Such an audit would not be able to produce information such as savings or collections — yet it, in the long run, could have a beneficial impact on the entire organization's performance.

Example of an Activity Report

Exhibit 19-2 is an annual activity report. The report also contains evaluations that round out the report.

This report may be submitted semiannually. In the opening it declares the department's internal audit objectives. It then shows audit days budgeted and expended. Senior management and the board are provided with composite assessments of the audit functions reviewed. The assessments are based on audit opinions expressed in "segments" of audit reports; one audit report might cover several segments. For example, a receiving department audit might include a segment on processing documentation, one on checking receipts, one on inspecting received material, and the like. Within one audit report, there may be varied opinions on the different segments. This tends to level out opinions on large audits and small audits.

The report analyzes audit disclosures and the causes of the weaknesses reported. It speaks of the special assistance provided to organization managers and the amounts both saved and recovered. The report concludes with the audit plans for the ensuing year.

Exhibit 19-2
Internal Audit Highlights - 20XX

Audit Objectives

The internal audit activity's objective is twofold: (1) to provide comprehensive, practical audit coverage of organization operations and (2) to assist organization management by conducting special reviews of organization problem areas; working with the organization's public accountants; and conducting reviews of claims, price proposals, and other data submitted by the organization's suppliers and licensees.

Summary Information

For the year 20XX, we expended about 3,200 audit days on our audit work. This represented 92 percent of the 3,500 audit days initially planned. We spent some 70 percent of our time on audit coverage of organization operations and the remainder in assisting management. We issued a total of 121 audit reports and audit memos — an average of 10 each month; 29 of those reports and 14 of those memos dealt with the results of our management assistance efforts.

Regular Audit Coverage
Summary Information

We based our 20XX audit coverage on our 20XX schedule, which we prepared after discussions with branch, program, and other management personnel and after review by the audit committee of the board of directors. We placed particular emphasis on sensitive control areas, or risk aspects, and on subjects covered in Corporate Policy Statement 5, "Business Ethics." We completed jobs covering significant activities for all major organization programs and involving all major functional areas and outside manufacturing locations. We also spent a significant part of our audit effort in monitoring the development of an integrated database. More specifically, we reviewed and reported upon 122 separate functions or audit segments:

Coverage	Audit Segments	Percent of Satisfactory Opinions
Audit Commercial Programs	33	52%
Results — Government Programs	15	53
Opinions Common Program Operations	26	65
General Systems	48	90
Totals	122	70%

At the midyear, we reported overall results showing only 65 percent satisfactory opinions. Although for the year overall results rose to 70 percent, that level reflects deterioration from prior year results. Audit results for 20VV were, in total, 84 percent, and for 20WW, 81 percent.

Exhibit 19-2 (Cont.)

Audit Results/Findings

We cited a total of 120 findings requiring corrective action in our 20XX audit reports. We regard one-half of those findings as having a significant effect on the satisfactory performance of the activity reviewed. Further analysis and study of those significant findings indicate that 60 percent of them dealt with the failure to follow established controls and that 40 percent of them dealt with shortcomings in the controls themselves. Before completing our audits, we discussed all of the findings cited with the management personnel responsible. And, in all cases, those people took corrective action that we considered satisfactory.

Underlying Causes

We believe that the failure to follow established controls is attributable in large measure to managers and supervisors not giving sufficient attention to training and motivating employees to do the work and not giving sufficient attention to monitoring the work. And we believe that shortcomings in controls are attributable for the most part to managers' lack of awareness of the need for controls. We did, however, find and report instances in which management decisions had been made to disregard — or to de-emphasize — acceptable practice.

Special Audit Coverage
Summary Information

During 20XX, we assisted management in undertaking a variety of assignments. We made reviews of supplier price and cost data, provided assistance to the organization's public accountants, made examinations of organization-sponsored employee organizations, and assisted organization personnel in the review of internal accounting controls. Other work we accomplished included a follow-up review of a subsidiary's financial reporting system, an examination of a customer's operations under an operating cost incentive program, an investigation of material shortages, and certain other management-requested audit and investigative effort.

$6,700,000 Saved and $131,000 Recovered

We issued 26 audit reports and five internal audit memos to report the results of our analysis of suppliers' price and cost data. Prices negotiated by material branch personnel using information we furnished them for 18 proposals we reviewed in 20XX and for eight proposals we reviewed in the prior year resulted in substantial savings. And the organization recovered a significant amount in connection with prior year audit work we performed on royalty payments.

Looking Ahead

Our plans for 20YY include organization operations by making qualified audit staff available for special assignments to key operating areas in the organization.

The report is notable for its brevity; it packs a good deal of material into a few pages and highlights significant matters in side comments. Hence, members of top management, the audit committee, and the board of directors can skim or read the report in a very short time. Some activity reports go into extensive narrative and quantitative detail. We question whether the executive readers of such reports would take the time to digest the extended comments and the detailed tables and schedules. Care must be taken to ensure that all of the comments in the report are factually supported by working papers. The report may, in fact, have its own working paper file. This material is also available if a reader desires more detail on a particular item in the report.

Some audit organizations supply the following general additional information in their summary reports of activities:

- The names and backgrounds of the internal auditors.

- A listing of work objectives, including new activities or organizations, sensitive areas to be audited, and other matters outside the normal routine.

- Means of promoting coordination of the internal and external auditing efforts. An example is the establishment of a "common user" file for flowcharts, form samples, and organization charts, to be consulted by both the external and internal auditors.

- Work on questionable payments and practices.

- Work on internal accounting and management controls to assure compliance with the provisions of the U.S. Foreign Corrupt Practices Act; the provisions of the Committee of Supporting Organizations (COSO) of the Treadway Commission; and similar organizations in countries other than the U.S.

- Work on audits involving equal employment opportunity and affirmative action.

- Reasons for any deviations from the long-range internal audit schedule, such as inability to recruit personnel, heavier than budgeted training, or increases in requests for special studies.

- The results of peer reviews of the internal audit function.

- Comments on audit philosophy and the broadening scope of internal auditing within the organization such as risk evaluation, environmental aspects, and ethics.

- Compliance with professional requirements such as the *Standards*.

Examples of Graphic Reports

Some organizations use graphs and charts to display the level of audit effort. Exhibit 19-3 shows audit accomplishment in terms of audit days and compares it with what was programmed. Exhibit 19-4 shows the number of written communications, both formal (internal audit reports) and informal (internal audit memorandums), as an indicator of audit accomplishment.

Supporting these charts are status reports (not reproduced here) that can describe such matters as:

- Expanded use of information systems and quantitative analysis.

- Extended use of visual presentations to management.

- Application of management techniques to solve management problems.

- Results of studies showing how to classify and investigate findings so as to disclose their cause and impact.

- Staff training sessions.

- Professional activities of the staff such as conferences, presentations, and publications.

- Conferences with executive management and the audit committee of the board of directors.

- Contacts with the external auditors.

- Cost savings.

- Titles of audit projects completed.

- Comments on audit productivity and the accomplishment of audit objectives.

- Acceptability of the audit process by management and by the general operating personnel.

- Examples of positive audit activity in emergency situations.

- Self-evaluation processes.

- Management consulting activities.

- Forensic activities.

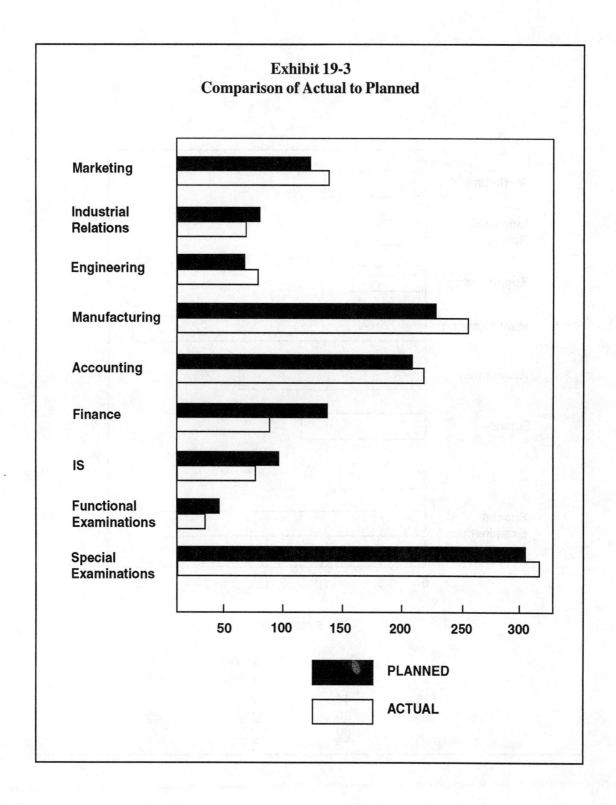

Exhibit 19-3
Comparison of Actual to Planned

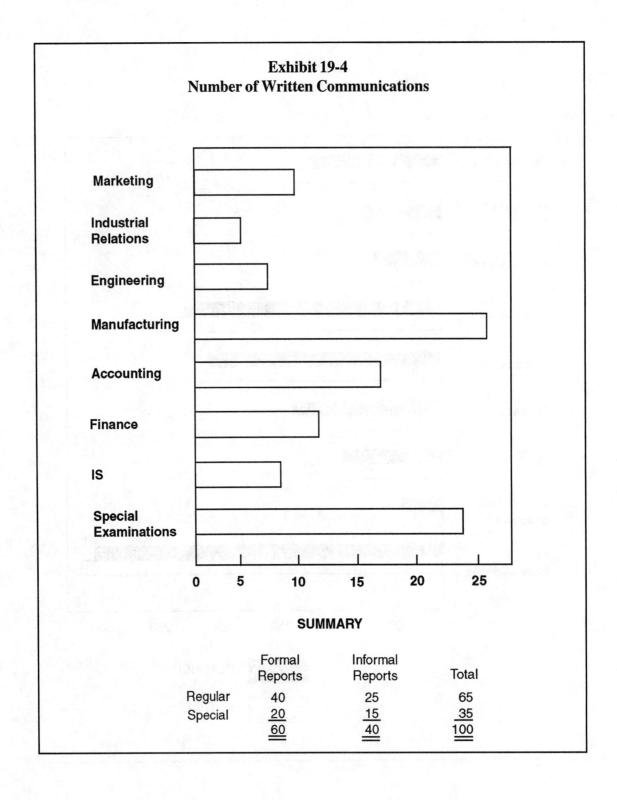

Exhibit 19-4
Number of Written Communications

SUMMARY

	Formal Reports	Informal Reports	Total
Regular	40	25	65
Special	20	15	35
	60	40	100

Judiciously prepared, reports of accomplishment can be of benefit to the auditors. The reports let management know that the auditors are evaluating themselves and measuring their own achievements in light of professional accomplishments and against approved standards. They point out that the auditors are carefully weighing what they have done and where they are going. The reports can be written in a simple style to make reading easy. They can be illustrated by charts and diagrams to improve understanding.

These reports are not easy to devise or to prepare. They encroach upon the busy auditor's schedule. They may be started with a flourish but abandoned after a few trials because keeping them up is an onerous task. But the auditor must remember that the reports will be read by management, and they will keep the auditor's efforts and accomplishments before management's eyes.

Evaluation Reports

Reports on the operational health of the organization can be of absorbing interest to management. These reports can be a powerful instrument and, hence, they must be used with discretion.

Management will see them as an indicator of administrative well-being or organizational illness. Thus they must be soundly and logically based. Conclusions drawn from a scattering of data can be misleading. A few random numbers will give incomplete and haphazard data. But the stability provided by high numbers on Likert scales can be a strong foundation on which auditors can build when they construct and present reports on the organization's operations.

Senior management does receive operating reports from operating management; these reports provide information on production, schedules, quality, backlogs, staffing, and the like. But these operating reports may be self-serving declarations. What senior management needs is an objective, educated, professional evaluation of what all the auditor's efforts have brought to light in terms of administering the organization's affairs. An ancillary activity is the internal auditor's review of the validity of the operational reports themselves.

This does not imply the direct evaluation of individuals, which can be a trap. Such evaluations are difficult to support and easy to dispute. What it does imply is the accumulation of individual audit findings and conclusions and the depiction of trends and variances. There are several units of measurement for such reports. Two of these are *audit opinions* and *audit findings*.

Summarizing Audit Opinions

Not all internal auditors express overall opinions on the results of their individual audits. Some are content to report findings and recommendations only; in some cases only findings.

Others, however, have taken the position that a professional opinion on the adequacy, efficiency, and effectiveness of the system of control, financial and operational, within the activities audited, provides useful and needed information to management. These internal auditors believe that opinions on operations are no less important than opinions on financial statements.

Looking at it from the viewpoint of senior managers, they, as well as the board, have a vital interest in knowing how well their controls can be relied on. This interest should be directed toward all the systems of controls in the organization — not only the internal accounting controls. After all, lack of control over production schedules or safety or quality or efficiency or effectiveness can be far more devastating to the organization than weaknesses in control over petty cash or trade discounts or travel expense vouchers.

Hence, both client management and the board need information — current, continuing, objective information — on how their internal auditors regard the existing systems of controls. With that information, the decision makers in the organization can take any action needed to correct control weaknesses or reverse adverse trends. Based on the audit information and on the corrective action taken, they will be able to make representations on their systems of control.

Internal audit opinions on specific operating activities audited are basically "satisfactory" or "unsatisfactory." There may be gradations, of course: highly satisfactory, satisfactory, qualified, poor, unsatisfactory. But this can be mere hair splitting. From management's point of view, the operation either measured up to standards or it did not. Either the job was being done or it was not — and if not, why not. Specific findings will support these opinions.

Therefore, audit reports should carry overall audit opinions. Also, those opinions should be summarized to provide management and the board with indications of the quality of both control and performance within an organization as viewed by the internal auditors.

Periodic summaries can show the total number of audit opinions expressed and the percentage and location and subject matters of those that were unsatisfactory. Management is thereby given an indication included in the findings as to whether — and if so, where — corrective action is needed.

Information on the status of the resolution of adverse opinions should also be included. Management should be advised as to:

- Clients' concurrence or nonconcurrence in the findings and in the adverse opinions.
- Clients' position on correction of conditions causing the adverse opinions.
- Situations where the conditions causing the adverse opinions have been resolved.
- Situations where there were mitigating circumstances.

Summarizing Findings

The summaries of findings that have resulted in unsatisfactory opinions will point out just where the corrective action should be taken. Findings may be divided into two classifications: major and minor. Guidelines should be set to differentiate between them. Here are some usable definitions (see Chapter 6):

A *major* finding is one that affects performance or control, preventing an activity, function, or unit from meeting a substantial part of its significant goals or objectives.

A *minor* finding is one that warrants reporting and requires corrective action, but that cannot be considered as preventing the accomplishment of a significant goal or objective.

Such rules need consistent and judicious interpretation on a case-by-case basis. All findings, therefore, should be evaluated by someone in authority so as to ensure consistency and due deliberation at an appropriate level.

Findings need one further breakdown if their reporting is to be used effectively. Put in simple terms, management has two basic responsibilities in carrying out its operations: The first is to tell its people what needs to be done. The second is to have them do it and to be sure that they do it right. Implicit in the first responsibility is providing criteria: systems, standards, directives, procedures, job instructions, and other means that come under the generic heading of control. Implicit in the second is carrying out activities in accordance with these means of control; this comes under the generic heading of performance. Findings, therefore, may be major or minor, and they may affect control or performance. Let us consider some simple examples of each:

Control/major. The procurement organization has not required competitive bids. Such a dereliction could seriously and adversely affect the organization and prevent it from reaching one of its primary objectives: getting required products or services at the best price. It affects control, rather than performance, since there is nothing to prevent buyers from obtaining bids. And, even if, without being told to do so, experienced buyers were obtaining bids, this would not minimize the seriousness of the deficiency. New buyers might enter the procurement organization and, in the absence of rules to the contrary, give all their orders to favored suppliers. Any buyers might succumb to the blandishments of unscrupulous vendors.

Performance/major. Procedures require competitive bids. Yet 50 percent of the 200 purchase orders examined, representing a substantial portion of the amounts committed for materials, were not bid competitively. The failure to obtain bids was not justified or otherwise documented. This is a performance deficiency because activities were not carried out in accordance with existing instructions. There may be a related control deficiency if the procurement instruction did not require supervisory review of the orders placed, but essentially we have a performance defect that could prevent the accomplishment of an important procurement objective.

Control/minor. Instructions on preparing a statistical report to senior management on procurement commitments do not provide for independent verification of the figures. It is assumed that supervisory review of the report would prevent gross errors from being reported to management, but the missing control violates precepts of good administration and should be corrected.

Performance/minor. Although instructions call for independent verification of the commitment report to executive management, a number of errors were found in the report, none of which exceeded $100. Employees should be cautioned to exercise greater care. The person who signs the report should make periodic tests of the report to ensure its accuracy. Certainly, the performance deficiency needs correcting — but it cannot be said that the errors adversely affected a significant goal or objective.

Normally, major findings are reported in audit reports. Minor findings are either summarized in the audit report or are included as a part of a management letter from the auditor to the client manager. This management letter does not relieve the client from responding to the minor findings. They are usually reviewed during the next audit and, if not resolved, the nonresolution can become a major finding in the subsequent audit report. Thus, the percentages of deficiency findings that are reported are considered to be percentages of major items, opinions, or performance.

With these definitions and guidelines known by all, reports on the volume and content of deficiency findings can be of considerable interest to management and can indicate either deterioration or improvement in the administration of the organization's activities. The information can prompt and guide management to take corrective action.

Charting Trends

Trends in opinions and deficiency findings should be charted to provide a useful indication of the organization's administrative health. Exhibit 19-5 contains charts that graphically chronicle the records of unsatisfactory major opinions. The opinions are shown separately for controls and performance. A final chart shows the combination of the two. The charts indicate a gradual deterioration of administration or the initiation or change in many of the operational aspects of the organization. They show a need to search for basic causes and to prompt management to take the action needed to reverse an unsatisfactory trend. However, the use of percentages is a dangerous practice without some qualifying information as to degree of importance and the risks and amounts of resources that are concerned. The use of the number of audit segments provides some of this information. Additional information would make the statistic more meaningful.

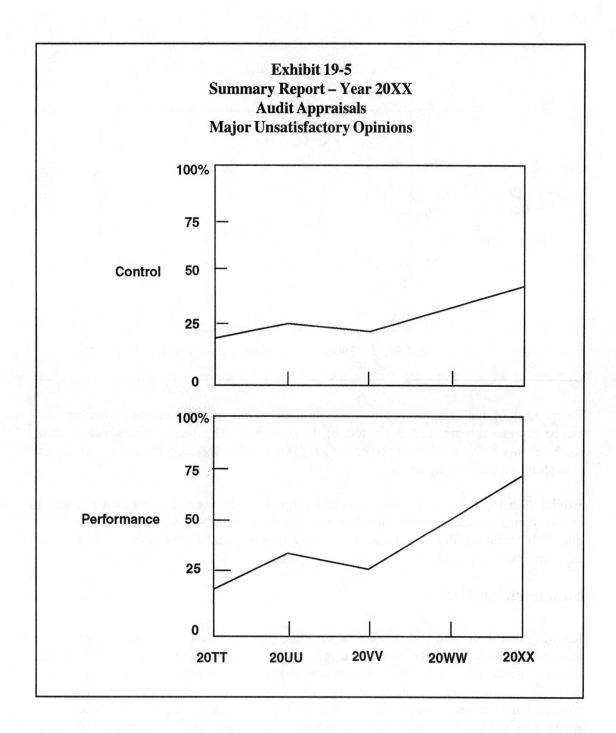

Exhibit 19-5
Summary Report – Year 20XX
Audit Appraisals
Major Unsatisfactory Opinions

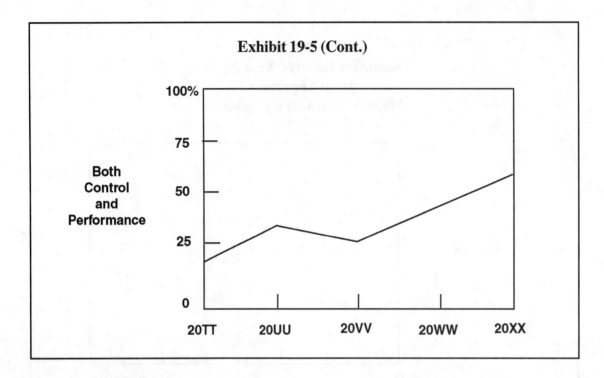

The number of audit segments, those discrete parts of an audit project for which opinions can be expressed, is set forth at the foot of the final chart. This provides information about the base on which the charts were constructed. Obviously, the base should be substantial enough to validate the report.

Exhibit 19-6 shows a similar chart. This one portrays the number of findings over a period of five years, and shows a condition that parallels that shown on the chart of opinions. The charts differentiate between control and performance, and between major and minor deficiencies.

Summarizing Causes

Knowing that things are bad is not enough. Management should know why. Probably the most helpful information the auditor can provide management is information on the causes of deficiencies. Know the cause and you are halfway to prescribing the cure. Reports of deficient conditions and unsatisfactory opinions can provide management with reason for concern, but the reports can be frustrating. The executive looks at the assessment of operational weaknesses and says, "I agree with you, internal auditor, that conditions are bad. But why are they bad? Until I know the causes, I'm not sure I can make things any better."

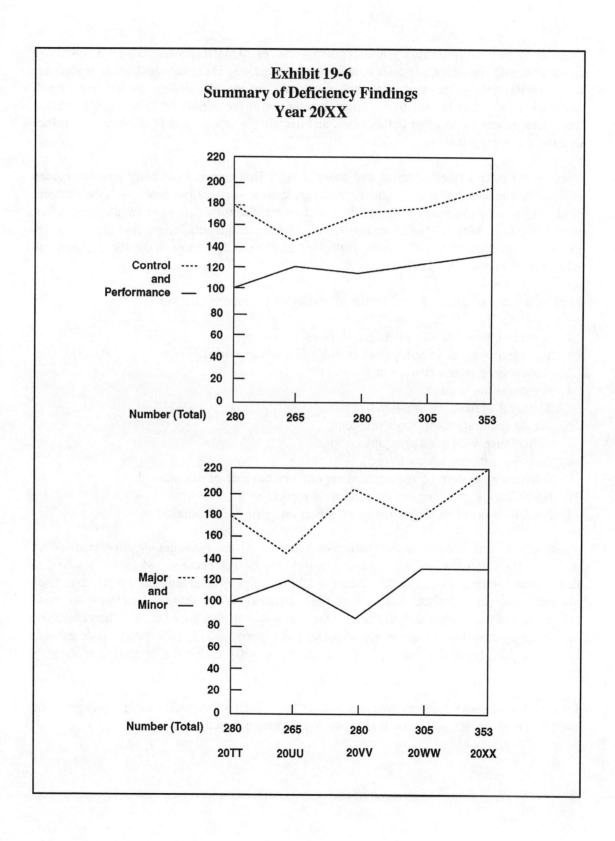

Exhibit 19-6
Summary of Deficiency Findings
Year 20XX

A good system of determining and reporting causes of deficiencies can go a long way toward helping the executive take broad corrective action. The individual audit reports set forth specific deficiencies that were then corrected. The individual deficiencies do not spell out tendencies. They do not provide management with the means of bringing a condition into focus, relating it to other deficiencies, and deciding which groups of deficient conditions deserve the most attention.

Spelling out causes takes planning and analysis. This first step is to identify possible causes of defects. This is a matter of judgment. A dozen internal auditors presented with the problem could argue *ad infinitum* on the subject and never come to full agreement. Each audit organization, working in slightly or entirely different environments, might find certain causes more relevant than others. The individual chief audit executive must make the decisions on what best suits the organization.

Here is one set of causes keyed to the hierarchy of management controls:

1. Suitable objectives and plans not devised.
2. Suitable resources of manpower or materials not provided.
3. Standards or other criteria not set.
4. Personnel not trained.
5. Approval system not provided.
6. Master (central) control not provided.
7. Compliance with standards not ensured.
8. Ongoing process not monitored.
9. Satisfactory system of records and reports not devised or maintained.
10. No action by management on receipt of reports.
11. No follow-up of implementation of action on prior deficiencies.

These causes are brought to the exclusive attention of the manager or supervisor of an activity. There is some validity to this hierarchy of causes because, when all is said and done, superb managers can make almost anything happen under any circumstances. They are restricted solely by the resources at their disposal. When these restrictions seriously affect them and are beyond their control, the cause will most likely be: (1) the failure (by senior management) to devise suitable objectives and plans, and (2) failure to provide suitable resources. The remaining causes cover matters generally under the operating manager's control.

Here is another set of causes that encompass the efforts of organizations, managers, and people. These causes are listed under four management functions:

A. Planning and Organizing
   1. Need for controls not recognized
   2. Appropriate authority not assigned
   3. Sufficient personnel not assigned
   4. Appropriate priority not assigned
   5. Adequate equipment not provided
   6. Means of coordination not provided
   7. Responsibility not assigned
   8. Adequate training not provided
   9. Operational strategy not designed

B. Directing and Controlling
   1. Schedules not set or met
   2. Adequate instructions not provided
   3. Standards not met
   4. Feedback about the ongoing process not obtained
   5. Prompt corrective action not taken
   6. Insufficient management attention
   7. Insufficient supervisory attention
   8. Management or supervisory attitude (control overrides)
   9. Employee attitude
   10. Human error
   11. Lack of communication
   12. Management decision to not take the required action
   13. Controls not updated
   14. Adequate basic training not provided

In addition to defining the cause, it becomes necessary to determine the nature of the deficiency. True, the cause may be, for example, the failure to take prompt corrective action. But this defect could happen all the time or part of the time. The action could be not timely or inaccurate. Finally, the action could be inconsistent. So, along with the cause, it is of interest to know whether the control or performance was:

   a. Incomplete.
   b. Lacking.
   c. Not timely.
   d. Inaccurate.
   e. Inconsistent.
   f. False.

It becomes abundantly clear, as efforts are made to assign causes, that, like boxes within boxes within boxes, there are causes behind causes behind causes. One can easily get lost in philosophical theorizing about the cause behind the cause. Carried far enough, the pursuit of cause winds up with humans' first fall from grace. But the essential cause — the cause that operating management is preoccupied with — is the cause that, upon removal, most directly corrects the condition. Hence it is significant, in assigning causes, to look both to the action that line management took to preclude the condition, correct the reported condition, and identify the nature of the deficiency.

This brings us to the use of a form that will help the auditor accumulate the data needed to prepare analyses of deficiencies for management. Exhibit 19-7 is an example of such a form. It provides space for identifying the deficiency for purposes of control. The identification can be made at the conclusion of each audit project. It also provides spaces for showing the project number and title, the date of the report that described the deficiency, and the supervisor and auditor-in-charge responsible for it. The functional area would be the broad organizational unit concerned, usually at the branch level of finance, administration, procurement, manufacturing, or quality control, to name a few. Some organizations, however, will require further breakdowns. For example, manufacturing may be subdivided among production control, tooling, and production.

The deficiency would be stated essentially as it was summarized in the report. The corrective action would be that taken or proposed. The cause (and impact) would be a narrative exposition of how the auditor — the one closest to the problem — perceived the cause (or impact) of the condition.

The identification of the finding helps accumulate statistical data on whether the finding concerned control or performance and is considered major or minor. If the same finding involves both control and performance, individual forms should be prepared for each category to make summarizing easy. This is proper since both the cause and the corrective action may be different.

For example: If an instruction was lacking on competitive bids in the procurement organization, the corrective action is to issue one. The cause is (A-1) "failure to recognize the need," and the nature of the deficiency is (b) "lacking." If, however, some buyers, because they were experienced and did not need to be told, were obtaining competitive bids while others were not, the entire situation changes. The corrective action, after the instruction has been issued, is closer supervisory control. The cause is (B-7) "insufficient supervisory attention," and the nature is (a) "incomplete." (See Exhibits 19-5 and 19-6.)

Exhibit 19-7
Causes of Deficiencies
Classification Record

Def. No. _____

Project No. _____   Title _____

Report Date _____   Supervisor _____   A/C _____

Functional Area _____

Deficiency: _____

_____

_____

_____

Corrective Action: _____

_____

_____

_____

Auditor's Statement of Underlying Cause: _____

_____

_____

	Major	Minor	Nature	Cause
Control	____	____	____	____
Performance	____	____	____	____

When these forms are faithfully prepared, they can readily be summarized into a report to management. Exhibit 19-8 is an example of a report of the auditor's analysis of deficiencies. The second set of causes, just listed, is used in the sample report.

Exhibit 19-8
Analysis of Deficiency Findings/Year 20XX

	Total Number	Percent	Contr.	Perf.	Major	Minor
Cause of Deficiency						
Planning and Organizing						
Need not recognized	78	22	110	14	60	24
Unauthorized decision by line management	37	11	22	20	30	12
Failure to update	18	5	21	—	12	4
Failure to assign appropriate priority	18	5	2	12	10	3
Failure to provide for coordination	14	4	6	4	5	5
Failure to assign responsibility	14	4	6	4	6	3
Failure to assign sufficient personnel	11	3	1	2	7	4
Failure to provide adequate training	11	3	2	3	10	5
Failure to provide adequate facilities	3	1	1	1		
Subtotal	204	58	171	60	140	60
Controlling						
Insufficient supervisory attention	75	21	16	32	31	37
Insufficient management attention	25	7	13	18	22	15
Failure to provide adequate instruction	21	6	3	16	8	3
Management/supervisory attitude	11	3	3	4	4	4
Employee attitude	7	2	2	3	6	6
Human error	3	1	2	5	5	4
Lack of communication	3	1	0	2	0	2
Other	4	1	1	2	4	2
Subtotal	149	42	40	82	80	73
Total	353	100	211	142	220	133
Nature of Deficiency						
Control or Performance:						
Incomplete	138	39	117	57	82	61
Lacking	110	31	72	38	76	32
Not timely	55	16	11	17	30	21
Inaccurate	36	10	6	18	10	9
Inconsistent	14	4	5	12	22	10
	353	100	211	142	220	133

The various administrative activities and reports just discussed may seem burdensome. When auditors work feverishly to meet the deadlines for such reports, they may bewail their tasks and berate their taskmaster. Still, the rewards are worth the effort. As senior management examines these reports, they can see the auditors as a continuing source of information that will help in guiding the entity. The auditor becomes more, not less, valued, strengthening audit's position as being a rightful member of executive senior management's council.

Special Communication[4]

An intolerable situation may endure when the internal auditor comes upon a serious situation and cannot obtain the support of any management level. If the auditor remains convinced that action is necessary, he or she must go directly to the audit committee. Understandably, this action might put the auditor's job "on the line." However, this risk goes with the territory and the auditor must be willing to accept it. On the other hand, the audit committee must clearly support the audit effort and make it clear that the auditor is a part of corporate management and that interference, either actual or implied, will not be tolerated.

One-page Audit Reports

Although audit reports are covered in Chapter 17, it might be appropriate to describe a specific audit report that has recently been innovated by several large organizations. The report is designed to conserve the time of busy executives and members of the board of directors. The report can be designed for a PowerPoint presentation or hard copy. The report is a one-page multi-color presentation that is supported by detailed references for areas in which the executive or board member is interested. A sample one-page report is shown in Figure 19-9.

This colorful report immediately gets the attention it deserves. Also, the areas of vulnerability and danger are immediately brought to the reader's or observer's attention. The comment section is a one- or two-sentence statement. If the reader wants more information, it is obtained by PowerPoint or by reference to a following section. This information is also abbreviated with the presenter supplying verbal details if requested. The presentation is supported by a traditional audit report electronically or on hard copy, as desired. The organizations that are using the presentation say that it has been well received by executives and board members.

Exhibit 19-9

Audit Title
Period Audited
Report Date

Title of Audit _____

Organization _____

Area Audited	Good (Green)	Status Fair (Yellow)	Bad Red	Comment	Report Reference
_____	_____	_____	_____	_____	_____
_____	_____	_____	_____	_____	_____
_____	_____	_____	_____	_____	_____
_____	_____	_____	_____	_____	_____

Lead Auditor _____   Chief Audit Executive _____

Caveats

Care should be taken to emphasize internal audit performance and to restrict data that are merely informational. Activity reports can become so voluminous that they defeat their purpose as summaries of accomplishments. They may be seen as merely a catalog of every activity the internal audit department undertakes. Some cautions should be considered in publishing the following types of reports:

Number and diversity of audit assignments. These reports may be considered informational only and not necessarily a good measure of performance. Besides, an increase in the number of departments audited may indicate that the audit staff is being spread too thin or that it is performing superficial audits.

Number of reports issued. Without explanation, an increase in the number of reports may imply shorter audits or smaller audit areas.

Number of other communications. The number of communications to management may not truly indicate the level of activity performed. But information on the number of follow-up memorandums might show any failure on the part of client managers to take appropriate corrective action on audit findings.

Suggestion adopted. These data may be misleading. Management may refuse to adopt a specific audit suggestion and yet correct a deficiency through means of its own devising. But combined with corresponding dollar savings, recoveries, or other improvements, these data may be a useful measure of audit effectiveness. However, the audit report may specify that some corrective action should be taken by the client, but no recommendations are provided by the auditor. If corrective action is taken by the client, there would be a positive impact on the report.

Consulting. Care should be taken in reporting the bald figures on consulting studies. Some years may involve a few long studies while other years may involve short studies or none, through no fault of the internal audit activity. Also, an excessive number of consulting studies might indicate a deterioration in carrying out the approved long-range audit schedule. Indeed, an excessive number of consulting studies might indicate that internal auditing is bowing too often to the desires of operating management, thereby casting a cloud on its independence and objectivity and its ability to perform discretionary or directed audits.

Investigations. This type of audit assignment is usually the result of an emergency. It would be difficult to classify such work. As a matter of fact, some investigations may be classified as containing restricted information. The statistics could contain data as to the source of the assignment, the type of investigation, the area of investigation, and the disposition such as: completed, turned over to security elements, in process, and unsuccessful.

These caveats do not mean that the related reports are necessarily invalid. Rather, they mean that the internal auditors should be careful in their activity reports not to give impressions that are counterproductive. Also, their activity should be guided by the implications inferred above.

References

[1] *IIA Today* (Altamonte Springs, FL: The Institute of Internal Auditors, March/April 1998), 7.
[2] *Internal Auditing Alert* (Boston, MA: Warren Gorham & Lamont, January 1995), 1-2.
[3] *Internal Auditing Alert* (Boston, MA: Warren Gorham & Lamont, October 1995), 1-2.
[4] Allison, Jr., Dwight, "Internal Auditors and Audit Committees," *Internal Auditor*, February 1994, 51.

Supplementary Readings

Apostolou, Nicholas G., and Richard A. Roy, *Financial Reporting Issues for Internal Auditors* (Altamonte Springs, FL: The Institute of Internal Auditors, 1990).

Bossle, Francis X., and Alfred R. Michenzi, "The Single Page Audit Report," *Internal Auditor*, April 1997, 37-41.

Danzinger, Elizabeth, "Communicate Up," *Journal of Accountancy*, February 1998, 67-69.

Didis, Stephen K., "Communicating Audit Results," *Internal Auditor*, October 1997, 36-38.

Hubbard, Larry D., "Talk First, Write Later," *Internal Auditor*, December 2000, 22-23.

Kintzele, Marilyn R., "The Use of Audit Committee Reports in Financial Reporting," *Internal Auditing*, Spring 1991, 16-24.

Leithead, Barry S., "In Touch with the Top," *Internal Auditor*, December 2000, 67-69.

Loss, James M., "The Communications Contract," *Internal Auditor*, December 2000, 88.

Parker, Susan, "The Role of the Audit Committee in Curbing Aggressive Financial Reporting," *Internal Auditing*, March/April 1999, 34-39.

Potla, Larry, "Audio Auditing," *Internal Auditor*, October 1999, 38-41.

Urbancic, Frank R., "A Content Analysis of Audit Committee Reports," *Internal Auditing*, Summer 1996, 36-42.

Multiple-choice Questions

Use the following information to answer questions 1 and 2.
After using the same public accounting firm for several years, the board of directors retained another public accounting firm to perform the annual financial audit in order to reduce the annual audit fee. The new firm has now proposed a onetime audit of the cost-effectiveness of the various operations of the business. The chief audit executive has been asked to advise management in making a decision on the proposal.

1. An argument can be made that the internal audit department would be better able to perform such an audit because:
   a. External auditors may not possess the same depth of understanding of the organization as the internal auditors.
   b. Internal auditors are required to be objective in performing audits.
   c. Audit techniques used by internal auditors are different from those used by external auditors.
   d. Internal auditors will not be vitally concerned with fraud and waste.

2. Additional criteria that should be considered by management in evaluating the proposal would include all of the following except:
   a. Existing expertise of internal audit staff.
   b. Overall cost of the proposed audit.
   c. The need to develop in-house expertise.
   d. The external auditor's required adherence to the single audit concept.

Use the following information to answer questions 3 and 4.
As an internal auditor for a multinational chemical company, you have been assigned to perform an operational audit at a local plant. This plant is similar in age, sizing, and construction to two other company plants that have been recently cited for discharge of hazardous wastes. In addition, you are aware that chemicals manufactured at the plant release toxic by-products.

3. Assume that you have evidence that the plant is discharging hazardous wastes. As a CIA, what is the appropriate reporting requirement in this situation?
   a. Send a copy of your audit report to the appropriate regulatory agency.
   b. Ignore the issue, the regulatory inspectors are better qualified to assess the danger.
   c. Issue an interim report to the appropriate levels of management.
   d. Note the issue in your working papers, but do not report it.

4. Identify your responsibility for detection of a hazardous waste discharge problem.
   a. You have no responsibility; it is the concern of the appropriate governmental agency.
   b. You are responsible for ensuring compliance with company policies and procedures.
   c. Operational audits do not require a determination of compliance with laws and regulations.
   d. You are required by the *Standards* to determine compliance with laws and regulations.

5. According to the *Standards*, an internal audit department's activity reports should:
   a. List the material findings of major audits.
   b. List unresolved findings.
   c. Report the weekly activities of the individual auditors.
   d. Compare audits completed with audits planned.

6. According to the *Standards*, activity reports submitted periodically to management and to the board should:
   a. Summarize planned audit activities.
   b. Compare performance with audit work schedules.
   c. Provide detail on financial budgets.
   d. Detail projected staffing needs.

PART 6

ADMINISTRATION

Chapter 20
Establishing the
Auditing Activity

The internal audit activity reflects the chief audit executive's philosophy. The executive's basic responsibilities. The audit charter. The Functions and Responsibility statement. The statement of audit policy. Emphasizing enterprise policy. Brochures to explain the internal audit function. Drafting job descriptions: chief audit executive, audit manager, audit supervisor, and senior auditor. The audit organization. A new organization strategy. Process auditing. Online auditing. Value-added concept. Developing audit manuals: Technical, administrative, and miscellaneous. Marketing the internal audit function. Specific ways of marketing internal auditing. Attributes of leadership in internal auditing. The elements of creativity. Marketing internal auditing through the problem-solving partnership. Environmental concerns. Outsourcing: reasons, advantages, and disadvantages. Internal audit mission statements. Acquisition and evaluation of external audit services. Responsibility for non-audit functions. Politics and the need for internal auditors to heed the politics and culture of the organization.

• •

Foundations for Successful Internal Auditing

The internal audit organization is anything the chief audit executive wants it to be — assuming top-level support. That support will depend on the perceived value of the product and the ability of the executive to market it.

The nature of the product can run the gamut from detailed verification of transactions to imaginative appraisals of all operations within the enterprise as well as special studies. The executive's philosophy of audit, with management's approval, will make the difference.

Of course, the executive has certain basic responsibilities. These are described in *Standard 2000*, "Managing the Internal Auditing Activity," of the *Standards for the Professional Practice of Internal Auditing* and Practice Advisory 2010-1. In general, the *Standards* call for the chief audit executive to develop a charter for the activity; to set goals, work schedules, staffing plans, financial budgets, and activity reports; to draft written policies and procedures;

to develop the activity's human resources; to coordinate with the external auditors; and to maintain a quality assurance program.

The foundation for internal auditing's independence, authority, and status within the organization is rooted in the activity's charter. The elements of the charter are usually found in two documents: The chief audit executive's statement of functions and responsibility and the statement of organization policy governing internal audit function, both are discussed and illustrated in the next section.

Preparing the Functions and Responsibility (F and R) Statement

Most organizations maintain a set of statements that establish the authority and responsibility of the major positions in the organization. These statements, along with related policy directives, set forth for the organization to see how senior management regards the purpose, mission, and authority of each major function within the enterprise. Internal auditors should make sure, therefore, that the charters for their organization provide frameworks within which they can function with the degree of independence that ensures complete objectivity.

The F and R statement must be carefully drafted so that it affords the auditors all the authority they need, yet does not assign responsibilities that jeopardize their objectivity or that they cannot conceivably carry out. The statement should not restrict auditors to matters of accounting and finance. Neither should it assign inappropriate functions — such as reconciling bank statements. On the other hand, the statement should not require the auditors to provide opinions on the effectiveness of technical or professional functions unless these are established criteria. For this reason, many statements stress the review of managerial controls rather than the appraisal of performance. The competent internal auditor can review administrative and managerial controls over any activity within the organization. This ability clearly cannot include the evaluation of professional performance or technical activities requiring specialized study and knowledge. But the auditors should not be barred in a consulting role from evaluating the performance of those financial and administrative activities that they are competent to judge.

An example of an authority and responsibility statement — a composite of several such statements in actual use — is shown in Exhibit 20-1.

Exhibit 20-1
The Chief Audit Executive
Statement of Authority and Responsibility

Authority
The chief audit executive is authorized to direct a broad, comprehensive program of internal auditing within the organization. Internal auditing examines and evaluates the adequacy and effectiveness of the systems of management control provided by the organization to direct its activities toward the accomplishment of its objectives in accordance with organization policies and plans. In accomplishing these activities, the chief audit executive and members of the audit staff are authorized to have full, free, and unrestricted access to all organization functions, records, property, and personnel.

Responsibility
The chief audit executive is responsible for:

Establishing policies for the auditing activity and directing its technical and administrative functions.

Developing and executing a comprehensive audit program for the evaluation of management controls provided over all organization activities.

Examining the effectiveness of all levels of management in their stewardship of organization resources and their compliance with established policies and procedures.

Recommending improvement of management controls* designed to safeguard organization resources, promote organization growth, and ensure compliance with government laws and regulations.

Reviewing procedures and records for their adequacy to accomplish intended objectives, and appraising policies and plans relating to the activity or function under audit review.

Authorizing the publication of reports on audits, including recommendations for improvement.

Appraising the adequacy of operating management's actions to correct reported deficient conditions; accepting adequate corrective action; continuing reviews with appropriate management personnel on action the chief audit executive considers inadequate until there has been a satisfactory resolution of the matter.

Conducting special audits as requested by management, including the reviews of representations made by persons outside the organization. Acting in a consulting capacity relative to the above areas of responsibility.

*"Management controls" is considered in this chapter to include all types of controls described in all chapters of this book.

Devising the Statement of Policy

Management support must be proclaimed clearly and categorically in the organization's highest policy statement. That statement should be specific and should spell out the scope and status of internal auditing within the enterprise, its objective to provide added value and to contribute to improved governance, its authority to carry out audits, issue reports, make recommendations, and evaluate corrective action. Exhibit 20-2 is a composite of several published policy statements. It sets forth a broad-gauged charter that is consistent with that in the original *Standards*.

The first eight missions enumerated in Exhibit 20-2 may be regarded as core responsibilities. They are essential to the performance of comprehensive, full-scope internal audits. The remaining missions have appeared in published policy statements of various enterprises. These define with greater particularity what executive management in those organizations expects of its internal auditors. Such missions may be regarded as optional in developing a policy statement. But the instruction stated in the final paragraph dealing with corrective action is essential if the internal auditor's findings and recommendations are to receive adequate consideration.

Not every organization is prepared to issue a policy statement concerning all these responsibilities. Some will restrict the internal auditor's scope and responsibility. Certainly, all internal audit activities must function within the environment in which they find themselves. But any reduction from the eight core responsibilities and the requirement for clients to respond adequately to audit reports adds to the risk of undetected, serious weaknesses. The effectiveness of the internal audit activity then becomes curtailed. Less reliance can be placed on its ability to function as an uninhibited monitor of the organization's controls and performance.

In seeking to secure organizational status and an effective charter, internal auditors should consider soliciting the aid of the external auditors. These independent accountants must be assured of the independence, objectivity, and unrestricted scope of the internal audit activity if they are to make maximum use of the internal auditor's work. The external auditors must never be apprehensive that internal auditors can be manipulated because of internal relationships or fear of reprisals, or that any internal operating weakness reported can go uncorrected. The external auditors, thus, have a stake in the internal audit function. Their willingness to rely on it will be diminished if the internal auditor's charter does not clearly set forth a comprehensive mission for the activity. Conversely, the internal auditors must be assured of the independence of the external auditors. Lack of such independence should be brought to the attention of the audit committee and the board.

Exhibit 20-2
Policy Statement

It is the policy of this organization to establish and support an internal audit organization as an independent appraisal function to examine and evaluate organization activities as a service to management and the board of directors. The internal audit activity reports administratively to executive management and functionally to the audit committee of the board of directors. In carrying out their duties and responsibilities, members of the internal audit activity will have full, free, and unrestricted access to all organization activities, records, property, and personnel.

The primary objective of the internal audit activity is to assist members of management and the board in the effective discharge of their responsibilities. To this end, internal auditing will furnish them with analyses, recommendations, counsel, and information concerning the activities reviewed.

The missions of the internal audit activity are:

1. Review organizations within the entity at appropriate intervals to determine whether they are efficiently and effectively carrying out their functions of planning, organizing, directing, and controlling in accordance with management instructions, policies, and procedures, and in a manner that is consonant with both organization objectives and high standards of administrative practice.

2. Determine the adequacy and effectiveness of the organization's systems of internal accounting and operating controls.

3. Review the reliability and integrity of financial and operating information and the means used to identify, measure, classify, and report such information.

4. Review the established systems to ensure compliance with those policies, plans, procedures, laws, and regulations that could have a significant impact on operations and reports, and determine whether the organization is in compliance. Suggest policy where required.

5. Review the means of safeguarding assets and, as appropriate, verify the existence of such assets.

6. Appraise the economy and efficiency with which resources are employed, identify opportunities to improve operating performance, and recommend solutions to problems where appropriate.

7. Review operations and programs to ascertain whether results are consistent with established objectives and goals and whether the operations or programs are being carried out as planned.

8. Provide adequate follow-up to make sure that appropriate corrective action is taken and that it is effective.

9. Coordinate audit efforts with those of the organization's independent accountants.

Exhibit 20-2 (Cont.)

10. Participate in the planning, design, development, implementation, and operation of major computer-based systems to determine whether: (a) adequate controls are incorporated in the systems; (b) thorough system testing is performed at appropriate stages; (c) system documentation is complete and accurate; and (d) the needs of user organizations are met. Conduct periodic audits of computer service centers and make post-installation evaluations of major data processing systems to determine whether these systems meet their intended purposes and objectives.

11. Participate in the planning and performance of audits of potential acquisitions with the organization's outside accountants and other members of the corporate staff. Follow up to assure the proper accomplishment of the audit objectives.

12. Review compliance with the organization's guidelines for ethical business conduct and see that the highest standards of personal and corporate performance are met.

13. Submit annual audit plans to the president and the board of directors, including the audit committee, for their review and approval.

14. Report every quarter to the board of directors (the audit committee, if so directed) as to whether:

- Appropriate action has been taken on significant audit findings.
- Audit activities have been directed toward the highest exposures to risk and toward increasing efficiency, economy, and effectiveness of operations.
- Internal and external audits are coordinated so as to avoid duplications.
- Internal audit plans are adequate.
- There is any unwarranted restriction on the staffing and authority of the internal audit activity or on access by internal auditors to all organization activities, records, property, and personnel.

15. Report to those members of management who should be informed or who should take corrective action, the results of audit examinations, the audit opinions formed, and the recommendations made.

16. Evaluate any plans or actions taken to correct reported conditions for satisfactory disposition of audit findings. If the corrective action is considered unsatisfactory, hold further discussions to achieve acceptable disposition. The operating division manager is responsible for seeing that corrective action on reported weaknesses is either planned or taken within 30 days from receipt of a report disclosing those weaknesses. The division manager is also responsible for seeing that a written report of action planned or completed is sent to the executive vice president. If a plan for action is reported, a second report shall be made promptly upon completion of the plan.

17. Evaluate the activities of the outside auditors as to their independence and compliance with generally accepted auditing standards.

Emphasizing Enterprise Policy

Policy statements describe management's apparent intentions. They do not necessarily give them urgency or prove management's unequivocal support of the policy. This is especially true for the internal audit activity. Many operating managers still regard internal auditing as a minor checking function; they do not perceive it as an extension of senior management or as an available resource. So they must be educated to that end. For professional internal auditing to be effective, senior management and the board must make it abundantly clear that they rely upon and support the internal audit activity.

Many large organizations underscore their policy statements with communications explaining their internal audit function. Properly done, these communications can be highly effective. Here are some excerpts from a brochure on internal auditing distributed to all operating managers in a large multinational corporation. The brochure is introduced by the following statement.* This brochure will help you understand the role we expect the internal audit activity to perform in the organization.

> Business, with its complexities both domestic and foreign, complicated by many external requirements, requires a staff of professionals concerned with every aspect of corporate activity. This group supports both management and the audit committee of the board of directors in the performance of their duties.

> Working closely with Alcoa's independent public accountants, and by developing a program of auditing that is responsive to both risk and cost effectiveness, the internal audit activity's purpose is to perform objective, independent appraisals and report on the adequacy of all internal controls throughout the organization and its subsidiaries.

> You should consider internal audit an additional resource to aid in ensuring that your systems are functioning adequately, identifying problems and providing recommendations for your consideration. You can help the internal auditors help you by assuring their complete access to all records, personnel, and properties.

> I expect that you will do everything possible to facilitate this work. Use this service and join me in providing full support.

> (Signed)
> Chairman of the Board
> and Chief Executive Officer

*Excerpts, printed with permission, from a brochure published by The Aluminum Company of America.

The brochure goes on to provide information under a number of subjects about the internal audit function. The subjects and summaries of the statements about them are as follows:

Statement of responsibilities. Discusses the authority of the internal audit activity, the activities that are affected, the scope of the audits, the relationship with the independent public accountants, the meaning of internal control, the responsibility of the internal auditors with respect to fraud, the responsiveness to management requests for special studies, and the professional standards under which the internal audit activity functions.

Specific responsibilities. The activity is responsible for evaluating the adequacy and effectiveness of both financial and operating internal control systems, including all assets; information systems; propriety of procedures; and compliance with plans, policies, and procedures.

Organization. The activity's organization is worldwide. The reporting relationship shows a solid line to executive management and a dotted line to the audit committee of the board of directors.

Audit committee. The chief audit executive of the internal audit activity has free access to the audit committee. The committee's activities include reviewing internal audit plans and objectives and the results of audits performed.

Objectivity. Objectivity is assured through organizational structure, training, and careful assignment of personnel.

Scheduling/scope. Assessment of risk, previous audit coverage, significance of exceptions, and need for regular contact are the primary considerations in audit scheduling. The scope of audit is adjusted to provide in-depth reviews in some activities and overviews in others. Audit scope is expanding because of government laws and regulations and management's growing responsibility to provide more specific information and to make this unique discipline available to all activities, not only the financial and regulatory areas.

Planning/execution. This portion of the brochure lists the common elements of an audit, from pre-audit announcement to closeout conference.

Audit reviews. Adequate communication between auditors and operating personnel is important. To that end, audit results are reviewed at the conclusion of audits to make sure that audit recommendations are based on factual information and are understood.

Audit reports. The audit reports, including executive summaries, are designed to communicate suggested improvements and operating management plans for their implementation; hence, they are jointly issued by the auditors and the managers of the functions audited.

Relationship with independent public accountants. The difference between the responsibilities of the internal and external auditors is explained as well as the means of coordinating the work of both.

Development/training/growth. Continuing education for the internal auditors is recommended and certification in internal auditing, accounting, and other appropriate areas is encouraged.

The future. To meet the challenge of change, internal auditors must demonstrate flexibility and provide constant review of the programs to produce a better product. The input of operating managers to that end is solicited.

The brochure seeks to remove the mystery from the internal audit activity and to prevent any potentially adversarial relationships with clients. The demonstrated support from management is the underpinning for a successful internal audit activity. Without it, auditing becomes a matter of grace to be accepted or rejected by management. With it, auditing becomes binding upon management, ensuring action when called for. Acceptance must be earned, of course; but the opportunity to earn it will not exist without a clear mandate from the highest management level in the organization, setting forth its support of the audit effort.

Drafting Job Descriptions

Statements of function and responsibility and management directives set the stage for the chief audit executives and provide the arena in which they will function. But they cannot function effectively without the right staff. The audit staff must therefore have adequate status in the organization in terms of hierarchical positions and salary grades. In most organizations, salary review boards set salary grades, making their determinations largely by reviewing job descriptions.

The job descriptions for the various levels may have a significant impact on the auditing organization. Modern internal auditing demands the highest level of audit effort. Only the best auditors perform successfully and carry out the promise that is held forth to management by the progressive chief audit executive. It has been abundantly demonstrated that it is much better to perform the internal audit function with fewer competent staff auditors than with many mediocre ones. Indeed the function will not be accomplished without people of intelligence, intuition, imagination, and initiative — to say nothing of understanding and the ability to deal with others. People with these qualities come high in the marketplace.

For this reason, the job descriptions should be drafted with care. They should set forth requirements that can be accomplished only by the best, not just average, auditors. Such descriptions will warrant the assignment of salary that will attract the best people, not only from the marketplace but from within the enterprise itself.

In large audit organizations with far-flung operations and locations, the hierarchy of jobs is usually:

1. Chief audit executive.
2. Manager.
3. Senior supervisor.
4. Supervisor.
5. Staff.

A typical description of the chief audit executive's function was presented earlier in Exhibit 20-1. Examples of job descriptions for the remaining positions, each a composite of several, are shown in Exhibits 20-3 through 20-5.

Exhibit 20-3
Position Description
Internal Auditing — Manager

Purpose

To administer the internal auditing activity of an assigned location or operation.

To develop a comprehensive, practical program of audit coverage for the assigned location or operation.

To accomplish the program in accordance with acceptable audit standards and stipulated schedules.

To maintain effective working relations with executive and operating management.

Authority and Responsibility

Within the general guidelines provided by the chief audit executive:

Prepares a comprehensive, long-range schedule of audit coverage for the location or operation to which assigned.

Identifies those activities subject to audit coverage, evaluates their significance, and assesses the degree of risk inherent in the activity in terms of cost, schedule, and quality.

Establishes the related activity structure.

Obtains, maintains, and directs an audit staff capable of accomplishing the internal audit function.

Assigns audit areas, staff, and budget to supervisory auditors.

Develops a system of cost and schedule control over audit projects.

Establishes standards of performance and, by review, determines that performance meets the standards.

Provides executive management within the assigned location or operation with reports on audit coverage and the results of the audit activity, and interprets those results so as to improve the audit schedule and the audit coverage.

Establishes and monitors accomplishment of objectives directed toward increasing the internal audit activity's ability to serve management.

Exhibit 20-4
Position Description
Internal Auditing — Supervisor

Purpose
To develop a comprehensive, practical program of audit coverage for assigned areas of audit.
To supervise the activities of auditors assigned to the review of various organizational and functional activities.
To ensure conformance with acceptable audit standards, plans, budgets, and schedules.
To maintain effective working relations with operating management.
To provide for and conduct research, develop manuals and training guides.

Authority and Responsibility
Under the general guidance of an internal auditing manager:
Supervises the work of auditors engaged in the reviews of organizational and functional activities.
Provides a comprehensive, practical schedule of annual audit coverage within general areas assigned by the internal auditing manager.
Determines areas of risk and appraises their significance in relation to operational factors of cost, schedule, and quality. Classifies audit projects as to degree of risk and significance and as to frequency of audit coverage.
Provides for flexibility in audit schedules so as to be responsive to management's special needs.
Schedules projects and staff assignments so as to comply with management's needs within the scope of the activity's overall schedule.
Coordinates the program with the organization's public accountant.
Reviews and approves the purpose, scope, and audit approach of each audit project for assigned areas of audit cognizance.
Directs audit projects to see that professional standards are maintained in the planning and execution and in the accumulation of evidentiary data.
Counsels and guides auditors to see that the approved audit objectives are met and that adequate, practical coverage is achieved.
Reviews and edits audit reports and, in organizations with the auditor-in-charge for the assigned project, discusses the reports with appropriate management.
Presents oral briefing to branch-level management.
Provides for and performs research on audit techniques.
Provides formal plans for the recruiting, selecting, training, evaluating, and supervising of staff personnel. Develops manuals and other training aids.
Accumulates data, maintains records, and prepares reports on the administration of audit projects and other assigned activities.
Identifies factors causing deficient conditions and recommends courses of action to improve the conditions, including special surveys and audits.
Provides for a flow of communication from operating management to the manager and to the chief audit executive.
Assists in evaluating overall results of the audits.

Exhibit 20-5
Position Description
Internal Auditor — Senior Supervisor

Purpose

To conduct reviews of assigned organizational and functional activities.

To evaluate the adequacy and effectiveness of the management controls over those activities.

To determine whether organizational units in the organization are performing their planning, accounting, custodial, or control activities in compliance with management instructions, applicable statements of policy and procedures, and in a manner consistent with both organization objectives and high standards of administrative practice.

To plan and execute audits in accordance with accepted standards.

To report audit findings, and to make recommendations for correcting unsatisfactory conditions, improving operations, and reducing cost.

To perform special reviews at the request of management.

To direct the activities of assistants.

Authority and Responsibility

Under the general guidance of a supervising auditor:

Surveys functions and activities in assigned areas to determine the nature of operations and the adequacy of the system of control to achieve established objectives.

Determines the direction and thrust of the proposed audit effort.

Plans the theory and scope of the audit, and prepares an audit program.

Determines the auditing procedures to be used, including statistical sampling and the use of electronic data processing equipment.

Identifies the key control points of the system.

Evaluates a system's effectiveness through the application of a knowledge of business systems, including financial, manufacturing, engineering, procurement, and other operations, and an understanding of auditing techniques.

Recommends necessary staff required to complete the audit.

Performs the audit in a professional manner and in accordance with the approved audit program.

Obtains, analyzes, and appraises evidentiary data as a base for an informed, objective opinion on the adequacy and effectiveness of the system and the efficiency of performance of the activities being reviewed.

Directs, counsels, and instructs staff assistants assigned to the audit, and reviews their work for sufficiency of scope and for accuracy.

Makes oral or written presentations to management during and at the conclusion of the examination, discussing deficiencies and recommending corrective action to improve operations and reduce cost.

Prepares formal written reports, expressing opinions on the adequacy and effectiveness of the system and the efficiency with which activities are carried out.

Appraises the adequacy of the corrective action taken to improve deficient conditions.

The Audit Activity Structure and Strategy

The Audit Organization

Most internal audit activities are divided into two or three segments. One segment is the line organization that comprises the auditors, supervisors, and managers who perform the audits: the field work, planning, supervision, client contacts, and report preparation. The other segment consists of two parts — administration and support. In some audit organizations they are combined. In smaller internal audit activities these two parts may be vested in the chief audit executive and possibly an assistant. Following is a brief outline of the functions included in each part of the segment:

- Administrative
  — Chief audit executive
  — Audit assistant executive
  — Personnel director

- Support

  Specialized staff
  — Policy and procedures
  — Information systems specialists
  — Actuarial specialists
  — Report processing (editing, illustrations, audiovisual)
  — Special staff coordinator (outsourcing and cosourcing)
  — Tax specialists

  Service staff
  — Financial (budgeting, accounting, asset control)
  — Payroll
  — Travel
  — Library (periodicals, books, information systems)

The operational segment of the audit organization is also frequently divided into parts. These parts relate to various classifications based on the subject matter of the audit. Examples are:

- Type of audit
  — Financial
  — Performance
  — Compliance

- Function
  - Purchasing
  - Production
  - Marketing

- Product
  - Product A
  - Product B
  - Product C

- Organization
  - Organization X
  - Organization Y
  - Organization Z

- Geographically
  - New York
  - Illinois
  - California

For audits of activities in all but the type of auditing, the staff should be multi-dimensionally experts. The specialization aspect of the other classifications results in knowledge of the operational aspects of the specialized area. However, unless there is periodic staff rotation, there is a tendency to become too familiar with the subject matter and to accept unusual situations rather than retaining a questioning approach. This also could result in accepting inefficiencies and ineffectiveness because, "it has always been that way," rather than questioning whether there is a better way to perform.

A New Organization Strategy[1]

Current trends regarding internal auditing organizations can be characterized as flattening the operation. There are several reasons for this:

1. The elimination of the supervisory levels needed for the "silo type function."
2. There is generally a shorter interim period between the end of the field work and report issuance.
3. There is a closer personal interrelation between the internal auditor and the client.
4. The internal audit staff becomes more knowledgeable as to the client operations and functions.

Also, the silo type organization uses staff who are specialists in specific types of auditing, e.g., financial, information systems, performance, etc. With the current innovational type of audit organization, auditors are trained to become relatively expert to all applicable audit elements. This concept does not preclude the use of activity specialists or outsourcing or cosourcing assistance for the auditing of important unique areas of operation.

An innovation of this arrangement is the use of a pool type of audit organization. Here, one or more pools are maintained. Auditors are drawn from the pool for specific audits. Coordination with clients is effected by supervisors who become client liaison on a permanent basis, thus giving clients a specific contact person for all audit problems. The pool concept endeavors to develop auditors who have broad general knowledge so that the client can look to an auditor to perform a balanced review of the work being reviewed. Also, the supervisors are trained well enough to allow them to review the draft reports and to issue them. Another group of audit managers are responsible for implementing strategic initiatives such as: control self-assessment, risk assessment best practices, audit automation, and auditing large enterprise systems within the organization.

The use of the pool arrangement results in a situation where the audit staff do not have a supervisor who is responsible for their intellectual and professional progress as well as their career progress. Thus, a mentoring program is used where a mentor — a senior staff member — is given this responsibility.

Several problems can be anticipated as a result of instituting this organizational strategy:

1. The competition in staff scheduling from the pools.
2. The clarity of supervisory roles.
3. Training in all of the areas where the staff is expected to perform.

Plans should be made to anticipate and accommodate these problems as a part of the strategy development.

Types of Auditing

Process Auditing

The evolution of subject matter internal auditing has progressed from the verification of the accountability of feudal lords and clerical officials to today's concepts of performance auditing and control self-assessment. There is another aspect of auditing that is capturing the imagination — and indeed the attention of progressive internal auditing shops.

This auditing approach is process auditing. Currently many internal audit activities are auditing products, organizations, financial accounts, or geographical locations of activity. This method is to audit processes. This audit cuts across organizational lines, geographical areas, and service units. The intent is to determine the status of the primary functions that are the major processes that comprise the entire organization.

The idea is not new. A similar internal audit pattern was used by the U.S. Atomic Energy Commission in the early 1950s. It was called "functional auditing" and the objective was the same — to determine the status of various functions within the Commission. The functions included purchasing, management of capital assets, budget formulation and execution, receiving and inspection, inventory management and warehousing, and the usual financial operations among others. There were 17 functions. The Commission had about 10 internal audit staffs throughout the country and when one of these functions was scheduled, all 10 of the staffs performed the audit based on a common program.

There is a difference between these functions or processes and the supporting operations such as cash management, accounts receivable, accounts payable, and payroll. Both types of audits can be scheduled; however, a modular program for the audit of supporting functions can be fit into many of the processes. These modular units that are interchangeable are programs that relate essentially to financial integrity and the presence of efficient and effective controls from a materiality standpoint. The processes are of the greatest importance because they are the activities that make the organization operate. The processes are simply the supporting functions; the integral activities that make the processes operative. An example:

Audit – Management of Capital Assets

Process Elements	Supporting Elements
Determination of Need	Management Budget Justification
Availability of Resources	Cash Management – Personnel, etc.
Acquisition of Assets	Accounts Payable – Cash Management
Utilization	Specific Surveys
Maintenance	Maintenance
Disposition	Surplus – Scrap – Accounts Receivable

The concept of controls varies also between processes and supporting audit areas. In the former, the controls are related to achievement of objectives, efficiency, and economy of operation. The controls and the supporting elements are related to fiscal propriety, although they also have elements of efficiency and effectiveness. There is basically the degree of importance and materiality of the former.

How would such an internal audit activity be organized? It is reasonable to believe that each process would have its own internal audit executive with an operational audit staff. These staffs would receive support from the office of a vice president for internal auditing, to whom the "process internal audit executives" would report. However, the internal audit report would be issued in a decentralized fashion by the respective internal audit supervisor.

Some of the benefits of this process auditing are:

- Internal audit reports normally relate to major activities of the organization; those that are essential to surviving and growing and of interest to top management.

- Familiarity of the internal audit staff with the process operations.

- A structure where internal audit findings are brought to senior management's attention. Less material findings are separately reported to responsible client management and to a lower tier of top management.

- There is a continuity of internal audit supervision so that client management has a focus point for the resolution of internal auditing issues. Also, the auditing activity provides a source to contact for advice and consultation relative to problems in the process.

- The decentralization and downsizing produces audit reports issued promptly after the completion of field work.

- A means of implementing less material findings relative to supporting activities at a lower level of support management.

- A cohesion between the internal audit staff and the process personnel developing into a unity of objective, the well-being and productivity of the process.

Online Auditing

In the normal evaluation of the processing of transactions through information systems operations, it became effective to establish what were called "edits." Systems were programmed to identify transactions that did not conform to established rules of procedures, or that exceeded certain limits. These exceptions were called to the attention of responsible workers who resolved the problems or who approved or modified the transaction.

This technique has been expanded to the point where the computer is actually auditing transactions as they are processed. An example of this is a situation where imbedded artificial intelligence serves as a review of specific processes. For example, in reviewing accounts receivables, a program could be set up that contained a series of variables or combinations of variables that would be used to evaluate accounts receivables charge-offs. Some of the variables might include:

- Age of the receivable.

- Evidence of collection letters.

- Evidence of attorney correspondence.

- Type of merchandise or service.

- Approvals of the charge-off.

- Amount of the charge-off.

- Other charge-offs with similar profiles.

Thus, the information system can be used to identify on a "by-difference" basis items that should be investigated and that do not conform to the normal configuration of the transaction or process. The online audit operations would be ongoing and would audit continuously. The artificial intelligence could also point to where the weak point in the controls existed and could even suggest a probable malefactor.

Value-added Concept

Senior management is interested in productivity in all functions and operations. This interest is also extended to internal auditing operations. In many organizations the auditing is traditional cyclical auditing that provides assurance that operations are compliant with procedures and policies and that controls are in place and are effective. However, the audits in may cases do not identify changes that could be made that would be cost effective, result in greater productivity, or help the organization operate more effectively.

The Institute of Internal Auditors, in considering the status of its current audit standards, convened a task force to provide guidance to The IIA's management and its Board of Directors. This task force emphasized the concept of "value added" in its discussions and believes that this concept should influence any planned restructuring of the standards.

This is not to say that the concept is totally new. The original *Standards* that were in effect until January 1, 2002, provided in the scope of general standards that the auditor should pay attention to the characteristics of efficiency and effectiveness. These characteristics have a direct impact on the adding of value to the organization's operations. Also, the practice of participative auditing that entails working directly with the client infer that this collaborative effort will enhance the client operation and thus "add value" to it.

We are also aware of many internal audit activities that function as an interchange of personnel from operating units of the organization. This migration of skilled operating personnel into the audit organization and the transfer of management-oriented internal auditors to operating units serve to stimulate the concepts of "how to do it better." This activity has been in effect for many years and has resulted in important contributions from the internal auditing activity.

However, an article by Gary Stern provides more detailed guidance resulting from a survey of several internal auditing activities.[2] Quoted from his article, the guidance is:

1. Become a catalyst for change.

2. Make auditing more collaborative.

3. Use self-assessment to buy-in.

4. Bring business staff into auditing.

5. Concentrate on business risk.

6. Aim to increase profits.

7. Attack problem areas, such as health-care costs.

8. Share technology with business units.

9. Align with customers.

10. Issue audit-advisories company wide.

11. Conduct preventive auditing.

12. Reduce external auditor costs.

13. Place auditors in special assignments.

14. Get the audit report out fast.

15. Go back to basics.

Though the concept is not new, the awakening interest of management on the potential contribution by the audit activity is. This does not portend an abandonment of financial audit activities nor attention to the effectiveness of controls, especially in areas of substantial risks, but it does awaken the audit staff to the need to become a prime factor in evaluating the organization's well-being.

Developing Audit Manuals

Chief audit executives communicate to their staff through audit manuals. These manuals instruct staff auditors how audit operations should be carried out. They provide for stability, continuity, standards of acceptable performance, and the means of coordinating the efforts of people or units within the auditing organization. But in modern internal auditing, the audit executive faces a dilemma: On the one hand is the need to provide instruction and to achieve uniformity in the organization. On the other is the possibility of inhibiting imagination and innovative auditing.

Despite the dangers of stifling independent thinking, however, the staff needs guidance to: (1) prevent individuals from going off in different and inconsistent directions; (2) establish standards that lift the level of performance; and (3) provide some assurance that the auditing activity's final product meets the executive's standards.

The audit activity's statements of policies and procedures must provide instructions and guidelines in several different areas. For convenience, this body of instructions to audit staff may be divided into the following groupings.

- Technical functions — seeing that the job of conducting internal audits meets acceptable standards.

- Administrative functions — seeing that the internal audit activity, as a unit, runs smoothly.

- Miscellaneous functions — providing answers to the complete spectrum of day-to-day problems that arise in the audit activity.

The audit manuals are a mirror of the philosophy of the individual audit activity and its executive. The manual in each audit organization, therefore, will be uniquely structured to carry out the ideas of the individual who charts the activity's course. Consideration also must be given to the structure of the activity, its size, and the complexity of the work performed. Instructions within small activities will obviously be less formal and extensive than those for large ones.

Technical Functions

The technical audit manual will guide the performance of an internal audit. Without limiting the matters that may properly be included, the following subjects are among those that should be considered to show in general how audits should be carried out.

Objectives of the audit. Establish the scope of the audit project so that an audit program can be written that will achieve the objective and that will delineate the audit area and normally prevent wandering off into avenues that are irrelevant to the central theme of the audit.

Theory of the audit. Establish the audit approach. Shall it be a review of an organization or of a function? What are the auditors trying to establish or accomplish? Is the idea to make a survey with little testing, or is it to select certain risk-prone functions for detailed examination? Are the auditors seeking to determine the degree to which the existing structure is effective or do they want to know whether established procedures are being carried out?

Scope of the audit. Describe audit scope. Will this be a compliance review to see if the rules, procedures, regulations, and laws are followed? Or will it be a management-oriented review where the following types of questions will be explored:

- Have responsibilities been adequately assigned?

- Is authority commensurate with responsibility?

- Have organizational or functional objectives been set?

- Do reports to higher management show progress in meeting established objectives?

- Are methods and procedures (systems of control) designed to help meet those objectives?

- Has the organization set measures of efficiency and effectiveness?

- Are objectives actually being met?

- Does management have a self-checking system to highlight deviations from acceptable performance?

Preliminary reviews. Provide guides on the matters to be considered in the initial phase of the audit: the review of prior working papers, the research of internal auditing literature on the activity to be reviewed, and the examination of organization charts, correspondence, and relevant organization reports and directives.

Preliminary discussions. Identify the levels of management where preliminary discussions should be held, the nature of the assistance the auditors may offer to management, and the explanations they should make of the audit objectives, approaches, and programs.

Preliminary surveys. Indicate the nature of the preliminary survey, the kind of information to be obtained, the ways in which it can be obtained, and the uses of the information (see Chapter 4).

Audit programs. Present the requirements for each segment of the audit program so as to be tailored to the particular assignment to determine operating objectives and related controls. Also, show the detail with which the programs should be prepared. Show the relationship to risk assessment and to the preliminary survey.

Budgets and schedules. Describe the controls to be exercised over the audit project to assist in the compliance with budget and schedule constraints.

Working papers. Establish standards for the structure of working papers, for methods of summarizing data, for indexing and cross-referencing work sheets, and for appropriate reviews.

Procedure for reviews with clients. Set forth policies on reviews of findings, obtaining corrective action, the evidence of corrective action needed to close a finding, and the levels at which findings should be discussed.

Report writing. Provide guidelines on the format of reports, their length, the philosophy of reporting (problems only, or comprehensive analysis of and opinions on the activity reviewed), and the levels of management to which reports should be directed.

Replies to reports. Provide instruction on how to deal with replies, what action to take if they are not acceptable, and how to close reports in which the internal auditor finds the replies acceptable.

Administrative Functions

Another volume of instructions is needed to provide guidance on those matters that are related to the business of performing internal audit engagements, but that are not an actual part of their performance. A separate manual, usually referred to as the administrative manual, is easier to handle. If combined with the audit manual, it tends to become unwieldy. The administrative manual often takes the form of a compilation of staff memos, each of which can be issued or revised whenever desired. Matters that can be the subject of staff memos are:

A. Administration
   1. Organization of the audit activity
   2. Audit office filing system
   3. Reference library
   4. Supplies
   5. Time reports
   6. Housekeeping
   7. Security requirements
   8. Miscellaneous correspondence
   9. Periodic administrative reports

B. Personnel
   1. Methods of recruiting
   2. Personnel records
   3. Code of conduct (may be a separate publication)
   4. Travel instructions and expense reports
   5. Staff evaluations
   6. Incentive awards
   7. Reporting injuries
   8. Jury duty
   9. Military duty
   10. Separation procedures

C. Audit Projects
   1. Assignment of the audit project
   2. Human relations — dealing with the client
   3. Permanent files for audit projects
   4. Budget estimates for audit projects
   5. Requests for program revisions or budget adjustments
   6. Uses of statistical sampling
   7. Uses of computers on audit projects (may be a separate publication)
   8. Preparation of and safeguarding working papers
   9. Destroying working papers
   10. Exit interviews with clients
   11. Closing audit projects

D. Audit Reports
   1. Interim or progress reports
   2. Supervisory review of audit reports
   3. Proofreading, reference checking, and processing final reports
   4. Distributing audit reports
   5. Requests for copies of audit reports

6. Report filing and retention
7. Handling classified audit material

Miscellaneous Functions

Auditors, like most other employees, are bombarded with many instructions over and above those appearing in the technical and administrative manuals. These instructions may amplify, explain, or restrict statements in those manuals or they may cover matters not germane to the information in technical and administrative regulations. But whatever their relationship, these instructions appear in an unending stream.

Usually, they are found in memoranda, formal or informal, from the audit executive's office. And since they were created by the same pen that wrote or approved the manuals, they generally have the same force and effect and require the same adherence.

Unfortunately, miscellaneous instructions, like comets, usually blaze across the departmental sky and then fall to rest in some correspondence file. There they lie to be revived only when they have been violated and are used to bludgeon the violator, or when they are vaguely remembered and take hours to locate. All such instructions, therefore, should be kept in an organized manner, capable of ready retrieval, in a miscellaneous manual.

The manual should be compiled and maintained so that: (1) only matters of continuing significance are included; (2) it is periodically and formally updated to incorporate new information and to delete superseded instructions; (3) the referencing system provides for easy revisions, additions, and deletions; and (4) the index is complete, easy to maintain, and permits prompt retrieval of information. With the advent of personal computers, these matters can be delivered in electronic form and thus be readily accessible to each auditor.

Clearly, each audit activity's miscellaneous manual will be different, and no strict format or table of contents can be devised to be universally applicable. One for a manufacturing organization would bear no recognizable relation to one for an insurance organization.

Each memorandum or instruction should be separately numbered according to the numbering system of the contents. For example, a memorandum providing information on how to budget for research projects might be numbered G.2.1. A subsequent memorandum setting forth budgeting for employee indoctrination might be numbered G.2.2, and so forth.

Marketing the Internal Audit Function

Nobody likes a critic. And in many organizations both managers and workers regard the internal auditor as the resident critic and hence the enemy. This makes for difficult audits; and so auditors should heed the old adage that the best way to destroy an enemy is to make him or her one's friend. Where the proposed friend is an internal auditor, that will take a good deal of marketing; but in the long range it is worth it. What follows are some thoughts on marketing internal auditing as a management-oriented resource, not a bean-counting or detective type of exercise:

Marketing Methods

Mann gives us some ideas on marketing the internal audit function.[3]

Brochures. An easily read nontechnical booklet can go a long way toward removing the mystery and hence the fear from internal auditing. One such brochure, sent to all operating managers, was described earlier in this chapter.

Bulletins/newsletters. Bulletins can highlight urgent, current findings. Newsletters can be anecdotal and hence easily understood without getting into internal audit jargon.

Organization publications. These often include human interest stories on employees. And a well-written story might be accepted and useful in showing the human side of internal auditors.

Organization programs. Many organizations sponsor civic or charitable activities. Helping to lead one of these will present internal auditors in a favorable light.

Open house/open door. Hosting an open house lets internal auditors meet operating personnel under relaxed circumstances.

Client vs. auditee. In both written and oral statements it is preferable to refer to the people being audited as "clients" or "customers."

Advisory board. To develop an interchange of information about organization reorganizations, changes, and developments, develop an advisory board of operating managers, chaired by the chief audit executive. Subjects discussed could relate to risk exposures and potential problems. The board is advisory only but can augment the approach to what and when to audit.

Preaudit meeting. Give greater care and thought to the preaudit meeting to use it as a way of explaining internal auditing and its true function — one that is more than the mysterious resident critic.

Risk-rating. This has generally been regarded as a one-dimension, internal audit function. But by promoting liaisons between internal auditors and selected operating people, it can be developed into a problem-solving partnership.

Postaudit questionnaire. Properly used, the questionnaire can be a valuable quality assurance tool. Client opinions can help fine-tune the audit process.

Client training. This can include courses for client personnel and a period of actually working in the internal audit activity for top-level new hires who are destined for management positions. This can offer hands-on training in assessing internal controls and valuable experience when the trainees take on the jobs they were hired for.

Quality programs. Internal auditors can be in the forefront of the quality quest sweeping the country. Audit reports receive wide distribution in the organization and should be quality-oriented to foster the attitude of doing it right the first time.

Leadership

Internal auditors have the reputation of cleaning up after the parade, not leading it. Leadership is not generally considered to be among the attributes of an internal auditor. But this is not necessarily true. It is a matter of attitude. And the verification-oriented role can be augmented by a leadership style if auditors are convinced of the capabilities within them.

A leadership temperament is as essential to the professional internal auditor as it is to a dynamic manager. Not only can it change the way internal auditors think and act, but it also can change others' perception of them. The qualities of leadership attributed to successful managers are shared by professional internal auditors: Intelligence . . .emotional maturity. . .initiative . . . communicative skills . . .confidence . . .perceptiveness.[4]

In identifying difficult problems, communicating them understandably, maintaining poise and confidence in their professional abilities, exhibiting perceptiveness in suggesting solutions to problems, and showing a mature understanding of what is good for the enterprise as a whole, internal auditors can readily demonstrate leadership qualities. If they convey those qualities with self-assurance to their clients and to top management, they are revealing the attributes of leaders and not followers.

Creativity

Creativity is not reserved to scientists and artists. It is employed in the business world all the time. It is sorely needed and can be developed. The days when internal auditors pointed to a problem and then walked away are gone. Now they are expected to be part of the solution. And they are fully capable of applying creativity to their daily tasks. Creativity can be fostered by:[5]

Skepticism. Refusing to accept existing practices as the ultimate and always reaching for something better.

Analysis. Analyzing activities and operations to determine their components and dynamics.

Amalgamation. Combining information to transform separate concepts into something new and better.

The Problem-solving Partnership

Include the client in the audit process. This can be done through pre-audit internal control questionnaires for the client to answer, a practice that has proved effective. By following the questionnaire, the client can identify problems even before the internal auditor. The process can also be accomplished by discussions that are problem oriented and that are participative in tenor. In many cases corrective action is begun before the audit is completed. Although significant findings are included in the audit report, the auditors give the client full credit for improving the operations.

This partnership goes a long way toward establishing the internal auditor as a working partner and a valuable resource, not as the enemy/critic.[6]

Further Concerns

The chief audit executive must keep up with what concerns the enterprise and be able to deal with emerging problems. The environment is an example. Environmental issues are creating enormous risk exposures. And where there is a risk to the enterprise, internal auditors have a vested interest. Many internal auditors are taking steps to examine how best to identify environmental risks and bring them to the attention of management.

In a 1992 Institute of Internal Auditors Research Foundation study, *The Role of Internal Auditors in Environmental Issues,* several environmental issues were examined, including definition of terms, U.S. and international environmental auditing trends, management practices, and regulations.[7] This subject is covered in Chapter 26.

Along those lines, Kamlet identifies for internal auditors some management-level commandments dealing with environmental problems. These can be used in determining whether management has properly dealt with the environmental issue.[8]

1. Scrutinize current waste management practices in the light of future liability implications.

2. Check to be sure that the client avoids spillage of waste to the environment, and when it occurs, cleans it up properly.

3. Make sure that there are federal or state discharge permits that address *all* pollutants with the potential to accumulate and persist in the environment.

4. Determine that there is integrated environmental management through clear lines of responsibility, accountability, and communication, including reporting necessary information timely to management.

5. Determine if there are inventories of waste streams to account for all outputs of waste.

6. Don't neglect to consider routine air and water permits.

7. Be sure that the client is a cautious participant in real estate transactions to make sure the organization is not buying property that contains leaking underground storage tanks, buried waste, asbestos materials, and the like.

8. Determine if there is filling in of wetlands without the proper permits.

9. Make sure that the organization is taking an orderly, systematic approach to identifying, evaluating, and controlling processes that involve hazardous chemicals.

10. Encourage the use of environmental compliance requirements as a means of gaining market advantage.

In many organizations environmental issues are attacked quite seriously. In one organization the chief audit executive sent eight of his auditors to a local university to become thoroughly aware of those issues and how to deal with them.

Outsourcing/Cosourcing

Outsourcing is generally defined as contracting out the internal audit or other function to others who are not employees of the organization. It can come in three forms:[9]

1. To supplement existing internal audit work, for example, to hire contract auditors for remote locations where language expertise is needed, or to add such expertise as EDP or environmental auditing. This activity is traditionally called outsourcing.

2. For audit consultation, where the existing public accountant is asked to help management define specific risk areas. This activity is sometimes known as cosourcing.

3. To replace the existing internal audit function, or to provide part-time internal audit work for small or mid-sized organizations. This activity is sometimes known as cosourcing.

The reasons for outsourcing are varied:[10]

1. An organization wants to start an internal audit function and wants immediate service.

2. The organization has an unpopular or ineffective internal audit function.

3. Management may perceive some audit time, such as training or juniors waiting to be assigned to a project as unproductive.

4. Small audit groups may not be able to afford adequate or effective training.

5. Small organizations do not see the need for a full-time audit staff.

6. A vacancy in the audit director position may disrupt operations and give management a reason to end an internal audit function.

7. Expertise is needed for a specific audit function.

There are both advantages and disadvantages to outsourcing, despite the opprobrium it attracts from professional internal auditors. For example:[11]

Advantages:

1. Contract auditors may be more independent and not affected by office politics.

2. Limited internal audit needs are less expensive.

3. Cost becomes a variable instead of a constant.

4. Using outside contractors can provide greater flexibility (subject and location).

5. Outsourcing is often performed by reputable professionals who can provide a reasonable degree of quality.

Disadvantages:

1. Internal auditors are more loyal to the organization.

2. They have a greater familiarity with the environment.

3. Internal audit departments provide a training ground for future operating managers.

4. Outsourcing lacks the long-range development that a stable internal audit activity provides. If executive management or the audit committee of the board does not have the requisite appreciation of internal auditing, the long-range focus could be limited.

One of the major public accounting firms has developed the concept of "cosourcing." It envisions situations where a well-conducted internal audit organization seeks assistance for a particular type of audit effort; several of which are described above. The "cosource" auditors will operate under the direction of the established audit directorate.

Chief audit executives must keep a lookout for the specter of outsourcing. For if it strikes them unexpectedly, they have only themselves to blame. Any internal audit activity that has failed to meet professional standards may be inviting its own replacement.[12] All internal audit executives should take a periodic look at their operations and see if they meet the kinds of critical success factors that will ensure tenure in the organization. Dymoski and Saake suggest some criteria that may be used for the self-evaluation of the internal audit activity.[13]

1. Human Resources
   a. Recruiting process
   b. Training
   c. Career development
   d. Leadership
       • Professionalism
       • Teamwork
       • Communication
   e. Image
       • Certification
       • Foreign language capabilities
       • Turnover/opportunities
       • Experience level

2. Audit Approach
   a. Communication with clients
   b. Industry knowledge
   c. Audit orientation (financial vs. operational)
   d. Audit risk — assessment process
   e. Value-added services
   f. Flexibility

3. Evolving Technologies
   a. Working paper automation
   b. Computer-assisted audit tools

   c. Audit retrievals
   d. New technology

4. Administration
   a. Audit plan/schedule
   b. Eliminating non-value added activities
   c. Coordination with external auditors
   d. Budgeting

Quality Mission Statements

Quality mission statements proclaim where audit executives are or should be heading. These can elevate auditing in the eyes of management and the board by demonstrating high resolve, quality, and professionalism.

Here are examples of mission statements that were developed by Alcoa and by Johnson & Johnson's internal audit activities:

Alcoa:*

Alcoa's internal audit team is dedicated to creating value through quality in satisfying the needs of a broad range of customers by providing:

- An objective and professional evaluation of the company's worldwide system of internal controls.

- Recommendations and advice on improvement in control systems, business processes, and the economical use of resources.

- The most cost-effective coordination of the audit effort with the company's independent public accountants.

- Significant training and development activities to enhance the personal and professional growth of our people in preparation for future opportunities.

*Used with the permission of Alcoa's Audit Team.

Johnson & Johnson:[14]

Our vision is excellence in fulfilling our responsibilities to our customers and leadership in our profession. Our goal is to create an environment that fosters:

- Leadership

We lead our profession in the use of technology, and will continue to update our audit approach for changes in the global business environment so that we can provide the corporation with quality audits. We create a participative environment that challenges our staff and allows it to fully utilize their talents.

- Image

We exemplify the highest degree of trust and integrity continually upholding the principles of our CREDO and professional standards. We are recognized for our professionalism and commitment to excellence in serving our customers. In return, we are respected and viewed as a source of highly trained and talented individuals for the Johnson & Johnson Family of Companies.

- Risk Taking

We encourage initiative and risk taking. We profit from a diversity of ideas. Recognition is bestowed on those who are innovative and accept responsibility for their actions. Mistakes are considered challenges from which we learn.

- Quality

We excel in everything we do by practicing the QUALITY IMPROVEMENT PROCESS. We enrich the activity's performance by delivering quality services and information to all our customers.

- Teamwork

Mutual respect, trust, and teamwork are a must! United we are the best activity ever by capitalizing on our strengths.

Acquisition and Evaluation of External Audit Services

The chief audit executive should serve the audit committee and the general management of the organization as an expert in the acquisition of external audit services and in the evaluation of these services relative to their compliance with generally accepted auditing procedures. Although the board, through its audit committee, normally bears the responsibility for the acquisition of these services, the chief audit executive should provide the technical and specialized knowledge to assist in this process. Practice Advisory 2050-2, "Acquisition of External Audit Services," recommends that this assistance include:

- Participation as a member of the selection team.
- Recommendation of criteria to be used in the selection process.
- Evaluation of fees.
- Identification of regulating or other governing requirements that should be considered.

The external audit services may include services, in addition to financial auditing, such as tax consulting, specialized internal audit cosourcing, valuation, appraisal, and actuarial services, legal work, and other temporary specialized activities.

The chief audit executive and appropriate staff should be used for: (1) the original provision of selection criteria; (2) the screening process; (3) the evaluation of candidates' attributes; and (4) the selection of recommended services to be used. The chief audit executive should also be used to monitor the work of the external auditors and should serve as an advisor to the audit committee and the board as to independence and the quality of technical services provided.

Responsibility for Non-audit Functions

In many organizations, both business and nonprofit, including government, internal auditors have provided a ready source of service for needed activities that are non-audit, operational, or general service. These assignments make sense to management and frequently are pressure oriented due to exigencies of the operation. They usually are emergencies but they also can result from the fact that the internal audit activity is not directly in the audited operational chain of the organization.

However, these assignments can impair the objectivity or independence of the internal audit activity especially when the assigned duties are related to operations that may be subject to normal internal auditing assessments. Practice Advisory 1130.A1-2, "Internal Audit Responsibility for Other (Non-Audit) Functions," cites the *Code of Ethics* and the *Standards* as requiring, in these cases, independence and objectivity and it recommends that the internal auditors:

- Avoid, if possible, the assignment.
- Disclose the potential impairment of independence and objectivity to appropriate parties.
- Consider that objectivity is impaired if the auditor provided assurance services within the previous year.
- Make it known that the non-audit work does not come under the mantle of internal auditing.

The internal audit staff should discuss the issues with management and the audit committee. Also, it should consider significance, length of the assignment, adequacy of separation of duties, scope of responsibility and potential impairment to objectivity and independence.

If the non-audit work must be performed, there are several options for the auditor to consider:

- Have the work performed by other auditors or audit organizations.
- Prevent the auditors performing the non-audit functions from participating in a related audit.
- Disclose the operational aspects of the function as to size, revenue, expenses, and relationship of the auditor to those ultimately auditing the function.
- Confirm the above in reports to the audit committee and to the related parties.

Politics

A highly professional staff and a progressive, state-of-the-art audit program will go a long way to avoid the perils of outsourcing. But an additional ingredient is necessary to ensure continuing stability of internal auditing within the enterprise. This ingredient is a combination of politics and culture. A shrewd knowledge of both is indispensable. One audit director was described as follows by an operating manager:[15]

> He is one of those rare individuals who can adapt very well to whatever the situation calls for. He can be a big bull in a china closet or he can wear the best velvet glove you've ever seen. He is the best politician that I have ever seen. He knows when to back his people and how to do it and how to get it done, but he also knows when to back off and when it is time to let things go.

If internal auditors are to survive in their organizations and make a difference, they must develop their political as well as their technical skills. They must use political skills to get things done outside the formal network, to promote the concepts and uses of internal auditing, and to avoid bruising and unproductive confrontations.

Technical auditing capabilities may be of no avail in the absence of an understanding of the politics and culture of an organization that permits the auditor to negotiate successfully the political corridors of the enterprise.[16]

References

[1]Herman, Joseph E., "Anheuser Busch Companies, Inc.: A New Audit Organization Strategy" in *Enhancing Internal Auditing Through Innovative Practices* (Altamonte Springs, FL: The Institute of Internal Auditors, 1996), 31-39.

[2]Stern, Gary M., "Fifteen Ways Internal Auditing Activities are Adding Value," *Internal Auditor*, April, 1994, 30-33.

[3]Mann, H.E., "Selling Internal Auditing," *Internal Auditor*, August 1989, 24-28.

[4]Sawyer, L.B., "The Leadership Side of Internal Auditing," *Internal Auditor*, August 1990, 16.

[5]Sawyer, L.B., "The Creative Side of Internal Auditing," *Internal Auditor*, December 1992, 57-62.

[6]Sawyer, L.B., "The Human Side of Internal Auditing," *Internal Auditor*, August 1988, 40.

[7]Thomson, R.P., T.E. Simpson, and C.H. Le Grand, "Environmental Auditing," *Internal Auditor*, April 1993, 19.

[8]Kamlet, K.S., "Environmental Management: Ten Commandments," *Internal Auditor*, October 1992, 36.

[9]Barr Jr., R.H., and S.Y. Chang, "Outsourcing Internal Audits, A Boon or Bane," *Managerial Auditing Journal*, 15.

[10]Ibid., 15, 16.

[11]Ibid., 16, 17.

[12]Courtemanche, Gil, "Outsourcing the Internal Audit Function," *Internal Auditor*, August 1991, 38.

[13]Dymoski, E.V., and P.H. Saake, "Strategic Planning," *Internal Auditor*, December 1992, 22.

[14]Ibid., 19.

[15]Stock, K.D., W.S. Albrecht, K.R. Howe, and D.R. Schueler, "What Makes an Effective Internal Audit Activity?" *Internal Auditor*, April 1988, 46.

[16]Sawyer, L.B., "The Political Side of Internal Auditing," *Internal Auditor*, February 1992, 27.

Supplementary Readings

Adamec, Bruce A., and Janet H. Zelenka, "Self-directed Audit Teams," *Internal Auditor*, April 1996, 36-43.

Aldhizer, III, George R., and James D. Cashell, "Cosourcing: An Alternative to Outsourcing," *Internal Auditing*, Summer 1997, 21-26.

Aldhizer III, George R., and James D. Cashell, "A Tale of Two Companies: The Decision to Outsource Internal Auditing," *Internal Auditing*, Winter 1996, 10-15.

Bonish, Peter, "CFIA Beams Up the Future," *Internal Auditor*, August 1999, 60-63.

Breakspear, Drew J., "Run It Like a Business," *Internal Auditor*, February 1998, 27-29.

Bridwell, John, "Developing a Successful Auditing Department – A Best Practice Approach," *Internal Auditing Alert*, August 1999, 5-6.

Burns, Stephen, "Reinforcing Internal Audit Value," *Internal Auditor*, October 2000, 80.

Burr, Thomas H., "Corporate Governance and Internal Audit Charters," *Internal Auditing*, November/December 2001, 25-28.

Calhoun, Charles, "Building An Audit Network in Cyberspace," *Internal Auditing Alert*, May 1998, 1-4.

Calhoun, Charles, "Revised Definition Mirrors World-class Internal Auditing Practices," *Internal Auditing Alert*, September 1999, 7-8.

Calhoun, Charles, "The Future of Modern Internal Auditing," *Internal Auditing Alert*, March 1999, 1-5.

Campbell, Jane E., and Nancy Mohan, *The Effect of Downsizing on the Internal Audit Function: The Case of Leveraged Buyouts (LBOs)* (Altamonte Springs, FL: The Institute of Internal Auditors, 1991).

Carcello, Joseph V., and Dana R. Hermanson, "Enhancing Internal Audit Department Credibility: Internal Auditors' Perceptions of Serving Two Customers," *Internal Auditing*, Spring 1997, 27-34.

Chadwick, William E., "Millennium Ready," *Internal Auditor*, 36-39.

Courtemanche, Gil, "Outsourcing The Internal Audit Function," *Internal Auditor*, August 1991, 34-39.

Cuzzetto, Charles E., "Lean, Mean, Auditing Machines," *Internal Auditor*, December 1994, 26-31.

Dame, Don R., "Strategic Use of Recovery Audit Services and Co-Sourcing," *Internal Auditing*, March/April 2000, 44-45.

Gibbs, Jeff, and Gil Courtemanche, "Inside Outsourcing," *Internal Auditor*, August 1994, 46-49.

Grand, Bernard, "Theoretical Approaches to Audits," *Internal Auditing*, November/December 1998, 14-19.

Hammer, Michael, "Just Do It," *Internal Auditor*, June 1998, 38-41.

Hinchliffe, Daniel A., and Alan H. Friedberg, "Capitalizing on Contingency Auditors," *Internal Auditor*, April 1998, 34-39.

Howard Jr., Clifford J., "Stretching the Narrow Band," *Internal Auditor*, April 1998, 64-68.

The IIA, "A Perspective on Outsourcing of the Internal Auditing Function," Professional Practices Pamphlet 98-1 (Altamonte Springs, FL: The Institute of Internal Auditors, 1998).

Jacka, J. Michael, "Auditing's Vision," *Internal Auditor*, June 1995, 46-49.

Kusel, Jimie, and James E. Gauntt, "Outsourcing: Dealing with an Outsourcing Proposal," *Internal Auditing*, Summer 1997, 52-56.

Lapelosa, Michael, "Outsourcing – A Vulnerability Checklist," *Internal Auditor*, December 1997, 66-67.

McNamee, David, and Georges Selim, "The Next Step in Risk Management," *Internal Auditor*, June 1999, 35-38.

Oliverio, Mary Ellen, "Is Internal Audit a Core Function?," *Internal Auditing Alert*, September 1999, 6-7.

Oliverio, Mary Ellen, "The SEC Chairman Challenge to the Financial Community: What are the Internal Auditors' Responsibilities?," *Internal Auditing Alert*, May 1999, 1-5.

Petravick, Simon, "Internal Auditor Outsourcing: Who and Why?" *Internal Auditing*, Winter 1997, 16-21.

Rittenberg, Larry, Wayne Moore, and Mark Covaleski, "The Outsourcing Phenomenon," *Internal Auditor*, April 1999, 42-46.

Sartori, Donald M., "High Performance in Hawaii," *Internal Auditor*, August 1998, 62-67.

Schubert, Darrel R., "Standardizing Multilocation Audits," *Internal Auditing*, Fall 1990, 68-71.

Seaberg, Gordon, "Smartsourcing," *Internal Auditor*, December 1996, 60-65.

Sears, Brian P., *Internal Auditing Manual* (New York: RIA, 2003.) (See Chapter C1, "Organizing and Planning the Internal Audit Function.")

Shedd, Timothy B., "Autonomy Issues," *Internal Auditing*, May/June 1999, 42-44.

Small, Lawrence M., "Respect and How to Get It," *Internal Auditor*, August 1998, 40-45.

Stern, Gary M., "Fifteen Ways Auditing Activities are Adding Value," *Internal Auditor*, April 1994, 30-33.

Walz, Anthony, "Adding Value," *Internal Auditor*, February 1997, 51-54.

Warrick, William W., "Outsourcing Internal Audit: The Strategic Questions," *Internal Auditing*, Spring 1997, 41-43.

White, Scott, Walter Fuller, and Timothy Dugan, "Uncharted Waters," *Internal Auditor*, February 1999, 55-58.

Williams, Satina V., and Benson Wier, "Creativity in Internal Auditing Departments," *Internal Auditing*, November/December 2000, 13-15.

Zhang, Charles, "A Checkup for Your Charter," *Internal Auditor*, October 1999, 42-43.

Ziegenfuss, Douglas, *Challenges and Opportunities of Small Internal Auditing Organizations* (Altamonte Springs, FL: The Institute of Internal Auditors Research Foundation, 1994).

Multiple-choice Questions

1. Independence permits internal auditors to render impartial and unbiased judgments. The best way to achieve independence is through:
   a. Individual knowledge and skills.
   b. Organizational status and objectivity.
   c. Supervision within the organization.
   d. Organizational knowledge and skills.

2. When faced with an imposed scope limitation, the chief audit executive should:
   a. Refuse to perform the audit until the scope limitation is removed.
   b. Communicate the potential effects of the scope limitation to the board of directors.
   c. Increase the frequency of auditing the activity in question.
   d. Assign more experienced personnel to the engagement.

3. A professional engineer applied for a position in the internal audit activity of a high technology firm. The engineer became interested in the position after observing several internal auditors while they were auditing the engineering activity. The chief audit executive:
   a. Should not hire the engineer because of the lack of knowledge of internal auditing standards.
   b. May hire the engineer in spite of the lack of knowledge of internal auditing standards.
   c. Should not hire the engineer because of the lack of knowledge of accounting and taxes.
   d. May hire the engineer because of the knowledge of internal auditing gained in the previous position.

4. To avoid being the apparent cause of conflict between an organization's top management and the audit committee, the chief audit executive should:
   a. Submit copies of all audit reports to both top management and the audit committee.
   b. Strengthen the independence of the activity through organizational status.
   c. Discuss all reports to top management with the audit committee first.
   d. Request board acceptance of policies that include internal auditing relationships with the audit committees.

5. Which of the items below would most likely reflect differences between the policies of a relatively small and relatively large internal audit operation? The policies for the large operation should:
   a. Spell out scope and status of internal auditing.
   b. Contain the authority to carry out audits.
   c. Be specific as to activities to be followed.
   d. Be in considerable detail.

6. The charter of the internal audit activity should:
   a. Authorize access to records, personnel, and physical properties relevant to the performance of audits.
   b. Provide recommended formats to report significant audit findings and recommendations.
   c. Describe audit programs to be carried out.
   d. Define the audit activity's work schedule, starting plan, and financial budget.

7. According to the *Standards*, the organizational status of the internal audit activity:
   a. Should be sufficient to permit the accomplishment of its audit responsibilities.
   b. Is best when the reporting relationship is direct to the board of directors.
   c. Requires the board's annual approval of the audit schedules, plans, and budgets.
   d. Is guaranteed when the charter specifically defines its independence.

8. An internal auditing charter would set forth which of the following items:
   a. Organizational structure of the internal audit activity.
   b. Annual internal audit plan.
   c. Internal auditing objectives.
   d. Purpose, authority, and responsibility of the internal audit activity.

9. Which of the following would be the best source of a chief audit executive's information for planning staffing requirements?
   a. Discussions of needs with executive management and the audit committee.
   b. Review of the audit staff education and training records.
   c. Review audit staff size and composition of similar sized organizations in the same industry.
   d. Interviews with existing audit staff.

10. Which of the following is most essential for guiding the audit staff in maintaining daily compliance with the activity's standards of performance?
    a. Quality control reviews.
    b. Position descriptions.
    c. Performance appraisals.
    d. Policies and procedures.

11. An internal auditor's objectivity would not be impaired by:
    a. Designing the computer operating systems.
    b. Installing application software.
    c. Recommending system control standards.
    d. Writing detailed operating procedures.

12. You have been selected to develop an internal audit activity for your organization. Your approach would most likely be to hire:
    a. Internal auditors each of whom possesses all the skills required to handle all audit assignments.
    b. Inexperienced personnel and train them the way the organization wants them trained.
    c. Degreed accountants since most audit work is accounting related.
    d. Internal auditors who collectively have the knowledge and skills needed to complete internal audit assignments.

13. Which of the following statements most correctly reflects the chief audit executive's responsibilities for personnel management and development as reflected in the *Standards*?
    a. The executive is responsible for selecting qualified individuals but has no explicit responsibility for providing ongoing educational opportunities for the internal auditor.
    b. The executive is responsible for performing an annual review of each internal auditor's performance but has no explicit responsibility for counseling internal auditors on their performance and professional development.

c. The executive is responsible for selecting qualified individuals but has no explicit responsibility for the preparation of job descriptions.

d. The executive is responsible for developing formal job descriptions for the audit staff but has no explicit responsibility for administering the corporate compensation program.

14. Select the most appropriate solution to resolve staff communication problems with clients:

a. Provide staff with sufficient training to enhance communication skills.

b. Review of trade publications.

c. Review of correspondence the entity has conducted with governmental agencies.

d. Meet with clients to resolve communication problems.

15. A charter is being drafted for a newly formed internal audit activity. Which of the following best describes the appropriate organizational status that should be incorporated into the charter?

a. The chief audit executive should report to the chief executive officer but have access to the board of directors.

b. The chief audit executive should be a member of the audit committee of the board of directors.

c. The chief audit executive should be a staff officer reporting to the chief financial officer.

d. The chief audit executive should report to an administrative vice president.

16. The *Standards* require written policies and procedures to guide the audit staff. Which of the following statements is false with respect to this requirement?

a. The form and content of written policies and procedures should be appropriate to the size of the activity.

b. All internal audit activity should have a detailed policies and procedures manual.

c. Formal administrative and technical audit manuals may not be needed by all internal audit activity.

d. A small internal audit activity may be managed informally through close supervision and written memos.

17. The chief audit executive for a large retail organization reports to the controller and is responsible for designing and installing computer application relating to inventory control. Which of the following is the major limitation of this arrangement?

a. It prevents the audit organization from devoting full time to auditing.

b. Auditors generally do not have the required expertise to design and implement such systems.

c. It potentially affects the executive's independence and thereby lessens the value of audit services.

d. Such arrangements are unlawful because the executive participates in incompatible functions.

18. The director of a newly formed internal audit activity is seeking management approval of a charter. What is the authoritative source for seeking such approval?
    a. The *Standards*, which clearly place that responsibility on the director.
    b. The appropriate Professional Standards Bulletin, which requires the director to take that course of action.
    c. The *Code of Ethics*, which requires internal auditors to document organization policy.
    d. According to the *Standards*, no approval is necessary.

19. The internal auditor customarily has a dual relationship with corporate management and the audit committee. This means that:
    a. Corporate management should help the internal auditors by revising and forwarding operational audit reports to the audit committee.
    b. The internal auditors should audit corporate operations and report directly to the audit committee, without corroborating the report with corporate management.
    c. The internal auditors should audit corporate operations, check the accuracy of the report with management, and then report to corporate management and the audit committee.
    d. Ideally, the internal auditor works under the audit committee, but reports to the chief operating officer on all operational audits.

20. The internal audit activity reports to the corporate controller. A report highly critical of the accounts payable function has just been issued. Based on the *Standards*, which of the following reflects this reporting problem?
    a. Reports critical of management should not be issued.
    b. Internal auditing should never report to the corporate controller.
    c. The organizational status of internal auditing should ensure appropriate action on audit recommendations.
    d. Audits of financial areas should be performed only by the external auditors.

21. The chief audit executive has assigned an auditor to perform a year-end review of payroll records. The auditor has contacted the director of compensation and has been refused access to necessary documents. According to the *Standards*:
    a. Access to records relevant to performance of audits should be specified in the activity charter.
    b. Internal auditing should be required to report to the president of the organization.
    c. By following the long-range planning process, access to all relevant records should be guaranteed.
    d. Audit committee approval should be required for all audit scope limitations.

22. According to the *Standards*, written policies and procedures relative to managing the internal audit activity staff should:
    a. Ensure compliance with activity performance standards.
    b. Give consideration to the structure of the activity and the complexity of the work performed.
    c. Result in consistent job performance.
    d. Prescribe the format and distribution of audit reports and the classification of deficiency findings.

23. An organization's charter for the internal audit activity includes the following items:
    I . . . .shall report to the controller. . . .
    II . . . .shall have direct access to the audit committee upon request. . . .
    III. . . .may access records with approval from client division manager. . . .
    IV. . . .must submit an annual audit plan to the board for approval. . . .
    Which of the above statements is in conflict with the *Standards*?

    a. I, II, III, and IV.
    b. I and III.
    c. I, III, and IV.
    d. III and IV.

24. Following a negative performance evaluation by a supervisor, a staff auditor went to the audit director to seek a change in the evaluation. The director was familiar with the auditor's performance and agreed with the evaluation. The director agreed to meet and discuss the situation. Which of the following is the best course of action for the director to take?
    a. Have the supervisor participate in the meeting, so that there is no misunderstanding about the facts.
    b. Have a human resources administrator present to ensure that improper statements are not made.
    c. Meet privately with the employee. Tell the employee of the director's agreement with the performance evaluation and express interest in any additional facts the employee may wish to present.
    d. Meet privately with the employee. Encourage discussion by asking for the employee's side of the issue and disclaiming any agreement with the supervisor.

Chapter 21
Selecting and Developing the Staff

The qualities of professional internal auditors: adaptability, understanding, and determination. Sources of new auditors: universities and colleges, CPAs, within the organization, IIA. How to select internal auditors: interviews, questions to ask, tests. Orientation: programs and guides. The art of mentoring. Training programs: individual study, promoting continuing education, new training course for senior internal auditors, staff meetings, research, IIA, Continuing Professional Development. An extensive in-house training program. Specialization comes to internal auditing. Staff evaluations. Evaluating accomplishments and traits. Various forms in use for evaluations. Audit assignments. Restructuring the human relations element. Strengths, conflicts, and violations. Examples of both. The development of the ethical culture.

• •

The Qualities of Professional Internal Auditors

Professional internal auditing requires a professional staff. The extended reach of modern internal auditing requires a broad knowledge of audit methods and techniques. These requirements set high standards for internal auditing — standards that should not be compromised. It is far better to be understaffed than to hire a single internal auditor who can destroy in one assignment the credibility that may have taken years to build. The chief audit executive must therefore consider certain attributes of professional knowledge, ability, and qualities of character when making personnel selections and retention decisions.

Education develops professional abilities; actual experience hones them. Education should develop the knowledge, skills, and disciplines essential to the performance of professional internal audit work. The broad scope of internal auditing makes complete knowledge of all its subjects almost impossible for any one individual. The auditing team as a whole, however, should possess the proficiency needed to carry out any audit engagements — or have access to that proficiency. The individual auditor should be proficient in certain core skills needed for broad-based internal auditing, have an understanding of others, and have an appreciation of the rest. *The Standards for the Professional Practice of Internal Auditing (Standards)* illustrated these terms and described their applicability. However, Practice Advisory 1210-1, "Proficiency," describes it well:

1. Each internal auditor should possess certain knowledge and skills as follows:

   (a) Proficiency in applying internal auditing standards, procedures, and techniques is required in performing engagements. Proficiency means the ability to apply knowledge to situations likely to be encountered and to deal with them without extensive recourse to technical research and assistance.

   (b) Proficiency in accounting principles and techniques is required of auditors who work extensively with financial records and reports.

   (c) An understanding of management principles is required to recognize and evaluate the materiality and significance of deviations from good business practice. An understanding means the ability to apply broad knowledge to situations likely to be encountered, to recognize significant deviations, and to be able to carry out the research necessary to arrive at reasonable solutions.

   (d) An appreciation is required of the fundamentals of such subjects as accounting, economics, commercial law, taxation, finance, quantitative methods, and information technology. An appreciation means the ability to recognize the existence of problems or potential problems and to determine the further research to be undertaken or the assistance to be obtained.

2. Internal auditors should be skilled in dealing with people and in communicating effectively. Internal auditors should understand human relations and maintain satisfactory relationships with engagement clients. Internal auditors should be skilled in oral and written communications so that they can clearly and effectively convey such matters as engagement objectives, evaluations, conclusions, and recommendations.

3. The chief audit executive should establish suitable criteria of education and experience for filling internal auditing positions, giving due consideration to scope of work and level of responsibility. Reasonable assurance should be obtained as to each prospective auditor's qualifications and proficiency.

4. The internal auditing staff should collectively possess the knowledge and skills essential to the practice of the profession within the organization. These attributes include proficiency in applying internal auditing standards, procedures, and techniques.

Certain qualities of character are needed to meet the demands made by modern internal auditing: adaptability, understanding, and determination, among others.

To cope with the diversity of internal auditing, auditors need adaptability to adjust to the ever-changing environment they encounter in their varied assignments. It calls for the facility to readily absorb the jargon that the activity has spawned, together with the ability to translate the information into plain English. It demands the agility to react quickly to new problems, new organization objectives, and new management viewpoints.

To deal successfully with people, auditors must have an understanding of what makes people react favorably or with hostility. They need empathy to comprehend people's problems and to be able to walk in their shoes for a while. They need a sensitivity as to what frustrates people, to how they feel about their jobs, their managers, and their organization. Auditors must have the tact to be able to ask productive questions without creating enmity.

To deal with difficult and novel problems internal auditors must be determined. They must be able to resist the pressures that would sway them from their goals. They must be able to insist that they and they alone can satisfy their own internal monitors before they stop pursuing the answers to their questions. And auditors must be willing to work as hard and as long as necessary to establish facts and to document them so that they will be impregnable to attack.

To be able to express professional opinions, auditors must have integrity, objectivity, and responsibility. They must develop a reputation for dealing only in facts, for placing the facts in perspective, for objectively evaluating the materiality of their findings, for having no personal axe to grind, for being absolutely trustworthy, and for being completely responsible, because they have the power to do serious injury through reported deficiencies.

Round these qualities out with the ability to communicate both orally and in writing with a strong, positive attitude that sells both the auditor and the audit, and with the imagination and initiative to find new ways of attacking old problems, and the modern internal auditor emerges.

Sources

Candidates for positions in internal auditing come from many sources. In addition, some auditing organizations have taken novel steps to use available talent possessed by other than professional auditors. Here are some of the sources and newer approaches:

Universities and colleges. A 1985 survey identified 44 schools that offered a single internal auditing course. But none had a formal program. Led by Louisiana State University, The Institute of Internal Auditors (IIA) developed a Target School Program to develop professional internal auditors. Under the program, courses were established or are in the process of development at over 50 U.S. and offshore universities. Students are attracted to the programs in sufficient numbers to justify administrative costs, and graduates are in high demand. One of the goals of the pilot schools is for students to achieve the Certified Internal Auditor designation.[1]

Another source of internal auditors is found in university-sponsored internship programs. These programs provide students with a onetime opportunity to gain practical experience and also receive academic credit. The full-time experience lasts anywhere from 10 weeks to six months, although 10 to 12 weeks is the norm. There are also some short-term internships of 20 to 40 hours that are a part of class assignments. One benefit is to help perform year-end procedures. Another is to assign interns to special projects that might not be otherwise performed because of lack of permanent staff. Some of the assignments for students have been:

- Analyzing internal controls.
- Analyzing account balances.
- Observing and reconciling physical inventories.
- Developing personal computer applications.
- Researching accounting and tax topics.
- Improving working paper organization.
- Performing small audits.

The internal auditing profession has not pursued top accounting students as aggressively as have public accountants. But internal auditing can be shown to possess greater challenges and excitement. Reaching out to interns can help the department on specific projects, but can also help evaluate candidates for full-time positions in the internal audit departments.[2]

One bank had a novel use for a student intern. The bank had been subject to a quality assurance review two years previously. The student was given a copy of the review report with the directive "Audit Us." Not being on the internal audit department payroll, the student had no pressures about trying to please the boss or mollify staff people and was able to provide a rigorous and objective view to the "audit."[3]

Certified Public Accountants (CPAs). Young accountants looking for new and exciting opportunities, who have put in an apprenticeship with a public accounting firm, can be fine prospects. Advertisements in the leading accounting journals can attract the attention of the young CPAs. They may be sold on the solid prospects of modern internal auditing rather than on a position of controller or chief accountant in a small organization. A useful sales approach is to cite those managers and executives who reached their present positions from the springboard of internal auditing.

Within the organization. Chief audit executives have an excellent source in their own backyards. They are in a position to obtain firsthand knowledge of the prospect in actual operation. The prospect already has a working knowledge of the organization's policies, methods, products, and management. The audit staff should be alert to people who have the basic equipment and who could be approached — through established channels, of course — for an interview.

The Institute of Internal Auditors. Internal Auditor, The Institute's professional journal, takes advertisements for auditors and has the advantage of being delivered to internal auditors throughout the world.

The Internet. Experienced personnel are constantly looking for new opportunities. Advertising, with the possibility of electronic discussions, can be an effective method to attract journeymen applicants.

How to Select Internal Auditors

Having attracted the prospect, the chief audit executive should then take two steps: first, interviewing; second, testing.

Interviewing

An interview with an applicant should be well-planned and well-organized. The prospect's resume and application should have been carefully read and the references called. Calling the references is better than writing to them. A former employer will be more free and candid on the telephone than on paper.

The interview should be set for a time when the pressure of other work will not interfere. Chief audit executives should screen the prospects first; if they seem to be likely candidates, some of the staff supervisors should assist in the prescreening.

Interviewing is an art and takes practice to develop. It should be a two-way street. The interviewer, normally a person who has a personnel background plus internal auditing experience, discusses the job, the organization or agency, the opportunities, and the nature of the work. The interviewees talk about themselves. Some people, when interviewed, need to be drawn out; some need to be guided.

Questions to ask experienced candidates include:

- What were some of the assignments you carried out?
- How did you approach them?
- What kinds of reports did you write?
- How have you kept up with your education?
- Why do you want to make a change?
- What do you like about internal auditing?
- What don't you like about it?
- What kinds of assignments do you like best?
- What are your personal goals?
- Give an example of one of the most difficult situations with which you were faced.

Questions to ask candidates with no experience include:

- What is your concept of internal auditing?
- How did you hear about it? Why do you think you'd like it?
- What kinds of assignments would you like best?
- Do you have any outside interests that might relate to internal auditing?
- What are your personal goals?

Keep records of all interviews in an organized manner so that they are readily available to compare the qualities and qualifications of different candidates for the same position. Exhibit 21-1 is an example of an applicant's interview record. Exhibit 21- 2 gives definitions of the qualities being explored and rated.

With so much hanging in the balance, auditing executives need every edge they can get when deciding whether to hire a prospect. Only time will tell whether the decision to hire was correct. There are no standard tests at this writing for internal auditors other than intelligence tests, aptitude tests, and the CIA examination. Having achieved the CIA designation, of course, may be test enough. But not all new hires are CIAs. So some auditing organizations have developed tests of their own to give an insight into the prospect's aptitude, writing ability, thought processes, logic, and personality.

It should be pointed out that some auditing executives are opposed to such tests. Others have used them with a fair degree of success and have validated them by comparing the grades on the tests with the evaluations subsequently given to the same employees on job rating sheets. These comparisons have shown reasonable correlations between test scores and their later evaluations.

Government laws and regulations forbid some tests for employment, but tests that bear a direct relation to the job being filled are often acceptable. Chief auditing executives should submit their proposed tests to their human resources officials for review and approval before use.

For the tests to be effective, the prospect should not be able to see them in advance. It would be unwise, therefore to use the exact tests shown in a book in general circulation, such as this one. Each auditing organization should develop its own tests or use sets of standardized tests that are printed in multiple editions. We have developed some ideas and shown some truncated examples for the preparation of such tests, rather than providing complete copies of those in actual use.

Exhibit 21-1
Interview Rating Sheet

Name _____ Age _____

Degrees _____

Last two employers _____

_____

Schools _____

_____

Certifications _____

Will travel? _____

	0	2	4	6	8	10
Attitude						
Appearance						
Maturity						
Sociability						
Self-expression						
Motivation						
Intelligence						
Persuasiveness						
Self-confidence						
Interest						
Potential						
Overall Evaluation						

Should we make this applicant an offer? _____

If so, for what position? _____

Comments _____

_____

Interviewer _____

Date _____

Exhibit 21-2
Interview Rating Sheet Definitions

Rating Factors

Attitude — Outlook in general.

Appearance — Physical appearance, neatness, posture.

Maturity — Behavior and apparent emotional stability.

Sociability — Apparent ability to get along with others; warmth, response.

Self-expression — Ability to express thoughts clearly, concisely, effectively.

Motivation — Drive, initiative, enthusiasm, energy, desire to succeed.

Intelligence — Mental ability, judgment, alertness, organization of thoughts.

Persuasiveness — Ability to influence others.

Self-confidence — Poise, interest in challenge.

Interest — Indication of sincere interest in internal auditing and our organization.

Potential — Your impression of the applicant's potential for a management position.

Overall Evaluation — Your general impression of the applicant.

Rating Scores

10 — Outstanding	Exceptional, clearly superior (applicable only in rare instances)
8 — Excellent	Considerably above average. Definitely stands out. Makes immediate and lasting impression.
6 — Satisfactory Plus	Well above average, a potential asset to the organization.
4 — Satisfactory	Normal for a person of this age, experience, and education.
2 — Satisfactory Minus	A marginal rating; doesn't quite meet minimum standards.
O — Unsatisfactory	Unsuitable for our work.

Test of writing ability. Provide applicants with a statement of an audit situation and ask them to write a report in a prescribed format, setting forth, for example: (a) background information; (b) the purpose of the audit; (c) the scope of the audit; (d) the auditor's opinion; and (e) the recommendations for corrective action. Here are examples of two such situations:

1. Envelopes are opened in the mail room by any one of several mail room employees. All remittances are put in a box until the end of the day. At that time, they are placed in an interdepartmental envelope and sent to the cashier.

2. Buyers in the purchasing department are permitted to develop their own lists of prospective bidders, prepare the requests for bids, mail them directly to the bidders solicited, and receive the completed bids directly from the mail room. They also make the selection of the successful bid.

The instructions to the applicants should tell them to write their reports on the above situations in nontechnical terms that would be plain to a manager who has no accounting or purchasing background. They should also be told that their reports will be evaluated according to standards of clarity, coherence (how they hang together), structure, and the use of appropriate language. (Note: The substance of the defects is not part of this test.)

The evaluation and grading of such tests presents a problem because there are no simple mathematical criteria to rely upon. Some measure of objectivity can be obtained, however, by assigning maximum numerical grades to each of four reporting standards and permitting two or more people to rate the test results independently of each other. The grading criteria might be:

Standard	Maximum Value	Grade
Clarity	35	( )
Coherence	35	( )
Structure	15	( )
Language	15	( )
Totals	**100**	( )

Test of ability to organize thoughts. Provide the applicant with a series of about 25 statements about an audit problem. The statements are numbered sequentially, but their logical order has been scrambled. Ask the applicant to rearrange the statement in a reasonable order under headings that have been provided. The headings may include Purpose, Scope, Control Findings, Performance Findings, Opinion, and Recommendations. An abbreviated example of the hashed statements is shown in Exhibit 21-3. The solution is shown in Exhibit 21-4.

The test can be graded by deducting from the perfect score of 100, two points each for every statement shown in wrong sequence under the correct heading, and four points each for every statement shown under the wrong heading.

Exhibit 21-3
Test of Ability to Organize Thoughts

INSTRUCTIONS: Insert, in the spaces provided, the proper numbers in their proper order.

Purpose	Scope	Control Findings	Performance Findings	Opinion	Recommendations
( )	( )	( )	( )	( )	( )
( )	( )	( )	( )	( )	( )
( )	( )	( )	( )	( )	( )
( )	( )	( )	( )	( )	( )
( )	( )	( )	( )	( )	( )

(1) We recommended that supervisors periodically check manuals to make sure they are kept up to date.
(2) It is our opinion that the system was working as intended except for the fact that some manuals were not up to date.
(3) Our test of the checked drawings showed that they had all been signed off by engineering supervisors before release.
(4) We reviewed systems and procedures by reading instructions and interviewing engineering personnel.
(5) Our test of the error reports showed them to be accurate and timely.
(6) We found an adequate supply of drafting manuals for all engineers, but 20 percent of the manuals were not up to date.
(7) We set out to determine whether the system was working as intended.
(8) We set out to evaluate the adequacy of the system of control over the accuracy of engineering drawings.
(9) Our test of 100 drawings showed that they had all been verified by drawing checkers.
(10) We found that all drawings must be verified by drawing checkers for accuracy.
(11) We found that after checking, the drawings must be reviewed by engineering supervisors before release.
(12) It is our opinion that the control system was adequate.
(13) We found that a drafting manual had been developed to provide detailed instructions to engineering draftsmen.
(14) We examined 100 engineering drawings in detail.
(15) Management had developed a system of reporting the number of drawing errors based on complaints from the production organization.
(16) We recommended that all manuals be brought up to date promptly.

Exhibit 21-4
Solution to Test of Ability to Organize Thoughts

Purpose

(8) We set out to evaluate the adequacy of the system of control over the accuracy of engineering drawings.

(7) We set out to determine whether the system was working as intended.

Scope

(4) We reviewed systems and procedures by reading instructions and interviewing engineering personnel.

(14) We examined 100 engineering drawings in detail.

Control Findings

(13) We found that a drafting manual had been developed to provide detailed instructions to engineering draftsmen.

(10) We found that all drawings must be verified by drawing checkers for accuracy.

(11) We found that after checking, the drawings must be reviewed by engineering supervisors before release.

(15) Management had developed a system of reporting the number of drawing errors based on complaints from the production organization.

Performance Findings

(6) We found an adequate supply of drafting manuals for all engineers, but 20 percent of the manuals were not up to date.

(9) Our test of 100 drawings showed that they had all been verified by drawing checkers.

(3) Our test of checked drawings showed that they had all been signed off by engineering supervisors before release.

(5) Our test of the error reports showed them to be accurate and timely.

Opinion

(12) It is our opinion that the control system was adequate.

(2) It is our opinion the system was working as intended except for the fact that some manuals were not up to date.

Recommendations

(16) We recommended that all manuals be brought up to date promptly.

(1) We recommended that supervisors periodically check manuals to make sure they are kept up to date.

Test of ability to differentiate between fact and conjecture. A fact is something that has actual existence, something that can be inferred with certainty, a proposition that is verified or verifiable. A conjecture is something suggesting insufficient evidence for it to be regarded as a fact. Auditors who cannot distinguish between the two need help because gathering facts, appraising them, and drawing conclusions from them — not just making conjectures — lie at the heart of the auditor's work.

The greatest barriers to appraising the truth or falsity of a proposition are taking things for granted, jumping to conclusions, and accepting plausible appearance for hard fact. The inexperienced auditor — and, quite often the old hand — may accept appearance for substance and come to improper conclusions. There is a subtle test, full of pitfalls for the unwary, that can be devised both to trip up the conclusion jumper and to provide some good education for any auditor. It brings home sharply that what appears factual on the surface is but a signal to an experienced auditor to ask more questions.

The test can be developed along the lines set forth in Exhibit 21-5. A score of 85 percent or better would be Excellent; 75 percent, Good; 60 percent, Fair; 50 percent, Poor; and less than that Unsatisfactory .The example shown has only five comments or questions. In practice, it is a good idea to present 25 to 30 questions.

As a result of current emphasis on performance auditing and the provision of consulting service for clients, less emphasis is being placed on a deep knowledge of accounting and more on concepts of efficient and effective operations. In many cases the internal auditor is not an accounting specialist, but may be a specialist in disciplines such as medicine or engineering. Also, an MBA education is becoming increasingly popular.

How to Provide Orientation

Orientation, as distinguished from training, means pointing the new auditor in the right direction. Its purpose is to provide staff members with the information they need to become productive as soon a possible.

The first days in a new organization can be traumatic. New employees want to like and respect their new environment. They want to feel that they can learn from the people around them, that these people are knowledgeable. They want to feel comfortable in their new jobs and in their new department. Their senses will be heightened to any ineptness or uncertainty. When they have been around a while, waiting for something to do is no strain; they know how to occupy themselves. But during their first day or days, any delay, confusion, or lack of organization will be accentuated in their minds and will create an undesirable reaction.

Exhibit 21-5
Distinguishing Between Fact and Conjecture

How to Take the Test
Shown below is a statement that you are to assume is completely true, although some parts are deliberately vague; so read the statement carefully. You may look back at the statement any time during the test.

Read the comments about the statement. Next to each comment indicate whether it is True (T), False (F), or Questionable (Q). Circle the letter you consider applicable. Circle T or F if you are quite sure of them. Circle Q if you are doubtful about the comment.

Answer each comment in turn. Do not change your answers once they are made. (In this example, the answers are shown in parentheses after each comment.)

Statement
XYZ Corporation's purchase order 30305, dated May 15, 2000, was issued to the ABC Organization for 10 castings at $10 each. The owner of the ABC Organization is a brother of Joe Blow, XYZ Corporation's casting buyer.

Comments
1. An order for 10 castings was placed with ABC Organization on May 15, 2000 (This is May 15, questionable, since we know only the date of the purchase order, not when the order was placed. It could have been placed by telephone at an earlier date.) T F Q
2. Joe Blow and the owner of ABC Organization are brothers. (This is true, being categorically stated.) T F Q
3. Joe Blow gave an order to his brother. (This is questionable; while Joe Blow was the castings buyer, the order could possibly have been placed by someone else. Joe might have been on vacation.) T F Q
4. Purchase order 30503 is dated May 15, 2000. (This is questionable. The purchase order in the statement that is numbered 30305 is dated May 15, 2000. We don't know the date of purchase order 30503, which mayor may not be May 15, 2000.) T F Q
5. The value of purchase order 30305 is $100, without considering discount terms. (This is true.) T F Q

Orientation of new employees should therefore be carefully planned and structured. One of the people in the auditing organization with a strong teaching instinct should be assigned the task of introducing the new auditors to their surroundings and guiding them through the maze of new requirements. The teacher should be thoroughly prepared with a specific program and with well-designed materials to do the job with ease and confidence.

Generally, the period of orientation should take at least three or four days and should be organized into five phases: Introduction to the staff; discussion of office policies and audit methods; reading of policies, procedures, audit reports, and working papers, electronic facilities and support; and feedback of what the new employee has learned. There should be a liberal portion of each phase, spaced so that the new auditor is neither overwhelmed nor bored.

The breadth and intensity of the orientation will, of course, depend on the new auditor's prior experience. The instructor should be familiar with that experience. Clearly, an employee transferred from within the organization, a newly graduated student, and an experienced auditor from another organization all require different orientation.

An orientation guide, providing general information about the organization and the internal audit department, can be an important means of furnishing general information for reference as needed. A guide should be made available immediately to the new auditor so as to provide early answers to any questions. Each organization must develop its own, of course, but to assist in its development, an outline of such a guide is shown in Exhibit 21-6.

The orientor needs a formal program to help remember all the matters to be covered during the orientation. Exhibit 21-7 is an example of such a guide as associated with a training program.

The Act of Mentoring[4]

One of the facets of staff development that is scarcely ever mentioned is the mentoring process. During an IIA Educators' Colloquium, a paper was read by Dr. Sridhar Ramamoorti, formerly of the University of Illinois and now with Ernst & Young LLP. The paper developed by the presenter along with Dr. Frederick L. Neumann and Julie K. Monroe, discussed the philosophy and early history of mentoring and applied the process to internal auditing.

The speaker quoted an expert connected with the Federal Express as stating that mentoring: helped develop the capacity to make sound professional judgments; enabled individual development; and enhanced the quality of professional experience gained. He then stated that mentoring assists to keep the profession "revitalized and relevant to an era of unprecedented change" and that is essentially important in developing an attitude of professional skepticism.

Exhibit 21-6
Orientation Guide

Purpose
To orient you, as a new member of the internal audit staff, to your new environment. To guide you through a review of pertinent administrative and technical matters before you are assigned to an audit organization.

Organization
Company
Provides an overview of the company organization and the names of key management people.

Internal Auditing
Shows where internal auditing stands in the organization. Supplies the names of the people most closely related to the audit function. Describes the functional responsibilities of the parts of the audit organization.

Administration

Hours of work	Nature of organization directives
Daily notification of location	Administrative manual
Delivery of paychecks	Audit manual
Time reports	Supplies
Security matters	Desk assignments

Electronic

Individual	Support Software

Benefits

Vacations	Military leave
Sick leave	Retirement plan
Holidays	Insurance
Jury Duty	

The speaker described the position of another source that views performance coaching as consisting of four sequential phases:

- Developing a synergistic relationship with employees,

- Using the four roles of performance coaching;
  - Training
  - Career coaching
  - Confronting
  - Mentoring

- Developing self-directed and self-esteeming employees, and

- Selecting rewards that build commitment and get results.

The four roles of performance coaching in more detail consist of:

- Training: Developing technical competence and problem-solving skills.

- Career coaching: Producing greater sense of commitment to his or her career and the organization.

- Confronting: Getting the employee to perform better regardless of current level of performance. It relates to the performance problem, not the person.

- Mentoring: Exerting a personal relationship with the mentee by sharing past experiences both good and bad, describing personal and professional history, building trust in the relationship and developing competence in the mentee.

The speaker quoted another source who stated that, "The ideal mentor creates an atmosphere of both stability and change in the presence of random noise," and that while knowledge, competence, integrity, and objectivity must remain unchanged, the kinds of knowledge and necessary competence may change and so will a greater sense of integrity and objectivity. Mentoring was described as building trust, competence, and loyalty in both senior and junior members of the profession. "It is the social glue that keeps the fabric of the profession from tearing apart."

The speaker spent a great deal of time to the developing by the mentor of professional skepticism. This characteristic or ability comes slowly during an auditor's normal experience. However, through the mentoring process and the exchange of experience and situations it can be expedited and related to current situations. Concurrently the development by the mentee of using sound professional judgment can be expedited by the mentor giving a "repertoire of analytical reasoning abilities and developing the skill to assess a difficult problem in an efficient manner." The mentee's reactions become intuitive resulting from the mentoring, rather than resulting from the long-term results of experience. The concept of professional skepticism is an attitude that, built on objectivity, intuition, curiosity, experience, and analysis, can serve as warning bell of areas that do not seem to meet the accepted patterns of professional and business practices.

To summarize, Dr. Ramamoorti inventoried the benefits of the mentoring process:

- "Easier assimilation into the organizational and professional cultures;

- Creation of a mentor protégé bond that builds trust and competence;

- Development of an appropriate attitude of professional skepticism and the ability to exercise sound professional judgment;

- Enhancement of technical and managerial skills, including problem-solving, interpersonal communication, and leadership;

- Cultivation of a strong sense of corporate loyalty and professional pride. ...;

- Access to the mentor's sagacious advice in negotiating the unavoidable uncertainties that arise in one's personal and professional life; and

- Accumulating professional experience and gaining necessary maturity to become a mentor himself or herself."

Training Programs

While an orientation program is designed to make a trained internal auditor productive as soon as possible, the constantly expanding scope and methodology of internal auditing requires continual training programs as well. The field is advancing far too quickly to let internal auditors rest on their laurels. Every internal audit activity should have a training program that will promote consistency and quality in the work of all professional employees while keeping them informed of what is new in the field. Such training programs should have as their prime objective the achievement of both individual and departmental goals.

Exhibit 21-7
Program for the Orientation
and Training of New Employees

The program provided here will supplement the orientation guide and help the training supervisor give the new auditors additional information on general administrative matters and on the more technical aspects of the activity's auditing approach. The program should be supplemented by any additional information considered desirable.

The orientation will take anywhere from three to five days, depending on the individual's background. The oral instructions and any tours provided should be interspersed between periods of reading so as to give some variety to the orientation period.

The Internal Auditing Activity
Introduce the new auditors to other members of the audit staff.
Discuss the auditing activity's objectives and how they are implemented.
Specifically cover opportunities for promotion and inform them of the organization's policies about management selection.
Supply the employees with copies of applicable manuals. Have them scan the manuals to familiarize themselves with their contents.
Discuss:
- The job duties and responsibilities of all members of internal auditing, from the chief auditing executive to the assistant auditor. Provide the new auditors with copies of their own job descriptions and answer any questions they may have about them.
- Discuss audit standards as they relate to audit coverage, audit examination, administrative records and reports, and communications.
- Discuss the charter.
Explain how the audit work is controlled:
- The long-range schedule.
- The basis for programmed jobs: areas which, by experience, require close review; chart of accounts; needs of management; and other.
- Discuss the various periodic reports to management.
- Discuss job assignments.
- Review the contents of the department's library.

The Organization
Have new employees attend any special orientation classes provided by the organization.
- Answer any questions raised by the new auditors as a result of the class instruction.
- Provide a tour of the plant, supplementing if necessary the tour given during the organization-provided classes.

Exhibit 21-7 (Cont.)

Have the new auditors scan:
- Organization charts.
- General information on the organization.
- The use of outsourcing.
- The latest corporate annual report.

Acquaint new auditors with the general ledger, subsidiary ledgers, and journal vouchers. Show them the chart and text of accounts.

Acquaint them with the work order system and with overhead accumulation and distribution.

Introduce them to management personnel with whom they may have contact on the job.

Internal Auditing

Bring to the new auditors' attention:
- The *Standards for the Professional Practice of Internal Auditing* (together with the Practice Advisories).
- The *Code of Ethics.*
- The activity's referenda file of the *Internal Auditor, Internal Auditing,* the *Bibliography of Internal Auditing,* and the supplements and research reports issued by The Institute of Internal Auditors.

Have new auditors read pertinent articles in *Internal Auditor* and other periodicals that relate to modern internal auditing in general.

Review the steps taken in planning an audit project.
- Explain the standard forms used in the organization.
- Explain the preliminary research undertaken, such as reviews of the relevant permanent files, the master program, organization charts, procedure manuals, and prior working papers.
- Describe the risk assessment procedure.
- Discuss professional skepticism.
- Discuss process auditing.
- Explain how and when the audit program should be prepared, emphasizing the identification of the activity's major objectives, plans, and controls.
- Discuss the survey approach to audits, flowcharting, sampling, and computer-assisted audits. Lead the new auditors through a selected set of working papers, showing them how the material is organized and how it is used to support the audit report. Discuss the preparation of a segment of working papers, which will normally include:
- General information: Include applicable directives, procedures, practices, work flow (supported by flowcharts), statistics, and key controls.

Exhibit 21-7 (Cont.)

- Purpose: The purpose should tie into the program and, if necessary, expand upon it. Try to cover cost, quality, and timeliness.
- Scope: Show what was done and how much, and give the source of information and data.
- Findings: The facts evidenced by the schedules documenting the audit tests. The findings should be responsive to the questions raised in the purpose. Many findings may relate to one purpose.
- Opinions: These are the conclusions that are based on the findings. There should be an "opinion" for each "purpose." The opinions should be specific; either favorable or unfavorable. "No exceptions" will not suffice.
- Test work sheets: The work sheets should support the findings. They should indicate scope and sufficiency of test or the reasons why tests were limited. They should be summarized, so that the reviewer has no difficulty tracing the findings to the detail in the test schedules.
- The preparation of computerized working papers and the applicable software. Use copies of client's records, reports, tabulations, etc., whenever possible to avoid unnecessary copying.

Discuss audit findings. They should be thoroughly documented. The documentary evidence should show:
- Just what is wrong.
- Whether the deficiency violates some directive or is just poor administrative practice.
- The significance of the deficiency and what effect it will have if it goes uncorrected.
- What evidence has been adduced to prove the existence and extent of the deficiency.
- Who or what is responsible.
- Whether the deficiency relates to control, performance, or both.
- The basic cause behind the deficient condition.
- What corrective action the auditor suggests.
- The client's opinion about the deficiency and what is proposed to be done to correct it.

Describe electronic audit operations:
- The auditor's electronic tools (including digital cameras).
- Support facilities available.
- Software for audit operations and control.

Exhibit 21-7 (Cont.)

- Electronic working papers: preparation and approval. Provide new auditors with copies of typical reports and explain the various report sections and their purpose and the different formats that are used. Discuss procedures in reviewing report drafts. Discuss responsibilities for the evaluation of corrective action and the closure of audit projects.

Evaluation and Follow-up
The training supervisor/mentor should keep in touch with the new auditors as they start on audit projects to see if they need answers to any of the questions that come up during early actual work on the job. In about a month, the supervisor should have a session with each new auditor, going over again the matters covered in this program and reinforcing those matters that may have been forgotten. One technique would be to use this program as a questionnaire to raise issues for the auditor to discuss or answer.

A comprehensive administrative program for training is composed of a number of different elements, including some that have already been discussed. Exhibit 21-7 also shows a summary of training elements common to most professional internal audit organizations. Following are administrative aspects on which they are based.

- Develop and secure top management approval of a charter that sets forth the duties, responsibilities, and authority of the internal audit activity. This represents the basic standards that all members of the auditing activity must meet. Training programs are designed to meet those standards.

- Obtain management support for an adequate number of auditors and for a salary structure that is competitive with others in the industry. An inadequate number leaves no time for training, and a low salary structure will keep the good people away.

- Restrict employment to people who have the technical, educational, and professional qualifications needed for the organization's long-range audit program.

- Insist that all internal auditors in the department be aware of, understand, and comply with the *Standards for the Professional Practice of Internal Auditing* and the *Code of Ethics* published by The Institute of Internal Auditors.

- Develop and disseminate an administrative policies and procedures manual covering such topics as job descriptions, rotation of personnel assignments, travel policies, and supervision of employees. This will promote consistent application of activity methods and techniques.

- Develop an in-house training program. Have the program designed and carried out by appropriate staff people. Teaching others is the surest way of developing oneself.

- Encourage and support participation in IIA chapter activities and seminars. Communication with others in the profession keeps internal auditors current with what is new and effective.

- Install a quality assurance program, including both internal and external independent reviews and evaluations to determine how well or how poorly professional standards are being met.

- Rotate the assignments of staff auditors through a variety of different types of activities, including assignments to non-audit organizations. Modern internal auditors should be generalists, not specialists. Variety broadens capability.

- Establish procedures for the evaluation, counseling, and training of staff members. People should know where they stand and where and when they need additional training.

Promoting Continuing Education

Too many people — auditors included — entertain the naive notion that education is something that happens to students in a classroom. The constant winds of change should dispel that foggy notion; but apathy, lack of imagination, and lack of direction can be frustrating and formidable barriers.

The torrents of technological changes in the business and operational communities should make it abundantly clear that the auditor must learn to breast the tide of new knowledge or remain high and dry on the shore. For those staff people not keeping up, audit management owes itself and them the duty of immersing them in the waters of continued learning.

Internal auditing especially — as a relatively young and growing product of management needs — must keep current to cope with the same changes that management itself must cope with. There is no excuse for a progressive auditing organization not to have formal, continuing programs of education for its staff people. There are many forms this education can take.

Individual Study

New ideas and theories found in professional journals give people a taste and a hint, but only formal university courses will provide a full meal. Now and again every auditor should take a formal course in a university or in an online course or in a correspondence school, if a university classroom is not available. There is a discipline about formal university courses — with their class discussions, homework, supervision, and grades — that induces an extra effort and comprehension that reading alone does not always generate.

And when auditors see that management regards such instruction as important, they will consider the possibilities seriously. Here are some of the steps management can take to motivate staff:

- Point to the benefit of becoming a CIA.

- Make available in the office the catalogs of resident and extension (online) courses from all local universities.

- Let it be known that a master's degree indicates education in many of the subjects useful to internal auditors both in their jobs and as a springboard to advancement.

- Ask staff auditors at the beginning of each year to prepare written statements of what they propose to do to improve their knowledge and ability.

- Discuss with staff auditors their own long-range and short-range plans for self-improvement.

- Post lists of staff members who are taking courses and indicate those who have completed them.

- Put the names of members of the audit organization on lists of those to be considered for management training courses sponsored by the organization.

- Let it be understood throughout the audit department that the organization thinks highly of, and provides opportunities for, those people who continue their education.

- Provide for the organization to provide financial support for formal education (based on grades achieved).

Such courses will benefit not only the individual attending; this knowledge can be passed on to others through staff meetings.

New Training Course for Senior Internal Auditors[5]

The Institute of Internal Auditors (IIA) has launched Vision University, a training program for new chief auditing executives. Formed in association with Louisiana State University's Center for Internal Auditing, Vision University is designed to provide new auditing executives with the tools to hit the ground running.

According to The IIA, participants will:

- Determine how to use new control models to manage risk.
- Explore best practices of leading-edge audit departments.
- Discover how internal auditing can partner with business strategies.
- Identify what is needed to become a core member of the executive management team.
- Learn about cosourcing and outsourcing.
- Expand their knowledge of emerging control evaluation tools and techniques.
- Pinpoint the audit issues, emerging technologies, electronic commerce, and the virtual organization.

John Fernandes, IIA's former director of Certification and Professional Development, explained that the new program addresses the necessity of organizational cross-training. 'The downsizing and reengineering of the past few years has resulted in a need for the organization's top performers to be multidisciplined and multidimensional," Fernandes commented.

"Many internal auditors are being tapped for leadership roles in other departments such as operations or finance and often, non-auditors who have proven themselves in other areas of the organization are brought in to head up the internal audit function," he added.

The six-day seminar is conducted at different times of the year in various parts of the country.

Staff Meetings

There are different types of staff meetings, each with a different purpose. They can be used to communicate or reinforce routine administrative matters, teach new techniques, or even to let off steam.

The meetings can be used to reinforce the understanding of existing administrative instructions and such bread-and-butter topics as report writing and audit programming. As more complex matters need study, the meetings can become classrooms to teach such techniques as the computer in sampling, model building, probability theory, risk assessment, and other operation research methods. They can also be used as safety valves. Staff can be given an opportunity to be heard on such matters as administrative procedures that are not working, promotion possibilities, salaries, lack of communication, and other potential sore points that should not be allowed to fester.

Staff meetings should be programmed formally. A certain amount of budget should be allotted to developing and attending meetings. Dates for the meetings and the personnel to conduct them should be established at the time the year's audit schedule is established. A double return can be obtained from educational staff meetings by assigning each one to staff auditors to research a subject, develop the lesson plan or presentation, and lead the meeting. A supervisor should be assigned so that staff people have someone to consult with, to remove roadblocks, and to see that objectives are being met.

Some of the topics that might be considered for staff meetings are:

- Audit programming.
- Working paper presentation.
- Outlining audit reports. Developing findings.
- Describing interesting findings. Selecting samples.
- Determining confidence levels and precision ranges.
- The use of process auditing.
- E-business auditing.
- Deciding on the sampling techniques to use under different circumstances.
- Surveys versus detailed examinations.
- What is acceptable evidence of corrective action.
- New organization products.
- New organization systems.
- Environmental problems.
- Presentations by people from other departments.
- Internal auditing quality control.
- Analytical auditing.
- Risk assessment.
- Process auditing.

The Institute of Internal Auditors (IIA)

The IIA provides opportunities for continuing education through its professional journal, *Internal Auditor*. Other publications contain information on what is new in the profession. The IIA also provides seminars and study courses in a broad spectrum of subjects.

Attendance at local chapter meetings of The IIA affords attendees with opportunities to hear speakers on auditing and related topics. Working as a committee head or an officer adds stature to the individual and provides an opportunity to make management decisions, try out new ideas, and widen the circle of professional colleagues.

Research

Research is a form of education with many side benefits. The researcher can become both student and teacher, educating both self and other people in the department.

Provision for research projects should be made in the annual plan. They should be given project numbers and project budgets. Researchers should be selected from among the staff, taking into account their ability, natural leanings, and how the research will benefit them.

Having been assigned their topics, the researchers should then present for audit management approval their research objectives, milestones by which to measure progress, and an estimate of the end result of the research — be it a report, a program, or a suggested course of action. Hours expended should be charged against the project, and requests for any extension of time and budget should be made as formally as those for normal audit projects.

Research can be original — the development of a brand new idea — or it can constitute the accumulation and arraying of information to determine whether the old ways are still valid. Research topics can cover any aspect of audit activity. For example:

- Information systems applications to audit processes
- Advanced program techniques for operational audits
- Simulation and game theory as audit tools
- Advanced working paper techniques
- E-business auditing
- Methods of evaluating human resources
- Methods of measuring administrative effort
- How best to audit a particular activity
- Development of a style manual for auditors
- Adapting operations research techniques to audit needs

A description of an actual research project, with an excerpt (one group) from the research report, is shown in Exhibit 21-8.

Continuing Professional Development

The Certified Internal Auditor (CIA) program requires continuing professional development. To maintain current continuing professional development status, a CIA must complete 100 hours of acceptable professional development during three successive years. Reporting periods end December 31 each year. Acceptable professional development includes:

1. Educational programs at colleges and seminars.
2. Speaker, discussion leader, or instructor.
3. Author of books and articles.

Exhibit 21-8
Research Report on Audits of Procurement

Foreword

Procurement accounts for the majority of all organization expenditures. These expenditures are committed by a large number of people working in many diverse procurement activities. Complete examinations of such activities and of the work of all the people currently is clearly unfeasible. Accordingly, the audit effort must be directed toward those areas where there is the greatest risk of potential exposure to the loss or dissipation of organization resources as a result of improper procurement activities.

To that end, we established a research project to determine how we could accomplish optimum coverage of the procurement activity by identifying actual or potential risks and indicating the related controls.

Purpose and Scope

The objectives of the research project were: (1) to identify the areas of major risk inherent in the procurement process, and (2) to suggest possible means of control designed to protect against such risks.

To accomplish our purpose, we used the "brainstorming" technique. The members of the research committee assembled for brainstorming sessions to list various risks, both actual and potential, that may be encountered in the procurement process. For each risk we attempted to suggest some form of control to provide protection against inadequate or improper procurement action.

We then sorted the various risk areas by major groups, and for each group we set forth the objectives of the activities and sufficient general information to give some background on how they function.

Exhibit 21-8 (Cont.)

Results of Research
Our research resulted in eight groupings and four sub-groupings of risk areas and associated control. The groupings were identified as:

    I. Bidding Procedures
   II. Noncompetitive Procurements
  III. Decentralized Ordering and Receiving Areas
       A. Procurement Activities at Outlying Locations
       B. Direct Deliveries of Purchased Materials and Supplies
       C. Non-stocked Inventory Plan
       D. Shipments of Organization-owned Materials from Suppliers to Third Parties
   IV. Outside Production
    V. Blanket Purchase Orders
   VI. Purchase Order Changes
  VII. Procurements Paid for from Imprest Funds
 VIII. Time and Material and Labor Hour Procurements

Lists of the risk areas and the suggested controls are included. Risk areas include not only actual risks ("selection of an unqualified supplier") but also areas of potential risk ("sole source procurement"). For simplicity we have designated them all as "risk areas." It will be observed that the same risk areas may appear more than once, in different groupings, since the identical risk can be equally applicable to two or more different groups. The same is true of the related controls.

We have concluded that the review and evaluation of these risk areas represent the least amount of audit effort that should be expended in examining procurement activities. We wish to emphasize that the lists should not be used as check sheets that will completely satisfy audit objectives because (1) there is no substitute for imaginative, innovative auditing; (2) the lists and the associated general information that were prepared as of the date of this research report are almost certain to change with the passage of time because of the advent of new circumstances, procedures, and systems; and (3) it is a virtual impossibility to succeed in listing every conceivable risk area inherent in so broad and complex an activity as procurement.

Properly used, however, the lists should represent reasonably satisfactory audit guidelines and should provide assurance of at least minimum audit coverage within the procurement organizations assigned for audit.

Exhibit 21-8 (Cont.)

Bidding Procedures

Purpose of Activity

To obtain, through competitive means, required materials, supplies, and services at the most favorable terms, giving due regard to quality, price, and schedule.

General Information

To provide assurance that materials and services will be obtained at acceptable prices on schedule from qualified suppliers, the following procedures are provided by established written directives:

- It is the policy of the procurement division to solicit competitive bids for all items to be purchased except under specified conditions when the solicitation of bids is considered to be impractical.
- In general, written quotations are to be obtained from all prospective suppliers. Written quotations are to be obtained without exception in connection with all procurements over $10,000.
- For procurements estimated to be in excess of $1,000, prior written supervisory approval is to be obtained of the prospective bidders.
- Buyers are to show on the applicable procurement request the number of bids solicited, whether the bids obtained were oral or written, and, when competitive bids are not obtained, the reasons for not obtaining them.
- Written quotations are to be obtained from the suppliers on Requests for Quotation (RFQ) forms whenever practical, and are to be controlled by the responsible purchasing agents.
- Buyers are to select the lowest bidder capable of performing the desired work on schedule, and they are to provide adequate reasons for not selecting the low bidder.

Because of numerous pressures of varying kinds, there often is an inducement to circumvent established procedures. The circumventions may often be found in the following risk areas.

Risk Areas	*Suggested Controls*
Incomplete or poor initial selection of proposed sources of supply.	The review and approval of bidders' lists by procurement supervisors and by quality control and finance personnel before completing and mailing the RFQs.

Exhibit 21-8 (Cont.)

Risk Areas	*Suggested Controls*
Authority for the same group both to select proposed suppliers and to type and mail the RFQs.	The typing and mailing of RFQs by an organization other than the buying group.
Authority for the buying group that originated RFQs to receive the bids directly from the mail room or from the supplier.	The receipt and retention of bids until the closing date by an organization other than the group.
The receipt from suppliers of bids on other than organization RFQ forms.	The analysis of terms and conditions to detect any conditions of sale that may conflict with "Terms and Conditions of Purchase."
The acceptance of oral, non-RFQ types of bids.	The review and approval of the use of this type of bid by appropriate supervision.
	The review and approval of the proposed sources of supply.
	The requirement that suppliers submit written confirmation of bids.
	The review of RTP and bid award by appropriate management level.
Awards based on fewer than three bids.	The provision for written explanations and justifications of awards based on fewer than three bids, and review of those reasons by appropriate supervision.
Awards to other than low bidders.	The provision for written justifications and for supervisory approvals.

Exhibit 21-8 (Cont.)

Risk Areas	*Suggested Controls*
The disclosure of bid information received from some suppliers to other favored suppliers.	Bids remain sealed until opening in the presence witnesses.
The pitting of favored suppliers against only those suppliers known to submit high bids.	Supervisory review and evaluation of list of bidders.
The submission to non-favored suppliers of specifications, or other matters, which affect cost, that are more stringent than those submitted to favored suppliers.	Data assembled, compared, and mailed by an organization other than the buying group.
The communication of extension of bid periods only to favored suppliers.	Extensions or changes typed and mailed by same organization (other than the buying group) that handled the original RFQs.
Collusive bidding among suppliers available or selected to bid.	Estimates from using organizations of what are selected to bid. reasonable prices.
	Review of trade periodicals for what are going prices.
	Communication by procurement supervision with their counterparts in kindred organizations to see what others are paying.
	Use of analytical comparisons on a historical basis.

As specific examples, credit may be allowed for home study courses in audit- related subjects; for writing articles about one's own internal audit department, so long as they are published; and for participating as a discussion leader of in-house training seminars for new audit staff. However, experience in the internal audit department is not regarded as education qualifying for Continuing Professional Development credit.

In-house Training Programs

One audit activity reviewed took a hard look at its training program and decided a new approach was necessary.[6]

Its first step was to survey management and staff and review the department's audit objectives. In addition, an analysis was made of the audit summary memos, written after each job was completed, for observations on subjects calling for further education. In addition, a training program was built that would qualify for Continuing Professional Education (CPE) credit for CPAs and CIAs.

Based on this information the activity developed a series of courses to fill those needs. The courses followed a standard format. Key learning objectives were identified and instruction manuals were developed. Three weeks a year were devoted to training at which time no audits were conducted. Finally, upon applying to a number of states, the organization was acknowledged as an accredited CPE sponsor in the categories of accounting, auditing, taxation, and computer sciences for its self-study courses.

Here are some of the courses relating to auditing:

Initial Staff Training:

Overall audit approach, internal control concepts, fraud awareness, analytical review, working paper automation, and review of selected auditing areas.

In-charge Training:

Management development, conflict management, motivating employees, effective delegation, dealing with management; review of selected auditing areas; handling meetings; handling sensitive issues; report writing; performance appraisal and counseling; and handling specialized audits.

Payroll/Executive
Compensation:

Review of key controls in payroll area, as well as executive compensation; audit programs, case studies.

Internal Controls:

Review of recommendations of the Treadway Commission, latest SASs and control objectives in various areas.

Auditing PCs and LANs:

LAN administration, data storing, security, and auditing.

Mergers and Acquisitions:

Background, trends, due diligence in auditing and in legal matters, review of audit approach, and reports.

Research and Development:

Controls over R&D projects, R&D facilities, and research grants; reviewing the project management system.

Construction Auditing:

Opportunities for cost recovery in such matters as fraud, kickbacks, overcharges, and conflicts of interest.

Advertising:

Controls over network TV placement and production, controls over print placement and production, terminology and industry practices, purchasing and payment processes.

According to the source, the feedback from these training programs — from staff, management, and operating activities — has been highly positive.

Specialization Comes to Internal Auditing[7]

Internal auditing is growing more complex yearly. Currently, two organizations are working to provide specialty designations besides the traditional Certified Internal Auditor (CIA). The IIA has developed its first specialty certification, a certification in control self-assessment (CCSA), and the Board of Environmental Auditor Certifications (BEAC) has also developed its first certifications.

"Clearly control self-assessment (CSA) is here to stay," said John Fernandes. "It's consistent with today's management models, and it encourages management — and everyone in the organization — to understand more completely their responsibility for control. The new certification program will identify the skill sets needed by successful practitioners, measure proficiency, and provide guidance and stability to CSA initiatives."

CCSA examination: The CCSA examination made its debut in the fall of 1998. Although The IIA handled conceptual development, Sylvan Learning Centers administers most other functions. The examination — which is a one-part, three-hour, computer-based test — is offered six days a week around the world.

In addition to passing the examination, CCSA applicants must demonstrate appropriate facilitation skills. Candidates will be observed in a facilitation setting, such as a seminar or roundtable, in which performance will be observed by a qualified observer. Applicants must meet other educational and experience requirements as well.

Green Auditor Program: Separately, BEAC has officially approved its Corporate Bylaws Code of Ethics, and Standards of Conduct, as well its examination/certification process.

BEAC is an independent, nonprofit corporation created as a joint venture of the Environmental Auditing Roundtable (EAR) and The IIA. BEAC offers a five-day training course titled "14000 Plus Training for Auditors." Candidates who pass the BEAC 14000 Plus examination and meet all other BEAC requirements will be designated Certified Professional Environmental Auditors (CPEAs).

Staff Evaluations

The chief objectives of staff evaluations is to advise employees as to the status of their work and to identify weaknesses and opportunities for them so as to improve their overall contribution to the department and to keep them informed of their strong points, their weak points, and their progress.

Where there is no frequent contact between staff and chief audit executive, a formal evaluation system has many advantages. Such a system should establish standards and provide consistent methods of gauging performance. The standards and evaluation methods for the program should be clearly set forth in a staff memorandum or directive that informs staff about the department's evaluation policies and the criteria by which staff performance will be measured. This step removes any element of surprise and lets each auditor know what is needed to achieve a satisfactory evaluation.

Evaluations should address the knowledge, skills, and disciplines needed to perform audit assignments. Among these, one of the most important is analytical ability, as displayed by logical and systematic problem solving. Still, the internal audit profession inherits special problems when it comes to evaluating audit staff: No two projects that an auditor carries out or assists in are the same. Some projects do not even stretch a person's abilities. Others may turn out to be beyond an individual's experience or potential.

Still other projects — those that had previously been performed in a pedestrian and unimaginative fashion — may be raised to unexpected heights because of an individual auditor's novel approach or innovative methods. All of these factors should be considered when structuring the evaluation system so as to be fair to the employee and useful to the activity.

Evaluations after each audit provide both staff auditor and audit management with immediate feedback on performance. It allows an exchange while the audit is fresh in the minds of all concerned. Through these periodic evaluations, an auditor with performance failings has the opportunity to correct them before any annual evaluations.

A staff auditor will typically work with more than one supervisor over the course of several audits. To offset the varying backgrounds and requirements of individual supervisors and because no two audit projects are the same, every evaluation system should be in two parts: first, evaluation after each project; second, an annual review by the chief audit executive to compensate for the different personal criteria of individual supervisors. Also, each staff auditor is entitled to a face-to-face meeting at least annually with an executive or audit manager to discuss the auditor's progress and future.

Many performance factors can be considered. These may include quantity of work, computer competence, quality of work, knowledge of auditing, audit aptitude, written and oral communication, knowledge of enterprise procedures, relations with clients, planning ability, and how well instructions are followed. Other matters that an audit manager or executive should consider are whether the auditor has improved since the last annual evaluation, how well the internal auditor is meeting personal goals and objectives, the auditor's experience and education, the auditor's participation in continuing education, and the complexity of the completed audit assignments.

Evaluators should seek to maintain a distinction between accomplishments and traits. Both are significant, but each has a different function. The rating of accomplishments should apply to the particular project completed, since each project has different problems. The evaluation of traits deals with the personal qualities that auditors bring with them into their working life.

Traits are harder to evaluate because the evaluator is applying subjective standards and because all people have built-in biases. But it is good for the manager or executive to be aware of significant traits, since these may affect decisions about audit assignments. For example, a project that will require contacts at high levels in the enterprise should not be assigned to an auditor who may be technically expert but who is not personable or articulate. Similarly, a project that requires a large number of assistants should not be assigned to an auditor who does not possess qualities of leadership.

Some of the factors that should be considered in evaluating traits are attitude, personality, leadership, judgment, initiative, self-confidence, and the ability to get along with other members of the audit staff. One program that has worked reasonably well — no one method is perfect where souls are bared — provides this pattern:

> At the conclusion of each audit assignment, the auditor-in-charge prepares a rating sheet for each assistant, and the supervisor prepares one for the auditor-in-charge. A rating for each assignment is necessary because of the variations among assignments. The actual numerical or adjectival ratings are not discussed, but a dialog is conducted on the strengths and weaknesses observed on that particular project.

> The dialog can work well or poorly, depending on how it is approached. The appraisal should be constructive. The climate of the interview should be empathetic and supportive. An often successful ploy is for the evaluator to open the conversation by asking the staff auditors how they themselves thought they had performed, what they felt they did well, what they felt they did poorly, what they learned from the job, and what areas of improvement they see for themselves. These dialogs are valuable because it is cruel to permit auditors to go to another assignment unaware of certain defects that adversely affect their performance and that will continue to plague their work unless they can identify their weaknesses and make a conscious effort toward improvement.

The supervisor or auditor-in-charge owes it to subordinates to help them identify their weaknesses. They also owe it to the employee to use tact and sympathy. Thus, to lead the auditor's self-evaluation toward the known defects can probably accomplish the most good. Most people like to talk about themselves, and getting staff people to do the exploring themselves can accomplish the objectives of the dialog with the least amount of abrasion.

At the end of a six-month or 12-month period, the chief auditing executive combines the various performance ratings of each auditor and discusses the results with them. In some organizations, the periodic discussions are held at the time of salary adjustments. The purpose is to bring home the significance of the rating. In other organizations, the periodic discussions are held separately from the salary adjustment interviews, thus placing the emphasis on improving the auditors, not on rewarding or punishing them.

These ratings and interviews are of extreme importance to the individual. In very large organizations, they may be the only opportunity during the year when the staff auditor has a chance for an eye-to-eye colloquy with the executive or manager. The meeting should be carried out in an unhurried atmosphere and be pervaded by a deep and sincere interest in the auditor's problems, goals, and assertions, and in his or her program to work the problems out.

Many styles of rating sheets are in use. Several of them that provide for evaluation of both accomplishments and traits have been reproduced in Exhibits 21-9 and 21-10, which provide numerical ratings on a large variety of subjects and qualities, and adjectival ratings to give meaning to the numbers. Exhibit 21-9 is a rating sheet for a staff auditor. Exhibit 21-10 is for a supervising auditor. Numerical ratings provide for quantitative comparisons among different auditors. The qualities being appraised on these sheets are self-explanatory. These forms also provide for an evaluation of the difficulty of the job: Class A is for a relatively simple job. Class B is for a job of normal difficulty. Class C is for a job of exceptional difficulty. These factors can be used to adjust total scores. Five percent is deducted for easy jobs and added for difficult ones.

Exhibit 21-9
Staff Rating Form — Staff Auditor

Total Score _____

Name: _____   Period: From _____ To _____

Job No.: _____   Job Title: _____

Class (A B C) _____   Signature: _____ Date: _____

Planning and Organizing	Excellent	Very Good	Good	Fair	Unsatisfactory
Understanding of the procedures and problems relating to the audit segments assigned.	80	72	64	48	32
Conformance to the instructions provided by the auditor-in-charge and by the departmental manuals — yet questioning what seems illogical or unreasonable in the instructions.	60	54	48	36	24
Organizing and programming the work assigned so as to provide for coverage of the key control points in proper depth.	60	54	48	36	24
Totals	200	180	160	120	80
Field Work					
Accuracy of working papers — computations, references, statistical analyses.	90	81	72	54	36
Thoroughness of examination — yet knowing when to suggest discontinuance of the investigations.	90	81	72	54	36
Appropriateness of tests to the transactions reviewed.	60	54	48	36	24
Adequacy of documentation for work performed — showing nature, scope, and results of examination.	60	54	48	36	24
Completion of required field work — leaving no loose ends.	40	36	32	24	16
Summarization of findings — to facilitate review.	40	36	32	24	16
Forming opinion — use of judgment in assessing significance.	60	54	48	36	24

Exhibit 21-9 (Cont.)

	Excellent	Very Good	Good	Fair	Unsatisfactory
Care in preparing and organizing working papers — properly indexed, cross-referenced, initialed, dated.	60	54	48	36	24
Totals	500	450	400	300	200
Clarity and conciseness of oral expression.	60	54	48	36	24
Effectiveness.	40	36	32	24	16
Totals	100	90	80	60	40
Writing Ability					
Use of clear, concise and appropriate language in working paper comments and in summaries and write-ups.	90	81	72	54	36
Organization of written material.	60	54	48	36	24
Totals	150	135	120	90	60
Administration					
Meeting the budget and the schedule for the work assigned.	50	45	40	30	20
Grand Totals	1,000	900	800	600	400
General Characteristics					
Place check mark under appropriate adjectival rating:					
Alertness, energy, and initiative.	—	—	—	—	—
Pleasantness, open-mindedness, tact, and cooperativeness.	—	—	—	—	—
Work habits — diligent application of effort to the job, and observation of organization working hours.	—	—	—	—	—
Readiness for In-charge Work					
Ability to carry out work successfully with only general supervision.	—	—	—	—	—
Additional Comments					
Discuss specific attributes that require strengthening so as to improve this auditor's ability to handle supervising assignments.					

Exhibit 21-10
Staff Rating Form — Supervising Auditor

Total Score _____

Name: _____   Period: From _____ To _____

Job No.: _____   Job Title: _____

Class (A B C) _____   Signature: _____ Date: _____

Planning	Excellent	Very Good	Good	Fair	Unsatisfactory
Understanding of procedures and problems relating to the activity under examination — awareness of objectives of activity under review, and relationship of those objectives to organization objectives.	40	36	32	24	16
Coverage in the audit program of all key control points — giving proper weight and emphasis to most significant control points.	50	45	40	30	20
Nature of planned tests — use of imagination and economy.	30	27	24	18	12
Extent of planned tests — use of appropriate sampling techniques.	30	27	24	18	12
Totals	150	135	120	90	60
Field Work					
Completion of required field work — coverage of all programmed steps; adequate reasons to eliminate steps.	20	18	16	12	8
Accuracy of working papers — computations, references, statistical analyses.	70	63	56	42	28
Thoroughness of examination — yet knowing when to discontinue investigation.	70	63	56	42	28
Appropriateness of tests to the transactions reviewed.	40	36	32	24	16
Adequacy of documentation for work performed — showing nature, scope, and results of examination.	45	41	36	27	18

Exhibit 21-10 (Cont.)

	Excellent	Very Good	Good	Fair	Unsatisfactory
Summarization of findings — to facilitate review.	25	22	20	15	10
Evaluation of findings in forming opinion — judgment in assessing significance of findings.	65	59	52	39	26
Working paper preparation and organization — properly indexed, cross-referenced, initialed, dated.	40	36	32	24	16
Totals	375	338	300	225	150
Report Draft					
Adequacy of support for report statements — ability of findings to withstand successful attack.	60	54	48	36	24
Proper treatment of findings according to relative significance — giving greater weight and space to more serious findings.	60	54	48	36	24
Organization — presenting material in a logical and orderly sequence.	50	45	40	30	20
Compliance with departmental instructions on reporting — following rules laid down in departmental manuals.	40	36	32	24	16
Clarity and appropriateness of report language — making findings clear to nontechnical reader.	50	45	40	30	20
Accuracy in preparation and review to eliminate errors.	40	36	32	24	16
Totals	300	270	240	180	120
Oral Communication					
Clarity and conciseness.	60	54	48	36	24
Persuasiveness.	40	36	32	24	16
Totals	100	90	80	60	40
Administration					
Meeting budget.	40	36	32	24	16
Meeting schedule.	35	31	28	21	14
Totals	75	67	60	45	30
Grand Totals	1,000	900	800	600	400

Exhibit 21-10 (Cont.)

General Characteristics	Excellent	Very Good	Good	Fair	Unsatisfactory
(Place check mark under appropriate adjectival rating)					
Alertness, energy, and initiative.	—	—	—	—	—
Pleasantness, open-mindedness, tact, and cooperativeness.	—	—	—	—	—
Work habits — diligent application of effort to the job and observation of organization working hours.	—	—	—	—	—

Additional Comments:

Exhibit 21-11 is a rating form that provides adjectival ratings only. The same form is used both for staff and for supervisors. But certain of the factors may be marked NA (not applicable) when appropriate, to distinguish between the two positions. Exhibit 21-12 provides explanations for the performance factors.

Exhibit 21-11
Performance Appraisal

Name _____ Assistant_____ Auditor in Charge _____
Assignment _____ Period Covered _____
Overall rating for this assignment

Desirability on Another Assignment
Desirable _____
Acceptable_____
Prefer Another Staff Member _____

Performance Factors*	O E S + S S - Na	**Personal Characteristics***	FA	NI
Quantity of Work	_____	Creativity	_____	
Quality of Work	_____	Initiative	_____	
Knowledge of Auditing	_____	Persistence	_____	
Auditing Aptitude	_____	Ability to work with others	_____	

Exhibit 21-11 (Cont.)

Performance Factors*		Personal Characteristics*	
O E S + S S - Na		FA NI	
Problem Analysis	_____	Judgment	_____
Decision-making	_____	Adaptability	_____
Planning	_____	Persuasiveness	_____
Follows Instructions	_____	Leadership	_____
Communications: Oral	_____	Self-confidence	_____
Written	_____	Attitude	_____

*See general instructions, Exhibit 21-12, for definitions and rating terms.

Attributes: Circle up to five adjectives that best describe the staff member's outstanding personal characteristics. They may be desirable and/or undesirable qualities. Extra blanks are provided for adjectives that you consider more descriptive.

aggressive	enthusiastic	lazy	self-assured
articulate	erratic	loud	shallow
careless	excitable	mature	sloppy
casual	flexible	naive	steady
cautious	flippant	neat	taciturn
clumsy	gullible	observant	tenacious
conceited	imaginative	officious	vacillating
deliberate	immature	open-minded	verbose
discreet	impulsive	overbearing	vigorous
discriminating	inarticulate	plodding	vulgar
dogmatic	indifferent	presumptuous	witty
dull	indiscreet	prim	
eager	inflexible	pushy	
energetic	inquisitive	resourceful	

Counseling: The completed appraisal report is confidential and should not be shown or read to the staff member even though it is required that performance on each assignment be discussed. Discuss the staff member's performance on each assignment during the course of the examination and in summary form at the end of the assignment. Please answer Yes, No, or Not Applicable (N/A) to these questions:

Have you discussed with the staff member at a meeting for that purpose:
(1) Good work done? _____
(2) Poor performance?_____
(3) Correctable deficiencies? _____

Exhibit 21-11 (Cont.)

(4) Means of correcting deficiencies? _____

Give the date of the meeting _____

Matters discussed with staff member and the reaction: _____

_____

_____

_____

_____

Comments: Comment on exceptionally outstanding performance or unsatisfactory ratings, as well as qualities not covered elsewhere. Do not include comments that are only a restatement of the various ratings; Specific illustrations are always more helpful than remarks of a general nature. Be concise.

Signature _____   Date _____

Exhibit 21-12
General Instructions

General Instructions: The purpose of the staff performance appraisal form is to obtain information on the level of work the audit staff member is qualified to perform as well as on prospects for advancement. The appraisal report is necessary for knowledgeable decisions on adjustments of compensation and on promotions, as well as a means of summarizing information to assist in effectively counseling and training the staff member. The completed appraisal report is confidential and should not be shown or read to the staff member, even though it is required that performance on the assignment be discussed. There is a difference between discussion of performance and reporting, since the latter includes grading and evaluating, while the former does not.

DEFINITIONS
Rating Factors
Performance Factors
Quantity of work — Accomplishments measured against the requirement of the position; results measured against goals. Timely completion of work for which the auditor is responsible.
Quality of work — The degree of excellence of the end results; thoroughness, accuracy, and overall caliber of completed assignments, including adequacy and clarity of working papers.

Exhibit 21-12 (Cont.)

Knowledge of auditing — Understanding basic auditing principles and organization operational policies and procedures.

Auditing aptitude — Understanding audit program objectives, and having the ability to analyze the systems of control to be audited.

Problem analysis — Recognizing problems and breaking problem situations into essential parts logically and systematically. Gathering facts and getting beneath the surface to discover their full meaning.

Decision-making — Screening facts, getting to the heart of the problem, and making sound and timely decisions.

Planning — Planning the work systematically and practically, and establishing logical priorities to do a more efficient audit job.

Following instructions — Having the ability to follow instructions exactly and conscientiously; being proficient in comprehending instructions; knowing when to question the instructions if they seem inappropriate in a given situation.

Communication skills — Expressing points of view clearly, logically, and convincingly in written and oral communications; and keeping superiors informed currently as the job progresses.

Personal Characteristics

Creativity — Ability to apply imagination and originality to the job so as to develop new and improved procedures or applications.

Initiative — Being a self-starter.

Persistence — Being persevering. Pursuing goals resolutely. Not being easily deterred from attaining audit objectives.

Ability to work with others — Ability to get along with people. Being tactful and diplomatic and aware of effect upon others.

Judgment — Ability to comprehend all facets of a problem and to assign values to each consideration in arriving at a decision.

Adaptability — Ability to adjust to change and to meet new situations.

Persuasiveness — Ability to influence others.

Leadership — Ability to motivate subordinates and associates to take desired action.

Self-confidence — Ability to remain at ease, self-assured, and poised.

Attitude — Enthusiasm for the job, loyalty to the organization, and the ability to accept constructive criticism.

Rating Terms
Performance Factors

0 — Outstanding	Exceptional, superior (would apply only in rare instances).
E — Excellent	Considerably above average; stands out; demonstrates rare ability
S+ — Satisfactory Plus	Above average.
S — Satisfactory	Exhibits an acceptable degree of performance under strong direction.
S- — Satisfactory Minus	A marginal rating; does not meet minimum accepted standards.
NA — Not Acceptable	

Personal Characteristics

NI — Needs Improvement	Definite improvement required to reach normally accepted standards.
FA — Fully Acceptable	Meets normally accepted standards in all respects.

A utility firm is experimenting with a unique evaluation form in two parts. The first part seeks to tie individual contribution and performance to the audit department's goals. The second deals with the employee's traits. The goals listed in the first part relate to Internal Controls, Environmental Quality, Total Quality Management, Regulatory Compliance, Contractors and Consultants, Non-utility Matters, and Professional Leadership. The qualities shown in the second part address Teamwork, Challenge, Candor, and Commitment.

The goals are listed in boxes with accompanying blank spaces for comments by the individuals on their own contributions. Auditors-in-charge and supervisors use similar forms to show their assessment of the auditors' contribution. Evaluator and auditor then compare the two forms and work out their differences. Exhibit 21-13 shows extracts from the form dealing with performance. Exhibit 21-14 shows the factors dealing with traits and qualities.

Exhibit 21-13
Audit Department Goals

✓ Internal Controls
✓ Environmental Quality
✓ Total Quality Management
✓ Regulatory Compliance

✓ Contractors & Consultants
✓ Non-utility
✓ Professional Leadership

Goals	Individual's Contributions
INTERNAL CONTROLS • Promotes improved financial management and reporting in line organizations. • Monitors and evaluates contract administration. • Supports communication/education programs within other organizations. • Conducts year-end expenditure reviews. • Evaluates controls and security of information systems and facilities. • Monitors adherence to *Standards of Conduct* and Corporate Policy Statements.	**Comments:**

Exhibit 21-13 (Cont.)

Goals	Individual's Contributions
ENVIRONMENTAL QUALITY • Completes 70+ audits/limited reviews. • Communicates environmental concerns to environmental audits manager. • Assists in compliance audit program. • Coordinates with law and environmental affairs.	**Comments:**

TOTAL QUALITY MANAGEMENT
 	
• Supports and participates in department TQM program as it applies to the following:
  - Customer satisfaction
  - Continuous improvement
  - Team building
  - Quality assurance
  - Measurement of results
  - Accuracy, timeliness, etc.
• Employs stop-and-go auditing concept.
• Contributes to the department's positive results in benchmarking studies.
• Recognizes the achievements of others through high-five nominations.
	Comments:

Exhibit 21-13 (Cont.)

Goals	Individual's Contributions
REGULATORY COMPLIANCE • Integrates utilization of regulatory compliance tracking system into audit program. • Identifies and evaluates high-risk areas and report to management. • Assists in correcting deficiencies to minimize disallowances. • Audits affiliated organization transactions.	**Comments:**
CONTRACTORS & CONSULTANTS • Monitors compliance with "blue book" guidelines. • Focuses coverage on areas of greatest risk/payback. • Reviews payments for inappropriate billings. Recovers $10+ million [2 times budget].	**Comments:**
NON-UTILITY • Expands coverage of Mission Energy's international projects. • Increases auditor involvement during business development cycle. • Conducts monthly management meetings with all Mission Organizations. • Establishes environmental compliance audit program.	**Comments:**

Exhibit 21-13 (Cont.)

Goals	Individual's Contributions
PROFESSIONAL LEADERSHIP	**Comments:**
• Demonstrates results in innovation & creativity.	
• Maintains an active role in continuous education.	
• Maintains/obtains professional certification(s).	
• Demonstrates leadership in the professional practice of internal auditing.	
• Demonstrates conformance to the *Standards for the Professional Practice of Internal Auditing.*	

NOTE: If you need additional space to write your comments, or if you contributed directly to a corporate goal not reflected in the department goals, please attach a separate piece of paper with your additional comments and cross reference appropriately.

The system does present an interesting departure from the customary numerical and adjectival forms of evaluations. Moreover, it calls upon both the evaluator and the one evaluated to give serious thought to the evaluations. A ticking off of numbers or adjectives won't do. Thoughtful narrative statements are much more revealing.

Exhibit 21-14

TEAMWORK

<u>Factors:</u>

- Contributes to achievement of team goals.
- Recognizes and supports contribution of others.
- Participates in maintaining a cohesive, supportive work environment.
- Shares information, ideas, and solutions.
- Enhances reputation and credibility of internal audit department.

<u>Comments:</u>

COMMITMENT TO VALUES
Challenge, Candor, Commitment

<u>Challenge</u>

- Challenges self to continuously improve own performance.
- Seeks out new ways to improve business processes and methods.
- Demonstrates innovation and creativity in all major aspects of work.

<u>Comments:</u>

<u>Candor:</u>

- Acts with honesty, openness, and integrity in all business relationships.
- Respects and responds with sincerity to the comments of others.
- Inspires an environment of trust.

<u>Comments:</u>

Exhibit 21-14 (Cont.)

COMMITMENT TO VALUES
Challenge, Candor, Commitment

Commitment:	**Comments:**
• Assures that all work contributes to organization value, quality, and productivity. • Enhances competitive performance through cost reductions.	

SIGNATURES AND EMPLOYEE COMMENTS

PLAN

Employee's Signature: _____ Date: _____
Manager's Signature: _____ Date: _____

☐ INTERIM REVIEW   ☐ ANNUAL REVIEW

Manager's Signature: _____ Date: _____
Second Level Reviewer's Signature: _____ Date: _____

EMPLOYEE'S COMMENTS: _____

_____

_____

Employee's Signature: _____ Date: _____

Employee's signature indicates document has been discussed with the employee and that he/she has received a copy. Signature does not necessarily indicate that the employee agrees with all aspects of the document.

Audit Assignments

Audit staff members are developed and their potentials made known by the audit assignments they are given. People should be made to stretch. But they should not be pushed beyond their capacity, for therein lies frustration and the loss of a potentially valuable resource. So audit management should consider certain factors when assigning audit staff to audit projects.

1. *The nature and complexity of the audit engagement.* Assignments should provide reasonable assurance that the members of the audit team collectively possess the knowledge, skills, and discipline to complete the audit in a professional manner.*

2. *The need for objectivity.* Auditors should not be placed in a position where their objectivity might be impaired or where a reasonable person would be given the perception of impairment. Assignments should take into account any potential for conflict of interest or bias.

3. *The desirability of rotating assignments.* Periodic rotations of assignments may enhance objectivity, since repeated audits by the same auditor of the same activities may develop undesirable attachments that might affect objectivity. Also, rotation of assignments among auditors with differing approaches and abilities provides a fresh look at and a new perspective on the engagement.

4. *The need for supervision.* All engagements should be supervised. The extent of that supervision will depend on the nature and complexity of the assignment as well as the experience, knowledge, and proficiency of the auditors.

5. *The need for developing and training staff auditors.* All audit staffs need development. The dynamic state of the profession can make accustomed routines obsolete as new methods and procedures become known in the auditing community. Providing experience through different types of assignments with varying degrees of complexity and subject matter and under different supervisors will lead to the development of a better audit staff.

*The IIA's *Code of Ethics* provides that: "Internal auditors shall engage only in those services for which they have the necessary knowledge, skills, and experience." (¶ 4.1, adopted June 17, 2000).

Restructuring the Human Relations Element[8]

The Aetna Life and Casualty Company, one of the largest insurance firms in the United States, during the early and mid-1900s made substantive changes in its personnel management philosophy. The organization was convinced that people want to do well and that it was the firm's responsibility to provide an environment that would assist.

Thus, the audit operation (first) emphasized staff and (second) emphasized innovation and productivity. It reasoned that motivated staff would perform quality work and that by so doing the employees would be better able to achieve their professional goals.

The philosophy consisted of five central focuses that served as the foundation of the work. The focuses:

- Develop partnerships with customers.
- Provide cost effective services.
- Strive for continuous improvement.
- Develop diversity, empowerment, innovation, and teamwork among staff members.
- Open communication in all directions.

The firm emphasized that the audit staff should act as owners of the function and to assume responsibility for improving quality. Also, staff should question current procedures to determine if they add value to the firm, or can be improved or dropped. The staff was encouraged to assume the concept of professional skepticism and the audit organization provided support for the exercise of the attitude.

The cornerstone of the restructuring was the development of the audit team concept. Team participation was based on staff preferences. However, there was also a rotation policy in order to accomplish diversion in approach. The team was responsible for:

- Planning.
- Staffing.
- Scheduling.
- Review.

Managers participated in the work as the audit progressed and thus improved quality as well as timeliness. This shift also allowed the audit activity to reduce its administrative staff from 10 to three members.

Another of the major changes was the shift of recruiting from the college campuses to the seeking of staff with demonstrated technical and interpersonal competence. Currently about one quarter of the staff has not had prior audit experience. Also, currently the teams as well as customers participate in the acquisition process.

Another facet of the changes was to use value-added adjustments. The audit staff is rewarded for increasing output, reducing costs, and improving quality.

The department required each staff member to outline a strategic plan for his/her career goals and strategies. To assist them, the department provided about 120 hours of training per year plus other educational projects as desired.

Finally the staff participated in an upward review process in which they review their managers. Managers are required to develop plans for responding to the reviews.

This approach resulted in a number of staff recommendations to cut costs. One of them was a reduction of office sizes. This alone saved about $500,000 per year. Another innovation was the use of a home page on the World Wide Web. This home page will serve as a communications device for the staff and others.

Over the years there was a steady trend of cost reduction. However, the largest part came from the management tier of staff and this was accomplished to the greatest degree by attrition.

The outcome of these and other improvements resulted in a series of positive outcomes.

- Customer service ratings improved 25 percent over an 18-month period and a corporate employee attitude survey showed that auditors were among the top in staff/management relations.

- A large number of staff have been recruited into the operating organizations of the firm.

- The firm itself is gearing up to employ the same philosophy that caused the very positive changes in the audit staff and its operations.

Strengths, Conflicts, and Violations

What distinguishes professional internal auditors from most other people within the enterprise is their objectivity and lack of bias. Non-audit employees and officers seeking to meet their responsibilities are usually working toward parochial goals and objectives. Senior management cannot be sure that the information such people provide is completely objective and unbiased. Therein lies the strength and the usefulness of the professional internal auditor: the comfort given to management that it can expect independent judgments and unmanipulated facts that can be completely relied upon.

This objectivity is rare and should not be compromised. To that end internal auditors should never place themselves or be placed in a position where that objectivity can be questioned. The internal auditor's *Code of Ethics* and *Standards* set forth certain rules to follow so they can avoid any imputation of lack of objectivity or presence of bias. Violations of these rules lay the internal auditors open to criticism and questions of lack of audit objectivity.

The *Code of Ethics* states that internal auditors have a responsibility to conduct themselves in a manner so that their good faith and integrity should not be open to question. They shall refrain from entering into any activity that may be in conflict with the interest of their employers or that would prejudice their ability to carry out objectively their duties and responsibilities.

The *Standards* states that internal auditors should be objective in performing audits. It describes objectivity as an independent mental attitude that internal auditors should maintain in performing audits. They are not to subordinate their judgment on audit matters to that of others.

In the course of internal audit assignments, conflicts are bound to arise. It is up to the chief audit executive, to supervisors, and to staff auditors to make sure that the rules of conduct binding on professional internal auditors are not violated and that no conflicts of interest or bias appear or can reasonably be inferred.

The kinds of circumstances that may arise are legion. Here are examples of but a sampling from the literature:

- An internal auditor who conveys information about an organization's financial condition is violating the *Code of Ethics*. Such action would warrant dismissal of the internal auditor.

- An internal auditor who discovers an illegal action by a corporate officer and brings the matter to the attention of a government agency is in an anomalous position. On the one hand, the auditor owes loyalty to the employer. On the other hand, he or she should not be party to any illegal act. Generally, the internal auditor's obligation to the *Code* is satisfied by bringing matters to the attention of senior management or the board of directors — not to outsiders.

- An internal auditor who reports information the basis of inadequate data is violating rules of conduct. The *Code* requires diligence in the audit and obtaining adequate factual evidence to warrant an audit opinion.

- Auditors who fail to report material deficiencies on the grounds that management is already aware of the defects are in violation of the *Code*, relative to revealing material facts in their audit reports, and the *Standards*, relative to subordinating audit judgment on audit matters to the judgment of others.

- Regular preparation of bank reconciliations by internal auditors should be avoided since that is an operating responsibility and, under the *Standards,* is presumed to impair audit objectivity.

- Chief audit executives may not place an auditor in a position where a conflict of interest may be inferred, even though the executive has confidence in the auditor's judgment and character. Such situations may include, but not be limited to, assigning an auditor to audit an activity for which the auditor had operating responsibilities less than a year previously, or making audits of areas in which the auditor has relatives or a financial interest.

- Internal auditors should not put themselves into positions where violations of confidentiality or a conflict of interest can be inferred. Examples would be misplacing working papers occasionally, using confidential information for personal gain, accepting a fee or a gift from a customer without the knowledge and consent of senior management, accepting frequent luncheons or otherwise socializing with suppliers of the employer, and purchasing stock in a corporation that the auditor proposed be acquired in a report to the board.

- Audit supervisors would be violating the *Standards* if they fail to report substandard work of a staff auditor.

Chapter 31 contains detailed material on the *Standards.*

Objectivity, as it has been said, is a state of mind. But two states of mind must be considered: that of the auditor and that of an observer. Objectivity is made of fragile stuff. An auditor may feel certain that so minor a matter as a lunch or a cup of coffee does not affect his or her objectivity. Yet that objectivity may be subconsciously touched whether the auditor knows it or not. Certainly, the internal auditor would have a different attitude toward a provider of a lunch than to a source of insulting language. And if the auditor had a high degree of moral character, it could well be that he or she might consciously or unconsciously lean over backward for, and deal less evenhandedly with, one who gave small favors — as opposed to one whom they found objectionable.

So the perception of the observer — a prudent, knowledgeable, reasonable observer — toward questioned conduct must be considered. How would such an observer regard the action? The rule of reason must prevail. Certainly not all interactions can be considered conflicts. For example, the following actions could not reasonably be considered capable of creating bias or loss of objectivity.

- Receiving a gift from a professional organization for services rendered without pay.

- Auditing an activity in which the auditor had been a key employee five years previously.

- Auditing a data processing center that the auditor had audited three times previously.

- Auditing a computer system for which the auditor had been internal auditing's representative on the design team.

Yet despite all efforts to maintain objectivity, the pressures of jobs and assignments can put an internal auditor in a quandary that must be dealt with carefully. Consider the case of a chief audit executive who is told by senior management to supervise and audit a special program, such as a political action committee or a charitable or social program. In such cases, the executive may be asking for contributions from management people who might refuse to contribute. Certainly, it could be perceived that those management people might not fare too well in the executive's audit evaluation of the program.

In such cases, unless the executive point-blank refuses the assignment and thereby brooks the wrath of executive management, the audit of the program would have to be assigned to someone else in the audit department. The executive should not only distance himself or herself from the audit project, but also should see that the resulting audit report makes clear the executive's relationship to the program.

Without a clear conception of the auditor's objectivity, all of the audit work, no matter how professionally carried out, may be considered suspect. And so, objectivity must be jealously guarded and any compromise studiously avoided.

The Development of the Ethical Culture of an Organization

In many organizations internal auditors have been selected to implement the ethics programs. The concept that the auditor is an evaluator between what is right operationally relative to the organization's basic objectives tends to carry over into the area of ethics. This philosophy cloaks the internal auditor with the authority and approach to be able to determine what is and is not in compliance with the organization's code of conduct. In many organizations the internal auditor is the author of the code and thus becomes the determining authority of acts relative to compliance with the code.

Practice Advisory 2130-1, "Role of the Internal Audit Activity and the Internal Auditor in the Ethical Culture of an Organization," addresses the above issue. It describes the organization's governance process and then shows how the process relates to its ethical culture. The advisory encourages internal auditors and the internal audit activity to take an active role in this process. It states that internal auditors "possess a high level of trust and integrity within the organization and the skills to be effective advocates of ethical conduct" and that they have the competence and capacity to encourage the organization's personnel to comply with ethical responsibilities.

The advisory suggests that the internal audit activity evaluate the effectiveness of a series of features of an enhanced ethical culture such as:

- A formal code of conduct.
- Communications of expected ethical attitudes and behavior.
- Strategies to enhance the ethical culture.
- Methods of reporting unethical activities.
- Regular employee declaration as to awareness of ethical requirements.
- A structure to operate the activities necessary to produce an ethical culture.
- Teaching employees to be ethical.
- Regular surveys to determine ethical climate.
- Reviews to identify processes that could lead to unethical activities.
- Background checks as a part of the hiring process.

References

[1]Brenner, V.C., and G.E. Sumners, "University-level Internal Audit Education Programs," *Internal Auditor,* June 1991, 43-46.

[2]Kimmell, D.L., and S.L. Kimmell, "Internal Auditing Internships," *Internal Auditor,* August 1988, 27- 30.

[3]Dittenhofer, M.A., D.R. Pack, and G.R. Wendt, "Internships Supplement Classroom Instruction," *Internal Auditor,* February 1990, 59-60.

[4]Ramamoorti, Sridhar, Frederick L. Newmann, and Julie K. Monroe, "The Value of Mentoring and Coaching in Internal Audit Setting," A paper presented at The Institute of Internal Auditors' Educators Colloquium at Dallas, Texas on June 14, 1998.

[5]*Internal Auditing Alert* (Boston, MA: Warren Gorham and Lamont, December 1997), 5.

[6]Hartman, B.E., "Building a World Class Training Program," *Internal Auditor,* April 1993, 48-51.

[7]*Internal Auditing Alert* (Boston, MA: Warren Gorham and Lamont, January 1998), 1.

[8]Gray, Glen L., and Maryann Jacobi Gray, *Enhancing Internal Auditing Through Innovative Practices* (Altamonte Springs, FL: The Institute of Internal Auditors, 1996), 19-24.

Supplementary Readings

Barrier, Michael, "Turnover: The Ebb and Flow," *Internal Auditor*, October 2001, 32-37.

Beeler, Jesse D., James E. Hunton, and Benson Wier, "Promotion Performance of Internal Auditors: A Survival Analysis," *Internal Auditing,* July/August 1999, 3-14.

Calhoun, Charles, "CIA Designation Celebrates 25 Years," *Internal Auditing Alert*, July 1999, 4-6.

Calhoun, Charles, "How to Evaluate Auditor Resumes," *Internal Auditing Alert*, September 1998, 1-3.

Calhoun, Charles, "New Core Competencies for Seasoned IA," *Internal Auditing Alert*, August 1998, 1-3.

Calhoun, Charles, "Resume Techniques for Auditors," *Internal Auditing Alert*, November 1997, 6-7.

Causa, Jack, "Taming Turnover," *Internal Auditor*, April 1999, 26-28.

Chau, Chak-Tong, "Career Plateaus," *Internal Auditor*, October 1998, 48-52.

Crumbley, D. Larry, and Glenn E. Sumners, "How Businesses Profit from Internships," *Internal Auditor*, October 1998, 54-58.

D'Amico, Karen L., and Bruce A. Adamec, "Coach," *Internal Auditor*, June 1996, 30-38.

Del Vecchio, Stephen C., and B. Douglas Clinton, "Cosourcing and Other Alternatives in Acquiring Internal Auditing Services," Internal Auditing, May/June 2003.

Dezoort, F. Todd, Richard W. Houston, and John T. Reisch, "Incentive-based Compensation for Internal Auditors," *Internal Auditor*, June 2000, 42-46.

Dittenhofer, Mortimer A., and John T. Sennetti, *Ethics and the Internal Auditor: Ten Years Later* (Altamonte Springs, FL: The Institute of Internal Auditors, 1995).

English, Denise, and Mark Pearson, "The Professor as Intern," *Internal Auditor*, October 1998, 60-61.

Figg, Jonathan, "Power Staffing 101," *Internal Auditor*, April 1999, 22-25.

Friedberg, Allan H., Paul Milici, and Steven J. Krouskos, "Benchmark Survey: Internal Auditor Training," *Internal Auditing*, Spring 1996, 54-59.

Galvin, Karen, "Leadership Today for the New Audit Manager," *Internal Auditing Alert*, November 1998, 4-5.

Greengard, Samuel, "Power Training Via the WEB," *Controller Magazine*, August 1998, 55-59.

Greenspan, James W., David C. Burns, and Susan Ligthle, "The Performance Evaluation Process: Results and Implications," *Internal Auditing,* Winter 1991, 4-10.

Hagen, Michael E., Jimie Kusel, James E. Gauntt, and Ralph Shull, "Best Practices Through Peer Networking, " *Internal Auditing*, Fall 1996, 56-58.

Harrington, Lawrence J., and Marcie Shepard, "Career Strategies for Turbulent Times," *Internal Auditor*, June 1996, 48-52.

Hinchliffe, Daniel A., and Alan H. Friedberg, "Capitalizing on Contingency Auditors," *Internal Auditor*, April 1998, 34-39.

Jeffords, Raymond, Greg M. Thibadoux, and Marsha Scheit, "Leadership Skills for Internal Auditors," *Internal Auditing*, September/October 2000, 17-21.

Jeffords, Raymond D., Nettie E. Bresee, and Cecelia D. Parsons, "Motivating Top Performance in the Internal Audit Department," *Internal Auditing*, Fall 1997, 52-56.

Jeffords, Raymond, Marsha Scheidt, and Greg M. Thibadoux, "Getting the Best from Staff," *Journal of Accountancy*, September 1997, 101-105.

Johnson, Veronica A., "Internal Audit Training," *Internal Auditor,* June 1991, 141-143.

Kattackal, Rose J., "Plugging In to Computer-based Training," *Internal Auditor,* December 1994, 32-37.

Luizzo, Anthony J., "Auditing Criminal History Records," *Internal Auditing Alert*, July 1999, 1-3.

Marks, Norman, "How Much is Enough?," *Internal Auditor*, February 2000, 28-34.

Marotta, Barbara L., "Internship for Internal Auditors," *Internal Auditing Alert*, June 1998, 1-3.

Marotta, Barbara, "Management Skills for the Internal Auditor," *Internal Auditing Alert*, February 1999, 1-4.

McDuffie, R. Steve, " A Better Way to Evaluate Internal Auditor Staff," *Internal Auditing,* Fall 1993, 53-57.

Mead, Kevin, "Net Work," *Internal Auditor*, June 1998, 65-67.

Messner, Max, "Capitalizing on Corporate Culture," *Internal Auditor*, October 2001, 38-45.

Myers, Patricia M., and Sridhar Ramamoorti, "Educating and Training Internal Auditors in the Use of Analytical Auditing Procedures," *Internal Auditing*, September/October 1999, 15-20.

Nash, Claire Y., and Dale L. Flesher, "Performance Management in Internal Audit," *Internal Auditing,* July/August 2001, 3-12.

Ramamoorti, Sridhar, Frederick L. Newman, and Julie K. Monroe, "The Value of Mentoring and Coaching in Internal Audit Settings," *Internal Auditing*, May/June 1999, 27-35.

Sears, Brian P., *Internal Auditing Manual* (New York: RIA, 2003.) (See Chapter C3, "Managing Human Resources and Other Resources and Records," and Chapter I6, "Career Development.")

Sears Campbell, Diane, "Training as a Retention Tool," *Internal Auditor*, October 2001, 47-51.

Siegel, Morton T., and Timothy R. Manholm, "Computer-based Training — The Payoff," *Internal Auditing,* Spring 1992, 84-88.

Sinason, David H., "Finding an Effective Audit Project Manager," *Internal Auditing,* July/August 2002, 22-26.

Williams, Satina V., and Benson Wier, "Creativity in Internal Auditing Departments," *Internal Auditing,* November/December 2000, 13-15.

Multiple-choice Questions

1. In objectively rating the performance of a staff auditor, the director should stress:
   a. Accomplishments.
   b. Traits.
   c. Abilities.
   d. Skills.

2. An organization has hired you to reorganize its internal audit department. According to the *Standards,* you need to know the educational qualifications of your staff to ensure:
   a. Accurate performance appraisals.
   b. Everyone is an accounting major.
   c. Audit responsibilities can be met.
   d. Minimum educational requirements can be met.

3. According to the *Standards,* internal auditors should possess all of the following except:
   a. Proficiency in applying internal audit standards.
   b. An understanding of management principles.
   c. The ability to exercise good interpersonal relations.
   d. The ability to conduct training sessions in quantitative methods.

4. According to the *Standards,* internal auditors should maintain their technical competence through continuing education. An internal auditor's continuing education:
   a. Should be contingent on time available in the audit schedule.
   b. May be obtained through participation in research projects.
   c. Must be reported annually to The IIA.
   d. Is the responsibility of the chief audit executive.

5. According to the *Standards,* internal auditors should be skilled in oral and written communications so they can clearly and effectively convey such matters as:
   a. Goals, budgets, and activities.
   b. Information gathered and techniques employed.
   c. Independence, coverage, and authority.
   d. Objectives, conclusions, and recommendations.

6. According to the *Standards,* the chief audit executive should establish a program for selecting and developing human resources for the internal audit department. Which of the following is not a provision of the *Standards?*
   a. Providing counsel to internal auditors on their performance and professional development.
   b. Training and providing continuing education opportunities for each internal auditor.
   c. Developing written job descriptions for each level of the audit staff.
   d. Developing specialists, as needed, among the audit staff.

7. According to the *Standards,* the chief audit executive is required to establish suitable educational and experience criteria for filling internal auditing positions. Select the most appropriate form for documenting such criteria.
   a. Department charter.
   b. *Code of ethics.*
   c. Staff evaluations.
   d. Position descriptions.

8. The chief audit executive has noticed that some staff auditors have become proficient in the use of personal computers while other auditors want nothing to do with them. The executive should:
   a. Disregard the differences.
   b. Provide training for those individuals interested in improving their skills.
   c. Discipline the individuals who display no self-starting abilities.
   d. Establish a program for developing the capabilities of the entire internal audit department.

9. A professional engineer applied for a position in the internal audit department of a high-tech firm. The engineer became interested in the position after observing several internal auditors while they were auditing the engineering department. The chief audit executive:
   a. Should not hire the engineer because of the lack of knowledge of internal auditing standards.
   b. May hire the engineer in spite of the lack of knowledge of internal auditing standards.
   c. Should not hire the engineer because of the lack of knowledge of accounting and taxes.
   d. May hire the engineer because of the knowledge of internal auditing gained in the previous position.

10. According to the *Standards,* the staff of a newly developed internal audit department should include:
    a. Members with bachelor's degrees in accounting and related fields.
    b. Members possessing appropriate professional designations.
    c. Members proficient in applying internal auditing standards, procedures, and techniques.
    d. Members with prior internal audit experience.

11. The best reason for establishing a code of conduct within an organization is that such codes:
    a. Are required by the Foreign Corrupt Practices Act.
    b. Express standards of individual behavior for members of the organization.
    c. Provide a quantifiable basis for personnel evaluations.
    d. Have tremendous public relations potential.

12. According to the *Standards,* an internal auditor should possess proficiency in:
    a. Management principles.
    b. The fundamentals of such subjects as accounting, economics, and finance.
    c. Computerized information systems.
    d. Applying internal auditing standards, procedures, and techniques.

13. Based on the *Standards,* an internal audit department's staff development program will be deficient if individual employees are:
    a. Given a large variety of tasks to perform.
    b. Expected to study current events on an independent basis.
    c. Assigned to a different supervisor on each job.
    d. Formally evaluated once every two years.

14. When hiring entry-level internal audit staff, which of the following will most likely predict the applicant's success as an auditor?
    a. Grade point average on college accounting courses.
    b. Ability to fit well socially into a group.
    c. Ability to organize and express thoughts well.
    d. Level of detailed knowledge of the organization.

15. Having been given the task of developing a performance appraisal system for evaluating the audit performance of a large internal auditing staff, you should:
    a. Provide for an explanation of the appraisal criteria methods at the time the appraisal results are discussed with the internal auditor.
    b. Provide general information concerning the frequency of evaluations and the way evaluations will be performed without specifying their timing and use.
    c. Provide primarily for the evaluation of criteria such as diligence, initiative, and tact.
    d. Provide primarily for the evaluation of specific accomplishments directly related to the performance of the audit program.

16. The key factor to the success of an audit organization's human resources program is:
    a. An informal program for developing and counseling staff.
    b. A compensation plan based on years of experience.
    c. A well-developed set of selection criteria.
    d. A program for recognizing the special interests of individual staff members.

17. You have been selected to develop an internal audit department for your organization. Your approach would most likely be to hire:
    a. Internal auditors who possess all the skills required to handle all audit assignments.
    b. Inexperienced personnel and train them the way the organization wants them trained.
    c. Degreed accountants since most audit work is accounting related.
    d. Internal auditors who collectively have the knowledge and skills needed to complete all internal audit assignments.

18. The internal audit department is considering hiring a person who has a thorough understanding of internal auditing techniques, accounting, and principles of management, but has nonspecialized knowledge of economics and computer systems. It would be appropriate to hire the person if:
    a. A professional development program is agreed to in advance of actual hiring.
    b. A mentor is assigned to ensure completion of an individually designed professional development program.
    c. Other auditors possess sufficient knowledge of economics and computer systems.
    d. The prospective employee could reasonably be expected to gain sufficient knowledge of these disciplines in the long run.

19. A chief audit executive is establishing the evaluation criteria for the selection of new internal audit staff members. According to the *Standards,* which of the following would be an inappropriate item to list?
    a. An appreciation of the fundamentals of accounting.
    b. An understanding of management principles.
    c. The ability to recognize deviations from good business practice.
    d. Proficiency in computerized operations and the use of computers in auditing.

20. Which of the following aspects of evaluating the performance of staff members would be considered a violation of good personnel management techniques?
    a. The evaluator should justify very high and very low evaluations because of their impact on the employee.
    b. Evaluations should be made annually or more frequently to provide the employee feedback about competence.
    c. The first evaluation should be made shortly after commencing work to serve as an early guide to the new employee.
    d. Because there are so many employees whose performance is completely satisfactory it is preferable to use standard evaluation comments.

21. As part of the process used in hiring new employees, a personnel clerk telephones the applicant's most recent employer, verifies prior employment, and initials the job application form. The most effective and efficient test to determine if the verification procedures are consistently followed is to select a sample from those recently hired and:
    a. Contact each applicant's last employer to confirm that an earlier verification had been performed.
    b. Verify that a personnel clerk had initialed each application form.
    c. Contact each applicant's last employer to verify previous employment.
    d. Check the computerized telephone logs from the clerk's phone for calls to each applicant's last employer.

22. As part of a company-sponsored award program, an internal auditor was offered a gift of significant monetary value by a division in recognition of the cost savings that resulted from the auditor's recommendations. According to The IIA's *Code of Ethics*, what is the most appropriate action for the auditor to take?
    a. Accept the gift since the audit is already concluded and the report issued.
    b. Accept the award under the condition that any proceeds go to charity.
    c. Inform audit management and ask for direction on whether to accept the gift.
    d. Decline the gift and write an informative memo to the division manager's superior.

23. An internal auditor would compare a department's staffing level with industry standards in order to reach a conclusion about the:
    a. Adequacy of controls over payroll processing.
    b. Current level of performance of the department.
    c. Adequacy of controls over hiring.
    d. Degree of compliance with human resources policies.

Chapter 22
Preparing Long-range Schedules

Need for planning and management involvement. Schedules as guides. Integration with audit strategy. Schedules justifying budgets. Schedules assisting to obtain management participation. Schedules helping to establish operating standards. Schedules as controls. Schedules ad external auditors. Structure of long-range schedules. Schedule budgets. Activities needing special audit emphasis. Risk analysis. Organization development objectives. Reviews with management. Small internal audit activities. Coordination with other control agencies.

• •

The Need for Planning and for Management Involvement

A good long-range audit schedule is an instrument of many uses. It is: (1) the auditor's guide; (2) support for budget requests; (3) a way of involving management and the board in the audit plans and obtaining their commitment to the scope of the audit philosophy and practice; (4) the standard by which auditors can measure their accomplishments; (5) a visible sign to management and the board that the audit activity is under competent control; and (6) a notice to the external auditors of proposed audit coverage.

As firms expand their definition of risk and as audit resources get stretched, a long-range plan becomes critically important. The plan causes the auditor to address critical issues that historically were taken for granted by the auditor. For example, what is maximum time that an auditor will allow a specific function/area to go without an outside review?

Long-range planning is not something a chief auditing executive can dismiss as a needless luxury. Practice Advisory 2010-1, "Planning," related to *Standard 2010* provides:

Planning for the internal audit activity should be consistent with its charter and with the goals of the organization. The planning process involves establishing:

Goals.
Engagement work schedules.
Staffing plans and financial budgets.
Activity reports.

The goals of the internal audit activity should be capable of being accomplished within specified operating plans and budgets and, to the extent possible, should be measurable.

They should be accompanied by measurement criteria and targeted dates of accomplishment.

Engagement work schedules should include the following:

What activities are to be performed.
When they will be performed; and
The estimated time required, taking into account the scope of the engagement work planned and the nature and extent of related work performed by others.

Matters to be considered in establishing engagement work schedule priorities should include:

The dates and results of the last engagement.
Undated assessments of risk and effectiveness of risk management and control processes.
Requests by senior management, audit committee, and governing body.
Current issues relating to organizational governance.
Major changes in enterprise's business, operations, programs, systems, and controls.
Opportunities to achieve operating benefits.
Changes to and capabilities of the audit staff. The work schedules should be sufficiently flexible to cover unanticipated demands on the internal audit activity.

External auditors and board audit committees are showing considerable interest in what internal auditing intends to audit. The long-range audit schedule is tangible evidence of that intention.

Long-range schedules should not be developed lightly. If they are to impress management with high-minded goals of the internal audit activity, they should demonstrate that the long-range goals of the organization have been taken into account. Also, they should identify the specific audit programs to be dealt with and the staff needed to accomplish those programs.

All management-oriented long-range audit schedules should be developed with certain standards in mind. For example:

- The schedule should be within the authority granted to the internal audit department by its charter and by management's needs. To that extent, the schedule should set specific goals, project the costs of running the department, and take into account the exposures and hazards implicit in the activities to be audited.

- The long-range schedule should include a financial budget for running the department and project any changes in staff that are needed to meet approved goals.

- Management's support of the schedule is essential to assure entry of the auditors into the areas scheduled for audit.

- With audit committees of the board facing greater risks in carrying out their functions, they will be interested in the coverage of the long-term schedule. It should therefore be prepared so that it would be readily understandable to them, indicating the protection it affords board members.

Every long-range schedule should contain certain basic elements. For example:

- All the operations of the organization should be analyzed for auditability and potential risks.

- Each organizational component should be analyzed as to specific objectives, performance standards, and controls. Proposed audit hours should be allocated to each of the identifiable elements constituting an audit project.

- Relative risks should be assessed, taking into account the objectives of internal control set forth in the *Standards* (2120.A1):

  - Reliability and integrity of information.
  - Compliance with internal and external rules and regulations.
  - Safeguarding of assets.
  - Economical and efficient use of resources.
  - Achievement of established organizational objectives and goals.

Audit effort should be directed to the needs of the organization and the concerns of management. To that extent, greater prompt efforts should be expended on activities that present special risks. Hence, internal auditors should employ some form of risk analysis to identify the hazards inherent in auditable activities. The reasons for risk analysis are:

- It is more efficient to give greater weight to activities prone to error or other exposure.

- The higher the risks, the greater the need for controls to guard against them.

- Internal auditors can deploy their resources most intelligently in exploring techniques to reduce or limit risks.

Hence, internal auditors must develop schedules that are flexible and subject to change with changing circumstances. They have, in effect, a contract with senior management and the board under which the audit activity will assist them in performing their oversight function.

Thus, changes to the audit schedule should be made only under conditions that would be acceptable to those who approved the original schedule. For example:

- New product lines or material changes in major operational components.
- Budget restraints or expansions.
- Anticipated legislation affecting the enterprise.
- Special problems that surfaced after the schedule was approved.
- Changes in top management and board philosophy.
- Changes in the technology of production.
- Changes in the degrees of risks in the activities to be audited.
- Loss of audit staff.
- New competitive pressures.
- Changes in the financial structure or operations of the organization.
- Relationships with outside auditors or questionable practices.

Changes should not be made at the request of operating managers who want audits postponed simply for their convenience. Changes can be made, however, with executive and/or audit committee approval to accommodate requests by client managers who identify problems that could be related to audit activity.

A well-constructed long-range schedule that meets professional standards, contains all the basic elements of a competent schedule, is responsive to the basic objectives of the audit organization, and takes appropriate risks into account has many uses and benefits for the internal audit activity. Among the chief benefits are those discussed in the following subsections of this chapter.

The Schedule as a Guide

By spelling out in detail the audit projects to be carried out, the long-range schedule gives evidence that, barring the emergence of risk-oriented situations, key functions are covered at planned intervals. It provides assurance that based on importance, no significant area worthy of audit will be overlooked.

The schedule simplifies the job of assuring that there will be adequate staff and it helps in assigning work to staff. Without a detailed schedule, the audit effort can be a haphazard groping, a repeated exercise of responding to random requests, or last-minute decisions about "what do we do next?" Further, the schedule provides information on quantities and skills of audit staff resources that will be needed.

In large audit organizations, the schedule can be allocated equitably to different supervisors or audit managers. They in turn can assign projects to their staff people in logical order. Also, a well constructed work schedule, stretching out for two, three, or five years, provides an air of permanence to the audit organization. It is evidence of long-term planning and the continued existence of the audit effort. Above all, it is a tangible demonstration internally and externally of the audit function as the keystone in the organization's management and its internal control structure.

In smaller organizations, the schedule relieves the internal auditing executives from constantly having to make decisions on audit coverage. It permits them to make those decisions early and to settle their scheduling problems — with provision for flexibility, of course — in advance of the year's work. For audits that are to be conducted by cosourcing, the long-range schedule provides for timely future arrangements for the resources that will be required.

Integration with Audit Strategy

As a part of its planning process the audit organization will have specified its mission and the objectives and goals that it believes will accomplish that mission. The long-range audit schedule should articulate into this pattern. Present also should be the elements of audit strategy that conceivably will assist to make this basic audit plan succeed. The long-range audit schedule should be related to these strategy aspects and will define its relationship to the various strategic elements. For example, the long-range schedule would describe the impact of a specific audit on:

Staffing:
It will indicate the numbers, areas of competence, timing of staff availability, and expected performance.

Audit Approach:
Audits will be organized by functional elements with attention to financial and/or operational aspects of each function.

Reporting:
Interim oral reports will be made weekly to higher level of management and to operating management of the unit being audited. Spot reports will be made immediately upon identification of significant elements needing timely attention.

Timing:
Auditing will be performed so as to cause the least conflict with client normal operations.

Funding:
Cost reports will be prepared on a weekly basis and compared with operational progress using CPM and/or PERT and PERT cost or other project management procedures.

The Schedule as a Justification for Budget

The long-range schedule should be specific and should describe in detail each audit project to be performed, while still providing for the unknown and unanticipated. Each project listed should indicate through its title the nature of the audit to be performed and should provide an estimate of the time and other resources required.

The total of the allotted time for the current year is a simple demonstration of the number of auditors needed. The total of audit days for each of subsequent years is a projection of changes to, or continuity of, staff levels. When accepted by senior management and the board, therefore, the schedule becomes a commitment to the number of auditors authorized. Simple arithmetic rather than rhetoric sustain the executive's request for maintaining or adjusting staff levels. And the accepted audit days, together with provision for administrative and training expense, travel expense, and related costs, and costs of outside expert assistance, represent management's consideration and provisional approval of a future budget for the audit organization.

The approved work schedule provides an additional and subtle function. It defends against one of the internal auditor's constant fears: being requested to perform non-audit functions — to be at the beck and call of middle management for "fire fighting" or expediting duties. When the audit schedule is adopted, it is tacit acknowledgment by senior management that the auditor's primary function is to carry out audit, and not line, activities. It is also a commitment to future projects in which senior management has a demonstrated interest. When such line activities become essential under emergency conditions, the auditor can properly request senior management's approval before doing the line work.

The Schedule as a Means of Obtaining Management Participation

All long-range work schedules should be reviewed up through the policy-making level of the organization. Schedule reviews at higher operating levels in the organization provide management with a preview of the audit coverage in their areas of responsibility. During these reviews, managers are given an opportunity to discuss each project and to comment on: (1) whether the scheduling is appropriate in light of the organization's present or projected activities; (2) whether other projects, different from those listed, should be covered; (3) whether some of the projects listed require more, less, or no coverage; (4) what difficulties the auditor should anticipate; (5) what specific problems management would like to see addressed; (6) whether the risk assessment conforms to management's estimates, and (7) what the thrust or scope of a particular audit should be. It should also provide management's views as to a provision for the unknown, the potential for situations that would require future audit assistance as a support to management. The schedule would also delineate the future audit relationships with outside auditors or with future outsource or cosource audit activities.

When senior managers accept the schedule, they are in effect potentially committed to it; they have provided the auditor with future entree into the organizations under their control and granted future authority to subject the organizations to the audits planned. Auditors then can plan to enter those areas and carry on their audit work with the full support of higher management — indeed, almost as a matter of a contract subject to future developments, with management.

Audit committees are taking a greater interest in internal auditing schedules. Previously, this concern was directed primarily to the audit programs of the independent public accountants. But as audit committees are faced with increased responsibilities and commitments, they begin to recognize the protection that internal auditing could afford. Thus, they became willing and eager to review and influence the scope and the depth of future internal audit coverage. An audit committee's even tentative approval of an internal audit long-range schedule is a powerful endorsement. It can also serve as an internal review of the efficacy of the external auditor's financial audit activity.

The Schedule as a Means of Establishing Standards

The long-range audit schedule gives executives of internal auditing a yardstick by which to measure their own accomplishments and those of their staffs. Current reports of work completed, in terms of audit days, provide a means of showing management and the audit committee whether the internal auditors accomplished what they had intended. The reports will also indicate reasons for variances such as situations requiring unanticipated audit attention. The comparison of audit days budgeted with audit days expended indicates and explains the degree of realization of audit goals. For example, overruns of budgeted audit days could point to shortcomings, either in budgeting or in accomplishment, and could indicate the need for improvement in one or the other. This may indicate that the budgets were unrealistic or that the audit projects were inadequately planned, programmed, or conducted or that unanticipated situations were discovered and resolved. Analysis of the variances can provide information to help in future scheduling or to point to needed changes in audit approach.

Further, in large audit organizations the work schedule can be used to a degree to measure the competence of audit managers or supervisors. At the beginning of the year the schedule may be divided among supervisors, and staff auditors may be assigned to them for specified periods. The performance of supervisors in carrying out their allotted share of the work with the staff assigned may be one indicator of their professional and managerial ability.

The Schedule as a Means of Control

Senior management is becoming more and more imbued with the concepts of objective- and goal-oriented administration, with adequate planning, and with sound administrative policies.

Management expects that all organizational units within its purview will also operate in an organized, well-administered manner.

Hence, the well-structured, well-considered, long-range work schedule, with periodic reports to show that the schedule was not just window dressing but a real management tool, is one of the benchmarks of a well-controlled audit organization. The schedule shows a setting of clear and quantifiable objectives and it implies a firm agreement with management on these objectives. Thus, when the cost-reduction itch starts, when ill-conceived and ineffective operational functions are subjected to rigorous cost-pruning, the demonstrated well-developed schedule of audits concentrating on key risk areas may be one of the best reasons for keeping the audit activity from being reduced or replaced.

The Schedule as Notice to the External Auditor

External auditors usually structure their own verification efforts to take into account the system of internal control. The long-range audit schedule provides them with insight into how internal control is being monitored — how the keystone of internal control, the internal audit, is operating — and permits them to pattern their own programs to complement or coincide with the internal audit schedule. The schedule can be the internal audit's part of an integrated overall audit process.

Through prearrangement, specific internal audit projects may be so scheduled that they will provide the external auditors with adequate assurances and permit them to limit their own tests of internal control. This form of cooperation may provide for a welcome reduction in the cost of the external audit.

The Long-range Schedule's Structure

The infinite variety of entity structures and purposes makes impossible a common form of work schedule. No two organizations or agencies are truly alike; in fact, most are quite different. While production control may be of great significance in one organization, it may be nonexistent in another. Inventory control will be more important to a retail store than it would be to an insurance organization.

Yet, certain factors are common to the development of most long-range schedules. The structure of the organization should be considered. Is it hierarchical with many levels, or flat with close control by higher management? How much or how little authority is delegated by senior management to operating managers? Does the form of delegation employ abdication or does senior management insist on adequate accountability from those to whom authority is delegated? How large are the auditable units? What is management's span of control? Is one buying supervisor responsible for so large a group of buyers that adequate reviews of purchases is a physical impossibility? If so, the risks rise. How different are the various auditable units? If they are comparable or homogeneous, this may influence the decision to make fewer audit assignments. How concerned is senior management with particular activities? The greater concern, the higher should be the sensitivity of the audit projects.

Identifying risks was discussed in Chapter 3, Risk Assessment. But with respect to the long-range schedule certain criteria should be considered in structuring the schedule in terms of risk: The materiality of the assets, revenues, or expenditures; the reliability of the control systems; the vulnerability to loss and the nature of the assets (are they subject to conversion loss or pilferage?). The number and significance of prior deficiency findings is an indicator of the nature of management control. Major organizational changes can breed confusion until matters settle down and people become comfortable with the changed circumstances. The ability to rely on external audit coverage will have a definite effect on the need for internal audit coverage. Specific requests by higher management will also have a significant influence on the degree and timing of the coverage.

Some audit risk software prepares long-range schedules. The schedules are based upon the risk score assigned to the area and the available internal audit resources available. These schedules can be updated as needed.

Hence, while no one long-range schedule will have universal applicability, an organized approach can meet the needs of many. Exhibit 22-1 gives the outline of a long-range schedule that provides a structure adaptable to most entities. In addition to the bare outline, a number — certainly nowhere near all — of potential areas of coverage are shown.

The schedule is divided into major areas of review. This example depicts a five-year span. But the span could be two, three, or four years, depending on the number of years between particular audits. If no area of coverage remains unreviewed for more than three years, then a longer span may not be applicable. Whatever the span, however, the schedule should be reevaluated every year to account for changes in entity structure, risk, management, product lines, stability of operation, and audit emphasis.

The first two columns in the schedule show, by project number and report date, the last time that the particular audit was performed. The third column lists the identification numbers of the applicable permanent or master program files. The fourth column describes the area of coverage. The fifth column shows the evaluation of the project in terms of risk from 1 (extreme risk) to 5 (least risk). The sixth column shows the frequency with which the audit should be made: every 1, 2, 3, 4, or 5 years. The next five columns show the years in which the audits should be made and the number of audit days allotted to each project.

In most cases, the budgets are for specific projects. In others, as in reviews of information systems, or follow-up reviews, or unidentified requests from management or the board, lump sum budgets are set out to be expended as circumstances warrant during the year.

Exhibit 22-1
Long-range Audit Schedule: Five-year Span

Audit Project Number	Report Date	Permanent File Number	Audit Project	Class	Frequency	Calendar Year Audit Days				
						2001	2002	2003	2004	2005
			MARKETING							
85-20	1-99	M-1	Advertising Department	3	3	40			40	50
86-18	2-00	M-2	Sales Department - Product A	3	3		50			
87-25	3-01	M-3	Sales Department – Product B	3	3			50		
86- 2	4-99	M-4	Branch X	3	3	30			30	
87- 4	5-00	M-5	Branch Y	3	3		30			30
87- 7	6-01	M-6	Branch Z	3	3			30		
84- 9	7-97	M-7	Customer Service Department	4	5	40				
87- 8	8-00	M-8	Contract Administration	2	3		40			40
			Total			110	120	80	70	120
			INDUSTRIAL RELATIONS							
86-13	9-98	IR-1	Safety Department	3	3	30			30	
85-19	10-99	IR-2	Personnel Records	4	4	40				40
88-20	12-01	IR-3	Employment	3	3			30		
			Employment							
			Total			70	—	30	30	40
			ENGINEERING							
85-15	1-99	E-1	Research & Development	2	3	50			50	
87-13	2-00	E-2	Drawings – Quality	2	2		60		60	
86-20	3-00	E-3	Drawings – Schedule	2	3			50		
87- 2	4-00	E-4	Technical Information & Data	3	4		50			50
85- 5	5-99	E-5	Engineering Files					50		
			Total			50	110	100	110	50

Exhibit 22-1 (Cont.)

Audit Project Number	Report Date	Permanent File Number	Audit Project	Class	Frequency	Calendar Year Audit Days 2001	2002	2003	2004	2005
			MFG. OPERATIONS							
86- 4	6-99	MO-1	Manufacturing Engineering	3	5	100	100	50	100	100
88- 1	7-00	MO-2	Procurement	1	1	60		100	60	
86- 9	8-99	MO-3	Quality Control	2	3		50	50		50
87- 5	9-00	MO-4	Production Control	2	3			40		50
87-12	10-00	MO-5	Material Control	2	2	50				
86-13	11-00	MO-6	Stores	2	3					
85-22	12-98	MO-7	Scheduling	2	4	30		40		30
86-17	1-98	MO-8	Receiving	3	4					
87-20	2-00	MO-9	Tooling	2	4		50		50	50
87-22	3-00	MO-10	Time Studies	4	5					
86- 3	4-99	MO-11	Traffic	3	4				30	
87- 6	5-00	MO-12	Shipping	3	5					
			Total			240	200	280	240	280
			ACCOUNTING							
88- 5	6-00	A-1	Budgets and Forecasts	1	1	40	40	40	40	40
88- 4	2-00	A-2	Cost Distribution	2	2		50		50	
88- 6	3-00	A-3	Inventories	2	2		40		40	
86-11	4-00	A-4	Timekeeping	3	3	30		50	30	50
87- 3	5-00	A-5	Payroll	2	2	50				30
88-12	6-00	A-6	Billing	1	1	30				
87- 9	7-97	A-7	Accounts Payable	2	2		30	30	30	50
87-19	8-00	A-8	Accounts Receivable	2	2	50	50	50	50	
87-21	2-00	A-9	General Accounting	3	3		40			40
			Total			200	250	170	240	210

Exhibit 22-1 (Cont.)

Audit Project Number	Report Date	Permanent File Number	Audit Project	Class	Frequency	Calendar Year — Audit Days				
						2001	2002	2003	2004	2005
			FINANCE							
87- 1	3-00	F-1	Mail Room	2	2	40		40		40
88- 3	4-00	F-2	Cash Receipts	1	1	30	30	30	30	30
88- 2	5-00	F-3	Cash Disbursements	1	1	20	20	20	20	20
86- 7	6-99	F-4	Credit	2	3	30			30	
88- 7	7-00	F-5	Cash Planning	2	2		30		30	
85-12	8-98	F-6	Insurance	2	2		20			
			Total			120	100	90	110	90
			ELECTRONIC DATA PROCESSING							
88- 8	8-00	EDP-1	Installation	1	1	50	50	50	50	50
88- 9	9-00	EDP-2	Maintenance	1	1	50	50	50	50	50
			Total			100	100	100	100	100
			FUNCTIONAL EXAMS							
87-14	10-00	FE-1	Conflict of Interest	2	3		50			50
88-11	11-00	FE-2	Rotate Employees in Key Positions	2	3			70		
86-16	12-99	FE-3	Incorporate of Engineering Changes	4	3	40			40	
			Total			40	50	70	40	50
			SPECIAL EXAMINATIONS							
Various		SE-1	Special Management Requests	1	1	100	100	100	100	100
Various		SE-2	Follow-up Audits	1	1	50	50	50	50	50
Various		SE-3	Audits of Supplies	1	1	100	100	100	100	100
Various		SE-4	Sensitive Control Areas	1	1	50	50	50	50	50
			Total			300	300	300	300	300
			Grand Total			1230	1230	1220	1240	1240

Exhibit 22-1 has been compressed for ease of understanding and applicability to a greater variety of organizations. For example, in some organizations, procurement, which is shown only as one line in the exhibit could very easily be expanded to include such matters as material requirements, shortage controls, scrap disposition, selection of suppliers, documentation of purchases, administration of subcontracts, audits of time and material contracts, and so forth.

An alternative schedule format is shown in Exhibit 22-2. This suggested long-range schedule, even more truncated for purposes of illustration, proposes a three-year span but allocates the coming year's budget to each of the four quarters. This format provides for spelling out deferred projects and the time allocated to those projects. Thus senior management obtains visibility on those areas of audit coverage that cannot be included in the three-year cycle, in light of current departmental budgets.

The allocated audit days, the scheduled frequencies, and the classification of priorities in the two schedules should not be regarded as suggestions for actual use. They are purely illustrative. Each audit organization must decide what priorities to assign to its audit projects and how many days to allocate to those projects.

Schedule Budgets

One approach to budgeting is to start with the authorized number of audit personnel. Multiply that number by the available work hours in the year. This base must then be reduced by allowances for vacation time, sick leave, employee training, staff meetings, and the like. The remainder is available for audit work.

What is left is broken down into scheduled and nonscheduled work. The amount of nonscheduled work is set aside — based on past experience, discussions with management, or the best available forecasts — for special requests from management, follow-up of prior audit findings, reviews of especially sensitive activities, research, and the like.

The time remaining is allotted to specific audit assignments. The budget assigned to each audit project is, in essence, what the director of auditing can afford to spend (or cannot afford to spend) on the particular audit. Some budgets are developed intuitively. Intuition is a personal matter incapable of precise analysis, but past experience can be recorded and preserved on a simple form to support the subjective decision.

An audit analysis form should be completed at the conclusion of each regularly scheduled audit assignment. It should be prepared by the person in the best position to provide the information — namely, the auditor in charge of that assignment; at that point he or she knows more about that audit activity than anyone else.

Exhibit 22-2
Long-range Audit Schedule: Three-year Span

Permanent File Number	Subject	Audit Frequency (Years)	Last Audit Date	Audit-Days Sch.	Audit-Days Act.	2001 (Quarters) 1	2	3	4	2002	2003	Defer
	AREA A											
A-1	Subject 1	3	5/00	20	22					20		
A-2	Subject 2	2	4/00	20	15		15					
A-3	Subject 3	3	4/00	10	11							10
	AREA B											
B-1	Subject 1	2	11/00	25	31				30			
B-2	Subject 2	3	6/00	35	26						25	
B-3	Subject 3	1	2/00	25	32			30				
	AREA C											
C-1	Subject 1	1	4/00	20	24	40						
C-2	Subject 2	3	1/00	25	20		20					
C-3	Subject 3	2	2/00	35	25							20
	AREA D											
D-1	Subject 1	3	10/99	10	11				10			
D-2	Subject 2	3	6/00	25	35					40		
D-3	Subject 3	2	10/00	40	39						30	
	Misc.			50	60		15	15	15	15	60	
	Special Mgm't Requests			40	80		20	20	20	20	80	

The audit manager should record on the form his/her conclusions as to the significance of the job (should it be repeated and, if so, how soon?); whether it can be combined with one or more other jobs; whether the audit thrust should be altered on future jobs; what is a reasonable budget for the job, either as a survey or as a full-scale audit assignment; what parts of the job absolutely must be done to protect the entire entity and what parts can be slighted without excessive risk; and what parts of the job should be followed up before the next regularly scheduled assignment. Exhibit 22-3 is one example of such a form.

Exhibit 22-3
Audit Analysis

Audit _____ Period Covered _____ Time Expended _____

Question	**Answer** (Give reasons)

Should this audit project be repeated?
If the answer is **yes** —
- How soon?
- Should it be combined with another project?
- What budget is recommended:
  (1) As a full-scale project?
  (2) As a survey?

What part of the audit project —
- Should be scheduled for an interim examination?
- Must be covered or warrant special attention in future examinations?
- Should be eliminated in future examinations?

What suggestions do you have for the auditor making the next examination in this area?

Audit Manager _____ Date _____

The executed form should be kept in the permanent file as assistance to the auditor in charge who next directs the job, and to the director of auditing or the audit managers who develop the long-range schedules.

Activities Needing Special Audit Emphasis

Certain activities within the entity are particularly susceptible to high risk: improprieties, manipulation, or significant loss. These are usually of serious concern to senior management. They should be of equal concern to the auditors. Like weak links in a chain, they are most susceptible to failure. When problems occur, the executive's lifted eyebrow is invariably turned toward the internal auditors. And the auditors who failed to identify the activities needing special audit emphasis have nobody but themselves to blame.

Each organization has its peculiar problem areas. That entity's internal auditors can best isolate and pinpoint them. These areas deserve special consideration and special assurance that they are being given proper audit scrutiny. These areas should be researched and listed, and the risk assessed. The list should be regularly reviewed and updated. Once identified, these sensitive areas should be prioritized, interwoven into the fabric of the regular audit programs, and audited when the related activities are reviewed. For example, an audit of deliveries bypassing the receiving department — often particularly susceptible to error or manipulation — can be performed as a part of the receiving department audit. The inherent dangers in such an activity demand assurances that direct deliveries will not be overlooked in the regular receiving audit. Also, authority to designate which units may use direct deliveries is usually vested in the receiving department.

Exhibit 22-4 is an example of a list of activities requiring special audit emphasis. It includes sensitive control areas common to many organizations. It can be expanded or reviewed to include areas peculiar to particular organizations. The exhibit lists the activities — the titles make them self-explanatory — along with the permanent file most applicable to that activity, the latest audit report (audit project number and report date), and the most recent result of risk analysis review, and the period scheduled for the next review. This period may coincide with the regular audit, or it may represent special scheduling for an interim or follow-up review.

The listing should be reviewed with management at the same time the long-range schedule is reviewed. This will offer management an opportunity to become aware of the high-risk areas and to add to the list, and to be alerted to the exposure from reducing the audit scope.

Risk Analysis

In developing the long-range audit plan, the chief audit executive must give special weight to risks and priorities. Chapter 3, Risk Assessment, covered the evaluation of risks within individual activities. Here we are concerned with the risk assessment of all activities within the audit universe.

Exhibit 22-4
Activities Requiring Special Audit Emphasis

Activity	Applicable Permanent File	Latest Report Number	Date	Scheduled for Next Review
Marketing				
No-charge sales	M-2	00-18	02-01	2004
Industrial Relations				
Authority to drive into plant	IR-1	00-13	02-01	2003
Vehicle inspection -- entering and leaving plant	IR-1	00-13	09-00	2003
Control of master keys	IR-1	00-13	09-00	2003
Conflict of interest	IR-2	99-19	09-00	2003
Wage and salary adjustments	IR-2	99-19	10-99	2003
			10-99	2003
Engineering				
Organization proprietary data	E-1	99-15	01-00	2003
Designation of sole procurement source	E-4	01-2	04-01	2005
Preparation of restrictive specifications	E-4	01-2	04-01	2005
Manufacturing Operations				
Deliveries bypassing receiving department	MO-8	00-17	01-01	2005
Scrap and salvage	MO-5	01-12	01-01	2003
Control over selection of suppliers	MO-2	01-1	07-02	2003
Control over purchase order changes	MO-2	01-1	07-02	2003
Transportation and routing of materials	MO-11	00-3	04-00	2004
Supplies susceptible to pilferage	MO-6	02-13	11-02	2005

Exhibit 22-4 (Cont.)

Activity	Applicable Permanent File	Latest Report Number	Date	Scheduled for Next Review
Accounting				
Approval and payment of overtime	A-5	01-3	10-01	2003
Payrolls	A-5	01-3	10-01	2003
Bank reconciliations	A-9	01-21	02-02	2004
Employee bonuses	A-5	01-3	10-01	2003
Credit memo forms	A-6	02-12	11-02	2003
Executive-approved invoices	A-7	02-9	12-01	2003
Payments to suppliers	A-7	01-9	12-01	2003
Accounts payable check mailing	A-7	01-9	12-01	2003
Fixed assets	A-9	01-21	02-01	2004
Finance				
Blank, void, and mutilated checks	F-3	02-2	05-02	2003
Undelivered checks	F-3	02-2	05-02	2003
Facsimile signature plate	F-3	02-2	05-02	2003
Cashiers funds	F-3	02-2	05-02	2003
Petty cash funds	F-3	02-2	05-02	2003
Cash receipts	F-2	02-3	04-02	2003
Credit approvals	F-4	02-7	06-00	2003
Travelers checks	F-3	02-2	05-02	2003
Metered postage	F-1	01-1	03-01	2003
Other				
Rotation and vacations of employees in key control positions	SE-4	01-25	3-02	2004

Many methods have been advanced for assessing risk in the audit universe. Some become extremely complicated and require the use of software. They involve mathematical formulae and computations of a number of variables, including but not limited to:

- Previous audit results.
- Assets controlled by the system.
- Confidentiality.
- System maturity.
- Changes to the system.
- Complexity of the system.
- Administrative controls.
- Employee turnover.
- Unit revenue and volume.
- Effect on competitiveness.
- Government regulations.
- Management concern.
- Performance indicators.
- Volume of production.
- Public relations.

These analyses can provide formidable documentation for the chief auditing executive who is defending the long-range audit plan and the priorities assigned to various projects. They can also be extremely time-consuming. Nevertheless, the executive should consider the elements of risk so as to have some reasonable basis for determining which audits to carry out, which to eliminate, and which priorities to assign.

The question arises whether the complicated computations are more valuable than the professional judgments of experienced internal auditors, amplified by discussions with operating managers. Whatever assessment the executive makes must start with certain subjective premises: "How much value do I assign to the risk inherent in an accounts payable audit or to an audit of a shipping department?" No matter what the numbers are, they are based on an estimate to begin with. Why, therefore, go through complex computations to arrive at a number based initially on a subjective estimate of each factor? Why not draw a final conclusion based on professional judgment and experience? In that way, all audit projects can be given simple numerical ratings running, say from 1 to 5. An audit project rated 1 has the highest risk and deserves the highest priority. An audit project rated 5 has the lowest risk and would be carried out only when higher rated projects have been completed and time is available. Where budget restrictions require a reduction in audit staff, all or some of the 5-rated projects or even the 4-rated projects may have to be eliminated or further delayed. Similarly, time intervals between audits can be based on the 1-to-5 ratings. An audit of accounts payable may be rated 1. An audit of time studies in a production area might be rated 5.

Nevertheless, many audit organizations believe it appropriate to spend considerable time and effort on risk assessment by applying detailed formulae. Exhibit 22-5 provides one method of evaluating priorities and assessing risk. Other methods can be found in the articles listed under "Supplementary Reading" at the end of this chapter or by reference to Chapter 3.

Exhibit 22-5
Audit Priorities

Weight			
35%	1.	Previous Audit Coverage	
		Previous year	1
		First prior year	2
		Second prior year	3
		Third prior year	4
		Other	5
35	2.	Yearly Expenditure Made or Dollars Controlled — Operation, Maintenance, or Capital Expenditures	
		50,000,001 +	5
		25,000,001 – 50,000,000	4
		5,000,001 – 25,000,000	3
		1,000,001 – 5,000,000	2
		1,000,000 or less	1
30	3.	Exposure (Risk) – A Subjective Measure of Potential Difficulties Relating to the Expected Internal Control in the Area	
		Most Exposure	5
			4
			3
			2
		Least Exposure	1
100%			

The planner ranks each auditable item in each category and multiplies that number by weighting percentage on the left. All products are summed for the total point ranking of the activity.

In all, these methods of risk analysis, the numbers assigned will call for auditor judgment in assessing the magnitude of risk involved resulting from changes in any particular element. For example, where a product line has been dropped from a previously active operation, the factor, say 1 to 5, should be lowered. Where there has been a change in management and a new team is installed, the added risk warrants a higher factor. A new information system is always a hazard until it has been debugged and personnel become familiar with it; this would warrant a factor indicating a high degree of risk. An investment of expensive assets and the undertaking of new ventures indicate risks and therefore warrant high risk factors. Also, the degree of potential liquidity should be considered.

The determination of the degree of risk is a matter of judgment. The internal auditors should apply the same judgment that a reasonable, prudent businessperson would employ in the same or similar circumstances.

Organization-development Objectives

An audit operation is no different from any other department in the organization. It cannot tie its lifeline to past experience alone. The rest of the enterprise, to be successful, is learning, adapting, expanding, and testing new ideas. Auditing executives cannot do less if they are to adequately serve their profession, their organization, and their people.

Admittedly, organization-development objectives are hard to fit into a busy audit schedule; but there is no choice. It is a case of improve or wither away. Such objectives must be more than wishful dreams. They must be implemented through the achievement of quantifiable goals and call for enumerated tasks. They must be controlled by set schedules. And of equal importance, the development goals should be keyed to certain continuing objectives that will lift auditors out of their daily routines and out of themselves, showing that they can make themselves better than they think they are.

First then, comes the setting of these continuing objectives — objectives that persist as long as the audit activity shall exist. These objectives must be set by the directors of auditing and should reflect the philosophy of what they consider most significant to the growth of the internal audit department. The objectives should be high-minded and should make mind-stretching demands.

It would not be amiss to key these objectives to three significant aims in the improvement of the profession, the organization, and people — stating the continuing objectives as:

- To make the audit activity the leader in the profession.
- To expand the service to management.
- To help the individual auditor achieve greater dimension and stature.

All organization-development projects could be keyed to these fundamental objectives. In this way, the development program has form and structure, and will be balanced among plans that concern each of the three objectives.

There is no end to the development projects that can be pursued. Annually, chief audit executives should ask their staff which projects they wish to undertake. Proposals for new projects should be screened to avoid duplication, as should frivolous excursions into unreality, exercises not worth the effort, or projects having no reasonable relation to the continuing objectives.

Once approved, each project should be controlled. The proposal should be accompanied by a schedule of specific milestones and a set of standards by which to measure accomplishments. Such standards or units of measurement might refer to a research report or a new manual or a new *pro forma* audit program. Or they might refer to a number of audit projects in which a particular new technique could be employed.

Development projects should be keyed to the needs of each individual audit organization. The examples in Exhibit 22-6 include a number of projects that were actually undertaken in one internal audit activity. The exhibit groups them according to the three prime objectives and shows the standards or units of measurement that can be applied.

Exhibit 22-6
Project Possibilities Related to Objectives

Project	Due Date	Standard of Measurement
To make the auditing organization the best in the profession.		
Expand the use of information systems in making sample selections.	Dec. 20XX	5 audits
Experiment with oral presentations and visual aids.	Dec. 20XX	10 audits
Develop a style manual for report writing.	Dec. 20XX	Completed manual
Experiment with the use of questionnaires to obtain data for audit examinations.	Nov 20XX	Two proposed questionnaires
Establish dollar budget control over various phases of audit examinations and reporting.	June 20XX	Research report

Exhibit 22-6 (Cont.)

Project	Due Date	Standard of Measurement
Expand the service to management.		
Develop or improve a system of classifying deficiency findings to afford management a basis for broad, corrective action throughout the organization, through analysis of causes.	July 20XX	List of deficiency causes
Develop or improve an annual summary report to management on the adequacy and effectiveness of its controls, based on audits made during the year.	Nov 20XX	Pro forma report
Perform research into the needs of various levels of management for audit assistance.	June 20XX	Research report
Develop or improve summary reports to management on audit results accumulated by families of jobs.	June 20XX	Two proposed summaries
Develop or improve a system of reporting significant findings in common areas as an aid to management in perceiving potential deficiencies, their causes, and the results if uncorrected.	Dec 20XX	Ten significant findings
Help auditors achieve greater dimension and stature.		
Encourage auditors to take outside courses.	Dec 20XX	Completion of 10 courses
Encourage participation in the professional organization of internal auditors.	June 20XX	Two new members One chapter officer One international officer
Develop or improve a program of counseling with staff auditors on their future education and training.	Dec 20XX	Annual counseling with all staff auditors
Establish and hold training programs for auditors on such subjects as:	Dec 20XX	Three training programs

- Use of EDP in audits
- Statistical sampling
- Report writing
- Flowcharting
- Audit programming
- Oral presentations
- Visual aids
- Referencing reports
- Office regulations

Each quarter, or at least semiannually, the chief audit executive should provide status reports on these projects. When the projects are completed, appropriate recognition should be accorded to those who accomplished their objectives. Also, the annual and semiannual reports to management on audit accomplishments should give prominent place to these accomplishments as well.

Reviews With Management

Management should become involved in the development of the long-range audit program. Reviewing the proposed program with management obtains both the involvement and the blessing of senior management. The review meetings provide for an interchange of ideas and an understanding by the audit staff of management's problems and needs.

These reviews should be undertaken first at the branch or division level; that is, in terms of Exhibit 22-1, the review would be undertaken with the directors or vice presidents of marketing, industrial relations, engineering, operations, accounting, and finance.

The internal auditors should carefully prepare for the reviews. They should provide copies of the proposed audit schedules (and rough programs) for each functional organization. They should come prepared to answer the questions that are bound to be asked and to take notes on the suggestions that the branch or division directors make. A record of these suggestions should be placed in the appropriate audit permanent or master file.

In preparation for the meeting, the auditors should accumulate copies of all relevant audit reports. In addition, they should prepare brief notes on the audit objectives of each of the audit projects. They should also have current assessments of risks in each of the purposed audit areas. In this way, they will have at their fingertips the answers to such questions as, "What problems did you encounter the last time in the audit of personnel records?" or "How do you propose to examine research and development activities?" and "What are the areas of risk and how imminent should you audit?"

Also, the auditors should inquire of management as to what impact new programs will have on operating activities, what aspect of current programs cause the operational or functional director or vice president the most problems, and which programs appear to be phasing out and do not warrant audit attention. Finally, the auditors should solicit advice from the operating directors as to the scheduling of the audits within their organizations — which projects should be postponed, which projects should be advanced, and which new projects should be added.

After the reviews at the operating level, the proposed program should be adjusted to accommodate the needs of management or to reflect new information obtained. At that point, it should be discussed with top entity executives at the organization president level, and with the audit committee of the board of directors. A summary of the program should be prepared to support the request for audit resources for the forthcoming year.

The presentation at the summit could be sparked by visual aids summarizing the last year's results, the proposed audit effort for the coming year, and the number of auditors and other resources required to accomplish the work.

Smaller Internal Audit Activities

A smaller audit organization is most likely to try to avoid the task of developing the long-range audit schedule. Yet it is the most likely to need the benefits of such schedules provide. The one- or two-auditor organizations are fair game for line assignments: help out in accounts payable when volume builds, reconcile bank statements, do legwork for external auditors, etc.

If management can be convinced that time away from audit projects increases risks, the likelihood of line assignments diminishes. But the campaign for a long-range schedule must be well thought out. Internal auditors will have to do more than list audit projects. They will have to convince senior management and the board that those audit projects are significant, that if the activities are not audited, the enterprise leaves itself open to risks, that there is no assurance of reliable systems of internal control, or that external audit costs might rise as a result of diminished audit activity. In short, "the uninspected inevitably deteriorates."

Thus, internal auditors should be specific about both the audit projects and the risks. For example, management might be told:

> "If we don't audit receiving, you might not know if you are paying for goods or services never received, received too early, or received damaged."

> "If we don't audit shipping and traffic, you might not know that we may be packaging goods improperly, using the wrong freight routings, sending goods to the wrong destinations, or incurring needless demurrage charges."

> "If we don't audit purchasing, you might not know that we may be paying too much for products, dealing with the wrong suppliers, facing the danger of improper buyer-vendor relations, buying too much or too little, or not receiving products on time."

> "If we don't audit marketing, you might not know if we are expending money on market research needlessly, placing ads in the wrong media, failing to compare actual with expected benefits, dealing with the wrong advertising agencies, losing track of expensive products loaned to the agencies, or paying exorbitant prices for sales promotion items."

The list can go on and on. Management often needs convincing. The convincer is a simple demonstration of an understandable risk resolved by an audit finding that saved the organization money or protected it from danger. If management has been clearly and convincingly warned and insists on accepting the risk, the auditor has done all that is necessary. If one of the enumerated risks mushrooms into a loss, the auditor cannot properly be held at fault. On the other hand, if management is refusing to accept normal business risks, the auditor can point the deleterious effect that such a position can have on the organization's well-being.

But the burden is on the auditor to aggressively make those risks clear and understandable. One auditor was taken to task for not having warned management of a risk that turned into a heavy loss. The auditor reminded the manager that he had indeed provided a warning of what could happen. Angrily, the manager retorted, "But you should have convinced me!"

One means of achieving internal audit objectives involves compromise — to provide formally for a certain amount of assistance to management. Internal auditors could set aside in their long-range program an agreed percentage of audit hours for whatever special services management needs. But internal auditors must make it clear that any appropriation to non-audit uses of the remaining audit hours could destroy the internal audit function as a viable entity, make it no longer credible as a management control, weaken the base on which external auditors rely, dissipate any basis for reliance upon internal auditing as a monitor of the organization's systems, and undermine its objectivity.

The need to keep an excessive number of audit hours from being spent on non-auditing activities applies to all internal audit activities. The smaller activities are the most vulnerable and need to jealously guard their auditing capability and capacity.

Coordination with Other Control Agencies in the Organization

Internal auditing does not stand alone as a monitor of control. In all large organizations there are other agencies that may be equally concerned with matters of control. Their interest may have a more technical aspect, but it may complement the internal auditor's interests in the administrative forms of control.

The security department is concerned with control over specific irregularities. The quality control department is concerned with control over product reliability and conformance to specifications and standards. The safety department is concerned with control over accident prevention. The industrial engineering organization is concerned with control over operating practices and procedures. Depending on the nature of the entity, other agencies may have comparable control functions and responsibilities.

The internal audit activity should keep open a line of communication to these agencies when planning its audits. Valuable information can be obtained, either to reduce any possibility of duplicate surveillance or to point to areas where special audit emphasis may be warranted.

There are many ways in which this coordination can be accomplished. The following approaches are representative:

Security. Hold periodic meetings with security personnel. Keep them informed of the ongoing audit projects. Solicit their suggestions on where manipulations or other improprieties have occurred or can occur. Offer to assist in reviewing records relating to ongoing security investigations; the auditor usually can locate the records more readily and accumulate the data more easily. Ask to be kept informed of ongoing investigations that indicate the possibility of control breakdowns.

Quality control. Exchange audit schedules and reports with the quality control agency. Seek to be kept informed of repetitive defects in suppliers' goods or in-house manufactured products; there may be administrative control weaknesses contributing to the difficulties.

Safety. Establish arrangements with the agency responsible for safety so that suspected dangers encountered in the audit can be immediately reported for investigation. Provide for feedback showing the nature of the corrective action.

Industrial engineering. Provide for a pattern of preliminary discussions with the industrial engineers before engaging in audits of production areas. Clear any findings and recommendations with the industrial engineers when areas within their cognizance are involved. With their technical expertise, the engineers may be able to point to matters that the auditors have overlooked in their findings and recommendations.

Supplementary Readings

Arnold, Elizabeth S., "A Risk Assessment Tool for Selecting Potential Audits: An Application for State Government," *Internal Auditing*, Spring 1997, 21-26.

Erenguc, Nur S., and S. Selcuk Erenguc, "Optimization-based Audit Planning: A Spreadsheet Modeling Approach," *Internal Auditing*, July/August 1998, 16-23.

Hubbard, Larry D., "Audit Planning," *Internal Auditor*, August 2000, 20-21.

Kann, Melvin M., "A Flexible Way to Plan Audits and Evaluate Internal Controls," *Bank Accounting & Finance*, Fall 1989, 9-18.

Kramer, Joel F., "Planning for World-class Audits," *Internal Auditor*, October 1999, 88.

Reding, Kurt F., and Kristine Kay DiGirolamo, "Allstate's Risk Assessment Approach to Selecting Operational Audit Topics," *Internal Auditor*, April 1994, 48-53.

Sittenfeld, Itamar, "Audit Planning with the Grid Model," *Internal Auditor*, February 1991, 32-37.

Urbanic, Frank R., "The Risk Assessment Approach to Internal Audit Scheduling," *Internal Auditing*, Summer 1993, 88-95.

Walz, Anthony P., "An Integrated Risk Model," *Internal Auditor*, April 1991, 60-65.

Ziegenfuss, Douglas E., and Otto B. Martinson, "An Activity-based Approach to Internal Audit Planning," *Internal Auditing*, Fall 1992, 45-52.

Multiple-choice Questions

1. An organization is identifying audits to be performed over the next three to five years. This is an example of a(n):
   a. Planned audit goal.
   b. Audit planning objective.
   c. Tactical audit plan.
   d. Strategic audit plan.

2. The requirements for staffing level, education and training, and audit research should be included in:
   a. The internal auditing department's charter.
   b. The internal auditing department's policies and procedures manual.
   c. The annual plan for the internal auditing department.
   d. Job descriptions for the various staff positions.

3. According to the *Standards*, the internal auditing department's goals should specify:
   a. Audit work schedules and activities to be audited.
   b. Policies and procedures to guide the audit staff.
   c. Measurement criteria and target dates for completion.
   d. Staffing plans and financial budgets.

4. Directors may use a tool called "risk analysis" in preparing work schedules. Which of the following would not be considered in performing a risk analysis?
   a. Financial exposure and potential loss.
   b. Skills available on the audit staff.
   c. Results of prior audits.
   d. Major operating changes.

5. The best means for the internal auditing department to determine whether its goal of implementing broader audit coverage of functional activities has been met is through:
   a. Accumulation of audit findings by auditable area.
   b. Comparison of the audit plan to actual audit activity.
   c. Surveys of management satisfaction with the internal auditing function.
   d. Implementation of a quality assurance program.

6. Which of the following factors serves as a direct input to the internal auditing department's financial budget?
   a. Audit work schedules.
   b. Activity reports.
   c. Past effectiveness of the internal auditing department in identifying cost savings.
   d. Auditing department's charter.

7. Risk models or risk analysis is often used in conjunction with development of long-range audit schedules. The key input in the evaluation of risk is:
   a. Previous audit results.
   b. Management concerns and preferences.
   c. Specific requirements of the *Standards*.
   d. Judgment of the internal auditor.

8. According to the *Standards*, activity reports submitted periodically to management and to the board should:
   a. Summarize planned audit activities.
   b. Compare performance with audit work schedules.
   c. Provide detail on financial budgets.
   d. Detail projected staffing needs.

9. Which audit planning tool is general in nature and is used to ensure adequate audit coverage over time?
   a. The long-range schedule.
   b. The audit program.
   c. The department budget.
   d. The department charter.

10. Which of the following is not a requirement of a long-range plan for the internal auditing department?
    a. To be consistent with the department's charter.
    b. To be capable of being accomplished.
    c. To include a list of auditable activities.
    d. To include the basics of the audit program.

Chapter 23
Controlling Audit Projects

Audit assignments. Controlling audit projects. Audit budgets and schedules. Integrating project control with payroll. Controlling time of audits. Budget revisions. Progress reports. The use of Program Evaluation Review Techniques (PERT). Schedule boards. Audit follow-up. Permanent files. Supervision. Using software. The Texaco audit software. Small internal audit activities.

Audit Assignments

A well-controlled, well-structured internal audit project has a far better chance of meeting its goals than one that is haphazard and formless. True, an audit demands creative thinking and calls for the auditor to beat new paths and stretch old boundaries. But without control of budgets, schedules, and progress reporting, and without clearly defined guides to get it going, the project will languish. It will suffer from lack of discipline. According to Performance Standard 2030, "Resource Management," "The chief audit executive should ensure that internal audit resources are appropriate, sufficient, and effectively deployed to achieve the approved plan."

Discipline, from without and within, is a hallmark of professional auditors. Their profession's stated criteria impose certain disciplines; their own well-developed standards provide the rest. These disciplines include a clear understanding of the value of the audit project in relation to the needs of the enterprise. They also include an understanding of the value of timeliness and of the staleness of yesterday's news.

The long-range schedule has allotted a budget and plan for the audit project assigned to the auditor. These budgets and schedules are part of the audit organization's master plan. They were established after contemplation of the value of the project to the enterprise and the timing most suitable to all concerned. Auditors must therefore fit their own audit budget and schedule into the plans mapped out by the master program.

The administration of internal audits includes these matters: controlling the audit project, meeting budgets and schedules, dealing with budget revisions, providing for progress reports on the job, maintaining an overview of the projects in process, reviewing permanent files, and devising ways of reminding auditors what they should do to launch a project on its way.

Controlling Audit Projects

The first step in controlling any audit project is to "get it on the books." This is no different from establishing a work order to authorize approved work and to permit the expenditure of money and effort on such work. A simple form, controlled by a register, should be devised for the purpose.

The form might show the number and title of the project; the assigned budget; the name of the auditor-in-charge, assistants, and supervisor; and other necessary information. The register will control the assignment of project numbers and will provide a historical record of projects for ready reference. The register will remain under the control of the central audit office; copies of the assignment records will be distributed to the auditor-in-charge, the supervisor, and the central office file.

Under broadening the internal auditing organization concept, the budgetary control may be delegated to the operating level and, thus, audit managers would be accountable for segmented portions of the internal auditing resources. Presuming the use of risk-oriented internal auditing activity, and assuming that the working level managers are responsible for the risk assessment, the actual assignments would be made at that level.

When devising forms like these, there is a tendency to provide for every conceivable contingency. The forms then get complicated and forbidding. Some of the called-for information gets omitted, and the system collapses of its own weight. Worst of all, if any prescribed procedure is neglected, contempt for other procedures tends to follow — resulting in incomplete records and impairment of office administration. Exhibit 23-1 is a simple assignment record that provides essentially all the information needed to authorize a project.

Exhibit 23-1
Project Assignment Order

Title _____   In Charge _____

Project No. _____   Supervisor _____

Permanent File _____   Start Date _____

No. _____

Programmed
Frequency _____

Programmed
Budget _____

Approved
Budget _____
(After audit program approved)

Client _____

Risk Assessment:
Identify the 6 greatest risks:

Description of Risk Area	Risk	Vulnerability
1._____	_____	_____
2._____	_____	_____
3._____	_____	_____
4._____	_____	_____
5._____	_____	_____
6._____	_____	_____

Objective — Scope_____

Criteria _____

Special Instructions _____

Authorized by _____

Date _____

Each audit organization will determine its own system of project numbering. A logical system would provide a simple means of showing: (l) the kind of project; (2) the year; and (3) the number of each project within each year's series. For example:

R0X-1. The first "regular" (R) project included in the long-range audit schedule for the year 200X. "(0X)"

M0X-2. The second project that was specifically requested by "management" (M) during 200X. "(0X)"

S0X-3. The third "special" examination — not included in the long-range program — undertaken by the audit organization because of special needs (S) due to unexpected circumstances.

I0X-4. The fourth "interim" project (I), conducted between regularly programmed reviews. Interim reviews may be designed to determine whether key controls or sensitive areas reviewed at prescribed intervals, are continuing to function as intended.

FU0X-5. The fifth "follow-up" project (FU) established to determine whether deficiencies have been corrected, whether corrected deficiencies have recurred, and whether the corrective action that had been instituted is still effective.

Res0X1. The first "research" project (Res) of 200X undertaken, for instance, to carry out plans for developing and expanding the effectiveness of the audit organization.

Separate series for projects can provide more precise control over the audit organization's budget. For example, audit days (or hours) expended on regular projects can be compared with the annual budget for those projects. The same is true for the budgets established for management requests, special work, research, and the rest. Where the assignments are made at the working level, the classification can alert internal audit management as to the overall character of the audit effort being expended.

Audit Budgets and Schedules

Creative souls abhor control. Modern internal auditing is largely a creative activity. The auditors engaged in that activity sometimes argue that budget and schedule constraints stifle creativity. Nonsense! Any business activity functions only so long as there are funds to pay for it, and every activity has its price tag. Even pure research in an organization engaged in scientific projects must be granted a budget and must have periodic evaluations of progress. True, the budgets may require adjustment when new conditions surface. It is also true that the project may be eliminated or halted when the budget limitations are reached or no return can be foreseen. Also, budgets may be increased when additional risks are disclosed.

In all audit activities, individual project budgets and schedules are essential. Without them, there is a tendency to dawdle, a tendency to give equal weight to all segments of an audit instead of determining which segments are the most significant and warrant the most attention, and a tendency to spend inordinate lengths of time "tying up loose ends" and covering all potential question areas, regardless of significance.

Accordingly, budgets and schedules for all assigned projects must become a normal way of life. To be effective, such controls must include a current recording and reporting system. The system should provide:

- A way for the audit manager and auditor-in-charge to allot budget to the various audits and segments of the audit project and to keep a record of the time spent on those segments and the results of the audit work.

- A way for each staff auditor to report time charges during the current period — could be a week or month — and a summary of the results.

- A way for the audit department to report currently — usually monthly — on the status of all its current audit projects.

Exhibit 23-2 is a suggested work sheet for controlling individual project budgets. It is submitted to audit management and a copy is kept in the working papers and provides for allocating the entire budget to the various segments of the project, beginning with initial planning and continuing through completion of the final report.

Exhibit 23-3 is the suggested time report for every employee in the department. The report requires an accounting for each hour in the current workweek. It provides for both programmed and non-programmed work and for vacations, holidays, administrative time, and sick leave. The reverse of the form on Exhibit 23-3 should contain:

   Results of current week work _____

   Plans for next week _____

Exhibit 23-2
Time Record

Project No. _____

TIME CHARGES IN HOURS FOR WEEK ENDED: _____

W/P Ref.		Budget		Total Act'l	First Week	Week	Cum.	Week	Cum.	Week	Cum.	Week	Cum.	Week	Cum.	Week	Cum.
		Orig.	Rev.														
Planning																	
Field Work																	
Audit Segment A																	
Audit Segment B																	
etc.																	
Total Field Work																	
Report Writing																	
Client Review																	
Total																	

Exhibit 23-3
Time Report

Name _____

Five-week Period Ended _____

	W/E						W/E				
Programmed Work:	M	T	W	T	F	S	M	T	W	T	F	S
Project Number												
Nonprogrammed Work:												
Abandoned projects												
Follow-up on completed proj.												
Special investigations (Describe)												
Other (Describe)												
Other Working Time:												
New employee training												
Staff meetings and training												
Research (Describe)												
Proofreading												
Supervisory and admins.												
IIA												
Secretarial and clerical												
Nonworking Time:												
Vacations												
Sick leave												
Approved time off												
Leave without pay												
Holidays												
Totals												

Exhibit 23-4 is a suggested monthly report that lists each project open at the end of the month, the allotted budget, the actual charges, the estimated date for completion of the field work, and the estimated date for the release of the final report. The audit manager should make an initial estimate of field work completion at least by the midpoint of the audit. This estimate should be based on an analysis of the various segments of the audit and assigning realistic time allowances, regardless of the cost impact and original time allotment.

Estimates of completion dates can be based on Program Evaluation and Review Technique (PERT); Critical Path Measurement (CPM); or some similar type of analytical and work projecting system. These systems can make it possible, using PERT-Cost, to project costs as well as work progress.

Exhibit 23-4
Status of Current Projects and Personnel Assignments Month Ended January 31, 200X

| **Supervisor A** | | Audit-Days | | | Due Date | |
Personnel Assigned	Project	Budget	To Date	To Complete	Field Work Completion	Report Issue
Auditor 1	Project Title	50	40	10	2-05-0X	
Ass't. Auditor	Project Number (date started)					
Auditor 2	Project Title Project Number (date started)	35	31	8	1-29-0X	2-15-0X
Auditor 3	Project Title Project Number (date started)	45	10	35	(*)	

Supervisor B
etc.
(*) Not yet determined.

Integrating Project Control with Payroll

The hours reported in Exhibit 23-3 should be used for integrating into a payroll system and a control system for audit reporting and for controls over non-audit activities. If computers are used, edits can:

- Assure the accuracy of employee identity.
- Identify hourly excess over normal working hours.

- Compute employee's weekly wage.
- Integrate approved deductions for each employee on a periodic and to-date basis.
- Compute employee's net pay.
- Transfer employee net pay to employee's bank (no checks to be written). Details of employee net pay available at a designated computer (password authorized) address.
- Maintain employees' earnings records.
- Accumulate computed audit costs by week by audit, and by type of audit activity.
- Prepare current "budget to actual" reports and show relationship of projected costs and hours to budget.
- Compute on a by-difference basis, budget vs. actual, auditor performance incidents greater than a stated percent (both plus and minus).

A computerized system such as the above can provide information for management decisions, audit activity, and personnel controls.

Controlling Time of Internal Audits[1]

A realistic approach to controlling time on internal audits starts with a careful estimate of the anticipated time. Although this could be considered as a part of the program development, it is important here. Following are some areas of consideration:

- Based on time spent in prior years.
- Analyze the forthcoming audit in terms of the prior year's scope.
- Estimate time requirements for field work, report drafting, conferences, and review supervision.

The budgeted time should be for work time and should not contain estimates for reserves. This is to prevent inefficiency. The time estimates should serve as a basis of staff assignments as well as providing guides for each staff member. Estimates should be compared with actual time during the audit and estimates should be modified as needed (with an impact on budgeted free time or time for other audits). The auditor time reports should identify specific staff assignments so that an analysis may be made for differences between the estimate and the actual.

Generally, the audits hours should be grouped into control categories that are emphasized based on the engagement risk analysis and other measures of importance. Even normal categories may be divided into subareas relative to the elements of activity making up the project.

Audit staff should prepare detailed time records in the same detail as are the budgets based on estimates. The subordinate classifications should be:

- Planning of the budget and program, also preliminary surveys.
- Field work — by major segments — including the time of all staff working on the segment.
- Supervisory reviews.
- Report writing through the initial draft.
- Management review, including report editing.

The budget should be allocated using a matrix: staff time by type of audit work with consideration of the normal business or operating cycles of the organization.

Monitoring consists of identifying variances between estimates and actual time spent and accounting for the variance. An important aspect here is to consider the impact on future audits of the variances disclosed in current audits. During interim monitoring it is necessary to project "time to complete" when a segment is in process. Time projections should be carefully established using a method such as PERT or CPM where possible.

Budget Revisions

While control through budgets is essential, that control should not be so rigid as to be self-defeating. The internal audit thrust is such that it cannot be reduced to a mechanical exercise. New projects, not previously undertaken, are constantly added to the schedule and some may be eliminated. Each old project either is attacked somewhat differently from the last audit or faces changes in organization or activity resulting from current activity. Thus, the budget system requires some flexibility without relinquishing formal control.

The rules for budget revision should be reasonable and simple. At the same time, they should not provide a cloak for incompetence or poor planning. Thus, budget adjustments should be entertained and approved as soon as it is determined that the audit project undertaken is not the same as the project planned in the long-range schedule. By and large, budgets should be appraised for potential revision — either up or down — immediately after the preliminary survey and the preparation of the audit program.

The preliminary survey (see Chapter 4) establishes the subject of the review, the theory of the audit approach, and the structure of the project. If the survey discloses new activities — different from those contemplated when the audit project was first programmed or if unusual disclosures are made such as the result of more recent risk assessment — appropriate budget adjustments should be requested and authorized. If the activities remain the same, any budget overruns that do occur should be explained — but not glossed over by extending the allotted budget.

For example, the present audit manager may have uncovered substantial deficiencies that required extended investigation, or the auditor may have been saddled with staff whose work had to be done over, or who required considerable attention. The audit tests may have required expansion to establish the reliability of the audit findings. Risks may have been disclosed that were not considered in the original planning. These matters, while legitimately taking more time, may have some effect on the original understanding in the long-range audit schedule. The activities subject to review may not always remain the same.

In effect, therefore, decisions to revise budgets should be made in terms of the long-term schedule, discussed in the previous chapter. The difficulties normally inherent in an internal audit project are simply matters for consideration when evaluating the auditor's accomplishments on that job. Accordingly, requests for budget revisions should clearly spell out the structural changes in the subject under review and the causes therefor. The requests should provide estimates of the additional time occasioned by those changes.

Similarly, where the survey and the resulting audit program indicate that coverage can appropriately be restricted or reduced, prompt downward adjustments should be made at that point. It would be naive to assume that audit managers will offer, with alacrity, to relinquish some of their treasured budget. Clearly, their jobs will be made easier if they can carry on a reduced audit with an unreduced allotment of audit-days. But in order to evaluate audit efforts, the budget should represent the time allotted for a reasonably proficient auditor to accomplish a particular examination. Accordingly, the supervisor or the audit manager should review the results of the survey and the proposed audit program to determine whether budget reductions, as well as increases, are in order.

Progress Reports

While more formal progress reports will be prepared monthly or quarterly, audit managers cannot wait that long to know how projects are proceeding. The supervisors or managers who are suddenly caught by surprise, when a budget has been used up or a schedule has slipped and the project is nowhere near completion, must turn their criticism inward.

Audit managers must function under the same rules that they expect operating managers to follow. Reduced to their essentials — and perhaps oversimplified — the guideposts of the good manager read "feedback," "follow-up," and "no surprises." Hence, audit managers should expect from their staff a simple weekly report that provides this information. Exhibit 23-5 is designed to show the allotted budget, the audit-days used through the prior week, the audit-days used in the week just ended, and the anticipated audit-days required to finish the job.

Exhibit 23-5
Weekly Status Report

Week ended _____

Audit Project _____ Project No. _____

Audit Days

Budget
Prior week's cumulative total   _____   _____
This week's total   _____
This week's cumulative total   _____
Budget still available   _____
Required to complete   _____

Audit Segments Over Budget

Audit-Days

Segment	Budgeted	Over	Reasons
1.	___	___	_____
2.	___	___	_____
3.	___	___	_____

Action Required to Recover   Estimate
1.   ___   _____
2.   ___   _____
3.   ___   _____

Potential Problems

_____
Audit Manager

Note: Submit this report to the supervisor by 10 a.m. each Monday.

The form should provide for comments on anticipated problems and information concerning when staff will be released. The latter information is quite important; it helps reduce staff standby time. The proper timing of assignments for assistants is a perennial problem; the sooner the people in charge of assignments are aware of the release of an assistant, the better they can schedule the staff assignments.

The Use of Program Evaluation Review Technique (PERT)

In internal auditing, as in any other activity that involves the commitment of valuable resources, in this case, personal services, money, and material, it is important to use a disciplined control process. Such a process is available in the procedure called Program Evaluation and Review Technique. This process can easily be applied to the internal audit activity and it provides an easily understood diagram or graphic network. The technique was developed by the U.S. Navy to expedite the development of the Polaris missile. It is very adaptable to computer operation.

In using PERT, the audit project is broken down into identifiable activity units, for example: the entrance conference, writing the audit program, compliance testing of certain aspects, substantive testing of these aspects, etc. Each unit has three estimated times: the best performance, the worst performance, and the most likely performance. Also, each unit has identified its dependence on preceding unit(s).

It should be understood that all activities are not performed in sequence. Some can be conducted concurrently, for example: the three segments of the preliminary survey; compliance testing of adherence to various regulations or procedures; and substantive testing of various activities.

Some activities, though necessary, are not in the critical path. Several examples could be research on a special problem, editing, cross-referencing, etc.

It is also necessary to determine whether time changes in one activity could impact on the time for performing another activity. The system must remain flexible so that changes, either to the events themselves or the estimated times, actually occurring or anticipated can be entered into the operation.

The times are entered into a model that relates probability to the estimates and produces a usable time factor. The events are then arrayed either manually or by the computer so that the entire audit process is displayed as an understandable diagram. As the audit progresses, actual times are inserted in place of the estimated times. The software will adjust the entire network for actual plus modified estimated time so as to arrive at a realistic estimate of the time necessary for completion.

The procedure can also be converted to what is called PERT-COST. The same techniques are used to compute estimated costs of the audit.

The details of the operation of this advanced procedure are beyond the confines of this text. Reference to a managerial science text or specialists should be made.

Schedule Boards

Scheduling staff assignments is no simple chore, at best. Slipped project schedules, unanticipated interruptions, and special requests from management complicate an already difficult task. Also, trying to get a clear picture of the current and downstream assignments of 20 or 30 auditors can boggle the mind. The project scheduler is well advised, therefore, to obtain some mechanical aid or software that is flexible and easy to update.

One device is a large board that makes use of assignment slips and numbered flags to show at a glance precisely what the scheduled assignments are, for periods up to a year. Exhibit 23-6 pictures such a board showing only the month of January. All the auditors in charge and all the assistants are grouped separately in alphabetical order. The supervisors are shown at the bottom of the board on differently colored markers to differentiate the jobs that are under their supervision.

The entire board covers a period of one year, and each of the spaces between vertical lines represent one week. The scheduled assignments for each auditor-in-charge are written on the board using the same color as that assigned to the supervisor of the job. Each assistant is assigned a number and is represented by a flag bearing that number. A string hanging vertically across the board — moved each week — indicates the current week.

To simplify explanations, Exhibit 23-6 shows the status of jobs for only one of the supervisors, Underwood. Her jobs are written in blue. The note on Exhibit 23-6 explains the assignments.

Information system controls can replicate such a device as shown in Exhibit 23-6 by the use of work sheets. The format can be modified to emphasize the work and progress by auditor, project, and by time element. Notes would be supplied by audit supervision. Through the use of work progress analysis (PERT), the software can project audit personnel availability for future work. Thus, there will be adequate time for mid-range planning of future auditing project.

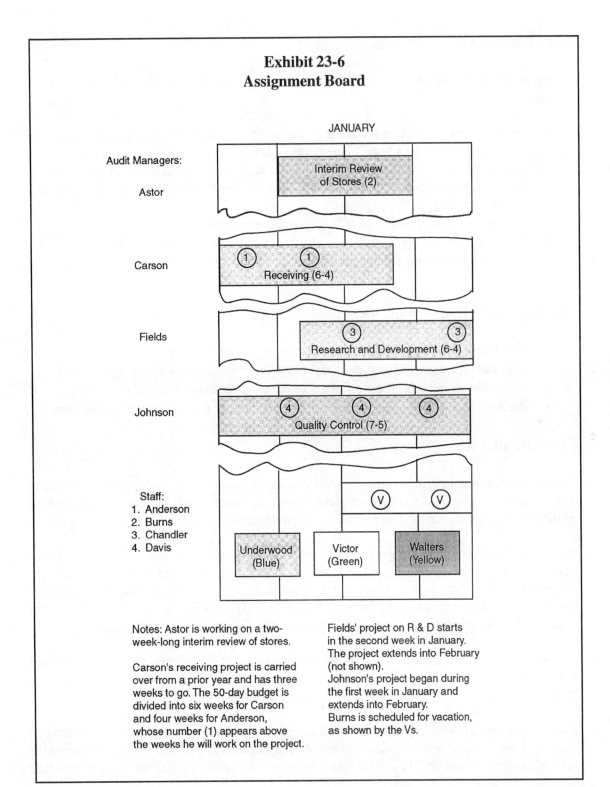

Exhibit 23-6
Assignment Board

JANUARY

Audit Managers:

Astor — Interim Review of Stores (2)

Carson — Receiving (6-4)

Fields — Research and Development (6-4)

Johnson — Quality Control (7-5)

Staff:
1. Anderson
2. Burns
3. Chandler
4. Davis

Underwood (Blue)   Victor (Green)   Walters (Yellow)

Notes: Astor is working on a two-week-long interim review of stores.

Carson's receiving project is carried over from a prior year and has three weeks to go. The 50-day budget is divided into six weeks for Carson and four weeks for Anderson, whose number (1) appears above the weeks he will work on the project.

Fields' project on R & D starts in the second week in January. The project extends into February (not shown).
Johnson's project began during the first week in January and extends into February.
Burns is scheduled for vacation, as shown by the Vs.

Audit Follow-up[2]

A method of managing of audit follow-up is to classify audit recommendations into three groups:

- Significant or immediate follow-up. The recommendations in this group should take no longer than 60 days to be implemented. It is possible that many of them will have been resolved during the audit or at least a start on the corrective action will be in process when the audit report is issued. The criteria is importance as defined by risk (frequency, magnitude, exposure).
- The less important would be 120-day implementation.
- No further follow-up is needed. These items are findings of the first and second types that have been completed as well as items that are so minor as to require no follow-up.

The follow-up technique should determine:

- That the recommended action has taken place or is in progress.
- That the recommended action is resolving the condition disclosed by the finding.
- That controls have been put in place to detect a recurrence of the condition.
- The benefits that have accrued to the organization as a result of the implementation.

Permanent Files

Permanent files for internal audits will vary to some extent from those used in financial audits. In financial audits, a consistent pattern in the conduct of the audit and the evaluation of the accounting data exists. The pattern in operating departments may not be that consistent.

Operating departments are subject to constant flux and change in their activities. Product lines change. As one activity becomes reduced, it may warrant consolidation with another. Organizations become restructured to accommodate changing conditions. The emphasis given to a particular function yesterday may be entirely different from what is called for today. Also the concept of risk analysis could materially modify the audit approach.

Accordingly, the permanent files should be flexible and useful, but economical. They should not be cluttered with matters that will not be of help, either in current audit or in planning the long-range schedule. Following are some of the matters that can be useful:

Prior audit reports and replies. Copies of all prior audit reports and replies and results of follow-up action provide a historical record of deficiencies, recommendations, and corrective action taken or proposed. They are a good index of the audit approaches used in previous years, the audit emphasis, and the audit findings. Where the record indicates a continuing trend of satisfactory opinions, in total or in part, the current audit programs may be structured accordingly, to reduce audit emphasis. Continuing difficulties, on the other hand, would be a signal for increased emphasis.

Audit reports from other organization divisions or branch offices. In multi-divisional audit organizations, where each unit issues its own audit reports under its own long-range schedule, copies of such reports give added insight into methods of attacking particular audit problems. Each internal auditor has his or her own techniques, preferences, and strengths; each can learn from the work of another. Unique deficiencies unearthed in one division may hint of audit techniques not considered at others.

Records of reviews with higher management. The long-range schedule reviews that are held with higher management often throw a sharp light on the needs and problems of management. These meetings can sometimes illuminate the dark corners of an audit subject and provide the auditor with a means of offering an improved service to management. Copies of the records of these reviews constitute an important part of the permanent file.

Post-audit reviews. Post-audit reviews (see Exhibit 22-3, the Audit Analysis form) provide conclusions and recommendations on audit approaches by the individual most qualified to make them — the audit manager who just completed the audit of the subject under consideration. These recommendations — if the information indicates they are still relevant — provide helpful guides for the current program.

Auditors' comments. All auditors, as part of their current reviews, learn of matters that are of interest to the audit organization but that may not be germane to their own current audit purposes. Where such matters speak of emergent circumstances, they may warrant the immediate opening of a special project or the expansion of a current one. But if the demand is not immediate, the matter should be informally recorded and the record made a part of the permanent file of the appropriate audit project.

Records of accounts and reports. In many audit organizations, a copy of the chart of accounts is referenced to appropriate audit projects. In this way, there is assurance that the operating matters relating to these accounts will be covered in the long-range program or the accounts will be analyzed, if appropriate. Each permanent file, therefore, should contain a reference to the related accounts and copies of recent account analyses.

Demographics of the audit environment. There should be information relative to:
Production of products or services.
Tables of organization.
Flow charts of materials, assemblies, and products; and documents.
Details of information system aspects of the operation.

Also, management looks to the auditor to assure validity and reliability of the management operations reports on which it leans when making day-to-day decisions. Errors or improprieties in such reports can have serious repercussions if they contribute to incorrect decisions. These management reports should be reviewed by the auditors, to the extent they consider necessary, when they engage in the audit of the particular activity. Records of these reports should likewise be referenced in the appropriate permanent files.

Miscellaneous matters. Considerable diversity of opinion exists among chief audit executives on what belongs in a permanent file. The miscellaneous matters that follow were also taken from responses to our inquiries concerning program or permanent file material. They are indicative, in some ways, of how closely the audit organization follows operating matters.

- A copy of each program and the related questionnaires applicable to a particular audit project, just so long as those programs and questionnaires remain applicable.
- Organization charts, which are to be replaced or corrected as changes occur.
- Contracts with labor unions, and copies of long-term contracts — such as those with concessionaires.
- Flowcharts and descriptions of operations and significant equipment and facilities.
- Wage earners' incentive plans.
- List of departments or cost centers, to help in the long-range planning and to assure coverage periodically.
- Historical financial information.
- Basic directives or instructions applicable to specific locations or activities.
- Important correspondence specifically related to the audit project.
- Audit time summaries, segregated by subject matter and program sections, as an aid in planning future audits.
- Summaries of test-checked periods (weeks, months, or quarters) to avoid repeating the same periods in subsequent audits.
- Operating routine summaries highlighting internal control points.
- Accounts receivable write-off summaries for use in future verifications.
- Obsolete equipment, facilities, and inventory summaries.
- Descriptions of major credit problems for use in future audit examinations.
- Photographs of locations and plats of plant layouts.
- Price lists and sales brochures.
- Identified risk aspects with assessments for a span of several periods. Also, audit activity relative to the highly rated evaluations and the results of those audits.
- For separately incorporated components: copies or digests of articles of incorporations; bylaws; minutes of board meetings; minutes of stockholders' meetings; capital stock authorizations; abstracts of changes in surplus accounts; abstracts of title to property; records of the last examination of public records for transfers of title; registration of mortgages, judgments, liens, and other relevant records of judicial

proceedings; lists of lands and buildings; reconciliations of changes in surplus with earnings reported for tax purposes; descriptions of pending tax assessments; and claims for tax refunds.

Note: For international audit assignments, complete information is needed relating to customs, economics, unique accounting standards, travel, living conditions, etc.

Supervision

No mechanical control can compare with knowledgeable accessible, concerned supervision. Professional, experienced auditors are likely to turn out professional audits; inexperienced auditors are not. Yet an audit activity's products must be consistently high. The equalizer is good supervision. A competent supervisor can warn of pitfalls, help in the audit planning, provide unbiased perspectives on audit findings, ensure the preparation of professional working papers, help maintain good auditor-client relations, monitor budgets and schedules and help reverse adverse trends, review audit reports, and see that essential elements are not missing from the audit project.

Standard 2340, "Engagement Supervision," and the related Practice Advisory advises as follows on the subject of supervision:

1. The chief audit executive is responsible for assuring that appropriate engagement supervision is provided.
2. Appropriate evidence of supervision should be documented and retained.
3. All internal auditing assignments, whether performed by or for the internal audit activity, remain the responsibility of the chief audit executive.
4. Supervision extends to staff training and development, employee performance evaluation, time and expense control, and similar administrative areas.
5. All engagement working papers should be reviewed to ensure that they properly support the engagement communications and that all necessary auditing procedures have been performed.

Experienced audit supervisors are a combination of teacher and monitor. They must therefore know the people they supervise. Experienced, competent staff people require less supervision than neophytes. At the same time, over-supervision retards growth. Unreasonably tight supervision develops excessive dependence. Staff auditors then adopt the unfortunate habit of asking for solutions instead of thinking through their problems and presenting alternative solutions to their supervisors.

Supervisors are not in an enviable position. They are the ones in the middle. On the one side is the manager; their subordinates are on the other. Management pressures the supervisor to see that audit projects are carried out efficiently, effectively, and economically. Subordinates, on the other hand, expect their supervisors to be the buffer between them and the audit manager. They expect supervisors to meet their needs for education, security, recognition, independence, and acceptance — and at the same time, to provide an environment in which they can grow and mature.

The supervisors-in-the-middle know all too well the power of management — the authority of those over them in the hierarchy. They also know the power of subordinates to withhold cooperation. In a professional organization, supervisors cannot treat their subordinates as vassals, so human relations become an important aspect of the supervisory function — good human relations can instill professionalism in the new auditor and support the experienced auditors while removing roadblocks from their paths.

The supervisor's job continues throughout the entire audit project. Supervisors must be involved in every phase of the audit work; for example:

Planning and introductions. Supervisors should offer their experience and their knowledge of management needs and desires as the audit project is planned. Their understanding of the way line managers like to deal with internal auditors can help the staff auditor over the difficult threshold of the initial meeting. Supervisors should attend those initial meetings, make the introductions, and lead or observe the introduction to the audit, depending on the experience of the auditor-in-charge.

Preliminary survey. Supervisors should approve the plans for the preliminary survey and visit the site to see that the proper information has been obtained. Where significant findings are observed, they should counsel the auditors on how to develop them through discussions with line or management people, use of interim report, development of audit programs, and determining the amount of evidence needed.

Audit programs. Audit managers should prepare the audit programs. Supervisors should approve both the initial program and any revisions to it. Supervisors should make sure, also, that the program steps are carried out or that adequate reasons are recorded for eliminating or changing any of them.

Field work. Supervisors should periodically visit the audit site and review the audit work that has been completed to date. This calls for a review of working papers. When staff auditors are aware that their papers will be reviewed, they are likely to take more care with them. Developing a high degree of respect in their subordinates for the importance of well-prepared working papers is one of the most important teaching functions supervisors can carry out. Auditors who have learned to develop professional working papers are usually those who worked under supervisors who set high standards of working paper preparation and insisted that those standards be met.

Supervisors should keep a wary eye on audit budgets and schedules, both through on-site observations and periodic time reports. In their reviews during the field work, supervisors should note all questions they may have about the audit, the working papers, the findings, the unanswered program steps, and the like. The auditors should respond to every point raised, recording their responses. These documents should become part of the working paper file.

Exit interviews. Exit interviews are extremely important, both in terms of corrective action, and auditor-client relations. Supervisors should attend these meetings if at all possible. If they have kept a watchful eye on the progress of the job, they should be able to contribute usefully to the meeting.

Reporting. Before auditors prepare their audit reports, they should have developed an outline for the draft. The supervisor should have reviewed it carefully and approved it during the audit and before the auditor started the final report writing. It is presumed here that much of the report writing is performed on an interim basis as findings are disclosed. The supervisor should ask the report writer to note, in the draft margin, the references to the applicable working papers. When reviewing the drafts, the supervisors should refer to the papers to make certain all statements are supported and can be authenticated.

Report reviews. Supervisors should try to attend all client audit report reviews with auditors. The objectivity they bring to bear can be useful if disputes develop. At the same time, supervisors can provide support for the auditor-in-charge if the client becomes difficult to deal with. The supervisor can also intervene if difficulties arise about the need for evidence of corrective action. Supervisors must be meticulous reviewers, and they must see to it that no errors or gaffes mar the final report.

Closing the project. Supervisors should review the working papers to see that they are complete before the papers are filed. They should see that all forms and administrative documents have been prepared. They should be satisfied that all corrective action needed has been taken before the project is closed.

Using Software

In departments with large audit staffs, manual controls over audit projects are time-consuming. Many internal audit activities have therefore turned to software to maintain timekeeping records and report the status of audit projects. A description of the characteristics of an integrated audit control software appeared earlier in the text.

Software is of particular use to internal audit activities that bill their costs to audited facilities — both direct charges and overhead. The software produces reports on audit-hours budgeted and used on each project, the dollar value of those hours, and an allocation of burden.

One governmental internal audit activity has described its use of software both for self-control and for management's information. The system turns out reports on internal audit status and progress.[3] The software provided one weekly and four monthly reports on audit assignments. Here are the reports of this system.

Completed assignments (Exhibit 23-7). Each audit assignment was given an individual number. The software listed all projects completed the previous month. For each project, the printout showed a comparison of audit days allotted and audit days worked. Also listed was the cost of each completed project, combining both direct charges and overhead.

Report of workload statistics (Exhibit 23-8). The monthly workload report summarized the status of all audit assignments for a 24-month period. The report showed the estimated available audit days for the two-year period, the assigned days for pending assignments, plus the assigned days for projects in progress, and the number of audit days committed to identified audit projects. Subtracting the committed days from available days yielded the audit days available for additional commitment. The report also gave an overview of the budget status. It shows whether staff had been over- or under-assigned — that is, whether more audit hours had been allotted to projects than were available. This information served as a guide when the chief audit executive was asked to accept new assignments and when additional staff time was being assigned.

Status of audit assignment (Exhibit 23-9). This report showed all open audit projects. The individual projects in progress were listed. For each project, the report showed project number, project description, month the project was last audited, name of the auditor, estimated audit days, audit days worked, audit days remaining, and the estimated date a report would be released.

Status of assignments by auditor (Exhibit 23-10). This monthly report listed the staff auditors in the audit activity and the projects to which they were assigned. The name of each auditor was followed by the number and description of the projects on which the auditor was working. For each project, the report showed estimated and actual audit days, the days remaining, and the estimated release date of the audit report and helped schedule requests from management. The list showed who was available for assignment and which projects might have had to be extended to fit top priority jobs into the overall schedule.

Review status (Exhibit 23-11). This report provided the auditors with information each Monday on the review status of audit reports that were under review the previous Friday. The status report showed the time allotted for the report reviewers to complete their work, and it highlighted the reports that were not meeting their target dates.

Exhibit 23-7
Florida Department of Transportation
Internal Audit Completed Assignments
Month of April 1980

Assignment No.	Date Completed	Description	Auditor	Audit-Days Estimate	Days Worked	Total Cost
010055	04/08/80	Follow-up on recommendations	Shook	10	15	$2,499.30
021410	04/30/80	Control of Purchases	Shook	55	23	3,832.26
022425	04/21/80	Rev. Tele. Credit Card Billings	Shook	15	21	3,599.02
022611	04/21/80	Payroll Processing – Inter. Cont	Hunter	15	10	1,666.20
060029	04/21/80	Right of Way Summary	Ellis	8	8	1,332.96
060034	04/08/80	Algd. Attempt to Defraud	Ellis	30	16	2,665.92
Total Count		6		133	93	$15,595.66

Exhibit 23-8

Internal Audit Report of Workload Statistics

as of April 30, 1980 — Report Status

GOAL THROUGH CURRENT MONTH	90	REPORTS	100%
ACTUAL THROUGH CURRENT MONTH	93	REPORTS	103%
ANTICIPATED AVERAGE AUDIT-DAYS PER REPORT		20.00	
ACTUAL AVERAGE AUDIT-DAYS FOR EACH REPORT		16.48	

WORKLOAD

ESTIMATED DAYS AVAILABLE FOR 24 MONTHS		4,095	100%
LESS ASSIGNED DAYS:			
73 ASSIGNMENTS IN PROGRESS	1,548	37	
72 ASSIGNMENTS PENDING	1,339	32	
AUDIT DAYS COMMITTED		2,887	69
DAYS AVAILABLE FOR ADDITIONAL ASSIGNMENTS		1,208	31

Exhibit 23-9
Internal Audit Status of Audit Assignments
as of April 30, 1980

Assign-ment No.	Description	Last Audited	Auditor	Audit-Days Estimate	Days Worked	Days Remaining	Estimated Release Date
020204	FDOT contract content review	1279	Goodwin	40		40	06/30/81
020205	Voucher procedures review	0280	Urbanek	15		15	04/30/81
021104	Construction – federal citations	0478	Goodwin	30	12	18	06/30/80
021105	Current billing review – federal	0679	Whigham	45		45	02/28/81
021307	Productivity survey		Langford	10	3	7	06/30/80
021403	Inventory proc-office eng & shop	0377	Moore	24		24	02/28/80
021409	Travel expense voucher review	0378	Shook	60	15	45	06/30/80
021415	Fiscal general audit section		Shook	18		18	11/30/80
021416	Fiscal accounting section		Shook	30		30	08/31/80
022201	Procurement office procedures	0577	Langford	30		30	07/31/81
022304	Review EDP function	1178	Hunter	45	23	22	11/30/80
022403	Admin services reproduction		Rollins	15	5	15	11/30/80
022410	Cafeteria vending audit	0478	Shook	5			07/31/80
022419	Employee fund – Central Office	0479	Geohagan	7		7	06/30/81
022420	Employee fund – District 1	0779	Price	7		7	06/30/81
022430	Telephone credit card billings		Shook	15		15	04/01/82
022612	Employment of Relatives	0778	Faircloth	25		25	09/30/81
022613	Payroll processing-int. control		Hunter	15		15	04/30/82
022702	Legal office review	0278	Faircloth	24		24	12/31/80
024001	Review of DOT vehicles control	0976	Adams	8		8	02/29/81
024003	Inventory procedures-buildings		Runyan	30		30	02/28/81
024019	Security – Central office		Lawrence	3		3	10/31/80
024026	Financial Management Summary	0380	Whigham	12		12	02/10/82
Total				513	58	455	

Exhibit 23-10
Internal Audit Status of Audit Assignments — by Auditor
as of April 30, 1980

Assign-ment No.	Description	Last Audited	Auditor Days	Auditor Days Worked	Auditor Days Remaining	Date Due From Auditor
Ellis						
060027	Right of Way — District II	0978	36	35	1	05/31/80
047020	EEO — Compliance		20		20	07/31/80
060043	Right of Way Special Assignment		8		8	10/31/80
060038	Right of Way — District IV		25		25	01/31/81
060041	Right of Way — District VI		25		25	01/31/81
060036	Right of Way — District I		25		25	04/30/81
Total Count	6		139	35	104	

Exhibit 23-11
Internal Audit Review Status — Internal Audit Reports
as of April 30, 1980

Assign-ment No.	Description	Review by	Under Reviewer	Date to from Reviewer	Date Due Late	Days Status	Comments
010059	Office procedures review – D-VI	O'Dell	04-30	05-30	000	F	
021104	Construction – Federal Citations	Brown	05-02	06-01	000	F	
034004	Rate structures – materials & rch.	Runyan	05-15	05-29	000	P	
041002	Rate structures – topographics	Runyan	05-21	06-04	000	P	
052017	Construction review – District V	Davis	04-17	05-17	000	T	
052023	Labor compliance summary	Brown	03-15	04-15	000	F	
052031	Keys bridges – construction	Brown	05-01	05-31	000	F	
060014	Outdoor ad. tag procedures	Davis	05-16	05-30	000	T	
092029	Sign shop procedural review	Brown	05-02	06-01	000	F	
092030	Weight stations review follow-up	Runyan	05-21	06-04	000	P	
400011	Marco Island bridge	O'Dell	04-11	05-12	000	F	
400020	Dade Co. Expressway	Levingston	05-21	06-04	000	A	
440001	Ft. Drum Citrus Shop	Runyan	05-21	06-04	000	P	

Status Code:
F = Field Review   P = Proofread   T = Typing   A = Administrative Review

Exhibit 23-12
Internal Audit Overdue Reports
as of April 30, 19XX

Assign-ment-No.	Description	Audit-Days Estimate	Auditor Days Worked	Auditor	Date Due From Auditor	Comments
060012	Algd. title organization fraud	12	7	Faircloth	05-31-77	Awaiting court action.
092019	Algd. Att. to falsify scale wt.	138	119	Faircloth	12-31-78	Litigation pending – Legal
092040	Mitchell maintenance contracts	120	30	Freaney	04-30-79	Pending arbitration – Legal
092044	Algd. misuse of equipment	18	119	Karseboom	06-30-79	Pending admin. action
092043	Construction operational-Dist. IV	25	8	Goodwin	11-30-79	Other invest.action required
052034	Algd. Rock Haul fraud	25	10	Faircloth	12-31-79	Info. needed from legal
092049	Public transportation – Dist. III	15	2	Hunter	12-31-79	Now under review
044002	Design engineer-consul. projects	20	3	Whigham	02-28-80	Insufficient staff time
092052	Preliminary engineering – Dist. IX	40	10	Lawrence	02-28-80	Other priorities
021409	Travel expense voucher review	60	15	Shook	04-28-80	Other priorities*

Although this reference is somewhat dated, the quality and completeness of its content are so good that it is repeated in this edition.

Overdue reports (Exhibit 23-12). This report identifies reports that are overdue, the auditor assigned to the project, and the reason why the report is delayed.

Each audit organization will have different reporting needs and different priorities. Each would have to devise computer programs to fit its individual needs. But in large auditing organizations where keeping track of budgeted, estimated, and actual audit days and due dates is desirable, the chore of maintaining records and issuing status reports can be eased by the computer.

Texaco Audit Software[4]

An article in *Internal Auditor* described a project of the internal audit staff of Texaco that was intended to improve work flows and reduce audit administrative time, provide a continuous review of audit work performed at remote locations, and increase sharing of information between audit offices.

The organization purchased templates from other organizations whose methods they planned to utilize. It reviewed the forms and reports of the other organizations to ensure that Texaco's needed information was available. It was then decided that specific databases of information would have to be modifications of the purchased templates.

"Texaco's 'Internal Audit Lotus Notes Database' contains several separate databases which are linked together to improve overall audit efficiency and effectiveness." They are all interrelated and changes in each are reflected in the others. The databases relating to the control of the audit work follows. Subsequently the other databases will be listed.

- Audit Universe Database contains the audit universe for all (6) offices. It includes:
  — Name of the audit.
  — Authorized days for the audit.
  — Last time the audit was performed.
  — Risk index.
  — Audit intervals.
- Workflow Database is the main database for audits in progress or completed. There is one workflow database for each year. Each audit has four automated sections:
  — Audit information, i.e., dates, personnel, etc., and time plans.
  — Audit planning:
    - Audit risk analysis.
    - Audit program.
    - Notification letter.
    - Assignment memorandum.
    - Management memorandums.

— Work papers, also including memoranda to the file and transmittal of audit findings.
— Wrap-up:
  - Audit report.
  - Management letters.
  - Executive summaries
  - Checklist of items that should have been completed.
  - Cash flow enhancement form.
  - Client feedback into quality assurance.
  - Risk index form, reassuring the risks associated with the audit.

The supervisory audit staff is required to electronically sign off as to each work paper. Unreviewed work papers continue to be listed until appropriate action is taken. Working papers are either signed off (approved) or returned to the auditor with electronic comments.
- Audit Reports Database contains the audit reports released during the last two years. The reports can be, "viewed under several options and categorized by":
  — Office.
  — Finding.
  — Repeat audit finding.
  — Open findings.

The databases that do not directly relate to the control of the audit process are:
- Standard Programs and Risk database.
- Self-assessment Review.
- Reference Manuals.

The article lists seven benefits:
- Time savings in setting up audits.
- Reduced number of audit management visits to sites.
- Reduced time to prepare for meetings of the audit committee and executive management.
- Lowered overall computing expense.
- Enhanced communication and sharing of work.
- More efficient and timely release of audit reports.
- A repository for electronic work papers and reference materials.

The system had been in effect for in excess one year at the time of the presentation. Texaco's statement, "We're pleased with our final product."

Smaller Internal Audit Activities

Small audit activities tend to be more informal than larger ones. Their administrative records are usually less comprehensive and their own internal control mechanisms are often faulty. They may justify loose procedures by citing their size and the fewer projects they deal with. This is not appropriate.

Senior management and the board of directors in smaller entities are, or should be, as much concerned with adequate administration as those in larger entities. External auditors no doubt share that concern. Reasonable administration of an internal audit activity is as necessary as the proper administration of an accounting department.

Thus, audit projects of small audit activities should also be formally controlled and budgets and schedules should be used. Time records should also be maintained. Permanent files should be installed and kept up. Reminder lists for projects should be developed and used, and audits should be supervised.

External auditors dealing with small internal audit activities will apply the same standards to them as to larger departments: the *Standards for* the *Professional Practice of Internal Auditing.* The internal audit work either can be relied upon or it cannot. Size makes no difference.

Certainly, supervision in a one-person auditing activity is not easy. A one-armed person has difficulty clapping hands. But this difficulty makes it all the more important to develop and use self-verification through checklists, reminder lists, and well-organized routines. Indeed, good administration that displays professionalism to both management and the external auditors becomes particularly important in small or one-person internal audit activities.

References

[1]*Internal Audit Alert* (Boston, MA: Warren Gorham & Lamont, September 1994), 3-4.
[2]*Internal Audit Alert* (Boston, MA: Warren Gorham & Lamont, September 1995), 1-2.
[3]Levingston, A.C., "How Well Are You Controlling Your Audit Assignments?" *The Internal Auditor,* December 1977, 36.
[4]Boffa, Mario P., and Michael Miller, "Audit Automation with Lotus Notes," *Internal Auditor*, June 1997, 15-17.

Supplementary Readings

Applegate, Dennis B., Lawrence G. Bergman, and Stephen K. Didis, "Measuring Success," *Internal Auditor*, April 1997, 62-67.
Crowell, David A, "Equipping a Mobile Audit Staff," *Internal Auditor*, August 1997, 50-56.

Erenguc, Nur S., and S. Selcuk Erenguc, "Optimization-Based Audit Planning: A Spreadsheet Modeling Approach," *Internal Auditing*, July/August 1998, 16-23.

Gotlob, David, James S. Moore, and Kim S. Moore, "Optimizing Internal Audit Resources: A Linear Programming Perspective," *Internal Auditing*, Fall 1997, 20-30.

Houck, Thomas P., "Improving Efficiency in Your Audit Department," *Internal Auditing*, Winter 1994, 32-37.

Jeffords, Raymond, Greg Thibadoux, and Marsha Scheidt, "Project Management Skills for Internal Auditors," *Internal Auditing*, November/December 1999, 12-17.

Johnston, Warren M., "Getting a Grip on Travel Costs," *Internal Auditor*, April 1996, 21-29.

Levingston, A.C., "How Well Are You Controlling Your Audit Assignments?" *The Internal Auditor,* December 1977, 36.

Newmark, Henry R., "Auditing Construction Projects," *Internal Auditor*, December 1997, 36-41.

Nourayi, Mahamoud M., and Ali N. Azad, "The Impact of Time Budget Pressure on Internal Auditors' Behavior," *Internal Auditing*, Summer 1997, 42-50.

Pelfrey, Sandra, and Eileen Peacock, "Updating Internal Auditor Productivity Criteria," *Internal Auditing*, Summer 1993, 25-32.

Sears, Brian P., *Internal Auditing Manual* (New York: RIA, 2003.) (See Chapter C2, "Controlling Audit Projects.")

Sinason, David H., "Project Management in an Audit Environment," *Internal Auditing,* March/April 2002, 3-9.

Sinason, David H., John E. McEldowney, and Arianna S. Pinello, "Improving Audit Planning and Control with Project Management Techniques," *Internal Auditing,* November/December 2002, 12-16.

Williams, Satina V., and Benson Wier, "Value-Added Auditing: Where Are the Efficiencies Realized," *Internal Auditing*, July/August 2000, 37-42.

Multiple-choice Questions

1. In a comprehensive audit of a not-for-profit activity, an internal auditor would be primarily concerned with the:
   a. Extent of compliance with policies and procedures.
   b. Procedures related to the budgeting process.
   c. Extent of achievement of the organization's mission.
   d. Accuracy of reports on the source and use of funds.

2. According to the *Standards*, audit planning should be documented and the planning process should include all the following except:
   a. Establishing audit objectives and scope of work.
   b. Obtaining background information about the activities to be audited.
   c. Collecting audit evidence on all matters related to the audit objectives.
   d. Determining how, when, and to whom the audit results will be communicated.

3. When assigning individual staff members to actual audits, internal audit managers are faced with a number of important considerations related to needs, abilities, and skills. Which of the following is the least appropriate criterion for assigning a staff auditor to a specific audit?
   a. The staff auditor's desire for training in the area.
   b. The complexity of the audit.
   c. The experience level of the auditor.
   d. Special skills possessed by the staff auditor.

4. Which of the following is a step in an audit program?
   a. The audit will commence in six weeks and include tests of compliance.
   b. Determine whether the manufacturing operations are effective and efficient.
   c. Auditors may not reveal findings to non-supervisory, operational personnel during the course of this audit.
   d. Observe the procedures used to identify defective units produced.

5. The chief audit executive is preparing the work schedule for the next budget year and has limited audit resources. In deciding whether to schedule the purchasing or the personnel department for an audit, which of the following would be the least important factor?
   a. There have been major changes in operations in one of the departments.
   b. The audit staff has recently added an individual with expertise in one of the areas.
   c. There are more opportunities to achieve operating benefits in one of the departments than in the other.
   d. The potential for loss is significantly greater in one department than it is in the other.

6. During an exit conference, an auditor and a client disagreed about a well-documented audit finding. Which of the following would describe an appropriate manner to handle the situation, assuming that it cannot be resolved prior to issuing the audit report?
   a. Present the finding giving all of the facts and conclusions resulting from the testing.
   b. Present both the audit finding and client's position on the finding.
   c. Defer reporting the item and plan to perform more detailed work during the next audit.
   d. Change the finding to agree with the client's position.

7. Which of the following best describes what should determine the extent of supervision required for a particular internal audit assignment?
   a. Whether or not the audit involves possible fraud on the part of management.
   b. Whether or not the audit involves possible violations of laws or government regulations.
   c. The proficiency of the internal auditors and the difficulty of the audit assignment.
   d. The audit organization's prior experience in dealing with the particular client.

8. Which of the following best describes audit supervision as envisioned by the *Standards*?
   a. The manager of each audit has the ultimate responsibility for supervision.
   b. Supervision is primarily exercised at the final review stage of an audit to ensure the accuracy of the audit report.
   c. Supervision is most important in the planning phase of the audit to ensure appropriate audit coverage.
   d. Supervision is a continuing process beginning with planning and ending with conclusion of the audit assignment.

9. What action should an internal auditor take upon discovering that an audit area was omitted from the audit program?
   a. Document the problem in the work papers and take no further action until instructed to do so.
   b. Perform the additional work needed without regard to the added time required to complete the audit.
   c. Continue the audit as planned and include the unforeseen problem in a subsequent audit.
   d. Evaluate whether completion of the audit as planned will be adequate.

10. According to the *Standards*, the documentation required to plan an internal auditing project should include evidence that the:
    a. Expected findings were clearly identified.
    b. Internal auditing activity's resources are effectively and efficiently employed.
    c. Planned audit work will be completed on a timely basis.
    d. Resources needed to perform the audit have been considered.

Chapter 24
Quality Assurance

The need for quality assurance reviews. The macro and micro approach to quality assurance. The IIA's Standard 1310, "Quality Program Assessments." *Expansion of the standard. The evolution of quality assurance reviews. The Institute's* Quality Assurance Review Manual. *A current quality control survey. Productivity in internal auditing. Evaluations of productivity in internal auditing. Who can audit the auditors? The use of supervision for quality assurance. The use of internal reviews and quality circles. The use of external reviews. Peer reviews and how they developed. Peer reviews of multi-site operations. Reviews by other professional organizations. Client evaluations. Southern California Edison's TQM program. Quality concerns of management and boards of directors. The concept of total quality management (TQM) applied to internal auditing. The use of "bench marking" as part of TQM. ISO 9000 standards.*

● ●

Introduction

"But who will guard the guards themselves?" mused Juvenal in the first century.[1] Not until the 20th century did internal auditors find much of the answer. The guards must guard themselves. The internal auditors must audit themselves. However, there are others who will supplement this self-examination, as this chapter will describe. All professions have recognized that a few incompetents can cast a shadow on the proficient, dedicated professionals and on the entire profession. And so, to forestall policing actions by the government, they opted for self-evaluation, or arranged for external evaluation, with penalties for those who did not meet standards.

In the 1980s, The Institute of Internal Auditors followed other professional organizations in developing means of objectively reviewing internal audit functions. These reviews were prompted by the publishing in 1978 of the *Standards for the Professional Practice of Internal Auditing (Standards)* and were given structure by procedures for both self-evaluations and external reviews. In this chapter, we shall explore the current state of who will guard the guards themselves.

The Macro and Micro Approach

Usually, the quality evaluation process is applied to the broad internal audit operation. A review is made of the entity's method of organization, the staffing methods, the professional development requirements, independence within the entire operating structure, planning the audit function, use of emerging technologies, employment of new methods, effective reporting, audit projects control, efforts to improve interpersonal relationships with clients, general communications, audit follow-up methods, and compliance with internal audit standards. This type of evaluation, in a macro sense, does provide much valuable information on the internal audit organization as a unit. Conceivably, if such an evaluation results in a positive picture of an efficient and compliant auditing unit, management should gain a sense of its dependability and beneficial operation.

However, the evaluation should go a step further; a giant step further. Examination and reviews should be made of the individual audit processes. An internal audit activity can perform efficiently and yet not effectively — and that is the essential quality. What impact have the audits had on the organization as a whole? Individual audits should have an objective and this objective should be measurable. These two elements should be a part of the basic audit program. They should be described and the audit, at its completion, should indicate the degree of accomplishment of this objective, based on the measurement criteria described in the program. Usually success is measured by the achievement of the client's goals and objectives.

The review of the individual audits should also examine and evaluate such aspects as:

- Evidence of the auditor's understanding of the operation being audited.

- Indications that the auditor is aware of client management's attitude as to the control factors related to compliance, efficiency, and effectiveness.

- The assessment of risk, vulnerability, and materiality in the client process.

- The extent of testing being performed that would result in productive audit results, yet conserve internal audit resources.

In addition to the above conceptual audit aspects, the review should examine the usual audit procedures to determine that they were conducted with imagination and professional skepticism. Essentially, were there signals of potential problems or areas of interest that escaped the auditor or the supervisory reviewer and which an intuitive review would have questioned? These procedures would include the preliminary survey, the development of the program, the preparation and content of working papers, the collection of evidence, and the types and results of tests that are conducted.

In summary, was the audit performed effectively and did it result in a package that left no significant questions unresolved?

The Standard on Quality Assurance

In 1978, with the publication of the *Standards*, The Institute of Internal Auditors took a definite position on both internal and external reviews. The following excerpt from those Standards sets the tone for these reviews. (Current nomenclature is being used.)

Quality Assurance

"The chief audit executive should establish and maintain a quality assurance program to evaluate the operations of the internal auditing activity.

"The purpose of this program is to provide reasonable assurance that audit work conforms with these *Standards*, the internal auditing activity's charter, and other applicable standards. A quality assurance program should include the following elements:

- Supervision
- Internal reviews
- External reviews

"Supervision of the work of the internal auditors should be carried out continually to assure conformance with internal auditing standards, activity policies, and audit programs.

"Internal reviews should be performed periodically by members of the internal auditing staff to appraise the quality of the audit work performed. These reviews should be performed in the same manner as any other internal audit.

"External reviews of the internal auditing activity should be performed to appraise the quality of its operations. These reviews should be performed by qualified persons who are independent of the organization and who do not have either a real or an apparent conflict of interest. Such reviews should be conducted at least once every three (now five) years. On completion of the review, a formal, written report should be issued. The report should express an opinion as to compliance with the *Standards for the Professional Practice of Internal Auditing* and, as appropriate, should include recommendations for improvement."

The current *Standard 1310,* "Quality Program Assessments," states:

"The internal audit activity should adopt a process to monitor and assess the overall effectiveness of the quality program. The process should include both internal and external assessments."

This new standard is augmented by Practice Advisory 1310-1 with the same title. The content of this latter document is essentially described in the following pages as it reiterates much of the material in the Red Book codification of both the original standard and Statement on Internal Auditing Standards No. 4 (December 1986) on the same subject. Pertinent material from SIAS No. 4 follows.

Quality assessment expanded on the specific standard and guidelines in the former *Standards.* It offered guidance for carrying out quality assurance programs for internal audit activities. Much of the philosophy in that publication is still appropriate for consideration. Some of the matters discussed are:

The people who should be given reasonable assurance of compliance with the *Standards* include senior management, the independent outside auditors, the board audit committee, and regulatory agencies.

Conformity with the *Standards* implies performing audits efficiently and effectively. Assessments of audit competence should be measured not only against the *Standards* but also against the audit activity's charter. Audit performance should meet the requirements of The Institute of Internal Auditors' *Code of Ethics*; the activity's own objectives, policies, and procedures; the organization's audit policies and procedures; applicable laws and regulations; long-range audit programs and risk assessments; and the plans, organization, and job requirements of the internal audit activity.

The Practice Advisory specifically suggests that internal audit should be perceived by stakeholders as adding value and improving the organization's operations. The assessment process of quality programs should include recommendations, if appropriate, relative to:

- Compliance with the *Standards* and *Code of Ethics.*
- Adequacy of the activity's charter, goals, objections, policies, and procedures.
- Contribution to risk management, governance, and control processes.
- Compliance with government laws, regulations, and industry standards.
- Effectiveness of operations.
- Addition to value and improvement of operations.

The results of the above assessment should be shared with the entities' stakeholders such as management, the board, and external auditors.

Supervision includes planning the audit assignments, assurance that audit programs are carried out, and documentation of the supervision exercised. Supervision should be conducted throughout the planning, examination, evaluation, reporting, and follow-up processes. It should extend, also, to training, employee evaluations, and such other administrative activities as time and expense control.

Formal internal reviews should be carried out to assure the chief audit executive that subordinates are complying with the *Standards* and other applicable criteria. The reviews should arrive at objective judgments and offer recommendations for improvement. Where formal internal reviews are not appropriate, the chief audit executive should see that tests are made of completed audits and feedback is obtained from clients. The IIA's *Quality Assessment Manual, Fourth Edition,* provides specific information on conducting internal reviews.

External reviews provide independent assurance of audit quality for senior management, the board audit committee, and the external auditors, as well as to any others who rely on the work of the internal audit activity. SIAS 4 defined "qualified individuals" competent to perform external reviews as people with the technical proficiency and educational background appropriate for the audit activities to be reviewed. The people may include internal auditors from outside the organization, outside consultants, and independent outside auditors.

The external review should be formally reported to the person who requested the review.

The *Standards* stated that external reviews should be conducted at least once every three years (current standards state every five years). Circumstances may dictate different intervals — for example, where: (1) there is significant monitoring by the board audit committee; (2) there are in-depth reviews by the independent public accountants; and (3) there is relative stability within the auditing activity.

Where external reviews are inhibited by scarce resources, more emphasis should be placed on supervision and internal reviews. SIAS 4 pointed out, however, that such methods cannot be expected to achieve the objectives of an external review.

More detailed guidance about external reviews is included in the *Quality Assessment Manual, Fourth Edition,* previously mentioned.

Evolution of Quality Assurance Reviews

As internal auditing assumes greater responsibility for evaluating entity operations, and senior managers and board audit committees rely more and more on their internal audit staffs to provide desired safeguards and information for management decisions, there is a need for increased assurance that management and the board are properly served by professional audit staffs. No self-serving declarations by the internal auditors themselves will do. Objective, believable assurances will be needed. These can be provided only by peer reviews or quality assurance reviews. Such reviews are designed to be independent analyses that identify whether:

- The audits are meeting the needs of those who depend on them.
- The audit operations are being performed correctly.
- The auditing can be done better. Whether more should be done.
- Maximum value is being received for each internal audit dollar of expense.
- Internal audits meet current professional standards.

Quality assurance reviews are essential in every profession. By the 1960s, the public had become increasingly aware that it could no longer assume that professional people are all professionally competent. They had to be put to the test. They had to be subjected to independent reviews and appraisals of performance. This was imperative where the public needed to be confident of the integrity and competence of those who served them.

During the 1970s, more and more professions were submitting themselves to self-regulation. For example, in the United States, the Office of the Comptroller of the Currency issued a *Comptroller's Handbook for National Bank Examiners* containing instructions for the review of a bank's internal audit function.[2] The U.S. General Accounting Office issued its Audit Standards Supplement Series No. 9, *Self-Evaluation Guide for Government Audit Organizations*.[3] The American Institute of Certified Public Accountants (AICPA) prepared a *Peer Review Manual*.[4] And in 1984, The Institute of Internal Auditors first published a *Quality Assurance Review Manual for Internal Auditing* and organized a Quality Assurance Review Service to perform peer reviews.[5] Currently, the total quality management (TQM) concept is being used in production and service organizations to make sure that operations are being performed more efficiently and more effectively. Also the *Quality Assurance Review Manual* has been updated. This activity is becoming a continuous element of the ongoing production and service functions and is not a postoperative evaluation.

The Institute's *Manual* benefited from both *A Framework for Evaluating an Internal Audit Function*[6] and the impressive research reported in *Quality Assurance for Internal Auditing*.[7]

The Institute's *Manual* is concerned with both internal and external reviews. Each has a different purpose. The internal review is to give the chief audit executive: (1) assurance that the activity is in compliance with the *Standards*; (2) confidence that activities not requiring the executive's personal involvement comply with policy and procedures; (3) identification as to the level of audit effectiveness and efficiency; (4) information for improving the operation; and (5) assistance in preparing for external reviews. The purpose of an external review is to provide an independent evaluation for management and the board audit committee. Here are some of the matters discussed in, and help provided by, the *Manual*:

Internal reviews. The *Manual* explains the need for an internal review and who decides to have one. It discusses review team selection, identifies the criteria for selecting team members, and describes team preparation. It points up the need for surveying clients and provides instructions for interview questions, a sample questionnaire, and a client survey.

The *Manual* provides questions to be used to assess the degree of compliance with the *Standards*. It offers a program for evaluating audits and shows how to assess both administrative activities and the information system controls of the internal audit activity.

Finally, the *Manual* provides instructions on reporting the results of the internal review. It stresses the need for follow-up and the desirability of documenting that follow-up to ensure that corrective action is taken and is effective.

External reviews. The *Manual* explains the purposes and benefits of an external review and who should request it. It describes an engagement letter, and discusses the qualifications and criteria to be used in selecting a review team and the origin of such teams. It discusses how to survey and interview clients and explains why they should be surveyed or interviewed. Extra audit steps are provided for decentralized audit activities.

The *Manual* lists items to be addressed by the team leader before the arrival of the review team. It clarifies the team's objectives, plans, and procedures as well as the review of self-study results and client surveys. It suggests interview topics for clients, external auditors, audit staffs, management, and audit committees.

The *Manual* contains specific evaluation modules covering eight internal auditing program activities. These are:

1. Planning.
2. Professional Proficiency.
3. Risk Analysis and Audit Planning.
4. Analysis of Audit Plan Accomplishment.
5. Individual Audit Review.
6. Special Project Review.
7. Audit Policies and Procedures.
8. Computer Audit Scope.

The review follows the format of the *Standards*. The *Manual* also provides, a systematic approach for evaluating an internal audit function and for conducting a closing conference.

The *Manual* concludes with instructions on complying with the reporting requirements set forth in the *Standards*.

The *Manual* is concerned primarily with adherence to The IIA's professional standards. While these are essential for any review of internal audit activities, Chadler and Salmon admonish us that other activities of the internal audit activity should also be kept in mind.[8]

Conformance to standards is no guarantee that an internal audit activity is accomplishing its mission. The internal auditors may be following rules impeccably, but they may not be operating at optimum effectiveness. They may not be performing in a way that will persuade senior management that the cost of the internal audit operation is far outweighed by the tangible benefits of improved controls and information for management performance. Indeed, some matters that are touched upon in the *Manual* need special attention:

- *The structure of the internal auditing activity:* How strong and comprehensive is management's mandate for internal auditing? What is the makeup of the audit committee and what is its relationship to the internal audit organization? How comprehensive and usable are the audit manuals? How conducive to self-respect and to good work are the physical facilities afforded the internal auditors?

- *The audit process and human relations:* The process is well defined in the *Standards* and The IIA's *Quality Assessment Manual*. But the process, no matter how well established in the internal audit function, will stumble in the absence of good human relations skills. Is there evidence that both of these skills are embedded in the auditors and used in the audits?

- *Management of the audit function:* Much is said in the *Standards* about managing the audit process. But not enough is said about the management of the audit function as a whole. How effective is the chief audit executive in terms of planning, organizing, directing, and controlling the internal auditing activity?

- *Evaluation of audit results:* How effective is the audit function? Are findings and recommendations being accepted? Are plans being carried out? Are client objectives and goals being met? What are the benefits gained by the audit activity as compared to its costs?

Current Quality Control in Internal Auditing

A survey by Gupta and Ray[9] of 482 industrial firms based in the 1990 rankings published by *Fortune* in its April 22, 1991, issue. The researchers received 145 usable responses, a satisfactory return rate of about 30 percent. The questionnaire covered various aspects of the audit effort related to quality control in the organizations. However, Part IV of the form related to the internal auditing organization itself. A table summarized this information and is shown on the following page:

Steps	Times Mentioned
Development of mission and vision statements and establishment of internal auditing activity objectives	47
Establishment and implementation of performance measures for various stages of the internal auditing process	43
Identification of customers of internal auditing department	38
Development and implementation of internal auditing customer satisfaction surveys and feedback systems	33
Benchmarking with other internal auditing departments	31
Introspective self analysis	30
TQM training and education of the internal auditing staff	15

One aspect of metrics related to the importance of optimum development of internal auditing performance measures was:

Phase		Yes
Planning	48	58%
Field Work	52	63%
Audit Report	62	76%

The authors stated that, "Most of the measures revolve around the comparison of actual vs. budgets, feedback from customers, etc." More needs to be learned about metrics development for each phase of the audit.

Although this chapter is essentially devoted to the reviews of quality control of the internal auditing activity itself, it is interesting to note that internal auditing is increasingly being used for this aspect of the entire organization. Internal auditors are being involved as systems developers, systems auditors, consultants and compliance auditors. It is moving beyond "operational auditing into proactive design and development of quality systems." Although this recognition of the competence of internal auditors could have adverse effects by impacting on the objectivity of the auditors when reviewing the systems and compliance.

Productivity in Internal Auditing

Recent articles on internal audit productivity emphasize such aspects as: (1) the total amount of dollars saved or collections made as a result of total audit activity; (2) number of audits completed; (3) number of audit findings; (4) number of audits completed within ± 5 percent of budget; etc. While such statistics are useful, they do not in themselves constitute the full measure of audit productivity that should be considered.

Characteristics and classification of the findings are a far more important measure. For instance, findings should be classified as to those that are material, moderately material, and not material. Materiality should be considered as the quality that has a major impact on the organization's operations and it may not have a direct relation to volume or value. The impact could be financial or operational, although the latter would normally also have a financial impact. Another measurement should be related to service. Thus, a finding could result in the provision of better service to customers, employees, vendors, or, in government and not-for-profit organizations, to beneficiaries or clients.

The concepts of improvement in audit quality and of provision of better service to internal auditing customers is also an aspect that should be considered. These measures are part of the total quality management concepts discussed elsewhere in this chapter.

One must not forget that productivity is a relationship between the input of resources, money, manpower, materials, and time, to output, which is identified as efficiency, and to outcome that is identified as effectiveness. Thus, a greater reported output is meaningless unless it can be related to outcome and to resource input. However, the theme that should run through the entire productivity measurement process is quality. All quality reviews, regardless of who makes them, should consider the productivity aspect.

Evaluating Audit Productivity

Productivity in service operations such as internal auditing is difficult to measure because:

- One may be unable to identify and quantify output and outcome.
- Internal auditors deliver their work internally making it difficult to value.
- Internal auditing is often a team effort with the team responsible for the output.
- Internal auditors generally have much discretion as to the selection of tasks to be performed, and when and how the work will be accomplished.

Steve Albrecht and his associates researched the internal audit function in 13 major firms. They requested that these organizations identify the qualities they believed should be included in the evaluation of productivity. The result in order of importance was:[10]

- Reasonable and meaningful findings and recommendations.
- Client's response and feedback.
- Professionalism of the internal auditing activity.
- Adherence to the audit plan.

- Absence of surprises.
- Cost effectiveness of the internal auditing activity.
- Development of people.
- External auditor's evaluation of the internal auditing activity.
- Operating management's feedback.
- Number of requests for audit work.
- Audit executive's report.
- Audit committee's evaluation of the internal audit activity.
- Quality of working papers.
- Results of internal review.
- Peer feedback.

A study of 92 chief audit executives to determine a definition of internal auditing productivity disclosed the following qualities:[11]

Quality	Number of Chief Audit Executives
Completing the audit within the time budget	29
Producing an end product efficiently and profitably	25
Creating a valuable finding	11
Audits or outputs/inputs or hours and expenses	8
Meeting organization's goals and objectives	6
Six other items	<u>13</u>
	<u><u>92</u></u>

The audit executive respondents were unable to agree as to assigning a quantitative performance measure to these qualitative aspects. However, it is suggested that clients be asked to evaluate the above Albrect qualities using a Likert scale. This evaluation might give an appropriate measure.

Who Can Audit the Auditors?

Each of the three elements of a quality assurance program, as stated in the original and the current *Standards*, has a different purpose and a different method. Thus:

Supervision is a continuing process. It focuses on individual audits and/or parts of audits. It provides assurance to the chief audit executive that staff auditors are doing what they are supposed to be doing in their ongoing projects. Supervision also evaluates the auditors' judgments, conclusions, and audit methodology. Care must be taken that supervision does not become a review of the mechanics of the audit process, but that it is an evaluative review of the propriety of the audit results. Supervision is performed by audit supervisors or managers who are responsible for assigned audit projects, but who do not themselves carry out the audit projects.

Internal reviews provide assurance to the chief audit executive that the entire staff, including the supervisors, is doing its traditional work properly. These reviews are also being made to provide special assurances, on specific assignments, that audit representations made are accurate and reliable. These reviews are carried out by independent internal staff auditors, supervisors, or managers.

External reviews are evaluations of the entire auditing activity. These reviews are designed to tell top management and the board whether they are being served by a professional staff of internal auditors whose work meets the criteria set by the *Standards*. These reviews must be performed by people outside the auditing activity.

According to the *Standards*, the evaluators must be independent of the object of review and without a real or apparent conflict of interest. Utter independence without even an apparent conflict of interest may be difficult or expensive to obtain. A number of sources for such evaluations are available, but each source has its benefits and drawbacks. Here are some of the possibilities:

Peer group within the enterprise. These peer groups may be auditors from headquarters who appraise internal auditing activities in subsidiary or regional organizations. These evaluators may be considered independent of their "clients." They have the benefit of a short learning experience because of the headquarters auditors' overall knowledge of the enterprise. It is doubtful that they could be considered independent of the environment in which internal auditors of the entire enterprise function.

The enterprise's external auditors. These auditors provide a greater degree of objectivity than internal auditors from within the enterprise. Their learning curve is not too steep because of their familiarity with the enterprise's accounting system. There may be a question of whether they are truly independent of the internal control system that they have accepted over the years, and there may be a question as to whether some are knowledgeable of internal auditing procedures outside the financial and accounting sphere. These evaluations may be expensive and, for audits of operations, they may miss the mark. Another questionable element of independence is the temptation to structure the evaluation so as to encourage outsourcing of the entire internal audit activity.

External auditors from another accounting firm. These external auditors represent a high degree of independence, but the learning curve is steep because of their unfamiliarity with the enterprise systems. They, too, may have difficulty in evaluating audits of nonfinancial operations. The question of outsourcing may also be a problem here.

Reciprocal evaluations between audit groups of different enterprises. These evaluators should represent no actual or apparent conflict of interest, but the evaluators should be competent in all kinds of internal audit operations. The learning curve should not be as steep as that for external auditors, and the expense should be less. Yet, management and the board may be understandably reluctant to permit a competitor's internal auditors to gain entry to trade secrets and operating methods. Also, there should be safeguards to assure that there is objectivity in fact and appearance.

Qualified consultants. These evaluators should be people with actual internal auditing experience who normally function at a management level and who can deal competently with executives and board members. They would normally have a steeper learning curve than headquarters auditors, but there would be no real or apparent conflict of interest. They should be comfortable in appraising audits of all types of operations within the enterprise.

The IIA Quality Auditing Service. The IIA has provided for this kind of service. It has established the position of Director of Quality Auditing Services, staffed by an experienced internal auditor. The Service makes use of volunteer practitioners to assist the director in carrying out peer reviews. Indeed, these practitioners are the only people who should perform "peer" reviews, since they are truly peers of the internal auditors being reviewed. In our opinion, this option is most likely to provide knowledgeable, professional, objective evaluations.

Supervision

Supervision will be dealt with here only as it relates to quality assurance. All work must be supervised. Internal audits — which appraise significant controls, the safeguarding of assets, reports of information to management, and crucial operating performance — are in special need of supervision to assure professional audit work. Supervision is discussed in Practice Advisory 1311-1, "Internal Assessments."

Supervisors must make sure that audit work is well planned, audit scope is appropriate, audit resources are economically deployed, appropriate technology is being used, serious defects are not being overlooked, minor matters are not being overstressed, audit representations are solidly and logically supported, significant deficiencies are thoroughly documented, audit opinions are buttressed by unassailable evidence, the audit effort is not dissipated by forays into irrelevant or insignificant matters, and staff auditors are properly trained and evaluated.

Internal audit supervisors should monitor audit assignments from start to finish. Audit managers or the chief audit executive should monitor the work of the supervisors. Audit managers or the chief audit executive should be satisfied that supervision is providing needed assurance of audit quality control. Where appropriate, these assurances should be documented. Here are some of the elements of proper audit supervision:

- Supervisors should discuss the thrust and scope of the audit before the preliminary survey. They should advise staff auditors on sources for research, on comparable audits performed elsewhere, and on management needs as they relate to the assigned audit project.

- Supervisors should approve in writing the audit program and any changes to it. They should suggest revisions to the program to eliminate what is not cost effective and to include areas of significant risk.

- Supervisors should be available during the audit to discuss with the staff the audit objectives, procedures, reporting, and any problems encountered.

- Supervisors should conduct reviews regularly. The extent of the reviews should be in proportion to the qualifications and experience of the audit staff.

- Supervisors should review audit working papers and provide evidence of such reviews.

- Supervisory reviews should provide assurance that the staff auditors conform to activity standards, that audit objectives are met, that the working papers support findings and logical conclusions, and that they provide adequate information for a meaningful audit report. More specifically, supervisors should see that the audit staff:

  - Obtains an understanding of the objectives of the audited entity before deciding on audit tests and procedures.

  - Follows up findings from the prior audit to determine whether appropriate measures have been taken and are effective.

  - Bases the extent of tests on the results of analytical auditing and on internal control and risk evaluations.

  - Directs audit tests toward achieving stated audit objectives.

  - Normally considers only those matters related to the audit objectives.

- Uses appropriate sampling plans and selection techniques.

- Interprets statistical sample results logically.

- Uses software in the audit where appropriate and economical.

- Completes all steps in the audit program or gives valid reasons for not doing so.

- Supervisors should see that significant findings are brought to the attention of operating management and that progress reports are realistic and are issued as needed.

- Supervisors should monitor budgets and schedules so they can help auditors-in-charge to reverse adverse work trends.

- Supervisors should attend important meetings with line and executive management; current reviews should keep supervisors aware of audit findings and enable them to discuss the findings knowledgeably.

- Supervisors should discuss proposed audit reports with their auditors-in-charge and approve report outlines.

- Supervisors should review drafts of reports in detail and see that they meet departmental policies and procedures. Lists should be made of questionable items in the working papers or report drafts. These items should be augmented by comments on their resolution. The lists with resolutions should be made a part of the working papers.

- Supervisors should attend draft reviews held with clients and with higher management, whenever possible.

- Supervisors should approve the adequacy of corrective action on audit findings.

- Supervisors should see that all administrative documents called for by department procedures have been completed: checklists, post-audit reviews, comparisons of budget and actual audit hours, project-closure recommendations, and the like.

- Supervisors should approve the filing or destruction of working papers in compliance with organization policy and procedure.

- Supervisors should meet at least once a week with audit managers or chief audit executive to discuss project status and any difficulties or problems encountered in the supervised projects.

Properly supervised audit projects are the first and, perhaps, the most important step in a program of quality assurance. When supervisors do their jobs properly in the first place, the internal and external reviews should disclose no serious defects in those matters that are under the direct control of the internal audit activity.

Internal Reviews

Internal reviews can provide both quality assurance to the chief audit executive and training for the audit staff. The reviews can take the form of verifications, internal reviews, and client evaluations. They can be done regularly or intermittently. Their frequency will depend on how concerned the chief audit executive is about the adequacy of the supervision of audit projects and on the amount of adverse feedback from clients. Internal reviews are conveyed in *Standard 1311* and Practice Advisory 1311-1, both titled "Internal Assessments."

The Practice Advisory suggests that there should be:

Ongoing reviews using checklists, feedback from audit customers and other stakeholders, analyses for performance metrics (e.g., cycle time and recommendations accepted), project budgets, cost recoveries, and other measures.

Periodic reviews performed by members of the internal audit activity who are CIAs or other internal competent audit professionals, and that use benchmarking and relevant best practice methodology of the internal auditing profession.

The Practice Advisory continues with conclusions as to the quality of performance and appropriate action to achieve improvements that should be developed and presented. The chief audit executive should establish a reporting and control procedure to ensure achievement of corrective activities and to advise appropriate persons and organizations outside the internal audit activity.

Verification

Chief audit executives or audit managers who sign audit reports have an understandable concern about the accuracy and propriety of what they are signing. Their professional reputations are at stake. Audit reports are often the result of extensive and complex accumulations of data, together with evaluations and judgmental decisions. Errors by internal auditors are not unheard of and can be extremely embarrassing. Those who assess blame should themselves be blameless. Yet auditors are human and a tendency to err is a fate that no human can escape.

To protect against this tendency and to ensure the highest degree of "blameless" reports, managers and chief audit executives should install a verification system designed to detect mechanical errors and faulty judgment that they are in no position to detect themselves. All drafts of internal audit reports should be subjected to an independent check. A staff auditor who was not assigned to the audit project should trace every number, date, name, and representation in the report to the working papers to make sure each one is thoroughly supported and documented.

All calculations should be recalculated. All footings and cross-footings should be footed and cross-footed again. All dates should be verified to source documents. All names and titles should be checked for spelling, accuracy, and current status. All findings should be verified to the working papers for cause, effect, significance, discussions, and evidence of corrective action. Judgment as to the audit methodology, conclusions based on raw data, logic, and method of presentation should also be reviewed.

The staff reviewer should then sign a quality review checklist as evidence of this independent verification.

Internal Review Program

Internal reviews of audit projects are just that. They are appraisals of how well auditors and supervisors have complied with the activity's policies and procedures and professional practice. Such internal reviews require more mature judgments than verifications. They encompass the work of both staff auditors and their supervisors. They are an assessment of a sample of audit reports and supporting working papers. They therefore require the attention of a senior staff auditor or a supervisor.

Such internal reviews can produce salutary results. First, of course, is the information supplied to the chief audit executive, information on how well procedures are followed and how well the audit work and the audit reports are documented. Second is the value to the external auditors. The tests of audit projects in an external review can be reduced if those evaluators see credible evidence of internal reviews of such projects.

Hence, the internal reviews of internal audits should be carried out with the formality and discipline of any audit examination. For example:

- A review project should be established with a budget and a schedule.

- A review program should be prepared that sets forth the steps the evaluator will take.

- An acceptable sample of audit projects should be selected that is representative of the activity's production.

- The evaluator should discuss any deficiencies found with the auditors and supervisors of the audit projects reviewed. (Here, tact will be extremely important.)

- The evaluator should prepare working papers documenting the internal review.

- The evaluator should also prepare a formal report on the result of the review.

The review program should be approved by the chief audit executive. It should comply with those *Standards* that deal with the performance of audit work. For example, the evaluator should be concerned with the following matters, which, because of their relevance, are referenced to the specific performance paragraphs in the original *Standards*:

How well the auditors planned the audit work. (410)

Were audit objectives and scope of work established?
Was background information obtained and was adequate research for the audit project performed?
Did the auditors perform sufficient review to:
    Determine the executive tone at the top?
    Become familiar with the business process?
Was an audit budget developed and was actual audit time charged?
Were appropriate client management personnel notified that the audit would take place?
Were they advised as to the audit objective?
Was a preliminary survey performed and were risk areas identified and assessed?
Was an audit program prepared and was the program approved by the audit management?

How well the auditor collected, analyzed, interpreted, and documented information to support audit results. (420)

Was the information collected relevant to the audit objectives?
Was the information collected sufficient, competent, relevant, and useful?
Did auditors use appropriate technology?
Did audit activity relate to areas of high risk?
Were all the steps in the audit program followed or were adequate reasons provided for not following them?
Were appropriate sampling techniques employed, and were the sample results logically interpreted?
Were working papers prepared that adequately demonstrated the collection, analysis, and interpretation of information?
Did the working papers bear evidence of supervisory review?
Were interim audit results communicated currently either orally or in writing?
Did the working papers evidence competent audit judgment?

How well the results of the audit work were reported. (430)

Was the report promptly prepared and issued?

Were interim or progress reports issued on significant findings?

Were conclusions and recommendations discussed at appropriate levels of client management before the final report was issued?

Were the report drafts carefully reviewed and verified?

Were the reports written in the format required by departmental procedures?

Did the reports receive all required reviews and approvals?

Were all matters reported adequately documented in the working papers?

Were audit findings properly structured so as to clearly present the basic elements and to encourage implementation of the necessary corrective action?

How well the auditor followed up to see that appropriate action was taken on reported findings. (440)

Was the corrective action adequately documented?

Was the corrective action complete and did it include provision for preventing a repetition of the reported weaknesses?

Was high-level approval obtained in all cases when corrective action was not taken?

The Institute's *Quality Assessment Manual* provides detailed questionnaires that include and expand on these questions.

Quality Circles

One of the methods that has been used effectively in improving quality and auditing productivity is the quality circle. Although efficiency and effectiveness can usually be easily defined, quality is a much more difficult term to describe. For one thing, quality is described differently by different people. Thus, to resolve this problem, organizations have developed quality circles. These groups of five to 15 workers are intimately familiar with the operation and its shortcomings, its strengths and weaknesses, and the possible solutions to the problems.

The approach is much like the peer review study as to structure and content. The quality circle studies the operation, makes recommendations, and frequently has the authority to implement them.

External Reviews

External reviews should be carried out by the peers of those to be reviewed. Just as the performance of doctors or academicians can best be evaluated by other doctors or academicians, so can the performance of internal auditors best be carried out by internal audit practitioners. They have the knowledge, training, and perspective that are difficult or impossible to attain by people from other professions. External reviews are usually called for by the level of management to which the audit organization reports: i.e., the audit committee, chief executive officer, an executive vice president, or a controller. External reviews are covered in *Standard 1312* and Practice Advisory 1312-1, both titled "External Assessments."

This Practice Advisory emphasized the requirement that assessments be made on a five-year or less rotational basis. It also prescribes in some detail as to qualifications of the external reviewers such as independence, integrity, and competence.

Independence: Freedom from obligation to or an interest in the subject audit activity or its personnel. Other than being a parting to reciprocal assessment reviews, absence of a real or apparent conflict of interest. Absence of control by the organization that controls the internal audit activity or influence resulting from present or past relationship.

Integrity and objectivity: Honesty, a candid approach, dedication to service and public trust, impartiality, intellectual honesty, and freedom of conflicts of interest.

Competence: Individuals performing assessments should be competent certified audit professionals, well versed and experienced, and have three recent years of practice at the management level. They should have information technology expertise and relevant industry experience. Also, individuals with other specialized audit related background can be used.

The scope of the assessment should include:

- Compliance with the *Standards* and the *Code of Ethics*.

- Compliance with the charter, plans, policies and procedures, and legal requirements.

- Consideration of the organization's expectations.

- The degree of integration of the internal audit activity into the total organization's fabric.

- The degree tools and techniques employed by the profession.

- The mix of knowledge, experience, and discipline of the internal audit staff.

- The degree of value added to the organization resulting from the internal audit activity.

The Practice Advisory brings in an important variation in the assessment process through its discussion of "Self-assessment with Independent Validation." It provides that the assessment process could be reviewed by individuals or organizations that comply with the basic provisions of the previously described assessment procedures.

The results of the assessment should be discussed with the chief audit executive and the communication should contain an opinion as to compliance with the *Standards*. Communication should be further transmitted to the official(s) who authorized the assessment. The communication to management should contain the responses of the chief audit executive and indications of corrective activity taken where appropriate.

Review Methodology

External reviews should be tailored to meet the function of the particular internal audit organization. The *Standards* point out that internal auditing around the world is performed in diverse environments that dictate the methodology and scope of the internal audit work.

Some internal audit activities have a broad charter. Their entree to any activity within the enterprise is without restriction. They are not hampered by any policy statement from complying fully with the *Standards*.

Other organizations may function under a variety of restrictions. Some may not have access to the board of directors, may report to a low-level executive, may be barred from reviewing nonaccounting operations, may not have the authority to require replies to their audit reports, may not be responsible for following up on a corrective action, or may not be authorized to review compliance with ethical business practices. The list could go on and on. Those internal auditors will be governed by their environment. They may not, therefore, be in compliance with all the concepts enunciated in the *Standards* and may not be regarded as carrying out the professional practice of internal auditing within the meaning of the *Standards*. Thus, their audit performance should not be measured by the full yardstick of the *Standards*. On the other hand, an unrestricted peer review may be able to bring to the attention of the board audit committee and to senior management the fact that the role of the internal auditors needs expansion before it can be regarded as meeting professional standards.

Earlier in this chapter, we mentioned briefly the scope of the external reviews set forth in The IIA's *Quality Assessment Manual* and the review service available through The IIA. Here, in somewhat greater detail, is the external review coverage the *Manual* presents.

1. Preparation

External reviews are usually decided on by the board audit committee, the person to whom the chief audit executive reports, and the chief audit executive. At the outset, these people should be informed that the purpose of the review is:

- To evaluate compliance with standards and organization policies and procedures.
- To appraise the quality of the activity's operations.
- To provide recommendations for improvement.

An engagement letter should be prepared to identify the scope of review; the audit activity's responsibility in the review (a self-study evaluation); the review team's responsibilities, including start and completion dates; a cost estimate; a save harmless clause to protect the review team from liability; and the names of the review team members.

Members of the review team should be selected with an eye toward independence and objectivity, experience, availability, and the specific expertise required (information technology, industrial engineering, accounting, etc.).

The review team should survey clients of the audited activity. This can be done by interviews or by a questionnaire that embraces these prime ingredients: anonymity, reader comprehension, and a representative sample. The *Manual* provides a sample questionnaire and cover letter. The transmittal letters and questionnaires seek to:

- Explain the survey process and its benefits to the respondents.
- Ensure anonymity of the respondent.
- Be brief.
- Concentrate on key areas.
- Contain headings conveying logical descriptions.
- Have each question relate to only one item.

The review team should interview those people for whom a questionnaire would not be appropriate: audit committee members and senior management.

Survey responses should be carefully analyzed. Software packages are available for statistical analysis of such responses.

The audited activity should be asked to prepare a self-study report that can help facilitate the review. It should seek information on:

- Essential documents, such as operating budgets, policy manuals, and the like.
- Statistical data about the organization, activity, and staff.

- Discussions about the activity — mission statements, its objectives, audit scope, personnel, and professional affiliations.
- Planning and budgeting methods.
- Relationship with executive management and the board.
- Relationship with external auditors and other oversight agencies.
- How the activity conducts internal audits.
- Specialized skills within the activity.
- The nature of quality control exercised by the chief audit executive.

2. Field Work

The team leader will make a preliminary visit to discuss the proposed review, the self-study, the people to be interviewed, the timing of the field work, and the selection of off-site offices for visits.

The team will obtain and review the self-study report, the client survey information, and any supporting documents. The team will interview audit staff members and others in the organization, such as the chief financial officer, controller, treasurer, operating management, the person to whom the chief audit executive reports, the external auditors, and the audit committee.

The team will review any specialized audit expertise, such as engineering, actuarial science, physics, etc.

The team will examine a representative sample of audit project working papers and reports and review administrative practices. These reviews should be directed toward the provisions of The IIA's *Standards*.

The *Manual* provides detailed audit steps for all phases of the peer review field work.

3. Reporting

The review team should prepare a written report at the conclusion of its examination. (See *Standard 1320* and Practice Advisory 1320-1, both titled "Reporting in the Quality Program.")

The draft of the report should be coordinated with the team members and provided to the chief audit executive for review. The final report should be addressed to the person or group requesting the review, with copies to the chief audit executive and the person to whom the executive reports administratively. The executive should respond in writing to the team's audit report.

Follow-up of any corrective action is always desirable for an objective determination that any reported deficiencies were indeed corrected. Such follow-up, in a peer review, will usually be made at the time of the subsequent review.

The *Manual* provides a sample report on the results of the external review.

An Example of a Peer Review

One of the first peer reviews made by internal auditors, rather than public accountants or consultants, followed *A Framework for Evaluating an Internal Audit Function*, the predecessor to *Quality Assurance Review Manual for Internal Auditing*. It was reported by J.K. Watsen, CIA, CPA, and is reported here because of its historical value.[12]

An ad hoc committee of internal audit practitioners performed a peer review of the internal audit department at Martin Marietta Corporation. After obtaining oral concurrence from the chief audit executive, the peer review team sent a proposal to the senior vice president and the chief financial officer of the firm, with a copy to the chairman of the audit committee. At the initial meeting, senior management expressed enthusiasm for the idea and asked only that the review be done by qualified practitioners with no holds barred.

The review team was made up of volunteers whose employers agreed to release them for the peer review. The reviewers and those who coordinated the review were at the internal audit manager level or higher.

Using the *Framework* with some modifications, the review was designed to measure the internal audit function against the *Standards* and against management expectations. The reviewers concentrated on what was wrong with the audit activity and therefore emphasized the negative. After the review, the team realized that this gave an unbalanced perspective to the review — unfair to the internal auditing activity. This was one of the lessons learned from the review. Actually, senior management was concerned with what could be improved, rather than with an overall appraisal; and so the team gave management just that. But hindsight convinced the team that a balanced approach would have been preferable.

The meeting with the chief audit executive, after the review, was surprisingly calm. He agreed with most of the observations, but pointed out errors in others.

The exit conference was held with the chief financial officers and the corporate controller. All findings were discussed. In particular, management was concerned about comments on the organizational status of the audit activity, the corporate audit charter, and the documentation of executive management's oversight of the audit function.

The most difficult part of the project was the audit report. The team finally decided to report its findings against the five general standards instead of the 25 specific standards, which were the criteria used in the peer review.

Watsen ends his article with a caveat: It is impractical to conduct a peer review of a large organization with an ad hoc group of volunteers. An answer to Watsen's concerns may be found in The IIA's Quality Assurance Review Service. While practitioners are recruited to assist in the reviews, each review is headed up by The IIA's director of Quality Auditing Service. He is therefore available to carry each project to a conclusion after the volunteers have returned to their regular jobs. The Service has since completed many other quality assurance reviews, including both government and corporate reviews.

The sample report included in the *Manual* gives some indication of the kinds of findings peer reviews can identify. For example:

- Internal auditors were performing some line functions.

- A formalized program for training and continuing education was needed.

- Thirty percent of the audit time was spent in the accounting department. Interviews with clients, supplemented by independent observations, impelled the conclusion that more time should be spent in operating areas outside the accounting function.

- No formalized project-reporting system was used to record hours budgeted and expended on each audit.

- In a number of cases, insufficient work had been done in the analysis of financial controls during the audits of financial activities.

- In 20 percent of the audit projects reviewed, there was a significant difference between work programmed and work accomplished. No supervisory approvals were in evidence to document the program changes.

- The working papers disclosed no evidence of supervisory review.

- The audit policy manual contained no instruction on audit planning, supervision, performance appraisals, project control, and continuing education.

At the same time, the report gave positive statements where the review indicated satisfactory performance.

Peer Reviews of Multi-site Operations

An interesting approach to the peer review operation of multi-site auditing operations is given in an article on a quality assurance program.[13] The writer describes the composition of the quality review team as consisting of "seasoned auditors with special skills relating to the various areas audited." In smaller organizations, staff for the team can be drawn from client specialists who were not members of the operations being reviewed.

In addition to the usual reviews of compliance with the internal audit standards, the quality control team should have as its other objectives:

- Monitoring independence.
- Providing a mobile reserve for exigencies, acquisition audits, and other high-risk situations.
- Disaster analysis to help analyze and prepare action plans.
- Providing technical support in specialized areas.

The peer review is conducted like an audit and covers a particular program and particular audits of the multi-site internal auditing activities. The areas evaluated should include:

- Organization.
- Business audit plan.
- Audit coverage.
- Staffing.
- Personnel administration.
- Field work.
- Working papers.
- Reports.
- Independence.
- Business perspective.
- Outside auditors.

Each of these classifications includes a number of subordinate items. All are evaluated to produce a summary score of the classification.

Reviews by Other Professional Organizations

An organization may want the quality evaluation to be performed by a professional organization such as a public accounting firm or a management consulting organization that specializes in internal auditing. It is important that the selection of such an outside organization be made so as to eliminate any benefits that would accrue to the firm as a result of an advance report. The letter of engagement covering such an evaluation should clearly state that if any consulting work is called for after the evaluation, or if outsourcing would be considered, that the evaluator would not be an eligible candidate.

The same review methodology described above for peer reviews should be used by the professional organization. However, the evaluator may present an alternative plan to the element of the organization that is calling for the quality evaluation. It is essential that the evaluating organization use personnel who are specialists in internal auditing from both a practical and a theoretical standpoint. Such personnel should be at a knowledge and skill level no lower than the chief audit executive or at the least, an audit manager.

The quality evaluation report should itself be patterned after an audit report and those elements usually supporting an audit finding should also support the comments in the report. One advantage of this type of evaluation is that the evaluating organization can make comparisons with other organizations that are successfully performing internal audit functions.

Client Evaluations

Although peer reviews of audit operations would normally request evaluations from clients on the quality of audit effort, the process of client evaluations is a technique that should be a part of every audit. At the conclusion of the audit, that is after the issuance of the audit report presumably with client comment within the body of the report and in an appendixed letter, the chief audit executive should request the manager of the audited organization to evaluate the audit functions. Comments that should be requested should include such questions as:

- How did the audit conform to your expectations as:
  - A positive assistance?
  - A negative detractor?

- Did the auditors conduct the audit in a professional manner?

- Did the auditors provide direct assistance to you at your request?

- Did the auditors' findings help achieve:
  - Improved compliance with policy and procedures?
  - Improved efficiency in operations?
  - Improved effectiveness in operations?

- Was the audit performed in a timely fashion?

- If so, to what degree? Did the audit disrupt your organization's normal operations?

- To what degree did the auditors display good behavioral relations?

- Would you consider the auditor as a valuable part of your management team?

- To what degree did the auditors direct their attention to aspects that you would consider material?

- What suggestions would you make to improve the audit operation?

The chief audit executive or a senior manager should review the evaluation with the audit team leader. Contested aspects of the evaluation should call for a written response by the audit team leader and possibly a further clarification by the client on an objective basis. The objective of the procedure should be a learning experience so as to improve relations and to make sure that one of the audit customers, the client, is satisfied.

Total Quality Management Implementation

The concept of total quality management (TQM) can be applied to internal audit operations.[14] The U.S. General Accounting Office, in a study outlined a series of steps, which although applicable to itself, can be applied to any internal audit organization.

Initial quality assessment. This element includes several steps:

- Identifying the organization's customers: i.e., top management, the audit committee, operations management, and individual client management.

- Establishing the needs of the customers.

- Setting priorities so as to best meet the customers' needs.

- Assessing the quality of the audit products as perceived by the audit customers as to timeliness, responsiveness, and cost. Cost analysis determines the "cost of quality." Poor quality is caused by: multiple reviews, rewrites, recycling of changes back to reviewers, and lost hours that could have been otherwise used.

- Interviewing customers so as to reveal pertinent information.

Top-level audit management awareness. Awareness training should stress the importance of quality management, using the results of the above quality assessment. The GAO approach is that audit management "must understand that quality management is a philosophy or an approach to management — not a program."[15]

Formation of a quality council. Next, the audit organization should form a quality council consisting of top audit managers and staff members from all levels of the audit organization. These council members should be interested in and knowledgeable of the principles of quality management. This council should report to the audit director. It should coordinate training, monitor and support prototypes, and study other audit organizations' approaches to successful practices.

The council should stand for excellence in its functions as an example to the audit organization. It should "demonstrate participative planning, open communication, and analytical problem solving."[16]

Fostering teamwork. The audit organization should, "establish a participative environment that fosters teamwork."[17]

Development of prototypes. As a means of convincing the skeptical, the audit quality council should demonstrate, "the practical value of new ways of organizing work with highly visible prototype quality and productivity initiatives."[18] These prototypes when tested and proven successful can convince the more cautious of the audit staff.

It should be possible to convince some of the more progressive audit managers to volunteer to have their organizations serve as prototype units. One way of performing this aspect is to select "one important cross-functional process" and have an evaluation team visit the prototype organizations to determine whether it is an "important strategic quality issue" and to appraise the efficiency of operation's payoff. Implementation steps could be:

- Awareness training described above.

- Selection of management objectives.

- Analysis of the existing process.

- Establishment of measurement standards.

- Implementation of a model for continuous improvement.

- Benchmarking to set criteria for methods of measurement and interim performance goals.

Celebration of success. The audit organization should publicize the achievements of the prototype organizations to encourage the cautious and hesitant staff.

Organizational implementation. Successful methods should be implemented by all units of the audit organization and appropriate recognition should be given for those units that are most successful.

Annual quality review. There should be an annual quality review as a technique for implementing the quality management process organization wide. The review, together with a rating system (the benchmarking process), will demonstrate the success of the implementation process.

Another dimension for the installation of total quality management in the audit organization was described in *Internal Auditing Alert.*[19] This article listed a series of elements:

- Determine the customers' current concept as to the quality of the audit.

- Maintain this concept of quality currently; updating it so as to maintain a current marketable product and service.

- Create an innovative environment by:
  - Allowing for creativity.
  - Challenging all staff members to question the status quo and suggest improvements.
  - Taking every staff suggestion seriously and implementing each, when appropriate.

- Review all audit activities, processes, and the audit structure as to purpose and benefits derived — as to usefulness and need. An example is the methodology of creating, organizing, cross-referencing, and maintaining working papers.

- Innovate in the audit office to determine how the basic techniques of setting audit objectives and scope, developing flexible programs, evaluating risk, testing compliance, and determining how efficiency and effectiveness can be best conducted.

- Be aware of and use "existing and emerging technological developments," especially in the computer area. Also, the audit staff must be consultants, advisors on internal controls, financial auditors, analysts of financial information, and fraud investigators, as needed.

Benchmarking. Probably one of the most important aspects of total quality management is the concept of benchmarking.[20] This methodology comprises the mechanics of measuring and evaluating those aspects of an operation that are considered vital and essential to a quality operation. The objective is to make comparisons with other organizations, with segments within the organization, and with standards that have been set by management and the quality councils. Measurements that are used are referred to as benchmark metrics because of their quantifiable nature. These metrics are a combination of quantity, quality, and cost measurements. Examples are:

- Quantity
  - Units per.
  - Calls per.
  - Trips per.
  - Hours per.
  - Pages per.

- Quality
  - Defects per.
  - Retests per.
  - Failures per.
  - Complaints per.

- Cost:
  - Cost per.

Other quality benchmarks include:

- Total quality costs as a percent of revenue.
- Prevention costs as a percent of total quality costs.
- Detection costs as a percent of total quality costs.
- Quality assurance department costs as a percent of revenue.[21]

The setting of benchmarks follows a normal analytical process. The council must:

- Decide what is to be measured.
- Determine the sources of the benchmark, internally and externally.
- Establish data collection methods.
- Set up analytical techniques together with methods to determine causes of deviations from goals or from top comparative units.
- Determine methods to resolve problems causing deviations.
- Follow-up to ensure progress in implementing corrective methods.

The concept of benchmarking is not new. Today it is becoming more extensive, more formal, and more disciplined.

The TQM Program of Southern California Edison Company

This public utility of about 17,000 employees and annual revenues of over $7 billion has an audit staff of approximately 80 employees.[22] The firm decided in 1993 to develop a TQM program and after some evolutionary activities finally in 1995 set up two groups of audit teams. The first group related to "Natural Work." Examples of the areas of interest were:

- Audit administration
- Contact and program
- Corporate organization
- Customer service
- Information technologies
- New business
- Nuclear and power production
- Power contracts and joint projects

The second group, the voluntary TQM teams included:

- TQM steering committee
- Team skills and education
- Special projects
- TQM measuring and reporting

The natural work teams in the first group were responsible, in addition to their normal audit responsibilities, for continuous improvement of processes, products, and client satisfaction. Membership on the teams resulted from the automatic assignment of people. The voluntary TQM teams were cross-functional teams that were responsible for implementing TQM strategies. Membership was voluntary.

The teams developed an eight-step development implementation management cycle. This cycle actually includes the activities that the teams should perform in each phase of the cycle and is a complete outline of a TQM engagement. The audit organization then developed a matrix establishing:

- Primary clients,
- Client and corporate expectations, and
- Audit department TQM strategy

The audit organization then designed a series of tools to be used in the quality-improvement evaluation:

- Benchmarking programs to collect information on audit quality and productivity from similar type organizations. This included information from The IIA's Global Auditing Information Network (GAIN).

- Client management satisfaction survey: These evaluations were provided after an audit engagement and covered the client's impression of the usefulness of the audit and the professionalism of the work.

- Annual self-assessment questionnaire: These anonymous questionnaires were submitted by individual audit activity members and included opinions on:
  - Audit activity strengths.
  - Auditor's natural work team strengths.
  - Improvements that could be made in the activity.
  - Improvements that could be made in the work team.

- Internal peer review checklist: This form completed by the TQM administrator, is to help managers identify their unit's strengths and weaknesses. The form covers information on the audit activity's compliance with:
  - The IIA *Standards*.
  - IIA and firms' *Code of Ethics*.
  - Audit activity, charter.
  - Audit activity's annual goals.
  - Firm's corporate strategic plan.

- Audit draft report quality evaluation form: This report rates the quality of 12 attributes of draft audit reports on a Likert scale (1 to 5). The characteristics are:
  - Grammar.
  - Clarity, readability, composition.
  - Graphics.
  - Accuracy of facts.
  - Ability of facts to support findings.
  - Objectivity.
  - Adequacy of supporting documentation.
  - Logic of conclusions.
  - Balance between positive and negative findings.
  - Value added.
  - Application of the "stop-and-go" audit technique.
  - Timeliness.

The report does not indicate causes of deficiencies nor potential improvements that could be made.

- Audit activity performance metrics: This report summarizes quantifiable activities of the audit organization. It covers:
  - Audits completed.
  - Investigations completed.
  - Cost/budget relationship.
  - Savings realized (cash and operational).
  - Attendance of staff.
  - Promotions.
  - Cross training.
  - TQM team activities.
  - Employee background (degrees, certifications).

- Semi Annual and annual reports on the status of the TQM program: This is a narrative report summarizing the prior period's quality related results.

- TQM newsletters: Published three to four times a year, the newsletters contain information from quality related groups and publications.

The program has had the desired outcome such as improved audit operations, better reporting, improved client attitudes, more credibility, and more requests for audit services.

Quality Concerns of Management and Boards of Directors

Beyond the requirements of the *Standards* are the real concerns of executive management and the audit committees of boards of directors. They need assurance that they can indeed rely on this safeguard that goes by the name of internal auditing. They sit in the shadow of the U.S. Foreign Corrupt Practices Act (FCPA) of 1977 — a law concerned with more than bribery. From 1978 to 1986, the Securities and Exchange Commission (SEC) brought 76 injunctive actions and 10 administrative proceedings to enforce the accounting provisions of the act.

A landmark court case, SEC v. Worldwide Coin Investments, has supported the SEC position.[23] In an extensive judicial opinion involving these accounting provisions, the court went into considerable detail in discussing the absence of internal control before it handed down a judgment against the defendant. The deterioration of the defendant's internal controls and accounting procedures constituted the primary thrust of the SEC's complaint. The SEC contended that the lack of internal controls placed the defendant organization in its precarious position at the time the lawsuit was filed. And the court pointed out that the failure to comply with internal controls caused the organization to decrease from 40 employees and assets of $2,000,000 to only three employees and assets of less than $500,000.

The court held that the efficiency of an internal control system cannot be evaluated without considering the organization's organizational structure, the caliber of its employees, the strength of its audit committee, the effectiveness of its internal audit operations, and a host of other factors that, while not part of the internal control system itself, have an impact on the functioning of the system.

In the light of this decision, it becomes quite clear that the effectiveness of any internal audit operation can best be demonstrated by adequate quality assurance programs — including peer reviews — carried out by and for the internal audit organization. The court held that the size of the organization was irrelevant in considering the applicability of the FCPA. It also held that the internal control provision of the act is not limited to material transactions or to those over a specific dollar amount.

ISO 9000 — A Challenge

A set of quality control standards has been developed during the last decade by European sources. These standards are to be used by manufacturing and service industries. They can also be used by internal auditing organizations. However, it has been stated in several recent articles that this is also an area in which internal auditors should be active.[24, 25]

The standards are the ISO 9000 series. The series comprises five individual but related standards on quality management and two in auditing and measuring (ISO 10,000 series). The series comprises:

- ISO 9001 — covering design, manufacturing, installation, and service systems.

- ISO 9002 — covering production and installation.

- ISO 9003 — covering final product inspection and testing.

- ISO 9004 — providing guidelines for producing the organization's own quality system.

- ISO 10011 — containing guidelines for auditing quality systems.

- ISO 10012 — containing quality assurance requirements for measuring equipment.

The standards are stated in user-friendly language. They are generic and have an easily understood format. However, they also involve technical aspects and would normally require technical expertise and basic industrial knowledge to be adequately used as audit criteria.

The standards are important for they must be met and certified to if U.S. firms are to sell to organizations in the European community. The official certification is to be made by a third party. However, as in financial operations, the review by internal auditors can assist greatly by reducing surprises to the third-party auditors. Up to this point there appears to be internal auditor resistance to the audit effort even though anecdotal stories evidence the considerable value, not only as to expansion of sales, but also as to improvements in internal operating techniques. This activity represents an opportunity for internal auditing organizations.

References

[1]Juvenal, Decimus Junius, Satires VI, line 347: "Sed quis custodiet ipso custodes?"

[2]*Comptroller's Handbook for National Bank Examiners* (Washington: Office of the Comptroller of the Currency, 1977).

[3]Audit Standards Supplement Series No. 9, *Self-Evaluation Guide for Governmental Audit Organizations* (Washington: Comptroller General of the United States, 1976).

[4]Division for CPA Firms, Private Companies Practice Section, *Peer Review Manual* (New York: American Institute of Certified Public Accountants, 1978).

[5]*Quality Assurance Review Manual for Internal Auditing — A Self-Assessment Workbook* (Altamonte Springs, FL: The Institute of Internal Auditors, 1984).

[6]Glazer, A.S., and H.R. Jacnicke, *A Framework for Evaluating an Internal Audit Function* (Altamonte Springs, FL: Foundation for Auditability, Research, and Education, 1980).

[7]Anderson, Urton, *Quality Assurance for Internal Auditing* (Altamonte Springs, FL: The Institute of Internal Auditors, 1983).

[8]Chadler, E.W., and E.R. Salmon, "The Framework and Beyond," *The Internal Auditor,* February 1982, 35-39

[9]Gupta, Parveen P., and Manesh R. Ray, *Total Quality Improvement Process and the Internal Auditing Function* (Altamonte Springs, FL: The Institute of Internal Auditors Research Foundation, 1995), 100-110.

[10]Albrecht, W. Steve, Keith R. Howe, Dennis R. Scheuler, and Kevin D. Stocks, *Evaluating the Effectiveness of Internal Audit Departments* (Altamonte Springs, FL: The Institute of Internal Auditors Research Foundation, 1988).

[11]Peacock, Eileen, and Sandra Pelfrey, "Measuring Internal Auditor Productivity," *Internal Auditing,* Spring 1991, 35-36.

[12]Watsen, J.K., "Peer Review at Martin Marietta," *The Internal Auditor,* February 1982, 40-43.

[13]DeMeo, Joseph C., "The Need for an Internal Audit Quality Assurance Program," *Internal Auditing,* Winter 1986, 14-22.

[14]U.S. General Accounting Office, *Quality Management Scoping Study* (Washington, DC: U.S. General Accounting Office, 1990), 36-40.

[15]Ibid., 37.

[16]Ibid., 38.

[17]Ibid., 26, 38.

[18]Ibid., 38.
[19]*Internal Auditing Alert,* Warren, Gorham & Lamont, March 1993, 5-6.
[20]Sears, Brian P., *Internal Auditing Manual* (New York: RIA, 2003).
[21]Ibid.
[22]Gray, Glen L., and Maryann Jacobi Gray, *Enhancing Internal Auditing Through Innovative Practices* (Altamonte Springs, FL: The Institute of Internal Auditors, 1996), 97-112.
[23]Securities and Exchange Commission v. Worldwide Coin Investments, Ltd., 5677 F. Supp. 724 (N.D. Ga. 1983).
[24]Stern, Gary M., "Sailing to Europe," *Internal Auditor,* October 1992, 29-32.
[25]DeMeulder, Roland, "Meeting the Challenge of ISO," *Internal Auditor,* April 1993, 24-30.

Supplementary Readings

Anderson, Urton L., "Quality Assurance, Total Quality Management, and the Evaluation of the Internal Audit Function," *Internal Auditing,* Fall 1991, 66-71.

Applegate, Dennis B., Lawrence G. Bergman, and Stephen K. Didis, "Measuring Success," *Internal Auditor,* April 1997, 62-67.

Clikeman, Paul M., "Improving Information Quality," *Internal Auditor,* June 1999, 32-33.

De Meulder, Roland, "Meeting the Challenge of ISO," *Internal Auditor,* April 1993, 24-31.

Dudley, Edward M., Michael R. Plumly, and Marie C. Knobloch, "How Do You Measure Success?," *Internal Auditor,* April 1999, 58-63.

Forrest, Jonathan S., and Edward Forrest, "Internal Audit and the Activity-based Management Connection," *Internal Auditing,* July/August 1999, 36-38.

Greenawalt, Mary Brady, and Faith B. Brownlee, "Value-added Auditing: Dollars and Sense," *Internal Auditing,* January/February 1999, 3-10.

Hagan, Michael F., Jimie Kusel, James E. Gauntt, and Ralph Shull, "Best Practices Through Peer Networking," *Internal Auditing,* Fall 1996, 56-58.

Hogan, William M., "How to Apply TQM to the Internal Audit Function," *Internal Auditing,* Winter 1994, 3-14.

The Institute of Internal Auditors, *Quality Assurance Review Manual for Internal Auditing* (Altamonte Springs, FL: The Institute of Internal Auditors, 1990).

Julien, Frederick W., and James C. Lampe, "Performance Measures in Internal Auditing," *Internal Auditing,* Fall 1993, 66-73.

Lampe, James C., and Steve G. Sutton, "Integrated Productivity and Quality Measures for Internal Audit Departments," *Internal Auditing,* Fall 1991, 51-65.

Lampe, James C., and Steve G. Sutton, *Developing Productivity in Quality Measurement Systems for Internal Auditing Departments* (Altamonte Springs, FL: The Institute of Internal Auditors Research Foundation, 1994).

Lynch, John J., "It's the Process," *Internal Auditor,* June 1996, 64-69.

Marsh, Treba, and Gene H. Johnson, "A Total Quality Management Approach to Environmental Auditing," *Internal Auditing,* Fall 1995, 3-8.

Reding, Kurt F., Craig H. Barber, and Kristine K. Digirolamo, "Benchmarking Against CFIA," *Internal Auditor,* August 2000, 41-46.

Ridley, Jeffrey, "Embracing ISO 9000," *Internal Auditor,* August 1997, 44-48.

Salierno, David, "The Right Measures," *Internal Auditor,* February 2000, 41-44.

Sherick, David, "ISO's Impact," *Internal Auditor,* June 1995, 30-33.

Sisaye, Seleshi, and George H. Bodnar, "TQM and Internal Auditing: A Synthesis," *Internal Auditing,* Summer 1994, 19-31.

Ziegenfuss, Douglas E., "Measuring Performance," *Internal Auditor,* February 2000, 36-40.

Multiple-choice Questions

1. The *Standards* require the performance of periodic internal reviews by members of the internal auditing staff. This function is designed to primarily serve the needs of:
   a. The audit committee.
   b. The chief audit executive.
   c. Management.
   d. The internal auditing staff.

2. The peer review process can be performed internally or externally. A distinguishing feature of the external review is its objective to:
   a. Identify tasks that can be performed better.
   b. Determine if audit activities meet professional standards.
   c. Set forth the recommendations for improvement.
   d. Provide an independent evaluation.

Use the following information to answer questions 3 through 5.
Upon being appointed, a new chief audit executive found an inexperienced audit staff that was over budget on most audits. A detailed review of audit working papers revealed no evidence of progressive reviews by audit supervisors. Additionally, there was no evidence that a quality assurance program existed.

3. As a means of controlling projects and avoiding time-budget overruns, decisions to revise time budgets for an audit should normally be made:
   a. Immediately after the preliminary survey.
   b. When a significant deficiency has been substantiated.
   c. When inexperienced audit staff are assigned to an audit.
   d. Immediately after expanding tests to establish reliability of findings.

4. Determining that audit objectives have been met is part of the overall supervision of an audit assignment and is the ultimate responsibility of the:
   a. Staff internal auditor.
   b. Audit committee.

    c. Internal auditing supervisor.

    d. Chief audit executive.

5. To properly evaluate the operations of an internal auditing department, a quality assurance program should include:

    a. Periodic supervision of internal audit work on a sample basis.

    b. Internal reviews, by other than the internal audit staff, to appraise the quality of department operations.

    c. External reviews at least once every three years by qualified persons who are independent of the organization.

    d. Periodic rotation of audit managers.

6. Which of the following aspects of evaluating the performance of staff members would be considered a violation of good personnel management techniques?

    a. The evaluator should justify very high and very low evaluations because of their impact on the employee.

    b. Evaluations should be made annually or more frequently to provide the employee with feedback about competence.

    c. The first evaluation should be made shortly after commencing work to serve as an early guide to the new employee.

    d. Because there are so many employees whose performance is completely satisfactory, it is preferable to use standard evaluation comments.

7. The best means for the internal auditing department to determine whether its goal of implementing broader audit coverage of functional activities has been met is through:

    a. Accumulation of audit findings by auditable area.

    b. Comparison of the audit plan to actual audit activity.

    c. Surveys of management satisfaction with the internal auditing function.

    d. Implementation of a quality assurance program.

8. Manufacturing operations that use just-in-time (JIT) inventory delivery must develop a system of total quality control (TQC) over parts and material. The objective of TQC is to:

    a. Provide an early warning system that detects and eliminates defective items.

    b. Statistically estimate the potential number of defective items.

    c. Detect and eliminate maintenance and processing problems which cause bottlenecks.

    d. Be sure that the "pull" exerted by each assembly stage includes correct quantities and specifications.

9. Having been given the task of developing a performance appraisal system for evaluating the audit performance of a large internal audit staff, you should:
   a. Provide for an explanation of the appraisal criteria methods at the time the appraisal results are discussed with the internal auditor.
   b. Provide general information concerning the frequency of evaluations and the way evaluations will be performed without specifying their timing and uses.
   c. Provide primarily for the evaluation of criteria such as diligence, initiative, and tact.
   d. Provide primarily for the evaluation of specific accomplishments directly related to the performance of the audit program.

10. Which of the following is most essential for guiding the audit staff in maintaining daily compliance with the department's standards of performance?
    a. Quality control reviews.
    b. Position descriptions.
    c. Performance appraisals.
    d. Policies and procedures.

11. Formal internal reviews of the internal audit department primarily serve the needs of:
    a. The board of directors.
    b. The audit staff.
    c. The chief audit executive.
    d. Executive management.

12. The interpretation related to quality assurance given by the *Standards* is that:
    a. Quality assurance reviews can provide senior management and the audit committee with an assessment of the internal audit function.
    b. Appropriate follow-up to an external review is the responsibility of the internal auditing director's immediate supervisor.
    c. The internal audit department is primarily measured against The IIA's *Code of Ethics*.
    d. Continual supervision is limited to the planning, examination, evaluation report, and follow-up process.

13. Which of the following is **not** ordinarily an objective of a quality assurance review? To determine compliance with:
    a. Applicable laws and regulations.
    b. The general standards for the professional practice of internal auditing.
    c. The specific standards for the professional practice of internal auditing.
    d. The goals of the internal audit function.

14. The use of teams in total quality management is important because:
   a. Well-managed teams can be highly creative and are able to address complex problems better than individuals can.
   b. Teams are quicker to make decisions thereby helping to reduce cycle time.
   c. Employee motivation is higher for team members than for individual contributors.
   d. The use of teams eliminates the need for supervision, thereby allowing a company to become leaner and more profitable.

PART 7

OTHER MATTERS RELATING TO INTERNAL AUDITING

Chapter 25
Principles of Management

Financial versus managerial auditing. Tracking the violations of management principles. Example of managerial auditing. The nature of management. Management principles. Management theories: classical, the early scientific managers; Fayol's 14 principles. Behavioral aspects — the human side of managing. Systems: input, processing, output, feedback. Quantitative, communication center, social systems. Management by objective. Integrating the theories: the contingency approach. Management models: autocratic, custodial, supportive, collegial. Management trends and techniques. Planning: forecasting, strategic and tactical planning, environmental scans, missions, objectives and goals, strategies, principles, policies, procedures, rules, standards, premises, budgets. Decision-making. Planning and the internal auditor — auditing the planning function. Organizing: approaches, organization charts, responsibility, authority, accountability, delegation, staff and line, functional authority, departmentalization and matrix organizations, decentralization, committees, informal groups. Staffing and human resources. Organizing and the internal auditor — auditing the organizing function. Directing: individual and group dynamics, styles of leadership, including the contingency theory; motivation and the expectancy theory, communication, MBO. Directing and the internal auditor — auditing the directing function. Controlling: quantitative and qualitative controls, responsibility for controls, standards, measurements, comparisons, evaluations, corrections, follow-up, approaches to control. Controlling and the internal auditor — auditing the controlling function. Managing to ensure an ethical environment.

• •

Understanding Management Principles

While financial auditing requires an understanding of management principles, internal auditing requires more in-depth understanding of these management principles. Virtually every defect the internal auditor unearths can be traced to a violation of some management principle; and, similarly, when internal auditors observe violations of management principles, they immediately become alert to the likelihood of defective performance.

Knowledge of sound management principles can be especially helpful when internal auditors find themselves on unfamiliar terrain. Even in the most esoteric operations, internal auditors can apply good management principles to conduct effective and useful examinations. An engineering-related example illustrates this point:

> An auditor was assigned to review the activities of an engineering department that evaluated and prescribed production processes. The work of the engineers was highly technical. Avoiding the trap of seeking to evaluate performance in so complex an area, the auditor concentrated on the manager's administration of the department. He learned that the manager had lost control over the hundreds of tasks the department was constantly being asked to perform.

> The manager had no firm grasp of the number of tasks requested. He had made no effort to determine which tasks had the highest priorities, nor did he evaluate whether or not the jobs should be done at all. Much of the efforts of the highly paid engineers were being wasted because they worked on many nonessential tasks. By bringing these defects to the department manager's attention, the administration of the engineering work was significantly improved. And by concentrating on management principles, many other administrative defects were brought to light and corrected.

Management principles are universal truths that can be used to solve management problems. Based on valid causal relationships developed from logical beliefs, successful experience, and repeated experiments, these principles have stood the test of time. They apply to all forms of organizations, including business, government, religious groups, educational institutions, and nonprofit organizations.

Management principles can be taught to anyone, but not everyone is blessed with a managerial temperament. The ability to move others toward desired goals and a knack for making reasonable decisions are sometimes elusive qualities. However, knowledge of management principles can help all managers avoid mistakes and point to the path most likely to lead to desired results.

The Nature of Management

Management deals with establishing objectives and seeing that they are met through the work of others. An art and a science includes creativity and intuition as well as an understanding of formal theories, laws, principles, and methodologies.

The complexities of modern enterprises have restructured and expanded the professional managers' responsibilities. Managers who once relied on their abilities to perform technical and functional activities must now be much more oriented toward establishing objectives, devising plans, developing organizations, allocating resources, directing people, identifying risks, and controlling events so that goals will be met. With the reduction of management layers that has occurred during the last decade, this orientation has become more important.

Theories

Several schools of thought have been developed by management theorists. Although each school has its advocates, none may provide the sole answer to what makes for successful management. The student of management should be aware of these theories, not because they are ultimate truths, but because each may have something to offer. Internal auditors should be sufficiently conversant with these theories so that they can adjust their thinking to that of the manager who is espousing a particular school. Well-known management theories include the classical, behavioral, systems, and quantitative schools, plus the communications center, social systems, management by objectives, and various integrated systems. Most recent theories are derivations of these core concepts.

Classical. The classical or scientific school began as a system of management in the 18th century. A number of brilliant minds developed the classical theory, which aimed to impose order on haphazard organizational structure.

Robert Owen, a Welsh industrialist, showed how productivity would increase under improved working conditions and good personnel management. Charles Babbage, a mathematician, proposed increased efficiency through division of labor. Max Weber concluded that an organizational hierarchy, a ruler with clear authority, task specialization, and discipline were the basis of successful management. Emile Durkheim, a French scholar, emphasized that group values and norms control the conduct of organizations. Frederick Taylor, a machinist and plant engineer, emphasized planning; and he maintained that intuition and guess work should be replaced by analyzing tasks, training workers scientifically, promoting the cooperation of workers and managers, and establishing more equal divisions of responsibilities among them.

Henri Fayol, a French industrialist, developed the functional sequence of planning, organizing, directing, and controlling, though he emphasized control as the basic function. In large part, his concepts are still relevant. Fayol's 14 principles of management were published in 1916:[1]

1. Division of work. Work should be divided so that individuals and groups can specialize in a particular task.

2. Authority and responsibility. Wherever authority is delegated, responsibility is exacted.

3. Discipline. Conformity to rules is essential.

4. Unity of command. Each worker should have one boss — single accountability.

5. Unity of direction. The organization should share one common goal.

6. Subordination of individual interests to the common good. The organization is more important than the individual.

7. Remuneration of personnel. A fair day's work should be rewarded with fair pay.

8. Centralization. Concentrating authority is cost effective.

9. Scalar chain. Authority and responsibility are delegated down the chain of command in a strict hierarchy.

10. Order. A place for everyone and everything should be a prevailing concept; human resources should be deployed according to organizational needs and the individual's abilities.

11. Equity. Employees should feel they are treated fairly.

12. Stability. A minimum of employee turnover is desired, since a stable organization has a better chance of success.

13. Initiative. Creativity and initiative — "additional self-motivated work effort undertaken for the good of the organization" — should be encouraged.

14. Esprit de corps. Harmony and good will among employees are desirable.

Ralph Currier Davis, a professor of industrial management, developed a unified theory of management and the concept of accountability. Henry Gantt, a pioneer of scientific management, developed charts to show the end product and the steps needed to achieve that product. The Gantt chart, named after him, is a scheduling device that shows output plotted against units of time. These contributors helped to create a growing awareness of the nature and potential of effective management.

Behavioral. Many observers of the management scene saw blind spots in the classical theory. Led by Elton Mayo and F.J. Roethlisberger, behaviorists in the 1930s and 1940s sought to bring attention to the human side of management. Extensive research was conducted to support the view that if the needs and desires of people are satisfied, productivity will increase.

The principal thrust of the behavioral school is participation of worker and superior in the decision-making process. Proponents contended that such participation leads to better decisions, greater employee involvement, and improved communication. Some researchers took the view that the behavioral approach canceled the concepts of the classical school of management, but many of the concepts of the classicists have defied the passage of time.

Behavioral management theories should be regarded as supplements to the classical management theory, not as substitutes or the last word in management theory.

Systems. In the systems theory of management, in the 1950s to 1970s every organization is regarded as a complex of integrated subsystems. Every system has elements of input, processing, and output. Each is affected by feedback and is governed by controls. Richard Johnson, Fremont Kast, and James Rosenzweig were among the foremost systems theorists.

A "closed system" acts independently of its environment, while an "open system" interacts with its environment. The closed system tends to deteriorate because it does not adjust to changes in the environment, while the open system is responsive to change. The manager's job is to deal with this change.

Systems theory orientation is obviously more mechanical than that of the behavioral school. It differs from the classical viewpoint in that the classicists regarded management as a closed system, ignoring most external elements to the organization.

"Operations research," one of the early applications of the systems approach, involves the construction of rational mathematical, economic, and statistical models of decision and control problems. "Program budgeting," another systems approach also known as "performance budgeting," identifies goals and alternate programs to achieve them. Projected costs are compared with projected benefits for each alternative.

Quantitative. The quantitative school, which can be traced to Frederick Taylor's scientific management concepts,[2] applies mathematical logic and techniques to quantify variables and relationships in the work place. It seeks to build quantitative models that can be used to analyze a given situation and find an optimum solution. The emergence and expanded capabilities offered by computers has enhanced the application of techniques such as simulation, PERT/CPM, probability theory, regression analysis, linear programming, Monte Carlo simulation, inventory theory, queuing theory, sensitivity analysis, game theory, dynamic programming, and exponential smoothing. Optimizing input-output is a characteristic of the quantitative measurement school. The systems and quantitative schools have much in common.

Social system. This system, which is related to the behavioral theory of management, regards the organization as a series of cultural interrelationships. It emphasizes cooperation as a tool for making decisions and solving problems and is also concerned with ethics — with what is morally right. In a world where unethical behavior makes business headlines every day, organizations become pressured by society to demonstrate their adherence to ethical precepts. No system will completely eliminate unethical behavior, but the social system urges the enterprise to show society that it has taken all reasonable steps to demonstrate commitment to ethical conduct.

Management by objective. Management by objective (MBO) is a term coined by management guru, Peter Drucker.[3] MBO in the 1950s to the 1970s seeks to integrate organization and individual objectives. The organization's objective is to achieve profits and growth. The individual's objectives may be to achieve self-development while contributing to organization objectives. According to Drucker, true MBO substitutes management by self-control for management by domination.

Some MBO implementation efforts have faltered, perhaps because managements haven't always approached MBO in an enlightened or fully committed way. The full title of Drucker's original treatise is Management by Objectives and Self-Control, but the last part of the title is sometimes ignored. In some instances, managers are not permitted to participate in setting objectives and goals, nor are they provided with the information they need to control themselves. Objectives and goals are not integrated throughout the organization. Quantitative goals may be overused and qualitative goals downgraded.

A successful MBO program should result in more cooperation among managers, improved communication between departments, more employee self-direction, and an improved sense of organizational purpose. Other MBO benefits can include enhancing communication between superior and subordinate, allowing people to participate in assigning tasks, forcing specification of quantifiable organizational objectives throughout the organization, and encouraging employee development.

Integrated. Many attempts have been made to integrate various theories. Some are closely related to Drucker's MBO concept. The fusion process points to the need for a coalescence of individual and organizational goals. The modified theory of management points to participation between the organization and the individual to dissipate the worker's alienation and, thereby, increase production. The organizational overlay school superimposes the informal organization on the formal organization chart and seeks to harness the power residing in groups and the flow of informal communication.

One of these integrating systems with much to commend it is the contingency approach. This theory holds that management cannot be governed by a single set of principles that are universally applicable. Situations vary, calling for different methods under different circumstances. The contingency approach uses ideas from many schools of thought in an effort to match the solution to the particular situation. It is a specific rather than a general approach to management.

It is also optimistic, in that it assumes all problems can be solved by the application of the appropriate management technique. Management is a complex and delicate process that can be affected by many factors: technology, people, and the environment, for example. Management must take all these factors or contingencies into account.

Models of Management

During the past two centuries, four distinct models of managers developed, roughly following the evolving theories of management. Each model has unique characteristics:

Autocratic. The autocratic model was based on the concept of military authority and the classical school. It is based on pure power; and until about 80 years ago, was almost universal. It has generally given way to more behavioral forms of management style, but is still practiced and is effective in some organizations.

Custodial. The custodial model, which emerged in the 1930s, was founded on the proposition that happy people are productive people. Custodial programs depended on material rewards for the worker; the workers were oriented toward the security blanket. Custodial model critics observe that, although people seemed happy, they were not fulfilled; and they were not necessarily productive. Rather they found a relaxed way to earn a living.

Supportive. The supportive model sought to avoid the shortcomings of both the autocratic and the custodial models. Workers are pointed toward performance, as opposed to the custodial emphasis on obedience and happiness. The drive to excel is awakened by participation and involvement. This model depends on leaders who have positive feelings toward their people — and on people who want to work, grow, and achieve.

Collegial. The collegial model is more likely to be encountered among professional groups. It is founded on feelings of mutual contribution among its members. The manager is oriented toward teamwork instead of toward a superior/subordinate relationship. Each member contributes to common goals. The results can be self-discipline, responsibility, self-fulfillment, and enthusiasm.

Internal auditors must adjust their approach to fit the specific management models encountered. Competent internal auditors will acquire a clear understanding of prevalent management theories and styles, both within and external to their organizations. Successful audits will also involve analysis of the various management models they encounter within audited units.

Trends and Techniques

In recent years, as competitive pressures and the pace of change have skyrocketed, managements have generally been far more willing to experiment with emerging theories, trends, and techniques. New books and concepts aimed at helping management find remedies to problems and opportunities for growth are launched in a steady cycle. Recently the COSO model has emerged. For various and sometimes complex reasons, some ideas catch on.

They capture the minds and imaginations of managers who are looking for a fix or an edge — strategies that will win the approval and allegiance of stakeholders, manage technology more effectively, enable the organization to attract and keep the best employees, improve the quality of products and services, capitalize on advantages, or outstrip competitors in other ways. While some critics have dubbed it "management by last book read," trends such as total quality management, quality circles, empowerment, reengineering, self-directed teams, learning organizations, and knowledge-based management can have dramatic impact.

In environments where management may have decided to implement a whole new "change model," the organization will almost certainly face tumult when the dynamics of the environment are overturned. Business process reengineering, for example, originated in the early 1990s as a concept for using information technology to link processes that cut across functional boundaries. Its architects, who included Michael Hammer and James Champy, argued that the value of computing was not simply in doing work more efficiently, but also in changing how work was done. By 1995, reengineering had become a $51 billion industry endorsed by some of the world's biggest organizations, management consultants, and information technology vendors. Shortly thereafter, reengineering faltered and fell, perhaps as a result of exaggerated promises and flawed implementation. In any case, the reengineering era was subsequently associated with massive layoffs, disillusioned workers, billions of dollars in costs, and high-risk restructuring that, in many instances, led to failure.

On the other hand, the reengineering emphasis on process has become a valued legacy in many quarters. Advocates point out that any organization that ignores its business processes or fails to improve them risks its future — although it is conceded that process improvement can occur without other, less positive elements of reengineering.

While management ultimately decides whether new ideas will be embraced and adopted, internal auditors may be able to provide assistance during the decision-making and transition processes. When internal auditors have won the role of trusted advisors and are closely attuned to strategic planning initiatives, they may be in a position to evaluate various implications of organizational innovation and consider how change should be managed. In any case, internal auditors who want to maximize their contributions will be students of emerging management trends; and they will be particularly interested in any theories with potential impact for their particular industry or type of organization. Internal auditors must keep pace with the constant developments in management thinking, and they must bolster their general knowledge with a precise understanding of their own management and its objectives.

Risk, Governance, and Control

Management concerns related to effective risk management have sparked many of the organizational changes of recent years. Expanding global competition and rampant change have been linked to escalating incidences of devastating fraud and scandal that have rocked organizations. Partly as a result of pressures from stakeholders, regulators, and enforcement agencies, issues related to risk management and effective governance and control have been pushed to the forefront in major organizations. Finding strategies for meeting obligations associated with effective risk management, control, and compliance has become a pressing, pervasive management issue.

Modern internal auditors have positioned themselves to provide essential support in these areas. In fact, the revised description of internal auditing promulgated by The Institute of Internal Auditors underscores this commitment: "Internal auditing ... helps an organization accomplish its objectives by bringing a systematic, disciplined approach to evaluate and improve the effectiveness of risk management, control, and governance processes." Internal auditing has shifted its emphasis from the past and the present to the future, and risk-based auditing is emerging as an integral part of professional practice. A part of this is the IIA study on "Corporate Governance and the Board – What Works Best." When internal auditors assist management in dealing with its most urgent concerns, such as those related to risk management, they clearly demonstrate their value to the organization.

The Functions of Management

Management's role is defined by four functions: planning, organizing, leading, and controlling. Internal auditors cannot perform these management functions because of their independence; but they can assist managers by identifying problems and suggesting improvements.

The four functions of management must be applied within the context of increasing globalization and technology. Major themes in larger entities that management must consider are:

1. Management is increasingly technology- and Internet-based.
2. Management of people is increasingly important.
3. Managers must manage change.
4. Teamwork is essential.
5. Diversity must be managed.
6. Managers much change organizational culture.[4]

Before internal auditors can maximize their assistance, however, they must fully understand each of the four management functions and how the work of internal auditors can provide vital support in each area.

Planning — The Manager's Perspective

Planning precedes all other management functions because organization, direction, and control flow from plans. Planning is the selection of the best choice from a number of options that can help the organization move from "where we are" to "where we ought to be." Effective planning cannot be accomplished haphazardly; it must be a rational and systematic process.

Planning calls for imagination, foresight, and thought from the top to the bottom of the organization. Successful plans should be cost effective and coordinated among functions. Every organization unit should be pointed at moving people toward planned objectives and goals. All controls should be designed to make sure that plans will be carried out effectively, efficiently, and economically.

Plans are decisions to take certain steps, but the plans should be flexible, adjusting to circumstances. Because plans are tentative and the premises on which they are based change, monitoring and reappraisals must be constant.

Planning differs from forecasting. Plans are goal oriented: This is what we intend to do. Forecasts are predictive: They represent the substance for premises on which management bases its plans. Management forecasts the demand for a product and the need for working capital; but it plans for technological advances, control systems, and diversification.

All planning is strategic or tactical. Strategic is long range; tactical is short range. Strategic planning is designed to assist managers in coping with future contingencies. It involves developing the organizational mission, objectives, and the means of accomplishing them. Strategic plans focus on taxes, capital budgets, personnel, and products. Tactical plans relate to the day-to-day operations, such as production scheduling.

All plans, whether strategic or tactical, are commitments to courses of action, not mere wishes. The risks associated with the plans must obviously be considered, along with the organizational risk management program. Management's planning activities must include an "environmental scan" of areas such as interest rates, employment levels, per capita spending, inflation, leisure time, quality of work life, cultural diversity, health, social responsibility, existing and proposed legislation, technology, the competition, customer needs, and the supply and cost of labor. Such elements must be factored into the premises.

Plans may be single-purpose or standing-purpose. Single-purpose plans apply to objectives of known duration, such as the installation of a new accounting system. Once the system is installed, the plan is completed. Standing-purpose plans are developed for the foreseeable future. For example, all purchases over $5,000 require at least three written bids; the plan continues until changed.

Management Activities

Plans and planning are umbrella terms that cover a number of different management initiatives. Although management structures obviously differ from one organization to another, the following areas represent universal aspects of management:

Missions. The mission is the basic function or task of an organization. It is the reason for being. Senior management's most crucial decision hinges on the questions, "What is our business?" and "What should it be?"

Objectives and goals. Objectives and goals guide the enterprise toward its mission. Although business language is sometimes ambiguous, objectives are generally considered to be long-range and general, while goals are short-range and specific. An objective might be to produce and sell a particular product or provide a specific service. A goal would be to sell a given number of those products or services by a given date.

Objectives and goals help to shape the structure, scope, and direction of the enterprise. Objectives and goals should be understandable, easily communicated, acceptable, attainable, and capable of being implemented by sub-plans such as procedures and rules. They should not conflict with laws, ethical standards, public policy, or other enterprise objectives.

Governance. Management is responsible to all stakeholders for providing authoritative direction and control of the organization. Risk management is an important aspect of the governance equation, especially since risks can be multifaceted and compounded in fast-changing, highly competitive environments.

Strategies. Strategies are broad, overall concepts that denote a general program of action and the deployment of resources. They are the tools for achieving objectives. A strategy might be a plan made in light of what a competitor is expected to do or not to do, for example. Strategic planning has a long-range rather than a short-range focus. Tactics denote how the strategy will be achieved.

Principles. Principles are general guides for action. They channel thinking and action in decision-making, but they allow a certain amount of discretion — otherwise, they would be rules.

Policies. Policies are general guides for action. They tend to pre-decide issues, help avoid repeated analysis, and give a unified structure to other types of plans. Policies permit managers to delegate authority while maintaining control. Like principles, they channel thinking and action in decision-making but allow a certain amount of discretion. The essential difference between a policy and a strategy is that a policy guides individual thinking and decision-making, while a strategy guides the actions for the entire organization.

Procedures. Procedures are specific guides that prescribe action but do not channel thinking. Procedures detail the exact manner in which a certain activity must be accomplished, often as a chronological sequence of events leading to the accomplishment of a task. Methods are specific techniques for accomplishing a task. Methods specify the manner in which a particular step of a procedure or tactic is to be accomplished.

Rules. Rules are the simplest plans. They allow for no discretion and must be followed as stated. A rule is a directive to act or not to act in a certain way in a given situation. In contrast, a procedure is a sequence of steps to accomplish a task.

Standards. Standards are norms against which activities are measured. They help determine whether actions comply with plans. When used to determine whether actions meet these norms, standards assume the attributes of controls.

Premises. Senior management should set premises, which are the assumptions on which plans are based. Everyone in the organization should use compatible premises to assure coordination of plans. Since premises are predictions, not facts, they cannot be certainties. They are founded on forecasts and historical information about the economy, society, government, and competition, as well as the enterprise's resources, strengths, and weaknesses.

Budgets. Budgets give quantitative expression to an entity's plans and compel an organization to identify its goals, the availability of resources, and methods of implementation. They are essential to the functioning of an enterprise or a function within the enterprise; yet they are almost inevitably a source of conflict. Responses to budgets are usually emotional and antagonistic. Antagonism can be reduced if budgets are based on realistic premises; if the people who are governed by them helped develop them; and if they are used to help managers help themselves.

Zero-based budgeting now infrequently used, is designed to force the annual justification of all costs and the examination of the cost/benefit trade-offs for alternative courses of action. Developing a zero-based budget requires a large investment of managerial time, and works best on fixed costs in relatively stable environments. Program budgeting is best characterized by the allocation of resources in ways that meet an organization's specific goals.

Decision-making. Decision-making is future-oriented problem solving. It involves rational selection of the best choice from among various options. The process includes the following steps:

- Recognize and define the problem.
- Gather pertinent information.
- Develop alternative courses of action.
- Select the best from among feasible alternatives.
- Take action.

Decisions can be programmable or non-programmable. For example, if more than two items from a batch do not meet standards, the programmable decision should be to reject the batch. Non-programmable decisions might be concerned with whether to add a specific new item to the product line.

The manager can make a decision alone and then require employees to implement them, or decisions might be based on discussions with those who will have to implement the decision. One important advantage of group decision-making is the creativity that often results from interaction of the group. Another is the greater likelihood that the decision will be accepted by the group that contributed to the decision.

Planning — The Internal Auditor's Perspective

Internal auditors no longer spend all their time looking back at completed transactions. They should look forward with management and assist in the planning process. In fact, internal auditors' broad perspectives can be particularly helpful, not only in assessing various planning initiatives, but also in evaluating how effectively the initiatives are integrated and supportive of the overall mission of the organization.

Internal Auditing Activities

No two managements are exactly alike, which means that specific internal auditing activities will vary somewhat from one organization to another. Regardless of these differences, all internal auditors can evaluate the overall planning process by determining whether plans, policies, and procedures meet certain standards of good management.

Standards for Management

Certain management standards are universal; they are based on management principles that are constant and consistent across organizations. Internal auditors can contribute to effective planning by confirming that:

- All plans, policies, and procedures are compatible with the organization's objectives.

- Plans anticipate problems and trouble spots that may arise.

- The premises for plans are based on accurate data and reasonable forecasting.

- The benefits of plans exceed the cost of preparation.

- Plans result in uniform action among interdependent organizations.

- Plans encourage initiative and are clearly communicated to those responsible for implementing them.

- Each plan includes a means of measuring success.

- Follow-up systems are devised to determine whether plans are carried out as intended.

Impediments to Plans

Not all plans are devised rationally. Sometimes plans are prepared in circumstances where failure is preordained; there is no chance of meeting goals. Often the planning mechanism itself is defective. Internal auditors should look for obstacles such as the following:

- Management is not committed to or involved in the plan.

- The grassroots people were not consulted.

- Plans are just not workable and may have been conceived by people out of touch with reality.

- Plans are not carried out; after being developed they are forgotten or are not monitored. The planners did not provide for feedback and control.

- Plans are based on inaccurate data and information.

- Plans do not consider contingencies; the planners did not ask themselves the "what if" questions.

- The plans are too rigid, allowing for no initiative.

- The planning is a subterfuge.

Bridging the Gap

Internal auditors are in a position to see the work of both the planner and the doer. They can therefore bridge the gaps that may exist between them. For example, internal auditors reviewing the accuracy of engineering drawings, which are essentially plans for production, can discuss them with production people to determine what problems might be encountered because of the drawings.

In all operating department audits, the review can be elevated to a management-oriented audit if the auditors concern themselves with the planning activity. For example, the auditor should:

- Get the manager's opinion with regard to the primary missions, purposes, and objectives of the department.

- Review the procedures designed to carry out department objectives and seek to identify those that are redundant, irrelevant, missing, or inconsistent.

- Talk to operating personnel and find out if they understand the objectives, the procedures, and the instructions.

- Make sure that the managers have a feedback system that informs them how well plans are being met.

A review of the development of plans, procedures, and programs can be helpful in determining whether managers considered certain key questions. For example, the following questions might be explored:

- Is it important for the plan to be carried out? Does the plan fill a real need?

- What has to be done to implement the plan? Is the most logical action being taken?

- Is the plan being carried out in the best place?

- Have schedules and due dates been set? Are specific milestones specified in long-range programs?

- Have specific individuals been given responsibility for carrying out the plans?

- Have procedures for carrying out the plans been clearly defined?

- Is there a monitoring process?

Change

Plans create change. People usually fear change as a threat to security, but change can be made acceptable under certain circumstances. Internal auditors can point out ways to ease the trauma of change:

- The need for change should be understood by operating personnel.

- Personnel should be assured that the change will not affect their security — assuming, of course, that the assurance is valid.

- Those affected should participate in planning the change.

- The change should result from a situation, not solely from management fiat.

- The change should follow a series of successful changes rather than a series of failures.

- The change should not be a part of many other changes all going on at once.

- The organization should be conditioned to accept change.

Procedures

Verifying adherence to procedures is a basic internal audit function. Managers often rely on internal audit analysis to tell them how well their people are following written procedures, but determining whether the procedures are useful and valid is of equal importance. Internal auditors can apply the following standards to the development and monitoring of procedures:

- Procedures should clearly indicate who is responsible for what. A provision for accountability should be included in each procedure.

- Procedures should not be empty hopes that are unsupported by adequate resources. Lack of people and equipment can prevent accomplishment of even the best procedures.

- Every job needs monitoring. Every procedure should provide for surveillance and progress reporting.

- Any forms that are developed to initiate the procedure should be designed so that everyone in the organization can use the same form. Paperwork should be kept to a minimum.

Budgets

Budgeting is an important managerial function, and internal auditors should conduct appropriate reviews related to budgets. Internal auditors are likely to be concerned with budgetary development and changes, the recording of actual costs, the reporting of performance, and management's use of performance reports. In auditing the budgeting and reporting process, the following criteria are likely to be relevant:

- The budget department should be authorized to obtain information from operating departments.

- Instructions and premises issued to those preparing the budgets should be understandable and consistent.

- The budget development process should be scheduled to show each of the specific steps required.

- To facilitate consolidation, the budget department should provide all contributing departments with the same format and premises for required information.

- Provision should be made for reviews of the budgets at higher levels in the organization.

- Information sent to the budget department should be adequately supported.

- Everyone whose work will be affected by the budget should be informed.

- Operating departments should adjust their operations to conform to budget changes.

- Significant variances between budgeted and actual amounts should be explained. Steps should be taken to correct the causes of excessive variances.

- Operating managers should receive adequate information to let them know how well they are meeting budgets.

- The measurement premises for the budget must conform to those of operations.

Substantial benefits can accrue from budget activity audits. Sound budget practices are vital to the success of an organization, and internal audit reviews can help to assure management that practices are effective and efficient.

Decision-making

Internal auditors can help managers in all but the final step of decision-making: the selection from among available choices. This is a management right and responsibility.

The internal auditor's role is to assist in identifying the problems and risks. Routine audits are directed to that end, and auditors can initiate the decision-making process by pointing to problems needing management attention.

In addition, internal auditors are often asked to perform management studies of significant problems. Wise internal auditors will proceed cautiously. They will first make sure that they have their fingers on the right problem, not necessarily on the one management has identified — sometimes hurriedly — as the problem.

Internal auditors are expert information gatherers. Often they can accumulate data, obtain varying views, and define expectations better than the managers themselves.

Internal auditors can offer alternative solutions to the decision-making process. Offering possible courses of action without prescribing which course to take is a normal audit function. Internal auditors can add to the choices management has developed, making sure that all or the most feasible of the alternatives are considered.

Internal auditors can evaluate possible choices by using mathematical techniques, modeling, or simulation. Management can thus be presented with alternatives that offer the greatest possibility of success.

Making the final choice, of course, is a step that must be left to line or senior management. If the internal auditor intrudes here, management may abdicate its responsibility and hold the internal auditor rather than itself accountable for results.

Management's action — its selection of the course to take — will usually require monitoring. Here internal auditors can offer safeguards by providing feedback on the results of the action taken as they carry out their regular audits. Since internal auditors were not responsible for the final choice, they are free to evaluate it.

Organizing — The Manager's Perspective

Organizing brings together people and processes in logical groupings to carry out plans and meet objectives. Good organization is no guarantee of success, but poor organization will almost inevitably bring about failure because it breeds conflict and frustration.

Approaches to Organization

Organizing can be accomplished through several means. The classical, behavioral, and contingency approaches are most common.

Classical. Also known as the traditional, structural, or formal approach, the classical approach leads to an autocratic organization. It creates squares and puts people into them. The person is selected to fill the job. The classical approach emphasizes the concepts of authority, responsibility, strict hierarchies, and prescribed spans of control.

Behavioral. The behavioral approach seeks to structure organizations so that the needs of both the people and the organization are meshed. It is concerned with the limits, strengths, and interests of the people available. It is less structured than the classical approach because group dynamics and the feelings of subordinates are considered.

Group dynamics, which emanated from Kurt Lewin's study of group behavior in an organizational setting,[5] focuses on the group's characteristics and how such groups function. The participants themselves provide information in defining their roles and structuring their jobs. The job is designed to fit the person, and the person helps design the job.

Contingency. The contingency approach, also called the modern approach, takes into account the unique situations in which the organization finds itself. In structuring the organization, the contingency approach considers the influence of the environment, technology, the existing work force, and the nature of the enterprise itself — its size, age, and capability.

The contingency approach is a synthesis of other management theories, including the classical and behavioral. Ideally, it involves the best features of each of the other theories.

Organization Charts

Although they depict only a small part of an executive's activities and interfaces, organization charts provide pictures of the enterprise. Since the pictures are static, they need constant revision if the organization is dynamic. In addition, the charts may make implications that are inaccurate, specifically with regard to the fact that departments on the same hierarchical line do not always have the same status. Some executives feel such charts do more harm than good because of their rigidity, the danger of misinterpretation, and the failure to record changing and complex relationships.

Organization charts do have benefits, however. They can show the chain of command — the hierarchy, accountability, and responsibility of the organization's executives. The charts provide a valuable overview of the organization and can be designed to show the basic function of each position. The very development of organization charts can be valuable because the task requires the planning of interrelationships within the enterprise. Some of the disadvantages of organization charts can be countered by periodic review and updating.

Responsibility

Responsibility is the obligation to perform. It is an unbroken chain from superior to subordinate to ultimate subordinate, and can never be relinquished. The chief executive remains responsible for every task in the organization, no matter how lowly placed that task may be. He or she is "the captain of the ship."

Responsibilities are grounded on tasks, and tasks are grounded on objectives. The clearer the understanding of one's objectives, the more likely it will be that responsibilities will be properly carried out.

Authority

Authority is the right to perform, to command, to enforce compliance. It derives from responsibility. The authority to carry out a task is meaningless when there is no responsibility for it. Many theories of organizational control, therefore, emphasize the parity between responsibility and authority.

Two forms of authority are exercised: formal or traditional authority and authority by acceptance. Formal authority stems from the right to give orders. It flourishes when jobs are scarce, because when workers need their jobs, they will follow orders even though they may disagree with them. Authority by acceptance is based on leadership. It works when the leader has convinced the workers that following directives will be in their own best interests. It is most desirable when workers are scarce and jobs are relatively secure. Workers may be independent enough to ignore the orders of the authoritative or positional leader, but they will follow a leader who has earned their respect and trust.

The sources of authority are varied. It may derive from:

- The virtue of the position — the legitimate power vested in the boss.

- The knowledge and experience of the leader; one who knows how and why is respected and followed.

- Friendship; we tend to do what people we like ask us to do.

- The ability to control rewards, or a matter of quid pro quo; you do for me and I'll do for you.

- Coercion; I can punish you for disobeying me.

- Referent powers: that is the power that comes from the leader's charismatic personality, causing people to cooperate because they admire the leader and wish to identify with him or her.

Accountability

Accountability is the obligation of workers and managers to give a reckoning for what they have accomplished. Accountability derives from responsibility. People cannot properly be held accountable when they have no relevant responsibility; and people should not be held accountable when their authority is not equal to the responsibility assigned. When responsibility is clear and authority is adequate, people should be asked to account for carrying out their responsibilities, for exercising the authority delegated to them, and for fulfilling their stewardship of the resources entrusted to them.

Delegation

Delegation includes assigning responsibility, granting authority, and exacting accountability. Obviously, only authority that is legitimately possessed can be delegated. However, delegation does not mean abdication. The superior remains responsible, and delegation must be accompanied by accountability and a mechanism for control and feedback.

Many superiors are reluctant to delegate and find it difficult to entrust tasks to others. They may fear that they will somehow be exposed or that someone else will take over their jobs. Understanding the following principles of delegation can help such reluctant managers:

- People must know what is expected of them.

- Each delegate must know his or her delegator; the chain of command must be clear.

- Once tasks are delegated, the delegate must carry through; evasion of responsibility should not be permitted.

- Authority to act must equal the responsibility to accomplish.

- Only those matters that are outside the authority delegated to the subordinates should be brought to the attention of superiors.

Span of Control

Span of control refers to the number of subordinates a supervisor can efficiently and effectively manage. Especially in periods of downsizing, the dominant view is to try to expand the span without destroying effective supervision; but no hard and fast rules prescribe how broad or narrow the span should be. An effective span of control will depend on a number of circumstances, including the skill of the manager, the skill and training of subordinates, the similarity of work performed, the complexity of the tasks, the physical proximity of subordinates, the difficulty of the technology employed, the motivation and attitude of the subordinates, and the nonmanagerial workload of the supervisor.

Staff and Line

Line people make "operational or line decisions." Staff people advise them. Line exists whenever an individual or group is responsible for an objective and makes decisions to that end. Staff exists whenever the individual or group is separated from the primary chain of command — the decision makers — to give them specialized service and support. Staff also provides support for the decision makers.

Thus, a computer programmer in a software organization, an auditor in an accounting firm, and a salesperson in a manufacturing organization would be line. But a computer programmer in a brokerage firm, a secretary in an accounting department, and an internal auditor in a public utility would be staff.

Staff and line must work together to produce results, but the seeds of conflict always exist. Staff is not authorized to make line decisions; and even if they were, such decisions would breed resentment and possibly encourage line people to shirk their responsibilities and become too dependent on staff people.

Conflicts are bound to erupt unless both line and staff make a concerted effort to develop and maintain reasonable working relations. Discord is usually rife where staff people assume authority over line activities. Communication breaks down between the two. Line stubbornly resists even reasonable, staff-recommended changes; and line fears punishment as a result of staff's critical reports. Staff exhibits abrasive and critical attitudes. Some conflicts seem to be consistent across organizations, such as manufacturing with quality assurance and engineering, product planning and inventory control with manufacturing, and sales with credit.

Several reasons for staff/line conflicts have been promulgated. Staff is concerned with ideas; line is more pragmatic and concerned with day-to-day operations. Line contributions are more easily measured than staff contributions; hence, staff may try overly hard to show what they managed to accomplish, often to the detriment of line. When staff feels that line does not appreciate their expertise, they may become resentful and punitive. Line may resent staff's expert status. Staff's perspective is typically limited to a narrow field; line may have to keep many balls in the air at one time.

While these may seem like irreconcilable conflicts, there are ways of reducing them. Management may:

- Replace incumbents with more compatible people.

- Insist on closer interaction.

- Provide training seminars.

- Emphasize closer cooperation.

- Clarify and delineate each function's authority.

- Ask the feuding parties to explore issues jointly and identify areas of agreement.

- Educate and encourage line managers to make more effective use of staff assistance.

- Negotiate more serious conflicts by using a higher-level manager as a mediator.

Functional Authority

Between line and staff is a twilight zone called functional authority, which exists out of necessity. Without it, the chief executive becomes overburdened. With it, chief executives can assign some of their authority to a staff organization or an individual.

Functional authority is the right and responsibility to prescribe processes, methods, or policies to line or other service groups. For example, a controller has the functional authority to issue instructions to all line and staff departments with regard to the kinds of accounting records they must keep. The controller has the special education, training, and expertise required for such tasks.

Departmentalization

Departmentalization divides the organization into distinct groupings to perform assigned tasks. Departmentalization can be based on function, territory, product, customer, or project. Most often, departmentalization is based on function. The most common departments include selling, production, and finance, extending upward to the chief executive.

Multinational or national firms with scattered locations often make their groupings by territory. Multi-line, large-scale firms group by product, which may be an outgrowth of functional departmentalization. Grouping by product grants greater authority to a division executive over a specific product or line. Public sector organizations normally make their groupings by program or service rendered.

Some activities in an organization, such as sales, or loan offices in large banks, may be divided according to customer. This kind of separation is rare at the top level of organizations.

For experimental or onetime activities, the project form of departmentalization can be used. Project departmentalization may be applicable in the construction of especially large projects, such as ships, buildings, or large design programs.

Matrix organizations are a combination of all these forms of groupings. They represent a compromise between functional and product departments. A manager for a particular product is chosen and is permitted to draw on personnel from different functions: production, sales, accounting, engineering, and the like. Matrix organizations have inherent difficulties because they violate the concept of unity of command. Employees report technically and functionally to the project manager, but administratively to the manager from whose organization they were drafted. To define the authority, responsibility, and accountability of the units involved is important so that confusion and employee dissatisfaction can be avoided.

Organizations may be "tall" or "flat." Tall organizations have a longer chain of command and a narrower span of control. They permit closer supervision but inhibit the development of self-reliant managers. Also, the communication process takes longer and is of poorer quality; "communication filtration" has a tendency to set in. Flat organizations have many groupings; they are set horizontally and report to a single superior.

Decentralization

Decentralization, which is increasing in usage, divides large complex organizations into smaller businesses that are relatively compact and simple. Each unit's management runs its own business and assumes responsibility for performance and accountability for results.

Committees

A committee is a group of people who are directed by competent authority to work together on some aspect of a management function. They reach decisions by consensus.

Committees are formed at all levels. At the highest level, standing committees include the board of directors and its committees, such as the audit committee. At lower levels, informal committees can be established to carry out a specific departmental task. These ad hoc committees are disbanded once the task has been completed.

Committee decision-making can often be slow and expensive. To arrive at a consensus, the committee members may settle for the lowest common denominator, thus achieving compromise instead of taking the best course. Committees are sometimes used as a burying place for projects that are unpopular or controversial. In such instances, the committee is usually doomed to inactivity and the project to extinction.

Conversely, committees bring together people with different experiences and training. The total can be greater than the sum of the parts because of the interchange of information and the resulting stimulation of ideas.

Informal Groups

For every formal group there is usually an informal one. Informal groups are composed of unstructured relationships among members who disregard the organization chart. Informal groups are not authorized, but they exist and cannot be ignored.

Informal groups are not necessarily negative. They fill social needs and generate a feeling of belonging. They can:

- Enhance employee feelings about the work environment.

- Develop effective, high-speed grapevines that management can use to transmit informal messages.

- Cause lazy individuals to shape up to the group's higher norms.

- Provide a safety valve for complaints that the organization itself cannot deal with.

- Aid in training.

- Perpetuate cultural values.

- Provide social satisfaction on and off the job.

- Foster creativity.

But informal groups can also cause problems. They tend to resist change, becoming protective of the status quo. They may engender role conflicts, diverting people from the objectives of the organization to the objectives of the group. The speed of the grapevine can spread false rumors as quickly as it spreads useful information. And conformity can work against the enterprise by forcing high performers to reduce productivity to meet lower group norms.

Staffing

Staffing is essential to organizing. In some classifications it assumes a fifth management function to the four currently being discussed. Staffing includes personnel planning and recruiting as well as selecting and developing people to operate the organization competently.

Program planning addresses job descriptions and specifications. Job descriptions define the duties, authority, and responsibility for positions. They provide guidance for new employees, the basis for job specifications, the means for reconciling grievances, tools for setting wage rates, and aids in organizing.

Job specifications describe the qualifications needed for acceptable performance in a particular job. They help in developing personnel advertisements, clarifying specific qualifications, analyzing promotions, and in carrying out overall personnel planning. They also establish responsibilities, authority, accountability, and the position of the job within the structure of the organization.

Planning can be enhanced by human resource accounting and manpower audits. Human resource accounting refers to assessments of the value of personnel available in the organization. Manpower audits generate the numbers, types, and quality of personnel that will be available or needed by a particular organization in the future. Management should also plan the personnel progression by closely linking succession planning with management training and development programs.

In searches for new employees, recruiters should be aware of several points:

Organization compensation policies. Salary ranges, the organization's fringe benefits, bonus or stock option plans, and opportunities for salary increases — including review periods — should be specified. The primary advantage of fringe benefits is to induce an individual to join an organization and stay with it.

Recruiting practices. Hiring the right people is an important issue in every organization. Costs associated with recruiting and training new employees can be enormous.

Specific matters of concern are often the colleges and universities to be visited, the campus interview procedures, and the ways of conducting interviews. Recruiters should also be aware of applicable government regulations, such as Equal Employment Opportunity, and organization-administered tests.

Many organizations began to use their Web sites as effective recruitment tools. Effective sites not only advertise vacancies, but they also provide extensive information about the organization and the position. In addition, surfing the Internet has become a widely used tool for job seekers and potential employers; and both management and internal auditors should be aware of the impact of technology on hiring practices. The cost-effectiveness of Internet recruitment can be an important factor in many organizations.

Manpower planning. Recruiters should be aware of the sequence of steps, from interview through final selection. They need to be aware of what to look for academically and technically as well as the importance of appearance, attitude, personality, and experience.

A dilemma for many organizations is whether to promote internal candidates or to consider external candidates for certain jobs. The advantage of promoting internal candidates includes lower training cost and time, morale boosts for employees, lower recruitment costs, greater knowledge of past performance, and organizational development that provides management with long-term talent. On the other hand, external candidates are sources of new ideas. They increase the breadth and depth of the organization's labor pool. Selection of external candidates also avoids organization politics, and there is increased opportunity to promote needed change.

Some organizations fall into traps in their compensation policies. For example, if the organization gives annual raises to everyone, the incentive for exemplary performance may be lessened. Meritorious performance and/or increased responsibilities should be rewarded.

Organizing — The Internal Auditor's Perspective

Internal auditors have no responsibility for designing organizations, but their knowledge of systems and controls can be of value to those who do. Sometimes questions that are central to good organization and natural to an experienced, management-oriented internal auditor would not occur to the designers of organizations and systems. The internal auditor's queries might include, for example:

- What are the objectives of the proposed operation?

- How do the objectives mesh with the organization's objectives?

- What controls exist, or should exist, to see that objectives will be met?

- How is development of the organization chart keyed to the organization's objectives?

Countless factors play into the overall effectiveness of organizing. Internal auditors who are informed and alert to them can offer their organizations invaluable perspectives.

Responsibility, Authority, and Accountability

Internal auditors are expected to determine what managers are responsible for, what they are authorized to do, and how they should account for their accomplishments and results. For example, when purchasing agents permit operating departments to deal directly with suppliers, they may be shirking their own responsibility for arms-length dealing. When other departments, with no right to do so, order supplies or services without consulting purchasing, they are violating the authority of the purchasing function to act as chief committer of organization funds. When executive management turns a blind eye to all this, it is relieving purchasing of its accountability.

In some organizations, management has given purchasing responsibilities to departments for good and valid reasons. Procurement cards are often issued, entitling the holder to make purchases up to specified dollar amounts. The control is at the back-end, when statements are scanned for unusual or irregular items. But it is internal auditing's job to confirm that such decisions have been made with a full understanding of the processes and controls involved. Purchasing cannot be held accountable or responsible unless it has authority.

So internal auditors have an interest in the responsibilities assigned and the authority delegated to the organizations they review. Where these are not carried out, the neglect represents weaknesses that need correcting. In some instances, auditors may find that responsibility is assigned but accountability is not required; senior management may have lost touch. Internal auditors should see that in any organization, responsibility, authority, and accountability are maintained.

Delegation

Delegation demands control as well as feedback to show how delegated tasks are carried out. Internal auditors can be the source of objective information on task accomplishment. For example, the receiving department delegates to certain organizations the authority, under specified conditions, to accept supplies or services directly, without going through receiving. Internal auditors can determine whether the conditions laid down by receiving were met.

In their analyses, internal auditors should seek answers to the following questions:

- Are the delegatees qualified to undertake their assignments?

- Do the delegatees understand their responsibilities?

- Does performance meet the standards set by the delegator?

- When the delegation was made, what form of control was developed to provide feedback to the delegator?

- Are the controls working as intended?

Staff and Line

Internal auditors have their own staff/line issues. They are responsible for identifying risks and other weaknesses. They have a commitment to assist line managers in solving problems, but they may not dictate the specific course of action. Although internal auditors may offer possible courses of action, the offer must be made with the distinct understanding that line makes the final decision, because line, not staff, must live with the action taken.

Yet the mildest suggestion made by an internal auditor may be seen as a direct order by line managers. So internal auditors should be careful with regard to the manner in which they couch their suggestions. The stress should always be on "You may want to consider" and not on "we suggest."

Internal auditors often audit staff work. Some of that work may be rendered by organization personnel, some by suppliers. Internal auditors can assist senior management in deciding whether particular staff services should be purchased or performed by organization personnel. Relevant issues might include:

- Comparative costs.

- The need for undivided staff attention.

- What to ask for in terms of services required.

- The ability of in-house managers to provide the needed services.

- Measuring the effectiveness of the acquired services.

Functional Authority

Better than most in the organization, internal auditors are in a position to determine whether functional authority is effective. For example, the human resources department may prescribe personnel appraisal forms for all departments in the organization, but they may be reluctant to make sure the forms are being used. The purchasing department may distribute procurement cards to ordering departments, but it may not know how those departments are guarding against misuse.

Line managers may perceive functional authority as intrusions into their own authority and reject questioning by the possessors of that authority. But they would be hard pressed to refuse to answer questions by internal auditors. One of the internal auditing responsibilities is to be sure the functional authority is effective. Internal auditors can bridge the gaps and be catalysts for corrective action.

Departmentalization

Internal auditors should not necessarily accept the current organizational structure. Departmentalization should also be questioned. Internal auditors should ask, for example:

- What activities are needed to carry out the department's objectives?

- How are the groupings balanced to meet departmental goals?

- Does departmentalization provide for adequate crosschecks of important activities to prevent errors and improprieties?

- How does the grouping of department activities facilitate the meeting of organization objectives?

- What are the key activities of an organization, and have they all been assigned to specific units or individuals?

- How well are departments or units integrated?

- Which ones seem to operate without surveillance or checks and balances?

Decentralization

Decentralization grants a great deal of autonomy to the decentralized units. These units act like separate businesses, yet they must be accountable to and guided by headquarters. They must conform with overall policies and procedures, such as accounting, that have been established by the head office.

Senior vice presidents responsible for the decentralized units may visit them rarely. When they do, the visits may be little more than social calls. Certainly, the executives cannot review them in depth, even if they wanted to. A major link to decentralized operations must be the knowledgeable internal auditor, giving senior management reasonable assurance that common objectives will be attained, efforts will be coordinated, and decisions on matters of high policy will be made visible.

Committees

Committees should not be above audit review. In fact, internal auditors are sometimes assigned as committee members so as to ensure conformance of committee action with organization policies.

In some instances committees may be established without determining whether their activities have already been assigned to other committees. In one organization an internal auditor identified a dozen standing committees that were concerned with safety. On a spreadsheet, the auditor captured the responsibilities of all of them, illustrating gross duplication in many activities.

Internal auditors can also be helpful in determining whether committees meet certain basic standards:

- The committee's charter should be in writing. The charter should define the committee's authority and responsibilities and should show to whom the committee is accountable.

- Committee members should have definite roles and not merely be observers. Their duties should be made clear.

- Committees should be large enough to provide varied viewpoints, but not so big as to be unwieldy.

- Committee members should have equal authority. None should feel dominated or fearful of expressing themselves.

- An agenda should be prepared for each meeting, and it should be transmitted to committee members in advance of the meeting.

- Minutes should be prepared for each meeting. Copies should be sent to the executives to whom the committees are responsible.

- Action items should be assigned to individuals, and due dates should be scheduled.

- The committee chair should follow up on assigned tasks.

- A committee's activities should not overlap those of other committees.

- A committee should be disbanded as soon as its mission is completed.

The simplest starting point to a committee audit is to ask the committee chair how the organization's standards are being met.

Informal Groups

Internal auditors should be sensitive to the informal organization that overlays the formal one. Informal groups have their own cultures, leaders, and forms of communication. By showing empathy and understanding, internal auditors can plug into the grapevine, which is the mode of communication for informal groups. This connection may help internal auditors understand why things work the way they do, including the causes for deviations from established procedures. It may also help them to identify problem areas that may not be evident in reviews of the system, but which need correction.

When they are performing audits in other countries, internal auditors must also be aware of informal groups and become attuned to the mores of the individual cultures. Setting up meetings during siesta time in Latin America would be useless. Getting upset for being kept waiting in countries where delays are a part of life would create antagonism that could abort a well-planned audit.

The informal organization is a fact of life. Managers have to effectively deal with it, and so do internal auditors.

Staffing

Internal auditors can be helpful in audits of staffing activities. Hiring and retaining the best people is widely considered to be one of the most important determinants for organizational success. In tight labor markets, sound staffing practices become even more vital. As a result, internal auditors should be concerned with hiring practices on a number of different levels.

Internal auditors should determine whether background checks are being made and see that a system exists for checking on the prior performance of new hires and rehires. Chances are good that the villains on board were villains in their former jobs. The following standards might be considered:

- The basis for the complement of a unit should be soundly supported.

- People should be in the proper position. An engineer should not be doing clerical work.

- Jobs should challenge people. If the turnover rate is high, the answer may be boredom.

While internal auditors will be concerned with overstaffing, handling this situation requires care. It is best for the statistics to speak for themselves: "This year the staff of 30 turned out 15,000 units. Last year, the same staff turned out 25,000 units."

Leading — The Management Perspective

Leading is the function of moving resources toward objectives and goals. Successful directing usually depends on motivating those directed. This function has historically been called directing. But as management has changed to recognize a major difference in the environment, we refer to it as leading to recognize the change in needs. Many complex factors, including background and training, colleagues, and the work situation itself, can affect motivation.

Early theories of directing were founded on the classical school and grew out of the military concept of orders issued by a commander. The advent of the behavioral school modified this theory, so that effective leadership was based on subordinates who accepted the leader and were willing to obey. Executives must find the link between the individual and the organization, creating a congruence of both needs. Authority is effective only if subordinates accept it.

Individual Dynamics

In his book, *Motivation and Personality,* Abraham Maslow laid down a hierarchy of needs that help to explain the actions of people.[6] According to Maslow's theory, lower needs normally must be satisfied before the higher needs could be met:

- Physiological. The fundamental requirements for sustaining human life: water, food, shelter, sleep, and sexual satisfaction.

- Security or safety. Freedom from physical or economic danger or loss.

- Acceptance. People need to be accepted by others and belong to groups. Hence, the importance of the informal organization.

- Esteem. People must be valued by themselves and by others. Needs are met by power, prestige, status, and even by self-confidence.

- Self-actualization. This is the top rung of the ladder. It is the inner drive to realize one's fullest potential.

Except for the physiological satisfactions, this hierarchy does not apply in all cases. People with different backgrounds will react differently. Cultural, professional, social, ethnic, and other factors strongly affect which level in the hierarchy a person can or will aspire to. In general, however, the tendency to move from the lowest to the higher hierarchies is inherent.

Group Dynamics

All enterprises are made up of groups and social arrangements. Group dynamics is a term used to describe the human behavior of these groups.

All groups have certain common characteristics, and they all have leaders — people who tend to rise to the top wherever they may be. The leaders usually set standards or norms for themselves and expect the members of the groups to meet those norms, be they high or low. Each group has its pecking order or status symbol, which may be based on skill, age, seniority, or personality. Each member of the group plays a role, following an expected pattern. The group has its own biases, values, and beliefs about the rest of the world.

Conflicts may emerge between groups because of the different roles they are expected to play. For example, the marketing department wants to keep inventories high so that customer needs can be quickly met, but the finance department wants to minimize inventory investment. Such structural goal conflicts are inherent in the objectives of the organizations and can be solved only through compromise, an understanding of each other's roles, and the optimum accommodation of the conflicting objectives.

Leadership

Leadership is the art of influencing and stimulating performance. Properly carried out, it can be the ability to make ordinary people do extraordinary things. Leadership stems from power, but that power can run the gamut from coercion to the charisma of the leader.

Defining the term leadership has never been simple, and specific traits have no hard-and-fast relationship to leadership skills. By and large, however, successful leaders usually demonstrate intelligence, maturity, interest in people, and status in the enterprise.

Despite the fact that leadership cannot be directly linked to personality traits or precise characteristics, four distinct styles of leadership have been identified:

- *Autocratic.* The manager orders people to perform, following the classical theory of management.

- *Consultative.* The manager has substantial trust in subordinates; provides motivational rewards and punishment, where appropriate; and exercises communication, both upward and downward. The manager listens to the employees but still makes the decisions.

- *Participative.* The employee has a role in providing input to the decision-making process. The manager includes the employees' views in the ultimate decisions.

- *Free-reign.* The manager adopts a laissez-faire attitude, and employees make their own decisions.

A contingency theory advanced by F.E. Fiedler in the mid-1960s emphasizes the situational factors that affect leadership.[7] The ability of the individual to react properly to a given situation permits the right person at the right time to emerge as a leader. The contingency model is founded on three different situations:

1. *The position.* Power can flow from the position held. In a formal organization, the position itself permits the leader to direct people toward the accomplishment of tasks.

2. *The task.* Power can flow from the way people's tasks are structured. Performance can more readily be directed when a person's tasks are clearly and carefully designed. In this situation, the path-goal theory of leadership is emphasized. The leader provides rewards and makes clear what the subordinates must do to earn them. Such leaders help subordinates achieve both enterprise and personal goals.

3. *The leader.* Power can flow from the way the leader and the followers interact. Power is linked to the degree people trust their leaders and are willing to follow them.

No one of these dimensions is always controlling. They are contingent on the situation.

Some managers have adopted an "open door" policy, where employees are welcome to enter their office with complaints and suggestions at any time. Although the concept may seem attractive on some levels, it doesn't always work. People may be intimidated by management. Where morale is low, people may just shrug and say, "What's the use?" They may be fearful about reprisals from immediate supervisors or the kind of reception they will receive and believe that the policy will change nothing.

These inhibitions can be countered, and the psychological barriers can be broken down by open communication. Management should respect its employees and demonstrate that respect. Management can give evidence of respect by actively asking for suggestions and rewarding the good ones. Suggestion boxes, surveys, and the appointment of an ombudsman have sometimes helped to dispel the suspicions and distrust of employees. Control self-assessments or other instruments have been used in some organizations to evaluate morale and levels of trust. Managements that truly respect their employees will want to know about serious impediments to a spirit of mutuality so that they can act on them; and since such assessments can be anonymous, employees are protected from repercussions.

Motivation

Every manager must motivate — move people toward some common goal. The old authoritarian method, the whip, may work for a while; but it is worthless when the boss's eye is turned away or when the job market for good people is open. The modern manager must understand people and know what motivates or offends them.

Many theorists have performed research and drawn conclusions about what motivates workers. The following names and theories are among the best known:

Douglas McGregor and the Theory Y and Theory X types of managers.[8] Theory Y managers believe people really want to accomplish something, while Theory X managers believe that all workers are lazy and must be driven.

Rensis Likert and the supportive manager.[9] Participation is the key to motivation.

Frederick Herzberg and the theory of dissatisfiers and satisfiers.[10] Dissatisfiers are factors that must be present but really do not motivate people, such as pay, interpersonal relations, supervision, organization policies, working conditions, status, and job security. Satisfiers that motivate the worker include recognition, achievement, and the potentials for growth and advancement.

Chris Argyris and integrating the needs of the individual with those of the organization.[11] Unresolvable conflicts arise when a mature, capable, creative person joins a structured, demanding, and limiting organization.

Many of these writers based their theories on the job itself as the one prime motivator. They postulate that by improving the job, managers can improve the desire of workers to perform. In job enrichment, a worker's assignments are made more fulfilling. In job enlargement, the variety and number of tasks are expanded and made more challenging. By having workers participate in structuring and planning their assignments, the jobs are enlarged and enriched. Workers then tend to perform according to their potential.

Victor Vroom's "expectancy theory"[12] refutes Herzberg's satisfier/dissatisfier concept on the basis that it is too dependent on the work itself. Vroom suggested that "motivation is the result of valence multiplied by expectancy." Valence is defined as the value of an individual's feeling about the possible outcome of a given situation, and expectancy refers to the probability that the individual assigns to the outcome. To be motivated, an individual must, therefore, have a reasonable or high expectancy that some desired rewards — valence — will occur.

Communication

Communication cannot occur without interaction and a shared, mutual understanding of ideas, facts, and courses of action. Because effective communication is widely regarded as one of the essential keys to successful management, understanding, assessing, and improving organizational and personal communications is a significant, though often overlooked, activity.

Every communication involves a sender, a means of transmission, a message, a receiver, and symbols. The sender wishes to convey what is in his or her mind to the mind of the receiver by couching the message in appropriate symbols. The best indicator of the effectiveness of a communication is a change in the receiver's behavior.

Formal communication is conducted through the formal structure of the organization, while informal communication operates outside formal structural channels. Informal communication is quicker and can be enhanced by the oral style and expression of the sender. Formal, written communication has its own benefits, however. For example, formal communications can be:

- Reviewed and edited, and more time can be allowed for absorbing the message.

- Documented for the future.

- Mass-produced.

- More complex, allowing the use of graphs and tables.

- Devoid of body language and physical gestures that may overpower the words.

Traditional or classical management functions by sending one-way communication from superior to subordinate, following the military model of management. Participative management functions in many directions. All parts of the organization are allowed and expected to communicate with each other for the benefit of the employee and the organization.

Feedback is an important aspect of successful communication because it determines the effectiveness of the communication. Without feedback, the sender has no assurance that communication was achieved. Feedback can prevent or modify the filtering process, where people in the hierarchical chain can withhold or alter unfavorable information that they do not want known by higher management.

The problems inherent in all communications include faulty transmission, poorly chosen words or phrases, careless omissions, lack of coherence, poor organization of ideas, jargon that is understandable only to a limited group, and the failure to clarify the meaning of what is to be communicated. All of these problems are related to perception — how the receiver perceives the message. Perception is conditioned by experience, knowledge, and intelligence.

The managers receive and transmit information on the basis of how they relate to themselves and others. They deal with four levels of communication:

- **Arena.** All information needed to carry on communication is known by the manager and other individuals.

- **Blind spot.** Information that is known to others is not known to the manager.

- **Facade.** Information is known by the manager and not by others.

- **Unknown.** Neither the manager nor others are aware of the information each knows.

This model is known as the "Johari Window" developed by Joseph Luft and Harry Ingram.[13]

Managers must not only understand communication processes and how they affect the organization and its units; they should also be committed to assessing and improving their own skills. Ineffective listening, for example, is one of the key inhibitors to full communication. Good listening requires objectivity, genuineness, empathy, caring, compassion, and patience. The speaker must be able to put himself or herself in the receiver's shoes, taking into account the listener's background, beliefs, values, and biases. Effective managers train themselves to listen closely and to evaluate what the person is saying and how the information can be used. They avoid interrupting; maintain steady, sincere eye contact; and don't do other things while they are listening. When the boss doesn't listen, it's not only demoralizing to employees; critical processes can break down.

Leading — The Internal Auditor's Perspective

Leading is people-oriented, not transaction-oriented; and internal audits of directing functions do not lend themselves to objective conclusions by documented numbers and facts. Still, internal auditors can provide counsel and assistance in the field.

Audits of leading can occur in any area of the organization. For example, in the human resources area, management-oriented audits can be performed by focusing on the department's objectives. Typically, these objectives will include identifying personnel needs, training and developing workers, and administering personnel programs and benefits. Internal auditors might want to employ standards such as the following:

- Jobs to be filled should be described clearly and completely.

- Uniform criteria should be used in classifying jobs.

- Job compensation should be keyed to particular classifications, competitive with jobs in other organizations, and comparable to those in other departments.

- Salary levels and compensation policies should be reevaluated periodically.

- Department heads should be consulted on current and future personnel needs.

- All significant jobs should have backup employees trained to fill them.

Operating managers develop and disseminate guidelines for employee orientation and training, such as information about employee rights and obligations and what the organization expects of its employees, encouragement to get additional training, tested training materials, and special training and certification for hazardous jobs.

Employee appraisals should be performed periodically to match compensation and performance within the employee's grade. Evaluations should be personally delivered with suggestions for improvement.

Employee turnover rates should be analyzed for trends, and investigations should be made to determine reasons for adverse trends.

Welfare and other services should be administered in a businesslike fashion. Often there is a tendency to be lax with such programs.

Exit interviews should be made in all separations, and the feedback should be evaluated for corrective action in problem areas.

Leadership and Motivation

Evaluating leadership and motivation is risky. Yet such audits, wisely carried out, can provide useful information to management. Some standards for such evaluations are:

- Good leaders exhibit confidence in their people, seeking and using their ideas.

- Subordinates are free to talk to their superiors about their jobs.

- The leader asks for employee participation.

- Corrective action, when needed, is immediate and addresses the inappropriate action or behavior.

- Employees are committed to achieving organizational goals.

- Subordinates have an open line to report their problems and accomplishments upward.

- People are clearly informed about the goals they are expected to meet.

- Leaders learn about and understand the subordinates' problems, difficulties, and frustrations.

- Employees are involved in the decision-making process.

- The basis and premise for decisions come from the top and from subordinates.

- The decision-making process motivates, rather than disaffects, employees.

- Goals are established by group action, not by command.

- Goal establishment does not result in employee resistance.

- The informal organization has the same goals as the formal one.

- Systems provide for self-control rather than imposed control.

Control self-assessments are often effective in gathering information in these areas. When internal auditors have developed the proper rapport, operating managers will be amenable to information about their performance in meeting these standards. Where operating managers will not heed cautions, and where the violations of such standards of conduct seriously affect performance, internal auditors may have to report their conclusions to senior management. Experience has shown that reports of this nature are more effective and less disruptive if they are conveyed to senior management orally and in strict confidence.

Communication

Internal auditors recognize that managers in large organizations make decisions largely on what they are told, rather than what they know on their own. Too often, reports from subordinates are self-serving statements and not scrupulously accurate accounts of conditions. The internal auditor, who has no ax to grind, can defend senior management from inaccurate and biased information. All reports on which significant management decisions are made should be reviewed for timeliness, accuracy, and usefulness.

Policies and procedures are forms of communication, as well as planning instruments. Internal auditors should determine in their audits whether policies and procedures can be easily understood, are relevant to current conditions, and are progressive.

Personnel policies are often linked to communication problems. However, it is not always the policy that presents the problem, but how employees perceive the policy. Audits can help to inform senior management about employee perceptions of personnel policies. Employees may be interviewed and asked questions such as the following:

- Has the policy been read?

- What is it perceived to mean?

- Does it seem reasonable?

- How would the employee restate the policy?

Internal auditors' perspectives of how — and how efficiently and effectively — communications flow through the organization may provide management with insights into significant problems and solutions. Audits of such areas often reveal surprises and opportunities for clearing away obstacles through improved methods.

Controlling — The Manager's Perspective

Evaluating the adequacy and effectiveness of control systems is central to the internal auditor's job. For that reason, Chapter 2, Control, provides a comprehensive survey of control from the viewpoint of the internal auditor. The manager's viewpoint of control overlaps in some areas, but it is obviously important for internal auditors to see and understand both perspectives.

Controlling is the process of making certain that directed action is carried out as planned to achieve some desired objective or goal. Controlling and planning are linked. Indeed, controlling cannot operate effectively without the tools provided by planning. Some devices, such as budgets, are used both to plan and to control.

Control is exercised by managers throughout the organization, from chief executive officer to floor supervisor. Various forms of control have been given labels such as management control, executive control, administrative control, financial control, accounting control, and systems control. They all function in the same way and differ only in the objectives they are designed to meet.

Controlling can be either quantitative or qualitative. Budgets and schedules are quantitative controls. Job instructions, quality control standards, and performance reviews are qualitative controls.

Control can be considered as a closed system consisting of a series of six elements:

1. Setting performance standards to provide a means of measuring and comparing events and establishing permissible variations.

2. Measuring performance or progress to accumulate information on existing conditions.

3. Analyzing performance or progress and comparing it with standards to determine variances.

4. Evaluating deviations and bringing them to appropriate attention to determine causes and effective corrective action.

5. Correcting deviations from standards to see that objectives and goals will be met.

6. Following up on corrective action to determine its effectiveness.

Controlling includes the other functions of management: planning, organizing, and directing. Management is responsible for establishing control systems; internal auditors are responsible for evaluating their adequacy and effectiveness.

The control system should be adapted to the formal organizational structure. It should be understandable to all administrators, and it should be oriented more toward anticipating future mistakes than correcting past ones.

Excessive control can be burdensome and unnecessarily expensive, and some parts of a system may not need to be under strict control. In establishing systems, managers should be concerned with the key control points. Although these points vary from one enterprise to another, they are always the areas or functions where activities tend to cluster and create bottlenecks. For example, in certain large manufacturing organizations, the president concentrates attention and appraisals on shipments, customer orders, inventories, production efficiency, and forecasts. Simple ratios can be worked out among key control points to highlight aberrations, focus attention, and conduct appraisals. Reports of comparisons and evaluations should be understandable and useful. They should include what is essential and avoid what is merely interesting.

When they select control points, managers should ask themselves:

- What will best measure performance?

- What will point out significant deviations?

- What will identify causes of problems?

- What will minimize the cost of correcting errors?

- What will be most efficient? (cost vs. outcome)

- What is the lowest practicable level in the organization at which the control point should be set?

Standards

Standards translate goals into specific measurable outputs or outcomes. They let people know what is considered to be acceptable performance. No objective measurement of performance is possible without standards.

All standards derive from plans, not from policies, rules, objectives, or principles. They should, therefore, be linked to plans and be relevant to various elements of performance. For example:

- *Quantity of output.* Output standards specify quantitative performance. They may be based on stipulations such as machine-hours or worker-hours per unit of output, units per day or week, or tonnage produced. Quality is prescribed.

- *Accuracy of quality.* Accuracy of quality standards specifies quality of performance, such as agreement with specifications, fastness of color, approvals required, or number of rejections.

- *Cost.* Cost standards specify benchmarks such as material costs per unit, overhead per direct labor hour, or direct and indirect costs per unit of production.

- *Timeliness.* Timeliness standards relate to production schedules, project completion, or meeting customer need dates.

- *Capital.* Capital standards apply monetary units to physical items. They deal with capital investments, not operating costs, so they relate more to the balance sheet than to the income statement. The standards include return on investment and ratios such as current assets, cash, and receivables, to current liabilities and turnover of receivables and inventory.

- *Revenue.* Revenue standards involve monetary values assigned to sales. They deal with measures such as revenue per airplane passenger mile, dollars per ton of sheet steel sold, and the average sale per customer.

Standards should be positioned at strategic control points. The earlier the point in a process, the greater assurance that deviations will be anticipated, or that they will be detected before too much time or money is expended.

Above all, performance standards should be related to the primary objectives of the activity; otherwise, the key measurements are not made. In a safety operation, for example, measurements can be made of the number of inspections conducted, differences reported, tests of equipment, number of operations observed, and accidents investigated. However, these will not show whether the activity is moving toward its prime objective of safe operations. More relevant standards might focus on reductions in accidents, reduction of machine downtime resulting from accidents, and lower worker's compensation insurance costs stemming from decreases in the number of accidents. Time and motion studies are often used in setting standards of measurement, but these are most relevant to repetitive work.

Measurements

Every end product or service can be measured. For some systems, the process of setting measurable standards can be frustrating. Each task has its productive purpose, or it should be eliminated. If that purpose can be defined and parsed out clearly, there should be some way of determining when the task has been achieved efficiently and effectively. When complete measurement is not desirable, as where destructive tests must be used, sampling is appropriate.

Measurement should be accurately recorded and promptly communicated. It should not only inform superiors, it should also assist the subordinates being measured. For example, factory foremen would be interested in cost analysis reports, labor distribution reports, and reports comparing budgeted and actual expenses. They would ordinarily have little interest in profitability forecast reports. Where an operating manager does not have the time to analyze reams of information, exception reporting is useful; only those matters requiring attention are brought to the manager's desk.

Although management may view certain controls and measurements as desirable, employees may regard them in a less kindly light. They may feel their self-esteem is damaged by controls that identify their personal weaknesses. They may believe that the standards and measurements are unfair. They may resent autocratic authority, or they may perceive the controls as conflicting with group norms.

Standards should, therefore, take into account the human factor. They should not be so loose that they present no challenge, or so tight that they are frustrating and unattainable. They should be acceptable to subordinates, and acceptability is improved if subordinates participate in setting the standards. For example, an MBO system will not be effective if the superiors alone establish and enforce standards and procedures, because the primary responsibility for exercising control rests with the employees charged with executing the plans. The need for controls should be explained to the employees involved and they should have a say in the standards by which they will be measured. To demonstrate fairness, standards should be reviewed periodically to ensure their continued applicability.

In considering the human factor, thought must be given to whether measurement should be performed by the people involved in the performance or by others. Each approach has its benefits and drawbacks. Self-measurement may create confidence and trust and permit fast feedback and correction. But it can also lead to distortions, concealment, and delays in reporting. Measurement by those not involved in the performance may create hostility and rebellion in those reported on. Objective measurement may minimize bias and suspicion of the reported measurements.

Comparisons

Once standards are set and tasks are measured, performance and standards must be compared. Care must be taken to compare items that are alike in terms of time, quantity, and quality. Decisions must be made with regard to how often data should be collected and how to spot significant deviations. Continuous comparisons are expensive and objectionable to subordinates. In determining significance, judgment is needed. A simple comparison between two sets of numbers is not enough. The data must be interpreted and evaluated rationally in terms of existing circumstances — the law of the situation.

Evaluations

Evaluation calls for an analysis of comparisons and a look at the standards. Were the goals really attainable? Did unanticipated factors prevent standards that seemed reasonable from being met? On the other hand, did luck play a part, so that the poorest of workers could have met the standards?

In automated control situations, the evaluation is relatively simple and reporting is clear. In personnel circumstances and other situations calling for mature judgment, the reporting and the resulting action may be more difficult and slower.

Evaluation should concentrate on the significant exceptions — those that do not conform with the standards. Concentrating on key control points will also be advantageous.

Correction

Correction means removing the roadblocks that prevent task accomplishment. Correction involves changing attitudes and reversing adverse trends. Significant variances require vigorous and immediate action. Effective control cannot tolerate needless delays, endless compromises, or excuses. Continuing and excessive exceptions should not be countenanced.

The people in charge of performance should take the corrective action. For maximum effect, the correction should be accompanied by fixed and individual responsibility. Holding an individual rather than a group responsible improves chances of correction. The best corrective action is remedial action. The root causes should be identified and removed to prevent recurrence.

Follow-up

Whenever superiors or systems prescribe corrective action, a means of follow-up should take over. The pressures of an ongoing system tend to push corrective action to the side. Effective follow-up sees to it that the need to take corrective action is not overlooked.

Follow-up includes surveillance of the control system itself. No control system can anticipate all possible events. Employees may unintentionally omit or intentionally distort the feedback provided under the system. Employees may resent the system and seek to subvert it. The "unknown unknowns" may render a system inoperative. Only supervisory surveillance can thwart these undreamed-of aberrations.

Approaches to Control

Control is either imposed, or it is achieved by self-control. Imposed control is traditional. It measures performance against imposed standards, takes corrective action through the people responsible, and follows up to see that the action works. This types of control has negative connotations.

Self-control avoids the negative and emphasizes the positive; it looks to the process of management and the function performed. Self-control attempts to improve the managerial process rather than merely to correct individual deviations. Management by objective programs, properly carried out, represent good examples of this approach.

Control self-assessment, which is also designed to encourage self-control, has emerged as an effective approach, especially in the area of soft controls. CSA involves employees in the processes of identifying control problems and suggesting solutions. CSA is covered in more detail in Chapter 10.

Feed-forward controls anticipate future performance problems so that appropriate action can be taken as soon as possible. Forecasting and budgeting are forms of feed-forward or future-directed controls. Practicing managers often neglect future-directed controls and rely instead on accounting and statistical reports. However, these data have inherent time delays, and using them to correct ongoing problems takes time.

Control Problems

Classical controls are like straitjackets. They tend to inhibit people and give rise to resentment. Individual employees may resent management's assignment of control authority over them to an outside person or group. The pressures of accountants to have people conform to budgetary controls may be deeply resented and cause a negative effect on performance, while the same control exercised by someone inside the budgeted organization may not have the same effect. Also, when informal group norms differ from control objectives, the group may resist the controls and sabotage them.

Different managers use different techniques in dealing with the resentment that controls sometimes engender. Such resentment can be minimized by:

- Having the employees participate in establishing the controls.

- Making sure the purpose of the controls is fully communicated.

- Developing general, rather than detailed, constricting controls.

- Using controls to achieve goals rather than to impose strict rules that trigger automatic censure or punishment.

Controlling — The Internal Auditor's Perspective

The internal audit of control systems to determine whether established objectives are being met is discussed in Chapter 2, Controls. Under another approach to controlling, useful both to management and the internal auditor, internal auditors determine how well managers exercise the principles of management control in handling their own operations. Internal auditors may want to use the following standards in evaluating controls:

Setting Standards and Developing Systems of Control

Provisions should be made for establishing and disseminating new standards of performance when the old ones are found to be inadequate or ineffective.

The systems of control should trigger feedback in a timely enough manner to warn managers of impending difficulties and enable them to appraise final results. The product of control should identify the location of the problem and the cause(s) of the variance.

Surveillance over the Operation

Periodic reviews should confirm that the lines of feedback communication are still open and functioning as intended.

A manager should have an up-to-date, documented program that identifies those methods, problems, and conditions that need to be implemented, improved, corrected, or eliminated — a program that shows the status of planned solutions and the corrective action required to meet the organization's objectives and standards.

Efforts should be made to eliminate or reduce the causes of exceptions and deviations rather than accepting such variances as "normal" and covering them with specially designed procedures.

Management should provide for periodic reviews of factors affecting costs of administration and operations and should see that timely and appropriate action will be taken to keep costs consistent with plans and objectives.

Training Personnel

The organization's objectives, standards, policies, procedures, and means of measuring performance should be communicated to all affected personnel. Periodic efforts should be made to reinforce organization-wide understanding, and employees should be provided with the results of feedback from downstream organizations.

Where existing practices represent interference with plans, provision should be made for prompt re-instruction of personnel.

Dealing with Deviations

Methods should be established for returning to the originator work that does not meet acceptable standards.

When existing policies and procedures interfere with the execution of plans, removing the interference must be subject to the approval of the same authority that prescribed those policies or procedures in the first place.

Establishing Master Controls

Management, in establishing its feedback system, should have brought to its attention only problems of importance, not all the routine actions of subordinates.

Where applicable, provision should be made for balancing and reconciling control records with subsidiary or detailed records, bringing variances and their reasons to the appropriate levels of management.

Management should not only provide for reports on all of its operations but also for prompt and effective action on deviations.

Compliance

Provision should be made for actual results to be evaluated with respect to the planned expectations or objectives, particularly for long-range objectives.

Provision should be made for a clear-cut assignment of responsibility for prompt expedition and feedback of information to management on variances between established budgets and schedules and actual accomplishments.

To ensure conformity with established requirements, provision should be made for periodic spot checks — in addition to normal monitoring — of work in process and completed work.

Provision should be made to inform personnel of their failure to comply with prescribed policies and procedures.

Maintaining Control over Processes and Operations

Provision should be made for management's attention to be given to exceptions at the most strategic control points in the system, instead of waiting until the ultimate objective has failed.

When complaints and recommendations are received from customers, provision should be made for all of them to be immediately recorded, evaluated, acted upon, and answered.

Provision should be made for all incomplete work to be systematically followed up in a timely manner to ensure removal of any interference with its completion.

Periodic status reports of work progress should be prepared for management review to determine whether work is progressing according to plan and whether established milestones are being reached.

The control system should provide assurance that all off-schedule and missed-schedule jobs are reported promptly to affected management for corrective action and/or establishment of measures to prevent future occurrences.

Control Specialists

Internal auditors' responsibilities as control specialists should be taken seriously. At the same time, internal auditors must also make every effort to see that managers and employees enhance their knowledge and appreciation of control and its benefit to the organization.

Managing to Ensure an Ethical Environment

As discussed in greater detail later in this text, ethical issues have become increasingly important. One ethics expert has stated:

> Unethical business practice involves the tacit, if not explicit, cooperation of others and reflects the values, attitudes, beliefs, language, and behavioral patterns that define an organization's operating culture. Ethics, then, is as much an organizational as a personal issue.[14]

Management's behavior is an important factor that influences ethical decisions. In today's environment, management's functions must be carried out to ensure an ethical environment. Behavior that may encourage unethical behavior includes:

- Telling staff to do whatever is necessary to achieve results.
- Overloading top performers to ensure work is accomplished.
- Looking the other way when wrongdoing occurs.
- Taking credit for others' accomplishments or shift blame.
- Playing favorites.[15]

Senior management must make sure that an ethical environment is important to the entity. In order to do so they must clearly establish that enforcement of the code of ethics is a major priority. The entity's emphasis on ethics must be communicated to employees, customers, suppliers, and other stakeholders.

Increased workforce diversity could cause senior management to spend additional time and resources on assuring an ethical environment. As one expert notes as immigrants flow across borders, "It may become harder to rely on a shared organizational culture to control ethical behavior. . . Because it is more difficult to infuse common values and beliefs in a diverse workforce, it may become more necessary to emphasize explicit rules, expectations, and ethical codes."[16] U.S. Federal Sentencing Guidelines now encourage management effort to ensure ethical behavior by basing fines to the effort expended.[17]

References

[1]Fayol, Henri, *General and Industrial Management* (London: Pitman, 1949), trans. from the French by Constance Storrs, 1949, originally published in 1916, Chapter 4.

[2]Taylor, Frederick Winslow, *Principles of Scientific Management* (New York: Harper & Brothers, 1911).

[3]Drucker, P.F., *Management: Tasks, Responsibilities, Practices* (New York: Harper & Row, 1954), 430-440.

[4]Dessler, Gary, *Management: Leading People and Organizations in the 21st Century, 2nd Edition* (Upper Saddle River, NJ: Prentice-Hall, 2001), xvii-xix.

[5]Lewin, Kurt, *Field Theory in Social Science* (New York: Harper, 1951).

[6]Maslow, Abraham H., *Motivation and Personality* (New York: Harper and Row, 1970), 2nd Edition, Chapter 4.

[7]Fiedler, Fred E., *A Theory of Leadership Effectiveness* (New York: McGraw-Hill, 1967), 15, 246-255.

[8]McGregor, Douglas, *The Human Side of Enterprise* (New York: McGraw-Hill, 1960), 33-34, 47-48.

[9]Likert, Rensis, *New Patterns of Management* (New York: McGraw-Hill, 1961) and *The Human Organization: Its Management and Value* (New York: McGraw-Hill, 1967).

[10]Herzberg, Frederick, *Work and the Nature of Man* (Cleveland, OH: World Publishers, 1966).

[11]Argyris, Chris, *Integrating the Individual and the Organization* (New York: John Wiley & Sons, Inc., 1964.)

[12]Vroom, Victor, *Work and Motivation* (New York: Wiley, 1964), 17-33, 121-147.

[13]Luft, Joseph, and Harry Ingram, *An Introduction to Group Dynamics* (Palo Alto, CA: National Press Books, 1963).

[14]Paine, Lynn Sharp, "Managing for Organizational Integrity," *Harvard Business Review*, March-April, 1994, 106.

[15]Brumback, Guy, "Managing Above the Bottom Line for Ethics," *Supervisory Management*, December 1993, 12.

[16]Dessler, Ibid., 76.

[17]For a further discussion, see "Management Antifraud Programs and Controls - Guidance to Help Prevent and Deter Fraud," Copyright 2002, by American Institute of Certified Public Accountants, Inc.

Supplementary Readings

Balkaran, Lal, "Corporate Culture," *Internal Auditor*, August 1995, 56-59.

Bhide, A., "How Entrepreneurs Craft Strategies That Work," *Harvard Business Review*, March-April 1994, 150-161

Collins, Rod, "Auditing in the Knowledge Era," *Internal Auditor*, June 1999, 26-31.

Crandall, William, Mark McCartney, and Chris Ziemnowicz, "Internal Auditors and Their Perceptions of Crisis," *Internal Auditing*, January/February 1999, 11-17.

Curtis, Mary B., "Executive Information Systems," *The EDP Auditor Journal*, 1995, 25-29.

Davenport, Thomas H., "The Fad That Forgot People," *Fast Company*, November 1995, 70.

DePree, Max, *Leadership is an Art* (New York: HarperCollins, 1998).

Doyon, Michel, "Tuned-in to Management," *Internal Auditor*, December 1996, 36-41.

Dubinsky, Joan E., "Business Ethics: A Set of Practical Tools," *Internal Auditing,* July/ August 2002, 39-45.

Gavin, Thomas A., "Auditing Business Process Change Initiatives," *Internal Auditing,* May/ June 1999, 8-19.

Gibbs, Jeff, "Auditing on the Edge," *Internal Auditor*, October 1999, 35-37.

Gibbs, Jeff, "Going Live with SAP," *Internal Auditor*, June 1998, 70-75.

Glover, Steven M., Douglas F. Prawitt, and Marshall B. Romney, "Implementing ERP," *Internal Auditor*, February 1999, 40-47.

Hammer, Michael, "Just Do It," interview by Christy Chapman, *Internal Auditor*, June 1998, 38-41.

Jeffords, Raymond, Greg M. Thibadoux, and Marsha Scheidt, "An Internal Auditor's Guide to Facilitating Organizational Change," *Internal Auditing*, July/August 1998, 37-41.

Jeffords, Raymond, Greg Thibadoux, and Marsha Scheidt, "Leadership Skills for Internal Auditors," *Internal Auditing*, September/October 2000, 17-21.

Klein, Gary, *Sources of Power: How People Make Decisions* (Boston: MIT Press, 1998).

Kreitner, Robert, *Management* (New York: Houghton Mifflin Company, 1995).

Leithead, Barry S., "Ensuring Audit Relevance," *Internal Auditor*, April 2000, 68-69.

McGarvey, Robert, "Now Hear This: Lend Your Employees an Ear - and Boost Productivity," *Entrepreneur Magazine*, June 1996, 87.

Noonan, Peggy, *Simply Speaking: How To Communicate Your Ideas with Style, Substance, and Clarity* (New York: HarperCollins 1998).

O'Shaughnessy, John, and McNamee, David, "The Internal Auditor and the Strategic Plan," *Internal Auditing*, Winter 1997, 53-58.

Ratliff, Richard L., and Beckstead, Stephen M., "How World-class Management is Changing Internal Auditing," *Internal Auditor*, December 1994, 38-45.

Sawyer, Lawrence B., "When the Problem is Management," *Internal Auditor*, August 1998, 33-38.

Sawyer, Lawrence, "Talk To Me, Please!" *Internal Auditor*, June 1997, 22-28.

Senge, P.M., *The Fifth Discipline: The Art and Practice of the Learning Organization* (New York: Doubleday, 1990).

Shedd, Timothy B., "Working with Management," *Internal Auditing*, January/February 1999, 37-39.

Stern, Carl W., editor, *Perspectives on Strategy* (New York: John Wiley & Sons, 1998).

Multiple-choice Questions

1. An approach to management based upon the assumption that the parts of an organization operate interdependently and that "the whole is greater than the sum of its parts" is called the:
   a. Universal process approach.
   b. Operational approach.
   c. Behavioral approach.
   d. Systems approach.

2. The managerial approach that seeks to determine, through research, which managerial practices and techniques are appropriate and can be generalized to specific situations is the:
   a. Contingency approach.
   b. Aldag/Dunham approach.
   c. Behavioral approach.
   d. Operational management approach.

3. An auditor was having trouble adjusting to a new supervisor. When a job-related problem arose, the auditor went directly to the audit director without consulting the supervisor. Identify Fayol's principle of management that the auditor violated:
   a. Order.
   b. Division of work.
   c. Scalar chain.
   d. Unity of direction.

4. Identify the management technique in which employees assist in setting goals, making decisions, solving problems, and designing and implementing organizational changes:
   a. Total quality control.
   b. Participative management.
   c. Kanban.
   d. Just-in-time technology.

5. Which situational leadership style would a superior use with a subordinate who possesses very low task maturity for a particular assignment?
   a. Achievement-oriented (delegating).
   b. Consultive (participating).
   c. Directive (telling).
   d. Supportive (selling).

6. A memo from the vice president for manufacturing to the manager of purchasing contained the following: "Effective immediately, parts used in manufacturing will be purchased only from suppliers who already have in place, or agree to implement, programs for statistical process control." This is an example of a(n):
   a. Policy.
   b. Procedure.
   c. Objective.
   d. Goal.

7. An internal auditor's involvement in reengineering should include all of the following except:
   a. Determining whether the process has senior management's support.
   b. Recommending areas for consideration.
   c. Developing audit plans for the new system.
   d. Directing the implementation of the redesigned process.

8. As part of a total quality control program, a firm not only inspects finished goods but also monitors product returns and customer complaints. Which type of control best describes these efforts?
   a. Feedback control.
   b. Feed-forward control.
   c. Production control.
   d. Inventory control.

9. Of the following, who would be responsible for formulating organization strategic long-range plans?
   a. Department manager.
   b. Division superintendent.
   c. Vice president of marketing.
   d. Manager of stockholder relations.

10. The traditional vertical orientation of organizational hierarchies is yielding to horizontal linkages based on need and convenience. The trend is best described as:
    a. Synthesis perspective.
    b. Decentralization.
    c. Networking.
    d. Self-reliance.

11. A vertically integrated organization is best described as one that:
    a. Owns all of its production facilities.
    b. Manufactures the component parts used in its product.
    c. Is departmentalized by product or service.
    d. Fosters very narrow span of control.

12. A Gantt chart is a graphical scheduling technique typically applied to production. The structure of the chart shows:
    a. Cost of dollars plotted against units of output.
    b. The sequencing and relationship of steps in a production process.
    c. Output plotted against units of time.
    d. The "critical path" in a chain of activities.

13. A matrix organization structure is probably most appropriate for which of the following business situations?
    a. A manufacturer producing a single product for only a few customers.
    b. A grocer operating a chain of stores nationwide.
    c. An automobile dealership.
    d. A construction organization with several large projects.

14. A "flat" organization structure is one with relatively few levels of hierarchy and is characterized by wide spans of management, while a "tall" organization has many levels of hierarchy and narrow spans of management. Which of the following situations is consistent with a flat organization structure?
    a. Tasks where little direction and control of subordinates is required.
    b. Work areas that are graphically dispersed.
    c. Tasks that are highly complex and varied.
    d. Subordinates who perform distinctly different tasks.

15. One of the keys to successfully redesigning jobs is:
    a. Creating autonomous work teams.
    b. Enlarging jobs by adding more tasks similar to those being performed.
    c. Rotating workers to different jobs to provide them with variety.
    d. Changing the content of jobs so that they fit workers' need for growth.

16. Planning is important in the business world:
    a. Because of limited resources and uncertain environments.
    b. Because of the need for emphasizing the short range over the long range.
    c. Because of the need for emphasizing the long range over the short range.
    d. Because it is necessary to mold policies and procedures.

17. An organization manufactures barbecue grills, steel mail carts, and aluminum screen door frames. Management recently instituted a practice that allows workers to choose which production line they want to work on each week, prioritize work orders according to urgency, inspect the quality of their output, and pack and label their work for shipping. The practice that management has installed is called:
    a. Job rotation.
    b. Management by objectives.
    c. Job enlargement.
    d. Job enrichment.

18. An organization has decided to build a multimillion-dollar plant to manufacture earth-moving equipment. Top management formed a committee of senior executives with experience in manufacturing, real estate, human resources, municipal law, transportation, and marketing to evaluate several potential plant sites and recommend one that seems best suited to the organization's needs. The committee will be disbanded after its recommendation has been made. Such a group is known as a(n):
    a. Steering committee.
    b. Ad hoc committee.
    c. Standing committee.
    d. Focus group.

19. A production worker in a plant often speaks for the entire workforce when problems arise between labor and management. Although this individual has the same level of authority and expertise as his co-workers, he seems to possess a degree of power that others do not have. What type of power does this individual apparently have?
    a. Coercive.
    b. Referent.
    c. Expert.
    d. Legitimate.

20. Managerial control can be divided into feed forward and feedback controls. Which of the following is an example of a feedback control?
    a. Quality control training.
    b. Budgeting.
    c. Forecasting inventory needs.
    d. Variance analysis.

21. "But I mailed the order four weeks ago giving the supplier plenty of time," said the parts manager when asked why a critical part was not available. The most likely reason for this failed communication between the parts manager and the supplier was:
    a. Lack of feedback.
    b. Confusing language.

    c. Inappropriate medium.

    d. Perceptual selectivity.

22. An organization's strategic plan calls for it "to achieve a 5 percent market share by 2001." Select the term best describing this statement:

    a. Goal.

    b. Budget.

    c. Principle.

    d. Policy.

23. A new auditor is being briefed on various types of audits by the audit supervisor. The supervisor states that some areas within the organization are more difficult to audit because the controls are generally not as clearly defined as in other departments. Select the type of control that is usually most difficult to assess:

    a. Operational.

    b. Hardware.

    c. Accounting.

    d. Physical security.

24. Some management scholars have credited Douglas McGregor with founding the field of organizational behavior by arriving at a modern set of assumptions about people. Identify the basic assumption(s) underlying McGregor's Theory Y.

    a. Employees are lazy and unambiguous.

    b. Employees are concerned only with higher wages.

    c. Employees are component parts of the organizational system.

    d. Employees are energetic and creative individuals.

25. The three basic components of all organizational control systems are:

    a. Objectives, standards, and an evaluation-award system.

    b. Plans, budgets, and organizational policies and procedures.

    c. Statistical reports, audits, and financial controls.

    d. Inputs, objectives, and an appraisal system.

26. Which of the following should be reviewed before designing any system elements in a top down approach to new systems development?

    a. Types of processing systems used by competitors.

    b. Computer equipment needed by the system.

    c. Information needs of managers for planning and control.

    d. Controls in place over the current system.

27. A means of limiting production delays caused by equipment breakdown and repair is to:
    a. Schedule production based on capacity planning.
    b. Plan maintenance activity based on an analysis of equipment repair work orders.
    c. Preauthorize equipment maintenance and overtime pay.
    d. Establish a preventive maintenance program for all production equipment.

28. Which of the following is true of benchmarking?
    a. It is typically accomplished by comparing an organization's performance with the performance of its closest competitors.
    b. It can be performed using either qualitative or quantitative comparisons.
    c. It is normally limited to manufacturing operations and production processes.
    d. It is accomplished by comparing an organization's performance to that of the best-performing organizations.

29. A flexible budget is a quantitative expression of a plan that:
    a. Is developed for the actual level of output achieved for the budget period.
    b. Is comprised of the budgeted income statement and its supporting schedules for a budget period.
    c. Focuses on the costs of activities necessary to produce and sell products and services for a budget period.
    d. Projects costs on the basis of future improvements in existing practices and procedures during a budget period.

30. An appropriate technique for planning and controlling manufacturing inventories such as raw materials, components, and subassemblies whose demand depends on the level of production is:
    a. Materials requirements planning.
    b. Regression analysts.
    c. Capital budgeting.
    d. Linear programming.

31. If a just-in-time purchase policy is successful in reducing the total inventory costs of manufacturing company, which of the following combinations of cost changes would be most likely to occur?
    a. An increase in purchasing costs and a decrease in stockout costs.
    b. An increase in purchasing costs and a decrease in quality costs.
    c. An increase in quality costs and a decrease in ordering costs.
    d. An increase in stockout costs and a decrease in carrying costs.

32. In an economic order quantity (EOQ) model, both the costs per order and the holding costs are estimates. If those estimates are varied to determine how much the changes affect the optimal EOQ, such analysis would be called a:
    a. Forecasting model.
    b. Sensitivity analysis.
    c. PERT/CPM analysis.
    d. Decision analysis.

33. All of the following are useful for forecasting the needed level of inventory except:
    a. Knowledge of the behavior of business cycles.
    b. Internal accounting allocations of costs to various segments of the company.
    c. Information about seasonal variations in demand.
    d. Econometric modeling.

Chapter 26
Environmental Auditing

Introducing the audit. The environmental auditing process. The benefits of environmental auditing. Customers of internal environmental auditing. Environmental auditing guidelines. Types of environmental audits. The management approach of the environmental audit. Environmental audit techniques and strategies. Who performs environmental auditing? Who is the environmental auditor? External environmental auditing. Auditing of environmental remediation liabilities. Assessing audit risk. Substantive audit procedures for remediation liabilities. Using specialists. Evaluating the specialists. Potential problems with environmental audits. Risks of the environmental audit. Internal control. Operational risks and exposures for audit review. Legal exposure. ISO 14000. Audit of the environmental management systems. Legal aspects of environmental audits. Conclusion.

● ●

Introducing the Audit

This book was not intended to provide instruction in the auditing of specific areas. Several contemporary works do this. The book is intended to provide information of a general nature and in appropriate depth for the conduct of progressive internal auditing organizations. Yet there seemed to be several areas where more explicit instruction was needed. These areas were:

- The auditing of computer produced material, and
- Auditing for fraud.

During the interim period between the 4th Edition (1996) and this 5th Edition (2003), two other areas have become so important operationally and in one case financially that the authors believed it to be expedient to develop two additional chapters that would apply to the auditing of these specific areas. These chapters deal with:

- Information systems auditing, and
- Environmental auditing.

The Institute of Internal Auditors (IIA) has taken the lead in this expansion and has, in the later case, established a section of the CIA exam to cover this specific area. The IIA has also created a section to cooperate with an organization that is specifically dedicated to environmental accounting and auditing. Thus, it seems appropriate to discuss the many aspects of the environmental auditing process.

Caring for the environment has assumed an important place in the American culture. We have become aware of the impact that the pollution of air, ground, and water can have on the quality of life, on the enjoyment of the earth's beauty, and on the physical well-being of its inhabitants. Because of this importance, federal, state, and local governments have entered the picture with laws and regulations that are intended to correct and cure the effects of past violations of good environmental practices, and designed to prevent future violations of good environmental disciplines.

Thus, there exists a wealth of material on the "do's" and "don'ts" of environmental activity. And, because the environment has become a matter of national interest, both the "do's" and the "don'ts" have sanctions related to actions that are not considered in the public well-being. So, it is not only an element of national ethics, but a matter of personal and organizational economic interest. Violation of the laws, statutes, and regulations can bring incarceration, fines, and, more importantly, the requirement to pay substantial sums for the costs necessary to clean up environmental messes.

The administrations of the environmental affairs of an organization are complex; this complexity requires the expertise of engineers, lawyers, scientists, accountants, and auditors. We are going to discuss the activities of the last specialist. Environmental auditing is probably more familiar than is environmental accounting, yet both are important and can render valuable service to most organizations whose activities impact on the environmental areas of consideration.

The Environmental Auditing Process

As a part of the management and internal control fabric of the organization, the internal auditor is interested in reviewing the compliance with regulations and statutes, determining the propriety of the accounting for environmental issues, and ensuring that proper disclosure is being made. However, the internal auditor is also interested in the controls that are in place or that should be in place to ensure that environmental problems are kept to a minimum, that environmental operations are efficient and effective, that waste management operations are proper, and that environmental decisions are based on factual information.

The audit team must be qualified for the operation. Thus, in addition to personnel with audit experience and ability, the team should have available to them qualified environmental engineers on a full time basis or as advisors when needed. The audit team should also have legal expertise available as needed. There should be independence and objectivity in the audit operation. The members of the internal audit team should be free from any organizational constraints and should have a direct reporting path to senior management.

The Benefits of Environmental Auditing

It is probably conventional wisdom that the principal benefit of the environmental audit is to ensure compliance with government regulations so as to preclude the threat of fines, penalties, and even criminal involvement. There is no question that this is the basic theme that impels the activity. However, many writers on the subject identify related benefits that have a residual effect on this most important exposure of the organization.

Below is a list of *potential* benefits as identified by four recent writers on the subject. The benefits shown by the first reference are in rank order as to the degree of benefit.

Benefit	Campbell[1]	Dye[2]	Marsh[3]	Thompson[4]
Reduction of fines for regulatory noncompliance	X	X		X
Early identification of problems before regulatory action	X	X		
Reduction of long-term environmental risk	X	X		
Increased assurance about compliance with organization environmental policy	X	X		
Increased management Awareness of environmental issues	X	X	X	
Enhanced reputation for environmental responsibility	X	X	X	
Cost saving from waste Minimization and pollution prevention	X	X	X	X
Increased employee awareness of environmental issues	X	X	X	X

Benefit	Campbell[1]	Dye[2]	Marsh[2]	Thompson[4]
Increased standardization of environmental protection practices	X	X		
Increased assurance of environmental liability accruals	X	X		
Plays a significant role in business planning				X
Employee development				X
Managing legislative and regulatory offers		X		
Ensures Environmental Management Systems are in place and effective		X		
Identifies unknown Liabilities and risks		X		
Provides opportunity for Information sharing between facilities				X
Prepares a facility for an inspection				X

The survey conducted by Campbell and Byington (first column above) contained interesting ratings by those responding. The mean rating for the first item mentioned was 6.12, with a maximum of 7.00. The lowest rating was 4.96. It would appear that those responding believed that there were many substantial benefits of the audit process. Also, there were three benefits that were mentioned in all four papers and three other benefits that were mentioned in three papers.

Campbell and Byington sum up the discussion by emphasizing that environmental auditing places the organization in a proactive rather than a reactive position. Thus, the organization anticipates problems to the degree possible and takes necessary action to prevent them from happening.

Unhee Kim, in her recent excellent book on the subject, also identified a series of benefits. They are reproduced with slight annotation from the detailed discussion that Ms. Kim provided:[5]

1. **International standards organization registration:** When properly performed the audit is evidence of excellence in the handling of environmental issues.

2. **Management division support data:** Provides essential information relative to environmental risks and as the use of resources in the correction of problems.

3. **Liability assurance:** Provides identification of liabilities relative to organizing operations and to future divestiture of the organization.

4. **Measurement tool:** Serves as a measurement tool for assessing performance. Assists in the integration of business and environmental goals.

5. **Compliance management:** Assists in the management of the numerous federal, state, and local laws and regulations vis a vis penalties for noncompliance.

6. **Educational process:** Helps to understand the issues, risks, and management aspects of the environmental function. Can also serve as an educational process for other personnel in the organization.

7. **Public relations and marketing:** Consumers and the public become aware of the organization's desire and activities so as to be a responsible corporate citizen.

8. **Securities and exchange commission:** Provides information for SEC required disclosures. Assists in the management of environmental liabilities and in the review of environmental management systems.

9. **Proactive management:** Provides early information as to incidents and noncompliance issues and allows time for effective remedial action. This can have both an economic and a reputational value.

Customers of Internal Environmental Auditing[6]

Internal auditing has two major customers: the client, the operating organization whose functions will be enhanced by the results of the audit; and management that needs intelligence on the operating units for which it is accountable. In order to accomplish these dual responsibilities, the audit operations should cover the seven areas described in a following section on "Types of Environmental Audits."

Attempts by the EPA to encourage and/or force the conduct of internal audits of environmental operations have had a difficult time primarily because the EPA often had used these audits to determine infractions. Industry and government have resisted such attempts by stating that the internal audit is more an internal management tool and is a means of internally determining and ensuring compliance. The aspect also is more completely covered later.

Environmental Auditing Guidelines

In 1994 The IIA published an Internal Auditor Tool Kit titled *Environmental Auditing: Risk Assessment Guidelines* by Herbert D. Glover and James C. Flagg. This publication will be of great value to audit organizations that are or will be active in the environmental areas. The authors have outlined a series of basic audit steps relative to a classification of three areas of audit activities. They are listed below.

> Pre-audit Activities
> > Select and schedule the facility to audit
> > Select the audit team members
> > Conduct the pre-assessment audit
> Activities at the Site
> > Review environmental management systems
> > Gather audit evidence
> > Evaluate audit findings
> > Report findings to the facility
> Post-audit Activities
> > Issue the draft report
> > Issue the final report
> > Prepare the action plan and implementation
> > Follow-up on the action plan.

The details of the activities in each of the above segments are shown in Exhibit 26-1. Glover and Flagg also have specified staff requirements for non-technically oriented internal auditors. These are shown in Exhibit 26-2.

As will be described next in the section, there are seven different types of environmental auditing:

1. Compliance
2. Environmental Management Systems
3. Transactions
4. Treatment, Storage, and Disposal Facilities
5. Pollution Prevention
6. Environmental Liability Accruals
7. Product

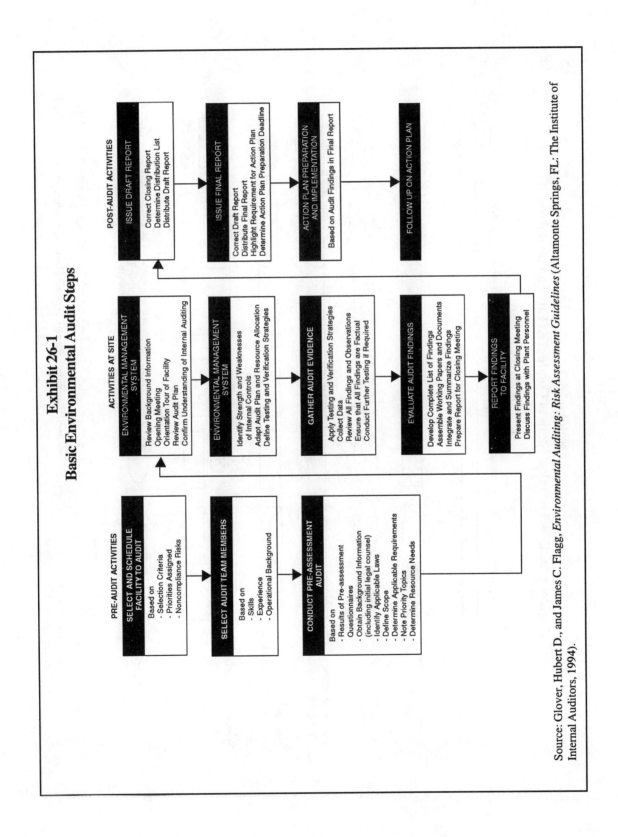

Exhibit 26-1
Basic Environmental Audit Steps

PRE-AUDIT ACTIVITIES

SELECT AND SCHEDULE FACILITY TO AUDIT

Based on
- Selection Criteria
- Priorities Assigned
- Noncompliance Risks

SELECT AUDIT TEAM MEMBERS

Based on
- Skills
- Experience
- Operational Background

CONDUCT PRE-ASSESSMENT AUDIT

Based on
- Results of Pre-assessment Questionnaires
- Obtain Background Information (including initial legal counsel)
- Identify Applicable Laws
- Define Scope
- Determine Applicable Requirements
- Note Priority Topics
- Determine Resource Needs

ACTIVITIES AT SITE

ENVIRONMENTAL MANAGEMENT SYSTEM

Review Background Information
Opening Meeting
Orientation Tour of Facility
Review Audit Plan
Confirm Understanding of Internal Auditing

ENVIRONMENTAL MANAGEMENT SYSTEM

Identify Strength and Weaknesses of Internal Controls
Adapt Audit Plan and Resource Allocation
Define Testing and Verification Strategies

GATHER AUDIT EVIDENCE

Apply Testing and Verification Strategies
Collect Data
Review All Findings and Observations
Ensure that All Findings are Factual
Conduct Further Testing if Required

EVALUATE AUDIT FINDINGS

Develop Complete List of Findings
Assemble Working Papers and Documents
Integrate and Summarize Findings
Prepare Report for Closing Meeting

REPORT FINDINGS TO FACILITY

Present Findings at Closing Meeting
Discuss Findings with Plant Personnel

POST-AUDIT ACTIVITIES

ISSUE DRAFT REPORT

Correct Closing Report
Determine Distribution List
Distribute Draft Report

ISSUE FINAL REPORT

Correct Draft Report
Distribute Final Report
Highlight Requirement for Action Plan
Determine Action Plan Preparation Deadline

ACTION PLAN PREPARATION AND IMPLEMENTATION

Based on Audit Findings in Final Report

FOLLOW UP ON ACTION PLAN

Source: Glover, Hubert D., and James C. Flagg, *Environmental Auditing: Risk Assessment Guidelines* (Altamonte Springs, FL.: The Institute of Internal Auditors, 1994).

Exhibit 26-2
Required Auditor Technical Skills to Conduct an Environmental Audit

Module

Skills	Compliance	EMS	Transactional	TSDF	Pollution Prevention	Liability	Product

Auditing:
Internal Audit Dept. Standards*

Environmental Laws and Regulation**

Applied Science and Engineering**

Industry Practices and Norms

Operating Facility Management Process

Operating Environment:
- Local
- National
- International

High
Medium
Low to Med.
Low

Varies
Very Low

*Skills expected per Standard 200 for each department/auditor to be proficient.
**Int. audit dept. may consider assistance of internal expert to join the environmental auditing team.
EMS = Environmental Management Systems
TSDF = Treatment, Storage, and Disposal Systems

Source: Glover, Hubert D., and James C. Flagg, *Environmental Auditing: Risk Assessment Guidelines* (Altamonte Springs, FL: The Institute of Internal Auditors, 1994).

For each of the audit areas, the writers have provided an introductory overview of the content and operation and then have listed normal objectives and detailed audit guidelines, including a questionnaire and a specific audit program. A classification for scoring results is also provided. The questions used in the scoring process generally come from material developed by acknowledged organizations such as the International Chamber of Commerce. The treatment of each of the audit areas is quite extensive and not appropriate for a chapter whose intent is to discuss generally the subject of environmental auditing. However, an example of steps recommended for one element of Transactional Audits is shown in Exhibit 26-3.

Exhibit 26-3
Steps Included in Typical Site Assessment

Phase I – Preliminary Assessment

Historical Review, for example:
   Land title and ownership history.
   Aerial photographs.
   Municipal directories and records.
   Regulatory governmental agency file.
   Personnel histories (on-site and off-site).

Walk-through Inspection, for example:
   Process and operations.
   Material and waste handling and storage.
   Neighboring properties.
   Underground storage tanks.
   Soil and vegetation damage.

Phase 2 – Detailed Investigation

   Subsurface surveying (soil stratigraphy and hydrogeology).
   Sample collection (solids, liquids, gases).
   Sample analysis (field instruments and laboratories).
   Data interpretation.

Exhibit 26-3 (Cont.)

Phase 3 – Remediation Alternatives

    Determination of cleanup requirements, standards.
    Identification of remediation alternatives.
    Evaluation and testing of alternatives.
    Cost estimation.
    Work plan and scheduling.

Steps Included in Typical Site Assessment

Operational Compliance Assessments

"Operational Compliance Assessments" is a term adopted in this report for investigations that primarily focus on the current adherence of specific operating plants and facilities or all of a company's operations with applicable environmental laws and regulations. The concerns of a lending institution or business acquirer typically extend beyond site cleanup liability to overall compliance with laws and regulations to day-to-day operations. Operational Compliance Assessments are frequently required when a buyer or lender needs to know if a company's operations are causing or likely to cause violations of environmental laws and regulations. These may ultimately result in costly fines, penalties, jail terms, or a suspension of operations.

Source: Glover, Hubert D., and James C. Flagg, *Environmental Auditing: Risk Assessment Guidelines* (Altamonte Springs, FL: The Institute of Internal Auditors, 1994).

The concept is to rate each segment of an audit area as to the risk involved in its function. These risks are converted to a rating score that becomes an indicator of segments that should receive early or even immediate attention.

Types of Environmental Audits[7]

The seven types of environmental audits referred to above have both internal and external objectives. Internal objectives include informing management whether or not:

1. "Operations are in compliance with regulations;
2. "Liability is associated with property transfers;
3. "Contract waste management operations are being performed competently;

4. "Environmental management decisions are being made on the basis of facts;
5. "Environmental liability accruals are appropriate; or
6. "Other activities that are being conducted are consistent and appropriate."

External environmental audits provide assurances to outsiders relative to the information relating to environmental activities that are included in or are a part of the usual financial statements (or that should be).

All environmental audits can be placed into these following seven types. The audits are most likely to be performed as internal audits, or can be contracted for by outside specialist organizations, or can be performed by external auditors — either in their own interests or for the internal auditors. The types are:

1. **Compliance audits:** Determine whether or not activities and operations are within the legal constraints imposed by regulations. They are detailed site-specific assessments of current, past, and planned operations. This classification includes three types of audit activities.

   a. Preliminary assessments that are used to provide insight into potential problem areas, especially where future audit activity should take place.

   b. Environmental audits that are more detailed audits focusing on operations. They include verification of compliance with permits and consent orders.

   c. Environmental investigations/site assessments that are time and labor-intensive assessments, conducted when the preceding phases indicate that there is a risk of contamination or other noncompliance. They include interpretation of technical analyses.

2. **Environmental management systems audits:** Focus on systems in place to ensure that they are operating properly to manage future environmental risks. The audits are conducted internally when the environmental auditing process matures.

3. **Transactional audits:** Also called: (a) acquisition and divestiture audits; (b) property transfer site assessments; (c) property transfer evaluations; and (d) due diligence audits. They are a risk management tool for banks, land buyers, lending agencies, and for any organization purchasing land for a facility site or accepting it as a gift or donation. The potential liability connected with an acquisition can easily exceed the market value of the asset.

4. **Treatment storage and disposal facility:** Audits involve the tracking of hazardous substances throughout their existence. All hazardous materials must be tracked from cradle to grave (creation to destination) and the "owners" of these materials have liability for them as long as the owners exist. The liability also accrues for leasing, managing, or for loaning funds.

5. **Pollution prevention audits:** Operational appraisals that serve to identify opportunities where waste can be minimized and pollution can be eliminated at the source rather than controlled at the end of the process.

6. **Environmental liability accrual audits:** Technical legal reviews involved with quantifying and reporting liability accruals for known environmental issues.

7. **Product audits:** Appraisals of the production process of a facility. The objective is to provide assurance that the product is in compliance with restrictions and with environmentally sensitive interests.

These audits may be exclusively performed by internal or external audit staffs. They can be performed individually or in combinations. They are of use to operating units, to senior management, and in the preparation of financial statements.

The Management Approach of the Environmental Audit

Much of this chapter is generally descriptive of various aspects of performing the environmental audit. However, this section is pointed toward considerations relative to starting and performing the audit. Here, we are guided by the excellent materials of Ralph Rhodes in his contribution to Kim's *Environmental and Safety Auditing.*[8] The basics of this aspect of the audit program are:

- Gaining management support.
- Developing a basic audit plan.
- Establishing a reasonable and solid starting operation.
- Selecting and training staff.
- "Minimizing mistakes."

Management may not always be enthusiastic about environmental auditing. For one thing it is an expensive operation because of the quality of the staff necessary to perform the audit. Not only are skilled auditors required, but environmental engineers and scientists and skilled and knowledgeable attorneys are also needed. Also necessary are travel, facilities, consultants, and, most important, as a by-product, funding for the disclosed potential cost of correcting the situations that the audit may identify.

The audit concept must be sold to management as a safety device. If properly performed, the audit will:

- Assist in compliance with laws and regulations.

- Identify areas where the organization is developing problems that could result in sizeable remediation costs and penalties; also possible criminal action against the organization and its individuals.

- Serve to improve community acceptance because of efforts to conform to safe, legal, and ethical practices.

- Assist in establishing liabilities needed for financial reporting.

- Create a closer relationship with the Environmental Protection Agency because of the aspect of self-policing.

There are other management benefits, mainly operational. However, the above seem to be those that would capture management's interest in agreeing to sponsor the activity. This support is important because the audit may not be popular with operating segments of the organization who will view the audit as dysfunctional and fraught with potential costs and possibly resulting in future complexity of operations.

In planning the early audits, the chief audit executive should ensure that the investigation is:

- In an area where management is supportive.

- A relatively non-complicated operation.

- A reasonably simple type of audit function.

Thus, success in the small early environmental audits is generally held in the audit community to be essential for developing credibility and a cooperative attitude on the part of clients.

The audit staff should, for credibility as well as performance, be experienced auditors who have been exposed to environmental situations. They should have a basic knowledge of the legal, engineering, and physical aspects of environmental activities. It may also be necessary to have specialists available to provide not only instructions but also advice and even direction to the audit teams.

One of the important aspects of the audit is the disclosure of information in working papers and reports. These communications can be used by governmental agencies as evidence of infractions and can be further used as the basis of governmentally assessed costs and penalties. Thus, lawyers to evaluate these communications are essential as a part of the audit teams.

Kim's Issues on the Environmental Audit[9]

The usual environmental audit starts somewhat similarly to the normal performance audit. However, because of the potential exposure to action by government regulatory agencies, there are some unique aspects. Kim has listed a series of "issues" that should be considered. Several of the special items deserve an additional brief comment. The unique issues that Kim identified are:

- Team selection and pre-audit preparation.

- Facility preparation.

- Protection of attorney-client privilege for audit reports.

- Legal review of audit information and information control.

- Scoring or ranking systems and the use of such systems.

- Corrective action plans and readiness plans.

- Defined use of audit information for senior management and facility management.

The objectives of the audit will set the stage for all of the audit activities that follow. This is not much different in character from the usual audit, but the contents do have a unique aspect. The characteristics of the audit will be responsive to the objectives. The latter should be analyzed and the audit should be designed to accomplish them. The content of working papers and reports will be very sensitive because of the potential exposure of information that could have an adverse legal compliance or financial effect.

Type and frequency of audits are similar to normal performance audits. The type should be one that will accomplish the program's objective. However, the frequency should be risk assessment driven.

The concept of scope in the usual performance audit includes integrity of information, efficiency and economy, effectiveness, internal control, and the safety of assets. In the environmental audit, scope has a topical relationship, although the audit contains appropriate operational breadth. The primary elements of the classification are environment, safety, industrial hygiene, compliance, and operational performances.

The team selection is especially important because of the previously mentioned unique areas of expertise that are needed. It is possible that some of the audit staff will be external specialists. As a matter of fact, if environmental auditing is performed on a sporadic basis, it would be far more economical to engage these specialists as needed. The alternative is to retain a core environmental audit staff, if continuous audits are anticipated. The specialty areas that would probably be needed are environmental engineering, environmental chemistry and physics, and environmental legislation and regulations.

Appropriate work experience for the environmental audit staff as defined by ISO 14012.2 is the development of skills and understanding in some or all of the following:

- Environmental science and technology

- Technical and environmental aspects of facility operations

- Relevant requirements of environmental laws, regulations, and related documents

- Environmental management systems and standards

- Audit procedures, processes, and techniques

To all of the above should be added good interpersonal relations, especially in this new audit area where the stakes are so high and the potential for problems is so possible.

The audit team should have preliminary meetings for indoctrination and to obtain familiarity with the objectives of the audit; to understand the method of auditing that will be used; to learn the responsibilities of each of the specialty areas; and to understand the coordination of the various team elements. There should be a team leader who is knowledgeable of the organization's culture and philosophy and who has a familiarity with all of the multifaceted aspects of the specifics of environmental auditing.

The actual audit activity should be similar to the usual performance audit. There should have been a preliminary survey that includes reviews of documents relating to the audit; interviews with personnel who are engaged in operations that may have an environmental impact; and a walk-through or physical observation of the audit area. Following these activities the audit team should develop an audit program after identifying the risk areas and assessing the degree of risk and thereby setting priorities for the audit process.

The reporting process is more complicated because of the complexity of the functions and their interdisciplinary aspects and also because of the potential legal and regulatory aspects of the disclosures. All audit programs, working papers, and especially the reports — including drafts — should be reviewed by legal counsel. This procedure helps to ensure an "Attorney-Client Privilege-Confidential," a degree of protection when disclosures could cause major problems. Kim suggests that the report should, "unambiguously summarize three important items:[10]

- "Compliance status of the facility as to federal, state, and local laws and regulations.

- "Facility conformance with company corporate policies, procedures, and goals.

- "The management system as it exists and its effectiveness in a manner appropriate to assist senior management and site personnel with decision and action plan implementation."

Environmental Audit Techniques and Strategies

The strategy for conducting an environmental audit is much like the strategy for conducting ordinary audits with the exception that the elements of the strategy are unique to the environmental area. It is to be presumed that both internal and external audit functions are well organized and integrated and that the audit staffs are knowledgeable as to the normal audit operations. Briefly, the elements of the strategic approach include:

1. Objective: The objective should be clearly stated as to whether it is to determine compliance, examine operations to establish methodology, propriety, determine costs, set up potential liability, or whatever.

2. Personnel: Based on the above objective, the audit team qualifications should be determined. This could include knowledgeable auditors, engineers, scientists, and legal talent.

3. Non-audit assistance: A description of the non-audit assistance that will be needed. This may include non-audit organizational staff and outside technical, legal, and scientific consulting organizations.

4. Audit scope: The scope of the audit as to the portions of the organization to be covered.

5. Documentation: Information should be collected as to government regulations and statutes, industry and government environment standards, and state-of-the-art technology for operations and for environmental aspects pertaining to the organization.

6. Plans: Plans should be established for the audit. These plans should include: (1) the interaction of the various disciplines; (2) the degree of testing and scientific exploration that will be necessary; (3) the methodology that will be used for cost estimating; (4) the techniques of audit control that will be used; and (5) a risk evaluation program.

7. Audit program: There should be a plan for a preliminary survey and the resultant audit program.

8. Scheduling: The segments of the audit should be scheduled as to time requirements and sequence.

9. Time element: Identification of the time element. How much time is to be required and what contingency plans are to be considered under specific identifiable conditions?

10. Facilities and equipment: Facilities and equipment that will be needed for the audit should be identified as well as indication of the planned sources and estimates of cost.

11. Cost estimates: Based on the above, calculation of the funding that will be required and indication of the potential sources of these funds in total and by time increments. Development of contingency plans for possible problems both temporary and in total. Problems may impact on the above elements of the strategy.

12. Criteria: Criteria for materiality, sampling precision, and other qualitative elements of the audit should be established.

13. Potential findings: Anticipation of the potential disclosures of the audit and plan for the implementation of the audit findings. This involves the commitment of top management and the knowledge by organizational management segments that corrective action may be required.

14. Plans for review: Plans for review by the client, by legal experts, by engineering and scientific experts, and by management should be set. Methods of resolution of differences should be set and agreed to.

15. Report: The report format should be set. Also plans should be made for establishing a rough outline of the report content as soon as the preliminary survey has been completed.

16. Report distribution: The distribution of the audit report should be established and approved by the audit and legal specialists and by senior management.

17. Media: Relations with media representatives should be planned. There should be a single spokesperson appointed and adequate notice given to all other parties to keep a strict silence. Consider the sensitivity of potential findings. Develop plans with legal assistance as to such aspects as media relations, working paper content, governmental relations, and internal security. Make provisions with legal assistance for the fully descriptive and complete working papers that support the audit effort so as to protect the organization in case of legal and/or regulatory problems.

18. Regulation update: A methodology should be established for keeping currently informed as to environmental regulations at all levels of government. Also, ensure that this information is distributed to organizational officials who have a need to know.

19. Recalcitrant clients: Develop plans for responding to recalcitrant clients. In this respect, ensure that top management is in full support of the audit effort in case that clients' problems do occur.

Each of the above areas should have contingency plans that will go into effect if the original plans are jeopardized and must be materially altered.

The chief audit executive is the normal contact and coordinator of the external audit operations and should, if cosourcing is needed, arrange with the external auditors or specialists as to their appropriate area of the strategic plan.

Who Performs Environmental Auditing?

Most of the writers on environmental accounting and auditing tend to mention the benefits of the auditing process. We can assume that there is value in the audit since it has become an integral part of many auditing programs and especially because of the requirements in most environmental legislation that audits be conducted. There is not complete agreement, however, as to who should perform the "audits." One would presume that the "audits" would be done by an internal auditing organization. However, such is not always the case, at least not universally so. Campbell and Byington in their survey of environmentally related industry groups reported that:[11]

Internal auditing had:				
No involvement	42.9%			
Slight involvement	22.3	}	}	}
Small involvement	19.4	} 41.7%	}	}
Moderate involvement	5.9		}	}
Considerable involvement	4.7		} 52.3%	}
Great involvement	2.4			}
Maximum involvement	2.4			} 57.1%
Total	100.0%			

Nevertheless, much of the literature that is evolving on the subject is originating in the field of internal auditing, even though the normal internal audit staff may not contain the several needed specialized areas of expertise. It can be assumed, however, that the auditing methods practiced by lawyers, engineers, and environmentalists will use the auditing techniques developed and practiced by internal auditors.

Who is the Environmental Auditor?

The preceding section provided statistics that showed that very little environmental auditing was performed by internal auditing organizations. It is possible that this situation is caused by the scarcity of environmental auditors on the internal auditing staffs. The question then arises — what is an environmental auditor and can the traditional internal auditor function as such?

A study by Kite, Louvens, and Radtke on industries that would normally utilize environmental auditing provided some interesting differences between the background characteristics of internal auditors and environment auditors.[12] They are listed on the following page.

- Environmental auditors have been with their employer 14.2 years compared to 9.5 for internal auditors. It could be that the organizations are using auditors with greater experience as environmental specialists. It would also be interesting to know how long the environmental auditors had been in an auditing capacity; although the next two items explain some of this.

- Environmental auditors have been in their current position 3.2 years compared to 2.9 for internal auditors. One explanation could be that the traditional internal auditing position in many organizations is an entry-level position for employees who are considered as being promotional into operating positions. It also could indicate that the environmental audit staff was more stable because of the specialist work they performed.

- Environmental auditors had 4.5 years of auditing experience compared to 7.8 for internal auditors. This supports a theory that many of them are specialists in disciplines other than traditional performance or financial auditing.

- Environmental auditors had .1 year experience in public accounting compared to 1.8 for internal auditors. This tends to support the position that the former are essentially specialists in fields other then performance auditing.

- 5.4% of the environmental auditors were CPAs while 42.3% of the internal auditors were certified. This measure also tended to support the theory that the former were specialists with technical backgrounds and experience.

- 20.8% of the environmental auditors had undergraduate business degrees compared to 96.2% of the internal auditors. This comparison also suggests that the environmental auditors have undergraduate technical or legal backgrounds.

- The environmental audit group had 41.1% graduate degrees compared to 34.1% for internal auditors. This statistic, when combined with the item immediately above, supports the contention that many of the environmental auditors are specialists who have later been taught how to audit.

Thus, it appears evident that the current environmental audit organizations are composed of technical specialists and of internal auditors who bring to the audit the traditional audit approach and more importantly the concept of "professional skepticism" that frequently is the key to important disclosures.

External Environmental Auditing

External auditors must be familiar with the environmental aspects of reviewing assets and liabilities; assets to determine: (1) that the valuation is proper; (2) that contamination has not reduced the carrying value of the assets; and (3) that the expending and capitalization of remedial costs have been recorded properly. The external auditors will also determine that financial statements reflect actual and potential liabilities of the organization. Here, the auditors must, either by themselves or with environmental experts, determine that the organization is complying with governmental regulations in the handling of emission of pollutants, the disposition of contamination and waste, and the detoxification of previously contaminated assets.

In addition, the external auditor must determine whether the client, as a result of the acquisition of new properties and assets, may be exposed to or actually have incurred liabilities as a result of the previous contamination of the acquired assets. The external auditor must also determine that proper disclosure in compliance with EPA and SEC regulations has been made.

Auditing of Environmental Remediation Liabilities[13]

The general guidance for auditing of environmental issues is based on current directives of the rule-making bodies concerned with the auditing in the public and private sectors. There is also specific guidance in that the content of these directives can be interpreted so as to apply to the environmental activity. With this direction in mind it becomes apparent that the audit staff engaged in these audits must have the skills necessary to address this complex and difficult subject. These staff requirements then infer that there be environmental specialists, engineers, scientists, and at times lawyers available on a full-time or an intermittent basis to address the technical issues that will arise during the audit.

Essentially the audit consists of planning, performing, and reporting in accordance with GAAS so as to conform to the requirements of applicable legislation. Following is an abstract from an AICPA SOP release on this environmental issue.

Planning. The auditor should obtain a level of knowledge about matters related to the nature of the entity's business, its organization, and its operating characteristics that will enable the auditor to plan and perform the audit in accordance was GAAS. Examples of such matters that pertain to environmental remediation liabilities include the following:

- What policies and procedures are in place to identify potential environmental remediation liabilities or related contingencies affecting the entity?

- Has the entity been designated as a potential responsible party (PRP) by the EPA under the Superfund laws or by state regulatory agencies under analogous state laws?

- If the entity has been designated as a PRP, are there any pending civil or criminal investigations or actions?

- Have regulatory authorities or environmental consultants issued any reports about the entity, such as site assessments or environmental impact studies?

- Are landfills or underground storage tanks used to store or dispose of environmentally hazardous substances?

- Is the entity required to have environmental permits, such as hazardous waste transporter permits or hazardous waste treatment, storage, and disposal permits?

- For property sold, abandoned, purchased, or closed, are there any requirements for site cleanup or for future removal and site restoration?

- Have there been any violations of environmental laws, such as the Superfund laws and the corrective action provisions of RCRA? (see Appendix A)

Assessing Audit Risk

Inherent risk. This element of the audit is prescribed by existing audit standards and directives. However, the above-mentioned release provides that certain transactions, such as past acquisitions involving real property (including acquisitions by a creditor pursuant to default by a debtor), may expose an entity to environmental remediation liabilities. Under the Superfund laws, current and former owners of land may be responsible for cleanup costs. Situations such as the following may indicate the existence of potential environmental remediation liabilities:

- Past or current ownership of property on which hazardous substances are being or were disposed of

- Recent purchases of property at prices that appear to be significantly below market

- Sales of contaminated land under arrangements whereby the seller retains responsibility for cleanup pursuant to indemnification clauses

- Aborted real estate sales transactions

- Sales of businesses involving the retention of real property by the seller

Control risk. The auditor should follow SAS 5 relative to the evaluation of the entities' control structure, i.e., the control environment, the accounting system, and the control procedures. Here, again, the auditor must view these control elements in the light of environmental operations and should perform such tests of the controls as are deemed necessary.

An organization in the UK has developed a method of rating environmental risk, acting as an outside consultant.[14] The rating allows organizations to present an evaluation of their environmental conditions on a quantitative series of scales. The rating is based on a report considering the following:

- Publicly available information

- Site and head office interviews

- Direct costs that are accumulated such as:
  - Compensation
  - Plant rebuilding and cleanup

- Indirect costs that are estimated:
  - Costs of loss of reputation
  - Loss of sales
  - Poor employee morale
  - Damaged relationships with governments, lenders, and investors

Third-party liabilities and the proceeds of insurance payments are offset and the adequacy and implementation for handling hazards are estimated. Comparisons are then made with the industry's best practices and ISO 9000 standards. The organization's environmental management system is reviewed and evaluated. The final report includes recommendations as to how conditions can be improved.

Substantive Audit Procedures for Remediation Liabilities[15]

The auditor may evaluate the reasonableness of estimates of environmental remediation liabilities by reviewing the process used by management to develop the estimate and by performing procedures to test it. This approach often is the most appropriate when the estimates are developed by or based on the work of an environmental specialist.

1. Identify whether there are controls over the preparation of accounting estimates and supporting data that may be useful in the evaluation. Some of the more common controls over the preparation of estimates of environmental liabilities that might be considered by the auditor include:

- The nature and extent of monitoring of the entity's consideration of environmental matters by senior management or the board of directors.

- The nature and extent of procedures in place for assessing compliance with applicable environmental laws and regulations and for evaluating possible violations.

- The nature and extent of procedures in place for monitoring the entity's environmental exposures, and in developing the estimates involving appropriate operating, financial, legal, and compliance personnel.

- The information systems used by the entity to compile and access data about the entity's waste generation, emissions, and other environmental impacts.

- The entity's use of environmental specialists, including its procedures for determining whether the specialists have the requisite competence in environmental remediation matters, knowledge of the entity's business, and understanding of the available methodologies for calculating environmental remediation cost estimates.

- The procedures in place for verifying that data about the nature, destinations, and volumes of hazardous substances or wastes are appropriately collected, classified, and summarized.

- The procedures in place for assessing the appropriateness of industry or other external sources of data used in developing assumptions (for example, information provided by other PRPs, regulatory authorities, and industry associations) and, where applicable, for substantiating such information.

2. Identify the sources of data and factors that management used in forming the assumptions, and consider whether such data and factors are relevant, reliable, and sufficient for the purpose, based on information gathered in other audit tests. Sources of data and factors used may include:

- Internal company records, such as those that accumulate payroll costs of employees dedicated to remediation efforts.

- Information from published sources about trends in socioeconomic or other factors that might affect environmental remediation liabilities, such as inflation rates, judicial decisions, and enacted changes in legislation affecting remediation methods or definitions of hazardous substances.

3. Consider whether there are additional key factors or alternative assumptions about the factors. Key factors that might be considered include:

- An entity's insurance coverage for environmental liabilities.

- Information about environmental remediation liabilities or contingencies included in the response to the inquiry of the entity's attorney.

- Studies or reports by environmental consultants.

- Reports, notices, or correspondence issued by regulatory authorities.

4. Evaluate whether the assumptions are consistent with each other, the supporting data, relevant historical data, and industry data.

- Allocations of remediation responsibilities (and consequently the attendant liabilities) among PRPs.

- Remediation techniques, including whether they are based on existing or proposed technologies and requirements, and the expected time frames.

- Post-closure monitoring requirements.

5. Analyze historical data used in developing the assumptions to assess whether the data are comparable and consistent with data of the period under audit, and consider whether the data are sufficiently reliable for the purpose.

6. Consider whether changes in the business or industry may cause other factors to become significant to the assumptions.

7. Review available documentation of the assumptions used in developing the accounting estimates and inquire about any other plans, goals, and objectives of the entity, and consider their relationship to the assumptions. Consider the following, for example:

- Practices concerning the resolution of environmental contingencies that may have a significant effect on the entity's ultimate liability (for example, a practice of vigorously contesting remediation plans proposed by regulators as opposed to a practice of tacitly accepting those plans).

- Plans to sell, dispose of, or abandon specific facilities.

8. Consider using the work of a specialist regarding certain assumptions.

9. Test the calculations used by management to translate the assumptions and key factors into the accounting estimate.

Using and Evaluating the Specialists

In several places in this chapter it has been indicated that, because of the complexity of environmental auditing, the audit team should be augmented (cosourced) by individuals or organizations who represent rather unique disciplines such as:

Attorneys, knowledgeable in environmental affairs.
Environmental engineers.
Environmental management specialists.
Environmental scientists.
Individuals who are specialists in governmental environmental laws, regulations, and required reporting.

The internal auditing organization should be responsible for assuring that the specialists (cosources) are competent to perform their contribution. The responsibility for the audit cannot be fragmented and the input of the specialists actually becomes material indigenous to the audit. If there are inaccuracies caused by the outsiders, they become those of the responsible auditor or audit organization.

The internal auditing organization should:

- Obtain independent references for similar work.

- Research the specialist in Dun & Bradstreet or another suitable reference.

- Ask the specialist for evidence disclosing prior similar work.

- Have interviews conducted by knowledgeable organization officials.

- Require the specialist to describe in a formal proposal the work that will be done.

- Contact industry or professional associations for references — or at least comfort letters.

- Contact governmental organizations relative to credibility and acceptance of work.

There are probably more; however, the above should provide good indications as to whether to engage the individual or firm. If one or more are being considered, the technical and professional aspects should be considered before money aspects are brought into the decision. The point to remember is that the specialist's work that is performed bears the impremature of the internal auditing activity. A good specialist may lend credibility. A bad specialist cannot be used as an excuse for poor work.

Potential Problems with Environmental Audits

The environmental audit process itself may be fraught with potential problems, most of them related to the uniqueness of the area being audited and also to the specialized approach that is characteristic of this type of auditing. Some of these exposures would include:

1. Inadequately defined organizational philosophy on environmental risk management. Thus, the audit group does not have a firm foundation on which to develop the audit process.

2. The audit staff may lack the expertise to perform an audit in the specialized environmental area. This expertise could include that of scientists, engineers, lawyers, and environmental specialists.

3. The audit organization may be using out-of-date audit tools.

4. The environmental audit report may not be accurate nor agree with the technical evaluations justified in working papers.

5. The report may not contain facts and may offer unsubstantiated opinions.

6. Dramatic and exaggerated items may be presented.

7. Because of the Freedom of Information Act and the required transmission of the audit report and associated working papers to the government, organization-sensitive information may be available to competition and to others.

8. The audit report (and supporting working papers) can be used as evidence of violations.

9. When audit recommendations are not implemented, problems can occur when the situation becomes known by the EPA.

The audit organization, together with legal counsel, should carefully review working papers and audit reports to reduce the vulnerability of the organization as much as possible. However, it must be kept in mind that nondisclosure of information discovered during an audit can also be considered by EPA and the SEC as (criminal) noncompliance with government regulations.

Risks of the Environmental Audit

There are risks associated with the environmental audit activity. These are risks apart from those environmental operating risks that are potentially harmful to persons or to the environment itself. Those risks have been described earlier. The risks relating to auditing arise from the audit process itself or as a result of an audit finding such as the reporting of noncompliance with environmental regulation. A listing of these risks includes:

1. Use of audit report against the organization in a regulatory action.*ø

2. Substantial cost; personnel and technical.*ø

3. Loss of public trust if problems are disclosed.*ø

4. Lack of financial or technical ability to solve problems.*ø

5. Self-reporting may not eliminate potential for civil penalties.ø

6. An environmental audit may be discoverable (legal) in an enforcement action or litigation.ø

7. Findings are so frequent or complicated that employees are overwhelmed.ø

---

*Campbell, op. cit.
øThompson, op. cit.

Regardless of these risks, the knowledge gleaned from the audit is valuable from a management standpoint. It will give information as to the effectiveness of the Environmental Management Program. However, the audit reporting should be coordinated with the legal staff so as to minimize any risks relating to reporting of noncompliance with laws or regulations, or risks resulting from operating activities in good faith that resulted in environmental conditions that were dangerous.

Internal Control

Both the internal and external auditors should review internal controls as related to environmental operations. The internal auditors are responsible for the general review of internal controls under Standard 2120. This section includes compliance reviews relative to procedures, laws, and regulations. External auditors are required to review internal controls by SAS 55. Their review should "focus on control procedures over the generation, transfer, elimination, and cleanup of toxic substances."[16]

These internal control audit procedures should extend themselves to the consideration and creation of liabilities for potential costs related to possible environmental agency sanctions, or for costs that will be incurred in cleanup and other remedial actions.

Both sets of auditors should hold discussions with management and ultimately with legal counsel, internal and external, covering these controls and as to potential litigation, claims, and assessments related to environmental activities and situations. Both audit groups should review an organization's legal fees with the intent of determining if there are any fees that are related to unrecorded litigation or to other undisclosed environmental related activity. If so, the auditors should fully investigate the situation and, based on this investigation, ensure that proper liabilities are established. In this connection, the auditors should determine the impact of such liabilities on the organization's resources or as to possible claims on these resources.[17] Correspondingly, there should be a consideration as to the entity's ability to continue as a going concern for a period of one year beyond the next balance sheet date (SAS 59).[18]

Operational Risks and Exposures for Auditor Review

What are the operational activities that internal and external auditors should review?

1. Does the organization use toxic materials in its production operation?

2. Does the organization, in its operation, emit hazardous materials into the environment?

3. Has or does the organization operate motor pools or similar operations that could contaminate the ground?

4. Does the organization's manufacturing operation create hazardous waste?

5. Does or has the organization operated on-site storage operations of hazardous supplies, materials, or waste?

6. Does the organization monitor the service contractor who disposes its hazardous waste or materials?

7. Has the organization had environmental studies made of properties and/or organizations that it has acquired?

8. Has the organization loaned money to other organizations that might be at environmental risk?

9. Has there been a violation of any of the federal, state, or local statutes or regulations other than those identified above?

10. Is there a possibility that the organization might be designated as a potential responsible party (PRP)?

11. Have actual and potential liabilities been identified and properly computed?

12. Does the organization have an adequate environment management operation? (Current literature contains articles that describe in detail the requirements for such an operation.)

13. Is there a potential for personal liability action?

14. Is there documented evidence of the possibility of environmental problems that have not been reviewed?

15. Is there a possibility that adjacent properties that may be contaminated have been acquired or are being considered for acquisition?

The above list probably does not comprise a complete list of the exposures. The auditor should be alert to similar types of situations and schedule for review those that are material. A method of establishing the priority of risks would be to assign an index for materiality and an index for probability. The combination of these two indexes can establish a priority measure. However, it should be recognized that some risks would require mandatory prompt attention.

Legal Exposure[19]

Organizations are vulnerable to environmental laws and regulations enacted by the federal government, by states or provinces, and by local governments. In the United States the major legislation is the 1980 Comprehensive Environmental Response, Compensation and Liability Act (CERCLA). The law was passed to curb the widespread disregard for the public, resulting from improper treatment of contamination and other situations. The act is very broad and contains the provision to coerce organizations to clean up sites that have hazardous wastes. However, if the organizations do not or cannot clean up, CERCLA will do it for them and charge for the service. The act establishes audit tests and procedures and prescribes the methods to be used in estimating cleanup costs. The Act is used as a model for general government regulation. The Resource Conservation and Recovery Act and the Toxic Substances Control Act are patterned after it, as are acts of several states. CERCLA also provides for strict record keeping relative to hazardous material storage and disposition. Fines and imprisonment can result from failure to perform as the act provides.

Liability is very broad and relates to individuals and organizations such as:

- Present and prior owners of the property.

- Any person or organization who transported or participated in the decision to use the site for disposal.

- Lenders.

- Lessees under long-term leases.

- Successor organizations whose predecessors would have been liable if they still existed.

There are provisions for potentially responsible parties (PRPs) to be able to escape the liability by showing that due care was taken to prevent a spill but that it occurred as a result of: (1) an act of God; (2) war; or (3) an omission of an unrelated third party. Also, if an organization acquires contaminated property and shows that it made "reasonable inquiry," it can escape liability.

ISO 14000, "The Audit of Environmental Management Systems"[20]

During the early 1990s, ISO 14000, a Publication of the International Organization for Standardization, stated that:

> "... achieving sound environmental performance requires organizational commitment to a systematic approach and to a continual improvement."[21]

It holds that one of the most important elements of the achievement of this condition is the organization and operation of an Environment Management System. It describes the system and then states that the system should be periodically audited to assure its efficiency. A summary of both of those aspects is given below.

The ISO sets 10 management principles for the environmental management systems:[22]

1. Recognition that the environment management system is one of the organization's highest priorities.

2. Establishment and maintenance of both internal and external communications.

3. Determination of the legislative and environmental aspects associated with activities, products, and services.

4. Development of commitments of all in the organization to environmental protection and the assignment of responsibilities and accountabilities.

5. Promotion of environmental planning in the products and processes.

6. Establishment of management discipline for targeted performance.

7. Provision of appropriate resources and timing to achieve performance targets.

8. Evaluation of performance against objectives, policy, and targets and developing improvements where possible.

9. Reviewing, monitoring, and auditing of the environmental management system to identify potential improvements.

10. Encouragement of vendors to establish environmental management systems.

Sayre goes on to say that, in compliance with the ninth item above, the operation should be audited "to determine conformance to requirements and agreements."[23] Implied in this provision is the need to assess the effectiveness of the system in precluding the occurrence of activities or events that could result in financial, cultural, or social deleterious impact. He provides a systems checklist that contains a series of areas to be reviewed:[24]

- Environmental policy: substance and objectives

- Environmental aspects and impacts: covering design, assignment of activities organizational interfaces, and production process planning

- Environmental objectives and targets

- Environmental plans and programs: includes legal aspects, production processes, and treatment of products

- Human, physical, and financial resources, including equipment calibration, resources, and training

- Organizational alignment and integration

- Accountability and responsibility of key personnel and of subcontractors

- Environmental values

- Knowledge skills and training

- Communication and reporting

- Documentation including procedures

- Records and information management

- Emergency preparedness and responsibilities, including plans, procedures, and training

- Measuring and monitoring, including performances indicators, monitoring of subcontractors, continuous monitoring of special processes that are critical to environmental exposure, and statistical control

- Review of the Environmental Management System on a periodic basis

- Corrective and preventive action and continual improvement, including nonconformance reporting

It is apparent that the environmental management system is a most important element of environmental protection. Each of the other types of environmental auditing would review an activity that would relate to a facet of the management overall responsibility. The amount of detail that would be included in the audit programs is prodigious. Reference should be made to ISO 14000 and its associated publications.

Sayre identifies a close relationship between ISO 14000 and ISO 9000 — quality control — especially relative to management procedures. He cites 10 such systems called for by ISO 9000 that he believes should also be the target of ISO 14000 audits. These characteristics and their relative weights are:[25]

System Element	Weight
Document Control	20
Design Control	12
Purchasing	10
Inspection & Testing	10
Process Control	8
Inspections	8
Contract Review	6
Corrective Actions	5
Management	4
Quality Records	3

Examples of findings for each of the above elements are shown in Exhibit 26-4.

Exhibit 26-4
Examples of Findings for System Elements

System Element	%	Common Issues
Document Control	20	• Documentation for a specific decision-making/ implementation process lacking • Documentation outdated and not available at relevant employee locations • Lack of non-falsifiable way of assuring that procedures and manuals actually followed at all times
Design Control	12	• Little/no documentation for engineering calculations and design assumptions • Outdated versions of engineering drawings not reliably eliminated from circulation • No adequate proof as to when certain changes/ modifications occurred
Purchasing	10	• Insufficient documentation regarding criteria used in purchasing process and lack of adherence to them • Insufficient validation that criteria used actually correlates to technical and quality requirements and specifications • Insufficient validation that purchasing personnel sufficiently trained to make certain decisions • Insufficient data regarding ability (and track record) of vendors and subcontractors to meet contractual requirements
Inspections & Testing	10	• Insufficient documentation that no incoming product was released before inspected or verified to conformity • Insufficient documentation as to inspection criteria to be utilized
Process Control	8	• Insufficient work instructions for employees and inadequate process monitoring during production and installation • Lack of specific criteria for workmanship in written form or by representative samples • Special and unique/proprietary processes not documented/validated sufficiently

---

Exhibit 26-4 (Cont.)

Inspection	8	• Insufficient records regarding timing and completeness of measuring control, calibration, and maintenance of measuring and test equipment • Inadequately defined procedures for testing and calibration • Insufficient assessment of causes incase equipment is found out of calibration and what remedial actions were taken • Insufficient environmental controls to assure fitness for use • Inadequate safeguarding of facilities, hardware and software from any action that would invalidate calibration
Contract Review	6	• Inability to demonstrate each contract was reviewed to assure capability to meet contract requirements
Corrective Action	5	• Inadequate documentation to provide investigation for cause, and corrective actions taken to eliminate problem • Lack of preventive action to deal with potential significant risks • Lack of ongoing controls to assure corrective actions implemented and remain effective
Management	4	• Inadequate verification that programs have actually been responsibly implemented • Employees not given adequate resources and training to carry out functions to necessary extent
Quality Records	3	• Lack of maintenance and retrievability of quality records • Lack of non-falsifiable proof that certain records were compiled on day/time indicated and by qualified and authorized personnel

---

The audit is intended to determine compliance with legal and procedural specifications, determine the efficiency and effectiveness of operations, provide information for management decision-making, and determine the validity of the financial aspects of the environmental activities of the organization.

The Structure of the Environmental Management System Audit[26]

As a part of the audit program, the auditors should analyze the gaps between the requirements of ISO 14001 and actual operations of the Environmental Management System. The auditor should classify the degree of implementation as follows:

0   Nothing.
1   Program exists but no implementation.
2   A program exists, is partially implemented but is uncontrolled.
3   A system exists and is implemented but does not meet the intent of ISO 14001.
4   The system is implemented and meets the requirements of ISO 14001.[27]

Based on the above, the auditor should develop recommendations relative to priorities and action items. In the process of developing these recommendations the auditor should assemble the substance of a series of factors.[28]

1. The size of the project. Will it be a major operation or merely a modification?
2. The size of each gap.
3. How can each gap be filled?
4. The availability of current information.
5. The nature and types of approvals needed.
6. Deadlines and timings.
7. Integrating with the organizations activities.
8. Resources required.

The environmental management system audit should be designed to determine that:

1. The environmental management system is compliant with regulations, good business practices, and ISO 14000.
2. The system is properly implemented and maintained.
3. The system provides for continual monitoring of emissions.
4. The system is operating effectively.
5. There is an active records retention component.

Organizations should determine the frequency and scope of the audits and the independence and reliability of the participants in the conduct of the audit. A follow-up procedure, preferably by individuals independent of the operation and, conceivably of the audit activity, should be in place.

Legal Aspects of Environmental Audits

During the 1999 IIA International Conference in Montreal, Canada, a presentation on environmental auditing was made by Robert Daigneault, an attorney in the Canadian firm, Lapointe Rosenstein. He discussed the legal aspects of the requirement for such audits and, although the recommendations were based on Canadian law, the material is important to consider, even for other countries' guidance.

He stated that audits should be performed for:

> Regulated undertakings (companies).
> Potentially hazardous undertakings (companies).
> Companies potentially liable.
> Others.

He then described the four classifications as:

Regulated Undertakings:

- "Means any undertaking subject to environmental rules, restrictions controls, and standards impressed by the law:
- "Compliance is the essence:
- "Presentation and corporate liability is the threat:
- "Due diligence is the minimum managerial requirement."

Potentially hazardous undertakings:

- "Usually but not necessarily regulated undertakings:
- "An incident may cause environmental prejudice and trigger environmental liability:
- "Prevention is the essence:
- "Costly corrective action is the threat as well as prosecution and liability:
- "Due diligence once again the requirement."

Companies potentially liable:

- "If not in the above categories, may still be liable through administrative liability:
- "Environmental liability often transferred to innocent persons such as lenders, purchasers, etc. ('administrative or statutory liability'):
- "Usually no escape if conditions for liability are met:
- "Foresight is the essence:
- "Costly corrective action is the threat:
- "Contingency planning is the requirement."

Others:

- "Nearly any business – even commercial – has some environmental effect:
  - ✓ Resource contamination such as energy, raw material:
  - ✓ Waste production:
  - ✓ Land use (buildings, parking lots storage areas all have environmental effects):
  - ✓ Nuisance (noise, dust, smell, etc.):
- "To be environment – friendly is the essence:
- "Negative corporate image is the threat:
- "Acting as a responsible citizen is the requirement."

He then described situations where liability under Canadian law would be established for regulated organizations and potentially hazardous organizations:

- "By virtue of the decision to enter the regulated field, the regulated person can be taken to have accepted certain terms and conditions of entry (R vs. Wholesale Travel Group Ltd):
- "This means that a person is deemed to know the rules regulating his activities and cannot argue that they are too restrictive or difficult to comply with."

And where Regulatory Rules are set ...

- "Liability may occur even when no environmental consequence results from noncompliance (compliance is the essence):
- "Environmental consequences will be relevant when determining the fine, or when setting the appropriate due diligence standards (the higher the probability for the extent of the prejudice, the higher the standards of care)."

Potentially hazardous organizations:

- "The *Environmental Quality Act* applies to all citizens. It is a law of general application. In the case of an unregulated Potentially Hazardous Undertaking, operations may be in compliance with rules of general applications and nonetheless be a cause of an illegal situation (e.g., pollution may occur through equipment failure like a suddenly leaking tank:
- "If someone knew (or should have known) that something illegal under its control could happen, and did not take reasonable care to prevent it from happening, that person would be liable of an offense:
- "Liability rests upon control and the opportunity to prevent, i.e., that the accused could have and should have prevented the pollution (R vs. Sault Ste Marie)."

His position is that the organization and those members who are responsible for its actions must exhibit "due diligence." His primary points are that due diligence:

- "Is taking all reasonable and appropriate measures to avoid breaking the law:
- "Applies to the operation as well as to the contingencies:
- "Applies to the staff as well as to the corporation:
- "Is to be proven by the defendant:
- "Is better proven through documentary evidence:
- "May result in an acquittal even though an offense has been committed."

Although these descriptions and their discussion are based on Canadian law, they provide an example of usual legal aspects that must be considered.

Conclusion

It is apparent that the area of environmental auditing is probably one of the most dynamic and important subjects to come to our recent attention. The exposure of organizations and individuals is unbelievably large. This exposure is not only financial but also can result in public censure fines or incarceration. It is a subject with which auditors, both external and internal, as well as accountants must become familiar. It is an enormous area under the influence of environmental protection organizations and departments of justice at all levels of government.

The important message is that of compliance with law and regulation and prevention of incidents. However, as with all worldly activities, there will be problems and, thus, auditing becomes a primary issue. Costs and associated liabilities must be established on an objective and realistic basis. Also, in the United States both the EPA and the SEC have strict requirements for disclosure. Keep in mind that this subject has both civil and criminal potentials.

Auditing by internal and external auditors must be the safety valve — the control that helps to ensure that there will be a minimum exposure to serious problems and that if the problems occur, that the requirements of the government agencies are met.

The task will not be easy. There is already a very large body of knowledge, many regulations, and case law with which one must be familiar. Knowledge of the sources of information will be an absolute requirement. Reliance on memory of the details will be dangerous because of the dynamics of the subject.

A suggestion — develop a literature data bank and keep it current. Use it continually on jobs and engagements. It can and must be done.

Appendix A
Major Legislation Affecting the Environment

- **The River and Harbor Act of 1899**
  This act prohibits the discharge or deposit of any refuse matter of any kind or description...into any navigable water or a tributary of navigable water in the United States. The requirements of this Act could have restricted any and all discharges from factories into waterways during most of its existence, but was narrowly interpreted to apply only when a discharge would impede navigation." (U.S. Code Title 33 Chapter 9)

- **The Oil Pollution Act of 1961 (Amended in 1973)**
  This act prohibits the discharge of oil or oily mixtures from a tanker or ship, "unless such discharge is for the purpose of securing the safety of the ship, presenting damage to a ship or cargo, or saving a life at sea." There are both criminal and civil penalties provided, with fines ranging up to $10,000. Persons who willfully discharge oil from a ship or tanker can be imprisoned for periods not to exceed one year. (1990 33 USCA 2701-2761)

- **The Clean Air Act of 1970**
  This Act originally provided for abatement orders and fines up to $50,000 per day for unlawful emissions of hazardous substances into the air. It has been amended several times, each time becoming more stringent. Numerous attempts to strengthen it further failed in the 1980s; it has not been amended since 1977. However, it is likely that amendments to strengthen the Act will pass Congress in the near future. President Bush's initiatives to clean up the air are expected to cost the industry $20 billion over the next 10 years. (42 USC 7401 Amended 1990)

  These initiatives include: (EPA 400K 93-0014/1993)

  - Requirements that auto makers build all new cars to meet California's tough standards for reducing tailpipe emissions for hydrocarbons/nitrogen oxide.

  - Force 107 of the Midwest's dirtiest industrial plants to drastically reduce sulphur dioxide emissions.

  - Mandate use of the best technology available to reduce emissions of 200 cancer-causing toxic substances.

  - Phase out during the next 10 years the production and use of fluorocarbons widely used in refrigeration and air conditioning systems.

- **The Water Quality Improvement Act of 1970 and the Clean Water Act of 1972**
  These two Acts expand the coverage of water discharges to include both oil and other hazardous substances. (USC 42 4371)

- **The Resource Conservation and Recovery Act (RCRA) of 1976**
  This major legislation was enacted in reaction to the public's fear of widespread health problems that might occur if there were other sites similar to Love Canal. The Act attempted to establish a "cradle to grave" tracking system to identify the generators, transporters, treaters, disposers, and storers of hazardous waste. It should be noted, however, that the definition of what constitutes hazardous waste may change over time. The Act was intended to initially establish a database of information related to hazardous waste sites and to regulate the disposal of hazardous wastes. In addition, the legislation was intended to mitigate an increasing problem of "orphaned waste sites." Such sites are defined as dump sites no longer currently in use and with no one ready to admit responsibility for having disposed waste at the abandoned site. Without such information, it is difficult for the EPA to identify and charge the polluters for the cleanup of the site.

  The RCRA significantly changed the emphasis of environmental protection toward identifying the parties responsible for pollution and establishing responsibility for cleaning up environmental damage. The RCRA is important because definitions of pollution change over time. A company that is in compliance with existing law at one point may be found retroactively responsible for cleaning up a site even if were in compliance of laws as they had existed at that one point. (USC 42 Chapter 82 Amended 1986)

- **The 1984 Hazardous and Solid Waste Amendments to RCRA**
  These amendments expanded owner responsibility for cleanup hazardous waste contamination at licensed waste facilities. The amendments also created the underground storage petroleum tanks. (USC 42 Chapter 82)

- **The Comprehensive Environmental Response, Compensation, and Liability Act of 1980 (Also referred to as the Superfund Act) (CERCLA)**
  The Act created a $1.6 billion fund (since increase) to give the EPA the authority and power to act quickly in cases of "imminent impairment" from hazardous substances. The fund is not intended to permanently absorb the costs of cleanup; if responsible parties are identified, they will be forced to reimburse the government for any costs incurred. The original fund was supported by taxes on the petrochemical industry. (USC 42 Section 9601)

- **Superfund Amendments and Reauthorization Act of 1986 (SARA)**
  This Bill increased the amount of the trust fund to $8.5 billion and reauthorized EPA authority for five years. The increased trust fund is supported by taxes on the petroleum industry, chemical industry, and general corporations. (USC 42 Section 9601)

The 1980 CERCLA legislation and the 1986 SARA legislation are together referred to as the Superfund laws. The acts give the EPA the authority to:

- Search for and identify potentially responsible parties (Peps) who will be made financially responsible for cleanup of hazardous waste sites.

- Coordinate cleanup activities.

- Recover costs of cleanup.

- Recover its own administrative costs from responsible parties.

A potentially responsible party is defined as:

- Current or past owners of vessels or facilities used to handle hazardous waste.

- Generators of waste.

- Transporters of waste.

- Any person who arranged for hazardous waste disposal by contract.

The legislation also created the Leaking Underground Storage Tank (LUST) trust fund to provide federal funding for state programs that clean up tank leaks and address contamination problems. The trust fund is limited, however, so the LUST legislation has implications for businesses such as service stations that must remove underground tanks and test surrounding soil for contamination. The fund is not intended to defray costs, but to provide an expedient method for the government to initiate action.

1. National Oil & Hazardous Substances Pollution & Contingency Plan (Part of the 1990 Act).
2. National Priorities List - Hazardous Ranking System.
3. Site Redemption Enforcement Under RCRA.

Source: Rittenberg, Larry E., Susan Fricano Haine, and Jerry K. Weggandt, "Environmental Protection: The Liability of the 1990s," *Internal Auditing*, Fall 1992.

Appendix B
Examples of Potential Environmental Liability Red Flags

Sources of information	Red Flag
Client inquiry/analytical review	
Auditor experience and familiarity with the industry, the lending environment (prime rate, etc.) and the real estate market.	➤ Client participated in real estate or corporate merger-consolidated transactions during the period in question.
Cash	➤ Client engaged in borrowing or lending activities with a higher-than-expected interest rate (possible "premium" charged to cover environmental risk).
Prepaid assets (insurance, etc.)	
Liabilities	➤ Client purchased land at a price significantly below local market (possible "bargain" sale due to environmental risk).
Notes receivable/payable	
Significant changes in other assets and liabilities	➤ A deal fell through that would have involved the client as a seller of real property.
Insurance expense	➤ Client made a piecemeal sale of assets (retaining real property).
Attorney-professional fees	
Loan losses	➤ An environmental audit was authorized or performed.
	➤ A risk assessment or estimate of cleanup costs was made.
	➤ Client was involved (as borrower-lender) in a transaction where the lender decided not to foreclose despite a default situation.

Sources of information	**Red Flag**
Review of corporate minutes	
Executive sessions	
Board of directors	
Shareholder meetings	
Review of legal documents	
Earnest money contracts	➤ Client agreed to provide an indemnity to another party or agreed to contractual allocations of potential liabilities.
Loan agreements	
Contracts for sale or purchase of land.	➤ Client agreed to obtain additional insurance coverage against environmental risks or liability to third parties.
Merger-acquisition documents	➤ Client became a fiduciary of a trust that includes land or stock of a closely held company among its assets.
Trust agreements	
Lease agreements	➤ Client agreed to perform periodic environmental audits or to restrict use of certain property.
Test of transactions	
Acquisition cycle	➤ Client purchased real property.
Payment cycle	➤ Client paid additional legal-professional fees relating to "deal" that fell through or to performance of environmental audit.

Sources of information	Red Flag
Audit of cash accounts	➢ Client set up new escrow accounts, letters of credit or set-asides.
Audit of notes receivable and payable	➢ Past due note: lending client has not foreclosed on property securing past-due note receivable or borrower client still has possession of real property securing a defaulted note payable.
Review of adequacy of insurance	➢ Client obtained additional insurance coverage against environmental risks or liability to third parties.

Source: Specht, Linda B., "The Auditor, SASSY and Environmental Violations," *Journal of Accountancy*, December 1992, p. 71.

Appendix C
What's Unique About Environmental Obligations

	Traditional Obligations	Environmental Obligations
• Time span involved	• Relatively well-defined short to medium-term.	• Ill-defined, more long-term (i.e., intergenerational)
• Degree of interdependence	• "Self-contained" liability	• High degree of interdependence — what other parties do or experience is critical
• Ease of estimation	• Relatively easy to estimate	• Inherently difficult to estimate
• Stewardship concept	• Traditional private property, shareholder stewardship concept	• Common property, stakeholder stewardship concept
• Contractual basis	• Explicit contract between known transacting parties, usually two-party contract with well-defined rights, benefits and obligations	• Implicit social contract with unknown, "invisible" parties, usually multi-faceted contract with ill-defined right, benefits and obligations
• Valuation basis	• Fair market transaction values	• Court-arbitrated values
• Philosophical orientation	• Economic orientation • Anthropocentric (center on human beings) • Entity specific	• Recognition of non-economical impact on other habitats • Multi-species orientation • Ecosystem specific

Source: Rubinstein, Daniel B., "Natural Capital and Invisible Interests in Natural Resources," *The CPA Journal*, (Canada) March 1992, p. 30.

References

[1]Campbell, Sharon N., and J. Ralph Byington, "Environmental Auditing: An Environmental Management Tool," *Internal Auditing*, Fall 1995, 13-15.

[2]Dye, Kenneth M., "Environmental Auditing," a presentation to the 11th Biennial Conference for Governmental Auditors, International Consortium of Government Financial Managers, September 1995.

[3]Marsh, Trela, and Gene H. Johnson, "A Total Quality Management Approach to Environmental Auditing," *Internal Auditing*, Fall 1995, 5-6.

[4]Thompson, Julie, "Environmental Auditing," a presentation to the class in "Applied Internal Auditing" at Florida International University, February 4, 1996.

[5]Kim, Umhee, *Environmental and Safety Auditing* (New York: Lewis Publishers, 1997), 9-14.

[6]Robbins, Nick, "Environmental Auditing - A Tool Whose Time Has Come," *Multinational Business*, No. 2, 1991, 20-21.

[7]Thompson, Rebecca P., Thomas E. Simpson, and Charles H. Le Grand, "Environmental Auditing," *Internal Audit*, April 1993, 20-21.

[8]Kim, Ibid., 83-101.

[9]Ibid., 87.

[10]Ibid.

[11]"Environmental Auditing: An Environmental Management Tool," *Internal Auditing*, Fall 1995, 17.

[12]Kite, Devan, Timothy J. Louwers, and Robin R. Radtke, "Environmental Auditing, an Emerging Opportunity," *Internal Auditing*, Winter 1997, 13.

[13]American Institute of Certified Public Accountants, *Environmental Remediation Liabilities*, SOP Exposure Draft, June 30, 1995.

[14]Barber, Jonathan, Frances Daly, and Martin Sherwood, "Rating Environmental Risk," *Certified Accountant* (UK), March 1997, 42-43.

[15]Ibid.

[16]Connell, David W., and Barbara Apostolou, "The Internal Auditor's Responsibility for Environmental Issues," *Internal Auditing*, Spring 1992, 51.

[17]Ibid., 55.

[18]Ibid.

[19]Hines, Dan R., and George S. Jackson, "Environmental Problems: How Far Must You Go?" *Practical Accountant*, March 1994, 52-54.

[20]Sayre, Don, *Inside ISO 14000* (Delray Beach, FL: St. Lucie Press, 1996).

[21]Ibid., 5.

[22]Ibid., 14-15.

[23]Ibid., 134.

[24]Ibid., 188-199.

[25]Ibid., 138.

[26]Voorhces, John, and Robert A. Woellner, *International Environmental Risk Management* (Boca Raton, FL: CRC Press, 1998), 225-26.

[27]Ibid., 196.
[28]Ibid., 197.

Supplementary Readings

Black, Ron, "A New Leaf in Environmental Auditing," *Internal Auditor*, June 1998, 24-27.

Cahill, Lawrence B., "The Value-Added Compliance Audit," *Internal Auditor*, June 1998, 28-31.

Holland, Linda K., "Health, Safety, & Well-being," *Internal Auditor*, August 1999, 88.

Kite, Devaun, Timothy J. Louvens, and Robin Radtke, "Environmental Auditing: An Emerging Opportunity," *Internal Auditing*, Winter 1997, 10-15.

Label, Wayne A., and Paulette R. Tandy, "ISO 14000 Environmental Management Systems: New Opportunities and Responsibilities for Internal Auditors," *Internal Auditing,* March/ April 1998, 3-8.

Picard, Robert R., "Environmental Management: What's Auditing Got To Do With It?," *Internal Auditor*, June 1998, 32-36.

Quirvan Mendoza, Carmen, and Alejandro Hazera, "A Survey of Environmental Management in Mexico," *Internal Auditing,* March/April 1998, 9-22.

Rezaee, Zabihollah, "ISO 14000," *Internal Auditor*, October 1996, 56-61.

Ross Coker, Diana, and Kathy S. Moffeit, "Evolving Standards for Environmental Liabilities," *Internal Auditing*, Fall 1996, 42-48.

Multiple-choice Questions

1. An auditor experienced in air quality issues discovered a significant lack of knowledge about legal requirements for controlling air emissions while interviewing the manager of the environmental, safety, and health (ESH) department. The auditor should:
   a. Alter the scope of the audit to focus on activities associated with air emissions.
   b. Share extensive personal knowledge with the ESH manager.
   c. Take note of the weakness and direct additional questions to determine the potential effect of the lack of knowledge.
   d. Report potential violations in this area to the appropriate regulatory agency.

2. Internal auditing in environmental operations is interested in:
   a. Compliance with governmental regulations.
   b. Accuracy of remediation liabilities.
   c. Operation of environmental management systems.
   d. All of the above.

3. An audit to determine whether an organization is organized to manage environmental risks is:
   a. A compliance audit.
   b. An environmental management audit.
   c. A transactional audit.
   d. None of the above.

4. Which of the following is not a unique issue in the performance of environmental audits?
   a. Audit team selection.
   b. Legal reviews of audit working papers and reports.
   c. Frequency.
   d. Protection of attorney-client privilege for audit reports.

5. The environmental audit field work is complete, the working papers have been assembled, and the report draft has been finished. Probably the most important reviews that should be made are that of:
   a. The legal staff.
   b. The audit policy board.
   c. The financial policy staff.
   d. The audit techniques staff.

6. An organization is being accused of improperly handling contaminated waste. The organization has reviewed its internal operations and finds them to be adequate. The internal auditors are called in to examine the operations. When might be the areas of greatest risk for the auditors to first examine:
   a. The contractor transporting the contaminated material.
   b. The storage of contaminated waste within the plant.
   c. The internal transporting system for the waste.
   d. The review operations conducting the survey.

7. State University has been deeded property within the industrial complex of City X. The property is very desirable for the expansion plans of the university. What should the university do?
   a. Accept the property. There is no indication of contamination.
   b. Accept the property. The grantor states it is free from contamination.
   c. Conditionally accept the property. Ask the grantor to have tests performed.
   d. Refuse the property.

8. Corporation X acquires Company ABC. Funds for the acquisition are provided by Bank XYZ. A year later the Environmental Protection Agency (EPA) finds that Company ABC has violated Federal EPA regulations and is liable for large fines and remediation costs. Which organization(s) is/are liable?
   a. Original owners of ABC.
   b. Original owners of ADC and Corporation X.
   c. Corporation X.
   d. Original owners of ABC, Corporation X, and Bank XYZ.

9. Inherent risk as to environmental costs can expose:
   a. A creditor acquiring property pursuant to default by a debtor.
   b. A bank financing an acquisition of a property later determined to be in violation of EPA regulation.
   c. A donee of property later determined to be contaminated.
   d. All of the above.

10. There are problems related to environmental audit. Which of the following is not now such a problem?
   a. Release of audit reports to the government may disclose confidential information to competitors.
   b. The audit report can be used as evidence of violations.
   c. The report if not implemented can be used by the EPA to cause problems.
   d. The audit staff may lack necessary expertise.

Chapter 27
Employee and Management Fraud

Nature of fraud. Definitions. Elements. Creating the proper environment. Conditions that spark fraud. Organized crime and fraud. Computer crimes. Forensics in fraud investigations. Risk analysis. Internal audit responsibility. History. Standards. Due professional care. Follow-up. Documentation. Reporting of fraud. Authority to probe. Three factors related to fraud. Difficulty of detection. Forms and indicators of fraud. Analytical auditing. Trend and proportional analyses. Verifying transactions. Access device fraud. Investigating fraud. Interviewing. Investigative process. Auditing for cyber fraud. Audit programs for fraud examiners. Hazards in interrogations: Libel and Slander. False imprisonment. Malicious prosecution. Compounding a felony. Confessions and admissions. Behavioral aspects of fraud. Prevention. Codes of conduct and hot lines. Created errors. Management fraud, reasons, actions to take, the symptoms. Controlling management fraud. U.S. Sentencing Commission Guidelines.

● ●

Nature

Wrongdoing by deceit goes by many names. It has been called fraud, white-collar crime, and embezzlement, among other things. None of these embraces the full spectrum of deceptive and illegal practices in the public and private sectors of society.

Fraud, briefly stated, is a false representation or concealment of a material fact to induce someone to part with something of value. This definition does not include employee peculations, extortion, or the conversion to one's own use of assets already in the custody of the wrongdoer. The Institute of Internal Auditors has referred to fraud as encompassing an array of irregularities and illegal acts characterized by intentional deception. It can be perpetrated for the benefit or to the detriment of the organization and by persons outside as well as inside the organization."[1]

White-Collar crime has been defined as a wrongful act or series of acts committed by nonphysical means and by concealment or guile to obtain money or property, to avoid payment or loss of money or property, or to obtain business or personal advantage.[2] But many forms of wrongdoing engaged in by employees and managers are not crimes and many are perpetrated by people who do not fit the category of white-collar workers.

Embezzlement is the unlawful conversion to personal use of property that is lawfully in the custody of the wrongdoer. This is a crime with a narrow meaning. It does not include such crimes as bribery, theft, fraud against the government, obtaining property by threats of violence or disclosure, or the like.

These three terms have special meaning for the ordinary lay reader that are more useful than the broader terms of deceit, wrongdoing, and impropriety. In this chapter, the gamut of wrong-by-deceit in the public and private sectors shall be referred to as employee and management fraud. It is distinguishable from outright theft by its active concealment of the wrongdoing.

The 1996 Report to the Nation on Occupational Fraud and Abuse estimated that firms lose six percent of their gross revenue to "occupational fraud and abuse" which is defined as "the use of one's occupation for personal enrichment through the deliberate misuse or misapplication of the employing organization's resources or assets."

Because of the enormous sums involved and the potentially disastrous effects of fraud and associated wrongdoing, internal auditors are being expected to put such unsavory activities under the spotlight of their audit surveillance.

Elements of Fraud

Fraud can take many forms. It may result from an intentional misrepresentation — the suggestion that something is true, when it is not, by someone who knows it is not. It may be a negligent misrepresentation — the assertion as a fact of that which is not true by one who has no reasonable grounds for believing it to be true. It includes concealment — the suppression of a fact by one who is bound to disclose it. It also includes false promises — a promise made with no intention to fulfill it.

The elements of legal fraud, or deceit as it was called in common law, are:[3]

- A false representation of a material fact, or in some cases an opinion.

- Made with the knowledge of its falsity or without sufficient knowledge on the subject to warrant a representation (often referred to as *scienter*).

- A person acting upon the representation.

- To his or her damage.

The elements of so-called white-collar crime are somewhat different. These have been described as:[4]

- Intent to commit a wrongful act or to achieve a purpose inconsistent with law or public policy.

- Disguise of purpose through falsities and misrepresentations employed to accomplish the scheme.

- Reliance by the offender on the ignorance or carelessness of the victim.

- Voluntary action by the victim to assist the offender as a result of the deceit practiced.

- Concealment of the crime.

The Federal Bureau of Investigation defines white-collar crime as "those illegal acts characterized by deceit, concealment, violation of trust, and not dependent upon the application or threat of physical force or violence. Such crimes are committed to obtain money, property, or services; or to secure personal or business advantage."[5]

Environment

Employee and management fraud is a poisonous weed that flourishes in a permissive climate where the seeds of fraud are helped and even invited to grow and mature.

The environment within an organization is generally developed and maintained by senior management and the board of directors. To deter fraud, the environment should be a rigorous one. Management should set forth clearly in written policies its commitment to fair dealing, its position on conflicts of interest, its requirement that only honest employees be hired, its insistence on strong internal controls that are well policed, and its resolve to prosecute the guilty.

The policy is an important first step in demonstrating the entity's resolve to reject fraud in all its forms. The policy should be carefully drafted, with input from the organization counsel. These elements should be considered in establishing the policy:[6]

- All illegal activity, including fraud for the benefit of the organization, is prohibited.

- The responsibility for conducting investigations will be clearly defined. Usually this is assigned to security or internal auditing or both.

- Any employee suspecting wrongdoing is required to notify immediately his or her superiors or those responsible for investigations.

- Any suspected wrongdoing will be investigated fully.

- All suspects and perpetrators will be treated consistently, regardless of position held or length of service.

- Managers are responsible for knowing exposures to wrongdoing and for establishing controls and procedures to deter and detect suspected wrongdoing.

- Managers are required to cooperate fully with law enforcement and regulators, including reporting to law enforcement and supporting prosecution.

- Cover-ups and retaliation against witnesses are strictly prohibited.

- All investigations of wrongdoing will be reported to the board of directors audit committee.

- All wrongdoing will be reported to the bonding organization, and bonding claims will be filed.

- A formal conflict of interest program will be established that requires annual statements by all appropriate personnel, including board members, of freedom from any actual or perceived conflicts.

In addition to a permissive climate, three other conditions combine to move people to commit fraudulent acts:

- *Situational pressures on employees.* Employees may be in debt or may be pressured (externally or internally) to improve their positions. Also, employees of organizations faced with lost sales, strong competition, rigorous schedules or specifications, harsh regulations, or falling profits, may do what is illegal or unethical to reverse their or their organization's position.

- *Uncontrolled access to assets, coupled with management's indifference.* One of the strongest deterrents to employee and management fraud is the certainty of detection and punishment. Strong controls and rigorous monitoring increase that certainty.

- *Personality traits that undermine personal integrity.* Some people have a tendency to take the crooked path. When others see no obstacles placed in that path, they are inclined to take it too.

Neither managers nor internal auditors can do much about an individual's situational pressures. These are not usually communicated readily. However, organizations can establish counseling programs and loan assistance facilities. Also, managers can reduce the perceived opportunities by installing appropriate controls, and internal auditors can evaluate controls.

One of the most effective ways of deterring dishonest conduct is by not hiring dishonest employees. The least management can do is to try to verify backgrounds. Too often, personnel departments fail to check references or contact former employers, even when employees are hired for sensitive positions. Senior management should insist on proper hiring practices; internal auditors should see whether those practices are carried out as intended.

Crime and Fraud

Employees may be induced to steal under the direction of organized crime. One method used to rob an organization is to have extra cartons, rolls, or other packages of merchandise loaded on a truck of a given purchaser. Organized crime takes the difference. The criminals refer to employees who help steal disposable merchandise as "10 percenters." The employees receive 10 percent of the value of the stolen goods.

Organized crime obtains lucrative gains from stolen credit cards. In one organization, strict control was maintained over credit cards from the time the blanks were purchased until the cards were sent to the post office for mailing to customers. A postal employee diverted the credit cards to an organized crime mailing address for the purpose of fraud. Organizations in the credit card business also suffer losses by reason of counterfeit credit cards. A comparison of identification numbers with a central record to detect duplication is an important form of protection.[7]

Officers and employees as well should be aware that fraudulent acts against the government would make them party to possible violation of four federal fraud statutes:

- The false statements statute, 18 U.S.C. 1001.
- The false claims statute, 18 U.S.C. 287.
- The mail fraud statute, 18 U.S.C. 1341.
- The conspiracy statute, 18 U.S.C. 371.

For example, officers and employees involved in improperly charging costs incurred under a fixed price contract to a government cost-plus contract may be violating the false statements statute that reads as follows:

Whoever, in any matter within the jurisdiction of any department or agency of the United States, knowingly and willfully falsifies, conceals, or covers up by any trick, scheme, or device a material fact, or makes any false, fictitious, or fraudulent statements or representations, or makes or uses any false writing or document knowing the same to contain any false, fictitious, or fraudulent statement or entry, shall be fined not more than $10,000 or imprisoned not more than five years, or both.

Federal law also provides remedies to organizations that have been victimized by fraud. The Racketeer Influences and Corrupt Organization (RICO) Act of 1970, 18 U.S.C. 1961, was designed initially to flush out crime from the channels of commerce. But the scope of RICO extends to white-collar bandits who have no connection to organized crime.

Under the act, organizations that have been victimized can sue for three times their losses plus attorney's fees and costs. Examples of the application of RICO are as follows:

- The manager of a regional office sells inventory for his own benefit and files false monthly sales reports with the home office (mail fraud). Once the second false report is filed, he has participated in the affairs of the enterprise through a pattern of racketeering activity and his action comes within the purview of RICO.

- A purchasing agent receives payoffs from suppliers. The payoffs are acts of commercial bribery and the supplier and the purchasing agent have conspired to participate in the affairs of the enterprise through a pattern of racketeering activity.

- A precision-tool manufacturer deliberately misrepresents the performance of parts by mail and in telephone conversations. The parts maker had conducted its affairs through a pattern of racketeering activity and had economically injured the enterprise.

Where such patterns of wrongdoing are uncovered, internal auditors should bring to the attention of management the enterprise's rights under the RICO Act.[8]

Computer Crimes

Computer crimes keep escalating. Only a small percentage of those committed are uncovered, and the amounts involved boggle the mind. The methods and means used to defraud enterprises and agencies are legion, and the detection of all computer frauds is but a wishful dream. The best protection against computer fraud is prevention. Preventive controls include such matters as:

- Personnel screening.
- Definition of duties.
- Segregation of duties.
- Dual access.
- Professional ethics.
- Licensing.

- System design controls.
- Physical-access security.
- Electronic-access security.
- Internal controls and edits.
- Fear of detection.

A recent authoritative book on fraud quoted material from the *AICPA Audit and Accounting Manual* relative to areas of vulnerability for fraud. The areas and recommended controls to offset the inherent risk are reproduced below.[9]

- "The computer functions are not fully segregated from users. For example, a using department may create source documents, enter them into the system, operate the computer, and produce output. This environment poses risks such as deliberately concealed errors, unauthorized master file changes, inadvertent input errors, and lost or corrupted data. Some controls to offset these risks include transaction and batch control logs, independent review of logs, use of passwords and other access supervision, rotation of user duties, a requirement that master files be altered only with applications programs that generate an internal log of all changes made and by who, and periodic comparison of vendor programs with the company's version.

- "The location of computers in the user's area gives rise to the following risks: unauthorized use of data files, unauthorized modification of programs, and misuse of computer resources. Controls suggested to offset these risks include password-protected menus, periodic review of usage history reports, and physical control over the system hardware, such as locks and read-only terminals.

- "Lack of computer department segregation of duties presents the following risks: unauthorized access to master files and programs, concealment of deliberate errors, and programs that are not representationally faithful to management's objectives. Controls to mitigate such risks include limited access to source code, periodic comparison of programs in use with authorized program versions, password protection to limit access to an as-needed basis, and management review of logs.

- "A lack of technical computer knowledge by computer supervisory personnel raises potential risks such as the inability of a supervisor to recognize failure to meet management objective and the inability to test and review the system effectively. Controls to offset these risks include use of documentation and checklists and recruitment of outside personnel to review program modifications.

- "Use of utility programs that bypass the system log to make master file and program modifications leads to several risks: unauthorized access to data and programs, undetected changes to files, and processing and concealment of unauthorized transactions. The primary means to control these risks are to require all program and master file modifications to be made through the relevant application program and to limit access to system utilities.

- "Diskettes pose a variety of risks because of the relative ease of concealment resulting from their size and data capacity. Risks include processing the wrong data files and bypassing error logs. Controls include restricted access to the control diskette library and the use of read-only terminals.

- "Terminals located throughout the company premises and offsite pose the risk of unauthorized access and unauthorized data entry. Controls include read-only terminals, terminals that can access only certain programs and files, and the physical security of hardware and access logs.

- "Readily available vendor software encourages suboptimization of management objectives. This happens because users find it more convenient to use programs that are already familiar to them, even though such packaged software may fall short of management objectives. Such programs often are not tested by authorized personnel before they are used and accepted. About the only control over this risk is to require that all user-acquired software be tested by system personnel to ensure that it complies with management objectives."

Fear of detection is enhanced by the presence of a knowledgeable internal audit group that is fully aware of potentials for computer abuse and that is involved in all phases of computer operation development and application. These matters are discussed more fully in Chapters 13-15.

Forensics in Fraud Investigations[10]

Forensics relates to information suitable for courts of law or for public discussion. We usually associate the term to the physical sciences such as chemistry, biology, psychiatry, and medicine. However, it can also apply to aspects of financial crimes such as fraud. The purpose of including this section in this chapter is to remind readers of the fact that there are aspects of the malfeasance that should be referred to forensic specialists. The most frequently used scientists for examining this type of evidence are forensic questioned document examiners, fingerprint specialists, and "forensic ink chemists."

Some of the areas where forensic specialists can assist are:

- Preparation and subsequent treatment of documents; in part or in entirety
- Authenticity of signatures
- Alteration of documents
- Variances in the use of ink
- Identification of the mechanical sources of documents produced by business machines such as:
    - Typewriters
    - Computers
    - Check protectors
    - Printers
- Use of correction fluids
- Copying of business papers
- Differences in paper used

The forensic expert is also trained to detect counterfeit documents using optical and nondestructive methods. Internal auditors should be aware of the potential assistance that can be provided by these experts and thus should maintain a skeptical attitude relative to accepting all business papers as valid.

Risk Analysis

Risk analysis (see Chapter 3) is generally considered to be related to the strategy of audit planning. Its intent is to direct audit effort to areas where the risk is the greatest and presumably where auditing can achieve the greatest productivity. However, risk analysis also can make a contribution to fraud auditing. It can identify those areas of an institution where the risk of loss resulting from fraudulent activity can be the greatest.

Risk is comprised of two elements: probability — the possibility of loss; and exposure — the amount of possible loss. The auditor should consider these two elements as related to potential fraudulent activity. Conventional wisdom is that each of the elements is given a quantitative evaluation and that operations with the highest score become the subject of early scrutiny relative to possible fraud. Thus, it stands to reason that liquidity, such as cash, and ease of conversion, such as accounts receivable, would become prime targets of potential fraud auditing.

It is reasonable to believe that a potential perpetrator will target an area where there is the least possibility of being caught. Consequently, these fraud attractive areas should become the object of strong audit scrutiny. Even pseudo audit activity in these high-risk areas can have a deterrent effect by indicating that they are constantly the objects of audit attention.

Responsibility

Historical Perspective

In early years, the attention of auditors was directed primarily to the detection of erroneous and fraudulent transactions. By and large, theirs was a policing action. Their function was protective and detective rather than constructive. No formal standards had been established that imposed a responsibility on internal auditors to prevent and detect fraud. But the courts had addressed the external auditor's responsibility for such prevention and detection. As far back as 19th century England, the courts applied the rule of reason: What can be expected of a reasonably proficient auditor. The same rule is equally applicable to internal auditors.

In the case of In re London and General Bank (No. 2), (1885, 2 Ch. 673), an auditor was required to pay to the Official Receiver of the London and General Bank, whose affairs were being concluded, the amount of certain dividends paid out on the basis of the auditor's certified balance sheet that did not properly state the provision for bad debts. Had provision properly been made, the dividends would never have been declared. In reversing the trial court and holding the auditor blameless with respect to one of the dividends, the appellate court said:

> An auditor. . . is not bound to do more than exercise reasonable care and skill in making inquiries and investigations. He is not an insurer . . . Such I take to be the duty of the auditor: he must be honest — that is he must not certify what he does not believe to be true, and he must take reasonable care and skill before he believes that what he certifies is true.

In the same vein, the court spoke as follows in the case of In re Kingston Cotton Mill Co., Limited (No. 2), (1896 2 Ch. 279):

> It is the duty of an auditor to bring to bear on the work he has to perform that skill, care, and caution that a reasonably competent, careful, cautious auditor would use . . . .An auditor is not bound to be a detective, or, as was said, to approach his work with suspicion or with a foregone conclusion that there is something wrong. He is a watchdog, but not a bloodhound. . . .If there is anything calculated to excite suspicion, he should probe it to the bottom, but in the absence of anything of that kind, he is only bound to be reasonably cautious and careful. . . .

History of the Standards

Nevertheless, for years internal auditors spent most of their time looking for suspicious transactions in financial records. This changed with the swing to operational auditing. The desire to show the constructive side of internal auditing resulted in a downplaying of attention to fraud. Then the business volcano erupted. In the flow that scorched a host of organizations were such major frauds as Equity Funding and National Student Marketing. The liability of corporate executives, board members, and external auditors grew heavier. Heads began to turn to the internal auditor — the so-called "eyes and ears of management." The internal auditor's responsibility for the prevention and detection of wrongdoing had to be reconsidered. It had to be set forth with particularity. This coincided with the issuing in 1978 of the *Standards for the Professional Practice of Internal Auditing (Standards)*. In Standard 280, The Institute set forth these responsibilities:

Internal auditors should exercise due professional care in performing internal audits.

Due professional care calls for the application of the care and skill expected of a reasonably prudent and competent internal auditor in the same or similar circumstances. Professional care should, therefore, be appropriate to the complexities of the audit being performed. In exercising due professional care, internal auditors should be alert to the possibility of internal wrongdoing, errors and omissions, inefficiency, waste, ineffectiveness, and conflicts of interest. They should also be alert to those conditions and activities where irregularities are most likely to occur. In addition, they should identify inadequate controls and recommend improvement to promote compliance with acceptable procedures and practices.

Due care implies reasonable care and competence, not infallibility or extraordinary performance. Due care requires the auditor to conduct examinations and verifications to a reasonable extent, but does not require detailed audits of all transactions. Accordingly, the internal auditor cannot give absolute assurance that noncompliance or irregularities do not exist. Nevertheless, the possibility of material irregularities or noncompliance should be considered whenever the internal auditor undertakes an internal auditing assignment.

When an internal auditor suspects wrongdoing, the appropriate authorities within the organization should be informed. The internal auditor may recommend whatever investigation is considered necessary in the circumstances. Thereafter, the auditor should follow up to see that the internal audit department's responsibilities have been met.

Currently, Standard 1210.A2 covers the aspect of Due Professional Care as it relates to responsibilities of the internal auditor's identification of fraud.

Statement on Internal Auditing Standards No. 3 expanded on the responsibilities of internal auditors with respect to fraud. The major conclusions of the Statement were:

Deterrence of fraud. This is the responsibility of management. Internal auditors are responsible for examining and evaluating the adequacy and the effectiveness of actions taken by management to fulfill this obligation.

Detection of fraud. Internal auditors should have sufficient knowledge of fraud to be able to identify indications that fraud might have been committed. If significant control weaknesses are detected, additional tests conducted by internal auditors should include tests directed toward the identification of other indicators of fraud. Internal auditors are not expected to have knowledge equivalent to that of a person whose primary responsibility is to detect and investigate fraud. Also, audit procedures alone, even when carried out with professional care, do not guarantee that fraud will be detected.

Investigation of fraud. Fraud investigations may be conducted by or involve participation by internal auditors, lawyers, investigators, security personnel, and other specialists from inside or outside the organization. Internal auditing should assess the facts known relative to all fraud investigations to:

- Determine if controls need to be implemented or strengthened.
- Design audit tests to help disclose the existence of similar frauds in the future.
- Help meet the internal auditor's responsibility to maintain sufficient knowledge of fraud.

Documentation

Fraud investigations differ from the usual auditing engagements in that the results must stand the scrutiny of judicial activity and possibly insurance investigation relative to the payment of claims. Following are aspects that should be covered.

1. What is the objective of the investigation?
2. Who are the parties concerned?
   Names
   Positions
   Background
   Economic aspects
   Behavioral aspects
3. How was the investigation performed?
4. How was the fraud or irregularity carried out?
   Sequence of events
5. What evidence has been collected?
   Identification
   Validity
   Security (compromise)
   Purpose
6. Economic aspects:
   Monies
   Property
   Securities

7. Results of:
Interviews
Interrogations
8. Results of clerical activities, testing?
9. Photographs
10. Computer aspects:
Controls: effective, ineffective
11. Analytical activities:
Indications of unusual situations
Projections
12. Relevant legal aspect

There should be copious notes, referencing to dependable sources, and cross-references.

Reporting of Fraud

A written report should be issued at the conclusion of the investigation phase. It should include all findings, conclusions, recommendations, and corrective action taken. (Practice Advisory 2410.A2-1, Par 10 & 11)

Current practice sets responsibilities that are not much different from the rules laid down in the English court cases in the 19th century. Internal auditors are monitors of their organization's control systems; they are not insurers against fraud, embezzlement, theft, and noncompliance with procedures. They must exercise ordinary prudence when devising audit programs and carrying them out. They are not responsible for anticipating or unearthing every devious, hidden defect that would escape an examination carried out in a professional manner.

Some frauds would be impossible to detect by even the best auditors. These are kickbacks, forgery, collusion, and other unrecorded transactions. Also, auditors cannot be charged with being handwriting experts. When skillfully prepared false documents are presented to auditors who have no reason to doubt their validity, it is reasonable for the auditors to rely on them.

When a system of control depends on separation of duties, the auditors have no way of knowing that the people charged with those duties have conspired to subvert the system. Neither can they be expected to detect collusion between people inside and outside the enterprise. Acceptable auditing techniques cannot provide assurance that there are no such transactions. How could auditors discover an unrecorded payable unless they requested confirmations from all potential creditors? Absolute certainty is no more an attainable goal of auditing than it is of any other professional endeavor.

Yet the responsibility remains to do more than accept representations from others. Certainly, an auditor who carefully reviews a reasonable sample of transactions cannot be held responsible for subsequently discovered fraudulent documents in the transactions not examined. And, unless the auditors have reason for suspicion, they may accept the truth of the representations made to them and the genuineness of the documents they inspect. But internal auditors are responsible for discoverable fraud discoverable by a reasonably skilled and prudent auditor and for any looseness of the system of control. Where suspicion is aroused or there are reasonable grounds for suspicion, internal auditors are responsible for going behind the documents and behind the numbers to track down improprieties. The comments of the court in State Street Trust Company vs. Ernst about the responsibility of accountants has equal applicability to internal auditors.[11]

> A representation certified as true knowledge of the accountants when knowledge there is none, a reckless misstatement, or an opinion based on grounds so flimsy as to lead to the conclusion that there was no genuine belief in its truth are all sufficient upon which to base liability. A refusal to see the obvious, a failure to investigate the doubtful, if sufficiently gross, may furnish evidence leading to an inference of fraud. In other words, heedlessness and reckless disregard of consequences may take the place of deliberate intention.

The dangers of fraud on the part of the auditor are too great, the risks too high to accept a passive role. As the current *Standards* say, the internal auditor must be alert. Hence, when an audit finding reveals the breakdown of controls, it is only the beginning of the deficiency's development. The evaluation of risk can highlight areas that are vulnerable and that should be given extra audit attention. For example: if approval requirements are not followed, if improperly developed shipping documents destroyed the control over merchandise, if billing of invoices was in arrears, if competitive bids were not obtained, if checks received in the mailroom were not listed, if one who maintains records also has control over the recorded assets, then the internal auditor should be alerted to the possibility of intentional wrongdoing and probe further.

Internal auditors may not merely report these control derelictions to operating management and move on. First of all, management may not be particularly control-oriented. Second, unit managers can very well be involved in wrongdoing themselves. Third, managers often find it difficult to believe that the very people they trusted could possibly be guilty of intentional wrongdoing. Hence the need to follow the dictates of the *Standards* when fraud is suspected, that "the appropriate authorities within the organization should be informed," and that "thereafter, the auditor should follow up to see that the internal auditing department's responsibilities have been met."

Fraud implies concealment. Its commission will not ring bells and flash lights. Nor are the signs of wrongdoing equally clear to all internal auditors. Some may overlook signs that would alert more capable auditors. Some auditors have the facility, the experience, and an undefinable intuitive sixth sense — professional skepticism — that put them on the alert and point them toward evidence of deception. Yet all internal auditors should learn from those with sharper eyes and keener instincts. The literature is replete with instances of fraudulent conduct. And professional internal auditors are responsible for keeping up with what is new in their profession. Thus, while they may not be insurers against fraud, their responsibility for due professional care will require an increasingly high level of alertness to the indicators of fraud, as those indicators find their way into the professional literature.

Authority

Responsibility for fraud detection can extend only as far as the authority to probe potential areas of fraud. Internal auditors cannot be expected to roam far afield if they are shackled by restrictions. Just as important, internal auditors cannot properly be held responsible for an obligation rightfully imposed on management or seek the authority to meet such an obligation. It is the responsibility of management to:

- Set the moral climate in which the enterprise functions.

- Provide for the organization to accomplish its plans and follow its policies.

- Establish and maintain internal controls.

- Determine the appropriate cost versus control ratios, keeping in mind the equation: exposure minus safeguards equals risks.

- Establish and maintain the lines of communication and systems of reporting within the organization and for knowing what is going on.

Internal auditors will be responsible for determining whether all these actions have been taken and whether they were carried out efficiently and effectively. But internal auditors can make those determinations only if management authorizes them to do so. Responsibility may not properly be imposed if coequal authority is not delegated.

Different organizations take different approaches to this authority. At a large bank holding organization, the internal auditors refer all suspected frauds to lawyers who are members of the internal audit activity. A separate security section of the internal audit activity in an insurance organization conducts fraud investigations. A special auditing section in a public utility deals both with fraud investigations and with special auditing assignments not a part of the regular audit program.

In some organizations, responsibility and authority have been made clear by high-level pronouncements. If internal auditors learn that top managers in their organization are committing fraudulent acts, they should have the authority, clearly spelled out, to consult with immediate supervision, outside directors, or public accountants. Without this specific authority, they would be unable to comply with the internal auditor's current *Code of Ethics*:

Code of Conduct

1.1 Internal auditing professionals shall perform their work with honestly and responsibility.

1.2 Internal auditing professionals shall report the law and shall make disclosure expected by the law and the profession.

1.3 Internal auditing professionals shall not knowingly be party to any illegal activity.

Hence, if internal auditors are to be held responsible for the investigation of potential wrongdoing at all levels in the organization, they should be authorized by the board of directors to carry out duties such as:

- Review and comment on annual reports from managers at all levels in the organization responsible for authorizing the payment of funds.

- Audit all consulting arrangements and evaluate both their documentation and justification.

- Analyze the organization's procedures and practices for opening and maintaining bank accounts. Recommend any needed controls.

- Review transactions that are approved at the executive level.

- Have access to actions of the board of directors.

- Review transactions with subsidiaries and associated organizations.

- Test the documentation supporting financial reports.

- Monitor compliance with the organization's record-retention policies.

- Ask managers whether there have been any illegal political contributions or questionable practices.

- Review the substance of legal expense accounts.

- Monitor the organization's conflict-of-interest policy, which questions an employee's possible relations with suppliers, contractors, and customers, including family alliances and outside business dealings.

Internal auditors will need broad authority because management, in desperation, looks increasingly to them for protection against fraud. Management will expect internal auditors to exert professional skepticism and to be especially alert to the risk of fraud in evaluating controls. And it will hold internal auditors responsible for detecting significant frauds that existed during the period covered by internal audits.

Frauds are often encountered in contracted work, especially where the contractor's profits increase with the cost of work. Cost-plus contracts, time-and-material purchase orders, and royalty agreements are all prime sources of knowing or unwitting overcharges. Some internal audit organizations can pay for the cost of the entire internal audit effort through recoveries under such contracts. But the internal auditors must have the authority to make such audits and to have access to the contractors' and subcontractors' or suppliers' records. Internal auditors should make sure, therefore, that the purchasing departments include in such purchase orders and contracts a right-to-audit clause similar to the one that follows:[12]

> **Records-Audit.** The contractor shall maintain, during the course of the work, and retain, not less than four years after completion thereof, complete and accurate records of all the contractor's costs that are chargeable to the organization in this contract. The organization shall have the right, at any reasonable time, to inspect and audit those records by authorized representatives of its own or of a public accounting firm selected by it. The records to be maintained and retained by the contract shall include (without limitation): (a) payroll records accounting for the total time distribution of the contractor's employees working full- or part-time on the work (to permit tracing to payrolls and related tax returns) as well as canceled checks or signed receipts for payroll payments in cash; (b) invoices for purchases, receiving and issuing documents, and all the other unit-inventory records for the contractor's stores stock or capital items; and (c) paid invoices and canceled checks for rental material purchased and for the subcontractor's and any other third-parties' charges.

The Three Factors Related to Fraud

It is generally agreed that there are three conditions that are present for fraud or embezzlement to take place. The three are collective and could exist in varying degrees. They are:

> A *situation of need:* This situation can be financial caused by expenses or other loss of funds that cannot be covered by an individual's normal source of financial resources. Examples are: illness in a family, gambling, living beyond one's means, extra marital affairs, investment losses, accidents, and educational needs. The need could also be psychological; for instance, the desire to "live dangerously," or to seek revenge for injustices. There is definitely a motivating influence that creates the state of mind that funds must be obtained, frequently considered as being borrowed, in other cases with no intent to repay.

An environment that invites defalcation: This is usually a situation where there are no controls, or where the controls are weak, or where there are controls but they are not functional. Frequently this condition becomes apparent through an accidental situation where the individual, through a mistake, realizes that he or she has received funds improperly, although unintentionally obtained, and that the controls that should have prevented it are missing or not functioning.

The behavioral characteristics of the individual: Both of the above conditions can exist, but if the individual has a high sense of honesty, fraud will not be perpetrated. However, extreme cases of the first element above, with the loose control situations mentioned second above, can overcome a person's basic moral repugnance and will open the door for impropriety.

It is interesting to suspect that the inability to pay bills or to default on obligations is considered a worse blemish on a person's character than the exposure to possible detection of conducting a fraudulent act. The internal auditor should keep these three factors in mind and realize that all three can exist in degrees from high to low. The figure below is illustrative of this condition.

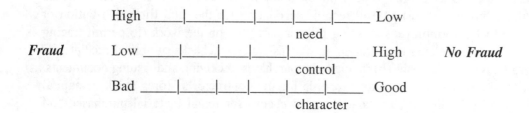

Thus, if the need is great and the controls are not too good, and if the sense of morality is not too high, the individual may rationalize and commit fraud, thinking that it is a temporary thing and that the funds will be repaid before the situation is discovered. It rarely is.

Detection

The Difficulties

A head teller in a bank managed to take more than $1 million over a three-year period by manipulating the bank's computer. The bank's normal internal controls did not detect the defalcations. He was apprehended simply because federal agents, investigating the activities of a known gambling place, found he was gambling as much as $30,000 a day. By following him, they found out where he was getting the money. The detection was by happenstance, not design. Some incidents based on dishonesty escaped as many as 15 examinations by independent public accountants. Others remained undiscovered for as long as 25 years despite regular state and federal examiners' efforts.[13]

If internal auditors are to be successful in detecting fraud, they will have to develop a great awareness of how it occurs and why. The first step is to devote more time determining what the systems of computer control are and what risks are being or should be guarded against. Then the auditors must determine whether control procedures are violated in actual practice.

Awareness

In addition to understanding control systems, auditors should be aware of the kinds of fraud that could be practiced. Exhibit 27-1 lists 40 common forms of fraud. These run the gamut from pilfering stamps for small amounts to dealing with favored suppliers who may increase contract prices by huge amounts and give kickbacks to a fraudulent purchasing agent. Exhibit 27-2 lists the telltale signs that should raise suspicion in the minds of internal auditors — from the open and constant borrowing of money from other employees to the surreptitious rewriting of records under the guise of making them look neat.

Exhibit 27-1
40 Common Forms of Fraud

1. Pilfering stamps.
2. Stealing merchandise, tools, supplies, and other items of equipment.
3. Removing small amounts from cash funds and registers.
4. Failing to record sales of merchandise, and pocketing the cash.
5. Creating overages in cash funds and registers by under-recording.
6. Overloading expense accounts or diverting advances to personal use.
7. Lapping collections on customers' accounts.
8. Pocketing payments on customers' accounts, issuing receipts on scraps of paper or in self-designed receipt books.
9. Collecting an account, pocketing the money, and charging it off; collecting charged-off accounts and not reporting.
10. Charging customers' accounts with cash stolen.
11. Issuing credit for false customer claims and returns.
12. Failing to make bank deposits daily, or depositing only part of the money.
13. Altering dates on deposit slips to cover stealing.
14. Making round sum deposits — attempting to catch up by end of month.
15. Carrying fictitious extra help on payrolls, or increasing rates or hours.
16. Carrying employees on payroll beyond actual severance dates.

Exhibit 27-1 (Cont.)

17. Falsifying additions on payrolls; withholding unclaimed wages.
18. Destroying, altering, or voiding cash sales tickets and pocketing the cash.
19. Withholding cash sales receipts by using false charge accounts.
20. Recording unwarranted cash discounts.
21. Increasing amounts of petty-cash vouchers and/or totals in accounting for disbursements.
22. Using personal expenditure receipts to support false paid-out items.
23. Using copies of previously used original vouchers, or using a properly approved voucher of the prior year by changing the date.
24. Paying false invoices, either self-prepared or obtained through collusion with suppliers.
25. Increasing amounts of suppliers' invoices through collusion.
26. Charging personal purchases to organization through misuse of purchase orders.
27. Billing stolen merchandise to fictitious accounts.
28. Shipping stolen merchandise to an employee or relative's home.
29. Falsifying inventories to cover thefts or delinquencies.
30. Seizing checks payable to the organization or to suppliers.
31. Raising canceled bank checks to agree with fictitious entries.
32. Inserting fictitious ledger sheets.
33. Causing erroneous footings of cash receipts and disbursement books.
34. Deliberately confusing postings to control and detail accounts.
35. Selling waste and scrap materials and pocketing proceeds.
36. "Selling" door keys or the combinations to safes or vaults.
37. Creating credit balances on ledgers and converting to cash.
38. Falsifying bills of lading and splitting with carrier.
39. Obtaining blank checks (unprotected) and forging the signature.
40. Permitting special prices or privileges to customers, or granting business to favored suppliers, for "kickbacks."

Exhibit 27-2
20 Danger Signs of Embezzlement

1. Borrowing small amounts from fellow employees.
2. Placing personal checks in change funds — undated, postdated — or requesting to others to "hold" checks.
3. Personal checks cashed and returned for irregular reasons.
4. Collectors or creditors appearing at the place of business, and excessive use of telephone to "stall off" creditors.
5. Placing unauthorized I.O.U.s in change funds, or prevailing on others in authority to accept I.O.U.s for small, short-term loans.
6. Inclination toward covering up inefficiencies by "plugging" figures.
7. Pronounced criticism of others so as to divert suspicion.
8. Replying to questions with unreasonable explanations.
9. Gambling in any form beyond ability to stand the loss.
10. Excessive drinking and nightclubbing or associating with questionable characters.
11. Buying or otherwise acquiring through "business" channels expensive automobiles and extravagant household furnishings.
12. Explaining a higher standard of living as money left from an estate.
13. Getting annoyed at reasonable questioning.
14. Refusing to leave custody of records during the day; working overtime regularly.
15. Refusing to take vacations and shunning promotions for fear of detection.
16. Constant association with, and entertainment by, a member of a supplier's staff.
17. Carrying an unusually large bank balance, or heavy buying of securities.
18. Extended illness of self or family, usually without a plan of debt liquidation.
19. Bragging about exploits, and/or carrying unusual amounts of money.
20. Rewriting records under the guise of neatness in presentation.

Analytical Auditing

Other indicators can be developed through analytical auditing procedures by experienced auditors. Some of these procedures come in the form of trend and proportional analyses: (Also see Chapter 12)

Trend analysis. Trend analysis is a diagnostic tool. The auditor charts operating data for prior years to evaluate the reasonableness of current income or expense. Here are some examples:

- An auditor charted sales and freight costs for a period of seven years. Sales had increased by 130 percent. But outbound freight, which was directly related to sales, was up by 300 percent. The auditor checked freight bills for several months and found they did not add up to the inflated amount. Investigation disclosed that expenditures purportedly for freight had been recorded and stolen.

- An auditor charted sales to customers and sales to employees. The first was increasing dramatically, mirroring the organization's excellent growth. The sales to the corresponding increase in employees were decreasing. Investigation disclosed no control over those sales. The office manager had been pocketing much of the cash received from employees.

Proportional analysis. Proportional analysis, like trend analysis, is a diagnostic tool. It is a method that appraises certain income and expense by relating them to other income and expense, or to other operating statistics. For example, the cost of shipping cartons should bear a proportional relation to the number of units sold and shipped.

Some proportional comparisons are based on ratios from other organizations or on industry averages. Trade associations often compile average costs and ratios for the information of their members. Several universities compile and issue valuable studies about certain industries. Often, personal experience provides indicators of what is reasonable or unreasonable. The Federal Department of Commerce also maintains operating statistics for specific industries.

Here are some examples of such comparisons.

- One auditor, within a few hours after his arrival at a brewery, discovered that the quantity of hops charged to costs was twice the amount necessary to produce the annual output of beer. Investigation disclosed that the thief was the treasurer. He was paying for hops delivered to another brewery in which he had an interest.

- A new manager took charge of a business and one of his first acts was to compare expense ratios with statistics compiled during his previous employment in the same industry. The comparisons revealed excessive payroll costs. Investigation showed that a cashier had been stealing $200 to $900 each week and concealing the thefts by overstating the totals of weekly payrolls.

Caveat on analyses. Internal auditors must be cautious in using these analyses. Variables and mitigating circumstances may enter into the calculations such as heavy overtime pay in one period and none in others. Moreover, most of these ratios are limited to relating only two variables to each other. But used cautiously, such analyses may provide useful indicators, with this additional caveat: Trend and proportional analyses do not produce substantive evidence. They do not show why. Like a divining rod in the hands of a dowser seeking water, these analyses merely show where to dig.

Verifying Transactions

Through the use of the computer, the auditor can verify transactions with elements within the organization that would normally be effected by those transactions. Some examples are:

1. Sales of manufactured products to the cost of materials used and the labor incurred. This comparison could disclose nonexistent sales and *in reverse* could disclose fraudulent material or labor costs.
2. Bad debts account debits to credits to accounts receivable for bad debts.
3. Purchases with increases in inventories (or sales).
4. Payroll costs with employee payroll tax reports.
5. Distribution costs to expenses paid for fuel for delivery costs.
6. Sales of surplus inventory to "open to buy" budgets.

This technique may be considered a part of analytical auditing. However, it is more a comparison of cause and effect and it can highlight unusual conditions.

Access Device Fraud[14]

As access devices (cards) are being more frequently used in organizations, both business and nonbusiness, they have expanded the exposure for their fraudulent use. Examples of such cards are:

- Bank or financial credit cards
- Retail cards
- Telephone cards
- Smart cards or integrated circuit cards

The use of access devices for potential fraudulent purposes includes the above types of cards plus:

- Check cards
- Credit cards
- False applications
- Account takeovers
- Mail theft, and
- Altered cards

Internal auditing activities in organizations that can be exposed to fraudulent activities that entail the use of any of these devices should have specialists who understand the details as to how this criminal action can take place. Knowledgeable authorities hold that this includes: (1) the mechanics of the crime; and (2) the scientific and technical aspects of the crime. To commence the investigation it is recommended that the following four questions be answered:

1. What aspects of the case are unusual?
2. What is the geographical history of the device?
3. Who is suspected?
4. What facts in the case require technical knowledge?

The authors of this unique study emphasize that the auditor should lose no time in the investigation, establish facts as to backgrounds of all persons related to the event(s), determine what details are important, conduct separate interviews of all persons in the case, do not waste time, obtain account documents and statements to show location and times of the events, obtain handwriting samples of all parties, ask for affidavits of fraud, and interview persons at all levels of the organization that were the locations of the fraudulent activity.

The investigator must know the usual actions and paths of the transactions so as to identify possible points of exposures to fraudulent treatment.

Integrate circuit cards that are one type of access devices are more sensitive to fraudulent use because of their competence to:

1. Authenticate parties.
2. Authorized transactions.
3. Execute the transaction.
4. Document the transaction.

The technical aspects of investigating fraud using these cards that could be considered as personal computers of limited use are considered beyond the areas of this text, although the subject is certainly relevant to this general area.

The Investigative Process

Some frauds are resolved simply by identifying inconsistencies and inquiring about them to a potential suspect who immediately confesses. Others are complex, hidden, and extensive; these require concerted effort to bring them to light and to justice. The internal auditors may not have a primary responsibility for the detection of wrongdoing. But the current *Standards* point out that once a wrongdoing is suspected, the internal auditors should notify appropriate investigators and follow up to see that the internal audit department's responsibilities have been met.

Kennish has listed the following objectives for an investigation into suspected fraud.[15]

- First and foremost, to protect the innocent, establish the facts, resolve the matter, and clear the air.

- Determine the basic circumstances quickly to stop the loss as soon as possible.

- Establish the essential elements of the crime to support a successful prosecution.

- Identify, gather, and protect evidence.

- Identify and interview witnesses.

- Identify patterns of actions and behavior.

- Determine probable motives that often will identify potential suspects.

- Provide accurate and objective facts upon which judgments concerning discipline, termination, or prosecution may be based.

- Account for and recover assets.

- Identify weaknesses in control and counter them by revising existing procedures or recommending new ones, and by applying security equipment when justified.

Clearly not all of these objectives can be met by internal auditors. Few will have the ability and experience to accomplish all of them. Hence, a successful investigation will usually require coordination among appropriate disciplines. Preferably, a small group comprising representatives from the security, internal auditing, legal, operations, and personnel departments, as well as a coordinating manager, would suffice. Preliminary information should be shared with senior management; but to the extent possible, information gained during the investigation should be kept confidential.

The first step in the investigative process is to establish that a loss has indeed occurred. The process should determine that an asset was accounted for at some point and then it was definitely missing at another. Once the time frame has been bracketed, it is relatively simple to determine which employees could have been implicated in the loss. If the missing asset cannot be firmly accounted for because the controls are weak, then the entity has learned an expensive lesson.

The next step is to establish the facts. Get as much information as possible from associated employees or informants. Interview all those who may have been involved in the control of or who had access to the asset during the bracketed period. Gather documents, organize data, examine documents for forgeries, and look for out-of-balance conditions. Don't stop at the documents themselves; go behind them to the facts they purport to establish. Look for relationships for things that don't make sense.

When a loss has been conclusively established, a determination should be made about how to go forward. Many approaches are open to the team and not every member is equipped to take them. Certain questions will have to be resolved by the auditors, security, and management, such as:

- What additional questions should be asked of people seemingly implicated in or knowledgeable of wrongdoing and by whom?

- How can evidence be immediately secured and legally cared for?

- At what point should a suspect be suspended pending outcome of the investigation?

- Should there be an interrogation and by whom?

- When should the authorities be informed?

- Where should professional investigative resources be applied and how would they be obtained?

Interviewing is a significant part of the investigative process. But since interrogations can trigger significant exposures to the organization — as we shall discuss later — hard-line interrogations should be left to the security people. Employees should be presumed to be innocent. And so, before any interrogation, questioners should make sure they have their facts straight.

Two members of the team should conduct the interview — one to speak and the other to witness. Questioners should speak calmly and avoid accusatory attitudes. They should show compassion and interrupt the suspect only to clarify points. If the suspect elects to be silent, the questioner should not threaten or intimidate. But the employee should not be allowed to return to the work area, because valuable evidence might be lost. Questioners should seek to obtain the subjects' confidence and encourage them to speak in their own words.

Only trained and experienced investigators can tell whether the person they are interrogating is lying or telling the truth. But Kennish tells us that much can be learned from body language. Here are some of his suggestions.[16]

> Watch carefully for unusual or specific indicators in response to "hot" questions that may suggest that the subject is less than truthful. These may include a dry mouth and lips that result in a clicking sound when speaking, avoiding eye contact or staring at the interviewer and then dropping the eyes down and away to the side as the question is answered, an unusual high pitch to the voice or rapid speech patterns, restlessness and shifting in the chair, crossing both arms and legs with the elbows kept tucked into the sides, abnormal eye blink rate, biting the lips or tongue, tightly squeezing the lips together, looking at or playing with fingernails, crying at inappropriate times, claiming memory failure or having remarkably keen memory, and smiling at inappropriate times or phony "over-smiling." Here are other key nonverbal signals: Rounding the shoulders with the elbows at the knees, dropping the head to look downward at the floor, and deep sighing. An experienced investigator will be aware of those signals and press the line of questioning accordingly.

Waltman and Golen talk about other nonverbal signals that can be assets for interviewers:[17]

- Kinetics. These are manual gestures and torso movements. The hand used to cover the mouth, the person talking through his or her fingers. Manipulation of clothing, such as tugging at the collar, or toying with the top button of a blouse. Picking lint or spots from clothes.

- Proxemics. This refers to the distance that one keeps from others. Moving away from the interviewer. Crossing arms and legs and leaning back. Placing a file or purse on the lap as a barrier between questioner and person being questioned.

When to approach security is a matter of judgment. The decision should be based on the nature and amount of the loss, the investigative ability available in-house, and the organization's relations with security. Generally, the police should be informed by security if the loss is substantial, the evidence is strong, and the employee either appears to be untruthful or makes an admission or confession. The decision is that of security not audit. Once charges are filed, the organization should not withdraw from its complaint without a recommendation from the prosecutor. Nor should charges be dropped in lieu of restitution; the organization will promptly lose the confidence of the police, the prosecutor, and the courts in future cases.

Intent is a legal matter best left to those trained in the law. Nevertheless, it would be well for internal auditors to be aware of the attitudes of the courts toward evidence that can be relied on to prove fraudulent intent. The courts have agreed that certain indicators can be acknowledged to show intent to deceive. For example, in Spies vs. United States, 317 U.S. 492, 499, 500 (1943), the court held:

By way of illustration, and not by way of limitation, we would think affirmative willful attempt may be inferred from conduct such as keeping a double set of books, making false entries or alterations, or false invoices or documents, destruction of books or records, concealment of assets or covering up sources of income, handling of one's affairs to avoid making the records usual in transactions of this kind, and any conduct, the likely effect of which would be to mislead or conceal.

In sum, auditing and investigating require different strategies. Auditing need not be in a hostile climate; indeed internal auditing literature suggests participation between auditor and client, absent any indication of wrongdoing. The investigation of fraud, however, is carried out in a hostile climate; deliberate deception is involved and the deceiver works hard to keep tracks and methods covered. Direct methods cannot be relied upon to determine scope and truth in a hostile environment. After all, the people don't want their depredations uncovered. Thus, when fraud is suspected, open audit methods are inapplicable and covert investigative methods are required.

Practice Advisory 1210.A2-1, "Identification of Fraud," summarizes the above by suggesting that when conducting fraud investigation, internal auditors should:

(a) Assess the probable level and the extent of complicity in the fraud within the organization. This can be critical to ensuring that the internal auditor avoids providing information to or obtaining misleading information from persons who may be involved.

(b) Determine the knowledge, skills, and disciplines needed to carry out the investigation effectively. An assessment of the qualifications and the skills of internal auditors and of the specialists available to participate in the investigation should be performed to ensure that it is conducted by individuals having the appropriate type and level of technical expertise. This should include assurances on such matters as professional certifications, licenses, reputation, and that there is no relationship to those being investigated or to any of the employees or management of the organization.

(c) Design procedures to follow in attempting to identify the perpetrators, extent of the fraud, techniques used, and cause of fraud.

(d) Coordinate activities with management personnel, legal counsel, and other specialists as appropriate throughout the course of the investigation.

(e) Be cognizant of the rights of alleged perpetrators and personnel within the scope of the investigation and the reputation of the organization itself.

Auditing for Cyber Fraud

One of the recent books on fraud auditing describes the subject as more of a mindset than a methodology. Yet, it contains much of the techniques of financial auditing. Its basic difference is that the auditor should think like a thief and be creative in designing the steps that he or she would use in:[18]

- Identifying the weakest areas (control-wise) that would be susceptible to manipulation.
- Determining how to attack them without drawing attention.
- Not destroying evidence of the action.
- Identifying the powers he/she would need to control the defalcation.
- Preparing plausible explanations if caught.

This is simply the old saying, "To catch a thief, think like the thief." A striking difference in fraud auditing is the lack of need for materiality of evidence in the auditing process. The amount of visible fraud is usually small but even the discovery of small items can possibly lead to the discovery of a large fraud incident. Success is usually the result of great effort and determination.

Probably at the beginning of the search would be the time to identify various objectives of the planned fraud incident, i.e.:

- To cover abstractions of cash
- To increase sales; percent of market
- To increase income
- To reduce liabilities
- To improve current ratio

The auditor would project methods that could be used by the malefactor to accomplish the objective and then explore to see if there was evidence that these methods were being used. Work could be coordinated with forensic experts to try to identify "how" and then further explore to determine the "who" element. That is, who would benefit and "how." Financial auditing also has a part in this effort — as a backdrop, to project possible financial methods that could be used.

For those internal audit activities that are organically associated with investigation units, as soon as it becomes evident that there is a possibility of fraud, the investigation should become a coordinated effort. Much of the general forensic effort would originate with the investigating unit.

Bologna and Shaw recommend that every organization have an "internal auditing game plan," starting with a board of directors' policy directive. The plan should include:

- What misconduct will trigger an investigation?
- To whom should the misconduct be reported?
- When should the investigation be initiated?
- Who should conduct the investigation?
- What should be the purpose of the investigation?
- What types of disclosures are mandatory?[19]

Audit Programs for Fraud Examiners[20]

George Manning has developed a general program for fraud examiners that should, at a minimum, include:

1. Collecting industry data: This includes general information as to how the industry performs relative to financial and nonfinancial operations.
2. Financial analysis: Included here is financial analytical data for the organization as compared to other organizations in the industry. Techniques that should be used are:
   - Ratio analysis
   - Vertical analysis (components of the whole)
   - Horizontal analysis (as to time periods)
   - Nonfinancial data (comparisons of different parts of statements, financial and operational, that should have a relationship)
   - Cash flow information
   - Net income adjustments:
     - Depreciation, Receivables, Inventories
     - Amortization, Payables
3. Reviewing of internal controls: The determination that:
   - Transactions are executed as per management authorization
   - Transactions are properly recorded
   - Safeguarding assets
   - Conformance of assets to records
4. Evidence gathering: Techniques to be used to gather evidence as to fraudulent activities. Examples are:
   - Interviewing
   - Internal control charts and visual comparisons
   - Document examination
   - Employee searches
   - Investigation (close supervision of suspects during an examination period)
   - Observation (spying or snooping; converting to media, if possible)

- Undercover (using an agent or informant; for major criminal acts; can be dangerous)
- Specific items; collection of specific evidence related to the fraud

5. Evaluating: Analysis of evidence to determine if fraud actually occurred
6. Reporting of findings to appropriate parties

Manning lists a series of fraud indicators that can alert the fraud investigator. Briefly they are:

1. Loose internal controls
2. Poor management philosophy
3. Poor financial position
4. Low employee morale
5. Ethics confusion
6. Lack of background checks on new hires
7. Lack of employee support programs
8. General conditions: high employee turnover, pending mergers, excess trust in key employees, etc.

Manning finally proposes that the fraud examiner should use the above as a guide, and should develop an array of conditions that could be red flags to alert the internal auditor as to the potential for fraudulent activities. Poor internal controls, he believes, is probably the most important element to use as a starting point.

Hazards in Interrogations

Interrogations are not only difficult; they can be hazardous to the interrogators and to their organizations. Employees, even when suspected of theft or fraud, have certain common law and statutory rights. If these are infringed upon — whether or not the employees are guilty — the suspects have a legal right to sue the interrogator and the organization. So every auditor needs to be aware of the legal dangers.

Libel and Slander

An accused employee can sue in civil action if the employer/defendant has made defamatory utterances. Libel is a written defamation. Slander is an oral defamation. A suit for defamation can be brought if:

- The defamatory words were communicated to someone other than the plaintiff/employee.

- The employee/plaintiff was actually damaged, losing money as a result of the defamation. The law states that some utterances are so defamatory that damage is conclusively presumed they are libelous or slanderous *per se.*

Sometimes the truth of the defamatory words is no defense; the employer/defendant would have to show that the utterance was not committed out of malice. Hence, open accusations should be avoided. To a certain extent, internal auditors' communications are privileged when they are justified or necessary under the circumstances for the performance of legitimate duties of the person (auditor) communicating the defamatory words. But an action of slander or libel can be brought if the communication of suspicion of a crime goes beyond that justified for investigation or for notification to management.

Thus, suspicions should not be broadcast. Written reports should be kept to a minimum and labeled "personal and confidential." It should be remembered that dictating a report to a secretary may be a "communication" within the meaning of libel statutes. Unnecessary "publication" [broadcasting] of defamatory statements can be construed as being malicious or vindictive.

False Imprisonment

An employer can be sued for false arrest or false imprisonment when he or she unreasonably restrains an employee's freedom of mobility. The restraint need not be a physical touching or a locking of a person in a room. Intimidating plaintiff/employees or telling them they cannot leave the room or even leave the city has been held to constitute false imprisonment.

Indeed, just causing great inconvenience can be the basis for a civil action. In one case, draining water from the employee's car radiator was considered false imprisonment. The employee could have emerged from the car, but he could not have taken it with him. No excessive restraint is necessary. According to one authority, "The imprisonment need not be more than an appreciable length of time and it is not necessary that any damage result from it, other than the confinement itself."[21] Placement in a room with the questioner between the employee and the entrance has been considered as restraint.

Malicious Prosecution

This action also called malicious use of process or abuse of process arises from the groundless institution of criminal or civil proceedings against the employee so as to cause damage. A suit against the employer can be brought when these elements of the civil wrong exist:

- The employer causes a criminal prosecution or a civil suit to be brought against an employee.

- The employer is motivated by malice. (The absence of probable cause for the suit is proof of malice.)

- The employee is acquitted of the criminal charge or prevails in the civil suit.

- The employee suffers damage to his or her person, property, or reputation.

It has been held that probable cause can be established by proof of good-faith reliance on the advice of counsel. A good rule for internal auditors to follow is to seek advice of counsel before proceeding with charges.

Compounding a Felony

The law in the United States provides that the right to punish or to forgive a criminal is reserved to the state. Defrauded employers cannot take those rights upon themselves. Agreeing for a consideration not to prosecute a criminal is itself a crime. It is called compounding a felony and can result in legal punishment for the employer, auditor, or both. In one state, for example, it is punishable by fines and maximum prison terms of three to five years. The elements of the crime are:

- A crime actually committed by one person.

- The receipt of something of value by another.

- Under an agreement not to prosecute for the crime, or to limit or handicap such a prosecution.

An employer may lawfully accept restoration of the amounts lost as a result of fraud or theft, but the employer may not lawfully bargain for the restoration by telling the employee no prosecution will take place. Consider this not unlikely scenario:

An employee defrauds an employer. The employee gives the employer a note promising to make good the loss. The employee is terminated. The note or an installment comes due but the employee does not pay. The wrathful employer sues on the note. The ex-employee, to whom the employer was quite benevolent, defends the suit by now claiming that the employer compounded a felony that the employer and the internal auditor who participated in the agreement should go to jail for their offense. The fact that the employer did not inform the police or prosecute the employee lends credence to the employee's claim of compounding a felony. Any determination not to prosecute an employee for fraud, theft, or other illegal actions should be under advice of counsel.

Confessions and Admissions

Confessions are not the most trustworthy form of evidence. They can be repudiated in court by showing mistake, bewilderment, or the fear of the interrogators; hallucination that he or she thought he or she had committed a crime when actually he or she had not; or coercion through brutality, threats, prolonged questioning, or any form of intimidation.

For a statement to constitute a confession, it must be made voluntarily after the offense, and it must be of such a nature that no inference, other than the guilt of the confessor, may be drawn from the confession.

A confession should be distinguished from an admission. A confession is a complete acknowledgment of being guilty of a crime. An admission is any other statement by the defendant of a fact that is relevant to the charge and that is offered against the defendant as evidence of the fact.

Behavioral Aspects of Fraud

A psychological approach to fraud and embezzlement attempts to relate the acts to a behavioral condition of the individual. A listing of some of these reasons includes:

1. My employer has not paid me what he should have. The funds I'm taking are only properly supplementing what I am receiving.
2. My employer is making tremendous profits but has not made reasonable distributions to employees. I'm getting mine this way.
3. I think I can beat the controls. I'm going to try. If I get caught, I'll say I was testing the controls.
4. I'm not sure that this is really wrong. In my opinion this is not illegal.
5. I really need the funds. I'll pay it back next week.
6. Sorry, I need the funds. I owe so much and I don't want to have my wages garnished. That would be too embarrassing.
7. I'm going to take a small amount and contribute it to my favorite charities. (Also a little bit for me.)
8. My employer is conducting illegal activities. This money I'm taking is for punishment that he should be getting.
9. I'm sorry, I'm in such bad shape that I have to do this.
10. What's wrong with this? If my employer isn't smart enough to set up controls, I'll take what I can get.

There are probably more approaches. However, the auditors should be aware of these potential approaches to fraud and should be sensitive to attitudes that may be evident in an organization.

Prevention

The Better Part of Valor

How much better it is not to lose something than to have to go to the trouble of finding it after it is lost. How much better to prevent a person from stealing than to detect the theft, recover the loss, and jail the miscreant. How much better to remove temptation than to punish someone of having succumbed to the temptation. How much better for the internal auditor to be regarded as a constructive consultant than as a police officer or a prosecutor.

For these reasons and more, these authors feel that it is far more profitable for internal auditors to concentrate on constructive and preventive services for their organizations than to track down miscreants whose thefts went undetected because of inadequate controls.

Every embezzler starts playing the game fully aware that he or she may be caught in due course. Those odds must be increased to the point where no matter how much of a gambler the potential thief, defalcator, or embezzler may be, the odds loom up as prohibitive. What increases the odds against the thief or embezzler is control and surveillance.

The Deterrent

Controls are important, but they are not complete insurance. They make the perpetration of fraud more difficult, but not impossible. Neither management nor internal auditors should be lulled into a sense of false security because certain controls are in force. Any barricade can be breached by a determined and crafty thief; but good controls make the job of the thief more difficult.

One of the strongest motivators for honesty is the fear of being caught. Make apprehension a certainty and inducement to steal dissipates. But even that certainty can be a foolish fancy. All one can hope for is deterrence.

Actually, the routine tests and checks in any audit program rarely turn up thefts. Many manipulatory thefts start as a mistake that does not get caught by the system. For example, a bookkeeper may make an error that results in a cash overage, assuming that sooner or later someone will detect the error and direct the disposition of the overage. But nobody does. The bookkeeper may then go back to find out what caused the overage and suddenly realize that if the mistake were made intentionally, nobody would know the difference. And so it starts. Had the control system thrown the spotlight on the error, the thought of manipulation might never have entered the bookkeeper's mind.

Honest People

Defense against fraud begins with hiring honest people determining their honesty as far as possible by checking backgrounds and references. It continues through systems of control and through a rigorous environment that makes honesty an essential attribute of the enterprise. Remove temptation. Install strict rules. Then refuse to tolerate that perfectly natural inclination to reduce the required surveillance out of human respect:

- The office manager who is reluctant to have petty cash audited on a surprise basis — a reflection on the cashier.

- The plant superintendent who will not have trash containers spot checked — a reflection on the maintenance people.

- The accounting people who do not supervise physical inventories — they see the inventories as the purchasing department's responsibility.

Misplaced confidence and the failure to install and maintain reasonable controls become allies of dishonest employees, or tempt honest ones to become dishonest. The results of good systems are to make thieves aware of greater odds against concealment. Fraud is perceived to be potentially more likely to be exposed at an early state. Data for business decisions are made more reliable. On the other hand, as an insurance executive pointed out, the lack of a system of internal controls may make an organization uninsurable — or the lack of controls may impose conditions that are difficult to live with, such as large deductibles or surcharged premiums.[22]

Minimum Controls

Certain minimum, well-established forms of control should always be in force. Embezzlement seldom builds to large sums unless the embezzler is able to cover peculations over long periods by manipulating accounting records. And so:

- Those responsible for the physical receipt of goods should not be responsible for paying for those goods.

- Those responsible for the custody of assets should not be responsible for maintaining the records of the assets.

- Those responsible for the collection of receivables should not be responsible for entries in the books of account.

- Those responsible for accounts receivable records should not be able to create noncash entries to reduce balances.

- Those responsible for issuing checks should not also be responsible for reconciling the bank statement to the books of account.

Nevertheless, internal auditors should be fully aware that the controls erected through such separation of duties can be circumvented by collusion between two or more people who represent the control. They are also circumvented when fellow employees are reluctant to tell on the perpetrator or do not want to get involved in a messy situation.

In reporting on a client's system of control, one public accounting firm made this statement in its report.[23]

There are inherent limitations that should be recognized in considering the potential effectiveness of any system of internal accounting control. In the performance of most control procedures, errors can result from misunderstanding of instructions, mistakes of judgment, carelessness, or other personal factors. Control procedures whose effectiveness depends upon segregation of duties can be circumvented by collusion. Similarly, control procedures can be circumvented intentionally by management with respect either to the execution and recording of transactions or with respect to the estimates and judgments required in the preparation of financial statements. Further, projection of any evaluation of internal accounting control to future accounting periods is subject to the risk that procedures may become inadequate because of changes in conditions and that the degree of compliance with the procedures may deteriorate.

This statement about internal control is equally applicable to internal administrative controls. In the absence of constant vigilance, they too can be rendered ineffective.

Practice Advisory 1210.A2-1, "Identification of Fraud," suggests that:

Internal auditors are responsible for assisting in the deterrence of fraud by examining and evaluating the adequacy and the effectiveness of the system of internal control, commensurate with the extent of the potential exposure/risk in the various segments of the organization's operations. In carrying out this responsibility, internal auditors should, for example, determine whether:

- The organizational environment fosters control consciousness.

- Realistic organizational goals and objectives are set.

- Written policies (e.g., code of conduct) exist that describe prohibited activities and the action required whenever violations are discovered.

- Appropriate authorization policies for transactions are established and maintained.

- Policies, practices, procedures, reports, and other mechanisms are developed to monitor activities and safeguard assets, particularly in high-risk areas.

- Communication channels provide management with adequate and reliable information.

- Recommendations need to be made for the establishment or enhancement of cost effective controls to help deter fraud.

Codes of Conduct and Hot Lines

Organizations have developed two, what might be called passive measures of fraud deterrence. One of them is specific provisions in codes of conduct. The other is telephone hot lines. These measures are described as follows:

Code of conduct: Organizations develop codes of conduct so as to provide employees with guides as to the organization's attitude relative to ethics, performance, attitudes, and relationships with vendors, customers, and other employees. These codes reflect the "tone at the top" and come to identify what is acceptable conduct. One of the aspects that is invariably present in the codes is the requirement for honesty in all activities, both internal and external. However, though this provision may be stated as an inflexible requirement, that isn't enough. The code must also state that any violation of these provisions will result in separation from the organization and in prosecution. The code must also explicitly provide that these conditions will be effected, even if the action is considered by the perpetrator to be in the organization's interest.

The code can refer to the Federal Sentencing Guidelines in identifying the potential penalties for misconduct. Anecdotal descriptions can make these warnings more dramatic and could increase the deterrent effect of the code.

The hot line: The "telephone hot line" is an arrangement for individuals to report observed irregularities to organization authorities without disclosing their identity. The information itself is not considered as evidence, but it serves as an alert to units such as internal auditing or security to investigate.

Both of these methods, if assiduously used, can have a definite dampening impact on employees who might consider wrongful activities for personal gain.

Inflexibility in enforcement is a must if the measures are to have any validity.

Created Errors

Another test of internal controls can be made through auditor-created errors, sometimes called custom-made frauds. The following kinds of improper documents are introduced into a system to determine the efficiency of the controls:

- Invoices marked paid or canceled.

- Purchase orders not approved.

- Requests to purchase not bearing proper authorization.

- A blank check prepared on a typewriter to a fictitious payee with a note attached saying, "Please rush — support will follow."

Proponents of the plan point out that the escalation of fraud and theft demands desperate remedies. They reason that if computerized systems are so tested (test decks), why shouldn't manual systems be tested in the same way?[24]

Opponents of the system cite the adverse effect the procedure will have on the internal auditor's reputation, the undue emphasis on employee fraud and the reputation of sneakiness on the part of management, the difficulty of controlling the management group that introduces the errors, the impossibility of keeping such plans secret, the alienation of honest employees, the objections by unions, and the accusation that the organization is practicing entrapment.[25]

All of these arguments against the use of created errors are valid, except the last. The defense of entrapment can be used by a defendant only when an officer of the law has actively induced and enticed a victim to commit some crime that the victim had no intention to commit and would not have committed except for the enticement. The defense is inapplicable when organization officials seek merely to test the effectiveness of a system of control.

It is possible, of course, for the management team or the individuals who introduce the errors to do so to their own advantage and, when caught, protest that they were only testing the system. This can be prevented. Three members of top management should be brought into the plan, including a personnel and a legal executive. They should initial the planned test and any changes to it. No deviations from the plan should be permitted. They should be kept informed currently of the results of the tests.

The enormity of thefts and embezzlements in some organizations may impel the use of created errors to test systems and the alertness of employees. If they are carried out, all of those participating in the plan should be made abundantly aware of the risks.

Publicity

Fear of punishment is a deterrent, but punishment is a matter of organization policy. That policy, if it is to be effective, should be publicized in advance to all employees. As a minimum, management should publicize these matters:

- If periodic credit checks are to be made on certain employees such as cashiers, claims adjusters, and buyers, those people should be told in advance that such checks go with the job.

- Employees should be told that security people or forensic investigators must be notified immediately of any suspicion of employee fraud.

- All employees are expected to cooperate with fraud investigations.

- Employees should be made abundantly aware that fraud will be vigorously investigated and prosecuted.

By these actions, management should publicize to its employees that dishonesty will not be tolerated and will be punished. Too often, management policy is simply to fire the dishonest employee and hope to recover from the bonding organization or from the employee the amounts stolen.

Management Fraud

Management fraud requires special consideration. It is a form of fraud that goes beyond the narrow legal definitions of embezzlement, fraud, and theft. It comprises all the forms of deception practiced by managers to benefit themselves to the detriment of the organization. Deception by managers — people in positions of power and trust — is not often talked about. It is more often concealed then revealed. It is usually covered up by its victims to avoid the adverse effects of publicity.[26]

Where It Takes Place

Management fraud can be found wherever managers have the opportunity and the need to better their purse, their status, or their ego through deception. The opportunity lies largely in the fiduciary position that managers have in the organization. In a position of trust, they command belief and respect — their motives are rarely questioned and their explanations are rarely disputed. Their respected roles as profit center managers — heads of autonomous units — place them above suspicion. They are often immune to the ordinary checks and balances imposed on their subordinates.

In decentralized organizations, division presidents, vice presidents, and general managers are vested with relatively complete authority. Their performance is judged by the central corporate executive group and by boards of directors. Such performance is generally portrayed in reports and financial statements. The artful imagination of the deceiver has little difficulty making red appear black.

The deception can continue for years. It goes on where there is no thoroughgoing surveillance. It goes on where group vice presidents who visit the decentralized organizations use those visits to make social calls, not to ask the hard questions. It goes on where there are no top-flight internal auditors who analyze and dissect both operations and reports. When it finally surfaces, or where suspicions trigger investigations, the harm is done and the miscreant usually moves on to graze in other pastures. The damage left behind can be incalculable.

The Reasons Behind Management Fraud

Different pressures push managers into deception. These pressures can be internal or external. The manager may have the inner drive to outperform all others, to exceed the performance displayed during the last fiscal year, to beat a rival to a coveted promotion, or to receive a larger incentive bonus. Reason and greed may exceed grasp. The goals set may be beyond the manager's capacity to achieve.

Similar pressures may come from superiors. Goals may be set by centralized management that are unrealistic. These goals filter down to subordinate managers who are forced to meet goals they had never committed to. Since they cannot achieve these goals fairly, they manage to appear to meet them through deception. A summary of some of the reasons behind management fraud is as follows:

> *Executives sometimes take rash steps from which they cannot retreat.* In one instance, the president of a large subsidiary in a conglomerate unthinkingly asserted before a group of financial analysts that profits for the current year would be X dollars a share. The assertion became an organization goal, and the independent public accountants were talked into writing off an inventory adjustment over a five-year period. The transaction increased the current year's profits, but it caused a distortion in the corporate financial statement. Corporate management was unaware of the deception until it was unearthed by consultants.

> *Organizations publicize to the financial markets estimates of future sales levels, market share, income, and stock performance.* When any of these performance measures cannot be reached, aggressive accounting is employed to achieve the desired results. An organization reclassified utility line rental payments as capitalized intangible assets so as to reduce current expenses. Outside accountants, under pressure and

facing loss of consulting fees (that exceeded auditing fees), temporized and overlooked the fraud. Internal audit disclosure was sublimated.

Profit centers may distort facts to hold off divestment. One profit center was running into hard times. Corporate management was looking only at the bottom line, judging the worth of the division by what it brought into the corporate coffers. When the line started turning from black to red, corporate executives started thinking about amputation. But the division comprised more than numbers and things; it was also made up of people. They were fully aware that poor performance could bring drastic action that their jobs, their status, their seniority, and their futures were in jeopardy. The first law of nature is self-preservation. Those with much to lose and the opportunity to protect themselves resorted to "cooking the books" to turn actual red into ostensible black.

Incompetent managers may deceive to survive. Nothing stands still. Ours is a galloping technology. Good managers keep abreast of change. Poor ones slip back. In a number of instances, consultants found that what some managers could not produce on merit, they spelled out in reports that puffed up their performance in defiance of the existing facts.

Performance may be distorted to warrant larger bonuses. Managers in many organizations participate in management incentive plans. The better the performance, the larger the bonus. In large organizations, performance is demonstrated by numbers in a report. The temptation dangles before all of us to put the best face on our accomplishments. When the size of the reward hangs on the size of the reported numbers, and where managers feel that they can manipulate the numbers without detection, some of them may succumb to temptation.

The need to succeed can turn managers to deception. Ambition is a worthy trait. It can move ordinary people to do extraordinary things. But when ambition drives with an unmerciful whip, and when self-advancement is more important than solid accomplishment, some managers will betray the stewardship of the resources entrusted to them. To the detriment of reasonable, long-range performance, some managers have shown superior short-range performance and then moved on before the long-range effects could catch up with them. Their methods included inadequate funding of research and development, so that the organization ultimately lost its share of the market; deterioration of machinery and equipment, so that ultimately production faltered; and the loss of good, well-paid people, replaced by low-salaried hacks.

Unscrupulous managers may serve interests that conflict. A manager should be loyal to one master only. That loyalty must never be fractioned. The chief engineer who requires all potential suppliers of goods to use a testing organization he or she personally owns, the purchasing agent who specifies products only a favored and compliant supplier will produce, the inspector who certifies a low-quality supplier for a price — all these contribute to the hiding or falsification of records that will hush the cry of conflict of interest.

Profits may be inflated to obtain advantages in the marketplace. The financial officers or executives who want their organization's stock to make a splash in the market, to cash-in stock options, or seek to obtain unwarranted credit lines may inflate profits unfairly. They take this path if they bow to temptation, have the opportunity, and are unafraid of being detected. Consultants have found that those who do deceive have insatiable greed and a supreme contempt for the abilities of those who have the job of detecting improprieties. Their belief of their own abilities transcends any fear of detection.

Each of these reasons for deception exists in abundance in the business world. But deceptions sprout only under the rains of opportunity. The umbrella against the downpour is constructed of good business practice, adherence to accepted principles of management, knowledge of what goes on in the enterprise, and reports that are independently reviewed by both external and internal auditors. Let any corporate executives forget their responsibility to manage — a responsibility they dare not delegate — and they reap a bitter harvest.

When Management Fraud Occurs

An immediate result of management fraud, after it is detected, is the cruel drain on the time and nervous systems of the senior executives or the members of the boards of directors who must excise the cancer and bind up the wound, unless they also are a part of the problem. All the cost and the time spent on curing will, most likely, exceed by far that which was needed for preventive medicine. All auditors and investigators who have worked on fraud cases will recall the pain that senior executives experience and exhibit (unless they themselves are also the miscreants) when they find that valued subordinates betrayed their trust. It is a trauma no executive seeks.

When management fraud occurs, executive management, in its outrage, may take swift and drastic action. This can be a fatal error. The tendency is to focus on the legal aspects, turn loose the authorities, dismiss the ostensible miscreant, and thus abort a methodical, thorough, productive investigation.

Corporate heads, including the boards of directors and audit committees, should regard the occurrence as a business problem, not a legal problem. The latter comes afterwards. Key personnel should not be dismissed before the problem is solved. There may be innocents among those considered guilty. Only a fair investigation can sort them out. Both the professional investigator and the internal auditors have a duty to protect the innocent as well as to identify the guilty.

Corporate heads should seek to minimize losses so that they can honestly tell the bonding organization that all efforts were exerted to prevent any extension of losses and mitigate damages.

They must look at a broader picture than that which focuses solely on the cancer within the body corporate. They must be concerned with the possible loss of credibility in the marketplace — the assessment that financial analysts will place upon the circumstances. They should be concerned with the premiums on new fidelity insurance and the impact on new coverage. And so they should be able to point out to the insurance carrier that the steps taken in the wake of the investigation will see to it that no more harsh surprises are in the offing.

They should concern themselves with the disruption of business. Herds of auditors and investigators descending on a profit center can have a devastating effect. Hence, an executive should be assigned to coordinate the efforts of all groups involved in the investigation. These efforts, among others, are:

External auditors. Have the external auditors verify financial reports. Request the external auditors to perform a "heavy review," as compared to an audit. Since the latter may result in litigation, the corporation legal staff should arrange to have access to the external auditors' working papers. Ensure that the external auditors are "independent" in fact as well as name.

Internal auditors. Have them supplement the work of the external auditors, analyze operating records and reports — as distinguished from financial records and reports — and support any consultants used in gathering information and helping to analyze data.

Legal counsel. Have corporate attorneys determine the need for disclosure and for compliance with Securities and Exchange Commission and other regulatory requirements. Premature disclosure, before it is determined with certainty that fraud exists and that there is adequate evidence to support the finding, may prejudice the organization's case and reputation. The attorneys can determine, as a matter of law, when the facts demand disclosure and when disclosure can properly be delayed. The attorneys should also evaluate the legal aspect of recoveries under any fidelity policies and what action may be taken against third parties whose negligence or participation contributed to the difficulties.

Outside consultants. Have consultants skilled in the identification of fraudulent acts carry out the delicate task of interrogating witnesses. Consultants can provide an aura of objectivity and neutrality needed to obtain the cooperation of witnesses. They can advise the internal auditors about which avenues to explore, what information to obtain, and what records to analyze. They can guide the analysis of third-party records — documents submitted by people outside the organization. They can help determine whether those documents are valid, and they can go behind supporting documents to dredge up the whole truth. Also, since they are external to the organization and may never again be seen, they can obtain information an insider might be denied. (See previous section, Forensics and Fraud Investigations.)

See Chapter 30, Relationships with Boards of Directors and Audit Committees, for comments resulting from misdeeds of corporate officers and "independent" public accountants that surfaced in 2001 and 2002.

The Symptoms of Management Fraud

Investigation consultants have identified a set of symptoms that are usually reliable indicators of an improper condition. The symptom is but a surface lesion. The cancerous condition lies below it, but the lesions have to be recognized for what they imply. Here are a few of these indicators, some explanations, and some examples:

Consistently late reports. Honest reports can usually be issued on time since their purpose is to inform, not deceive. But in order for a deceiver to know where figures need to be plugged, he or she must analyze the reported data to know just where the data is to be manipulated. These analyses take time. Continuing late reports cry for in-depth investigations and a search for the reasons for delays.

Managers who regularly assume subordinates' duties. In one organization, a vice president of administration never relinquished the comptrollership function. The nominal comptroller was a flunky. The vice president also overrode the credit manager and acted as warehouse manager. Even worse, he preempted the cash manager's responsibilities and took deposits to the bank. Some of the purported deposits, most of them in cash, were never made to the organization's account. An alert internal audit department might have detected the symptoms and done some digging. But the organization, large enough to generate $400,000,000 in sales, apparently did not feel that it needed any internal auditors.

Noncompliance with corporate directives and procedures. A chief financial officer of a subsidiary was directed by corporate executives to install a standard cost system. He gave excuse after excuse for the delay. Three years went by while he was able to hide the cost problems that a standard cost system would have exposed.

Payments to trade creditors supported by copies instead of originals. One subsidiary had a practice of doctoring the support for payments to its creditors. Some of the payments were supported with an original invoice but a copy of a receiving memo. Others it supported with an original receiving memo but a duplicate invoice. The duplicates and the originals were artfully mixed so as to avoid a pattern that might have alerted the external auditors. The organization employed no internal auditors.

Because of the clever mixture of originals and copies, and the absence of the deterrent effect of competent internal auditors, duplicate payments and kickbacks flourished.

Negative debit memos. At one profit center, credit memos were generated by the computer. When the financial officer wished to write off a credit memo, he would generate a negative debit memo. The external auditors were dutifully provided with all credit memos. They were not made aware of the debit memos.

Commissions not in line with increased sales. In one corporation, sales skyrocketed. But most of the increase was the result of cranking fictitious contracts into the computer. At the same time, commissions to salespeople were valid and accurate. The sales and commissions were supposed to be interrelated. So the picture was there for anyone to see: contracts escalating but commissions hardly rising.

In all the cases just described, the symptoms were visible. The indicators could be plotted and the data behind them could be verified. An alert internal audit group could have been able to determine the types of indicators needed for top management surveillance.

Controlling Management Fraud

The cornerstone in the structure designed to control management fraud is an environment created by the organization's policy makers. It is an environment that fosters morality and high business ethics. Let sharp practices flourish at the top — income smoothing, "aggressive accounting," lavish entertainment, bribes to officials — and the seeds for management fraud are sown.

Senior management must also understand that the manager of a profit center has autonomy and opportunity. The greater the freedom, the easier it is to fall into temptation. Without constricting managers to the point that imagination and innovation are squeezed out of them, the systems should provide checks and balances and reports that cause flares to streak across the corporate sky if improprieties are practiced. Some of the control measures that executive managers should install are:

- Establish standards, budgetary and statistical, and investigate all material deviations.

- Use quantitative and analytical techniques (time series analyses, regression and correlation analyses, and random sampling) to highlight aberrant behavior. Develop indicators such as space used, time required, weight limitations imposed, and usage and output compared. Where possible, develop management information systems that supply the data needed for such analyses.

- Compare performance with industry norms as well as with the performance of comparable profit centers within the organization.

- Identify critical process indicators: melt loss in smelting, death loss in feedlots, rework in manufacturing and assembly, and gross profit tests in buy-sell or retail operations.

- Carefully analyze performance that looks too good as well as performance that does not meet standards.

- Establish a professional internal audit department. Provide it with a charter, signed by the chief executive officer and approved by an independent professional audit committee of the board of directors, which gives it independence of the activities it audits, guarantees objectivity, authorizes the periodic review of all operations, and demands the appropriate consideration of all reported deficiency findings and recommendations for corrective action.

U.S. Sentencing Commission Guidelines

In closing this chapter it might be well to briefly discuss the U.S. Sentencing Commission Guidelines.[27] Organizations are vulnerable for acts of their employees. If an employee commits an act for which the organization could be held culpable, some degree of relief can be available if the organization can prove that it had an effective compliance program in effect before the act was committed. The benefits of having this program in effect include:

1. Lowering of fines.
2. Easier prosecution.
3. Reduction of liability of officers and directors.
4. Lower costs of legal defense.
5. Prevention of damage to the reputation of the organization.

A compliance program is based on, among other things, an effective internal auditing program that comprises in total what is described as "organizational due diligence." These items are briefly:

1. Compliance standards and procedures.
2. Assignment at a high level of responsibility for compliance with the standards.
3. Use of due care in preventing authority by questionable personnel.
4. Communication of the standards and procedures to employees and others along with suitable training.
5. Achieving compliance through maintaining and auditing systems and hot lines.
6. Consistent enforcement of the standards, including proper disciplinary action when necessary.
7. Making appropriate changes in the above when there are indications of failure.

Thus, it appears that the auditing for fraud that should be an element of all internal auditing programs here has, relative to the "Sentencing Guidelines," a dual benefit, i.e., the protection of assets of the organization; and protection of the organization and its officers from the punitive aspects of federal action where federal criminal law has been violated.

References

[1]*Statement of Internal Auditing Standards No. 3,* "Deterrence, Investigation, and Reporting of Fraud" (Altamonte Springs, FL: The Institute of Internal Auditors, May 1985).

[2]U.S. Department of Justice, *The Investigation of White Collar Crime* (Washington, DC: Government Printing Office, April 1977), 4.

[3]Prosser, W.L., and W.P. Keeton, *Prosser and Keeton on Torts,* 5th Ed. (St. Paul, MN: West Publishing Co., 1984), 728.

[4]*The Investigation of White Collar Crime,* 123.

[5]Kelley, C.M., "Accountants and Auditors vs. White Collar Crime," *The Internal Auditor,* June 1976, 35.

[6]Thompson, Jr., C.M., "Fighting Fraud," *Internal Auditor,* August 1992, 23.

[7]Niestrath, D.B., "Catch That Thief," *The Internal Auditor,* January/February 1974, 67.

[8]Horn, Stephen, "A Unique Remedy for Business Loss," *The Internal Auditor,* February 1974, 22.

[9]Davia, H.R., P.C. Coggins, J.C. Widman, and J.T. Kastantin, *Accountant's Guide to Fraud Detection and Control* (New York: John Wiley and Sons, Inc., 2000), 153-154.

[10]Iannacci, Jerry, and Ron Morris, *Access Device Fraud and Related Financial Crimes* (New York: CRC Press, 2000), 66.

[11]State Street Trust Company v. Ernst, 15 N.E. 2nd 416, 1938.

[12]Steele, H.T., "Investigating Alleged Fraud," *The Internal Auditor,* October 1982, 22.

[13]Henderson Jr., W.E., "Employee Thefts and Fidelity Bonding," *The Internal Auditor,* November/December 1974, 24.

[14]Iannacci, 27-40.

[15]Kennish, J.W., "The Investigative Process," *The Internal Auditor,* April 1985, 20.

[16]Ibid., 22.

[17]Waltman, J.L., and S.P. Golen, "Detecting Deception During Interviews," *Internal Auditor,* August 1993, 61-63.

[18]Bologna, Jack, and Paul Shaw, *Auditing Cyber Fraud in Small Businesses* (New York: John Wiley & Sons, Inc., 2000), 153-4.

[19]Ibid., 159.

[20]Manning, George A., *Financial Investigating and Forensic Accounting* (New York: CRC Press, 1999), 369-390.

[21]Prosser, 48.

[22]Henderson Jr., W.E., "Employee Thefts and Fidelity Bonding," *The Internal Auditor,* November/December 1974, 31.

[23]Russel, H.F., *Foozles and Frauds* (Altamonte Springs, FL: The Institute of Internal Auditors, 1977), 146.

[24]"Readers Problem Clinic," *The Internal Auditor,* Fall 1961, 68-69.

[25]"Readers Problem Clinic," *The Internal Auditor,* Spring 1961, 71-76.

[26]Sawyer, L.B., A.A. Murphy, and Michael Crossley, "Management Fraud: The Insidious Specter," *The Internal Auditor,* April 1979, 11-25.

[27]Bologna, 49-53.

Supplementary Readings

Albrecht, W. Steve, Edwin A. McDermott, and Timothy L. Williams, "Reducing the Cost of Fraud," *Internal Auditor*, February 1994, 28-35.

Albrecht, W. Steve, and Timothy L. Williams, "Understanding Reactions to Fraud," *Internal Auditor*, August 1990, 45-51.

Albrecht, W. Steve, "Employee Fraud," *Internal Auditor*, October 1996, 26-37.

Allen, Robert, and Marshall B. Romney, "Lessons from New Era," *Internal Auditor*, October 1998, 40-47.

Allen, Robert D., and D. Ray Strong, "Are We Giving Fraud Perpetrators a License to Steal?," *Internal Auditing,* September/October 1999, 3-6.

Beasley, Mark S., Joseph V. Carcello, and Dana R. Hermanson, "Prevention and Detection of Financial Statement Fraud," *Internal Auditing*, May/June 2001, 8-12.

Bologna, G. Jack, Robert J. Lindquist, and Joseph Wells, *The Accountant's Handbook of Fraud & Commercial Crime* (New York: John Wiley and Sons, Inc., 1992).

Burke, Jacqueline, and Anthony N. Dalessio, "Highlights of SAS N° 82 for the Internal Auditor," *Internal Auditing*, November/December 1998, 40-44.

Colbert, Janet L., and C. Wayne Alderman, "Auditing Standards on Fraud: SIAS 3 and SAS 82," *Internal Auditing*, May/June 1998, 3-8.

Collier, Paul Arnold, Robert Dixon, and Claire Lesley Marston, "Computer Fraud: Research Findings from The UK," *Internal Auditor*, August 1991, 49-52.

Cowan, Neil, "Company-Wide Fraud Offensive," *Internal Auditor*, 88.

DeHaven Sr., David L., "Detecting and Reporting Illegal Acts," *Internal Auditor*, August 1990, 52-54.

Ehlers, Helen, "Building a Case," *Internal Auditor*, October 1996, 38-43.

Figg, Jonathan, "Whistleblowing," *Internal Auditor*, April 2000, 30-37.

Green, Brian Patrick, and Thomas G. Calderon, "The Role of Collusion in Management Fraud," *Internal Auditing,* September/October 2001, 3-16.

Grieshober, William E., "Old Dogs, New Tricks," *Internal Auditor*, August 2001, 77-79.

Grieshober, William E., "A Thief Among Us," *Internal Auditor*, December 2000, 71-73

Hancox, David R., "Could the Equity Funding Scandal Happen Again?" *Internal Auditor*, October 1997, 28-34.

Holter, Norma C., and W. Michael Seganish, "Identity Fraud: A New Frontier in Risk Assessment," *Internal Auditing*, July/August 2000, 3-10.

Kolman, Mark R., "What Constitutes Fraud?," *Internal Auditor*, June 1999, 88.

Leinicke, Linda Marie, W. Max Rexroad, and Jon D. Ward, "Computer Fraud Auditing: It Works," *Internal Auditor*, August 1990, 26-34.

Loescher, Barbara A., "No Friend Indeed," *Internal Auditor*, February 2001, 73-75.

Lovret, Robert, "Fidelity Insurance Claims," *Internal Auditor*, April 2000, 58-61.

Martin, Dale R., George R. Aldhizer, III, John L. Campbell, and Terry A. Baker, "When Earnings Management Becomes Fraud," *Internal Auditing*, July/August 2002, 14-21.

Pearson, Thomas C., Terry Gregson, and John Wendell, "A Primer for Internal Auditors Considering Whistle-blowing," *Internal Auditing*, May/June 1998, 9-19.

Rezaee, Zabihollah, "Internal Auditors' Roles in the Prevention, Detection, and Correction of Financial Statement Fraud," *Internal Auditing*, May/June 2002, 13-20.

Rudloff, Robert W., "Casino Fraud," *Internal Auditor*, June 1999, 44-49.

Sears, Brian P., *Internal Auditing Manual* (New York: RIA, 2003). (See Chapter H1, "Business Fraud and Business Ethics," Chapter H2, "Financial Reporting Fraud," and Chapter H3, "Procurement Fraud.")

Strand, Carolyn A., and Jeffrey W. Strawser, "Help for Internal Auditors: SAS N° 82 Identifies Risk Factors for Misappropriation of Assets," *Internal Auditing*, January/February 2000, 9-14.

Thomas, C. William, and Curtis E. Clements, "The Internal Auditor's Role in the Detection and Prevention of Fraud," *Internal Auditing*, July/August 2002, 3-13.

Thompson, Jr., Courtenay M., "Fighting Fraud," *Internal Auditor*, August 1992, 18-23.

Thompson, Courtenay, "The Incentive to Defraud," *Internal Auditor*, October 2000, 63-65.

Thompson, Courtenay, "Snag in the New Subsidiary," *Internal Auditor*, June 2000, 71-73.

Thompson, Courtenay, "Whose Mercedes is That?," *Internal Auditor*, February 2000, 61-63.

Thompson, Courtenay, "Exposing Financial Statement Fraud," *Internal Auditor*, October 1999, 69-71.

Thornhill, William T., "The Importance of Internal Control in Fraud Prevention," *Internal Auditing*, Fall 1996, 50-54.

Verschoor, Curtis C., "SEC Hopes New Rules Will Stop Financial Fraud," *Internal Auditing*, March/April 2000, 38-40.

Welch, Sandra T., Sarah A. Holmes, and Robert H. Strawser, "The Inhibiting Effect of Internal Auditors on Fraud," *Internal Auditing*, Fall 1996, 23-32.

Wells, Joseph T., and Richard B. Carozza, "Corruption in Collegiate Sports," *Internal Auditor*, April 2000, 38-45.

Wells, Joseph T., "An Unholy Trinity," *Internal Auditor*, April 1998, 28-33.

Zeune, Gary, "Are You Teaching Your Employees to Steal?," *Internal Auditing*, May/June 2001, 33-35.

Multiple-choice Questions

1. Which of the following would indicate that fraud may be present in a marketing department?
   a. There is no documentation for some fairly large payments made to a new vendor.
   b. A manager appears to be living a lifestyle that is in excess of what could be provided by a marketing manager's salary.
   c. To encourage creativity, management has adapted a control environment that can best be described as very loose.
   d. All of the above.

2. Which of the following might be considered a "red flag" indicating possible fraud in a large manufacturing organization with several subsidiaries?
   a. The existence of a financial subsidiary.
   b. A consistent record of above average return on investment for all subsidiaries.
   c. Complex sales transactions and transfers of funds between affiliated organizations.
   d. Use of separate bank accounts for payrolls by each subsidiary.

3. An organization hired a highly qualified accounts payable manager who had been terminated from another organization for alleged wrongdoing. Six months later, the manager diverted $12,000 by sending duplicate payments of invoices to a relative. A control that might have prevented this situation would be to:
   a. Adequately check prior employment backgrounds for all new employees.
   b. Not hire individuals who appear overqualified for a job.
   c. Verify educational background for all new employees.
   d. Check to see if close relatives work for vendors.

4. A subsidiary president terminated a controller and hired a replacement without the required corporate approvals. Sales, cash flow, and profit statistics were then manipulated by the new controller and president via accelerated depreciation and sale of capital assets to obtain larger performance bonuses for the controller and the subsidiary president. An approach that might detect this fraudulent activity would be:
   a. Analysis of overall management control for segregation of duties.
   b. Required exit interviews for all terminated employees.
   c. Periodic changes of outside public accountants.
   d. Regular analytical review of operating divisions.

5. According to the *Standards*, a fraud report is required:
   a. At the conclusion of the detection phase.
   b. At the conclusion of the investigation phase.
   c. At the conclusion of both the detection and the investigation phases.
   d. Neither at the conclusion of the detection phase nor at the conclusion of the investigation phase.

6. Experience has shown that certain conditions in an organization are symptoms of possible management fraud. Which of the following conditions would **not** be considered an indicator of possible fraud?
   a. Managers regularly assuming subordinates' duties.
   b. Managers dealing in matters outside their profit center's scope.
   c. Managers not complying with corporate directives and procedures.
   d. Managers subject to formal, regular performance reviews.

7. An employee was reimbursed for expenses in which receipts were being altered by adding a 1 to the amount (e.g., $29.00 raised to $129.00). A means of detection is to:
   a. Verify copies of receipts from vendors to the amount submitted by the employee.
   b. Require proper supervisory approval.
   c. Require the controller to approve all expense reports.
   d. Require both supervisory and controller approvals of all expense reports.

8. A personnel department is responsible for processing placement agency fees for new hires. A recruiter established some bogus placement agencies and, when interviewing walk-in applicants, the recruiter would list one of the bogus agencies as referring the candidate. A possible means of detection or deterrence is to:
   a. Process all personnel agency invoices via a purchase order through the purchasing department.
   b. Verify new vendors to firms listed in a professional association catalog and/or verify the vendor name and address through the telephone book.
   c. Monitor the closeness of the relationships of recruiters with specific vendors.
   d. Require all employees to sign an annual conflict of interest statement.

9. Purchases from two new vendors increased dramatically after a new buyer was hired. The buyer was obtaining kickbacks from the two vendors based on sales volume. A possible means of detection is:
   a. Periodic vendor surveys regarding potential buyer conflict of interest or ethics violations.
   b. The receipt of an invoice to put new vendors on the master file.
   c. The use of purchase orders for all purchases.
   d. The use of change analysis and trend analysis of buyer or vendor activity.

10. Because of the small staff, one remote unit's petty cash custodian had responsibility for the impress fund checking account reconciliation. The cashier concealed a diversion of funds by altering the beginning balance on the monthly reconciliations sent to the group office. A possible audit test to detect this would be to:
    a. Compare monthly balances and use change and trend analysis.
    b. Require additional monitoring by headquarters whenever improper segregation of duties exists at remote units.

  c. Determine if any employees have high personal debt.

  d. Determine if any employees are leading expensive lifestyles.

11. In an organization that has a separate division that is primarily responsible for fraud deterrence, the internal audit department is responsible for:

  a. Examining and evaluating the adequacy and effectiveness of that division's actions taken to deter fraud.

  b. Establishing and maintaining that division's system of internal controls.

  c. Planning that division's fraud deterrence activities.

  d. Controlling that division's fraud deterrence activities.

12. Internal auditors must exercise due care if they are to meet their responsibilities for fraud detection. Thus, the existence of certain conditions should raise "red flags" and arouse auditors' professional skepticism concerning possible fraud. Which of the following is most likely to be considered an indication of possible fraud?

  a. A new management team installed as a result of a takeover.

  b. Rapid turnover of financial executives.

  c. Rapid expansion into new markets.

  d. An Internal Revenue Service audit of tax returns.

13. An internal auditor has detected probable employee fraud and is preparing a preliminary report for management. The report should include:

  a. A statement that an internal audit conducted with due professional care cannot provide absolute assurance that irregularities have not occurred.

  b. The auditor's conclusion as to whether sufficient information exists to conduct an investigation.

  c. The results of a polygraph test administered to the suspected perpetrator(s) of the fraud.

  d. A list of proposed audit tests to help disclose the existence of similar frauds in the future.

14. When conducting fraud investigations, internal auditing should:

  a. Clearly indicate the extent of internal auditing's knowledge of the fraud when questioning suspects.

  b. Assign personnel to the investigation in accordance with the audit schedule established at the beginning of the fiscal year.

  c. Perform its investigation independent of lawyers, security personnel, and specialists from outside the organization who are involved in the investigation.

  d. Assess the probable level and the extent of complicity of fraud within the organization.

15. For internal auditors to be able to recognize potential fraud, they must be aware of the basic characteristics of fraud. Which of the following is **not** a characteristic of fraud?
    a. Intentional deception.
    b. Taking unfair or dishonest advantage.
    c. Perpetration for the benefit or detriment of the organization.
    d. Negligence on the part of executive management.

16. Internal auditing is responsible for assisting in the prevention of fraud by:
    a. Informing the appropriate authorities within the organization and recommending whatever investigation is considered necessary in the circumstances when wrongdoing is suspected.
    b. Establishing the systems designed to ensure compliance with the organization's policies, plans, and procedures, as well as applicable laws and regulations.
    c. Examining and evaluating the adequacy and the effectiveness of control, commensurate with the extent of the potential exposure/risk in the various segments of the organization's operations.
    d. Determining whether operating standards have been established for measuring economy and efficiency, and whether these standards are understood and are being met.

17. A significant employee fraud took place shortly after an internal audit. The internal auditor may **not** have properly fulfilled the responsibility for the deterrence of fraud by failing to note and report that:
    a. Policies, practices, and procedures to monitor activities and safeguard assets were less extensive in low-risk areas than in high-risk areas.
    b. A system of control that depended upon separation of duties could be circumvented by collusion among three employees.
    c. There were no written policies describing prohibited activities and the action required whenever violations were discovered.
    d. Divisional employee had not been properly trained to distinguish between bona fide signatures and cleverly forged ones on authorization forms.

18. An internal auditor is preparing a report that discusses the possibility of employee fraud by a specifically named employee. The auditor should be careful that distribution of the report be limited on a "need-to-know" basis. Failure to follow this caveat may result in the auditor and his or her employer being found liable for:
    a. Libel.
    b. Slander.
    c. Compounding a felony.
    d. Malicious prosecution.

19. After completing an investigation, internal auditing has concluded that an employee has stolen a significant amount of cash receipts. A draft of the proposed report on this finding should be submitted for review to:
    a. Legal counsel.
    b. The audit committee of the board of directors.
    c. The president of the organization.
    d. The organization's outside auditors.

20. Fraud may be most properly defined as:
    a. False representation or concealment of a material fact to the benefit or detriment of an individual or the organization.
    b. Extortion in which the threat of physical violence is used to coerce someone to part with something of value.
    c. The use of organization assets for one's own personal purposes.
    d. The outright theft of organization assets without falsification of records to conceal the act.

21. According to the *Standards*, an internal auditor's responsibility for reporting fraud includes which of the following guidelines?
    a. Notify management of fraud when the auditor has exhausted reviewing the data related to the fraud.
    b. Issue a written report at the conclusion of the investigation and not sooner.
    c. Notify management if fraud has been established to a reasonable certainty.
    d. Provide a draft of the report only to senior management.

22. Fraud may be perpetrated with the intent to benefit an organization. Which of the following is an example of such a fraud?
    a. Acceptance of bribes or kickbacks by a purchasing agent.
    b. Claims submitted for services or goods not provided to the organization.
    c. Sale or assignment of fictitious or misrepresented assets.
    d. Diversion to an employee or outsider of a transaction that would normally generate profits for the organization.

23. One of the elements of fraud includes a representation made with the knowledge of its falsity or without sufficient knowledge on the subject to warrant a representation. This is commonly referred to as:
    a. Undue influence.
    b. Scienter.
    c. Estoppel.
    d. Unconscionable advantage.

24. Which of the following would be used by internal auditors to indicate the possible existence of fraud?
   a. Analytical review.
   b. Confirmations.
   c. Inquiry.
   d. Test of detailed transactions.

25. Which of the following is most likely to be considered an indication of possible fraud?
   a. The replacement of the management team after a hostile takeover.
   b. Rapid turnover of the organization's financial executives.
   c. Rapid expansion into new markets.
   d. A government audit of the organization's tax returns.

26. Which of the following fraudulent entries is most likely to be made to conceal the theft of an asset?
   a. Debit expenses, and credit the asset.
   b. Debit the asset, and credit another asset account.
   c. Debit revenue, and credit the asset.
   d. Debit another asset account, and credit the asset.

Use the following information for the next two questions.

An audit of an international nonprofit organization established to finance medical research revealed the following amounts (in millions):

	Current Year	Past Year
Revenue	$ 500	$425
Investments (average balance)	$ 210	$185
Medical research grants made	$ 418	$325
Investment income	$ 16	$ 20
Administrative expense	$ 10	$ 8

27. Which of the following possible frauds or misuses of organization assets should be considered the area of greatest risk if controls are only marginal?
   a. A senior manager using company travel and entertainment funds for activities that might be unauthorized.
   b. Supplies purchased from fictitious vendors.
   c. Grants made to organizations that might be associated with the president or not for purposes dictated in the organization's charter.
   d. A payroll clerk adding fictitious employees.

28. Before an audit report is issued, a front-page article appears in a newspaper alleging that the president has been using the organization's funds for personal purposes. The auditor has enough information to confirm the allegations made in the newspaper article. The auditor is contacted by a reporter for the newspaper to confirm the facts. Which of the following would be the best response by the auditor?
    a. Respond truthfully and fully since the auditor is able to confirm the facts concerning the president, not the organization.
    b. Direct the inquiry to the audit committee of the board of directors.
    c. Provide information "off the record" so that the article does not state who gave the information.
    d. Respond that the investigation is not complete.

29. The audit committee of a charitable organization suspects that a senior manager may be taking major contributions and depositing them in alternative accounts or soliciting contributions to be made in the name of another organization. Which of the following audit procedures would be most effective in detecting the existence of such improper activities?
    a. Use generalized audit software to take a sample of pledged receipts not yet collected and confirm the amounts due with the donors.
    b. Select a sample that includes large donors for the past three years and a statistical sample of others and request a confirmation of total contributions made to the organization or to affiliated organizations.
    c. Select a discovery sample of cash receipts and confirm the amounts of the receipts with the donors. Investigate any differences.
    d. Use analytical review procedures to compare contributions generated with those of other comparable institutions over the same period of time. If the amount is significantly less, take a detailed sample of cash receipts and trace to the bank statements.

30. Which of the following would not be considered a condition that indicates a higher likelihood of fraud?
    a. Management has delegated the authority to make purchases under a certain dollar limit to subordinates.
    b. An individual has held the same cash-handling job for an extended period without any rotation of duties.
    c. An individual handling marketable securities is responsible for making the purchases recording the purchases, and reporting any discrepancies and gains/losses to senior management.
    d. The assignment of responsibility and accountability in the accounts receivable department is not clear.

31. Which of the following statements is correct regarding the deterrence of fraud?
    I. The primary means of determining fraud is through an effective control system initiated by top management.
    II. Internal auditors are responsible for assisting in the deterrence of fraud by examining and evaluating the adequacy of the control system.
    III. Internal auditors should determine whether communication channels provide management with adequate and reliable information regarding the effectiveness of the control system and the occurrence of unusual transactions.
    a. I only.
    b. I and II only.
    c. II only.
    d. I, II, and III.

32. A CIA, working as the director of purchasing, signs a contract to procure a large order from the supplier with the best price quality and performance. Shortly after signing the contract, the supplier presents the CIA with a gift of significant monetary value. Which of the following statements regarding the acceptance of the gift is correct?
    a. Acceptance of the gift would be prohibited only if it were non-customary.
    b. Acceptance of the gift would violate The IIA's Code *of Ethics* and would be prohibited for a CIA.
    c. Since the CIA is not acting as an internal auditor, acceptance of the gift would be governed only by the organization's code of conduct.
    d. Since the contract was signed before the gift was offered, acceptance of the gift would not violate either The IIA's *Code of Ethics* or the organization's code of conduct.

33. An adequate system of internal controls is most likely to detect an irregularity perpetrated by a:
    a. Group of employees in collusion.
    b. Single employee.
    c. Group of managers in collusion.
    d. Single manager.

34. During the course of a bank audit, an auditor discovered that one loan officer had approved loans to a number of related but separate organizations in violation of regulatory policies. The auditor believes the action may have been intentional because the loan officer is related to one of the primary owners or the corporate group that controls the related organizations. The auditor should:
    a. Inform management of the conflict of interest and the violation of the regulatory requirements and suggest further investigation.
    b. Report the violation to the regulatory agency because it constitutes a significant breakdown of the bank's control structure.

c. Not report the violation if the loan officer agrees to take corrective action.

d. Expand the audit work to determine if there may be fraudulent activity on the part of the loan officer and report the findings to management when the follow-up investigation is complete.

35. Which of the following situations would be a violation of The IIA's *Code of Ethics?*
   a. An auditor was subpoenaed in a court case in which a merger partner claimed to have been defrauded by the auditor's company. The auditor divulged confidential audit information to the court.
   b. An auditor for a manufacturer of office products recently completed an audit of the corporate marketing function. Based on this experience, the auditor spent several hours one Saturday working as a paid consultant to a hospital in the focal area that intended to conduct an audit of its marketing function.
   c. An auditor gave a speech at a local IIA chapter meeting outlining the contents of a program the auditor had developed for auditing electronic data interchange connections. Several auditors from major competitors were in the audience.
   d. During an audit, an auditor teamed that the company was about to introduce a new product that would revolutionize the industry. Because of the probable success of the new product, the product manager suggested the auditor buy additional stock in the company, which the auditor did.

36. Even though a chief audit executive referred a case of potential fraud to the security department, the suspected perpetrator continued to defraud the organization until discovered by a line manager two years later. What should the chief audit executive have done?
   a. The executive's actions were correct.
   b. The executive should have periodically checked the status of the case with the security department.
   c. The executive should have conducted a fraud investigation.
   d. The executive should have discharged the perpetrator.

37. According to the *Standards,* which of the following is the correct listing of the information that must be included in a fraud report?
   a. Purpose, scope, results, and, where appropriate, an expression of the auditor's opinion.
   b. Criteria, cause, condition, and effect.
   c. Background, findings, and recommendations.
   d. Findings, conclusions, recommendations, and corrective action.

38. Which of the following payroll fraud control activities is an appropriate responsibility of the human resources department?
    a. Distributing payroll checks.
    b. Controlling overtime throughout the organization.
    c. Authorizing payment master-file additions and deletions.
    d. Receiving unclaimed payroll checks and retaining them until final disposition.

Chapter 28
Dealing with People

How clients regard internal auditors. Staff-line conflicting objectives. Reasons for low esteem. Churchill and Cooper's study. Mints' study. Fears stemming from the line/staff relations. Negative connotations of control. The potential misuse of power. Using motivational needs to improve audit relationships. Learning to manage constraints resulting from change. How to react to conflicts in the audit process. Resolving conflict. The use of motivation. Roles, role conflicts, stress, and how to accommodate them. Why good relations can lead to good audits. Auditor/client relations. Suggestions for improving relations. Client feedback. The internal auditor as a consultant. The client's perception of the auditor. Dealing with fraud. Dispelling fear and mistrust. Dealing with the intransigent client. The importance of learning to listen. Aggressive listening. Barriers to listening. Means of concentrating. Effective use of interview questions. Communication. Meetings. Obtaining participation from the client. Traditional versus participative auditing. Participative auditing. Problem-solving partner vs. investigator. Dealing with operating managers but issuing reports on their work.

Introduction

Financial auditors usually deal with figures, sometimes with management processes. Management oriented internal auditors deal extensively with people. To obtain the information they need and to ensure corrective action on their audit findings, internal auditors must develop and maintain good relations with clients. Yet internal auditors can find themselves buffeted by conflicting objectives that appear to be in complete opposition. The problem is a knotty one:

- On the one hand, to secure cooperation from clients; on the other hand, to be alert to the possibility of fraud and inefficiency and to root it out when it becomes evident.

- On the one hand, to gain the confidence of an operating manager; on the other hand, to record deficiency findings in a report going to the manager's superior.

- On the one hand, to be on the chief executive officer's payroll; on the other hand, to report to the board of directors derelictions in an enterprise for which the CEO has complete responsibility.

Meeting these conflicting aims can be difficult; yet they must be met if internal auditors are to carry out the responsibilities assigned to them. This chapter discusses the problems and explores solutions; specifically:

- How clients regard auditors.
- The causes of low esteem.
- The importance of developing and maintaining good auditor/client relations.
- Handling change, power, and conflict.
- The use of motivational needs.
- The impact of roles and stress.
- The need for and importance of good relations.
- Some suggestions for improving relations.
- Listening.
- Communication.
- Participative auditing.
- Special problems in audit relationships.

Attitudes Toward Internal Auditors

Early studies on the relationships between internal auditors and those who were audited indicated that the latter, the objects of the audit effort, in most cases, bore no friendly attitudes toward the former. Not only that, responses to questions as to effectiveness, contribution, and problem solving resulting from internal audit effort brought disappointing results. On the other hand, senior management and board of directors seemed to recognize their need for internal audit assistance in the management and direction of the organization.

This attitude has changed materially as a result of the change in the attitude of the internal auditors themselves toward their work. Most audit staffs see their functions as a cooperative approach with the objective of contribution to the organization audited. The result is the increasing number of operating managers who are requesting assistance from the internal audit staff so as to improve their operations as to both efficiency and effectiveness.[1, 2, 3, 4]

Reasons and Causes for Low Esteem

Staff/Line Conflicts

The staff/line relationship is inherently prone to conflict. The very aspect of most staff operations is not endearing to line personnel. Staff people are usually younger. They generally have a better formal education. They are more individualistic. They frequently use a business casual dress mode. They report to higher echelons than do line personnel. Being specialists in their field, they may believe their answers are the only answers. They tend to discount the difficulty line personnel face if called upon to act on a staff person's ideas. And line personnel may feel that they must point out defects to prove themselves to senior management.[5] Finally, they do not have to implement their own recommendations.

Under such circumstances, line personnel most likely regard staff with animosity. The aspect of the staff person is but one reason for the animosity; line people also have reason to fear staff. They fear being shown up for not having thought of the improvements themselves. They fear that proposed changes may disrupt comfortable routines and existing cliques. They fear that revised methods may expose inefficiencies and/or forbidden practices. In a sense, they fear change. This aspect is discussed in more detail later.

Internal auditors are staff. And line people — in this sense, all clients — are likely to regard internal auditors the same way they regard other staff people. Chris Argyris could have been talking about internal auditors in his study of conflicts between budget staff personnel and operating line personnel.[6] Budget personnel, like internal auditors, can perceive their role as being "watchdogs" for the organization. Their gain is somebody else's loss. Their identification of faults and weaknesses shows management they are doing their job well. It also implies, however, that the line personnel are doing theirs badly. Budget personnel — and internal auditors — hold up their findings for all the world to see. At the same time, the line personnel are left naked and shivering before the cold glare of senior management. As Argyris summed it up, ". . .to add insult to injury, the entire incident is made permanent and exhibited to top officials by being placed in a formal report circulated through many top channels."

The above attitudes are being changed. Many internal auditing organizations are emphasizing a cooperative approach. The intent is to focus the work as a helpful device where findings are not termed as deficiencies but more as practices that can be improved by modifications jointly developed by the client and the auditor working together. The intent is to provide assistance to operating managers to perform more efficiently and effectively and thus to improve their stature in the management hierarchy.

An example of this change in attitude is the widespread usage by audit organizations of client evaluations of the audit functions. Questions put to clients are such as: (see "Feedback by the Client" later in this chapter)

- Has the audit made a meaningful contribution to your operating function?
- Did the auditors display a participative approach to the audit?
- Were the audit recommendations a result of joint effort by you and the auditors?
- Were the auditors careful not to disrupt your operations?
- Did the auditors display respect for the operating expertise of you and your specialists?

The evaluation of such questions and others can have two impacts. First, this provides evidence to the client that audit management intends to develop a harmonious and helpful relationship. And, second, the audit staff member is alerted that these attitudes are important to his or her supervisors and managers and that these elements are used as support for his or her performance evaluations.

Suffice to say, it is not always "peaches and cream." Some clients do not respond to this sort of treatment. The recalcitrant client intends to disrupt the audit and create friction on the method of audit and thus to keep the auditor defensive of the methods being used and hopefully (on the client's part) to curtail or limit the audit function. The client's attitude is, "We won't cooperate — you're the auditor — you find the deficiencies and if you are wrong, we'll take you up to top management for poor auditing." In these cases, the client must be told by top management that this is in effect an affront to top management for whom the auditors are working and that it will not be tolerated.

Control

Line personnel may bow to control, but they do not have to like it. Control has negative connotations. Line personnel regard internal auditors as part of the control system. Indeed, internal auditors have made no attempt to downplay that role. The original *Statement of Responsibilities* declared at the outset that internal auditing "is a managerial control which functions by measuring and evaluating the effectiveness of other controls." The Statement is no longer in effect, but the impact of the idea continues. People almost universally dislike both control and those who exert control over them. Control therefore breeds antagonism as a result of client perception of, or personal experience with, audits. Mints points out the causes of antagonism, based on his research findings:[7]

- Fear of criticism stemming from adverse audit findings.

- Fear of changes in day-to-day working habits because of audit recommendations.

- Punitive action by superiors prompted by reported deficiencies.

- Insensitive audit practices — reports that are overly critical, reports that focus on deficiencies only, the air of mystery cloaking some audits, and the perception that auditors gain personally from reporting deficiencies.

- Hostile audit style — a cold and distant aspect, a lack of understanding of the client's problems, an absence of empathy, an air of smugness or superiority, an excessive concentration on insignificant errors, a prosecutorial style when asking questions, and a greater concern with parading defects than helping constructively to improve conditions.

Many internal auditors contribute to these perceptions through their failure to understand why people act as they do in the presence of an auditor. Nearly all conscious behavior is motivated or caused. Internal auditors who have no understanding of motivational theory will cause behavior that places roadblocks in front of their audit objectives. People receive motivation from their underlying needs and act in a way to satisfy those needs. They react negatively and hostilely when those needs are threatened. Motivation is discussed in more detail later.

Douglas R. Carmichael has shown that internal control systems usually make the assumption that "employees have inherent mental, moral, and physical weaknesses."[8] He also showed that these assumptions can be self-fulfilling. They cause the employee to behave in the same undesirable manner that the system sought to prevent. Employees may feel threatened because internal audit findings will result in punishment, loss of personal goals, and deprivation of need satisfaction. Hence, they may resort to dishonesty to meet standards, or they may bury their errors and inefficiencies in the hope that the internal auditor will not find them.

The Handling of Power, Change, and Conflict

Power

Within any organization, people fear or respect power. They fear the power of an autocratic boss. They respect the power of a knowledgeable, charismatic leader. Internal auditors enjoy power. But their ability to deal with people will depend on the kind of power they exercise. For that reason, auditors should be aware of the power that is available to them.

Taylor discusses seven sources of power:[9]

Positional. Power comes from the position itself. Internal auditors have it when they enjoy sufficient organizational status and have the authority to report findings and to express independent opinions.

Expertise. Power depends on knowledge, skills, background, education, wisdom, and information. Professional internal auditors with a broad knowledge of organization operations and audit techniques have this form of power.

Charismatic. Power is based on personality, charm, and an aura of confidence. Internal auditors who develop this form of power, the concept of professional confidence, and the expressed desire to help, gain their ends through the personal relationships they form with clients.

Influential. Power comes from the ability to do favors and give rewards. The objectivity required of internal auditors precludes the complete exercise of this form of power. But internal auditors who assure clients that any voluntary assistance in the audit process and devising and performing corrective action taken on deficiency findings will be duly mentioned in audit reports are, in effect, wielding influential power.

Coercive. Power comes from the ability to withhold favors — the ability to direct, to threaten, and to actually force desired behavior. Internal auditors are advised to refrain from wielding this form of power, since it inevitably breeds resentment and destroys any favorable auditor/client relations.

Applied pressure. The owners of such power can apply sanctions and impose punishment. This may entail borrowing power from others to strengthen the owner's power base. Internal auditors may have that power as a result of their inherent characteristics, and their organizational and reporting status. But like coercive power, it should be exercised with great discretion.

Raw force. This is the final and ultimate power. It usually resides in those having a line position over others. Internal auditors are in staff positions in relation to clients. Raw force, therefore, would seldom if ever be available or appropriate.

The skills needed to wield internal audit power are: technical, interpersonal, and conceptual. For internal auditors, the technical ability lies in their knowledge of principles of control and of good administration, and the capacity to analyze the most complex activities and draw logical conclusions from them. Interpersonal skills depend on the ability to deal with people, a knowledge of their needs, and the use of technical skills to help people achieve those needs. Conceptual skills come from the ability to relate activities audited to the objectives and goals of the individual, his or her organization, and the entire entity.

When internal auditors develop the skills to exercise the appropriate forms of power, their ability to achieve their own goals without unnecessarily upsetting clients is greatly enhanced.

Management of Change

Change is feared by some and welcomed by others. Internal auditors are concerned by the former and delighted by the latter. It is the former that poses the problem in the implementation of the internal audit recommendations. Also, at times it causes rejection of the audit effort and of the auditor as being the originator of the change.

The auditor must be prepared to manage the impact of change resulting from recommendations or those that are anticipated by the client. Following are several causes for client concern together with suggestions for successful action by the audit staff:

1. Fear of the unknown can be neutralized by explaining to the degree possible the impact on current operations that the change will make and clearly describing the potential advantages and risks of the change.

2. Conflicts with present operations can be explained by describing the positive results that the change will make and the credits that will accrue to client management.

3. Ego problems can be resolved by bringing client management into the decision process so that the change actually becomes the product of present client management.

4. Bureaucratic problems, including the need for vertical and horizontal realignments, can be reduced by working with all involved to outline the integrated changes that will be needed and by working with the horizontal and vertical units involved.

5. If the change is not cost beneficial or results in a less efficient operation, explain the positive results the benefits of which exceed the apparent losses.

The changes should be reasonable, should not violate moral values or good business practice, should be capable of accomplishment, should be in the client's interest, be communicable, and to the degree possible should be cost-beneficial.

Conflict

Conflict is present in all organizations and shows itself in varying degrees. In most organizations it is kept reasonably under control. Conflict is caused by differences between people or organizations relative to:

- Methods of performance of activities.
- Turf problems — areas of responsibility.
- Commitment of resources.
- Ideology and ethics.

Auditor-client conflicts are common. As a matter of fact, the auditor acting in an adversarial position constitutes the basic aspect of conflict. Conflict can be resolved by arbitration, mediation, or compromise. It can also be eliminated, though not resolved, by direction. The concept of compromise is greatly to be desired. To the degree possible, both auditor and client should give way so that the greatest possible benefit for the organization can be achieved.

Resolving Conflict[10]

Some suggestions from an article in *Internal Auditor* hold much promise relative to the resolution of conflicts. Resolution in this case infers that the conflict no longer exists and that the parties agree to certain conditions, understandings, and action. The article proposes two essential activities: first, understanding the conflict; and second, negotiating a resolution.

Understanding the conflict involves three questions that must be answered.

- Is the conflict real? Could it be a misunderstanding or poor communication?

- What is the conflict? The real conflict must be disclosed so as not to be concerned about "secondary issues."

- What is the cause of the conflict? The source of the problem should be identified as soon as possible. It could be that the parties are arguing about results of conflict, not the cause of it.

Negotiating a resolution can be enhanced by concentrating on six activities. These activities are:

- *Concentrate on people issues.* This issue involves treating the "other side" as human beings rather than obstacles. Empathy is important and the recognition that the discussion could generate progressive results.

- *Separate the individuals from the context of the conflict.* Auditors should not attack people, but should isolate the issues and discuss them.

- *Consider the opposition's view of the conflict.* Viewing the conflict through the eyes of the opposition can lead to resolution that can be compatible to the opposition. The ensuing discussion should not take an accusatory tone.

- *Involve the opposition in the decision-making process.* Participation is a great leveler, assuming the objective is a position desired by both parties.

- *Discuss emotions openly.* Emotions should be recognized and freely discussed. The fact that stakes and reputations are threatened should be acknowledged and resolution should be pointed toward mutual satisfaction. Emotional outbursts should be tolerated without retribution or retaliation. After the release of the emotions, levelheaded discussion should be resumed.

- *Communicate.* Each side should listen and try to comprehend. This aspect also infers that the auditors adequately plan their statements that should not be inflammatory to the degree possible.

The article then suggests that the parties develop alternative options. There must be a degree of flexibility on both sides. There also are three obstacles that must be overcome:

- "Premature judgment,"
- "Fixation on a single answer," and
- "Assumption of a fixed solution."

These obstacles can be overcome if the parties mutually:

- "Brainstorm other options,"
- "Separate the creation process from the decision-making process,"
- "Consider all options," and
- "Look for mutual gain."

The basis for resolution is for agreement to be reached in establishing objective criteria on which both parties can agree. Though the article shuns "bargaining" it seems reasonable to believe that compromise can still be used to produce a "win-win" result. Regardless of the ideal methodology that is being used, such as described above, the element of emotions and even an earnest belief in the validity of one's position, some element of compromise is bound to creep in. Also, this may not be too bad a solution because at a later date, after the interim experience, another go can be held at a further resolution of the remaining elements of the conflict.

The Use of Motivational Needs

Earlier, the subject of motivation was mentioned as a benign force that causes clients to accept the audits as a stimulus for improvement. How does this work? We generally recognize Maslow's series of needs that motivate humans. These needs vary from the physical — air, food, and water — to the complicated need to believe that one is performing the work that one was destined to perform. Two other needs, security, both physical and economic, and the need for recognition can serve to stimulate the client to:

- Bring suspected problems to the auditor's attention.
- Cooperate with the auditor in the conduct of the audit.
- Implement the auditor's recommendations.

How are these motivational needs served? By disclosing in the audit report that the client so performed and that it was because of that client's cooperative action that the audit was successful.

Management recognition and the recognition by the client's peers can impact favorably on the client's economic condition and can bring recognition as being knowledgeable of the facets of good management and as being management-minded in accepting change in the interest of the organization's well-being.

The Impact of Roles and Stress

People play many roles in the conduct of their normal lives. Roles consist of attitudes and the resulting conduct resulting from various situations. Both the auditor and the client play roles relating to business and to their personal lives. The roles can be roughly classified as: (no horizontal relationships)

	Auditor	**Client**
Traditional	Police officer	Ignore
	Watchdog	Intimidate
	Detective	Cooperate
Professional	Auditor	Client
	Supervisor	Manager
	Manager	
Personal	Parent	Parent
	Spouse	Spouse
	Teacher	Teacher
	Student	Student

At times there are conflicts between the requirements of the various roles. For instance, overtime work as an auditor or a client may conflict with the requirements and responsibilities as a parent or a spouse. These role conflicts constitute the greatest causes of stress on the part of both the auditor and the client.

Other causes of stress are situations regarding ethical conduct, beliefs as to inadequacy, travel requirements, time constraints, and situations where the organization's short-term wellness conflicts with issues of morality and honesty.

The resolution of role conflicts and stress is not easy. Probably the setting of priorities and the evaluation of effects of activities are two of the best methods.

The lesson for the auditor is to recognize that the client is subject to as many of the role conflicts and stress issues as is he or she. In many cases the auditor is or may become aware of these client problems. This is not to say that the auditor must become a counselor or an advisor, but he or she can modify the audit effort on a short-term basis to accommodate these personal client problems.

To close this discussion, the auditor should prevent his or her role conflicts or stress issues from interfering with the audit to the greatest degree possible. Recognizing the problems and prioritizing the issues should be a basic requirement.

The Need For and Importance of Good Relations

Assuming that the behaviorists are right, that line people are adverse to staff people in general and internal auditors in particular, and that controls — especially in the form of an internal auditor — may cause people to be fearful, defensive, and dishonest, does it matter? Isn't it the job of internal auditors to carry out their audits despite difficulties? Isn't it their job to exhume what was covered up, to disclose errors, poor judgment, and poor work? Isn't it their job to report what they found?

The answer to all these questions is "yes." But why make the job more difficult than necessary? Why do in a spirit of animosity what can be carried out in a spirit of cooperation and helpfulness?

The conflict is compounded with the auditor's move into operations. Even though clients' fears and distrust may not keep a financial auditor in an accounting area from achieving audit objectives, the audits of operations present different and usually more personalized problems.

When internal auditors perform comprehensive audits of operations, they cannot possibly be as well informed about such operations as a financial auditor in a financial department. Operating processes may be unfamiliar, complex, and bewildering. The operating people may be speaking a language and using terms that are foreign to the auditor's knowledge and experience. Then too, the corrective action required is likely to demand the wholehearted commitment of operating personnel if it is to be effective. Yet operating personnel are less accustomed to internal auditors and to the audit process, and are less likely to accept the auditors and their recommendations.

Stephen Keating, president of Honeywell, Inc., saw clearly the importance of cooperation between auditor and client when he said, ". . . real progress cannot be made in an environment of conflict and friction . . . Finding the trouble is only half the battle — the other half is putting recommendations to work. This requires understanding and confidence."[11]

W.G. Phillips, also a corporate president, said that the auditor ". . . must approach his job in a constructive manner, realizing that mistakes are guides for improvement, not crimes . . . He must consider himself a partner with those involved in the audit, not an adversary."[12]

The ability to deal effectively with others goes beyond pleasant relations. It goes beyond people being nice to each other. It means the ability to get a job done with the least adverse effect on others.

Harmeyer cites a study by psychologists of 4,000 employees who had been discharged.[13] The study showed, surprisingly, that only 38 percent had been discharged for technical incompetence. Almost two-thirds, 62 percent, had been discharged for social unsuitability. Yet most organizations — including The Institute of Internal Auditors — spend about 95 percent of the time concentrating on technical skills.

What profits the auditor to develop a sound audit finding only to see it bitterly contested by operating management because the auditor, wittingly or unwittingly, created a feeling of conflict and distrust?

The Effects of Auditor/Client Relations

Mints' research study amassed abundant evidence of the importance of conducting audits without animosity. His study included test audits in which some audit teams used a cool, superior, impersonal style and other teams used a participative, teamwork approach. After each audit, clients were asked to evaluate the auditors in terms of their audit style. For example, did they regard the auditor as a police officer or a teacher? After the audits had been made, after the auditors had been evaluated, and after sufficient time had elapsed for the effect of the audits to be known, one of the general auditors involved in the study wrote to the researcher:[14]

> Within six months of the completion of an audit, the clients send a memo to the corporate controller and division manager in which they report action taken or otherwise. We noted a direct correlation between the client ratings of the auditors and these replies. When the auditors were highly rated, action was normally taken on practically all items, and vice versa. Since motivating personnel is one of our major objectives, I'd say this is a most important finding, which substantiates our need to improve auditor acceptance by client.

The research study demonstrated, as clinically as such studies can, that poor relations defeat the audit purpose and good relations promote it. Two examples from the study offer evidence of this conclusion:[15]

> One auditor who used the cold, aloof style performed an audit that was professional and technically outstanding. It was characterized by imaginative and potentially profitable work. Yet eight months after the audit, the operating organization had not implemented the audit recommendations. The operating people were apparently seething over the methods that the auditor had used.

On the other hand, in an audit that followed — in which the cooperative approach was used — the controller of the division audited called the director of auditing to compliment him and to say that the operating people were enthusiastic about implementing the suggestions. The audit director was convinced that the differences in style were responsible for the diverse results.

Another auditor also evaluated the results of the audits conducted for the research study. He was able to say without reservation that the results obtained from the warm, empathetic style were significantly better than those obtained from the cold, reserved style. He also said that one of the sad things coming out of his correlation was that, from a technical point of view, the works performed by the reserved auditors was judged superior in some respects to that performed by the empathetic auditors. Yet the results from the empathetic audit group showed that management accepted and implemented their ideas readily. He concluded:[16]

> Putting it another way, the results of our audits depend a good deal on how we are perceived by others, rather than how we perceive ourselves. Further, we can positively influence the "how we are perceived by others" by getting ourselves involved with the clients, by having empathy with them, and by considering what's best for them rather than us.

Internal auditors should not think that high status in the organization will shield them from the effects of poor client/auditor relations. Macher reports a study of 21 executives who were fired or forced to retire. The chief reason cited was poor interpersonal relations. The three most frequently named factors were "insensitivity to others," "cold/aloof," and "betrayal of trust."[17]

There seems little doubt that intelligent, imaginative internal audit work, in and of itself, is not enough to ensure improvement in operations. Clients must want to implement audit recommendations. So audit style may be as important as technical competence.

Suggestions for Improving Relations

Relations between auditor and client may improve if the auditor, the expert on control, appreciates the differences between imposed controls and self-directed control. The principle of self-directed control requires that a staff group never be the instrument for policing — being the conduit through which the control procedures developed by upper echelons flow down on the heads of operating managers and people.

Rather, they should act, and be perceived, as a means of transmitting the reasons for needed procedures. They should seek to help managers control themselves. This help includes informing operating people when they are out of line; but it also includes helping them get themselves back in line and motivating them to want to do so. Internal auditors are in the middle. They find themselves between senior management controls on the one hand and those who are being controlled on the other. The way they conduct themselves — as helpful buffers or abrasive forces — may make the difference between effective and ineffective audits.

Feedback From the Client

Before internal auditors can improve their image within the organization, they must know how they are regarded. Ferrier suggests that a review of internal auditors by clients is a feasible step toward improving client/auditor relations. Reporting the results of feedback to both internal auditors and senior management helps ensure accountability for the internal audit function. Reports of feedback can provide benefits such as:[18]

- A means of judging internal audit performance.

- A means of making future audits better by recognizing the areas in which the internal audit service can be improved.

- A way of encouraging harmonious relations with clients by creating a deeper atmosphere of participation.

- A means of reducing the conflicts arising from the "them and us" syndrome where clients are continually on the defense against the "management spies."

- A way of exposing clients to some of the problems and difficulties encountered by auditors in evaluating the performance of others. A better appreciation of, and closer identification with, the internal audit function would result.

Many internal audit organizations use a questionnaire for clients to complete at the conclusion of audits. This subject is covered in greater degree in Chapter 24, Quality Assurance. Exhibit 28-1 is an example of such an evaluation form.

Exhibit 28-1
Internal Audit Evaluation

Activity or department evaluated: _____

Date prepared: _____

Preparer: _____

Department or activity: _____

	Rating (10-highest, 1-lowest)	No Basis

1. Technical Knowledge.
   How well did the internal auditors exhibit an understanding of the objectives and the functions of your department or activity?
2. Range of Service.
   How well did they provide a service?
3. Professional Knowledge.
   How well did they exhibit a professional knowledge of the principles and techniques of internal auditing?
4. Relations.
   How well did the auditors get along with: Management? Employees?
5. Communications.
   How well did they communicate with management and operating personnel?
6. Responsiveness.
   How responsive were they to your needs?
7. Professionalism.
   Did the internal audit personnel appear to be well trained and professional?
8. Confidentiality.
   Did the internal auditors treat the information they obtained with appropriate confidentiality?
9. Attitude.
   Did the internal auditors exhibit a professional, helpful, and positive attitude toward you and your people?

Exhibit 28-1 (Cont.)

	Rating (10-highest, 1-lowest)	No Basis

10. Creativity.
    To what extent were they creative in helping to solve problems?
11. Productivity.
    How productive did you consider the internal auditors to be?
12. Significance.
    How significant were the findings reported?
13. Helpfulness.
    How helpful were the auditors in suggesting corrective action?
14. Return.
    Would you want these internal auditors to return for another engagement?
15. Overall.
    What is your overall rating of the internal audit team (not necessarily an average of the ratings already given)?

Any additional comments and recommendations that you would like to bring to the attention of internal auditing or senior management?

Consultative Attitudes

A favored behavior solution to line and staff, and therefore to client/auditor relations, is the adoption of a consulting rather than a policing attitude. If staff specialists, including internal auditors, are to succeed in achieving their objectives, they must demonstrate that their knowledge and their efforts can work to the benefit of the operating people. Participation can succeed where imposition will not. Exhibit 28-2 compares the traditional (hard line) and the participative audit approaches.

Internal auditors will have to emphasize to operating managers their constructive, participative role. This calls for continued, innovative methods to bring the message to operating people. The importance of the proper perception by the client is highlighted in a statement by

Comptroller General Elmer B. Staats on July 25, 1978, to a congressional committee in connection with the Inspector General (IG) Act of 1978. Dr. Staats said:[19]

> I cannot stress too strongly to you the need to revise the inspector general's title in this bill. This may seem a minor point, but I can assure you that what this subcommittee does in the matter is going to have far-reaching consequences in the years to come. We believe that the name of the organizations established by the bill will set the tone for how they operate. If you call them "office of inspector general" you are going to find that future hiring of personnel for those offices will be concentrated on persons with investigative backgrounds, and future operations will increasingly be centered on investigations for the purpose of detecting fraud. . .what the federal agencies need are strong internal controls to minimize the opportunities to defraud the government.

Dr. Staats' warning was very appropriate. The appointments of many inspectors general of the major departments and agencies has emphasized attorneys and investigators rather than auditors or specialists in control systems.

Currently, the dual relationship of auditor and consultant has received much attention. The specter of loss of independence by the auditor has raised its head. However, internal auditors whose basic charter is to add value to the organization can hardly operate only in an assurance capacity. Inevitably, the auditor will observe practices where changes will result in cost savings on operational improvements. To ignore those potential value benefits would be improper. Consequently, the auditor must include them along with the assurance findings. This is consulting, nevertheless the auditor can provide a series of recommendations to preclude acting in a managerial capacity. Clients can and will choose the best recommendation to accept or, with further study of the situation, develop expanded action that will further improve the auditor's disclosure.

This consultive posture can and should be performed with the assistance of the client. The joint endeavor will not only be more effective and probably more efficient, but it also will ensure the client's interest and support because of the joint ownership of the potential improved operation.

This procedure does not violate an independent approach as long as the client is the ultimate decision-maker as to the change to be made.

Exhibit 28-2
Audit Approach Comparisons

Traditional	Participative
Reduced costs and improved efficiency are the traditional audit objectives.	Providing better means by which managers can reduce costs and improve efficiency are the participative audit objectives.
Procedures and controls are imposed from above and policed by the internal auditors.	Procedures and controls belong to operating managers. The internal auditor is a professional consultant dedicated to helping managers improve their controls and procedures.
The internal auditor sets the standards by which operations will be managed. The manager provides only the knowledge of operations.	Both the manager and the internal auditor agree on the standards of measurement and how the standards will be applied.
The internal auditor issues reports describing deficiencies only, reporting audit recommendations to top management.	The internal auditor issues balanced reports and describes what line management is doing to improve operations and to correct any weaknesses found.
Improved conditions will result from focusing on deficiencies disclosed by the internal auditor.	Improved conditions will result from corrective action in which both auditor and client participate.
The internal auditor sees that all of the procedures and policies are strictly adhered to.	The internal auditor examines procedures and policies for relevance, viability, and good sense; proposes appropriate changes and controls; and points out to operating managers and their employees the desirability of following acceptable policies and procedures.
The internal auditor acts as an outside expert.	The internal auditor acts as an internal consultant.

Exhibit 28-2 (Cont.)

Traditional	**Participative**
The internal auditor, through examination, discloses deficient controls and points them out in the audit report.	The client with the internal auditor develop a control self assessment procedure that results in the client staff identifying control problems that they have observed.
The internal auditor maintains tight follow-up on recommendations.	The internal auditor helps the client to establish controls to assure corrective implementation of findings.

Conflicting Demands Relating to Fraud

Fraud prevention and detection are important. The losses resulting from fraud are enormous. Their effect on enterprises can be staggering, and internal auditors have a responsibility to be alert for the existence of fraud and to take appropriate action when it is suspected (see Chapter 27). In short, internal auditors must act as a capable manager acts.

The fact that an admirable manager will not countenance reprehensible conduct does not make him or her less admirable to desirable employees. We believe that the internal auditors' rooting out wrongdoing when wrongdoing occurs should not affect the way they are regarded if, in their regular audits, they function in a participative manner.

Indeed, in some internal audit organizations, separate internal audit groups are employed for the protective and the constructive audit phases. Thus, those performing the regular internal audit functions not related to fraud are not identified with investigative tactics. They are free to carry out participative audits with no tinge of an adversary relationship. As a matter of fact, the inspectors general (IG) of the federal government and those of state and local governments have a staff of investigators for this purpose. These investigators are usually individuals with some type of law enforcement experience. Also, the associated IGs maintain training courses for them and they also participate in FBI and other forensic training sessions.

Considering the Audit Impact

Internal auditors who seek cooperation will have to plan their approach carefully. They will have to recognize that definite behavioral effects surface in three different steps in the audit: the anticipation of the audit, the conduct of the audit, and the reports of the audit.

The anticipation of the audit and the mystery attached can be defused by positive steps on the part of the internal auditors. They can keep surprise audits to a minimum, restricting them to such activities as handling cash and negotiable securities or where fraud is suspected. They can provide information in advance to clients, explaining the audit process and how to prepare for it. They can explain to the clients the positive results of the audit and the benefits the clients can expect. Jarvis describes an approach that was used in a multi-branch bank.[20] An article was designed to give branch employees a capsule view of what internal auditors do and don't do and thus put them at ease when they see that "here come the auditors."

Similarly other organizations have produced brochures describing the internal auditing function, the experience and background of staff, its contribution to the organization's well-being, and its normal method of operations. These booklets also tell how to prepare for the audit and how to work with the auditors so as to make the audit experience a mutually productive event.

During an audit, people are given a feeling of importance if they are asked people-type rather than control-type questions. For example:

- What tasks do you perform?

- What tasks does your immediate supervisor perform?

- What tasks do the people directly under your supervision perform?

- Which of the people in your own work group do you see most often outside of work?

- When you want a job done in a hurry to whom do you turn?

This type of inquiry has additional benefits. It provides a window to the information organization. It shows the network of relationships that overlays the formal, structured organization chart, and it helps the internal auditor understand not only how things are supposed to work, but also how they actually do work.

Burnett regards auditor/client relationships in terms of the two motivators: fear and recognition.[21] In these relationships, the client has fears of losing his or her job, of receiving an adverse evaluation, and of the unknown — the mysterious audit. Internal auditors can counter these fears by explaining the audit process and removing the mystery from it. They can counter the fears of bad evaluations or losing one's job by demonstrating fairness and objectivity and by putting all findings into perspective, balancing the bad with the good; also, by giving client staff credit for contributions to the audit process.

To provide recognition, auditors should take into account Maslow's Hierarchy of Needs. This aspect has been discussed in some detail earlier. Operating managers have probably satisfied their needs for the basic necessities, for safety, and for belonging. They need to satisfy the needs for recognition and for self-actualization. The answer is to sell the findings before the report is issued and to document them in a framework that shows an understanding of management's needs, motivations, and styles and that describes client assistance in the audit.

By understanding management style, the auditor can judge which matters to explore and which to downplay. When a manager is detail-oriented, the auditor may be wasting time in auditing details. When the manager is long-range oriented, the details need review. Also, when findings are coupled with management style, they are easier for the client to accept.

The Management View

During the audit, internal auditors should take a managerial approach to deficiencies. They should downplay the insignificant findings, search for the causes of significant ones, and work with operating managers to correct weaknesses. Internal auditors should keep in mind that operating people usually have a pretty good idea of what is going on. No matter what ideas the auditors may have about improvement, chances are that the operating people have already considered them. Relations are improved immeasurably when the internal auditors openly adopt these ideas, filter them through their own experience, and then present them as the result of a team effort between the auditor and client.

During the reporting phase, no deficiency finding should be formally reported that has not been thoroughly discussed with operating management. No weakness should be overstated. No nitpicking findings should appear in the formal report. Also, credit for outstanding achievements by the client should find a place in the report.

The Investigative Audit

Not all audits can be carried out in the participative mode. Some are frankly critical or problem-finding audits. Even here, the behavioral aspects should be considered:[22]

- Be sure the nature and scope of the investigation are understood in advance by those being audited, if at all possible.

- Be sure the examination or investigation is supported by higher management and that this support has been communicated to those concerned.

- Before the work starts, meet with the responsible manager in charge of the functions being audited to discuss the range and scope of the audit, the time required, and the work to be done.

- Conduct the audit with the least possible disruption of day-to-day operations without compromise of audit work that must be performed.

- If the audit is prolonged, keep operating management currently informed of progress.

- At the end of the audit, report as fully as may be permissible to the manager involved.

Meeting Hostile Opposition

Despite all the good will in the world, internal auditors are still bound to find antagonism. The auditors may seek reasonably and logically to present their point of view, but the client will remain adamant, unhearing, unconvinced, and completely negative. These confrontations happen. They are bound to happen, now and again, so long as people remain people. It is the closed-mind syndrome, and there is no master key.

This client opposition may be reflected in several ways:

- Client management does not deign to attend conferences, but sends a lower level individual to be his or her representative.

- The client manager questions all audit activities as being unnecessary and improper. The auditor is forced to justify each action and then in some cases is met by a refusal to cooperate or accept the activity.

- The client accuses the auditor of interfering with the work of the audit area. Each test or other audit action must be approved by the client on the basis of eliminating interference.

- The client refuses to discuss interim findings, telling the auditor that he or she is "on their own" and that they "better be right" or that they will be "creamed" to top management.

- The client manager downgrades and ridicules potential findings as not material and insignificant to the client operation.

- The client accuses the auditor of improprieties but refuses to support the accusation.

- The client management refuses to participate in exit conferences but sends an insignificant representative who listens but makes no comment.

These suggestions may be useful:

- *Select the right time.* Do not try to open the closed mind to reason when the owner is angry, tired, or distracted.

- *Never take a locked-in-concrete position.* All that does is seal the closed mind from any possible penetration.

- *Don't rely on logic.* Logic never opened a closed mind. If it were agreeable to logic, it could not be characterized as a closed mind.

- *Never paint yourself into a corner.* Never take a position from which you cannot gracefully retreat.

- *Avoid force and embrace persuasion.*

- *At the outset, find a point of agreement.* Opposition is useless; agreement is the opening wedge. There must be some things on which auditor and client agree, even if it is that you are in disagreement.

- *Invite the clients to spell out their position.* Listen and try to understand — really listen. Don't be closed-minded yourself.

- *Make an active effort to put yourself in their place.* Sincerely try to understand.

- *Help them to be right.* That is what the closed mind wants above all. When you understand where they stand, when you have put yourself in their shoes, try to make them feel the position you want them to take is the position they themselves want to take.

When all else fails, when the deficiency or weakness is serious, when the risks are great and correction cannot be compromised, the internal auditors must remember their responsibilities and carry the matter to higher authority. The time bombs of potential risk to the organization must be defused.

But it is best to try persuasion first. Internal auditors must remember that one day they may have to return to deal with the closed mind again.

Listening

Audit derives from the Latin auditus — to hear. Initially, it meant a judicial hearing of complaints, a judicial examination. Later, it meant an official examination of accounts with verification by reference to witnesses and vouchers. Accounts were originally oral. Later auditing practices increased the reliance on written records and decreased the weight given to oral witness.

The wheel has turned. In audits of operations, the emphasis is on people as much as it is on documents. Auditors have been adept at analyzing, comparing, and evaluating the written words and numbers; they are not, however, equally adept at evaluating the spoken word. That is not necessarily their fault. Little has been written and less has been taught about listening. Nichols reported that 12 months of research on the subject disclosed that 3,000 scientific and experimental researchers had been published on reading. Only one had been published on listening.[23]

Most of schooling is spent in teaching students reading, writing, and arithmetic. Little if any is spent on teaching listening, and yet this is how we spend almost half of our waking day. The obvious question here is, "So what?" Is lack of formal listening training such a problem?

The answer is yes. An experiment by Professor Harry Jones of Columbia University proved that we recall but 50 percent of what we have just heard. In two weeks, we recall only 25 percent.[24] This presents a problem to all people, but it is especially serious for internal auditors. They must gain their understanding of operations chiefly by listening to people — really listening.

A sales maxim has it that "the foolish salesman would sell me with his reasons; the wise salesman with my own." How does the wise salesman — or the wise internal auditor — learn "my own" reasons? By listening, not by talking.

Listening, then, is as important to an internal auditor as is the ability to verify, compare, and evaluate. Indeed, those very abilities can be used in aggressive, attentive listening. First, however, internal auditors should know the barriers to good listening — the bad habits that bar a comprehension of what was heard.

Dr. Nichols carried out a research project at the University of Minnesota that identified 10 bad listening habits. Other studies at Michigan State University and in Colorado confirmed his findings. Here are some of the barriers to good listening that are of particular interest to the internal auditor.[25]

Criticizing the speaker's delivery. Internal auditors must often listen, for their very livelihood, to people who are dull, who fail to come to the point, who wander, and who murder the

King's English. Yet among all the chaff may be kernels that will be significant to an effective audit.

Getting overstimulated. Evaluation should be withheld until comprehension is complete. The internal auditors' naturally critical faculties impel them to criticize and rebut, but if the mind is on rebuttal, there is no listening and no comprehension.

Listening only for the facts. The inept listener tries to absorb the many facts a speaker uses to support the central ideas being conveyed. In the mad scramble to remember the facts, the poor listeners lose the central concept — the hook on which the facts hang. The good listener is the idea listener. The facts tend to be appended to the threads connected to the ideas.

Trying to write down everything. Most inept listeners will try to write down everything the speaker says. Good listeners seek out the central premises and record those, spending the rest of the time listening for how well the speaker will support these premises.

Letting emotion-laden words get in the way. An emotion-laden word can have such an impact on the listener that the speaker is completely tuned out. Aggressive listening can overcome this tendency to concentrate on the hated words rather than on what the speaker is trying to say.

Wasting the differential between speech and thought speed. People speak at about 125 words a minute. But thought cruises along easily at 400 words a minute. For college-educated people, the cruising speed is well over 800 words a minute. Most internal auditors have a college education or its equivalent. This differential can be a liability if it lets the listener randomly tune out and back into the speaker. Important information may be lost. This liability can be converted to an asset by three mental forms of concentration:

1. *Anticipate the speaker's next point.* Run ahead of the speaker mentally. Try to guess the point that will be made. Then compare your guess with that point. Learning is thereby reinforced. One of the oldest laws of learning is to contrast or compare one fact or idea with another.

2. *Identify evidence.* The speaker's points should not be accepted at face value. They are not true merely because they have been asserted. They should be supported by facts. The time differential can be used to identify the facts.

3. *Recapitulate periodically as you listen.* The good listener will tune the speaker in, listen hard for four or five minutes, and then take a quick mental time out. In that interval the listener, with that enormous thought speed, can summarize in 10 seconds what was said in five minutes. Several of these summaries increase the ability of the listener to understand and recall what was heard.

The Effective Use of Interview Questions[26]

Auditing, both internal and external, has traditionally built its information-seeking on the technique of asking questions. The internal control questionnaire is a long-used example and its use continues. However, three writers have identified expanded use of questions as:

- Focusing attention on key issues and motivating immediate action.
- Minimizing conflicts.
- Facilitating negotiation.
- Defusing emotional reactions.
- Assisting to persuade the questionee of the soundness of the questioners' recommendations.

These appear to be prerequisites to effective communication such as:

- "Always ask for specifics."
- "Pay attention to what is not said." Do not use open-ended questions.
- "Guard against unwarranted assumptions." Get the specifics.
- "Pay attention to the meaning of words."

Minimizing conflicts:

- Do not use questioning behavior that is aggressive, i.e., tone of voice, attitude, critical approach, sarcasm, etc.
- Consider compromise.
- Try to resolve conflicts; get at the root cause
  - over facts
  - involving feelings and perceptions
  - involving personalities
  - involving values

Persuasion and negotiating:

- Use questions to guide the client to come to the conclusion that the auditor is trying to sell.
- Act as a salesperson by creating confidence and, through questions, to lead the client to independently come to the position that auditor is trying to sell.
- Determine, through questions, the reasons the client may not want to come to the auditor's conclusion; then, again through questions, try to weave these reasons into a fabric that will resolve the situation the auditor believes should be corrected.

The subject article emphasizes effective listening by understanding the significance and meaning of the speaker's words. Use nonverbal behavior through close attention and neutral body language and listen for feelings as well as facts. Be noncritical and nonjudgmental. Learn to listen reflectively and to periodically summarize what the speaker has said for two reasons: to show you were listening and also to ensure that you understand the facts. Finally, listen with an open mind.

The referenced article is far more definitive than this description, is instructional, and well worth the reader's attention. It can be used, through questions, to build trust, obtain cooperation, resolve conflicts, and attain audit-directed objectives.

Communication

Internal auditors listen to obtain information. They communicate to impart information. Communication is the transfer of thoughts from the mind of one person to the mind of another. Complete communication is an utter impossibility. No two people have the same history, education, training, parents, teachers, and colleagues. And all this background will affect how listeners perceive what they heard.

Only when internal auditors truly understand the difficulty of good communication can they begin to achieve some reasonable degree of communication. Meetings with the client, either to convey findings or to impart the results of the audit, can go well or badly — depending on how the internal auditor prepares for them.

First of all, internal auditors should know what they are going to talk about and come fully prepared on the subject. They should prepare agendas, review them, and rehearse them. Small desktop flip charts in the form of three-ring binders can be very useful to hold the attention of the clients and to give the internal auditors control of the meeting. The meeting should be theirs, or else control passes to the client.

Scheduling the meeting at the right time is important. A meeting certainly should be avoided immediately before or after lunches or vacations. Also, the past history of meetings between the two can affect the present meeting. If prior meetings were cordial, the participants can continue in the same vein where they left off. If they were less than cordial, a special effort should be made to change the atmosphere. An honest interest in the clients and their operations can be helpful.

The message that the internal auditors are seeking to impart can be divided into five categories: set, sequence, support, emphasis, and polish.[27]

Setting the Message

Setting the message has three dimensions: credibility, climate, and content. The auditor's credibility is needed for the client to listen and pay attention. That source of credibility is: (1) professional — for instance, professional certification; (2) organizational — the status of internal auditing in the organization; and (3) personal — appearance, manner, communication and language skills, personality, technical ability, and preparation. Of the three dimensions, personal is the most important. The others are meaningless if the listener has no respect for the internal auditor as an individual. Internal auditors have some control over the climate by controlling the setting of the meeting. Even more important, however, are voice intonation, relaxed attitude, confident bearing, and nonverbal signs such as posture, gestures, and facial expressions. The content is controlled by the agenda, either formal or informal.

Sequence

Most of the meetings involve complicated matters that must be clarified and simplified so as to be understood. The client will have great reluctance in agreeing with something he or she does not understand. The message should therefore be given in logical sequence. The auditor should not assume that the client has the same familiarity with the situation or condition that the auditor has. Hence, the sequence should follow much the same pattern that is used in developing a finding:

- A brief identification of the problem.
- A brief statement of the principles or procedures governing the problem.
- Existing conditions.
- A comparison of conditions with the principles or procedures.
- Audit conclusions.
- Audit recommendations.

The recommendations should not have the force and effect of a directive. This would usurp a management prerogative. Also, auditors spend only a small fraction of the time that the client spends in the audited operations, so the auditors cannot possibly have the detailed knowledge and expertise of the operating personnel. Still, the auditors are experts in analysis and the development of findings. They bring a measure of independence and objectivity to the operation. They also bring knowledge and perspective of overall goals and objectives. If internal auditors develop mutual respect with the clients, their findings will be accepted, or at least considered.

By giving due respect to the client's knowledge, the auditors will concentrate on what they are best at: the analysis and development of findings. They should leave to the client the details of the recommendations for curing any problems unearthed. Clients convinced against their will, will still stay of the same opinion. Rather, solutions should be tentative and general and the auditor should invite the clients to present their views of how conditions could be specifically improved — joining the clients in a problem-solving partnership. However, if the auditor acts in a consultant relationship, suggestions relative to implementation may be appropriate.

Benjamin Disraeli said: "Next to knowing when to seize an opportunity, the most important thing in life is to know when to forego an advantage." Internal audit effectiveness in dealing with people is greatest when the auditors concentrate on helping the manager solve the problems — not forcing solutions on them.

It is politic for the auditor to seek to have a good-news message precede any bad-news message. If the first subject of an audit reveals a reportable problem, the auditor is advised to withhold discussing it until some satisfactory conditions have been encountered and can be presented first.

Support

Support, such as documentation or a record of discussions with knowledgeable people, will help achieve acceptance of the message. The support should be sufficient to be convincing, but not so overwhelming as to be intimidating — unless the circumstances dictate the desirability of intimidation.

Emphasis

In any communication, some messages come through more clearly than others. If there are key points, number them. Graphic illustrations can be helpful. Gestures, raising and lowering the projection of the voice, or repeating the key messages all help to emphasize what the auditor is seeking to convey.

Polish

Polish is a matter of attention to detail. Good grammar, word selection, neat appearance, careful preparation, and good listening habits and polished questions all make an impressive presentation and elevate the client's estimation of the auditor. Planning and practice increase polish. Most people are not born with it; they must develop it.

Other Aspects

Feedback. Without adequate feedback, both client and auditor may be confused as to whether the objectives of the meeting were met. If the purpose of the meeting was informational, the auditor may ask the client to summarize the more significant points: "As you see this matter, what do you consider to be its most important aspects?" If the objective is to get action started or completed, ask for a commitment — who will be responsible for the action and when can it be expected to be completed.

Presentation. Oral presentations should be professional, interesting, and persuasive. In developing a presentation, internal auditors should be concerned with content, organization, and delivery.

The *content* must, of course, be technically correct and error-free. It should be sufficiently complete so that all major points are included, but not so long as to wear out the listeners. The audience should be considered and the detail should be appropriate to their perception. All illustrations should be relevant and simple, not merely interesting. And the point of view presented should be abundantly clear.

In the *organization* of the presentation, sufficient background information should be included to set the stage and show the purpose of the presentation. The organization should be obvious so that it can be followed easily. Try to lead the listeners and never lose them in a marsh of excessive detail. The presenter should move clearly from point to point, emphasizing when a new subject is being brought up. The conclusions should not surprise the listeners but be clearly related to the body of the presentation.

The *delivery* should be made in an assured manner so that the presenter is always in command. Movements and gestures should be natural and not distracting. The presenter should not have his or her head buried in notes, but rather maintain eye contact as much as possible. The presenter should speak loudly enough, clearly enough, and slowly enough. The delivery should be varied in projection, emphasis, and volume so as not to get monotonous. The presenter should be dressed appropriately for the audience.

Participative Auditing

People are willing to assist others when they feel they will share in the benefits — when they are all working toward the same goal. Operating people have less animosity toward budgets when they participate in establishing them. People work more enthusiastically toward goals when they help set the goals. Line looks more kindly toward staff when it sees staff as an aid and not a control.

The same is true of internal auditing. The fear, the distrust, the mystery are dissipated when auditor and client work together in a spirit of cooperation and self-evaluation.

Mints urges some methods of establishing teamwork relationships so that clients may feel a real share and interest in the audit projects. Specifically he suggests:[28]

> For example, the truly participative auditor might do such things as: (1) take the clients into his confidence at the beginning of the examination by discussing his program along with his objectives and the reasoning behind his approach; (2) solicit suggestions and assistance from them; (3) discuss all findings currently with those directly concerned and actively seek their help in developing proposed solutions; (4) provide the clients with interim reports of findings so that steps toward implementation of corrective action might be taken before issuance of the final report; and (5) review his reports with all those concerned at each level and carefully consider their suggestions for modification before going to the next higher level. When he does not agree with their suggestions for changes, he would explain his views and attempt to persuade them of the reasonableness of his position.

The conduct Mints suggests in performing audits would appear basic to establishing a useful relationship between auditor and client. We believe, however, that, under some situations, a truly participative audit could imply that operating personnel will personally take part in the audit itself.

The internal auditors must always guide and direct the audit since the audit opinion, in the final analysis, is theirs. Their direction is essential to ensure independence and objectivity. But within that framework, participation can still take place. It calls for an aggressive program of involving the client personnel in the gathering of information, the identification of weaknesses, and the correction of defects. This can be done and has been done with some success:[29]

An organization president requested the audit of research and development (R&D) activities. The people assigned to the audit reviewed R&D methods and interviewed scientists and engineers in other divisions and organizations. As a result, the auditors were able to construct a body of standards that, if met, would provide evidence that the R&D activities were being carried out in a professional, businesslike manner. Here, for example, are two of such standards from about 30:

1. The technological requirements for R&D should be identified, and the personnel responsible for the work should have the requisite knowledge and skills in their technologies.

2. Managers should be provided with adequate systems of financial control to assist them in accomplishing their goals and missions within allocated budgets.

Once the standards were developed, the auditors met with client personnel and convinced them of the desirability of a teamwork approach: The clients would contribute their technical knowledge; the auditors would contribute their administrative and management knowledge.

The clients then gathered pertinent and useful information about each of the 30 standards. The information was provided by accumulating such things as procedures, instructions, manuals, statistics, job descriptions, employee histories, and the like. In accordance with the agreement, the auditors validated the information gathered, making such independent checks as they deemed necessary.

During their gathering of information, the clients found deviations from acceptable standards. Without any prompting, they initiated corrective action. Before the audit was completed, most of the weaknesses had been strengthened and most of the deviations had been corrected. Client and auditor worked together in harmony to achieve mutual goals. The exercise in participative auditing paid off.

One of the important aspects of participative auditing is to acknowledge the assistance in audit reports and in other communications. This assistance then becomes an element of satisfying for the client one of Maslow's "needs" — the achievement of recognition. The auditor should not fear a diminution of his or her competency — on the other hand such treatment indicates skill in interpersonal relations as well as in the technical aspects of the audit.

With the increasing complexity of enterprise systems, and with the broadening of the scope of internal audit work to include all manner of operations within the enterprise, such participative audits may become the norm rather than the exception. A wedding of technical expertise contributed by the client and the management expertise contributed by internal auditors may be the only effective way to make thorough audits of complex, technical activities.

Special Problems in Audit Relationships

Internal auditors find themselves torn by conflicting forces and faced by duties and responsibilities that may seem completely irreconcilable.[30] They owe a duty to senior management, whose activities they appraise and whose pay they accept; they also owe a duty to keep the audit committee informed of serious weaknesses that are detected during their appraisals.

Auditors are encouraged to be problem-solving partners of operating managers and help the managers improve their operation; yet auditors have a duty to be the watchdogs of the enterprise — alert for management inefficiency, ineptitude, and even fraud. They are urged to work together in participative teamwork with operating managers, yet are required to report deficiencies to the manager's superiors.

These operating claims on the auditor's loyalties and responsibilities can create audit schizophrenia. The solutions may not be simple, but solutions will have to be found so auditors can do their jobs with the least possible friction.

The Partner vs. the Watchdog

In recent years, the stress in the internal auditing profession has been on having a concern for, and dealing openly and fairly with, people. Present auditor/client relations still reflect some basic conflicts and hostility. These attitudes limit the auditor's ability to contribute to overall organizational goals.

Many senior managers see the internal auditor's role as more than a detector of wrongdoing. They want their internal auditors to be a part of a problem-solving team, working shoulder-to-shoulder with operating managers to correct weaknesses and deficiencies.

But senior managers also want to be assured of the internal auditor's protective role. Internal auditors must make sure that systems are properly controlled and protected. The *Standards* requires internal auditors to be alert to the possibility of intentional wrongdoing, errors, omissions, inefficiency, waste, ineffectiveness, and conflicts of interest. Further, when internal auditors suspect wrongdoing, they should inform appropriate authorities within the organization. The internal auditor does have a watchdog function and must be aware of the ever-present danger of management fraud.

No internal auditor can be so naive as to think every manager is a model of probity and rectitude. Too often, managements' operating reports are self-serving declarations by the operating manager instead of precise statements of fact. Some managers, including those holding high positions, have been known to be less than ethical in their transactions and representations. The events at the close of the 20th century— Enron, World Com, and others — are epics of this corporate malfeasance.

The quandary is painful but clear: The behaviorists admonish us to improve staff/line relations; yet there is the responsibility to identify risks and be alert for wrongdoing and failures. Again, the internal auditors must go back to their charter in the organization, to the statement of their *Standards*, and to their professionalism.

The charter must provide internal auditors with free access to all persons, records, systems, and facilities. This provision is for access, not suspicion. The first approach, the first contacts, the preliminary surveys — without prior indicators of malfeasance, misfeasance, or nonfeasance — should be carried out openly and cordially. The purpose here is to gather information. And, particularly where the activities are esoteric, internal auditors will need the assistance of operating managers and their subordinates to familiarize themselves with the objectives, procedures, controls, and standards that have been set. If there is naught to persuade otherwise, the auditors may continue their role of problem-solving partners and complete the audit in that manner.

But what if all is not well? What if the indicators of impropriety begin to raise their heads? Then the internal auditors must heed the requirements of their *Standards*. Although they are not responsible as insurers against fraud or misfeasance, they must be alert to what may be shown by the indicators as possible wrongdoing.

The steps to be taken will vary with the circumstances. The requirements of the situation will dictate the program to follow. Here are some suggestions:

- Seek out or assist in establishing standards, both budgetary and operational, and investigate all material deviations.

- Use quantitative and analytical techniques (time series analyses, regression and correlation analyses, and random sampling) to highlight aberrant behavior: What stands out like a candle in the darkness? Develop benchmarks such as space used, time required, weight limitations imposed, and wage and output compared.

- Compare performance with industry norms as well as with performance in comparable profit centers within the organization.

- Identify critical process indicators — melt loss in smelting, death loss in feedlots, rework in assembly, scrap in manufacturing, and gross profit tests in buy-sell operations.

- Analyze carefully not only performance that does not meet standards, but also performance that looks too good.

Then, if the indicators proclaim aberrant behavior, the internal auditor has no choice but to follow Practice Advisory 1210.A2-1, "Identification of Fraud," which provides that the appropriate authorities within the organization should be informed. The internal auditor may recommend whatever investigation is considered necessary in the circumstances. Thereafter, the auditor should follow up to see that the internal auditing activity's responsibilities have been met.

When senior management, made aware of the problem, is coping with it, the internal auditor should wait a seemly time to make sure it is corrected. This may not be the appropriate time to notify the audit committee or the board or suggest that senior management do so. Every organization has its problems. The internal auditors should not cry wolf each time they see a problem.

But if management is not taking care of the difficulty in a timely manner, further audit action may be necessary. The internal auditor should heed Ward Burns, who said that internal auditors must have guts. They must have the fortitude to stand up and be heard — even if it means going to the top.[31] That top may be the chief executive officer or the audit committee of the board, depending on the circumstances.

Knowing to whom to go, and when to go, calls for professionalism. Here too, resolving the dilemma is dependent on status, an unequivocal charter, professional conduct, and fairness to all.

Operating Managers and Their Superiors

The commandment to employ humanistic behavior toward the client is not only to show that the internal auditor is a human being. It is also to provide an atmosphere of candor, trust, and fair dealing.

But fair dealing must not equate with whitewashing. No matter how pleasant the relations with the manager and no matter how charming the manager is personally, a significant deficiency in his or her shop is still a deficiency. It must, therefore, be brought up to the cold light of day, and it cannot be hidden until it is corrected. However, steps being taken to resolve the problem can be reported.

What happens when the internal auditor sees on the one side a hard-working accounts payable manager who has been helpful and pleasant during the audit, and then sees on the other side an unacceptable series of inadvertent duplicate payments of significant amounts? It depends on how the internal auditor handles the situation. The overpayments can cause financial failure or they can create an opportunity for auditor and client to roll up their sleeves, mutually resolve the problem, and with illustrations, say to the client's superiors, "We fixed it!"

Such a relationship has to be developed early and nurtured carefully. It starts at the preliminary meeting. It points out the way the internal auditor operates — fairly and objectively. For example, the auditor could say:

> I'm going to keep my audit open and above board. Absent fraud, which vitiates everything, you'll be kept currently aware of all my findings, both good and bad. If I or my assistants come up with some minor deviation or haphazard human error,

we'll point it out to the individual who caused the error and we'll not bother reporting it. But let's face it, significant deviations occur in the best-run organization. If we find one or a series that will continue to hurt our organization if not corrected, then we must report it. My charter and my professional code require that I report it and discuss it with whomever I feel should know.

This I will do for you: You'll be the first to know. We'll discuss it in whatever depth you wish. We'll present you with all the evidence we gathered. If you like, we'll show you our working papers. We'll search together for the causes. We'll explore together the effect, both actual and potential.

I'll offer my counsel, based on my experience, on how to correct the difficulty and solve the problem. The corrective action will, of course, be yours, not mine. If I receive evidence of action taken or action begun with a due date for completion, I will stress that to your superiors and I certainly will not exaggerate the matter in my report. Can I be fairer than that and still do my job?

Most operating managers will welcome this attitude, this openness and sincerity. The fact that defects will be communicated to superiors need not be fatal to the problem-solving partnership. But it is a sad fact of internal auditing life that some managers will not respond to this offer of good working relations. Where these mangers are encountered, the internal auditor must maintain professionalism.

If all managers are educated to know what to expect, then the results do not come as a surprise. Unnecessary surprises are unfair. Operating managers have a right to be treated fairly, but they have no right to have the deficiencies in their shops hidden from the light of day. Internal auditors are bound to uncover the hidden defects by their charter, by their *Standards for the Professional Practice of Internal Auditing.* Internal auditors must be prepared to look both ways. They must deal openly and fairly with operating managers, yet they must disclose and help drive out chicanery, inefficiency, and wrongdoing. They must seek out defects in operations, while also helping managers correct them so that superiors do not visit unfair punishment on their subordinates as a result of audits.

References

[1]Churchill, N.C., and W.W. Cooper, "A Field of Study of Internal Auditing, " *The Accounting Review,* October 1965, 267-281.
[2]Mints, F.E., *Behavioral Patterns in Internal Audit Relationships, Research Committee Report 17* (Altamonte Springs, FL: The Institute of Internal Auditors, 1972), 37.
[3]Clancy, D.K., Frank Collins, and S.C. Rael, "Some Behavioral Perceptions of Internal Auditing," *The Internal Auditor,* June 1980, 50.

[4]Mautz, R.K., Peter Tiessen, and R.H. Colon, *Internal Auditing: Directions and Opportunities* (Altamonte Springs, FL: The Institute of Internal Auditors Research Foundation, 1984), 120-124.

[5]Dalton, Melville, "Conflicts Between Staff and Line Managerial Officers," *American Sociological Review,* Vol. 15 (1950), 342-351.

[6]Argyris, Chris, *The Impact of Budgets on People* (New York: Controllership Foundation, 1952).

[7]Mints, F.E., "Cooperative Auditing: The Key to the Future," *The Internal Auditor,* November/December 1973, 35.

[8]Carmichael, D.R., "Behavioral Hypothesis of Internal Control," *The Accounting Review,* April 1970, 235-245.

[9]Taylor, H.R., "Power at Work," *Personnel Journal,* April 1986, 42-49.

[10]Johnson, Gene H., Tom Means, and Joe Publis, "Managing Conflict," *Internal Auditor,* December 1998, 54-59.

[11]Keating, S.F., "How Honeywell Management Views Operational Auditing," *The Internal Auditor,* September/October 1969, 43-51.

[12]Phillips, W.G., "The Internal Auditor and the Changing Needs of Management," *The Internal Auditor,* May/June 1970, 55-56.

[13]Harmeyer, W.J., "Some of My Best Friends Are Auditors, But . . ." *The Internal Auditor,* January/February 1973, 8.

[14]Mints, Behavioral Patterns, 60.

[15]Ibid., 67.

[16]Ibid.

[17]Macher, Ken, "The Politics of People," *Personnel Journal,* January 1986, 50-53.

[18]Ferrier, R.J., "One Step Beyond Peer Review," *The Internal Auditor,* October 1985, 35-38.

[19]DeZerne, W.R., "Will the IG Act Improve Internal Auditing in Federal Agencies?" *The Internal Auditor,* June 1980, 100.

[20]Jarvis, J.E., "Here Come the Auditors," *The Internal Auditor,* August 1980, 43.

[21]Burnett, R.R., "Does Management Style Matter?" *The Internal Auditor,* June 1983, 16-19.

[22]Butler, J.J., "Human Relations in Auditing," *The Internal Auditor,* Spring 1963, 66.

[23]Nichols, R.G., "Listening Is Good Business," *The Internal Auditor,* March/April 1970, 32.

[24]Ibid., 33-34.

[25]Ibid., 38-42.

[26]Jeffords, Raymond, Greg Thabadoux, and Marsha Scheidt, "Utilizing Questions in the Audit Interview," *Internal Auditing,* January/February 2003, 14-20.

[27]Ratliff, R.L., and A.W. Switzler, "Preplanned Meetings Reap Dividends, *The Internal Auditor,* February 1984, 47-52.

[28]Mints, Behavioral Patterns, 86.

[29]Sawyer, L.B., "Tomorrow's Internal Auditor," *The Internal Auditor,* June 1978, 20-23.

[30]Sawyer, L.B., "Janus, or the Internal Auditor's Dilemma," *The Internal Auditor,* December 1980, 19-27.

[31]Burns, Ward, "What Management Expects of Internal Audit Now!" *The Internal Auditor,* May/June 1975, 23.

Supplementary Readings

Akers, Michael D., and Don E. Giacomino, "Personal Values of Certified Internal Auditors," *Internal Auditing*, January/February 1999, 19-27.

Allen, Robert D., "Managing Internal Audit Conflicts," *Internal Auditor*, August 1996, 58-61.

Calhoun, Charles, "Five Tips for Improving Performance Through Professional Relationships," *Internal Auditing Alert*, December 1998, 1-3.

Carlozzi, Catherine L., "Make Your Meetings Count," *The Journal of Accountancy*, February 1999, 53-55.

Collins, Rod, "Auditing in the Knowledge Era," *Internal Auditor*, June 1999, 26-31.

Cook, Ethel, "The IA as Detective: How to Get the Information You Need Quickly and Painlessly," *Internal Auditing Alert*, September 1998, 1-5.

Filak, Alicia J., "Changing Perceptions," *Internal Auditor*, October 2001, 80.

Flesher, Dale L., and Jeff Zanzig, "Audit Customers Express a Desire for Change in the Functioning of Internal Auditing," *Internal Auditing*, November/December 1999, 18-29.

Jeffords, Raymond, Greg M. Thibadoux, and Marsha Scheidt, "An Internal Auditor's Guide to Facilitating Organizational Change," *Internal Auditing*, July/August 1998, 37-41.

Jeffords, Raymond, Greg M. Thibadoux, and Marsha Scheidt, "Understanding Social Styles for Internal Auditors," *Internal Auditing*, September/October 2001, 17-24.

Jeffords, Raymond, Greg M. Thibadoux, and Marsha Scheidt, "Utilizing Questions in the Audit Interview," *Internal Auditing*, January/February 2003, 14-20.

Kimbrough, Jr., Ralph B., "Facilitating Trust," *Internal Auditor*, August 1997, 64-66.

Kreuter, Eric A., and John J. Kennedy, "Safeguarding your Employees' Assets," *Internal Auditing Alert*, April 1997, 1-2.

Levy, Joel F., and Abba Z. Krebs, "Performance Audits to Control Cost of Lost Time," *Internal Auditing Alert*, April 1998, 1-4.

Luizzo, Anthony J., "Auditing Investigative Techniques," *Internal Auditing Alert*, November 1998, 1-3.

Madigan, Carol Orsag, "Removing the Skeptic's Hat," *Controller Magazine*, August 1998, 50-53.

Mautz, R.K., et al., *Internal Auditing: Directions and Opportunities* (Altamonte Springs, FL: The Institute of Internal Auditors Research Foundation, 1984).

Mints, F.E., *Behavioral Patterns in Internal Audit Relationships*, Research Committee Report 17 (Altamonte Springs, FL: The Institute of Internal Auditors, 1972).

Nolen, William E., "Reading People," *Internal Auditor*, April 1995, 48-51.

Nouri, Hossein, and Kathleen Bird, "Matching Internal Auditor's Tasks with their Personality Type as Assessed by Myers-Brigg Type Indicator," *Internal Auditing*, July/August 1999, 32-35.

Ratliff, Richard L., and James W. Brackner, "Relationships," *Internal Auditor*, February 1998, 37-43.

Tavel, Greer, "Less Stress for Internal Auditors," *Internal Auditing Alert*, September 1999, 1-3.

Wilson, James A., and Donna J. Wood, *Stress and Mental Health in Internal Auditing* (Altamonte Springs, FL: The Institute of Internal Auditors, 1989).

Wilson, James A., and Donna J. Wood, *Roles and Relationships in Internal Auditing* (Altamonte Springs, FL: The Institute of Internal Auditors, 1989).

Wilson, James A., Donna J. Wood, and Edward C. Holub, *Professionalism in Internal Auditing* (Altamonte Springs, FL: The Institute of Internal Auditors, 1989).

Multiple-choice Questions

1. An example of an appropriate "interpersonal" role carried out by a manager in an organization would be:
   a. Designing and initiating changes within the organization.
   b. Transmitting selected information to subordinates.
   c. Participating in negotiating sessions with other parties (vendors, unions, etc.).
   d. Motivating subordinates to get the job done properly.

2. A personnel manager in a manufacturing firm, whose department is responsible for recruiting employees, has delegated the task of recruiting new entry-level production workers to an assistant. Which of the following statements best describes the relationship that has been created as a result of the delegation?
   a. The manager has transferred ultimate responsibility for recruiting the workers to the assistant.
   b. The assistant is accountable to the manager for the recruiting of the workers but the manager is ultimately responsible.
   c. The assistant has the authority and the sole responsibility for recruiting the workers.
   d. The assistant has the authority to recruit the workers but is not accountable for results.

3. Behavior modification is an attempt to get people to do the right things more often and the wrong things less often by systematically managing environmental factors. One factor that is managed is the consequences associated with behavior. Behaviorists claim that in the long run, the consequence that is most effective for behavior modification is:
   a. Positive reinforcement.
   b. Negative reinforcement.
   c. Money.
   d. Punishment.

Use the following information to answer questions 4 through 7.
In an effort to revitalize the organization, senior management engaged a human resources consultant to study the overall pay and benefit structure. The consultant has spent several weeks reviewing conditions at the organization and surveying other organizations within

the same industry. The consultant's report to management recommends that one of the following pay plans be adopted:

All salary — No bonuses are awarded. Both management and nonmanagement employees are paid an annual salary based on contractually established rates with step increases based upon years of service.

Skill-based evaluation — Pay is based on certifications held, degree(s) earned, or skills exhibited.

Profit sharing — Each employee has an annual salary. In addition, every employee shares in the organization's profit.

Lump-sum salary increases — Each employee is awarded a lump-sum salary increase based on merit.

Cafeteria benefits — Each employee is given a specified organization employee-benefit contribution but personalizes his or her benefits from an array of available choices.

4. Which plan reduces the discretionary power of management over pay increases?
    a. Skill-based.
    b. Lump-sum salary increase.
    c. All salary.
    d. Cafeteria benefits.

5. Identify the pay plan for which greater visibility of pay increases to the individual employee is most obvious:
    a. All salary.
    b. Lump-sum salary increases.
    c. Cafeteria benefits.
    d. Profit sharing.

6. Which plan promotes flexibility for the individual employee?
    a. Profit sharing.
    b. All salary.
    c. Lump-sum salary.
    d. Cafeteria benefits.

7. Which pay plan is likely to lead to organization-wide improvements?
    a. Cafeteria benefits.
    b. Skill-based evaluation.
    c. Profit sharing.
    d. Lump-sum salary increases.

8. A consumer product manufacturer is organized into five major departments: production, engineering, marketing, finance, and administration. In addition, to ensure coordination for each product, there is a product management department. This organization structure is an example of:
   a. Matrix organization.
   b. Decentralization.
   c. Product-service departmentalization.
   d. Organic organization.

Use the following information to answer questions 9 and 10.
The president of a firm asked for help to clearly define the managerial approach the firm should take. The following four statements were among the responses:

1. Management is the same in all organizations and includes the functions of organizing, staffing, directing, and controlling.
2. For us to remain competitive, we must focus on using our resources efficiently and effectively. That is the key to managerial success.
3. Employees are important. To be successful, we must make sure that they are properly trained and motivated, and we must keep the communication channels open.
4. Organizations are complex, dynamic, integrated organisms. We need to recognize this fact and focus our attention on developing synergistic interrelationships.

9. Which statement reflects the operational approach to management?
   a. 1.
   b. 2.
   c. 3.
   d. 4.

10. Which statement reflects the behavioral approach to management?
    a. 1.
    b. 2.
    c. 3.
    d. 4.

11. When faced with the problem of filling a newly created or recently vacated executive position, organizations must decide whether to promote from within or to hire an outsider. One of the disadvantages of promoting from within is that:
    a. Internal promotions can have a negative motivational effect on the employees of the firm.
    b. Internal promotions are more expensive to the organization than hiring an outsider.
    c. It is difficult to identify proven performers among internal candidates.
    d. Hiring an insider leads to the possibility of social inbreeding within the firm.

12. Both Maslow and Herzberg have developed popular motivational theories. Select the statement that best distinguishes Herzberg's theory.
    a. Job performance improves as job satisfaction increases.
    b. Job performance improves as physiological needs are met.
    c. Job esteem improves as physiological needs are met.
    d. Job esteem improves as job satisfaction increases.

13. A salesperson has been told that he can earn up to $20,000 more per year if he changes from straight salary to straight commission and works at least three evenings a week. Select the motivational theory that is being employed in this scenario.
    a. Herzberg's theory.
    b. Theory Z.
    c. Maslow's theory.
    d. Expectancy theory.

14. To explain a preliminary audit finding to the manager of personnel, an auditor comments as follows: "We believe that our statistical sample documents a breakdown in the review of updates to the personnel master file by the immediate supervisor. The expected error rate of our attributes sample was one percent but the actual error rate was between four and six percent. The result was a rejection of the sample hypothesis. We, therefore, recommend that the importance of complying strictly with existing review procedures be reemphasized." The manager of personnel disputes the validity of the finding. The communications barrier presented above is best described as:
    a. Poor environment.
    b. Technical jargon.
    c. Inappropriate communication method.
    d. Poor timing.

15. To motivate an auditor-in-charge to improve the work of the staff auditors assigned to an audit, an internal audit supervisor sent the following memo: "I want you to initial and date every working paper. You are to check all work and get these people to conform to department procedures." At the end of the audit, the supervisor was shocked to discover that the audit budget was grossly exceeded, working paper quality was poor, and audit focus was on low risk and unproductive areas. The failure in the communication chain was most likely due to:
    a. Noise.
    b. Audience.
    c. Environment.
    d. Method.

16. An auditor was having trouble adjusting to a new supervisor. When a job-related problem arose, the auditor went directly to the audit director without consulting the supervisor. Identify Fayol's principle of management that the auditor violated:
    a. Order.
    b. Division of work.
    c. Scalar chain.
    d. Unity of direction.

17. As part of a Total Quality Control program, a firm not only inspects finished goods but also monitors product returns and customer complaints. Which type of control best describes these efforts?
    a. Feedback control.
    b. Feed forward control.
    c. Production control.
    d. Inventory control.

Use the following information for questions 18 and 19.
A multinational firm was attempting to buy a controlling interest in a medium size ($10 million annual sales) Brazilian metal working firm. Their negotiator in Brazil sent the following telegram: "They won't deal unless 51 percent ownership."

The executive committee of the multinational firm, not wanting a minority interest, then canceled the deal. Upon returning to the multinational firm, the negotiator pointed out that the Brazilian firm wanted to sell no more than 51 percent ownership, so they could retain at least 49 percent. Thus, the deal could have been made.

18. The telegram received by the executive committee was faulty. In terms of the links in the communications process, the error occurred due to:
    a. Noise in the communication chain.
    b. The sender's perception.
    c. Message encoding.
    d. The choice of transmission medium.

19. The faulty telegram led to a communications error by the executive committee of the multinational firm. Their error was in:
    a. Decoding of the message.
    b. Choice of transmission medium.
    c. Understanding of the message.
    d. Response to the message.

20. Fredrick Herzberg postulated a two-factor theory of human behavior that included satisfiers and dissatisfiers. Identify the dissatisfier from the following:
    a. Promotion to another position.
    b. Salary.
    c. Challenging work.
    d. Responsibility.

21. Perception is a vital part of communication and is made up of which three subprocesses:
    a. Selectivity, organization, and interpretation.
    b. Sending, receiving, and feedback.
    c. Physical, semantic, and psychosocial.
    d. Listening, writing, and speaking.

22. Identify the condition managers are working under when they make decisions based on incomplete, but reliable, information.
    a. Uncertainty.
    b. Certainty.
    c. Synectics.
    d. Risk.

Use the following information for questions 23 through 30.
An insurance claims processing department consists of 20 employees. The department manager is considering several possible actions in order to increase employee motivation. Before acting, however, the manager wants to identify the motivational effect according to current theories. Maslow's Hierarchy of Needs includes five levels:

    a. Physiological.
    b. Safety.
    c. Love.
    d. Esteem.
    e. Self-actualization.

For each of the possible actions listed in questions 23 through 30, use "a" through "e" above to identify the need level addressed:

23. Pay for continuing education courses.
24. Provide a beneficial suggestion system.
25. Provide ergonomically designed chairs.
26. Improve lighting in the work area.
27. Establish an "employee of the month" award.
28. Hold a departmental holiday party.

29. Provide transportation services for after-hour workers.
30. Publicly praise employees for good work.

31. An organization manufactures barbecue grills, steel mail carts, and aluminum screen
    door frames. Management recently instituted a practice that allows workers to choose
    which production line they want to work on each week, prioritize work orders according
    to urgency, inspect the quality of their output, and pack and label their work for shipping.
    The practice that management has installed is called:
    a. Job rotation.
    b. Management by objectives.
    c. Job enlargement.
    d. Job enrichment.

32. The manager responsible for 40 order-taking clerks tells you: "I don't want creativity; I
    want conformance to established procedures." Your best counter-argument in favor of
    creativity is:
    a. Creativity is necessary to solve problems and make decisions.
    b. Environmental changes make creativity essential for long-term survival.
    c. There will never be anything new in the department without creativity.
    d. Creativity is so easy to get and manage that it is foolish not to do so.

33. During a production department audit in a large manufacturer of plastic containers,
    managers frequently mentioned low worker morale and control difficulties. You are
    considering suggesting implementation of quality circles. One of the benefits you can
    cite for quality circles would be:
    a. Increased accounting control.
    b. Cross-training of employees.
    c. Decrease training costs.
    d. Improved worker-management relations.

34. A manager recently transferred from a manufacturing organization to a service-oriented
    affiliate. When the manager unexpectedly announced a set of production standards, two
    of his employees quit on the spot, three others transferred out within a week, and the
    remainder were openly hostile. Select the best method for resolving this dysfunctional
    conflict situation:
    a. Conflict triggering.
    b. Forcing.
    c. Smoothing.
    d. Problem solving.

35. The expectancy model of motivation theory relates motivational strength to:
    a. Need for safety.
    b. Dissatisfiers.
    c. Supervision.
    d. Perceived probability of reward.

36. Many organizations make concerted efforts to make sure that job titles have no negative connotations. Attainment of a job title that is perceived to be prestigious addresses which of the following needs:
    a. Physiological.
    b. Esteem.
    c. Love.
    d. Safety.

37. During the first week on the job, a new assembler's output exceeded the group norm by 10 units per day. By the end of the second week, the assembler's output had dropped to that of the group norm. This phenomenon, characteristic of informal work groups, is referred to as:
    a. Group cohesiveness.
    b. Conformity.
    c. Synergy.
    d. Satisfying.

38. A competent manager will employ various means to achieve organizational objectives. Three effective means are to:
    a. Depend on a mentor, balance efficiency and economy, and think about the next job.
    b. Work with and through others, balance effectiveness and efficiency, and get the most out of limited resources.
    c. Think fundamentally, analyze specific performance problems, and remain aloof.
    d. Play politics, get the most out of employees, and adapt to varying situations.

39. Some management scholars have credited Douglas McGregor with founding the field of organizational behavior by arriving at a modern set of assumptions about people. Identify the basic assumption(s) underlying McGregor's Theory Y.
    a. Employees are lazy and unambiguous.
    b. Employees are concerned only with higher wages.
    c. Employees are component parts of the organizational system.
    d. Employees are energetic and creative individuals.

Use the following information for questions 40 and 41.

A personnel director asked an assistant to write a management-training casebook. "The cases must be real-world oriented and totally realistic," the director said. The assistant submitted a preliminary draft with cases that were fictitious but based on realistic situations. "I said I wanted real-world stuff instead of fictionalized junk," the director told the assistant. "I followed up with memos, calls, and meetings to verify that you understood me. What more do I have to do to get through to you?" "But my cases are real-world oriented," the assistant countered. "They illustrate situations that I've seen countless times in this organization! Just because I didn't abstract them from a magazine doesn't mean they're not realistic!"

40. Which of the following links in the communication chain caused this communication failure?
    a. Noise.
    b. Choice of media.
    c. Feedback.
    d. Encoding/decoding.

41. The assistant does not have time to rewrite the casebook in addition to performing regular duties. Also, the assistant believes that abstracting cases from current business literature will require copyright clearance and the payment of permission fees. Which communication medium would be most appropriate to convince the personnel director to use the cases as originally submitted?
    a. Face-to-face conversation.
    b. Memo.
    c. Formal report.
    d. Telephone call.

42. The internal auditor assigned to audit a vendor's compliance with product quality standards is the brother of the vendor's controller. The auditor should:
    a. Accept the assignment, but avoid contact with the controller during field work.
    b. Accept the assignment, but disclose the relationship in the audit report.
    c. Notify the vendor of the potential conflict of interest.
    d. Notify the chief audit executive of the potential conflict of interest.

Chapter 29
Relationships with
External Auditors

Introduction. Differing objectives, accountability, qualifications, and activities. Changing relationships. Improved internal audit professionalism. The effect of economics. More aggressive audit committees. Importance and benefits of internal/external auditor coordination. Historical barriers to internal/external auditor relationships. Values of internal/external auditor coordination. Internal auditor assistance in the expansion of the scope of external audits. A critical approach to former SAS No. 9. The issuance of SAS No.65, its philosophy and content. Summarizing external auditor philosophy. External audit evaluations — substitute for external reviews. Preparation for the external auditor review. The evolution of the IIA position, SIAS No. 5 interpreting IIA Standard 550. The philosophy of coordination and the coordination of audit effort. Acquisition of external audit services. External auditor independence requirements for providing internal audit service. Internal auditors' participation in external audits. How internal auditors view external auditors. Internal auditors' opinions of the external auditors. Means of coordination: the "unified audit" concept; outsourcing and cosourcing; coordinating total audit coverage. The bridge of trust; and the exchange of information.

• •

Introduction

External and internal auditors pursue different objectives, owe a different accountability, possess different qualifications, and engage in different activities. But they have mutual interests that call for coordination of their talents for the benefit of the enterprise.

The internal auditor's objective is determined by senior management and the board and by professional standards: usually, that objective is to review the efficiency and effectiveness of the operation, compliance, and the adequacy and effectiveness of internal controls throughout the enterprise. The external auditor's objective is that required by statute or as determined by the representatives of shareholders — members of boards of directors — who hire them; usually, the objective is to express an opinion on the fairness with which financial statements have been prepared and presented.

Internal auditors are most often accountable to senior management, although more recently there has developed a dual accountability to senior management and the audit committee of the board. The external auditors are accountable to the representatives of the shareholders; and statutes often reinforce independence by excluding some individuals as external auditors and precluding some ancillary functions such as internal auditing and consulting.

Internal auditors' qualifications are those that management deems appropriate, and run the gamut from certification down to nothing more than on-the-job training — although individual internal audit departments may demand more professional backgrounds for all their internal auditors. The qualifications of external auditors are generally set by statute and usually require membership in a professional body.

Internal auditors are concerned with all aspects of enterprise activities — both financial and nonfinancial. External auditors are concerned primarily with the financial aspects of the organization.[1]

In early years, internal auditors work closely paralleled that of the external auditors. This was often in a subordinate role, to assist in the analysis of accounting records, under the supervision of external auditors. For the most part, that was the extent of the coordination practiced by the two disciplines. But studies have found that coordination practices between internal and external auditors have changed considerably in recent years. Internal and external audit executives are working closely together to identify more cost-effective methods to reduce duplication in total audit coverage. What has elevated the internal auditor from a subordinate role to a partnership can be attributed to two factors: one, the improved professionalism of internal auditors; two, the economics of auditing.

Internal audit professionalism gives the external auditors more confidence in an audit partnership. Indeed, in one study, what stood out more than anything else was the high praise the external auditors voiced for the professionalism, competency, and objectivity of the internal audit staffs.[2]

Because of the changing economics of auditing and legislation, audit committees are taking an expanded position, that they have the right to review and approve the audit fees required by external auditors, to monitor the hours expended by the external auditors, and to review audit coverage. Audit committees have taken a more aggressive negotiating stance, with the assistance of internal auditors. And they look to greater coordination between the two disciplines to eliminate duplication and overlap.[3]

Audit committees are helped in this effort by the dramatic increase in the status and ability of internal auditing staffs. This has created a more favorable environment in which external auditors can rely on the work of internal auditors. Increased independence, with internal auditors reporting to higher levels of management and having unrestricted access to audit committees, further improves the chances of creating a cooperative partnership between internal and external auditors. In fact, both audit staffs could be viewed as one pool of auditors available for assignment to a given audit under the supervision of either an external or an internal auditor.[4]

Some large corporations are adopting an aggressive strategy to control total corporate audit costs. Often, the aim is the complete elimination of duplicate or overlapping audit coverage. Audit committees are negotiating for their internal auditors to take over the audit of additional areas that do not have to be audited exclusively by the external auditors. Indeed, the CPAs are being asked to demonstrate why some of their audits cannot be done by the internal auditors. Moreover, certain corporate audit committees have stated bluntly that some CPA firms are now faced with the possibility of losing a client if they are not willing to cooperate in working toward cost-effective total audit coverage that requires audit coordination between internal and external auditors.[5]

There are some dissenting views to close cooperation. In one study, an internal audit respondent declared that the worst possible use of an internal audit group is to hold down external audit fees. The respondent stated that the two groups should complement each other; there should be little, if any, duplication of effort. And as much as possible, the financial auditing should be left to the external auditors and the operational controls to the internal audit group. Besides, added the respondent, when the internal audit group does work for the external auditors, the fee reduction is minimal.

All of this does not mean a lack of involvement with the external auditors. The respondent said that the internal auditors watch the external audit fees, question the need for some audit work, and challenge the billing for certain audit work if the internal auditors consider it excessive.[6]

The Sarbanes-Oxley Act of 2002 dramatically curtailed many of the non-audit functions of external auditors, further expanding and strengthening the position of the internal auditor. This subject is more specifically described in Chapter 30.

To expand upon these matters, we shall discuss the importance and benefits of coordination, some prerequisites for coordination, the assessment of internal audit qualifications, and some means of coordination — including the unified audit concept.

Importance and Benefits of Coordination

Coordination between external and internal auditors is important because of the potential to increase the economy, efficiency, and effectiveness of the total audit activity for the enterprise. Neither form of auditing can replace the other. But in many ways, they impinge on each other. If the two audits are uncoordinated, there will be overlaps and duplication that unnecessarily increase audit costs and confuse audit responsibilities.

The need for coordination becomes more pressing with each passing day. Both the business and the public sector are becoming more complex. Financial reporting standards have stretched the coverage needed for financial audits. Inflation has increased the personnel costs of public accounting firms. Fees have risen accordingly, and the increased costs have not gone unnoticed by management and boards of directors. Hence, internal and external auditors should coordinate their work as much as possible.

Rising costs are not the only reasons for coordination. The U.S. Foreign Corrupt Practices Act placed rigorous requirements on organizations to ensure adequate systems of internal accounting control. The penalties attached to violations of the act give impetus to a united effort from both disciplines to comply with the law. The advanced technique developed by independent accounting firms, melded to internal audit expertise and intimate knowledge of the organization, can provide greater comfort to management and the board.

The primary objective is not merely economic; it is to obtain maximum efficiency and effectiveness of the total audit effort. Efficiency is enhanced when each group's audit results are made available to the other group, on time, and as needed.

The expanded responsibilities of boards of directors and their audit committees add pressures that demand the assurance of no surprises. A well-coordinated effort by professional external and internal auditors can provide nervous board members and senior management with welcome and needed assurances that financial and operation reports and statements are proper and that weaknesses in control systems will be detected and that failures to comply with adequate systems will be promptly brought to light.

A historic research study conducted for The IIA by Brink and Barrett appraised relations between external and internal auditors. As a part of their study, they questioned chief financial officers (CFOs), chief executive officers (CEOs), and chairmen of audit committees (CACs). Questions included their perception of the internal audit services currently provided and desired in two areas: assuring sound internal financial control and assisting external auditors.

Respondents were asked for their rating of the desirability of these services on a scale of 1 to 5, with 1 equaling the lowest and 5 equaling the highest rating. A rating of 3.1 was considered moderately high; 4.0 to 5.0 was considered very high. The ratings by CFOs, CEOs, and CACs were as follows:[7]

Internal Audit Service:	Current Evaluation by			Optimum Evaluation by		
	CFOs	CEOs	CACs	CFOs	CEOs	CACs
Assure sound internal financial controls	4.3	4.4	4.4	4.8	4.7	4.7
Assist external auditors	3.5	3.8	3.9	3.8	4.0	4.0

Clearly, there was a high degree of interest in assuring sound internal control. At the CEO and CAC levels particularly, there was a strong desire to see internal auditors cooperate with external auditors.

Other studies perceive some barriers to completely satisfactory relationships. The acceptance of each other's work, the perceptions of each other's needs, and the willingness to subordinate each group's goals to the greater good of the enterprise will have to be improved for useful relationships to take hold. Mautz et al. disclosed a significant interpersonal difficulty.[8] The researchers asked internal auditors to rank, from a list of 10, the three most appealing and the three least appealing job features. Relationships with (cooperating with) external auditors fared next to the least, after travel. Interestingly enough, far and away the two most appealing job features were, first, the variety of assignments and, second, the intellectual challenge. It is not hard to see that the internal auditors found little variety or challenge to the analysis of accounts, which is what internal auditor usually do for external auditors.

Yet internal auditors can affect the scope of external audit work by decreasing the extent and the need to perform detailed tests. This is supported by Wallace's 1984 study.[9] She found that an increase by internal auditors of the estimated percent of total assets audited, total income audited, and total cost of sales audited is related to statistically lower external audit fees. Also, a higher allocation of internal audit hours to operational audits is likewise related to lower external audit fees. Moreover, more experienced internal audit managers are associated with lower external audit fees, and so is the formal coordination of internal and external auditors.

Wallace determined that internal audit departments, on the average, allocate only five percent of the total available audit hours to assisting the external auditor. As a consequence, fees are reduced about 10 percent. Subsequent studies included later in this chapter provide a different picture as to participation.

But useful coordination goes far beyond the reduction of external audit fees. Berry concluded that internal auditors can also use the work of the external auditors. This exchange can become significant because of the rising cost of internal auditing. Berry found that in some organizations the hourly audit rates of the internal auditors were approaching those of the external auditors. These increased rates reflect a higher quality of internal audit staff in terms of education, skill, and performance level.[10]

Because of the improved level of internal audit competency, each group can rely on the other in more ways than account analysis. Ward and Robertson pointed out some of these ways:[11]

Value to External Auditors

- External auditors get a better insight into client operations in specialized areas within the organization through the internal auditors' experience in those areas.

- Client relations are improved because of a feeling of involvement through cooperation and coordination of effort.

- External auditors are allowed to concentrate on more significant areas to rotate audit emphasis.

- External auditors receive beneficial training from coordinating and managing an audit team that includes internal auditors.

Value to Internal Auditors

- The training of internal auditors is enhanced through an interchange of new and different audit techniques, procedures, ideas, and information.

- Areas of further internal audit work and procedures for accomplishing that work are identified.

- Internal auditors obtain a better understanding of independence, audit standards, and audit objectives and are encouraged to become more professional.

- The external auditors' appraisal of the effectiveness of internal audit functions can be helpful.

The enterprise can gain in additional ways by coordinating the work of special projects that the external auditors undertake. A survey by the accounting firm of Peat Marwick revealed more than 400 examples of nonaccounting assertions being audited — other than cost-based financial statements.[12]

But there are boundaries to this form of "attestation." The external audit attestees must have a good understanding of the subject matter and how it relates to the particular client. In the current litigious climate, auditors might resist expanding their scope of audit. And so they would welcome a partnership with the internal auditors to help avoid the unknowns within a particular organization. Here are some of the attestation engagements listed by Peat Marwick with which a mature internal audit organization could provide assistance:

- Financial forecasts and projections.
- Information systems software and hardware performance.
- Internal controls at service and fiduciary organizations.
- Reorganization and bankruptcy plans. Antitrust case data.
- Contract costs.
- Compliance with contract terms.
- Compliance with government regulations.
- Lease payment contingencies.
- Management audits.
- Royalties.
- Occupancy, enrollment, and attendance statistics.
- Political contributions and expenditures.
- Cost reimbursement.
- Productivity indicators.

Historical Barriers to Coordination

The relationship between internal and external auditors should be based on coordination and cooperation. External auditors can get a good deal of help from the work of the internal auditors. But there have been bars to complete coordination. These were spelled out in the *Statement on Auditing Standards No. 9 (SAS No. 9)*, issued by the American Institute of Certified Public Accountants (AICPA).[13] *SAS No. 9* superseded AICPA's *Statement on Auditing Standards No. 1*, Section *320.74*. *SAS No. 9* has now been supplemented (1991) by *Statement on Auditing Standards No. 65*.

SAS No. 9 flatly stated that, "The work of internal auditors cannot be substituted for the work of the independent auditor." This blanket denial was puzzling to those internal auditors who came from public accounting and who were well equipped by training, experience, and continuing education to perform acceptable financial audits. *SAS No. 9* continued by saying that, in determining the nature, timing, and extent of their own auditing procedures, independent auditors should consider the procedures, if any, that internal auditors perform. Yet the prohibition against substitution remained.

Berry's study disclosed criticism of *SAS No. 9* on the grounds that it was outdated, in light of the changes that have taken place in practice.[14] More specifically, the criticisms were:

- *SAS No. 9* did not recognize the contribution of internal auditing as a profession.

- *SAS No. 9* did not recognize the significant advancement of internal auditing as a competent discipline.

- *SAS No. 9* assumed that external auditors relinquished their independence and increased audit risk when they relied on internal auditors' work.

- Because of its vagueness, external auditors were applying the provisions of *SAS No. 9* inconsistently in their audits. Despite the statement that "the work of the internal auditors cannot be substituted for the work of the independent auditor," Berry found that, in the 14 organizations he studied, the work of internal auditors was being substituted to a large degree.

- *SAS No. 9* did not address the subject of coordination in a systematic fashion and then only from the external auditor's point of view.

In practice, therefore, *SAS No. 9* seemed honored in the breach; external auditors felt confident about the professionalism of the particular internal auditors with whom they dealt and upon whom they relied. And according to research that had been done, there appeared to be a high level of professionalism in the larger internal audit departments. Clay and Haskin sent 100 questionnaires to chief financial officers of Fortune 500 organizations, seeking to determine the degree of professionalism of their internal audit staffs.[15] The results of the 60 responses were very positive and showed a high level of internal audit competency.

Clay and Haskin concluded from their survey that there was justification for the expanded use of internal audit departments by external auditors of large U.S. firms.

The Issuance of *SAS No. 65* — A New Contract

SAS No. 9 was the guiding regulation from its issuance in 1975 to 1990. It was generally agreed that it had value. However, as internal auditing began to be recognized as a responsible discipline, also as its techniques became more sophisticated and effective, and as its members' competence was recognized as progressive and encompassing modern state-of-the-arts concepts, it became obvious that the cautious, negative approach of *SAS No. 9* was no longer appropriate. Also, it was recognized that the *SAS No. 9* general approach needed more specificity to provide more direction as to the qualities that the external auditors needed to consider in the process of accepting the work of the internal auditor.

Finally, it became apparent that the new directive needed to include a more cooperative tone relative to the prospective interactivity of both sets of auditors in assisting with the responsibilities of each other. This concept of mutuality is evidenced by the fact that the AICPA recalled its first exposure draft so as to reevaluate its content and to reissue a draft that would be more appropriate to the interface with the newly recognized competency of the internal audit profession.

The SAS No. 65 Philosophy. SAS No. 9 provided very general guidelines for the external auditors' consideration of the objectivity and competence of the internal audit operation. Detailed guidance is now provided by *SAS No. 65*, "The Auditor's Consideration of the Internal Audit Function in the Audit of Financial Statements." The *SAS*, as its name implies, relates to financial statement audits and it describes in more specific terms the evaluation that must be made of the internal audit function so as to define the extent to which internal audit work can impact on the external auditors' procedures. It should be recognized that the audit of financial statements itself has expanded to be more searching as a result of the issuance of the new "expectation gap." *SAS's* in the 50 series are more rigorous and demanding. Thus, the use of internal audit, especially in reviews of internal controls and in expanded compliance and substantive testing, should be a welcome addition.

To accommodate to the provisions of *SAS No. 65,* the external auditor must:[16]

- Determine the relevancy of the internal audit function.

- Evaluate the internal auditor's objectivity and competency.

- Consider the effects of the internal auditor's work on the financial audit being conducted by the external auditor, including necessary audit procedures.

- Evaluate and test the effectiveness of the work performed by the internal auditor.

The SAS 65 Content. SAS No. 65 provides instruction in the same seven areas that were included in *SAS No. 9*. These areas are:

1. Auditor and internal auditor roles.
2. Internal audit function.
3. Internal auditor competence and objectivity.
4. Extent of effect of internal audit work.
5. Auditor/internal auditor coordination.
6. Auditor evaluation of internal audit work.
7. Direct assistance by internal auditors.

It is understandable that there was a need to develop specific directions as to how these seven areas were to be considered and the evaluations that should be made by the external audit staff. The sections below provide the details with which the internal auditor should be familiar.

External and internal auditor roles. Internal auditor work can be considered as an element of the auditor's internal control process. However, the work of the internal auditor cannot be substituted for that of the external auditor. *SAS No. 65* has expanded the above concept to say that the external auditor must maintain independence from the client and the internal auditor should maintain objectivity from the client units. (This latter provision is GAAS for both organizations.)

Internal audit function. Both *SAS No. 9* and *SAS No. 65* provide that the external auditor acquire an understanding of the internal audit function. However, the latter explains how it should be done. Thus, the external auditor should inquire into these items:

- The internal auditor's organizational status. This could be a measure of independence and objectivity.

- The degree to which the internal auditor applies professional audit standards (IIA, government, etc.). This could be a measure of reliability.

- The contents of the annual internal audit plan and the degree to which it is followed.

- The extent of access to records and to personnel and the amount of constraints exerted over the scope of the internal auditor's work.

- The content of the internal auditor's charter or similar directive and the degree with which it is complied.

The external auditor, based on the above evaluations, must determine the relevancy of the internal auditor's work as related to internal control structure and its impact on financial statements or on potential misstatements of financial data. The degree of relevancy can be obtained from a review of prior years' audits and the content of internal audit reports.

Assessing the Competence and Objectivity of the Internal Auditors. SAS No. 65 provides that internal audit competence can be judged based upon:

- Educational levels and professional experience.
- Professional certification and continuing professional education.
- Audit policies, programs, and processes being used.
- Practices regarding staff assignments.
- Supervision and review of audit activities.
- Quality of working paper documentations, reports, and recommendations.
- Evaluation of audit performance generally.

Internal audit objectivity should be judged based on:

- Organizational status as to reporting and administration.
- Policies that prevent internal auditors from auditing in areas where their objectivity would be compromised by personal constraints.

Extent of Effect of Internal Audit Work. Internal audit work can impact on the external auditor's:

- Understanding of the internal control structure.
- Risk assessments in areas of material misstatements.
- Performance of substantive tests.

The extent to which external auditors should use the work of internal auditors depends on:

- The materiality of financial statements involved.
- The inherent and control risks of the material assertions.
- The degree of subjectivity involving evaluation of audit evidence.

External Auditor/Internal Auditor Coordination. SAS No. 65 expanded on the statements of SAS No. 9 relative to coordination. The activities outlined include:

- Periodic meetings between internal and external auditors.
- The development of a coordinated audit schedule.
- Access by the external auditor to internal audit working papers and reports. (Internal auditors do have access to external auditor reports; a belief is generating that access to external auditor working papers should also be available.)
- Discussion of potential accounting issues.

Full frank and candid discussions between both audit groups, including feedback from the external auditors can assist the internal auditors to perform more effectively.

Auditor Evaluation of Internal Audit Work. Here, SAS No. 65 does not add materially to the provisions of SAS No. 9. These provisions were that if internal audit work would have an impact on external audit work, that the documentary evidence should be tested and that the external auditor should consider:

- Is the scope of the work appropriate?
- Are the audit programs adequate? Do working papers adequately document the work performed?
- Are conclusions appropriate?
- Are prepared reports consistent with work performed?

Direct Assistance by Internal Auditors. After having determined that the internal auditor's competence and objectivity is adequate, the external auditor may request direct assistance. This assistance may be:

- Assistance in understanding the internal control structure.
- Performance of tests of control.
- Performance of substantive tests.

The external auditor, in addition to assessing competence and objectivity, should review, test, and evaluate the work of the internal auditor. When performing work for the external auditor, the internal auditor should be informed as to the appropriate responsibilities, objectives, and procedures so as to perform effectively. This instruction should also include information on accounting and auditing issues.

There should be no need for unusual activity on the part of internal auditors who are already complying with The IIA's *Standards*. The provisions in *SAS No. 65* could well be taken from the *Standards* themselves. *SAS No. 65*'s requirements could well be termed, "Compliance with The IIA's *Standards*." Nevertheless, it is important that chief audit executives be aware of the areas that will be reviewed so that they can establish operational controls over those areas and produce periodic reports as to the audit organization's status in each. Some of the sensitive information is:

- Qualifications of personnel:
  - Education.
  - Experience.
  - Certifications.
- Training programs.
- Continuing education programs.
- Organization charts.
- Procedures manuals.
- Working paper files.
- Supervisory procedures.
- Audit report files.
- Quality control procedures.

It is hoped that *SAS No. 65* is encouraging a closer relationship between internal and external auditors, especially relative to the coordinated scheduling of audits and segments of audits. *SAS No. 65* also must imply more candid disclosure by the external auditors of the substance of their work. This could include access to their working papers. The advantage to the client could be substantial in preventing duplication of audit effort, early disclosure by the external auditors of areas that the internal auditors should review in depth, and the educational advantage of the disclosure of professional audit techniques.

Conversely, there is also the possibility of disclosure of substandard external audit effort. This is a service that the internal auditors should provide to the audit committee and the board of directors.

Sears sums up the impact of the issuance of *SAS No. 65* by stating that the substance of *SAS No. 9* and *SAS No. 65* is not much different. The "fundamental message" is that the external auditor must rely on his own judgment. He concludes that:[17]

". . .*SAS No. 65* conveys this message in light of the advanced professional status of internal auditing and the expectation gap faced by external auditors. It is more studied and reasoned and, as a result, establishes an improved basis for advancing the relationship between internal auditors."

He also faults *SAS No. 65* in that it, "omitted guidance as to how the external auditor might use the work of the internal auditor to reduce detection risk, that is, the risk that the external auditor will not detect material misstatements in the financial statements under audit."[18]

A Summary of the External Auditor Philosophy[19]

Much internal audit effort is not relevant to the work of the external auditor. The very difference in audit objectives between the two groups could render much internal audit work that is intended to assess compliance, efficiency, and effectiveness to have little application to the determination of the fairness of presentation of financial statements.

On the other hand, reviews of internal controls that are a basic procedure for internal auditors could, in many cases, hold a high degree of relevance to the external audit process. If the external auditors believe that some of the internal audit work is useful or if they wish to have the assistance of the internal audit staff, they must plan to assess the competence and objectivity of the internal audit staff. Generally speaking, the assistance can be in the areas of:

- Understanding the design of internal control and determining if the controls are effective.
- Reduction of risk assessment if the internal auditors perform relevant procedures.
- Reduction of the performance of substantive testing when the internal auditors have performed similar work on an interim basis.

It is important to realize that the external audit is an independent examination. In areas of high risk, the external auditors must rely on their own work and subjective decisions. They must remember that they alone are responsible for the audit opinion and that the responsibility cannot be shared.

External Audit Evaluations — A Substitute for the External Auditor Reviews

The IIA audit standards 1311 and 1312 provide for quality assurance reviews of the internal audit activity. The reviews can be:

- Internal assessments.
- External assessments.

Sumners and Toerner provide their belief that, ". . .the external quality assurance review has the potential to satisfy the requirements of *SAS No. 65* and to increase external auditor reliance on internal auditors."[20] The authors describe the areas in each of the IIA *Standards* that the external auditors would normally review and then relate these specific areas of review to the requirements of *SAS No. 65* that call for evaluations of the internal audit function's competence, objectivity, and effectiveness. For example, in the competence area, items that the external reviewers would examine and that also are covered by *SAS No. 65* are:

- Educational level and professional experience of IIA staff members.
- Continuing education program.
- Assignment of staff members to engagements and supervision of staff members' work.
- Professional certifications held by staff members.
- Quality of internal audit policies, working papers, reports, recommendations, and performance.

The areas of objectivity and effectiveness are similarly structured.

The writers hold that because of the similarities between the external reviews and the requirements of *SAS No. 65*, external auditors could well reduce the amount of time spent in the internal audit function's evaluation. Also, they perceive that because both groups will be evaluating from a common body of standards, the results would be materially the same. As a matter of fact, the writers believe that the external review could build more confidence on the part of the external auditor than the review by the external auditors themselves.

Preparation for the External Auditors' Review

Chief audit executives should, in preparation for reviews by external auditors, have available in documented form the following material:

Understanding the Internal Audit Functions[21]

SAS No. 65 Requirements

- Organizational status within the entity
- Application of professional standards.
- Audit plans.
- Access to records; any scope limitations.

Assessing Competency and Objectivity[22]

SAS No. 65 Requirements

- Educational level and professional experience.
- Professional certification and continuing education.
- Audit policies, programs, and procedures.
- Practices regarding assignment of internal auditors.
- Supervision and review of internal audit activities.
- Quality of working paper documentation, reports, and recommendations.
- Evaluation of internal auditor performance re *SAS No. 65* requirements.

The Evolution of the Institute of Internal Auditors' Position

In 1987, The Institute of Internal Auditors issued *Statement on Internal Auditing Standards No. 5*, "Internal Auditors Relationships with Independent Outside Auditors." This statement was written when *SAS No. 9*, issued by the AICPA, was in force and was responsive to the restricted provisions of that issuance. The statement interpreted former Standard 550, "External Auditors," which stated:[23]

> **The director of internal auditing (chief audit executive) should coordinate internal and external audit efforts. (parentheses added)**
> .01 The internal and external audit work should be coordinated to ensure adequate audit coverage and to minimize duplicate audit efforts.
> .02 Coordination of audit efforts involves:
> .1 Periodic meetings to discuss matters of mutual interest.
> .2 Access to each other's audit programs and working papers.
> .3 Exchange of audit reports and management letters.
> .4 Common understanding of audit techniques, methods, and terminology.

The Institute's Audit Standards Committee in 1987 recognized the need to expand the above skeletal provisions of the standard in the light of the many inquiries made of it and because of the confusion between it and the AICPA's *SAS No. 9*.[24] Here is a summary of the substance of *SIAS 5*:

- To the extent that professional and organizational responsibilities allow, internal auditors should conduct examinations in a manner that allows for maximum audit coordination and efficiency.

- The chief audit executive should make regular evaluations of the coordination between internal and independent outside auditors.

- A sufficient number of meetings should be scheduled to discuss audit activities planned by both internal and independent outside auditors to ensure appropriate coordination of audit work; that duplicate efforts are kept to a minimum; that audit effort activities are efficient and timely; and that the scope of planned audit work is appropriate.

- Internal auditors need reasonable access to programs, working papers, audit reports, and management letters of independent outside auditors and conversely should provide the independent outside auditors reasonable access to internal audit programs, working papers, and audit reports.

- The chief audit executive should ensure that the independent outside auditors' techniques, methods, and terminology are sufficiently understood by the internal auditors and conversely he/she should provide sufficient information to enable the independent outside auditors to understand the internal auditors' techniques, methods, and terminology.

The Philosophy of Coordination. The *SIAS* described the underlying philosophy of the coordination effort by:

- Identifying the differences in scope of the normal internal audits and external audit efforts and relating the latter to the requirements of the AICPA standards.

- Stating that the oversight of the work of the external auditor was generally the responsibility of the audit committee. Actual coordination should be the responsibility of the chief audit executive, with the support of the audit committee.

- Providing that the chief audit executive should make sure that the scope of internal audits did not duplicate the work of external auditors. Internal audits should allow for maximum audit coordination and efficiency.

- Explaining that internal auditors may perform work for external auditors. If so, the internal auditor's work will conform to The IIA's *Standards.*

- Stating that the chief audit executive should make periodic evaluations of the coordination between the internal and external auditors. The evaluations may include an assessment of the efficiency of both audit staffs including aggregate audit cost.

- Asserting that the audit committee may request the chief audit executive to assess the performance of the outside auditors. The assessment should be based on sufficient evidence of the efficiency and effectiveness of the work.

The Coordination of Audit Effort. The *SIAS* described the coordination of audit effort in the following detail:

- The periodic meetings should have the following effects:
  - Planning to coordinate audit coverage.
  - Efficient and timely completion of the audit.
  - Determinations as to whether findings to date require audit scope revisions.

- There should be access to each others' audit programs and working papers for the determination of the degree of reliance on the others' work. Access on both parts to carry with it the respect for confidentiality of the working papers.

- Exchange of audit reports and management letters would be necessary for:
  - External auditors' consideration of management's response and subsequent internal audit follow-up so as to assist in potential scope modifications.
  - Internal auditors to plan for areas to emphasize in future audit work. Also, the chief audit executive should make sure that needed corrective action by management or the board of directors has been followed up.

- Common understanding of audit techniques, methods, and terminology would include:
  - Understanding the scope of work planned by external auditors and determining that it, plus the internal auditors' work, fulfilled the requirements of IIA *Standard 300,* "Scope of Work." The understanding required knowledge of the external auditors' consideration of materiality and the nature and extent of planned procedures.
  - The chief audit executive's determination that the internal auditors' understanding of the outside auditors' techniques, methods, and terminology would be such that:
    * The work of both staffs could be coordinated.
    * The work of the external auditors could be evaluated.
    * Effective communication could be made relative to assisting external auditors.
  - The provision by the chief audit executive's of sufficient information for the external auditors' reliance on the internal auditors' assisting work.
  (Note: It may be more efficient if similar techniques, methods, and terminology are used by both staffs.)

It should be noticed that there was a thread of direction and emphasis in the *SIAS* relative to the proactive responsibility of the chief audit executive to evaluate the efficiency and effectiveness of the external auditors' work. This approach is probably the result of: (1) the U.S. General Accounting Office evaluation in 1986 of CPA firms' work in auditing government programs and finding it wanting; and (2) the rash of litigation relative to reported substandard audit work at that time on the part of external auditors in the private sector.

IIA *Standard 2050,* "Coordination," and Practice Advisory 2050-1, "Coordination," paragraphs 1 to 5 and 10 describes this current coordinative aspect:

"Internal and external auditing work should be coordinated to ensure adequate audit coverage and to minimize duplicate efforts. The scope of internal auditing work encompasses a systematic, disciplined approach to evaluate and improve the effectiveness of risk management, control, and governance processes. The scope of internal auditing work is covered by Section 2100 of the *Standards.* On the other hand, the external auditors' ordinary examination is designed to obtain sufficient evidential matter to support an opinion on the overall fairness of the annual financial statements. The scope of the work of external auditors is determined by their professional standards, and they are responsible for judging the adequacy of procedures performed and evidence obtained for purposes of expressing their opinion on the annual financial statements.

"Oversight of the work of external auditors, including coordination with the internal audit activity, is generally the responsibility of the board. Actual coordination should be the responsibility of the chief audit executive. The chief audit executive will require the support of the board to achieve effective coordination of audit work.

"In coordinating the work of internal auditors with the work of external auditors, the chief audit executive should ensure that work to be performed by internal auditors in fulfillment of Section 2100 of the *Standards* does not duplicate the work of external auditors which can be relied on for purposes of internal auditing coverage. To the extent that professional and organizational reporting responsibilities allow, internal auditors should conduct engagements in a manner that allows for maximum audit coordination and efficiency.

"The chief audit executive may agree to perform work for external auditors in connection with their annual audit of the financial statements. Work performed by internal auditors to assist external auditors in fulfilling their responsibility is subject to all relevant provisions of the *Standards for the Professional Practice of Internal Auditing.*

"The chief audit executive should make regular evaluations of the coordination between internal and external auditors. Such evaluations may also include assessments of the overall efficiency and effectiveness of internal and external auditing functions, including aggregate audit cost.

"Coordination of the audit efforts involves periodic meetings to discuss matters of mutual interest.

(a) *Audit Coverage.* Planned audit activities of internal and external auditors should be discussed to assure that audit coverage is coordinated and duplicate efforts are minimized. Sufficient meetings should be scheduled during the audit process to assure coordination of audit work and efficient and timely completion of audit activities, and to determine whether observations and recommendations from work performed to date require that the scope of planned work be adjusted.

(b) *Access to each other's audit programs and working papers.* Access to the external auditors' programs and working papers may be important in order for internal auditors to be satisfied as to the propriety for internal audit purposes of relying on the external auditors' work. Such access carries with it the responsibility for internal auditors to respect the confidentiality of those programs and working papers. Similarly, access to the internal auditors' programs and working papers should be given to external auditors in order for external auditors to be satisfied as the propriety, for external audit purposes, of relying on the internal auditors' work.

(c) *Exchange of audit reports and management letters.* Internal audit final communications, management's responses to those communications, and subsequent internal audit activity follow-up reviews should be made available to external auditors. These communications assist external auditors in determining and adjusting the scope of work. In addition, the internal auditors need access to the external auditor's management letters. Matters discussed in management letters assist internal auditors in planning the areas to emphasize in future internal audit work. After review of management letters and initiation of any needed corrective action by appropriate members of management and the board, the chief audit executive should ensure that appropriate follow-up and corrective action have been taken.

(d) *Common understanding of audit techniques, methods, and terminology.* First, the chief audit executive should understand the scope of work planned by external auditors and should be satisfied that the external auditors' planned work, in conjunction with the internal auditors' planned work, satisfies the requirements of Section 2100 of the *Standards*. Such satisfaction requires an understanding of the level of materiality used by external auditors for planning and the nature and extent of the external auditors' planned procedures.

Second, the chief audit executive should ensure that the external auditors' techniques, methods, and terminology are sufficiently understood by internal auditors to enable the chief audit executive to (1) coordinate internal and external auditing work; (2) evaluate, for purposes of reliance, the external auditor's work; and (3) ensure that internal auditors who are to perform work to fulfill the external auditors' objectives can communicate effectively with external auditors.

Finally, the chief audit executive should provide sufficient information to enable external auditors to understand the internal auditors' techniques, methods, and terminology to facilitate reliance by external auditors on work performed using such techniques, methods, and terminology. It may be more efficient for internal and external auditors to use similar techniques, methods, and terminology to effectively coordinate their work and to rely on the work of one another."

Acquisition of External Audit Services

The Institute of Internal Auditors believed it appropriate to further expand *Standard 2050* relative to coordination between internal and external audit operations so as to ensure proper coverage and minimize duplication of effort. Thus, it issued Practice Advisory 2050-2, "Acquisition of External Audit Services." The objective was to provide that the internal auditors have a "role in the selection or retention of external auditors and in the definition of scope of work."

The Practice Advisory covers such areas as:

- The establishment of regular periodic requests for proposals for external audit services regardless of whether or not there is satisfaction as to the performance of the current external auditor.

- The development of appropriate policies for reduction or retention of external audit services such as:

  - Nature and types of services.
  - Policy approvals.
  - Duration of contracts and retention aspects.
  - Solution and evaluation teams.
  - Evaluation criteria.
  - Fee aspects.
  - Unique regulatory aspects.

- Types of services other than financial audits that might be offered such as:*

  - Tax services.
  - Consulting services.
  - Internal audit outsourcing and cosourcing services.
  - Special services:
    * Valuation.
    * Appraisal.
    * Actuarial.
  - Temporary financial assistance.
  - Legal services.

- Appropriate documentation as to solicitation or retention.

- Development of plans for selection including:

  - Selection committee participants.
  - Deliverables.
  - Target dates.
  - Candidates.
  - Services to be requested.
  - Methods of dissemination of information to participants.

- Use of two-phased requests for screening purposes and content of methodology for each phase. (performance and financial)

- Development of analytical methodology.

- Service agreement documentation.

- Change-over procedures when new providers are engaged.

- Methods of monitoring ongoing external audit service providers including their independence and contract terms compliance.

---

*Subject to the restrictions in the Sarbanes-Oxley Act.

External Auditor Independence Requirements for Providing Internal Audit Services

The Institute has issued Practice Advisory 2030-2, "SEC, External Auditor Independence Requirements," for providing internal audit services. This Advisory is essentially informational in character. It relates to organizations subject to SEC requirements and provides information relative to the determination as to the independence of present or proposed providers of internal audit services. The SEC amendments are related to:

- Investments by auditors or their family members in audit clients.

- Employment relationships between auditors and their family members and audit clients.

- The scope of services provided by audit firms to their audit clients.

Those SEC amendments, effective February 5, 2001, provide more restrictive provisions that are described in great detail in the Advisory as well as requiring disclosure as to such arrangements. Specialized transaction dates in 2002 are provided for implementing the new rules. The SEC rules state that the auditor is not independent if the external auditor, at any point during the audit period, provided to the audit client, subject to "criteria exemptions and limitations" explained in the rules:

- Bookkeeping or other accounting service related to the client's financial statements.

- Financial information systems design and implementation.

- Appraisal or valuation services or fairness opinions.

- Actuarial services.

- Internal audit services.

- Management functions.

- Human resources.

- Broker dealer services.

- Legal services.

The Practice Advisory detailed related SEC rules, one of which provides that independence is impaired if the external auditor provides internal audit services in an amount greater than 40% of the client's total hours of internal audit service, (not including "operational internal audit service unrelated to the internal accounting controls, financial systems or financial statements"). The Advisory further delineates exceptions, one of which is the provision of a competent employee or employees within the senior management to be responsible for the internal audit function. Another is evaluation by the client's management of the accountant's findings and results. A third is the determination by the client of the scope risk and frequency of the accountant's internal audit activities. Finally, "the audit client's management does not rely on the accountant's work as the primary basis for determining the adequacy of internal controls."

The remainder of the Advisory relates to the chief audit executive's responsibility for communications, the administration, and the documentation of the arrangements with the external auditors. A series of examples, definitions, and computations are also presented and explained. There is considerable discussion of the computation of the above-mentioned 40 percent limit.

Internal Auditors' Participation in External Audits[25]

This chapter has thus far discussed the internal-external auditor relationships and the qualities that the external auditors look for in determining the degree of assistance to be obtained from the internal audit staff. It has also identified the internal auditors' approach to assistance. However, what is the amount of time actually spent by internal auditors in assistance and what tasks are performed? A study published in *Internal Auditing,* Winter 1991, attempts to answer these questions. A sample of 170 responses was used from 501 randomly selected organizations in the 1987 *Forbes 500*. This response rate was 33.9 percent. The study was indeed a significant addition to professional information.

Several questions were asked; we will provide only summary information so as to establish a general picture.

Extent of Participation

Of the 170 responses, 10 did not participate. Consequently the following statistical presentation will cover only the responses of the 61 *limited* participation responses and the 99 *considerable* responses. The separation into the two groups was based on the respondents' replies. The separation is useful as it allows for a rough comparison based on the respondents' concept of their participation.

	Number	%
Did not participate	10	5.9
Participated to a *limited* extent	61	35.9
Participated to a *considerable* extent	99	58.2
	170	100.0

Internal Auditors' Contribution to External Audit

The *limited* group disclosed that internal auditors provided very little assistance in 16 percent of the engagements. However, internal auditors did provide more than 100 hours in 83.6 percent of the cases. Reference to the next table for the 40 respondents who specified the number of hours provided, indicated that substantial assistance was provided in 60 percent of the engagements (over 500 hours). In 14 cases, 35 percent, the assistance was from 1,000 hours to 10,000 hours. This could be classed as substantial assistance.

| | Extent of Participation | | | | |
| | Limited | | Considerable | | |
	Number	%	Number	%	Total
No more than 50 hours	1	1.6	0	0.0	1
From 50 to 100 hours	9	14.8	0	0.0	9
More than 100 hours	51	83.6	99	100.0	150
Total	61	100.0	99	100.0	160

Hours of Participation in External Audit Related Tasks

Of the 61 participating to a limited extent, only 40 provided specific hours spent; of the 99 who participated to a considerable extent, 76 gave specific hours.

| | Extent of Participation | | | |
| | Limited | | Considerable | |
	Number	%	Number	%
No more than 500 hours	16	40.0	7	9.2
501 to 999	10	25.0	10	13.2
1,000 to 4,999	12	30.0	43	56.6
5,000 to 9,999	2	5.0	9	11.8
10,000 to 17,250	0	0.0	7	9.2
Total	40	100.0	76	100.0

The mean for the considerable extent was 3,530 hours.

Hours of Participation in External Audit of Combined Groups

The mode for the groups responding was the time classification from 1,000 to 4,999 hours. On a rough computation, if we could postulate that the mean was 3,000 hours and assume that the external audit engagement was about six weeks, this would equate to 500 hours per week and assuming a 50 hour week (40 hours plus 10 hours overtime), we would average about 10 internal audit staff members per engagement.

	Number	%
Fewer than 1,000 hours	43	37.1
From 1,000 to 4,999	55	47.4
From 5,000 to 9,999	11	9.5
10,000 or more hours	7	6.0
Total	116	100.0

Portion of Total Internal Audit Hours Contributed to External Audit

The next question was, what was the portion of the total internal audit hours that was contributed to the external auditors? In the *limited* group 92 percent reported that they contributed 10 percent or less to the external auditors. However, in the *considerable* group a much larger percentage of contribution was made. Almost 50 percent of the respondents indicated that they devoted 11 percent or more with 20 percent of the respondents exceeding 20 percent of their staff time. This is a substantial contribution and raises questions as to the quantity and quality of internal audit work that could then be performed on an as-directed or discretionary basis.

| | Extent of Participation | | | | | |
| | Limited | | Considerable | | Total | |
	Number	%	Number	%	N	%
No more than 10 percent	56	91.8	49	49.5	105	65.6
11 to 20 percent	4	6.6	29	29.3	33	20.6
More than 20 percent	0	0.0	19	19.2	19	11.9
No response	1	1.6	2	2.0	3	1.9
Total	61	100.0	99	100.0	160	100.0

The Percentage of the External Audit Performed by Internal Auditors

It would appear that in many cases a substantial portion of the audit — about 27 percent — was performed by the internal auditors. This is a welcome sign of improved cooperation between the two staffs and should result in a favorable economic impact relative to fees and a greater awareness on the part of internal auditors as to the financial condition of the organization.

| | Extent of Participation | | | | | |
| | Limited | | Considerable | | Total | |
	Number	%	Number	%	N	%
No more than 10 percent	47	77.1	20	20.2	67	41.8
11 to 20 percent	12	19.7	31	31.3	43	26.9
More than 20 percent	1	1.6	42	42.4	43	26.9
Qualified/No response	1	1.6	6	6.1	7	4.4
Total	61	100.0	99	100.0	160	100.0

Nature of Tasks Performed by Internal Auditors

The responses as to the general nature of the work performed by the internal auditors showed that most assisted in the three major audit areas: internal control reviews, compliance testing, and substantive testing. This is the first indication of the extent of such employment and it is valuable information.

	Extent of Participation					
	(n=61) **Limited**		**(n=99)** **Considerable**		**(n=160)** **Total**	
	Number	%	Number	%	N	%
Reviewed internal control	44	72.1	91	91.9	135	84.4
Performed compliance tests (now tests of control)	47	77.0	92	92.9	139	86.9
Performed substantive tests	44	72.1	88	88.9	132	82.5

It is obvious here that the internal auditors performed work in more than one of these task areas.

Specific Tasks Performed by Internal Auditors

This is probably one of the first extensive indications available as to the specific tasks that are performed by internal auditors who assist the external auditors. It is encouraging to see that much of the work is beyond the "number crunching" chores that have been characterized as the lot of many of the internal auditor participants. The 20 complete audits of branches and units, although only 12.5 percent, are an indication of confidence by the external auditors.

	Extent of Participation					
	(n=61) **Limited**		**(n=99)** **Considerable**		**(n=160)** **Total**	
	Number	%	Number	%	N	%
EDP related tasks	13	21.3	16	16.2	29	18.1
Accounts receivable confirmations	8	13.1	6	6.1	14	8.8
Analytical review	4	6.6	8	8.1	12	7.5
Inventory observations and counts	5	8.2	5	5.1	10	6.3
Complete audits of branches/units	5	8.2	15	15.2	20	12.5
Report preparation	1	1.6	4	4.0	5	3.1
Management letter preparation	0	0.0	3	3.0	3	1.9

Note: Although there were 77 who added additional tasks, the extent of participation is related to the total group.

Assessment of Cooperation During Last Annual Audit

This positive indication of the effectiveness of cooperation during the audit (84.4 percent) is a very encouraging sign of the cooperative stature of the combined audit effort.

	Extent of Participation					
	(n=61)		(n=99)		(n=160)	
	Limited		**Considerable**		**Total**	
	Number	%	Number	%	N	%
Two groups cooperated:						
Very effectively	48	78.7	87	87.9	135	84.4
In a minimally effective manner	12	19.7	8	8.1	20	12.5
Problems developed	1	1.6	4	4.0	5	3.1
Total	61	100.0	99	100.0	160	100.0

How Internal Auditors View External Auditors[26]

A survey of internal auditors' attitudes toward external auditors was conducted shortly after the issuance in 1987 of *SIAS 5*, "Internal Auditor's Relationships With Independent Outside Auditors," but before the issuance in 1991 by the AICPA of *SAS No. 65*, "The Auditors Consideration of the Internal Audit Function in the Audit of Financial Statements." This survey probably was the result of several previous surveys that indicated general dissatisfaction on the part of internal auditors with the evaluation of: (1) the internal audit function; and (2) the working relationships during the audit. Also, the external auditor's comments in the management letters.

The survey was limited to the Detroit, Michigan, industrial area and was well organized and representative. Following are the responses to 10 statements provided by chief audit executives and staff auditors:

	Executives	Staff
1. I do not have to train the external auditors.	55%	52%
2. I receive appropriate credit for work I do on the external audit.	75%	37%
3. I feel that the external auditors' deadlines are reasonable.	68%	49%
4. Working with the external auditors is rewarding.	37%	28%
5. I learn from the external auditor.	33%	33%
6. I document/evaluate internal control for the external audit.	61%	66%

	Executives	Staff
7. I feel that the external auditor is using my expertise to the fullest.	40%	33%
8. I see and comment on the management letter.	61%	34%
9. I have access to the organization's audit committee.	86%	39%
10. Management values and listens to its internal auditors.	77%	69%

To generalize from the above responses (four additional questions that relate to professional status of the internal auditor were not quoted here), it would appear that:

	Response No.
1. Much work needs to be done by external auditors in interpersonal relations.	2, 4
2. Technical relationships are fair.	3, 5, 6, 8
3. Quality of the external auditor is rated as fair.	1, 7
4. Internal audit relationships with internal management are good.	9, 10

The picture was not bright and if this condition still exists, it would appear that much work needs to be done. It is hoped that *SAS No. 65* is having a beneficial impact on these conditions.

Internal Auditors' Opinions of the External Audit[27]

The survey quoted above, conducted in the Detroit area, of audit directors and their staffs also evaluated the performance of the external auditors who audited their organizations. The ranking of the external auditors by the internal audit staff using a five-point scale showed:

Quality	Mean Score
Knowledge of industry	3.5
Knowledge of the organization	3.3
Knowledge of the accounting system	3.7
Knowledge of accounting	4.0
Ability to organize the audit:	
Task delegation	3.4
Schedule work assignments	3.3
Interpersonal relations with other	
external auditors	3.8
Interpersonal relations with internal	
auditors	3.5
Communication skills (written)	3.5

The previous ratings are not outstanding. They display a degree of adequacy, nothing more. The percentage of excellent and good ratings was disappointing: five of the qualities had 10 percent of the respondents who were so rated, one (knowledge of accounting) had 20 percent. The predominant percentages were in the "good" rating — lots of room for improvement.

Practice Advisory 2050-1, "Coordination," paragraphs 6 and 7, provide the following directive:

"In exercising its oversight role, the board may request the chief audit executive to assess the performance of external auditors. Such assessments should ordinarily be made in the context of the chief audit executive's roles of coordinating internal and external auditing activities, and should extend to other performance matters only at the specific request of senior management or the board. Assessments of the performance of external auditors should be based on sufficient information to support the conclusions reached. Assessments of the external auditors' performance with respect to the coordination of internal and external auditing activities should reflect the criteria described in this Practice Advisory.

"Assessments of the performance of external auditors extending to matters beyond coordination with the internal auditors may address factors, such as:

- Professional knowledge and experience.
- Knowledge of the organization's industry.
- Independence.
- Availability of specialized services.
- Anticipation of and responsiveness to the needs of the organization.
- Reasonable continuity of key engagement personnel.
- Maintenance of appropriate working relationships.
- Achievement of contract commitments.
- Delivery of overall value to the organization."

As to the involvement of the internal auditors in the conduct of the external audit, the internal auditors indicated their activity as:

	Average Percentage of Internal Auditing Staff Participating
Planning:	
Deciding the nature of testing	33%
Deciding on the staff to do the testing	56
Deciding the timing of the tests	45
Internal Control:	
Reviewing internal control	50

	Average Percentage of Internal Auditing Staff Participating (Cont.)
Documenting internal control	51%
Interim testing performed on:	
Cash receipts	52
Cash disbursements	54
Sales	42
Purchases	52
Payroll	52
Year-end testing:	
Bank reconciliations	41
Confirmation of receivables	52
Inventory	52
Analytic reviews	18

The above disclosure indicates that the internal auditors believe that they are participating materially in the external audits. Even in the planning stage, the internal auditors are surprisingly performing a substantial portion of the work. The effort devoted to internal control reviews and the interim testing comes as no surprise. Much of this could be part of the internal audit normal review of the organization's operation. What does come as a surprise is the predominance of work on cash, receivables, and inventories, and the small amount of work on analytic reviews, an area where the internal auditor probably is more knowledgeable than the external auditors.

The authors conclude that the chief audit executives see the external auditors making full use of the internal audit staff (92 percent.) The staff (38 percent) does not agree. The authors believe that the staff may view its abilities higher than do its executives; and the staff members do not fully understand financial statement auditing (fewer than 25 percent had public accounting experience).

The research does give a good description in a general sense of the internal-external auditor relationships and the types and quantities of work performed by the internal audit staffs. Unfortunately, there is no recent research on this subject. It is our opinion, however, that there is increased participation because of the improved technical proficiency of internal audit staffs, and because of economic pressures on external audit fees.

Means of Coordination

Berry's study of 14 corporations impelled the conclusion that the coordination of total audit coverage has changed significantly in recent years. It was then in a state of flux and will probably continue to change more in the future. Two factors appear to have contributed to change: One is the elevated professionalism of internal auditors, which provides greater confidence on the part of the external auditors to rely on internal audit work. The other is the increased cost of total audit coverage, which was and has become significant and of increasing concern to corporate management.[28]

The "Unified Audit" Concept

Much of the coordinated work as described earlier involves a division of labor between the external and internal auditors. This is often unplanned and haphazard. As a result, much of the work done by the two groups overlaps and results in a certain amount of redundancy. The answer to these inefficient and uneconomical methods is what has been termed the "single audit." Because of the federal government's use of the term "single audit" to designate an audit performed by one audit organization for all other federal agencies, this concept will be termed the "unified audit." Once the internal and external auditors are regarded as equals, both audit staffs could be viewed as one pool of auditors available for assignment to a given audit segment under the supervision of either an internal or external auditor.[29]

When competency has been accepted by both groups, the work of one can be accepted by the other without duplicative testing. In one organization that Berry studied, the chief internal audit executive said that the external auditors accepted 99.9 percent of the internal audit work without testing the working papers to the hard-copy documentation; the external auditor concurred.[30]

In the "unified audit" concept, all financial statements, entities, and functions should be audited only once during a given period, no matter which group does it. Indeed, external auditors should work cooperatively with the internal auditors to see if external audit work should be done — not so much to reduce costs but because of the special expertise the particular group can bring to the audit. For example, the external auditors will usually have greater expertise in foreign tax audits than the internal auditors.

Logistics also play a part. Where one group is making an audit in an off-site location, it can take on the responsibilities of the other group by continuing on with complete audits at that site. Also, audit risk is reduced. By working together and making use of the internal auditor's knowledge of the industry and the organization, audit risks are minimized. Proper planning is essential to successful coordination and "unified audit" execution. Exhibit 29-1 gives a picture of the planning and coordination practices employed. Following are some of the key decisions and actions that should take place during the planning meetings:[31]

- Determine the extent of external audit activity in planned internal audit areas since the previous internal audit.

- Discuss the state of internal controls, accounting records, procedures, and personnel.

- Identify areas/locations planned to be audited by external auditors.

- Compare with areas/locations planned to be audited by internal auditors.

- Identify the audit areas/locations to be audited exclusively by external auditors.

- Agree on areas of external audit where the internal auditors can assume responsibility to audit.

- Decide on the areas of the internal audit where the assistance of external auditors is required, including an estimate of the number of external auditors and work days needed.

- Decide on the areas of the external audit where the assistance of internal auditors is required, including an estimate of the number of internal auditors and work days needed.

- Agree on the dates and the timing for all parts of the joint audit plan.

- Develop the external auditor fee budget.

- Agree on the approach for preparing a joint audit program.

- Agree on the format of working papers for joint audit work.

- Agree on joint training.

- Complete the audit plan and reduce it to writing; have it reviewed and approved by senior management and the audit committee of the board.

Both groups should follow some basic rules in the execution and controlling of the coordinated audit plan. Internal auditors can be a source of useful information that external auditors might have difficulty obtaining for themselves. The external auditors can accumulate facts, but they might not have the same depth of understanding that internal auditors have about systems, organizations, and people. The cost of obtaining such information can be reduced by appropriate coordination and communication between the audit staffs.

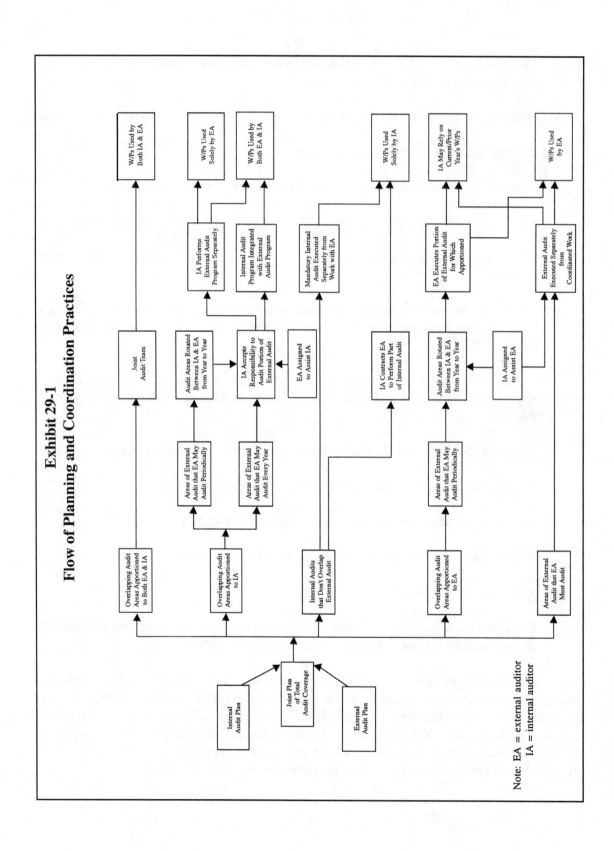

Exhibit 29-1
Flow of Planning and Coordination Practices

Note: EA = external auditor
IA = internal auditor

The coordination must be based on mutual respect and integrity. Each group must be able to regard the other as professionals of equal competence. Each must be able to respect the other's independence. Moreover, the internal auditors should not be dragged off at the peremptory call of management to leave the external auditor high, dry, and alone.

Outsourcing and Cosourcing

Outsourcing of internal auditing functions in one form or another has been on the internal audit scene for the last 20 years. Specifically it is the performance of an organization's function by another organization that is not integrally a part of the basic organization structure. Tax work, insurance, risk management, market research, research and development, and even accounting have been targets of the outsourcing organizations. The shrinking number of CPA clients as a result of consolidations and mergers; normal economic trends causing the costs of public accounting to rise, resulting in dwindling profits from audit work; the profitability of the consulting practice (of which internal auditing is a part); and the ability to use staff in normally quiet periods in the public accounting work cycle have forged a deep interest in both small practitioners and in the large regional and national CPA firms, and especially the "Big Four" international accounting giants.

In the internal auditing area outsourcing comes in these patterns:

- The outsourcing firm takes over the entire internal auditing function. The chief audit executive is an official of the outside accounting organization and reports to senior management of the organization.

- The outsourcing firm provides all of the internal auditing functions. However, there is an auditing organization managing structure between the outsourcing operation and the organization's senior management.

- The organization engages staff from the external accounting firm to perform internal auditing on a specific assignment basis. This basis could be functional, program, geographical, or other basis. The firm's internal auditors report following the normal channels of the organization's internal auditing activity. This method is called cosourcing.

Independence has been an issue ever since the practice started. One of the basic elements is a situation where an organization's external auditor also performs as an internal auditor. The question as to the evaluation of the outsourced internal auditing activity, a part of a normal external audit engagement, becomes very tricky. Even when two external auditing firms are concerned, the performance of true independence and dual criticism could have disastrous results later, if the tables were to be turned.

In instances where the external auditor performed both attest services, the American Institute of Certified Public Accountants (AICPA) previously held under ruling 17, under rule 101 of the Independence of the AICPA Code of Professional Conduct, that the auditor could perform both provided that the extended service was an extension of normal audit procedures normally conducted during the annual audit. However, as a result of a growing uneasiness of the U.S. Securities and Exchange Commission, the AICPA overruled Ruling 97 and replaced it with rulings 103, 104, and 105 under rule 101. The new ruling says that independence would not be impaired with attest firms as long as:

- The auditor does not act "in a capacity equivalent to a member of 'client' management or as an employee;"
- The auditor does not possess nor control organization assets;
- The auditor does not control activities that will affect the execution of business transactions; or
- Perform processes that relate to the quality control function.

The SEC still has problems and suggests that it would be better from an actual point of operation as well as credibility, if the extended service function were to be conducted by a firm not engaged to attest.

There is a wealth of material, both in periodical articles and issuances from major firms engaged in the outsourcing process. These publications outline the advantages and disadvantages to both the accounting firms and most importantly to the client organization as a result of the outsourcing process.

Cited advantages to the client organization are, for example:

- An industry perspective.
- Elimination of the need to organize and manage a nonproductive operation.
- The availability of multi-skilled specialists.
- Global coverage without the need for travel and international audit problems.
- Access to current state of the arts developments.
- The ability to convert fixed-cost staff with variable-cost staff and to accommodate fluctuating requirements.

Cited disadvantages to the client organization are, for example:

- The audit staff are not loyal employees.
- The audit staff are motivated by aspects of the external auditor operations.
- The external auditor may in times of stress pull internal audit personnel for other higher priority work.

- The audit staff is not flexible so as to accommodate emergency situations.
- Potential turnover of external audit staff with extensions of the learning curve for new auditors.
- Lack of familiarity with the organization.

The internal-external audit relationships are important primarily in the third variation of the operation, the cosourcing where the internal auditing is still a requirement of a chief audit executive and his or her staff. There are a series of aspects that should be considered. For example:

- An engagement letter outlining responsibilities.
- Lines of control and authority.
- Structure and expertise of the external staff.
- Relationships with the external audit staff.
- Handling of classified information.
- Methods of reporting.
- Aspects of client relationships.
- Handling of findings that have a material external audit significance.
- Quality of staff and tenure.
- The use of risk assessment and its relationship to client management.
- Mandatory and self designated audits and the use of cyclical audit schedules.
- Methods of achieving independence:
  — From external audit organization.
  — From client.
  — From management influences.
- Methods of evaluation of the outsourcing operation.

There are probably more aspects that could be identified for internal audit consideration. There should be a designated high-level internal audit official responsible for the monitoring of the cosourcing operation. Deviations should be immediately brought to the attention of the chief audit executive, and in extreme cases, to the attention of senior management and the audit committee.

Coordinating Total Audit Coverage[32]

A recent (1998) survey of the relationships between internal and external auditors, sponsored by The Institute of Internal Auditors Research Foundation showed that perceptions of internal and external auditors as to the relationship ranges from one where there is complete coexistence to one where there is "partnering." This arrangement is understandable. However, the opinions of the respondees to all four identified classifications tend to disclose a preponderance toward "coordination." The positions of the 114 internal auditors and 113 external auditors who responded were distributed as follows:

	Internal Auditors	External Auditors
Coexistence	18.4%	4.4%
Coordination	62.3	69.0
Integration	8.8	15.0
Partnering	10.5	11.5
	100.0%	99.9%

There tended to be agreement between both groups that there was "coordination." Also, reasonable agreement exists that there was "partnering." The interesting disclosure was that 21 internal auditors compared to five external auditors classified the relationship as "coexistence." Also, in contrast, that 10 internal auditors compared to 17 external auditors classified the relationship as "integrated."

As to the current conditions, there seemed to be agreement that coordination has been moderate, that it was contributing to some degree to total audit coverage, and that it was significantly effective in minimizing duplicate efforts. As to the aspects of coordination, the survey also explored the frequency of annual formal and informal meetings, scheduling and planning activities, access to reports and working papers, understanding of external audit operations, training activities, and appraisal activities.

Formal meetings:

Internal auditors	4.58 meetings
External auditors	7.22 meetings

This difference could be a lack of clarity as to the "formality" of the meeting. The point is that there *were* at least four, almost five, formal meetings each year.

Informal meetings

	Internal Auditors	External Auditors
Daily	7	4
Weekly	21	40
Monthly	31	43
Quarterly	31	19
Less frequently than quarterly	16	5

This pattern replicates that of the formal meetings in that the external auditors observed that coordination was effected on a much more frequent basis, than did the internal auditors. There could be some confusion as to the definition of "informal meetings.

Scheduling and Planning

	Internal Auditors	External Auditors
Work together in scheduling audit work	.94	1.33
Coordination is ongoing throughout the year	1.14	1.40
Work together in planning audit coverage	.89	.89
A coordinated audit plan is used to assess total audit effort	.63	.80
A coordinated plan is developed jointly	.20	.34

Scale: 2: strongly agree; 1: slightly agree; 0: neither

The fact that all of the above are positive is an indication that there *is* coordination in planning and scheduling. There is some disagreement as to how continuously the coordination is effected.

Access to Reports and Working Papers

	Internal Auditors	External Auditors
Working papers access		
Internal auditors' working papers to external auditors	1.82	1.76
External auditors' working papers to internal auditors	1.11	1.39
Report access		
Internal auditors' report to external auditors	1.97	1.96
External auditors' report to internal auditors	1.61	1.88

Scale: 2: strongly agree; 1: slightly agree; 0: neither

Agreement appears on both sides that there should be reasonably free access. The interesting aspect is the large degree of favor on the part of external auditors in providing their working papers as well as their reports and management letters to the internal auditors. The authors of the survey propose that this sharing of working papers and reports can result in a better total audit effort.

Understanding of External Audit Activities

	Internal Auditors	External Auditors
Internal auditors understand the level of materiality used by external auditors	1.25	.60
Internal auditors understand the nature and extent of external audit procedures	1.23	.97

Scale: 2: strongly agree; 1: slightly agree; 0: neither

The results of this comparison tend to conflict with the results of the previous comparison on access to working papers and reports. Also, there is a substantial gap between the perceptions of the two groups of auditors. This seems to be an area where further communication could bear important results.

Training Activities	Internal Auditors	External Auditors
Internal auditors participate in training activities of external auditors	-.61	-.33
External auditors participate in training activities of internal auditors	-.61	-.45

Scale: 2: strongly agree; 1: slightly agree; 0: neither; -1: slightly disagree; -2: strongly disagree

The results of this query are that there is little (but some) mutual participation in training activities. This may be a reasonable approach as the objectives and methodology of the two organizations have significant differences.

Appraisal Activities	Internal Auditors	External Auditors
External auditors <u>formally</u> appraise the effectiveness of internal auditors	-.21	-.33
Internal auditors <u>formally</u> appraise the effectiveness of external auditors	-.88	-.43
External auditors <u>informally</u> appraise the effectiveness of internal auditors	.94	.92
Internal auditors <u>informally</u> appraise the effectiveness of external auditors	.58	.65

Scale: 2: strongly agree; 1: slightly agree; 0: neither; -1: slightly disagree; -2: strongly disagree

The results of this comparison are that although there is some formal evaluations of the others' effectiveness, there tends to be much more informal evaluations and appraisals. It is interesting to note that external auditors may not be aware of the internal auditors formal evaluations of their work. Both groups tend to favor the informal appraisals that seem to be somewhat common.

The Bridge

Trust must be a keystone of the cooperative bridge. Neither should try any tricks on the other. Neither should be ashamed or reluctant to admit to not having been especially clever in the way they handled a particular task. With the feeling of mutual respect and trust, they can soundly construct that all-important bridge. Here are some of the building blocks that can help make it strong:

- Awareness of each other's plans requires close coordination at the very outset, but the internal auditor must accept the fact of some surprises. External auditors must have the right to keep some audit features to themselves until they are ready to carry them out. If both are aware of each other's understanding of this prerogative, such surprises should not be fatal to a wholesome relationship.

- External auditors should be kept informed of any conditions that may affect the qualifications, independence, and competence of the internal audit staff.

- The client's system of internal controls is the foundation on which all independent audits are built. The external auditors must be absolutely certain they have reliable, unbiased information about the system. Hence, it has been suggested that the internal auditors fill out the independent auditor's control questionnaires. The internal auditors must accept it as professional practice for the external auditors to test the information the internal auditors give them so that they are in a position to make independent judgments and express independent opinions. This form of cooperation leads to "common user" files that contain internal control questionnaires, flowcharts, audit programs, records of weaknesses and of corrective action, and similar matters. Of course, with increased confidence in the internal auditors' competence and independence, such tests will be reduced.

- Both groups could make use of the same or similar statistical sampling techniques and of software designed to extract statistical samples and compute statistical results.

- Internal and external auditors should pool their knowledge of systems installations and applications. Each should be aware of the organization's systems for making sure that the proper information goes into the system, the information is correctly processed by the system, the information that comes out of the system is controlled and dealt with properly, and the system hardware and software are secure.

- External auditors can be particularly helpful to internal auditors by supplying an outsider's viewpoint, unobstructed by the close contact internal auditors have with the affairs of their organization, by providing advice on current developments in accounting and financial auditing, by supporting internal audit recommendations, and by supporting the internal auditor's need for a sufficiently high status in the organization to ensure independence.

- Most important is close and constant communication between the groups. Internal auditors can be particularly helpful to external auditors by exchanging ideas and providing an informed viewpoint on conditions and developments in the organization, by conducting plant tours and explaining processes and procedures, and by providing briefings on audit activities and findings.

Along these lines, Berry's study pointed out the types of information needed to develop an effective communication system:[33]

- Completion of major tasks assigned — information on working papers, reports, internal control weaknesses, recommendations to top management, and management letters.

- Detection of audit needs — internal auditors sharing information with the external auditors even when it is sensitive.

- Exchanging ideas — a procedure to routinely exchange viewpoints on organization operations.

- Identification of unexpected problems or issues affecting coordination.

- Disclosure of modification of plans as circumstances dictate.

- Discussion of significant developments that could affect the independent auditor's opinion on the financial statements.

- Identification of new developments in auditing and accounting discovered by either group.

- Discussion of any weaknesses in the coordination system.

References

[1]Ferrier, R.J., "Developing a Working Relationship With Your External Auditor," *The Internal Auditor,* December 1981, 26.

[2]Berry, L.E., *Coordinating Total Audit Coverage: Trends and Practices* (Altamonte Springs, FL: The Institute of Internal Auditors Research Foundation, 1983), 3.

[3]Ibid., 8.

[4]Ibid., 11.

[5]Berry, L.E., "The Internal and External Auditor's New Coordinated Environment," *The Internal Auditor,* October 1985, 58.

[6]Wallace, W.A., *A Time Series Analysis of the Effect of Internal Audit Activities on External Audit Fees* (Altamonte Springs, FL: The Institute of Internal Auditors Research Foundation, 1984), 167.

[7]Barrett , M.J., and V.Z. Brink, *Evaluating Internal/External Audit Services and Relationships,* Research Report 24 (Altamonte Springs, FL: The Institute of Internal Auditors, 1980), 26.

[8]Mautz, R.K., Peter Tiessen, and R.H. Colson, *Internal Auditing: Directions and Opportunities* (Altamonte Springs, FL: The Institute of Internal Auditors Research Foundation, 1984), 105.

[9]Wallace, 198.

[10]Berry, *Coordinating Total Audit Coverage,* 10.

[11]Ward , D.D., and J.C. Robertson, "Reliance on Internal Auditors," *Journal of Accountancy,* October 1980, 62-73.

[12]Elliott, R.K., "Auditing in the 1990s: Implications for Education and Research," *California Management Review,* Summer 1986, 89-97.

[13]*Statement on Auditing Standards No. 9,* "The Effect of an Internal Audit Function on the Scope of the Independent Auditor's Examination" (New York: The American Institute of Certified Public Accountants, 1975).

[14]Berry, *Coordinating Total Audit Coverage,* 16-19.

[15]Clay, R.J., and D.L. Haskin, "Can Internal Auditors Reduce External Audit Costs?" *The Internal Auditor,* April 1981, 62-69.

[16]McDuffie, R. Steve, and Ken W. Brown, "SAS No. 65: A Suggested Response," *Internal Auditing,* Spring 1993, 21.

[17]Sears, Brian P., *Internal Auditing Manual* (New York: RIA, 2003).

[18]Ibid.

[19]Colbert, Janet L., "Perspective: SAS 65, The Other Side of SAS 65," *The Internal Auditor,* April 1992, 54-56.

[20]Sumners, Glenn E., and Michael C. Toerner, "External Quality Assurance Reviews Can Positively Affect the Application of SAS 65," *Internal Auditing,* Winter 1993, 34-40.

[21]Braiotta, Jr., Louis, and Hugh L. Marsh, "Developing a Constructive Relationship Under the Guidance of SAS No. 65," *Internal Auditing,* Fall 1992, 7.

[22]Ibid., 9.

[23]The Institute of Internal Auditors, *Standards for the Professional Practice of Internal Auditing* (Altamonte Springs, FL: The Institute of Internal Auditors, 1978).

[24]See also comment at the end of this section.

[25]Olivanio, Mary Ellen, and Bernard H. Newman, "Internal Auditor Participation in External Audits, *Internal Auditing,* Winter 1991, 57-67.

[26]Pelfrey, Sandra, and Eileen Peacock, "How Internal Auditors View External Auditors," *Internal Auditing,* Fall 1990, 12-21.

[27]Peacock, Eileen, and Sandra Pelfrey, "How Internal Auditors View the External Audit," *The Internal Auditor,* June 1989, 48-54.

[28]Berry, *Coordinating Total Audit Coverage,* 7.

[29]Berry, *Coordinating Total Audit Coverage,* 10.

[30]Ibid., 11-12.

[31]Ibid., 39-40.

[32]Felix, William L., Audrey A. Gramling, and Mario J. Maletta, *Coordinating Total Audit Coverage* (Altamonte Springs, FL: The Institute of Internal Auditors, 1998).

[33]Berry, *Coordinating Total Audit Coverage,* 43-45.

Supplementary Readings

Barrett, M.J., and V.Z. Brink, *Evaluating Internal/External Audit Services and Relationships,* Research Report 24 (Altamonte Springs, FL: The Institute of Internal Auditors, 1980).

Beeler, Jesse D., James E. Hunton, and Benson Wier, "Does Participative Goal-Setting Work Well in Audit Practice?" *Internal Auditing,* Winter 1997, 39-46.

Brody, Richard G., Steven P. Golen, and Philip M.J. Reckers, "The Effect of SAS 65 on the Use of Internal Auditors," *Internal Auditing,* January/February 1999, 28-36.

Calhoun, Charles, "Making a Case for Cooperation Between Internal and External Auditors," *Internal Auditing Alert,* August 1998, 7-8.

Clikeman, Paul, "It's Internal Auditing's Turf," *Internal Auditor,* April 1998, 112.

Colbert, Janet L., "State Regulation of External Auditors: What Internal Auditors Need to Know," *Internal Auditing,* September/October 2002, 42-48.

Colbert, Janet L., "The Impact of the New External Auditing Standards," *Internal Auditor*, December 2000, 46-50.

Colbert, Janet L., "A Consolidated Consulting Approach," *Internal Auditor*, June 1999, 58-67.

Colbert, Janet L., "Internal Auditors and Assurance Services," *Internal Auditing*, July/August 1998, 29-36.

Dodd, James C., and Thomas A. Doucet, "Cycle Times Benchmarks for the Year-End Audit," *Internal Auditing*, Summer 1997, 15-20

Engle, Terry J., "Managing External Auditor Relationships," *Internal Auditor*, August 1999, 65-69.

Engle, Terry J., "Revisiting Independence," *Internal Auditor*, December 1996, 66-70.

English, Tom, "Independent or Not?" *Internal Auditor*, December 1996, 84-85.

Felix, Jr., William L., Audrey A. Gramling, and Mario J. Maletta, "Internal Audit's Coordination of Internal and External Audit Efforts," *Internal Auditing,* September/October 1999, 7-15.

Janiga, John M., and Barbara Brockie Leonard, "The Impact of Limited Liability Partnerships on Internal Audit Function," *Internal Auditing*, Fall 1996, 33-41.

Lapelosa, Michael, "Outsourcing: A Vulnerability Checklist," *Internal Auditor*, December 1997, 66-67.

Oliverio, Mary Ellen, "Internal Auditor and External Auditors: A Cooperative Effort Adds Value," *Internal Auditing Report*, July 2000, 7-8

Sears, Brian P., *Internal Auditing Manual* (New York: RIA, 2003). (See Chapter I1, "Relationships with Third-Party Users of Internal Auditing Work Products.")

Tacket, James, and Peter Woodlock, "Efforts to Preserve External Auditor Independence: In Fact and in Appearance," *Internal Auditing*, November/December 1999, 3-11.

Taylor, Martin E., Vicki S. Peden, and Judith K. Welch, "Internal Auditor Use: Different Perceptions," *Internal Auditing*, Spring 1997, 35-39.

Thomas, C. William, and John Parish, "Co-Sourcing: What's in It for Me?," *The Journal of Accountancy*, May 1999, 85-88.

Thornhill, William T., "Defenses Against Outsourcing," *Internal Auditing*, Winter 1995, 47-52.

Turetsky, Howard, and Susan Parker, "Going-Concern Reporting: Assessing Financial Distress," *Internal Auditing*, March/April 2000, 35-40.

Multiple-choice Questions

1. Which of the following most seriously compromises the independence of the internal audit department?
   a. Internal auditors frequently draft revised procedures for departments whose procedures they have criticized in an audit report.
   b. The chief audit executive has dual reporting responsibility to the firm's top executive and the board of directors.

c. The internal audit department and the firm's external auditors engage in joint planning of total audit coverage to avoid duplicating each other's work.

d. The internal audit department is included in the review cycle of the firm's contracts with other firms before the contracts are executed.

2. Which of the following reporting structures would best depict the internal audit organizational guidelines contained in the *Standards*?

   a. Administratively to the board of directors, functionally to the chief executive officer.

   b. Administratively to the controller, functionally to the chief financial officer.

   c. Administratively to the chief executive officer, functionally to the board of directors.

   d. Administratively to the chief executive officer, functionally to the external auditor.

Use the following information to answer questions 3 and 4.

After using the same public accounting firm for several years, the board of directors retained another public accounting firm to perform the annual financial audit to reduce the annual audit fee. The new firm has now proposed a onetime audit of the cost-effectiveness of the various operations of the business. The chief audit executive has been asked to advise management in making a decision on the proposal.

3. An argument can be made that the internal audit department would be better able to perform such an audit because:

   a. External auditors may not possess the same depth of understanding of the organization as the internal auditors.

   b. Internal auditors are required to be objective in performing audits.

   c. Audit techniques used by internal auditors are different from those used by external auditors.

   d. Internal auditors will not be vitally concerned with fraud and waste.

4. Additional criteria that should be considered by management in evaluating the proposal would include all the following except:

   a. Existing expertise of internal audit staff.

   b. Overall cost of the proposed audit.

   c. The need to develop in-house expertise.

   d. The external auditor's required adherence to the single audit concept.

5. To improve audit efficiency, internal auditors can rely upon the work of external auditors if it is:

   a. Performed after the internal audit.

   b. Primarily concerned with operational objectives and activities.

   c. Coordinated with the internal audit.

   d. Conducted in accordance with The IIA's *Code of Ethics*.

Use the following information to answer questions 6 and 7.
You are the chief audit executive of a parent organization that has foreign subsidiaries. Independent external audits performed for the parent organization are not conducted by the same firm that conducts the foreign subsidiary audits. Since your department occasionally provides direct assistance to both external firms, you have copies of audit programs and selected working papers produced by each firm.

6. The foreign subsidiary's audit firm would like to rely on some of the work performed by the parent organization's audit firm, but they need to review the working papers first. They have asked you for copies of the parent organization's audit firm working papers. Select the most appropriate response to the foreign subsidiary's auditors:
   a. Provide copies of the working papers without notifying the parent organization's audit firm.
   b. Notify the parent organization's audit firm of the situation and request that either they provide the working papers or authorize you to do so.
   c. Provide copies of the working papers and notify the parent organization's audit firm that you have done so.
   d. Refuse to provide the working papers under any circumstances.

7. The foreign subsidiary's audit firm wants to rely on an audit of a function at the parent organization. The audit was conducted by the internal audit department. To place reliance on the work performed, the foreign subsidiary's auditors have requested copies of the working papers. Select the most appropriate response to the foreign subsidiary's auditors:
   a. Provide copies of the working papers.
   b. Ask the parent organization's audit firm if it is appropriate to release the working papers.
   c. Ask the audit committee for permission to release the working papers.
   d. Refuse to provide the working papers under any circumstances.

8. Accounts payable schedule verification may include the use of analytical evidence. Which of the following is most appropriately described as analytical evidence?
   a. Comparing the items on the schedule with the accounts payable ledger or unpaid voucher file.
   b. Comparing the balance on the schedule with the balances of prior years.
   c. Comparing confirmations received from selected creditors with the accounts payable ledger.
   d. Examining vendors' invoices in support of selected items on the schedule.

9. The *Standards* require that the chief audit executive seek the approval of management and acceptance by the board of a formal written charter for the internal audit department. The purpose of this charter is to:
   a. Protect the internal audit department from undue outside influence.
   b. Establish the purpose, authority, and responsibility of the internal audit department.
   c. Clearly define the relationship between internal and external auditing.
   d. Establish the executive's status as a staff executive.

10. Coordination of internal and external auditing can reduce the overall audit costs. According to the *Standards*, who is responsible for coordinating internal and external audit efforts?
    a. Chief audit executive.
    b. External auditor.
    c. Audit committee of the board of directors.
    d. Management.

Chapter 30
Relationships with Boards of
Directors and Audit Committees

Board responsibilities, then and now. Audit committee history. Further SEC requirements. The Sarbanes-Oxley Act of 2002. The audit committee charter. Chief audit executive and the board. Relationships with the audit committee. The structure of the audit committee. The interfaces of the audit committee with management, external auditors, and internal auditors. Reporting and oversight relationships of the audit committee. Presentations to the audit committee. What the audit committee expects of the internal auditor. What worries audit committees. Educating the audit committee.

• •

Responsibilities of Boards of Directors

In 1962, Lord Boothby said to a group of Yorkshire clubwomen, concerning board membership:[1]

> No effort of any kind is called for. You go to a meeting once a month in a car supplied by the organization. You look both grave and sage, and on two occasions say "I agree," say "I don't think so" once, and if all goes well you get 500 pounds a year. If you have five of them, it is total heaven, like having a permanent hot bath.

That hot bath has chilled considerably in recent years. Courts are heaping more and more liability on directors. In one case, experienced directors agreed to a merger deal which, as it turned out later, was sound and advantageous to the stockholders. The deal had been worked out carefully by a highly qualified director. But the matter was accepted in a board meeting after only two hours spent reading the agreement. Stockholders sued and the court held that two hours of study did not indicate an informed decision on the part of the directors [Smith v. Van Gorkom, Del. Supr. 488 A. 2d 858, (1985), (Del) 488 ALR 4th 821]. A similar ruling of alleged director negligence is recorded in Hanson Trust PLC v. ML SCM Acquisition, Inc., 781 F. 2d 264 (2nd Cir. 1986).

The lot of today's directors is not a happy one. Their responsibilities are becoming more demanding. The courts are looking to them to protect the shareholders and to make informed business judgments instead of rubber-stamping the decisions of executive management.

This changing attitude toward directorship responsibility will require boards to take a closer look at management proposals than was envisioned by Lord Boothby. K.N. Dayton, himself a chief executive officer and a board member, said ". . . the board of directors is the Achilles heel of the American corporation. Every time you find a business in trouble, you find a board of directors either unwilling or unable to fulfill its responsibilities."[2]

Until 2002, no specific responsibilities that had the force and effect of law had been established for directors. The issue was, however, addressed by a number of writers. Peter Drucker sees these three tasks as being central to an effective board.[3]

1. *To be a review organ.* Without such an organ, top management has no way to control itself.

2. *To remove top management when it fails to perform.* A board capable of removing nonperforming top management has real power.

3. *To be a public relations and community relations organ.* The board needs easy and direct access to the various publics and constituents.

The prestigious Business Roundtable, made up of top business executives in the United States, adds a fourth task.[4]

4. *To develop policy and implement procedures necessary to limit conflicts of interest and to ensure compliance with both the law and ethical principles at all levels of the enterprise.*

The Conference Board recently suggested another task that has gained prominence.[5]

5. *Ensure that corporate compliance programs are in place.*

This was added because of recent case law that changed the traditional view of boards as only policy-making. This is the result of important legislation and legal decisions that have effectively overturned the traditional view of the board as a policy-making body to one that is also expected to react to issues that come to its attention. In the United States, the Federal Organizational Sentencing Guidelines provide for sentencing following convictions based upon the degree of monitoring that was in place. Hence it encourages entities to ensure proper monitoring. The significant legal decision in this area has held that the board is obligated "to exercise a good faith judgment that the corporation's information and reporting system is, in concept and design, adequate to assure that appropriate information will come to its attention in a timely manner as a matter of ordinary operations."[6]

The courts usually follow the "business judgment rule" in evaluating decisions that directors make. Under this rule, there is "a presumption that in making a business decision, the director of a corporation acted on an informed basis, in good faith and in the honest belief that the action taken was in the best interests of the company."[7]

But the courts have begun to articulate more explicitly what has been referred to as a "threshold requirement" before the business judgment rule would apply. This is the requirement that the directors' decision resulted from the exercise of an informed business judgment. Some courts ask that a "reasonable investigation" be made or that "advice" be obtained.[8] In other words, the courts will allow the protection of the business judgment rule when the record has shown the directors hired expert advisers to obtain information for them or obtained information themselves. But there is no protection for directors who have made an unintelligent or unadvised judgment.[9]

Objective information, secured directly for the board by its qualified internal auditors, would in our judgment pass the tests now used by many courts concerning what constitutes an informed judgment. Indeed, the use of insiders to obtain information was suggested by one court, which held that: "Often insiders familiar with the business of a going concern are in a better position than are outsiders to gather relevant information: and under appropriate circumstances, such directors may be fully protected in relying in good faith upon the valuation reports of their management."[10] It would seem that the courts would give even greater credibility to information obtained for the board by internal auditors reporting directly to the board.

Recent cases have further defined the importance of the business judgment rule. For shareholders to prevail in a case claiming a lack of due care in a board making business decisions, they must show, for example, that "(a) the directors did not in fact rely on the expert; (b) their reliance was not in good faith; (c) they did not reasonably believe that the expert's advice was within the expert's professional competence; (d) the expert was not selected with reasonable care by or on behalf of the corporation, and the faulty selection process was attributable to the directors; (e) the subject matter…that was material and reasonably available was so obvious that the board's failure to consider it was grossly negligent regardless of the expert's advice or lack of advice; or (f) that the decision of the board was so unconscionable as to constitute waste or fraud."[11]

In evaluating actions of a board, care must be taken in considering the appearances presented. In evaluating the Chancery Court decision on a dismissal motion, the Delaware Supreme Court stated, "This is potentially a troubling case on its merits. On the one hand, it appears from the Complaint that (a) the compensation and termination payout for Ovitz was exceedingly lucrative, if not luxurious, compared to Ovitz's value to the Company; and (b) the processes of the boards of directors in dealing with the approval and termination of the Ovitz Employment Agreement were casual, if not sloppy and perfunctory. On the other hand, the Complaint is so artfully drafted that it was properly dismissed under our pleading standards for derivative suits. From what we can ferret out of this deficient pleading, the processes of the Old Board and the New Board were hardly paradigms of good corporate governance practices. Moreover, the sheer size of the payout to Ovitz, as alleged, pushes the envelope of judicial respect for the business judgment of directors in making compensation decisions. Therefore, both as to the processes of the two Boards and the waste test, this is a closed case."[12] Hence, courts may be willing to expand their review of the business judgment rule.

The Private Securities Litigation Reform Act of 1995 was designed to reduce abusive practices associated with private securities class action litigation. Among the practices identified by the Conference Committee on the bill was "the targeting of deep pocket defendants, including accountants, underwriters, and individuals who may be covered by insurance, without regard to their actual culpability"[13] (Joint Explanatory Statement of the Committee of Conference, H. R. Conf. Rep. No. 104-369). However, litigation, in fact, increased. The Securities Litigation Standards Act of 1998, also called the Uniform Standards Act, was passed to reduce the litigation. The Act prohibits the prosecution of any "covered class action based upon the statutory or common law of any State or subdivision thereof...in any State or Federal court by any private party" that basically alleges violations of SEC's Rule 10b-5. There are four limitations of the Act. One of the limitations is that the Act applies only to a covered class action. The Act does not apply to a single plaintiff or to a group of less than 50 plaintiffs. Another limitation is that it applies only to securities registered with the SEC and traded on a national market. The third limitation is that it does not apply to plaintiffs who are only state or local governments or their pension plans. The fourth and potentially most significant limitation is that the Act does not apply where an investor brings an action under a state law duty of candor.

The importance of this last limitation is shown in a Delaware Supreme Court decision that "it is well-established that the duty of disclosure represents more than the well-recognized proposition that directors of Delaware corporations are under a fiduciary duty to disclose fully and fairly all material information within the board's control when it seeks shareholder action."[14] The same court has also held that "whenever directors communicate publicly or directly with shareholders about the corporation's affairs, with or without a request for shareholder action, directors have a fiduciary duty to shareholders to exercise due care, good faith and loyalty."[15] In addressing whether the plaintiffs were subject to federal statutes and regulations of the SEC, the court stated that "the claim appears to be made by those who did not sell and, therefore, would not implicate federal securities laws which relate to the purchase or sale of securities."[16]

Even before what is now being referred to as the "Enron Era," there were substantial settlements involving directors and officers. Some of these include the $2.83 billion settlement involving Cendant, the $457+ million settlement involving Waste Management, and the $230 million settlement involving Computer Associates.

Audit Committees

History

Boards of directors are increasingly recognizing the value of audit committees as instruments of control and as a means of improving the quality of an organization's financial reporting practices. This recognition is relatively recent, brought about by pressures from the Securities and Exchange Commission (SEC), New York Stock Exchange (NYSE), the American Institute of Certified Public Accountants (AICPA), and the Securities and Exchange Commission (SEC):

> In the NYSE, a report of the Subcommittee on Independent Audits and Audit Procedures of the Committee on Stock List, accepted by the Board of Governors on August 23, 1939, said: "Where applicable, the selection of the [independent] auditors by a special committee composed of directors who are not officers of the company seems desirable."

> The AICPA Executive Committee's statement of July 20, 1967, published in the Journal of Accountancy, September 1967, said in part: "The executive committee of the American Institute of Certified Public Accountants recommends that publicly owned corporations appoint committees composed of outside directors . . . to nominate the independent auditors . . . and to discuss the auditors' work with them.

> "Audit committees can assist their full board of directors in matters involving financial statements and control over financial operations. They can also strengthen the positions of management by providing assurance that all possible steps have been taken to provide independent reviews of the managements' financial policies and operations. This is good for the company and good for the public."

> In Canada, Section 182(1) of the 1970 Business Corporations Act prescribed that the directors of a corporation offering securities to the public should establish audit committees composed of not fewer than three directors. A majority must be outside directors.

> In the U.S., SEC Accounting Series Release No. 123, March 23, 1972, "Standing Audit Committees Composed of Outside Directors," states in part: ". . .The Commission. . .endorses the establishment by all publicly held companies of audit committees composed of outside directors. . . ."

> In a White Paper published in 1973, the NYSE said: "The Exchange first suggested the concept of an audit committee back in 1940. The Securities and Exchange Commission and the AICPA subsequently added their support. The Exchange believes

that the idea no longer represents a corporate luxury but has become a necessity, and we strongly recommend that each listed company form an Audit Committee."

In January 1977, the NYSE adopted an "Audit Committee Policy Statement" that said in part: "Each domestic company with common stock listed on the Exchange, as a condition of listing and continued listing of its securities on the Exchange, shall establish no later than June 30, 1978 and maintain thereafter an Audit Committee comprised solely of directors independent of management and free from any relation that, in the opinion of the Board of Directors, would interfere with the exercise of independent judgment as a committee member."

The U.S. Foreign Corrupt Practices Act of 1977 makes concern for good internal controls an imperative for audit committees. In April 1977, in the case of SEC vs. Killearn Properties, Inc., a United States District Court judge handed down a final judgment and order that decreed that (a) the majority of the board of directors are not to be employees of Killearn, (b) the board maintain an audit committee of outside directors, the audit committee become involved in internal control and improvement suggested both by the independent auditor and the internal staff, and the committee meet at least twice a year with the organization's financial staff and discuss with them the scope of internal accounting and auditing procedures in effect and the extent to which recommendations made by the independent accountants and the internal staff have been implemented.

Today, professional guidance from The Institute of Internal Auditors outlines various duties and responsibilities for chief audit executives in relationship to audit committees. With further SEC requirements instituted in 2000 and the passing of the Sarbanes-Oxley Act of 2002, audit committees of publicly held companies are also charged with specific responsibilities regarding the internal audit function. These duties and responsibilities are discussed later in this chapter. Additional procedures and responsibilities can be expected as we progress further in the post-Enron era.

Further SEC Requirements

The SEC required additional audit committee disclosures effective January 2000. These rules and amendments:

Require that companies' independent auditors review the financial information included in the companies' Quarterly Reports prior to the companies filing such reports with the SEC.

Extend requirements to a wider range of companies at fiscal year end appropriate reconciliations and descriptions of any adjustments to the quarterly information previously reported.

Require that companies include reports in their proxy statements as to whether their audit committees: (i) reviewed and discussed the audited financial statements with management; (ii) discussed with the independent auditors the matters required to be discussed by Statement on Auditing Standards No. 61; (iii) received from the auditors disclosures regarding the auditors' independence required by Independence Standards Board Standard No. 1 as may be modified or supplemented, and (iv) discussed with the auditors the auditors' independence.

Require that the report of the audit committee also include a statement by the committee whether, based on the review and discussions noted above, the committee recommended to the Board of Directors that the audited financial statements be included in the company's Annual Report for the last fiscal year for filing with the Commission.

Require that companies disclose in their proxy statements whether their Board of Directors has adopted a written charter for the audit committee, and if so, include a copy of the charter as an appendix to the company's proxy statements at least once every three years.

Require that companies disclose in their proxy statements whether the audit committee members are "independent" as defined in the applicable listing standards and disclose certain information regarding any director on the audit committee who is not "independent.

Require that companies, including small business issuers whose securities are not quoted on Nasdaq or listed on the AMEX or NYSE that have an audit committee, disclose in their proxy statements whether the members are "independent," as defined in the NASD's, AMEX's, or NYSE's listing standards.

The Sarbanes-Oxley Act

The Public Company Accounting Reform and Investor Protection Act of 2002, the Sarbanes-Oxley Act, adds additional responsibilities to the audit committee to which the chief audit executive must be alert. Under the Sarbanes-Oxley Act, the audit committee, as a committee of its board, is responsible for the appointment, compensation, independence, and oversight of the outside independent auditor. This includes resolution of financial reporting disagreements between management and the auditor. The Act also provides that the auditor shall report directly to the audit committee.

The Act requires that work of a registered public accounting firm providing audit services be approved by the audit committee in advance. It further requires that a registered public accounting firm providing audit services to a client cannot perform any of the following non-audit services to that client:

1. Bookkeeping or other services related to the accounting records or financial statements of the audit client
2. Financial information systems design and implementation
3. Appraisal or valuation services, fairness opinions, or contribution-in-kind reports
4. Actuarial services
5. Internal auditing outsourcing services*
6. Management functions or human resources activities
7. Broker or dealer, investment adviser, or investment banking services
8. Legal services and expert services unrelated to the audit

The Act gives a newly organized Public Company Accounting Oversight Board the authority to designate any other service that it, the Board, considers impermissible.[17]

The Sarbanes-Oxley Act also requires the auditing firm to report on a timely basis to the audit committee about:

1. All critical accounting policies and practices to be used.
2. All alternative treatments of financial information within generally accepted accounting principles that have been discussed with management officials relative to the issues, ramifications of and use of such alternative aspects, disclosures, and treatments, including the treatment of such issues preferred by the firm.
3. Other material written communications between the registered public accounting firm and the management of the issuer, such as any management letter or schedule of unadjusted differences.[18]

The Act also requires that each member of the audit committee be independent, which includes not accepting any consulting, advisory of other compensatory fee from the company. The company must also disclose whether at least one audit committee member is considered a "financial expert." If no member of the audit committee is a financial expert, the company must disclose the reasons why no member is a financial expert. Factors that will be considered in determining whether an individual is a financial expert are:"

> Whether a person has, through education and experience as a public accountant or auditor or a principal financial officer, comptroller, or principal accounting officer of an issuer, or from a position involving the performance of similar functions —

---

*The Act does not preclude cosourcing. Thus, the public accounting firm could, as a cosource provider, conduct auditing that more appropriately be conducted by the organization's organic internal audit activity.

(1) An understanding of generally accepted accounting principles and financial statements;
(2) Experience in:
    a. The preparation or auditing of financial statements of generally comparable issuers; and
    b. The application of such principles in connection with the accounting estimates, accruals, and reserves;
(3) Experience with internal accounting controls; and
(4) An understanding of audit committee functions.[19]

The audit committee also must establish procedures for:
(1) The monitoring of internal controls;
(2) The receipt, retention, and treatment of complaints regarding internal accounting controls and auditing matters;
(3) The confidential, anonymous submission by employees of concerns regarding questionable accounting or auditing matters.

The Act also requires that filings with the SEC contain an internal control report that states management responsibility for maintaining an adequate internal control structure and procedures for financial reporting and contains an assessment of the effectiveness of the internal control structure and procedures for financial reporting. The external auditor is also required to attest to the assessment.

Personal loans to executives and directors are also prohibited unless specifically exempted.[20] A code of ethics for senior financial officers is also required by the Act. The code is defined to include standards that are reasonably necessary to promote:

(1) Honest and ethical conduct, including the ethical handling of actual or apparent conflicts of interest between personal and professional relationships.
(2) Full, fair, accurate, timely, and understandable disclosure in reports filed by the company.
(3) Compliance with applicable governmental rules and regulations.[21]

These requirements are expected to have a substantial impact on the functioning and characteristics of an effective audit committee.

The Audit Committee Charter

The *Standards for the Professional Practice of Internal Auditing (Standards)* provide that "the purpose, authority, and responsibility of the internal audit activity should be formally defined in a charter consistent with the *Standards*, and approved by the board." Practice Advisory 1000-1 identifies that the charter should:

Establish the internal audit activity's position within the organization;
Authorize access to records, personnel, and physical properties relevant to the performance of engagements; and
Define the scope of internal audit activities.

Sample Audit Committee Charter

The following sample charter, suggested by The IIA, captures many of the best practices used today. Of course, no sample charter encompasses all activities that might be appropriate to a particular audit committee, nor will all activities identified in a sample charter be relevant to every committee. Accordingly, this charter must be tailored to each committee's needs and governing rules.

Audit Committee Charter

PURPOSE

To assist the board of directors in fulfilling its oversight responsibilities for the financial reporting process, the system of internal control, the audit process, and the company's process for monitoring compliance with laws and regulations and the code of conduct.

AUTHORITY

The audit committee has authority to conduct or authorize investigations into any matters within its scope of responsibility. It is empowered to:

Appoint, compensate, and oversee the work of any registered public accounting firm employed by the organization.

Resolve any disagreements between management and the auditor regarding financial reporting.

Pre-approve all auditing and non-audit services.

Retain independent counsel, accountants, or others to advise the committee or assist in the conduct of an investigation.

Seek any information it requires from employees — all of whom are directed to cooperate with the committee's requests — or external parties.

Meet with company officers, external auditors, or outside counsel, as necessary.

COMPOSITION

The audit committee will consist of at least three and no more than six members of the board of directors. The board or its nominating committee will appoint committee members and the committee chair.

Each committee member will be both independent and financially literate. At least one member shall be designated as the "financial expert," as defined by applicable legislation and regulation.

MEETINGS

The committee will meet at least four times a year, with authority to convene additional meetings, as circumstances require. All committee members are expected to attend each meeting, in person or via tele- or video-conference. The committee will invite members of management, auditors, or others to attend meetings and provide pertinent information, as necessary. It will hold private meetings with auditors (see below) and executive sessions. Meeting agendas will be prepared and provided in advance to members, along with appropriate briefing materials. Minutes will be prepared.

RESPONSIBILITIES

The committee will carry out the following responsibilities:

Financial Statements

- Review significant accounting and reporting issues, including complex or unusual transactions and highly judgmental areas, and recent professional and regulatory pronouncements, and understand their impact on the financial statements.

- Review with management and the external auditors the results of the audit, including any difficulties encountered.

- Review the annual financial statements, and consider whether they are complete, consistent with information known to committee members, and reflect appropriate accounting principles.

- Review other sections of the annual report and related regulatory filings before release and consider the accuracy and completeness of the information.

- Review with management and the external auditors all matters required to be communicated to the committee under generally accepted auditing standards.

- Understand how management develops interim financial information, and the nature and extent of internal and external auditor involvement.

- Review interim financial reports with management and the external auditors before filing with regulators, and consider whether they are complete and consistent with the information known to committee members.

Internal Control

- Consider the effectiveness of the company's internal control system, including information technology security and control.

- Understand the scope of internal and external auditors' review of internal control over financial reporting, and obtain reports on significant findings and recommendations, together with management's responses.

Internal Audit

- Review with management and the chief audit executive the charter, plans, activities, staffing, and organizational structure of the internal audit function.

- Ensure there are no unjustified restrictions or limitations, and review and concur in the appointment, replacement, or dismissal of the chief audit executive.

- Review the effectiveness of the internal audit function, including compliance with The Institute of Internal Auditors' *Standards*.

- On a regular basis, meet separately with the chief audit executive to discuss any matters that the committee or internal audit believes should be discussed privately.

External Audit

- Review the external auditors' proposed audit scope and approach, including coordination of audit effort with internal audit.

- Review the performance of the external auditors, and exercise final approval on the appointment or discharge of the auditors.

- Review and confirm the independence of the external auditors by obtaining statements from the auditors on relationships between the auditors and the company, including non-audit services, and discussing the relationships with the auditors.

- On a regular basis, meet separately with the external auditors to discuss any matters that the committee or auditors believe should be discussed privately.

Compliance

- Review the effectiveness of the system for monitoring compliance with laws and regulations and the results of management's investigation and follow-up (including disciplinary action) of any instances of noncompliance.

- Review the findings of any examinations by regulatory agencies, and any auditor observations.

- Review the process for communicating the code of conduct to company personnel, and for monitoring compliance therewith.

- Obtain regular updates from management and company legal counsel regarding compliance matters.

Reporting Responsibilities

- Regularly report to the board of directors about committee activities, issues, and related recommendations.

- Provide an open avenue of communication between internal audit, the external auditors, and the board of directors.

- Report annually to the shareholders, describing the committee's composition, responsibilities and how they were discharged, and any other information required by rule, including approval of non-audit services.

- Review any other reports the company issues that relate to committee responsibilities.

Other Responsibilities

- Perform other activities related to this charter as requested by the board of directors.

- Institute and oversee special investigations as needed.

- Review and assess the adequacy of the committee charter annually, requesting board approval for proposed changes, and ensure appropriate disclosure as may be required by law or regulation.

- Confirm annually that all responsibilities outlined in this charter have been carried out.

- Evaluate the committee's and individual members' performance on a regular basis.

Extracted from The IIA's Web site at www.theiia.org on April 24, 2003.

The Chief Audit Executive and the Board

The Institute of Internal Auditors has published Standard 2060, "Reporting to the Board and Senior Management." This standard provides:

> "The chief audit executive should report periodically to the board and senior management on the internal audit activity's purpose, authority, responsibility, and performance relative to its plan. Reporting should also include significant risk exposures and control issues, corporate governance issues, and other matters needed or requested by the board and senior management."

The standard is augmented by Practice Advisory 2060-1, "Reporting to the Board and Senior Management," which recommends:

> "The chief audit executive should submit activity reports to senior management and to the board annually or more frequently as necessary. Activity reports should highlight significant engagement observations and recommendations and should inform senior management and the board of any significant deviations from approved engagement work schedules, staffing plans, and financial budgets, and the reasons for them.

> "Significant engagement observations are those conditions that, in the judgment of the chief audit executive, could adversely affect the organization. Significant engagement observations may include conditions dealing with irregularities, illegal acts, errors, inefficiency, waste, ineffectiveness, conflicts of interest, and control

weaknesses. After reviewing such conditions with senior management, the chief audit executive should communicate significant engagement observations and recommendations to the board, whether or not they have been satisfactorily resolved.

"Management's responsibility is to make decisions on the appropriate action to be taken regarding significant engagement observations and recommendations. Senior management may decide to assume the risk of not correcting the reported condition because of the cost or other considerations. The board should be informed of senior management's decision on all significant observation and recommendations.

"The chief audit executive should consider whether it is appropriate to inform the board regarding previously reported, significant observations and recommendations in those instances when senior management and the board assumed the risk of not correcting the reported condition. This may be necessary; particularly when there have been organization, board, senior management, or other changes.

"The activity reports should also compare (a) performance with the internal audit activity's goals and audit work schedules and (b) expenditures with financial budgets. They should explain the reason for major variances and indicate any action taken or needed."

Communication is extremely important. As Practice Advisory 1110-1, "Organizational Independence," states:

"The chief audit executive should be responsible to an individual in the organization with sufficient authority to promote independence and to ensure broad audit coverage, adequate consideration of engagement communications, and appropriate action on engagement recommendations.

"Ideally, the chief audit executive should report functionally to the audit committee, board of directors, or other appropriate governing authority, and administratively to the chief executive officer of the organization.

"The chief audit executive should have direct communication with the board, audit committee, or other appropriate governing authority. Regular communication with the board helps assure independence and provides a means for the board and the chief audit executive to keep each other informed on matters of mutual interest."

The Advisory goes on to point out that "direct communication occurs when the chief audit executive regularly attends and participates in meetings of the board, audit committee, or other appropriate governing authority which relate to its oversight responsibilities for auditing, financial reporting, organizational governance, and control." The Advisory also suggests that the chief audit executive meet privately at least annually with the board or its audit committee.

Relationships with the Audit Committee

In December 2002, The IIA issued Practice Advisory 2060-2, "Relationship with the Audit Committee," that further defines appropriate relationships between audit committees and internal auditing. The Advisory explains that there may be other oversight groups in organizations that carry out the usual functions of audit committees but that bear other names and that those groups should be considered as audit oversight entities and for which the chief audit executive should:

Assist to ensure that their charters, activities, and processes are appropriate.

Ensure that the charter, role, and activities of internal audit are clearly understood and responsive to the needs of the audit committee and the board.

Maintain open and effective communications with the audit committee and the chairperson.

The Advisory identifies a series of activities where the chief audit executive can act in an advisory capacity for committees such as:

Reviewing the audit committee's charter at least annually and advise the committee whether the charter addresses all responsibilities directed to the committee in any terms of reference or mandates from the board of directors.

Reviewing or maintaining a planning agenda for the audit committee's meeting that details all required activities to ascertain whether they are completed and that assists the committee in reporting to the board annually that it has completed all assigned duties.

Draft the audit committee's meeting agenda for the chairman's review, facilitate the distribution of the material to the audit committee members, and write up the minutes of the audit committee meetings.

Encourage the audit committee to conduct periodic reviews of its activities and practices compared with current best practices to ensure that its activities are consistent with leading practices.

Meeting periodically with the chairperson to discuss whether the materials and information being furnished to the committee are meeting their needs.

Inquiring from the audit committee if any educational or informational sessions or presentations would be helpful, such as training new committee members on risk and controls.

Inquiring from the committee whether the frequency and time allotted to the committee are sufficient.

The internal audit activity should also assist the committee so as to ensure that it understands, supports, and reviews all needed assistance from the internal audit function. Elements of this assistance are:

Requesting the committee review and approve the internal audit charter on an annual basis.

Reviewing with the audit committee the functional and administrative reporting lines of internal audit to ensure that the organizational structure in place allows adequate independence for internal auditors.

Incorporating in the charter for the audit committee the review of hiring decisions, including appointment, compensation, evaluation, retention, and dismissal of the chief audit executive.

Incorporating in the charter for the audit committee to review and approve proposals to outsource any internal audit activities.

Assisting the audit committee in evaluating the adequacy of the personnel and budget, and the scope and results of the internal audit activities, to ensure that there are no budgetary or scope limitations that impede the ability of the internal audit function to execute its responsibilities.

Providing information on the coordination with and oversight of other control and monitoring functions (e.g., risk management, compliance, security, business continuity, legal, ethics, environmental, external audit).

Reporting significant issues related to the processes for controlling the activities of the organization and its affiliates, including potential improvements to those processes, and provide information concerning such issues through resolution.

Providing information on the status and results of the annual audit plan and the sufficiency of department resources to senior management and the audit committee.

Developing a flexible annual audit plan using an appropriate risk-based methodology, including any risks or control concerns identified by management, and submitting that plan to the audit committee for review and approval as well as periodic updates.

Reporting on the implementation of the annual audit plan as approved, including as appropriate any special tasks or projects requested by management and the audit committee.

Incorporating into the internal audit charter the responsibility for the internal audit department to report to the audit committee on a timely basis any suspected fraud involving management or employees who are significantly involved in the internal controls of the company. Assist in the investigation of significant suspected fraudulent activities within the organization and notify management and the audit committee of the results.

Audit committees should be made aware that quality assessment reviews of the internal audit activity be done every five years in order for the audit activity to declare that it meets The IIA's *Standards*. Regular quality assessment reviews will provide assurance to the audit committee and to management that internal auditing activities conform to the *Standards*.

The Advisory also describes the communications with the committee as being open and candid. The chief audit executive should consider providing the following:

Audit committees should meet privately with the chief audit executive on a regular basis to discuss sensitive issues.

Provide an annual summary report or assessment on the results of the audit activities relating to the defined mission and scope of audit work.

Issue periodic reports to the audit committee and management summarizing results of audit activities.

Keep the audit committee informed of emerging trends and successful practices in internal auditing.

Together with external auditors, discuss fulfillment of committee information needs.

Review information submitted to the audit committee for completeness and accuracy.

Confirm there is effective and efficient work coordination of activities between internal and external auditors. Determine if there is any duplication between the work of the internal and external auditors and give the reasons for such duplication.

Structure of the Audit Committee

The responsibilities of the audit committee should be specified in a formal written charter approved by the full board of directors. To meet the test of independence and objectivity, the audit committee should be made up solely of directors from outside the organization.

This objectivity, both in appearance and fact, is essential when, during the course of their work with both public- and private-sector organizations, internal auditors may bring to light errors or deficiencies. Audit committees composed of directors from within the organization may be affected by their direct involvement with the matters reported. Hence, an audit committee made up of outside directors would more likely be impartial and objective, while at the same time bringing a wide range of experience to the decision-making process.

The number of members on the audit committee should be determined by the size of the board of directors and the size of the organization. Usually, the audit committee has three to five members.

Interfaces of the Audit Committee

The audit committee will interface with management, with the external auditors, and with the internal auditors. A sophisticated audit committee can make these contacts and meetings highly successful. An inept audit committee can create serious conflicts or, at best, waste the time of all three groups.

More effective interface with all three groups can be achieved if the following steps are taken:

- Provide committee members and those with whom they will meet full agendas for meetings well in advance of those meetings.

- See to it that the meetings are informative and candid.

- See to it that all relevant financial reports and SEC documents are regularly distributed to committee members.

- Make continuing efforts to familiarize committee members with organization operations and financial affairs that significantly affect financial and operational reporting.

- Obtain objective information from the external and internal auditors.

- Provide adequate resources for effective functions.

Reporting and Oversight Relationships of the Audit Committee

Reporting relationships. The effective discharge of internal audit responsibilities in matters relating to financial reporting, corporate governance, and corporate control will require a reporting relationship with the board audit committee This relationship should ensure the chief audit executive's unrestricted access to the committee. Only if such a relationship exists does internal auditing have any recourse in cases of misconduct or fraud involving senior management itself.

Oversight relationships. The audit committee should exercise an active oversight role with respect to internal audit activities.

The audit committee's monitoring function should go beyond a determination that the internal auditors are performing reviews of financial and accounting records, reports, and systems. It should also monitor the organizational framework of the internal audit activity and its procedures so as to ensure a comprehensive scope. Without such a framework and adequate performance auditing procedures, the internal auditors remain engrossed with assessing traditional control systems, to the exclusion of grappling with the control problems flowing from growth and complexity.[22] To make sure that the internal audit function is balanced, the committees should consider:

- Corporate auditing philosophy.
- Corporate auditing independence.
- Logistical matters, such as size and location of staff.

Philosophy. Is the philosophy narrow and restricted to accounting matters, and does it help the external auditors, or is it a comprehensive philosophy covering operational and management areas? The committee could ask the external auditors or peer audit groups for a written assessment of the internal auditing philosophy.

Independence. Internal auditing should be responsible to the board/audit committee or an executive who can assure independence, objectivity, and the implementation of audit recommendations. In its meetings with the internal auditors, the committee should ask the executive whether he or she is free from organizational or external or internal pressures.

Logistical matters. Management will have different auditing needs depending on the nature, size, complexity, and diversity, both technical and geographical, of the corporate entity. Audit committees should review the cost/benefit evaluations as to centralization or decentralization.

Aside from reviews of audit programs and accomplishments, the audit committee should be satisfied with the following attributes of the internal audit function:

- The selection process for internal auditors
- The professional qualifications and educational background of internal auditors
- The professional development program
- The performance appraisal and evaluation system

Presentations to the Audit Committee[23]

Presentations to the audit committee consist of two general classifications:

- Presentations on the operations and status of the internal audit organization
- Reports of specific audits in which the audit committee has an interest

Topics that might be covered in the former classification would include:

- Scope of planned audit coverage:
  - Master audit schedule
  - Planned regular audit coverage
  - Headquarters coverage
  - Special security coverage
  - Other reviews

- Review of policies and procedures:
  - Audit philosophy
  - Policy reviews
  - Procedure reviews
  - Typical audit procedures

- Trends in audit practice.

The chief internal audit executive would also make presentations in the latter classification such as:

- Summary of audits by location and function.
- Review of selected audits.
- Freedom of activity reports:
  - Access to information and people.
  - Access to the board, audit committee, and top management.
  - Independence in report preparation.

What the Audit Committee Expects of the Internal Auditor[24]

Speaking in a general way, the chairman of one of the nation's largest pharmaceutical firms states that the primary information needed relates to:

- What — What parts of the auditing agenda need to be changed? Are the internal auditors providing evidence relative to internal controls, compliance, efficiency, effectiveness, and the work of the external auditor?

- Why — Control is critical; the internal audit staff provides the information for its development and use.

- When — Urgency is Great: The When is Now.

- How — The use of imaginative and innovative auditing methodology.

- Where — Where is whenever change is occurring.

- Who — Who is the entire organization. All are audit partners. However, their partnership must be won by fair treatment. Also, the who should be well trained.

The writer says that this format must be followed if the committee is to provide integrity, ethical values, a control environment, and clear management objectives.

What Worries Audit Committees

To help audit committees, internal auditors should be aware of what it is that keeps the committee members up at night. Here are some of these worrisome matters:[25]

Legal actions. The possibility of some sort of legal action when directors fail to exercise due diligence or to employ an informed business judgment.

Information systems. The adequacy of the corporation's management information systems.

Standards. The corporation's compliance with ethical and legal standards.

Capital items. Requests for capital expenditures.

Compliance. Not following the requirements of governmental regulations.

Performance. Unsatisfactory performance by the chief executive officer.

Organization background. Unfamiliarity with the organization background.

Audit committee members, according to one source, should see The IIA's *Standards* as an answer to a prayer. It makes clear that internal auditing is a service to the organization, not only to management. Mautz continued by saying that, if he were a member of a corporate audit committee, he would ask the chief audit executive two questions:

- Do you accept these [IIA] *Standards*?
- Can you meet them?

Educating the Audit Committee

If internal auditors are to bring care and comfort to audit committees, they will have to take the initiative in educating the committees on what internal auditing can offer.

The first step in developing the right relationship with the committee is getting the matter on the table. That calls for the draft of a proposed internal audit charter, if there is none, or of a revised charter that makes it quite clear that internal auditing has unrestricted access both to the activities it needs to audit and to the ear of the committee. This charter should contain the internal auditor's bill of rights: the right to inquire, the right to obtain information, the right to be heard, and the right to the resources needed to do all three.

In many cases, the improvement of the internal audit activity can be attributed to the committee itself. The mature committee will ask: Does the internal audit activity need strengthening? Does the chief audit executive have ready access to the board through the audit committee?

Many internal audit units have embarked on courses of education for audit committee members, bringing to their attention, especially for new members, what the internal audit activity is now doing and what it is capable of doing. The results are greater support, increased status, and improved effectiveness for the auditors and correspondingly greater comfort to the audit committees.

Another course of action is for the chief audit executive to work with the organization's finance committee, attorneys, and external auditors to promote discussions with the audit committee on matters such as:

- SEC and similar legal and regulatory requirements.
- The professional stature of internal auditing.
- Education and qualifications of the internal audit staff.
- The *Standards for the Professional Practice of Internal Auditing.*

- The *Code of Ethics.*
- Peer reviews and the external auditor's review of the internal audit program.

Properly presented, this action will emphasize the fact that internal auditing is a professional, quality function vital to the oversight process.

References

[1]Herzel, Leo, Richard Shepro, and Leo Katz, "Next to Last Word on Endangered Directors," *Harvard Business Review*, January/February 1987, 38.
[2]Dayton, K.N., "Corporate Governance: The Other Side of the Coin," *Harvard Business Review*, January-February 1984, 34-37.
[3]Drucker, P.F., *Management: Tasks, Responsibilities, Practices* (New York: Harper & Row, 1974), 631.
[4]"Core Functions of a Board," *Harvard Business Review*, September-October 1978, 26.
[5]The Conference Board, Executive Action, February 2002, 1.
[6]Caremark International Inc. Civ A 670 (1996).
[7]Smith v. Van Gordom, 488 A. 2d. 858 (1985).
[8]46 ALR 4th 886.
[9]Mitchell v. Highland-Western Glass, Del Ch., 167 A. 831 (1933)*
[10]Cheff v. Mather, Del. Supr., 199 A. 2d, 548, 556 (1964).
[11]Brehm v. Eisner Dkt No 469 (Del Supr. Feb 9, 2000).
[12]Brehm v. Eisner Dkt No 469 (Del Supr. Feb 9, 2000).
[13]Joint Explanatory Statement of the Committee of Conference, H. R. Conf. Rep. No. 104-369
[14]Zirn v. VLI Corp., Del Supr., 681 A.2d 1050 (1996).
[15]Malone v. Brincat Del Supr, 459, (1997).
[16]Malone v. Brincat Del Supr, 459, (1997).
[17]Sec 204, Auditor Reports to Audit Committees.
[18]Sec 407, Disclosure of Audit Committee Financial Expert.
[19]Sec 402, Enhanced Conflict of Interest Provisions.
[20]Sec 406, Code of Ethics for Senior Financial Officers.
[21]Braiotta, Jr., Louis, "How Audit Committees Monitor Internal Auditing," *The Internal Auditor*, April 1982, 27-29.
[22]Wilson, James D., and Steven J. Root, *Internal Auditing Manual* (Boston, MA: Warren Gorham & Lamont, 1989), 10-15 to 10-19.
[23]Horn, Karen N., "An Audit Committee Member Looks at Internal Auditing," *The Internal Auditor,* December 1992, 32-36.
[24]Mautz, R.K., *First Conference on Audit Committees* (Altamonte Springs, FL: The Institute of Internal Auditors, 1977), 182.
[25]Sawyer, Lawrence B., "The Political Side of Internal Auditing," *The Internal Auditor*, February 1992, 32-33.

Supplementary Readings

Allison Jr., Dwight L., "Internal Auditors and Audit Committees," *Internal Auditor*, February 1994, 50-55.

Apostolou, Barbara, and Raymond Jeffords, *Working with the Audit Committee* (Altamonte Springs, FL: The Institute of Internal Auditors, 1990).

Braiotta, Jr., Louis, *The Audit Committee Handbook, Third Edition* (New York: John Wiley and Sons, Inc. 1999).

DeZoort, F. Todd, Alan H. Friedberg, and John T. Reisch, "Implementing a Communications Program for Audit Committees," *Internal Auditing*, July/August 2000, 11-18.

The Institute of Internal Auditors, Sarbanes-Oxley Act Webcast Series on CD-ROM 1-4, (Altamonte Springs, FL: The Institute of Internal Auditors, 2002).

The Institute of Internal Auditors Research Foundation and PriceWaterhouseCoopers, *Audit Committee Effectiveness – What Works Best, 2nd Edition* (Altamonte Springs, FL: The Institute of Internal Auditors, 2000).

The Institute of Internal Auditors Research Foundation and PriceWaterhouseCoopers, *Corporate Governance and the Board – What Works Best* (Altamonte Springs, FL: The Institute of Internal Auditors, 2000).

Metz, Mary S., "Inside The Audit Committee," *Internal Auditor*, October 1993, 42-48.

Research Report prepared by Price Waterhouse, *Improving Audit Committee Performance: What Works Best* (Altamonte Springs, FL: The Institute of Internal Auditors Research Foundation, 1993).

Sears, Brian P., *Internal Auditing Manual* (New York: RIA, 2003). (See Chapter C4, "Relating to the Audit Committee.")

Vanasco, Rocco R., *The Audit Committee: An International Perspective* (Altamonte Springs, FL: The Institute of Internal Auditors, 1995).

Verschoor, Curtis C., *Audit Committee Briefing 2001: Facilitating New Audit Committee Responsibilities* (Altamonte Springs, FL: The Institute of Internal Auditors, 2001.)

Verschoor, Curtis C., *Audit Committee Briefing: Understanding the 21st Century Audit Committee and its Governance Roles* (Altamonte Springs, FL: The Institute of Internal Auditors, 2000.)

Multiple-choice Questions

1. Audit committees are responsible for:
   a. Selecting the chief audit executive.
   b. Developing the internal auditing plan and budget.
   c. Reviewing and approving the internal audit charter.
   d. Selecting the independent accountants.

2. The status of the internal audit function should be free from the impact of irresponsible policy changes by management. The most effective way to make sure of that freedom is to:
   a. Have the internal audit charter approved by both management and the board of directors.
   b. Adopt policies for the functioning of the auditing department.
   c. Establish an audit committee within the board of directors.
   d. Develop written policies and procedures to serve as standards of performance for the department.

3. Audit committees are most likely to participate in approving:
   a. Staff promotions and salary increases.
   b. Internal audit report findings and recommendations.
   c. Audit work schedules.
   d. Appointment of the internal auditing director.

4. The audit committee can serve several important purposes, some of which directly benefit internal auditing. The most significant benefit provided by the audit committee to the internal auditor is:
   a. Protecting the independence of the internal auditor from undue management influence.
   b. Reviewing annual audit plans and monitoring audit results.
   c. Approving audit plans, scheduling, staffing, and meeting with the internal auditor as needed.
   d. Reviewing copies of the internal control procedures for selected organization operations and meeting with organization officials to discuss them.

5. The *Standards* state that the chief audit executive should have direct communication with the board. Such communication is often accomplished through the board's audit committee. Which of the following best describes why the charter for internal auditing should provide for direct access to the audit committee?
   a. Such access is required by law for publicly traded organizations.
   b. Direct access to the audit committee tends to enhance internal auditing's independence and objectivity.
   c. With direct access, the chief audit executive is in a better position to affect policy decisions.
   d. The audit committee must authorize implementation of audit recommendations that involve financial reporting.

6. The audit committee of an organization has charged the chief audit executive with bringing the department into full compliance with the *Standards*. The chief audit executive's first task is to develop a charter. Identify the item that should be included in the statement of objectives:
   a. Report all audit findings to the audit committee every quarter.
   b. Notify governmental regulatory agencies of unethical business practices by organization management.
   c. Determine the adequacy and effectiveness of the organization's systems of internal controls.
   d. Submit departmental budget variance reports to management every month.

7. To avoid being the apparent cause of conflict between an organization's top management and the audit committee, the chief audit executive should:
   a. Submit copies of all audit reports to both top management and the audit committee.
   b. Strengthen the independence of the department through organizational status.
   c. Discuss all reports to top management with the audit committee first.
   d. Request board acceptance of policies that include internal auditing relationships with the audit committee.

8. An audit committee of the board of directors of a corporation is being established. Which of the following would normally be a responsibility of the committee?
   a. Approval of the selection and dismissal of the chief audit executive.
   b. Development of the annual internal audit schedule.
   c. Approval of internal audit programs.
   d. Determination of findings appropriate for specific internal audit reports.

9. Which of the following would not be an appropriate member of an audit committee?
   a. The vice president of the local bank used by the organization.
   b. An academic specializing in business administration.
   c. A retired executive of a firm that had been associated with the corporation.
   d. The firm's vice president of operations.

10. Audit committees are most likely to participate in approving:
    a. Staff promotions and salary increases.
    b. Internal audit report findings and recommendations.
    c. Audit work schedules.
    d. Appointment of the internal audit director.

11. According to the *Standards*, the organizational status of the internal audit department:
    a. Should be sufficient to permit the accomplishment of its audit responsibilities.
    b. Is best when the reporting relationship is direct to the board of directors.
    c. Requires the board's annual approval of the audit schedules, plans, and budgets.
    d. Is guaranteed when the charter specifically defines its independence.

12. A charter is being drafted for a newly formed internal audit department. Which of the following best describes the appropriate organizational status that should be incorporated into the charter?
    a. The chief audit executive should report to the chief executive officer but have access to the board of directors.
    b. The chief audit executive should be a member of the audit committee of the board of directors.
    c. The chief audit executive should be a staff officer reporting to the chief financial officer.
    d. The chief audit executive should report to an administrative vice president.

13. The chief audit executive for a large retail organization reports to the controller and is responsible for designing and installing computer applications relating to inventory control. Which of the following is the major limitation of this arrangement?
    a. It prevents the audit organization from devoting full time to auditing.
    b. Auditors generally do not have the required expertise to design and implement such systems.
    c. It potentially affects the chief audit executive's independence and thereby lessens the value of audit services.
    d. Such arrangements are unlawful because the director participates in incompatible functions.

14. Which of the following will best promote the independence of the internal audit function?
    a. A quality control system within the internal audit function designed to make sure that departmental objectives are met.
    b. Direct lines of communication between the audit committee and the chief audit executive.
    c. A written charter that reflects the concepts contained in the *Statement of Responsibilities of Internal Auditing.*
    d. Direct reporting responsibilities to the organization's chief financial officer.

15. The charter of a newly formed internal audit department contains the following statement: "The organizational status of the internal audit department will be sufficient to permit the accomplishment of its audit responsibilities." Select the best reporting lines from the following relationships that would promote the accomplishment of the intended organizational status. Solid line to:
    a. Board of directors, dotted line to vice president of finance.
    b. President, dotted line to board of directors.
    c. Controller, dotted line to board of directors.
    d. Vice president, finance, dotted line to board of directors.

16. Which of the following audit committee activities would be of the greatest benefit to the internal audit department?
    a. Review and approval of audit programs.
    b. Assurance that the external auditor will rely on the work of the internal audit department whenever possible.
    c. Review an endorsement of all internal audit reports prior to their release.
    d. Support for appropriate follow-up of recommendations made by the internal audit department.

17. Which of the following relationships best depicts the appropriate dual reporting responsibility of the internal auditor? Administratively to the:
    a. Board of directors, functionally to the chief executive officer.
    b. Controller, functionally to the chief financial officer.
    c. Chief executive officer, functionally to the board of directors.
    d. Chief executive officer, functionally to the external auditor.

Chapter 31
Standards for the Professional Practice of Internal Auditing and Code of Ethics

• •

This chapter is comprised of material developed by the authors and material taken from three documents that preceded the issuance in January 2001 of the revised *Standards for the Professional Practice of Internal Auditing*.

1. "Development of the Proposed *Standards for the Professional Practice of Internal Auditing*" by Urton Anderson, Ph.D., CIA, Professor, University of Texas at Dallas, Member of the Internal Auditing Standards Board, December 2000.

2. "Where We're Going" by Jack L. Krogstad, Ph.D., Professor, Creighton University, Graduate Task Force (GTF) Research Director; Anthony J. Ridley, CIA, GTF Chairman, Former General Auditor, Ford Motor Company; and Larry L. Rittenberg, Ph.D. CIA, IIA Vice-Chairman of Professional Practices, Professor, University of Wisconsin - Madison; *Internal Auditor*, October 1999.

3. Letter providing the "Internal Auditing Standards Board Progress" issued by Wayne G. Moore, CIA, Chairman of the Internal Auditing Standards Board, and Auditing Manager, Du Pont Chemical Company.

The material from these sources clearly illustrates the information appropriate to this chapter, and with just minor editing, it is properly descriptive. It is considered that rewriting would lose the excellent approach embodied in the three documents.

An Addendum to the chapter covers proposed changes to the *Standards* as this book goes to press.

Introduction

The internal auditing profession has changed dramatically during the six decades since it was originally defined in the *Statement of Responsibilities of Internal Auditing*. During that period the profession's narrow scope of measuring and evaluating the effectiveness of controls was expanded to a much broader spectrum of activities. Spurred on by challenges from outside providers and management, internal auditors now also place significant emphasis on working with clients to improve operations and add continuous value to their organizations.

Such changes have created an opportunity for the profession to reexamine its fundamental premises. In 1997, The Institute of Internal Auditors (IIA) established a Guidance Task Force (GTF) to review the status of guidance provided to internal audit practitioners and to recommend actions for continually improving and updating such guidance. The GTF's 22 recommendations and supporting rationale were recently published by The IIA as a monograph, *A Vision for the Future: Professional Practices Framework for Internal Auditing.*

The GTF's initial recommendation urged The IIA's Board of Directors to adopt a broader definition of internal auditing, effectively expanding the boundaries within which guidance could be issued. As a result, a new definition was proposed and was widely exposed. After all comments to the exposure draft were considered, the definition was revised for a final time. The IIA's Board of Directors unanimously approved the new definition at its June 1999 meeting.

Background of the Original *Standards*

In June 1978, The Institute of Internal Auditors issued its first standards for internal auditing. The work was the culmination of the efforts of a board of internal auditing specialists who had worked for about two years in their development. The standards were titled *Standards for the Professional Practice of Internal Auditing (Standards)*. The development of these standards was influenced by the earlier standards for government auditing issued in 1972 by the U.S. Comptroller General through the General Accounting Office. This latter body of standards was a far reaching and progressive body of standards that embodied many of the concepts that The IIA was promoting and thus it appeared appropriate for The IIA to publish a body of standards several years later to provide guidance in the progressive aspects that it was endorsing.

The IIA's *Standards* were augmented through the years by a series of issuance titled *Statements on Internal Auditing Standards* (SIAS). These statements expanded various areas of the *Standards* and were developed by an Internal Auditing Standards Board. Subsequently, The IIA began to combine the original standards and the statements into a single document, a codification titled the "Red Book," (the preceding government auditing standards were known as the "Yellow Book"). As time went on the SIAS were integrated into the several issuances of the Red Book in an orderly manner and served The IIA well.

The new definition and the activity preceding its issuance and approval by the Board are more completely discussed in Chapter 1, *The Nature of Internal Auditing.*

The Audit Standards Process

The development of the new *Standards* is part of the process of creating the Professional Practices Framework. When the Framework is complete, three categories of guidance will be available to the profession:

- *Ethics and Standards.* This includes the *Code of Ethics* and the *Standards for the Professional Practices of Internal Auditing.* All mandatory guidance is submitted for review by the entire profession through the exposure draft process and is considered to be essential for the professional practice of internal auditing.

- *Practice Advisories.* Practice Advisories are the equivalent of the non-mandatory guidelines that represented the bulk of what was contained in the *Red Book.* The Professional Issues Committee is developing these into Practice Advisories and creating new ones in areas not previously covered. Although not mandatory, Practice Advisories represent best practices endorsed by The IIA as way to implement the *Standards.* In part, Practice Advisories may help to interpret the *Standards* or to apply them in specific internal auditing environments. While some Practice Advisories may be applicable to all internal auditors, others may be developed to meet the needs of a specific industry, a specific audit specialty, or a specific geographic area. All Practice Advisories are reviewed by The IIA's Professional Issues Committee. Significant portions of the guidance formerly found in the Red Book and in the *Professional Standards Practice Releases* will be converted to Practice Advisories. These Practice Advisories are available on The IIA's Web site at www.theiia.org.

- *Development and Practice Aids.* Development and Practice Aids include educational products, research studies, seminars, conferences, and other aids related to the professional practice of internal auditing. Development and Practice Aids are developed and/or endorsed by The IIA, but do not meet the criteria for inclusion as a Standard or a Practice Advisory. Development and Practice Aids provide internal auditing practitioners with the views of various expert authors and sources commissioned by The IIA to present techniques and processes for the development of internal auditing staff and related processes.

In its first phase of the process of revising the *Standards*, the Internal Auditing Standards Board sought to achieve the following objectives.

- Recast the current *Standards* (the *Red Book)* into the new Professional Practices Framework developed by the Guidance Task Force.

- Modify the *Standards* of the *Red Book* to be consistent with the new Definition of Internal Auditing.

- Integrate into the *Standards* concepts from risk management, control, and governance models such as COSO, CoCo, and Cadbury to reflect advancements made in the understanding of the application of these concepts to internal auditing.

- Update the current *Standards* to reflect changes in service delivery structures.

- Clarify several issues the Guidance Task Force had identified as challenges in the *Red Book*.

Standards Development

Within the new framework, the Guidance Task Force called for the development of three sets of standards: Attribute, Performance, and Implementation Standards. The Attribute Standards address the attributes of organizations and individuals performing internal audit services. The Performance Standards describe the nature of internal audit services and provide quality criteria against which the performance of these services can be measured. The Attribute and Performance Standards apply to all internal audit services. The Implementation Standards expand Attribute and Performance Standards so as to prescribe standards applicable in specific types of engagements across the broad spectrum of assurance and consulting activities offered by internal auditors. These standards ultimately may deal with industry-specific, regional, or specialty types of auditing services.

At this point, the Attribute and Performance Standards are essentially complete, and some Implementation Standards have been developed for assurance services. Phase I was restricted to Implementation Standards for assurance services because the first objective was to revise information in the *Red Book* in conformance with the new framework, and the *Red Book* only provided guidance at the implementation level for assurance services. Therefore, the Implementation Standards for consulting services were not addressed in the Phase I revision of the *Standards*.

In many cases, the language from the *Standards* in the *Red Book* was maintained. However, in some instances, the Board considered the information within the Guidelines portion of the *Red Book* of such significance that it needed to be raised to the level of a standard. In several other cases, the Board believed a gap existed and that a new standard needed to be developed. In addition, there were places where changes to the way the internal auditing profession is practiced resulted in the need for modification of the language used in the *Red Book*.

With the completion of Phase 1, the Internal Auditing Standards Board now turns its attention to developing additional implementation standards. Its next task will be to develop additional implementation standards for assurance services and implementation standards for consulting services. Potential for a limited number of new Attribute and Performance Standards also exists, particularly in some areas of risk management and in governance, which were previously not specifically addressed by the *Red Book.*

The development of additional guidance is also under way, in the form of Practice Advisories and Development and Practice Aids. This additional guidance will initially be linked to the *Standards* by an interactive, Web-based delivery mechanism scheduled for introduction by March 31, 2001.

The Standards are presented in Appendix A.

Practice Advisories

As described earlier, selected material has been abstracted from the *Red Book* to assist internal auditors by augmenting the new standards. Each of the Advisories is related to one or more *Red Book* references and/or to a Professional Standards Practice Releases reference. The *Practice Advisories* currently relate to Attribute Standards and Performance Standards and at this point refer only to the assurance aspects of the *Standards*. It is planned that the Standards Board will subsequently develop Implementation Standards and associated guidance for the consulting aspect of the audit process.

A list of the Practice Advisories appears in Appendix B to this chapter.

Changes in Language and Content

One change in language that occurs in the new *Standards* is the use of the term "internal audit activity." This term is used in place of "internal audit department," which no longer reflects the structure of many internal audit organizations. In addition, the term "chief audit executive (CAE)" is now used rather than "director of internal auditing."

One of the issues that the Guidance Task Force identified as needing clarification was the concept of independence. Although taking the essence of the *Red Book's* specific standards 100, 110, and 120, the wording is changed to clarify the concept that independence is an attribute of the internal audit function and objectivity an attribute of the individual auditor. The Board also added an additional standard (1130) that addresses cases of impairment to either independence or objectivity.

The new *Standards* require the establishment of a quality assurance and improvement program for the internal audit activity. The objectives of this program are to ensure that the internal audit activity adds value and improves its organization's operations and to ensure compliance with the *Standards* and The Institute of Internal Auditors' *Code of Ethics. Standards 1320, 1321, 1322,* and *1330* are new standards that elevate to the level of a standard some of the guidance contained in the *Red Book* regarding recording and communicating quality assurance policies and procedures and monitoring the process. *Standard 1340* adds requirements on the use of the phrase "conducted in accordance with the *Standards for the Professional Practice of Internal Auditing.*"*

The nature of internal audit activity or scope of work is discussed in *Standard 2100* and represents a significant departure from the 300 standard in the *Red Book*. *Standard 2100* reflects the new definition of internal auditing, stating the internal audit activity should add value and evaluate and improve the organization's risk management, control, and governance processes.**

Standard 2110 states that internal audit should assist the organization in managing risk by (1) identifying and evaluating significant exposures to risk and (2) contributing to the improvement of risk management and control systems. *Standard 2120* states that internal audit should evaluate the effectiveness and efficiency of the organization's control processes. *Standard 2130* describes the role of internal audit in the governance process. Internal audit should assist the organization by evaluating and improving the process through which (1) values and goals are established and communicated, (2) the accomplishment of goals is monitored, (3) accountability is ensured, and (4) values are preserved.

Standards 2200 to *2500* follow the *Red Book's* 400 section, breaking the specific engagement into planning (2200 corresponding to 410), performing (2300 corresponding to 420), communicating the results (2400 to 430), and follow-up (2500). In this section selected guidelines have been raised to the level of a standard. Wording has also been generalized so as to apply to the full range of services. For example, a written report is not required under 2400, only that results be appropriately communicated. While guidance for assurance services will likely suggest a written or formal report, this may not be true for consulting activities or control self-assessment. A new standard (2430) requires specific disclosure when engagements are not conducted in accordance with the *Standards*.

When used in these *Standards*, the term "board" is defined as a board of directors, audit committee of such boards, head of an agency or legislative body to whom internal auditors report, board of governors or trustees of a nonprofit organization, or any other designated governing body of an organization.

---

*The standards numbers were subsequently changed to 1310, 1311, 1312 and 1320. *Standard 1340* became *1330* and a new *Standard 1340* was used for "Disclosure of Noncompliance."

**The elements of the former Scope General Standard (300) in the *Red Book* relating to the determination of integrity of information, efficiency and economy of operation, achievement of effectiveness of operations and the protection of assets are included in new *Standard 2100*, "Nature of Work." The internal auditor is to determine the effectiveness of governance process in achieving these characteristics. The authors suggest that in future revisions, more emphasis be given this aspect. It was one of the basic provisions of the original standards and served to materially differentiate internal (performance auditing) from financial auditing.

Organization and Content of the *Standards*

The newly adopted framework calls for the development of three sets of *Standards*: Attribute Standards, Performance Standards, and Implementation Standards. The Attribute Standards address the characteristics of organizations and individuals performing internal audit services. The Performance Standards describe the nature of internal audit services and provide quality criteria against which the performance of these services can be measured. The Attribute and Performance Standards apply to internal audit services in general. The Implementation Standards apply the Attribute and Performance Standards to specific types of services (for example, a compliance audit, a fraud investigation, or a control self-assessment project). Thus while there is one set of Attribute and Performance Standards, there are multiple sets of Implementation Standards, a set for each of the major types of internal audit activity.

Within the new framework, a new numbering system is used for the *Standards*. Attribute Standards comprise the 1000 series and Performance Standards the 2000 series. Thus, the Attribute Standard titled "Proficiency and Due Professional Care" is 1200, with more specific discussion of proficiency in 1210. The Implementation Standards are covered under the related Attribute and Performance Standards and indicated by a letter. For example, the implementation Standards for assurance activities are numbered nnnn.A1, nnnn.A2, etc., and the Implementation Standards for consulting activities are numbered nnnn.C1, etc. An example of an Assurance Implementation Standard is 1130.A2, "Impairments to Independence."

> **1130.A2 -** The internal auditing activity should report to alternate independent management if performing assurance services for functions for which the chief audit executive has operating responsibility.

With the adoption of the new definition and framework, The Internal Auditing Standards Board began the process of revising the *Standards for the Professional Practice of Internal Auditing* (the "Red Book") to reflect these changes as well as other recommendations from the Guidance Task Force's report. The first phase of this process was to take the existing standards and guidelines in the "Red Book" and place them in the new framework. The Internal Auditing Standards Board then issued an Exposure Draft which completed the initial step of redistributing the guidance in the "Red Book" to the new Attribute and Performance Standards and Implementation Standards for Assurance Activities. In many cases, the language from the original five General Standards or 25 Specific Standards was kept. However, in some instances, the Board determined that the information previously contained within the Guideline portion of the "Red Book" was of such significance that it needed to be raised to the level of a standard. In several other cases, the Board believed a gap existed and that a new standard needed to be developed. In addition, there were places where changes to the way the internal auditing profession is practiced, which resulted in the need for modification of the language used in the "Red Book."

Commentary on the *Standards*

The concept of auditing standards has a tendency over time to expand itself through augmentation and to become procedural in nature and content. The original standards of The IIA that were issued in 1978 suffered from this malaise. The *Statements on Internal Auditing Standards* issued subsequently and integrated with the *Standards* through the *Red Book* codification resulted in this type of a product. The *Standards* became lost in a plethora of procedure that had a tendency to obscure the basic thrust of the original *Standards*.

The reissuance of the *Standards* tends to again identify the basic thrust of the new concept of internal auditing as covered by its revised definition and to emphasize those areas that currently are important.

The *Code of Ethics*

The IIA's International Ethics Committee, in an effort to modernize the presentation of The IIA's philosophy of ethics and to a degree influenced by the Guidance Task Force, has over the last few years modernized the presentation of the *Code of Ethics*. Actually no new elements were added to the Code; however, the organization was expanded to include three sections:

- Introductory Comments
- Fundamental Principles
- Code of Conduct

The Fundamental Principles relate to five elements:

- Integrity
- Objectivity
- Confidentiality
- Professionalism
- Competency

Each of these elements is described and then, in the *Code of Conduct* Section, a series of ethical directives, 15 in all, support each, other than Professionalism, which underlies the entire code.

Probably the most important change in the new Code is its application to all "internal auditing professionals" rather than to "Members and CIAs," as did the replaced Code. This is an appropriate modification based on the global aspects of internal auditing and the growing utilization of outsourcing and cosourcing of internal audit effort.

The reorganization of and presentation of the body of ethics is well described by Ziegenfuss in a recent article as, "express(ing) both the spirit of the code as stated in general principles and the letter of the law as stated in the code of conduct."[1]

The revised *Code of Ethics* is presented in Appendix C.

---

[1]Ziegenfuss, Douglas E., "Revised Standards for Internal Auditors for the IIA," *Internal Auditing*, March/April 2000, 26-34.

Appendix A
Standards for the Professional Practice of Internal Auditing*

Introduction

Internal auditing is an independent, objective assurance and consulting activity designed to add value and improve an organization's operations. It helps an organization accomplish its objectives by bringing a systematic, disciplined approach to evaluate and improve the effectiveness of risk management, control, and governance processes.

Internal audit activities are performed in diverse legal and cultural environments; within organizations that vary in purpose, size, and structure; and by persons within or outside the organization. These differences may affect the practice of internal auditing in each environment. However, compliance with the *Standards for the Professional Practice of Internal Auditing (Standards)* is essential if the responsibilities of internal auditors are to be met.

The purpose of the *Standards* is to:

1. Delineate basic principles that represent the practice of internal auditing as it should be.
2. Provide a framework for performing and promoting a broad range of value-added internal audit activities.
3. Establish the basis for the measurement of internal audit performance.
4. Foster improved organizational processes and operations.

The *Standards* consist of Attribute Standards (the 1000 Series), Performance Standards (the 2000 Series), and Implementation Standards (nnnn.Xn). The Attribute Standards address the characteristics of organizations and individuals performing internal audit activities. The Performance Standards describe the nature of internal audit activities and provide quality criteria against which the performance of these services can be measured. The Attribute and Performance Standards apply to internal audit services in general. The Implementation Standards apply the Attribute and Performance Standards to specific types of engagements (for example, a compliance audit, a fraud investigation, or a control self-assessment project).

There is one set of Attribute and Performance Standards, however there may be multiple sets of Implementation Standards: a set for each of the major types of internal audit activity. Initially, the Implementation Standards are being established for assurance activities (noted by an "A" following the *Standard* number, e.g., 1130.Al) and consulting activities (noted by a "C" following the *Standard* number, e.g., nnnn.C1).

---

*Effective January 1, 2002.

The *Standards* are part of the Professional Practices Framework. This framework was proposed by the Guidance Task Force and approved by The IIA's Board of Directors in June 1999. This framework includes the Definition of Internal Auditing, the *Code of Ethics*, the *Standards,* and other guidance.

The *Standards* incorporate the guidance previously contained in the "Red Book," recasting it into the new format proposed by the Guidance Task Force and updating it as recommended in the Task Force's report, *A Vision for the Future.*

The *Standards* employ terms that have been given specific meanings that are included in the Glossary.

ATTRIBUTE STANDARDS

1000 - Purpose, Authority, and Responsibility

The purpose, authority, and responsibility of the internal audit activity should be formally defined in a charter, consistent with the *Standards*, and approved by the board.[1]

> **1000.A1** - The nature of assurance services provided to the organization should be defined in the audit charter. If assurances are to be provided to parties outside the organization, the nature of these assurances should also be defined in the charter.

> **1000.C1** - The nature of consulting services should be defined in the audit charter.

1100 - Independence and Objectivity

The internal audit activity should be independent, and internal auditors should be objective in performing their work.

1110 - Organizational Independence

The chief audit executive should report to a level within the organization that allows the internal audit activity to fulfill its responsibilities.

> **1110.A1** - The internal audit activity should be free from interference in determining the scope of internal auditing, performing work, and communicating results.

---

[1]When used in these *Standards*, the term "board" is defined as a board of directors, audit committee of such boards, head of an agency or legislative body to whom internal auditors report, board of governors or trustees of a nonprofit organization, or any other designated governing body of an organization.

1120 - Individual Objectivity
Internal auditors should have an impartial, unbiased attitude and avoid conflicts of interest.

1130 - Impairments to Independence or Objectivity
If independence or objectivity is impaired in fact or appearance, the details of the impairment should be disclosed to appropriate parties. The nature of the disclosure will depend upon the impairment.

> **1130.Al -** Internal auditors should refrain from assessing specific operations for which they were previously responsible. Objectivity is presumed to be impaired if an auditor provides assurance services for an activity for which the auditor had responsibility within the previous year.

> **1130.A2 -** Assurance engagements for functions over which the chief audit executive has responsibility should be overseen by a party outside the internal audit activity.

> **1130.Cl -** Internal auditors may provide consulting services relating to operations for which they had previous responsibilities.

> **1130.C2 -** If internal auditors have potential impairments to independence or objectivity relating to proposed consulting services, disclosure should be made to the engagement client prior to accepting the engagement.

1200 - Proficiency and Due Professional Care
Engagements should be performed with proficiency and due professional care.

1210 - Proficiency
Internal auditors should possess the knowledge, skills, and other competencies needed to perform their individual responsibilities. The internal audit activity collectively should possess or obtain the knowledge, skills, and other competencies needed to perform its responsibilities.

> **1210.Al -** The chief audit executive should obtain competent advice and assistance if the internal audit staff lacks the knowledge, skills, or other competencies needed to perform all or part of the engagement.

> **1210.A2 -** The internal auditor should have sufficient knowledge to identify the indicators of fraud but is not expected to have the expertise of a person whose primary responsibility is detecting and investigating fraud.

1210.C1 - The chief audit executive should decline the consulting engagement or obtain competent advice and assistance if the internal audit staff lacks the knowledge, skills, or other competencies needed to perform all or part of the engagement.

1220 - Due Professional Care

Internal auditors should apply the care and skill expected of a reasonably prudent and competent internal auditor. Due professional care does not imply infallibility.

1220.A1 - The internal auditor should exercise due professional care by considering the:

- Extent of work needed to achieve the engagement's objectives.
- Relative complexity, materiality, or significance of matters to which assurance procedures are applied.
- Adequacy and effectiveness of risk, management, control, and governance processes.
- Probability of significant errors, irregularities, or noncompliance.
- Cost of assurance in relation to potential benefits.

1220.A2 - The internal auditor should be alert to the significant risks that might affect objectives, operations, or resources. However, assurance procedures alone, even when performed with due professional care, do not guarantee that all significant risks will be identified.

1220.C1 - The internal auditor should exercise due professional care during a consulting engagement by considering the:

- Needs and expectations of clients, including the nature, timing, and communication of engagement results.
- Relative complexity and extent of work needed to achieve the engagement's objectives.
- Cost of the consulting engagement in relation to potential benefits.

1230 - Continuing Professional Development

Internal auditors should enhance their knowledge, skills, and other competencies through continuing professional development.

1300 - Quality Assurance and Improvement Program

The chief audit executive should develop and maintain a quality assurance and improvement program that covers all aspects of the internal audit activity and continuously monitors its effectiveness. The program should be designed to help the internal auditing activity add value and improve the organization's operations and to provide assurance that the internal audit activity is in conformity with the *Standards* and the *Code of Ethics*.

1310 - Quality Program Assessments

The internal audit activity should adopt a process to monitor and assess the overall effectiveness of the quality program. The process should include both internal and external assessments.

1311 - Internal Assessments

Internal assessments should include:

- Ongoing reviews of the performance of the internal audit activity: and
- Periodic reviews performed through self-assessment or by other persons within the organization, with knowledge of internal auditing practices and the *Standards*.

1312 - External Assessments

External assessments, such as quality assurance reviews, should be conducted at least once every five years by a qualified, independent reviewer or review team from outside the organization.

1320 - Reporting on the Quality Program

The chief audit executive should communicate the results of external assessments to the board.

1330 - Use of "Conducted in Accordance with the *Standards*"

Internal auditors are encouraged to report that their activities are "conducted in accordance with the *Standards for the Professional Practice of Internal Auditing.*" However, internal auditors may use the statement only if assessments of the quality improvement program demonstrate that the internal audit activity is in compliance with the *Standards*.

1340 - Disclosure of Noncompliance

Although the internal audit activity should achieve full compliance with the *Standards* and internal auditors with the *Code of Ethics*, there may be instances in which full compliance is not achieved. When noncompliance impacts the overall scope or operation of the internal audit activity, disclosure should be made to senior management and the board.

PERFORMANCE STANDARDS

2000 - Managing the Internal Audit Activity

The chief audit executive should effectively manage the internal audit activity to ensure it adds value to the organization.

2010 - Planning

The chief audit executive should establish risk-based plans to determine the priorities of the internal audit activity, consistent with the organization's goals.

2010.Al - The internal audit activity's plan of engagements should be based on a risk assessment, undertaken at least annually. The input of senior management and the board should be considered in this process.

2010.Cl - The chief audit executive should consider accepting proposed consulting engagements based on the engagement's potential to improve management of risks, add value, and improve the organization's operations. Those engagements that have been accepted should be included in the plan.

2020 - Communication and Approval

The chief audit executive should communicate the internal audit activity's plans and resource requirements, including significant interim changes, to senior management and to the board for review and approval. The chief audit executive should also communicate the impact of resource limitations.

2030 - Resource Management

The chief' audit executive should ensure that internal audit resources are appropriate, sufficient, and effectively deployed to achieve the approved plan.

2040 - Policies and Procedures

The chief audit executive should establish policies and procedures to guide the internal audit activity.

2050 - Coordination

The chief audit executive should share information and coordinate activities with other internal and external providers of relevant assurance and consulting services to ensure proper coverage and minimize duplication of efforts.

2060 - Reporting to the Board and Senior Management

The chief audit executive should report periodically to the board and senior management on the internal audit activity's purpose, authority, responsibility, and performance relative to its plan. Reporting should also include significant risk exposures and control issues, corporate governance issues, and other matters needed or requested by the board and senior management.

2100 - Nature of Work

The internal audit activity evaluates and contributes to the improvement of risk management, control and governance systems.

2110 - Risk Management

The internal audit activity should assist the organization by identifying and evaluating significant exposures to risk and contributing to the improvement of risk management and control systems.

2110.Al - The internal audit activity should monitor and evaluate the effectiveness of the organization's risk management system.

2110.A2 - The internal audit activity should evaluate risk exposures relating to the organization's governance, operations, and information systems regarding the:
- Reliability and integrity of financial and operational information.
- Effectiveness and efficiency of operations.
- Safeguarding of assets.
- Compliance with laws, regulations, and contracts.

2110.Cl - During consulting engagements, internal auditors should address risk consistent with the engagement's objectives and should be alert to the existence of other significant risks.

2110.C2 - Internal auditors should incorporate knowledge of risks gained from consulting engagements into the process of identifying and evaluating significant risk exposures of the organization.

2120 - Control

The internal audit activity should assist the organization in maintaining effective controls by evaluating their effectiveness and efficiency and by promoting continuous improvement.

2120.Al - Based on the results of the risk assessment, the internal audit activity should evaluate the adequacy and effectiveness of controls encompassing the organization's governance, operations, and information systems. This should include:
- Reliability and integrity of financial and operational information.
- Effectiveness and efficiency of operations.
- Safeguarding of assets.
- Compliance with laws, regulations, and contracts.

2120.A2 - Internal auditors should ascertain the extent to which operating and program goals and objectives have been established and conform to those of the organization.

2120.A3 - Internal auditors should review operations and programs to ascertain the extent to which results are consistent with established goals and objectives to determine whether operations and programs are being implemented or performed as intended.

2120.A4 - Adequate criteria are needed to evaluate controls. Internal auditors should ascertain the extent to which management has established adequate criteria to determine whether objectives and goals have been accomplished. If adequate, internal auditors should use such criteria in their evaluation. If inadequate, internal auditors should work with management to develop appropriate evaluation criteria.

2120.C1 - During consulting engagements, internal auditors should address controls consistent with the engagement's objectives and should be alert to the existence of any significant control weaknesses.

2120.C2 - Internal auditors should incorporate knowledge of controls gained from consulting engagements into the process of identifying and evaluating significant risk exposures of the organization.

2130 - Governance

The internal audit activity should contribute to the organization's governance process by evaluating and improving the process through which (1) values and goals are established and communicated, (2) the accomplishment of goals is monitored, (3) accountability is ensured, and (4) values are preserved.

2130.A1 - Internal auditors should review operations and programs to ensure consistency with organizational values.

2130.C1 - Consulting engagement objectives should be consistent with the overall values and goals of the organization.

2200 - Engagement Planning

Internal auditors should develop and record a plan for each engagement.

2201 - Planning Considerations

In planning the engagement, internal auditors should consider:
- The objectives of the activity being reviewed and the means by which the activity controls its performance.
- The significant risks to the activity, its objectives, resources, and operations and the means by which the potential impact of risk is kept to an acceptable level.

- The adequacy and effectiveness of the activity's risk management and control systems compared to a relevant control framework or model.
- The opportunities for making significant improvements to the activity's risk management and control systems.

> **2201.Cl -** Internal auditors should establish an understanding with consulting engagement clients about objectives, scope, respective responsibilities, and other client expectations. For significant engagements, this understanding should be documented.

2210 - Engagement Objectives

The engagement's objectives should address the risks, controls, and governance processes associated with the activities under review.

> **2210.Al -** When planning the engagement, the internal auditor should identify and assess risks relevant to the activity under review. The engagement objectives should reflect the results of the risk assessment.

> **2210.A2 -** The internal auditor should consider the probability of significant errors, irregularities, noncompliance, and other exposures when developing the engagement objectives.

> **2210.C1 -** Consulting engagement objectives should address risks, controls, and governance processes to the extent agreed upon with the client.

2220 - Engagement Scope

The established scope should be sufficient to satisfy the objectives of the engagement.

> **2220.Al -** The scope of the engagement should include consideration of relevant systems, records, personnel, and physical properties, including those under the control of third parties.

> **2220.Cl -** In performing consulting engagements, internal auditors should ensure that the scope of the engagement is sufficient to address the agreed-upon objectives. If internal auditors develop reservations about the scope during the engagement, these reservations should be discussed with the client to determine whether to continue with the engagement.

2230 - Engagement Resource Allocation

Internal auditors should determine appropriate resources to achieve engagement objectives. Staffing should be based on an evaluation of the nature and complexity of each engagement, time constraints, and available resources.

2240 - Engagement Work Program

Internal auditors should develop work programs that achieve the engagement objectives. These work programs should be recorded.

2240.A1 - Work programs should establish the procedures for identifying, analyzing, evaluating, and recording information during the engagement. The work program should be approved prior to the commencement of work, and any adjustments approved promptly.

2240.C1 - Work programs for consulting engagements may vary in form and content depending upon the nature of the engagement.

2300 - Performing the Engagement

Internal auditors should identify, analyze, evaluate, and record sufficient information to achieve the engagement's objectives.

2310 - Identifying Information

Internal auditors should identify sufficient, reliable, relevant, and useful information to achieve the engagement's objectives.

2320 - Analysis and Evaluation

Internal auditors should base conclusions and engagement results on appropriate analyses and evaluations.

2330 - Recording Information

Internal auditors should record relevant information to support the conclusions and engagement results.

2330.A1 - The chief audit executive should control access to engagement records. The chief audit executive should obtain the approval of senior management and/or legal counsel prior to releasing such records to external parties, as appropriate.

2330.A2 - The chief audit executive should develop retention requirements for engagement records. These retention requirements should be consistent with the organization's guidelines and any pertinent regulatory or other requirements.

2330.C1 - The chief audit executive should develop policies governing the custody and retention of engagement records, as well as their release to internal and external parties. These policies should be consistent with the organization's guidelines and any pertinent regulatory or other requirements.

2340 - Engagement Supervision

Engagements should be properly supervised to ensure objectives are achieved, quality is assured, and staff is developed.

2400 - Communicating Results

Internal auditors should communicate the engagement results promptly.

2410 - Criteria for Communicating

Communications should include the engagement's objectives and scope as well as applicable conclusions, recommendations, and action plans.

2410.A1 - The final communication of results should, where appropriate, contain the internal auditor's overall opinion.

2410.A2 - Engagement communications should acknowledge satisfactory performance.

2410.C1 - Communication of the progress and results of consulting engagements will vary in form and content depending upon the nature of the engagement and the needs of the client.

2420 - Quality of Communications

Communications should be accurate, objective, clear, concise, constructive, complete, and timely.

2421 - Errors and Omissions

If a final communication contains a significant error or omission, the chief audit executive should communicate corrected information to all individuals who received the original communication.

2430 - Engagement Disclosure of Noncompliance with the *Standards*

When noncompliance with the *Standards* impacts a specific engagement, communication of the results should disclose the:
- *Standard(s)* with which full compliance was not achieved,
- Reason(s) for noncompliance, and
- Impact of noncompliance on the engagement.

2440 - Disseminating Results

The chief audit executive should disseminate results to the appropriate individuals.

2440.A1 - The chief audit executive is responsible for communicating the final results to individuals who can ensure that the results are given due consideration.

2440.C1 - The chief audit executive is responsible for communicating the final results of consulting engagements to clients.

2440.C2 - During consulting engagements, risk management, control, and governance issues may be identified. Whenever these issues are significant to the organization, they should be communicated to senior management and the board.

2500 - Monitoring Progress

The chief audit executive should establish and maintain a system to monitor the disposition of results communicated to management.

2500.A1 - The chief audit executive should establish a follow-up process to monitor and ensure that management actions have been effectively implemented or that senior management has accepted the risk of not taking action.

2500.C1 - The internal audit activity should monitor the disposition of results of consulting engagements to the extent agreed upon with the client.

2600 - Management's Acceptance of Risks

When the chief audit executive believes that senior management has accepted a level of residual risk that is unacceptable to the organization, the chief audit executive should discuss the matter with senior management. If the decision regarding residual risk is not resolved, the chief audit executive and senior management should report the matter to the board for resolution.

Glossary

Add Value - Organizations exist to create value or benefit to their owners, other stakeholders, customers, and clients. This concept provides purpose for their existence. Value is provided through their development of products and services and their use of resources to promote those products and services. In the process of gathering data to understand and assess risk, internal auditors develop significant insight into operations and opportunities for improvement that can be extremely beneficial to their organization This valuable information can be in the form of consultation, advice, written communications, or through other products all of which should be properly communicated to the appropriate management or operating personnel.

Adequate Control - Present if management has planned and organized (designed) in a manner that provides reasonable assurance that the organization's risks have been managed effectively and that the organization's goals and objectives will be achieved efficiently and economically.

Assurance Services - An objective examination of evidence for the purpose of providing an independent assessment on risk management, control, or governance processes for the organization. Examples may include financial, performance, compliance, system security, and due diligence engagements.

Board - A board of directors, audit committee of such boards, head of an agency or legislative body to whom internal auditors report, board of governors or trustees of a nonprofit organization, or any other designated governing bodies of organizations.

Charter - The charter of the internal audit activity is a formal written document that defines the activity's purpose, authority, and responsibility. The charter should (a) establish the internal audit activity's position within the organization; (b) authorize access to records, personnel, and physical properties relevant to the performance of engagements; and (c) define the scope of internal audit activities.

Chief Audit Executive - Top position within the organization responsible for internal audit activities. In a traditional internal audit activity, this would be the internal audit director. In the case where internal audit activities are obtained from outside service providers, the chief audit executive is the person responsible for overseeing the service contract and the overall quality assurance of these activities, reporting to senior management and the board regarding internal audit activities, and follow-up of engagement results. The term also includes such titles as general auditor, chief internal auditor, and inspector general.

Code of Ethics - The purpose of the *Code of Ethics* of The Institute of Internal Auditors (IIA) is to promote an ethical culture in the global profession of internal auditing. A code of ethics is necessary and appropriate for the profession of internal auditing, founded as it is on the trust placed in its objective assurance about risk, control, and governance. The *Code of Ethics* applies to both individuals and entities that provide internal audit services.

Compliance - The ability to reasonably ensure conformity and adherence to organization policies, plans, procedures, laws, regulations, and contracts.

Conflict of Interest - Any relationship that is or appears to be not in the best interest of the organization. A conflict of interest would prejudice an individual's ability to perform his or her duties and responsibilities objectively.

Consulting Services - The range of services, beyond internal audit's assurance services, provided to assist management in meeting its objectives. The nature and scope of work are agreed upon with the client. Examples include facilitation, process design, training, and advisory services.

Control - Any action taken by management, the board, and other parties to enhance risk management and increase the likelihood that established objectives and goals will be achieved. Management plans, organizes, and directs the performance of sufficient actions to provide reasonable assurance that objectives and goals will be achieved.

Control Environment - The attitude and actions of the board and management regarding the significance of control within the organization. The control environment provides the discipline and structure for the achievement of the primary objectives of the system of internal control. The control environment includes the following elements:

- Integrity and ethical values.
- Management's philosophy and operating style.
- Organizational structure.
- Assignment of authority and responsibility.
- Human resource policies and practices.
- Competence of personnel.

Control Processes - The policies, procedures, and activities that are part of a control framework, designed to ensure that risks are contained within the risk tolerances established by the risk management process.

Engagement - A specific internal audit assignment, task, or review activity, such as an internal audit, control self-assessment review, fraud examination, or consultancy. An engagement may include multiple tasks or activities designed to accomplish a specific set of related objectives.

Engagement Objectives - Broad statements developed by internal auditors that define intended engagement accomplishments.

Engagement Work Program - A document that lists the procedures to be followed during an engagement, designed to achieve the engagement plan.

External Service Provider - A person or firm, independent of the organization, who has special knowledge, skill, and experience in a particular discipline. Outside service providers include, among others, actuaries, accountants, appraisers, environmental specialists, fraud investigators, lawyers, engineers, geologists, security specialists, statisticians, information technology specialists, external auditors, and other auditing organizations. The board, senior management, or the chief audit executive may engage an outside service provider.

Fraud - Any illegal acts characterized by deceit, concealment or violation of trust. These acts are not dependent upon the application of threat of violence or of physical force. Frauds are perpetrated by individuals and organizations to obtain money, property or services; to avoid payment or loss of services; or to secure personal or business advantage.

Governance Process - The procedures utilized by the representatives of the organization's stakeholders (e.g., shareholders, etc.) to provide oversight of risk and control processes administered by management.

Impairments - Impairments to individual objectivity and organizational independence may include personal conflicts of interest, scope limitations, restrictions on access to records, personnel, and properties, and resource limitations (funding).

Internal Audit Activity - A department, division, team of consultants, or other practitioner(s) that provides independent, objective assurance and consulting services designed to add value and improve an organization's operations. The internal audit activity helps an organization accomplish its objectives by bringing a systematic, disciplined approach to evaluate and improve the effectiveness of risk management, control, and governance processes.

Objectivity - An unbiased mental attitude that requires internal auditors to perform engagements in such a manner that they have an honest belief in their work product and that no significant quality compromises are made. Objectivity requires internal auditors not to subordinate their judgment on audit matters to that of others.

Risk - The uncertainty of an event occurring that could have an impact on the achievement of objectives. Risk is measured in terms of consequences and likelihood.

Appendix B
Audit Standards Practice Advisories

Practice Advisory 1000-1: Internal Audit Charter

Practice Advisory 1000.C1-1: Principles Guiding the Performance of Consulting Activities of Internal Auditors

Practice Advisory 1000.C1-2: Additional Considerations for Formal Consulting Engagements

Practice Advisory 1100-1: Independence and Objectivity

Practice Advisory 1110-1: Organizational Independence

Practice Advisory 1110.A1-1: Disclosing Reasons for Information Requests

Practice Advisory 1110-2: Chief Audit Executive (CAE) Reporting Lines

Practice Advisory 1120-1: Individual Objectivity

Practice Advisory 1130-1: Impairments to Independence or Objectivity

Practice Advisory 1130.A1-1: Assessing Operations for Which Internal Auditors were Previously Responsible

Practice Advisory 1130.A1-2: Internal Audit Responsibility for Other (Non-Audit) Functions

Practice Advisory 1200-1: Proficiency and Due Professional Care

Practice Advisory 1210-1: Proficiency

Practice Advisory 1210.A1-1: Obtaining Services to Support or Complement the Internal Audit Activity

Practice Advisory 1210.A2-1: Identification of Fraud

Practice Advisory 1210.A2-2: Responsibility for Fraud Detection

Practice Advisory 1220-1: Due Professional Care

Practice Advisory 1230-1: Continuing Professional Development

Practice Advisory 1310-1: Quality Program Assessments

Practice Advisory 1311-1: Internal Assessments

Practice Advisory 1312-1: External Assessments

Practice Advisory 1320-1: Reporting on the Quality Program

Practice Advisory 1330-1: Use of "Conducted in Accordance with the Standards"

Practice Advisory 2000-1: Managing the Internal Audit Activity

Practice Advisory 2010-1: Planning

Practice Advisory 2010-2: Linking the Audit Plan to Risk and Exposures

Practice Advisory 2020-1: Communication and Approval

Practice Advisory 2030-1: Resource Management

Practice Advisory 2030-2: SEC External Auditor Independence Requirements for Providing Internal Audit Services

Practice Advisory 2040-1: Policies and Procedures

Practice Advisory 2050-1: Coordination

Practice Advisory 2050-2: Acquisition of External Audit Services

Practice Advisory 2060-1: Reporting to Board and Senior Management
Practice Advisory 2060-2: Relationship with the Audit Committee
Practice Advisory 2100-1: Nature of Work
Practice Advisory 2100-2: Information Security
Practice Advisory 2100-3: Internal Audit's Role in the Risk Management Process
Practice Advisory 2100-4: Internal Audit's Role in Organizations Without a Risk Management Process
Practice Advisory 2100-5: Legal Considerations in Evaluating Regulatory Compliance Programs
Practice Advisory 2110-1: Assessing the Adequacy of Risk Management Processes
Practice Advisory 2120.A1-1: Assessing and Reporting on Control Processes
Practice Advisory 2120-A1-2: Using Control Self-assessment for Assessing the Adequacy of Control Processes
Practice Advisory 2120.A4-1: Control Criteria
Practice Advisory 2130-1: Role of the Internal Audit Activity and Internal Auditor in the Ethical Culture of an Organization
Practice Advisory 2200-1: Engagement Planning
Practice Advisory 2210-1: Engagement Objectives
Practice Advisory 2210.A1-1: Risk Assessment in Engagement Planning
Practice Advisory 2230-1: Engagement Resource Allocation
Practice Advisory 2240-1: Engagement Work Program
Practice Advisory 2240.Al-1: Approval of Work Programs
Practice Advisory 2310-1: Identifying Information
Practice Advisory 2320-1: Analysis and Evaluation
Practice Advisory 2330-1: Recording Information
Practice Advisory 2330.Al-1: Control of Engagement Records
Practice Advisory 2330.A1-2: Legal Considerations in Granting Access to Engagement Records
Practice Advisory 2330.A2-1: Retention of Records
Practice Advisory 2340-1: Engagement Supervision
Practice Advisory 2400-1: Legal Considerations in Communicating Results
Practice Advisory 2410-1: Communication Criteria
Practice Advisory 2420-1: Quality of Communications
Practice Advisory 2421-1: Errors and Omissions
Practice Advisory 2440-1: Disseminating Results
Practice Advisory 2440-2: Communications Outside the Organization
Practice Advisory 2500-1: Monitoring Progress
Practice Advisory 2500.A1-1: Follow-up Process
Practice Advisory 2600-1: Management's Acceptance of Risks
Practice Advisory 2600-2: Communicating Sensitive Information and Whistleblowing

Appendix C
Code of Ethics

Introduction

The purpose of The Institute's *Code of Ethics* is to promote an ethical culture in the global profession of internal auditing.

> *Internal auditing is an independent, objective assurance and consulting activity designed to add value and improve an organization's operations. It helps an organization accomplish its objectives by bringing a systemic, disciplined approach to evaluate and improve the effectiveness of risk management, control, and governance professes.*

A code of ethics is necessary and appropriate for the profession of internal auditing, founded as it is on the trust place in its objective assurance about risk, control, and governance. The Institute's *Code of Ethics* extends beyond the definition of internal auditing to include two essential components:

1. Principles that are relevant to the profession and practice of internal auditing.
2. Rules of Conduct that describes behavior norms expected of internal auditors. These rules are an aid to interpreting the Principles into practical applications and are intended to guide the ethical conduct of internal auditors.

The *Code of Ethics* together with The Institute's *Professional Practices Framework* and other relevant Institute pronouncements provide guidance to internal auditors serving others. "Internal Auditors" refer to Institute members, recipients of our candidates for IIA professional certifications, and those who provide internal auditing services within the definition of internal auditing.

Applicability and Enforcement

This *Code of Ethics* applies to both individuals and entities that provide internal auditing services.

The Institute members and recipients of or candidates for IIA professional certifications, breaches of the *Code of Ethics* will be evaluated ad administered according to The Institute's Bylaws and Administrative Guidelines. The fact that a particular conduct is not mentioned in the Rules of Conduct does not prevent it from being unacceptable or discreditable, and therefore, the member, certification holder, or candidate can be liable for disciplinary action.

Principles

Internal auditors are expected to apply and uphold certain fundamental principles.

Integrity

The integrity of internal auditors establishes trust and thus provides the basis for reliance on their judgment.

Objectivity

Internal auditors exhibit the highest level of professional objectivity in gathering, evaluating, and communicating information about activity or process being examined. Internal auditors make a balanced assessment of all the relevant circumstances and are not unduly influenced by their own interests or by others in forming judgments.

Confidentiality

Internal auditors respect the value and ownership of information they receive and do not disclose information without appropriate authority unless there is a legal or professional obligation to do so.

Competency

Internal auditors apply the knowledge, skills, and experience needed in the performance of internal auditing services.

Rules of Conduct

1. Integrity

Internal auditors:

1.1 Shall perform their work with honesty and responsibility.

1.2 Shall observe the law and make disclosures expected by the law and the profession.

1.3 Shall not knowingly be party to any illegal activity, activities that are discreditable to the profession of internal auditing or to the organization.

1.4 Shall respect and contribute to the legitimate and ethical objectives of the organization as appropriate.

Addendum to Chapter 31
Proposed Changes to the *Standards*
(New and Amended)

During the mid 1990s, The IIA developed a Guidance Task Force that met numerous times internationally to assist in determining the directions that The IIA should take to respond to the changing environment in which its members functioned. The Task Force's recommendations resulted in a revised Body of Ethics and a substantial revision of the *Standards* originally issued in 1978. Both of these revisions have now been in effect for several years. However, the revision of the *Standards* was essentially a restructuring of the then existing standards to modernize them and to bring into being the concept that internal auditing was not only assurance (attribute and performance) related but now also consultive as well.

The Guidance Task Force in its deliberations had also discussed the changes within the basic organizational and functional operations that internal auditing should be designed to treat as well as the modifications in internal auditing philosophy that would be important in meeting these changes. This activity has been an evolutionary process and currently the Auditing Standards Board, in an Exposure Draft dated January 15, 2003, is proposing additional changes and additions to the *Standards* to accomplish coverage of these important areas.

It goes without saying that the recent unfortunate events of corporate and organization malfeasance, misfeasance, and nonfeasance have stimulated The IIA and the Board to meet the challenge and to expedite the placing of new directives to address them.

The modifications proposed at this time are addressed to cover:

- Information technology risks.
- Computer-assisted audit tools.
- Contributions to the governance process.
- Broadening ethics-related responsibilities.
- Closer communications with internal and external clients.
- Assurance that audits conform to the *Standards*.
- Assessing the implications of the release of audit results.
- Identification of consulting opportunities resulting from assurance audits.

A new paragraph is proposed to be added to the *Introduction of the Standards*. It is reproduced below.

> *Assurance services involve the internal auditor's objective assessment of evidence for the purpose of providing an independent opinion regarding a process, system, or other subject matter. There are generally three parties involved in assurance services: (1) the person or group directly involved with the process or system — the process owner, (2) the person or group making the assessment — the auditor, and (3) the person or group using the assessment to make decisions — the user. Consulting services are advisory and other non-assurance activities delivered by the internal auditor generally at the specific request of an engagement client, while not assuming management responsibility for the engagement results. Consulting services involve two parties, the auditor and the client. Unlike assurance services engagements where the internal auditor determines the nature and scope, in consulting the nature and scope are subject to agreement with the client. Consulting services, like assurance services, are intended to add value and improve the organization's governance, risk management, and control processes.*

Proposed changes to the *Standards* are shown below. Where there are major changes, the old standard is also presented.

1210 Proficiency

> *1210.A3 - Internal auditors should have general knowledge of key information technology risks and controls and available technology-based audit techniques. However, not all internal auditors are expected to have the expertise of an internal auditor whose primary responsibility is information technology.*

1220 Due Professional Care

> *Internal auditors should apply the care and skill expected of a reasonably prudent and competent internal auditor. Due professional care does not imply infallibility.*

1220.A1 - Internal auditors should exercise due professional care by considering the:

- Extent of work needed to achieve the engagement's objectives.
- *Use of computer-assisted audit tools and techniques. [new]*
- Relative complexity, materiality, or significance of matters to which assurance procedures are applied.
- Adequacy and effectiveness of risk management, control, and governance processes.
- Probability of significant errors, irregularities, or noncompliance.
- Cost of assurance in relation to potential benefits.

2130   Governance

[old]

The internal audit activity should contribute to the organization's governance process by evaluating and improving the process through which (1) values and goals are established and communicated, (2) the accomplishment of goals is monitored, (3) accountability is ensured, and (4) values are preserved.

[new]

The internal audit activity, consistent with the organization's structure, should contribute to the governance process by proactively assisting management and the board in fulfilling their responsibilities by:

- *Assessing and promoting strong ethics and values within the organization.*
- *Assessing and improving the process by which accountability is ensured.*
- *Assessing the adequacy of communications about significant residual risks within the organization.*
- *Helping to improve the board's interaction with management and the external and internal auditors.*
- *Serving as an educational resource regarding changes and trends in the business and regulatory environment.*

Also:

[old]

2130.Al - Internal auditors should review operations and programs to ensure consistency with organizational values.

[new]

2130.Al - The internal audit activity should evaluate the design, implementation, and effectiveness of the organization's ethics-related programs and activities.

2200   Engagement Planning

[old]

Internal auditors should develop and record a plan for each engagement.

[new]

Internal auditors should develop and record a plan for each engagement, including its scope, objectives, and resource allocations.

Also:

[new]
2200.A1 *- Internal auditors should understand the activities under review and identify the risks and related controls that impact the achievement of the activities' objectives to develop the engagement plan.*

2201 Planning Considerations

[new]
2210.A1 *- When planning the engagement that includes clients outside the organization, internal auditors should establish a written understanding with them about objectives, scope, respective responsibilities, and other expectations.*

2210.A2 *- When planning an engagement of which the results will be released to parties outside the organization, internal auditors should consider the potential uses of the results.*

2220 Engagement Scope

[new]
2220.A2 *- When significant consulting opportunities arise within an assurance engagement, an agreement on objectives should be reached and the results communicated in accordance with consulting standards.*

2410 Criteria for Communicating

[new]
2410.A3 *- When releasing results to clients or other parties outside the organization, the communication should include limitations on distribution and use of the results. If the internal audit activity meets the conditions for use, reference should be made that "the engagement was conducted in accordance with the Standards for the Professional Practice of Internal Auditing."*

2440 Disseminating Results (Recipients of Engagement Results)

[new]
2440.A2 *- When releasing results to parties outside the organization, the chief audit executive should:*

- *Assess the potential risk to the organization.*
- *Control dissemination.*
- *Obtain the approval of senior management and/or legal counsel prior to release.*

The Auditing Standards Board also has proposed some changes in terms related to the *Standards*. These changes are intended to "clarify meanings or improve understanding." They are classified as editorial changes and are not expected to have a significant impact on the application of the *Standards*. These changes follow:

Current Standard or Glossary Term	Proposed Edited Standard or Glossary Term
1300 - Quality Assurance and Improvement Program	**1300 - Quality Assurance and Improvement Program**
The chief audit executive should develop and maintain a quality assurance and improvement program that covers all aspects of the internal audit activity and continuously monitors its effectiveness. The program should be designed to help the internal auditing activity add value and improve the organization's operations and to provide assurance that the internal audit activity is in conformity with the *Standards* and the *Code of Ethics*.	The chief audit executive should develop and maintain a quality assurance and improvement program that covers all aspects of the internal audit activity and continuously monitors its effectiveness. *This program includes periodic internal and external quality assessments and ongoing internal monitoring. Each part of the program* should be designed to help the internal auditing activity add value and improve the organization's operations and to provide assurance that the internal audit activity is in conformity with the *Standards* and the *Code of Ethics*.
2100 - Nature of Work	**2100 - Nature of Work**
The internal audit activity evaluates and contributes to the improvement of risk management, control, and governance systems.	The internal activity *should* evaluate and contribute to the improvement of risk management control, and governance *processes using a systematic and disciplined approach.*
2110.Cl - During consulting engagements, internal auditors should address risk consistent with the engagement's objectives and should be alert to the existence of other significant risks.	**2110.C1** - During consulting engagements, internal auditors should address risk consistent with the engagement's objectives and *be* alert to the existence of other significant risks.
2120.Cl - During consulting engagements, internal auditors should address controls consistent with the engagement's objective and should be alert to the existence of any significant control weaknesses.	**2120.C1** - During consulting engagements, internal auditors should address controls consistent with engagement's objectives and *be* alert to the existence of any significant control weaknesses.

2210 - Engagement Objectives	**2210 - Engagement Objectives**
The engagement's objectives should address the risk, controls, and governance processes associated with the activities under review.	*Objectives should be established for each engagement.*
2210.A1 - When planning the engagement, the internal auditor should identify and assess risks relevant to the activity under review. The engagement objectives should reflect the results of the risk assessment.	**2210.A1 -** *Internal auditors should conduct a preliminary risk assessment relevant to the activity under review.* Engagement objectives should reflect the results of *this assessment and should be communicated to the management of the activity under review.*
2240.A1 - Work programs should establish the procedures for identifying, analyzing, evaluating, and recording information during the engagement. The work program should be approved prior to the commencement of work, and any adjustments approved promptly.	**2240.A1 -** Work programs should establish the procedures for identifying, analyzing, evaluating, and recording information during the engagement. The work program should be approved prior to *its implementation,* and any adjustments approved promptly.
2300 - Performing the Engagement	**2300 - Performing the Engagement**
Internal auditors should identify, analyze, evaluate, and record sufficient information to achieve the engagement's objectives.	Internal auditors should *use a systematic and disciplined approach in identifying, analyzing, evaluating, and recording* sufficient information to achieve the engagement's objectives.
2400 - Communicating Results	**2400 - Communicating Results**
Internal auditors should communicate the engagement results promptly.	Internal auditors should communicate the engagement results *appropriately.*
2600 - Management's Acceptance of Risks	**2600 - *Resolution of* Management's Acceptance of Risks**
When the chief audit executive believes that senior management has accepted a level of residual risk that is unacceptable to the organization, the chief audit executive should discuss the matter with senior management. If the decision regarding residual risk is not resolved, the chief audit executive and senior management should report the matter to the board for resolution.	When the chief audit executive believes that senior management has accepted a level of residual risk that *may be* unacceptable to the organization, the chief audit executive should discuss the matter with senior management. If the decision regarding residual risk is not resolved, the chief audit executive and senior management should report the matter to the board for resolution.

The Board is also recommending changes relating exclusively to the Glossary as follows:

Current Text of Glossary Term	Editorial Change to Glossary Term
Add Value - Organizations exist to create value or benefit to their owners, other stakeholders, customers, and clients. This concept provides purpose for their existence. Value is provided through their development of products and services and their use of resources to promote those products and services. In the process of gathering data to understand and assess risk, internal auditors develop significant insight into operations and opportunities for improvement that can be extremely beneficial to their organization This valuable information can be in the form of consultation, advice, written communications, or through other products all of which should be properly communicated to the appropriate management or operating personnel.	**Add Value -** *Value is provided by satisfying management and board needs, improving opportunities to achieve organizational objectives, identifying operational improvement, or reducing risk exposure through both assurance and consulting services.*
Board - A board of directors, audit committee of such boards, head of an agency or legislative body to whom internal auditors report, board of governors or trustees of a nonprofit organization, or any other designated governing bodies of organizations.	**Board -** A board *is the governing body such as a board of directors,* audit committee of such boards, *supervisory board,* head of an agency or legislative body, board of governors or trustees of a nonprofit organization, or any other designated bodies of organizations *to whom the chief audit executive may report functionally.*

Chief Audit Executive - Top position within the organization responsible for internal audit activities. In a traditional internal audit activity, this would be the internal audit director. In the case where internal audit activities are obtained from outside service providers, the chief audit executive is the person responsible for overseeing the service contract and the overall quality assurance of these activities, reporting to senior management and the board regarding internal audit activities, and follow-up engagement results. The term also includes such titles as general auditor, chief internal auditor, and inspector general.	**Chief Audit Executive -** Top position within the organization responsible for internal audit activities. *Normally,* this would be the internal audit director. In the case where internal audit activities are obtained from outside service providers, the chief audit executive is the person responsible for overseeing the service contract and the overall quality assurance of these activities, reporting to senior management and the board regarding internal audit activities, and follow-up engagement results. The term also includes such titles as general auditor, chief internal auditor, and inspector general.
Code of Ethics - The purpose of the *Code of Ethics* of The Institute of Internal Auditors (IIA) is to promote an ethical culture in the global profession of internal auditing. A code of ethics is necessary and appropriate for the profession of internal auditing, founded as it is on the trust placed in its objective assurance about risk, control, and governance. The *Code of Ethics* applies to both individuals and entities that provide internal audit services.	**Code of Ethics -** The *Code of Ethics* of the Institute of Internal Auditors (IIA) *includes Principles relevant to the profession and practice of internal auditing, and Rules of Conduct that describe behavior norms expected of internal auditors.* The *Code of Ethics* applies to both individuals and entities that provide internal audit services. The purpose of the *Code of Ethics* is to promote an ethical culture in the global profession of internal auditing.
Compliance - The ability to reasonably ensure conformity and adherence to organization policies, procedures, laws, regulations, and contracts.	**Compliance -** *Conformity and adherence to* polices, plans, procedures, laws, regulations, contracts, *or other requirements.*
Conflict of Interest - Any relationship that is or appears to be not in the best interest of the organization. A conflict of interest would prejudice an individual's ability to perform his or her duties and responsibilities objectively.	**Conflict of Interest -** *A condition in which an individual duty of loyalty to an organization is challenged by an opposing duty or opportunity.*

Consulting Services - Advisory and related client service activities, the nature and scope of which are agreed upon with the client and which are intended to add value and improve an organization's operations. Examples include counsel, advice, facilitation, process design, and training.	**Consulting Services -** Advisory and related client service activities, the nature and scope of which are agreed upon with the client and which are intended to add value and improve an organization's *governance, risk management, and control processes while not assuming management responsibility.* Examples include counsel, advice, facilitation, process design, and training.
Control - Any action taken by management, the board, and other parties to enhance risk management and increase the likelihood that established objectives and goals will be achieved. Management plans, organizes, and directs the performance of sufficient actions to provide reasonable assurance that objectives and goals will be achieved.	**Control -** Any action taken by management, the board, and other parties to *manage* risk and increase the likelihood that established objectives, and goals will be achieved. Management plans, organizes, and directs the performance of sufficient actions to provide reasonable assurance that objectives and goals will be achieved.
External Service Provider - A person or firm, independent of the organization who has special; knowledge, skill, and experience in a particular discipline. Outside service providers include, among others, actuaries, accountants, appraisers, environmental specialists, fraud investigators, lawyers, engineers, geologists, security specialists, statisticians, information technology specialists, external auditors, and other auditing organizations. The board, senior management, or the chief audit executive may engage in outside service provider.	**External Service Provider -** A person or a firm *outside* of the organization, who has special knowledge, skill, and experience in a particular discipline.
Governance Process - The procedures utilized by the representatives of the organization's stakeholders (e.g., shareholders, etc.) to provide oversight of risk and control processes administered by management.	**Governance Process -** *The procedures used by the governing body* to provide oversight of risk and control processes administered by management.

[No previous definition]	*Independence - Independence is the freedom from significant conflicts of interest that threaten objectivity. Such threats to objectivity must be managed at the individual auditor level, the engagement level, and the organizational level.*
Objectivity - An unbiased mental attitude that requires internal auditors to perform engagements in such a manner that they have an honest belief in their work product and that no significant quality compromises are made. Objectivity requires internal auditors not to subordinate their judgment on audit matters to that of others.	**Objectivity -** An unbiased mental attitude that *allows* internal auditors to perform engagements in such a manner that they have an honest belief in their work product and that no significant quality compromises are made. Objectivity requires internal auditors not to subordinate their judgment on audit matters to that of others.
[No previous definition]	*Preliminary Risk Assessment - A risk assessment performed during engagement planning to establish the scope and objectives of the engagement.*
[No previous definition]	*Residual Risks - The risk remaining after management takes action to reduce the likelihood and impact of an adverse event, including control activities in responding to a risk.*
Risk - The uncertainty of an event occurring that could have an impact on the achievement of objectives. Risks are measured in terms of consequences and likelihood.	**Risk -** The uncertainty of an event occurring that could have an impact on the achievement of objectives. Risk is measured in terms of *impact* and likelihood.
[No previous definition]	*Risk Management - A process designed to identify, manage, and control potential events to provide reasonable assurance regarding the achievement of the organization's objectives.*
[No previous definition]	*Standard - A statement that delineates the requirements for the professional practice of internal auditing, provides a framework for performing and promoting a broad range of value-adding internal audit activities, and establishes the basis for the evaluation of internal audit performance.*

[No previous definition]	**Unacceptable Residual Risk** - *Exists when control activities are not adequately designed, not properly executed, or ineffective at reducing a risk to a prudently acceptable level.*

As this edition goes to press, the above material is presented to readers as potential changes. Responses to the Exposure Draft are not due until May 15, 2003; thus final action by the Board and subsequently by The IIA's directors will not occur until after this edition is published.

Supplementary Readings

Barbier, Etienne, "Audit Committees a la Française," *Internal Auditor*, June 1998, 77-80.

Bean, Jr., James W., "The Audit Committee Road Map," *The Journal of Accountancy*, January 1999, 47-54.

Barr, Stephen, "Watchdogs or Lapdogs?," *CFO Magazine*, May 1999, 44-60.

Bishop III, William G., Dana R. Hermanson, Paul D. Lapides, and Larry E. Rittenberg, "The Year of the Audit Committee," *Internal Auditor*, April 2000, 46-51.

Calhoun, Charles, "The Expanding Role of the Audit Committee," *Internal Auditing Alert*, February 1999, 1-3.

Dezoort, F. Todd, Alan H. Friedberg, and John T. Reisch, "Implementing a Communications Program for Audit Committees," *Internal Auditing*, July/August 2000, 11-18.

Forrest, Edward, and Jonathan S. Forrest, "Trinity," *Internal Auditing*, May/June 2000, 35-37.

Hermanson, Dana R., Paul D. Lapides, and Wenying Lu, "What Internal Auditors Should Know About Corporate Governance," *Internal Auditing*, September/October 2000, 9-12.

Horton, Thomas R., "Assisting the Board," *Internal Auditor*, October 2000, 53-57.

McEnroe, John E., "The Auditing Standards Board and the Auditing Standard-Setting Process," *Internal Auditing*, July/August 2000, 25-31.

Parker, Susan, "The Role of the Audit Committee in Curbing Aggressive Financial Reporting," *Internal Auditing*, March/April 1999, 34-39.

Rezaee, Zabihollah, "Corporate Governance and Accountability: The Role of Audit Committee," *Internal Auditing*, Summer 1997, 27-41.

Ridley, Anthony J., "An Audit Committee Event Matrix," *Internal Auditor*, April 2000, 53-56.

Sears, Brian P., *Internal Auditing Manual* (New York: RIA, 2003). (See Chapter B4, "Standards for the Professional Practice of Internal Auditing.")

Steinberg, Richard M., and Deborah Pojunis, "Corporate Governance: The New Frontier," *Internal Auditor*, December 2000, 34-39.

Tidrick, Donald E., "A Conversation with David M. Walker, Comptroller General of the U.S.," *Internal Auditing*, May/June 2000, 39-45.

Urbancic, Frank R., "A New Perspective on the Code of Ethics for Internal Auditors," *Internal Auditing,* January/February 2001, 3-7.

Urbancic, Frank R., "A Content Analysis of Audit Committee Reports," *Internal Auditing*, Summer 1996, 36-42.

Verschoor, Curtis C., "New Audit Committee Responsibilities Provide Governance Opportunities for Internal Auditing," *Internal Auditing*, September/October 2000, 35-38.

Verschoor, Curtis C., "SEC Demands Better Corporate Reporting: An Opportunity for Internal Auditors," *Internal Auditing*, November/December 1998, 45-48.

Wolitzer, Phillip, "Improving the Effectiveness of Audit Committees," *Internal Auditing Alert*, June 1999, 5-7.

Woodlock, Peter, "The Audit Committee's Implementation of the Treadway Commission's Good Practice Guidelines," *Internal Auditing*, March/April 1999, 41-46.

Index

Unless otherwise indicated, "auditors" are internal auditors; "auditing" is internal auditing.

-A-

Abandoned approaches, 381
Abstracts, 364, 365, 367
Acceptance
    of authority, 1072
    of decisions, 1065
    by external auditors, 1302
    as human need, 1085
    of recommendations, 692–94, 788–91
    of residual risk, 143, 1369, 1384, 1388, 1389
Access
    to assets, 1166
    of auditors, 1256
    to computer systems, 544, 563–67, 614, 1169, 1170
    and external auditors, 1286, 1289, 1309–10, 1312
    to working papers, 391, 392, 394, 409–13, 1309
Account analyses, 991
Account balances, 124–25, 497–98
Accountability
    auditor role, 1079–80, 1354, 1365
    of auditors, 1272
    auditor view, 1079–80
    and controls, 68, 79, 104
    for decisions, 1070
    description, 1072–73
    for environment, 1142
    of external auditors, 1272
    for inventory, 271
    in job specs, 1078
    for performance, 83
    for resources, 79
    for working papers, 674
Accountants
    coordination with, 847, 867
    as external auditors, 1276–77
    recruiting, 882
    training for, 910
Accounting
    basic principles, 85
    controls, 61–62, 90–92
    entry verification, 290
    and FCPA, 206, 1324
    human resource, 1078

proficiency, 880
reconciliations, 934
Accounts, chart of, 991
Accounts payable, 228, 290–91, 581–82
Accounts receivable
    auditing software, 634, 635
    fraud, 1198–99
    monitoring, 853–54
    risk, 126
    sampling, 460
Accuracy
    of data, 592–94
    of reports, 701, 743
    of transactions, 598, 1185
    verification, 1024–25
Accusations, 1193–94
Acquisition(s)
    of external auditors, 1290–91
    funding, 127
    of real estate, 864, 1123, 1133, 1140–42, 1154–56
Act of God, 1142
Activities audited, 807–88
Activity reports, 803, 806–17
    examples, 811–12, 815, 816
Add value. *See* Value-added
Administration. *See also* Continuing education;
        Coordination; Management, of auditing;
        Marketing; Quality assurance; Scheduling;
        Supervision; Training
    Aetna approach, 930–32
    audit assignments, 930, 934
    of audit projects (*see* Audit projects)
    board authorization, 840–45
    budgeting, 903
    computer-assist, 631–35, 673–78, 853–54, 995–1004
        (*see also* Audit tools)
    continuing objectives, 965–68
    documentation, 847, 856–60, 858–60
    evaluation of, 1016
    external auditors, 813, 814, 840, 864–67, 869
    functions and responsibilities, 839–40
    job descriptions, 846–48
    management support, 899, 947
    manuals, 856–60, 900
    marketing, of auditing, 860–64, 965–70
    mentoring, 892–95
    non-audit functions, 869–70, 934, 950, 969, 970

(non)scheduled work, 957
organizational structure, 849–51
politics, 870, 899
of process auditing, 853
productivity, 653, 655, 809–10, 854–56, 1017–19
in rating form, 917
records, 976–84, 990–93
risk analysis, 960–65, 983
self-assessment, 866–67, 1029
software for, 995–1004
staff evaluation, 912–15, 924–29
    forms, 916–23
staffing (*see* Staffing)
staff meetings, 902–3
Standards, 837–39
time reports, 978–82
and TQM, 1017, 1036–42
verification system, 1024–25
visibility, 45, 803–17, 822–31, 843–45, 854–56
Administrative controls, 232. *See also* Control(s);
    Organizational audits
    questionnaire, 183
Admissions, 1196
Advance notice, 188
Advertising
    audit objectives/procedures, 227
    testing, 237–39
    training about, 911
Advisory boards, 861
Aetna Corp., 930–32
Affirmative action, 813
Agency theory, 74
Air, 864, 1151
Aircraft example, 275
Alarm devices, 227
Alcoa, 867
Alcohol, 634–35
Allstate, 129–30
Alternative search engines, 639
Alternatives, search for, 1231
Ambiguity, 244–45, 733
Ambition, 1204
American Institute of Certified Public Accountants
    (AICPA)
    on auditors, 1277–85
    on board communication, 895–96
    on continuous auditing, 329
    and controls, 206
    on controls, 61–63, 90–92
    on environment, 1132–33
    and FCPA, 87–88, 90
    on fraud, 1169–70

on independence, 1306
and risk, 120, 122, 126–27, 161
Analysis
    ability for, 887–90, 894–95
    and control self-assessment, 430
    and creativity, 863
    description, 288–90
    of engagements, 957–59
    proportional, 1184–85
    reverse what-if, 657
Analytical evidence, 325
Analytical procedures. *See also* Operations research
    computer-assisted (*See* Audit tools)
    critical path methods, 507–11
    decision trees, 522
    dynamic programming, 522
    electronic spreadsheets, 657
    exponential smoothing, 523
    for financial analysis, 1192
    fraud detection, 1184–85, 1192, 1208–9
    game theory, 523
    Gantt charts, 511
    key concepts, 493
    learning curves, 272, 520–21
    linear programming, 504–6
    networks, 507–11
    outsourcing, 525–26
    probability theory, 507
    queuing theory, 515–19
    ratio analysis, 497–98
    real-time, 644–45
    regression analysis, 498–503
    sensitivity analysis, 519–20
    simulation, 521–22
    Standards, 492, 494
    and supervision, 1022
    in training, 897
    transaction verification, 1185
    trend analysis, 497–98
Analytical reviews, 316–19
Animosity, 1224–27, 1234–35, 1244–45
Annotation, electronic, 658, 661
Annual reports, 1178
Anticipation
    of audit, 1242
    in listening, 1247
Anxiety, 1242–43
Application controls
    audit trails, 582, 601–3
    in distributed system, 613
    in EDI, 666
    failures, 591–92

input, 592–95
output, 599–601
processing, 595–99
Application interaction, 655, 657, 658
Application software, 544–45, 596
Approaches, 30–32
    abandoned, 381
Approvals
    of audit program, 221, 246, 250
    and data entry, 594
    and enterprise-wide software, 328
    of reports, 716–17
    of work programs, 1384
Arena, 1090
Argyris, Chris, 1088, 1225
Arthur Andersen, 277–78
Articles of incorporation, 992
Artificial intelligence, 672–73
Asbestos, 864
ASCII, 543
Assertions, 124–25, 126, 128
Assets
    access to, 1166
    capital, 298
    conversion loss, 953
    disposal of, 227
    and environmental audits, 1132, 1154
    fixed, 317
    piecemeal sale, 1054
Assignment boards, 988–89
Assignments
    to audits, 930, 934
    and ethics, 930, 1102
    non-audit, 950, 969, 970
    status of, 996–1003
    tracking, 988–89
Association controls, 666
Assumptions
    about computer systems, 636
    for budget, 1069
    in COSO model, 69
    and environment, 1135–36
    of internal control, 1227
    in operations research, 503, 523, 524, 525
    responsibility for, 1064
Assurance audits, 31, 1379, 1382
Assurance services, 1353, 1360, 1370, 1380
Attestation, 1276–77, 1306
Attitude, of auditors. *See also* People skills
    in analytic approach, 495
    in communication, 881, 1230, 1248, 1250–51
    consultative, 1238–41

and evidence, 259–60, 321, 322, 323
and external auditors, 1275, 1298–1301
and findings, 359
flexibility, 880–81, 1232–33
in functional audits, 300–301
ideal, 213
problem-solving, 881
in questioning, 191, 285
rating, 917, 920, 921, 923, 928–29
in report reviews, 777–79, 786–88
in reports, 701–2, 704, 716, 723, 737, 741
risk taking, 868
skepticism, 863, 894–95, 897, 1175–79, 1247
toward clients, 169–70, 712, 1245
Attitude, of clients
    audit activity, 33–34, 687–88
    toward auditors, 1224–27
    and audit reports, 692
    and change, 786–88, 1226, 1228–29
    and computer data, 608, 613
    and control, 81–82, 1099, 1226–27
    in control self assessment, 429–30
    and criticism, 860–62
    of executives, 712–13, 717–18, 805
    expectation gap, 60
    and fraud, 1165–67, 1179–83, 1196
    of management, 60, 687–88, 692, 1041, 1165–66
    in TQM, 1036, 1037, 1041
Attorney-client privilege, 412–13, 1126
Attribute sampling, 454–60, 481
Attribute Standards, 1352, 1355, 1359–62
Audit committees
    accountability to, 1272
    and audit plan, 1335–36
    charter, 1328–32, 1334
    concerns, 1340–41
    and control self-assessment, 427
    evaluation of, 1332, 1338
    expectations, 1340
    and external auditors, 869, 1272–73, 1286, 1331,
        1335, 1336–39
    and fraud, 1205–6
    history of, 1323–24
    independence, 1325, 1326
    interfaces, 1326, 1331–32, 1334–36, 1337–39
    organizational level, 1076
    presentations to, 1339
    reporting relationships, 1338
    responsibilities, 829, 1324–27, 1329–32
    role, 829, 1324–27, 1328–32, 1338–39
    and scheduling, 951
    structure, 1337

and whistleblowing, 40, 829
Audit coverage, 1273–74, 1289, 1307–11, 1339
    redundancy, 1273, 1302
Audit objectives. *See also under* Objectives
    and audit program, 226–30
    documentation, 857
    and field work, 260, 268–73
    and findings, 354
    and productivity, 809–10
    in reports, 708
    responsibility for, 846, 847
    and sampling, 440, 445, 454, 470–72
    and supervision, 1022
    and TQM, 1038
    vs. operating objectives, 267
    in worksheets, 389
Audit opinions. *See* Opinions
Audit plan
    and audit committee, 1335–36
    and controls, 60
    evaluation of, 60
    and risk assessment, 121
Audit procedures, 226, 268–73
Audit programs
    ambiguity, 244–45
    approvals, 221, 246, 250
    audit procedures, 226–30
    background information, 230–31
    benefits, 220
    and budget, 248, 984–85
    changes, 246, 673–74
    client input, 222–23, 248
    criteria, 249–50
    custom *vs.* general, 221, 231, 240, 243–44, 249
    detail level, 250
    documentation of, 231, 247, 858
    for environmental audits, 1128
    examples, 233–35, 241–44
    and final report, 246
    flowcharts, 248
    for fraud examiners, 1192–93
    management discussions, 222–23, 858
    objectives
        of audit, 226–30, 232
        of operation, 225–30
    and permanent file, 992
    preparation
        guidelines, 248–49
        responsibility, 994
        steps, 248–49
    pro forma, 221, 243–44
    for purchasing, 232–36

    purpose, 219–20
    and quality reviews, 1026
    responsibilities, 221
    revisions, 246, 250
    risk prioritization, 236
    scope, 223–24, 226, 248
    for small staff, 247
    software, 221
    steps, 249, 377, 393–94
    summaries in, 385–86
    supervision of, 246, 847–48, 850–51, 853, 994,
        1022
    testing, 221
    time factors, 221, 246, 248
    training about, 897
    in unified audit, 1303
    and working papers, 236, 247, 248
    work steps, 249
Audit projects. *See also* Engagements; Supervision
    budget control, 978–82
    client evaluations, 1035–36
    closing, 995
    demographics, 991
    emergent circumstances, 991
    evaluation of, 1010–13
        (*see also under* Quality assurance)
    follow-up, 990
    forms for, 976–78
    interim reviews, 978
    multi-site, 1034
    and payroll, 982–85
    quality reviews, 1024–27
    records, 976–84, 990–93
    risk analysis, 960–65, 983
    small, 1005
    software for, 995–1004
    status reports, 985–86, 996–1003, 1023
    time controls, 979, 983–84
Audit risk
    account balance, 124–26
    of environmental audits, 1133–34, 1139
    financial statements, 123–24
    and other risks, 128–29
    software, 953
    and unified audit, 1302
Audit supervisors. *See* Supervision
Audit teams
    Aetna approach, 930–32
    expertise, 850–51, 879, 880
    self-directed, 264–65
Audit tools
    database management, 640–42

desktop publishing, 672
electronic working papers, 391–92, 643–44, 671,
     674–76
and environmental audits, 1138
expert systems, 644–46, 645–46, 672–73
fraud detection, 635–39
Internet resources, 639–43
mainframe-based
    data testing, 636
    generalized audit software (GAS), 633–35,
       673
    integrated test facility (ITF), 637
    mapping, 638
    process testing, 636
    simulation, 637–38
    snapshot, 638–39
PC-based
    application interaction, 655
    desktop publishing, 672
    due diligence reporting, 723
    expert systems, 644–46, 672–73
    flow-charting, 662–67
    graphics, 669–71
    mainframe downloads, 673
    multitasking, 653–55, 656, 659
    presentation software, 671, 726
    project management software, 667–69
    scheduling, 988–89
       (see also PERT)
    spreadsheets, 656–58
    training about, 898–99
    word processing, 658–62
project management, 995–1004
and Standards, 1379, 1380
TQM approach, 1038
Audit trails, 582, 601–3, 613
Auditors. See also under Attitude, of auditors;
    Auditors, role of; External auditors; Image;
    Internal auditing
accountability of, 1272
attitudes toward, 1224–27
from branches/divisions, 991
characteristics of, 862–63, 870, 880–81, 913–15
    rating forms, 917, 920, 921, 923, 928–29
    (see also Objectivity)
environmental, 1130–31
evaluation of, 912–15, 1225–26, 1236
    forms, 916–23, 1237–38
in external audits, 1293–98
from within organization, 882, 934, 991
prior experience, 931
staff/line issues, 1081

Auditors, role of. See also Administration; Consulting
    services
accountability, 1079–80, 1354, 1365
added value, 855, 867
    (see also Value-added)
and audit trails, 602–3
and board information, 1320–21
in computer-assisted audit, 635
consultative approach, 1238–41
and controls, 1364–65
in control self-assessment, 427–28
and corrective action, 714–15, 793–97
and deficient conditions, 705
in draft report review, 783–91
engagement analysis, 957–59
enhancement of, 822–29
and enterprise-wide software, 330–31, 605–7, 644
in environmental audits, 1139–40
ethical culture, 935–36
in external audits, 1293–98, 1300–1301
F and R statement, 838–39
and findings, 351
and fraud, 1172–79, 1199–1200, 1360
in functional audits, 300–301
and goals, 198
in governance, 1363, 1365, 1381, 1383
in human resources, 1078
IIA view, 1061
and information systems, 602–3, 620–21, 623–24
and management fraud, 1206
and management reports, 817
marketing, 860–64
non-audit functions, 869–70, 934, 950, 969, 970
    consulting, 304–7
in operating decisions, 1069–70
in organization, 34–41, 1079–84
in organizational audits, 301–3
in participative audit, 1253–54
partner vs. watchdog, 1254–57
in planning, 1065–70
procedure monitoring, 1068
and quality, 862, 925, 971
and report replies, 793–97
and risk, 16, 35, 142–43, 200–203, 807, 970
    in Standards, 1364–66, 1383
and risk management, 163, 1060–61, 1364
security, 562
Standards, 1354, 1379
and stress, 1232–33
TQM approach, 1038
unsupportive management, 829
and values, 1354, 1365, 1381

Authority
    of audit committee, 1328–29, 1335
    of auditor
        establishment of, 838
        in fraud, 1177–79
        over replies, 793–97
    auditor view, 1079–80
    and audit scope, 223
    in CoCo model, 68
    of committees, 288
    communication of, 678
    and corrective action, 370–71
    delegated, 83
    description, 1072
    to discontinue audit, 265
    formal *versus* acceptance, 1072
    and fraud, 1177–79
    functional, 1075, 1081
    of internal audit activity, 837–42
        of managers/supervisors, 846–48
    in job specs, 1078
    of management, 83
    for objectives and standards, 198
    over audit team, 262
    over policies/procedures, 1100
    for purchasing, 235
    and responsibility, 1073
    and systems
        changes, 582–83, 584
        development, 558
    and transaction processing, 591, 594
Authorizations, 1170, 1200
Autocratic management, 1059, 1086
Automated systems. *See also* Enterprise-wide systems
    and controls, 71
    working papers, 390–91
Automobile emissions, 1151

-B-

Babbage, Charles, 1055
Background
    in audit program, 230–31
    environmental issues, 1132–33, 1134–37, 1142
    for fraud investigation, 1192
    of new hires, 936, 1084, 1167
    for presentations, 1257
    in reporting, 707–8, 738
    in report reviews, 784–85
    training about, 897
Backups
    of data, 573–74, 579, 609, 610, 615

        and laptop computers, 676
        software for, 671
        for employees, 1091
Bad debts account, 126
Balances, 124–25, 497–98
Balancing (data entry), 594
Bank accounts, 1178
Bank reconciliations, 934, 1199
Banks
    analytical procedures, 497
    example report, 753–62
    inherent risk, 126, 127
    safe deposit audit, 243–44
    system conversion, 556
Banks v. Lockheed-Georgia, 411
Barrett, M. J., 1274–75
BASIC, 613
Batch processing, 546–47, 592–93, 611
Behavior
    audit effect, 1241–43
    ethical, 1102
    fraud justification, 1196
    in investigations, 1243–44
    while questioning, 1248
Behavioral management, 1056–57
Behavioral organization, 1071
Bell Canada, 132–33
Bell curve, 449–50, 453–54
Benchmarking. *See also* Comparisons
    and control self-assessment, 427
    in field work, 277–78
    and quality assurance, 1017
    of software packages, 605
    in TQM, 1038–39
Benford's Law, 646
Bennett, George E., 61
Berry, L. E., 1275, 1277–78, 1302
Best evidence, 320, 326
Best practices, 162, 277–78. *See also* Practice
        Advisories
Bias
    in fieldwork, 259
    and opinion evidence, 322
    perceptions of, 15
    in sampling, 442, 444, 480
Bibliography of Internal Auditing, 897
Billing, for overhead, 295, 312
Binns, James, 286–87
Binomial distribution, 476
Biometric access, 564
Birkett, William, 16
Blind spot, 1090

Boards. *See also* Assignment boards; Audit committees
  activity reports, 803, 806–17
    examples, 810–12, 815–16
  and audit charter, 14
  and benchmarking, 278
  communication with, 803–10, 1332–34
    example, 810–17
  conflicts of interest, 1166
  and control self-assessment, 427
  definitions, 1370, 1372
  and environmental issues, 1135
  evaluation reports, 803–4, 817–20
  and fraud, 1165, 1178, 1205–6, 1256–57
  internal audit support, 840–45
  and long-range schedule, 947, 950–51
  personal loans, 1327
  quality concerns, 1042–43
  reports, 810, 1332–34
  responsibility of, 1319–22, 1384
  role, 1320
  in *Standards,* 813, 1354, 1384
Boards, assignment, 988–89
Body language, 192, 1189
Bologna, Jack, 1192
Bonding claims, 1166
Bonuses, 1204
Brainstorming, 45, 1231
Branch offices, 991, 1034
Bredice v. Doctors Hospital, 410
Bribery, 1168
Brink, V. Z., 1274–75
Brochures, 843–45, 861, 992
Brown, Dudley E., 687–88
Budgeting
  for advertising, 237
  and audit committee, 1335
  audits of, 298, 1068–69
  billing software, 995
  change, 984–85
  and conflict, 1064
  contingency, 264
  for continuing education, 903
  and control, 85–86
  criteria for, 1068–69
  for engagements, 248, 264, 858, 978–82, 984–85
  monitoring of, 1023
  by operating management, 1068–69
  overruns, 984
  for preliminary survey, 214
  responsibility for, 85
  reviews, 1068–69
  revisions, 984–85
  and schedule, 950, 951, 957–59, 978–82, 984–85
  for special work, 978
  variances, 1069, 1101
  zero-based, 1064
Building. *See* Construction
Burlington Northern, 411
Burnett, R. R., 1242–43
Burns, Ward, 1257
Business Corporations Act, 88–89
Business judgment rule, 1320–22
Business process reengineering, 1060
Business systems, 75–76
Byington, J. Ralph, 1115–16

-C-

Cadbury, 422–23
Calibration, 1146
Cameras, 898
Campbell, Sharon N., 1115–16, 1139
Campfield, W. M., 789–90
Canada
  audit committees, 1323
  Business Corporation Act, 88–89
  control model, 67–69
  control self-assessment, 422–23
  environmental auditing, 1148–50
  legislation, 88–89, 1148–50
Canadian Institute of Chartered Accountants, 329–32
Capital assets, 298
Capital standards, 1095
Cards, 1185–86
  access, 563–64, 614
  for PC security, 609
Carmichael, Douglas R., 1227
Carolina Power and Light, 273
Carpet example, 284–85
Carrying costs, 512
Cars, 318
Cash audits
  announcement of, 188, 1242
  environmental red flags, 1156
  and questioning, 285–86
Cash receipts
  commingling, 353
  control of, 92
  fraud example, 1184
  inherent risk, 126
  risk assessment, 140–42
Cathode ray tubes, 544
Causes
  of calibration loss, 1146

of conflict, 1229
in findings, 356–57
    example, 812, 824–25
    summarizing, 812, 822–29
of fraud
    by employees, 1166–67, 1179–83, 1196
    by management, 1203–5
of hostility, 1224–27
identification of, 80, 792–93, 822–29
and regression analysis, 503
CD-ROM, 599–600, 609, 674, 677
Central Limit Theorem, 449
Central processing units (CPUs), 542, 545, 653
centralization, 1338
CERCLA, 1133, 1141–42, 1152–53
Certification. *See also* Examinations
and contracts, 311
in control self-assessment, 29, 912
credits, 28, 29
eligibility, 27
for environmental auditing, 912, 1113–14
and experience, 29
grandfathered, 26
international aspect, 27, 28
professional development, 904–10
and recruiting, 884
requirement for, 11
for specialties, 29, 32
study material, 11
Chadler, E. W., 1016
Challenge
and employee turnover, 1084
response to, 928
Champy, James, 1060
Change(s)
to audit programs, 246, 673–74
to budget, 984–85
of certification exams, 27, 28
CFIA on, 16421
and contracts, 310, 312, 313
and controls, 81
and CSA, 421
fear of, 786–88, 1226, 1228–29
in information systems (*see under* Information
    systems)
learning curve, 520–21
management of, 616, 1228–29
and operations research, 519–20, 525
planning for, 1067–68
policies/procedures, 84, 1100
in products, 203, 297–301
and report reviews, 780, 786–87

response to, 16
to schedule, 947–48, 968–69
sensitivity analysis, 519–20
to working papers, 391
Characteristics
of auditors, 862–63, 870, 880–81, 913–15
    rating, 917, 920, 921, 923, 928–29
    testing for, 886–90
    (*see also* Objectivity; Skepticism)
of engagements, 930
Charisma, 1227
Charities, 935
Charter
access guarantees, 1256
of audit committee, 1328–32, 1334
and consulting, 44
definition, 1370
and follow-up, 363
for internal auditing, 837–40, 1335
and quality reviews, 1028, 1029
and training, 899
and whistleblowing, 40
Charts
of accounts, 991
for Boards
    in activity reports, 813–17
    deficiency summary, 823
    in evaluation reports, 820–22
of finding trends, 820–22
Gantt, 511, 1056
of organization, 992, 1071
in word processing, 660
Check digits, 594
Check issuers, 1199
Checklists
audit reminder list, 171–73
and computer security, 1169
environmental, 1143–44
quality reviews, 1024, 1025
in TQM, 1041
Chemical plant example, 289–90
Chemicals, hazardous, 864
Chief audit executive
and audit committee, 1334–36
characteristics, 33–34, 45
definitions, 1370, 1386
and emerging problems, 863–64
and external auditors, 869, 1130, 1285–90, 1286
and external reviews, 1029, 1031, 1032–33
independence, 1333–34, 1335, 1338, 1355, 1359
and politics, 870, 899, 935
qualifications, 45

responsibilities
  audit assignments, 934
  to audit committee, 1334–36
  to boards, 804, 1332–34, 1384, 1385
  communication, 697, 1332–36, 1363, 1368–69, 1382
  for development, 965–68
  environmental audits, 1130
  for follow-up, 368, 1369
  outsourced services, 316
  for quality, 1383
      (*see also* Quality assurance)
  for records, 1367
  reports, 697, 700, 717, 1332–34, 1363
  for staff evaluation, 913, 915, 993, 1286
  staffing, 879–80, 883, 884, 1360
  Standards on, 837, 1362–63, 1368–69
  statement of, 837–42
  for supervision, 993
  for training, 993
and risk acceptance, 1369, 1384
Circumstantial evidence, 321
Claims processing, 269–70, 271, 291
Classical management, 1055–56, 1089
Classical organization, 1070
Clean Air Act, 1151
Cleanup, 1133, 1141–42, 1152, 1154
Clerical errors, 352–53
Clients. *See also* Customers
  attitude of (*see* Attitude, of clients)
  attitude toward, 169–70, 712, 1245
      (*see also* People skills)
  audit impact on, 1241–43
  and audit program, 222–23, 248, 249
  communication with, 356, 359, 370, 700–701, 712–16, 1379, 1382
  evaluation by, 1035–36, 1225–26
  external, 1382
  and findings, 356, 358–59, 370
  identification of, 1017
  line and staff, 794, 1224–26
  motivational needs, 1231–32, 1254
  (non)concurrence, 791–92, 818
  outsiders as, 1382
  and outsourcing, 316
  in participative audit, 1251–54
  quoting, 787–88
  relationship with, 14–15, 169–70, 854–56, 1233–40, 1244–45, 1254–58
      (*see also* Control self-assessment (CSA))
  report input, 737, 777–82, 788–89
  role-related stress, 1232–33

  terminology, 861
  testimonial evidence, 324
  training, 862
  uncooperative, 264, 1129, 1244–45
Closed systems, 75–76, 1057
Closing, of engagement, 794–97
Cluster sampling, 444, 481
Coaching, 265, 851, 892–95
Code of ethics. See also Ethics
  applicability, 1375
  on assignments, 930
  and consulting, 45
  on deficiency reporting, 933
  definitions, 1370–71, 1386
  on evidence, 933
  evolution of, 14–15
  and fraud investigation, 1177–78
  and new employees, 897
  on non-audit functions, 869–70
  noncompliance, 1362
  and objectivity, 932–33, 1376, 1377
  principles, 1376
  and training, 899
  updates, 1351, 1356–57
  and whistleblowing, 40, 933
Codes of conduct, 1200, 1375, 1376–77
Coercion, 1228, 1245
Cohen, Fred., 614
Cold sites, 570, 571
Collegial management, 1059
Collusion, 1175, 1199
Color, 829–30
Comments, 991
Commingling, 353
Commissions, 1208
Commitment
  in CoCo model, 68
  to corrective action, 693, 790
  to environment, 1142
  rating, 928–29
  of senior management, 950–51
Commitment reports, 233
Committee of Sponsoring Organizations (COSO)
  audit approach, 96–98
  and boards, 813
  on control, 63, 65–66
  control self-assessment, 267, 420, 422
  description, 1059–60
  on risk, 119–20, 136, 151–57
Committees
  analysis of, 288–89
  audits of, 1082–83

and control self-assessment, 427
description, 1076–77
overlap of, 288–89
safety/disaster, 276, 288
Common Body of Knowledge, 16, 27
Common-size statements, 497, 498
Common user files, 1312
Communication. *See also* Detail, level of; Feedback;
    Questions; Report(s)(ing); Writing
  ambiguity, 244–45, 733
  with audit committee, 829, 1334–37, 1339–42
    (*see also* Audit committees)
  of audit program, 222–23, 248
  with audit staff, 856–60
  with boards, 803–10, 1332–34
    example, 810–17
  charting, 816
  by chief audit executive, 697, 1332–36, 1363,
    1368–69, 1382
  with clients, 356, 359, 370, 700–701, 712–16,
    1379, 1382
  by computer, 390, 663–66, 739
  concurrent, 782–83
  and consulting, 43–44, 45, 47, 831, 1366, 1369
  and controls, 67, 68, 103, 152
    example, 81–82
  of deviations, 1101
  emphasis, 1251
  of engagement status, 739, 837–45, 861–62, 870,
    996–1003
  of ethics, 936, 1102
  evaluation of, 917, 919, 1092–93
  with executives (*see under* Executives)
  with external auditors (*see under* External
    auditors)
  in external reviews (*see under* External reviews)
  of findings (*see under* Findings)
  of fraud (*see under* Fraud)
  graphic aids, 1251
  of grave deficiency, 829
  hierarchical, 1089
  of illegal activities (*see under* Illegal activities)
  (in)formal, 1089
  in interviews, 190–93
    (*see also* Interviews)
  Johari window, 1090
  in leadership, 1089–90, 1092–93
  listening, 192, 1090, 1246–49
  with management (*see under* Operating
    management)
  in meetings, 1250–52
  message setting, 1250

  nonverbal, 192, 1189, 1249
  open door policy, 1087, 1090
  of opinions, 712–16
  oral, 724–26, 738–39, 1250–52
    (*see also* Presentations)
  and organization structure, 85, 1089
  outside organization, 179, 724, 1382
  and outsourcing, 316
  in participative auditing, 1250–51
  of policies, 83
  polish, 1251
  and preliminary survey, 213
  privilege, 410–11, 717
    attorney-client, 412–13, 1126
  of procedures, 84, 286–87
  of recommendations (*see under*
    Recommendations)
  reports, 688–99
    in reviews of, 700–701
    (*see also* Writing)
  of responsibility, 796–97
  of risk, 143, 738
  sequence, 1250–51
  as skill, 880
  Standards on, 348–49, 1354, 1368–69
  tone of, 881, 1230, 1248, 1250–51
  of values, 68
Comparisons. *See also* Benchmarking
  accomplishment *vs.* schedule, 807, 815, 951, 982,
    996, 1101
  across organizations, 498
  in activity reports, 807
    example, 815
  of computer programs, 584, 1169
  for control, 1097
  for data validation, 593
  in environmental audits, 1134
  for fraud detection, 1184–85, 1190, 1192, 1209
  with historical data, 494, 521, 593
  intraorganizational, 498
  of line items, 492–93
  in listening, 1247
  in performance, 86
  for quality assurance, 1017
  between time frames, 494, 497
  trend analysis, 497
Compensating controls, 71
Compensation
  of auditors, 264–65, 899
  of employees, 1078, 1091
  of executives, 911
  as motivation, 1088, 1091

and recruiting, 899, 1078
Competence. *See also* Expertise; People skills; Staff
        evaluations
    Aetna approach, 931
    AICPA view, 1280, 1285
    in analytical auditing, 495
    of audit committee, 1326–27
    of audit management, 951
    of auditors, 301–3, 495, 539–41, 913–15
        characteristics, 862–63, 870, 880–81, 914–15
    basic characteristics, 880–81
    in certification test, 27
    CoCo model, 68
    in *Code of ethics,* 1376, 1377
    of computer supervisors, 1169
    in computer systems, 539–41, 603, 632–33
    for consulting, 43, 1137–38
    and controls, 78
    in COSO model, 153–54
    for environmental audit, 1114, 1120, 1125–27,
        1128, 1130–31
    of evidence, 325–26
    of external auditors, 1284
    fraud detection, 1173–74, 1181–83
    and information systems, 1380
    of new staff, 931, 1078
    in planning, 301–3
    quality reviews, 1028
    and scheduling, 668–69
    standards, 16–22
    in *Standards,* 1360–61
    of supervision, 951
Competency Framework for Internal Auditing (CFIA),
    9, 16–22, 27
Competition
    analytical techniques, 523
    and audit scheduling, 948
    and contracts, 311
    and E-commerce, 603
    and fraud, 1166
    and purchasing, 233, 269, 279, 476–79, 819–20
        cause analysis, 826
        example, 905–9
        sampling, 476–79
Competitive advantage, 547, 929
Compliance
    as control tool, 1101
    definitions, 1371, 1386
    environmental, 864, 925, 1114, 1127, 1135
    ethical, 935–36
    with procedures, 1068
    and quality reviews, 1028

    with regulations, 926
    Sarbanes-Oxley Act, 1327
    and TQM, 1038
Compliance auditing
    definition, 30
    environmental, 292, 1123
    and investigation, 292
Compliance objectives, 139
Compliance programs, 1209–10, 1320
Compliments, 213, 713, 716, 1251
    example, 757
Comprehensive auditing, 30, 240
Computations
    in electronic spreadsheets, 658
    testing, 636, 637
Computer Assisted Audit Techniques (CAAT), 280,
        391, 1380. *See also* Audit tools; Internal
        auditing
Computer centers, 564–66, 670
Computer crime, 1168–70, 1191–92
Computer models, 525
Computer systems
    controls
        in conversion s, 556
        distributed systems, 610, 612, 614
        documentation of, 617
        end-user computing, 608–9
        fire, 564, 565, 568
        firewalls, 329, 643, 671
        power interruption, 565
        risk management, 72, 151
    operating environment, 653–56, 662–63
    program changes, 581–84, 603, 1169–70
    technical services, 550, 568
    terminal locations, 544, 1170
    utilization review, 568
Computers. *See also* Audit tools; Information systems;
        Mainframes; Minicomputers; Personal
        computers; Software
    analytical reviews, 319
    building for, 568
    and control self-assessment, 425
    equipment checks, 585
    and evidence, 325, 326
    and findings status, 739
    hardware, 541–44, 554, 566–69
    maintenance, 566–67
    and sampling, 437–38
Concentration risk, 160
Conclusions
    in findings, 358, 712–14
    report example, 754

and working papers, 383
Conclusive evidence, 321
Conditions
    in findings, 356
    in working papers, 383
Conduct, 1200, 1375, 1376–77
Conferences, 23
Confessions, 1196
Confidence interval, 446–48
Confidence level, 446, 453
Confidentiality
    of application output, 600
    in *Code of ethics,* 1376, 1377
    in control self-assessment, 267
    disk erasure, 609
    and investigations, 831, 1187, 1193–94
    tape disposal, 574–75
    violations, 933, 934
Conflict of interest
    and boards, 1320, 1332
    and consulting, 44
    definitions, 1371, 1386
    detection, 298, 1178
    and facilitators, 428, 432
    formal statement, 1166
    inference of, 934
    and management fraud, 1204–5
    training on, 911
Conflict resolution
    and audit opinions, 791–92, 818
    cause and effect, 792–93
    communication in, 786–88
    and consulting, 45
    in environmental audits, 1129
    between groups, 1086
    with hostile clients, 1244–45
    irreconcilable difference, 787–88
    and outsourcing, 316
    over budget, 1064
    questions, 1248
    and report reviews, 781, 785–90
    and roles, 1232–33
    as skill, 1229–31
    staff *vs.* line, 1074–75
Conjecture, 890, 891
Consistency
    of data, 615
    and manuals, 900
    of policies, 83
    of reports
        content, 743
        distribution, 717

format, 705–6
    in writing, 733
    and wrongdoers, 1166
Conspiracy statute, 1167
Constraints, 206–7
Construction
    analytical procedures, 496
    contracts, 310–11, 313
    training about, 911
Consultants. *See also* External auditors
    dealing with, 315, 525–26
    and environmental audits, 1125–27, 1128, 1132, 1135
    evaluation of, 1137–38
    forensic specialists, 1170–71
    and management fraud, 1206–7
    monitoring, 525–26, 926
Consultative approach, 31, 1238–41
Consultative management, 1086
Consulting services
    for auditing evaluation, 1021
    and boards, 814, 831
    communication, 43–44, 45, 47, 831, 1366, 1369
    and control weakness, 1383
    documentation, 1366
    due professional care, 46–47, 1361
    fieldwork, 303–7
    guiding principles, 44–47
    and independence, 43, 44, 46, 1360
    objectives/scope, 1366
    objectivity, 43, 46
    for operations research, 525–26
    opportunities for, 1379
    reports, 47
    and risk, 43, 44, 47, 1383
    risk management, 1364, 1369
    standards, 42–44
    in *Standards,* 45, 304, 1361, 1364, 1365, 1366, 1367
        definition, 1371, 1387
        proposed change, 1380
    types of, 46
Contingency organization, 1071
Contingency plans
    and environmental audits, 1129
    evaluation of, 276–77
    and fieldwork, 264
    for information systems, 569–71, 583, 615
    for telecommunications, 579
Contingency theory, 1058, 1087
Continuing education. *See also* Training
    for control self-assessment, 912

environmental auditing, 912
home study, 910
IIA role, 902, 903–4
in-house programs, 910–11
motivation for, 901
professional development, 904–10
research projects, 904
example, 905–9
scheduling for, 965–68
for senior auditors, 902
and staff evaluation, 913
staff meetings, 902–3
Continuing objectives, 965–68
Continuous auditing, 329–32
Contract audits, 310–14
Contracts
categories, 310–14
data processing, 295
environmental context, 1157
with federal government, 1167–68
fraud, 1179
monitoring, 926
record retention, 1179
reviews of, 1146
risks, 311–12
Contributions, 935
Control(s). *See also* Application controls; Fraud;
Internal control(s); Prevention
in accounting, 61–62, 90–92
adequacy, 1370
administrative, 232
questionnaire, 183
attitude toward, 81–82, 1099, 1226–27
auditing of, 89–90, 95–104, 194–95, 199–200,
824–26, 1099–1102
Standards, 1364–65
automated, 330
benefits, 64, 73–74, 77
characteristics, 79–82
CoCo model, 68, 69
communication of, 67, 68, 103, 152
example, 81–82
components, 82–86
for computers (*see* Application controls; Computer
systems; Electronic data interchange (EDI);
Information system audits; Information
systems; Internet; Personal computers;
Security)
corrective, 72–73
COSO model, 66–67, 96–98, 151–57
criteria for, 59
in CSA, 433–34

cycles, 90–92
definitions, 61–64, 67, 69–71, 1371, 1387
detective, 72, 73, 150–51
embedded, 635
excessive, 101–2, 104, 1094
and executives, 103, 1320
failures, 80–82, 102–4, 678, 1176
feedback from, 1099–1100
feed forward, 1098–99
guidelines, 95–96
human element, 73, 81–82, 102–4
imposed *vs.* self-directed, 1235–36
levels of, 57–58
master, 1100–1101
objectives of, 78, 81–82, 95–96
placement, 80
preventive, 72, 150–51
primary and secondary, 149–50
prioritization, 91
and probability, 73, 1171, 1202
in process auditing, 852–53
questionnaire, 183–84
and regulation, 87–88
reliability, 73, 78, 79
responsibility for, 68, 77
and risk, 121–22, 141–42, 200–205
matrix analysis, 137, 148–50, 203–5, 249
(*see also* Control risk)
self-directed, 1235–36
span of, 1073
Standards, 57–58, 1139–40
standards for, 59, 78–79, 276–77, 1095–96
in telecommunications, 578
time factor, 79, 1099–1100
in virtual organization, 94–95
weakness, 1332–33
Control environment
components, 70–71
in COSO model, 66
definition, 1371
SAC model, 70–71
Control framework, 70–71
Control matrix, 137, 148–50, 203–5, 249
Control points, 1094, 1095, 1101
Control procedures, 71
Control processes, 1371
Control records, 597
Control risk
in audits, 95, 98
calculation of, 645–46
description, 127
and EDI, 135–36

in environmental audits, 1134
levels of, 135–36
and other risks, 128
Control self-assessment (CSA)
    background, 419–22
    certification, 29, 912
    communication, 428, 434
    and conventional auditing, 428–29
    description, 31–32, 266–67, 422–24, 1098
    facilitators, 424–26, 428, 429–34
    implications, 427
    management, 427
    of morale/trust, 1087
    and outside resources, 427
    pitfalls, 430–31
    reports, 90, 267, 434
    and risk, 426–27, 429
    and safety, 277
    training, 427, 431
    and value-added, 855
    verification of, 429
    workshops, 31–32, 267, 424–26, 430
        preparation for, 432
Control systems, 74–77, 95–96, 1093–99
    evaluation of, 1099–1102, 1364–65
Controlling function
    approaches, 1098–99
    auditor view, 1099–1102
        (see also under Control(s))
    basic concepts, 1093–98
    and R&D, 101
Cooperation. See also Participative auditing
    with external auditors, 1275–77, 1286, 1293–98,
        1311–13
        (see also under Coordination)
    importance of, 1233–40
    lack of, 264, 1129, 1244–45
Coordination
    of audit coverage, 1307–11
    and boards, 813
    common user files, 813, 1312
    cosourcing, 32–33, 864–67, 1026, 1305–7
    with external auditors, 1272–78
        AICPA views, 1277–85
        and audit committee, 1336
        coverage, 953, 1273, 1336
        IIA views, 1285–93
        responsibility for, 869, 1130, 1285–90, 1363
        and schedule, 952
        statement of policy, 840
        total coverage, 1302–13
        unified audit, 1302–5

of fraud investigation, 1188–90
with industrial engineering, 970, 971
of internal controls, 970–71
against management fraud, 1206
with other control groups, 14, 970, 971
of personal computers, 608
Practice Advisory on, 1300
with quality control, 970, 971
responsibility for, 1363
with safety, 970, 971
with security, 970–71
weakness and problems, 1313
Copies, 1207–8
Core functions, 33–34
Corporate culture
    and auditing function, 33
    and CSA, 433–34
    ethics, 935–36
    fraud deterrence, 1166–67
    as inherent risk, 127
    and internal auditing, 870
Corporations, separate, 992–93
Corrective action
    adequacy criteria, 368–70
    assurances of, 189
    auditor authority, 793–97
    client input, 700
    for controls, 90, 97
    control self-assessment, 424, 425–26
    as control tool, 1097–98
    in data processing, 600
    and environmental audits, 1129, 1138, 1146
    for environmental infractions, 292, 1133
    in executive summary, 699
    in findings, 358, 1023, 1146
    form for, 826
    lack of, 1333
    in participative audit, 1254
    and preliminary surveys, 188–89, 213, 370–71
    recommendations for, 294–95, 692–94, 778–79
    in report, 751, 831
    responsibility for, 358, 751, 778–79, 794–97,
        839–40, 848, 1333, 1369
    scrap management, 299–300
    and suggestions, 350
    and supervisors, 1023
    timeliness, 1098, 1101
Corrective controls, 72–73
Correlation coefficient, 501
Correspondence. See Memos
Corroborative evidence, 321, 325

Cosourcing, 315–16, 866, 1128, 1307, 1326n. *See also* Consultants; Expertise; External auditors
Cost(s)
    of audit activity, 929, 932, 949–50
    of cleanup, 1133, 1141–42, 1154
    of engagements, 846, 982
    of environmental audits, 1126, 1129
    of environmental liability, 1134
    evaluation of, 279
    of information systems, 619–21
    inventory-related, 515
    and preliminary survey, 176–77
    in purchasing, 279, 512
    queuing theory, 515–19, 1057
    of recruiting, 1078
    reductions, 176–77
    standards of, 1095
Cost benefit studies, 308, 1057
Cost-effectiveness
    and accounting, 85
    of assurance, 1380
    in audit coverage, 1273–75, 1288, 1303
    and audit programs, 231
    of consulting services, 1361
    and controls, 72, 79, 80, 142
    of (de)centralization, 1338
    of encryption, 624
    of internal auditing, 806–7, 809, 814
        example, 812
    of material records, 319
    of new process, 272
    of operations research, 524
    of PC acquisition, 653
    of procured items, 234
    in program audits, 308
    of risk management, 150, 157–59, 161, 206
    of self-directed audit teams, 264–65
    of system creation, 554
    and telecommunication, 578
Cost-plus contracts, 310–11, 312, 314, 1167–68, 1179
Cost recovery, 911
Counsel. *See* Lawyers
Counterfeit documents, 1170–71
Court decisions
    SEC v. Worldwide Coin Investments, 1042–43
    on working paper access, 409–12
Courtney, Robert, 157–58
Cover-ups, 1167–68
Created errors, 1201
Creativity, 862–63, 928
    versus controls, 978
    and TQM, 1038

Credibility
    dimensions of, 1250
    and environmental audits, 1125
    of findings, 366–67
    and measurement, 1097
    and outsourcing, 1306
    and report reviews, 700, 701, 786
Credit
    letters of, 1156
    and permanent file, 992
    and risk, 126, 127
    by seller, 496
Credit cards, 1167, 1185–86
Credit union auditing, 32
Crime. *See also* Environmental audits, legal factors; Fraud
    with computers, 1168–70, 1191–92
    organized, 1167–68
    testing for, 1201
    white-collar, 1163, 1165, 1168
Criteria
    for environmental audits, 1129
    in findings, 354–56
Critical path, 507–11, 508
Criticism, 704, 785, 860–62, 1246–47. *See also* People skills; Recommendations
Cross-referencing, 386–88, 392
Cultural factors, 1085
Cumulative monetary amount, 465–70
Custodial management, 1059
Customers. *See also* Clients
    and enterprise-wide software, 331
    of environmental audits, 1117
    and internal auditing, 855
    revenue standards, 1095
    in TQM, 1036, 1037, 1041
Cyberspace, 1191–92

-D-

Daigneault, Robert, 1148–50
Data
    anomalous, 646
    for comparisons, 1097
    computed, 636, 637
    corruption, 584
    encryption of, 609
    environmental, 1135–36
    industry-wide, 1192, 1209
    missing, 584
    numerical, 593, 594, 596
    for operations research, 524

residual, 609
security of, 559–61
    (*see also under* Security)
testing, 636
transmission of, 577–78, 611, 667
    (*see also* Telecommunications)
uniformity, 615
validation, 592–94, 612
for working papers, 383, 388
Data entry
    batch mode, 592–94
    in EDI, 666
    in enterprise-wide system, 328, 605
    memoposting, 546–47
    real time, 547
    single entry, 642
Data processing
    batch processing, 546–47, 611
    contract, 295
    controls, 541, 547–52, 556
    distributed system, 611–15
    documentation of, 615–18
    modification utilities, 613
    risk, 547–49
Data storage
    devices, 542–43, 599–600
    environment, 565
    and packaged software, 605
    precautions, 550–51, 556, 572–75
    training about, 911
    working paper archives, 677
Database management systems, 640–42
Databases
    and audit programs, 674–75
    as audit tool, 642
    of controls, 328
    in distributed system, 615
    environmental data, 1150
    of hazardous waste, 1152
    project management, 1003–4
    relational, 640–42
    testing, 636–38
    and working papers, 675
Date checks, 596
Davis, Ralph C., 1056
Decentralization, 1076, 1082
Decision trees, 522
Decisions
    and accounting, 85, 491
    auditor role, 36–37, 1069–70
    by boards, 1319–22
    by committees, 1076–77

conflict in, 523, 1230
consequences of, 522
due diligence audits, 723–24
equipment acquisition, 621
and financial statements, 491
by groups, 1065
influences, 1063
make-or-buy, 233, 554, 555, 604–7
management type, 1056–57, 1086–87
(non-)programmable, 1065
responsibility for, 1069–70
simulations, 521–22
software acquisition, 233, 554, 555
source documents, 610
spreadsheets, 610
steps, 1064
time frame, 522
Deferred projects, 957
Deficiencies. *See also* Findings
    causes, 792–93, 822–29
    communication of
        to Board, 808, 822–29
            form, 827
        and good news, 1251
        to operating manager, 1243
        over operating manager, 1257–58
        Standards, 933
        time factor, 1245, 1251
    sampling for, 470–72
    unreported, 933
    urgent, 829, 1245
Definitions
    of ambiguous terms, 245
    glossary (of *Standards*), 1370–72
    of internal auditing, 8–10, 1372
Delegation, 83, 1073, 1080
Demographics, 991
Department stores, 126
Departmentalization, 1075–76, 1082
Design control, 1145
Detail, level of
    in audit programs, 250
    for boards, 804–5, 812–13, 829–31
    in control feedback, 1100–1101
    and documentation, 1251
    in environmental audits, 1123
    for executives, 698–99, 812–13, 829–31
    in findings, 355–56, 371, 786, 1257–58
    in oral reports, 726
    in presentations, 371
    in procedures, 84
    and process management, 853

in reports, 696–97, 703–4, 714, 790, 1243
 draft reviews, 786
 example, 749–51, 757–62
in system design, 555
in working papers, 395
Detection risk, 128
Detective controls
 description, 72–73
 and risk management, 150–51
 in virtual organization, 94
Development projects, 965–68
Deviations, 1100
Dial-back systems, 579
Dicksee, L. R., 61
Difference estimation, 462
Direct evidence, 321, 325
Directed sample, 438
Directing function. *See also* Leadership
 auditor view, 1090–93
 leadership concepts, 1085–90
 and morale, 1087
 open-door policy, 1087, 1090
 and organizational audits, 302
 preliminary survey, 194
 R&D example, 100
Disagreement, irreconcilable, 787–88. *See also* Conflict resolution
Disaster planning, 264, 276–77, 564, 569–71. *See also* Contingency plans
Disaster recovery, 569–70, 571
Disclosure
 and board lawsuits, 1322
 of *Code of ethics* noncompliance, 1362
 in environmental audits, 1125, 1138, 1150
 and external auditors, 1282
 of plan changes, 1313
 of restricted information, 717–18
 of risk, 160–61
 Sarbanes-Oxley Act, 1327
 of *Standards* noncompliance, 697, 1362, 1368
Discovery sampling, 459–60, 481
Disk drives, 543
Disk management, 573–75
Diskettes, 1170
Dissatisfiers, 1088
Distributed processing, 611–15
Distribution
 Benford's Law, 646
 of budget, 1069
 of environmental regulations, 1129
 of reports, 697
  consistency, 717

in environmental audits, 1129
 examples, 746, 755, 763
 software, 576
Diversity, 1085, 1102
Documentary evidence, 323, 324, 325, 326
Documentation. *See also* Manuals; Records; Working papers
 of activities audited, 807–8
 for audit personnel, 847, 856–60
 and audit programs, 231, 247, 858
 of audit replies, 794
 for audit reporting, 738, 858
 for computer systems, 599, 617–18, 1169 (*see also* Logs)
 of consulting services, 1366
 and control, 71, 78
 counterfeit, 1170–71
 of engagements, 857–60, 976–78, 1023, 1366, 1367, 1372, 1381
 environmental, 1128, 1136, 1141, 1145
 of error-handling, 596, 600
 as evidence, 320, 323, 324, 326
 of FCPA compliance, 409
 of findings, 786
 of follow-up, 968
 of human resources, 859
 of information system audit, 618
 of information systems, 615–18, 620, 621, 624
 of interviews, 193
 inventory control, 271, 289–90
 of investigations, 1174–75
 of memos, 305–7
 for new employees, 892, 893
 of operations research models, 523–24
 of organization, 83
 planning for, 263
 of policies, 83
 for preliminary survey (*see under* Preliminary surveys)
 of procedures, 84, 286–87
 of processing interruptions, 600
 of regulation compliance, 89
 of reports, 738, 858, 859–60
 of reviews, 782, 857
 and risk, 127
 for standards, 610
 and supervision, 900
 as support, 1251
 of telecommunications, 580
 of testing, 738
 word processing, 658–62
 working papers, 858

of work instructions, 1145
Dollar-unit sampling, 465–70
Downsizing
    auditor role, 1084
    of audit staff, 850–51, 853, 931, 932
    and control, 93–94
    and control self-assessment, 421
    and training, 902
Drag and drop editing, 658, 660
Drucker, Peter, 1058
Drugs, 634–35
Due diligence, 911, 1150
Due diligence auditing, 723–24, 1123
Due professional care
    in consulting, 46–47, 1361
    environmental issues, 1142
    and fraud detection, 1173, 1176–77
    and operating standards, 355
    risk perception, 201
    Standards, 1361, 1380
    and standards, 198
Duplication. *See also* Redundancy
    of activities, 1083
        of internal and external auditors, 953, 1273,
            1285–86, 1336
    of process checks, 585
Durkheim, Emile, 1055
Duties, segregation of
    and advertising, 238
    and cash receipts, 286
    collusion, 1175, 1199
    and computers, 1169
    as control, 82, 95
    downsizing effect, 95
    as fraud deterrent, 1198–99
    and information systems, 550–51, 576, 598, 612,
        614, 620
Dye, Kenneth M., 1115–16
Dymoski, E. V., 866–67
Dynamic programming, 522, 1057

-E-

Eavesdropping, 578
EBCDIC, 543
E-commerce, 133–35, 331–32, 603, 646
Economic order quantity (EOQ), 512–15
Economy, 224. *See also* Cost-effectiveness
Economy audits, 197, 357, 718
Edison, 265–66
Education, 881–82, 900, 901. *See also* Continuing
    education; Training

Effect, 357–58
Effectiveness
    of controls, 1354
        (*see also* Control(s))
    definition, 225
    of new program, 272
    and TQM, 1038
Efficiency
    of audit coverage, 1274
    and controls, 103
    definition, 225
    in information systems, 618–21
    in manufacturer audit, 271–72
    of service organizations, 515–19
    and TQM, 1038
Efficiency audits, 197, 357, 718
Egyptians, 4
Electromagnetic noise, 566
Electronic data interchange (EDI)
    controls, 137, 663, 666–67
    flowchart example, 663–65
    risks, 135–37, 331, 332, 663
    software, 665
    transactions, 663–66
    trusted third party, 663, 665, 667
    and vendor invoices, 94–95
Electronic voting, 425
Electronic working papers, 391–92, 643–44, 671, 674–
    76
    training about, 899
Elements, of findings, 263, 353–59, 709–15
Embezzlement
    conditions for, 74, 1198–99
    danger signs, 1183
    definition, 1164
    testing for, 1201
    verification example, 291
Emergencies. *See also* Backups; Contingency plans
    and audit activity, 814
    coping with, 276–77
    program changes, 583, 584
    reporting on, 831
Emergent circumstances, 991
Emissions, 1151
Emotions, 1230, 1247
Empathy. *See also* People skills
    in auditors, 787–88, 881, 1232–35, 1241–43,
        1245
        lack of, 1226
    in conflict resolution, 1230
    in facilitators, 431

Encryption
    cost factors, 624
    in data transmission, 578
    description, 609
    in EDI, 667
    of PC files, 611
Engagements. *See also* Audit projects; Prior audits;
    Supervision
    acceptance of, 1363
    analysis of, 957–59
    approaches, 857
        abandoned, 381
    assignments to, 930, 934
    attestation, 1276–77, 1306
    behavioral impact, 1241–43
    closing, 793–97
    control of (*see* Audit projects)
    deferred, 957
    definition, 1371
    discontinuation, 213, 265
    documentation, 857–60, 976–78, 1023, 1366,
        1367, 1372, 1381
    evaluation of, 1010–11
    management/supervision, 846–48, 1367
    objectives of, 1365, 1366, 1371, 1383
    phases, 1354
    planning, 261–62, 1365–66, 1381–82
    prioritization, 265–66
    quality rating, 734–35
    records of, 1367
    reporting on, 803–10, 848
        to board, 830, 1332–33
    resources for, 261–62, 930, 934, 948, 1366
    risk assessment, 1384, 1388
    scheduling, 946, 947, 949
    scope, 857, 1366
    segments, 822, 858, 983
    staffing, 261–62, 930, 934, 948, 1078, 1366
Engineering drawings, 396–407
Engineering services, 295
England, 4–5
Enterprise-wide systems
    and control, 605, 644–46
    description, 327–32
    (dis)advantages, 644–46
    and fraud, 330–31
    and sampling, 437
Entrapment, 1201
Environment. *See also* Control environment
    controls, 1134–35
    for data storage, 565
    for ethics, 1102, 1199–1200

and fraud, 1165–67, 1180, 1190, 1197, 1199–
    1200, 1202
legislation, 1129, 1135, 1138, 1141–42, 1151–53
recycling, 202, 285
responsibility for, 864, 1132–35, 1141, 1142,
    1152, 1153
and risk, 1117, 1140–41
standards, 1142–47
    ISO 14000, 1142–44
unique obligations, 1157
Environmental Auditing Roundtable, 32
Environmental audits
    benefits, 1115–17, 1124–25
    certification, 912, 1113–14
    checklist, 1143–44
    customers, 1117
    equipment, 1128
    and ethics, 912
    example findings, 1145–46
    frequency, 1126
    and internal control, 1139–40
    internal *vs.* external, 1122–23
    legal factors, 1125, 1129, 1138–39, 1140, 1148–
        50
    liability, 1117, 1123, 1124, 1134–37, 1140, 1141,
        1148–50
        red flag, 1154–56
    outsourcing, 1114, 1120, 1125–28, 1130–32, 1135
    planning, 1125, 1128–30, 1132–33
    potential problems, 1138
    potential responsibility, 1132–35, 1141
    qualifications, 1114, 1120
    rating schemes, 1134, 1147
    real estate transactions, 864, 1123, 1133, 1140–42,
        1154–56
    records, 1132, 1135–36
    as red flag, 1154
    reports, 1125, 1127, 1129, 1138
    reviews, 1129
    risk assessment, 1126, 1127, 1132–34, 1139–41
    sampling, 1129
    scheduling, 1128
    staffing, 1114, 1120, 1126–27, 1128, 1130–32,
        1130–33, 1137–38
    steps, 1118–22
    structure, 1147
    techniques, 1128–30
    types, 1122–24
    working papers, 1125–26, 1129, 1138
        access to, 412
Environmental protection
    audit objectives/procedures, 227

auditor roles, 863–64
  evaluation of, 925, 926
Environmental Protection Agency, 1152
Equal opportunity, 813
Equipment. *See also* Computers
  calibration, 1146
  and contracts, 311, 312
  for control self-assessment, 425
  for environmental audits, 1128
  for information systems, 621
  ISO guidelines, 1043–44
  in permanent file, 992
  purchasing, 234
  retired office, 289
  for testing/research, 202–3
Errors
  clerical, 352–53
  handling of, 1257–58, 1368
  and permanent file, 992
  in procurement report, 820
  in reports, 697, 717, 743, 744
    verification system, 1024–25
  in sampling, 454–60, 467, 475–76, 480
  as tests, 1201
  transaction processing, 585, 592–95, 600, 604
Escrow accounts, 1156
Estimation risk, 160
Ethical culture, 935–36, 1165–67
Ethics. *See also Code of ethics*
  and boards, 1320
  CoCo model, 68
  communication of, 936, 1102
  and control self-assessment, 428
  and environmental auditing, 912
  management role, 1102
  in management theories, 1057
  and professional identity, 11
  prohibited activities, 10
  responsibility for, 1379
  Sarbanes-Oxley Act, 1327
Ethnic factors, 1085
Europe, ISO 9000, 1043–44
Evaluation. *See also* Staff evaluations
  of audit activity, 1010, 1018–19, 1021, 1361–62
    reciprocal, 1021
    (*see also* Activity reports)
  of audit committees, 1332, 1338
  of audit management, 951, 1013–21
  of audit managers, 951
  of auditors, 912–15, 1225–26, 1236
    forms, 916–17, 920–23, 1237–38

  substandard, 934
  of audit plan, 60
  of audit supervisors, 918–23, 951
  by clients, 1035–36, 1225–26
  of consultants, 1137–38
  of contingency plans, 276–77
  as control, 1097
  of control system, 1099–1102, 1364–65
  of engagements, 1010–11
  of environmental impact, 1157
  of environmental liability, 1132–37
  and external auditors, 1137–38, 1283–90, 1300,
    1311
  in field work, 279–80, 293–95
  focus of, 1097
  of human resources, 866
  by lawyers, 1125
  of leadership, 1090–93
  and listening, 1247
  of loss, 1188
  of management
    auditor role, 30
    constraints, 206–7
    decision-making, 1070
    organizing, 1079–90
    planning, 1065–70
  of morale, 1087
  of operations research, 523–25
  in program audits, 308
  self-, 866–67
  of software, 606–7, 611
  of specialists, 1137–38
  of standards, 1099
Evaluation reports, 803–4, 817–20
Event concept, 603
Evidence. *See also* Legal evidence
  audit, 319–20, 324–26
  confessions as, 1196
  of environmental infraction, 1141
    (*see also under* Working papers)
  of fraud, 1192–93
  handling, 326–27, 392
  (in)adequacy, 933
  legal, 319–24
  physical, 324
  recognition of, 890, 891, 894–95
  and reporting, 701
  responsibility for, 847, 848
  and risk assessment, 128
  standards for, 325–26
  working papers as, 378

Examinations
    for certification, 27
    content, 28–29
    earliest, 12
    format, 28
    and professions, 11
Examples. *See also* Forms
    memo report, 763–65
    of peer review, 1032–33
    of reports, 746–51, 753–62
    of TQM, 1040–42
Exceptions, 1099–1100
Executive summaries, 698–99, 807–8
    one-page report, 829–30
Executives
    abuse by, 717–18
    commitment of, 950–51
    communication with, 698–99, 712–16, 805, 817–
        18, 968, 1332–33
    compensation of, 911
    and consulting services, 304–5
    and controls, 103, 1320
    and environmental issues, 1135
    expectations, 712–13, 805
    and fraud, 1165, 1177–78, 1202–9, 1256–57
        by corporate officer, 933
    interference by, 264
    involvement of, 950–51, 968–69
    loans to, 1327
    and premises, 1064
    presentations to, 371
    quality concerns, 1042–43
    removal of, 1320
    reports on, 717–18
    reports to, 803
    special requests, 935
Exit interviews, 995, 1032–33
Expectancy theory, 1088
Expectation gap, 60
Expectations
    of audit committees, 1340
    and control self-assessment, 430
    and delegation, 1073
    deviations from, 493, 496
    of executives, 712–13, 805
    and motivation, 1088
    and operations research, 501, 524
Expected value, 159
Expenditure cycle, 90, 91, 224
Expenses
    legal, 1178
    pension, 126

    travel, 460, 900
Experience
    of environmental auditors, 1131
    and scheduling, 957
    and staffing, 883–84, 931
Expert systems, 644–46, 672–73
Expert witnesses, 322
Expertise
    of audit committee, 1326–27
    of audit staff, 850–51, 879, 880, 1380
    and boards, 1320–21
    in computer systems, 603
    and continuous auditing, 329
    for control self-assessment, 427
    in distributed systems, 615
    for engagements, 261–62
    and environmental audits, 1114, 1120, 1125–27,
        1128, 1130–31, 1135
    evaluation of, 1137–38
    forensic specialists, 1170–71
    of operating personnel, 855
    in operations research, 525–26
    and outsourcing, 261, 315–16, 603, 865
    in participative audit, 1253–54
    as power, 1227
Exponential smoothing, 523, 1057
Extended records, 639
External auditors. *See also* Cosourcing; Outsourcing
    accountability, 1272
    acquisition, 869, 1290–91
    attitude toward, 1275, 1298–1301
    and audit committee, 869, 1272–73, 1286, 1331,
        1335, 1336–39
    as auditor reviewers, 1020–21
    and benchmarking, 278
    communication with, 1287, 1289–90, 1309, 1312
    as consultants, 303
    and continuous auditing, 329–30
    coordination with (*see under* Coordination)
    differences, 7–8
    in environmental audits, 1126, 1128, 1130, 1132,
        1139–40
    evaluation, 1137–38, 1283–90, 1300, 1311
    evolution of, 12
    flowchart sharing, 662–63
    focus, 30
    IIA views, 1274–75, 1285–93
    and independence, 1291–93, 1312
    and internal controls, 1283
    and management fraud, 1206
    mission, 6
    non-audit functions, 1291, 1326

objectivity, 1020
oversight, 1282, 1286
and politics, 870
Practice Advisories, 869
quality assurance, 1283–84
responsibility for, 869, 1285–90
reviews of, 1283–85
and schedule, 950, 952, 1309
service types, 1291
and small activity, 1005
Standards, 1283–93
training, 1310
unified audit, 1302–5
and working papers, 394
External audits, 1293–98, 1300–1301
External clients, 1382
External financial reporting cycle, 91
External reviews
communication, 1029, 1031, 1032–33, 1035
by consultants, 1021
by external auditors, 1020–21
frequency, 1013, 1362
by peers, 1020, 1021, 1027–33
Practice Advisories, 1028–29, 1031
by professional organizations, 1021, 1034–35
reciprocal, 1021
Standards, 1028–29, 1031, 1383
External service providers, 1372, 1387. *See also*
Consultants; External auditors

-F-

Facade, 1090
Facilitators, 424–26, 428, 429–34
Facilities
abandoned, 1136
and environmental audits, 1128, 1136
environmental issues, 1123–24, 1127
in permanent file, 992
tours of, 208–9
Facts
listening for, 1247
in reports, 701, 743, 933
vs. conjecture, 890, 891
False arrest, 1194
False claims statute, 1167
False statements statute, 1167–68
Fayol, Henri, 1055–56
Fear
of audit, 1242–43
of change, 1226, 1228–29
of punishment, 1226

Feasibility
and efficiency, 619
in system life cycle, 553, 554, 558
Federal Organizational Sentencing Guidelines, 1320
Federal Trade Commission, 410
Feedback. *See also* Evaluation
on auditors, 912–15, 1225–26, 1235, 1236
forms, 916–23, 1237–38
and controls, 1099–1100
forms for, 916–23, 1237–38
and leadership, 1089
of meetings, 385, 1252
timeliness, 1099–1100
Fees
and ethics, 934
and external auditors, 1272, 1273, 1275
for legal services, 1154, 1155
as red flag, 1054, 1055
Felonies, compounding, 1195
Fernandes, J. J., 902, 912
Fiedler, F. E., 1087
Field checks, 593
Field work. *See also* Evidence; Testing; Working
papers
accountability for, 674
analysis, 288–90
(*see also* Analytical procedures)
analytical reviews, 316–19
benchmarking, 277–78
for consulting, 303–7
contingency plans, 264
continuous auditing, 329–32
for contract audits, 310–14
in control self-assessment, 266–67
definitions, 259, 260
and enterprise-wide software, 327–32
evaluation, 279–80, 293–95
in fraud investigation, 1192–93
for functional audits, 297–301
for integrated auditing, 314–15
for management studies, 303–7
measurement in, 260, 276
methods, 262–63, 1384
for activity types, 271–73
for process evaluation, 282–95
in organizational audits, 301–3
preparation for, 260–64
procedure selection, 267–73
program audits, 308–10
quality review of, 1031
questioning, 285–87
(*see also* Questions)

rating forms, 916–17, 918–19
reminder list, 172–73
SMART auditing, 273–74
standards, 275–77, 281
in stop-and-go audit, 265
supervision of, 918–19, 994
and technology, 315–16, 327–33
timing/sequence, 262
verification, 290–91
File balancing, 600, 614
File libraries, 50–51
Files. *See also* Data; Records; Retention
backups, 573–74, 579, 609, 610, 615
and laptop computers, 676
software for, 671
changes to, 674, 675, 1169
common user, 813, 1312
deletion of, 609
footing, 635
labels, 594, 596
linking, 659
master, 1170
names, 573
parameter, 597
payroll, 635
permanent, of audits, 990–93
read-only, 674
system control, 596
tracking, 573
versions, 596
word processing, 659, 661
Financial analysis, 1192
Financial auditing, 29, 30, 139, 382
Financial information, 497, 933, 1326, 1330
Financial ratios, 497–98
Financial reports, 139, 1178
Financial statement assertions, 124–26, 128
Financial statements
assertions, 124–26, 128
and audit committees, 1325, 1329–30
audit risk, 123–24
and decisions, 491
environmental issues, 1132
and external auditors, 1313
inherent risk, 126–27
Financing. *See* Credit
Financing cycles, 91
Findings
abstracts, 364, 365, 367
adding value, 351–52
(*see also* Value-added)
charting, 820–22

charts, 820–22
client views, 356, 359, 370, 700–701
communication of
to board, 807–8, 822–29
charts, 820–22
concurrent, 782–83
detail level, 352–53, 819–20, 826
examples, 747–51, 756–57, 764–65, 807–8,
808, 1145–46
good news, 1251
graphic aids, 371
over manager, 1257–58
preparation for, 359, 364, 365, 370, 407
before report, 777–79
Standards, 348–49, 1354, 1368–69, 1379,
1382
status, 739
summary reports, 367, 807–8
(*see also under* Summaries)
timing, 705, 1243, 1245, 1251, 1384
of control self-assessment, 426, 434
control *vs.* performance, 819–20
credibility, 366–67
detail level, 355–56
effect in, 357–58
elements of, 263, 353–59, 709–15
of environmental audits, 1129, 1145–46
follow-up, 367–71
and goals, 354–55
(in)significant, 352–53
and judgment, 351
major *vs.* minor, 819–20, 826
materiality, 1018, 1129
memos, 364, 365, 367, 695
Practice Advisories, 348–49
of prior audits, 382
and purpose, 898
and recommendations, 358–59, 366, 715
records of, 360–65, 367
in reports, 350, 353–54, 367, 371, 692, 698
to board, 819–20
examples, 747–51, 756–57, 764–65
short reports, 738
responsibility for, 848
reviews of, 366–67
and service, 1018
suggestions, 349–50
supervisor role, 366–67, 1023
support for, 1026
terminology, 347–48
training on, 898
and working papers, 383

worksheet, 711
Fines, 1102
Fire
    and data security, 564, 565
    hazard depiction, 670
Firewalls, 329, 643, 671
Fixed assets, 317
Fixed-price contracts, 310, 311–12, 1167–68
Flagg, James C., 1118
Flexibility
    and audit administration, 870
    of auditors, 880–81, 1232–33
    of budget, 984
    and conflict resolution, 1231
    and controls, 80
    and external auditors, 1313
    in management, 1058
    of organization, 83
    in presentations, 726
    in report reviews, 788
    and risk, 127
    of scheduling, 947–48, 1232–33
    TQM approach, 1038
Flip charts, 724–26
Flowcharts
    in audit program, 248
    description, 144–47
    electronic data interchange, 663–65
    packages, 662
    in permanent file, 991, 992
    in preliminary survey, 209–12
    of purchasing, 211–12
    sharing, 662–63
    symbols, 210
    table format, 211
    in training, 897
    of unified audit, 1304
    and working papers, 383
Focus, 7
Follow-up
    of audit projects, 990, 1022
    of change procedures, 584
    as control tool, 1098
    of delegation, 83
    documentation, 968
    guidelines, 791
    monitoring, 694, 1369
    of peer reviews, 1032
    postaudit questionnaire, 862
    quality reviews, 1027
    of recommendations, 790–91, 990
    reporting on, 738–39

responsibility for, 367–71, 1022, 1369
    Standards, 368
Force, 1228, 1245
Ford Motor Company, 94
Forecasting, 1062, 1064
Foreclosures, 1156
Foreign Corrupt Practices Act (FCPA)
    accounting controls, 206, 1324
    and audit committees, 1324
    and boards, 806, 813, 1042–43
    description, 87–89
    and working papers, 378–79, 409
Forensic auditing, 32
Forensics, 814, 1170–71
Forewords, of report, 707–8
Forgery, 1170–71, 1175
Format
    of computer output, 600
    of data, 593
    of EDI messages, 665
    of exams, 28
    of reports, 691, 705–6, 734–35
    of working papers, 379, 380, 382–84, 395
Forms. *See also* Worksheets
    audit analysis, 957–59, 991
    corrective action, 826
    deficiency causes, 826–27
    design of, 1068
    employment interview, 885, 886
    for engagements, 957–59, 976–78, 986
    for feedback, 916–23, 1237–38
    staff evaluation, 916–17, 920–23
        of supervisors, 918–23
    teamwork, 928
    time record, 980
    time report, 981
    use of, 1068
Fraud. *See also* Illegal activities; Investigations;
        Management fraud
    and analytic procedures, 496
    analytic tools, 1184–85
    auditor role, 1172–77
    audit program, 1192–93
    authority issues, 1177–79
    awareness of, 1181–83
    behavioral aspects, 1196
    communication of, 15, 717–18, 933, 1165, 1175–
        79, 1187, 1193–94, 1200, 1256–57, 1332,
        1336
    with computers, 638, 1168–70
    in contracts, 1179
    contributing factors, 1166–67, 1179–80

controls, 1165–67, 1173, 1197–1200, 1202
    as indicators, 1192, 1193
by corporate officers, 933
counterfeit documents, 1171–72
in cyberspace, 1191–92
definitions, 1163, 1164, 1372
detection, 635–39, 1173, 1176–77, 1201, 1256–57, 1360
E-commerce, 332
and enterprise-wide software, 330–31
evidence-gathering, 1192–93
and executives, 1165, 1177–78, 1202–9, 1256–57
against government, 1167–68
and information systems, 547, 581–82, 646
organizational liability, 1209–10
planning for, 264
Practice Advisories, 1190, 1199–1200, 1256–57
prevention, 1168–70, 1171, 1197–1200, 1208–9
probability factor, 1171, 1202
reduction, 84, 646
responsibility for, 1172, 1209–10
and Sentencing Guidelines, 1209–10
Standards, 1173
training about, 911
traps for, 1201
types, 1181–82
via access devices, 1185–86
victims of, 1168
Freedom of activity, 1339
Freedom of Information Act, 1138
Freight. *See* Transportation
Fringe benefits, 492–94
Functional auditing, 297–301, 851–53
Functional authority, 1075, 1081
Functional specifications, for system design, 555, 558
Functions/responsibilities, 838–39. *See also* Responsibility
Future. *See also* Planning; Program auditing
    feed-forward control, 1098
    personnel needs, 1078–79

-G-

Game plan, 1192
Game playing, 102
Game theory, 523, 1057
Gaming auditors, 32
Gantt charts, 511, 1056
Gelprin, David, 553
General Accounting Office (GAO)
    and operations research, 492
    and program audits, 37

on recommendations, 692–94, 790–91
and state auditor generals, 11
General auditor. *See* Chief audit executive
Generalized audit software, 633–34, 636, 673
Gibbs, Jeff., 94
Gifts, 934, 935
Global Auditing Information Network (GAIN), 1041
Globalization, 1060–61
Glover, Herbert D., 1118
Goals
    of audited activity, 196, 197, 354–55
    of auditing, 945–46
    of auditing (worksheet), 924–29
    and cooperation, 1252
    definition, 198, 1063
    of economy audits, 197
    of efficiency audits, 197
    of employer, 7
    and fraud, 1199, 1203
    of individuals, 932
    and information systems, 619
    measurability, 945–46
    of organization, 1354, 1365
    and program audits, 309
    responsibility for, 198–99
    and scheduling, 949
    vs. objectives, 196
Golen, S. P., 1189
Governance
    auditor role, 1363, 1365, 1381, 1383
    definition, 1372, 1387
    as management function, 1063
Government auditors, 29, 36
    software for, 634–35
Governments. *See* Canada; Legislation; State governments; United States
Grammar checking, 659
Grandstand, K., 805
Granger v. National Railroad...., 412
Graphical user interfaces (GUIs), 670–71
Graphics
    in communication, 1251
    as evidence, 324
    Gantt charts, 511, 1056
    networks, 507–11
    in presentations, 371, 724–26, 727
        of schedule, 969
    for project management, 669
    in reporting, 718, 813–17, 820–22, 829–30
    scanning, 390, 669–70
    three-dimensional, 662
    in word processing, 660

Greeks, 4
Grocery stores, 127
Group dynamics, 1065, 1071, 1086
Groups
    conflicts between, 1086
    informal, 1077, 1084
    and responsibility, 1098
Growth, provision for, 558
Guidance Task Force (GTF)
    and approaches, 31
    auditing definition, 9–10, 1350
    and consulting, 42
    and *Standards,* 24, 1350, 1379
Gulf Canada Resources, Ltd., 421–22
Gupta, Parveen P., 1016–17

-H-

Hammer, Michael, 1060
Hand recognition, 564
Hanson Trust v. ML SCM Acquisition, 1319
Haphazard sampling, 444–45
Hardware. *See also* Minicomputers; Personal
    computers; Telecommunications
    acquisition, 568, 608, 610, 621
    auditing, 551–52, 558, 561, 567–69, 585, 608,
        610, 621
    description, 541–44
    error detection, 584–85
    in feasibility study, 554
    mainframes, 542, 544, 631–33, 1170
    maintenance, 566–67
    personal computers, 607–11
    scanners, 669–70
    security, 584–85
    and software packages, 605
    software with, 575–76
Hardy v. New York News, 411
Harmeyer, W. J., 1234
Hash totals, 593
Hazardous materials, 1123–24, 1135
Hazardous waste, 864, 1133, 1140, 1141–42, 1152
    example, 292
Hearsay evidence, 322–24
Herzberg, Frederick, 1088
Hetzel, William, 553
Hierarchy, 1070, 1071, 1076, 1089
Hierarchy of needs, 1085
Hiring, 318, 936, 1167. *See also* External auditors;
    Human resources; Personnel; Staffing
History, 3–5, 12, 1172
Hospitals, 271, 502–3

Hostility, 1224–27, 1234–35, 1244–45
Hot lines, 1200
Hot links, 657, 671
Hot sites, 569–70, 571
Human element
    and controls, 73, 81–82, 102–4
    and procedures, 84
    and standards, 1096–97
Human nature, 1085
Human relations. *See* People skills
Human resource accounting, 1078
Human resources. *See also* Personnel; Staffing
    Aetna approach, 930–32
    analytic reviews, 318
    and audit objectives, 227, 272
    audits of, 1078
    background checks, 936, 1167
    in CoCo model, 68
    diversity, 1085, 1102
    documentation, 859
    evaluation of, 866
    hiring, 318, 1167
    new employees, 84, 886–90, 910
    and preliminary survey, 207–8
    promotions, 1079
    recruiting, 881–83, 899, 931, 1078–79
    standards for, 1090–91
    testing, 884–90
Humidifiers, 566, 567

-I-

Illegal activities. *See also* Crime; Fraud; Investigations
    and boards, 1320, 1332
    communication of, 15, 717–18, 933, 1165, 1175–
        79, 1187, 1193–94, 1200, 1256–57, 1332,
        1336
    computer crime, 1168–70, 1191–92
    by corporate officers, 933
    federal laws, 1167–68
    not prosecuting, 1195
    policies on, 1165
    political, 1178
    in reports, 1175–79, 1193–94, 1332
    and sales, 1168
    suspicion of, 1165
Image, 213, 866, 868, 881
Implementation Standards, 1352–53, 1355, 1358
Improvement
    environmental, 1143
    in internal auditing, 1018
    scheduling for, 965–68

suggestions for, 349–50, 715, 1335
Independence
    AICPA on, 1306
    of audit committee, 40, 1325, 1326
    and audited activity, 8
    and audit trails, 602
    of chief audit executive, 1333–34, 1335, 1338, 1355, 1359
    and consultative approach, 1239
    and consulting, 43, 44, 46, 1360
    definition, 1388
    and external auditors, 1291–93, 1312
    impairments, 1292–93, 1360, 1372
    of information systems, 550–51
    of internal auditing, 840
    and management, 8, 38
    and non-audit functions, 869–70, 970
    and outsourcing, 1305–6
    in quality reviews, 1028
    of reviewers, 1020
    SEC on, 1292–93
    Standards, 1359–60
    types of, 39
    and whistleblowing, 15, 39–41
Indexing, 388, 661–62
Industrial engineering, 970, 971
Industrial Revolution, 4–5
Influence, 1228
Informal groups, 1077, 1084
Informal reporting, 719–22
Information. *See also* Background; Data; Disclosure
    amalgamation of, 863
    in audit program, 250
    board responsibility, 1320–21
    communication types, 1090
    from comparisons, 492–94
    controls, 67, 69, 102, 152
    dissemination model, 1090
    for environmental audits, 1150
    financial, 497, 933, 1326, 1330
    from functional audits, 300
    item relationships, 493
    legal factors, 622–24, 1138
    for operations research, 524
    for preliminary survey, 193–96
    and program audits, 309
    proprietary, 717
    quality reviews, 1026
    restricted, 717–18
    security of, 739–40
        (*see also under* Data)
    sensitive, 634, 1138, 1312

sharing, 1311–13
Information centers, 564–69, 608
Information system audits. *See also* Audit tools; Information systems
    change management, 584
    computer-assisted, 631–35
        (*see also* Audit tools)
    data entry, 593–95, 612
    data storage, 574–75
    disasters, 564, 569–75
    distributed systems, 614–15
    documentation, 617–18
    efficiency, 620–21
    hardware, 551–52, 558, 561, 567–69, 585, 608, 610, 621
    mapping, 638
    new systems, 558
    and objectivity, 935
    operating system, 58, 59, 576–77
    organization, 551–52
    output, 600–601
    personal computers, 610–11
    processing controls, 597–98
    security, 562, 642–43
    software for, 633–35
    training for, 911
    transaction tracing, 602–3
    vendor-supplied software, 606–7
Information systems. *See also* Hardware; Software; Telecommunications
    access to, 563–67, 614, 1169, 1170
    in audit project file, 991
    backups (*see* Backups, of data)
    batch and real time, 546–47, 592–94
    change management, 557, 577, 581–84, 614
        documentation, 616
        event concept, 603
    controls, 71, 541, 547–52
    cost accounting, 619–21
    data storage (*see* Data storage)
    dependence on, 570, 579–80
    distributed processing, 611–15
    documentation of, 615–18, 620, 621, 624
    efficiency, 618–21
    and enterprise-wide planning, 328
    for environmental data, 1135
    evidence database, 326
    expertise in, 1380
    and external auditors, 1312
    and fraud, 547, 581–82, 646
    functional groups, 549–50
    high-level languages, 613

and Internet, 642–43
legal factors, 622–24
maintenance, 566
management of, 553–54, 558–59, 617, 619
operating system, 58, 59, 544, 575–77
operator, 596–97
output, 599–601
program audits, 37
program comparisons, 584, 1169
reports on, 584
responsibility for, 551, 556
risks
    distributed processing, 612–13
    hackers, 609
    inherent, 547
    management of, 149–51, 547–52
    personal computers, 607–8
    real-time transactions, 644–45
    types, 547, 578, 591–92
    vendor-supplied software, 604–7
    viruses, 671
sampling, 470–72
scheduling, 620, 621
security, 544, 559–69
    application level, 561
    and internet, 642–43
    responsibility for, 739–40
standards, 550, 614
STEP evaluation, 553
system life cycle, 552–57, 605, 639
testing, 571, 631–46
    (*see also* Contingency plans)
user role, 619
zoning, 563–64
Ingram, Harry, 1090
Inherent risk
    description, 126–27, 128–29
    in environmental audits, 1133
    evaluation software, 645–46
    in information systems, 547
Initiative, 868, 928
Input controls, 592–94
Input-output, 1057
Insignificant findings, 352–53
Inspections, 1145, 1146
Inspector general. *See* Chief audit executive
Institute of Internal Auditors (IIA). *See also*
    Certification; *Code of Ethics; Competency*
    Framework for Internal Auditing (CFIA);
    Guidance Task Force (GTF); *Standards;*
    Systems Auditability and Control (SAC)
    added value, 854

alliances, 32
on auditor role, 1060–61
and benchmarking, 1041
Board of Regents (BOR), 29
certification program, 11
Common Body of Knowledge, 16
continuing education role, 902, 903–4
and control self-assessment, 419
environmental issues, 863, 1113–14
external auditors, 1274–75, 1285–93
founding, 5–6
information systems, 540
integrated auditing, 315
professional identity, 11
    definition, 8–10
quality, 1014–16, 1021, 1029–33
specialties, 32
staffing, 883
Standards board, 25
Target School Program, 881–82
Web site, 171
whistleblowing, 40–41
working paper access, 412
Insurance
    and contracts, 311
    and environmental liability, 1136, 1154, 1155,
        1156
Insurance companies, 203, 269–71, 291
Integrated auditing, 314–15
Integrated test facility, 637
Integrity
    of auditors, 881, 928
    of audit program, 673–74
    in *Code of ethics,* 1376
    and controls, 78
    in quality reviews, 1028
    and report reviews, 786
    and virtual organization, 94–95
Interest, 126
Interest rates, 127, 496
Interim Audit Memorandum (IAM), 695, 722. *See also*
    Memos
Interim reports, 698, 705, 719–22
Internal auditing. *See also* Administration;
    Engagements; Non-audit functions
    as added value, 854–56, 861
        (*see also* Value-added)
    administration of (*see* Administration)
    AICPA views, 1277–85
    approaches, 30–32
    benefits, 806–7
    best practices, 17–22, 277–78

categories, 29–30
computer-assisted, 673–78, 853–54, 897
    (*see also* Audit tools)
continuous, 329–32
as core function, 33–34
definitions, 8–10, 1372
dilemma, 38–41
evolution of, 3–5, 12
focus, 7
goals, 9240927
key roles *(CFIA),* 20
management support, 899, 947
marketing, 687–88, 860–64, 965–70
    (*see also* Marketing)
mission, 6–7, 841–42
in multi-site operations, 991, 1034
online, 853–54
organizational structure, 849–51
organization-development, 849–51, 899, 965–68
outsourced, 32–33, 864–67, 1026, 1305–7
    (*see also* Cosourcing; External auditors)
perceptions of, 1274–75
as profession, 10–17
research projects, 904
scope, 34–38, 837–42, 1354, 1363–65
sequence of activities, 219–20
status of, 33–34
visibility, 45, 803–17, 830–31, 843–45, 854–56
Internal Auditing Standards Board (IASB), 25
Internal auditors. *See* Auditors; Auditors, role of;
    Characteristics; Competence
Internal control(s)
accounting, 206, 1324
adequate, 1370
and audit committee, 1330
in audit staff evaluation, 924
CoCo model, 67–69
concepts, 1093–99
and consulting services, 1383
coordination of, 970–71
COSO model, 66–67, 267
database of, 328
and deficiencies, 824–26
definitions, 61–63
and downsizing, 91–92
and environmental audits, 1139–40
evaluation of, 1099–1102
and external auditors, 1283, 1311–12
key points, 992
objectives of, 223–24
in permanent file, 992
questionnaires, 147–48, 1311–12

and regulation, 87–88
SAC definition, 69–71
and SEC, 1042–43, 1327
standards for, 78–79, 137, 276–77, 1095–96
and supervision, 1022
training about, 911
Internal Revenue Service, 409–10
Internal reviews, 1020, 1024–27, 1362, 1383
International Standards Organization (ISO 14000), 32
Internet. *See also* Firewalls; World Wide Web
controls, 642–43
fraudulent use, 1191–92
as recruiting tool, 883, 1078
Interval sampling, 442–43, 481
Interviews. *See also* Questions
in audit program, 248
body language, 1189
and evidence, 324
exit, 995, 1032–33
hazards of, 1193–96
in investigations, 1188–90
legal factors, 1194
note-taking, 1247
in preliminary survey, 189–93
question types, 1242
in recruiting, 883–86
scheduling, 190
worksheets, 389
Intuitive filling, 658
Inventories
analytical procedures, 496
audit objectives/procedures, 227, 271
blank-check, 202
computerized auditing, 635
cost reduction, 512–15
illegal sales, 1168
model, 514
pallet recycling, 285
and permanent file, 992
in preliminary survey, 202
of risk, 129–30
sampling, 460–65
shortages, 512
theft, 271
transfers, 271, 289–90
turnover analysis, 318
Inventory theory, 1057
Investigations
access device misuse, 1185–86
versus auditing, 291–93, 1190
audit program, 1192–93
behavioral aspects, 1243–44

created errors, 1201
of cyberspace fraud, 1191–92
documentation of, 1174–75
of emergencies, 831
evidence, 1174–75, 1189–90
forensics, 1170–71
game plan, 1192
hazards of, 1193–96
interviews, 1188–90
liability, 1193–96
loss determination, 1188
of management fraud, 1205–7
objectives, 1187–88
and participative approach, 1241
responsibility for, 1165, 1175–79
staffing, 1174, 1241
steps, 1188, 1190
time frame, 1188
Investments, 1095, 1292
ISO 9000, 1043–44, 1134, 1144–46
ISO 14000, 1142–47
ISO 10,1000, 1043–44

-J-

Jarvis, J. E., 1242
Job control language, 582, 583
Job descriptions
for audit manager, 846
for audit supervisors, 847–48
and motivation, 1088
staff and line, 1074–75, 1081
and staffing, 900, 1078, 1091
Job specifications, 1078, 1091
Johnson, Richard, 1057
Johnson & Johnson, 868
Jones, Harry, 1246
Journals
and continuing education, 903
earliest, 12
and new employees, 897
and professions, 11
Judgment
business judgment rule, 1320–22
and comparisons, 1097
and deficiency revelation, 933
development of, 894–95
and enterprise-wide software, 319
and evidence, 325
executive expectations, 712–13
versus facts, 395
in field work, 294

and findings, 351
and risk analysis, 960–65
and sampling, 445, 470–72, 480, 481
in *Standards,* 933
testing, 887–90
Judgment sampling, 445, 470–72, 480, 481
Just-in-time audits, 35, 169

-K-

Kamlet, K. S., 863–64
Kast, Fremont, 1057
Keating, Patrick, 94
Keating, Stephen, 1233
Kendig, W. L., 788–89
Kennish, J. W., 1187, 1189
Keyes v. Lenoir Rhyne College, 411
Keystroke verification, 594
Kickbacks, 911, 1175
Kim, Unhee, 1117
Kingston Cotton Mill, 1172
In re Kingston Cotton Mill, 1172
Kite, Devan, 1130–31
Krogstad, Jack L., 1349

-L-

Land acquisition, 227, 1155
Landfills, 1133
Language
jargon, 880–81
in writing, 731–34
Languages, fourth generation, 613, 634
LANs (local area networks), 541
Lapointe Rosenstein Co., 1148–50
Lapse time, 668–69
Lasky, Joseph, 744
Lawyers, 1125–26, 1129, 1195, 1206
Leadership. *See also* Directing function
as auditor trait, 862
audits of, 1090–93
in communication, 1089–90, 1092–93
contingency model, 1087
group dynamics, 1071, 1085
individual needs, 1085, 1088
motivation, 1088
in quality, 868
rating, 917, 927
styles of, 1086–87
training for, 902
Learning curve, 272, 520–21
Leaseway case, 410

Least squares, 499–500

Legal evidence
  in environmental audits, 1125–26, 1138
  in fraud investigations, 1174–75, 1189–90
  types, 319–24

Legal expenses, 1178

Legal factors
  entrapment, 1201
  environmental, 1125, 1129, 1138–39, 1140, 1148–
      50
  and information systems, 622–24, 1138
  libel and slander, 1193–94
  proficiency, 880
  prosecution decisions, 1194–96

Legal fees, 1154, 1155

Legislation
  and audit schedule, 948
  Canadian
      Business Corporations Act, 88–89
      environmental, 1148–50
  compliance with, 89
  and employment testing, 884
  environmental, 1129, 1135, 1138, 1141–42, 1151–
      53
  and risk assessment, 120
  United States
      and audit committees, 1325–27
      environmental, 1141–42, 1151–53
      Foreign Corrupt Practices Act, 87–89
          (see also Foreign Corrupt Practices Act
              (FCPA))
      fraud and crime, 1167–68
      and information, 622–24, 1138
      on litigation, 1322
      and non-audit functions, 1273
      Sarbanes-Oxley Act, 1273, 1291, 1324,
          1325–27
      and whistleblowing, 41

Lenders, 1142

Lessees, 1142

Letters of credit, 1156

Lewin, Kurt, 1071

Liability
  of directors, 1319–22
  and environmental audit, 1117, 1123, 1124, 1132–
      37, 1141, 1148–50
  for environmental infractions, 1142, 1148–50
  for fraud, 1209–10
  in investigations, 1193–96
  of lenders, 1140, 1142
  time factor, 313

Libel, 1193–94

Library documentation, 616

Licensure, 11

Likert, Rensis, 1088

Line items, 492–93

Line personnel, 1074–75, 1081, 1224–26

Linear programming, 504–6

Listening skills, 192, 1090, 1246–49

Litigation
  against directors, 1319, 1322
  and environmental audits, 1140
  and investigations, 1193–96
  legislation, 1322

Littleton, A. C., 495

Loans
  to employees, 1167
  environmental liability, 1140, 1142, 1154, 1156
  to executives, 1327

Local area networks (LANs)
  administration of, 612
  auditing, 580–81
  and controls, 610
  description, 541–42, 612
  training about, 911

Location zoning, 563

Locations, remote, 181, 221, 244–45

Lockheed-Georgia, 411

Log offs, 646

Logistics
  analytic reviews, 318
  of audits, 1302
  and contracts, 312
  inventory, 227, 271
  lead time, 241
  questionnaire, 183
  receiving function, 270

Logs, 566–67, 568, 596, 620

London and General Bank, 1172

In re London and General Bank, 1172

Long-range scheduling. *See* Scheduling

Losers' Clubs, 284

Loss
  determination of, 1188
  restoration of, 1195

Lot sizes, 523

Lotus Notes, 1003–4

Louisiana State University, 881–82

Louvens, Timothy J., 1130–31

Luft, Joseph, 1090

Lump-sum contracts, 310, 311–12

-M-

Macher, Ken, 1235
Macros, 657, 659
Magnetic tape drives, 542–43, 572–75
Mail fraud, 1167, 1168
Mail merge, 661
Mainframes
    access controls, 544
    description, 542
    for IS audits, 631–33
    terminal locations, 544, 1170
Maintenance
    of computers, 566–67, 568
    of fixed assets, 317
    of operating systems, 575–76
    in system life cycle, 557
    and vendor software, 606–7
Major findings, 353, 819–20, 826
Malicious prosecution, 1194–95
Management. *See also* Management, of auditing;
        Management fraud; Management functions;
        Operating management
    basic responsibility, 819
    concepts, 1070–76
    constraints, 206–7
    consultative, 1086
    contingency approach, 1058
    level of, 789, 794
        (*see also* Boards; Executives; Hierarchy)
    participative, 1087, 1088, 1096–97
    and programs, 308–10
    standards, 276–77, 1065–66
    theories/styles, 1055–59, 1086–88
    trends (*see* Committee of Sponsoring
        Organizations (COSO))
Management, of auditing. *See also* Administration;
        Engagements
    and audit committee, 1337
    and audit scope, 222–23
    authority/responsibility, 846
    budget, 957
    evaluation of, 951, 1013–21
    marketing, 860–64, 965–70
    mission, 949
    and operating management, 950–51, 968–69
    and politics, 870
    program approvals, 221, 246, 250
    project management, 667–69, 676
    responsibilities, 846–48, 850
    scheduling, 946–65
        examples, 954–56, 958, 959, 961–62, 964

    staffing, 899
        (*see also* Staffing)
    Standards, 837–39, 1362–63
    training, 910
    value-added approach, 931–32
Management by objective, 1058, 1096–97, 1098
Management fraud
    causes, 1203–5
    control of, 1208–9
    impact, 1205–6
    investigation of, 1205–7
    reporting, 1256–57
    as risk, 138–39
    symptoms, 1207–8
Management functions. *See also* Planning
    and authority, 83
    control, 64, 1093–99
        auditor role, 89–90, 98–104, 194–95, 199–
            200, 824–26, 1099–1102
        R&D example, 101
    directing, 1085–90
        auditor role, 37, 100, 1090–93
    environmental issues, 1123, 1124, 1142–47
    ethical environment, 1102
    fraud deterrence, 1173, 1202
    and law enforcement, 1166
    organizing, 100, 1070–79
        auditor role, 37, 1079–84
    planning, 99, 1062–70
        auditor role, 37, 1065–70
    untenable constraints, 206–7
Management-oriented auditing
    definition, 30
    scope, 857
    vs. management auditing, 30
Management principles, 880
Management studies, 303–7
Management style, 127, 1243
Mann, H. E., 861–62
Manning, George, 1192–93
Manpower audits, 1078
Manual systems, 71
Manuals. *See also* Documentation
    for auditors, 856–60, 900
    quality assessment, 1014–16, 1029–33
    work instructions, 1145
Manufacturers
    audit case, 298–300
    audit objectives, 271–72
    and control, 76
    cost analysis, 516–19
    lot size, 523

management fraud, 1209
output analysis, 504
risk, 203
Mapping, 638
Marketing
  analytical procedures, 523
  of auditing, 687–88, 860–64, 965–70
  and audit program, 239
  of audit reports, 692
  and environmental audit, 1117, 1124–25
  field work, 297–301
  objectives, 236
  questionnaire, 186–87
Marsh, Trela, 1115–16
Maslow, Abraham, 1085, 1243, 1254
Master controls, 1100–1101
Master files, 1170
Material costs, 319, 1179, 1184
Materiality, 1018, 1129, 1380
  of external auditors, 1310
Matrix analysis, 137, 148–50, 203–5, 249
Matrix organization, 1076
Mautz, R. K., 38–39, 1275
Maynard, Gregg R., 162
Mayo, Elton, 1056
McGregor, Douglas, 1088
McNamee, David, 121–22
Meals, 934
Mean-per-unit, 462, 463
Measurement
  for benchmarking, 1039
  for budgeting, 1069
  calibration, 1146
  as control, 1096–97
  and goals, 945–46
  human factor, 1096–97
  in inspections, 1146
  of performance, 198, 275, 1017, 1024, 1043, 1096
  of productivity, 809–10
  and standards, 260, 275, 1096–97
  and TQM, 1037
Media, 1129
Medical contributions, 227
Meetings. See also Reviews
  of audit committee, 1329
  with audit committee, 1334–37
  of audit staff, 902–3, 1127
  communication in, 1250–52
  draft report review, 700, 779–88, 1023
  with external auditors, 1308–9
  of IIA chapters, 903–4

preaudit, 861
preliminary, 188–89, 370, 1127, 1257–58
presentation software, 671, 726
scheduling, 1249
summaries of, 385, 1252
supervisor role, 994, 995, 1023
Memo posting, 546–47
Memos
  for audit administration, 858–60
  closing, 794–97
  engineering drawing examples, 407
  and external auditors, 1289
  on findings, 364, 365, 367, 695
  Interim Audit, 695, 722
  for management studies, 305–7
  negative debit, 1208
  number of, 831
  in permanent file, 992
  for report transmittal, 706–7, 788–89
    of draft, 782, 784
    example, 763–65
    reply request, 793–94
Mentoring, 851, 892–95, 899
Mergers and acquisitions
  board negligence, 1319
  and consulting, 44, 46
  due diligence audits, 723–24
  and environment, 1155
  training about, 911
Message sequencing, 578, 1250–51
Message setting, 1250
Microfiche, 599
Middle Ages, 4
Mileage, 318
Minicomputers, 542, 544, 596–97, 611
  reorganization of, 542, 544, 596–97, 611
Minor findings, 353
Mints, F. E., 1226, 1234, 1253
Minutes, corporate, 1155
Mission, 6–7, 1063
Mission statements, 841–42, 867–68
  and quality, 1017
  and scheduling, 949
Mistakes, 868. See also Errors
Mitigating circumstances, 818
Modeling, 1070
Monetary unit sampling, 465–70
Monitoring. See also Quality assurance
  of auditing quality, 1012, 1019–21, 1362, 1383
    (see also Quality assurance)
  by audit manager, 846

auditor role, 35
of audit projects, 976–82, 976–84
and boards, 1320
budgets/schedules, 1023
in CoCo model, 69
computer-assisted, 853–54
with computerized auditing, 635
computer systems, 567–69, 1168–70
    log-in/log-offs, 646
of consultants, 525–26, 926
consulting services, 44, 47
of contracts, 926
of controls, 78
in COSO model, 67, 153
data security, 562–63
of decision-making, 1070
E-commerce, 646
of environmental matters, 1135, 1140, 1143
of expert systems, 645
of external auditors, 1286
of follow-up, 694, 1369
for fraud, 1178, 1200
of lump-sum contracts, 312
of operations, 1100
and operations research, 524, 525–26
of procedure adherence, 1068
and reports, 86, 797
and safety, 277
of schedule, 1023
spot checks, 1101
standards for, 277
telecommunications, 579, 580
of transaction processing, 646
Monroe, J. K., 892–95
Monte Carlo simulation, 522, 1057
Moore, Wayne G., 1349
Morale
    and communication, 1090
    and control self-assessment, 430
    and fraud detection, 1201
    and open door policy, 1087, 1090
    in preliminary surveys, 178
Motivation
    of clients, 1231–32, 1243, 1254
    for continuing education, 901
    theories of, 1085, 1088
Motor pools, 1140
Multi-site operations, 1034
Multitasking, 654–55, 656
Murphy, J. E., 412–13

-N-

Nations Bank, 390–91
Natural disasters, 564, 569–71
Negative debit memos, 1208
Negotiation
    in conflict resolution, 1230–31, 1248–49
    of prosecution, 1195
Network-monitoring software, 579
Networks, 507–11, 580–81
    global auditing information (GAIN), 1041
    security, 644
Neumann, F. L., 892–95
New York Stock Exchange v. Sloan, 411
Newsletters, 672, 1042
Nichols, R. G., 1246
No audit decisions, 213
Non-audit functions. See also Consulting services
    avoidance of, 950, 969, 970
    bank reconciliations, 934
    coping with, 869–70, 978
    of external auditors, 1291, 1326
    legislation, 1273, 1292
    problem studies, 1069–70
    scheduling, 869–70, 934, 950, 970
    Standards, 869–70, 934
Noncompliance
    with Code of ethics, 1362
    with corporate directives, 1207
    with Standards, 90, 697, 1362, 1368
Nonstatistical sampling, 439, 4724
Nonverbal communication, 192, 1189, 1249
Norms, 319
Note-taking, 1247
Not-for-profit activity, 228
Numeric data, 593, 594, 596
    computations, 636, 637

-O-

Object code, 545, 613
Object program, 545
Objectives. See also Audit objectives; Operating
    objectives
    of auditing activity, 813
        continuing audit, 965–68
        and scheduling, 949, 951–52, 965–68
    auditor role, 198–99
    continuing, 965–68
    of controls, 67, 78, 81–82, 95, 96
    definition, 1063

development, 965–68
of due diligence audits, 723
of engagements, 1365, 1366, 1371, 1383
environmental audits, 1122–23, 1127, 1128
of external auditors, 1271
of fraud investigations, 1187
of internal controls, 223–24
management by (MBO), 1058, 1096–97, 1098
of presentations, 727
and program audits, 309
and responsibilities, 1071–72
    (*see also under* Responsibility)
and risk assessment, 139–42
of risk management, 143
and standards, 1096
of testing, 280
vs. goals, 196
Objectivity
AICPA view, 1280–81
auditor image, 881
boards, 803–5, 817
Code of ethics, 932–33, 1376, 1377
and consulting, 43, 46
in control self-assessment, 424, 428
definition, 1372, 1388
of external auditors, 1020
failure examples, 932–34
impairments, 1360, 1372
of internal auditing, 838, 840, 930
and management reports, 817
and measurement, 1097
and non-audit functions, 869–70, 934, 970
perception of, 934–35
prohibited activities, 15
quality assurance, 1013–16
in quality reviews, 1028
in reports, 701–2, 723, 737
as responsibility, 14
in reviewers, 1020
in *Standards,* 932–33, 934, 1359–60
and summaries, 384–86
Observation(s)
facility tours/walk-throughs, 208–9
role of, 283–85
significant, 1332–33
vs. analysis, 283
Obsolescence, 126
Oil well example, 496
Oliverio, Mary Ellen, 33–34
Omissions, 697, 717–18, 1368
Online auditing, 853–54
Open door policy, 1087, 1090

Operating controls, 98–101
Operating management. *See also* Management
    functions
attitude of, 60, 687–88, 692, 1041, 1165–66
and audit schedule, 950–51
bypassing, 829
communication with
    caveats, 830–31
    detail level, 355–56
    on faulty procedures, 355–56
    of findings, 370–71, 705
        (*see also under* Findings)
    Johari window, 1090
    management studies, 305–7
    preliminary discussions, 858, 861, 994, 1257–58
    in reports, 688–99, 705, 719–22, 830–31
    responsibility for, 846, 847, 994
    of risk assessment, 1384
    and scheduling, 949, 950–51, 968–70
    and subordinates, 1087, 1089–90
    timing, 705, 1243, 1245
constraints on, 206–7
evaluation by, 1065–70, 1079–90
evaluation of, 30, 206–7, 1070
and information security, 739–40
planning by, 1062–65
and productivity, 302–3
and programs, 309
relationship with, 7, 8, 13–14, 13–15, 15, 789–90,
    1238–41, 1252–58
reports by, 817, 1207
style of, 1243
unsupportive, 829
Operating objectives
administrative, 232
and audit benefits, 969–70
and audit schedule, 968–69
and budgets, 85
and controls, 64, 66–68
definition, 225–26
and findings, 353
and fraud, 1199
internal auditor role, 7
of internal control systems, 223–24
of marketing, 236
and operating controls, 98
and policies, 83
in preliminary survey, 196, 197
procedures for, 225–30, 268–70
of purchasing, 231
and risk assessment, 139

for specific areas, 227–30
vs. audit objectives, 267
and working papers, 395
Operating standards
and field work, 260
in findings, 354–55
sources, 77–78, 355
Operating systems
and accounting, 85
audit of, 58, 59, 576–77
controls, 64, 98–101
description, 57–58, 544, 575–76
file management, 573
in virtual organization, 94
Operational auditing, 30, 297–301, 851–53
Operations department, 549–50
Operations documentation, 616
Operations research, 490–92, 519–20, 523–26, 1057
Operations risk, 160
Operators, 596–97, 599
Opinions
auditor comments, 991
disputed, 791–92, 818
as evidence, 322
and facts, 791–92
overall, 709, 712–14, 734–35, 817–18
and purpose, 898
reports to board, 808, 817–18
summarizing, 817–18
and training, 898
trend charting, 820–22
Optical character recognition, 669–70
Optical disks, 599–600
Oral reports, 724–26, 738–39, 949, 1250–52
Oral testimony, 320, 321, 325
in working papers, 380
Ordering costs, 512
Organization(s)
comparisons between, 277–78, 498
contingency, 1071
control departments, 970–71
as control means, 82–83
ethical culture, 935–36
fraud liability, 1209–10
goals, 1354, 1365
governance, 1063, 1365, 1372, 1379
hierarchy, 1070, 1071, 1076, 1089
interface with, 179, 724–27
multi-branch, 991, 1034
planning in, 104, 825
politics in, 870, 899
potentially hazardous, 1148–50

preliminary survey, 179, 194
professional, 1021, 1034–35
recruiting within, 882
risk, 159–61
service-providing (*see* Service organizations)
small audit, 969–70
successor, 1142
types of, 1070–71, 1076, 1089
virtual, 94–95
Organization charts, 992, 1071
Organization function. *See also* Accountability;
    Authority; Responsibility
auditor role, 37, 1079–84
basic concepts, 1070–76
charts, 1071
committees, 1076–77, 1082–83
informal groups, 1077, 1084
in R&D, 100
staffing, 1074–75, 1077–79
    (*see also* Staffing)
Organizational audits, 301–3
Organizational culture. *See* Corporate culture
Organizational development, 965–68
Organizational risk, 160–61
Organizational status, 837–42, 870
Organizational structure. *See also* Duties, segregation
    of
and audit committees, 1076
auditor role, 37, 899, 1082
branches/divisions, 991, 1034, 1075–76
and budgets, 86
and communication, 85
and controls, 70, 128, 1094
departmentalization, 1075
flat, 850–51, 1076
hierarchical, 1070, 1071, 1076, 1089
of internal auditing, 261–62, 849–51
and long-range schedule, 952–53
matrix, 1076
multibranch, 991, 1034
project-oriented, 1076
self-direction, 264–65
separate corporations, 992–93
standards for, 276–77
time factors, 850, 853
types, 1070–71
virtual organizations, 94–95
Organized crime, 1167–68
Orientation, 890–92, 896–99
Outlines, 660, 728–29
Outsourcing. *See also* External auditors
of auditing, 32–33, 864–67, 1026, 1305–7

and auditor reviewers, 1020
communication, 316
(dis)advantages, 865–66, 1305–7
and environmental audits, 1114, 1120, 1125–28,
    1130–32, 1135
operations research, 525–26
responsibility for, 316
specialist evaluation, 1137–38
in strategic planning, 261
uses, 315–16, 865
Overcontrolling, 101–2, 104, 1094
Overflow checking, 593
Overhead, billing for, 295, 312
Overstaffing, 1084
Overstatements, 465–70
Owen, Robert, 1055

-P-

Page layout, 672
Pallet example, 285
Parallel processing, 557
Parallel simulation, 637–38
Parameter files, 597
Parker, Xenia Lee, 134–35
Participative auditing. *See also* Control self-assessment
    (CSA)
    benefits, 1238–43
    communication in, 1250–51
    definition, 30–31
    exceptions, 1243–44
    and marketing, 861, 863
    and safety, 277
    teamwork relationship, 1253–54
Participative management, 1087, 1088, 1096–97
Partnering, 1307–8
Passwords, 559–60, 614, 667, 674, 1169
Payables. *See* Accounts payable
Payments
    of claims, 269
    for EDI transactions, 666
    fraud detection, 1178
    questionable, 813
    records of, 1207–8
Payoffs, 1168
Payroll
    analysis of, 492–94
    audit objectives/procedures, 228–29
    audit project integration, 982–85
    data processing, 546
    file testing, 635
    fraud example, 1185

risks and controls, 205
tape management, 572–74
training about, 911
Peat Marwick, 1276–77
Peer-coupled systems, 615
Peer reviews, 1020, 1021, 1027–33
    example, 132–33
    in multi-site operations, 1034
Pension expenses, 126
People skills. *See also* Conflict resolution; Empathy;
        Participative auditing
    animosity
        causes, 1223–27
        coping with, 1224–27, 1234–35, 1244–45
    anxiety, 1242–43
    change management, 1228–29
    competence, 880–81
    compliments, 213, 713, 716, 1251
        example, 757
    consultative approach, 1238–41
    credit acknowledgment, 712
    effective approaches, 1234–40
    in environmental audits, 1127
    in investigations, 1241, 1243–44
    listening, 192, 1090, 1246–49
    motivation, 1086, 1088, 1231–32, 1242–43
    openness, 1257–58
    personnel management, 930–32
    persuasion, 1245, 1248–49
    and power, 1227–28
    and quality, 1016
    questions, 1242, 1248–49
        (*see also* Questions)
    role conflicts, 1232–33
Perceptions
    of auditors, 1235, 1238–39
    of bias, 15, 1360
    of external audit role, 1275, 1293–1301, 1307–8
    of internal auditing, 1274–75
Performance. *See also* Evaluation
    accountability for, 83
    of auditing, 830–31, 846, 1017
        substandard, 934
    and controls, 74
    and environment, 1143
    of management, 98–99, 838, 951
    and management fraud, 1204, 1209
    measurement of, 198, 275, 1017, 1024, 1043,
        1096
    misrepresentation of, 1168
    monitoring, 69
    quantitation of, 198, 1017, 1024

reporting on, 86, 830–31
reviews of, 85
Performance budgeting, 1057
Performance Standards, 1352, 1355, 1362–69
Permanent files, 990–93
Permits, 864, 1133
Personal computers
    as audit tools, 652
    coordination, 608
    cost-effectiveness, 652–53
    in distributed processing, 611–12
    as hardware, 541–42, 544
    laptop and desktop, 653, 676, 677
    in local networks (LANs), 610, 612
    risks and controls, 607–11
    software, 608, 609
    training (for audits), 911
Personnel. *See also* Duties, segregation of; Human
        resources; Staffing
    Aetna approach, 930–32
    audit objectives/procedures, 272
    background checks, 936, 1167
    backups for, 1091
    change, 421, 1067–68
    diversity, 1085, 1102
    excessive, 1084
    investigation of, 1188–90
    line and staff, 1074–75, 1081, 1224–26
    mentoring, 851, 892–95, 899
    morale, 1087
    nonmanagerial, 90
    from operating areas, 855
    rotation of, 234, 930
    salaries, 1078, 1091
    security, 202
    turnover, 318, 328, 1084
Persuasion, 1245, 1248–49
PERT, 507–11, 949, 987, 1057
PERT-Cost, 982, 987
Pharmacy example, 502–3
Phillips, W. G., 1233
Photographs, 324, 718, 992
Physical evidence, 324
Physical inspection, 1127
Planning
    analytical approach, 491, 495
    assumptions, 1064
    for change, 1067–68
    deficiency causes, 825
    for development, 965–68
    failure causes, 1066
    versus forecasting, 1062

long range, 945–48
and malfeasance, 264
as management function, 99, 1062–65
    auditor view, 1065–70
and new employees, 897
for orientation, 892
and outsourcing, 316
preliminary information, 104
quality reviews, 1026
rating forms, 916, 918
record access, 412–13
of research projects, 904
reviews of, 1026, 1067
risk assessment, 121, 139–42
risk management, 1062
single-purpose, 1062
software for (*See* Enterprise-wide systems)
and staffing, 1078–79, 1091
standing-purpose, 1062
strategic *versus* tactical, 1062, 1063
supervision of, 994
vs. accomplishment, 807, 951, 982, 996, 1101
    example, 815
Planning, of audit. *See also* Contingency plans;
        Scheduling
    auditor role, 37, 1065–70
    of consulting services, 47
    documentation, 856–60
    for documentation, 263
    environmental audits, 1125, 1128–30, 1132–33
    with external auditors, 1302–5, 1309
    field work strategy, 260–64
    long range, 945–48
    mid-range, 988
    organizational audits, 301–2
    Practice Advisories, 222, 945
    and prior audits, 992
    for R&D, 99
    reminder list, 171–73, 172
    for report, 263
    risk assessment, 139–42, 1384, 1388
    Standards, 222, 945, 1363, 1365–66
        changes to, 1381–82
    strategic approach, 270–64
    for testing, 281–82
    for working papers, 858
Poisson distribution, 466, 467
Policies
    and audit programs, 248
    and boards, 1320
    changes, 1100
    computer storage, 669

and control, 83–84
definition, 1063
on fraud, 1200
noncompliance, 1101
and risk, 127
Policy statements, 840–42
Political action committees, 935
Political contributions, 1178
Politics, 870, 899
Pollution, 864, 1123–24, 1151, 1152
Positional power, 1227
Positive-sum game, 523
Post-its, electronic, 658, 661
Potential responsible parties (PRPs), 1132–35, 1141, 1153
Powell case, 409
Power, 1227–28. *See also* Authority
Power supply, 565
Practice Advisories
    on analytical auditing, 492
    on audit committee, 1334–36
    on audit quality, 1012
    on board reporting, 1332–33
    on chief audit executive, 1333–134
    for consulting, 42–44
    on control, 59–60
    on coordination, 1300
    description, 1351
    on ethical culture, 935–36
    on external auditors, 869
    on external reviews, 1028–29, 1031
    on findings, 348–49
    on follow-up, 368, 791
    on fraud, 1190, 1199–1200, 1256–57
    fraud investigation, 1175
    on independence, 1292–93, 1333
    on internal reviews, 1024
    listing of, 1372–74
    and new employees, 897
    on non-audit functions, 869–70
    on planning
        of audit, 222
        long-range, 945
    on proficiency, 879–80
    on reporting, 714, 724, 804
    result dissemination, 777
    on risk, 122, 143, 161, 200
    on supervision, 993, 1013
    updates, 1353
    Web site, 1351
Precision
    and environmental audits, 1129

in presentations, 726
in reports, 702
Predictions, 490–91, 501–3
Preliminary risk assessment, 1384, 1388
Preliminary surveys
    and budgeting, 214, 984–85
    and controls, 194–95, 199–200
        questionnaire, 183–84
    and corrective action, 188–89, 213, 370–71
    documentation
        cost reductions, 176–77
        impressions, 177–79
        questionnaires, 180–87
        reminder list, 171–74
        staff instruction, 858
        table of contents, 174–76
    for environmental audits, 1127, 1129
    flow-charting, 209–12
    goals and objectives, 196–99
    information gathering, 193–209
    initial study, 170–71
    interviews, 189–93
    meeting, 188–89, 370
    no audit outcome, 213, 265
    physical observation, 208–9
    and prior audits, 248
    red flags, 195, 202
    reporting, 213
    and risk, 206
    standards, 196–99
    supervision of, 994
    time for, 214
    uses, 169–70
Premises, 1064, 1069
Presentations
    to audit committee, 1339
    communication tips, 1250–52
    to executives, 371
    of long-range schedule, 968–69
    material retention, 739
    one-page audit report, 829–30
    preparation, 727
    software for, 671, 726, 738–39
    timeliness, 726
    uses, 724–26, 738–39
Pressure, 1228
Prevention
    as added value, 351–52, 855
    of calibration loss, 1146
    of conflict of interest, 934
    employee backups, 1091
    environmental, 1117, 1124

against fraud, 646, 1171, 1197–1200, 1208–9
    with computers, 1168–70
for information security, 739–40
and laptop loss, 677
of non-audit assignments, 950, 969, 970
of schedule deviations, 1101
of unethical activity, 935–36
of viruses, 671
Price lists, 992
Pricing, 229
Principles, 1063
Printers, 543, 612
    integrated, 657, 660
Prior audits
    analysis role, 494
    and objectivity, 934–35
    and preliminary survey, 248
    records of, 990–91
    reports from, 730
    and schedule, 946, 953, 957, 968–69, 983
    and supervision, 1022
    working papers from, 381
Prioritization. See also Evaluation
    in audit program, 250
    in audit scheduling, 946, 947, 960–65
    of audit steps, 676
    and controls, 91
    of engagements, 265–66
    environmental issues, 1142
    in reports, 741
    and risk, 236, 807, 947–48, 953, 960, 968, 983
    Standards, 1380
Privacy, 622
Private Securities Litigation Reform Act, 1322
Privileged communication, 410–11, 717
    with attorney, 412–13, 1126
Probability
    binomial distribution, 476
    and fraud deterrence, 198, 1171, 1197
Probability ratio, 507
Probability theory, 507, 1057
Probes, 292
Problem areas
    and audit program, 249
    with consulting services, 303
    emergent, 991, 992
    identification of, 880
    in preliminary survey, 195–96
    reporting on, 714
    and schedule, 948, 960
    in self-directed audit, 265
    studies of, 1069–70

Problem-solving
    attitude toward, 881
    board visibility, 814
    for management, 37–38
    management theories, 1057
    participative, 1250–51
    partners in, 861, 863
    steps, 356–57
Procedures. See also Audit procedures; Industrial
        engineering; Work programs
    and audit programs, 248
    changes, 1100
    and control, 84
    critical indicators, 1209
    database of, 328, 669
    definition, 1064
    environmental, 1135
    error-handling, 596, 598, 600
    and evidence reliability, 325
    of external auditors, 1310
    human element, 84
    instructions for, 1145
    noncompliance, 1101
    for operating objectives, 225–30, 268–70
    questionnaire, 286–87
    for reviews, 858
    and risk, 127
    and standards, 355
    for system changes, 557
Process auditing, 297–301, 851–53, 897
Process control, 1145, 1209
Process instructions, 1145
Process reengineering, 1060
Procurement. See also Purchasing departments;
        Receiving
    by operating departments, 1079–80
    product testing, 234, 1145
    research example, 905–9
    and schedule, 234, 957
Production
    audit objectives/procedures, 229
    and audit scheduling, 948
    environmental issues, 1124
    information systems, 549–50
    questionnaire, 183, 184
Production cycles, 91
Productivity
    of audit activity, 1017–19
    auditor role, 36, 302–3
    of auditors, 653, 655, 809–10, 854–56
    measurement, 809–10
    and organizational audits, 302–3

output standards, 1095
in program audits, 308–9
Products
	change in, 203, 297–301
	departmentalization by, 1075–76
	environmental issues, 1124, 1142, 1143
	incoming, 1145
	misrepresentation of, 1168
Professional development. *See also* Continuing
		education; Training
	of auditing activity, 965–68
	of auditors, 904–10, 930, 993
	Standards, 1351, 1361
Professional identification, 10–12
Professional organizations, reviews by, 1021, 1034–35
Professional recognition credit (PRC), 29
Professional Standards Bulletins (PSBs), 26
Professional Standards Practice Releases (PSPRs), 26
Professions, characteristics of, 10–11, 14
Proficiency, 879–81, 1361–62. *See also* Competence;
		Expertise
Profit centers, 1204, 1208, 1209
Profitability, 1095
Program auditing, 31, 37, 308–10, 1078
Program budgeting, 1057
Program documentation, 616
Program planning, 1078
Project life cycle, 550, 552–57, 605, 639
Project management
	of audits, 668–69, 676
		(*see also* Audit projects)
	critical path methods, 507–11
	software for, 667–69, 995–1004
Project organization, 1076
Property transfer audits, 1123
Proportional analysis, 1184–85
Proprietary information, 717
Prosecution, 1195
Prototypes, 1037–38
Proxy statements, 1325
Public relations
	board role, 1320
	brochures, 1242
	and environmental audits, 1117, 1129
Publicity, 1129, 1202, 1203–4
Punishment, 1226, 1228
Purchasing departments
	accounting controls, 90–91
	analytical procedures, 496
	audit benefits, 969
	auditor role, 36–37
	audit scope, 224

bypassing, 1079–80
competitive bidding, 233, 269, 279, 476–79, 819–
		20
computer equipment, 568, 608, 610, 621
computerized auditing, 635
controls, 232–36
documentation, 1145
EDI role, 663–67
evaluation example, 279–80
evasion of, 235
flowcharts, 211–12
major findings, 819–20
minor findings, 820
objectives/procedures, 229, 231–35
	audit *vs.* operating, 269–71
propriety verification, 290
questionnaire, 185–86
repeat transactions, 235
risk, 204, 232
sampling, 476–81
time and material, 1179
truck repairs, 292–93
in virtual organization, 94
Purpose
	and findings, 898
	in report, 763
	in working papers, 395, 8989

-Q-

Qualifications. *See* Competence; Expertise
Quality
	auditor role, 229, 271–72, 862, 925, 971
		evaluation of, 925
	awareness of, 1037
	in evaluation, 279
	and findings, 354
		example, 1145–46
	focus on, 13
	of internal auditing, 867–68, 931
		reviewers, 1019–21, 1027–34
	ISO 9000, 1043–44
	in manufacturing, 271–72
	in program audits, 308–9
	in purchasing, 279
	questionnaire, 184
	and receiving department, 270
	standards, 1043–44, 1095
	total quality management (TQM), 1017, 1036–39
Quality assurance
	computer systems, 582
	of engagements, 1010–11, 1024–32

client evaluations, 1035–36
rating, 734–35
verification system, 1024–25
and environment, 1144–46
of external auditors, 1283–84
of internal auditing
    IIA manual, 1014–16
    macro and micro, 1010–11
    productivity, 1017–19
    reviews
        external (*see* External reviews)
        internal, 1020, 1024–27, 1362
        by professional organizations, 1034–35
        TQM, 1038
    and *SEC v. Worldwide Coin,* 1043–44
    Standards, 1011–13, 1019–20, 1024, 1352–
        54, 1361–62, 1383
    survey, 1016–17
ISO guidelines, 1043
Practice Advisory, 1012–13
records, 1146
supervision, 1019–20, 1021–24
Quality circles, 1027
Quality control, coordination with, 970, 971
Quality councils, 1037, 1039
Quantitative management, 1057
Quantitative techniques. *See also* Analytical
    procedures; Measurement
appreciation of, 880
for decisions, 1070
for fraud detection, 1208
performance metrics, 198, 275, 1017, 1024, 1037,
    1043, 1096–97
of risk, 157–59, 960–65
Quarterly Reports, 1324
Questionnaires
administrative controls, 183
and control self-assessment, 431
of external auditors, 1311–12
internal control, 147–48, 1311–12
post-audit, 862
in preliminary surveys, 180–87
purchasing department, 185–86
quality, 184
resources, 183
risk management, 147–48
standard operating procedures, 286–87
transmittal memo, 182
Questions
in audit programs, 249
in interviews, 191–92, 285–87
in investigations, 1188–89

people-type, 1242
in presentations, 727
for program audits, 309–10
uses of, 1248–49
Queuing theory, 515–19, 1057
Quoting, of clients, 787–88

-R-

r, 501
Racketeer Influences and Corrupt Organization Act
    (RICO), 1168
Radtke, Robin R., 1130–31
Ramamoorti, S., 892–95
Random number sampling, 441–42, 481
Random samples, 438
Rapport, 861–62
Ratio analysis, 317, 497–98, 1184–85
Ratio estimation, 463
Ratios, capital, 1095
Ray, Manesh, R., 1016–17
Real estate transactions. *See under* Transactions
Real-time systems, 546–47, 592–94, 644–45
Reasonable assurance, 206
Reasonable inquiry, 1142, 1173, 1175
Reasonableness, 493–94, 501
and data entry, 593
and objectivity, 934–35
Receiving department, 270, 960, 969, 1198
Recognition, need for, 1231–32, 1243, 1254
Recommendations
acceptance of, 692–94, 788–91, 1233–35
characteristics, 693, 736–37, 789–91
by clients, 788–89
communication of, 305, 692–94, 712, 714–15,
    736–37
    examples, 757–62, 764–65
for corrective action, 294–95, 692–94, 778–79
and findings, 358–59, 366, 715
follow-up on, 790–91, 990
GAO on, 692–94
key, 694, 791
post-audit, 957–59, 991
repercussions, 358–59
responsibility for, 294–95, 848
Reconciliations, 594, 934, 1199
Record of Audit Findings (RAF), 360–65, 367, 387
Record retention, 642, 1178, 1179
Records. *See also* Files
access to, 412–13, 1367
accounting, 382

of audit (*see* Record of Audit Findings (RAF);
       Working papers)
of cash receipts, 92
of computer systems, 561, 582, 599
       (*see also* Logs)
and consulting services, 43
and contracts, 312
and control, 78
of engagements, 976–84, 990–93, 1367
       environmental audits, 1132, 1135–36
       prior audits, 453
as evidence, 323
of findings, 360–65, 367
of hazardous material, 1141
of interviews
       in audit, 193
       for employment, 884
material distribution, 319
of memos, 306–7
of payments, 1207–8
permanent, 990–93
of previous audits, 953
of purchasing departments, 1145
of quality, 1146
regulations, 87–88
retention/release, 43, 642, 1178, 1179, 1367
and sampling, 282
staff evaluation, 916–23
Records audits, 1179
Recovery, 94
Recycling, 202, 285. *See also* Scrap
Red flags
       in analysis, 493
       of embezzlement, 1183
       environmental liability, 1154–56
       of fraud, 1181–82, 1192–93, 1198
              by management, 1207–8
       in preliminary surveys, 195, 202
Redundancy. *See also* Duplication
       of audit coverage, 1273
       of character checks, 584
       elimination of, 1302–5
Reengineering
       of business processes, 1060
       and controls, 93–94
       and enterprise-wide software, 328, 605
       training for, 902
Regression analysis, 317, 498–503, 1057
Regulations. *See* Legislation
Relationships. *See also* Auditors, role of; People skills
       with audit committee, 1326, 1331–32, 1334–36,
              1337–39, 1341–42

with clients, 14–15, 169–70, 854–56, 1233–40,
       1244–45, 1254–58
with employers, 7, 15
with external auditors, 813, 814, 840, 864–67,
       952, 953, 1272–78, 1275
       surveys, 1298–1301, 1308–10
and independence, 1292
between information items, 493
with operating management, 7, 8, 13–15, 789–90,
       1238–41, 1252–58
between risks, 128–29
between variables, 499–501, 503
Relevance
       of evidence, 326
       and working papers, 380–81, 409
Reliability level, 446
Remote locations, 181, 221, 244–45
Rental property, 229
Repair shop example, 313
Report(s)(ing). *See also* Communication; External
       financial reporting cycle; Reviews, of reports;
       Writing
       access to, 1309
       approvals, 716–17
       by audit committees, 1331–32, 1338
       to audit committees, 1326, 1339–42
       and audit program, 246
       on audit status, 985–86, 996–1003, 1023
       and background, 707–8, 738
       and benchmarking, 278
       to boards, 810, 1332–34
       caveats, 830–31
       and chief audit executive, 697, 700, 717, 1332–34,
              1363
       client input, 737, 777–82, 788–89
       closure, 794
       computer-generated
              data processing output, 599–601
              of review notes, 675–76
              validation of, 35, 36
       on consulting, 47
       content, 707–16, 790
       and control, 86, 89–90, 101–2, 150
       control self-assessment, 90, 267, 434
       and corrective action, 751, 831
       cross-referencing, 366–88, 392
       on deficiencies, 780
              lack of, 779
       design, 263
       distribution, 697, 717
              (*see also* Results, dissemination of)
       documentation of, 738, 858, 859–60

drafts, 730–31, 1041, 1127
of emergencies, 831
of environmental audits, 1125, 1127, 1129, 1138
errors and omissions, 697, 717–18
examples, 746–51, 753–62
exceptional, 737–38
on executives, 717–18
to executives, 803, 1332–34
by external auditors, 1325
facts and evidence, 791
final audit, 371
on findings (*see under* Findings)
focus points, 712–14, 741
on follow-up, 738–39
format, 691, 705–6, 714, 734–35
graphics and color, 718, 829–30
"How to Read" page, 753
indexes, 388
informal, 719–22
interim, 698, 705, 719–22, 949
    (*see also* Memos)
libel, 1193–94
operational, 817, 1207
outside the enterprise, 15, 724
perspective, 701–2, 716, 723
planning for, 263
Practice Advisories, 714, 724, 804
purposes, 688–89
quality
    rating, 734–35
    reviews, 1027, 1031–32, 1035
    TQM status, 1042
recommendations in, 692–94, 712, 714–15, 736–37
    example, 757–62, 764–65
replies to, 778–79, 793–97, 858
of risks, 143, 738
short, 738–39
    memo type, 763–65
        (*see also* Memos)
    one-page, 829
Standards, 697, 705, 706, 714, 718, 737–38, 779, 803, 1354
summaries, 698–99, 706–7, 734
    examples, 747–48, 763
    (*see also* Summaries)
supervision, 690–91, 739, 847, 919, 995, 1023
support for, 785–86
tables in, 737
timeliness, 86, 694–95, 704, 739, 949, 1207, 1326
tone, 704, 737, 741
Reputation. *See* Credibility; Image; Perceptions

Requirements
    compliance with, 1101
    for systems, 555, 558
Research and development (R&D)
    audit objectives/procedures, 230, 272
    controls, 99–101
    participative audit, 1253–54
    training about, 911
Research grants, 911
Research projects, 904
    example, 905–10
Reserves, 983
Residual risk, 143, 1369, 1384, 1388, 1389
Resource Conservation and Recovery Act (RCRA), 1152
Resource time, 668–69
Resources
    access to, 70, 79
    for auditing, 170–71, 264, 1363
    controls, 79
    for engagements, 261–62, 930, 934, 948, 1366
    for feasibility studies, 554, 619
    of operating departments, 1335
    questionnaire, 183
    responsibility for, 74, 1363
    usage analysis, 504
Responsibility. *See also* Statement of responsibility
    and accountability, 83, 1072–73
    for assumptions, 1064
    of audit committees, 829, 1324–27, 1329–32
    of audit managers/supervisors, 846–48, 850
    of audit organization, 790
    of auditors, 221, 1172, 1175–76, 1254–58
        in audit team, 262, 264, 294–95
    auditor view, 1079–80
    for audit program, 994
    for audit projects, 976
    of boards, 1319–22, 1384
    and budget, 85
    for bypassing management, 829
    of chief audit executive (*see under* Chief audit executive)
    in CoCo model, 68
    communication of, 796–97
    for controls, 68, 77
    for coordination, 1363
    for corrective action, 358, 751, 778–79, 794–97, 839–40, 848, 1098, 1333, 1369
    for decisions, 1069–70
    definitions, 83, 1071–1972
    delegation of, 83, 1073

for environment, 864, 1132–35, 1141, 1142, 1152, 1153
for ethics, 1379
for external auditors, 869, 1285–90
of facilitators, 428
for follow-up, 367–71, 1022, 1369
for fraud, 1166–67, 1172, 1173, 1209–10
for goals and objectives, 198–99, 846, 847
individual *versus* group, 1098
for information systems, 551, 556, 739–40
in job specifications, 1078
of management, 819
    (*see also* Management functions)
for non-audit functions, 869–70, 970
for outsourced services, 316
for program evaluation, 309–10
and reporting, 86
for resources, 74, 1363
for result dissemination, 697, 1382
for reviews, 848
for risk management, 1063
for schedule, 846, 847
for staffing, 846, 847, 880
for standards, 198–99, 846, 848
of supervisors, 850, 993–95, 1019–24
for testing system, 556
Results, dissemination of, 697, 777, 1379, 1382, 1384
Retail stores, 271
Retention
    of audit files, 990–93
    of external auditors, 1290, 1291
    of presentations, 739
    of records, 43, 642, 1178, 1179, 1367
    of working papers, 408–9, 1023
Retina scanning, 564
Return on investment, 1095
Revenue cycles, 91, 92
Revenue standards, 1095
Reverse what-if, 657
Reviewers, 1019–21, 1027–34
Reviews. *See also* Quality assurance; Staff evaluations
    analytical, 316–19
    of audit charters, 1334, 1335
    of auditing activity, 1011–13
    of audit projects, 1010–11
    of budgeting, 1068–69
    of change procedures, 584
    of *Code of ethics,* 1351
    of control self-assessment, 427
    documentation of, 857
    in environmental audits, 1129
    external (*see* External reviews)

of external auditors, 1283–85
of findings, 366–67
interim, 978
internal, 1020, 1024–27, 1362, 1383
legal, 1126
of long-range schedule, 950–51, 953, 968–69, 991
by peers (*see* Peer reviews)
of performance, 85
of planning, 1026, 1067
post-audit, 957–59, 991, 1023
preliminary, 857
procedures for, 858
by professional organizations, 1034–35
responsibility for, 848
time factors, 1013, 1022, 1038
upward, 932
of working papers, 382, 392–94, 675–76, 993, 994, 1022
    TQM approach, 1038
Reviews, of reports
    cause and effect, 792–93
    and change, 780, 786–87
    concurrent, 782–83
    conference, 783–88
    conflict resolution, 785–88
    of deficiencies, 780
    of drafts, 700, 779–88, 1023
    for editorial purposes, 691, 740–44
    instructions for, 780, 781
    objectives, 778–79
    reviewers, 779–82
    revisions, 793
    of satisfactory conditions, 779–80
    status of, 996
    supervisor role, 995, 1023
    time factors, 782–83, 789
Revisions
    of audit programs, 246, 250
    to reports, 793
Rework, 1209
Ridley, Anthony J., 1349
Risk(s)
    administrative, 232
    of audit (*see* Audit risk)
    and audit marketing, 969–70
    audit role, 16, 35, 142–43, 200–203, 807, 970, 1060–61
    communication of, 143, 738
    and consulting services, 43, 44, 47, 1364, 1369, 1383
    and contracts, 311–12
    and controls, 121–22, 141–42, 200–205

matrix analysis, 137, 148–50, 203–5, 249
definition, 1372, 1388
detection of, 128, 200–203
disclosure of, 160–61
of E-commerce, 133–35, 331–32, 603
of EDI, 135–36, 331, 332, 663
of engagements, 1384, 1388
    (*see also* Audit risk)
and enterprise-wide software, 327–31
environmental, 1117, 1140–41
    (*see also under* Liability; Risk assessment)
exposure examples, 202, 1140–41
and financial statements, 123–24, 126–27
and follow-up, 368
industry-wide, 127
in information systems (*see under* Information
    systems)
inherent, 126–27, 128–29, 547, 1133
inventory of, 129–30
organizational, 160–61
of personal computer use, 607–8
Practice Advisories, 122, 143, 161, 200
prioritization, 236, 807, 947–48, 953, 960, 968
in procurement, 905–9
relationship between, 128–29
residual, 143, 1369, 1384, 1388, 1389
in sampling, 438
Standards, 1364–66, 1383
in telecommunications, 578
time factor, 160–61
Risk analysis, 947–48, 960–65, 983, 1171
Risk assessment
    and AICPA, 120, 122, 126–27, 161
    analytical procedures, 495
    assertions, 124–25, 126, 128
    auditor role, 122–23
    of audit risk, 123–24
    benchmarking, 277–78
    in CoCo model, 68
    computer-assisted, 677–78
    and control, 59, 66
    and control self-assessment, 429
    in COSO model, 66, 119–20, 152
    Courtney method, 157–58
    dollar value, 157–59
    of EDI, 135–37
    of electronic commerce, 133–35
    and environmental audits, 1126, 1127, 1132–34,
        1139, 1140–41
    factors, 131–32
    impact evaluation, 132–33
    and Internet, 643

of management fraud, 138–39
organizational evaluation, 159–60
in permanent files, 992
planning for, 121, 139–42
preliminary, 206, 1384, 1388
quantitation, 157–59, 960–65
versus risk analysis, 960
and scheduling, 947–48, 953
users of, 120–21
worksheets, 155–57
Risk-based auditing, 121–22
Risk control, 142
Risk financing, 142
Risk management
    activities, 121–22
    auditor role, 142, 163, 1060–61, 1364
        Standards, 1364–66, 1383
    best practices, 162
    and communication, 143
    and consulting services, 1364, 1369
    and control self-assessment, 426–27
    COSO method, 151–57, 161
    cost-effectiveness, 150, 157–59, 161, 206
    definition, 1388
    flowcharts, 144–47, 161
    management role, 1062, 1063
    matrix analysis, 137, 148–50, 203–5, 249
    organizational approaches, 159–60
    and planning, 1062
    questionnaires, 147–48
    of real estate transactions, 1123, 1140–42
    responsibility for, 1063
Risk-rating, 861
Risk taking, 868
Rittenberg, Larry L., 1349
River and Harbor Act, 1151
Robertson, J. C., 1275–76
Roethlisberger, F. J., 1056
Roles, 1232–33. *See also* Audit committees; Auditors,
    role of; Boards; Duties, segregation of
Rolling stock, 318
Romans, 4
Rosenzweig, James, 1057
Royalties, 1179
Rules, defined, 1064

-S-

Saake, P. H., 866–67
Safety
    committees for, 276, 288
    field work type, 297–301

standards for, 276–77
Safety department, 970, 971
Salaries. *See* Compensation
Sales
    audit objectives/procedures, 230
    commissions, 1208
    criminal, 1168
    E-commerce, 331–32
    forecasts, 523
    fraud example, 1184
    revenue standards, 1095
Sales brochures, 992
Salmon, E. R., 1016
Salvage, 202
Sampling. *See also* Statistical sampling
    for attributes, 454–60, 481
    and audit objectives, 440, 445, 454, 470–72
    Central Limit Theorem, 449
    cluster, 444, 481
    combined attributes variables (CAV), 465–70
    confidence level, 446–48, 453
    definition, 437
    discovery, 459–60, 481
    dollar estimation, 460–65
    dollar-unit, 456–70
    and environmental audits, 1129
    error rate, 454–59, 467, 475–76, 480
    and external auditors, 1312
    for fraud/gross error, 459–60
    interval, 442–43, 481
    judgment, 445, 470–72, 480, 481
    large-value items, 465–70
    method selection, 282, 439–45, 480–81
    normal distribution, 449–50, 453–54
    for overstatement, 465–70
    populations, 438–39, 448–50, 480–81
        infinite, 455–56
        no variability, 470–72
        proportion of, 476–80
        small clean, 457–59
        subpopulations, 440
    precision, 446–48, 1129
    quality of, 1026
    random number, 441–42, 481
    reporting on, 737
    result evaluation, 475–76
    risk, 438
    sample size, 443, 445, 448–49, 454
    selection principles, 439–41
    and simulation, 521–22
    standard deviation, 451–53, 460, 466, 476
    stop-and-go, 457–59, 481

    stratification, 443–44, 448, 466, 480–81
    subpopulations, 440
    supervision of, 1023
    for system deficiencies, 470–72
    theory, 446–54
    in training, 897
    variability, 448–49, 450
    variables sampling, 460–65, 481
    vs. whole population, 437–38
Sampling proportionate to size (SPS), 465–70
Sampling risk, 438
Sarbanes-Oxley Act, 1273, 1291, 1324, 1325–27
Satisfactory reports, 779
Satisfiers, 1088
Sayre, Don, 1143–44
Scaling, 657
Scanners, 669–70
Scatter diagrams, 498–99
Scheduling
    assignment boards, 988–89
    of auditor evaluations, 914–15
    and auditor expertise, 851
    basic elements, 947
    benefits, 948–52, 969–70
    and budget, 950, 951, 953, 957–59, 978–82, 984–85
        of budget development, 1069
    changes, 947–48, 968–69
    completion estimates, 982
    critical path methods, 507–11
    of development objectives, 965–68
    deviations, 807, 815, 951, 982. 996, 1101, 1313
    deviations from, 813, 979
    documentation of, 858
    environmental audits, 1128
    in evaluation, 280
    with external auditors, 1309
    flexibility, 947–48, 1232–33
    and fraud, 1166
    Gantt charts, 511
    horizon, 948–49, 953
    of information systems, 620, 621
    of interviews, 190
    just-in-time, 35, 169
    of logistics, 241
    of meetings, 1249
    and mission statement, 949
    monitoring of, 1023
    non-audit functions, 869–70, 934, 950, 970
    by operating activity, 952–58
    PERT, 987
    and prior audits, 946, 953, 957, 968–69, 983

prioritization, 946, 947, 952–58, 960–65
of procurement, 234
and purchasing, 280
reserve estimates, 983
responsibility for, 846, 847
reviews of, 950–51, 953, 968–69, 991
and risk, 947, 948, 950, 960–65
software for, 668–69, 953
standards, 946–47
and technology, 948
training, 910, 965–68
in turnkey systems, 596–97
vs. accomplishment, 807, 951, 982, 996, 1101
   example, 815
Schnee, E. J., 412
Schott v. McDonald, 411
Scope
analytical approaches, 495
of auditor expertise, 34–38
in audit program, 223–24, 226, 248
of engagements, 857, 1366
in environmental audits, 1126, 1128
and external auditing, 1287
of internal auditing, 837–42, 1354, 1363–65
   versus external, 1286
management-oriented auditing, 857
in reports, 708–9
   examples, 756, 763
Standards, 1287, 1366
and TQM, 1038
in working papers, 383, 395, 898
Scrap
disposal of, 272–73
excessive, 302–3
functional audit example, 298–300
and manufacturer quality, 272
and preliminary survey, 202
Search engines, 639
Searches, of employees, 1192
Sears, Brian P., 1282–83
Secondary evidence, 320
Securities and Exchange Commission (SEC)
and audit committees, 1324–25
and environmental audits, 1117, 1138
and independence, 1292–93, 1306
and quality assurance, 1042–43
Securities Litigation Standards Act, 1322
Security
of audit program, 673–74
against computer crime, 1168–70
of data
   application level, 560–61

audit of, 562–63, 570–71, 574–75
description, 559–61
disaster plans, 569–71
in distributed environment, 613, 614
in enterprise-wide software, 329, 644
and Internet, 643
and operating system, 576
physical factors, 563–67
responsibility for, 739–40
risk priority, 35–36
software for, 560–61
storage, 550–51, 572–75
tape disposal, 574–75
transmission, 578–81
   (*see also* Application controls)
of hardware, 563–69, 584–85
incomplete log-off, 646
as motivational need, 1231–32
of networks, 644
personal computers, 607–11
program changes, 581–84, 603, 1169–70
in telecommunications, 578
in virtual organization, 94
and working papers, 391, 392, 394, 643–44, 674–75
Security audits
announcement of, 188
data storage, 574–75
disaster plans, 570–71
of hardware, 563–69
Security department, 570–71
Security personnel, 202
Security trading firms, 126
SEC v. Worldwide Coin Investments, 1042–43
SEC vs. Killearn Properties, 1324
Segments
of audit organization, 849–50
of audit programs, 858
of engagement, 822, 858, 983
of working papers, 897–98
Self-assessment. *See under* Administration; Control self-assessment (CSA)
Self-checking, in data transmission, 578
Self-control, 1098
Self-critical analysis, 410
Self-directed audit teams, 264–65
Self-directed control, 1235–36
Self-evaluative privilege, 410–12
Self-measurement, 1097
Selim, Georges, 121–22
Seminars, 902
Sensitivity analysis, 519–20, 1057

Sequence
  in communication, 1250–51
  in data security, 593
Sequence checking, 593
Servers, 541
Service organizations, 515–19
Services
  environmental issues, 1142
  and findings, 1018
  level of, 515–19
Set-asides, 1156
Shalin, Peder, 663
Sharaf, H. A., 38–39
Shaw, Paul, 1192
Shipping, 969
Short reporting, 738–39
Shortage, of inventory, 512
Signature plates, 202
Signatures
  electronic, 665, 1004
  on reports, 716–17
  verification before, 1024–25
  verification of, 564
Significance, 1380
Significant observations, 1332–33
Simmons, Mark, 96–98
Simulation
  continuous and intermittent (CIS), 638
  and decisions, 1070
  description, 521–22
  Monte Carlo, 522, 1057
  parallel, 637–38
Single audit, 1302–5
Single-purpose plans, 1062
Skepticism, 863, 894–95, 897, 1175–79, 1247
Skills, 668–69
Slack, 508
Slander, 1193–94
Small audits, 247, 1005
SMART auditing, 273–74
Smith v. Van Gorkom, 1319
Snapshots, 638–39
Social system management, 1057
Socializing, 934
Society, 1057
Software. See also Application controls; Enterprise-
    wide systems; Operating systems
  and analytical reviews, 317
  application, 544–45
  for auditing, 633–35, 636, 673
    training about, 898
  for audit programs, 221

  for audit project management, 995–1004
  audit risk, 953
  for backups, 671
  data anomalies, 646
  data change utilities, 613
  for data security, 560–61
  downloaded, 643
  for EDI, 665
  enterprise resource planning, 327–29
  expert systems, 672–73
  fourth-generation languages, 545
  for information system audit, 633–37
  for LANs, 612
  master copy, 609
  for network security, 644
  off-the-shelf (see Vendor packages)
  for one-page audit report, 829
  optical character recognition, 669–70
  page layout, 672
  for personal computers, 608, 609
  for presentations, 671, 726, 738–39
  project management, 667–69, 995–1004
  regression analysis, 501–2
  report distribution, 576
  for residual data, 609
  and sampling, 437, 458
  for scheduling, 668–69, 953
  source code, 545, 583
  spreadsheet, 656–58
  statistical, 634, 1312
  systems, 544, 545–46
  telecommunications, 579
  U. S. government, 634–35
  utilities, 613
  virus protection, 671
  word processing, 658–62
  for working papers, 390–91
Source code, 545, 583
Southern California Edison, 1040–42
Span of control, 1073
Specialization, 32
Specification files, 597
Specifications
  for jobs, 1078
  for systems, 555, 558
Spies vs. United States, 1189–90
Spreadsheets
  electronic, 656–58
  linking, 656
  standards for, 610
Staats, Elmer B., 1239
Staff and line, 1074–75, 1081, 1224–26

Staff evaluations
    description, 912–15
    forms, 916–23, 924–27
    forms for, 916–17, 920–23
        managers/supervisors, 918–23
    goal-oriented, 924–29
    managers/supervisors, 951
Staff meetings, 902–3
Staff personnel, 794, 1074–75, 1081, 1224–26
Staffing. *See also* Supervision
    of audit activity, 899
    audit job types, 849–51
    auditor role, 1084
    and audit programs, 247
    and boards, 813
    of engagements, 261–62, 930, 934, 948, 1078,
        1366
        and scheduling, 949, 950
    of environmental audit, 1114, 1120, 1126–28,
        1130–32, 1137–38
    excessive, 1084
    for fieldwork, 261, 264
    of fraud investigations, 1174, 1241
    interviews, 883–87
    mentoring, 892–95, 899
    with operating personnel, 855
    orientation, 890–92, 896–99
    planning for, 1078–79, 1091
    pool strategy, 850–51
    proficiency requirements, 879–81
    recruiting, 881–83, 931, 1078–79
    responsibility for, 846, 847, 880
    screening, 886–90
    Standards, 897
Standard deviation, 451–53, 460, 466, 476
Standard operating procedures, 286–87
Standards. *See also* Norms
    of audit evidence, 325–26
    and audit program, 248
    for committees, 1083
    of competency, 17–22
    for consulting, 42–44
    for controls, 59, 78–79, 137, 276–77, 1095–96
    of cost, 1095
    definitions, 197, 1064, 1388
    development of, 198, 276–77
    for documentation, 610
    for EDI transactions, 665
    for environmental management, 1142–47
    evaluation of, 1099
    for field work, 275–77, 281
    for file names, 573

    and fraud detection, 1172–73
    and group dynamics, 1086
    human element, 1096–97
    for human resource activity, 1090–91
    for human resources, 1090–91
    and information systems, 550, 614
    for investments, 1095
    ISO 9000, 1043–44
    for long-range schedules, 946–47
    for management, 276–77, 1065–66
    and measurement, 260, 275, 1096–97
    and monitoring, 277
    operating, 77–78
    for operations research models, 523–25
    for organizational structure, 276
    for output, 1095
    of profitability, 1095
    and program audits, 309
    of quality, 1043–44, 1095
    and reporting, 86
    responsibility for, 198–99, 846, 848
    and risk, 160–61
    for safety, 276–77
    and sales, 1095
    and scheduling, 951
    setting, 198
    for spreadsheets, 610
    for system development, 558–59
    for testing, 281
    for timeliness, 1095
    training in, 1100
Standards
    accordance with, 813, 1362, 1379, 1382
    on analytical auditing, 492, 494
    application of, 25
    on audit management, 837–39, 1362–63
    on auditor role, 1364–66, 1383
    and boards, 813, 1354, 1384
    changes/updates, 25–26
        numbering system, 1354*n*, 1355
        process, 1351–53, 1355–56, 1379
        proposed, 1379–89
        terminology, 1353–54, 1383–85
    and consulting, 45, 304, 1361, 1365, 1366, 1367
        definition, 1371, 1387
        proposed change, 1380
    on control, 57–58, 1139–40, 1364–65
    and deficiency revelation, 933
    definitions, 1370–72
    on engagements, 1354
    on environmental audits, 1139–40
    and external auditors, 1283–84, 1285–93

on external reviews, 1028–29, 1031, 1383
on findings, 348–49, 1354, 1368–69, 1379, 1382
on follow-up, 368
and fraud, 1173
on independence, 1359–60
on judgment, 933
and new employees, 897
on non-audit functions, 869–70, 934
noncompliance with, 90, 697, 1362, 1368
and objectivity, 932–33, 934, 1359–60
origins of, 23–24, 1009, 1350–56
on planning, 222, 945, 1363, 1365–66
on proficiency, 879–80
purpose, 1358
on quality assurance, 1011–13, 1019–20, 1024, 1352–54
on reporting, 697, 705, 706, 714, 718, 737–38, 779, 803, 1354
responsibility, 13–14
and risk, 201
on scope, 1287, 1366
for small activity, 1005
on supervision, 993, 1005, 1011, 1368
and training, 899
types, 1352–53, 1355, 1358–69
and whistleblowing, 40
Standing-purpose plans, 1062
State governments
    auditor generals, 11
    audits of, 230
    environmental issues, 1132
    tax revenue, 230
    whistleblowing laws, 41
Statement of responsibility
    and animosity, 1226
    in audit charter, 838–39
    earliest, 12
    evolution of, 13–14
    and *Standards,* 13–14
Static electricity, 566
Stationery usage, 319
Statistical sampling. *See also* Sampling; sampling
    basic concepts, 446–54
    classical, 465, 466
    and external auditors, 1312
    and risk, 438
    vs. nonstatistical, 472–74
Statistical software, 634, 1312
Statistical summaries, 385
Statistics
    software for, 634, 1312
    workload, 996

Status
    of internal auditing, 33–34
    reports on, 985–86, 996–1003, 1023
Stern, Gary, 855
Stewardship, 1157
Stock purchases, 934
Stop-and-go auditing, 265–66, 1041
Stop-and-go sampling, 457–59, 481
Storage tanks, 864, 1133, 1153
Strategic planning
    of audit, 260–64
    and controls, 64
    for individuals, 932
    versus tactical, 1062, 1063
Strategies
    description, 1063
    for environmental auditing, 1128–30
    and investigations, 1190
Stratified sampling, 443–44, 448, 466, 480–81
Stress, 1232–33
Substance use, 634–35
Substitutes, 1091
Sufficiency, of evidence, 325
Suggestions, 349–50, 715, 831
    from subordinates, 1087, 1090
Summaries
    of activities audited, 807–8
    of audit opinions, 817–18
    in audit programs, 385–86
    of audit segments, 385
    of audit workload, 996
    of causes, 812, 822–29
    in control self-assessment, 425
    of findings, 386, 387, 756–57, 819–20
        of causes, 828
        examples, 387, 747–51, 756–57, 808, 830
    in listening, 1247
    of meetings, 385, 1252
    and objectivity, 384–86
    in permanent file, 992
    of preliminary surveys, 213
    of recommendations, 757–58
    of reports, 698–99, 706–7, 734
        examples, 747–48, 763
    statistical, 385
    of testing, 385
    in working papers, 384–86
Summary reports, 698–99
Sumners, Glenn E., 1284
Superfund laws, 1133, 1141–42, 1152–53
Supervision
    analytic procedures, 1022

of auditing activity, 847–48
audit programs, 246, 847–48, 850–51, 853, 994, 1022
of computers, 1169
and contracts, 312
and control, 79
delegation, 83, 1073
documentation of, 900
of engagements
    evaluation of, 951
    field work, 918–19, 994
    and findings, 366–67, 1023
    job descriptions, 847, 848
    levels of, 261–62, 930
    new auditors, 899
    Practice Advisories, 993, 1013
    rating form, 918–20
    reports, 690–91, 739, 847, 919, 995, 1023
    responsibilities, 850, 993–95, 1019–24
    staff evaluations, 913
    Standards, 993, 1005, 1011, 1368
    substandard auditors, 934
    training for, 910
    and working papers, 378, 382, 392–94, 993, 994, 1004
evaluation of, 918–23
of planning, 994
preliminary impressions, 179
and quality assurance, 1019–20, 1021–24
responsibility, 846–48, 850, 993–95, 1019–24
of sampling, 1023
of small staff, 1005
span of control, 1073
trends, 850–51, 1023
Supply usage, 319
Surprise audits, 188, 190, 1242
Suspicion, 1175–76, 1193–94, 1256–57
System control files, 596
System life cycle, 552–59, 605, 639
Systems
    design of, 555, 558
        vendor alternatives, 544–45, 554, 555
    manual, 71
Systems Auditability and Control (SAC), 69–71, 540
Systems management theory, 1057

-T-

Tables
    in reports, 737
    in word processing, 661
Taboos, 428

Tactical planning, 1062, 1063
Tape drives, 542–43
Tape management systems, 572–75
Tape recorders, 193
Taxes
    in permanent files, 992–93
    and state governments, 230
Taylor, Frederick, 1055
Taylor, H. R., 1227–28
Taylor, M. E., 412
Teams. *See* Audit teams
Teamwork, 868, 879, 880, 930–32. *See also*
    Participative auditing
    rating form, 928
    and TQM, 1037
Technology
    auditor role, 35–36
    and feasibility studies, 554, 619
    and field work, 315–16, 327–33
    and long-range schedule, 948
    and obsolescence, 126
    and productivity, 653
    proficiency with, 880
    risk, 126, 547, 1379
    and sampling, 437–38
    TQM approach, 1038
Telecommunications
    auditing, 579–81, 615
    cable modems, 672
    contingency planning, 571
    controls, 578–79
Telephone cards, 1185–86
Telephones
    analytical reviews, 319
Terminals, 544, 1170
Terminology
    ambiguous, 244–45
    of clients, 861
    definitions, 1370–72
    of findings, 347–48
    Standards updates, 1353–54, 1383–84
Test data, 636
Test equipment, 202–3
Test transaction techniques, 636
Testimonial evidence, 324
Testing
    of advertising, 237–39
    for auditor traits, 886–90
    of audit programs, 221
    computer-assisted, 635–39
    documentation of, 738
    for employment, 884–90

of engineering drawings, 400–407
of entered data, 592–94
for fraud, 1201
of information systems, 631–46
   contingency plan, 571
      (*see also* Contingency plans)
   new systems, 556, 557
integrated, 635, 637
for inventory control, 271
for manufacturer efficiency, 272
network security, 644
new systems, 556, 557
objectives, 280
planning for, 281–82
population selection, 282
of procured items, 234, 1145
for purchasing department, 233–36
sampling methods, 282
and software packages, 604, 1170
standards for, 281
summaries of, 385
supervision of, 1022
in system life cycle, 556
and TQM, 1038
for traffic program, 241–42
of transaction processing, 636–39, 646
and working papers, 381, 383, 400–407
worksheets, 898
Texaco Corp., 1003–4
t factors, 455
Theft, 271, 1167, 1197, 1201. *See also* Fraud
Theory X, 1088
Theory Y, 1088
Thesauri, 659
Third parties (in EDI), 663, 665, 667
Thompson, Julie, 1115–16, 1139
Thought processes, 887–90
Thurston, John B., 6
Time, usage of
   and analytic reviews, 318
   in engagements, 979, 983–84, 987
Time and material, 1179
Time checks, 596
Time frame(s)
   for area coverage, 953
   and audit program, 221, 246, 248
   of board reporting, 810
   comparisons, 494, 497
   and decisions, 522
   environmental, 1126, 1157
   of external audit participation, 1294–98
   in field work, 262

and hostile clients, 1245
of investigation, 1188
of management response, 791
of meetings, 1249
for observation, 283
PERT analysis, 507–11
for preliminary survey, 214
in project management, 668–69
report design, 263
of report reviews, 782
of reviews, 1013, 1022, 1038
of risk, 160–61
and variables, 503
of work program approval, 1384
Time records, 978–82
Time zoning, 563
Timeliness
   of audits, 931, 949
   of controls, 79
   of corrective action, 1098, 1101
   in evaluation criteria, 280
   of feedback, 1099–1100
   of findings communication, 705, 1243, 1245,
      1251, 1384
   of liability recognition, 313
   in oral presentations, 726
   and organization structure, 850, 853
   and purchasing, 280
   of reports, 86, 694–95, 704, 739, 949, 1207, 1326
      review process, 780, 782, 789
   standards of, 1095
Tools example, 479–80
Total checks, 596
Total quality management (TQM), 1017, 1036–39
   example, 1040–42
Traffic department, 241–42
Training. *See also* Continuing education; Professional
   development
   analytical procedures, 897
   and audit assignments, 930
   for audit managers, 910
   of auditors, 540, 813, 814, 857–58, 867, 881–82
      of managers/supervisors, 910
      new hires, 895–900, 910
      responsibility for, 993
   of clients, 862
   on construction, 911
   as control, 1100
   for control self-assessment, 427, 431
   for employees, 84
      backups for, 1091
   on ethics, 936

with external auditors, 1310
and findings, 898
in-house programs, 910–11
for investigators, 1241
orientation, 890–92, 896–99
PC audits, 911
PC use, 610, 657, 660
and professions, 10
for reporting, 691
scheduling, 910, 965–68
for senior internal auditors, 902
and software, 606, 898
Standards, 899
in standards, 1100
TQM, 1017, 1037
for unified audit, 1303
Transaction controls, 666
Transaction processing. *See also* Application controls;
    Data processing; Flowcharts
audit trails, 602–3
and control, 78, 87–88, 90–91
and data security, 560–61
in EDI, 94–95, 135–37, 663–67
embedded auditing, 635
errors
    detection, 585, 595
    notification of, 600
    and packaged software, 604
    prevention, 592–94
examination techniques, 282–95
monitoring, 646
with new system, 557
purchasing, 235
real-time, 644–45
simulation, 637–38
snapshots, 638–39
testing, 636–39, 646
Transaction trails, 598
Transactional audits, 1123
Transactions
    (un)authorized, 1170, 1200
    computer validation, 853–54
    in electronic data interchange, 663–66
    fraud detection, 1178
    real estate, 864, 1123, 1133, 1140–42, 1154–56
        rentals, 229
    repeat, 235
    unrecorded, 1175
    verification of, 1185
    via access devices, 1185–86
Transmission controls, 667

Transportation
    analytic reviews, 318
    audit benefits, 969
    cost analysis, 504–6
    and environment, 1140
    example report, 746–51
    fraud example, 1184
Travel
    and laptop computers, 676, 677
    policies/procedures, 900
Travel vouchers, 460
Treadway Report, 419–20
Trend analysis, 317–498, 497, 1184
Trends
    of accountability, 1272
    and boards, 820–22
    findings and opinions, 820–22
    in management, 1055–61
    organizational, 1076
    in organization structure, 850–51
    quality assurance, 1014
    in supervision, 850–51, 1023
    total quality management, 1017, 1036–42
Truck repair example, 292–93
Trust
    atmosphere of, 1257–58
    and CoCo model, 68
    and CSA facilitators, 428, 429–30
    and ethics, 14–15
    evaluation of, 1087
    and external auditors, 1311
    and leadership, 1086
    in rating form, 928
Trusts, 1155
TRW Corp., 410, 695
Turnkey systems, 596–97
Turnover
    of inventory, 318
    of personnel, 1084

-U-

Unannounced audits, 188, 190
Unified audit, 1302–5
Uniform Standards Act, 1322
United States. *See also under* Legislation
    Atomic Energy Commission, 852
    auditing history, 4–5
    government, and working papers, 409–14
    government software, 634–35
    Sentencing Commission, 1209–10
United States v. Powell, 409

Unit-price contracts, 311, 312
University auditors, 32
University programs, 12, 881–82
User documentation, 617
Utilization review, 568

-V-

Valence, 1088
Validation
of data, 592–94, 612
of transactions, 853–54
Value-added, 854–56
Aetna example, 931–32
and CSA, 855
definitions, 1370, 1385
in findings, 351–52
guidelines, 854–56
and quality, 867, 1028
Value-added networks, 581
Value analysis, 235. *See also* Cost-effectiveness
Values
of auditing, 928–29
auditor role, 1354, 1365, 1381
communication of, 68
and ethics, 1102
Variability, 448–49, 450
Variables, relationships between, 499–501, 503
Variables sampling, 460–65, 481
Variances
from budget, 1069, 1101
communication of, 1101
from schedules, 807, 815, 951, 982, 996, 1101, 1313
from standards, 1099–1100
Vendor packages
auditing software, 633–34, 636
code change, 607
customization, 544–45, 605, 607, 611
desktop publishing, 672
(dis)advantages, 604–5
for due diligence reporting, 723
for enterprise-wide planning, 605–7
evaluation of, 606–7, 611
for flow-charting, 662–67
graphics for, 670–71
with hardware, 575–76
illegal copies, 610
for information system scheduling, 620
make-or-buy decision, 233, 554, 555
operating system hooks, 575
for personal computing, 608

presentation tools, 671, 726
releases, 583, 604, 605, 606–7
for tape management, 572–73
testing, 604, 1170
Vendors
environmental factors, 1143
payoffs from, 1168
socializing with, 934
Verification, 290–91
Video display terminals, 544
Virtual organizations
control in, 94–95
Viruses, 671
Visibility
of auditing function, 45, 803–17, 830–31, 843–45, 854–56
of continuing education, 901, 965–68
of ethical culture, 935–36
Vision statements, 1017
Vision University, 902
Voice recognition, 564
Vroom, Victor, 1088

-W-

Walk-throughs, 208–9, 1127
Wallace, W. A., 1275
Waltman, J. L., 1189
War, 1142
Ward, D. D., 1275–76
Warehouse space, 318
Waste, 7, 1332. *See also* Efficiency
Waste management, 863–64, 1114, 1123–24, 1132, 1135. *See also* Hazardous waste
Water, 864, 1151–53
Watsen, J. K., 1032–103
Web sites, for audit resources, 171
Webb v. Westinghouse Electric, 411
Weber, Max, 1055
Wetlands, 864
What-if analysis, 657
Whistleblowing
by auditor, 829, 933
by employees, 1165
hot lines, 1200
IIA position paper, 40–41
Standards, 40
Wide area networks, 580–81
Wiretapping, 578
Word processing, 658–62, 672
spreadsheet links, 657
Work areas, 179. *See also* Facilities

Work instructions, 1145
Work programs, 1367, 1372, 1384
Workflow, 670
Working habits, 178
Working papers
    access to, 391, 392, 394, 409–13, 1309
    accountability for, 674
    archives, 677
    in audit programs, 236, 247, 248
    automated management, 390–91
    changes, 391
    content, 379–80, 381, 395
    cross-referencing, 386–89, 392
    data sources, 383, 388
    documentation for, 858
    electronic, 391–92, 643–44, 671, 674–76
        training about, 899
    for environmental audits, 1125–26, 1129, 1138
    examples, 395–406
    for financial audits, 382
    format, 379, 380, 382–84, 395
    indexing, 388
    information system, 390–91
    ownership, 409–14
    parts of, 897–98
    pictures in, 669–70
    planning for, 858
    from prior audits, 381
    quality of, 1026
    reference numbers, 383, 386
    and reports, 785–86
    responsibility for, 382, 392–94, 675–76, 993
    retention, 408–9, 1023
    reviews of, 382, 392–94, 675–76, 993, 994, 1022
        TQM approach, 1038
    software for, 390–91
    style, 380, 382, 408
    summaries, 384–86
    supervision, 378, 382, 392–94, 993, 994, 1004, 1022
    templates, 389–90, 408
    and testing, 381, 383, 400–407
    "to do" list, 381–82
    in training, 897–98
    types, 327
    in unified audit, 1302, 1303
    uses, 377–79
    verification of, 1025
Workload statistics, 996

Worksheets. *See also* Forms
    audit department goals, 924–29
    for audit projects, 980, 981
    dollar unit sampling, 471
    for findings, 711
    risk assessment, 155–56
    scheduling, 954–58, 959
    status report, 986
    for testing, 898
    in training, 898
    and working papers, 381, 389
Workshops. *See* Control self-assessment (CSA)
World Wide Web
    audit resource site, 171
    communication via, 932
    employee usage, 643
    and fraud, 1191–92
    recruiting via, 883, 1078
    searching, 639
    security issues, 643
WORM, 599–600
Writing. *See also* Detail, level of
    acronyms, 736
    checklist, 742
    drafts, 730–31, 1041, 1127
    editing, 740–41
    friction causes, 690–91
    guidelines, 731–34, 735–37
    outlines, 728–29
    proofreading, 741–44
    rating form, 917
    report style, 687–88, 691–92, 701–4, 714
    test for, 886–87
    titles, 735
    vs. listening, 1247
    of working papers, 408

-Z-

Zap programs, 576
Zero-based budgeting, 1064
Zero-sum game, 523
Z factors, 455
Ziegenfuss, Douglas E., 1357
Zoning (information systems), 563